A GRAMMAR

OF THE

KANNADA LANGUAGE

IN ENGLISH

A GRAMMAR

OF THE

KANNADA LANGUAGE

IN ENGLISH

COMPRISING THE THREE DIALECTS OF THE LANGUAGE
(ANCIENT, MEDIAEVAL AND MODERN)

BY

THE REV. DR. F. KITTEL

GYAN

Published by

GYAN

Gyan Publishing House
5, Ansari Road
Daryaganj, New Delhi-110002
Phone: 011-47034999, 9811692060
E-mail: books@gyanbooks.com

Distribution Network
gyanbooks.com
India, USA, Canada, UK, Australia

ISBN: 978-93-6208-451-4 (HB)
First Published, 1903

2nd Impression 2024

Printed at: Gyan Press, Delhi.

A GRAMMAR OF THE KANNADA LANGUAGE IN ENGLISH
Author: DR. F. KITTEL

A GRAMMAR

OF THE

KANNAḌA LANGUAGE

IN ENGLISH

COMPRISING THE THREE DIALECTS OF THE LANGUAGE

(ANCIENT, MEDIÆVAL AND MODERN)

BY

THE REV. DR. F. KITTEL

MANGALORE

BASEL MISSION BOOK AND TRACT DEPOSITORY

1903

PREFACE.

The present Grammar is chiefly based on Kêšava's Šabdamaṇidarpaṇa. The terminology of this his Grammar is simple, and fit for the three dialects of Kannaḍa. At the same time it will be interesting to learn the general way of an ancient native scholar's teaching Kannaḍa grammar.

In Kêšava's age most of the rules of Kannaḍa grammar were fixed. That before him there had been grammarians who had not deserved that name, seems to follow from his quoting a part of a Kanda verse that is fully quoted in the Šabdânušâsana (under its sûtra 469), from which we translate it as follows— 'Remain, O daughter! Could the unprofitable grammarian (šushkavaiyâkaraṇa), the unprofitable sophist and the rustic have as (their) subject matter the gem of poetical composition which is the subject matter of the assemblage of very clever poets?'

Some specific statements of Kêšava concerning his predecessors or contemporaries are the following—

He considered it a matter of necessity to caution literary writers against using final ḷ in several Kannaḍa words, as only rustics would do so (§ 228).

He teaches (§ 252) that if there exist Tadbhavas of two words compounded, both words ought to be in their Tadbhava form. In this respect he quotes an instance from his great predecessor Haṁsarâja (of A. D. 941, according to Mr. B. Lewis Rice), *viz.* taravêḻ mâṇikyabhaṇḍârada puṭikĕgaḷaṁ, which, he says, is a mistake (tappu), as mâṇikabhaṇḍârada would be right (šuddha).

He says that in satisaptami (§ 365) which always refers to two subjects, the letter ŏ is to be used; by some (of his predecessors or contemporaries) al has, without hesitation, been employed for it; clever people do not agree to that. Then he quotes two sentences with al, and calls them wrong (abaddha).

He states (very probably in order to counteract a tendency of that kind) that to form kâṇikŏ, tĕraḷikĕ, pûṇikĕ of kâṇ, pûṇ, tĕraḷ (which formations are frequently found at least in the mediæval dialect) is faulty, as the suffix ikĕ should not be added to verbs ending in a consonant (see § 243, *A*, 5).

When introducing the suffix tana, he teaches that it is not to be used for Saṁskṛita words, as *e. g.* ârôhakatana would be wrong (abaddha, § 243, *A*, 14). That he certainly has done so for the above-mentioned reason becomes evident by the fact that the Šabdânušâsana (under its sûtra 431) adduces unnatatana and pannatatana as instances of ancient usage.

He states that to form a causative verb, *e. g.* khaṇḍisisu, to cause to cut, from khaṇḍisu, to cut, a verb derived from a Saṁskṛita noun, is not allowed (§ 150, remark), which statement probably also opposes a tendency of grammarians (or poets) towards doing so.

He says that nouns ending in a consonant do not insert in before the a of the genitive, except pagal and iruḷ; to form *e. g.* bĕmarina, maṇalina, mugalina is a fault (dôsha, § 121, *a* 6). It follows from his opposition to such forms as bĕmarina that they had already come or were coming into use.

He states that forms like nôḍidapaṁ, mâḍidapaṁ are not used as declinable kṛilliṅgas (§ 194, remark 2); but according to the Šabdânušâsana (sûtras 447. 448. 544) they were used as such, because its author Bhaṭṭâkalaṅkadêva adduces nôḍidapanaṁ, kûḍidapanaṁ, mâḍidapaṅgĕ, irdapana as ancient formations.

He says (see § 240, remark) that some (grammarians or poets) who are fond of a practice that is connected with grass (satṛinâbhyavahârigaḷ), do not consider that abnormity does not enter in poetical prose, and use a short letter followed by an initial letter which is a compound with rêpha, as šithila; such disgustful persons (arôčigaḷ) do put it in poetical prose without calling it a blame (tĕgaḷ).*

The author hopes that the remarkable fact that Kannaḍa and the other Draviḍa languages have no relative pronoun (§ 174), has been satisfactorily explained and established by him (§ 330), and that the origin of the negative form of the verb in Draviḍa has been made evident by him (§ 210), two subjects which (he may remark) used to puzzle European scholars. See also his explanation of the participles (§§ 169. 185) and of the infinitive (§ 188).

As to the age of Kannaḍa poets Mr. Rice's Introduction to his edition of the Šabdânušâsana (p. 11 *seq.*) should be consulted.

---

* Here the remark may be added that according to the Šabdânušâsana (under its sûtra 288) the pronoun nâṁ (which is not mentioned by Kêšava, § 137) was agreed to by some of the great poets of the northern way, whereas those of the southern one were siding with âṁ. According to Nṛipatuṅga's Kavirâjamârga (1, 36) of the 9th century the region in which Kannaḍa was spoken, extended from the Kâvêri as far as the Gôdâvari.

Regarding the comparison of Draviḍa languages see 'A Comparative Grammar of the Dravidian or South-Indian Family of Languages, by the Rev. R. Caldwell, D. D., LL. D, etc., 2nd edition, 1875, London, Trübner & Co.' Dr. Caldwell in his work is inclined to think that Draviḍa exhibits close traces of relationship to the languages of the Scythian group.

The Publications consulted for the present grammar are, besides the Šabdamaṇidarpaṇa, the following—

1. The Karṇâṭaka Šabdânušâsana (see p. 4, note).

2. Nuḍigaṭṭu. A Kannaḍa Manual of School-Grammar, by Dhondo Narasiṁha Mulbagal, Kannaḍa Teacher, Training College. 2nd edition. Mangalore, Basel Mission Press, 1894.

3. Kannaḍa Schoolbooks, by native authors. Bombay, the Department of Public Instruction. Printed at the Basel Mission Press, Mangalore, 1882—1898.

4. An Elementary Grammar of the Kannaḍa Language, by the Rev. Thomas Hodson, Wesleyan Missionary. 2nd edition. Bangalore, 1864.

5. A Practical Key to the Canarese Language, by the Rev. F. Ziegler. 2nd edition. Mangalore, Basel Mission Press, 1892.

6. Nâgavarma's Karṇâṭaka Bhâshâbhûshaṇa (of about the beginning of the 12th century), edited by B. Lewis Rice, M. R. A. S., etc. Bangalore, 1884.

7. A Kannaḍa-English Dictionary, by the Rev. F. Kittel. Mangalore, Basel Mission Press, 1894.

8. Very valuable Inscriptions published in the Indian Antiquary and Epigraphia Indiça, by J. F. Fleet, PH. D., C. I. E., etc.

9. Elements of South-Indian Palæography, by A. C. Burnell, HON. PH. D. of the University of Strassburg, etc. Mangalore, Basel Mission Press, 1874.

10. A Sanskrit Grammar for Beginners, by Professor Max Müller, M. A., London, 1866.

Special thanks are due to the SECRETARY OF STATE FOR INDIA for his generous aid by ordering a certain number of copies of the forthcoming Grammar for the Home Department in Calcutta and by inducing the Governors of Madras and Bombay and the Governments of Mysore and of His Highness the Nijam to take a considerable number of copies of the work in advance whereby the Publishers have been enabled to carry it through the Press.

The author would also gratefully acknowledge the encouragement he has received from the interest that several gentlemen have taken in his composing the present Grammar, of whom he may mention Mr. B. Lewis RICE, C. I. E., M. R. A. S., Director of the Archæological Researches in Mysore; the Rev. G. RICHTER, late Inspector of Schools in Coorg; Dr. E. HULTZSCH, Government Epigraphist, Bangalore; Dr. J. F. FLEET, BO. C. S., M. R. A. S., C. I. E., and Professor R. GARBE, PH. D., Tübingen.

As the author lived in Germany, the printing was carried on in India, and proof-sheets could not be sent to him for correction, there occurs an unusual number of misprints; but a corrected list of the errata will enable the student to set them right before perusing the Grammar.

Finally the author quotes for his work the words of Kêšava (sûtra and vṛitti 4)—"If there are any mistakes (dôsha) in this (my) Šabdamaṇi-darpaṇa, may the learned (first) thoughtfully listen, and (then) with mercy combined with gladness of heart rectify them."

Tübingen, 5th February 1903.

TABLE OF CONTENTS.

A

GRAMMAR

OF THE

KANNAḌA LANGUAGE

I. Introductory observations

1. The term Kannaḍa (ಕನ್ನಡ), the Canarese of European writers, is formed from Kar-nâḍu (ಕರ್-ನಾಡು), the black cultivated country, referring to the black soil, commonly called cotton soil, which characterises the plateau of the Southern Dekkan (ದಕ್ಷಿಣ). In the Saṁskṛita language the term appears as Karṇâṭa (ಕರ್ಣಾಟ) and Karṇâṭaka (ಕರ್ಣಾಟಕ). Kannaḍa is the appellation of the Canarese country and its language.[1)]

2. Kannaḍa is spoken throughout Mysore, the Southern Mahratta country, in some of the western districts of the Nijam's territory (as far north as Bidar), and partly in North Canara on the western coast. The people that speak the Kannaḍa language are estimated at about nine millions.

3. The Kannaḍa language belongs to a group of languages which has been called the Dravidian (*i.e.* ದ್ರವಿಡ or ದ್ರಾವಿಡ) family by European writers. The chief members of this family are Kannaḍa, Tĕlugu (ತೆಲುಗು), Tamiḻ (ತಮಿೞ್), Malayâḷa (ಮಲಯಾಳ), Tuḷu (ತುಳು), Koḍagu (ಕೊಡಗು), and Baḍaga (ಬಡಗ, on the Nîlagiri).

4. The so-called Dravidian languages have borrowed a great many words from Saṁskṛita, especially such as express abstract ideas of philosophy, science, and religion, together with the technical terms of the more elegant arts, etc. (*cf.* § 369); but their non-Saṁskṛita portion is considerable, and once was sufficient for ordinary conversation. Chiefly by a comparison of their grammatical structure with that of Saṁskṛita the essential independence of the

[1)] The district of Canara (a corrupted form of Kannaḍa) on the Western coast got that name because it was subjected for centuries to the rule of Kannaḍa princes, and the Carnatic (*i. e.* Karṇâṭaka), the country below the Eastern Ghauts on the Coromandal coast, was (by a misapplication of terms) called by that name first by the Muhammedans.

Dravidian languages of Saṁskṛita can satisfactorily and conclusively be established.

5. The earliest written documents of the Kannaḍa language are inscriptions on walls and pillars of temples, on detached stone-tablets and monumental stones, and on copper-plates of the Canarese country. The inscriptions are often dated; if they have no date, the form of the letters used and historical references to dated inscriptions serve to ascertain their age.

6. As regards the forms of the Old and Modern Kannaḍa alphabets, they are varieties of the so-called Cave-character, an alphabet which was used for the inscriptions in the cave hermitages of Buddhists in India (*e. g.* at Salsette, Kânhêri, Nâsik, Sahyâdri, Ajanta), and rests on the Southern Aśôka character. This character was about 250 B. C. employed in the Edicts of the Buddhist king Aśôka. Different forms of the letters used for the Kannaḍa inscriptions appear at different periods, the earlier forms differing in the greatest degree from those of the Modern Kannaḍa alphabet[1]. At the time of the composition of the Basavapurâṇa 1369 A. D. the old alphabet had become already out of use, as the author of that work mentions the letters of Old Kannaḍa (ಪೞಗನ್ನಡಲಿಪಿ) as belonging to the past.

7. The Kannaḍa language in the old inscriptions (of the Kadamba, Gaṅga, Čâlukya, Râshṭrakûṭa and other kings) of which specimens exist that belong to about 600 A. D., is not the same as that of the present day; it is what is called Old Canarese. This Old Canarese is also the language of the early Kannaḍa authors or the literary style. It may be said to have continued in use to the middle of the 13th century (see § 109), when by degrees the language of the inscriptions and literary compositions begins to evince a tendency to become Modern Canarese or the popular and colloquial dialect of the present time. A characteristic of the literary or classical style of the early authors is its extraordinary amount of polish and refinement. The classical authors were Jainas. One of them was Nṛipatuṅga, who wrote the Kavirâjamârga (a treatise on

[1] The earliest authentic specimens of writing in India are the edictal inscriptions of the Buddhist king Aśôka (also called Dharmâśôka and Priyadarśi) who was the grandson of the Maurya king Čandragupta at Pâṭaliputra (the modern Patna), and ruled from the extreme north-west of India as far as Magadha in the East and Mahishmaṇḍala (Mysore) in the South. These inscriptions are written in two different alphabets. The alphabet which is found in the inscription that is at Kapurdigiri (near Peshawar), is written from right to left, and is clearly of Phenician or old Semitic (Aramaic) origin (it has been called Khanôshṭi); the Southern inscriptions that are found in numerous places from Girnâr in Gujerat to Siddâpura in the Chitaldroog district of Mysore (these last ones discovered by Mr. B. L. Rice), are written from left to right, and the alphabet employed in them is the source of all other Indian alphabets. It has been thought by some scholars (Professors Weber, Bühler and others) that the character of the Southern inscriptions also may be traced back to a Phenician prototype.

alaṅkâra) in the 9th century; another was Pampa or Hampa who composed his Bhârata (an itihâsa more or less based on Vyâsa's Mahâbhârata) in 941 A. D.; and a third one was Argaḷa who finished his Purâṇa in 1189 A. D.[1]

8. The grammatical treatises on Kannaḍa were constructed on the Saṁskṛita plan. Their Jaina authors took Pâṇini and others as their guides. The earliest grammarian, whose works have come down to us, is Nâgavarma who appears to belong to the first half of the 12th century. Kêśirâja or Kêśava, the author of a well-known grammar, lived about one hundred years later, in the 13th century. The above-named authors treat on the Old Canarese language, illustrating it by quotations from the writings of former (or contemporary) poets. Nâgavarma wrote his first grammar, an epitome, in Kanda verses and Old Canarese, and embodied it in his treatise on the art of poetry, the Kâvyâvalôkana (in Old Canarese); his second grammar, the Karṇâṭakabhâshâbhûshaṇa, is in Saṁskṛita prose sûtras, each accompanied by a vṛitti or explanatory gloss also in Saṁskṛita. Kêśirâja's grammar, the Śabdamaṇidarpaṇa, is composed wholly in Kanda verses and Old Canarese (each verse having its prose vṛitti), and is the fullest systematic exposition of that language[2].

9. The ancient Kannaḍa grammarians held the study of grammar in high esteem, as may be learned from the following words of the author of the Śabdamaṇidarpaṇa: — "Through grammar (correct) words originate, through the words of that grammar meaning (originates), through meaning the beholding of truth, through the beholding of truth the desired final beatitude; this (final beatitude) is the fruit for the learned" (sûtra 10 of the Preface).

---

[1] The Kavirâjamârga was edited in 1898 by K. B. Pâṭhak, B. A., Assistant to the Director of Archæological Researches in Mysore, the Bhârata also in 1898 by Lewis L. Rice, C. I. E., M. R. A. S., Director of Archæological Researches in Mysore. (Mysore Government Central Press, Bangalore.)

[2] Nâgavarma's Karṇâṭakabhâshâbhûshaṇa was edited by B. Lewis Rice, M. R. A. S., Director of Public Instruction (Bangalore, Mysore Government Press, 1884). It contains 10 paričchêdas, viz. sañjñâvidhâna, sandhividhâna, vibhaktividhâna, kârakavidhâna, śabdarîtividhâna, samâsavidhâna, taddhitavidhâna, âkhyâtanigamavidhâna, avyayanirûpaṇavidhâna, and nipâtanirûpaṇavidhâna, in 280 sûtras. An edition of Kêśirâja's Śabdamaṇidarpaṇa was printed at Mangalore (Basel Mission Press, 1872). His work has 8 sandhis or chapters and 322 sûtras. A short summary of its contents is as follows: — I. Sandhi or euphonic combinations of letters. 1) aksharasañjñâprakaraṇa or the section of the signs used as letters. *a*) the letters of the alphabet; *b*) the vowels in particular; *c*) the consonants in particular. 2) sandhiprakaraṇa or the section of combination of the mentioned letters. *a*) combination of vowels; *b*) combination of consonants. II. Nâma or nominal themes. *a*) liṅgas or declinable bases, *aa*) kṛits or bases formed from verbs by means of suffixes, *bb*) taddhita-bases formed from nouns and verbs by means of certain other suffixes, *cc*) samâsas or compound bases, *dd*) nâmas or ready nouns (distinguished as rûḍha, anvartha and aṅkita; they include the so-called adjectives, pronouns, numerals, and themes from Saṁskṛita, altered or unaltered); *b*) genders; *c*) the seven cases in the singular; *d*) the two numbers; *e*) the augments of the plural; *f*) particularities regarding

II. On the form of the signs that are used as Letters

(aksharar̂upa, aksharasañjñâkâra, aksharasañjñârûpa, varṇasañjñĕ, varṇâṅka, *cf.* §§ 217-241), etc.

10. Kêšava, the author of the Šabdamaṇidarpaṇa, remarks on the origin of articulate sound: — "By the wish of the individual soul, by means of suitable (vital) air, at the root of the navel, like a trumpet, the substance of sound (šabdadravya) originates which is white (svêta, dhavala); its result is (articulate, aksharâtmaka) sound (šabda)"; and: — "The body is the musical instrument, the tongue is the plectrum, the individual soul is the performer; on account of the operation of his mind (articulate) sound (šabda) originates which is of a white colour (dhavalavarṇa) and has the form of letters (akshararûpa)."

Inarticulate (anaksharâtmaka) sounds, as thunder from the clouds or the roar of the sea, have no representations in grammatical alphabets.

11. There is a distinct letter for each sound, and therefore every word is pronounced exactly as it is spelt; thus the ear is a sufficient guide

---

declension; *g*) uses of the cases; *h*) remarks on number, gender, construction, etc.; *i*) declension of pronouns; *j*) change of gender; *k*) change of letters. III. Samâsa or composition of words, compound bases. 1) augment, elision, and substitution. 2) the six classes of Saṁskṛita compounds. 3) the compounds called kriyâsamâsa, gamakasamâsa, and vîpsâsamâsa. IV. Taddhita-bases formed from nouns and verbs by means of certain suffixes. V. Âkhyâta or verbs and their conjugation. VI. Dhâtu or verbal roots (or themes). VII. Tadbhava (Apabhraṁša) or words corrupted from the Saṁskṛita language. VIII. Avyaya or adverbs, etc.

Besides the Karṇâṭakabhâshâbhûshaṇa there is another grammar of the Old Canarese language in Saṁskṛita sûtras, etc., the Karṇâṭakašabdânušâsana, written by the Jaina Bhaṭṭâkalaṅka, dated A. D. 1604. It was edited by B. Lewis Rice, C. I. E., M. R. A. S., Director of Archæological Researches in Mysore, late Director of Public Instruction in Mysore and Coorg (Bangalore, Mysore Government Central Press, 1890). According to its learned editor it treats, in the order given, of the alphabet; avyayas; sandhi; nipâtas; gender; tadbhavas; case affixes; compound words; uses of personal pronouns; uses of the singular and plural numbers and numerals; taddhitas; verbs and verbal affixes.

The first grammar of the Canarese language which appeared in English, was compiled by John McKerrell Esq., M. C. S., who dedicated his work to the *King* (George IV), Madras, November the 16th, 1820. He calls it "A Grammar of the Carnâṭaka Language". In his Preface he states: "In the course of my labours I have derived much information from a very scarce and accurate treatise upon the ancient dialect, which was compiled, about seven centuries ago, by an Indian author named *Césheva*, and by him termed ಶಬ್ದಮಣಿದರ್ಪಣಂ, or 'The mirror of verbal gems'..... I feel myself under considerable obligations to..... Edward Richard Sullivan, Esq., of the Civil Service, for his kindness in procuring for me from His Highness the Rajah of Mysoor, the work of Céshava" McKerrell's work has 211 pages.

in orthography. After the exact sounds of the letters have been once acquired, every word can be pronounced with perfect accuracy.

The accent falls on the first syllable.

12. The name of a pure, true letter (šuddhâkshara) is **akshara, akkara,** or **varṇa.**

13. Each letter has its own form (âkâra) and sound (šabda); by the first it becomes visible (čâkshusha), by the other audible (šrâvaṇa).

14. Kannaḍa is written from left to right.

15. The **Alphabet** (called aksharamâlĕ, akkaramâlĕ in the old and later dialect and also ônâma in the later one), as an instruction for the youthful (bâlašikshĕ), consists of 57 letters, in which case the so-called Saṁskṛita and Prâkṛita **kshaḷa** (the vedic letter ಳ್ಹ of certain schools) is also counted, though its form and sound are the same as that of the so-called Kannaḍa **kuḷa.**

Of the 57 letters forty-eight (in various forms) are notorious on the "sea-girdled" earth, *i. e.* throughout India, and the order in which they are read (pâṭhakrama) is as follows: — ಅ ಆ ಇ ಈ ಉ ಊ ಋ ೠ ಌ ೡ ಏ ಐ ಓ ಔ ಕ್ ಖ್ ಗ್ ಘ್ ಙ್ ಚ್ ಛ್ ಜ್ ಝ್ ಞ್ ಟ್ ಠ್ ಡ್ ಢ್ ಣ್ ತ್ ಥ್ ದ್ ಧ್ ನ್ ಪ್ ಫ್ ಬ್ ಭ್ ಮ್ ಯ್ ರ್ ಲ್ ವ್ ಶ್ ಷ್ ಸ್ ಹ್ ಳ್. The letter ಳ್ in this list is called kshaḷa in order to distinguish it from the true Kannaḍa kuḷa. In Saṁskṛita the kshaḷa is a substitute for the letter ಡ್ (*cf.* § 230); in Kannaḍa it is a substitute for the Saṁskṛita letter ಲ್ (see § 31).

The other nine letters are: — ಎ ಒ ಱ್ ಳ್ ೞ್ ಂ ಃ ೱ ೲ. Of these ಎ ಒ ಱ್ ಳ್ ೞ್ are peculiar to the Kannaḍa country (dêšîya), and this letter ಳ್ is the kuḷa.

The four letters ಂ ಃ ೱ ೲ, together with the above-mentioned forty-eight, form the Saṁskṛita alphabet of 52 letters.

In true Kannaḍa (aččagannaḍa) there are 47 indigenous letters (šuddhagĕ), *viz.* **(the vowels)** ಅ ಆ ಇ ಈ ಉ ಊ ಎ ಏ ಐ ಒ ಓ ಔ; (the **anusvâra**) ಂ; (and the **consonants**) ಕ್ ಖ್ ಗ್ ಘ್ ಙ್ ಚ್ ಛ್ ಜ್ ಝ್ ಞ್ ಟ್ ಠ್ ಡ್ ಢ್ ಣ್ ತ್ ಥ್ ದ್ ಧ್ ನ್ ಪ್ ಫ್ ಬ್ ಭ್ ಮ್ ಯ್ ರ್ ಱ್ ಲ್ ವ್ ಸ್ ಹ್ ಳ್ ೞ್.

16. The consonants (§ 25) that in the preceding paragraph appear with the top-mark ್ (ಕ್, ಖ್, etc.) which indicates that they are to be pronounced without any vowel after them (asvaravidhi, vyañjanavidhi),

are commonly printed with the sign ◡ (a sort of crest, nowadays called talĕkaṭṭu) added to the top (ತ, ಗ, etc.), in order to point out that the short Kannaḍa vowel a (ಅ) is to be sounded after them.

In the case of ten consonants (ಖ ಙ ಜ ಝ ಞ ಣ ಬ ಲ ಱ ಳ), however, the crest does not appear on the top, as it is so to say incorporated with them. It is supposed that the sign ◡ is a secondary form of the Kannaḍa vowel a (ಅ, *see* § 24); but why are certain other vowels (u, û, ಉ, ಊ, etc.) united with crested consonants? See § 37.

17. The following is **a tabular view of the forms of the 57 letters** of **the Alphabet** as they are written and printed nowadays (*cf.* § 6), the consonants bearing the sign ◡ (the talĕkaṭṭu, see § 16). Their sounds are expressed in Roman characters with the aid of some diacritical marks, and illustrated, as well as possible, by English letters (the illustrations being given according to English authors of Kannaḍa, Tĕlugu, Tamiḻ and Malayâḷa grammars): —

ಅ. a. This letter has the sound of the English initial a in 'about', 'around', or of the English final a in 'era', 'Sophia', 'Victoria', or of the English u in 'gun', 'cup'. (There is no letter in Kannaḍa to represent the sound of the English a in such words as 'pan', 'can', 'sat', 'hat').

ಆ (ಅಾ). â. This letter has the sound of the English a in 'half', 'father', or of the English final a in 'papa'.

ಇ. i. This letter has the sound of the English i in 'pin', 'in', 'gig', 'folio'.

ಈ. î. This letter has the sound of the English i in 'machine', 'ravine', 'pique', or of the English ee in 'eel', 'feel'.

ಉ. u. This letter has the sound of the English u in 'full', 'pull', 'put', or of the English oo in 'book'.

ಊ. û. This letter has the sound of the English u in 'rule', 'crude', or of the English oo in 'fool', 'root', 'shoot'.

ಋ. ṛi. The sound of this letter can only be learned from the mouth of an efficient teacher. (Rustics pronounce it like the English ri in 'rich', or also like the English roo in 'rook'.)

ೠ (ಋೂ). ṛî. The sound of this letter is that of lengthened ಋ.

ಌ. lṛi. The sound of this letter can only be learned from an educated native. (Rustics pronounce it like the English loo in 'look'.)

ೡ. lṛî. The sound of this letter is that of lengthened ಌ. (The letter is a mere invention of grammarians.)

ಎ. ĕ. This letter has the sound of the English e in 'end', 'leg', 'beg', 'peg'.

ಏ. ê. This letter has the sound of the English a in 'ache', 'fate', 'late'.

ಐ. **ai.** This letter has the sound of the English **ai** in 'aislo', of the English **ei** in 'hoight', or of the English word 'eye'.

ಒ. **ŏ.** This letter has the sound of the English **o** in 'police', 'polite', 'romance', 'produced', 'potential' 'located'. (There is no sound in Kannaḍa to represent the sound of the English **o** in such words as 'on', 'hot', 'got', 'object'. Uneducated Canarese people use to pronounce this English **o**, ಆ (â) making, *e. g.* lost ಲಾಸ್ಟು, hot ಹಾಟು, top ಟಾಪು.)

ಓ. **ô.** This letter has the sound of the English **o** in 'gold', 'old', 'sold', 'ode'.

ಔ. **au.** This letter has the sound of the English **ou** in 'ounce', 'out', 'mount'.

ಂ. **ṁ.** This letter, when it is final, has the sound of the English **m** in 'botom', 'bartram'. (When in the middle of a word it is followed by a consonant, its sound depends on the character of that consonant, as in the words ಶಂಕ, ಶಂಖ, ಸಂಗ, ಸಂಘ, ಅಂಚ, ಉಂಛ, ಅಂಜನ, ಕಂಟಕ, ಕಂಠ, ಖಂಡ, ಚುಂಢಿ, ಬಂಣ, ಕಂತಿ, ಕಂಥೆ, ಕಂದ, ಕಂಧ, ಸಂನ, ಸಂಪದ್, ಸಂಬಲ, ಸಂಮತ, ಸಂಯಮ, ಸಂರಕ್ಷಣ, ಸಂಲಾಪ, ಸಂವತ್, ಸಂಶಯ, ದಂಷ್ಟ್ರ, ಸಂಸಾರ, ಸಂಹತಿ; *cf.* §§ 34. 39. 40.)

ಃ. **ḥ.** This aspirate has the sound of the English initial h in 'hat', 'head', or 'hiss', the aspiration proceeding directly from the chest. (Rustics, in reciting the alphabet, use to pronounce it **aḥa** the **a** having the sound of the Kannaḍa letter ಅ.)

ೱ. **ḫ.** This aspirate is used only before the letters ಕ (ka) and ಖ (kha), and then pronounced like the letter ಃ (ḥ).

ೲ (ೲ). **ṟh.** This aspirate is used only before the letters ಪ (pa) and ಫ (pha), and then has a sound somewhat similar to that of the letter ಃ (ḥ). (In Saṁskṛita it is often represented by the letter ಷ್, sh.)

ಕ. **ka.** This letter has the sound of the English initial **k** pronounced with the Kannaḍa letter ಅ (a) after it.

ಖ. **kha.** This letter has the sound of the preceding one, but aspirated, the aspiration proceeding directly from the chest.

ಗ. **ga.** This letter has the sound of the English initial **g** in 'gold', 'good', pronounced with the Kannaḍa letter ಅ (a) after it.

ಘ. **gha.** This letter has the sound of the preceding one but aspirated.

ಙ. **ṅa.** This letter has the sound of the English letter **n** before **g** in 'king', 'ring', 'long', 'song' with the Kannaḍa letter ಅ (a) after it.

ಚ. **ča.** This letter has a sound similar to that of the English **ch** in 'charity', 'charm', 'chase', 'child', 'church', pronounced with the Kannaḍa letter ಅ (a) after it.

ಛ (ಛ). **čha.** This letter has the sound of the preceding one but aspirated.

ಜ. **ja.** This letter has a sound similar to that of the English **j** in 'judge', 'join', 'jar', 'jackal', pronounced with the Kannaḍa ಅ (a) after it.

ಝ. jha. This letter has the sound of the preceding one but aspirated.

ಞ. ña. This letter has a sound which is something like that of the English ni in 'opinion', 'onion' (the n being nasalised), pronounced with the Kannaḍa letter ಅ (a) after it.

ಟ. ṭa. This letter has the sound of an English letter t that is formed by curling back the tongue, forcibly striking the under part of it against the roof of the mouth, and pronouncing the Kannaḍa letter ಅ (a) after it. (It differs essentially from the true English t, for which there is no letter in Kannaḍa. Natives, however, use to represent the English t by ಟ.)

ಠ. ṭha. This letter has the sound of the preceding one but aspirated.

ಡ. ḍa. This letter has the sound of an English letter d that is formed by curling back the tongue, forcibly striking the under part of it against the roof of the mouth, and pronouncing the Kannaḍa letter ಅ (a) after it. (It differs essentially from the true English d, for which there is no letter in Kannaḍa. Natives, however, use to represent the English d by ಡ. See also sub-letter ಠ, ra.)

ಢ. ḍha. This letter has the sound of the preceding one but aspirated.

ಣ. ṇa. This letter has the sound of an English n that is formed by curling back the tongue, forcibly striking the under part of it against the roof of the mouth, and pronouncing the Kannaḍa letter ಅ (a) after it. (No English letter answers to it; see under letter ನ, na.)

ತ. ta. This letter has the sound of an English letter t that is formed by bringing the tip of the tongue against the very edge of the upper front teeth, and pronouncing the Kannaḍa letter ಅ (a) after it. (There is no corresponding letter in English; see under letter ಟ, ṭa.)

ಥ. tha. This letter has the sound of the preceding one but aspirated.

ದ. da. This letter has the sound of the English letter d that is formed by bringing the point of the tongue against the very edge of the upper front teeth, and pronouncing the Kannaḍa letter ಅ (a) after it. (There is no English letter which answers to it; see under letter ಡ, ḍa.)

ಧ. dha. This letter has the sound of the preceding one but aspirated.

ನ. na. This letter has the sound of the English letter n that is formed by placing the tip of the tongue against the very edge of the upper front teeth, and pronouncing the Kannaḍa letter ಅ (a) after it. (There is no corresponding English letter. Natives, however, use to represent the English n by ಣ, ṇa.)

ಪ. pa. The sound of this letter answers to that of the English initial p pronounced with the Kannaḍa letter ಅ (a) after it.

ಫ. pha. This letter has the sound of the preceding one but aspirated.

ಬ. **ba.** The sound of this letter is the same as that of the English initial b pronounced with the Kannaḍa letter ಅ (a) after it.

ಭ (ಫ಼. ಬ಼). **bha.** This letter has the sound of the preceding one but aspirated.

ಮ. **ma.** The sound of this letter is like that of the English **m** pronounced with the Kannaḍa letter ಅ (a) after it.

ಯ. **ya.** The sound of this letter is the same as that of the English initial **y** in 'yard', 'young', 'you', 'yonder' pronounced with the Kannaḍa letter ಅ (a) after it.

ರ. **ra.** The sound of this letter nowadays has an indefinite character like the Saṁskṛita r (which Canarese people occasionally mistook for their letter ಱ); in ancient times it was formed by placing the point of the tongue against the very edge of the upper front teeth, producing a trilled, delicate sound of the English letter **r**, and pronouncing the Kannaḍa letter ಅ (a) after it. At present the sound may be said to resemble that of the English initial letter r in 'ring', 'risk' with the Kannaḍa letter ಅ (a) sounded after it. (English people often used to represent the Kannaḍa letter ಡ, by their r, as in Canara, Coorg, Dharwar = ಕನ್ನಡ, ಕೊಡಗು, ಧಾರವಾಡ.)

ಱ. **ṟa.** This letter has the sound of a very harsh English letter r pronounced with the Kannaḍa letter ಅ (a) after it. Nowadays it is not unfrequently represented by a double Kannaḍa ರ, *i. e.* ರ್ರ (see § 39).

ಲ. **la.** This letter has the sound of the English letter **l** that is formed by bringing the tip of the tongue against the very edge of the upper front teeth, and pronouncing the Kannaḍa letter ಅ (a) after it. (The Kannaḍa letter ಲ has neither the same sound as the Saṁskṛita ಲ nor that of the English l. The Saṁskṛita letter ಳ is very often represented in Kannaḍa by the so-called Kshaḷa; see §§ 15. 31.)

ವ. **va.** The sound of this letter resembles that of the initial letter ವ in 'wife', 'woman', the Kannaḍa letter ಅ (a) being pronounced after it.

ಶ. **śa.** The sound of this sibilant letter cannot be represented by any English letter; it is to be learnt by hearing an efficient teacher pronounce it. (Englishmen, however, have represented it by the s in 'sure' and 'session'.)

ಷ. **sha.** This letter has the sound of an English initial **sh** (as in 'shoe', 'shun') that is formed by placing the tongue near the roof of the mouth, and pronouncing the Kannaḍa letter ಅ (a) after it.

ಸ. **sa.** This letter has nearly the sound of the English initial letter **s** in 'sat', 'sin', 'so', the Kannaḍa letter ಅ (a) being pronounced after it.

ಹ (ಹ). ha. The sound of this letter is something like that of the English initial letter h in 'horse', 'husband', 'hoop', the Kannaḍa letter ಅ (a) being pronounced after it.

ಳ. ḷa. This letter has the sound of the English letter l that is formed by curling back the tongue, forcibly striking the under part of it against the roof of the mouth, and pronouncing the Kannaḍa letter ಅ (a) after it. (It represents two letters, *viz.* the kshaḷa and kuḷa; see §§ 15. 31.)

ಳ. ḷa. See the preceding letter.

ೞ. ḻa. The sound of this letter l is formed by curling back the tongue and pronouncing the English letter r, *e.g.* in the word 'farm', in a rather liquid manner (Dr. Caldwell) with the Kannaḍa letter ಅ (a) after it.

18. Of the above-mentioned 57 letters sixteen are vowels (svara).

19. The initial forms of the vowels are as follows:—

Kannaḍa		Present Tamiḻ		Present Malayâḷa		Dêvanâgarî	
ಅ	a	அ	a	അ	a	अ	a
ಆ	â	ஆ	â	ആ	â	आ	â
ಇ	i	இ	i	ഇ	i	इ	i
ಈ	î	ஈ	î	ഈ	î	ई	î
ಉ	u	உ	u	ഉ	u	उ	u
ಊ	û	ஊ	û	ഊ	û	ऊ	û
ಋ	ṛi	—		ഋ	ṛi	ऋ	ṛi
ೠ	ṛî	—		ൠ	ṛî	ॠ	ṛî
ಌ	lṛi	—		ഌ	lṛi	ऌ	lṛi
ೡ	lṛî	—		ൡ	lṛ	ॡ	lṛî
ಎ	ĕ	எ	ĕ	എ	ĕ	—	
ಏ	ê	ஏ	ê	ഏ	ê	ए	ê
ಐ	ai	ஐ	ai	ഐ	ai	ऐ	ai
ಒ	ŏ	ஒ	ŏ	ഒ	ŏ	—	
ಓ	ô	ஓ	ô	ഓ	ô	ओ	ô
ಔ	au	ஔ	au	ഔ	au	औ	au

20. Seven of the vowels are **short** (hrasva), *viz.* ಅ, ಇ, ಉ, ಋ, ಌ, ಎ, ಒ; and nine are **long** (dîrgha), *viz.* ಆ, ಈ, ಊ, ೠ, ೡ, ಏ, ಐ, ಓ, ಔ.

Short vowels have one measure (mâtrĕ or prosodical instant) or are êkamâtraka; long vowels have two or are ubhayamâtra or dvimâtra. A consonant (ಕ್, ಖ್, etc.) is said to last half the time of a short vowel.

Occasionally a vowel is lengthened to three measures in pronunciation or becomes trimâtraka or protracted (pluta). See §§ 140, *a* and 215, 6, letter *k*.

In prosody a short or light vowel is called laghu, and a long or heavy vowel guru. Such a long vowel is long either by nature, or by position (*i.e.* being followed by a double or compound consonant; see § 38).

21. Vowels are again divided into ten **monophthongs** (samânâkshara):— ಅ ಆ, ಇ ಈ, ಉ ಊ, ಋ ೠ, ಌ ೡ, of which each pair is of the same class of letters (savarṇa) whether its letters be read in regular order (anulôma) as ಆ ಅ, ಇ ಈ, etc., or out of the usual order (vilôma) as ಆ ಅ, ಈ ಇ, etc., or as ಅ ಅ, ಆ ಆ, ಇ ಇ, ಈ ಈ, etc.; and (in Saṁskṛita) into four diphthongs (sandhyakshara): ಏ ಐ ಓ ಔ. The vowels ಏ ಐ ಓ ಔ, however, are no real diphthongs in true Kannaḍa; in this language the radical forms of ಐ are ಅಯ್, ಅಯಿ, and those of ಔ are ಅವ್ರು, ಅವ (see § 217).

Also the vowels ಎ ಏ ಒ ಓ are such as belong to one class, or are savarṇa.

22. By the way it is observed that, in so far as Samskṛita is concerned, the true Saṁskṛita vowels (§ 15), except a and â, *i. e.* 12 of them, are subject to the peculiar changes called guṇa and vṛiddhi (see § 217). Though the terms are mentioned by the grammarians Nâgavarma and Kêśava, their use is not stated. The same is to be said with regard to the term nâmi which they mention, and which in Saṁskṛita denotes all the true Saṁskṛita vowels, except a and â, as changing a dental into a cerebral. The Upêndravajra verse cited by Nâgavarma and Kêśava (probably from a Purâṇa), in which the terms guṇa, vṛiddhi and nâmi occur together, is in praise of the 12 Âdityas.

23. In pure Kannaḍa the vowels ಋ ೠ ಌ ೡ are not indigenous; they are found only in words borrowed from Saṁskṛita.

24. If the initial vowels mentioned in § 18, follow a consonant, each of them uses a secondary form that is always compounded with one of the consonant forms (see §§ 36. 37).

The initial forms of the vowels together with their secondary ones appear in the subjoined table:—

Initial forms	Secondary forms
ಅ	(See § 16)
ಆ	ಾ
ಇ	ಿ
ಈ	ೀ
ಉ	ು
ಊ	ೂ
ಋ	ೃ (ೃ)
ೠ	ೄ
ಌ	ೢ
ೡ	ೣ
ಎ	ೆ
ಏ	ೇ
ಐ	ೈ
ಒ	ೊ (ೊ)
ಓ	ೋ (ೋ)
ಔ	ೌ

Remark.

The form of the long initial vowel ಏ, and the sign ೕ (see § 37) nowadays regularly used to mark a long secondary vowel form, are somewhat uncommon in Kannaḍa manuscripts of the 18th century. Initial ಏ is written ಯೆ (euphonical ಯ್ + ಎ) in them, but to be pronounced ಏ, *e. g.* ಯೆಕಾನ್ತ = ಏಕಾನ್ತ; only occasionally we find ಎೕ for ಏ. Initial ಈ appears as ಯೀ in them (euphonical ಯ್ + ಿ + the sign ೕ). The existence of the sign ೕ at the time that the manuscripts were written, becomes further certain *e. g.* by the form of the verb ಮೀಱು (mîṟu), to transgress, *etc.* repeatedly used in them, a form which is used also nowadays (ಮೀಱು for ಮೀಱು). ಈ, ಏ and ಓ however in vowelled compound-syllables (see § 36) are generally not marked as long by the sign ೕ in the manuscripts, *e. g.* ತೊಱುವ stands for ತೋಱುವ, ದೆವತೆ for ದೇವತೆ, ನಿತಿ for ನೀತಿ, ಪಿಠ for ಪೀಠ, ಪ್ರಿತಿ for ಪ್ರೀತಿ, ಬೆಟ for ಬೇಟ, ಹೊಗು for ಹೋಗು, *etc. Cf.* also § 41.

25. The consonants (vyañjana, bilakkara) of the alphabet are thirty-seven in number. Bearing the sign which indicates that they are sounded with the short vowel ಅ (a) after them (see §§ 16. 17. 36), they are the following: —

ಕ ಖ ಗ ಘ ಙ
ಚ ಛ ಜ ಝ ಞ
ಟ ಠ ಡ ಢ ಣ
ತ ಥ ದ ಧ ನ
ಪ ಫ ಬ ಭ ಮ
ಯ ರ ಱ ಲ ವ ಶ ಷ ಸ ಹ (ಳ, the kshaḷa) ಳ ೞ

The same in present Tamiḻ :—

க ங
ச ஜ ஞ
ட ண
த ந ன
ப ம
ய ர ற ல வ ஷ ஸ ஹ ள ழ

The same in present Malayâḷa: —

ക ഖ ഗ ഘ ങ
ച ഛ ജ ഝ ഞ
ട ഠ ഡ ഢ ണ
ത ഥ ദ ധ ന
പ ഫ ബ ഭ മ
യ ര റ ല വ ശ ഷ സ ഹ ള ഴ

The same in Dêvanâgarî, as far as they exist therein: —

क ख ग घ ङ
च छ ज झ ञ
ट ठ ड ढ ण
त थ द ध न
प फ ब भ म
य र ल व श ष स ह ळ

26. It will be observed that 25 consonants are horizontally arranged in sets having five letters (pañčaka) in each. Such a set is called a series or **class** (varga), and a letter belonging to it a **classified letter** (vargâkshara, vargîyâkshara).

27. The five classes (pañčavarga), each from their first letter, are distinguished as kavarga (ಕವರ್ಗ), čavarga (ಚವರ್ಗ), ṭavarga (ಟವರ್ಗ), tavarga (ತವರ್ಗ), and pavarga (ಪವರ್ಗ).

The remaining 12 (11) consonants are **unclassified** (avarga, avargîya).

28. The letters of the first perpendicular column (called vargaprathama or vargaprathamâkshara) are hard, those of the second one (called vargadvitîya or vargadvitîyâkshara) hard and aspirated, those of the third one (called vargatṛitîya or vargatṛitîyâkshara) soft, those of the fourth one (called vargačaturtha or vargačaturthâkshara) soft and aspirated; those of the fifth one (called vargapañčama or vargapañčamâkshara) are the particular nasals (anunâsika) of each class, which are used as such when, in combination, they precede a consonant of their respective class; see § 220, and *cf.* §§ 39. 40.

The difference between hard and soft consonants is not expressed in words in the old Kannaḍa grammars. By the way it may be remarked that modern Kannaḍa grammars call hard ones karkaŝavarṇa or parushavarṇa, and soft ones mṛidûvarṇa or saraḷavarṇa.

29. Kannaḍa grammars distinguish between consonants with slight breathing or weak aspiration (alpaprâṇa), *viz.* ಕ್ ಚ್ ಟ್ ತ್ ಪ್ ಗ್ ಜ್ ಡ್ ದ್ ಬ್, and consonants with hard breathing or strong aspiration (mahâprâṇa), *viz.* ಖ್ ಛ್ ಠ್ ಥ್ ಫ್ ಘ್ ಝ್ ಢ್ ಧ್ ಭ್; but practically alpaprâṇa is an **unaspirated** letter, and mahâprâṇa an **aspirated** one (see § 218). Nowadays some call an aspirated letter gaṇḍakkara (male letter) and an unaspirated one hĕṇṇakkara (female letter).

30. In pure Kannaḍa the consonants ಶ and ಷ do not occur; they are found only in words borrowed from Saṁskṛita.

31. The letter ೞ in paranthesis in § 25 is called kshaḷa (§ 15) by the grammarian Kêŝava. It is, in fact, identical as to form and pronunciation with the kuḷa, as Kêŝava terms it, or the true Kannaḍa ೞ (§ 15); and it is, therefore, unnecessary to make it a separate letter. It is often used by Kannaḍa people as a substitute for Saṁskṛita ಌ, the sound of which in the Saṁskṛita language apparently bears a dubious character for them, one that is neither their ಲ nor their ಳ; this ಳ is Kēšava's kshaḷa. *Cf.* §§ 227. 228.

32. The consonants ಱ and ೞ have become, at the present period, obsolete (although they are of intrinsic value for Dravidian philology). Already the grammarian Kēšava had to state in which words the ೞ was used according to previous authors (see § 233). In bygone times ೞ was occasionally changed into ರ್ (see § 236), occasionally into ಳ್, occasionally into the letter which it preceded; in the mediaeval dialect and nowadays it is as a rule represented by ಳ್ (see § 228), is exceptionally converted into a following letter (as ಬಿದ್ದು, for ಬಿೞ್ದು or ಬಿದುಱ್) or disappears also altogether (as ಬದುಕು, for ಬೞ್ದುಂಕು or ಬದುಱ್ಕು)[1]. ಱ, in the modern dialect, appears as ರ್ or as a double ರ್ (ರ್ರ). ೞ and ಱ are up to this time in common use among the Tamiḻ, Malayâḷa and Baḍaga people; ಱ occurs still in the present Tĕlugu (see § 3). The letter ಱ appears still in Kannaḍa literature of the 18th century.

In the course of this work the ancient original forms have been retained.

---

[1] Some historical dates regarding the ೞ್ (based chiefly on the very valuable inscriptions or šâsanas published by Dr. Fleet in the *Indian Antiquary* are the following (*cf.* § 109).

1. From about 600 to about 900 A. D. the ೞ್ was throughout in use; in that period we find *e. g.* ಗೞ್ದೆ, a paddy field, ಏೞ್ನೂರ್ವರ್, seven hundred persons, ಎೞ್ಪತ್ತು, seventy, ಅೞಿ, to destroy, ಇೞ್, to be (could this be the ಇೞು, to stay, to be, of the Dictionary?), ಕೞ್ಚು, to wash.

We meet also with the strange forms ಕೆೞಗೆ (for ಕೆಳಗೆ), below, ೞೋಕ (for ಲೋಕ), the world, ಗೆೞ್ದು (for ಗೆಲ್ದು), having gained or overcome.

2. From about 900 till about 1200 A. D. a transition of the ೞ್ into ಱ and ಳ್, is observed, as we find ಅಳ್ತು, pleasure, and ಪದಿನೇಳು (for ಪದಿನೇೞು), seventeen, ಪೇಳ್ (for ಪೇೞ್), to speak, in a šâsana of 929 A. D.; ಕೞ್ಚು and ಕಳ್ಚು, to wash, in one of 951 A. D.; ಅದ್ದಿಱದುದು (for ಅೞ್ದಿದುದು), it immersed, ಬಿದ್ದಱ (for ಬಿೞ್ದು), having fallen, ಏಳು (for ಏೞು), seven, ಏಳ್ಗೆ (for ಏೞ್ಗೆ), increase, ಗದ್ದೆ (for ಗೞ್ದೆ), a paddy field, in one of 1019 A. D.; ಬಳಿ (for ಬೞಿ), place, etc., ಗಳೆ (for ಗೞೆ), staff, and ಗೞ್ದೆ a paddy field, in one of 1048 A. D.; ನೆಗೞ್ and ನೆಗಳ್, to shine, ಬಳಿ (for ಬೞಿ), place, etc., ಕಳ್ಚು (for ಕೞ್ಚು), to wash, in one of 1075 A. D.; ಇೞ್, to be, and ಏಳು (for ಏೞು), seven, ಅಳಿ (for ಅೞಿ), to destroy, ಉಂಬಳಿ (for ಉಂಬೞಿ), a rent-free grant, in one of 1076 A. D.; ನೆಗೞ್, to shine, ಪೞ್ದಲ್, N. of a place, ಇೞ್, to be, and ಪದ್ದಱಲ್ (for ಪೞ್ದಲ್), ಪೊಗಳ್ (for ಪೊಗೞ್), to praise, ನೆಗತ್ತೆ (for ನೆಗೞ್ತೆ), fame, ಪಾಳ್ (for ಪಾೞ್), waste, ಅಳಿ (for ಅೞಿ), to ruin, in one of 1084 A. D.; ಮಾಳ್ಕೆ (for ಮಾೞ್ಕೆ), may he make, ಅಗಳ್ (for ಅಗೞ್), to dig, ಅಗಳ್ (for ಅಗೞ್), a ditch, ಪೊಗಳ್ (for ಪೊಗೞ್), to praise, ನೆಗಳ್ (for ನೆಗೞ್), to shine, ನೆಗಳ್ತೆ (for ನೆಗೞ್ತೆ), fame, ಪೊಗಳ್ತೆ (for ಪೊಗೞ್ತೆ), praise, ನೆಗತ್ತೆ (for ನೆಗೞ್ತೆ), fame, in one of 1123 A. D.; ಪಸ್ತುೞ್ವೆ, N. of a place, ಬೞಿ, place, etc., ಪೇೞ್, to speak, ನೋೞ್, to see, ಮಾೞ್, to make, and ಕರ್ಚು (for ಕೞ್ಚು), to wash, ಅಳಿ (for ಅೞಿ), to destroy, ಪೊಗಳ್ತೆ (for ಪೊಗೞ್ತೆ), praise, ನೆಗಳ್ತೆ (for ನೆಗೞ್ತೆ), fame, in one of 1181 A. D.; ಪೊಗಳ್ (for ಪೊಗೞ್), to praise, ನೆಗಳ್ (for ನೆಗೞ್), to shine, ಏಳ್, ಏಳು (for ಏೞ್, ಏೞು), seven, in one of 1183 A. D.; ಇಳಿಗುಂ (for ಇೞಿಗುಂ), he will descend, in one of 1187 A. D. *Cf.* § 228; § 160, 1.

33. The throat (kaṇṭha, kŏral), the palate or roof of the mouth (tâluka, tâlugĕ, galla), the head or skull (śira, mastaka, mûrdhan), the teeth (danta, pal), the lips (ôshṭha, tuṭi), the nose (nâsikĕ), the chest (ura, ĕrdĕ), and the root of the tongue (jihvâmûla, nâligĕya buḍa) are **the eight places (sthâna, tâṇa) or organs of the letters.**

The letters pronounced from the throat are **guttural** (kaṇṭhya); they are ಅ ಆ ಕ ಖ ಗ ಘ ಙ ಹ (ೱ). Those formed by means of the palate are **palatal** (tâlavya); they are ಇ ಏ ಐ ಚ ಛ ಜ ಝ ಞ ಯ ಶ; (ಏ and ಐ have been called also kaṇṭhya-tâlavya). Those coming from the head are **cerebral** (mûrdhanya); they are ಋ ೠ ಟ ಠ ಡ ಢ ಣ ರ ಱ ಷ ೞ; (sometimes these letters are called lingual). The letters formed by the aid of the teeth are **dental** (dantya); they are ಌ ೡ ತ ಥ ದ ಧ ನ ಲ ಸ ಳ. Those pronounced with the lips are **labial** (ôshṭhya); they are ಉ ಊ ಓ ಔ ಪ ಫ ಬ ಭ ಮ ವ ೲ; (sometimes ಓ ಔ are called kaṇṭhôshṭhya, and ವ has been called dantôshṭhya). The letters uttered through the nose are **nasal** (anunâsika, nâsikya); they are ಙ ಞ ಣ ಮ ಂ; (ಂ has been called also kaṇṭhya-nâsikya). The letters ಯ ಲ ವ (called semi-vowels) are **not nasal** (anunâsika, niranunâsika) **and,** under certain circumstances, **nasal** (anunâsika, see § 219); there is no mark in Kannaḍa to show the difference. The letter pronounced in the chest or **pectoral** letter (urasya) is ಃ. That uttered from the root of the tongue or the **tongue-root sibilant** (jihvâmûlîya) is ೱ.

When two consonants are produced in the same place or by the same organs, they are called êkasthâni (see §§ 238. 239).

34. The labial sibilant (or aspirate) ೲ is called **upadhmânîya,** *i. e.* a letter that is to be pronounced with a forcing out of breath; it only occurs before the consonants ಪ and ಫ. The nasal ಂ is called **anusvâra** or after-sound, as it always belongs to a preceding vowel; from its form that in Saṁskṛita is a dot, it is called bindu, and from its form in Kannaḍa where it is represented by a circle or cipher, it is called **śûnya** or **sŏnnĕ;** it is a substitute for a nasal letter, and when it does not stand at the end of a word (where it is pronounced like the English **m,** *cf.* § 215, 8), its sound depends on the following consonant (see under letter ಂ in § 17; §§ 39. 40). The sibilant (or aspirate) ಃ is called **visarga** or **visarjanîya** either from its being pronounced with a full emission of breath or from its liability to be rejected; if followed by another letter, it is frequently changed and occasionally dropped. The tongue-root sibilant (or aspirate) **jivhâmûliya** X can only stạnd before the consonants ಕ and ಖ.

35. The šûnya (sŏnnĕ or bindu) ಂ and visarga ಃ are **semi-vowels** (svarâṅga) and **semi-consonants** (vyañjanâṅga). They and the upadhmânîya oo and jihvâmûlîya X are so to say semi-letters, and as such form the 4 so-called **yôgavâha letters,** *i. e.* letters always appearing in connection with, or depending on, **others.**

Visarga, upadhmânîya and jihvâmûlîya do not occur in pure Kannaḍa, but are used only in words borrowed from Saṁskṛita.

36. As has been stated in §§ 16 and 25 the crested consonants (including ಖ ಙ ಜ ಞ ಟ ಣ ಬ ಲ ಱ ೞ) are always sounded with the short vowel ಅ (a) after them. When any of the secondary forms of the vowels given in § 24 is united with the consonants to form **vowelled compound-syllables,** the consonants partly retain the shape they have when the vowel ಅ (a) is sounded after them, but mostly lose their talĕkaṭṭu or crest. Here follows a tabular view of them:—

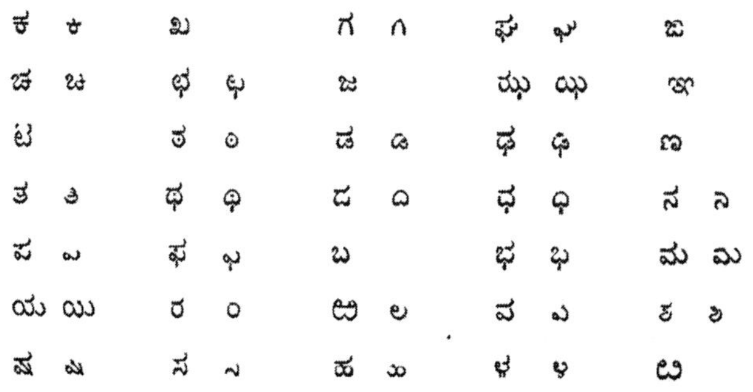

When the union has taken place, the vowels, like the short ಅ (a), are pronounced after the consonants to which they are attached.

37. In the Southern Mahratta country the vowelled compound-syllables are called kâ-guṇitâkshara, *i. e.* syllables that are multiplied or increased in number after the manner of **kâ,** this being the first of them; and a series of them is called baḷḷi. In writing and reading the series of the kâ-guṇita-syllables it is customary to place the consonant after which the short ಅ (a) is sounded, at the beginning of each series.

A table exhibiting the union of vowels with consonants is given on the following two pages:—

ಕ ka	ಕಾ kâ	ಕಿ ki	ಕೀ kî	ಕು ku	ಕೂ kû	ಕೃ kṛi	ಕೄ kṛî
ಖ kha	ಖಾ khâ	ಖಿ khi	ಖೀ khî	ಖು khu	ಖೂ khû	ಖೃ khṛi	ಖೄ khṛî
ಗ ga	ಗಾ gâ	ಗಿ gi	ಗೀ gî	ಗು gu	ಗೂ gû	ಗೃ gṛi	ಗೄ gṛî
ಘ gha	ಘಾ ghâ	ಘಿ ghi	ಘೀ ghî	ಘು ghu	ಘೂ ghû	ಘೃ ghṛi	ಘೄ ghṛî
ಙ ṅa	ಙಾ ṅâ	ಙಿ ṅi	ಙೀ ṅî	ಙು ṅu	ಙೂ ṅû	ಙೃ ṅṛi	ಙೄ ṅṛî
ಚ ča	ಚಾ čâ	ಚಿ či	ಚೀ čî	ಚು ču	ಚೂ čû	ಚೃ čṛi	ಚೄ čṛî
ಛ čha	ಛಾ čhâ	ಛಿ čhi	ಛೀ čhî	ಛು čhu	ಛೂ čhû	ಛೃ čhṛi	ಛೄ čhṛî
ಜ ja	ಜಾ jâ	ಜಿ ji	ಜೀ jî	ಜು ju	ಜೂ jû	ಜೃ jṛi	ಜೄ jṛî
ಝ jha	ಝಾ jhâ	ಝಿ jhi	ಝೀ jhî	ಝು jhu	ಝೂ jhû	ಝೃ jhṛi	ಝೄ jhṛî
ಞ ńa	ಞಾ ńâ	ಞಿ ńi	ಞೀ ńî	ಞು ńu	ಞೂ ńû	ಞೃ ńṛi	ಞೄ ńṛî
ಟ ṭa	ಟಾ ṭâ	ಟಿ ṭi	ಟೀ ṭî	ಟು ṭu	ಟೂ ṭû	ಟೃ ṭṛi	ಟೄ ṭṛî
ಠ ṭha	ಠಾ ṭhâ	ಠಿ ṭhi	ಠೀ ṭhî	ಠು ṭhu	ಠೂ ṭhû	ಠೃ ṭhṛi	ಠೄ ṭhṛî
ಡ ḍa	ಡಾ ḍâ	ಡಿ ḍi	ಡೀ ḍî	ಡು ḍu	ಡೂ ḍû	ಡೃ ḍṛi	ಡೄ ḍṛî
ಢ ḍha	ಢಾ ḍhâ	ಢಿ ḍhi	ಢೀ ḍhî	ಢು ḍhu	ಢೂ ḍhû	ಢೃ ḍhṛi	ಢೄ ḍhṛî
ಣ ṇa	ಣಾ ṇâ	ಣಿ ṇi	ಣೀ ṇî	ಣು ṇu	ಣೂ ṇû	ಣೃ ṇṛi	ಣೄ ṇṛî
ತ ta	ತಾ tâ	ತಿ ti	ತೀ tî	ತು tu	ತೂ tû	ತೃ tṛi	ತೄ tṛî
ಥ tha	ಥಾ thâ	ಥಿ thi	ಥೀ thî	ಥು thu	ಥೂ thû	ಥೃ thṛi	ಥೄ thṛî
ದ da	ದಾ dâ	ದಿ di	ದೀ dî	ದು du	ದೂ dû	ದೃ dṛi	ದೄ dṛî
ಧ dha	ಧಾ dhâ	ಧಿ dhi	ಧೀ dhî	ಧು dhu	ಧೂ dhû	ಧೃ dhṛi	ಧೄ dhṛî
ನ na	ನಾ nâ	ನಿ ni	ನೀ nî	ನು nu	ನೂ nû	ನೃ nṛi	ನೄ nṛî
ಪ pa	ಪಾ pâ	ಪಿ pi	ಪೀ pî	ಪು pu	ಪೂ pû	ಪೃ pṛi	ಪೄ pṛî
ಫ pha	ಫಾ phâ	ಫಿ phi	ಫೀ phî	ಫು phu	ಫೂ phû	ಫೃ phṛi	ಫೄ phṛî
ಬ ba	ಬಾ bâ	ಬಿ bi	ಬೀ bî	ಬು bu	ಬೂ bû	ಬೃ bṛi	ಬೄ bṛî
ಭ bha	ಭಾ bhâ	ಭಿ bhi	ಭೀ bhî	ಭು bhu	ಭೂ bhû	ಭೃ bhṛi	ಭೄ bhṛî
ಮ ma	ಮಾ mâ	ಮಿ mi	ಮೀ mî	ಮು mu	ಮೂ mû	ಮೃ mṛi	ಮೄ mṛî
ಯ ya	ಯಾ yâ	ಯಿ yi	ಯೀ yî	ಯು yu	ಯೂ yû	ಯೃ yṛi	ಯೄ yṛî
ರ ra	ರಾ râ	ರಿ ri	ರೀ rî	ರು ru	ರೂ rû	ರೃ rṛi	ರೄ rṛî
ಱ ṟa	ಱಾ ṟâ	ಱಿ ṟi	ಱೀ ṟî	ಱು ṟu	ಱೂ ṟû	ಱೃ ṟṛi	ಱೄ ṟṛî
ಲ la	ಲಾ lâ	ಲಿ li	ಲೀ lî	ಲು lu	ಲೂ lû	ಲೃ lṛi	ಲೄ lṛî
ವ va	ವಾ vâ	ವಿ vi	ವೀ vî	ವು vu	ವೂ vû	ವೃ vṛi	ವೄ vṛî
ಶ ša	ಶಾ šâ	ಶಿ ši	ಶೀ šî	ಶು šu	ಶೂ šû	ಶೃ šṛi	ಶೄ šṛî
ಷ sha	ಷಾ shâ	ಷಿ shi	ಷೀ shî	ಷು shu	ಷೂ shû	ಷೃ shṛi	ಷೄ shṛî
ಸ sa	ಸಾ sâ	ಸಿ si	ಸೀ sî	ಸು su	ಸೂ sû	ಸೃ sṛi	ಸೄ sṛî
ಹ ha	ಹಾ hâ	ಹಿ hi	ಹೀ hî	ಹು hu	ಹೂ hû	ಹೃ hṛi	ಹೄ hṛî
ಳ ḷa	ಳಾ ḷâ	ಳಿ ḷi	ಳೀ ḷî	ಳು ḷu	ಳೂ ḷû	ಳೃ ḷṛi	ಳೄ ḷṛî
ೞ ḻa	ೞಾ ḻâ	ೞಿ ḻi	ೞೀ ḻî	ೞು ḻu	ೞೂ ḻû	ೞೃ ḻṛi	ೞೄ ḻṛî

ಕೢ klṛi ಕೣ klṛî ಕೆ kĕ ಕೇ kê ಕೈ kai ಕೊ kŏ ಕೋ kô ಕೌ kau
ಖೢ khlṛi ಖೣ khlṛî ಖೆ khĕ ಖೇ khê ಖೈ khai ಖೊ khŏ ಖೋ khô ಖೌ khau
ಗೢ glṛi ಗೣ glṛî ಗೆ gĕ ಗೇ gê ಗೈ gai ಗೊ gŏ ಗೋ gô ಗೌ gau
ಘೢ ghlṛi ಘೣ ghlṛî ಘೆ ghĕ ಘೇ ghê ಘೈ ghai ಘೊ ghŏ ಘೋ ghô ಘೌ ghau
ಙೢ ṅlṛi ಙೣ ṅlṛî ಙೆ ṅĕ ಙೇ ṅê ಙೈ ṅai ಙೊ ṅŏ ಙೋ ṅô ಙೌ ṅau
ಚೢ člṛi ಚೣ člṛî ಚೆ čĕ ಚೇ čê ಚೈ čai ಚೊ čŏ ಚೋ čô ಚೌ čau
ಛೢ čhlṛi ಛೣ čhlṛî ಛೆ čhĕ ಛೇ čhê ಛೈ čhai ಛೊ čhŏ ಛೋ čhô ಛೌ čhau
ಜೢ jlṛi ಜೣ jlṛî ಜೆ jĕ ಜೇ jê ಜೈ jai ಜೊ jŏ ಜೋ jô ಜೌ jau
ಝೢ jhlṛi ಝೣ jhlṛî ಝೆ jhĕ ಝೇ jhê ಝೈ jhai ಝೊ jhŏ ಝೋ jhô ಝೌ jhau
ಞೢ ńlṛi ಞೣ ńlṛî ಞೆ ńĕ ಞೇ ńê ಞೈ ńai ಞೊ ńŏ ಞೋ ńô ಞೌ ńau
ಟೢ ṭlṛi ಟೣ ṭlṛî ಟೆ ṭĕ ಟೇ ṭê ಟೈ ṭai ಟೊ ṭŏ ಟೋ ṭô ಟೌ ṭau
ಠೢ ṭhlṛi ಠೣ ṭhlṛî ಠೆ ṭhĕ ಠೇ ṭhê ಠೈ ṭhai ಠೊ ṭhŏ ಠೋ ṭhô ಠೌ ṭhau
ಡೢ ḍlṛi ಡೣ ḍlṛî ಡೆ ḍĕ ಡೇ ḍê ಡೈ ḍai ಡೊ ḍŏ ಡೋ ḍô ಡೌ ḍau
ಢೢ ḍhlṛi ಢೣ ḍhlṛî ಢೆ ḍhĕ ಢೇ ḍhê ಢೈ ḍhai ಢೊ ḍhŏ ಢೋ ḍhô ಢೌ ḍhau
ಣೢ ṇlṛi ಣೣ ṇlṛî ಣೆ ṇĕ ಣೇ ṇê ಣೈ ṇai ಣೊ ṇŏ ಣೋ ṇô ಣೌ ṇau
ತೢ tlṛi ತೣ tlṛî ತೆ tĕ ತೇ tê ತೈ tai ತೊ tŏ ತೋ tô ತೌ tau
ಥೢ thlṛi ಥೣ thlṛî ಥೆ thĕ ಥೇ thê ಥೈ thai ಥೊ thŏ ಥೋ thô ಥೌ thau
ದೢ dlṛi ದೣ dlṛî ದೆ dĕ ದೇ dê ದೈ dai ದೊ dŏ ದೋ dô ದೌ dau
ಧೢ dhlṛi ಧೣ dhlṛî ಧೆ dhĕ ಧೇ dhê ಧೈ dhai ಧೊ dhŏ ಧೋ dhô ಧೌ dhau
ನೢ nlṛi ನೣ nlṛî ನೆ nĕ ನೇ nê ನೈ nai ನೊ nŏ ನೋ nô ನೌ nau
ಪೢ plṛi ಪೣ plṛî ಪೆ pĕ ಪೇ pê ಪೈ pai ಪೊ pŏ ಪೋ pô ಪೌ pau
ಫೢ phlṛi ಫೣ phlṛî ಫೆ phĕ ಫೇ phê ಫೈ phai ಫೊ phŏ ಫೋ phô ಫೌ phau
ಬೢ blṛi ಬೣ blṛî ಬೆ bĕ ಬೇ bê ಬೈ bai. ಬೊ bŏ ಬೋ bô ಬೌ bau
ಭೢ bhlṛi ಭೣ bhlṛî ಭೆ bhĕ ಭೇ bhê ಭೈ bhai ಭೊ bhŏ ಭೋ bhô ಭೌ bhau
ಮೢ mlṛi ಮೣ mlṛî ಮೆ mĕ ಮೇ mê ಮೈ mai ಮೊ mŏ ಮೋ mô ಮೌ mau
ಯೢ ylṛi ಯೣ ylṛî ಯೆ yĕ ಯೇ yê ಯೈ yai ಯೊ yŏ ಯೋ yô ಯೌ yau
ರೢ rlṛi ರೣ rlṛî ರೆ rĕ ರೇ rê ರೈ rai ರೊ rŏ ರೋ rô ರೌ rau
ಱೢ ṟlṛi ಱೣ ṟlṛî ಱೆ ṟĕ ಱೇ ṟê ಱೈ ṟai ಱೊ ṟŏ ಱೋ ṟô ಱೌ ṟau
ಲೢ llṛi ಲೣ llṛî ಲೆ lĕ ಲೇ lê ಲೈ lai ಲೊ lŏ ಲೋ lô ಲೌ lau
ವೢ vlṛi ವೣ vlṛî ವೆ vĕ ವೇ vê ವೈ vai ವೊ vŏ ವೋ vô ವೌ vau
ಶೢ šlṛi ಶೣ šlṛî ಶೆ šĕ ಶೇ šê ಶೈ šai ಶೊ šŏ ಶೋ šô ಶೌ šau
ಷೢ shlṛi ಷೣ shlṛî ಷೆ shĕ ಷೇ shê ಷೈ shai ಷೊ shŏ ಷೋ shô ಷೌ shau
ಸೢ slṛi ಸೣ slṛî ಸೆ sĕ ಸೇ sê ಸೈ sai ಸೊ sŏ ಸೋ sô ಸೌ sau
ಹೢ hlṛi ಹೣ hlṛî ಹೆ hĕ ಹೇ hê ಹೈ hai ಹೊ hŏ ಹೋ hô ಹೌ hau
ಳೢ ḷlṛi ಳೣ ḷlṛî ಳೆ ḷĕ ಳೇ ḷê ಳೈ ḷai ಳೊ ḷŏ ಳೋ ḷô ಳೌ ḷau
ೞೢ ḻlṛi ೞೣ ḻlṛî ೞೆ ḻĕ ೞೇ ḻê ೞೈ ḻai ೞೊ ḻŏ ೞೋ ḻô ೞೌ ḻau

At school the mark ಿ used for the vowel ಇ and the mark ೆ used for the vowel ಎ are called ಗುಡಸು, ಗುಡಿಸು or ಗುಡುಸು, the mark ು used for ಉ is called ಕೊಮ್ಬು, the mark ಾ that descends from a consonant as the sign for the long vowels ಆ and ಈ (as in ಕಾ, etc., and in ಬಾ and ಯಾ) is called ಇಲಿ, and the name for the mark ೕ is ದೀರ್ಘ. ಕೊ ಕೋ ಗೊ ಗೋ etc. may be written also ಕಾ ಕಾೕ ಗಾ ಗಾೕ etc.

38. If a consonant is followed immediately by another consonant or by more than one, the two or more consonants are written in one group (saṁyôga), and thus **double or compound consonants** (dvitvâkshara, ŏttakkara, daḍḍa, daḍḍakkara) are formed (*cf.* §§ 20. 240).

When two consonants are compounded, the latter consonant is written underneath the former one or is subscribed; when three consonants are united in one group, the third is written underneath the second one; and when four are compounded, the fourth is subscribed to the third. In true Kannaḍa a combination of more than two consonants does not occur.

In reading, the upper consonant that is crested (including ಖ ಙ ಜ ಞ ಟ ಣ ಬ ಲ ಱ ೞ, § 36) is pronounced like a half consonant, and the short vowel ಅ (a) is sounded with the lower consonant; if three consonants are compounded, the second one too is pronounced like a half consonant, and the short vowel ಅ (a) is sounded with the lowest one; and so on.

39. The subscribed consonants, as a rule, have the uncrested shape that is used for the union of consonants with vowels (§ 36); but in the case of seven letters the shape is different, namely ತ appearing as ್ತ, ನ as ್ನ, ಮ as ್ಮ, ಯ as ್ಯ, ರ as ್ರ, ಲ as ್ಲ, and ಷ as ್ಷ. ರ often takes also the form of ೯, in which case it is written after the following consonant, but sounded before it; the same is to be said concerning ಱ.

The following are some examples of double and compound consonants:—

ಕ್ಕ kka, ಕ್ಖ kkha, ಕ್ಚ kča, ಕ್ಛ kčha, ಕ್ತ kta, ಕ್ತ್ಯ ktya, ಕ್ತ್ರ ktra, ಕ್ತ್ರ್ಯ ktrya, ಕ್ತ್ವ ktva, ಕ್ನ kna, ಕ್ನ್ಯ knya, ಕ್ಮ kma, ಕ್ಯ kya, ಕ್ರ kra, ಕ್ರ್ಯ krya, ಕ್ಲ kla, ಕ್ವ kva, ಕ್ವ್ಯ kvya, ಕ್ಷ ksha, ಕ್ಷ್ಮ kshma, ಕ್ಷ್ಯ kshya, ಕ್ಷ್ವ kshva; ಖ್ಯ khya; ಗ್ಗ gga; ಘ್ನ ghna; ಙ್ಕ ṅka; ಚ್ಚ čča; ಜ್ಜ jja, ಜ್ಞ jña; ಞ್ಚ ńča; ಟ್ಟ ṭṭa, ಟ್ಣ ṭṇa; ಣ್ಡ ṇḍa, ಣ್ಡ್ರ್ಯ ṇḍrya; ತ್ಕ tka, ತ್ತ tta, ತ್ಥ ttha, ತ್ನ tna; ನ್ನ nna; ಪ್ಪ ppa; ಬ್ಬ bba; ಭ್ಯ bhya; ಮ್ಪ mpa, ಮ್ಬ mba, ಮ್ಮ mma, ಮ್ರ mra, ಮ್ಲ mla; ಯ್ಯ yya; ರ್ಕ rka, ರ್ತ rta; ಱ್ಛ ṟčha; ಲ್ಪ lpa; ವ್ವ vva; ಶ್ಚ šča; ಷ್ಟ shṭa, ಷ್ಟ್ರ್ಯ shṭrya; ಸ್ಕ ska, ಸ್ತ sta, ಸ್ತ್ರ stra; ಸ್ಥ stha, ಸ್ಮ sma; ಹ್ನ hna.

Instead of ರ್ಕ, ರ್ತ, ರ್ಥ, etc., ರ್ಭು, ರ್ಮು, etc., the forms ಕ೯, ತ೯, ಥ೯, etc., ಭು೯, ಮು೯, etc. may be used. The upper nasals (for the sake of convenience in writing) may take the form of the circlet called sŏnnĕ (§ 34), so that ಙ್ಕ, ಞ್ಚ, ಣ್ಟ, ಣ್ಡ, ನ್ತ, ನ್ಥ, ನ್ದ, ನ್ಧ, ನ್ನ, ಮ್ಪ, ಮ್ಬ, ಮ್ಮ may appear as ಂಕ, ಂಚ, ಂಟ, ಂಡ, ಂತ, ಂಥ, ಂದ, ಂಧ, ಂನ, ಂಪ, ಂಬ, ಂಮ, *e. g.* in ಅಂಕ, ಪಂಚ, ಬಂಟ, ಗಂಡ, ಪಂತ, ಅಂಥ, ಬಂದ, ಅಂಧ, ನಿಂನ, ಕಂಪಣ, ಎಂಬ, ಅಂಮ. See § 220.

40. If one of the secondary forms of the vowels (§ 24) is to form a part of a compound consonant, it is attached to the upper consonant. In reading, it is sounded after the lower consonant, or if more than two are compounded, after the lowest one, just as the short vowel ಅ of § 38.

The following instances may be given, in which also the way of attaching the vowels appears in case the sŏnnĕ represents an upper nasal (§ 39):—

ಅಕ್ಕಿ akki; ಅಪ್ಪಿ appi; ಅಪ್ಪು appu; ಅಮ್ಮೆ or ಅಂಮೆ ammĕ; ಇನ್ದು or ಇಂದು indu; ಇಮ್ಬು or ಇಂಬು imbu; ಇರ್ಮೆ or ಇಮೆ೯ irmĕ; ಒಟ್ಟಿ ŏṭṭi; ಒಣ್ಟೆ or ಒಂಟೆ ŏṇṭĕ; ಕಙ್ಕಿ or ಕಂಕಿ kaṅki; ಕಞ್ಚಿ or ಕಂಚಿ kañči; ಕುಕ್ಷಿ kukshi; ಕುನ್ತಿ or ಕುಂತಿ kunti; ಕೋಳ್ದು kôḷdu; ತನ್ದೆ or ತಂದೆ tandĕ; ಬಣ್ಡಿ or ಬಂಡಿ baṇḍi; ಸ್ತ್ರೀ strî; ಸ್ತೋತ್ರ stôtra; ಸ್ಥಾನ sthâna; ಹೊನ್ನು or ಹೊಂನು, hŏnnu. See § 220.

41. Many Kannaḍa people pronounce and write the initial vowels ಇ ಈ ಉ ಊ ಎ ಏ ಒ ಓ ungrammatically, prefixing ಯ್ to ಇ ಈ ಎ ಏ, and ವ್ to ಉ ಊ ಒ ಓ, thus: ಯಿ ಯೀ ಯೆ ಯೇ; ವು ವೂ ವೊ ವೋ. Regarding initial ಎ they use also, instead of ಯೆ, ಯ *e. g.* ಯತ್ತು, ಯಮ್ಮೆ for ಎತ್ತು, ಎಮ್ಮೆ. Initial ಏ may appear as ಯಾ, *e. g.* ಯಾಲಕ್ಕಿ (=ಏಲಕ್ಕಿ), ಯಾಕೆ (=ಏಕೆ, see § 125; § 265), also when attached to an initial consonant, *e. g.* ದ್ಯಾವ (=ದೇವ), ಮ್ಯಾಲೆ (=ಮೇಲೆ). Initial ಒ is vulgarly changed into ವ, *e. g.* ವಲ್ಲನು for ಒಲ್ಲನು, and ವ into ಒ, *e. g.* ಒನ್ದಿಸು for ವನ್ದಿಸು. *Cf.* also remark under § 24.

42. With the exception of jihvâmûlîya, upadhmânîya, anusvâra and visarga, all **vowels and consonants** (the latter compounded with the talĕkaṭṭu or with any secondary form of the vowels) **are named in four ways**: 1) by simply using their sounds, *e. g.* ಅ, ಆ, etc., ಕ, ಕಾ, etc.; 2) by adding ಕಾರ, 'making', to their sounds, *e. g.* ಅಕಾರ, ಆಕಾರ, ಇಕಾರ, ಕಕಾರ, ಗಕಾರ, ಗೆಕಾರ, ತುಕಾರ, ತೆಕಾರ, ದುಕಾರ, ದೆಕಾರ, ಪಿಕಾರ, ಪುಕಾರ, ಮೆಕಾರ, ಔಕಾರ, ಲಿಕಾರ, ಸುಕಾರ; 3) by adding ತ್ವ to their sounds, *e. g.* ಅತ್ವ, ಆತ್ವ, ಇತ್ವ, ಕತ್ವ, ತೆತ್ವ, ರತ್ವ, ಲಿತ್ವ, ಸುತ್ವ; and 4) by adding ವರ್ಣ, 'letter', to their sounds, *e. g.* ಅವರ್ಣ, ಇವರ್ಣ, ಉವರ್ಣ, ಋವರ್ಣ, ಎವರ್ಣ.

The letter ರ (ರ್, ೯) is generally called ರೇಫ or ರೇಫೆ, also when the ೯ is a substitute of ಱ್.

43. The system of punctuation in Kannaḍa manuscripts is the same as the Saṁskṛita one, *viz.* in prose at the end of a sentence the sign । is used, and at the end of a longer sentence, the sign ॥ ; in poetry the sign । is placed at the end of a half verse, and at the end of a verse, the sign ॥ . (In certain prose writings, as in Dêvarasa's Sânandačaritra, the sign । is put not only at the end of a sentence, but also after single words or a number of words.)

44. The Kannaḍa figures used to express numbers (aṅkĕ, lĕkka, saṅkhyĕ) or the **numerical figures** are:—

೧	೨	೩	೪	೫	೬	೭	೮	೯	೦
1	2	3	4	5	6	7	8	9	0

They have been adopted from the Saṁskṛita, wherein they first appear in the 5th century A. D. The Arabs who borrowed them from the Hindus, introduced them into Europe, where they were called Arabic figures.

III. On roots or verbal themes

45. Before introducing the chapter on declinable bases (IV.) the author thinks it desirable to treat of the so-called verbal roots (dhâtu), as very many nominal bases are derived from them (§ 100).

46. "A (verbal) root (dhâtu)", the grammarian Kêšava says "is the basis of a verb's meaning (kriyârthamûla) and has no suffixes (pratyaya, vibhakti)", or, in other words, a root is the crude form of a verb.

47. Ancient Kannaḍa grammars based on literary writings, distinguish between **monosyllabic** (êkâksharadhâtu) and **polysyllabic roots** (anêkâksharadhâtu). These roots have been collected by Kêšava in his 'root-recital' (dhâtupâṭha) or list of roots.

In this list there appear as **monosyllabic** roots *e. g.* ಈ, ಏಾ, ಇರ್, ಗೆಯ್, ಕೊಯ್, ಕೊಲ್, ಕೊಳ್, ತಿನ್, ಕೇಳ್, ತಾಳ್, ಬೇಳ್, ಕೂನ್, ಸೀನ್, ಸೋಲ್; as **dissyllabic** ones *e. g.* ಅರಿ, ಪರಿ, ಕುಸಿ, ಮುರಿ, ಎರೆ, ನಡೆ, ಒಕ್ಕು, ಕೊಂಕು, ಕಿಟ್ಟು, ಕುಟ್ಟು, ಕಿಡು, ಕುಡು, ಕೆತ್ತು, ಕಮೞ್, ಪಮೞ್, ಕೊಮೞ್, ತೀಮೞ್, ನುಣ್ಚು, ಕೊಬೞ್, ಪಬೞ್, ಅಳುರ್, ತಳಿರ್, ಕುಳಿರ್, ಆಗು, ತೂಗು, ಪೋಗು, ನೋಡು, ಬೇಡು; as **trisyllabic** ones *e. g.* ಅಡಕು, ಅಡಂಗು, ಒಱಗು, ತಿರುಪು, ತಿಳಿಪು, ತಡವು, ಗರವು,

ಕಿನಿಸು, ಬಳಸು, ಅಲರ್ಚು, ನಿಮಿರ್ಚು, ಸುಗುಳ್ಚು, ಪಳಂಚು, ನಮ್ಬಿಸು, ಬಿಡಿಸು, ಕೊಣ್ಡಾಡು, ಬೇಸಾಡು, ಊಳಿಡು; as quadrisyllabic ones *e. g.* ಕೊಕ್ಕರಿಸು, ಬೆಚ್ಚಳಿಸು, ಒಡಮ್ಬಡು, ಕೊಱಿಚಾಡು; and as **quinquesyllabic** ones *e. g.* ಕದಕದಿಸು, ಕಳವಳಿಸು, ಗುಡುಗುಡಿಸು, ತಡವರಿಸು, ಉಬ್ಬಸಮ್ಬಡು, ಹೊಲಬುಗಿಡು, ಒಲವರಂಗೊಳ್.

48. It is a striking peculiarity of modern Kannaḍa that it apparently has no roots ending in a consonant without a vowel, so that *e. g.* the above mentioned roots ಇರ್, ಗೆಯ್, ಕೊಯ್, ಕೊಲ್, ಕೊಳ್, ತಿನ್, ಕೇಳ್, ತಾಳ್, ಕೂನ್, ಸೀನ್, ಸೋಲ್, ಅಳುರ್, ತಳಿರ್ ಕುಳಿರ್, by the addition of the vowel ಉ as a help to enunciation, have the forms of ಇರು, ಗೆಯ್ಯು, ಕೊಯ್ಯು, ಕೊಲ್ಲು, ಕೊಳ್ಳು, ತಿನ್ನು, ಕೇಳು, ತಾಳು, ಕೂನು, ಸೀನು, ಸೋಲು, ಅಳುರು, ತಳಿರು, ಕುಳಿರು in it (*cf.* § 54; § 61, remark; § 166; the present-future participle in § 181, and also the imperative ಕೊಯಿ for ಕೊಯ್ etc. in § 205, 2 and 3); further that such monosyllabic roots as ಈ, ಸಾ and ಬೇ, appear as ಈಯು, ಸಾಯು and ಬೇಯು in it (§§ 162. 163).

But we have, in the modern language, *e. g.* the past participles ಅನ್ದು (of ಅನ್ನು), ತಿನ್ದು (of ತಿನ್ನು), ಕೊಯ್ದು (of ಕೊಯ್ಯು), ಗೆಯ್ದು (of ಗೆಯ್ಯು, § 155), ತನ್ದು (of ತರು), ಬನ್ದು (of ಬರು), ನಿನ್ತು (of ನಿಲ್ಲು), ಅಸತ್ತು (of ಅಸಱು), ಬೇಸತ್ತು (of ಬೇಸಱು, § 160), ತೆತ್ತು (of ತೆಱು, § 161), ಬೆನ್ದು (of ಬೇಯು, § 162), ಉಣ್ಡು (of ಉಣ್ಣು), ಕಣ್ಡು (of ಕಾಣು), ಕೊಣ್ಡು (of ಕೊಳ್ಳು, § 164), which forms prove the existence of roots with originally final consonants in it too (ಅನ್, ತಿನ್, ಕೊಯ್, etc.).

49. When carefully examining Kêšava's list of roots, one finds that the English term 'root', in many instances, does not properly express the meaning of the term 'dhâtu'. The verbs ನಮ್ಬಿಸು and ಬಿಡಿಸು in § 47, for instance, are formed by means of the suffix ಇಸು, from ನಮ್ಬು and ಬಿಡು, ಅಲರ್ಚು and ನಿಮಿರ್ಚು, by means of the suffix ಚು, from ಅಲರ್ and ನಿಮಿರ್ (see § 149 seq.); ಕೊಣ್ಡಾಡು is composed of ಕೊಣ್ಡು and ಆಡು, ಒಡಮ್ಬಡು of ಒಡವ್ and ಪಡು, ಹೊಲಬುಗಿಡು of ಹೊಲಬು and ಕಿಡು, ಒಲವರಂಗೊಳ್ of ಒಲವರಂ ಕೊಳ್, and so on. Such verbs are, according to European notions, no roots. Kêšava's term 'dhâtu' may here and there denote a root *i. e.* the primary element of a verb or primitive verbal theme, but often stands also for a secondary verbal theme and a compound verb. His definition of dhâtu, therefore, is that it is the crude form of any verb which is not always a real root.

50. In further discussing the subject of dhâtus let us use the general term of '**verbal themes**' for them.

51. There are a good many **monosyllabic verbal themes** in ancient Kannada the vowels of which are short, *e. g.* ಇರ್, ಉಣ್, ಉಳ್, ಎನ್, ಒಲ್, ಕೆಯ್ (or ಗೆಯ್), ಗೆಲ್, ನಿಲ್, ಬಯ್, ಬಿಲ್, ಮುಳ್; other monosyllabic verbal themes have long vowels, *e. g.* ಆಳ್, ಕಾಯ್, ಕೇಳ್, ತೀರ್, ಪಾಯ್, ಪಾರ್, ಪೇರ್, ಪೂೞ್, ಪೇಲ್, ಪೇೞ್, ಪೋರ್, ಪೋಲ್.

52. Some monosyllabic verbal themes appear with short and long vowels, *e. g.* ಅೞ್ and ಆೞ್, ಅಱ್ and ಆಱ್, ಇೞ್ and ಈೞ್, ಎೞ್ and ಏೞ್, ಕಿೞ್ and ಕೀೞ್, ತರ್ and ತಾರ್, ತಳ್ and ತಾಳ್, ಬರ್ and ಬಾರ್, ಬೞ್ and ಬಾೞ್, ಬಿೞ್ and ಬೀೞ್, ಸಲ್ and ಸಾಲ್. It may be supposed that the short vowels are original, and the long verbal themes secondary. (About ತಾರ್ and ಬಾರ್ see § 210.)

53. Because some monosyllabic verbal themes with a long vowel change, in the past participle, their long vowel into a short one, as ಈ makes its past participle ಇತ್ತು (§ 163), ಕಾಣ್ ಕಣ್ಡು (§ 164), ನೋ ನೊನ್ದು, ಬೇ ಬೆನ್ದು, ಮೀ ಮಿನ್ದು (§ 162), and ಸಾಯ್ ಸತ್ತು (§ 163), it is reasonable to think that their primitive vowel has been short (regarding ಕಾಣ್ *cf.* ಕಣ್, ಕಣಿಸು, ಕಣ್ಬು in the Dictionary). A similar lengthening of a vowel is also seen in the verbal themes ತೋ and ನಾನ್, as they have also the form of ತುಯ್ and ನನೆ. (See also the remark under § 59.) In such cases too we may consider the long themes to be secondary.

54. In § 48 it has been indicated that nowadays there are no monosyllabic verbal themes in modern Kannaḍa, the vowel ಉ, as a help to enunciation, being added to make them dissyllabic. A similar tendency to lengthen an originally monosyllabic verbal theme with a short vowel by the addition of the euphonic vowel ಇ is observed already in ancient literary works in which we find *e. g.* ಒಲಿ for ಒಲ್, ಕಲಿ for ಕಲ್, ಗೆಯಿ for ಗೆಯ್, ಗೆಲಿ for ಗೆಲ್, ಬಲಿ for ಬಲ್, ಬಿಲಿ for ಬಿಲ್, ಮೆಲಿ for ಮೆಲ್, and also ಕದಿ for ಕಳ್.

Concerning the lengthening of an originally monosyllabic verbal theme with a short vowel by adding the vowel ಉ it may be remarked that this practice too, now and then, took place already in ancient literature; thus, for instance, ಕೊಲ್ and ಕೊಲು, ಗೆಲ್, and ಗೆಲು, ಮೆಲ್ and ಮೆಲು were used therein.

Also monosyllabic themes with a long vowel were in ancient literature occasionally made dissyllabic by the addition of ಉ, as *e. g.* ಕೇೞ್ was written ಕೇೞು, ನೇಲ್ ನೇಲು, and ಸೋಲ್ ಸೋಲು (*cf.* § 166).

55. There are several seemingly dissyllabic verbal themes, with a short vowel in the first syllable, that end in ಡು, as ಅಡು, ಇಡು, ಉಡು, ನಡು, ಪಡು, ಬಿಡು, ಸುಡು. Were these originally monosyllabic, the final ಉ being merely euphonic or a help to enunciation? No doubt, for their past participles ಅಟ್ಟು, ಇಟ್ಟು, ಉಟ್ಟು, ನಟ್ಟು, ಪಟ್ಟು, ಬಿಟ್ಟು and ಸುಟ್ಟು are formed by adding the formative syllable ತು (which by assimilation becomes ಟು, § 164, 4) immediately to ಅಡ್, ಇಡ್, ಉಡ್, etc., which thus represent the primitive themes.

56. A small number of seemingly dissyllabic verbal themes having a short vowel in the first syllable and ending in ಱು, represents itself in ಉಱು, (ಎಱು), ಕಿಱು, ಗಿಱು, (ಜಿಱು), ತಱು, ತಿಱು, ಪೆಱು and ಪೊಱು. Like the ಉ of the themes ಅಡು, ಇಡು, etc. in § 55 that of ಉಱು, etc. too is a euphonic addition, as their past participles are ಉತ್ತು, ಕಿತ್ತು, ಗೆತ್ತು (instead of ಗಿತ್ತು), ತತ್ತು, ತೆತ್ತು (instead ತಿತ್ತು), ಪೆತ್ತು and ಪೊತ್ತು, the formative syllable ತು having been attached directly to the radical ಱ್, which by assimilation was changed into ತ್ (§ 160, 4; § 161). They are, therefore, originally monosyllables, and as such primitive themes. (For the past participle of ಎಱು and ಜಿಱು we have as yet no grammatical or other references.)

57. Also the verbal themes ಇಸು, ಪಸು and ಬಿಸು are not radically dissyllabic, as their past participles are ಎಚ್ಚು (for ಇಚ್ಚು), ಪಚ್ಚು, and ಬೆಚ್ಚು (for ಬಿಚ್ಚು), the formative syllable ತು having been added immediately to the radical ಸ್ with the proper euphonic change of consonants (§ 164, 9. 10).

58. We have now to examine another class of verbal themes that (like those in §§ 55. 56. 57) are customarily pronounced as if they were dissyllables. They have their first syllable long, and their second syllable is ಡು. Three of them are ನೋಡು, ಬೇಡು and ಮಾಡು, and the final ಉ of these is simply euphonic, as they appear also as ನೋೞ್, ಬೇೞ್ and ಮಾೞ್ (§ 183, 4). They are, therefore, true monosyllables and as such primitive themes. (According to the Šabdânušâsana, sûtra 85, there are also ಮೂೞ್ಗಿಂ of ಮೂಡು, ಕೊೞ್ಗಿಂ of ಕೊಡು, sûtra 514 ಸೂೞ್ಪು of ಸೂಡು, and sûtra 545 ಅೞ್ಕೆ of ಅಡು, ಮಾೞ್ಕೆ of ಮಾಡು.) *Cf.* § 234.

Others are ಆಡು, ಊಡು, ಓಡು, ಕಾಡು, ಕೂಡು, ಪಾಡು, etc. Although no direct monosyllabic form of them exists to show the merely euphonic character of their final ಉ (but see the Šabdânušâsana's ಆಱ್ಕುಳಿ in § 58), they apparently are monosyllables, because their verbal nouns (bhâvavačanas) ಆಟ, ಊಟ, ಓಟ, ಕಾಟ, ಕೂಟ and ಪಾಟ are formed exactly like ನೋಟ of ನೋಡು, ಬೇಟ of ಬೇಡು, and ಮಾಟ of ಮಾಡು. *Cf.* § 242.

59. A further number of verbal themes similar to those mentioned in § 58 are the following:—ಆೞು, ಊೞು, ಏೞು, ಕಾೞು, ಕೀೞು, ಕೇೞು, ತಾೞು, ತೀಱು, ತೂೞು, ತೋೞು, ದೂೞು, ನಾಱು, ಪಾೞು, ಪೀೞು, (ಪೇೞು), ಬೀೞು, ಮಾೞು, ವಿಾೞು, ಸಾೞು, ಸೀಱು. The difference is that they have ೞು as their second syllable. As a rule their past participle shows the formative vowel ಇ (ಊೞಿ, etc. § 166), and the ೞು remains before the formative syllable ವ of the present-future participle relative (ಊೞುವ, etc., § 180, 3); but there are exceptions. Thus we have ಆೞ್ತು (ಆೞ್ + ತು, § 160, 4), ಆೞ್ಪ (ಆೞ್ + ಪ, ಪ = ವ, § 183, 2); ಕಾೞಿ and ಕಾೞ್ದು (ಕಾೞ್ + ದು, § 166); ತೂೞುವ and ತೂೞ್ವ (ತೂೞ್ + ವ, § 180 6); ತೋೞಿ, ತೋೞ್ದು (ತೋೞ್ + ದು, § 166), ತೋೞುವ and ತೋೞ್ಪ (ತೋೞ್ + ಪ, § 183, 2); ನಾಱುವ, ನಾಱ್ವ (ನಾಱ್ + ವ, § 180, 6) and ನಾಱ್ಪ (ನಾಱ್ + ಪ, § 183, 2); ಪಾೞಿ, ಪಾೞ್ದು (ಪಾೞ್ + ದು, § 166), ಪಾೞುವ and ಪಾೞ್ವ (ಪಾೞ್ + ವ, § 180, 6); ಬೀೞಿ, ಬೀೞ್ದು (ಬೀೞ್ + ದು, § 166), ಬೀೞುವ, and ಬೀೞ್ವ (ಬೀೞ್ + ವ, § 180, 6); ಮಾೞುವ, ಮಾೞ್ಪ (ಮಾೞ್ + ಪ, § 183, 2) and ಮಾೞ್ವ (ಮಾೞ್ + ವ, § 180, 6); ವಿಾೞಿ and ವಿಾೞ್ದು (ವಿಾೞ್ + ದು, § 166). At the same time we have the verbal nouns ಏತ (for ಏೞ್ತ of ಏೞು), ತಾೞ್ (for ತಾೞು), ಮಾೞ್ (for ಮಾೞು), and the past participle ನಾತು (for ನಾೞ್ತು of ಸಾೞು, § 159). It must, therefore, be concluded that the final ಉ of the verbs is nothing but a help to enunciation, and that they are originally monosyllabic themes.

It may be remarked that the long vowel of ನಾಱು, ಪಾೞು and ಮಾೞು is short in the nouns ನೞು, ಪೞು and ಮೞು.

60. As has been stated in the preceding paragraphs (51 *seq.*) there are many and various monosyllabic verbal themes in Kannaḍa.

As examples of **dissyllabic verbal themes** may be adduced *e. g.* ಅಗಿ, ಬಿಗಿ, ಒಗೆ, ಬಗೆ, ಇಡಿ, ಕಡಿ, ಕೆಡೆ, ನಡೆ, ಮಣೆ, ಅಣೆ, ಕುದಿ, ಒದೆ, ಹನಿ, ಸನೆ, ಸಮೆ, ಅರಿ, ಕರೆ, ಅಱಿ, ಎಱೆ, ಅಲೆ, ಕವಿ, ಬಸಿ, ತಿಳಿ, ಅಳೆ, ಉೞಿ; but with respect to their finals ಇ and ಎ it is to be said that they are not radical (see § 157; § 165, letter *a*, 3. 4. 5; § 172; § 180, 5; § 243, 16. 18. 21. 23. 34. 25. 26. 27), and in the vulgar dialect some of the themes may become monosyllabic (§ 151, *a*, 4; § 158; § 165, *a*, 7).

61. Another class of verbal themes which in Kêšava's list are introduced as trisyllabic ones with the final syllable ಱು, are really dissyllables, which by several of them can be proved, *e. g.* by ಒಳಱು, ಕೆದಱು, ಗಜಱು, ಪೆಳಱು and ಬೆದಱು, as these occasionally add the participial syllables ದು and ವ (see § 59), with elision of the merely euphonic vowel ಉ, immediately to ಱ್ (ಒಳಱ್ದು, ಕೆದಱ್ದು, etc., ಗಜಱ್ವ, ಬೆದಱ್ವ, § 166; § 180, 6), by ಅಟ್ಕಱು and ಬೆಳ್ಕಱು, as they always attach the participial syllable ತು directly to ಱ್ (ಅಟ್ಕಱ್ತು, ಬೆಳ್ಕಱ್ತು), and by ಎಚ್ಚಱು, ಆಸಱು, ತೆಪ್ಪಱು and ಬೇಸಱು, as they do the same, changing the ಱ್ into ತ್ (ಎಚ್ಚತ್ತು, ಆಸತ್ತು, etc., § 160, 4).

Let it be remarked here that dissyllabic themes with the final consonants ರ್, ಲ್, ೞ್ and ಱ್, such as ಅಡರ್, ಉದಿರ್, ಬೆಮರ್, ಅಟಿಲ್, ತೊಟಿಲ್, ಬಟಿಲ್, ತಗುೞ್, ಅಗುಱ್, are never written as trisyllables in the ancient dialect, although they are occasionally trisyllabic in the mediæval dialect, and always so in the modern one (see §§ 48. 166). An exception is formed by a few ancient themes when they suffix the particle ಇಸು, for which see § 151, letter *a*, 2.

62. Some instances of verbs that are always trisyllabic, are the following:—ಅಡಕು, ಕುಡುಕು, ಬರ್ದುಂಕು, ಮಲಗು, ಕುನುಂಗು, ನಿಮಿರ್ಚು, ಬೆರಂಜು, ಸುರುಙ್ಚು, ಕಲಡು, ಮುದುಡು, ಪರಡು, ಹೊರಡು, ತಣಿವು, ಕಲುಮ್ಬು, ಎಳವು, ಅಟಿಸು, ನಮ್ಬಿಸು; and some instances of such as are always **quadrisyllabic** are: ಓಸರಿಸು, ಗಬ್ಬರಿಸು, ನಿಗುಮ್ಬಿಸು; **quinquesyllabic** verbs are *e. g.* ಕದಕದಿಸು, ಉಬ್ಬಸಮ್ಬಡು.

Two trisyllabic verbs with final ಡು, *viz.* ಬೆಗಡು and ಬಿಸುಡು, appear also as dissyllabic when their forms become ಬೆಗಱ್ and ಬಿಸುಱ್ (see § 183, 4).

More or less of the trisyllabic verbs can be derived from monosyllabic or dissyllabic themes. Of the above-mentioned terms ಬರ್ದುಂಕು is another form of ಬಱ್ದುಂಕು, which has sprung from ಬಱ್, to live. ಅಡಕು has arisen of ಅಡೆ, to fill, etc.; ಕುಡುಕು of ಕುಡು, to beat; ಮಲಗು of ಮಣಿ, to bend or be moved out of a straight or standing position; ಕುನುಂಗು of ಕುನಿ, to bend; ನಿಮಿರ್ಚು of ನಿಮಿರ್, to be stretched; ಬೆರಂಜು of ಬೆರೆ, to join; ಸುರುಙ್ಚು of ಸುರುೞ್, to contract; ಕಲಡು of ಕಲಿ, to be mixed; ಪರಡು of ಪರೆ,

to spread; ತಣಿಪು of ತಣಿ, to grow cool; ಕಲುಮ್ಬು of ಕಲಿ, to be mixed; ಎಳವು of the noun ಎಣೆ, adjustment, compared with the verbal theme ಪೆಣೆ, to be joined, etc.; ಅಱಿಸು of ಅಱಿ, to learn to know; ನಮ್ಬಿಸು of ನಮ್ಬು, to trust (*cf.* § 49).

Of the above-mentioned quadrisyllabic verbs ಓಸರಿಸು comes from the noun ಓಸರ, ನಿಗುಮ್ಬಿಸು from ನಿಗುಮ್ಬು; ಗಬ್ಬರಿಸು may be connected with ಕಪ್ಪು, to dig.

Of the above-mentioned quinquesyllabic verbs ಉಬ್ಬಸಮ್ಬಡು is composed of ಉಬ್ಬಸಂ and ಪಡು (*cf.* § 49); regarding ಕದಕದಿಸು see § 211, remark 2.

63. We have seen that the vowels ಇ (§ 54) and ಉ (§§ 48. 54-59. 61) at the end of verbal themes are often simply euphonic, also ಐ and ಎ when they seemingly belong to them (§ 60).

64. Kêšava says that there are no Kannaḍa verbs which end in aspirated consonants (mahâprâṇâkshara), the nasals ಙ್ and ಞ್, the consonants ಶ್, ಷ್ and ಹ್, and the double consonant ಕ್ಷ್. With regard to ಹ್ it is to be observed that his statement was true only for his own time, as in a later period many verbal themes with final ಹ್ (ಹು) were in use, this letter often taking the place of ಪ್ (ಪು); see *e. g.* ಅಱಿಹು, ಇಱಿಹು, ಉಱುಹು, ಕಳುಹು, ಕೊಡಹು, ತಿರುಹು in the Dictionary. *Cf.* § 223.

65. Kêšava's list of verbs (§ 47) is so arranged that the alphabetical order shows itself in the final letters, ಱ್ and ೞ್ coming after ಸ್.

Of verbs that form a single vowel, he adduces only two, *viz.* ಈ and ಓ, and of such as consist of one consonant with a long vowel, twelve, *viz.* ಕಾ, ಕೀ, ಕೇ, ತೀ, ತೋ, ನೋ, ಪೂ, ಬಾ, ಬೀ, ಬೇ, ಮಾ and ಮೇ.

The final consonants and syllables of the verbs in his list are the following:—

ಕು, ಂಕು; ಗು, ಂಗು; ಚು, ಂಚು (ಇಚು); ಜು, ಂಜು; ಟು, ಣ್ಟು; ಡಿ, ಡು, ಡೆ; ಣ್, ಣಿ, ಣೆ; ತು; ದಿ, ದು, ದೆ; ನ್, ನಿ, ನೆ; ಪು; ಬು, ಮ್ಬು; ಮು, ಮೆ; ಯ್; ರ್, ರಿ, ರೆ; ಲ್, ಲೆ; ವಿ, ವು; ಸಿ, ಸು, (ಇಸು), ಸೆ; ಱ್, ಱು, ಱೆ; ೞ್, ೞ, ೞೆ; ಳ್, ಳಿ, ಳೆ. (*Cf.* §§ 149-151.)

The finals often are essential parts of the verbal theme. That they are not always radical, but sometimes mere formatives, *e. g.* ಕು, ಂಕು, ಗು, ಂಗು, ಜು, ಂಜು, ಟು, ಣ್ಟು, appears to a certain extent from the §§ 62 and 63. We add as a peculiarity that what may be called the root of verbs of frequentative action, is seen in the first form of reduplication, as in ಮುಱಿ ಮುಱಿಂಗು (§ 211, 6), ತೊಳ ತೊಳ ತೊಳಗು, ಬೆಳ ಬೆಳ ಬೆಳಗು (§ 211, 10).

66. A peculiarity of some verbal themes is that they change their root vowels. This, in the ancient dialect, is especially seen in the past participle, in which ಇಸು takes the form of ಎಚ್ಚು, ಬಿಸು that of ಬೆಚ್ಚು (§ 164, 10), ಕಿಡು that of ಕೆಟ್ಟು (§ 164, 8), ಕಿಱು that of ಕೆತ್ತು, ಗಿಱು that of ಗೆತ್ತು, ತಿಱು that of ತೆತ್ತು (§ 161), ಉಗು that of ಒಕ್ಕು, ಪುಗು that of ಪೊಕ್ಕು (§ 164, 12), ಕುಡು that of ಕೊಟ್ಟು, ತುಡು that of ತೊಟ್ಟು (§ 164, 7). ಇಸು, in the later dialect, has become ಎಸು and ಎಸೆ, ಕಿಡು ಕೆಡು, ಕುಡು ಕೊಡು, ತುಡು ತೊಡು, ತಿಱು ತೆಱು, ಉಗು ಒಗು, ಪುಗು ಪೊಗು, and ಬಿಸು ಬೆಸು and ಬೆಸೆ. ಇಱ್, already in Kêšava's time, appeared as ಎಱೆ, ಉಡಿ as ಒಡೆ, ಉಳ್ as ಒಳ್; ಕೊಲ್ must originally have been ಕುಲ್, as ಕುಲಿ (not ಕೊಲಿ) is 'a killer', and ಕೊಳ್ಳು, to take, ಕುಳ್, as the verbal noun ಕೊಳು exists also as ಕುಳು. Observe, further, that ಉಯ್ appears also as ಒಯ್, ಕುಯ್ as ಕೊಯ್, ತುಯ್ as ತೊಯ್, ಪುದಿ as ಪೊದೆ, ಕಯ್ as ಕೆಯ್, ಇದಿರ್ಚು as ಎದರಿಸು, and that several themes have a long and short vowel (§§ 52. 53). Observe also the change of ಇ into ಈ, ಎ and ಏ and that of ಉ into ಊ and ಓ in § 101; that of ಉಳ್ of the locative into ಒಳ್, and that of ಎ of the instrumental into ಇ in § 109; that of ಇ into ಎ, ಏ and ಉ, that of ಉ into ಒ in § 247, *d*, 9. 10. 13. 17. 18. 21. 22, and that of ಏ into ಇ in § 251.

IV. On declinable bases

67. According to grammar there are words called **bases** (liṅga, prakṛiti). Such a base is defined as follows: "It does not express verbal action (kriyĕ), has no case-terminations (vibhakti, *cf.* § 105 *seq.*), but embodies meaning (artha)."

68. According to the grammarian Kêšava **bases are first of four** kinds, *viz.*

1, **verbal bases** (kṛit, kṛilliṅga), *i. e.* such as are formed directly from verbs by the so-called kṛit-suffixes attached to the relative present and past participle (kṛit, see § 102, 8. *e*; §§ 177. 180. 185. 253, 9, *d*; 254), *e. g.* to ಬೇಡುವ, ಪಾಡುವ, ಪೊಯ್ವ; ಮಾಡಿದ, ಬೇಡಿದ, ಪಾಡಿದ, ನೋಡಿದ, ಕೂಡಿದ, ನಲಿದ; ಧರಿಸುವ; ಭಾಗಿಸಿದ, ಭಂಗಿಸಿದ, ರಂಗಿಸಿದ; ಓಸರಿಸಿದ, ಒಸೆದ;

2, **bases with other suffixes** (taddhita, taddhitaliṅga), *i. e.* such as are formed by the so-called taddhita-suffixes (ಇಗ, ವಳ, ವಳ್ಳ, ಅಳ, ಅಯ್ತ, etc., see § 243) from nouns and verbs, *e. g.* ಕಬ್ಬಿಗ, ಗಡ್ಡಿಗ, ಅಡಪವಳ, ಮಡಿವಳ, ಅಟ, ಕಟ್ಟಿ;

3, **compound bases** (samâsa, samâsaliṅga), *i. e.* such as are compounded of two (or more) words, *e. g.* ತೆಂಗಾೞಿ, ಇಮ್ಮಾವು, ಕುಡುವಿಲ್ಲ, ಮುಂಗೆಯ್; ಪುರವನ, ನೀಲೋತ್ಪಲ, ತ್ರಿಶೂಲ, ಸದಯ (*cf.* No. 4, *b;* see § 244 *seq.*);

4, **nominal bases** (nâma, nâmaliṅga, nâmaprakṛiti) or crude nouns (see § 242) which include

a) words not etymologically derived by the public, but commonly known and used in a conventional sense (rûḍhanâma, diṭanâma, niščitanâma), *e. g.* ನೆಲ, ಪೊಲ, ಜಲ, that by their number of syllables (aksharavṛitti), also without being compounds in the generally accepted meaning (asamâsatĕ), may be monosyllabic, etc., and even quinquesyllabic, as ಪೂ, ಮರ, ಪೊತ್ತಗೆ, ಕವೞಿಗೆ, ಕಟ್ಟವತ್ತಿಗೆ;

b) words whose meaning is intelligible in themselves (anvarthanâma), expressing either quality (guṇânurûpa) of beings, as ದಾನಿ, ದಯಾಪರ, ಅತ್ಯಭಿಮಾನಿ, ಪರಾಕ್ರಮಿ, or circumstance and condition (arthânurûpa) of beings, as ಪೆರ್ಗಾಲ, ನಿಡಿಮೂಗ (or ನಿಡುಮೂಗ), ಕುಸಿಗೊರಲ (*cf.* No. 3, so that Kêśava enlarges the compass of nominal bases by including also compound bases, and, we may say, also all the others);

c) words by which one of a species is pointed out (aṅkitanâma) or proper names, as ಕಾಟಿ, ಕಸವ, ಮಾಚ, ಮಾರ, which though occasionally without a clear meaning (sârthakam alladuvu), are current everywhere in Kannaḍa and other languages.

Besides these four kinds of declinable bases there are three others, which will be given in § 90.

Remarks.

1, When a verb (kriyĕ) stands at the end of the description of the character of a person, it too has been called a kṛilliṅga by poets, *e. g.* (with case-termination) ನಮೋಸ್ತುಗಳ್ ಇರ್ಪ ಅನ್ದದಿನ್ ಇರ್ದಂ, he who was as Jainas are.

2, When a series of words (vâkyamâlĕ) is considered as a whole, as in attributes, poets have called such a series too a nominal base, *e. g.* (with case-terminations) ಅಹಿಂಸಾ ಪರಮೋ ಧರ್ಮಮೆಂಬುದನೀ ಸವಿತುವರ್ಗರೇಣ್ಯರ್ ಆಬೂದರ್; ತೋಳ್ಗೆಷ್ಪ ನಾಳ್ದರ ಕೆಯ್ದುವೊತ್ತರ ದೇವಂ; ಗುಣಕ್ಕೆನಲ್ಲಗಣೇಶಂ; ಸೊಕ್ಕಾನೆಗಳಂಕಂ.

69. A word is termed ಶಬ್ದ or ಪದ in grammar. ಪದ, however, has two additional meanings, signifying also either a nominal base (§ 68) with a case-termination (vibhakti) attached to it (nâmapada) or a verbal theme (dhâtu, § 50) with a personal termination (vibhakti) attached to it (âkhyâtapada, kriyâpada, §§ 144. 192).

70. Not only Kannaḍa words do belong to the nominal bases or crude nouns (liṅga, nâmaliṅga, nâmaprakṛiti), but, as seen in § 68, also words that have been adopted from Saṁskṛita. These often exhibit the form they have in Saṁskṛita dictionaries, in which case they are called ಸಮಸಂಸ್ಕೃತ terms, *e. g.* ಕಾಮ, ಭೀಮ, ರಾಮ, ಕುಮಾರ, ಮುಖ, ಕಮಲ, ಭುವನ, ಭವನ, ನಲಿನ, ಶಯನ, ಶ್ರುತಿ, ಸ್ಮೃತಿ, ಶುದ್ಧಿ, ಸಿದ್ಧಿ, ಕವಿ, ರವಿ, ಅರಿ, ಗಿರಿ, ಲಿಪಿ, ಕಪಿ, ಧ್ವನಿ, ಮುನಿ, ಪಶು, ಶಿಶು, ರಿಪು, ಭಾನು, ಧೇನು, ಸೇತು, ಕೇತು, ಬನ್ಧು, ಸಿನ್ಧು, ದಾರು, ಭೀರು.

71. Another series of nominal bases called ತತ್ಸಮ terms which have not been borrowed from Saṁskṛita, but of which nearly all exist in the same shape in Kannaḍa as well as in Saṁskṛita, are ಅಂಕ, ಅಂಗಣ, ಅಟ್ಟ, ಕಂಕಣ, ಕೋಣ್ಟೆ (ಕೋಟೆ or ಕೋಟ್ಟೆ), ಗಣ್ಡ, ಗಲ್ಲ, ಗಾಳ, ಗೋಣಿ, ತಳ, ತೋರಣ, ಪಟ್ಟ, ಬಣ್ಡಿ, ಬಲ, ಬಿಲ, ಮಂಚ, ಮಣಿ, ಮಲ್ಲ, ಮಾಲೆ (ಮಾಲಾ), ಲತೆ (ಲತಾ), ಸಬಳ (*cf.* § 252, 3). Also the nominal bases ಘಟ್ಟಾಘಟ್ಟಿ, ಮಲ್ಲಾಮಲ್ಲಿ are tatsamas.

72. Saṁskṛita particles (avyaya) as ಅನ್ತರ್, ಬಹಿರ್, ಪುನರ್, or Saṁskṛita pronouns (sarvanâma) as ತ್ಯದ್, ತದ್, ಯದ್, or Saṁskṛita participles ending in ಅತ್ (śatṛiṅanta) as ಕ್ವಣತ್, ಝುಣತ್, ಭ್ರಮತ್, cannot form by themselves declinable bases in Kannaḍa; but compound bases (samâsaliṅga) with a final vowel, of which they form the first member, are declinable, *e. g.* ಅನ್ತರ್ಮುಖ, ಬಹಿರಂಗ, ಪುನಃಪಾಕ; ತ್ಯತ್ಕಥನ, ತದ್ವಚನ, ಯತ್ಸುಖ; ಕ್ವಣತ್ಕಂಕಣ, ಝುಣನ್ನೂಪುರ, ಭ್ರಮದ್ಭ್ರಮರ.

73. The Saṁskṛita numerals (saṅkhyâvâĉi) ಏಕ, ದ್ವಿ, ತ್ರಿ, ಚತುರ್, ಪಂಚ (ಪಂಚನ್, see § 86), ಷಟ್, ಸಪ್ತ (ಸಪ್ತನ್), ಅಷ್ಟ (ಅಷ್ಟನ್), ನವ (ನವನ್), ದಶ (ದಶನ್) are indeclinables; but with suffixes (pratyaya) in the form of ದ್ವಿತಯ, ತ್ರಿತಯ, ಚತುಷ್ಕ, ಪಂಚಕ, ಷಟ್ಕ, ಸಪ್ತಕ, ಅಷ್ಟಕ, ನವಮ, ದಶಮ, and in compounds (samâsa), as ಏಕಾಂಗ, ದ್ವಿಮುಖ, ತ್ರಿಲೋಕ, ಚತುರ್ವೇದ, ಪಂಚಭೂತ, ಷಟ್ಕರ್ಮ, ಸಪ್ತದ್ವೀಪ, ಅಷ್ಟಭುಜ, ನವನಿಧಿ, ದಶಪ್ರಕರಣ (of which they form the first member), they are declinable bases in Kannaḍa.

74. Saṁskṛita words with final ಆ, *e. g.* ಮಾಲಾ (which is one of the tatsamas in § 71), ಬಾಲಾ, ಶಾಲಾ, ಅಲಕಾ, ನಿದ್ರಾ, ರೇಖಾ, change this ಆ into ಎ to become declinable bases in Kannaḍa, in which case they appear as ಮಾಲೆ, ಬಾಲೆ, ಶಾಲೆ, ಅಲಕೆ, ನಿದ್ರೆ, ರೇಖೆ, or are ಎಕಾರಾನ್ತ terms.

75. As an exception to rule 74 the Saṁskṛita words ಕನ್ಧರಾ, ಉಪತ್ಯಕಾ, ಕರುಣಾ, ಅಧಿತ್ಯಕಾ, ದಂಷ್ಟ್ರಕಾ, ವಾಲುಕಾ and others change their final ಆ into ಅ to become declinable bases in Kannaḍa, appearing therein as ಕನ್ಧರ, ಉಪತ್ಯಕ, etc. or being ಅಕಾರಾನ್ತ terms.

76. When the Saṁskṛita words ಗ್ರೀವಾ and ಭಿಕ್ಷಾ are used as declinable bases in Kannaḍa, they appear as ಗ್ರೀವ or ಗ್ರೀವೆ, ಭಿಕ್ಷ or ಭಿಕ್ಷೆ.

77. Some Saṁskṛita words with final ಅ (ಅಕಾರಾನ್ತ terms), *viz.* ವಧ, ಅಭಿಲಾಷ, ಉದಾಹರಣ, ದರ್ಪ, ಪ್ರಶ್ನ, ಊಹ and ಅಲಕ (*cf.* § 74), change this ಅ into ಎ to become declinable bases in Kannaḍa, and then appear as ವಧೆ, ಅಭಿಲಾಷೆ, etc.

78. Saṁskṛita words with final ಈ (ಈಕಾರಾನ್ತ terms), *e. g.* ಲಕ್ಷ್ಮೀ, ಗೌರೀ, ಸರಸ್ವತೀ, ಕಾಮಿನೀ, ನಾರೀ, always change their ಈ into ಇ to become declinable bases in Kannaḍa, and then appear as ಲಕ್ಷ್ಮಿ, ಗೌರಿ, etc.

79. Saṁskṛita polysyllabic words (ಅನೇಕಾಕ್ಷರಶಬ್ದ) with final ಊ (ಊಕಾರಾನ್ತ terms), *e. g.* ಸರಯೂ, ಕಣ್ಡೂ, ಖರ್ಜೂ, ಸ್ವಯಮ್ಭೂ, ಖಲಪೂ, change their ಊ into ಉ to become declinable bases in Kannaḍa, and then appear as ಸರಯು, ಕಣ್ಡು, etc.

80. All Saṁskṛita monosyllabic terms (ಏಕಾಕ್ಷರಶಬ್ದ), *e. g.* ಜ್ಯಾ, ಮಾ, ಪ್ರಾ, ಶ್ರೀ, ಸ್ತ್ರೀ, ಭೀ, ಭ್ರೂ, ಕೂ, remain unchanged when used as declinable bases in Kannaḍa.

81. As a rule Saṁskṛita words ending in ಋ (ಋಕಾರಾನ್ತ terms), *e. g.* ಪಿತೃ, ಸವಿತೃ, ನಪ್ತೃ, ಕರ್ತೃ, ನೇತೃ, ಹೋತೃ, ಜಾಮಾತೃ, ದುಹಿತೃ, ಮಾತೃ, ಧಾತೃ remain unchanged when used as declinables in Kannaḍa.

ಧಾತೃ, however, often takes the form of ಧಾತ, also in ಮಾನ್ಧಾತ, and that of ಧಾತ್ರ in ವಿಧಾತ್ರ. For the ಋ in ಪಿತೃ the substitute ಅರ (ಅರಾದೇಶ) may be used, so that ಪಿತೃ appears as ಪಿತರ.

82. The declinable base of ಸಖಿ may become ಸಖ in Kannaḍa.

83. The second class of Saṁskṛita words that are used as nominal bases in Kannaḍa are such as end in consonants (ವ್ಯಂಜನಾನ್ತ terms); but before they become Kannaḍa declinables, they have to undergo various changes, as will be seen from §§ 84-89.

84. The Saṁskṛita words ದಿವ್, ಸ್ರಿಜ್, ಚತುರ್, ಮರುತ್, ಬುಧ್, ಕಕುಭ್, ವೇದವಿದ್, ಪುರ್, ಮುದ್, ಸಮವಯಸ್, ಗುಣಭಾಜ್, ವಿಹಾಯಸ್, ಸಮ್ಪದ್ and others add ಅ (ಅತ್ವ) to their finals, and become ದಿವ, ಸ್ರಜ (*cf.* § 85), ಚತುರ, etc.

85. The Saṁskṛita words ಅಪ್, ಕ್ಷುತ್ (ಕ್ಷುಧ್), ಪ್ರತಿಪತ್ (ಪ್ರತಿಪದ್), ಋಕ್ (ಋಚ್), ದಿಕ್ (ದಿಶ್), ಯಜುಸ್, ವಿದ್ಯುತ್, ವಿಪತ್ (ವಿಪದ್), ಮಹತ್, ಬೃಹತ್, ತ್ವಕ್ (ತ್ವಚ್), ಸಮ್ಯಕ್ (ಸಮ್ಯಚ್), ಸ್ರಕ್ (ಸ್ರಜ್, *cf.* § 84), ದ್ವಿಟ್ (ದ್ವಿಷ್), ಪ್ರಾವೃಟ್ (ಪ್ರಾವೃಷ್), ವಾಕ್ (ವಾಚ್) and others double their final consonant (or take ದ್ವಿರ್ಭಾವ) and add ಉ, *e. g.* ಅಪ್ಪು, ಕ್ಷುತ್ತು, ಪ್ರತಿಪತ್ತು, ಋಕ್ಕು, etc.

86. The Saṁskṛita words ರಾಜನ್, ಮೂರ್ಧನ್, ಪೂಷನ್, ಅರ್ಯಮನ್, ಕರಿನ್, ಕರ್ಮನ್, ಬ್ರಹ್ಮನ್ and others drop their final (or take ಅನ್ತ್ಯಲೋಪ), *e. g.* ರಾಜ, ಮೂರ್ಧ, etc.

But ಸೀಮನ್ and ಊಷ್ಮನ್ dropping their ನ್ become ಸೀಮೆ and ಊಷ್ಮೆ.

87. The Saṁskṛita words ಯಶಸ್, ತೇಜಸ್, ವಯಸ್, ಪಯಸ್, ಮನಸ್, ಶ್ರೇಯಸ್ either drop their final consonant, or double it and attach ಉ, in which case they appear in Kannaḍa as ಯಶ or ಯಶಸ್ಸು, ತೇಜ or ತೇಜಸ್ಸು, ವಯ or ವಯಸ್ಸು, ಪಯ or ಪಯಸ್ಸು, ಮನ or ಮನಸ್ಸು, ಶ್ರೇಯ or ಶ್ರೇಯಸ್ಸು.

88. The Saṁskṛita word ವಾರ್ remains as it is; ಗೀರ್ (ಗಿರ್) does so too, but appears also as ಗಿರೆ.

89. Lastly, the nominative plural in Saṁskṛita of some Saṁskṛita words, after having dropped its visarga, is used as a nominal base, *e. g.* ಶ್ವಾನ (of ಶ್ವನ್), ಯುವಾನ (of ಯುವನ್), ಅಧ್ವಾನ (of ಅಧ್ವನ್), ಸಖಾಯ (of ಸಖಿ), ಜ್ಯಾಯಾಂಸ (of ಜ್ಯಾಯಸ್), ಕನೀಯಾಂಸ (of ಕನೀಯಸ್), ವಿದ್ವಾಂಸ (of ವಿದ್ವಸ್), ಭಾಸ್ವನ್ತ (of ಭಾಸ್ವತ್), ಶ್ರೀಮನ್ತ (of ಶ್ರೀಮತ್), ಹನುಮನ್ತ (of ಹನುಮತ್).

Remark.

The grammarian Kêšava does not class the apabhraṁša or tadbhava words (§ 370) with the words given in §§ 74-79. 81. 82. 84-89, probably because he did not consider the changes they undergo in order to become declinable bases so essential as those of the tadbhavas.

90. In § 68 it has been stated that first there are four classes of declinable bases (liṅgas) in Kannaḍa, *viz.* ಕೃಲ್ಲಿಂಗ, ತದ್ಧಿತಲಿಂಗ, ಸಮಾಸಲಿಂಗ, ನಾಮಲಿಂಗ.

Besides these we have a fifth class called ಸರ್ವನಾಮ, pronouns, *e. g.* ಅದು, ಇದು, ಉದು, ಆವುದು, ಎಲ್ಲದು, ಪೆಜಿತು, ಏನ್, together with the ಉಕ್ತ, words, ಆಂ, (ನಾಂ), ನೀಂ, ತಾಂ (see § 102, 8, letters *a* and *b;* § 137, *a*, 1, § 255 *seq.*); a sixth class called ಗುಣವಚನ, ಗುಣವಾಚಿ or ಗುಣೋಕ್ತಿ, attributive nouns or adjectives, *e. g.* ಒಳ್ಳಿತು, ಮೆಲ್ಲಿತು, ಬಸಿದು, ಆಸಿದು, ಒಳ್ಳಿತ್ತು, ಮೆಲ್ಲಿತ್ತು (see § 273, *seq.*); and a seventh class called ಸಂಖ್ಯೆ or ಸಂಖ್ಯಾವಾಚಿ, numerals and appellative nouns of number, *e. g.* ಒನ್ದು, ಎರಡು, ಮೂಱು, ನಾಲ್ಕು, ಒರ್ವ, (and, with the termination of the nominative plural, ಇರ್ಬರ್, ಮೂವರ್, etc., and also ಪಲವು, ಕೆಲವು, ಪಲವರ್, ಕೆಲಬರ್, see § 278, 4).

Thus there are 7 classes of declinable bases in Kannaḍa.

A subdivision of the numerals may perhaps be adduced as an 8th class, *viz.* the four words ಅನಿತು, ಇನಿತು, ಉನಿತು, ಎನಿತು, ಎಲ್ಲದು that express indefinite quantity (nirvišêshapavaṇ; see § 278, 3. 4).

Regarding the avyayaliṅgas or adverbial declinable bases see § 281.

91. What has been said regarding verbal themes (§§ 47. 51 *seq.*) that they are monosyllabic, dissyllabic, etc., applies also to the Kannaḍa nominal bases or crude nouns (nâmaliṅga) of the ancient dialect.

92. In modern Kannaḍa all monosyllabic true Kannaḍa nominal bases with a final consonant generally appear as dissyllabic, and all dissyllabic ones as trisyllabic; in the mediæval dialect the two kinds are optionally used as dissyllables and trisyllables. The lengthening, as a rule, is done by the addition of a euphonic ಉ to facilitate pronunciation (*cf.* §§ 48. 54 *seq.*); monosyllabic nominal bases ending in ಯ್ may likewise use the vowel ಇ to become dissyllabic (*cf.* the euphonic ಇ of § 54; see § 93), doubling or not doubling their final.

93. Monosyllabic true Kannaḍa nominal bases of the ancient dialect end in consonants (or are ವ್ಯಂಜನಾನ್ತ terms), these consonants being ಣ್,

ನ್, ಯ್, ರ್, (ಱ್), ಲ್, ಳ್, and ೞ್ (*cf.* § 61), *e.g.* ಕಣ್, ಮಣ್, ಗೇಣ್, ಪೊನ್, ಬೆನ್, ಜೇನ್, ಸೀನ್, ಕೆಯ್, ಮೆಯ್, ನಾಯ್, ನಾರ್, ತೇರ್, ಬೇರ್, (ಏಱ್), ಕಲ್, ನೆಲ್, ಪಾಲ್, ಪುಲ್, ಬಿಲ್, ಕೋಲ್, ಒಳ್, ಕಳ್, ಮುಳ್, ತೋಳ್, ಬಾೞ್, ಸೂೞ್, ತೇೞ್ (ಚೇೞ್). See some exceptional forms in § 121, *a*, and *cf.* the remark under § 96.

In mediæval Kannaḍa the above terms are also dissyllabic, *viz.* ಕಣು, ಕಣ್ಣು, ಮಣ್ಣು, ಗೇಣು, ಪೊನ್ನು, ಬೆನ್ನು, ಜೇನು, ಸೀನು, ಕೆಯ್ಯು, ಮೆಯಿ, ನಾಯಿ, ನಾರು, ತೇರು, ಬೇರು, ಕಲು, ಕಲ್ಲು, ನೆಲ್ಲು, ಪಾಲು, ಪುಲು, ಪುಲ್ಲು, ಬಿಲು, ಬಿಲ್ಲು, ಕೋಲು, ಒಳು, ಕಳ್ಳು, ಮುಳು, ಮುಳ್ಳು, ತೋಳು, ಬಾೞಿ, ಸೂೞಿ, ತೇೞಿ (ಚೇೞಿ).

In modern Kannaḍa they are dissyllabic (as far as they are used therein); but see the exceptional forms in § 120, *c*.

94. **Dissyllabic** true Kannaḍa **nominal bases** of the ancient dialect **ending in consonants** are *e.g.* ಉಸಿರ್, ತಳಿರ್, ತೆಮರ್, ಪೆಸರ್, ಎಡಱ್, ಕೆಸಱ್, ತುನ್ತುಱ್, ಕುತ್ತುಱ್, ಪೆಸಱ್, ಬಸಿಱ್, ಹಗೞ್, ನೇಸಱ್, ಎಚ್ಚಿಱ್, ಅವಲ್, ಕೊರಲ್, ಮಣಲ್, ತನ್ದಲ್, ಕರುಳ್, ಕುರುಳ್, ತಿರುಳ್, ಪುರುಳ್, ಅಗೞ್, ನೆಗೞ್, ಉಗುೞ್, ಇಕ್ಕುೞ್, ಪೊಕ್ಕುೞ್, ಬಾಸುೞ್. See a few exceptional forms in § 121, *a*.

In mediæval Kannaḍa the above terms may become trisyllables by adding a euphonic ಉ; in modern Kannaḍa they always are such (as far as they are used in it), *e.g.* ಉಸಿರು, ತಳಿರು, ಕೆಸಱು.

Observe that ancient ಬೇಸಱ್ becomes ಬೇಸಱ, and ancient ಅಚ್ಚಱ್ becomes ಅಕ್ಕಱ in modern Kannaḍa.

95. There are a few **trisyllabic** true Kannaḍa **nominal bases** with a **final consonant** in the ancient dialect, *e.g.* ಇಱಿಸಿಲ್, ಪುೞಿಚಿಲ್, ಪೊಸನ್ತಿಲ್. The last term occurs in the mediæval dialect also as ಹೊಸತಿಲು (with the euphonic ಉ), *i. e.* quadrisyllabic; but in the same dialect and in modern Kannaḍa is trisyllabic too, *viz.* ಹೊಸ್ತಿಲು.

96. **Dissyllabic** true Kannaḍa **nominal bases ending in vowels** (ಸ್ವರಾನ್ತ terms) are used in the same shape as well in ancient and mediæval as in modern Kannaḍa (as far as they occur in it). The final vowels are ಅ, ಇ, ಉ and ಎ. With regard to the bases with final ಉ it is to be observed that, in this case (see the contrary in § 97), this vowel may somehow originally have been euphonic, as it is nearly always elided before a following vowel in sandhi (see § 213 *seq.*, also the optional use in § 215, 4), and as we have ಕಾೞ್ for ಕಾಡು, and ಕೋೞ್ for ಕೋಡು.

We give the following instances: ಮುಗ, ತಡ, ಕುಱಿ, ಕೊಳ, ತೆರ, ನರ, ನೆರ, ಬರ, ನೆಲ, ಪೊಲ, ಮೊಲ, ನೊಳ, ತೋಳ; ನರಿ, ಮಱಿ, ಕಿಡಿ, ಕುಱಿ, ಪುಲಿ, ಸುೞಿ, ಕೇರಿ, ಕೋಡಿ; ತುತ್ತು, ಎಱ್ತು (ಎತ್ತು), ಪೊಱ್ತು (ಪೊತ್ತು), ಮಾವು, ಕೂಸು, ಮಾಸು; ಎಮ್ಮೆ, ಕಟ್ಟೆ, ಕಡೆ, ಕಱ್ತೆ (ಕತ್ತೆ), ಮರೆ, ಮಱೆ, ಮೞೆ, ನೆರೆ, ನೆಱೆ, ಎಱೆ, ಪೊೞೆ, ಪುಲ್ಲೆ.

Observe that ಮಾವು occurs also as ಮಾ, ತೆರ as ತೆರವು, ನರ as ನರವು, ನೆರ as ನೆರವು, ನೊಳ as ನೊಳವು, ಬರ as ಬರವು, ಒಳ as ಒಳವು, the unradical ಉ being suffixed by means of a euphonic ವ್.

Remark.

Kêšava in the sûtras and vṛittis of his Šabdamaṇidarpaṇa (but not in the instances given) occasionally adds a final euphonic ಉ to the suffixes ಅರ್ and ಅಲ್, so that they appear as ಅರು and ಅಲು (see pages 120. 121. 123. 124. 147. 278. 296 of the Mangalore edition) and treats them according to the rule laid down in § 215, 4. Also with regard to the suffixes ಅದು, ಉವು, ಇತು, ಇತ್ತು, ಅತ್ತು he does so (pages 264. 265). Compare also the ಅರು (for ಅರ್) in § 110, *a*, 1; the ಅಲು (for ಅಲ್) in §§ 109, *a*, 7; 120, *a*, 7; 121, *a*, 1; 187, 1; the ಒಳು (for ಒಳ್) in § 109, *a*, 7; see ಇದುವೆ ಭೇದಂ in a verse quoted in § 271.

97. There are a number of true Kannaḍa **dissyllabic nominal bases with final ಉ in which this vowel is not euphonic but radical,** and are, therefore, never elided before a following vowel in sandhi, in this respect resembling the final ಉ of the Saṁskṛita nominal bases ಗುರು, ಪಶು, ಭಾನು, ರಿಪು, ವಿಷ್ಣು, etc. Such bases are *e. g.* ಅಸು, ಕರು, ಕಱು, ಕಳು, ತಣು, ತಳು, ತುಱು, ಪೞು, ಪುೞು, ಮಡು (see § 128), and their euphonic letter in sandhi is ವ್ (§ 215, 3, *d*).

98. **Trisyllabic** true Kannaḍa **nominal bases which end in the vowels** ಅ, ಇ, ಉ and ಎ, the ಉ being like that of § 96, are *e. g.* ಮುಱ್ತಿಗ, ಕುಱುಮ್ಬ, ಬೆಜ್ಜರ, ಬಾೞಿಕ; ಕರಡಿ, ಪುರುಳಿ, ಕಜ್ಜಳಿ, ಕೊತ್ತಳಿ, ಪೊಲದಿ; ಈಗಡು, ಆಗಡು, ಮುಗುವು, ನಿಲವು, ಕುಡುಹು, ಮುನಿಸು, ತುಱುಮ್ಬು, ಪೊಲಮ್ಬು, ಮೊಱಿಗು, ಸೆಱಿಗು, ನೆಲಹು, ಪೊಳವು (see also ತೆರವು etc. in § 96); ಕುದುರೆ, ತೊಡಮ್ಬೆ, ಬಗಸೆ, ಹಸುಳೆ, ಪಸಲೆ, ಕಱಿಲೆ, ಕಱ್ತಲೆ (ಕತ್ತಲೆ).

The bases ಎರಡು and ಕಿವುಡು are also dissyllabic, appearing as ಎರೞ್ and ಕಿವುೞ್.

99. As **quadrisyllabic** true Kannaḍa **nominal bases** which are not plain taddhitaliṅga words (§ 68, 2) may be mentioned ಬಗರಗೆ and ತರುವಲಿ (see also § 95). **Quinquesyllabic** and **sexisyllabic** Kannaḍa **words,** as ಅಗಡುತನ, ನೆಱೆಯುವಿಕೆ, ಕಳುಹಿಸುವಿಕೆ, ತರುವಲಿತನ, are plain taddhitaliṅga terms.

Taddhitaliṅga terms will be treated of separately in § 243.

100. As will be seen from the Kannaḍa-English Dictionary very many true Kannaḍa nominal bases (liṅgas) are identical as to form with verbal themes (or are ಸಹಜಧಾತು terms), *e. g.* ಅಟ್ಟು, pursuing; ಅಡಕು, piling; ಅಡು, cooking; ಅಪ್ಪು, embrace; ಅರಲ್, flower; ಅರೆ, ground state; ಅಲೆ, wave; ಅವುಂಕು, pressing firmly; ಅಳಿಪು, hankering after; ಅಳ್ಕು, fear; ಅೞಿವು, destruction; ಆಗು, coming to pass; ಆಡು, motion; ಇಡು, putting; ಈಸು, swimming; ಉಗುೞ್, spittle; ಉಚ್ಚು, making loose; ಉಡಿ, fragment; ಉಬ್ಬು, swelling; ಉರಿ, burning; ಉರ್ಕು, rising; ಉೞುಂಗು, crookedness; ಉಲಿ, sound; ಉೞಿ, remaining; ಊಳ್, outcry; ಎಚ್ಚೞ್, waking; ಎತ್ತು, raising; ಎಱೆ, pouring; ಏಱು, rising; ಒಣಗು, drying; ಒಪ್ಪು, fitness; ಓದು, reading; ಕಟ್ಟು, binding; ಕಡಿ, cutting; ಕಳ್, theft; ಕಾಯ್, unripe fruit; ಕುಕಿಲ್, cuckoo; ಕುಟ್ಟು, blow; ಕುಳಿರ್, coolness; ಕೂಂಟು, limping; ಕೇಗು, crying as a peacock does; ತಡೆ, obstacle; ತಿರ್ದು, training, etc.; ತೆಗೞ್, blame; ತೇಗು, belching; ತೊಡಕು, entanglement; ದಾಂಟು, passing over; ನಡೆ, walk; ನೋಡು, looking on, etc.; ಪೂ, flowering; ಪೆರ್ಚು, increase; ಪೆಳೞ್, fear; ಬಿತ್ತು, seed; ಬೆಸು, soldering; ಬೆಳೆ, crop; ಮೆಚ್ಚು, fondness; ಸೊರ್ಕು, infatuation; ಸೊಲ್, saying, word; etc., etc. See § 242.

Such nominal bases represent the true ಭಾವವಚನ or ಭಾವವಾಚಿ terms or verbal nouns, signifying the abstract notion of a verb either as to state or action. Regarding bhâvavačanas see § 243 and the paragraphs quoted there.

Other nominal bases are formed by adding *e. g.* ಅ or ಎ to the verbal theme, as ನೀಳ (from ನೀಳ್), ಸಾಲ (from ಸಾಲ್), ಕೊಲೆ (from ಕೊಲ್), ಕಟ್ಟೆ (from ಕಟ್ಟು); these and other formatives will be treated of in § 243.

Several nominal bases have a form in the ancient dialect that differs from that which they have in the mediæval and modern one, *e. g.* ಎೞ್ತು, ಕೞ್ತೆ, ಪೊೞ್ತು, ಬಿೞ್ತು (see § 233).

101. Kannaḍa nominal bases derived from verbal themes by altering their radical vowel (*cf.* § 66 and see § 242), are *e. g.* ಈಡು (from ಇಡು), ಬೀಡು (from ಬಿಡು), ಸೂಡು (from ಸುಡು), ಕೇಡು (from ಕಿಡು), ಏಸು (from ಇಸು), ತೋಡು (from ತುಡು), ಕೋಡು (from ಕುಡು).

Others alter that vowel and add a formative vowel to the final consonant, as ಕೆೞೆ (from ಕಿೞ್), ತೆೞೆ (from ತಿೞ್), ನೆಲೆ (from ನಿಲ್), ಬೆಲೆ (from ಬಿಲ್).

102. (Theoretically) it may be said (the grammarian Kêšava teaches) that, according to properties and qualities, there are eight genders (liṅgas) for the seven declinable bases (liṅgas, prakṛitis, §§ 67. 68. 90), and that there is also, as a ninth kind, a gender of particles (avyayaliṅga). Compare § 116. (Remark that the term 'liṅga' thus has two distinct grammatical meanings.)

The nine genders are the following:—

1, The masculine gender (puṁ, pulliṅga, purusha). It is seen in the names of men, male deities and demons, *e. g.* ಅಣ್ಣ, ತಮ್ಮ, ನರ, ಅರಸ, ದೇವ, ಸುರ, ಅಸುರ, and in those of some animals, *e. g.* ಹರಿಣ, ಕೋಣ, ಹಂಗ, ಹಸುಬ, ಸರ್ಪ, ಗರುಡ, ಕೂರ್ಮ, ಕಮಠ), ವೃಷಭ, ಬಸವ.[1]

2, The feminine gender (strî, strîliṅga). It appears in the names of the female sex of the human race, of deities and of demons, *e. g.* ತಾಯ್, ಅಕ್ಕ, ಅಮ್ಮ, ಅವ್ವ, ಅರಸಿ, ದೇವಿ, ಗೌರಿ, ಮಾತೆ, ರಾಕ್ಷಸಿ.

3, The neuter gender (nappu, napuṁsaka, napuṁsakaliṅga). To this belongs everything which is destitute of reason whether animate (čêtana) or inanimate (ačêtana), *e. g.* ಪುಲಿ, ಭೃಂಗ, ತುರಂಗ, ಹಯ, ಗಜ (but see Nos. 1 and 5); ಗಿಡ, ಕಳಸ, ಕನ್ನಡಿ, ಜಿಡೆ, ಕೊಡೆ.[2]

4, The masculine-feminine, *i. e.* common or epicene gender (puṁstrîliṅga). This is seen in the plural of nouns and demonstrative (see No. 8, remark pronouns (ಅವಂ, ಇವಂ, ಉವಂ) wherein the same suffix ಅರ್ (ಇರ್) is added to masculines and feminines without regard to sex, *e. g.* ಇವರ್ ಪುರುಷರ್, ಇವರ್ ಸ್ತ್ರೀಯರ್; ಅವರ್ ಗಣ್ಡರ್, ಅವರ್ ಪೆಣ್ಡಿರ್; ಉವರ್ ದೇವರ್, ಉವರ್ ದೇವಿಯರ್. *Cf.* §§ 119. 132. 134.

It is seen also in the singular, namely in that of ತೊತ್ತು, which term by itself is masculine and feminine. *Cf.* § 243, *B*, 7.

5, The masculine-neuter gender (punnapuṁsakaliṅga). This is found in the nouns ರವಿ (or ಸೂರ್ಯ), ವಿಧು (or ಚನ್ದ್ರ), ಮಂಗಲ, ಬುಧ, ಬೃಹಸ್ಪತಿ, ಶುಕ್ರ, ಶನಿ, ರಾಹು, ಕೇತು (the nine planets, navagraha), ಆಳ್ (see § 120), ಬಸನ್ತ, ಚೈತ್ರ, ಮಲಯಾನಿಲ, ಕಾಮ and ವರಾಹ, which are used either as masculines or neuters.

---

[1] The Kannaḍa grammar called Nuḍigaṭṭu (p. 122) says that *e. g.* ತೋಳನು, ಮಂಗನು have their verb in the neuter, *e. g.* ಆ ಅಡವಿಯಲ್ಲಿ ಒನ್ದು ತೋಳನು ಇತ್ತು; ಮಂಗನು ಹಲ್ಲು ಕಿಸಿಯುತ್ತದೆ; but that animals, if they are introduced as speaking, have their verb in the masculine, as ವ್ಯಾಘ್ರನು ಇನ್ತೆನ್ದನು, or in the feminine, as ಬಹುಲೆ ಇನ್ತೆನ್ದಳು.

[2] With regard to masculine and feminine terms the Nuḍigaṭṭu (p. 122) says that in disdain (ತಿರಸ್ಕಾರ) they may be used as neuters, *e. g.* ನಿನ್ನ ಗಣ್ಡ ಏನು ಮಾಡುತ್ತದೆ? ಏನು ಮಾಡೀತು? ಮೂಲೆಯಲ್ಲಿ ಕೂತಿದೆ. ಮುದುಕಿ ಎಲ್ಲಿ ಅದೆ? ಅದು ನೋಡು, ಅಲ್ಲಿ ನಿನ್ತದೆ. In a Bombay schoolbook we find likewise: ಈ ಹುಡಿಗೆ ಎಷ್ಟು ಹೊಲಸು ಕಾಣಿಸುತ್ತದೆ!

The Nuḍigaṭṭu (p. 120) says that such is also done in ignorance (ಅಜ್ಞಾನ), *i. e.* if the concerned ones are ignorant, *e. g.* ಹುಡುಗರು ಆಡುತ್ತವೆ; ಹುಡುಗ ಬನ್ತು; ಹುಡುಗಿ ನಗುತ್ತದೆ; ಹೊತ್ತಲ್ಲದ ಹೊತ್ತಿನಲ್ಲಿ ತೊತ್ತು ಮೈನ್ನೆರೆಯಿತು; ಇವರ ಮನೆಯಲ್ಲಿ ಒನ್ದು ವರನು ಅದೆ, ಇವರಲ್ಲಿ ಒನ್ದು ಕನ್ನೆ ಅದೆ. In a Bombay schoolbook we find likewise: ನಿನ್ನ ವರ್ಗದಲ್ಲಿ ಎಷ್ಟು ಹುಡುಗರು ಅವೆ?

6, The feminine-neuter gender (strînapuṁsa, strînapuṁsakaliṅga). This is used for the nouns ಪೆಣ್, ಕನ್ನಿಕೆ, ಸಿರಿ, ಸರಸ್ವತಿ and ದೇವತೆ, which are treated either as feminines or neuters.

7, The masculine-feminine-neuter gender (triliṅga). This is employed *e. g.* for the words ಆಂ, ನೀಂ, ತಾಂ (see No. 8, letter *a*, *cf.* § 256), and the nouns ಶಿಶು, ಹಸುಳೆ, ಮಗುವು, ಕೂಸು, ಸೊಣ್ಡಿ, ಪಗೆ, ಕೆಳೆ, ಅರಸು, ತರುವಲಿ, which are either of the masculine or feminine or neuter gender.

8, The adjective gender (vâčyaliṅga) or the gender that depends on the word which is to be distinguished or defined (viśêshyâdhînaliṅga).

This gender comprises

a) the words (ukti, šabda) ಆಂ (ನಾಂ), ನೀಂ, ತಾಂ (§ 90).

Remark.

Neither Kêšava nor Nâgavarma (sûtra 99) reckon ಆಂ, ನೀಂ, ತಾಂ among the pronouns (sarvanâma), though Europeans would call the first two the personal pronouns, and the last one the reflexive (reciprocal) pronoun. In order to distinguish them from the pronouns mentioned under letter *b* let us call the three words simply 'pronouns' here.

b) the pronouns (sarvanâma, § 90)[1], *viz.* ಅದು, ಇದು, ಉದು, ಆವುದು, ಎಲ್ಲದು, ಪೆಱತು, ಪೆಱವು (neuter)[2]; ಏನ್ (masculine, feminine, neuter, see §§ 255. 262); ಅವಂ, ಇವಂ, ಉವಂ, ಪೆಱಂ (masculine); ಅವಳ್, ಇವಳ್, ಉವಳ್, ಪೆಱಳ್ (feminine); ಆತಂ, ಈತಂ, ಊತಂ (masculine); ಆಕೆ, ಈಕೆ, ಊಕೆ (feminine); *cf.* also ಆ, ಈ, ಊ in § 264.

Remark.

Both Kêšava and Nâgavarma (sûtras 42. 49. 66. 102) call these terms sarvanâma. ಅದು, ಇದು, ಉದು, ಪೆಱತು, ಪೆಱದು, ಎಲ್ಲದು, ಅವಂ, ಇವಂ, ಉವಂ, ಪೆಱಂ, ಅವಳ್, ಇವಳ್, ಉವಳ್, ಪೆಱಳ್, ಆತಂ, ಈತಂ, ಊತಂ, ಆಕೆ, ಈಕೆ, ಊಕೆ are what Europeans call demonstrative pronouns, and ಆವುದು, (ಆವಂ, ಆವಳ್, ಯಾವದು, ಯಾವನು, ಯಾವಳು), ಏನ್ are what they call interrogative pronouns. To distinguish these pronouns from those under letter *a* we may term them 'adjectival pronouns' in this place.

---

1) In Saṁskṛita ಸರ್ವನಾಮ means originally 'a class of words beginning with ಸರ್ವ (ಸರ್ವ ವಿಶ್ವ, ಉಭ, etc.)' under which native grammarians have included also the real pronouns (ಅಹಂ, I, ತ್ವಂ, thou, ಸಃ, he, etc.).

2) As seen in the Dictionary under ಅದು, the Basavapurâṇa and Jaiminibhârata occasionally use the pronoun ಅದು in combination with masculine terms (see § 270). The Nuḍigaṭṭu (p. 122) says that in disdain (ತಿರಸ್ಕಾರ) ಅದು, ಇದು and their plurals ಅವು, ಇವು are used for males and females, *e. g.* ಅದು (for ಅವನು or ಅವಳು) ಕೂತಿದೆ; ಅವು (for ಅವರು) ಕೆಲೆದಾಡುತ್ತವೆ.

It (p. 162) further says that in order to express positiveness (ನಿಶ್ಚಯಾರ್ಥ) ಅದೇ and ಇದೇ are combined with masculine terms and feminine terms, *e. g.* ಅದೇ ಮನುಷ್ಯರನ್ನು ನಾನು ಕಣ್ಡೆನು; ಅದೇ ಜನರಲ್ಲಿ ಈ ನಡತೆಯುಣ್ಟು; ಅದೇ ಹೆಂಗಸು ಮಾಡುತ್ತಾಳೆ; ಅದೇ ನಾನು ಈಗ ಬಿಕ್ಕೆಯ ಬೇಡುತ್ತೇನೆ; ಅದೇ ನೀನು ಈಗ ನನ್ನ ಹಗೆಯಾದೆ; ಅದೇ ಅವನು ನನ್ನ ಕೇಳಿದನು; ಇದೇ ಇವನೇ ನನ್ನ ಗೆಳೆಯನು; ಇದೇ ಇವನೇ ನಮ್ಮ ಮಾವನ್ದಿರು; ಇದೇ ಹೆಂಗಸು ನಿನ್ನೆ ಕುಣಿದಳು; ಇದೇ ಜನರು ಅಲ್ಲಿದ್ದರು. (In such a case ಆ and ಈ might be used instead; thus: ಆ ಮನುಷ್ಯನನ್ನೇ ನಾನು ಕಣ್ಡೆನು; ಈ ಹೆಂಗಸೇ ನಿನ್ನೆ ಕುಣಿದಳು; ನಾನೇ ಈಗ ಬಿಕ್ಕೆಯ ಬೇಡುತ್ತೇನೆ.)

About possessive pronouns see § 272, and about indefinite ones § 290.

c) so-called Kannaḍa adjectives (guṇavačana, § 90, clearly formed in this case from nouns by means of pronominal suffixes, see § 276), such as ನೇರಿದಂ (masculine), ನೇರಿದಳ್ (feminine), ನೇರಿತು or ನೇರಿತ್ತು (neuter); ಇನಿಯಂ (m.), ಇನಿಯಳ್ (f.), ಇನಿದು (n.), and Saṁskṛita adjectives (which partly are used also as nominal bases, § 68, 4, *b*), *e. g.* ಗುರು, ಲಘು, ಪಟು, ಸಾಧು. ಅಭಿಮಾನಿ, ದಾನಿ, ಭೋಗಿ, ಸುಖಿ.

d) so-called adjective compounds (bahuvrîbi, § 249), *e. g.* ವಿಮಲಮತಿ, ಕಡು ಚಾಗಿ, ಕಡುಗೇಡಿ.

e) verbal bases (kṛit, kṛilliṅga), *e. g.* ಪಾಡಿದಂ (of ಪಾಡಿದ, masculine), ಪಾಡಿದಳ್ (of ಪಾಡಿದ, feminine), ಪಾಡಿದುದು (of ಪಾಡಿದ, neuter); ಪಾಡುವಂ (of ಪಾಡುವ, m.), ಪಾಡುವಳ್ (of ಪಾಡುವ, f.), ಪಾಡುವುದು (of ಪಾಡುವ, n.). See §§ 68, 1. 177. 180. 185. 198, 3. 7, remark 1; 253, 2, c; 254.

f) bases with certain suffixes (taddhita, taddhitaliṅga, § 68, 2), *e. g.* ಓದಾ ಳಿ, ಜೂದಾಳಿ, ಮಾತಾಳಿ, ಆಯ್ಕುಳಿ, ಪೇಂಕುಳಿ, ಮಱುಕುಳಿ (see § 243).

g) numerals (saṅkhyŏ, § 90), *e. g.* ಸಾಯಿರ (ಸಾಸಿರ, ಸಾವಿರ), because it is put before nouns in the plural whether these are masculines, feminines or neuters. See § 278, 1.

9, The gender of particles (avyayaliṅga), although they are unchangeable (avikâra, avikṛita). It appears in words like ಕಮ್ಮಿದಂ (masculine), ಕಮ್ಮಿದಳ್ (feminine), ಕಮ್ಮಿತು (neuter), in which from the particle (avyaya) ಕಮ್ಮ (*cf.* § 273), by adding ಇ + ದ್ + ಅಂ, ಇ + ದ್ + ಅಳ್ and ಇ + ತು (see § 276), a masculine, feminine and neuter term has been formed, so that one may say that ಕಮ್ಮ in such a case represents three genders;—and then in the particles or adverbs themselves (avyaya, nipâta, §§ 212. 281) used to modify the sense of a verb, *e. g.* ಭೋಂಕನೆ, ತೊಟ್ಟನೆ, ಕಮ್ಮನೆ, ಸಿಯ್ಯನೆ, ಕೆಚ್ಚನೆ, which so to say are of the gender of the agent (kartṛi, § 344) of the verb to which they belong, the agent (whether actually given or only understood by the verbal termination) being either masculine, feminine or neuter, and being in any of the three grammatical numbers (vačanatraya, vačanatritaya, § 107).

103. Although the nine genders (Kêšava continues) mentioned in § 102 are occasionally accepted and used (kvačitprayôga), practically there are only three genders (liṅgatraya) in Kannaḍa, *viz.* the masculine, feminine and neuter. Words denoting males (purushavâčaka) are of the masculine gender, *e. g.* ಶಿವ, ರಾಮು, ಭೀಮು, ಅರಸ; words denoting females (strîvâčaka) are of the feminine gender, *e. g.* ಪಾರ್ವತಿ, ಲಕ್ಷ್ಮಿ, ಸರ ಸ್ವತಿ, ಶಚಿ, ರೋಹಿಣಿ, ಕಾಮಿನಿ, ಭಾಮಿನಿ, ರಮಣಿ, ಅತ್ತೆ, ತಾಯ್; and all other words, whether Saṁskṛita or Kannaḍa, are of the neuter gender, *e. g.* ವೃಕ್ಷ, ಪ್ರೀತಿ, ಧರೆ, ನದಿ, ಮತಿ, ಕುಲ, ಲೋಕ, ಮರ, ಗಿಡು, ಬಳ್ಳಿ, ಪುಲ್, ಪೊದಪ್, ಪುಲಿ, ಕರಡಿ, ಗಟ್ಟ, ಬೆಟ್ಟ, ಜೆಡೆ, ಕೊಡೆ, ಕನ್ನಡಿ, ಕಳಸ. *Cf.* §§ 115. 116.

Remark.

If it happens to be necessary to distinguish the sex of any animal, (tree, river, etc.), ಗಣ್ಡು, male, and ಪೆಣ್. (ಪೆಣ್ಣು, ಹೆಣ್, ಹೆಣ್ಣು). female, are prefixed.

104. As a special rule it is to be stated that the terms ಜನ, ಮಹಾಜನ, and ಲೋಕ (in the sense of 'man', 'men') are neuter in Kannaḍa, whereas the terms ದುರ್ಜನ, ಸಜ್ಜನ, and ಸುಜನ are masculine; but ಸಜ್ಜನ, if it denotes a woman of good family (kulastrî), is neuter. Likewise ಕಲತ್ರ, wife, and ಅಪತ್ಯ, child (whether male or female) are of the neuter gender.

In metaphorical diction (rûpaka) a substantive (viśêshya) in the neuter may represent a feminine noun, as ನೆಲ, the earth, may mean ಧರಾವನಿತೆ, the earth considered as a woman (§ 239); or an attribute (viśêsha), *e. g.* ಜಗದ್ವರ್ಣ, may be masculine, feminine or neuter according to the gender of the noun to which it refers (§ 239).

105. For the seven (or eight declinable bases (liṅga, prakṛiti) adduced above (§§ 68. 90) there are **seven** (sapta) **cases** (vibhakti) and **case-terminations** (vibhakti, nâmavibhakti, pratyaya).

106. **The names of the seven cases** are ಪ್ರಥಮೆ or the English nominative, ದ್ವಿತೀಯೆ or the E. accusative, ತೃತೀಯೆ or the E. instrumental, ಚತುರ್ಥಿ or the E. dative, ಪಂಚಮಿ or the E. ablative, ಷಷ್ಠಿ or the E. genitive, and ಸಪ್ತಮಿ or the E. locative. (About the vocative see § 140.)

107. Kannaḍa declinable bases have **two** numbers (vačana), *viz.* the singular (êkavačana, êkatĕ, êkatva, êkôkti) and the plural (bahuvačana, bahutĕ, bahutva).

A third number, the dual (dvitva, dvivačana), may be thought of with propriety (učita, aučitya), that is when two persons forming a pair are so introduced that the first one is without a case-termination and the second one has a termination of the plural, *e.g.* ಭೀಮಾರ್ಜುನರ್, ರಾಮಲಕ್ಷ್ಮಣರ್, ನಕುಲಸಹದೇವರ್; or when objects are mentioned that exist as pairs in nature, *e.g.* ಕಣ್ಗಳ್, ತೊಡೆಗಳ್, ತೋಳ್ಗಳ್ (see § 102, 9).

108. The case-terminations are attached to the end of a declinable base, and therefore are **suffixes**.

109. The instances of the case-terminations (or their series, vibhaktimâlĕ) are taken from writings of the three periods; if from inscriptions (śâsanas), they are marked by 'in a śâsana'. The period of the written ancient dialect extends from about 600 to 1250 A. D., that of the mediæval dialect from about 1250 to 1600 A. D., and that of the modern one from about 1600 A. D. to the present time. Compare § 32, note.

The terminations for the singular of neuter bases ending in ಅ are the following:—

a) in the ancient dialect

1, Nominative ಂ, *e. g.* ಮರಂ (of ಮರ), ಪೊಲಂ (of ಪೊಲ), ನೆಲಂ (of ನೆಲ), ಬಿಲಂ (of ಬಿಲ), ಬೆಟ್ಟಂ (of ಬೆಟ್ಟ), ಕುಲಂ (of ಕುಲ).

The ಂ or ಸೊನ್ನೆ when followed by a vowel, becomes ನ್, ಮ್, or ವ್ (see § 215, 8).

2, Accusative ಅಂ, *e. g.* ಮರನಂ (of ಮರ), ಪೊಲನಂ (of ಪೊಲ), ನೆಲನಂ (of ನೆಲ), ಬಿಲನಂ (of ಬಿಲ), or ಬೆಟ್ಟಮಂ (of ಬೆಟ್ಟ), ಗಟ್ಟಮಂ (of ಗಟ್ಟ), ಹಳ್ಳಮಂ (of ಹಳ್ಳ), ಕೊಳ್ಳಮಂ (of ಕೊಳ್ಳ), ಬಳ್ಳಮಂ (of ಬಳ್ಳ).

It will be observed that in this kind of accusative either the augment (âgama) ನ್ or the augment ಮ್ is, for the sake of euphony, inserted between the base and termination.

In true Kannaḍa words it is optional which of the two augments may be employed; but in Saṁskṛita words the ಮ್ is always required, *e. g.* ಕುಲಮಂ (of ಕುಲ), ಚಲಮಂ (of ಚಲ), ಅವಲೇಪನಮಂ (of ಅವಲೇಪ).

3, Instrumental ಇಂ, ಇನ್ದಂ, ಇನ್ದೆ, ಎ, *e.g.* ಮರದಿಂ (of ಮರ), ಮನದಿಂ (of ಮನ); ಭಯದಿನ್ದಂ (of ಭಯ), ಸ್ಮಯದಿನ್ದಂ (of ಸ್ಮಯ); ಭಯದಿನ್ದೆ (of ಭಯ), ರಾಗದಿನ್ದೆ (of ರಾಗ), ವ್ಯಾಕರಣದಿನ್ದೆ (of ವ್ಯಾಕರಣ); ಕ್ರಮದೆ (of ಕ್ರಮ), ನಯದೆ (of ನಯ), ಭಯದೆ (of ಭಯ).

In this case the terminations are annexed to the base by means of the augment ದ, that is the secondary termination of the genitive, *q. v.*, the final ಅ of ದ losing its sound when it coalesces with the terminations or in sandhi (§ 213 *seq.*).

ಇನ್ದಂ and ಇನ್ದೆ are forms of ಇಂ lengthened by the addition of the suffixes ಅಂ (in the later dialect ಅ) and ಎ, and stand for ಇನಂ and ಇನೆ, the ದ್ being simply euphonic or a help to enunciation.

The first three terminations of the instrumental are often used also for the ablative, *e. g.* ಮಸ್ತಕದಿಂ, ಉತ್ತಮಾಂಗದಿಂ, ಅಭ್ರದಿಂ, ತಿಳಿಗೊಳದಿನ್ದಂ, ತಿಳಿಗೊಳದಿನ್ದೆ. See § 352 4 *a*, 1 *seq.*

4, Dative ಕೆ, ಕ್ಕೆ, *e. g.* ಮರಕೆ or ಮರಕ್ಕೆ (of ಮರ), ನೆಲಕೆ or ನೆಲಕ್ಕೆ (of ನೆಲ), ಪೊಲಕೆ or ಪೊಲಕ್ಕೆ (of ಪೊಲ), ಬನಕೆ or ಬನಕ್ಕೆ (of ಬನ), ಕುಲಕೆ or ಕುಲಕ್ಕೆ (of ಕುಲ).

The doubling is optional (see § 371 regarding it). ಕ್ (= ಗ್, § 117, *a*, 4) with the vowel ಎ (or with the vowels ಅ, ಒ, ಓ) conveys the meaning of pointing at or exciting attention to. *Cf.* ಅ-ಕ, ಅ-ಕೊ, ಅ-ಕ್ಕ, ಇ-ಕೊ, ಇ-ಕೋ, ಇ-ಕ್ಕೋ in the Dictionary, and see also in § 265 the ಕೆ of ಆಕೆ, ಈಕೆ, ಊಕೆ.

5, Ablative ಅತ್ತಣಿಂ, ಅತ್ತಣಿನ್ದಂ, ಅತ್ತಣಿನ್ದೆ, *e.g.* ಮರದತ್ತಣಿಂ (of ಮರ), ಮನದತ್ತಣಿಂ (of ಮನ); ಬೆಟ್ಟದತ್ತಣಿನ್ದಂ (of ಬೆಟ್ಟ); ಗಟ್ಟದತ್ತಣಿನ್ದೆ (of ಗಟ್ಟ).

The suffixes ಅತ್ತಣಿಂ, ಅತ್ತಣಿನ್ದಂ, ಅತ್ತಣಿನ್ದೆ are the ablative of ಅತ್ತ, that side, meaning 'from that side' (see § 123, *a*, 5). They are attached to the base that has the secondary ದ of the genitive.

In the dialect of the present time ದೆಸೆಯಿನ್ದ or ಕಡೆಯಿನ್ದ, both meaning 'from the side', are occasionally used to imitate the form of this so-called case.

The terminations ಇಂ, ಇನ್ದಂ, ಇನ್ದೆ of the instrumental are, as has been stated under No. 3, often employed for the ablative.

6, Genitive ದ, ದಾ, *e. g.* ಮರದ (of ಮರ), ಮನದ (of ಮನ); ನರಕದಾ (in a śâsana between 597-608 A. D.), ವರ್ಷದಾ, ಶೀರ್ಥದಾ (in śâsana of 804 A. D.).

The suffix ದ is not the primitive termination of the genitive. It is composed of ದ್, a letter of euphony facilitating pronunciation, and ಅ, the real termination of the sixth case (see § 120, *a*, 6). ದಾ is ದ್ + ಆ, *i. e.* a long form of ಅ. *Cf.* the lengthening of the genitive in §§ 117, *a*, 6; 119, *a*, 6; 120, *a*, 6; 128, *a*, 6; 130, *a*, 6; 131, *a*, 6; that of the accusative in 122, *a*, 2. About the ದ್ see also § 119, *a*, 1; and compare also the euphonic ಯ್ in § 130, *a*, 6.

If 'ಪದನ' of the word, in the Šabdamaṇidarpaṇa, page 53, is not a mistake for ಪದದ, the existence of the termination ನ (*i. e.* euphonic ನ್ + ಅ, = ದ್ + ಅ) of the mediæval and modern period is proved already for the ancient period; *cf.* the ನ in ಹೊಲನಲ್ಲಿ under the locative, and ನೆಲನೊಡೆಯ (ನೆಲನ + ಒಡೆಯ) in § 243, *B*, 23.

Regarding the augments ದ್ and ನ್ compare the augments ಅಣ್ and ಅಱ್ in § 122, *a*, 6.

7, Locative ಉಳ್, ಒಳ್, ಒಳು, ಒಳಗೆ, ಅಲ್, ಅಲು, ಅಲ್ಲಿ, ಇ, *e. g.* ವಾರಣಾಶಿವ ದುಳ್ (in a śâsana of 689-696 A. D.), ಪೂರ್ಣಮಾಸದುಳ್, ವಿಷುಪದುಳ್, ಗಾಣದುಳ್ (in a śâsana of 707 A. D.); ಮರದೊಳ್, ಮನದೊಳ್, ಕೊಳದೊಳ್; ತಪದೊಳು, ಭುವನದೊಳು (in a śâsana of 1084 A. D.), ದೇಶದೊಳು, ವಂಶದೊಳು (in a śâsana of 1123 A. D.); ಬನ ದೊಳಗೆ; ಅರ್ಥದಲ್ (in a śâsana of 1181 A. D.); ಬೃಹಸ್ಪತಿವಾರದಲು, ಪಶ್ಚಿಮಭಾಗದಲು (in a śâsana of 1132 A. D.); ತೇಂದಾಳದಲು, ಆದಿವಾರದಲು, ಸ್ಥಳದಲು (in a śâsana of 1182 A. D.); ಕೊಳದಲ್ಲಿ, ಬನದಲ್ಲಿ; ಹೊಲನಲ್ಲಿ (which form occurs in a śâsana of 1186 A. D.); ಕುರು ಕ್ಷೇತ್ರದಿ (in a śâsana of 1187 A. D.).

The suffixes ಉಳ್, ಒಳ್, ಒಳು, ಒಳಗೆ mean 'inside', 'within', and ಅಲ್, ಅಲು (*cf.* remark in § 188), ಅಲ್ಲಿ mean 'place', 'in a place'; ಅಲ್ಲಿ is composed of ಅಲ್ and the termination ಇ; the ಉ of ಒಳು and ಅಲು is a help to enunciation or euphonic (*cf.* 92. 96, remark). The suffixes are added to the base by means of the ದ (*i. e.* ದ್ + ಅ) or ನ (*i. e.* ನ್ + ಅ) of the genitive.

b) in the mediæval dialect

1, Nom. ಂ, ನು, ವು, and (the nominal base itself without any termination, *i. e.*) the crude base, *e. g.* ಮರಂ (of ಮರ), ಕೊಳಂ (of ಕೊಳ), ತೆಱಂ (of ತೆಱ); ನೊಗನು (of ನೊಗ), ನೆಣನು (of ನೆಣ), ನೊಣನು (of ನೊಣ), ಮರನು (of ಮರ), ಹೆಣನು (of ಹೆಣ), ಮೊಱನು (of ಮೊಱ); ಕಸವು (of ಕಸ), ಗುಣವು (of ಗುಣ), ಮೊತ್ತವು (of ಮೊತ್ತ), ಇಱಿಸುಹವು (of ಇಱಿಸುಹ), ಕೊಳ ಗವು (of ಕೊಳಗ); ದಿವಸ, ದಿನ, ಮರ, ಮನ, ಹಳ್ಳ, ಕೊಳುಹ, ಇಸ್ಪ್ರಚಾಪ.

In ನು and ವು the ಂ or ಸೊನ್ನೆ has been changed into ನ್ and ವ್, to which the euphonic ಉ has been added (regarding which see *e. g.* the locative under letter *a*; §§ 92. 111. 112. 113. 119. 121. 125. 126).

Compare the crude base for the nominative in the ancient dialect in §§ 110. 120. 121. 122. 123. 125. 126. 127. 128.

2, Acc. ಅಂ, ಅನು, ಅ, ಅನ್ನ, *e. g.* ಮರನಂ, ಕೆಱನಂ; ಧೂಪಮಂ; ಬೇಟೆವಂ, ಬೋನವಂ, ಕಸವಂ, ಭಸಿತವಂ, ಅಂಗವಂ, ಫಸವಂ; ಅಭಯವನು, ಬೋನವನು; ಕೊಳನ, ಆಶ್ರಯನ; ಉದಕವ, ದೋಷವ, ಕುಲವ, ರಸವ, ಸನ್ದೇಹವ; ಗುಗ್ಗಳವನ್ನ.

The euphonic augments ನ್, ಮ್ and ವ್ are inserted between the base and the terminations. ಅನು is ಅಂ with the euphonic ಉ; in ಅನ್ನ the termination ಅನು has taken the form of ಅನ, and its final has been doubled on account of euphony.

Concerning ಅ compare the ಅ of the genitive (§ 120, *a*, 6), and see the remark on the accusative in the ancient dialect in § 117, *a*, 2.

3, Instr. ಇಂ, ಇನ್ದಂ, ಇನ್ದೆ, ಇನ್ದವು, ಇನ್ದ, ಇ, *e. g.* ನಿನದದಿಂ; ಚಿತ್ತದಿನ್ದಂ, ನಿಯಮದಿನ್ದಂ; ಓಲಗದಿನ್ದೆ; ನಿಶ್ಚಯದಿನ್ದವು, ವಿಕಲ್ಪದಿನ್ದವು; ಅನ್ದದಿನ್ದ, ಸತ್ಕ್ರಿಯದಿನ್ದ; ಅನ್ದದಿ, ಪ್ರಕಾರದಿ, ಆಸುರದಿ, ಅಕ್ಷರತ್ರಯದಿ.

In ಇನ್ದವು (*i. e.* ಇಂ + ದ್ + ಅವು) the ಅಂ has been changed into ಅವ್ to which the euphonic ಉ has been added; ಇನ್ದ has dropped the ಸೊನ್ನೆ. The ಇ is another form of the ancient ಎ of the instrumental. *Cf.* the note under ಇ 2 in the Dictionary and see also § 151, *b*, 2, and the close of § 282.

4, Dat. ಕೆ, ಕ್ಕೆ, *e. g.* ಮರಕೆ, ಮನ್ದಿರಕೆ; ಮರಕ್ಕೆ, ಲಗ್ನಕ್ಕೆ.

5, Abl. ಅತ್ತಣಿಂ, ಅತ್ತಣಿನ್ದಂ, ಅತ್ತಣಿನ್ದೆ, ಅತ್ತಣಿನ್ದ, *e. g.* ಬೆಟ್ಟದತ್ತಣಿನ್ದ, in which the ಸೊನ್ನೆ has been dropped.

6, Gen. ದ, ನ, *e. g.* ಮರದ; ಕೊಳನ, ಜೇಂಕೊಡನ, ಮೊಱನ.

The augment ನ್, like ದ್, is euphonic. Compare the ನ್ of the genitive in §§ 109, *a*; 117, *a*, *b*, *c*.

7, Loc. ಒಳ್, ಒಳು, ಒಳಗೆ, ಅಲು, ಅಲ್ಲಿ, ಅಲಿ, ಇ, *e. g.* ಕಟಕದೊಳು, ಸಮಯದೊಳು; ಉದರದೊಳಗೆ; ಕಾಲದಲು (in a śâsana of 1509 A. D.), ಗುರುವಾರದಲು (in a śâsana of 1533 A. D.); ಬೇಗದಲಿ, ಭಾಗದಲಿ, ತುಪ್ಪದಲಿ; ಪುರದಿ.

ಅಲಿ is a curtailed form of ಅಲ್ಲಿ.

For the augment ದ್ occasionally ನ್ is used, as in ಮರನಲ್ಲಿ.

c) in the (later and) modern dialect

1, Nom. ನು, ವು, and (most frequently) the crude base, *e. g.* ಮೊಲನು (of ಮೊಲ), ಬಱನು (of ಬಱ), ಮರನು (of ಮರ), ಗಿಡನು (of ಗಿಡ); ಪುಸ್ತಕವು (of ಪುಸ್ತಕ), ವಿಷವು (of ವಿಷ), ಗಿಡವು (of ಗಿಡ), ಮರವು (of ಮರ), ಹನ್ದರವು (of ಹನ್ದರ), ಕಾಳಗವು (of ಕಾಳಗ); ಗಿಡ, ಮರ.

2, Acc. ಅನು, ಅನ್ನು, ಅ, ಆ, and (most frequently) the crude bases, *e. g.* ಸಂಗವನು, ಜಗವನು, ದೇಹವನು, ಬೆಲ್ಲವನು; ಕಾಗದವನ್ನು, ಕಷ್ಟವನ್ನು, ಸಾವಿರವನ್ನು, ಗಿಡವನ್ನು, ಮರವನ್ನು; ಮೊಲನ, ಹೆಣನ, ನೆಲನ; ವಿಷವ, ಕೆಲಸವ, ಗಿಡವ, ಮರವ, ತಡವ, ತವವ; ಅನ್ನಾ (of ಅನ್ನ), ಕಾಟಾ (of ಕಾಟ), ಪಾಠಾ (of ಪಾಠ), ಭೇದಾ (of ಭೇದ), ಮೊಱಾ (of ಮೊಱ), ಹಣಾ (of ಹಣ), ಹಳ್ಳಾ (of ಹಳ್ಳ); ಗಿಡ, ಮರ.

The euphonic augments are ವ್ and ನ್; in ಅನ್ನು the final of ಅನು has been doubled for the sake of euphony; the ಆ is attached to the crude base.

3, Instr. ಇನ್ದ, ಇ, *e. g.* ಮನದಿಂದ, ಕುತ್ತದಿಂದ; ಅತಿಶಯದಿ, ಕುಶಲದಿ, ಕೊಟತನದಿ, ಕೃತ್ಯದಿ, ಧ್ಯಾನದಿ, ಹಸನದಿ.

4, Dat. ಕೆ, ಕ್ಕೆ, *e. g.* ಕುಲಕೆ, ಕ್ಷಣಕೆ, ಉತ್ತರಕೆ; ಮರಕ್ಕೆ, ಆಲಕ್ಕೆ, ಸಾಲಕ್ಕೆ.

5, Abl. ಇನ್ದ, *e. g.* ಮರದಿನ್ದ, ಕೆಱದಿನ್ದ; ಮರನಿನ್ದ, ನೆಲನಿನ್ದ.

The augment ನ್ is the same as ದ್.

6, Gen. ದ, ದಾ, ನ, *e. g.* ಮರದ; ನಾರಾಯದಾ, ಧರ್ಮದಾ, ಕರ್ಮದಾ; ಕೊಡನ, ನೆಲನ.

The lengthened ದಾ appears frequently in poetry.

7, Loc. ಒಳಗೆ, ಅಲ್ಲಿ, ಅಲಿ, ಇ, *e. g.* ಗ್ರಾಮದೊಳಗೆ; ಮರದಲ್ಲಿ; ಬಲದಲಿ, ವಿನೋದದಲಿ, ಸದ್ಮದಲಿ, ಸೊಸ್ತದಲಿ; ಬನದಿ, ಮನದಿ, ಕಾನನದಿ, ಸ್ಥಳದಿ, ವಳದಿ, ವೇಳ್ಯದಿ.

110. In ancient Kannaḍa no nominal bases receive the ೦ or ಸೊನ್ನೆ in the nominative singular, except masculine, a few feminine (see § 102, ೭), and neuter bases with final ಅ.

Words of which the crude base forms the nominative singular, are *e. g.* ಕಣ್, ಬೆನ್, ಕಡಲ್, ಕಲ್, ಕಾಲ್, ಪುಲ್, ಬಿಸಿಲ್, ಪೊದಱ್, ನೇಸಱ್, ತಳಿರ್, ಬಿದಿರ್, ಸಿಡಿಲ್, ಊರ್, ನೀರ್, ಬೇರ್, ಕುರುಳ್, ಮರುಳ್, ಮುಳ್, ಪೊಕ್ಕುೞ್, ನಾಯ್, ಬಾಯ್, ಗಿಡು, ಕಱು, ಮೞ, ಬಳ್ಳಿ, ಪುಲಿ, ಕರಡಿ, ಎರಲೆ, ಕರೆ, ತೆರೆ, ಕೞಿ, ಕೇೞಿ, ಕೊಲೆ, ಮೞೆ; ಕವಿ, ಪತಿ, ಮನ್ತ್ರಿ, ದೇವಿ, ದೇವತೆ, ಪ್ರಕೃತಿ, ಪ್ರೀತಿ, ಗುರು, ಪಶು; ಪೂ, ಗೋ. See some exceptions in § 111, and § 109 under *b* 1.

111. In the mediæval dialect, as has been stated in §§ 93 and 94, nominal bases ending in a consonant may receive a final euphonic ಉ, in which case their nominative singular shows such an ಉ, *e. g.* ಕಣು, ಕಣ್ಣು, ಕಲು, ಕಲ್ಲು, ಬೆನ್ನು, ಪುಲು, ಪುಲ್ಲು, ಮುಳು, ಮುಳ್ಳು.

Exceptionally this is the case in the ancient dialect too, as we find in a śâsana of about 778 A. D. also ಮಗಳು (for ಮಗಳ್), in one of 1048 A. D. ಕಲ್ಲು (for ಕಲ್), in one of 1084 A. D. ಊರು (for ಊರ್), in one of 1123 A. D. ಸೊಡರು (for ಸೊಡರ್), in one of 1182 A. D. ಪೋಲು, ಸಿಡಿಲು (for ಪೋಲ್, ಸಿಡಿಲ್), and in one of 1187 A. D. ಮುತ್ತರು (for ಮುತ್ತರ್).

112. In modern Kannaḍa, as will be seen from the same paragraphs, nominal bases with a final consonant generally receive the euphonic ಉ, and their nominative singular, therefore very often ends in such an ಉ.

113. A strange peculiarity of modern Kannaḍa writings, especially of school-books, which begins to appear already in mediæval works, is that also to nominal bases with the final vowels ಇ, ಈ, ಉ, ಎ, ಊ, ಋ, ೠ, ಓ, ಔ, the nominative singular of which in the ancient dialect has no termination at all (see § 110), an ಉ is annexed, at option, as the termination of the nominative singular, by means of the letters ಯ್

and ವ್, these ಯ್ and ವ್ being merely a help to enunciation, e. g. ಪತಿಯು, ಗಿಳಿಯು, ತಾಯಿಯು, ನುಡಿಯು; ಹೇಡಿಯು, ಬಳ್ಳಿಯು, ಸ್ತ್ರೀಯು, ಅಪ್ಪೆಯು, ಸಭೆಯು; ಕಱುವು, ಗಿಡುವು, ಗುರುವು, ಪೂವು, ಪಿತೃವು, ಖೂವು, ಗೋವು, ಗೌವು. See §§ 128. 129. 130, and compare letters *b* and *c* in § 109.

114. As very many ancient true Kannaḍa nominal bases have no nominative case-sign in the singular (see § 110), as already in the mediæval dialect neuter and masculine bases with final ಅ too occasionally appear without it (see § 109, letter *b* and § 117, letter *b*), and as in later Kannaḍa such neuter, masculine and feminine bases are most frequently used without it (see § 109, letter *c* and § 117, letter *c*), the thought arises that the ancient ಂ (sŏnnĕ), the termination of the nominative singular of neuters (§ 109), masculines and feminines (§ 117) ending in ಅ, of which ನ್, ಮ್, ವ್, ಸು and ವು are but other forms, originally may have been a sign introduced by grammarians, partly for the sake of euphony in sandhi (§ 215, 8) in order to avoid an hiatus (*e. g.* ಮರನ್ ಇರ್ದುದು for ಮರ ಇರ್ದುದು, ಅರಸನ್ ಒಪ್ಪಿದಂ for ಅರಸ ಒಪ್ಪಿದಂ) and partly as a help to the formation of the oblique cases, especially the accusative and genitive, it forming also therein the euphonic letter (*e. g.* ಮರ+ನ್+ಅಂ, ಮರ+ನ್+ಅ; ರಾಜ+ನ್+ಅಂ, ರಾಜ+ನ್+ಅ). Let it be added that Tuḷu, one of the sister-languages of Kannaḍa, never uses a nominative case-sign for neuter bases ending in ಅ.

115. Kannaḍa grammarians teach that by the suffix ಅ (which means 'he', as we learn from § 193) true Kannaḍa masculine nominial bases are formed. The application of this rule appears *e. g.* in the following instances, in which the formative ಅ is annexed to the ಅ of the genitive (§ 109, letter *a*, 6), the two letters ಅ being euphonically joined (§ 214, *seq.*):—

ಕೇಸಡಿ, a reddish foot, Gen. ಕೇಸಡಿಯ (§ 130); ಕೇಸಡಿಯ+ the formative suffix ಅ, or joined and forming the crude base 'ಕೇಸಡಿಯ', and combined with the nominative case-sign ಂ ಕೇಸಡಿಯಂ, a man of or with reddish feet;—ಇನಿ, charm, Gen. ಇನಿಯ (§ 130); ಇನಿಯ+ಅ, or joined and forming the crude base 'ಇನಿಯ', and combined with the nominative case-sign ಂ ಇನಿಯಂ, a man of charm, a charming man;—ಅಲರ್ಗಣ್, a flower-like eye, Gen. ಅಲರ್ಗಣ್ಣ (§ 120); ಅಲರ್ಗಣ್ಣ+ಅ, or joined and forming the crude base 'ಅಲರ್ಗಣ್ಣ', and combined with the nominative case-sign ಂ ಅಲರ್ಗಣ್ಣಂ, a man of or with flower-like eyes;—ಪೊನ್, gold, Gen. ಪೊನ್ನ (§ 120); ಪೊನ್ನ+ಅ, or ಪೊನ್ನ, or ಪೊನ್ನಂ, a man of gold, a very precious man;—ಬಿಲ್, a bow, Gen. ಬಿಲ್ಲ (§ 120); ಬಿಲ್ಲ+ಅ, or ಬಿಲ್ಲ, or ಬಿಲ್ಲಂ, a man of the bow, an archer;—ಮೂಡ, the east, Gen. ಮೂಡಣ (§ 123); ಮೂಡಣ+ಅ, or ಮೂಡಣ, or ಮೂಡಣಂ, a man of the east;—ಕೆಲ, the side, Gen. ಕೆಲದ (§ 109); ಕೆಲದ+ಅ, or ಕೆಲದ, or ಕೆಲದಂ, a man of or on the side;—ಎಳೆ, youth, Gen. ಎಳೆಯ (§ 130); ಎಳೆಯ+ಅ, or ಎಳೆಯ, or ಎಳೆಯಂ, a man of youth, a youthful man;—ಬಱು, vainness, Gen. ಬಱುವ (§ 128); ಬಱುವ+ಅ, or ಬಱುವ, or ಬಱುವಂ, a vain man;—ಕಱುಬು, envy, Gen. ಕಱುಬ (§ 122); ಕಱುಬ+ಅ, or ಕಱುಬ, or ಕಱುಬಂ, a man of envy, an envious man;—ಕೞ್, theft, Gen. ಕೞ (§ 120); ಕೞ + ಅ, or ಕೞ, or ಕೞಂ, a man of theft, a thief;—ಗಣ್ಮು strength, Gen. ಗಣ್ಮ (§ 122); ಗಣ್ಮ + ಅ, or ಗಣ್ಮ, or ಗಣ್ಮಂ, a man of strength, a powerful man. *Cf.* §§ 224; 243, *B*, remark; 249.

Analogously the formation of the true Kannaḍa masculine nominal bases ಅಣ್ಣ, ತಮ್ಮ, ಕಬ್ಬಿಲ, ಕುಱುಬ, ಪೊಸಮ್ಮ, ಹಱಬ, etc. may have taken place, although the themes to the genitive of which the formative ಅ was attached, are nowadays out of use.

116. But the form of true Kannaḍa crude bases with final ಅ, used in books and the language of ordinary conversation for the nominative singular, *e. g.* ಮರ, ಪೊಲ, ನೆಲ, ಅಲಗಣ್ಣ, ಗಣ್ಮ, ಹೊನ್ನ, does not by itself indicate the gender of them (see also § 102). Likewise ಂ (the sŏnnĕ), the grammatical sign of the nominative singular of bases ending in ಅ (§ 114), does not express distinction of gender; thus, for instance, the neuters ಮರಂ, ಪೊಲಂ, ನೆಲಂ, ಬೆಟ್ಟಂ cannot, by their sŏnnĕ, be distinguished as to gender from the masculines ಅಣ್ಣಂ, ತಮ್ಮಂ, ಗಣ್ಮಂ, ಹೊನ್ನಂ, or from the feminine tadbhavas ಅಕ್ಕಂ, ಅವ್ವಂ (§ 117).

This impossibility of discerning the gender by the sŏnnĕ appears also in the oblique cases of neuter bases ending in ಅ, because they show, with regard to their final ಂ or sŏnnĕ, frequently the same forms as such masculine bases do (see §§ 109. 117), *e. g.* Nom. ಮರನ್ (*i. e.* ಮರಂ before a following vowel; *cf.* its vocative ಮರನೇ and the vocative ಕೊಳನೆ in § 140), ಅಣ್ಣನ್ (*i. e.* ಅಣ್ಣಂ before a following vowel) or also ಮರನು, ಅಣ್ಣನು; Acc. ಮರನಂ, ಅಣ್ಣನಂ; ಪೊಲನಂ, ಅಣ್ಣನಂ; ಕೊಳನ, ಅಣ್ಣನ; Gen. ಕೊಳನ, ಅಣ್ಣನ; Abl. ಮರನಿನ್ದ, ಅಣ್ಣನಿನ್ದ; Loc. ಮರನಲ್ಲಿ, ಅಣ್ಣನಲ್ಲಿ.

Hence it is to be stated as a general rule that all Kannaḍa nominal bases with final ಅ are, in the singular, destitute of a particular sign to express their gender, except in the nominative when it has the euphonic ನ್, in the genitive when it is formed by means of the euphonic ದ್ (§ 109), and in the dative ending in ಕೆ or ಕ್ಕೆ (§ 109).

When the grammarian Kêšava says that there are eight or nine genders in the Kannaḍa language (§ 102), he does not found their difference on outward signs in the nominal bases, but on their distinguishing properties and qualities. It is a fact that in Kannaḍa no nominal crude base in the singular, whether ending in ಅ, ಇ, ಉ and ಎ, or in a consonant, shows a difference of termination expressive of the distinction of male, female and neuter, except in the feminine pronominal suffixes ಅಳ್, ಅಳು (§§ 120. 121), in the neuter pronominal suffixes ತು, ತ್ತು and ದು (§§ 122. 169), in the neuter pronouns ಅದು, ಇದು, ಉದು (§ 122), and in the feminine suffixes ಇತಿ, ಇತ್ತಿ and ತಿ (*e. g.* ಕನ್ನಡಿಗಿತಿ, ಅಕ್ಕಸಾಲಿತಿ, ಗಾಣಿಗಿತ್ತಿ, ಪೆಣ್ಣತಿ), although also these suffixes and words do not bear such terminations as specify absolutely their gender by themselves.

The termination ಅ has above been treated of as to the impossibility of its expressing by itself a distinction of gender. The same absence of an outward sign of gender is seen in the final vowels ಇ, ಉ and ಎ, as there are *e. g.* ಸೊಣ್ಣಿ, a profligate, ತಂಗಿ, a younger sister, ಕೆಳದಿ, a female friend, ಮನ್ದಿ, male or female persons, ಪನ್ದಿ, a hog, ಕುಱಿ, a sheep, ಗಱಿ, a feather; ಗಣ್ಡಸು, a male person, ಗಣ್ಡು, a male person, ಹೆಂಗಸು, a female, ಪೆಣ್ಣು (ಹೆಣ್ಣು), a female, ಕೂಸು, a child, ಎತ್ತು, an ox, ತುಱು, a cow, ಕತ್ತು, the neck; ಎಱೆ, a master, ತನ್ದೆ, a father, ಊಮೆ, a dumb man, ಆವೆ, who? which? ಅನ್ನೆ, such a woman as, ಆಕೆ, that woman, ನೀಱೆ, a damsel, ಪಾಣ್ಬೆ, a whore, ಆನೆ, an elephant, ಕೆಱೆ, a tank, ತೆರೆ, a wave, ಪೆಱೆ, the crescent;—and in final consonants, as there are *e. g.* ಆಳ್ (ಆಳು), a person (masc., fem. and neuter), ಪೆಣ್, a female, ಕಲ್, a stone, ತೇರ್, a chariot, ಚೇಳ್, (ಚೇಳು), a scorpion, ಬಾಳ್ (ಬಾಳು), life.

Let it be added that also in the plural no terminations exist by which the gender is fixed (see §§ 118. 119. 131. 132. 134. 135); also ಅವು, ಇವು, ಉವು (§ 136), the plurals of ಅದು, ಇದು, ಉದು, do not show such forms as at once distinguish them from the singular of the neuters ಕೆಳವು, ಉಱುವು, ಅಱುವು, etc.

117. In § 109 the case-terminations for the singular of neuter bases with final ಅ have been given according to the forms they have in the three periods of the language; here follow the case-terminations for the singular of masculine and feminine bases with final ಅ, *viz.*

a) in the ancient dialect

1, Nom. ಂ, *e. g.* ಕಾಟಂ (of ಕಾಟ), ಕೇಸವಂ (of ಕೇಸವ), ಭೀಮಂ, ವೇದವಿದಂ, ದೇವಂ, ಮಾಡಿದಂ, ಬೇಡುವಂ, ಅಲರ್ಗಣ್ಣಂ, ಕೇಸಡಿಯಂ, ಅಡಪವಳಂ, ಅವಂ, ಆವಂ, ಒಳ್ಳಿದಂ, ತೆಳ್ಳಿದಂ, ಮೆಲ್ಲಿದಂ, ಬೆಟ್ಟಿದಂ, ತೋರಿದಂ, ಎಲ್ಲಿವಂ, ಅಸಿಯಂ; ಅಕ್ಕಂ, ಅಮ್ಮಂ, ಅವ್ವಂ.

ಆವಂ appears also as ಆವೊಂ (*cf.* §§ 119 and 120, letters *a*; 122, letter *a*; § 193, 1 and remarks).

2, Acc. ಅಂ, ಅನು, (ಅ), *e. g.* ಅರಸನಂ (of ಅರಸ), ಮಾಣವಕನಂ (of ಮಾಣವಕ), ಮಾಡಿದನಂ, ಅಡಪವಳನಂ, ಅವನಂ, ಆವನಂ; ಅಕ್ಕನಂ, ಅಮ್ಮನಂ, ಅವ್ವನಂ; ದೇವನನು (in a śâsana of 1182 A. D.).

ಆವನಂ appears also as ಆವೊನಂ (Šabdânuśâsana sûtra 175).

The augment ನ್ is euphonic like that of neuter bases in the accusative § 109, letters *a* and *b*).

In ಅನು the euphonic ಉ has been added to the sonnĕ of ಅಂ.

The termination ಅ in the parenthesis refers to a quotation in the Šabdamaṇidarpaṇa (page 164), *viz.* ಎಲವೋ, ನೀನ್ ಎನ್ನ ಕೊನ್ದಯ್ (oh, thou killedst me), in which, as Kêšava supposes, the ಎನ್ನ (of ಆಂ, I, § 137) is the genitive used instead of the accusative ಎನ್ನಂ. Kêšava appears to be wrong; our opinion is that in this case ಎನ್ನ is the accusative with final ಅ that so frequently occurs in the neuter, masculine and feminine singular of the mediæval and modern dialects (*cf.* ನಾಟ and ತುಱುವ್ವು in § 122, *a*, 2; § 352, 1, *b*).

Likewise when Bhaṭṭâkalaṅka in his grammar under sûtra 231 thinks that in ಎನ್ನ ಮಱೆದಂ (he forgot me) the genitive is used for the accusative, we believe that in this case too ಎನ್ನ is the accusative with final ಅ.

Another similar instance of Kêšava that belongs to a neuter noun with final ಉ, is ಪೂಱುವ (of ಪೂಱು) in the obscene sentence ಪೂಱುವ ಕೇೞ್ (Šabdamaṇidarpaṇa page 75; see § 215, 6, remark 3); it too is the accusative of the mediæval and modern dialects.

It is reasonable to think that the accusative ending in ಅ existed already in the colloquial dialect of the ancient period, but had not been generally accepted by classical writers.

3, Instr. ಇಂ, ಇನ್ದಂ, ಇನ್ದೆ, *e. g.* ಪಾರ್ವನಿಂ (of ಪಾರ್ವ), ಜನನಿಂ (of ಜನ), ಮಾಡಿದನಿಂ, ಅಕ್ಕನಿಂ, ಅಪ್ಪನಿಂ; ಜನನಿನ್ದಂ; ಜನನಿನ್ದೆ, ಗೋವಳನಿನ್ದೆ.

The terminations are attached to the genitive, the final ಅ of which disappears in sandhi (§ 213 *seq.*).

4, Dat. (ಗೆ), ಂಗೆ, *e. g.* (ವಲ್ಲಭಗೆ, in a šâsana of 1123 A. D., if the reading be right; ನಿಮಿರ್ಚಿದಗೆ in the stanza under rûpaka in § 239); ಅರಸಂಗೆ, ಕೆಳೆಯಂಗೆ, ಬ್ರಾಹ್ಮಣಂಗೆ, ಮಾಡಿದಂಗೆ, ಅಡಪವಳಂಗೆ, ಅವಂಗೆ; ಅಕ್ಕಂಗೆ, ಅಪ್ಪಂಗೆ.

ಗೆ is the true termination; the sŏnnĕ before it is merely euphonic (*cf.* § 137, *a*, 4). ಗ್ + ಎ has the same meaning as ಕ್ + ಎ (see § 109); *cf. e. g.* ಅ-ಗೊ, ಇ-ಗೊ in the Dictionary.

5, Abl. ಅತ್ತಣಿಂ, ಅತ್ತಣಿನ್ದಂ, ಅತ್ತಣಿನ್ದೆ, *e. g.* ಮಾಣವಕನತ್ತಣಿಂ, ಅಡಪವಳನತ್ತಣಿಂ, ಮಾಡಿದನತ್ತಣಿಂ, ಆಳ್ದನತ್ತಣಿಂ, ಅವನತ್ತಣಿಂ; ಅಕ್ಕನತ್ತಣಿಂ, ಅಪ್ಪನತ್ತಣಿಂ; ಆಳ್ದನತ್ತಣಿನ್ದಂ; ಆಳ್ದನತ್ತಣಿನ್ದೆ.

The terminations are added to the genitive the final ಅ of which disappears in sandhi (§ 213 *seq.*); those of the instrumental are optionally used for the ablative. See § 352, 4 *a*, 1 *seq.*

6, Gen. ಅ, ಆ, *e. g.* ಕರ್ಣನ (of ಕರ್ಣ), ನೃಪನ, ಮಾಡಿದನ, ಅಡಪವಳನ, ಅವನ; ಅಕ್ಕನ, ಅಪ್ಪನ; ಮೃಡನಾ, ರಾಮನಾ, ಕೈಲಪನಾ, ಇಲ್ಲದನಾ, ಜಿನನಾ.

The augment ನ್ is a letter of euphony facilitating pronunciation; *cf.* the ದ್ and ನ್ of the genitive in § 109, letters *a*, *b* and *c*. About the lengthening of ನ see § 109, *a*, 6.

7, Loc. ಒಳ್, (ಒಳಗೆ), ಅಲ್ಲಿ, *e. g.* ಅರಸನೊಳ್, ಮಾಡಿದನೊಳ್, ಅಡಪವಳನೊಳ್, ಅವನೊಳ್; ಅಕ್ಕನೊಳ್, ಅಪ್ಪನೊಳ್; (ಅರಸನೊಳಗೆ); ಅರಸನಲ್ಲಿ, ಅಕ್ಕನಲ್ಲಿ.

The terminations are added to the genitive according to the rule of sandhi.

b) in the mediæval dialect

1, Nom. ಂ, ನು, and (the nominal base itself without any termination, *i. e.*) the crude base, *e. g.* ಅರಸಂ, ಅವಂ, ಆವಂ; ಅಕ್ಕಂ; ಅಧಿಪನು, ಕಿಂಕರನು, ಅಯ್ಯನು, ಒಡೆಯನು, ಕ್ಷತ್ರಿಯನು, ಮಾಳ್ಪವನು; ಅವ, ಮಗ, ರಾಮಯ್ಯ, ಮಾದರಸ, ವಸಿಷ್ಠಪುತ್ರ, ಮಾವನ್ತ, ಶುನಕ, ಆತ.

In ನು the sŏnnĕ has been changed into ನ್ before the euphonic vowel ಉ.

2, Acc. ಅಂ, ಅನು, ಅನ್ನು, ಅ, *e. g.* ಧನಿಕನಂ (of ಧನಿಕ); ಅಕ್ಕನಂ; ಅಭಿಷಿಕ್ತನನು, ಚೋರನನು, ವಾರ್ಯ್ಕನನು, ಧೂರ್ಜನನು; ಮಂಗಳನನ್ನು; ಸತ್ತವನ.

In ಅನ್ನು the ನ್ has been euphonically doubled.

3, Instr. ಇಂ, ಇನ್ನಂ, ಇನ್ದೆ, (ಇನ್ದವೃ, ಇನ್ದ)[1], *e.g.* ಕಷ್ಟನಿಂ; ಅಯ್ಯನಿನ್ದಂ; ಶಂಕರನಿನ್ದೆ.

4, Dat. ಗೆ, ಂಗೆ, *e.g.* ಅಯ್ಯಗೆ, ಶಿವಗೆ, ಅವಗೆ, ಈತಗೆ; ತನೂಜಂಗೆ, ಪಾರ್ವರಂಗೆ, ಬಸವಂಗೆ, ತಿಲಾಡಂಗೆ, ಈತಂಗೆ.

5, Abl. (ಅತ್ತಣಿಂ, ಅತ್ತಣಿನ್ದಂ, ಅತ್ತಣಿನ್ದೆ), **the terminations of the instrumental.**

6, Gen. ಅ, *e.g.* ರಾಜನ; ಅಪ್ಪನ.

7, Loc. ಒಳ್, ಒಳು, (ಒಳಗೆ), ಅಲ್ಲಿ, (ಅಲಿ, see § 109, letter *b*), *e.g.* ಅಜನೊಳ್; ಶಂಕರನೊಳು; ಅಣ್ಣನಲ್ಲಿ; ಅಕ್ಕನಲ್ಲಿ.

c) in the (later and) modern dialect

1, Nom. ನು, **frequently the crude base,** *e.g.* ಹುಡುಗನು, ಹೋಪವನು, ಅವನು, ಇವನು, ಯುವನು; ಅಕ್ಕನು, ಅಪ್ಪನು; ಅಪ್ಪ, ನೃಪ, ಮೂರ್ಖ, ಮುಖಾವ, ಅಳಿಸುವವ, ಹೊರೆವವ, ಅವ, ಇವ; ಅಪ್ಪ.

2, Acc. ಅನು, ಅನ್ನು, ಅ, ಅನ್ನ, *e.g.* ಅಜನನು, ತಿಮ್ಮಪ್ಪನನು, ಶಯನನನು; ಹುಡುಗನನ್ನು, ಆತನನ್ನು, ಅವನನ್ನು; ಅರಸನ, ಮೂರ್ಖನ, ಹಾರುವನ, ಹುಡುಗನ, ಅವನ; ಮಗನ್ನ, ಬಾವನ್ನ, ಬ್ರಹ್ಮರಾಕ್ಷಸನ್ನ, ಕೃಷ್ಣನ್ನ, ವಿಠಲನ್ನ; ಅಕ್ಕನ್ನ.

3, Instr. ಇನ್ದ, *e.g.* ಹುಡುಗನಿನ್ದ, ಅವನಿನ್ದ, ಈತನಿನ್ದ, ಅಕ್ಕನಿನ್ದ, ಅಪ್ಪನಿನ್ದ.

4, Dat. ಗೆ, ನಗೆ, ನಿಗೆ, *e.g.* ಈಶ್ವರಗೆ, ಭಕ್ತಗೆ, ಶೂಕರಗೆ, ಅಣ್ಣಗೆ, ಅವಗೆ; ಅಕ್ಕಗೆ; ಮರುಳನಗೆ, ಹುಚ್ಚನಗೆ; ಅರಸನಿಗೆ, ಅಳಿಯನಿಗೆ, ಹುಡುಗನಿಗೆ, ಮಗನಿಗೆ, ಅವನಿಗೆ; ಅಪ್ಪನಿಗೆ.

The augments ನ and ನಿ and other forms of the euphonic sŏnnĕ, to which the vowels ಅ and ಇ are joined for the sake of euphony, so that ನಗೆ and ನಿಗೆ stand for ಂಗೆ.

5, Abl. ಇನ್ದ, *e.g.* ಅರಸನಿನ್ದ, ಅವನಿನ್ದ; ಅಕ್ಕನಿನ್ದ.

6, Gen. ಅ, ಆ (especially in poetry), *e.g.* ಹುಡುಗನ, ಅವನ; ಅಕ್ಕನ; ಗಣ್ಡನಾ, ಮೂರ್ಖನಾ, ಕೊಡುವವನಾ.

7, Loc. ಒಳಗೆ, ಅಲ್ಲಿ, ಅಲಿ, *e.g.* ಅರಸನೊಳಗೆ; ಹುಡುಗನಲ್ಲಿ, ಅವನಲ್ಲಿ; ಅವನಲಿ; ಅಕ್ಕನಲಿ.

118. The case-terminations for the plural of neuter nominal bases with final ಅ. (*Cf.* §§ 131. 132.)

a) in the ancient dialect

1, Nom. ಗಳ್, ಂಗಳ್, ಂಗಳು, ಂಗಳಿರ್, *e.g.* ಮರಗಳ್, ಪೊಲಗಳ್, ಕೆಲಗಳ್; ಮರಂಗಳ್, ಪೊಲಂಗಳ್, ಕೆಲಂಗಳ್; ಗುಣಂಗಳ್, ಮನಂಗಳ್, ದೇಶಂಗಳ್; ನಗರಂಗಳು (in a śâsana of 1123 A. D.); ಸುರಸಾಲಯಂಗಳಿರ್, ಸುರತರುನನ್ದನಂಗಳಿರ್.

ಗಳ್ is the true termination; in ಂಗಳ್ the sŏnnĕ is euphonic, likewise the ಉ in ಂಗಳು. The ಂಗಳಿರ್ is composed of ಂಗಳ್ and ಇರ್ which is another termination of the plural (see § 119).

Either ಗಳ್ or ಂಗಳ್ are added to true Kannaḍa bases. Saṁskṛita bases according to grammar always use to receive ಂಗಳ್ or ಂಗಳಿರ್ (*cf.* 109, *a*, 2); in a śâsana of 1076 A. D., however, we find ತೀರ್ಥಗಳೊಳು and ಧರ್ಮಗಳನ್.

---

[1] The absence of instances for certain terminations in parenthesis in this and other cases, only means to say that instances with them have not been met with by the author, although they do exist; see *e.g.* ಇನ್ದವು in § 119, *b*; ಇನ್ದ in § 120, *b*.

2, Acc. ಅಂ, *e. g.* ಮರಗಳಂ, ಮರಂಗಳಂ; ವಚನಂಗಳಂ.

The terminations are attached to those of the nominative. A final ಉ, as in ಂಗಳು, disappears then in sandhi (§ 213 *seq.*).

3, Instr. ಇಂ, ಇನ್ದಂ, ಇನ್ದೆ, *e. g.* ಮರಗಳಿಂ, ಕೆಲಂಗಳಿಂ; ಗುಣಂಗಳಿಂ.

The terminations are added to the genitive, the ಅ of which disappears in sandhi (§ 213 *seq.*).

4, Dat. ಗೆ, ಇಗೆ, *e. g.* ಮರಗಳ್ಗೆ, ಮರಂಗಳ್ಗೆ; ದೇಶಂಗಳ್ಗೆ; ಧರ್ಮಗಳಿಗೆ (in śâsana of 1076 A. D.).

The ಇ in ಇಗೆ is euphonic.

5, Abl. ಅತ್ತಣಿಂ, ಅತ್ತಣಿನ್ದಂ, ಅತ್ತಣಿನ್ದೆ, *e. g.* ಮರಗಳತ್ತಣಿಂ, ಮರಂಗಳತ್ತಣಿಂ; ದೇಶಂಗಳತ್ತಣಿಂ.

The terminations are attached to the genitive.

6, Gen. ಅ, *e. g.* ಮರಗಳ, ಮರಂಗಳ; ದೇಶಂಗಳ.

7, Loc. ಒಳ್, ಒಳು, (ಒಳಗೆ), ಅಲ್ಲಿ, *e. g.* ಮರಗಳೊಳ್, ಮರಂಗಳೊಳ್; ದೇಶಂಗಳೊಳ್, ಬನಂಗಳೊಳ್; ತೀರ್ಥಗಳೊಳು (in a śâsana of 1076 A. D.); ಮರಗಳಲ್ಲಿ, ಮರಂಗಳಲ್ಲಿ; ದೇಶಂಗಳಲ್ಲಿ.

The terminations are added to the genitive.

b) in the mediæval dialect

1, Nom. ಗಳ್, ಗಳು, ಂಗಳ್, ಂಗಳು, ಗಳಿರ್, (ಂಗಳಿರ್), *e. g.* ಮರಗಳ್; ಮರಂಗಳ್; ಕರ್ಮಗಳು, ಸೇನಾಂಗಗಳು; ಮರಂಗಳು, ಉಪಕರಣಂಗಳು; ಮರಗಳಿರ್.

2, Acc. ಅಂ, ಅನು, ಅ, *e. g.* ಫಲಂಗಳಂ, ಪರಿಚರಿಯಂಗಳಂ; ಫಲಂಗಳನು, ಕುತೂಹಲಗಳನು, ರಸಾಯನಗಳನು; ಪದಾರ್ಥಗಳ, ರಸಾಯನಂಗಳ.

3, Instr. ಇಂ, ಇನ್ದಂ, ಇನ್ದೆ, ಇನ್ದ, (ಇನ್ದವು), *e. g.* ಆಟಂಗಳಿಂ, ಸ್ಥಳಗಳಿಂ; ವಿಮಾನಗಳಿನ್ದಂ; ಅಕ್ಷರಂಗಳಿನ್ದೆ; ವಿಭವಂಗಳಿನ್ದ.

4, Dat. ಗೆ, ಇಗೆ, *e. g.* ಮರಗಳ್ಗೆ, ಮರಂಗಳ್ಗೆ, ವೃಕ್ಷಂಗಳ್ಗೆ; ಉಪಚಾರಂಗಳಿಗೆ, ಕೆಲಸಂಗಳಿಗೆ, ಗೃಹಂಗಳಿಗೆ, ಧರ್ಮಂಗಳಿಗೆ, ವಾದ್ಯಂಗಳಿಗೆ, ಚರಣಂಗಳಿಗೆ, ಕುಜಂಗಳಿಗೆ.

5, Abl. ಅತ್ತಣಿಂ, ಅತ್ತಣಿನ್ದಂ, ಅತ್ತಣಿನ್ದೆ, (ಅತ್ತಣಿನ್ದ); the terminations of the instrumental.

6, Gen. ಅ, *e.g.* ನರಗಳ, ಮರಂಗಳ; ವಿಧಂಗಳ.

7, Loc. ಒಳ್, ಒಳು, ಒಳಗೆ, ಅಲ್ಲಿ, ಅಲಿ, *e.g.* ಗೃಹಂಗಳೊಳ್; ಜನಂಗಳೊಳು; ಬೆಟ್ಟಂಗಳೊಳಗೆ, ವನವಾಸಂಗಳೊಳಗೆ; ಯುಗಂಗಳಲ್ಲಿ, ವೃಕ್ಷಂಗಳಲ್ಲಿ; ಆಲಿಂಗನಗಳಲಿ, ಪ್ರತ್ಯಯಂಗಳಲಿ, ಭಕ್ಷಣಂಗಳಲಿ.

c) in the modern dialect

1, Nom. ಗಳು, *e.g.* ಗಿಡಗಳು, ಮರಗಳು, ಕರ್ಮಗಳು, ದೋಷಗಳು.

2, Acc. ಅನು, ಅನ್ನು, ಅ, *e.g.* ತರ್ಪಣಗಳನು, ಕರಗಳನು, ವಸನಗಳನು; ಗಿಡಗಳನ್ನು, ಮರ್ಗಗಳನ್ನು; ಪುರಗಳ, ಗಿಡಗಳ, ಉಪಕಾರಗಳ.

3, Instr. ಇನ್ದ, *e.g.* ಗಿಡಗಳಿನ್ದ, ಕರ್ಮಗಳಿನ್ದ.

4, Dat. ಇಗೆ, *e.g.* ಗಿಡಗಳಿಗೆ, ಕರ್ಮಗಳಿಗೆ.

5, Abl. ಇನ್ದ, *e.g.* ಗಿಡಗಳಿನ್ದ, ಕರ್ಮಗಳಿನ್ದ.

6, Gen. ಅ, *e.g.* ಗಿಡಗಳ, ಕರ್ಮಗಳ, ರಸ್ತೆಗಳ.

7, Loc. ಒಳಗೆ, ಅಲ್ಲಿ, ಅಲಿ, *e.g.* ಗಿಡಗಳೊಳಗೆ; ಗಿಡಗಳಲ್ಲಿ, ಕಮಲಗಳಲ್ಲಿ; ಅಮ್ಬರಗಳಲಿ.

119. The case-terminations for the plural of masculine, feminine and epicene (§ 102, 4) bases with final ಅ, including also some bases that occur only in the plural. (*Cf.* §§ 131. 132. 134. 135. 137.)

a) in the ancient dialect

1, Nom. ಂಗಳ್, ಕಳ್, ಅರ್, ಅರು, ಒರ್, ಬರ್, ಂಬರ್, ವರ್, ಅರ್ಕಳ್, ಅರ್ಗಳ್, ಇರ್, ಅರಿರ್, ಂಗಳಿರ್, ಅರ್ಕಳಿರ್, ಂದಿರ್, ಂದಿರಿರ್, ಂದಿರ್ಗಳ್, *e.g.* ಅಣ್ಣಂಗಳ್, ಅಯ್ಯಂಗಳ್, ಆತಂಗಳ್, ಈತಂಗಳ್, ಊತಂಗಳ್, ಭಾವಂಗಳ್, ಮಾವಂಗಳ್; ಅಕ್ಕಂಗಳ್, ಅವ್ವಂಗಳ್; ಮಕ್ಕಳ್, (of ಮಗ); ಅರಸರ್, ಸಾಮನ್ತರ್, ಪಾರ್ವರ್, ಮಾಡಿದರ್, ಎರೆವರ್, ನುಡಿವರ್, ಪೆಂಡಿರ್, ಅವರ್, ಇವರ್, ಉವರ್, ಒಳ್ಳಿದರ್, ಮೆಲ್ಲಿದರ್, ನೇರಿದರ್, ಇನಿಯರ್, ಪಿರಿಯರ್, ಮಣಿಗಾರರ್, ಇರ್ಬರ್, ಪಲರ್, ಕೆಲರ್, ಎಲ್ಲರ್, ಅನಿಬರ್; ಅರಸರು, ತೆಲ್ಲಿಗರು (both in a šâsana of 1123 A. D.), ಶಿಷ್ಯರು, ದೇವರು, ಸಧರ್ಮರು, ತಾಪಸರು (the four terms in a šâsana of 1182 A. D.), ನಾಯಕರು, ಗೊಂಕರಸರು (both in a šâsana of 1187 A. D.); ಕಾನ್ದಜೋರ್ (in a šâsana between 680 and 696 A. D.), ಇಬ್ಬೊರ್ (in a šâsana of 866 A. D.), ನೂರ್ಪದಿನ್ಬೊರ್ (in a šâsana of 916 A. D.); ಇರ್ಬರ್, ಅನಿಬರ್, ಇನಿಬರ್, ಎನಿಬರ್, ಪಲಬರ್, ಕೆಲಬರ್; ಪಲಮ್ಬರ್, ಕೆಲಮ್ಬರ್; ಎಲ್ಲವರ್, ಇರ್ವರ್, ಮೂವರ್, ನೂರ್ವರ್, ಸಾಸಿರ್ವರ್, ಪಲವರ್; ಬುಧರ್ಕಳ್, ಗೋವರ್ಕಳ್, ಪುರುಷರ್ಕಳ್, ಅಹಿತರ್ಕಳ್, ಮೂವರ್ಕಳ್; ಕಾದಲರ್ಗಳ್, ಅವರ್ಗಳ್, ಇವರ್ಗಳ್, ಉವರ್ಗಳ್; ಪೆಣ್ಡಿರ್; ನಣ್ಬರಿರ್, ನಲ್ಲರಿರ್, ಪುರುಷರಿರ್, ಪಣ್ಡಿತರಿರ್, ನೇರಿದರಿರ್; ಅಕ್ಕಂಗಳಿರ್; ಬುಧರ್ಕಳಿರ್; ಅಣ್ಣನ್ದಿರ್, ಭಾವನ್ದಿರ್, ಮಾವನ್ದಿರ್, ಅಯ್ಯನ್ದಿರ್, ಇವನ್ದಿರ್, ಅವನ್ತಿರ್, ಉವನ್ದಿರ್; ಅಕ್ಕನ್ದಿರ್; ಮೂವನ್ದಿರಿರ್; ಇವನ್ದಿರ್ಗಳ್.

ಅರು is ಅರ್ and a euphonic ಉ (*cf.* § 96 remark); ಒರ್ is another form of ಅರ್ (*cf.* § 117, letter *a*). In ಬರ್, ಂಬರ್ and ವರ್ the letters ಬ್, ಂಬ್ and ವ್ are euphonic augments; ಅರ್ಕಳ್, ಅರ್ಗಳ್ are composed of ಅರ್ and ಕಳ್ and ಗಳ್; ಅರಿರ್ is composed of ಅರ್ and ಇರ್, and ಅರ್ಕಳಿರ್ of ಅರ್, ಕಳ್ and ಇರ್; in ಂದಿರ್ the sŏnnĕ is euphonic; ಂದಿರಿರ್ is ಂದಿರ್ and ಇರ್; ಂನ್ದಿರ್ಗಳ್ is composed of ಂದಿರ್ and ಗಳ್; ದಿರ್ is composed of a euphonic ದ್ and ಇರ್ (*cf.* the euphonic ದ್ of the genitive in § 109, *a*, 6; that of ದಿರ್ in §§ 132, *a*. 134, *a*; that of ಅಲ್ಲಿದಂ, etc. in § 243, *B*, remark; that of ಒಳ್ಳಿದಂ in § 276).

2, Acc. ಅಂ, ಅನು, *e.g.* ಅಣ್ಣಂಗಳಂ; ಮಕ್ಕಳಂ; ಅಕ್ಕಂಗಳಂ, ಅರಸರಂ, etc.; ಕೂಲರನು (in a šâsana of 1182 A. D.).

ಅನು is ಂ (ನ್) and a euphonic ಉ.

3, Instr. ಇಂ, ಇನ್ದಂ, ಇನ್ದೆ, *e.g.* ಅಣ್ಣಂಗಳಿಂ; ಮಕ್ಕಳಿಂ; ಅಕ್ಕಂಗಳಿಂ; ಧೀರರಿಂ; ಧೀರರ್ಕಳಿಂ; etc.

The terminations are added to the genitive according to the rule of sandhi (§ 213 *seq.*).

4, Dat. ಗೆ, ಗ್ಗೆ, ಇಗೆ, ಕೆ, *e.g.* ಅಣ್ಣಂಗಳ್ಗೆ; ಮಕ್ಕಳ್ಗೆ; ಅಕ್ಕಂಗಳ್ಗೆ; ದೇವರ್ಗೆ or ದೇವರ್ಗ್ಗೆ, ಬುಧರ್ಗೆ or ಬುಧರ್ಗ್ಗೆ, ಬಾನ್ಧವರ್ಗೆ or ಬಾನ್ಧವರ್ಗ್ಗೆ, ಎರೆವರ್ಗೆ or ಎರೆವರ್ಗ್ಗೆ, etc.; ದೇವರಿಗೆ (in a śâsana of 1123 A. D.), ಭೀತರಿಗೆ, ಬ್ರಾಹ್ಮಣಂಗೆ (both in a śâsana of 1181 A. D.); ದೇವರ್ಕೆ (in a śâsana between 597 and 608 A. D.).

ಗ್ಗ occurs optionally after the rêpha; such a doubling of a consonant after it is very frequent. *Cf.* §§ 132, *a*; 155; 240, under 5; 246, under *a*; § 371, 1.

The ಇ before ಗೆ is a euphonic prefix.

5, Abl. ಅತ್ತಣಿಂ, ಅತ್ತಣಿನ್ದಂ, ಅತ್ತಣಿನ್ದೆ; the terminations of the instrumental, *e. g.* ಅಣ್ಣಂಗಳತ್ತಣಿಂ, etc.

6, Gen. ಅ, ಆ, *e. g.* ಅಣ್ಣಂಗಳ; ಮಕ್ಕಳ; ಅಕ್ಕಂಗಳ; ಪೆಣ್ದಿರ; etc.; ವೆಡೆವಳ್ಳಿಯರಾ (in a śâsana between 680 and 696 A. D.), ಭಟಾರರಾ (in a śâsana of 804 A. D.).

ಆ is simply a euphonically lengthened ಅ. See § 109, *a*, 6.

7, Loc. ಒಳ್, (ಒಳಗೆ), ಅಲ್ಲಿ, *e. g.* ಅಣ್ಣಂಗಳೊಳ್; ಅಕ್ಕಂಗಳೊಳ್; ದೇವರೊಳ್, ರಸಿಕರೊಳ್, ಕಾದುವರೊಳ್; etc.

b) in the mediæval dialect

1, Nom. the same case-terminations as in the ancient dialect; further ಗಳ್, ಗಳು, ಂಗಳು, ಕಳು, ಕಳುಗಳ್, ಬರು, ಂಬರು, ಅರುಗಳ್, ಅರುಗಳು, ಅರುಗಳಿರ್, ದಿರ್, ದಿರು, ಂದಿರು, *e. g.* ಈತಗಳ್; ದೇವಗಳು; ಪರಿಜನಂಗಳು; ಅಕ್ಕಂಗಳಿರ್; ಮಕ್ಕಳು; ಮಕ್ಕಳುಗಳ್; ಅವರ್; ದೇವರು, ಭಕ್ತರು, ನರರು, ಮಾನವರು, ಊರವರು, ಕೆಲರು; ಕೆಲಬರು; ಕೆಲಮ್ಬರು; ಭಕ್ತರುಗಳ್, ಮುಗ್ಧರುಗಳ್, ಹಿರಿಯರುಗಳ್, ಹೋದವರುಗಳ್; ಭಕ್ತರುಗಳು, ಅವರುಗಳು; ಜಡರುಗಳಿರ್; ಅವದಿರ್, ಅವದಿರು; ತಮ್ಮನ್ದಿರು.

The terminations show a free use of the euphonic ಉ and an occasional omission of the euphonic sŏnnĕ.

2, Acc. ಅಂ, ಅ, *e. g.* ಹಿರಿಯರುಗಳಂ; ಮೂವರಂ; ಅಯ್ಯಗಳ, ಅವರುಗಳ, ಲೋಗರ, ಅನಿಬರ.

3, Instr. ಇಂ, ಇನ್ದಂ, ಇನ್ದೆ, ಇನ್ದವು, *e. g.* ಮತಿವನ್ತರಿನ್ದಂ; ವಿದ್ವಾಂಸರಿನ್ದೆ, ಇವರಿನ್ದೆ; ಬಲ್ಲವರುಗಳಿನ್ದವು.

4, Dat. ಗೆ, ಇಗೆ, ಇಂಗೆ, *e. g.* ಭಕ್ತರ್ಗೆ, ಇನಿಯರ್ಗೆ, ಎಲ್ಲರ್ಗೆ; ಅಯ್ಯಂಗಳಿಗೆ, ಒಡೆಯರಿಗೆ, ಅರಸರಿಗೆ, ಗಣ್ಡರಿಗೆ, ಪ್ರಮಥರಿಗೆ, ಮನುಜರಿಗೆ, ಮಾನವರಿಗೆ, ಅವರಿಗೆ, ಎಲ್ಲರಿಗೆ, ವೇದಿಸುವರಿಗೆ, ಪರರುಗಳಿಗೆ, ಭಕ್ತರುಗಳಿಗೆ, ಶಿಷ್ಯರುಗಳಿಗೆ, ಅವರ್ಗಳಿಗೆ; ಅವರಿಂಗೆ.

The ಇ and ಇಂ are euphonical prefixes.

5, Abl. ಅತ್ತಣಿಂ, ಅತ್ತಣಿನ್ದಂ, ಅತ್ತಣಿನ್ದೆ; the terminations of the instrumental.

6, Genitive ಅ, *e. g.* ಅಯ್ಯಗಳ, ದೇವರ್ಕಳ, ಅವರ್ಗಳ, ಹೋದವರುಗಳ, ಮೂವರ, ಪಲರ, ಅವನ್ದಿರ.

7, Loc. ಒಳ್, ಒಳು, ಒಳಗೆ, ಅಲ್ಲಿ, (ಅಲಿ), *e. g.* ಶರಣರುಗಳೊಳ್; ಎಲ್ಲರೊಳು; ಅವರೊಳಗೆ, ಇವರೊಳಗೆ, ನರರೊಳಗೆ, ಆಢ್ಯರುಗಳೊಳಗೆ, ಅವರಲ್ಲಿ.

c) in the modern dialect

1, Nom. ಗಳು, ಕಳು, ಕಳಿರು, ಅರು, ಬರು, ವರು, ಂದರು, ಂದಿರು, *e. g.* ಅಕ್ಕಗಳು; ಮಕ್ಕಳು; ಮಕ್ಕಳಿರು; ಹುಡುಗರು, ಹೆಣ್ಡಿರು, ಅವರು, ಇವರು, ಹಲರು; ಹಲಬರು, ಇಬ್ಬರು; ಹಲವರು, ಕೆಲವರು, ಮೂವರು; ಬಾವನ್ದರು; ತಮ್ಮನ್ದಿರು, ಅಣ್ಣನ್ದಿರು, ಹೆಣ್ಣನ್ದಿರು.

ಕಳಿರು is ಕಳು (= ಕಳ್) and ಇರು (= ಇರ್).

Another plural is formed by adding ಅವರು, the nominative plural of the pronouns ಅವ or ಅವಳು, to the nominative singular, *e. g.* ಅಪ್ಪನವರು (ಅಪ್ಪಂ or ಅಪ್ಪನ್ + ಅವರು), ಅವ್ವನವರು, ಅಯ್ಯನವರು, or to the nominative plural, *e. g.* ಸಾಹೇಬರವರು. *Cf.* § 131, *c*, 1, and see § 258.

2, Acc. ಅನು, ಅನ್ನು, ಅನ್ನ, ಅ, ಆ, *e.g.* ಕಳ್ಳರನು, ಹೆಣ್ಣರನು; ಹುಡುಗರನ್ನು; ಯಾರನ್ನ (§ 135); ಎಲ್ಲರ, ಯಾರ (§ 135); ಭ್ರಷ್ಟರಾ.

3, Instr. ಇನ್ದ, *e.g.* ಹುಡುಗರಿನ್ದ.

4, Dat. ಅಗೆ, ಇಗೆ, *e.g.* ಇಬ್ಬರಗೆ; ಅಧಮರಿಗೆ, ಹುಡುಗರಿಗೆ.

The ಅ and ಇ before ಗೆ are euphonic additions.

5, Abl. ಇನ್ದ, *e.g.* ಹುಡುಗರಿನ್ದ.

6, Gen. ಅ, ಆ, *e.g.* ಹುಡುಗರ, ಮೂವರ, ಹಲವರ, ಎಲ್ಲರ; ಅವರಾ, ಒಬ್ಬರಾ, ಹೆಣ್ಣರಾ.

7, Loc. ಒಳಗೆ, ಅಲ್ಲಿ, (ಅಲಿ), *e.g.* ನೃಪರೊಳಗೆ; ಹುಡುಗರಲ್ಲಿ.

120. The case-terminations for the singular of neuter and feminine bases (and of one that is either masculine or neuter in the ancient language, *viz.* ಆಳ್, § 102, 5) **ending in consonants.**

a) in the ancient dialect

1, Nom. **the crude base,** *e.g.* ಕಲ್, ಬಿಲ್, ಕಳ್, ಮುಳ್, ಕೆಯ್, ಕಾರ್, ಕಾಲ್, ಕೋಲ್, ಕುರುಳ್, ಅಗಡ್, ಬಾಸುಟ್, ತಿಮಿರ್, ಮೊಸರ್, ಪವಣ್; ಪೆಣ್, ತಾಯ್; ಅವಳ್, ಇವಳ್, ಉವಳ್, ಆವಳ್, ಪೆಱಳ್, ಇನಿಯಳ್, ಕರಿಯಳ್, ಒಳ್ಳಿದಳ್, ಒರ್ವಳ್, ಒರ್ಬಳ್; ಆಳ್; ಅಗಲ್, ಪೊಗಬಲ್; ನುಡಿಯಲ್, ಪೇೞಲ್ (see § 187, 1).

ಆವಳ್ appears also as ಆವೊಳ್ (Šabdânušâsana sûtra 175).

2, Acc. ಅಂ, ಆಂ, the crude base, *e.g.* ಕಲ್ಲಂ, ಬಿಲ್ಲಂ, ಮುಳ್ಳಂ, ಕೆಯ್ಯಂ, ಕಾರಂ, ಕಾಲಂ, ಕೋಲಂ, ಕಾಯಂ, ಬಾಯಂ, ಕುರುಳಂ, ಅಗಡಂ, ಮೊಸರಂ, ಅವಳಂ, ಇವಳಂ, ಉವಳಂ, ಆವಳಂ; ಕಲ್ಲಾಂ, ಬಿಲ್ಲಾಂ; ಬೀಡ್ (in ಬೀಡ್ ಕೊಳ್), ಕೋಡ್ (in ಕೋಡ್ ಕುಟ್ಟು), ಊಳ್ (in ಊಳ್ ಇಡು).

ಆವಳಂ appears also as ಆವೊಳಂ (Šabdânušâsaṇa sûtra 175).

The doubling of the consonant of monosyllabic bases with a short vowel takes place on account of euphony (*cf.* § 215, 7, *d*).

Kêšava (page 297) gives the following quotation (see § 365); ಬಯ್ಗಿನ ಕೆಮ್ಬಿಸಿಲೆಳಸಲ್ ಎಸೆದುವು ಆಶ್ರಯದ ತರುಗಳ್, and remarks that the ಅಲ್ in ಎಳಸಲ್ is wrong (abaddha), as it ought to be ಎಳಸೆ or ಎಳಸಲೊಡಂ or ಎಳಸಲೊಡನೆ, because a new agent or subject is introduced, *viz.* ತರುಗಳ್, ಕೆಮ್ಬಿಸಿಲ್, therefore, is the crude base and stands for the accusative. A translation is:—'When (they, certain people) desired the purple sunshine of the evening, the trees of the hermitage appeared'. *Cf.* the ancient accusatives ಐ in § 125, ಮೂಡಲ್ in § 126, ಅನ್ನು in § 127, ಗೆ in § 130, *a*, 2, especially also the Kriyâsamâsa (§ 253, 1, *a*) in which the crude base represents the accusative, and § 352, 6, *b*.

3, Instr. ಇಂ, ಇನ್ದಂ, ಇನ್ದೆ, *e. g.* ಕಲ್ಲಿಂ, ಕಲ್ಲಿನ್ದಂ, ಕಲ್ಲಿನ್ದೆ, ಕಾರಿಂ, ಕೋಲಿಂ, ಬೇರಿಂ, ಬದಿರಿಂ, ತುಱುಗಲಿನ್ದೆ.

The terminations are attached to the genitive according to the rule of sandhi (§ 213 *seq.*). *Cf.* the ಇಂ in the Dictionary, Additions, p. 1711.

4, Dat. ಕೆ, ಗೆ, *e. g.* ನುಡಿಯಲ್ಕೆ, ಪೇೞಲ್ಕೆ, ಕಾೞ್ಕೆ, ಕೋೞ್ಕೆ, ನಾಡ್ಕೆ; ಕಲ್ಗೆ, ಪುಲ್ಗೆ, ಬಿಲ್ಗೆ, ಮುಳ್ಗೆ, ಕೆಯ್ಗೆ, ಕಾಲ್ಗೆ, ತೋಳ್ಗೆ, ಸೂೞ್ಗೆ, ಅಗೞ್ಗೆ, ಬಾಸುೞ್ಗೆ, ಪವಣ್ಗೆ; ಅವಳ್ಗೆ, ಇವಳ್ಗೆ.

5, Abl. ಅತ್ತಣಿಂ, ಅತ್ತಣಿನ್ದಂ, ಅತ್ತಣಿನ್ದೆ, the terminations of the instrumental *e. g.* ಕಲ್ಲತ್ತಣಿಂ, ಕೆಯ್ಯತ್ತಣಿಂ, ಕಾಲತ್ತಣಿಂ.

6, Gen. ಅ, ಆ, *e. g.* ಕಲ್ಲ, ಬಿಲ್ಲ, ಕಳ್ಳ, ಕೆಯ್ಯ, ಕಾಲ, ಕೋಲ, ತೋಳ, ನಾಯ, ಸೂೞ, ಕುರುಳ; ಪೆಣ್ಣ, ತಾಯ; ಅವಳ, ಇವಳ, ಉವಳ, ಆವಳ, ಒರ್ವಳ; ಆಳ; ಊರಾ (in a śâsana of about 750 A. D.).

Here we have the primitive form of the genitive, *viz.* ಅ. About the doubling see the Accusative.

7, Loc. ಉಳ್, ಒಳ್, (ಒಳಗೆ), ಅಲ್, ಅಲು, ಅಲ್ಲಿ, *e. g.* ತಿಂಗಳುಳ್ (in a śâsana of 707 A. D.); ಎಳ್ವೊಳ್ (of ಎಳ್), ಕೆಯ್ಯೊಳ್, ಬೆನ್ನೊಳ್, ಕಾಲೊಳ್, ತೇರೊಳ್, ಸೂೞೊಳ್; ಕೆಯ್ಯಲ್ (in a śâsana of 971 A. D.); ಕೋಲಲು (in a śâsana of 1187 A. D.); ಕಣ್ಣಲ್ಲಿ, ನೀರಲ್ಲಿ.

The terminations are added to the genitive according to rule.

b) in the mediæval dialect

1, Nom. the crude base, *e.g.* ಕಲ್, ಕಾಲ್; ಹೆಣ್; ಅವಳ್, ಇವಳ್, ಆವಳ್, ಒರ್ಬಳ್, ಒರ್ವಳ್; ಈಗಳ್.

2, Acc. ಅಂ, ಅ, the crude base, *e. g.* ಕಲ್ಲಂ, ಕಾಲಂ; ಮಗಳಂ; ಹೆಣ್ಣ; ಕಲ್ಲ, ಪಾಲ, ಹಾಲ; ಊಳ್ (in ಊಳ್ ಇಡು), ಬೇರ್ (in ಬೇರ್ ಊಱು), ಬೇಳ್ (in ಬೇಳ್ ಮಾಡು), ಮೆಯ್ (in ಮೆಯ್ಯ್ ಇಕ್ಕು).

3, Instr. ಇಂ, (ಇನ್ದಂ), ಇನ್ದೆ, (ಇನ್ದವು), ಇನ್ದ, *e. g.* ಕೆಯ್ಯಿಂ, ನೀರಿಂ, ಕೆಯ್ಯಿನ್ದೆ, ಕೆಯ್ಯಿನ್ದ, ಕೊರಳಿನ್ದ.

4, Dat. ಕೆ, ಗೆ, *e. g.* ಈಗಳ್ಕೆ; ಹರಸಲ್ಕೆ, ಅಗಲ್ಕೆ, ಅಯ್ದಲ್ಕೆ; ಊರ್ಗೆ, ಬಾಯ್ಗೆ, ಕಲ್ಗೆ.

5, Abl. ಅತ್ತಣಿಂ, ಅತ್ತಣಿನ್ದಂ, ಅತ್ತಣಿನ್ದೆ, the terminations of the instrumental.

6, Gen. ಅ, *e. g.* ಕಲ್ಲ, ಕೆಯ್ಯ, ಮಣ್ಣ, ಹುಲ್ಲ, ಊರ, ಕಾಯ; ತಾಯ (or ತಾಯ್ಯ); ಅವಳ, ಇವಳ, ಆವಳ, ಒರ್ಬಳ; ಆಳ.

7, Loc. ಒಳ್, ಒಳು, ಒಳಗೆ, ಅಲು, ಅಲ್ಲಿ, ಅಲಿ, ಇಲಿ, *e. g.* ಕಲ್ಲೊಳ್, ಕೆಸಱೊಳ್, ಪಾಲೊಳ್; ನೀರೊಳು, ಬಾಗಿಲೊಳು; ಒಡಲೊಳಗೆ, ಕೊರಲೊಳಗೆ, ಬಿಸಿಲೊಳಗೆ; ಕೆಯ್ಯಲು; ಕೆಯ್ಯಲ್ಲಿ, ಕೊರಳಲ್ಲಿ; ಕಣ್ಣಲಿ, ಕಲ್ಲಲಿ, ಕಾಲಲಿ, ನೀರಲಿ, ಕೊರಳಲಿ, ಪೆಸರಲಿ, ಮೊಸರಲಿ, ಹೊಱವಾಱಲಿ; ಕಲ್ಲಿಲಿ.

In ಇಲಿ the auxiliary augment ಇನ್ of § 121 appears to have been mutilated.

c) in the modern dialect

In §§ 92. 93 and 112 it has been stated that, in general, all ancient nominal bases with a final consonant appear with a euphonic final ಉ or ಇ in modern Kannaḍa; but there are exceptions, that is especially when such bases are immediately connected with another noun or verb, *e. g.* ಕಲ್-ದೋಣಿ, ಕಲ್-ನಾರು, ಕಲ್-ಹೂವು, ಕಾಲ್-ಕುಪ್ಪಸ, ಕಾಲ್-ನಡೆ, ಕೆಯ್-ಕೆಳಗೆ, ಕೆಯ್-ಗುದ್ದಲಿ, ಮೆಯ್-ಬಣ್ಣ, ಮೆಯ್-ಮೇಲೆ,

ಬಯಲ್-ಕಡೆ, ಕಾಲ್ ತೆಗೆ, ಕೆಯ್ ಕೊಡು, ಕೆಯ್ ಕೊಳ್ಳು. ಮೆಯ್ ಬರು, or also when they are in union with case-terminations, *e. g.* ಕಾಯು; ಬಾಯಿನ್ದ, ಕೆಯ್ಯಿನ್ದ; ಕೆಯ್ಗೆ, ಮೆಯ್ಗೆ; ತಾಯು, ನಾಯು; ಮೆಯ್ಯಲ್ಲಿ, ಬಾಯಲ್ಲಿ; ಮೆಯ್ಯೊಳಗೆ, ಬಾಯೊಳಗೆ. See also ಕೆಯ್ಯ and ಬಾಯಿಂ (of ಬಾಯ್) in § 121, and ಕೆಯ್, ಬಾಯ್ in a proverb under ಕೆಸಱು in the Dictionary.

121. The case-terminations for the singular of neuter and feminine bases (and of the base ಅಳು that is masculine-feminine-neuter in the modern dialect) **ending in ಉ, this vowel being merely euphonically suffixed** to ancient bases ending in consonants (see §§ 92. 93. 94. 96 remark). Such bases appear nowadays chiefly in the mediæval and modern dialects; but there are proofs of their existence also in the ancient one, namely in its dative and genitive, and in the words ಮಗಳು (for ಮಗಳ್), ಕಲ್ಲು (for ಕಲ್), ಪೋೞಲು, ಸಿಡಿಲು, ಮತ್ತರು, ಅಳಿಯಲು (ಅೞಿಯಲು), ರಕ್ಷಿಸಲು, ನಿರೀಕ್ಷಿಸಲು. *Cf.* § 187, 1.

a) In the ancient dialect

1, Nom. ಉ, *i. e.* the crude base, *e. g.* ಮಗಳು (in a śâsana of about 778 A. D.), ಕಲ್ಲು (in one of 1048 A. D.), ಪೋೞಲು, ಸಿಡಿಲು (in one of 1182 A. D.), ಮತ್ತರು (in one of 1187 A. D.), ಅಳಿಯಲು (in one of 1076 A. D.), ರಕ್ಷಿಸಲು (in one of 1123 A. D.), ನಿರೀಕ್ಷಿಸಲು (in one of 1182 A. D.).

4, Dat. ಇಂಗೆ, ಕೆ, *e. g.* ಅಗಳಿಂಗೆ, ಈಗಳಿಂಗೆ; ಊರಿಂಗೆ (in a śâsana of 1084 A. D.), ಸೊಡರಿಂಗೆ (in a śâsana of 1123 A. D.); ಪೊಗಳಲುಕೆ (for ಪೊಗೞಲುಕೆ), ಅಗಲುಕೆ (in one of 1123 A. D.).

The grammatical bases of the terms ಅಗಳಿಂಗೆ, ಈಗಳಿಂಗೆ, ಊರಿಂಗೆ, ಸೊಡರಿಂಗೆ, ಪೊಗಳಲುಕೆ, ಅಗಲುಕೆ are ಅಗಳ್, ಈಗಳ್, ಊರ್, ಸೊಡರ್, ಪೊಗಳಲ್, ಅಗಲ್. According to rule their dative ought to be ಅಗಳ್ಗೆ, ಈಗಳ್ಗೆ, ಊರ್ಗೆ, ಸೊಡರ್ಗೆ, ಪೊಗಳಲ್ಕೆ, ಅಗಲ್ಕೆ (see § 120); but they have been treated as if they were ಅಗಳು, ಈಗಳು, ಊರು, ಸೊಡರು, ಪೊಗಳಲು, ಅಗಲು, analogously to the ancient ಅಗಡು and ಈಗಡು (§ 122), for which ಇಂಗೆ is the grammatical termination of the dative, and somewhat analogously *e. g.* to the modern ಮಾಡಲು and ಹೋಗಲು, for which ಇಕೆ is the grammatical termination of the dative (see under letter *c*). Thus the forms ಅಗಳ್, ಈಗಳ್, ಊರ್, ಸೊಡರ್, ಪೊಗಳಲ್, ಅಗಲ್ have existed with the euphonic suffix ಉ of the mediæval and modern dialect already in ancient times, and have been used like the bases with final ಉ in § 122. Observe that ಏೞ್ and ಏೞು, seven, appear in these two forms in the ancient dialect.

ಇಂಗೆ consists of the euphonic augment ಇಂ and the termination of the dative ಗೆ (see § 120). The ಉ before ಕೆ is simply euphonic.

6, Gen. ಇನ, *e. g.* ಇರುಳಿನ, ಪಗಲಿನ, ಸೂೞಿನ, ಅಗಳಿನ, ಈಗಳಿನ.

The bases of these terms are ಇರುಳ್, ಪಗಲ್, ಸೂೞ್, ಅಗಳ್, ಈಗಳ್, and the grammatical forms of the genitive would be ಇರುಳ, ಪಗಲ, ಸೂೞ, ಅಗಳ, ಈಗಳ (see § 120). Kêśava remarks that ಇರುಳಿನ and ಪಗಲಿನ are optionally used for ಇರುಳ and

ಪಗಲ, which goes to show that ಇರುಳು and ಪಗಲು, forms with the euphonic ಉ, were together with ಸೂಡು, ಆಗಳು, ಈಗಳು, in common use at his time and in the time preceding. Kêšava adds that it is wrong (dôsha) to use such forms as ಬೆಮರಿನ, ಮಣಲಿನ, ಮುಗಲಿನ, etc. He evidently opposes the too free use of forms of ordinary conversation, which presuppose the existence of many bases with the euphonic final ಉ (§ 122), in the present case of ಬೆಮರು, ಮಣಲು and ಮುಗಿಲು.

ಇನ is ಅ, the termination of the genitive, and the euphonic augment ಇಂ (ಇನ್).

b) in the mediæval dialect

1, Nom. ಉ *i. e.* the crude base, *e. g.* ಎಳ್ಳು, ಕಲು, ಕಲ್ಲು, ಊರು, ಕಾಲು, ಪಾಲು, ಮಿನು, ಸೂಡು, ತಿಂಗಳು, ಮೊಸರು, ಸೊಡರು, ಸೆಡಲು; ಅವಳು, ಇವಳು, (ಆವಳು), ಒರ್ವಳು, ಒಬ್ಬಳು; ಈಗಳು, ಆಗಳು, ಆಗಲು; ಅಳು.

2, Acc. ಅಂ, ಅ, the crude base, *e. g.* ತಿಂಗಳಂ; ಬಯಲಂ, ಅವಳಂ; ಕಲ್ಲ, ಮಿನ, ಮೇಲ; ಆಳ; ಮರುಳು.

It is impossible to settle whether ತಿಂಗಳಂ, ಬಯಲಂ, ಅವಳಂ, ಕಲ್ಲ, ಮಿನ, ಮೇಲ, ಆಳ are the accusative of bases with final consonants (§ 120, letter *b*) or of bases with the euphonic ಉ.

3, Instr. ಇಂ, (ಇನ್ದಂ, ಇನ್ದೆ, ಇನ್ದ), ಇನಿನ್ದ, *e. g.* ಕಲ್ಲಿಂ, ಊರಿಂ, etc.; ಕಂಕುಡಿನಿನ್ದ.

It is possible that in such forms as ಕಲ್ಲಿಂ, ಊರಿಂ, etc. the bases are ಕಲ್, ಊರ್, etc. (see § 120, letter *b*).

ಇನಿನ್ದ is ಇನ್ದ attached to ಇನ of the genitive.

4, Dat. ಇಂಗೆ, ಇಗೆ, ಇಕೆ, *e. g.* ಕಣ್ಣಿಂಗೆ, ಬಿಲ್ಲಿಂಗೆ, ಊರಿಂಗೆ, ನೀರಿಂಗೆ, ಪಾಲಿಂಗೆ, ಬೇರಿಂಗೆ, ಮೇಲಿಂಗೆ, ಸೂಡಿಂಗೆ, ಬೆರಳಿಂಗೆ, ಹೆಗಲಿಂಗೆ; ಊರಿಗೆ, ಬೇರಿಗೆ, ಸೂಡಿಗೆ, ಕೊರಳಿಗೆ, ಸೆಡಲಿಗೆ; ಈಗಳಿಕೆ.

Like the ಇಂ the ಇ that precedes the terminations ಗೆ and ಕೆ, is a euphonic augment.

5, Abl. (ಅತ್ತಣಿಂ, etc.), the terminations of the instrumental.

6, Gen. ಅ, ಇನ, *e. g.* ಎಳ್ಳ, ಮಣ್ಣ, ಊರ, ಕಾಲ, ಕೊರಳ, ಮಳಲ; ಅವಳ, ಇವಳ, (ಆವಳ), ಒರ್ವಳ, ಒಬ್ಬಳ; ಆಳ; ಬಿಲ್ಲಿನ, ಹಾಲಿನ, ತೊಗಲಿನ, ಇರುಳಿನ.

ಎಳ್ಳ, ಮಣ್ಣ, etc. may be referred also to ಎಳ್, ಮಣ್, etc. (see § 120, letter *b*).

7, Loc. ಇನೊಳ್, ಇನಲ್ಲಿ, *e. g.* ಗೇಣಿನೊಳ್; ಹಾಲಿನಲ್ಲಿ.

c) in the modern dialect

1, Nom. ಉ, *i. e.* the crude base, *e. g.* ಎಳ್ಳು, ಕಲ್ಲು, ಊರು, ಕೊರಳು, ಮಾಡಲು, ಹೋಗಲು, ನೋಡಲು; ಹೆಣ್ಣು; ಅವಳು, ಇವಳು, ಯಾವಳು, ಒಬ್ಬಳು; ಆಗಲು, ಈಗಲು; ಆಳು.

2, Acc. ಅನು, ಅನ್ನು, ಅ, ಅ, the crude base, *e. g.* ಹೆಣ್ಣನು, ಕೊರಳನು, ನೀರನು; ಹೆಣ್ಣನ್ನು, ಕಲ್ಲನ್ನು, ಹೊನ್ನನ್ನು, ಬೇರನ್ನು, ಕೆಸರನ್ನು; ಅವಳನ್ನು, ಇವಳನ್ನು; ಆಳನ್ನು; ಹಲ್ಲ, ಊರ, ಕಾಲ, ಕೂದ, ತೇರ, ಮಿನ, ನೇಗಿಲ, ಬಾಗಿಲ; ಕೆಚ್ಚಲಾ, ಬಚ್ಚಲಾ, ನೆತ್ತರಾ; ಕಲ್ಲು, ಬೇರು.

It is impossible to decide whether ಹಲ್ಲ, ಊರ, etc., also in this case, are formed from ಹಲ್ಲು, ಊರು, etc. or from ಹಲ್, ಊರ್, etc. (see § 120, letter *c*).

3, Instr. ಇನ್ದ, ಇನಿನ್ದ, *e. g.* ಮೇಲಿನ್ದ; ಕಲ್ಲಿನಿನ್ದ, ನೀರಿನಿನ್ದ, ಹಾಲಿನಿನ್ದ.

ಮೇಲಿನ್ದ may come from ಮೇಲು or ಮೇಲ್.

4, Dat. ಇಕೆ, ಇಕ್ಕೆ, ಇಗೆ, *e. g.* ಮಾಡಲಿಕೆ or ಮಾಡಲಿಕ್ಕೆ, ಹೋಗಲಿಕೆ or ಹೋಗಲಿಕ್ಕೆ (see § 370, 4); ಹೆಣ್ಣಿಗೆ, ಇವಳಿಗೆ, ಅವಳಿಗೆ; ಆಳಿಗೆ; ಕಲ್ಲಿಗೆ, ಬಯ್ಲಿಗೆ, ಹಣ್ಣಿಗೆ, ಹಲ್ಲಿಗೆ, ಊರಿಗೆ, ನೀರಿಗೆ, ಬಾೞಿಗೆ, ಮೊಸರಿಗೆ, ಮುಗಿಲಿಗೆ.

5, Abl. ಇನ್ದ, ಇನಿನ್ದ, *e. g.* ಊರಿನ್ದ, ಮೇಲಿನ್ದ; ಊರಿನಿನ್ದ, ಮೇಲಿನಿನ್ದ, ಕೆಸಱಿನಿನ್ದ.

ಊರಿನ್ದ, ಮೇಲಿನ್ದ may, also in this case, come from ಊರು or ಊರ್, ಮೇಲು or ಮೇಲ್.

6, Gen. ಅ, ಇನ, *e. g.* ಕಣ್ಣ, ಕಲ್ಲ, ಬಿಲ್ಲ, ಕಾಲ, ಹಾಲ, ಕೊರಳ, ಮುಗಿಲ; ಅವಳ, ಇವಳ, ಯಾವಳ; ಹೆಣ್ಣಿನ; ಕಣ್ಣಿನ, ಕಲ್ಲಿನ, ಮಣ್ಣಿನ, ಹಣ್ಣಿನ, ತೇರಿನ, ನೀರಿನ, ಮೀನಿನ, ಹಾಲಿನ, ಮೇಲಿನ, ಕೆಸಱಿನ, ಮುಗಿಲಿನ; ಆಳಿನ.

ಕಣ್ಣ, ಕಲ್ಲ, etc. may, also in this case, come from ಕಣ್ಣು, ಕಲ್ಲು, etc. or from ಕಣ್, ಕಲ್, etc.

7, Loc. ಒಳಗೆ, ಅಲ್ಲಿ, ಅಲಿ, ಇನಲ್ಲಿ, ಇನಲಿ, ಇಲಿ, ಲಿ, *e. g.* ಊರೊಳಗೆ; ಕಲ್ಲಲ್ಲಿ, ನೀರಲ್ಲಿ, ಹಾಲಲ್ಲಿ, ಬಿಸಲಲ್ಲಿ, ಮೊಸರಲ್ಲಿ; ಇವಳಲ್ಲಿ, ಅವಳಲ್ಲಿ; ಗಣ್ಟಲಲಿ; ಊರಿನಲ್ಲಿ, ಕಣ್ಣಿನಲ್ಲಿ, ಕಲ್ಲಿನಲ್ಲಿ, ತೇರಿನಲ್ಲಿ, ಹಾಲಿನಲ್ಲಿ, ಕೆಸಱಿನಲ್ಲಿ; ಕಣ್ಣಿನಲಿ; ಕಣ್ಣಿಲಿ, ಕಾಲಿಲಿ, ಬಾಯಿಲಿ, ಹೊನ್ನಿಲಿ; ಹೆಸರ್ಲಿ, ಕೆಯ್ಲಿ.

ಊರೊಳಗೆ, ಕಲ್ಲಲ್ಲಿ, etc. may, also in this case, be referred to bases with final consonants.

In ಲಿ the ಅಲಿ or ಇಲಿ has been mutilated (*cf.* § 130, letter *c*).

122. The case-terminations for the singular of dissyllabic and trisyllabic neuter bases, (of the masculine bases ಗಣ್ಡಸು, ಗಣ್ಡು, of the feminine base ಹೆಂಗಸು, and of the masculine-feminine-neuter bases ಅರಸು, ಕೂಸು) **always ending in the euphonic ಉ in the ancient, mediæval and modern dialect** (see §§ 96. 98). See ಅನ್ದು, ಇನ್ದು, ಉನ್ದು, ಎನ್ದು in § 127.

Concerning the terminations ತು, ತ್ತು and ದು in ಒಳ್ಳಿತು, ಒಳ್ಳಿತ್ತು, ಬೆಟ್ಟಿತು, ಬೆಟ್ಟಿತ್ತು, ಕಿಱಿದು, ನೇರಿದು, etc. (which are classed with the so-called adjectives, § 102, 8, *b. c.*; §§ 273. 276) the grammarian Kêśava teaches only that they are their base-terminations. They are pronominal forms; ತು we find again in ಎತ್ತಣ್ತು (§§ 123, *a*; 272), in ಅತುರ್ಗ (§§ 135. 270. 272 under 2), in ಎನ್ತು, ನಿನ್ತು, ತನ್ತು (§ 272, 2), in ಏತು (§ 125), in ಅಲ್ತು (§ 212), in past participles (§§ 166. 168. 169), in ಉಣ್ಟು (§ 194), in a personal termination (§§ 193. 198. 199), in the formation of the pronouns ತಾ (§ 138, *d*, 3) and ಅತ, etc. (§§ 138, *d*, 3; 265), in ಪಿನ್ತು, ಮುನ್ತು (§ 243, *A*, remark *b*), and ದು in past participles (§§ 166. 168. 169) and in the modern ನೋಡಿದ್ದು, ಮಾಡದ್ದು, etc. (§ 254, 1, *a* and remark 3).

ತು, ತ್ತು (euphonically doubled) and ದು represent the letters ತ್, ತ್ತ್, ದ್ದ್, the primitive signs which point to an object in a general way, with a euphonic ಉ. When the vowels ಅ, ಇ, ಉ (other forms of ಆ, ಈ, ಊ, see § 264) are prefixed to ದು (ಅದು, ಇದು, ಉದು which are the commonly used demonstrative neuter pronouns) the direction becomes distinct; ಅತು, ಅತ್ತು, (which are substitutes for ಅದು) are met with in combination with ಎನ (of me), etc. as ಎನತು, ಎನತ್ತು, etc. (§ 137, *a*, 6; § 272, 2), ಅತ್ತು, ಇತು, ಇತ್ತು (= ಇದು) as personal terminations (§ 193), ಉತು

(= ಉದು) in combination with ಎಮ್ಮ (of us), etc. as ಎಮ್ಮುತು, etc. (§ 272, 2, and ಉತ್ತು as a participial termination, § 173). Compare also § 124, ಉ, 4; § 265.

Regarding the neuter plural of ಒಳ್ಳಿತು, etc., ಕಿಱಿದು, etc., ಅದು, etc. see § 136.

The case-terminations are

a) in the ancient dialect

1. Nom. ಉ, *i. e.* the crude base, *e. g.* ಒತ್ತು, ಎಬ್ಬು, ಪೊಱಬ್ಬು, ಕೊಸು, ಪಾವು, ನಾಡು, ತುಱುಮ್ಬು, ಮಾತು, ಕಡುಪು, ಈಗಡು, ಆಗಡು, ನಾಡಿದು, ಸೆಱಂಗು, ಒಳಗು, ಕೆಳಗು, ಮೇಗು, ಪಿನ್ಬು, ಮುನ್ದು, ಪಿನ್ತು, ಮುನ್ತು, ಪೊಱಗು, ಅನಿತು, ಬಿಟ್ಟಿತು, ಒಳ್ಳಿತು, ಬಿಟ್ಟಿತ್ತು, ಒಳಿತ್ತು, ಇದು, ಅದು, ಉದು, ಆವುದು, ಪೆಱತು, ಎಲ್ಲದು, ಕಿಱಿದು, ಇನಿದು, ಒನ್ದು, ಎರಡು.

ಅದು appears also as ಒದು (in a śâsana between 594 and 608 A. D.; *cf.* § 117, letter *a*).

2, Acc. ಅಂ, (ಅ), ಆಂ, *e. g.* ಒಳ್ಪಂ, ಕೊಪ್ಪಂ, ಪಾವಂ, ನಾಡಂ, ಮಾತಂ, ಪದಪಂ, ಸೆಱಂಗಂ, ಅನಿತಂ, ಒಳ್ಳಿತಂ, ಅದಂ, ಆವುದಂ, ಕಿಱಿದಂ, ಒನ್ದಂ, ಎರಡಂ, ಅಯ್ದಂ, ಮೇಲುದಂ; (ನಾಡ, ತುಱುಮ್ಬು); ಇದಾಂ (in a śâsana between 680 and 696 A. D., in one of somewhat after 732 A. D., and in one of 750 A. D.).

The ಅ in parenthesis refers to ನಾಡ and ತುಱುಮ್ಬ. We take ನಾಡ to be the accusative in the sentence quoted by Kêśava (page 164) in ತೆಂಕನಾಡ ಮಱೆಯಲ್ಕೆ ಎನ್ದುಂ ಮನಂ ಬರ್ಕುಮೆ (could it ever come to (my) mind to forget the southern country?). He, however, supposes that ನಾಡ is the genitive used for the accusative. ತುಱುಮ್ಬ stands (according to a Mdb. Ms.) in the passage quoted by Kêśava in page 288:—ಬೆರಣ್ಪವು ಪೊಕ್ಕುಬನ್ ಉಗುರಿಸಿದುವು ತುಱುಮ್ಬ (they scratched the (*i. e.* his or her or its or their) navel and clawed the hair-knot). *Cf.* the note under the ancient accusative in § 117, and see § 352, 1, *b*. Regarding the lengthening *cf.* § 109, *a*, 6.

3, Instr. ಇಂ, ಇನಿಂ, ಇನ್ದೆ, ಇನಿನ್ದೆ, ಅಱಿಂ, *e. g.* ಮಾತಿಂ, ಕಡುಪಿಂ; ಮಾತಿನಿಂ, ಕಡುಪಿನಿಂ; ಒಳ್ಪಿನ್ದೆ, ಚೆಲ್ವಿನ್ದೆ, ರೂಪಿನ್ದೆ; ಪಾಂಗಿನಿನ್ದೆ; ಅದಱಿಂ, ಆವುದಱಿಂ, ಒನ್ದಱಿಂ, ಎರಡಱಿಂ, ಮೂಱಱಿಂ, ಅನಿತಱಿಂ, ಎನಿತಱಿಂ, ಮೇಲುದಱಿಂ.

4, Dat. ಇಂಗೆ, ಅಕ್ಕೆ, ಅಱ್ಕೆ, *e. g.* ಮಾತಿಂಗೆ, ಲೇಸಿಂಗೆ, ರೂಪಿಂಗೆ, ಕೂಸಿಂಗೆ, ಆಗಡಿಂಗೆ, ಈಗಡಿಂಗೆ, ನಾಡಿದಿಂಗೆ; ಮೇಗಣ್ಗೆ, ಕೆಳಗಣ್ಗೆ, ಮುನ್ದಣ್ಗೆ, ಪಿನ್ದಣ್ಗೆ, ಪಿನ್ತಣ್ಗೆ, ಒಳಗಣ್ಗೆ; ಅದರ್ಕೆ, ಇದರ್ಕೆ, ಆವುದರ್ಕೆ, ಕಿಱಿದರ್ಕೆ, ಒನ್ದರ್ಕೆ, ಎರಡರ್ಕೆ, ಎಣ್ಬರ್ಕೆ, ಪತ್ತರ್ಕೆ, ನೂಱರ್ಕೆ, ಅನಿತರ್ಕೆ, ಎನಿತರ್ಕೆ, ಬಿಟ್ಟಿತರ್ಕೆ, ಮೇಲುದರ್ಕೆ.

The terminations are ಗೆ and ಕೆ; ಇಂ, ಅಕ್ and ಅಱ್ are euphonical augments.

5, Abl. ಇನತ್ತಣಿಂ, ಇನತ್ತಣಿನ್ದಂ, ಇನತ್ತಣಿನ್ದೆ, ಅಣಿಂ, ಅಱಿತ್ತಣಿಂ, the terminations of the instrumental, *e. g.* ಮಾತಿನತ್ತಣಿಂ; ಮೇಗಣಿಂ, ಕೆಳಗಣಿಂ, ಮುನ್ದಣಿಂ, ಪಿನ್ದಣಿಂ, ಪೊಱಗಣಿಂ, ಒಳಗಣಿಂ; ಆವುದಱತ್ತಣಿಂ; ಮುಳಿಸಿನ್ದೆ, ತಳಿರ್ವಾಸಿನಿನ್ದೆ.

6, Gen. ಅ, ಇನ, ಅಣ, ಅಱ, *e. g.* ನಾಡ, ತುಱುಮ್ಬ; ಎಬ್ಬನ, ಓದಿನ, ಮಾತಿನ, ಸೊಬಗಿನ, ಕೊಸಗಿನ, ಹೊರಸಿನ, ಬಯ್ಗಿನ, ಮುತ್ತಿನ, ಆಗಡಿನ, ಈಗಡಿನ, ನಾಡಿದಿನ; ಕೆಳಗಣ, ಮೇಗಣ, ಮುನ್ದಣ, ಪಿನ್ದಣ, ಪಿನ್ತಣ, ಪೊಱಗಣ, ಒಳಗಣ; ಅದಱ, ಇದಱ, ಆವುದಱ, ಮಾಡಿಮುದಱ, ಒನ್ದಱ, ನಾಲ್ಕಱ, ಅಯ್ಪಱ, ಆಱಱ, ಅನಿತಱ, ಎನಿತಱ.

ಇನ is the euphonic augment ಇಂ (ಇನ್) and ಅ, the true termination of the genitive; in ಅಣ the augment is ಅಣ್, and in ಅಱ it is ಅಱ್. Compare the augments ದ್ and ನ್ in § 109, letter *a*, and see § 141, remark under Dative.

7, Loc. ಇನೊಳ್, ಇನೊಳು, ಇನೊಳಗೆ, ಇನಲ್ಲಿ, ಅಱುಳ್, ಅಱೊಳ್, ಅಱಲ್ಲಿ, *e. g.* ಪೆಮ್ಮಿನೊಳ್, ಮಾತಿನೊಳ್, ಮಾವಿನೊಳ್, ಪಾಸಿನೊಳ್, ಕರ್ವಿನೊಳ್; ನೆಲೆವೀಡಿನೊಳು (in a šâsana of 1123 A. D.); ಬಣ್ಣಿನೊಳಗೆ; ಕಾವಿನಲ್ಲಿ; ಈರೆಪ್ಪತ್ತಱುಳ್ (in a šâsana between 680 and 696 A. D.); ಇದಱೊಳ್, ಅಪ್ಪುದಱೊಳ್, ಎರಡಱೊಳ್, ಎಣ್ಬಱೊಳ್, ಕೀೞ್ದಱೊಳ್, ಇನಿತಱೊಳ್, ಎನಿತಱೊಳ್; ಅದಱಲ್ಲಿ, ಅಯ್ದಱಲ್ಲಿ.

b) in the mediæval dialect

1, Nom. ಉ, *i. e.* the crude base, *e. g.* ಎತ್ತು, ಒತ್ತು, ಪೊತ್ತು, ಹಿನ್ದು, ಹೊಱಗು, ಅದು, ಇದು, ಉದ್ದಿತು, ಒಳ್ಳಿತು, ಒಳಿತು, ಬಟ್ಟಿತು, ಕಿಱುಮು, ಒನ್ದು, ಎರಡು, ಐಱು, ಅಷ್ಟು, ಐಸು, ಮೇಲುದು.

2, Acc. ಅಂ, ಅ, the crude base, *e. g.* ಒತ್ತಂ, ಕನಸಂ, ಮಾತಂ, ಒಳ್ಳಿತಂ, ಇನಿದಂ, ಕಿಱಿದಂ, ಅದಂ, ಐಱಂ, ಐಸಂ; ಉರ್ಕ, ಕನ್ದ, ಕಿಚ್ಚ, ಕುಱುಪ, ಕೇಡ, ತಪ್ಪ, ಹಿನ್ದ, ಅದ, ಇದ, ಒನ್ದ; ಕಾಪು, ಕೇಡು, ಕಿಱುಮು, ಪಿರಿದು.

3, Instr. ಇಂ, ಇನಿಂ, ಇನಿನ್ದಂ, ಇನಿನ್ದೆ, ಇನ್ದಂ, ಇನ್ದವು, ಇನ್ದ, ಅಱಿಂ, ಅಱಿನ್ದೆ, ಅಱಿನ್ದವು, ಅಱಿನ್ದ, *e. g.* ಕಡುಪಿಂ, ಕಡುಹಿಂ; ಕಡುಹಿನಿಂ, ಹಮ್ಮಿನಿಂ; ಕೊರಡಿನಿನ್ದಂ; ಕಿಚ್ಚಿನಿನ್ದೆ, ಹಮ್ಮಿನಿನ್ದೆ; ಬಲುಹಿನ್ದಂ; ಜೂಜಿನಿನ್ದವು; ಕಿಚ್ಚಿನ್ದ, ಒಲವಿನ್ದ, ಕಳವಿನ್ದ, ಮುಸುಡಿನ್ದ; ಅದಱಿಂ; ಅದಱಿನ್ದೆ; ಅದಱಿನ್ದವು; ಅನಿತಱಿನ್ದ.

4, Dat. ಇಂಗೆ, ಇಗೆ, ಇಕೆ, ಇಕ್ಕೆ, ಇಂಕೆ, ಅಱಿಕ್ಕೆ, ಅಕ್ಕೆ, ಅಕೆ, *e. g.* ಮಾತಿಂಗೆ, ಹೊತ್ತಿಂಗೆ; ಮಾತಿಗೆ, ಮುದ್ದಿಗೆ, ಲೇಸಿಗೆ, ತಪ್ಪಿಗೆ, ಗೆಲವಿಗೆ, ಹಸಿವಿಗೆ, ಬಿಳಿದಿಗೆ; ಕೆಳಯಿಕೆ; ಕೆಳಯಿಕ್ಕೆ; ಒಳಯಿಂಕೆ; ಒನ್ದರ್ಕೆ, ಅನಿತರ್ಕೆ; ಅನಿತಕ್ಕೆ, ಐಸಕ್ಕೆ, ಎರಡಕ್ಕೆ, ಮೂಱಕ್ಕೆ, ಎಣ್ಬಕ್ಕೆ, ಒಳಿತಕ್ಕೆ, ಒಳ್ಳಿತಕ್ಕೆ; ಮುನ್ದಕ್ಕೆ, ಹಿನ್ದಕ್ಕೆ, ಮೇಲಕ್ಕೆ; ಅದಕೆ, ಇದಕೆ, ಅನಿತಕೆ; ಮುನ್ದಕೆ, ಹಿನ್ದಕೆ, ಮೇಲಕೆ.

ಇಂಗೆ, ಇಗೆ, ಇಂಕೆ, ಇಕೆ, ಇಕ್ಕೆ are ಗೆ, ಕೆ, ಕ್ಕೆ, the terminations of the dative, and the euphonic augments ಇಂ and ಇ. In ಕೆಳಯಿಕೆ, ಕೆಳಯಿಕ್ಕೆ, ಒಳಯಿಂಕೆ the final letter ಗು of ಕೆಳಗು and ಒಳಗು has been changed into ಯು. ಅಕ್ಕೆ, ಅಕೆ generally are mutilated forms of ಅಱಿಕ್ಕೆ. ಮೇಲಕೆ, ಮೇಲಕ್ಕೆ, ಮುನ್ದಕೆ, ಮುನ್ದಕ್ಕೆ, ಹಿನ್ದಕೆ, ಹಿನ್ದಕ್ಕೆ either stand for ಮೇಲಣ್ಕೆ, ಮುನ್ದಣ್ಕೆ, ಹಿನ್ದಣ್ಕೆ (see letter *a*), or for ಮೇಲರ್ಕೆ, ಮುನ್ದರ್ಕೆ, ಹಿನ್ದರ್ಕೆ, ಮೇಲರ್ಕ್ಕೆ, etc.

5, Abl. (ಇನತ್ತಣಿಂ, etc.), the terminations of the instrumental.

6, Gen. ಅ, ಇನ, ಅಣ, ಅಱ, *e. g.* ಚಲುವ, ಹಾವ, ಅರಸ, ಮೇಲುದ; ಒತ್ತಿನ, ಓದಿನ, ತಪ್ಪಿನ, ಬೆಳ್ಪಿನ, ತುಱುಬಿನ, ಕಱಿದಿನ, ಬಿಳಿದಿನ, ಅರಸಿನ, ಮೇಲುದಿನ; ಕೆಳಗಣ, ಮೇಗಣ, ಮುನ್ದಣ, ಹಿನ್ದಣ, ಪೊಱಗಣ, ಹೊಱಗಣ, ಒಳಗಣ, ಸುತ್ತಣ, ಮೂಱಣ; ಅದಱ, ಅಷ್ಟಱ, ಇಷ್ಟಱ, ಐಸಱ, ಒನ್ದಱ, ಎರಡಱ, ಮೂಱಱ, ನಾಲ್ಕಱ, ಒಳ್ಳಿತಱ, ಬಿಳಿದಱ, ದೊಡ್ಡಿತ್ತಱ, ಬಟ್ಟಿತಱ.

The Basavapurâṇa, exceptionally, has ಹಿನ್ದಣದ; see § 123, letter *c*, 4. 5. 6.

7, Loc. ಇನೊಳ್, ಇನೊಳು, (ಇನೊಳಗೆ), ಇನಲ್ಲಿ, ಇನಲಿ, ಅಱೊಳ್, ಅಱೊಳು, ಅಱೊಳಗೆ, ಅಱಲ್ಲಿ, ಅಱಲಿ, *e. g.* ಒತ್ತಿನೊಳ್, ಕಿಚ್ಚಿನೊಳ್, ಬೇವಿನೊಳ್, ಕೆಳಗಿನೊಳ್, ಕಱಿದಿನೊಳ್, ಕಿಱಿದಿನೊಳ್, ಬಿಳಿದಿನೊಳ್, ಅರಸಿನೊಳ್; ಕಬ್ಬಿನೊಳು, ಎತ್ತಿನೊಳು; ಒತ್ತಿನಲ್ಲಿ, ಬಱಿಹಿನಲ್ಲಿ, ಕಿಱಿದಿನಲ್ಲಿ, ಬಿಳಿದಿನಲ್ಲಿ, ಹಟುವಿನಲ್ಲಿ, ದೊಡ್ಡಿತ್ತಿನಲ್ಲಿ; ಒತ್ತಿನಲಿ, ಕಿಚ್ಚಿನಲಿ, ಕುಱುಹಿನಲಿ, ಜಿನುಗಿನಲಿ; ಇನಿತಱೊಳ್, ನಾಲ್ಕಱೊಳ್; ಐಱಱೊಳು; ಒನ್ದಱೊಳಗೆ; ಎರಡಱಲ್ಲಿ, ಸೂಜಱಲ್ಲಿ, ಒಳಿತಱಲ್ಲಿ, ಬಿಳಿದಱಲ್ಲಿ, ಉದ್ದಿತಱಲ್ಲಿ,

ದೊಡ್ಡಿತಱಲ್ಲಿ, ಬೆಟ್ಟಿತಱಲ್ಲಿ; ಅನಿತಱಲಿ, ಒನ್ದಱಲಿ, ನಾಲ್ಕಱಲಿ, ಅಯ್ದಱಲಿ. ಆಱಱಲಿ, ಎಣ್ಟಱಲಿ, ಹತ್ತಱಲಿ, ಒಳಿತಱಲಿ.

c) in the modern dialect

1, Nom. ಉ, *i. e.* **the crude base,** *e. g.* ಎತ್ತು, ಬೆಕ್ಕು, ಕೂಸು, ಕನಸು, ಬೆಳಗು, ಬರವು, ಅದು, ಇದು, ಒನ್ದು, ಅಷ್ಟು, ಹಿನ್ದು.

2, Acc. ಅನು, ಅನ್ನು, ಅನ, ಅನ್ನ, ಅ, ಆ, ಅಱಿನ್ನು, **the crude base,** *e. g.* ಚೆಲುವನು, ಸೊಪ್ಪನು, ಮಾತನು, ಅದನು, ಇದನು, ಒನ್ದನು, ನಾಲ್ಕನು; ಹೆಂಗಸನ್ನು, ಗಣ್ಡಸನ್ನು, ಕೇಡನ್ನು, ಆದನ್ನು, ಇದನ್ನು, ಯಾವದನ್ನು, ಅಷ್ಟನ್ನು, ಒನ್ದನ್ನು, ನಾಲ್ಕನ್ನು, ಹತ್ತನ್ನು; ಆದನ; ಅದನ್ನ; ಕನ್ದ, ಕೂಸ, ತಪ್ಪ, ಮಾತ, ಹಾವ, ತುಱುಬ; ಗುರ್ತಾ; ಆದಱನ್ನು, ಯಾವದಱನ್ನು, ಒನ್ದಱನ್ನು, ಹತ್ತಱನ್ನು; ಕನಸು, ಕೂಸು.

About ಅನು, etc. see *e. g.* § 109, letters *b*, c; § 117, *b*, *c*. In the vulgar ಅಱನ್ನು the ಅನ್ನು is attached to the ಅಱ of the genitive.

3, Instr. ಇನ್ದ, ಇನ್ದೆ, ಇನಿನ್ದ, ಅಱಿನ್ದ, *e. g.* ನಾಡಿದಿನ್ದ, ಹಿನ್ದಿನ್ದ, ನೂಱಿನ್ದ; ಹಿನ್ದಿನ್ದೆ; ನಾಡಿದಿನಿನ್ದ, ಕೆಮ್ಮಿನಿನ್ದ, ಕೂಸಿನಿನ್ದ, ಬರವಿನಿನ್ದ, ಹಿನ್ದಿನಿನ್ದ; ಅಷ್ಟಱಿನ್ದ, ನೂಱಱಿನ್ದ.

4, Dat. ಇಗೆ, ಅಕ್ಕೆ, ಅಕೆ, *e. g.* ತೆಂಗಿಗೆ, ಸಿಟ್ಟಿಗೆ, ಹೊತ್ತಿಗೆ, ಕಾಡಿಗೆ, ಸಾವಿಗೆ, ಬರವಿಗೆ, ಬೆಳಗಿಗೆ, ಗಣ್ಡಿಗೆ, ಗಣ್ಡಸಿಗೆ, ಹೆಂಗಸಿಗೆ, ನೂಱಿಗೆ; ಅದಕ್ಕೆ, ಅಷ್ಟಕ್ಕೆ, ಎಱಕ್ಕೆ, ಹತ್ತಕ್ಕೆ, ನೂಱಕ್ಕೆ, ಹಿನ್ದಕ್ಕೆ, ಮುನ್ದಕ್ಕೆ, ಮೇಲಕ್ಕೆ; ಅದಕೆ, ಅಷ್ಟಕೆ, ಒನ್ದಕೆ, ಮುನ್ದಕೆ, ಹಿನ್ದಕೆ, ಮೇಲಕೆ, ಕೆಳಯಕೆ, ಒಳೀಕೆ.

ಕೆಳಯಕೆ comes from ಕೆಳಗು, and ಒಳೀಕೆ (for ಒಳಿಯಕೆ) from ಒಳಗು (see letter *b*).

5, Abl. **the terminations of the instrumental,** *e. g.* ಒಳಗಿನ್ದ, ಹೊಱಗಿನ್ದ, ಕೆಳಗಿನ್ದ; ಒಳಗಿನಿನ್ದ, ಹೊಱಗಿನಿನ್ದ, ಮುನ್ದಿನಿನ್ದ; ಹತ್ತಱಿನ್ದ.

6, Gen. ಅ, ಆ, ಇನ, ಅಣ, ಅಳ, ಅಱ, *e. g.* ಕೆಮ್ಮ, ತಪ್ಪ, ಬೆಳಗ, ಕಾಡ, (ನೂಱ); ನೂಱಾ; ಗಣ್ಡಿನ, ಕೂಸಿನ, ಕೆಮ್ಮಿನ, ತೆಂಗಿನ, ಬೆಕ್ಕಿನ, ಕನಸಿನ, ಬೆಳಗಿನ, ನೂಱಿನ, ಕೆಳಗಿನ, ಒಳಗಿನ, ಹೊಱಗಿನ, ಮುನ್ದಿನ, ಹಿನ್ದಿನ; ಕೆಳಗಣ, ಮೇಲಣ, ಒಳಗಣ, ಹೊಱಗಣ, ಮುನ್ದಣ, ಹಿನ್ದಣ, ಸುತ್ತಣ; ಮೇಗಳ, ಹಿನ್ದಳ; ಆದಱ, ಇದಱ, ಅಷ್ಟಱ, ಎಷ್ಟಱ, ಒನ್ದಱ, ನೂಱಱ.

ಅಳ is another form of ಅಣ.

7, Loc. ಅಲ್ಲಿ, (ಅಲಿ), ಇನೊಳಗೆ, ಇನಲ್ಲಿ, ಇಲಿ, ಅಱೊಳಗೆ, ಅಱಲ್ಲಿ, ಅಱಲಿ, *e. g.* ಕಾಡಲ್ಲಿ, ನೂಱಲ್ಲಿ; ಕಾಡಿನೊಳಗೆ, ಕಬ್ಬಿನೊಳಗೆ; ಉಪ್ಪಿನಲ್ಲಿ, ಕಾಡಿನಲ್ಲಿ, ಕೂಸಿನಲ್ಲಿ; ಕಳವಿಲಿ, ಕಾವಿಲಿ, ಮೂಗಿಲಿ; ಅವಱೊಳಗೆ, ಅಷ್ಟಱೊಳಗೆ; ನಾಡಿದ್ದಱಲ್ಲಿ, ಅಷ್ಟಱಲ್ಲಿ, ಒನ್ದಱಲ್ಲಿ, ಮೂಱಱಲ್ಲಿ, ನೂಱಱಲ್ಲಿ; ಒನ್ದಱಲಿ,

123. **Eight neuter nominal bases with final ಅ** (words denoting direction. digvâčaka, digvâči), which, in the ancient and mediæval dialect, and partly also in the modern one, **are declined like some bases with the final euphonic of ಉ § 122.** (Their lengthened form appears in § 126).

a) in the ancient dialect

1, Nom. ಅ, *i. e.* **the crude base,** *viz.* ಅತ್ತ, ಇತ್ತ, ಉತ್ತ, ಎತ್ತ, ತೆಂಕ, ಪಡುವ, ಬಡಗ, ಮೂಡ.

4, Dat. ಅಗ್ಗೆ, *e. g.* ಅತ್ತಗ್ಗೆ, ಇತ್ತಗ್ಗೆ, ತೆಂಕಗ್ಗೆ, ಪಡುವಗ್ಗೆ, ಬಡಗಗ್ಗೆ, ಮೂಡಗ್ಗೆ.

5, Abl. ಅಣಿಂ, ಅಣಿನ್ದಂ, ಅಣಿನ್ದೆ, ಅಣತ್ತಣಿಂ, *e. g.* ಅತ್ತಣಿಂ, ಅತ್ತಣಿನ್ದಂ, ಅತ್ತಣಿನ್ದೆ; ಎತ್ತಣಿಂ, ತೆಂಕಣಿಂ, ಬಡಗಣಿಂ, ಮೂಡಣಿಂ; ಮೂಡಣತ್ತಣಿಂ.

6, Gen. ಅಣ, ಅಣ್, *e. g.* ಅತ್ತಣ, ಇತ್ತಣ, ತೆಂಕಣ, ಪಡುವಣ, ಬಡಗಣ, ಮೂಡಣ.

The simple ಅಣ್ appears in ಎತ್ತಣ್ಮು, that stands for the full form ಎತ್ತಣಮು (see § 272 under No. 2).

b) in the mediæval dialect

1, Nom. ಅ, i. e. the crude base, e. g. ಅತ್ತ, ಇತ್ತ, ಎತ್ತ.

4, Dat. (ಅಣ್ಗೆ).

5, Abl. ಅಣಿಂ, (ಅಣಿನ್ದಂ), ಅಣಿನ್ದೆ, ಅಣಿನ್ದ, e. g. ಮೂಡಣಿಂ; ಎತ್ತಣಿನ್ದೆ; ಅತ್ತಣಿನ್ದ

6, Gen. ಅಣ, ಅಳ, e. g. ಇತ್ತಣ, ಎತ್ತಣ, ತೆಂಕಣ, ಪಡುವಣ, ಬಡಗಣ, ಮೂಡಣ; ಎತ್ತಳ.

c) in the modern dialect

1, Nom. ಅ, i. e. the crude base, e. g. ಅತ್ತ, ಇತ್ತ.

4, Dat. ಅಣಾಕೆ or ಅಣಾಕ್ಕೆ, ಕೆ or ಕ್ಕೆ, e. g. ತೆಂಕಣಾಕೆ or ತೆಂಕಣಾಕ್ಕೆ; ಬಡಗಕೆ or ಬಡಗಕ್ಕೆ.

In ತೆಂಕಣಾಕೆ, ತೆಂಕಣಾಕ್ಕೆ the augment ಅಣ್ has received an ಅ, and as ಅಣ has become a part of the base, which is declined like a neuter base with final ಅ (§ 109). In ಬಡಗಕೆ, ಬಡಗಕ್ಕೆ no augment appears, and ಬಡಗ is treated as a neuter base with final ಅ.

5, Abl. ಅಣಿನ್ದ, ಅಣಾದಿನ್ದ, ಇನ್ದ, e. g. ತೆಂಕಣಿನ್ದ; ಮೂಡಣಾದಿನ್ದ; ಅತ್ತಿನ್ದ, ಇತ್ತಿನ್ದ.

For ಮೂಡಣಾದಿನ್ದ the base ಮೂಡಣಾ has been formed like that of ತೆಂಕಣಾ of the dative, and has been declined like a neuter base ending in ಅ (§ 109); cf. the ಹಿನ್ದಣಾದ in § 122 under letter b.

The bases for ಅತ್ತಿನ್ದ, ಇತ್ತಿನ್ದ seem to be ಅತ್ತು, ಇತ್ತು (ಅತ್ತ, ಇತ್ತ with final ಉ, § 122).

6, Gen. ಅಣ, ಅಣಾದ, e. g. ತೆಂಕಣ, ಪಡುವಣ, ಮೂಡಣ.

Regarding ಅಣಾದ see the ablative and locative.

7, Loc. ಅಣಾದಲ್ಲಿ, ಅಲ್ಲಿ, e. g. ಪಡುವಣಾದಲ್ಲಿ; ಬಡಗದಲ್ಲಿ.

The bases are ಪಡುವಣಾ and ಬಡಗ, that are declined like neuter bases with final ಅ (§ 109).

124. Remarks on the employment of the augments ಅಱ್ and ಅಣ್ of §§ 122 and 123. (See also the declension of the pronoun ಏನ್ in § 125 and that of the plural of ಅದು, etc. in § 136).

ಅಱ್ is used

1, in numerals (sankhyê), e. g. ಒನ್ದು, ಎರಡು, ಮೂಱು, ನಾಲ್ಕು, ಅಯ್ದು, ಆಱು, ಏಱು, ಎಣ್ಟು, ಒಮ್ಬತ್ತು, ಪತ್ತು (ಹತ್ತು), ನೂಱು;

2, in pronouns (sarvanâma), e. g. ಅದು, ಇದು, ಉದು, ಆವುದು, ಯಾವದು, ಪೆಱತು;

3, in terms denoting quantity (pramâṇavâči, pavaṇ), their finals ತು, ತ್ತು, (ಸು, ಟು) being pronominal forms (see § 122), e. g. ಅನಿತು, ಇನಿತು, ಎನಿತು, ಅನಿತ್ತು, ಆಸು, ಈಸು, ಏಸು, ಆಟು, ಈಟು, ಏಟು, ಅಷ್ಟು, ಇಷ್ಟು, ಎಷ್ಟು; (the ಆಸು is probably another form of ಅನಿತು; ಆಟು one of ಅಷ್ಟು; ಅಷ್ಟು one of ಆಸುತು, the ತು having taken the form of ಟು and the ಆ having become short);

4, in the so-called adjectives (guṇavačana), their finals ತು, ತ್ತು, ದು being pronominal forms, and the pronoun ಅದು, e. g. ಒಳ್ಳಿತು, ಒಳ್ಳಿತ್ತು, ಕಿಱಿದು, ಅಸಿದು; (modern) ದೊಡ್ಡದು, ಸಣ್ಣದು, ಚಿಕ್ಕದು;

5, in verbal bases (kṛit), their end-syllables ಉದು or ಅದು being neuter pronouns, e. g. ಮಾಡಿದುದು, ಕೊಡಿದುದು, ಮಾಳ್ಪುದು, ಕೊಡುವುದು, ಮಾಡಿದಮು, (ಮಾಡಿದ್ದು), ಮಾಡುವದು;

6, in the term ಮೇಲುದು, it being composed of ಮೇಲ್ and the neuter pronoun ಉದು.

The Šabdânušâsana under its sûtra 269 states that ಎಲ್ಲ (ಎಲ್ಲಂ), which is one of the words which express indefinite quantity (§ 90), exceptionally receives the augment ಅಱ್ in the neuter forms ಎಲ್ಲಱಿಂ, ಎಲ್ಲರ್ಕೆ, ಎಲ್ಲಱ, ಎಲ್ಲಱೊಳ್. The dative ಎಲ್ಲಕ್ಕೆ appears in the Šabdamaṇidarpaṇa, and ಎಲ್ಲಕೆ, ಎಲಕ್ಕೆ in the mediæval and modern dialect, in which forms the rêpha has disappeared. See the neuter plural of ಎಲ್ಲ in § 136, its epicene plural in § 119; *cf.* § 266.

ಅಣ್ is used

in nominal bases denoting direction (digvâčaka, digvâči), *e.g.* ಮೇಗು, ಕೆಳಗು, ಪೊಱಗು, ಅತ್ತ, ಇತ್ತ, ತೆಂಕ, ಬಡಗ. Compare the terms ನಡು, ಕಡೆ, ಎಡೆ, ಅಲ್ಲಿ, ಇಲ್ಲಿ, ಉಲ್ಲಿ, ಎಲ್ಲಿ in § 139.

125. Declension of the interrogative pronoun ಏನ್ (ಏಂ, *cf.* §§ 262. 269. 301), the augment being ಅಱು. This is not directly attached to ಏಂ or its crude form, but to ಏತು, *i. e.* ಏ and the pronominal form ತು (§ 122), literally meaning 'what-it'.

a) in the ancient dialect

1, Nom. ಂ, the crude base, *i. e.* ಏಂ; ಏ.

2, Acc. ಅಂ, the crude base, *i. e.* ಏನಂ; ಏ.

3, Instr. ಅಱಿಂ, *i. e.* ಏತಱಿಂ.

4, Dat. ಅಱ್ಕೆ, ಅಕೆ, ಕೆ, *i. e.* ಏತರ್ಕೆ; ಏತಕೆ; ಏಕೆ.

ಏತಕೆ is a mutilated form of ಏತರ್ಕೆ; compare the mutilated forms of the dative of the mediæval and modern dialect in § 122 and in this paragraph. Such forms, therefore, must have existed in ancient times. In ಏಕೆ the termination ಕೆ has been suffixed directly to ಏ. See also § 124 ಎಲ್ಲಕ್ಕೆ, ಎಲ್ಲಕೆ for ಎಲ್ಲರ್ಕೆ, ಎಲ್ಲರ್ಕೆ.

5, Abl. ಅಱತ್ತಣಿಂ, *i.e.* ಏತಱತ್ತಣಿಂ.

6, Gen. ಅಱ, *i. e.* ಏತಱ.

7, Loc. ಅಱೊಳ್, *i. e.* ಏತಱೊಳ್.

b) in the mediæval dialect

1, Nom. ಂ, ನು, the crude base, *i. e.* ಏಂ; ಏನು; ಏ, (ಯಾ).

ಏನು is ಏಂ (ಏನ್) and the euphonic ಉ. ಯಾ is another form of ಏ (see § 41).

2, Acc. ಅಂ, ಅ, the crude base, *i. e.* ಏನಂ; ಏನ; ಏ.

3, Instr. ಅಱಿಂ, *i. e.* ಏತಱಿಂ, (ಯಾತಱಿಂ).

4, Dat. ಅಕ್ಕೆ, ಅಕೆ, ಕೆ, *i. e.* ಏತಕ್ಕೆ or ಏತಕೆ, ಯಾತಕ್ಕೆ or ಯಾತಕೆ; ಏಕೆ, ಯಾಕೆ.

5, Abl. (ಅಱತ್ತಣಿಂ), the termination of the instrumental.

6, Gen. ಅಱ, *i. e.* ಏತಱ, ಯಾತಱ.

7, Loc. ಅಱೊಳ್, ಅಱೊಳು, ಅಱೊಳಗ, ಅಱಲ್ಲಿ, ಅಱಲಿ, *e. g.* ಏತಱಲಿ.

c) in the modern dialect

1, Nom. ನು, the crude base, *i. e.* ಏನು; ಯಾ.

2, Acc. ನು, ಅನು, ಅ, the crude base, *i. e.* ಏನು; ಏನನು; ಏನ.

3, Instr. ಅದರಿಂದ, *i. e.* ಯಾತರಿಂದ.

4, Dat. ಅಕ್ಕೆ, ಅಕೆ, ಕೆ, *i. e.* ಯಾತಕ್ಕೆ or ಯಾತಕೆ; ಯಾಕೆ.

5, Abl. ಅದರಿಂದ, *i. e.* ಯಾತರಿಂದ.

6, Gen. ಅದು, *i. e.* ಯಾತರ.

7, Loc. ಅದರೊಳಗೆ, ಅದರಲ್ಲಿ, (ಅದರಲಿ), *e. g.* ಯಾತರಲ್ಲಿ.

126. Concerning the eight nominal bases with final ಉ mentioned in § 123 it is to be stated that in the nominative, accusative, and locative they may receive the termination ಅಲ್ or ಅಲು; ಅಲ್ or ಅಲು appears also in the ablative of the mediæval dialect, and ಅಲು in the ablative, genitive, and locative of the modern one. **The declension of the lengthened bases** is the following.

a) in the ancient dialect

1, Nom. the crude base, ಉ, *e. g.* ಮೂಡಲ್, ಪಡುವಲ್, ಅತ್ತಲ್; ಬಡಗಲು (in a sâsana of 1123 A. D.).

In this case the ಅಲ್ means 'place' (see § 109, letter *a*, Locative). The question arises whether *e. g.* ಮೂಡಲ್ may not be ಮೂಡ, the genitive of ಮೂಡು, the east (see the genitive with ಅ in §§ 120. 122), and ಅಲ್, *i. e.* the place of the east. For ಅತ್ತಲ್, ಇತ್ತಲ್, ಉತ್ತಲ್, ಎತ್ತಲ್, however, no base ending in ಉ has as yet been established; but see the curious modern ablative ಅತ್ತಿಂದ, ಇತ್ತಿಂದ in § 123, letter *c*.

2, Acc. the crude base, *e. g.* ಮೂಡಲ್, ಪಡುವಲ್, ಅತ್ತಲ್.

Here we have an accusative represented by the crude base; *cf.* the ancient accusative in §§ 120. 125. 127.

7, Loc. the crude base, *e. g.* ಮೂಡಲ್, ಪಡುವಲ್, ಅತ್ತಲ್.

In this case ಅಲ್ means 'in the place'. It is not impossible that ಅಲ್ has been suffixed to the genitive of ಮೂಡು and ಪಡುವು; but, as remarked above, a base ending in ಉ for ಅತ್ತಲ್, etc. is still to be established.

b) in the mediæval dialect

1, Nom. the crude base, ಉ, *e. g.* ಮೂಡಲ್, ಇತ್ತಲ್; ಮೂಡಲು, ಇತ್ತಲು.

5, Abl. ಇಂ, *e. g.* ಅತ್ತಲಿಂ.

7, Loc. the crude base, ಉ, *e. g.* ಮೂಡಲ್; ಮೂಡಲು.

c) in the modern dialect

1, Nom. ಉ, *i. e.* the crude base, *e. g.* ತೆಂಕಲು, ಬಡಗಲು, ಅತ್ತಲು.

5, Abl. ಇಂದ, *e. g.* ಅತ್ತಲಿಂದ, ಇತ್ತಲಿಂದ.

6, Gen. ಅ, *e. g.* ಬಡಗಲ, ಅತ್ತಲ.

7, Loc. ಅಲ್ಲಿ, *e. g.* ಮೂಡಲಲ್ಲಿ, ಪಡುವಲಲ್ಲಿ, ಬಡಗಲಲ್ಲಿ.

127. Declension of four nominal bases always ending in the euphonic ಉ (see § 122) that express time (kâlavâčaka, kâlavâči), *viz.* ಅನ್ದು, ಇನ್ದು, ಉನ್ದು, ಎನ್ದು, the nominative, accusative, and locative of which have the same form, though the locative may receive also the terminations ಇನೊಳ್, ಇನಲ್ಲಿ. (*Cf.* the declension of ನಾಳೆ, etc. in § 139.)

a) in the ancient dialect

1, Nom. the crude base, *i. e.* ಅನ್ದು, ಇನ್ದು, ಉನ್ದು, ಎನ್ದು.

2, Acc. the crude base, *i. e.* ಅನ್ದು, ಇನ್ದು, ಉನ್ದು, ಎನ್ದು.

3, Instr. ಇಂ, *e. g.* ಅನ್ದಿಂ, ಇನ್ದಿಂ.

4, Dat. ಇಂಗೆ, *e. g.* ಅನ್ದಿಂಗೆ, ಇನ್ದಿಂಗೆ.

5, Abl. ಇನತ್ತಣಿಂ, *e. g.* ಅನ್ದಿನತ್ತಣಿಂ, ಇನ್ದಿನತ್ತಣಿಂ.

6, Gen. ಇನ, *e. g.* ಅನ್ದಿನ, ಇನ್ದಿನ.

7, Loc. the crude base, ಇನೊಳ್, ಇನಲ್ಲಿ, *e. g.* ಅನ್ದು, ಇನ್ದು, ಉನ್ದು, ಎನ್ದು; ಅನ್ದಿನೊಳ್; ಅನ್ದಿನಲ್ಲಿ,

b) in the mediæval dialect

1, Nom. the crude base, *i. e.* ಅನ್ದು, ಇನ್ದು, ಎನ್ದು.

An instance for ಉನ್ದು has not been found by the author.

2, Acc. the crude base, *i. e.* ಅನ್ದು, ಇನ್ದು, ಎನ್ದು.

3, Instr. the terminations of the ablative.

4, Dat. ಇಂಗೆ, ಇಗೆ, *e. g.* ಇನ್ದಿಂಗೆ, ಎನ್ದಿಂಗೆ; ಎನ್ದಿಗೆ.

5, Abl. ಇನಿಂ, ಇನಿನ್ದ, ಇನ್ದ, *e. g.* ಅನ್ದಿನಿಂ; ಎನ್ದಿನಿನ್ದ; ಎನ್ದಿನ್ದ.

6, Gen. ಇನ, *i. e.* ಅನ್ದಿನ, ಇನ್ದಿನ, ಎನ್ದಿನ.

7, Loc. the crude base, *i. e.* ಅನ್ದು, ಇನ್ದು, ಎನ್ದು.

c) in the modern dialect

1, Nom. the crude base, *i. e.* ಅನ್ದು, ಇನ್ದು, ಎನ್ದು.

2, Acc. the crude base, *i. e.* ಅನ್ದು, ಇನ್ದು, ಎನ್ದು.

3, Instr. the termination of the ablative.

4, Dat. ಇಗೆ, *i. e.* ಅನ್ದಿಗೆ, ಇನ್ದಿಗೆ, ಎನ್ದಿಗೆ.

5, Abl. ಇನಿನ್ದ, *e. g.* ಅನ್ದಿನಿನ್ದ, ಇನ್ದಿನಿನ್ದ.

6, Gen. ಇನ, *e. g.* ಅನ್ದಿನ, ಇನ್ದಿನ.

7, Loc. the crude base, ಇನಲ್ಲಿ, *e. g.* ಅನ್ದು, ಇನ್ದು, ಎನ್ದು; ಅನ್ದಿನಲ್ಲಿ.

128. The case-terminations for the singular of nominal bases with a radical final ಉ (see § 97), whether masculine, feminine, or neuter (see § 139 regarding ನಡು).

The bases comprise Kannaḍa and Saṁskṛita words. They can easily be distinguished from those in §§ 121, 122, and 127, as their final ಉ never unites with a following vowel without the euphonic augment ವ್ being inserted. For instance, we say ನಾಡಿವಾಯಿತು (ನಾಡು ಆಯಿತು), ಮುತ್ತಾ

ಯಿತು (ಮುತ್ತು ಆಯಿತು), but we cannot say, as every intelligent teacher knows, ಕುರಾಯಿತು, ಮಡಾಯಿತು, but must say ಕುರುವಾಯಿತು (ಕುರು-ವ್-ಆಯಿತು), ಮಡುವಾಯಿತು (ಮಡು-ವ್-ಆಯಿತು). See § 215, 3, *d*.

The case-terminations are suffixed by means of a euphonic ವ್, except in one form of the dative.

a) in the ancient dialect

1, Nom. ಉ, *i. e.* **the crude base,** *e. g.* ಅನು, ಉಡು, ಎಲು, ಕರು, ಕಱು, ಕೞು, ಕೆಯ್ಯು, ಕುರು, ತಣು, ತೞು, ತುಱು, ನಡು, ಪಱು, ಪುೞು, ಬಱು, ಬೆಟ್ಟು, ಮಡು; ಗುರು, ತನು, ಪರಶು, ಪಶು, ಭಾನು, ರಿಪು, ವಧು.

2, Acc. ಅಂ, *e. g.* ಕುರುವಂ (ಕುರು-ವ್-ಅಂ), ಪಱುವಂ (ಪಱು-ವ್-ಅಂ); ಗುರುವಂ (ಗುರು-ವ್-ಅಂ).

3, Instr. ಇಂ, ಇನಿಂ, ಇನ್ದಂ, ಇನಿನ್ದಂ, ಇನಿನ್ದೆ, *e. g.* ಮಡುವಿಂ, ನಡುವಿಂ, ಗುರುವಿಂ, ಮನುವಿಂ; ಮಡುವಿನಿಂ, ಗುರುವಿನಿಂ, ಮನುವಿನಿಂ; ಗುರುವಿನ್ದಂ; ಮಧುವಿನಿನ್ದಂ; ಮಧುವಿನಿನ್ದೆ.

4, Dat. ಗೆ, ಇಂಗೆ, *e. g.* ಮಡುಗೆ, ನಡುಗೆ, ತನುಗೆ; ಮಡುವಿಂಗೆ, ಗುರುವಿಂಗೆ.

5, Abl. ಇನತ್ತಣಿಂ, ಇನತ್ತಣಿನ್ದಂ, ಇನತ್ತಣಿನ್ದೆ, **the terminations of the instrumental,** *e. g.* ಧಾತುವಿನತ್ತಣಿಂ.

6, Gen. ಅ, ಆ, ಇನ, *e. g.* ಮಡುವ, ಕೆನ್ನುವ, ಗುರುವ, ವಧುವ; ವಧುವಾ; ಮಡುವಿನ, ಗುರುವಿನ, ಮನುವಿನ.

7, Loc. ಒೞ್, (ಅಲ್ಲಿ), ಇನೊೞ್, ಇನಲ್ಲಿ, *e. g.* ಗುರುತ್ತೊೞ್, ಸ್ವಕರ್ತೃವೊೞ್; ಮಡುವಿನೊೞ್, ಗುರುವಿನೊೞ್; ಮಡುವಿನಲ್ಲಿ.

b) in the mediæval dialect

1, Nom. ಉ *i. e.* **the crude base,** ಉ, *e. g.* ಗಿಡು, ತುಱು, ಗುರು, ತನು; ಕಱುವು, ಗಿಡುವು, ಮೇರುವು (see § 113, and *cf.* § 130, letter *b*).

2, Acc. ಅಂ, (ಅನು), ಅ, *e. g.* ಅನುವಂ, ಕಱುವಂ, ಕೆಯ್ದುವಂ, ತುಱುವಂ, ಶಮ್ಭುವಂ; ಅನುವ, ಎಲುವ, ಕೆಯ್ದುವ, ತೞುವ, ನಡುವ, ಪಶುವ.

3, Instr. ಇಂ, ಇನಿಂ, *e. g.* ಪರುಶುವಿಂ; ಅನುವಿನಿಂ.

4, Dat. ಗೆ, ಇಗೆ, (ಇಂಗೆ), *e. g.* ಶಮ್ಭುಗೆ, ಸಿಸುಗೆ; ಗುರುವಿಗೆ, ತನುವಿಗೆ.

5, Abl. (ಇನತ್ತಣಿಂ, etc.), **the terminations of the instrumental.**

6, Gen. (ಅ), ಇನ, *e. g.* ಅನುವಿನ, ಉಡುವಿನ, ಕಱುವಿನ, ಕೆಯ್ದುವಿನ, ಗುರುವಿನ, ತುಱುವಿನ, ಶಮ್ಭುವಿನ.

7, Loc. (ಒೞ್), ಇನೊೞ್, ಇನೊಳು, ಇನೊಳಗೆ, ಇನಲ್ಲಿ, ಇನಲಿ, *e. g.* ತನುವಿನೊೞ್, ಬೆಟ್ಟುವಿನೊೞ್; ಅನುವಿನೊಳು, ತನುವಿನೊಳು; ತನುವಿನೊಳಗೆ; ಕೆಯ್ದುವಿನಲ್ಲಿ, ಸ್ವಕರ್ತೃವಿನಲ್ಲಿ; ಅನುವಿನಲಿ, ತುಱುವಿನಲಿ.

c) in the modern dialect

1, Nom. ಉ *i. e.* **the crude base,** ಉ (see § 113), *e. g.* ಗುರು; ಗುರುವು, ಹಸುವು.

2, Acc. ಅನ್ನು, ಅ, ಇನ, ಇನನ್ನು, **the crude base,** *e. g.* ಗುರುವನ್ನು, ಹಸುವನ್ನು; ಹಸುವ; ಗುರುವಿನ; ಗುರುವಿನನ್ನು; ಹಸು.

The strange forms ಗುರುವಿನ, ಗುರುವಿನನ್ನು are given in his 'Outlines of Kanarese Grammar', page 17, by Venkat Rango Katti, Kanarese Translator, E. D., Bombay, 1886.

Forms of the modern dialect like ಸಂಪತ್ತುವನ್ನು (of ಸಂಪತ್ತು) and ಹೊತ್ತುವನ್ನು (of ಹೊತ್ತು) in which the final ಉ is wrongly treated as if it were radical, are modern licenses in literature.

3, Instr. ಇನ್ದ, ಇನಿನ್ದ, *e. g.* ಗುರುವಿನ್ದ; ಗುರುವಿನಿನ್ದ.

4, Dat. ಇಗೆ, *e. g.* ಅಸುವಿಗೆ, ಕಱುವಿಗೆ, ಗುರುವಿಗೆ, ಹಸುವಿಗೆ.

5, Abl. ಇನ್ದ, ಇನಿನ್ದ, *e. g.* ಗುರುವಿನ್ದ, ಹಸುವಿನ್ದ; ಗುರುವಿನಿನ್ದ, ಹಸುವಿನಿನ್ದ.

6, Gen. ಅ, ಇನ, *e. g.* ಹಸುವ; ಗುರುವಿನ, ಹಸುವಿನ.

7, Loc. ಅಲ್ಲಿ, ಇನಲ್ಲಿ, *e. g.* ಹಸುವಲ್ಲಿ; ಮಡುವಿನಲ್ಲಿ, ಗುರುವಿನಲ್ಲಿ, ಹಸುವಿನಲ್ಲಿ.

129. There are some **nominal bases ending in** ಊ, ಋ, ೠ, ಓ, and ಔ which in the singular are declined like those in § 128, *e. g.* ಪೂ, ಹೂ, ಪಿತೃ, ಮಾತೃ, ೠ, ಭೂ, ಗೋ, ಗ್ಲೌ.

a) in the ancient dialect

1, Nom. **the crude base,** *e. g.* ಪೂ, ಪಿತೃ, ೠ.

2, Acc. ಅಂ, *e. g.* ಪೂವಂ, ಪಿತೃವಂ, ಗೋವಂ, ಗ್ಲೌವಂ.

In Šabdamaṇidarpaṇa p. 67 there is ೠವಿತ್ತಂ or the crude base. *Cf.* letter c.

3, Instr. ಇಂ, ಇನ್ದೆ, ಇನ್ದಂ, ಇನಿಂ, *e. g.* ಪೂವಿಂ, ಪಿತೃವಿಂ; ಪೂವಿನ್ದೆ; ಪೂವಿನ್ದಂ; ಪೂವಿನಿಂ, ಪಿತೃವಿನಿಂ.

4, Dat. ಗೆ, ಇಂಗೆ, *e. g.* ಪೂಗೆ, ಪೂವಿಂಗೆ, ಗೋವಿಂಗೆ.

5, Abl. ಇನತ್ತಣಿಂ, *e. g.* ಪೂವಿನತ್ತಣಿಂ.

6, Gen. ಅ, ಇನ, *e. g.* ಗೋವ, ಗ್ಲೌವ; ಪೂವಿನ, ಕರ್ತೃವಿನ, ಪಿತೃವಿನ, ೠವಿನ, ಗೋವಿನ, ಗ್ಲೌವಿನ.

7, Loc. ಒಳ್, ಇನೊಳ್, *e. g.* ಗೋವೊಳ್; ಪೂವಿನೊಳ್, ಕರ್ತೃವಿನೊಳ್, ಗೋವಿನೊಳ್.

b) in the mediæval dialect

1, Nom. **the crude base,** ಉ, *e. g.* ಪೂ; ಪೂವು.

2, Acc. ಅಂ, *e. g.* ಪೂವಂ.

6, Gen. ಇನ, *e. g.* ಪೂವಿನ, ಹೂವಿನ.

c) in the modern dialect

1, Nom. **the crude base,** ಉ, *e. g.* ಹೂ, ಗೋ; ಹೂವು, ಗೋವು.

2, Acc. ಅನ್ನು, **the crude base,** *e. g.* ಹೂವನ್ನು; ಹೂ.

4, Dat. ಇಗೆ, *e. g.* ಹೂವಿಗೆ.

6, Gen. ಇನ, *e. g.* ಹೂವಿನ.

130. The case-terminations for the singular of masculine, feminine and neuter **bases ending** in ಇ, ಈ and ಎ. (Regarding some exceptions see § 139.)

The terminations are suffixed by means of a euphonic ಯ್, except in the dative (*cf.* the ದ್ in § 109, *a, c*).

a) in the ancient dialect

1, Nom. ಇ, ಈ, ಎ, *i. e.* **the crude base,** *e. g.* ಪುಲಿ, ಕರಡಿ, ದಾಸ, ಕಪಿ, ತರುಣ, ಶ್ರೀ, ಸ್ತ್ರೀ; ಮನೆ, ಆಕೆ, ಈಕೆ, ಊಕೆ, ಸೀತೆ.

2, Acc. ಅಂ, **(the crude base),** *e. g.* ಪುಲಿಯಂ, ಗಾಳಿಯಂ, ದಾಸಿಯಂ, ಕಪಿಯಂ, ಪಸಿಯಂ, ರುಚಿಯಂ, ಅರಾತಿಯಂ, ತರುಣಿಯಂ; ಸ್ತ್ರೀಯಂ; ಮನೆಯಂ, ಆನೆಯಂ, ಆಕೆಯಂ. ಈಕೆಯಂ, ಸೀತೆಯಂ.

The crude base is seen, *e. g.* in the following instance of Kêšava:—ಗಿಳಿ ಸೋವಾಕೆಗಳ್. See § 120, *a*, 2.

3, Instr. ಇಂ, ಇನ್ದಂ, ಇನ್ದೆ, ಎ, *e. g.* ಕಿವಿಯಿಂ, ಜನಪತಿಯಿಂ, ಬಕಾರಿಯಿಂ, ಕೊಡಲಿಯಿಂ, ಕದೆಯಿಂ, ಗದೆಯಿಂ, ಸಿಡುಗೆಯಿಂ, ಅಕ್ಕಸಾಲೆಯಿಂ; ನದಿಯಿನ್ದಂ, ಪಸುರ್ವಿಡಿಯಿನ್ದಂ; ನಿರ್ದಯೆಯಿನ್ದೆ, ನದಿಯಿನ್ದೆ; ಅಬ್ಬೆಯೆ (in a šâsana of 929 A. D.; Pampa Bhârata 1, 140; see Nṛipatuṅga's Kavirâjamârga, edited by K. B. Pathak, B. A., introduction p. 2).

4, Dat. ಗೆ, *e. g.* ಕಿವಿಗೆ, ಮಣಿಗೆ, ಕವಿಗೆ, ಅಬ್ಬೆಗೆ, ಸವತಿಗೆ, ಕಡೆಗೆ, ಮಱಿಗೆ, ಸೀಱೆಗೆ, ಆಕೆಗೆ.

5, Abl. ಅತ್ತಣಿಂ, ಅತ್ತಣಿನ್ದಂ, ಅತ್ತಣಿನ್ದೆ, *e. g.* ಸ್ವಾಮಿಯತ್ತಣಿಂ, ತೆಂಗಾಳಿಯತ್ತಣಿಂ, ಕಱಿಯತ್ತಣಿಂ, ಪಗೆಯತ್ತಣಿಂ, ರಮ್ಭೆಯತ್ತಣಿಂ; ಕೆಱೆಯತ್ತಣಿನ್ದಂ; ಕೆಱೆಯತ್ತಣಿನ್ದೆ, ಜಾದಿಯತ್ತಣಿನ್ದೆ.

6, Gen. ಅ, ಆ, *e. g.* ಗಾಳಿಯ, ಗಿಳಿಯ, ಸ್ವಾಮಿಯ, ರಕ್ಕಸಿಯ, ಕಾಗೆಯ, ಕಡೆಯ, ಕೆಱೆಯ, ಕುದುರೆಯ, ಆನೆಯ, ಈಕೆಯ, ಆಕೆಯ; ಪುಲಿಯಾ, ಕಿರಾತಯಾ, ನೇತ್ರೆಯಾ, ಗಂಗೆಯಾ. See under § 109, *a*, 6, about the lengthening.

7, Loc. ಉಳ್, ಒಳ್, ಒಳು, ಒಳಗೆ, ಅಲ್, ಅಲು, ಅಲ್ಲಿ, *e. g.* ವಾರಣಾಸಿಯುಳ್ (in a šâsana of 707 A. D.), ಬಾರಣಾಸಿಯುಳ್ (in a šâsana of 866 A. D.); ಕಿವಿಯೊಳ್, ಕೊಡಲಿಯೊಳ್, ಭೂತವತಿಯೊಳ್, ಇಳೆಯೊಳ್, ಎಡೆಯೊಳ್, ಧರೆಯೊಳ್, ಸಭೆಯೊಳ್; ತ್ರಾಹೆಯೊಳು, ಗುಡಿಗೆಱೆಯೊಳು (both in a šâsana of 1076 A. D.), ಧರಿತ್ರಿಯೊಳು (in a šâsana of 1123 A. D.); ಉಡಿಯೊಳಗೆ, ಮನೆಯೊಳಗೆ; ಅವಧಿಯಲ್ (in a šâsana of 1186 A. D.); ಪುರಿಗೆಱೆಯಲು (in a šâsana of 1076 A. D.), ಹೆಬ್ಬಟ್ಟೆಯಲು (in a šâsana of 1123 A. D.), ಯಾತ್ರೆಯಲು (in one of 1182 A. D.); ಕಿವಿಯಲ್ಲಿ, ಸಭೆಯಲ್ಲಿ.

b) in the mediæval dialect

1, Nom. ಇ, ಈ, ಎ, *i. e.* **the crude base, the augment** ಉ (see § 113), *e. g.* ತಾಯಿ, ಕೇರಿ; ಸ್ತ್ರೀ; ಮನೆ; ವಿಧಿಯು, ಅನ್ವೆಯು, ಸಭೆಯು, ಶಿಲೆಯು.

The augment ಉ, like that of § 128 and § 129, is in reality not euphonic or a help to enunciation, and is so to say, a superfluous addition. Like that of § 128 and § 129 it disappears in sandhi (§ 213 *seq.*).

2, Acc. ಅಂ, ಅನು, ಅ, *e. g.* ಭಕ್ತಿಯಂ, ಕವಿತೆಯಂ, ಅನ್ವೆಯಂ; ಪ್ರಸಿದ್ಧಿಯನು, ಆಜ್ಞೆಯನು, ಚರಿತೆಯನು; ಮಹೀಪತಿಯ, ಇಲಿಯ, ಕೃತಿಯ, ತನ್ತ್ರಿಯ, ಮತಿಯ, ಗಣ್ಣೆಯ.

3, Instr. ಇಂ, ಇನ್ದಂ, ಇನ್ದೆ, ಇನ್ದ, *e. g.* ಅರ್ತಿಯಿಂ, ಪ್ರೀತಿಯಿಂ, ಮಾಱ್ಕೆಯಿಂ; ವಾಣಿಯಿನ್ದಂ, ಭ್ರಾನ್ತಿಯಿನ್ದಂ, ಹತಿಯಿನ್ದಂ; ಅಡಿಯಿನ್ದೆ, ಉಕ್ತಿಯಿನ್ದೆ, ಪರಿಯಿನ್ದೆ, ಮತಿಯಿನ್ದೆ, ಪ್ರವರ್ತನೆಯಿನ್ದೆ; ಕಠಾರಿಯಿನ್ದ, ನನ್ನಿಯಿನ್ದ, ಚಮ್ಮಟಿಗೆಯಿನ್ದ.

4, Dat. ಗೆ, *e. g.* ನನ್ನಿಗೆ, ತಾಯಿಗೆ, ಭಕ್ತಿಗೆ, ಮೂರ್ತಿಗೆ, ತನ್ದೆಗೆ, ಆಕೆಗೆ, ಸುತೆಗೆ, ಶಿಲೆಗೆ.

5, Abl. (ಅತ್ತಣಿಂ, etc.), ಇನ್ದವು, **the terminations of the instrumental,** *e. g.* ತುದಿಯಿನ್ದವು; ಎದೆಯಿನ್ದ.

6, Gen. ಅ, *e. g.* ಹತ್ತಿಯ, ತಂಗಿಯ, ಆನೆಯ, ಮನೆಯ, ತನ್ದೆಯ, ಆಕೆಯ, ಈಕೆಯ.

7, Loc. ಒಳ್, ಒಳು, ಒಳಗೆ, ಅಲು, ಅಲ್ಲಿ, ಅಲಿ, *e. g.* ಕ್ಷಿತಿಯೊಳ್, ಬೀದಿಯೊಳ್, ಇಳೆಯೊಳ್, ಎಚ್ಚರಿಕೆಯೊಳ್; ಅವನಿಯೊಳು, ಧರಣಿಯೊಳು, ಪ್ರೌಢವಿಯೊಳು, ಕಡೆಯೊಳು, ವೇಳೆಯೊಳು; ರಾಸಿಯೊಳಗೆ, ಅವನಿಯೊಳಗೆ, ಪ್ರೌಢವಿಯೊಳಗೆ, ಕತ್ತಲೆಯೊಳಗೆ, ಕಥೆಯೊಳಗೆ, ವಿಗಡಿಗೆಯೊಳಗೆ; ಆದಿಯಲು; ಹಿಡಿಯಲ್ಲಿ, ಚೆಣ್ಡಿಕೆಯಲ್ಲಿ; ಗೋಷ್ಠಿಯಲಿ, ಜೀರ್ಕೊಟವಿಯಲಿ, ಪರಿಯಲಿ, ಭಕ್ತಿಯಲಿ, ತಲೆಯಲಿ, ಬೆಣ್ಣೆಯಲಿ, ಮಟಿಯಲಿ, ಸಜ್ಝೆಯಲಿ, ಸನ್ನೆಯಲಿ, ಸೇವೆಯಲಿ.

c) in the modern dialect

1, Nom. ಇ, ಈ, ಎ, *i. e.* the crude base, the augment ಉ (see § 113), *e. g.* ತಂಗಿ, ಕಪಿ, ಕವಿ; ಸ್ತ್ರೀ; ಕೆನ್ನೆ, ಬೆಣ್ಣೆ; ಗಿಳಿಯು, ನುಡಿಯು, ಪಕ್ಷಿಯು, ಸ್ತ್ರೀಯು, ಕ್ರಿಯೆಯು, ವಿದ್ಯೆಯು, ಆಕೆಯು.

2, Acc. ಅನು, ಅನ್ನು, ಅ, ಅನ, lengthening of the final vowel, the crude base, *e. g.* ದಾರಿಯನು, ಬೇಲಿಯನು, ಬುದ್ಧಿಯನು, ಸೇವೆಯನು; ಪ್ರೀತಿಯನ್ನು, ಮುನಿಯನ್ನು, ಎಮ್ಮೆಯನ್ನು, ಅಱಿವೆಯನ್ನು; ದನಿಯ, ಮತಿಯ, ಮುನಿಯ, ಹೆಣ್ಡತಿಯ, ಬೆಳೆಯ, ಕಱಿಕೆಯ, ಕೀರ್ತನೆಯ; ತಂಗೀನ, ತಾಯೀನ, ಹುಡುಗೀನ, ಅತ್ತೇನ, ಸೊಸೇನ; ಅಂಗೀ, ಕೊಳ್ಳೀ, ಗಾಳೀ, ಕಪೀ, ಚಾಡೀ, ಬಾವೀ, ಅಡಿಕೇ, ಕಾಗೇ, ಕೊಟ್ಟಿಗೇ, ತಪ್ಪಲೇ, ತಲೇ, ತೆಱಗೇ, ಮನೇ, ಮನ್ದೇ, ಸೋಗೇ; ಕನ್ನಡಿ, ಗುಗ್ಗರಿ, ಆನೆ, ಮನೆ.

ಅನ is ಅನು with a final ಅ, and ತಂಗೀನ, ಅತ್ತೇನ, etc. stand for ತಂಗಿಯನ, ಅತ್ತೆಯನ, etc. The forms ಅಂಗೀ, etc., ಅಡಿಕೇ, etc., stand for ಅಂಗಿಯ, etc., ಅಡಿಕೆಯ, etc.

3, Instr. ಇನ್ದ, *e. g.* ಮುನಿಯಿನ್ದ, ನುಡಿಯಿನ್ದ, ತನ್ದೆಯಿನ್ದ, ಮಱಯಿನ್ದ.

4, Dat. ಗೆ, *e. g.* ಮುನಿಗೆ, ನುಡಿಗೆ, ತಾಯಿಗೆ, ನಾಯಿಗೆ, ಸ್ತ್ರೀಗೆ, ಅತ್ತೆಗೆ, ಸೊಸೆಗೆ, ತನ್ದೆಗೆ, ಆಕೆಗೆ, ಮನೆಗೆ, ಆನೆಗೆ.

5, Abl. ಇನ್ದ, *e. g.* ಮುನಿಯಿನ್ದ, ದೊರೆಯಿನ್ದ, ನರಿಯಿನ್ದ.

6, Gen. ಅ, ಆ, lengthening of the final vowel, *e. g.* ಮುನಿಯ, ನಾಯಿಯ, ಸ್ತ್ರೀಯ, ತನ್ದೆಯ, ಸೊಸೆಯ, ಆಕೆಯ, ಈಕೆಯ, ತಲೆಯ, ಕೋಗಿಲೆಯ; ಬಟ್ಟೆಯಾ, ಹಾದಿಯಾ; ತಾಯಾ, ಕಾಯಾ, ಗಾಳೀ, ನೆಲ್ಲೀ, ಹಳ್ಳೀ, ಕೊಱಚೀ, ಹಿತ್ತಾಳೀ, ತನ್ದೇ, ಆನೇ, ಕುದುರೇ, ಕೆಱೇ, ಕೊಟೇ, ಬೋರೇ, ಬಾಟೇ, ಮೋಜೇ, ಮನೇ, ಸಾಲೇ.

ತಾಯಾ, etc., ತನ್ದೇ, etc. stand for ತಾಯಿಯ, etc., ತನ್ದೆಯ, etc.

7, Loc. ಒಳಗೆ, ಅಲ್ಲಿ, ಅಲಿ, ಈಲಿ, ಎಲಿ, ಲಿ, *e. g.* ಪ್ರೌಢವಿಯೊಳಗೆ, ಸಭೆಯೊಳಗೆ, ಮಟಿಯೊಳಗೆ; ಮುನಿಯಲ್ಲಿ, ಮನೆಯಲ್ಲಿ; ದಿಟ್ಟಿಯಲಿ, ಕಡೆಯಲಿ, ಸಭೆಯಲಿ, ಮಮತೆಯಲಿ; ಬಾವೀಲಿ, ಹಸ್ತೀಲಿ, ಹಾದೀಲಿ; ಇಚ್ಚೇಲಿ, ಕಡೇಲಿ, ತಿಪ್ಪೇಲಿ, ಮನೇಲಿ; ಕೇರಿಲಿ, ದಾರಿಲಿ, ನೆತ್ತಿಲಿ, ಬೀದಿಲಿ, ಸಂಗತಿಲಿ, ಎಣ್ಣೆಲಿ.

ಬಾವೀಲಿ, etc., ಇಚ್ಚೇಲಿ, etc. stand for ಬಾವಿಯಲಿ, etc., ಇಚ್ಚೆಯಲಿ, etc.; and ಕೇರಿಲಿ, etc. are corrupted forms of ಕೇರಿಯಲಿ, etc. (*cf.* § 121, letter *c*).

131. The case-terminations of the plural of neuter bases with final ಅ are given in § 118, and those of the plural of masculine and feminine (and epicene) bases with final ಅ in § 119.

Here follow the case-terminations for the plural of neuter bases, (the feminine bases ತಾಯ್, ಪೆಣ್, and the masculine-neuter base ಆಳ್) ending in consonants (§ 120), in the vowel ಉ that, occasionally also in the ancient dialect, is euphonically suffixed (§ 121), and in the euphonical vowel ಉ that in each dialect is always suffixed (§ 122), and further those for the plural of masculine, feminine and neuter bases ending in the radical vowel ಉ (§ 128), in ಊ, ಋ, ೠ, ಓ and ಔ (§ 129), and in ಇ and ಎ (§ 130), the case-terminations nowhere indicating the gender (see § 132 wherein the gender, to some extent, appears from the terminations of the plural).

The case-terminations are

a) in the ancient dialect

1, Nom. ಗಳ್, ಕಳ್, ಗಳು, *e. g.* ಕಣ್ಗಳ್, ಪುಲ್ಗಳ್, ಊರ್ಗಳ್, ಕಾಲ್ಗಳ್, ಕೇಱ್ಗಳ್, ಗೇಣ್ಗಳ್, ತೋಳ್ಗಳ್, ಅಗಲ್ಗಳ್, ಬಾಸುಲ್ಗಳ್, ಮುಗುಳ್ಗಳ್, ಕುರುಳ್ಗಳ್, ಕನರ್ಗಳ್, ಕೆಸರ್ಗಳ್, ಅಳ್ಗಳ್, ತಾಯ್ಗಳ್, ಪೆಣ್ಗಳ್; ಕೋಟ್ಕಳ್, ನಾಟ್ಕಳ್; ಕಲ್ಲುಗಳ್ (in a śâsana of 1187 A. D.); ಅರಸುಗಳ್, ನಾಲ್ಕುಗಳ್, ಆಯ್ದುಗಳ್, ನೂಱುಗಳ್, ಕರ್ಪೂರಗಳ್, ಕೂರ್ಪುರಗಳ್, ಬೆಳ್ಪುಗಳ್; ಗುರುಗಳ್, ತುಱುಗಳ್, ತರುಗಳ್, ಮಧುಗಳ್; ಪೂಗಳ್, ಪಿತೃಗಳ್, ಭ್ರಾತೃಗಳ್; ಕಲಿಗಳ್, ಕವಿಗಳ್, ಚಾಗಿಗಳ್, ಪಾಪಿಗಳ್, ಸ್ವಾಮಿಗಳ್, ಉಕ್ತಿಗಳ್, ಕಿಪಿಗಳ್; ತನ್ದೆಗಳ್, ಅತ್ತೆಗಳ್, ಆಕೆಗಳ್, ಎಡೆಗಳ್, ತೊಡೆಗಳ್, ದೆಸೆಗಳ್, ಮನೆಗಳ್, ಕುದುರೆಗಳ್; ಗುರುಗಳು, ಸ್ವಾಮಿಗಳು (both in a śâsana of 1182 A. D.).

2, Acc. ಅಂ, *e. g.* ಕಾಲ್ಗಳಂ, ಊರ್ಗಳಂ; ತುಱುಗಳಂ; ಕೇಶಿಗಳಂ; ಮೊಳೆಗಳಂ.

3, Instr. ಇಂ, (ಇನ್ದಂ, ಇನ್ದೆ), *e. g.* ಕಾಯ್ಗಳಿಂ, ಪಣ್ಗಳಿಂ, ತಳಿರ್ಗಳಿಂ; ಆಕೆಗಳಿಂ, ಆಜ್ಞೆಗಳಿಂ, ಉದಾಹರಣೆಗಳಿಂ.

4, Dat. ಗೆ, ಉಗೆ, *e.g.* ಊರ್ಗಳ್ಗೆ; ಕಿವಿಗಳ್ಗೆ; ಶತ್ರುಗಳುಗೆ (in a śâsana of 1187 A. D.).

The ಉ in ಉಗೆ is merely euphonic.

5, Abl. (ಅತ್ತಣಿಂ, ಅತ್ತಣಿನ್ದಂ, ಅತ್ತಣಿನ್ದೆ), the terminations of the instrumental, *e. g.* ಕೋಟ್ಕಳಿಂ; ಕುಡಿಯಳ್ಳೆಗಳಿನ್ದೆ.

6, Gen. ಅ, ಆ, *e. g.* ಕಣ್ಗಳ, ಮೆಯ್ಗಳ, ಕುರುಳ್ಗಳ; ಗುರುಗಳ, ತುಱುಗಳ; ಪೂಗಳ; ಬಿರಯಿಗಳ, ಸ್ವಾಮಿಗಳ; ಗುರುಗಳಾ.

7, Loc. ಒಳ್, (ಅಲ್ಲಿ), *e. g.* ಕಣ್ಗಳೊಳ್; ಚಾಗಿಗಳೊಳ್; ಸಮ್ಪಗೆಗಳೊಳ್.

b) · in the mediæval dialect

1, Nom. ಗಳ್, ಗಳು, *e. g.* ಹೆಣ್ಗಳ್, ಪುಲ್ಗಳ್; ಪೂಗಳ್; ತಾಯಿಗಳ್, ಮಱಿಗಳ್, ಬಳ್ಳಿಗಳ್, ಗಣ್ಡುಗಳ್, ತನ್ದೆಗಳ್, ಗಟ್ಟಿಗಳ್; ತಾಯ್ಗಳು, ಕಾಲ್ಗಳು; ನೆಲ್ಲುಗಳು, ಮುಗುಳುಗಳು; ಎತ್ತುಗಳು; ಕಱುಗಳು, ವಸುವುಗಳು; ತಾಯಿಗಳು, ಕುದುರೆಗಳು.

In ವಸುವುಗಳು the termination ಗಳು has been appended to the euphonic ಉ of the nominative singular (see § 128, letter *b*).

2, Acc. ಅಂ, ಅನು, ಅ, *e. g.* ಕಾಲ್ಗಳಂ; ಒಡಲುಗಳಂ, ಆಳುಗಳಂ; ಅನುಗಳಂ, ಕಱುಗಳಂ; ವ್ರತಿಗಳಂ, ಮಾಲೆಗಳಂ; ನೆಲೆಗಳನು, ಮಹಿಮೆಗಳನು; ಕಲ್ಲುಗಳ, ಕೋಲುಗಳ, ಸರಳುಗಳ, ಮಾತುಗಳ, ಕೆಯ್ದುಗಳ, ವಸ್ತುಗಳ, ಆಲಿಗಳ, ಉಕ್ತಿಗಳ, ಮಿಳಿಗಳ, ಗಡ್ಡೆಗಳ.

3, Instr. ಇಂ, ಇನ್ದಂ, ಇನ್ದೆ, ಇನ್ದ, ಇ, *e. g.* ಶ್ರುತಿಗಳಿಂ, ಸ್ತುತಿಗಳಿಂ; ಧ್ವನಿಗಳಿನ್ದಂ; ಕೆಯ್ದುಗಳಿನ್ದೆ, ಉಕ್ತಿಗಳಿನ್ದೆ, ಸೂಕ್ತಿಗಳಿನ್ದೆ; ಕೆಯ್ದುಗಳಿನ್ದ, ವಿಧಿಗಳಿನ್ದ, ವೀಣೆಗಳಿನ್ದ; ಮಾಯೆಗಳಿ.

For the ಇ in ಮಾಯೆಗಳಿ see § 109, letters *b* and *c*.

4, Dat. ಗೆ, ಇಗೆ, *e. g.* ಅರ್ಥಿಗಳ್ಗೆ; ಕಾಲ್ಗಳಿಗೆ, ತಳಿರುಗಳಿಗೆ, ಅರಸುಗಳಿಗೆ, ಗುರುಗಳಿಗೆ, ಜೀವಿಗಳಿಗೆ, ಅದಿಗಳಿಗೆ, ಕಿವಿಗಳಿಗೆ, ಸುಱಿಗಳಿಗೆ, ವಿಷ್ಣುಗಳಿಗೆ.

5, Abl. (ಅತ್ತಣಿಂ, etc.), **the terminations of the instrumental**, *e. g.* ಮನೆಗಳಿಂ.

6, Gen. ಅ, *e. g.* ಕಾಲ್ಗಳ; ಅರಸುಗಳ, ಎತ್ತುಗಳ, ಮುತ್ತುಗಳ; ಧೇನುಗಳ, ಪಶುಗಳ; ಪೂಗಳ; ತಾಯಿಗಳ.

7, Loc. ಒಳ್, (ಒಳು), ಒಳಗೆ, ಅಲ್ಲಿ, ಅಲಿ, *e. g.* ಗಣ್ಣುಗಳೊಳ್; ಕಪ್ಪುಗಳೊಳಗೆ, ದೆಸೆಗಳೊಳಗೆ; ನಾಯ್ಗಳಲ್ಲಿ; ಮತಿಗಳಲಿ, ಮನೆಗಳಲಿ, ದೊಣ್ಣೆಗಳಲಿ, ವೇಳೆಗಳಲಿ, ಸಭೆಗಳಲಿ, ಹಡೆಗಳಲಿ.

c) in the modern dialect

1, Nom. ಗಳು, *e. g.* ಕಣ್ಣುಗಳು, ಮುಳ್ಳುಗಳು, ಹಣ್ಣುಗಳು, ಕಾಲುಗಳು, ಹೆಸರುಗಳು, ಆಳುಗಳು; ಎತ್ತುಗಳು, ಕೂಸುಗಳು, ಮಾತುಗಳು; ಗುರುಗಳು, ವಸ್ತುಗಳು, ಹಸುಗಳು; ಪೂವುಗಳು, ಗೋಗಳು, ಕರ್ತೃಗಳು; ತಾಯಿಗಳು, ಮುನಿಗಳು, ಕುನ್ನಿಗಳು, ಇಲಿಗಳು, ಕಾಯಿಗಳು; ತನ್ದೆಗಳು, ದೊರೆಗಳು, ಮೊಲೆಗಳು, ಮೊಳೆಗಳು.

Another plural is formed by adding the plural of the pronouns ಅವ or ಅವಳು, *viz.* ಅವರು, to the nominative plural, *e. g.* ದೊರೆಗಳವರು, ಶ್ರೀಗಳವರು, or to the nominative singular, *e. g.* ಚಕ್ರವರ್ತಿನಿಯವರು. *Cf.* § 119, *c*, 1.

2, Acc. ಅನ್ನು, ಅ, *e. g.* ಕಲ್ಲುಗಳನ್ನು, ಹಣ್ಣುಗಳನ್ನು, ಕಾಲುಗಳನ್ನು, ಆಳುಗಳನ್ನು; ಎತ್ತುಗಳನ್ನು, ಮಾತುಗಳನ್ನು, ಒಡ್ಡುಗಳನ್ನು; ಗುರುಗಳನ್ನು, ವಸ್ತುಗಳನ್ನು; ಮುನಿಗಳನ್ನು, ಇಲಿಗಳನ್ನು, ಕಾಯಿಗಳನ್ನು, ರೂಪಾಯಿಗಳನ್ನು; ತನ್ದೆಗಳನ್ನು, ಎಲೆಗಳನ್ನು; ಕೂಸುಗಳ, ಗುರುಗಳ, ಮುನಿಗಳ.

3, Instr. ಇನ್ದ, *e. g.* ಕಾಲುಗಳಿನ್ದ, ಉಗುರುಗಳಿನ್ದ; ಎತ್ತುಗಳಿನ್ದ, ಕೂಸುಗಳಿನ್ದ; ಗುರುಗಳಿನ್ದ; ಮುನಿಗಳಿನ್ದ, ಕಡ್ಡಿಗಳಿನ್ದ, ಗಱಿಗಳಿನ್ದ; ದೊರೆಗಳಿನ್ದ, ಗೆರೆಗಳಿನ್ದ.

4, Dat. ಇಗೆ, *e. g.* ಬಾಗಿಲುಗಳಿಗೆ; ಎತ್ತುಗಳಿಗೆ, ಕೂಸುಗಳಿಗೆ, ನಾಡುಗಳಿಗೆ; ಗುರುಗಳಿಗೆ, ಕಱುಗಳಿಗೆ; ಪಿತೃಗಳಿಗೆ; ಮುನಿಗಳಿಗೆ, ಪ್ರಾಣಿಗಳಿಗೆ; ಪಾತ್ರೆಗಳಿಗೆ, ಹಲಗೆಗಳಿಗೆ.

5, Abl. **the termination of the instrumental.**

6, Gen. ಅ, *e. g.* ಕಲ್ಲುಗಳ, ಬೇರುಗಳ; ಕೂಸುಗಳ, ಬೆಕ್ಕುಗಳ; ಗುರುಗಳ, ಕಱುಗಳ; ಪಿತೃಗಳ; ಮುನಿಗಳ, ನಾಯಿಗಳ, ಇಲಿಗಳ; ತನ್ದೆಗಳ, ಗೋಡೆಗಳ.

7, Loc. ಒಳಗೆ, ಅಲ್ಲಿ, ಅಲಿ, *e. g.* ಕಲ್ಲುಗಳೊಳಗೆ, ನಾಡುಗಳೊಳಗೆ, ಕಣಿಗಳೊಳಗೆ; ನಾಡುಗಳಲ್ಲಿ, ಗುರುಗಳಲ್ಲಿ, ಮುನಿಗಳಲ್ಲಿ, ಕುಱಿಗಳಲ್ಲಿ, ನಾಯಿಗಳಲ್ಲಿ, ಅಡವಿಗಳಲ್ಲಿ, ಟೊಂಗೆಗಳಲ್ಲಿ; ನದಿಗಳಲಿ.

132. As has been remarked in § 131 there are such plural case-terminations for nominal bases as indicate their gender, but only to a certain extent; for these **terminations are of an epicene character** (*cf.* § 102, 4), and besides in poetical diction are appended even to neuter objects. (*Cf.* the terminations in §§ 118. 119. 134.)

The terminations that are affixed to bases ending in ಇ, ಈ, (ಉ, *e. g.* in ತೊಟ್ಟು), ಋ, ಎ, (ಯ್, in ತಾಯ್), (ಲ್, *e. g.* in ಮುಗಿಲ್), **are the following:—**

a) in the ancient dialect

1, Nom. ಅರ್, ಇರ್, ಗಳಿರ್, ಅರಿರ್, ಅರ್ಕಳ್, ಅರ್ಕಳಿರ್, ದಿರ್, ದಿರ್ಕಳ್, ವಿರ್, ವಿರಿರ್, ವಿರ್ಕಳ್, ವಿರ್ಗಳ್, *e. g.* ತನ್ದೆಯರ್, ಅತ್ತೆಯರ್, ದೇವಿಯರ್, ಸ್ತ್ರೀಯರ್, ಪಣ್ಡಿತಿಯರ್, ಕಾನ್ತೆಯರ್, ಸೂಳೆಯರ್; ತೊಟ್ಟರ್ (of ತೊಟ್ಟು); ಮುಗಿಲ್ಗಳಿರ್, ದೆಸೆಗಳಿರ್; ದೇವಿಯರಿರ್, ಸ್ತ್ರೀಯರಿರ್; ತನ್ದೆಯರ್ಕಳ್, ಅತ್ತೆಯರ್ಕಳ್, ಕಾಮಿನಿಯರ್ಕಳ್, ಸ್ತ್ರೀಯರ್ಕಳ್; ದೇವಿಯರ್ಕಳಿರ್; ತನ್ದೆದಿರ್, ತಾಯ್ದಿರ್, ತಂಗಿದಿರ್, ಅಕ್ಕದಿರ್, ಸೊಸೆದಿರ್; ತನ್ದೆದಿರ್ಕಳ್, ಅಕ್ಕದಿರ್ಕಳ್; ತನ್ದೆವಿರ್, ತಾಯ್ವಿರ್, ಭ್ರಾತೃವಿರ್, ಅತ್ತೆವಿರ್.

ಸೊಸೆವಿರ್, ಅಕೆವಿರ್, ಈಕೆವಿರ್; ಅತ್ತೆವಿದಿರ್; ತನ್ದೆವಿರ್ಕಳ್, ಅತ್ತೆವಿರ್ಕಳ್, ಈಕೆವಿರ್ಕಳ್; ಅಕ್ಕೆವಿಗಳ್, ಆಕೆವಿಗಳ್, ಈಕೆವಿಗಳ್.

The ಯ್ in ತನ್ದೆಯರ್, etc. is euphonic or a help to enunciation. ಗಳಿರ್ consists of ಗಳ್ and ಇರ್, ಅರಿರ್ of ಅರ್ and ಇರ್, ಅರ್ಕಳ್ of ಅರ್ and ಕಳ್, ಅರ್ಕಳಿರ್ of ಅರ್ and ಕಳ್ and ಇರ್, ದಿರ್ಕಳ್ of ದಿರ್ and ಕಳ್, ವಿರಿರ್ of ವಿರ್ and ಇರ್, ವಿರ್ಕಳ್ of ವಿರ್ and ಕಳ್, ವಿಗಳ್ of ವಿರ್ and ಗಳ್. In ದಿರ್ and ವಿರ್ the ದ್ and ವ್ are euphonic (*cf.* § 119, *a*).

2, Acc. ಅಂ, *e. g.* ಸ್ತ್ರೀಯರಂ.

3, Instr. ಇಂ, (ಇನ್ದಂ, ಇನ್ದೆ), *e. g.* ಕಾಮಿನಿಯರ್ಕಳಿಂ.

4, Dat. ಗೆ, ಗ್ಗೆ, *e. g.* ಸ್ತ್ರೀಯರ್ಗೆ or ಸ್ತ್ರೀಯರ್ಗ್ಗೆ, ಕಾನ್ತೆಯರ್ಗೆ or ಕಾನ್ತೆಯರ್ಗ್ಗೆ, ಸೂಳೆಯರ್ಗೆ or ಸೂಳೆಯರ್ಗ್ಗೆ. See § 119, *a*, 4 as to the doubling.

5, Abl. (ಅತ್ತಣಿಂ, etc., the terminations of the instrumental).

6, Gen. ಅ, *e. g.* ತನ್ದೆಯರ.

7, Loc. (ಒಳ್, ಅಲ್ಲಿ).

b) in the mediæval dialect

1, Nom. ಅರ್, ಇರ್, ಗಳಿರ್, ಅರು, ಆರ್, *e. g.* ತನ್ದೆಯರ್, ಕೆಳದಿಯರ್, ಮಾತೃಕೆಯರ್, ತೊತ್ತರ್ (of ತೊತ್ತು); ತೊತ್ತಿರ್ (of ತೊತ್ತು); ಮುನಿಗಳಿರ್, ಸುಮತಿಗಳಿರ್, ಅವ್ವೆಗಳಿರ್; ಕನ್ನೆಯರು, ದೇವತೆಯರು, ಅರಸಿಯರು, ವಿಲಾಸಿನಿಯರು, ಅವ್ವೇರು; ಕುಲಚ್ಛಣಿಯಾರ್.

ಅವ್ವೇರು stands for ಅವ್ವೆಯರು. The ಆರ್ in ಕುಲಚ್ಛಣಿಯಾರ್ has been adopted from Tamiḻ (by the Basavapurâṇa).

6, Gen. ಅ, *e. g.* ಸೂಳೆಯರ.

7, Loc. (ಒಳ್), ಒಳು, (ಅಲ್ಲಿ), *e. g.* ಸತಿಯರೊಳು.

c) in the modern dialect

1, Nom. ಅರು, ಂದಿರು, *e. g.* ತಂಗಿಯರು, ಮಡದಿಯರು, ಸ್ತ್ರೀಯರು, ಸೊಸೆಯರು, ಸೂಳೆಯರು, ಅಕ್ಕಸಾಲೆಯರು; ಓರಗಿತ್ತೀರು, ಬಡಿಗೇರು; ಸೊಸೆನ್ದಿರು.

ಓರಗಿತ್ತೀರು, ಬಡಿಗೇರು stand for ಓರಗಿತ್ತಿಯರು, ಬಡಿಗೆಯರು.

133. Let it be remarked here that many declinable bases are optionally pluralised in Kannaḍa, 1, neuters expressing the idea of genus, species or kind (jâti), as ಆನೆ, ಕುದುರೆ, ಕಾಲಾಳ್, ಹಂಸೆ, ಸೋಗೆ, ಕೋಗಿಲೆ, ತುಮ್ಬಿ, ಎರಳೆ, ಪುಲ್ಲೆ; 2, neuters of numerical character (saṅkhyêya, saṅkhyânavastu), as ದೆಸೆ, ಲೋಕ, ಯುಗ; 3, numerals (saṅkhyĕ, saṅkhyâna), as ನಾಲ್ಕು, ಅಯ್ದು, ನೂಱು; and 4, abstract neuters (bhâva), as ಕೂರ್ಪು, ಬೆಳ್ಪು, ಕರ್ಪು. See § 354, I.

134. The case-terminations of the plural of feminines of which the singular in the ancient dialect ends in ಅಳ್, in the mediæval dialect in ಅಳ್ or ಅಳು, and in the modern dialect in ಅಳು. (Regarding their singular see §§ 120, 121, and regarding the plural of their masculine bases, § 119.)

a) in the ancient dialect

1, Nom. ದಿರ್, (and with the elision of ಅಳ್) ಅರಾ, ಕಳ್, *e. g.* ಅವಳ್ದಿರ್ (of ಅವಳ್), ಇವಳ್ದಿರ್ (of ಇವಳ್), ಉವಳ್ದಿರ್ (of ಉವಳ್), ಆವಳ್ದಿರ್, ಪೆಱಳ್ದಿರ್, ಕರಿಯಳ್ದಿರ್, ಬಿಳಿಯಳ್ದಿರ್.

ಎಳೆಯಳ್ವಿರ್, ಪಟಿಯಳ್ದಿರ್, ಎರಡನೆಯಳ್ವಿರ್, ಮೂಱನೆಯಳ್ದಿರ್, ಪತ್ತನೆಯಳ್ದಿರ್, ಮಗಳ್ವಿರ್; ಅವರ್, (of ಅವಳ್), ಇವರ್ (of ಇವಳ್), ಉವರ್ (of ಉವಳ್), ಆರ್ (of ಆವಳ್). ಪೆಱರ್ (of ಪೆಱಳ್), ಇನಿಯರ್ (of ಇನಿಯಳ್), ಕರಿಯರ್ (of ಕರಿಯಳ್); ಮಕ್ಕಳ್ (of ಮಗಳ್).

ಆರ್ stands for ಆವರ್ (see § 135). The case-terminations for the oblique cases are identical with those of the plural of the masculine bases.

b) in the mediæval dialect

1, Nom. ಅರ್, ಅರು, *e. g.* ಅವರ್, ಇವರ್, ಒರ್ಬರ್, ಒರ್ವರ್, ಆರ್; ಅವರು, ಇವರು, ಆರು.

c) in the modern dialect

1, Nom. ಅರು, *e. g.* ಅವರು, ಇವರು, ಒಬ್ಬರು, ಯಾರು.

135. In the preceding paragraph we have met with the forms ಆರ್, ಆರು and ಯಾರು as the nominative plural of feminines with final ಅಳ್ and ಅಳು. It is to be added here that the same forms of the plural are also those of the masculine interrogative pronouns ಆವಂ, (ಆವನು). ಯಾವನು, ದಾವನು, their singular being declined like that of masculine bases with final ಅ (§ 117). *Cf.* § 270.

a) in the ancient dialect

1, Nom. ಆರ್ .

ಆರ್ is a contraction of ಆವರ್ (see § 265).

2, Acc. ಆರಂ.

4, Dat. ಆರ್ಗೆ.

6, Gen. ಆರ, ಆರ್.

ಆರ್ occurs only in ಆರ್ತು for ಆರತು or ಆರದು, of whom it? whose (is) it? (§ 270).

b) in the mediæval dialect

1, Nom. ಆರ್.

2, Acc. ಆರಂ.

4, Dat. (ಆರ್ಗೆ), ಆರಿಗೆ, ಆರಿಂಗೆ.

6, Gen. ಆರ.

c) in the modern dialect

1, Nom. (ಆರು), ಯಾರು, ದಾರು.

2, Acc. ಯಾರನ್ನು, ದಾರನ್ನು: ಯಾರ, ಯಾರನ್ನ.

4, Dat. ಯಾರಿಗೆ, ದಾರಿಗೆ.

6, Gen. ಯಾರ, ದಾರ.

136. The plural of the neuter pronouns ಅದು, ಇದು, ಉದು, ಏವುದು, ಪೆಱಿತು, ಎಲ್ಲದು (§ 102, 8, *b*. *c*), ಯಾವದು, ದಾವದು, and of the neuter pronominal bases (so-called adjectives, § 102, 8, *c*) with final ತು, ತ್ತು and ದು (*cf.* §§ 116. 122. 276), such as ಒಳ್ಳಿತು, ಒಳ್ಳಿತ್ತು, ಮೆಲ್ಲಿತು, ಮೆಲ್ಲಿತ್ತು, ಬೆಟ್ಟಿತು, ಬೆಟ್ಟಿತ್ತು, ತೆಳ್ಳಿತು, ತೆಳ್ಳಿತ್ತು, ನೇರಿತು, ನೇರಿತ್ತು, ಅಸಿದು, ಬಸಿದು, ಇನಿದು, ಪಿರಿದು,

ಕಡಿದು, ನಿಡಿದು, ಕಿಱಿದು, ಬಿಳಿದು, ಕರಿದು. Regarding their singular see §§ 122. 124, and regarding their masculine and feminine or epicine, plural §§ 119. 134).

a) in the ancient dialect

1, Nom. ಅವು, ಇವು, ಉವು, ಆವುವು, ಪೆಱವು, ಎಲ್ಲವು; ಒಳ್ಳಿದುವು, ಮೆಲ್ಲಿದುವು, ಬೆಟ್ಟಿದುವು, ತೆಳ್ಳಿದುವು, ತೋಱಿದುವು, ನೇರಿದುವು; ಅಸಿಯುವು, ಬಸಿಯುವು, ಇನಿಯುವು, ಪಿರಿಯುವು, ಕಡಿಯುವು, ನಿಡಿಯುವು, ಕಿಱಿಯುವು, ಬಿಳಿಯುವು, ಕರಿಯುವು.

In ಆವುವು ಉವು is attached to the base ಆವ (§ 117), and in ಪೆಱವು, ಎಲ್ಲವು ಅವು to ಪೆಱ, ಎಲ್ಲ; in ಒಳ್ಳಿದುವು, etc. (of ಒಳ್ಳಿತು, etc.) the ಉವು is joined to a euphonic ದ್ (*cf.* the masculine bases ಒಳ್ಳಿದ, ಮೆಲ್ಲಿದ, ತೆಳ್ಳಿದ, etc. in § 117); in ಅಸಿಯುವು, etc. the pronominal ದು (§ 122) has been dropped and ಅವು (for ಉವು) been suffixed to the original base ಅಸಿ, etc. by means of a euphonic ಯ್, or to their genitive (see § 276). Regarding the ವು compare the plural signs ವ್ and ವು in §§ 137. 193, remarks.

2, Acc. ಅವಂ, ಇವಂ, ಉವಂ, (ಆವುವಂ, ಪೆಱವಂ, ಒಳ್ಳಿದುವಂ, ಅಸಿಯುವಂ), ಎಲ್ಲವಂ, ಎಲ್ಲಮಂ.

3, Instr. ಅವಱಿಂ, ಇವಱಿಂ, ಎಲ್ಲವಱಿಂ, (ಪೆಱವಱಿಂ, ಒಳ್ಳಿದುವಱಿಂ, ಅಸಿಯುವಱಿಂ).

4, Dat. ಅವರ್ಕೆ, ಇವರ್ಕೆ, ಎಲ್ಲವರ್ಕೆ, ಪೆಱವರ್ಕೆ, (ಒಳ್ಳಿದುವರ್ಕೆ, ಅಸಿಯುವರ್ಕೆ).

5, Abl. (ಅವಱತ್ತಣಿಂ, ಅವಱಿಂ).

6, Gen. ಅವಱ, ಇವಱ, ಪೆಱವಱ, ಎಲ್ಲವಱ, (ಒಳ್ಳಿದುವಱ, ಅಸಿಯುವಱ).

7, Loc. ಅವಱೊಳ್, ಇವಱೊಳ್, ಪೆಱವಱೊಳ್, ಎಲ್ಲವಱೊಳ್; ಅವಱಲ್ಲಿ, ಇವಱಲ್ಲಿ.

b) in the mediæval dialect

1, Nom. ಅವು, ಇವು, ಆವುವು, ಎಲ್ಲವು.

The plurals ಪೆಱವು, ಒಳ್ಳಿದುವು, etc. have not been found by the author.

2, Acc. ಅವಂ, ಇವಂ; ಎಲ್ಲವುಂ, ಎಲ್ಲವ.

3, Instr. (ಅವಱಿಂ).

4, Dat. ಅವಕ್ಕೆ or ಅವಕೆ, ಇವಕ್ಕೆ or ಇವಕೆ.

5, Abl. (ಅವಱತ್ತಣಿಂ, ಅವಱಿಂ).

6, Gen. ಅವಱ, ಇವಱ.

7, Loc. ಅವಱಲ್ಲಿ; ಎಲ್ಲವಱಲ್ಲಿ.

c) in the modern dialect

1, Nom. ಅವು, ಇವು, ಯಾವವು, ದಾವವು, ಎಲ್ಲವು; ಅವುಗಳು, ಇವುಗಳು, ಯಾವವುಗಳು, ಎಲ್ಲವುಗಳು.

In ಅವುಗಳು, etc. the termination ಗಳು (see it *e. g.* in § 131) has been added to ಅವು, etc.

2, Acc. ಅವನು, ಇವನು; ಅವನ್ನು, ಇವನ್ನು; ಅವುಗಳನ್ನು, ಇವುಗಳನ್ನು.

3, Instr. ಅವುಗಳಿಂದ, ಇವುಗಳಿಂದ.

4, Dat. ಅವಕ್ಕೆ or ಅವಕೆ, ಇವಕ್ಕೆ or ಇವಕೆ; ಅವುಗಳಿಗೆ, ಇವುಗಳಿಗೆ.

5, Abl. ಅವುಗಳಿಂದ, ಇವುಗಳಿಂದ.

6, Gen. ಅವುಗಳ, ಇವುಗಳ.

7, Loc. ಅವುಗಳೊಳಗೆ, ಇವುಗಳೊಳಗೆ; ಅವುಗಳಲ್ಲಿ, ಇವುಗಳಲ್ಲಿ.

137. Declension of the personal pronouns and of the reflexive pronoun (see § 102, 7, 8, *a*).

a) in the ancient dialect

Singular.

1, Nom. ೦ (ನ್ before vowels), *viz.* ಆಂ (ಆನ್), (ನಾಂ, ನಾನ್); ನೀಂ (ನೀನ್); ತಾಂ (ತಾನ್).

According to some ancient poets also ನಾಂ (ನಾನ್) is used (Šabdânušâsana sûtra 288; see the plural.

The long vowel of the crude form of the above terms, as will be seen, presents itself as short in the oblique cases of the singular as well as of the plural.

2, Acc. ಅಂ, *viz.* ಎನ್ನಂ, ನಿನ್ನಂ, ತನ್ನಂ; (ನನ್ನಂ); (ಎನ್ನ, see § 352, 1 *b*).

The ನ್ is an augment; its doubling is euphonic (see *e. g.* § 109, *b* and *c*).

3, Instr. ಇಂ, ಇನ್ದಂ, ಇನ್ದೆ, *viz.* ಎನ್ನಿಂ, ನಿನ್ನಿಂ, ತನ್ನಿಂ; ಎನ್ನಿನ್ದಂ, ನಿನ್ನಿನ್ದಂ. ತನ್ನಿನ್ದಂ; ಎನ್ನಿನ್ದೆ, ನಿನ್ನಿನ್ದೆ, ತನ್ನಿನ್ದೆ; (ನನ್ನಿಂ, etc.).

4, Dat. ಂಗೆ, *viz.* ಎನಗೆ, ನಿನಗೆ, ತನಗೆ; (ನನಗೆ).

The forms are irregular, as after the euphonic augment ನ್ (ಂ) the letter ಅ has been inserted; ಎನಗೆ, etc. stand for ಎಂಗೆ, etc. (*cf. e. g.* letter *c* and § 117, *a*).

5, Abl. ಅತ್ತಣಿಂ, etc., *e. g.* ಎನ್ನತ್ತಣಿಂ, ನಿನ್ನತ್ತಣಿಂ, ತನ್ನತ್ತಣಿಂ; (ನನ್ನತ್ತಣಿಂ, etc.).

6, Gen. ಅ, *viz.* ಎನ, ನಿನ, ತನ; ಎನ್ನ, ನಿನ್ನ, ತನ್ನ; (ಎನ್, ನಿನ್, ತನ್); (ನನ, etc.).

The not doubling of the augment ನ್ appears when the pronouns ಅತು, ಅತ್ತು (substitutes for ಅದು, see § 122) are added to the genitive. *e. g.* ಎನತು, (ನನತು), ಎನತ್ತು, (ನನತ್ತು). Exceptionally the pronominal form ತು (see § 122) is suffixed to ಎನ್, ನಿನ್, ತನ್, *e. g.* ಎನ್ತು (see § 272, 2).

7, Loc. ಒಳ್ (ಅಲ್ಲಿ), *viz.* ಎನ್ನೊಳ್, ನಿನ್ನೊಳ್, ತನ್ನೊಳ್; (ನನ್ನೊಳ್, ನನ್ನಲ್ಲಿ).

Plural.

1, Nom. ೦ (ಮ್ before vowels), ವು, ಂಗಳ್, *viz.* ಆಂ (ಆಮ್), ನೀಂ (ನೀಮ್), ತಾಂ (ತಾಮ್); (ನಾಂ); ನಾವು (in a šâsana of 1181 A. D.), ತಾವು (in a šâsana of 1123 A. D.); ಆಂಗಳ್, ನೀಂಗಳ್, ತಾಂಗಳ್.

The change of the sŏnnĕ into ಮ್ and ವು (see also the mediæval and modern forms) reminds one of the ವ್ as a sign of the plural in ಅವು, etc. (§ 136) and of that of the plural of the personal terminations (§ 193). *Cf.* § 265.

2, Acc. ಅಂ, *viz.* ಎಮ್ಮಂ, ನಿಮ್ಮಂ, ತಮ್ಮಂ; (ನಮ್ಮಂ).

3, Instr. ಇಂ, etc., *e. g.* ಎಮ್ಮಿಂ, ನಿಮ್ಮಿಂ, ತಮ್ಮಿಂ; (ನಮ್ಮಿಂ, ನಮ್ಮಿನ್ದೆ, ನಮ್ಮಿನ್ದಂ).

4, Dat. ಂಗೆ, *viz.* ಎಮಗೆ, ನಿಮಗೆ, ತಮಗೆ; (ನಮಗೆ).

Regarding the form see the remark under the dative singular. In the often-used form of reduplication ತಮ ತಮಗೆ the ತಮ is an abbreviation of ತಮಗೆ.

5, Abl. (ಅತ್ತಣಿಂ, etc., *e. g.* ಎಮ್ಮತ್ತಣಿಂ, etc.); (ನಮ್ಮತ್ತಣಿಂ, ನಮ್ಮತ್ತಣಿನ್ದೆ, ನಮ್ಮತ್ತಣಿನ್ದಂ).

6, Gen. ಅ, *viz.* ಎಮ, ನಿಮ, ತಮ; ಎಮ್ಮ, ನಿಮ್ಮ, ತಮ್ಮ; (ನಮ್ಮ).

The not doubling of the augment ಮ್ appears when the pronouns ಅತು, ಅತ್ತು are added to the genitive, *e. g.* ಎಮತು, ಎಮತ್ತು. In the often-used form of reduplication ತಮ್ ತಮ್ಮ the ತಮ್ is an abbreviation of ತಮ or ತಮ್ಮ. *Cf.* § 250.

7, Loc. ಒಳ್, (ಅಲ್ಲಿ), *viz.* ಎಮ್ಮೊಳ್, ನಿಮ್ಮೊಳ್, ತಮ್ಮೊಳ್; (ನಮ್ಮೊಳ್, ನಮ್ಮಲ್ಲಿ).

b) **in the mediæval dialect**

Singular.

1, Nom. ಂ, ನು, **the crude base,** *viz.* ಆಂ (ಆನ್), ನೀಂ (ನೀನ್), ತಾಂ (ತಾನ್); ನಾಂ (ನಾನ್); ಆನು, (ನೀನು), ತಾನು; ನಾ, ನೀ, ತಾ.

2, Acc. ಅಂ, *viz.* ಎನ್ನಂ, ನಿನ್ನಂ, ತನ್ನಂ; ಎನ್ನುವಂ, ನಿನ್ನುವಂ, ತನ್ನುವಂ.

In ಎನ್ನುವಂ, etc. a euphonic ಉ has been added to ಎನ್ನ್, etc. which has been treated as if it were radical (see § 128).

3, Instr. (ಇಂ), ಇನ್ದಂ, ಇನ್ದೆ, ಇನ್ದ, *e. g.* (ಎನ್ನಿನ್ದಂ), ನಿನ್ನಿನ್ದಂ; ನಿನ್ನಿನ್ದೆ; ತನ್ನಿನ್ದ.

4, Dat. ಂಗೆ, *viz.* ಎನಗೆ, ನಿನಗೆ, ತನಗೆ.

5, Abl. (ಅತ್ತಣಿಂ, etc.).

6, Gen. ಅ, *viz.* ಎನ್ನ, ನಿನ್ನ, ತನ್ನ.

7, Loc. ಒಳ್, ಒಳು, ಒಳಗೆ, (ಅಲ್ಲಿ), *e. g.* ತನ್ನೊಳ್; ನಿನ್ನೊಳು, ತನ್ನೊಳು; ತನ್ನೊಳಗೆ.

Plural.

1, Nom. (ಂ or ಮ್), ವು, *viz.* (ಆಂ, etc.); ಆವು, ನಾವು, ನೀವು, ತಾವು.

2, Acc. ಅಂ, *viz.* ಎಮ್ಮಂ, (ನಮ್ಮಂ), ನಿಮ್ಮಂ, ತಮ್ಮಂ; ಎಮ್ಮುವಂ, ನಿಮ್ಮುವಂ, ತಮ್ಮುವಂ.

3, Instr. (ಇಂ), ಇನ್ದಂ, (ಇನ್ದೆ), *e. g.* ಎಮ್ಮಿನ್ದಂ, ನಮ್ಮಿನ್ದಂ.

4, Dat. ಂಗೆ, *viz.* ಎಮಗೆ, ಎವಗೆ, ನಮಗೆ, ನಿಮಗೆ, ತಮಗೆ, ತವಗೆ.

The ವ್ in ಎವಗೆ and ತವಗೆ is an optional substitute for ಮ್; see § 225. In the often-used ತಮ ತಮಗೆ and ತವ ತವಗೆ the ತಮ and ತವ are abbreviations of ತಮಗೆ and ತವಗೆ.

5, Abl. (ಅತ್ತಣಿಂ, etc.).

6, Gen. ಅ, *e. g.* ತಮ; ಎಮ್ಮ, (ನಮ್ಮ), ನಿಮ್ಮ, ತಮ್ಮ.

7, Loc. (ಒಳ್), ಒಳು, etc., *e. g.* ತಮ್ಮೊಳು.

c) in the modern dialect

Singular.

1, Nom. ನು, **the crude base,** *viz.* ನಾನು, ನೀನು, ತಾನು; ನಾ, ನೀ, ತಾ.

2, Acc. ಅನು, ಅನ್ನು, ಅ, *viz.* ನನ್ನನು, ನಿನ್ನನು, ತನ್ನನು; ನನ್ನನ್ನು, ನಿನ್ನನ್ನು, ತನ್ನನ್ನು; ನನ್ನ, ನಿನ್ನ, ತನ್ನ.

3, Instr. ಇನ್ದ, *viz.* ನನಿನ್ದ, ನಿನಿನ್ದ, ತನಿನ್ದ; ನನ್ನಿನ್ದ, ನಿನ್ನಿನ್ದ, ತನ್ನಿನ್ದ.

4, Dat. ಂಗೆ, ಇಗೆ, *viz.* ನಂಗೆ, ನಿಂಗೆ, ತಂಗೆ; ಎನಗೆ, ನನಗೆ, ನಿನಗೆ, ತನಗೆ; ನನಿಗೆ, ನಿನಿಗೆ, ತನಿಗೆ.

In ನನಿಗೆ, etc. the euphonic ಇ of § 117, letter *c*, has been inserted. ಎನಗೆ is occasionally used in proverbs.

5, Abl. **the termination of the instrumental.**

6, Gen. ಅ, *viz.* ನನ, ನಿನ, ತನ; ನನ್ನ, ನಿನ್ನ, ತನ್ನ; (ನನ್, ನಿನ್, ತನ್).

ನನ್ in ನನ್ಮಗ, ನನ್ದಸ, ನಿನ್ in ನಿನ್ಮಗ, ನಿನ್ಮನೆ, and ತನ್ in ತನ್ದು (*i. e.* ತನ್ ಅಮು) are abbreviations of ನನ, ನಿನ, ತನ (see § 272, 2).

7, Loc. (ಒಳಗೆ), ಅಲ್ಲಿ, ಅಲಿ, *viz.* ನನಲ್ಲಿ, ನಿನಲ್ಲಿ, ತನಲ್ಲಿ; ನನ್ನಲ್ಲಿ, ನಿನ್ನಲ್ಲಿ, ತನ್ನಲ್ಲಿ; ನನಲಿ, ನಿನಲಿ, ತನಲಿ; ನನ್ನಲಿ, ನಿನ್ನಲಿ, ತನ್ನಲಿ.

Plural.

1, Nom. ವು, *viz.* ನಾವು, ನೀವು, ತಾವು.

2, Acc. ಅನು, ಅನ್ನು, ಅ, *viz.* ನಮ್ಮನು, ನಿಮ್ಮನು, ತಮ್ಮನು; ನಮ್ಮನ್ನು, ನಿಮ್ಮನ್ನು, ತಮ್ಮನ್ನು; ನಮ್ಮ, ನಿಮ್ಮ, ತಮ್ಮ.

3, Instr. ಇನ್ದ, *viz.* ನಮಿನ್ದ, ನಿಮಿನ್ದ, ತಮಿನ್ದ; ನಮ್ಮಿನ್ದ. ನಿಮ್ಮಿನ್ದ, ತಮ್ಮಿನ್ದ.

4, Dat. ಂಗೆ, *viz.* ನಮಂಗೆ, ನಿಮಂಗೆ, ತಮಂಗೆ.

For ತಮ ತಮಂಗೆ, which is often used, see under letter *b*.

5, Abl. the termination of the instrumental.

6, Gen. ಅ, *viz.* ನಮ, ನಿಮ, ತಮ; ನಮ್ಮ, ನಿಮ್ಮ, ತಮ್ಮ.

ನಮ್ in ನಮ್ಮಗ, ನಮ್ಮಕ್ಕಳು, ನಮ್ಮನೆ, ನಿಮ್ in ನಿಮ್ಮನೆ, and ತಮ್ in ತಮ್ಮಮ್ಮ are abbreviations of ನಮ, ನಿಮ, ತಮ.

7, Loc. (ಒಳಗೆ), ಅಲ್ಲಿ, ಅಲಿ, *viz.* ನಮ್ಮಲ್ಲಿ, ನಿಮ್ಮಲ್ಲಿ. ತಮ್ಮಲ್ಲಿ; ನಮಲ್ಲಿ, ನಿಮಲ್ಲಿ, ತಮಲ್ಲಿ; ನಮ್ಮಲಿ, ನಿಮ್ಮಲಿ, ತಮ್ಮಲಿ; ನಮಲಿ, ನಿಮಲಿ, ತಮಲಿ.

138. As it is possible to trace the origin of the personal pronouns and the reflexive pronoun almost with certainty, the following etymological remarks on them may not be out of place.

a) Forms of their nominative singular in the five chief Draviḍa languages.

Kannaḍa ಆಂ (ಆನ್), ನಾಂ (ನಾನ್), ನಾನು, ನಾ;
Malayâḷa ಞಾನ್;
Tamiḻ ಯಾನ್, ನಾನ್;
Tuḷu ಯಾನ್;
Tĕlugu ಏನು, ನೇನು, ಏ, ನೇ.

Kannaḍa ನೀಂ (ನೀನ್), ನೀನು, ನೀ;
Malyâḷa ನೀ;
Tamiḻ ನೀ;
Tuḷu ಈ;
Tĕlugu ನೀವು, ಈವು.

Kannaḍa ತಾಂ (ತಾನ್), ತಾನು, ತಾ;
Malayâḷa ತಾನ್;
Tamiḻ ತಾನ್;
Tuḷu ತಾನ್;
Tĕlugu ತಾನು, ತಾ.

b) Its crude forms.

The finals ಂ, ನ್, ನು, ವು are not radical, as is learned from the forms ನಾ, ನೇ, ಏ; ನೀ, ಈ; ತಾ; they are signs of the nominative singular. *Cf.* § 114.

Without them the bases are ಆ, ನಾ, ಞಾ, ಯಾ, ಏ, ನೇ; ಈ, ನೀ; ತಾ. (*Cf.* also the interrogative ಏ in § 265.)

c) The forms used for the oblique cases.

In the oblique cases the long vowels are, as a rule, short. If we accept the long vowels to be primitive, the shortening rests on nothing else but euphonism employed in attaching the case-terminations (*cf.* ಎಲ್ಲಿ = ಆವಲ್ಲಿ, ಏ + ಅಲ್ಲಿ in § 265).

Kannaḍa ಆ appears as ಎ, ನಾ as ನ, Malayâḷa ಞಾ as ಎ and ಇ (this occasionally in the dative), Tamiḻ ಯಾ, ನಾ appear as ಎ, Tuḷu ಯಾ appears as ಯ and following a consonant as ಎ, Tĕlugu ಏ, ನೇ appear as ನಾ (in the genitive and dative) and as ನ (in the accusative). The forms of the oblique cases for the first person are, therefore, ಎ, ಇ, ನ, ನಾ.

Kannaḍa and Malayâḷa ನೀ appear as ನಿ, Tuḷu ಈ appears likewise as ನಿ, Tĕlugu ನೀ appears as ನಿ (in the accusative) and as ನೀ (in the genitive and dative), Tamiḻ ನೀ appears as ನಿ, ನು, ಉ. Thus the forms for the oblique cases of the second person are ನೀ, ನಿ, ನು, ಉ.

The form for the oblique cases of ತಾ, the **reflexive** pronoun (the pronoun of the third person), is ತ in Kannaḍa, Malayâḷa, Tamiḻ, Tuḷu, and Tĕlugu.

d) Probable origin of the three pronouns.

1, That of the first person.

The vowels used in the formation of this person are ಆ, ಅ, ಇ, ಎ, ಏ. The exceptional ಇ of the dative of Malayâḷa may be dismissed from further consideration, as the regular vowel of its dative too is ಎ; it may be added that ಇ and ಎ frequently interchange in Kannaḍa (see *e. g.* § 66; § 109, *b*, 3).

The short ಅ and ಎ of the oblique cases have been taken to be the shortened forms of ಆ and ಏ (above letter c); if the reverse be accepted, no material difference will proceed from it. Let the radical vowels be ಆ and ಏ.

Which of the two vowels has been leading in the formation of the pronoun of the first person? We may say the one or the other, because they are related and occasionally interchanged, *e. g.* Kannaḍa ಆ, ಏ, ಓ! (see § 140); ಆ, ಏ, what? which? ಆರ್, ಏರ್, a pair of oxen yoked to the plough; ಆಳ್, ಏಳ್ to be possible; ಸಾರ್, ಸೇರ್, to be or become near; Tamiḻ, Tĕlugu ಆ, ಏ, ಓ; Tamiḻ ಆಱು, Tĕlugu ಏಱು, a river. (Regarding the interchange of short ಅ and ಎ *cf.* *e. g.* ಅ, ಎ, ಓ! (see § 140); ಅನ್, ಎನ್, to say; ಕಯ್, ಕೆಯ್, the hand; ತಲೆ, ತೆಲೆ the head; ಅರ್ಕ, ಎಕ್ಕೆ, swallow-wort).

If we take ಏ (or ಆ) as the leading vowel, the idea which underlies the formation of the pronoun of the first person, is that of calling the attention of another or others to one's self or the 'I', the particle ಏ (or ಎ) being commonly used in calling, or calling to, a person near or at a distance (see § 140). ಏಂ (or ಆಂ) thus is the person that desires to be taken notice of, '**the-o-here**'!

But what about the initial consonants ಯ್, ಞ್ and ನ್? Do they in any way influence the meaning of ಏಂ (ಆಂ) or in other words are they essential?

The answer must be in the negative already on account of their not appearing in Kannaḍa ಆಂ, Tĕlugu ಏನು, ಏ, and, as a rule, in the oblique cases.

In order to explain this we add that the letter ಯ್ (like the Saṁskṛita ಯ್) is a semi-vowel in Kannaḍa, and especially Kannaḍa and Tĕlugu people very often use it euphonically as a help to pronouncing the initial vowels ಇ, ಈ, ಎ, ಏ (§ 41; *cf.* also the euphonic ಯ್, *e. g.* in §§ 113. 130. 132); only exceptionally it has disappeared in the tadbhavas ಆಮಳ್ (=ಯಮಳ) and ಉಗ (=ಯುಗ); in the tadbhavas ಎತಿ (=ಯತಿ), ಎತ್ನ (=ಯತ್ನ), ಎವೆ (=ಯವ) the initial ಎ, when not preceded by a consonant or a consonant with a euphonic ಉ, is pronounced ಯೆ. Also before ಆ the ಯ್ is euphonically sounded, *e. g.* ಆ, ಯಾ, what? which?, ಆರ್ ಯಾರ್, who?, Tamiḻ ಆರ್, ಯಾರ್, who?, ಆನೆ, ಯಾನೆ, an elephant, Tĕlugu ಏನ, ಯಾನ wild, which is likewise done when an initial ಏ appears as ಯಾ, *e. g.* ಏಲಕ್ಕಿ, ಯಾಲಕ್ಕಿ, cardamoms, ಏತ, ಯಾತ, a picotta, ಏ, ಯಾ, what? which?, ಏಕೆ, ಯಾಕೆ, why? (or when an initial short ಎ appears as ಯ, *e. g.* ಎಣ್ಣೆ, ಯಣ್ಣೆ, oil, ಎಮ್ಮೆ, ಯಮ್ಮೆ, a female buffalo, Tĕlugu ಎವರು, ಯವರು, who?). Thus the initial ಯ್ of the nominative singular of the pronoun of the first person must be declared to be unessential or simply euphonic, when at the same time one considers that occasionally it has no place there, that ಞ್ and ನ್ are used in its stead, and that it is not found in the oblique cases.

ಞ್ is never initial in a true Kannaḍa and Tĕlugu word; but is found as the initial of some Tamiḻ, Malayâḷa and Tuḷu terms. The form ಞಾನ್ of the first pronoun is Malayâḷa. ಞ್ is another form of ನ್; thus Tamiḻ ಞಾಯಿಱು, ನಾಯಿಱು are Kannaḍa ನೇಸಱ್, the sun; Tamiḻ ಞಾಲು, ನಾಲು are Kannaḍa (ನೆಱಲ್), ನೇಲ್, to be suspended; Tamiḻ ಞಮಲಿ, ನವಿರ are Kannaḍa ನವಿಲ್, Tĕlugu ನೆಮ್ಮಿ, ನೆಮಲಿ, ನೆವಲಿ, a peacock. Besides, as apparently in the first person of the pronoun, it makes its appearance as a vowel (ಎ or ಏ) also in other words, as does likewise its co-ordinate and substitute ನ್. For instance for Tamiḻ ಞಾಲು, ನಾಲು and Kannaḍa ನೇಲ್, to be suspended, there is the ancient Kannaḍa ಎಱಲ್ (Tĕlugu ವೇಲು); Tĕlugu ನೆಮ್ಮಿ, a peacock, appears also as ಎಮ್ಮಿ; Tamiḻ ಞೆಣ್ಡು, ಞಣ್ಡು, ನಣ್ಡು, a crab, are ಏಡಿ in Kannaḍa and ಎಣ್ಡ್ರ in Tĕlugu (in Kannaḍa there is also the primitive form ಎಸಡಿ, a crab); Kannaḍa ನಾಳೆ, Tamiḻ ನಾಳೈ, Malayâḷa ನಾಳೆ, to-morrow, are ಎಲ್ಲಿ in Tĕlugu and ಎಲ್ಲೆ in Tuḷu. There is, therefore, no reason for considering the ಞ್ to be an essential part of the nominative of the pronoun of the first person, as it bears the same character as the semi-vowel ಯ್; it is used to facilitate pronunciation by a small section of the Draviḍa people.

ನ್ bears no character in the pronoun different from that of its substitutes ಞ್ and ಯ್, the last occurring in Tamiḻ side by side with ನ್; it too is simply euphonic (*cf.* the ನ್ of the second person), although it has been, and still is, often used in the nominative of the pronoun and its oblique cases by a large number of the Draviḍas. By the bye, in a few tadbhavas ನ್ appears as a direct substitute of ಯ್, *e. g.* in Kannaḍa ನೊಗ (=ಯುಗ), a yoke, and in Tamiḻ ನಮು, ನೆಮು (=ಯಮು), Yama.

2, That of the second person.

The vowels used in the formation of the second person are ಈ, ಇ, and ಉ.

That the initial consonant ನ್ is not essential, but euphonic, follows from its absence in Tuḷu ಈ, Telugu ಈವು in the nominative, and Tamiḻ ಉ in the oblique cases (*cf.* the ನ್ of the first person).

The leading vowel is ಈ, this, the proximate demonstrative particle, expressing that a person (or any object) is situated in front of another; the original meaning of the pronoun is 'next (to me) one'! This ಈ appears also as short *e. g.* in ಇದು, ಇವ.

In the oblique cases of the Tamiḻ pronoun the leading vowel presents itself as ಉ, a short form of ಊ, the intermediate demonstrative pronoun, denoting, in the present case, a person who is intermediate between the left and right and directly faces the speaker in being addressed, the primitive meaning being 'right opposite (to me) one'! This ಊ is also short *e. g.* in ಉದು, ಉವ.

3, That of the pronoun of the third person or of the reflexive pronoun.

The vowels employed for the formation of this pronoun are ಆ and ಅ, the first appearing in the crude base ತಾ, the second in ತ, the base used for the oblique cases. ಆ is shortened into ಅ, both demonstrative particles which mean 'that' (§ 264), *i. e.* he, she, it, being used for all the three genders; ಅ, as we have seen in § 115, has got also the specific meaning of 'he'.

ಆ and ಅ are attached to the pronominal syllable ತು (ತ್ + euphonic ಉ, § 122), another form of ಅತು or ಅದು, the demonstrative neuter pronoun, by means of sandhi (§ 213 *seq.*), the ಉ disappearing. The ತು in this case points back to the agent or subject, and ತಾ (ತು + ಆ), ತ (ತು + ಅ) originally mean 'that-that', *i. e.*, according to circumstances, 'that-he', 'that-she', 'that-it'. (The same ತು + ಅ appears also in ಅತ, ಈತ, ಊತ, 'that-it-he', 'this-it-he', 'this-intermediate-it-he'; see § 265.)

Remark.

It seems proper here to refer to the connection that exists between the pronouns of the first, second and third person and the personal terminations of the verb. Regarding the vowels ಅ, ಆ, ಎ, ಏ of the pronoun of the first person compare the ಅ, ಅಂ, ಆ of the first person plural of the imperative in § 205 and the ಎ, ಎಂ, and ಎನು of the first person singular and its ಎಂ, ಎವು in the plural in § 193; regarding the vowels ಇ, ಈ of the pronoun of the second person compare the ಇ, ಎ and ಅಯ್ of the second person singular in § 193, the ಇರ್, ಇರಿ of the second person plural in § 193, and the ಇ, ಇಂ, ಇರಿ of the second person plural of the imperative in § 205; and regarding the ಅ and ಆ of the pronoun of the third person compare the ಅ, ಅಂ, ಅನು of the third person singular in § 193.

139. Peculiarities in the declension of some nominal bases are still to be adduced. In § 122 there are some terms of direction with final euphonic ಉ, and in § 123 some such terms with final ಅ of which the genitive singular, etc. are formed by the help of the augment ಅಣ್ (see § 124). This augment is used likewise in the ancient declension of the following words when they express direction:— ನಡು, ಕಡೆ, ಎಡೆ. ನಡು, a term of direction with radical ಉ (§ 128); instrumental and ablative ನಡುವಣಿಂ, dative ನಡುವಣ್ಗೆ, genitive ನಡುವಣ. ಕಡೆ, a term of direction with final ಎ (§ 130); instr. and abl. ಕಡೆಯಣಿಂ, dat. ಕಡೆಯಣ್ಗೆ, gen. ಕಡೆಯಣ. ಎಡೆ, a term of direction with final ಎ (§ 130); gen. ಎಡೆಯಣ. If the three words are not used as terms of direction, their declension follows that of §§ 128. 130, *e. g.* ನಡುವಿನ, ಕಡೆಯ, ಎಡೆಯ.

The use of the same augment is seen also in the genitive singular of ಅಲ್ಲಿ, ಇಲ್ಲಿ, ಉಲ್ಲಿ and ಎಲ್ಲಿ, terms of direction with final ಇ (§ 130), chiefly in the ancient dialect, *viz.* ಅಲ್ಲಿಯಣ, ಇಲ್ಲಿಯಣ, ಉಲ್ಲಿಯಣ, ಎಲ್ಲಿಯಣ. The common declension, however, of ಅಲ್ಲಿ, ಇಲ್ಲಿ, and ಎಲ್ಲಿ, is *a*) in the ancient dialect *e. g.* dative ಅಲ್ಲಿಗೆ, ಎಲ್ಲಿಗೆ, ablative ಅಲ್ಲಿಂ, ಅಲ್ಲಿನ್ದೆ, ಅಲ್ಲಿನ್ದಂ, genitive ಅಲ್ಲಿಯ; *b*) in the mediæval dialect *e. g.* dat. ಅಲ್ಲಿಗೆ, ಅಲ್ಲಿಂಗೆ, ಇಲ್ಲಿಗೆ, ಎಲ್ಲಿಗೆ, abl. ಅಲ್ಲಿನ್ದೆ, ಅಲ್ಲಿನ್ದ, gen. ಅಲ್ಲಿಯ, ಇಲ್ಲಿಯ, ಎಲ್ಲಿಯ; *c*) in the modern dialect dat. ಅಲ್ಲಿಗೆ, ಇಲ್ಲಿಗೆ, ಎಲ್ಲಿಗೆ, abl. ಅಲ್ಲಿನ್ದ, ಇಲ್ಲಿನ್ದ, ಎಲ್ಲಿನ್ದ. gen. ಅಲ್ಲಿಯ, ಇಲ್ಲಿಯ, ಎಲ್ಲಿಯ, ಇಲ್ಲಿನ.

ಆಚೆ and ಈಚೆ, terms of direction with final ಎ, are generally declined like terms ending in ಎ (§ 130), *e. g.* genitive ಆಚೆಯ (in the mediæval and modern dialect); but in the modern dialect we find also *e. g.* ಈಚಿಗೆ (for ಈಚೆಗೆ) and ಈಚಿನ (for ಈಚೆಯ).

Further, in the same manner as the nominal bases always ending in a euphonic ಉ in § 127 which express time, ನಾಳೆ, ನಿನ್ನೆ and ಮೊನ್ನೆ, terms with final ಎ which relate to time, are declined, *viz.* *a*) in the ancient dialect *e. g.* nom. (the crude base) ನಾಳೆ, dat. ನಾಳಿಂಗೆ, gen. ನಾಳಿನ; ನಿನ್ನೆ, ನಿನ್ನಿಂಗೆ, ನಿನ್ನಿನ; ಮೊನ್ನೆ, ಮೊನ್ನಿಂಗೆ, ಮೊನ್ನಿನ; *b*) in the mediæval dialect *e. g.* ನಾಳೆ, ನಾಳಿನ, ನಾಳಿನಲಿ; *c*) in the modern dialect *e. g.* ನಾಳೆ, ನಾಳಿಗೆ, ನಾಳಿನ್ದ, ನಾಳಿನಿನ್ದ, ನಾಳಿನ; ನಿನ್ನೆ, ನಿನ್ನಿನ; ಮೊನ್ನೆ, ಮೊನ್ನಿನ.

Besides, two terms with final ಅ that relate to time, are declined like bases with final euphonic ಉ (§ 122), *viz.* ಆಗ and ಈಗ. In the mediæval dialect we have *e. g.* ಆಗಿನ, and in the modern one ಆಗಿನ್ದ, ಆಗಿನಿನ್ದ, ಆಗಿನ; ಈಗಿಗೆ, ಈಗಿನಿನ್ದ, ಈಗಿನ. The mediæval form ಮುನ್ನಿನ may be referred to ಮುನ್ನ, also a term ending in ಅ.

In the ancient dialect the genitive of the term ಮುತ್ತೆ is ಮುತ್ತಿನ.

140. The vocative (sambôdhana, sambuddhi, âmantraṇa) is not considered as one of the cases by Kannaḍa grammarians, who enumerate only seven (§ 106). It is used in addressing, calling or calling to (âmantraṇa, abhimukhîkaraṇa) objects that are inanimate or destitute of reason (jaḍavastu, as posts, pots, flowers, trees, bees, etc.), idols (dêvapratimĕ), persons which are different from one's self (lôkântara), and one's own self (âtmîyačitta).

The forms of the vocative are as follows:

a) in the ancient dialect

Singular.

1, The first form of the vocative is **the crude base,** *e. g.* ದೇವ! ಅರಸ! ಕುಸುಮಾಯುಧ! ಮಾಧವ! ಗಣಪ! ಸರ್ವೇಶ! ಗನ್ಧವಾಹ! ವಿದ್ಯಾಚಕ್ರವರ್ತಿ! ಸತಿ! ಉರ್ವಶಿ! ಮೇನಕಿ! ಮಂಜುಘೋಷಿ! ತುಮ್ಬಿ! ಅಭಿಮನ್ಯು! ವಧು! ರಮ್ಭೆ! ತಿಲೋತ್ತಮೆ! ಕೋಗಿಲೆ!

This form is called short emphatical speech (hrasvakâku).

2, In its second form **the vowel** of the base **is lengthened,** *e. g.* ದೇವಾ! ಜಿನೇನ್ದ್ರಾ! ಭಾನುತನುಜಾ! ಕುರುಪತೀ! ಅಭಿಮನ್ಯೂ!

This form is called long emphatical speech (dîrghakâku). A pluta form of this vocative is *e. g.* ರಾಮಾ (§§ 20. 215, 6, letter *k*).

3, In its third form **the vocative particle** ಎ **is suffixed** either immediately to bases with a final consonant, or by the help of a euphonic letter to bases ending in a vowel, *e. g.* ನಲ್ಲಳೆ (of ನಲ್ಲಳ್)! ಉಯ್ಯಲೆ (of ಉಯ್ಯಲ್)! ತಳಿರೆ (of ತಳಿರ್)! ಮಾವೆ (of ಮಾವು)! ಕಳಸವೆ (of ಕಳಸ)! ಕೊಳನೆ (of ಕೊಳ)! ಚನ್ದ್ರನೆ (of ಚನ್ದ್ರ)! ಮದಾಳಿಕುಲಮೆ (of ಮದಾಳಿಕುಲ)! ದೇವನೆ (of ದೇವ)! ಅರಸನೆ (of ಅರಸ)! ಹೃದಯಮೆ (of ಹೃದಯ)! ತುಮ್ಬಿಯೆ (of ತುಮ್ಬಿ)! ಕೂಸೆ (of ಕೂಸು)! ಅಭಿಮನ್ಯುವೆ (of ಅಭಿಮನ್ಯು)! ವಧುವೆ (of ವಧು)! ಮನುವೆ (of ಮನು)! ತಾವರೆಯೆ (of ತಾವರೆ)! ನೀಲಕುನ್ತಲೆಯೆ (of ನೀಲಕುನ್ತಲೆ)! ಹಂಸಯಾನೆಯೆ (of ಹಂಸಯಾನೆ)!

The euphonic augments, as will be observed, are ನ್, ಮ್, ಯ್, ವ್.

4, In its fourth form, instead of the ಎ and in the same manner, **the vocative** particle ಏ **is attached,** *e. g.* ಉಯ್ಯಲೇ! ಮಾವೇ! ತಮ್ಬುಲರೇ! ಮರನೇ! ದೇವನೇ! ಕೂಸೇ! ಮನುವೇ! ಕೋಗಿಲೆಯೇ! ನೀಲಕುನ್ತಲೆಯೇ! ಹಂಸಯಾನೆಯೇ!

Plural.

1, The first form simply is **the nominative plural,** *e. g.* ಉಗ್ರಾಂಗಳ್! ಗುರುಗಳ್! ದೇವರ್!

2, In its second form **the vocative particle** ಅ is added to the nominative, *e. g.* ಮುಗಿಲ್ಗಳಿರ! ನನ್ದನಂಗಳಿರ! ನಣ್ಬರಿರ! ನಲ್ಲರಿರ! ಬುಧರಿರ! ದೇವರಿರ! ದೇವಿಯರಿರ! ಬುಧರ್ಕಳಿರ! ದೇವರ್ಕಳಿರ! ದೇವಿಯರ್ಕಳಿರ! ಲತೆಗಳಿರ! ದೆಸೆಗಳಿರ! ಮಾವನ್ದಿರಿರ! ಅತ್ತೆವಿರಿರ!

3, In its third form **the vocative particle** ಆ is added to the nominative, *e. g.* ದೇವರಿರಾ! ದೇವಿಯರಿರಾ! ದೇವರ್ಕಳಿರಾ!

4, In its fourth form the vocative particle ಎ is added to the nominative, *e. g.* ಭಟ್ಟರೆ! ದೇವರೆ! ದೇವರ್ಕಳೆ! ಗುರುಗಳೆ! ಮಾವನ್ದಿರೆ!

5, In its fifth form the vocative particle ಏ is added to the nominative, *e. g.* ದೇವರೇ! ದೇವರ್ಕಳೇ!

b) in the mediæval dialect

Singular.

1, ದೇವ! ಅಪ್ಪ! ಅವ್ವ! ಅಕ್ಕ! ಒಡೆಯ! ಸ್ವಾಮಿ! ಪಿನಾಕಿ! ಸೆಟ್ಟಿ! ತಂಗಿ! ದೇವಿ! ನಾಯಿ! ಗುರು! ತನ್ದೆ! ಮುತ್ತವ್ವೆ! ವನಿತೆ! ಚಂಗಳೆ! ತರಳೆ!

2, ದೇವಾ! ರಾಜಾ! ಕಲ್ಲಿನಾಥಾ! ಅಪ್ಪಾ! ಮೂರ್ತೀ!

3, ತಾಯೆ! ಮುತ್ತಗವೆ! ಮಲಹಲರನೆ! ನಾಯಿಯೆ! ಗುರುವೆ! ಶಮ್ಭುವೆ!

4, ಅತ್ತಿಯೇ! ಕಾನ್ತನೇ! ಒಡೆಯನೇ! ತನಯನೇ! ಗುರುವೇ!

Plural.

2, ಮರಗಳಿರ! ಅವ್ವೆಗಳಿರ! ಅಕ್ಕಂಗಳಿರ! ಮುನಿಗಳಿರ! ದುರುಳರಿರ!

3, ಅಜ್ಞಾನಿಗಳಿರಾ! ಜಡರುಗಳಿರಾ! ಮತಿಗೆಟ್ಟವನ್ದಿರಾ! ವಾಹಕರಿರಾ!

4, ದೇವರೆ! ನೀವೆ!

5, ದೇವರೇ! ಗುರುಗಳೇ!

c) in the modern dialect

Singular.

1, ಅಮ್ಮ! ಮನುಜ! ಸ್ವಾಮಿ! ಭೂದೇವಿ! ಗುರು!

2, ಅಪ್ಪಾ! ಅವ್ವಾ! ಮಾವಾ! ರಂಗಾ! ಸ್ವಾಮೀ! ತಂಗೀ! ರಘೂ! ಶಾಮೂ! ಗುರೂ!

3, ನೀನೆ! ಸರ್ವೋತ್ತಮಳೆ! ಹುಡುಗನೆ! ಗಿಡವೆ! ಸತಿಯೆ! ಮುನಿಯೆ! ಸ್ತ್ರೀಯೆ! ಗುರುವೆ!

4, ಊರೇ! ಹಗಲೇ! ಮಗಳೇ! ಮಗನೇ! ಹುಡುಗನೇ! ಗಿಡವೇ! ಮುನಿಯೇ! ಸ್ತ್ರೀಯೇ! ಗುರುವೇ!

Plural.

1, ದೇವರು! o master!

3, ವಿದ್ಯಾರ್ಥಿಗಳಿರಾ! ಮಕ್ಕಳಿರಾ!

4, ಹುಡುಗರೆ! ಅರಸುಗಳೆ!

5, ಮರಗಳೇ! ಗುರುಗಳೇ! ರಾಯರೇ! ಹುಡುಗರೇ!

141. Here follows an enumeration of the terminations and augments of the seven cases.

1. Singular.

Nom. 1, the crude base (§§ 109, *b*, *c*; 117, *b*, *c*; 120; 121; 122; 123; 125; 126; 127; 128; 129; 130; 137, *b*, *c*; 139); 2, ಂ or the sŏnnĕ (§§ 109. 117); 3, a euphonic ಉ added to the sŏnnĕ, in which case it appears as ನ್ or ಮ್ (§§ 109, *b*, *c*; 117, *b*, *c*); 4, a euphonic ಉ added, by means of an enunciative ಯ್ or ವ್, to the vowels ಇ, ಈ, ಉ, ಊ, (ಋ, ೠ, ಓ, ಔ) and ಎ (§§ 128, *b*, *c*; 129, *b*, *c*; 130, *b*, *c*).

Acc. 1, the crude base with or without a vowel (§§ 109, *c*; 120; 121, *b*, *c*; 122, *b*, *c*; 125; 126; 127; 128, *c*; 129, *c*; 130, *c*); 2, ಅ (§§ 120, *b*, *c*; 121, *b*, *c*; 122); 3, ಅ preceded by a euphonic ನ್ (§§ 109, *b*, *c*; 117, *b*, *c*), or ಯ್ (§ 130, *b*, *c*), or ವ್ (§§ 109, *b*, *c*; 128, *b*, *c*); 4, ಅಂ (§§ 120, *a*, *b*;

121, *b*; 122, *a*, *b*); 5, ಅಂ preceded by a euphonic ನ್ (§§ 109, *a*, *b*; 117, *a*, *b*; 125, *a*, *b*), or ಯ್ (§ 130, *a*, *b*), or ನ್ (§§ 128, *a*, *b*; 129, *a*, *b*); 6, a euphonic ಉ suffixed to ಅಂ, the sŏnnĕ of ಅಂ becoming ನ್ or ನ್ನ್ (*i. e.* ಅನು, ಅನ್ನು, §§ 109, *b*, *c*; 117; 121, *c*; 122, *c*; 125, *c*; 128, *c*; 129, *c*; 130, *b*, *c*); 7, ಅ added to ಅಂ, its sŏnnĕ becoming ನ್ or ನ್ನ್ (*i. e.* ಅನ, ಅನ್ನ, §§ 109, *b*; 117, *c*; 122, *c*; 130, *c*; 135, *c*); 8, ಅ (§§ 109, *c*; 121, *c*; 122, *c*); 9, ಅಂ (§§ 120, *a*; 122, *a*); 10, the euphonic ಉ of No. 6 added to ಅಂ and suffixed to the base by the insertion of the augment ಅಱ್ (*i. e.* ಅಱನ್ನು, a quite vulgar form, § 122, *c*).

Instr. 1, ಇ (§ 109, *b*, *c*); 2, ಎ (§§ 109, *a*; 130, *a*); 3, ಇಂ (§§ 109, *a*, *b*; 117, *a*, *b*; 120, *a*, *b*; 121, *b*; 122, *a*, *b*; 127, *a*; 128, *a*, *b*; 129, *a*; 130, *a*, *b*; 137, *a*); 4, ಇಂ extended in length either by the final augments ದ, ದಂ, ದವು, ದೆ (*i. e.* ಇನ್ದ, etc., §§ 109; 117; 120, *a*, *b*; 121, *c*; 122; 127, *b*; 128, *a*, *c*; 129, *a*; 130; 137), or by ಇನ್ದ, ಇನ್ದಂ, ಇನ್ದೆ, by means of ಇನ, the genitive of ಇಂ or ಇನ್ (*i. e.* ಇನಿನ್ದ, etc., §§ 121, *b*, *c*; 122; 127, *b*, *c*; 128, *a*, *c*), or by ಇಂ through ಇನ, the genitive of ಇಂ (*i. e.* ಇನಿಂ, §§ 122, *a*, *b*; 127, *b*; 128, *a*, *b*; 129, *a*); 5, ಇಂ, ಇನ್ದ, ಇನ್ದಂ, ಇನ್ದೆ preceded by the augment ಅಱ್ through its genitive ಅಱ (*i. e.* ಅಱಿಂ, etc., §§ 122; 125).

The terminations and their augments presuppose the genitive.

Dat. 1, ಕೆ (§§ 109; 120; 121, *a*; 123, *c*; 125); 2, ಗೆ (§§ 117; 120; 128, *a*, *b*; 129, *a*; 130); 3, ಕ್ಕೆ (§§ 109; 123, *c*); 4, ಗೆ preceded by a euphonic sŏnnĕ (*i. e.* ಂಗೆ, § 117, *a*, *b*; *cf.* § 137); 5, ಗೆ preceded by a euphonic ನ which is to represent the sŏnnĕ (*i. e.* ನಗೆ, § 117, *c*); 6, ಗೆ preceded by a euphonic ನಿ which is to represent the sŏnnĕ (*i. e.* ನಿಗೆ, § 117, *c*); 7, ಗೆ preceded by a euphonic ಇ (*i. e.* ಇಗೆ, §§ 121, *b*, *c*; 122, *b*, *c*; 127, *b*, *c*; 128, *b*, *c*; 129, *c*; 137, *c*); 8, ಗೆ preceded by a euphonic ಇಂ (*i. e.* ಇಂಗೆ, §§ 121, *a*, *b*; 122, *a*; *b*; 127, *a*, *b*; 128, *a*; 129, *a*); 9, ಕೆ preceded by a euphonic ಇ (*i. e.* ಇಕೆ, §§ 121, *b*, *c*; 122, *b*); 10, ಕ್ಕೆ preceded by a euphonic ಇ (*i. e.* ಇಕ್ಕೆ, §§ 121, *c*, 122, *b*); 11, ಕೆ preceded by a euphonic ಇಂ (*i. e.* ಇಂಕೆ, § 122, *b*); 12, ಕೆ preceded by the euphonic augment ಅಂ್ (*i. e.* ಅಬ್ಕೆ, §§ 122, *a*, *b*; 125, *a*); 13, ಗೆ preceded by the euphonic augment ಅಱ್ (*i. e.* ಅಱ್ಗೆ, §§ 122, *a*; 123, *a*). 14, ಕೆ or ಕ್ಕೆ preceded by the euphonic augment ಅಱ (*i. e.* ಅಱಕೆ, ಅಱಕ್ಕೆ, which is a vulgar form, § 123, *c*); 15, ಅಕ್ಕೆ, *i. e.* a mutilated form of ಅಱ್ಕೆ (§§ 122, *b*, *c*; 125, *b*, *c*); 16, ಅಕೆ, *i. e.* a mutilated form of ಅಱ್ಕೆ (§§ 122, *b*, *c*; 125).

Remark.

That the letter ಱ್ is another form of ದ್ becomes a fact when the Tuḷu dialect is compared (see Kannaḍa Dictionary p. XVI, note 1, sub 7); further, ಱ್ appears as ಣ್ in Tuḷu (see the same note, sub 5), and ಣ್ as ನ್ in Tĕlugu (*e. g.* Tĕlugu ಕನು, ಕನ್ನು = Kannaḍa ಕಣ್, ಕಣು, ಕಣ್ಣು, the eye; *cf.* also § 222). Hence it may be concluded that the letters ಱ್, ದ್, ಣ್ and ನ್ are closely related in Draviḍa and change places in the dialect. The augments ದ್ and ನ್ of the genitive (§§ 109; 117), ಯ್ of the genitive (§ 130; *cf.* 243, *B*, remark), ಇ್ and ಣ್ of the dative and genitive, and to some extent the sŏnnŏ ೦ (ನ್) are, therefore, ultimately the same euphonic letters (*cf.* ದ್, ನ್, and ಣ್ in § 176; see also the ದಾ in § 265). The vowel ಅ sounded before ಇ್ and ಣ್ (*i. e.* ಅ-ಇ್, ಅ-ಣ್) apparently is a help to enunciation.

Abl. 1, the terminations of the instrumental except ಎ; 2, ಇಂ, ಇನ್ದ, ಇನ್ದಂ, ಇನ್ದೆ preceded by the augment ಅಣ್ through its genitive ಅಣ (*i. e.* ಅಣಿಂ, etc., §§ 122, *a*; 123); 3, ಇನ್ದ preceded by the augment ಅಣ through its genitive ಅಣದ (*i. e.* ಅಣದಿನ್ದ, § 123, *c*); 4, ಇಂ, ಇನ್ದ, ಇನ್ದಂ, ಇನ್ದವು, ಇನ್ದೆ preceded by ಅತ್ತಣ, the genitive of ಅತ್ತ (§ 123, *i. e.* ಅತ್ತಣಿಂ, etc., §§ 109, *a*, *b*; 117, *a*; 120, *a*; 123, *a*); 5, ಇಂ preceded by ಅಇ, the genitive of the augment ಅಇ್, and ಅತ್ತಣ (*i. e.* ಅಇತ್ತಣಿಂ, etc., §§ 122, *a*; 125, *a*); 6, ಇಂ, ಇನ್ದ, ಇನ್ದೆ preceded by ಇನ, the genitive of ಇನ್, and ಅತ್ತಣ (*i. e.* ಇನತ್ತಣಿಂ, etc., § 122, *a*).

The terminations and their augments presuppose the genitive.

Gen. 1, ಅ (§§ 120, *a*, *b*; 121, *b*, *c*; 122; 126, *c*; 137); 2, ಅ preceded by the euphonic augment ದ್ (*i. e.* ದ, § 109); 3, ಅ preceded by the euphonic augment ನ್ (*i. e.* ನ, §§ 109. 117); 4, ಅ preceded by the euphonic augment ಇನ್ (*i. e.* ಇನ, §§ 121. 122. 127); 5, ಅ preceded by the euphonic augment ಅಣ್ (*i. e.* ಅಣ, §§ 122. 123); 6, ಅ preceded by the euphonic augment ಅಳ್, this being another form of ಅಣ್ (*i. e.* ಅಳ, §§ 122, *c*; 123, *b*); 7, ಅ preceded by the euphonic augment ಅಣದ್ (*i. e.* ಅಣದ, which is a vulgar form, § 123, *c*); 8, ಅ preceded by the euphonic augment ಅಇ್ (*i. e.* ಅಇ, §§ 122. 125); 9, ಅ preceded by the euphonic augment ಯ್ (*i. e.* ಯ, § 130); 10, ಅ preceded by the euphonic augment ವ್ (*i. e.* ವ, §§ 128; 129, *a*); 11, ಇನ (ಇನ್+ಅ, *i. e.* No. 4) preceded by the euphonic augment ವ್ (*i. e.* ವಿನ, §§ 128. 129); 12, ಅ preceded by the euphonic ಯ್ and forming with the final ಇ and ಎ of the base a long syllable (*i. e.* ಈ or ಏ, § 130, *c*); 13, ಅ preceded by the euphonic augments ದ್, ನ್, ಯ್ and ವ್ (*i. e.* ದಾ, ನಾ, ಯಾ and ವಾ, §§ 109, *a*, *c*; 117, *a*, *c*; 128, *a*; 130, *a*, *c*); 14, ಅ (§§ 120, *a*; 122, *c*).

Loc. 1, ಉಳ್ (§§ 109, *a*; 120, *a*; 122, *a*; 130, *a*); 2, ಒಳ್ (§§ 109, *a*, *b*; 117, *a*, *b*; 120, *a*, *b*; 121, *b*; 122, *a*, *b*; 125, *a*, *b*; 127, *a*; 128, *a*, *b*; 129, *a*; 130, *a*, *b*; 137, *a*, *b*); 3, ಒಳು (§§ 109, *a*, *b*; 117, *b*; 120, *b*; 122, *a*, *b*; 125, *b*; 128, *b*; 130, *a*, *b*; 137, *b*); 4, ಒಳಗೆ (§§ 109; 117, *c*; 120, *b*; 121, *c*; 122, *a*, *c*; 125, *b*, *c*; 128, *b*; 130; 137, *b*); 5, ಅಲ್ (§§ 109, *a*; 120, *a*; 130, *a*); 6, ಅಲು (§§ 109, *a*, *b*; 120, *a*, *b*; 130, *a*, *b*); 7, ಅಲ್ಲಿ (§§ 109; 117; 120; 121, *b*, *c*; 122; 123, *c*; 125, *b*, *c*; 126, *c*; 127, *a*, *c*; 128; 130; 137, *c*); 8, ಅಲಿ (§§ 109, *b*, *c*; 117; *c*; 120, *b*; 121, *c*; 122, *b*; 125, *b*; 128, *b*; 130, *b*, *c*; 137, *c*); 9, ಇಲಿ (§§ 120, *b*; 121, *c*; 122, *c*); 10, ಲಿ (§§ 121, *c*; 130, *c*); 11, ಇ (§ 109); 12, the crude base (§§ 126. 127).

The terminations are suffixed to the genitive with and without its augments.

2. *Plural.*

Nom. 1, ೦ (ವ್, § 137, *a*); 2, a euphonic ಉ added to the sönnĕ, in which case this is changed into ವ್ (*i. e.* ವು, § 137; *cf.* § 136); 3, ವು (*i. e.* No. 2) lengthened by the addition of ಗಳು (*i. e.* ವುಗಳು, § 136, *c*); 4, ಕಳ್ (§§ 119, *a*; 131, *a*; 134, *a*); 5, ಕಳ್ with a euphonic ಉ (*i. e.* ಕಳು, § 119, *b*, *c*); 6, ಕಳು lengthened by the addition of ಗಳ್ (*i. e.* ಕಳುಗಳ್, § 119, *b*); 7, ಕಳ್ with the augment ಇರು (*i. e.* ಕಳಿರು, § 119, *c*); 8, ಗಳ್ (§§ 118, *a*, *b*; 131, *a*, *b*); 9, ಗಳ್ with a euphonic ಉ (*i. e.* ಗಳು, §§ 118, *b*, *c*; 119, *b*, *c*; 131); 10, ಗಳ್ with the augment ಇರ್ (*i. e.* ಗಳಿರ್, §§ 118, *b*; 132, *a*, *b*); 11, ಗಳ್ preceded by a euphonic sönnĕ (*i. e.* ಂಗಳ್, §§ 118, *a*, *b*; 119, *a*, *b*; 137, *a*); 12, ಗಳು preceded by a euphonic sönnĕ (*i. e.* ಂಗಳು, §§ 118, *a*, *b*; 119, *b*); 13, ಗಳಿರ್ preceded by a euphonic sönnĕ (*i. e.* ಂಗಳಿರ್, §§ 118, *a*; 119, *a*, *b*); 14, ಅರ್ (§§ 119, *a*, *b*; 132, *a*, *b*; 134, *a*, *b*); 15, ಅರ್ with a euphonic ಉ (*i. e.* ಅರು, §§ 119; 132, *b*, *c*; 134, *b*, *c*); 16, ಅರ್ lengthened by the addition of ಕಳ್ (*i. e.* ಅರ್ಕಳ್, §§ 119, *a*; 132, *a*); 17, ಅರ್ lengthened by the addition of ಕಳಿರ್ (*i. e.* ಅರ್ಕಳಿರ್, §§ 119, *a*; 132, *a*); 18, ಅರ್ lengthened by the addition of ಗಳ್ (*i. e.* ಅರ್ಗಳ್, § 119, *a*); 19, ಅರು lengthened by the addition of ಗಳ್ (*i. e.* ಅರುಗಳ್, § 119, *b*); 20, ಅರು lengthened by the addition of ಗಳು (*i. e.* ಅರುಗಳು, § 119, *b*); 21, ಅರು lengthened by the addition of ಗಳಿರ್ (*i. e.* ಅರುಗಳಿರ್, § 119, *b*); 22, ಅರ್ lengthened by ಇರ್ (*i. e.* ಅರಿರ್, §§ 119, *a*; 132, *a*); 23, ಇರ್ (§§ 119, *a*; 132, *a*, *b*); 24, ಇರು (see Nos. 29. 30); 25, ಇರ್ preceded by a euphonic ದ್ (*i. e.* ದಿರ್, §§ 119, *b*; 132, *a*; 134, *a*); 26, ಇರ್ preceded by a euphonic ಂದ್ (*i. e.* ಂದಿರ್, § 119, *a*); 27, ಂದಿರ್ lengthened by the addition of ಇರ್ (*i. e.* ಂದಿರಿರ್, § 119, *a*); 28, ಂದಿರ್ lengthened by the addition of ಗಳ್ (*i. e.* ಂದಿರ್ಗಳ್, § 119, *a*); 29, ಇರು preceded by a euphonic ದ್ (*i. e.* ದಿರು, § 119, *b*); 30, ಇರು preceded by a euphonic ಂದ್ (*i. e.* ಂದಿರು, §§ 119, *b*, *c*; 132, *c*); 31, ಅರು (*i. e.* No. 15) preceded by a euphonic ಂದ್ (*i. e.* ಂದರು, § 119, *c*); 32, ದಿರ್ (*i. e.* No. 25) lengthened by the addition of ಕಳ್ (*i. e.* ದಿರ್ಕಳ್, § 132, *a*); 33, ಇರ್ preceded by the euphonic ವ್ (*i. e.* ವಿರ್, § 132, *a*); 34, ವಿರ್ lengthened by the addition of ಇರ್ (*i. e.* ವಿರಿರ್, § 132, *a*); 35, ವಿರ್ lengthened by the addition of ಕಳ್ (*i. e.* ವಿರ್ಕಳ್, § 132, *a*); 36, ವಿರ್ lengthened by the addition of ಗಳ್ (*i. e.* ವಿರ್ಗಳ್, 132, *a*); 37, ಅರ್ preceded by a euphonic ಬ್ (*i. e.* ಬರ್, § 119, *a*); 38, ಅರ್ preceded by a euphonic ಂಬ್ (*i. e.* ಂಬರ್, § 119, *a*); 39, ಅರ್ preceded by a euphonic ವ್ (*i. e.* ವರ್, § 119, *a*); 40, ಅರು (*i. e.* No. 15) preceded by a euphonic ಬ್ (*i. e.* ಬರು, § 119, *b*, *c*); 41, ಅರು preceded by a euphonic ಂಬ್ (*i. e.* ಂಬರು, § 119, *b*); 42, ಅರು preceded by a euphonic ವ್ (*i. e.* ವರು, § 119, *c*); 43, ಅರ್ (§ 132, *b*).

Acc. 1, ಅ (§§ 118, *b*, *c*; 119, *b*, *c*; 131, *b*, *c*; 135, *c*); 2, ಅಂ (§§ 118, *a*, *b*; 119, *a*, *b*; 131, *b*, *c*; 135, *c*); 3, a euphonic ಉ attached to ಅಂ, the sönnĕ becoming ನ್ or ನ್ನ್ (*i. e.* ಅನು, ಅನ್ನು, §§ 118, *b*, *c*; 119, *a*, *c*; 131, *b*, *c*;

135, c); 4, ಅ added to ಅಂ, the sŏnuĕ becoming ನ್ (i. e. ಅನ್ನ, § 119, c; 135, c); 5, ಆ (§ 119, c).

Regarding the augments see the nominative.

Instr. 1, ಇ (§ 131, b); 2, ಇಂ (§§ 118, a, b; 119, a; 131, a, b; 132, a; 137, a); 3, ಇಂ lengthened by the final augments ದ, ದಂ, ದತ್ತು, ದೆ (i. e. ಇನ್ದ, etc., §§ 118; 119; 131, b, c; 137, b, c); 4, ಇಂ preceded by the augment ಅಱ್ (i. e. ಅಱಿಂ, § 136, a).

Dat. 1, ಗೆ (§§ 118, a, b; 119, a, b; 131, a, b; 132, a; 135, a); 2, ಗ್ಗೆ (§§ 119, a; 132, a); 3, ಗೆ preceded by a euphonic sŏnnĕ (i. e. ಂಗೆ, § 137); 4, ಗೆ preceded by a euphonic ಇ (i. e. ಇಗೆ, §§ 118; 119; 131, b, c; 135, b, c; 136, c); 5, ಗೆ preceded by a euphonic ಇಂ (i. e. ಇಂಗೆ, §§ 119, b; 135, b); 6, ಗೆ preceded by a euphonic ಉ (i. e. ಉಗೆ,, § 131, a); 7, ಗೆ preceded by a euphonic ಅ (i. e. ಅಗೆ, § 119, c); 8, ಕೆ (§ 119, a); 9, ಕೆ preceded by the euphonic augment ಅಱ್ (i. e. ಅಱ್ಕೆ, § 136, a); 10, ಅಕ್ಕೆ, a mutilated form of ಅಱ್ಕೆ (§ 136, b, c); 11, ಅಕೆ, a mutilated form of ಅಱ್ಕೆ (§ 136, b, c).

Abl. 1, ಇಂ, ಇನ್ದಂ, ಇನ್ದೆ preceded by the genitive of ಅತ್ತ (i. e. ಅತ್ತಣಿಂ, etc., §§ 118 a; 119, a); 2, the terminations of the instrumental.

Gen. 1, ಅ (§§ 118; 119; 131; 132, a, b; 135; 136, c); 2, ಅ preceded by the euphonic augment ಅಱ್ (i. e. ಅಱ, § 136, a, b); 3, ಆ (§§ 119, a, c; 131, a).

Loc. 1, ಒಳ್ (§§ 118, a, b; 119, a, b; 131, a, b; 137, a); 2, ಒಳು (§§ 118, a, b; 119, b; 132, b; 137, b); 3, ಒಳಗೆ (§ 118, b, c; 119, b, c; 131, b, c; 136, c); 4, ಅಲ್ಲಿ (§§ 118; 119; 131, b, c; 136, c); 5, ಅಲಿ (§§ 118, b, c; 131, b, c; 137, c); 6, ಒಳ್ and ಅಲ್ಲಿ preceded by the augment ಅಱ್ (i. e. ಅಱೊಳ್ and ಅಱಲ್ಲಿ, § 136, a, b).

142. Looking back on the declension of bases (§§ 109. 117-137. 139) one observes **twelve more or less distinct modes of declension.**

1. The first mode comprises neuter bases with final ಅ, e. g. ಗಿಡ, ಮರ, ನೆಲ, ಬೆಟ್ಟ, ಕೊಡ, ಕೊಳ, ಮೊಲ. Their singular appears in § 109, their plural in § 118.

2, The second comprises masculine and feminine bases ending in ಅ, e. g. ಕೂಟ, ಕಸವ, ಭೀಮ, ದೇವ, ಅರಸ; ಮಾಡಿದ, ಬೇಡುವ; ಅವ, ಇವ, ಉವ, ಆತ, ಈತ, ಊತ, ಆವ, ಯಾವ; ಅಕ್ಕ, ಅಮ್ಮ, ಅವ್ವ. Their singular is given in § 117, their plurals appear in §§ 119. 135.

3, The third comprises neuter and feminine bases ending in consonants (and one that is used either as masculine or neuter in the ancient dialect, *viz.* ಆಳ್), e. g. ಕಣ್, ಕಲ್, ಬಿಲ್, ಮುಳ್, ಊರ್, ಕಾರ್, ಕೇರ್, ಕೆಸಱ್; ತಾಯ್, ಪೆಣ್; ಅವಳ್, ಇವಳ್, ಉವಳ್, ಒರ್ಬಳ್, ಒರ್ವಳ್, ಆವಳ್, ಪೆಱಳ್, ಕರಿಯಳ್, ಬಿಳಿಯಳ್; ಆಳ್. Their singular is given in § 120, their plurals appear in §§ 131. 134. Regarding ಆಗಳ್, ಈಗಳ್ see § 121.

4, The fourth comprises two kinds of bases

a) neuter and feminine bases (and one that is either masculine, feminine, or neuter in the modern dialect, *viz.* ಆಳು) which, occasionally also in the ancient dialect, optionally in the mediæval one, and always in the modern one are formed from bases with final consonants (see No. 3) by the addition of a euphonic ಉ, *e. g.* ಎಳ್ಳು, ಕಣ್ಣು, ಕಲು, ಕಲ್ಲು, ಊರು, ಕಾಲು, ಕೊರಳು, ತಿಂಗಳು; ಅವಳು, ಇವಳು, ಯಾವಳು, ಒರ್ವಳು, ಒಬ್ಬಳು; ಈಗಳು; ಆಳು. Their singular appears in § 121; their plurals are given in §§ 131. 134.

b) neuter bases (and two masculine ones *viz.* ಗಣ್ಡಸು, ಗಣ್ಡು, one feminine one *viz.* ಹೆಂಗಸು, and two masculine-feminine-neuter ones *viz.* ಅರಸು, ಕೂಸು) always (with option only in two numerals) ending in a euphonic ಉ in the ancient, mediæval and modern dialect, *e. g.* ಎಱ್ತು, ಎತ್ತು, ಪೊಱ್ತು, ಪೊತ್ತು, ಹೊತ್ತು, ತಪ್ಪು, ಜೆಂಗು, ಕೆಮ್ಪು, ನಾಡು, ಕೇಡು, ಬೆಳಗು; ಅದು, ಇದು, ಉದು, ಪೆಱತು, ಎಲ್ಲದು, ಆವುದು, ಯಾವದು; ಒಳ್ಳಿತು, ಮೆಲ್ಲಿತು, ಅಸಿದು, ಬಸಿದು, ಕಱಿದು, ಕಿಱಿದು; ಒನ್ದು, ಎರಡು, ಮೂಱು, ನಾಲ್ಕು, ಅಯ್ದು, ಆಱು, ಏೞು, (or also ಏೞ್), ಎಣ್ಟು, ಹತ್ತು, ನೂಱು (or also ನೂಱ್); ಅನಿತು, ಇನಿತು, ಉನಿತು, ಎನಿತು, ಆಸು, ಈಸು, ಏಸು, ಅಷ್ಟು, ಇಷ್ಟು, ಎಷ್ಟು; ಒಳಗು, ಪೊಱಗು, ಹೊಱಗು, ಪಿನ್ದು, ಹಿನ್ದು, ಮುನ್ದು, ಕೆಳಗು, ಮೇಗು, ಸುತ್ತು. Their singular is given in § 122 (*cf.* 124), their plurals appear in §§ 131. 136.

5, The fifth comprises

a) masculine, feminine, and neuter bases ending in a radical ಉ, *e. g.* ಅನು, ಉದು, ಕೆಱು, ತುಱು, ಮದು, ಗುರು, ವಧು, ಪಶು. Their singular appears in § 128, their plural in § 131.

b) masculine, feminine, and neuter bases ending in ಊ, ಋ, ೠ, ಓ and ಔ, *e. g.* ಪೂ, ಹೂ, ಪಿತೃ, ಮಾತೃ, ಋೂ, ಗೋ, ಗ್ಲೌ. Their singular appears in § 129, their plural in § 131.

6, The sixth comprises masculine, feminine and neuter bases ending in ಇ, ಈ, ಏ, *e. g.* ಕವಿ, ತಾಯಿ, ತಂಗಿ, ಕಪಿ, ಇಲಿ, ಕೇಱಿ; ಸ್ತ್ರೀ; ತನ್ದೆ, ಅತ್ತೆ. ಅವ್ವೆ, ಸೂಳೆ, ಆಕೆ, ಈಕೆ, ಊಕೆ, ಮನೆ, ಆನೆ. Their singular is given in § 130, their plurals appear in §§ 131. 132.

7, The seventh comprises eight neuter bases of direction with final ಅ, *e. g.* ಅತ್ತ, ಇತ್ತ, ತೆಂಕ. Their declension is given in § 123.

8, The eighth comprises the bases of the seventh mode when the suffix ಅಲ್ or ಅಲು is attached, *e. g.* ಅತ್ತಲ್, ಅತ್ತಲು, ಮೂಡಲ್, ಮೂಡಲು. See § 126.

9, The ninth comprises four bases expressing time that end in the ಉ of No. 4, letter *b*, *viz.* ಅನ್ದು, ಇನ್ದು, ಉನ್ದು, ಎನ್ದು. See § 127.

10, The tenth is formed by the pronoun ಏಂ (ಏನ್), ಏನು. See § 125.

11, The eleventh is formed by the singular and plural of the personal pronouns and of the reflexive pronoun, *viz.* ಆಂ, ನಾಂ, ನೀಂ, ತಾಂ, ಆನು, ನಾನು, ನೀನು, ತಾನು. See § 137.

12, The twelfth mode comprises a number of terms that express direction and time, *viz.* ನಡು, ಕಡೆ, ಎಡೆ, ಅಲ್ಲಿ, ಇಲ್ಲಿ. ಉಲ್ಲಿ, ಆಚೆ, ಈಚೆ, ನಾಳೆ, ನಿನ್ನೆ, ಮೊನ್ನೆ, ಆಗ, ಈಗ. ಮುನ್ನ, (ಮತ್ತೆ). See § 139.

V. On verbs (see §§ 313—315)

143. In chapter III (§ 45 *seq.*) verbal roots or themes (dhâtu) have been already treated of. We have seen that Kêšava calls the crude form (prakṛitisvarûpa, dhâtusvarûpa) of any verb its root, whether it be the primary element (primitive theme) or a secondary theme.

He gives the rule (sûtra 216) that the crude form or theme is found by dropping the pronominal termination (vibhakti) ಉಂ of the negative (see § 209, text and note 2). This rule, however, is (to say the least) insufficient, as it does not enable a student to make a distinction between themes ending in ಉ (which alone are contained in Kêšava's instances, (as ಕೂಡು, ನೋಡು, ತೀಡು) and themes ending in consonants (as ಎನ್, ಗೆಯ್, ಕೊಯ್, ತಾಳ್, ಬಾಚ್, ಸೋಲ್), and as it does not take notice of the doubling of final consonants in the negative (§ 215, 7, *f*), of the euphonic ಯ್ of themes ending in ಇ and ಎ (§§ 170. 209), and of themes that lengthen their vowel (§ 209), thus presupposing the grammarian's list of dhâtus (§ 47).

144. Ancient Kannaḍa grammarians call a verb ಕ್ರಿಯೆ or ಆಖ್ಯಾತ; its action, or the general idea expressed by any verb, they term ಕ್ರಿಯೆ too.

They do not distinguish between mood (mode) **and tense.** Kannaḍa has so to say only one mood, the indicative, for which, however, it uses no particular word. *Cf.* § 314.

Tense they call ಕಾಲ.

A conjugated verb, *i. e.* one ending in a personal termination, is called ಪದ, ಆಖ್ಯಾತಪದ or ಕ್ರಿಯಾಪದ (§§ 69. 189. 192).

145. The name of **the present tense** is ವರ್ತಮಾನ or ಭವತ್, or ಭವತ್ಕಾಲ, or ವರ್ತಮಾನಕಾಲ, or ವರ್ತಿಪ ಕಾಲ, or ಸಮ್ಪ್ರತಿ; that of **the past tense** is ಭೂತ, or ಭೂತಕಾಲ, or ಭೂತವತಿ, or ಪೋದ ಕಾಲ; that of **the future tense** is ಭವಿಷ್ಯತ್, or ಭವಿಷ್ಯನ್ತಿ, or ಭವಿಷ್ಯತ್ಕಾಲ, or ಬರ್ಪ ಕಾಲ, or ಭಾವಿ. The **comprehensive term for the three times or tenses** is ಕಾಲತ್ರಯ.

146. The action of the imperative, or **the imperative**, is called ವಿಧಿ ಕ್ರಿಯೆ, or ವಿಧಿ, or ವಿಧ್ಯರ್ಥ. The negative form of the verb, or **the negative**, is termed ಪ್ರತಿಷೇಧ.

147. A person of the verb is called **ಪುರುಷ.** The name of the first person (*i. e.* the third person in European grammars) is ಪ್ರಥಮ or ಪ್ರಥಮ ಪುರುಷ, or also ಅನ್ಯ, ಅನ್ಯಪುರುಷ; that of the second is ಮಧ್ಯಮ or ಮಧ್ಯಮ

ಪುರುಷ; and that of the third (*i. e.* the first in European grammars) is ಉತ್ತಮ or ಉತ್ತಮಪುರುಷ. *Cf.* § 192.

If occasionally the term ಕ್ರಿಯೆ is added to ಪ್ರಥಮ, ಮಧ್ಯಮ and ಉತ್ತಮ, or to ಪ್ರಥಮಪುರುಷ, ಮಧ್ಯಮಪುರುಷ and ಉತ್ತಮಪುರುಷ, it is to say that no other persons are meant than those who regulate the action of a verb in grammar.

The comprehensive term for the three persons is ಪುರುಷತ್ರಯ.

148. The grammarians Nâgavarma and Kêšava do not use a word to distinguish a transitive from an intransitive verb; they mentally saw such a distinction themselves, and expected others to do the same. The sûtra about the so-called passive voice in the Šabdamaṇidarpaṇa wherein the term ಸಕರ್ಮಕ, transitive, occurs, is an interpolation (ಅನುಕ್ತಸೂತ್ರ).

About 400 years afterwards Bhaṭṭâkalaṅka in his Šabdânušâsana (sûtra 443) introduced by name transitive verbal themes, ಸಕರ್ಮಕಧಾತು, and intransitive verbal themes, ಅಕರ್ಮಕಧಾತು.

Voices, *i. e.* active and passive (see § 315), are not mentioned by Nâgavarma and Kêšava, and the terms parasmaipada and âtmanêpada which have been introduced from Saṁskṛita into Kannaḍa by modern writers, are not used by them.

149. Causation is called ಹೇತು. A verb that expresses causation or is causal (ಹೇತುಕ), is formed from an intransitive or transitive one by adding the particle ಇಸು (or also, as we shall see in § 151, ಸು, ಚು, ಇಚು, ಅಸು), *e. g.* ನಗಿಸು, to cause (somebody) to laugh (from ನಗು), ಅಡಿಸು, to cause (somebody) to cook (from ಅಡು), ನುಡಿಯಿಸು, to cause (a person) to speak (from ನುಡಿ), ಮುಡಿಯಿಸು, to cause (a person) to put (something) into the hair (from ಮುಡಿ), ಕಡೆಯಿಸು, to cause (a person) to churn (from ಕಡೆ), ಈಯಿಸು, to cause (a person) to give (from ಈ), ತೇಯಿಸು, to cause (a person) to grind (from ತೇ), ನೋಯಿಸು, to cause (a person) to feel pain (from ನೋ), ಮೇಯಿಸು, to cause (cattle) to eat grass (from ಮೇ), ಅಲರಿಸು, to cause (a flower) to open (from ಅಲರ್), ಕಾಣಿಸು, to cause (something) to appear (from ಕಾಣ್).[1]

The agent (*cf.* § 344) that causes another to do something or causes something to be done or happen, is called ಹೇತುಕರ್ತೃ, ಅನ್ಯಕರ್ತೃ, ಪರಕರ್ತೃ, or ಭಿನ್ನಕರ್ತೃ.

---

[1] It may be remarked that a causative verb may also be formed by the verb ಮಾಡು, to make, and an infinitive ending in ಅ (§ 187, 2), *e. g.* ಅವನನ್ನು ಓದ ಮಾಡು, make him read (= ಓದಿಸು).

150. But if a verb is formed by means of ಇಸು (etc., § 149) that is used in the sense of doing that which the word expresses, the agent is termed ನಿಜಕರ್ತೃ, ಸ್ವಕರ್ತೃ, or ಸ್ವಯಂಕರ್ತೃ. Such verbs may be intransitive or transitive, *e.g.* ನಿಟ್ಟಿಸು, to look, to stare; ತುಟ್ಟಿಸು, to decrease in power; ದಳ್ಳಿಸು, to become greater in bulk; ಮಿಳ್ಳಿಸು, to move about, to float; ಭ್ರಮಿಸು, to roam or wander about; — ಖಂಡಿಸು, to break, to crush; (or effecting a useful object, ಪ್ರಯೋಜನವಸ್ತು) ಚಿತ್ರಿಸು, to draw (sketches, figures, pictures); ಮುದ್ರಿಸು, to affix a seal to (see § 151, remark); ಪೊಂಗಿಸು, to extend, to widen; ಸೊಪ್ಪಿಸು, to slacken (*v. t.*). *Cf.* § 215, 1, *b.*

Remark.

It is not allowed to form causative verbs from such verbs, *e. g.* to form ಖಂಡಿಸಿಸು from ಖಂಡಿಸು would be wrong.

151. The suffix ಇಸು appears also as ಸು, ಚು, ಇಚು, and ಅಸು; compare some of the finals mentioned in § 65. It is more than probable that the ಇ in ಇಸು and ಇಚು, and the ಅ in ಅಸು are euphonic (*cf.* the ಇ of §§ 63. 168).

It has been supposed that ಇಸು and ಇಚು are the same as ಇಸು, ಈಸು, to permit, etc.; but that is wrong, as ಇಸು, ಈಸು are formed from ಈ, to give, etc., by means of ಸು which is another form of ಇಸು; see letter *b*, 3 in this paragraph and § 316, 14.

We further state

a) that ಇಸು is suffixed

1, to verbal themes which originally are monosyllabic, and end in consonants if they have not received a euphonic ಉ (see § 54), *e. g.* ಇರಿಸು, ಉಣಿಸು, ಎನಿಸು, ಏಱಿಸು, ಕಾಣಿಸು, ಕಾಯಿಸು, ಕೇಳಿಸು, ಕೊಲಿಸು, ಕೊಳಿಸು, ತರಿಸು, ತಿನಿಸು, ತೀರಿಸು, ಪಾಯಿಸು, ಪೋಲಿಸು, ಬರಿಸು, ಬಾಱಿಸು, ಸೊಲ್ಲಿಸು, ಸೋರಿಸು, ಸೋಲಿಸು. See exceptions under letter *b*, 1, letter *c*, 1, and letter *e*.

2, to verbal themes that originally are dissyllabic and end in consonants, but are made trisyllabic by the addition of a euphonic ಉ, *e. g.* ಅಗಲಿಸು, ಅಲರಿಸು, ಅಱಿಲಿಸು, ಉದಿರಿಸು, ಉರುಳಿಸು, ಕಱಿಲಿಸು, ತಗುಳಿಸು, ತೊಡರಿಸು, ನಿಗುರಿಸು, ನೆಗಱಿಸು, ಪೊಣರಿಸು, ಬಱಿಲಿಸು, ಸಡಲಿಸು, ಮಗುಱಿಸು, ಹೊರಳಿಸು. To this class belong also the ancient ಒಡರಿಸು, ಅಗುಱಿಸು, ತೆಗಱಿಸು, ಪೊಗಱಿಸು. See the common ancient forms under letter *c*, 2; and exceptions under letter *d*.

In ತುಟ್ಟಿಸು, ದಳ್ಳಿಸು, ನಿಟ್ಟಿಸು and ಮಿಳ್ಳಿಸು (§ 150) no verbal or nominal theme nowadays appears to which ಇಸು is added. ಓರಣಿಸು, ದಟ್ಟಿಸು, ಪವ್ವಳಿಸು, and similar terms are derived from nouns by means of ಇಸು.

3, to themes that appear as dissyllables and trisyllables in the ancient, mediæval and modern dialect and end in ಉ, *e. g.* ಆಗಿಸು, ಆಡಿಸು, ಒಪ್ಪಿಸು, ಓಡಿಸು, ಓದಿಸು, ಕಾಸಿಸು, ಕುಟ್ಟಿಸು, ಕೂಡಿಸು, ಕೊಡಿಸು, ತಪ್ಪಿಸು, ತುಮ್ಬಿಸು, ನಾಣ್ಚಿಸು, ನೂಕಿಸು, ನೋಡಿಸು, ಪಣ್ಣಿಸು, ಪತ್ತಿಸು, ಪೊಂಗಿಸು, ಪೋಗಿಸು, ಹಾಕಿಸು; ಅಡಂಗಿಸು, ನಿಗುಮ್ಬಿಸು, ಪೊಚ್ಚಱಿಸು, ಬದುಕಿಸು, ಮಲಂಗಿಸು, ಹುಡುಕಿಸು. See an exception under letter *e*.

4, to themes that are dissyllabic and end in ಇ and ಎ, to which, especially in the ancient and mediæval dialect, ಇಸು is attached by means of a euphonic ಯ್, *e. g.* ಅಳಯಿಸು (ಅಳಿಯಿಸು), ಅಱಿಯಿಸು, ಎಱೆಯಿಸು, ಕಡಯಿಸು, ಕರೆಯಿಸು, ತೆಗೆಯಿಸು, ತೊಳಯಿಸು, ನಡಯಿಸು (ನಡೆಯಿಸು), ನುಡಿಯಿಸು, ನೆಱಿಯಿಸು (ನೆಱೆಯಿಸು), ಪೊಡಯಿಸು (ಪೊಡೆಯಿಸು), ಬೆಳಯಿಸು (ಬೆಳೆಯಿಸು), ಮಱಿಯಿಸು. See exceptions under letter *b*, 2 and *c*, 3.

Regarding the dropping of the final vowel of some themes *cf.* letter *b*, 2; §§ 60; 157; 165, letter *a*, 3. 4. 5; 165, *b*, 2; 172; 180, 5.

5, to monosyllabic themes that are a vowel or end in one, to which it is attached by means of a euphonic ಯ್, *e. g.* ಈಯಿಸು, ತೇಯಿಸು, ತೋಯಿಸು, ನೋಯಿಸು, ಬೇಯಿಸು, ವಿಾಯಿಸು, ಮೇಯಿಸು. The forms occur also in the modern dialect. See exceptions under letter *b*, 3.

b) that ಸು is suffixed

1, to themes that end in the consonants ಯ್ and ಲ್, *e. g.* ಕಾಸು, ಪಾಸು (in the three dialects), ಕೊಲ್ಸು (only in the mediæval one). *Cf.* letter *a*, 1.

2, to dissyllabic themes ending in ಇ and ಎ, in the three dialects, *e. g.* ಅಡ್ಡಸು, ಅಳಸು (ಅಳಿಸು, ಅಳಿಸು, ಅಳುಸು), ಅಱಿಸು, ಇಱಿಸು, ಉರಿಸು (ಉರಸು, ಉರುಸು), ಉಱಿಸು (ಉಱಿಸು, ಉಱುಸು), ಎಣಿಸು (ಎಣಸು, ಎಣುಸು), ಎಱಿಸು, ಕವಿಸು, ಕುಡಿಸು, ತಡಸು (ತಡಿಸು), ತಿಳಿಸು, ತುಱಿಸು (ತುಱಿಸು, ತುಱುಸು), ತುಱಿಸು, ತೆಗಸು (ತೆಗೆಸು, ತೆಗಿಸು), ತೊಳಸು (ತೊಳಿಸು), ನಡಸು (also in a śâsana of 1076 A. D., ನಡೆಸು, ನಡಿಸು), ನುಡಿಸು, ಪೊಡಸು, ಪೊದಿಸು, ಬೆರಸು (ಬೆರಿಸು), ಬೆಳಸು (ಬೆಳಸು, ಬೆಳಿಸು), ಮಡಿಸು (ಮಡಸು), ಮಱಿಸು (ಮಱಿಸು), ಸುಲಿಸು, ಹನಿಸು. See letter *a*, 4 and *c*, 3.

ಪಱಿಸು, ಹಱಿಸು are derived from nouns by means of ಸು.

About the dropping of the final vowel of some themes see letter *a*, 4, about the change of ಎ into ಇ § 109, *b*, 3 (*cf.* § 66), and about that of ಇ into ಉ §§ 165, *a*, 5; 247, *d*, 13. 14.

3, to monosyllabic themes that are a vowel or end in one, *e. g.* ಈಸು (or ಇಸು, of ಈ § 316, 14; *cf.* its past participle ಇತ್ತು), ಕೋಸು,

ತೋಸು, ಬೇಸು, ವಿಾಸು, ಮೇಸು. The forms are common to the three dialects. *Cf.* letter *a*, 5.

c) that ಚು is suffixed

1, to monosyllabic long themes ending in the consonant ರ್, *e.g.* ತೀರ್ಚು, ಸಾರ್ಚು, ಸೋರ್ಚು. *Cf.* letter *a*, 1.

ನಾಣ್ಚು is derived from a noun with a long vowel by means of ಚು. Themes like ಪೆರ್ಚು, ಬಿರ್ಚು, ಮುಂಚು are derived from nouns with short vowels which they retain.

2, to dissyllabic themes ending in the consonants ರ್, ಲ್, ಳ್ and ೞ್, in the ancient and mediæval dialect, *e.g.* ಅಮರ್ಚು, ಅಲರ್ಚು, ಉಡಿರ್ಚು, ಒಡರ್ಚು, ತಳಿರ್ಚು, ತೆರಳ್ಚು, ತೊಡರ್ಚು, ನಿಗುರ್ಚು, ನಿಮಿರ್ಚು, ಪೊಣರ್ಚು, ಬಿದಿರ್ಚು; ಅಗಲ್ಚು, ಅಬಿಲ್ಚು, ಕಬಿಲ್ಚು, ಬಬಿಲ್ಚು, ಸಡಿಲ್ಚು; ಉರುಳ್ಚು, ಕೆರಳ್ಚು, ತಗುಳ್ಚು, ಪೊರಳ್ಚು; ಅಗುೞ್ಚು, ನೆಗೞ್ಚು, ಮುಗುೞ್ಚು. *Cf.* letter *a*, 2 and letter *d*.

3, to dissyllabic themes ending in ಇ and ಎ, *e.g.* ಅಡಚು, ಅೞಿಚು, ಎಬಿಚು, ಕವಿಚು, ಕಳಚು, ಕೊಡಚು, ಮಡಚು. The forms appear more or less in the three dialects. *Cf.* letter *a*, 4 and *b*, 2.

About the dropping of the final vowel of some themes see also letter *a*, 4 and *b*, 2.

d) that occasionally ಇಚು is suffixed to the themes mentioned under letter *a*, 2, *e.g.* ಉರುಳಿಚು, ಒಡರಿಚು, ಕೆರಳಿಚು, ತೆರಳಿಚು, in the mediæval dialect.

e) that occasionally ಅಸು is suffixed to the themes mentioned under letter *a*, 1 and 3, *e.g.* ಎನಸು, ಬರಸು, ಹಾಕಸು, in the modern dialect.

Remarks.

As will be seen from § 150 ಇಸು is also used to form verbs from Saṁskṛita nouns, *e.g.* ಖಣ್ಡಿಸು, ಚಿತ್ರಿಸು, ಮುದ್ರಿಸು, ಶಬಿಸು, ವರ್ಧಿಸು, ರಕ್ಷಿಸು, ಭೋಗಿಸು, ಭಾವಿಸು, ಕಾಮಿಸು ಭುಂಜಿಸು, ಅಶಿಸು, ನಮಿಸು, ಭ್ರಮಿಸು, ರಮಿಸು, ಗಮಿಸು, ಜಪಿಸು, ಓಲಗಿಸು. Such verbs occur in the three dialects. *Cf.* § 215, 1, letter *b*.

Sometimes, in the ancient and mediæval dialect, also a euphonic ಯ್ is used in suffixing the ಇಸು, *e.g.* ಶುದ್ಧಯಿಸು, ತಾರಯಿಸು, ನಿರ್ಣಯಿಸು, ಪೂರಯಿಸು, ಮೇಳಯಿಸು, ನಮಿಯಿಸು, ಭ್ರಮಿಯಿಸು, ರಮಿಯಿಸು, ಗಮಿಯಿಸು, ಜಪಿಯಿಸು, (ಓಲಯಿಸು). *Cf.* § 215, 2, letter *c*.

Occasionally, chiefly in the ancient and mediæval dialect, the ಇ of ಇಸು is dropped, and we get such forms as ತಾರಯ್ಸು, ಪೂರಯ್ಸು; in ಓಲಗಿಸು the ಗ್ is changed into ಯ್, and ಓಲಯ್ಸು is produced. Also in Kannaḍa words that dropping takes place, so that ಕೋರಯಿಸು appears as ಕೋರಯ್ಸು (or ಕೋರೈಸು), ತೆಲ್ಲಯಿಸು as ತೆಲ್ಲಯ್ಸು (or ತೆಲ್ಲೈಸು), ತೇರಯಿಸು as ತೇರಯ್ಸು (or ತೇರೈಸು), ದಟ್ಟಯಿಸು as ದಟ್ಟಯ್ಸು, ಸೂಳಯಿಸು as ಸೂಳಯ್ಸು, ಹಾರಯಿಸು as ಹಾರಯ್ಸು, ಹೊಲ್ಲಯಿಸು as ಹೊಲ್ಲಯ್ಸು (ಹೊಲ್ಲೈಸು, see § 217).

In the mediæval dialect the euphonic ಯ್ in ಯಿಸು changes also into ವ್, *e. g.* ಓಲವಿಸು, ತರ್ಕವಿಸು, ತಾಱವಿಸು, ಪೂರವಿಸು, ಮೇಳವಿಸು, ಸೂಳವಿಸು, ಹಾರವಿಸು. *Cf.* § 215, 3, letter *a*.

152. In § 148 it has been stated that verbs are transitive and intransitive, and in § 149 that there are causal verbs too. There are no frequentative verbs in Kannaḍa; no verbal theme (dhâtu) can be turned into a frequentative one. But though **frequentative or iterative action** is never contained in a particular shape of a Kannaḍa verbal theme, it is expressed either by simple repetition (yugalôččaraṇa, dviḥprayôga) or triple repetition (triprayôga); see § 165, 211, and 339. Regarding **a sort of reflexive verb** see § 341.

153. In Kannaḍa not only verbal themes (dhâtu) are conjugated, but also declinable bases (liṅga, §§ 68. 90), that is to say nouns (nâmaliṅga), *e. g.* ಪೆಣ್ಡತಿ, ದೌಹಿತ್ರ, compound bases (samâsaliṅga), *e. g.* ಕವಿಕೇಶವ, ಮಲ್ಲಿಕಾರ್ಜುನಸುತ, ಕಲಾಪಣ್ಡಿತ, pronouns (sarvanâma), *e. g.* ಪೆಱ, attributive nouns or adjectives (guṇavačana) whether Kannaḍa or Saṁskṛita, *e. g.* ಒಳ್ಳಿದ, ಕೂಱಿದ, ನೇಱಿದ, ಅಸಿಯು, ಪಿಱಿಯು, ಉದ್ಧತ, ವೃದ್ಧ, and appellative nouns of number (saṅkhyĕ), *e. g.* ಒರ್ವ. See § 197.

When bases like the mentioned ones are conjugated they have been called, by Europeans, **appellative verbs or conjugated appellatives.** Kannaḍa grammarians use no name for them.

The author of the present grammar has not met with any instance of such a conjugated base in the mediæval dialect; in the modern dialect no conjugation of nouns, etc. is in use.

154. There are two different forms of the Kannaḍa verb that have been called **verbal participles or gerunds** by Europeans.

The first is **the preterit or past verbal participle** (bhûtakâlakriyĕ, pûrvakâlakriyĕ, pûrvakriyĕ, §§ 155—171); the second is **the present verbal participle** (vartamânakâlakriyĕ, vartamânakriyĕ, §§ 172. 173). See § 361.

155. **The first kind of the past participle is formed by suffixing the syllable** ದು to verbal themes (dhâtu, prakṛiti) ending in consonants (vyañjanânta), in the vowel ಇ (ikârânta), and in the vowel ಎ (ĕkârânta) without altering the themes, *e. g.* ಪೂಣ್ದು (of ಪೂಣ್), having admitted, ಮಾಣ್ದು (of ಮಾಣ್), having ceased, ಅನ್ದು (of ಅನ್, the later ಅನ್ನು), having said, ಎನ್ದು (of ಎನ್, the later ಎನ್ನು), having said, ತಿನ್ದು (of ತಿನ್, the later ತಿನ್ನು), having eaten, ಕೊಯ್ದು (of ಕೊಯ್, the later ಕೊಯ್ಯು), having cut,

ಗೆಯ್ದು (of ಗೆಯ್, the later ಗೆಯ್ಯು, *cf.* § 48), having tilled, ಪಾಯ್ದು (of ಪಾಯ್), having jumped, ಪೀರ್ದು (of ಪೀರ್), having sucked, ಸೋರ್ದು (of ಸೋರ್), having dropped, ಗೆಲ್ದು, having gained, ಮೆಲ್ದು, having chewed, ನೇಲ್ದು, having swung, ಕಳ್ದು, having stolen, ಮುಳ್ದು, having become angry, ಕೇಳ್ದು, having heard, ಸೀಳ್ದು, ಅಱ್ದು, ಬಾಱ್ದು, ಅಮರ್ದು, ಒಸರ್ದು, ತೊಡರ್ದು, ಪೊಡರ್ದು, ಬೆಮರ್ದು, ಅಗಲ್ದು, ಕನಲ್ದು, ಸಿಡಿಲ್ದು, ತಗುಳ್ದು, ನೆಗಱ್ದು; ಇಡಿದು (of ಇಡಿ), ಕುಡಿದು, ಕುಣಿದು, ಮುನಿದು, ಇಱಿದು, ಬಲಿದು, ಕುಸಿದು, ತಿಳಿದು, ಇೞಿದು; ನಡೆದು (of ನಡೆ), ಪಡೆದು, ನೆನೆದು, ಕರೆದು, ಒಲೆದು, ಒಸೆದು, ಕಳೆದು, ಎಱೆದು. Regarding the etymological explanation and original meaning see § 169.

Themes ending in ರ್ optionally double the ದ್ of ದು, *e. g.* ಪೀರ್ದ್ದು, ಸೋರ್ದ್ದು, ಅಮರ್ದ್ದು, ಒಸರ್ದ್ದು, ತೊಡರ್ದ್ದು, ಪೊಡರ್ದ್ದು (see § 371, 2; *cf.* § 119, *a*, 4).

The same formation of the past participle by means of ದು takes place also when verbal themes consist of one consonant with a long vowel, *e. g.* ಕಾದು (of ಕಾ), ಕೇದು (of ಕೇ), ಕೋದು (of ಕೋ), ತೇದು, ತೋದು, ಬಾದು, ಮೇದು, ಸೋದು.

Remark.

The grammarian Kêšava states that the syllable ದು consists of the vowel ಉ (ukâra) added to the augment (âgama) ದ. About ದ see §§ 175. 189.

156. In the formation of the second kind of the past participle the only difference is that in several themes **ತು is substituted for** ದು, *e. g.* ಅನ್ತು (of ಅನ್), ಕೂನ್ತು, ಕೂರ್ತು, ಕಲ್ತು, ನಿಲ್ತು, ಬಲ್ತು, ನೇಲ್ತು, ಪೋಲ್ತು, ಸೋಲ್ತು, ಅಱ್ತು, ಉಱ್ತು, ಕಿಱ್ತು, ಚಿಗುರ್ತು, ಬೆಮರ್ತು, ಕವಲ್ತು; ಆಱಿತು (of ಆಱಿ), ಕಲಿತು, ತಣಿತು, ಬಲಿತು, ಬಿಲಿತು, ಚಳಿತು; ಅೞಿತು (of ಅೞಿ), ಒೞಿತು, ಮೞಿತು; ಓತು (of ಓ), ಕೀತು (of ಕೀ), ಪೂತು, ಬಾತು, ಬೀತು.

A list of themes that form their past participle by means of ತು is given in sûtra 507 of the Šabdânušâsana, *viz.* ಕವಲ್, ಮಡಲ್, ಬಲ್, ಕಲ್, ಪೋಲ್, ಸಾಲ್, ಸೋಲ್, ಪೇಲ್, ನೂಲ್, ಕೂರ್, ಕಸರ್, ಕನರ್, ಕೊನರ್, ತಳಿರ್, ಬಿಳಿರ್, ಚಿಗುರ್, ಬೆಮರ್, ಅಱ್, ಉಱ್, ಕಿಱ್, ಚಳಿ, ಮೊಳೆ, ಅಱು, ಆಱಿ, ಕುಱಿ, ಬಾ, ಕೀ, ಪೂ, ಬೀ, ಓ, ಕೂನ್, ಪೇನ್, ಸೀನ್, ಅನ್, ನೋನ್, ಈನ್, to which it adds ಒೞಿ, ಅೞಿ in sûtra 508, ನಿಲ್ in sûtra 509, and ನೇಲ್ in sûtra 510, remarking that one may use ನೇಲ್ತು or ನೇಲ್ದು; under sûtra 553 it has also ಈತು (of ಈ).

In some instances **the use of** ದು and ತು **is optional,** *e. g.* ನೇಲ್ದು, ನೇಲ್ತು; ಬೆಮರ್ದು, ಬೆಮರ್ತು; ಮುಗುಳ್ದು, ಮುಗುಳ್ತು; ಆಱಿದು, ಆಱಿತು; ತಣಿದು, ತಣಿತು; ಮೞಿದು, ಮೞಿತು; ಬಲಿದು, ಬಲಿತು; ಬಾದು, ಬಾತು.

The use of suffixing ದು or ತು to themes with a final consonant has partly disappeared in the mediæval dialect, and still more so in the modern one, on account of a euphonic ಉ being added to the themes. See § 166.

157. The third kind of the past participle differs in so far from the first and second one, as in themes ending in a vowel this vowel (ು or ಇ) may be altered or dropped before ದು and ತು. In the ancient, mediæval and modern dialect **the vowel ು may be converted into the vowel ಅ**, *e. g.* ಎಱದು (= ಎಱಿದು), ಎಱದು (= ಎಱಿದು), ಒಡದು, ಒರದು, ಕಳದು, ನಡದು (in a šâsana between 750 and 814 A. D.), ನೆರದು (in a šâsana of 929 A. D.), ಪೊರದು (in a šâsana of 804 A. D.), ಬೆಳದು, ಹೊಳದು, ಬೆರತು, ಕೊಱತು; in the modern dialect **the vowel ಇ too may be changed into the vowel ಅ**, *e. g.* ಕಡದು (= ಕಡಿದು), ದುಡದು, ಸರದು, ಸಿಡದು, ಸುಲದು, ಹುರದು, ಹುಱತು. (*Cf.* §§ 60; 151, *a*, 4; 151, *b*, 2; 151, *c*, 3; 165, *a*, 3. 4. 5; 172; 180, 5.)

158. The fourth kind of the past participle is formed by eliding the final vowel (ು or ಇ) of the theme, producing a theme ending in a half consonant, and then suffixing ದು or ತು, *e. g.* ಅರ್ತು (= ಅಱಿತು of ಅಱಿ), ಉರ್ದು (= ಉರಿದು of ಉರಿ), ಎಸ್ತು (= ಎಸೆದು of ಎಸೆ), ಒದ್ದು (= ಒದೆದು), ಒನ್ತು (= ಒನೆದು), ಕಿಸ್ತು (= ಕಿಸಿದು), ಕುದ್ದು (= ಕುದಿದು), ಕೊಸ್ತು (= ಕೊಸೆದು), ನುಸ್ತು (= ನುಸಿದು), ಪೊದ್ದು (= ಪೊದೆದು), ಬಸ್ತು (= ಬಸಿದು), ಮಸ್ತು (ಮಸೆದು), ಮಿತ್ತು (= ಮಿದಿದು), ಸದ್ದು (= ಸದೆದು), ಸಸ್ತು (= ಸಸಿದು), ಹದ್ದು (= ಹದಿದು), ಹಸ್ತು (ಹಸಿದು), ಹೊತ್ತು (= ಹೊದೆದು), ಹೊದ್ದು (= ಹೊದೆದು), ಹೊಸ್ತು (= ಹೊಸೆದು). *Cf.* § 165, letter *a*, 7.

The mentioned past participles occur only in the modern dialect except ಪೊದ್ದು which is found likewise in the mediæval one, and ಮಿತ್ತು which, according to the Šabdânušâsana sûtra 482, is met with in the ancient one.

159. The fifth kind of the past participle is formed by eliding the final consonant of themes before the termination ದು or ತು. This formation is nearly wholly restricted to the modern dialect. We have

1, the elision of ನ್, *e. g.* ಆತು (= ಆನ್ತು), ನಾತು or ನಾದು (= ನಾನ್ದು), ನೋತು (= ನೋನ್ತು), ಸೀತು (= ಸೀನ್ತು), for which there is the instance ಈದು (of ಈನ್) in the ancient dialect (*cf.* the ಈತು of ಈ in § 156);

2, the elision of ಯ್, *e. g.* ಆದು (= ಆಯ್ದು), ಮಾದು (= ಮಾಯ್ದು). ಹಾದು (= ಹಾಯ್ದು); *cf.* ನೇದು (= ನೆಯ್ದು);

3, the elision of ಱ್, *e. g.* ನಾತು (of ನಾಱ್);

4, the elision of ಲ್, *e. g.* ಜೋತು (=ಜೋಲ್ದು), ನೂತು (=ನೂಲ್ತು), ನೇತು (=ನೇಲ್ತು), ಸಾತು (=ಸಾಲ್ಟು), ಸೋತು (=ಸೋಲ್ತು, used also in the mediæval dialect), ಹೇತು (=ಹೇಲ್ತು), ಹೊತು (=ಹೊಲ್ತು);

5, the elision of ರ್ of the ancient theme ಕುಳಿರ್, *i. e.* ಕುಳಿತು (=ಕುಳಿದುಱ್);

6, the elision of ರ್ together with the preceding vowel ಇ of the ancient theme ಕುಳಿರ್, *i. e.* ಕುಳ್ತು (=ಕುಳಿದುಱ್), a form used in the mediæval dialect;

7, the elision of ರ್ of ಕೂರ್, a theme formed from the ancient ಕುಳಿರ್, *i. e.* ಕೂತು (=ಕುಳಿದುಱ್).

160. **The sixth kind of the past participle is formed by changing or converting the final consonant** into another one **before** ದು **and** ತು. This changing takes place in the ancient, mediæval, and modern dialect. We find

1, the conversion of ಟ್ into ಱ್ before ದು, *e. g.* ಎದುಱ್ (=ಎಟ್ಟು), ಬಿದುಱ್ (=ಬಿಟ್ಟು) in the ancient dialect, and ಅದುಱ್ (=ಅಟ್ಟು), ಬಿದುಱ್ (=ಬಿಟ್ಟು) in the mediæval one (*cf.* § 236);

2, the conversion of ಟ್ into ತ್ before ತು, *e. g.* ಅತ್ತು (=ಅಟ್ಟು), ಉತ್ತು (=ಉಟ್ಟು), ಕಿತ್ತು (=ಕಿಟ್ಟು) in the mediæval and modern dialect;

3, the conversion of ದ್ into ತ್ before ತು in ಮುತ್ತು (of ಮುದು) of the ancient and mediæval dialect;

4, the conversion of ಟ್ (or ಟ್ with the euphonic ಉ, *i. e.* ಟು) into ತ್ before ತು, *e. g.* ಉತ್ತು (=ಉತುಱ್, of ಉಟ್ or ಉಟು), ಎಚ್ಚಿತ್ತು (of ಎಚ್ಚಿಟ್ or ಎಚ್ಚಿಟು), ಅಸತ್ತು, ತೆಪ್ಪತ್ತು, ಪೆತ್ತು, ಪೊತ್ತು, ಬೇಸತ್ತು of the ancient and mediæval dialect, and ಅಸತ್ತು, ಎಚ್ಚತ್ತು, ತೆಪ್ಪತ್ತು, ಬೇಸತ್ತು, ಹೆತ್ತು, ಹೊತ್ತು of the mediæval and modern dialect; ತತ್ತು (of ತಟ್ = ತಟು) occurs in the Jaimini Bhârata; exceptions to this rule in the ancient dialect are *e. g.* ಅಟುತು, ಬಿಟುತು, ಅತುಱ್, ಆತುಱ್, ಅಟ್ಕಿತುಱ್, ಬೆಳ್ಕತುಱ್;

5, the conversion of ಲ್ into ತ್ before ತು in ನಿತ್ತು (=ನಿಲ್ತು) of the modern dialect;

6, the conversion of ಱ್, the subsitute of ಟ್ (see No. 1), into ದ್ before ದು, *e. g.* ಅದ್ದು (=ಅಟ್ಟು, ಅದುಱ್), ಎದ್ದು (=ಎಟ್ಟು, ಎದುಱ್), ಬಿದ್ದು (=ಬಿಟ್ಟು, ಬಿದುಱ್) in the mediæval dialect, and ಎದ್ದು (=ಎಟ್ಟು, ಎದುಱ್), ಬಿದ್ದು (=ಬಿಟ್ಟು, ಬಿದುಱ್) in the modern one;

7, the conversion of an original ರ್ into ದ್ before ದು in ಇದ್ದು (=ಇದುಱ್) in the mediæval and modern dialect;

8, the conversion of ಲ್ into ದ್ before ದು in ಗೆದ್ದು (=ಗೆಲ್ದು) of the mediæval and modern dialect, and in ಮೆದ್ದು (=ಮೆಲ್ದು) of the modern one;

9, the conversion of ಳ್ into ದ್ before ದು in ಕದ್ದು (= ಕಳ್ದು) of the mediæval and modern dialect;

10, the conversion of ರ್ into ನ್ before ದು in ತನ್ದು (of ತರ್, ತರು) and ಬನ್ದು (of ಬರ್, ಬರು) of the ancient, mediæval and modern dialect;

11, the conversion of ಲ್ into ನ್ before ದು in ಕೊನ್ದು (of ಕೊಲ್, ಕೊಲ್ಲು), ನಿನ್ದು (of ನಿಲ್, ನಿಲ್ಲು), and ಸನ್ದು (of ಸಲ್, ಸಲ್ಲು) of the ancient, mediæval and modern dialect;

12, the conversion of ಲ್ into ನ್ before ತು in ನಿನ್ತು (= ನಿಲ್ತು) of the mediæval and modern dialect;

13, the conversion of the ಳ್ of ಕುಳ್, a mutilated form of the ancient ಕುಳಿರ್ (see § 159, No. 6), into ನ್ before ತು in ಕುನ್ತು (= ಕುಳ್ತು, *i. e.* ಕುಳಿರ್ದು) of the modern dialect.

161. The seventh kind of the past participle is formed **by changing not only the final consonant** of the theme before the termination ತು, **but also its initial vowel.**

To this kind belong only the three themes ಕಿಱ್ (ಕಿಱು), ಗಿಱ್ (ಗಿಱು), ತಿಱ್ (ತಿಱು) of the ancient and mediæval dialect, which convert their initial vowel ಇ into ಎ and their ಱ್ into ತ್, so that their participles are ಕೆತ್ತು, ಗೆತ್ತು, ತೆತ್ತು (see § 66).

ತೆತ್ತು occurs likewise in the modern dialect wherein its theme, however, appears as ತೆಱು, which is found also in the mediæval one.

162. The eighth kind of the past participle is formed by **changing,** *i. e.* shortening, **the vowel** of the theme and **inserting** a euphonic ನ್ before the termination ದು.

The themes which do so, are ಬೇ, ಮೀ, ನೋ; their participles are ಬೆನ್ದು, ಮಿನ್ದು, ನೊನ್ದು in the ancient and mediæval dialect, and also in the modern one, though their themes herein are ಬೇಯು, ಮೀಯು and ನೋಯು (see § 48).

163. The ninth kind of the past participle is formed by **changing,** *i. e.* shortening, **the vowel** of the theme and **inserting** a euphonic ತ್ before the termination ತು.

The themes are ಈ and ಸಾ (ಸಾಯ್), and their participles are ಇತ್ತು and ಸತ್ತು in the ancient and mediæval dialect, and also in the modern one, though the themes herein appear as ಈಯು and ಸಾಯು.

Remark.

The form of ಸಾ is in sûtras 477. 566 of the Śabdânuśâsana; it is not given in the Karṇâṭakabhâshâbhûshaṇa which adduces only the past participle ಸತ್ತು:—

the Šabdamaṇidarpaṇa under sûtra 48 clearly gives the form of ಸಾಯ್; under sûtra 240 it has ಸಾಯಿಸಾ, which may be either ಸಾಯ್ ಈ or ಸಾ ಈ; it has neither ಸಾಯ್ nor ಸಾ in its dhâtupâṭha. The present-future participle generally is ಸಾವ, instead of ಸಾಯ್ವ, in the ancient and mediæval dialect (§ 180, 1, remark).

164. From § 155 up to § 163 the syllables ದು and ತು underwent no changes when they were used as suffixes for the past participle; in the present paragraph instances of the tenth kind of the past participle will be adduced, that is to say instances of the participle in the formation of which the suffixes ದು and ತು are changed. Namely

1, ದು is converted into ಡು after the theme ಉಣ್ (ಉಣ್ಣು), the past participle of which is ಉಣ್ಡು in the ancient, mediæval and modern dialect;

2, ದು is converted into ಡು after the theme ಕಾಣ್ (ಕಾಣು), its vowel being shortened, so that its past participle is ಕಣ್ಡು in the ancient, mediæval and modern dialect;

3, ದು is converted into ಡು after the theme ಕೊಳ್ (ಕೊಳ್ಳು), the final ಳ್ being changed into ಣ್, and ಕೊಣ್ಡು becomes the participle for the three dialects;

4, ತು is converted into ಟು after the themes ಅಡು, ಇಡು, ಉಡು, ನಡು, ಪಡು, ಬಿಡು, ಮಡು, ಸುಡು and ಬಿಸುಡು, their final ಡು being changed into ಟ್, so that ಅಟ್ಟು, ಇಟ್ಟು, ಉಟ್ಟು, ನಟ್ಟು, ಪಟ್ಟು, ಬಿಟ್ಟು, ಸುಟ್ಟು are the participles for the three dialects, and ಮಟ್ಟು, ಬಿಸುಟ್ಟು those for the ancient one.

In the ancient dialect ಬಿಸುಟ್ಟು is written also ಬಿಸುಟು, a form that is common in the mediæval one.

The original forms of the past participles of the modern dialect ಬಿಸಾಟು (of ಬಿಸಾಡು = ಬಿಸುಡು) and ಹೊಱಟು (of ಹೊಱಡು) must have been ಬಿಸಾಟ್ಟು (ಬಿಸಾಡು + ತು) and ಹೊಱಟ್ಟು (ಹೊಱಡು + ತು); *cf.* No. 6;

5, the past participle ಹೊಱಟು, mentioned under No. 4, is, by contraction, vulgarly changed into ಹೊಣ್ಟು;

6, the past participle ಬೆರಣ್ಟು is identical in form with the theme, *i. e.* ಬೆರಣ್ಟು (Šabdamaṇidarpaṇa sûtra 241); the participle's original form must have been ಬೆರಣ್ಟು, *i. e.* ಬೆರಣ್ಟು with the termination ತು which was converted into ಟು;

7, ತು is converted into ಟು after the ancient and mediæval themes ಕುಡು and ತುಡು, these changing their initial vowel ಉ into ಒ and taking the forms ಕೊಟ್ and ತೊಟ್, so that the past participles become ಕೊಟ್ಟು and ತೊಟ್ಟು.

The themes ಕುಡು and ತುಡು occasionally appear as ಕೊಡು and ತೊಡು in the mediæval dialect, and always so in the modern one; the participles remain ಕೊಟ್ಟು, ತೊಟ್ಟು;

8, ತು is converted into ಟು after the ancient theme ಕಿಡು, this changing its initial vowel ಇ into ಎ and taking the form ಕೆಟ್, so that the past participle becomes ಕೆಟ್ಟು.

In the mediæval and modern dialect the theme is ಕೆಡು; the participle remains ಕೆಟ್ಟು;

9, ತು is converted into ಚು, after the ancient theme ಪಸು which becomes ಪಚ್, so that the past participle is ಪಚ್ಚು;

10, ತು is converted into ಚು after the ancient (and mediæval) themes ಇಸು and ಬಿಸು, these changing the initial vowel ಇ into ಎ and taking the forms ಎಚ್ and ಬೆಚ್, so that the participles become ಎಚ್ಚು and ಬೆಚ್ಚು.

In the mediæval dialect the themes generally are ಎಸು, ಬೆಸು; the participles remain ಎಚ್ಚು, ಬೆಚ್ಚು;

11, ತು is converted into ಕು after the themes ನಗು, ಮಿಗು (and ancient ತಗು, Šabdamaṇidarpaṇa under sûtra 241) of the ancient, mediæval and modern dialect, and ಸಿಗು of the mediæval and modern one, the themes taking the forms ನಕ್, ಮಿಕ್, (ತಕ್), ಸಿಕ್, so that the past participles become ನಕ್ಕು, ಮಿಕ್ಕು, (ತಕ್ಕು), ಸಿಕ್ಕು; *cf.* § 165, letter, *a*, 7;

12, ತು is converted into ಕು after the themes ಉಗು and ಪುಗು of the ancient and mediæval dialect, the themes changing their initial vowel ಉ into ಒ and taking the forms ಒಕ್ and ಪೊಕ್, so that the past participles become ಒಕ್ಕು and ಪೊಕ್ಕು.

The themes ಉಗು and ಪುಗು appear also as ಒಗು and ಪೊಗು in the mediæval dialect, the participles remaining ಒಕ್ಕು, ಪೊಕ್ಕು. In the modern dialect ಪೊಗು has taken the form of ಹೊಗು which occurs also in the mediæval one; the past participle is ಹೊಕ್ಕು; *cf.* § 165, letter *a*, 7;

13, ತು is converted into ಪು after the ancient theme ತವು, this taking the form ತಪ್, so that the past participle becomes ತಪ್ಪು; see an instance in § 165 under *b*, 1.

165. From § 155 to § 164 we have seen how the Kannaḍa past participle is formed in various ways when the syllables ದು and ತು are suffixed to the theme; now its eleventh kind follows, a short form which appears without ದು and ತು, is often identical as to shape with the verbal theme (which at the same time often is a verbal noun), and may be considered to be a

verbal noun (see § 100 compared with § 60; § 169). Compare the short past participle with final ಇ in § 168.

This short participle occurs only when a verb directly follows it which shows that the sense of the past participle is meant, as it does not bear the characteristic mark of a participle itself. See, however, § 198, 6, where the third person neuter singular is directly formed from it.

It is used in the ancient, mediæval and modern dialect.

It includes **two classes,** it being put either before a verb that differs from that from which it has been formed, or before a verb that is identical; in the second case it is repetition (§§ 152. 211).

a) **The short participle used before verbs that are not the same as that from which it has been formed,** chiefly before ಕೊಳ್ (ಕೊಳ್ಳು, *cf.* § 341) and ತರ್ (ತರು):

1, Instances with regard to **unaltered verbal themes with a final consonant,** are *e. g.* ಎೞ್ ತರ್ (=ಎೞ್ದು ತರ್), ಕಾಯ್ ತರ್ (=ಕಾಯ್ದು ತರ್), ಪಾಯ್ ತರ್ (=ಪಾಯ್ದು ತರ್), ಬೞ್ ತರ್ (=ಬೞ್ದು ತರ್), ಸಾರ್ ತರ್ (=ಸಾರ್ದು ತರ್), ಸೀೞ್ ಕೆಡಹು (=ಸೀೞ್ದು ಕೆಡಹು), ಹೊಯ್ ಕೊಳ್ (=ಹೊಯ್ದು ಕೊಳ್).

2, Instances with regard to **unaltered themes with a final vowel,** are *e. g.* ಇೞಿ ತರ್ (=ಇೞಿದು ತರ್), ಉಗು ತರ್ (=ಒಕ್ಕು ತರ್), ಒಗೆ ತರ್ (=ಒಗೆದು ತರ್), ಕಱೆ ತರ್ (=ಕಱೆದು ತರ್), ಕೞಿ ತರ್, ಕವಿ ತರ್, ಕುಸಿ ಬೀೞ್, ತವು ತರ್, ತಿರಿ ತಿನ್, ತಿೞಿ ತರ್, ತಿವಿ ಕೊಳ್, ತೆಗೆ ತರ್, ದೊರೆ ಕೊಳ್, ನಡೆ ತರ್, ಪದೆ ಪೋಯ್, ಪರಿ ತರ್, ಪಿಡಿ ತರ್, ಪಿಡಿ ಪಡೆ, ಪಿಡಿ ಪೆಱು, ಪುಗು ತರ್, ಬಿಡು ತರ್, ಬಿಲಿ ತರ್, ಸುರಿ ತರ್, ಹರಿ ತರ್, ಹಿಡಿ ತರ್.

3, Instances with regard to **themes that have changed their final vowel** ಎ **into** ಅ (which often are verbal nouns and occasionally appear in the mediæval dialect and frequently in the modern one), are *e. g.* ಎೞ ಕೊಳ್ (=ಎೞೆದು ಕೊಳ್), ಎಱ ಕೊಳ್ (=ಎಱೆದು ಕೊಳ್), ಎೞ ತರ್ (=ಎೞೆದು ತರ್), ಒಡ ಕೊಳ್, ಒರ ಕೊಳ್, ಕರ ಕೊಳ್, ಕರ ತರ್, ಕೞ ತರ್, ಕಳ ಕೊಳ್, ಕೆರ ಕೊಳ್, ಕೊಱ ಕೊಳ್, ತಡ ಕೊಳ್, ತೆಗ ತರ್, ತೆೞ ಕೊಳ್, ತೊಡ ಕೊಳ್, ತೊಳ ಕೊಳ್, ದೊರ ಕೊಳ್, ನಡ ಕೊಳ್, ಬಡ ಕೊಳ್, ಬೆಳ ಕೊಳ್, ಹೊಡ ಕೊಳ್. *Cf.* § 157.

4, Instances with regard to **themes that have changed their final vowel** ಇ **into** ಅ (which often are verbal nouns and not unfrequently occur in the modern dialect), are *e. g.* ಇಡ ಕೊಳ್ (=ಇಡಿದು ಕೊಳ್), ಇಱ ಕೊಳ್ (=ಇಱಿದು ಕೊಳ್), ಉಱ ಕೊಳ್ (=ಉಱಿದು ಕೊಳ್), ಕಡ ಕೊಳ್, ಕಸ ಕೊಳ್, ಕುಡ ಕೊಳ್, ತೞ ಕೊಳ್, ತಿಳ ಕೊಳ್, ತುಱ ಕೊಳ್, ದಣ ಕೊಳ್, ದುಡ ಕೊಳ್, ನಸ

ಕೊಳ್, ಬೞಿ ಕೊಳ್, ಬಿರ ಕೊಳ್, ಮುಡ ಕೊಳ್, ಮುಱಿ ಕೊಳ್, ಸರ ಕೊಳ್, ಸುಱಿ ಕೊಳ್, ಸುಲ ಕೊಳ್, ಹಱಿ ಕೊಳ್, ಹಿಡ ಕೊಳ್, ಹಿಡ ತರ್, ಹೊಲ ಕೊಳ್. *Cf.* § 157.

5, **Instances with regard to themes that have changed their final** ಇ **into** ಉ (which partly are verbal nouns and occasionally occur in the modern dialect), are *e. g.* ಇಡು ಕೊಳ್ (=ಇಡಿದು ಕೊಳ್), ಇೞು ಕೊಳ್ (=ಇೞಿದು ಕೊಳ್), ಉೞು ಕೊಳ್ (=ಉೞಿದು ಕೊಳ್), ಕವು ಕೊಳ್ (=ಕವಿದು ಕೊಳ್), ಕುಡು ಕೊಳ್, ತಿಳು ಕೊಳ್, ದಣು ಕೊಳ್, ದುಡು ಕೊಳ್, ನಸು ಕೊಳ್, ಬಡು ಕೊಳ್, ಬೞು ಕೊಳ್, ಬಿರು ಕೊಳ್, ಮುಡು ಕೊಳ್, ಮುೞು ಕೊಳ್, ಸುೞು ಕೊಳ್, ಹಿಡು ಕೊಳ್, ಹೊಲು ಕೊಳ್. *Cf.* § 151, letter *b,* 2.

6, **Instances with regard to themes that have dropped their final syllable,** are ಅಯ್ (=ಅಯ್ದಿ of ಅಯ್ದು) ತರ್ (used in the ancient and mediæval dialect), ಪೋ (=ಪೋಗಿ of ಪೋಗು) ತರ್ (used in the ancient dialect), and ಮಲ (=ಮಲಗಿ of ಮಲಗು) ಕೊಳ್ (used in the modern dialect). *Cf.* letter *b,* 3.

Here may be adduced the vulgar ಉಡು ತೊಡಿಸು (=ಉಡಿಸಿ ತೊಡಿಸು; **see** § 166). *Cf.* ಪಱ ಪಱೂಸು **undor** *b,* 4.

7, **Instances with regard to themes that have dropped the vowel of their final** ಗಿ, ಗು **or** ಗೆ **and converted the remaining consonant** ಗ್ **into** ಕ್ before the verbs ಕೊಡು and ಕೊಳ್ (ಕೊಳ್ಳು), are *e. g.* ಅಕ್ (=ಅಗಿದು of ಅಗಿ) ಕೊಳ್, ಒಕ್ (of ಒಗೆ) ಕೊಡು, ಒಕ್ (of ಒಗೆ) ಕೊಳ್, ತೆಕ್ (of ತೆಗೆ) ಕೊಳ್, ನಕ್ (of ನಗು) ಕೊಳ್, ಬಕ್ (of ಬಗೆ) ಕೊಳ್, ಬಿಕ್ (of ಬಿಗಿ) ಕೊಳ್, ಮೊಕ್ (of ಮೊಗೆ) ಕೊಳ್, ಸಿಕ್ (of ಸಿಗು) ಕೊಳ್. The instances occur only in the modern dialect. *Cf.* § 158; § 164, 11. 12.

b) **The short participle used before verbs that are identical with that from which it has been formed,** *i. e.* **in repetition** (§ 211):—

1, Instances with regard to themes that, **in an unaltered form,** precede an identical verb, are *e. g.* ಕಡಿ ಕಡಿ (=ಕಡಿದು ಕಡಿ), ಕವಿ ಕವಿ (=ಕವಿದು ಕವಿ), ಕಾಯ್ ಕಾಯ್ (=ಕಾಯ್ದು ಕಾಯ್), ಕರೆ ಕರೆ (=ಕರೆದು ಕರೆ), ಕಱೆ ಕಱೆ (=ಕಱೆದು ಕಱೆ), ಕುಡಿ ಕುಡಿ (=ಕುಡಿದು ಕುಡಿ), ಕುಣಿ ಕುಣಿ, ಕುನಿ ಕುನಿ, ಜಡಿ ಜಡಿ, ಜಿಗಿ ಜಿಗಿ, ತಱಿ ತಱಿ, ತಿಳಿ ತಿಳಿ, ತಿವಿ ತಿವಿ, ತುೞಿ ತುೞಿ, ತೆಗೆ ತೆಗೆ, ನನೆ ನನೆ, ನಲಿ ನಲಿ, ನೆಗೆ ನೆಗೆ, ನೆನೆ ನೆನೆ, ಪರಿ ಪರಿ, ಪಿಡಿ ಪಿಡಿ, ಪೊಗೆ ಪೊಗೆ, ಬಗಿ ಬಗಿ, ಬಡಿ ಬಡಿ, ಬಿರಿ ಬಿರಿ, ಮಡಿ ಮಡಿ, ಮಣಿ ಮಣಿ, ಮಿಡಿ ಮಿಡಿ, ಮುಱಿ ಮುಱಿ, ಮೊಗೆ ಮೊಗೆ, ಮೊರೆ ಮೊರೆ, ಸಿಡಿ ಸಿಡಿ, ಸುಱಿ ಸುಱಿ, ಸುಲಿ ಸುಲಿ, ಸುೞಿ ಸುೞಿ, ಸೆಳೆ ಸೆಳೆ, ಹಿಡಿ ಹಿಡಿ, ಹಿರಿ ಹಿರಿ, ಹೊಗೆ ಹೊಗೆ, ಹೊಡೆ ಹೊಡೆ.

It is to be observed that the instances always presuppose the second verb to be in the form of the past participle ending in ದು (§ 155) or also in the past tense, as ಕಡಿ ಕಡಿದು, ಕವಿ ಕವಿದು, etc. (see § 211, 4). They are found in the three dialects. In Abhinavapampa 13, 53 there is ತವು ತಪ್ಪು ದುವುಭಯಬಳದ . . . ಸೈನ್ಯಂ.

2, Instances with regard to themes that have lost their final vowel before an identical verb (which are found in the mediæval and modern dialect), are *e. g.* ಕಳ (*i. e.* ಕಳೆದು of ಕಳೆ) ಕಳೆ, ತೆಗ (= ತೆಗೆದು of ತೆಗೆ) ತೆಗೆ, ನೆಗ ನೆಗೆ, ಬೆಳ ಬೆಳೆ, ಮೊಗ ಮೊಗೆ, ಸೆಳ ಸೆಳೆ, ಹೊಡ ಹೊಡೆ, ಹೊಸ ಹೊಸೆ, ಹೊಳ ಹೊಳೆ. *Cf.* § 151, letter *a*, 4 and *b*, 2.

Remark.

In such an instance the short participle may be doubled, *e. g.* ಬಡ ಬಡ ಬಡೆ, also when another verb follows, *e. g.* ಬಡ ಬಡ ಕೊಳ್. See § 211, 8.

3, Instances with regard to themes that have dropped their last syllable before an identical verb, are *e. g.* ತಿರ (of ತಿರಗು) ತಿರಗು, ತಿರಿ (of ತಿರಿಗು) ತಿರಿಗು, ತಿರು ತಿರುಗು, ತೊಲ ತೊಲಗು, ತೊಳ ತೊಳಗು, ನಿಲಿ ನಿಲಿಕು, ಬೆಳ ಬೆಳಗು, ಮುಱು ಮುಱುಗು, ಮೊಗ ಮೊಗಸು, ಮೊಱ ಮೊಱಗು, ಸೊಗ ಸೊಗಸು. *Cf.* letter *a*, 6. The instances belong to the three dialects. See § 211, 7.

Remarks.

In such an instance the short participle may be doubled, *e. g.* ತೊಳ ತೊಳ ತೊಳಗು, ನಡ ನಡ ನಡುಗು (or ನಡುಗು), ಬೆಳ ಬೆಳ ಬೆಳಗು (used in the ancient dialect, see § 211, 10. See also § 339, 8.

Also in the repetition of nouns the last syllable has been dropped, as in ತಿಂಗ ತಿಂಗಳು, ಮೊದ ಮೊದಲ್ (see § 303, 1, *a. b. c. d*).

4, An instance in which the vowel of the penultima too has been lost before an identical verb, is ಪಱ ಪಱೊಸು (= ಪಱೊಸಿ ಪಱೊಸು, of the mediæval dialect). *Cf.* ಉಡು ತೊಡಿಸು under *a*, 6.

166. Hitherto the formation of the past participle of verbal themes ending in consonants and the vowels ಇ and ಉ has been treated of; it still remains to be introduced the formation of the twelfth kind of the past participle. It concerns the themes which end in the vowel ಉ in the three dialects.

Their past participle is formed by suffixing the vowel ಇ, in the ancient, mediæval and modern dialect. The final ಉ is treated as a euphonic letter, disappearing before the ಇ according to the rule of sandhi (§ 213, *seq.*).

Instances are ಅಳ್ಕಿ (of ಅಳ್ಕು), having feared, ಒಗ್ಗಿ (of ಒಗ್ಗು), having met together, ನಚ್ಚಿ (of ನಚ್ಚು), having trusted, ಮೆಚ್ಚಿ (of ಮೆಚ್ಚು), having liked,

ಕುಟ್ಟಿ (of ಕುಟ್ಟು), ಮುಟ್ಟಿ, ಒಡ್ಡಿ, ಹಿಣ್ಣಿ, ಎತ್ತಿ, ಮುತ್ತಿ, ಪೊರ್ದಿ, ಆಗಿ, ಹೋಗಿ, ಪೋಗಿ, ಚಾಚಿ, ಮಾಜಿ, ಆಡಿ, ಪಾಡಿ, ಕಾಱಿ, ಪಾಱಿ, ಬೀೞಿ, ಸಾಱಿ, ಪಾಸಿ, ಉಡಿಸಿ, ಒಡಱಿ, ಕೆದಱಿ, ಗದಱಿ, ಬೆದಱಿ, ನಗಿಸಿ, ಕಾಣಿಸಿ, ಓದಿಸಿ, ಅಲರ್ಚಿ, ಇದಿರ್ಚಿ, ನಿಗುಮ್ಬಿಸಿ, ಓಸರಿಸಿ, ಕಳವಳಿಸಿ.

ಆಗು, ಪೋಗು, ಹೋಗು form also the irregular past participles ಆಯ್, ಪೋಯ್, ಹೋಯ್, used for the third person neuter singular of the past tense (see § 199, and *cf.* § 176). ಆಯ್ appears also as ಅಯ್, regarding which see § 176, and compare ಅಗು (= ಆಗು) in the Dictionary[1].

Themes with final ಱು generally form their past participle by means of the vowel ಇ; but if the ಱು is changed into ಱ್, which occasionally and in some instances always is done (§§ 59. 61. 160, 4), they suffix ದು or ತು (§§ 155. 156), *e. g.* ಕಾರ್ದು (of ಕಾಱ್ = ಕಾಱು), ತೋರ್ದು, ಪಾರ್ದು, ಬೀರ್ದು, ಮೀರ್ದು, ಒಳರ್ದು, ಕೆದರ್ದು, ಪೆಳರ್ದು, ಬೆದರ್ದು; ಅರ್ತು, ಆರ್ತು, ಅಟ್ಟಿರ್ತು, ಬೆಳ್ಕರ್ತು, and before the syllable ತು their final ಱ್ is sometimes converted into ತ್ (ಎಬ್ಬಿತ್ತು, etc., § 160, 4).

In the mediæval dialect a theme that in the ancient one ends in a consonant, is not unfrequently made to end in ಉ, in which case the vowel ಇ is used to form its past participle, *e. g.* ಜೋಲಿ (= ಜೋಲ್ದು), ಊಳಿ (= ಊಳ್ದು), ಕೇಳಿ (= ಕೇಳ್ದು), ತಾಳಿ, ಪೇೞಿ, ಹೂೞಿ, ಹೇೞಿ, ಹೋರಿ, ಅದರಿ, ಕೊನರಿ, ಚಿಗುರಿ, ನಿಗುರಿ, ಅಗಲಿ, ಕನಲಿ, ತೊೞಲಿ, ಬೞಲಿ, ಸಡಲಿ, ಉರುಳಿ, ಉಗುೞಿ; this, as a rule, is done in the modern dialect. *Cf.* §§ 48. 181, 1. 198, 4. 5.

167. The thirteenth kind of the past participle which, as it would appear, occurs only in the mediæval dialect, **is formed by means of the syllable ಇದು.** This is, instead of ದು (§ 155), suffixed to themes that in the ancient dialect, without exception, end in consonants, but in later times have optionally received a euphonic ಉ (*cf.* the close of § 166), *e. g.* ಕೇಳಿದು (of ಕೇಳು, = ಕೇಳ್ದು), ತೂಳಿದು (of ತೂಳು, = ತೂಳ್ದು), ಸಾರಿದು

[1] Dr. J. F. Fleet draws the author's attention to some copper-plate grants in which ಅಯ್ and ಆಯ್ have been used directly for ಅಗಿ and ಆಗಿ in the forms ಮೂಡಯ್, ಮೂಡಾಯ್, ತೆಂಕಯ್, ತೆಂಕಾಯ್, etc. (for ಮೂಡಗಿ, ಮೂಡಾಗಿ, ತೆಂಕಗಿ, ತೆಂಕಾಗಿ, etc., to the east, to the south, etc.). He writes: "With one exception, noted further on, I have found these forms in only some of the spurious copper-plate grants of the Western Gaṅga series, from Mysore. These grants claim to be of various dates from A. D. 248 upwards. But there are strong reasons for fixing the eleventh century as the period when most of them were fabricated." The one exception occurs in a stone inscription at Bannûr in the Tiruma-Kûḍlu-narasîpura tâluka, Mysore district, which appears to include the word ಪಡುವಾಯ್ (or ಪಡುವ್ಪೋಯ್?), and may belong to about A. D. 920. *Cf.* § 281. We remark that ಅಗಿ appears as ಅಯಿ in Telugu.

(of ಸಾರು, =ಸಾರ್ದು), ಸೀೞಿದು (of ಸೀೞು, =ಸೀೞ್ದು), ಸೂರುೞಿದು (of ಸೂರುೞು, =ಸೂರುೞ್ದು), ಹೋರಿದು (of ಹೋರು, =ಹೋರ್ದು), ಹೋಱಿದು (of ಹೋಱು, =ಹೋಱ್ದು), ಬಱಲಿದು (of ಬಱಲು, =ಬಱಲ್ದು), ಮರೞಿದು (of ಮರೞು, =ಮರೞ್ದು). In a śâsana of A. D. 1123 we find ಗೆಲುದು (for ಗೆಲ್ದು) in which a euphonic ಉ is used for ಇ.

Towards the end of the mediæval period (*e. g.* in the Kannaḍa Râmâyaṇa) here and there we meet with forms in which the ಇದು has been used to form the past participle even of verbal themes that end in ಉ in the three dialects (§ 166), *e. g.* ಚಾಚಿದು (of ಚಾಚು, =a ಚಾಚ್ದು), ಮೆಟ್ಟಿದು (of ಮೆಟ್ಟು, =a ಮೆಟ್ಟು), ನೋಡಿದು (of ನೋಡು, =a ನೋಡ್ದು). Also the curious past participle ನಿನ್ದಿದು (=ನಿಸ್ದು, of ನಿಲ್ಲು) occurs in the Râmâyaṇa.

The vowel ಇ in ಇದು in this case is, of course, nothing else but a euphonic letter employed before the real termination ದು.

168. The question naturally arises how the vowel ಇ of § 166 came to represent the suffix for the past participle of verbal themes ending in ಉ in the three dialects. It appears to be certain that ಇ originally was a euphonic or enunciative augment put before ದು (§ 155 *seq.*) in order to avoid forms like ಪಾಡ್ದು (of ಪಾಡು), having sung (actually used in the Jaimini Bhârata 21, 57), ಮಾಡ್ದು (of ಮಾಡು), having made (used in the Dharmaparîkshĕ, edited by the Rev. G. Würth in his ಪ್ರಾಕ್ಕಾವ್ಯಮಾಲಿಕೆ vačana 1301), ಕುಟ್ದು, ನಜ್ದು, ಮುಜ್ದು, etc. Such forms, certainly, are clumsy and cacophonous, and led people to use the enunciative augment ಇ between the theme and ದು, as they actually did in the forms ಕೇೞಿದು, ತೂೞಿದು, etc. and then in the forms ಚಾಚಿದು, ಮೆಟ್ಟಿದು, ನೋಡಿದು, which, probably as a remnant of by-gone times, we find in § 167. This is corroborated by the fact that in the so-called relative past participle (§ 175, *e. g.* ಪಾಡಿದ, ಮಾಡಿದ, ಕುಟ್ಟಿದ, ಮುಟ್ಟಿದ, ನಜ್ಜಿದ, ಮುಜ್ಜಿದ), in the ancient and mediæval present tense (§ 194, *e. g.* ಪಾಡಿದಪೆಂ, ಮಾಡಿದಪೆಂ, ಕುಟ್ಟಿದಪೆಂ, ನಜ್ಜಿದಪೆಂ), and in the imperfect tense (§ 198, *e. g.* ಪಾಡಿದೆಂ, ಕುಟ್ಟಿದೆಂ, ನಜ್ಜಿದೆಂ) the ದು, in the form of ದ (§ 178), is always used. (In the contingent present-future tense the participle with ಇ is generally added directly to ಎನು, etc.).

We are, therefore, compelled to think that **the past participle with final ಇ is another particular kind of the short participles** treated of in § 165. About its representing verbal nouns **see** § 169.

In passing it may be observed that in the future tense (§ 200) the trisyllabic forms ಮಾಡುವೆಂ, ನೋಡುವೆಂ, when they are to become dissyllabic, do not appear as ಮಾಡ್ವೆಂ, ನೋಡ್ವೆಂ, but as ಮಾಬ್ಪೆಂ, ನೋಬ್ಪೆಂ, the ಬ್ in combination with ಪ being used to avoid a hardness of the pronunciation, which is avoided in the past participles ಪಾಡ್ದು, ಮಾಡ್ದು by the insertion of an enunciative ಇ before ದು and finally dropping the ದು.

Remark.

Nâgavarma and Kêšava call the ಇ an augment (âgama), and Kêšava states that this ಇ and the ಉ in ದು are vowels which are substitutes for the personal terminations (kriyâvibhaktyâdêšasvara). See the personal terminations in § 193.

169. Is it possible to find out the original meaning of the past participle in Kannaḍa?

In § 165 it has been stated that the short past participles, namely those without ದು and ತು, are often identical as to shape with their verbal themes which at the same time are verbal nouns, so that the participles themselves appear as verbal nouns and finally must be such, *e. g.* ಎೞ್, a rising, ಪಾಯ್, a running, ಸೀಳ್, a splitting, ಹೊಯ್, a striking; ಇೞಿ, ಕವಿ, ಕುಸಿ, ತವು, ತಿರಿ, ತಿೞಿ, ತಿವಿ, ತೆಗೆ, ದೊರೆ, ನಡೆ, ಪಡೆ, ಪರಿ, ಪಿಡಿ, ಪುಗು, ಬಿಡು, ಬಿಲಿ, ಹರಿ, ಹಿಡಿ; ಎಱ, ಒಡ, ಒರ, ಕಳ, ಕೊಱ, ತಡ, ತೆಱ, ನಡ, ಬೆಳ, ಹೊಡ; ಇಱಿ, ಉಱಿ, ಕಡ, ಸರ; ಇಱು, ಉಱು, ಕುಡು, ದಣು, ನಸು, ಬಱು, ಬಿರು, ಮುಡು, ಹಿಡು; ಪೋ. If we thus consider the short participles to be verbal nouns, their meaning before ಕೊಳ್ and ತರ್ is as follows:— ಹೊಯ್ ಕೊಳ್, to take (*i. e.* to apply) a blow (or blows, to one's self); ಎೞ್ ತರ್, to bring a standing up (to a certain place, *i. e.* to come); ಪಾಯ್ ತರ್, to give a running (*i. e.* to run); ತಿವಿ ಕೊಳ್, to take (*i. e.* to apply) a stabbing (to one's self); ನಡೆ ತರ್, to bring a walking (*i. e.* to come); etc.

We believe that analogously the past participles ending in ದು and ತು are nouns, namely verbal nouns augmented by the pronominal suffixes ತು and ದು (§ 122; *cf.* §§ 178 and 298, 3). Thus, for instance, ಇೞಿ, a descending, has become ಇೞಿದು, a descending-it; ನಡೆ, a walking, ನಡೆದು, a walking-it; ಬಿಲಿ, a selling, ಬಿಲಿತು, a selling-it; ಮೊಳೆ, a germinating, ಮೊಳೆತು, a germinating-it (*cf.* our explanation of ಅದೆ in § 171, of ಉತ್ತುಂ, etc. in § 173, of ಅದ in §§ 178. 179, of ಪು, ವು and ಹು in §§ 185. 186, of the infinitive in § 188, of ಗು and ಕು in § 204, and of the second and third person of the imperative in § 205). The suffixes ದು and ತು are so to say redundant. The special idea of the past ('a having descended-it', 'a having walked-it', or having descended, having walked, etc.) has, only by usage, been attached to the forms with ದು and ತು (*cf.* ಅದ in § 273). A similar indefinite character as to time has been actually preserved in the verbal forms produced by suffixing the syllables ಕುಂ and ಗುಂ (see § 203), in the negative participle and conjugated negative (see §§ 170. 171. 209. 210), and in the verbal forms (participles) produced by the syllables ವ, ಬ, ಪ, and ಹ (see §§ 180-185). Further the use of the past participle ಎನ್ದು in combination with ಒಡೆ or ಅರೆ (ಎನ್ದೊಡೆ, ಎನ್ದರೆ), *e. g.* in §§ 322-329 and that of the infinitive with final ಅಲು (ಅಲ್) in combination with ಇಲ್ಲ (§ 316, 2) will assist to elucidate such an original indefiniteness as to time. *Cf.* also § 313, 4 about the combination of the past participle and verbal nouns in the past.

In § 168 the short past participles with a final enunciative ಇ which remained after the dropping of ದು, have been introduced. With their ದು they are obvious verbal nouns, and they are therefore to be considered as verbal nouns also without ದು. This is established by the fact that they in combination with ಇಲ್ಲ are used identically with other verbal nouns in combination with ಇಲ್ಲ in § 316, 2 (*e. g.* ಮಾಡಿಲ್ಲ, ಆಗಿಲ್ಲ = ಮಾಡಿದುದಿಲ್ಲ, ಆದುದಿಲ್ಲ).

170. The fourteenth kind of the past participle is the so-called negative one (pratishêdhakriyĕ, vilômakriyĕ, abhâvakriyĕ). It is formed by putting ಅದೆ to the short form of the so-called infinitive (kriyârtha, see § 187), *i. e.* to the form of the verb that is conventionally used to denote object, design, purpose, or future of intention of action (before another verb), expressing the idea of the English infinitive preceded by 'to', 'for to', 'about to', 'ready to', 'yet to' (see § 188). This short form of the infinitive ends in the vowel ಅ, *e. g.* ಇರ (of ಇರ್, ಇರು), to be or stay, about to be or stay, going to be or stay, yet to be or stay. When ಅದೆ is put to ಇರ, the form of the participle becomes either ಇರ ಅದೆ, or, with the application of sandhi (§ 214), ಇರದೆ, 'not actually being or staying' or 'not having actually been or stayed'. The idea of the past is secondary, depending on circumstances (see § 209, and *cf.* § 169). Both forms, ಇರ ಅದೆ and ಇರದೆ, were used in the ancient dialect; in the mediæval and modern one only ಇರದೆ is in use. Other instances are ಅಲ್ಲದೆ (of ಅಲ್), not being fit or not having been fit, ಇಲ್ಲದೆ (of ಇಲ್), not being present or not having been present (§ 338), ಅಂಜದೆ (of ಅಂಜು), not fearing or not having feared, ಕಟ್ಟದೆ (of ಕಟ್ಟು), not tying or not having tied, ಉಡದೆ (of ಉಡು), ಕಿಡದೆ (of ಕಿಡು), ಆಗದೆ, ತೀರದೆ, ಬೇಡದೆ, ಮಾಡದೆ, ಎಸಾಬಿದೆ, ಹೋಗದೆ, ಕೇಳದೆ,

ಪೇೞದೆ, ಆಗಲದೆ, ಉಗುೞದೆ, ತಗುಳದೆ, ಬಗುಳದೆ, ಬಿಸುಡದೆ, ಒಡಮ್ಬಡದೆ, ಪರಿಹರಿಸದೆ. *Cf.* §§ 208. 209. 210. (212, 7).

If verbal themes end in ಇ, ಎ, ಆ, ಈ, ಏ, or ಓ, the infinitive inserts a euphonic ಯ್ between the theme and ಅ when ಅದೆ is attached, *e. g.* ಇೞಿಯದೆ (of ಇೞಿ), ಉೞಿಯದೆ (of ಉೞಿ), ಕುಡಿಯದೆ (of ಕುಡಿ), ತಿಳಿಯದ (of ತಿಳಿ), ನಡೆಯದೆ (of ನಡೆ), ಪಡೆಯದೆ (of ಪಡೆ), ಬಗೆಯದೆ (of ಬಗೆ), ಕಾಯದೆ (of ಕಾ), ಈಯದೆ (of ಈ), ಬೀಯದೆ (of ಬೀ), ಕೇಯದೆ (of ಕೇ), ನೋಯದೆ (of ನೋ). The theme ಓ exceptionally inserts a euphonic ವ್, and the negative participle becomes ಓವದೆ.

Monosyllabic themes ending in ಣ್, ನ್, ಯ್, ಲ್, and ಳ್, and having a short initial vowel or consonant, form the negative participle by doubling their final consonant before the ಅ of the infinitive and suffixing ಅದೆ, *e. g.* ಉಣ್ಣದೆ (of ಉಣ್), ಎನ್ನದೆ (of ಎನ್), ಒಲ್ಲದೆ (of ಒಲ್), ಕೊಳ್ಳದೆ (of ಕೊಳ್), ಬಯ್ಯದೆ (of ಬಯ್). As an exception there is ಕಳದೆ (of ಕಳ್) in the ancient dialect. In the mediæval one we find exceptionally ಉಣದೆ (of ಉಣ್), ಗೆಲದೆ (of ಗೆಲ್); as the modern one uses to double the finals of monosyllabic themes already before a euphonic ಉ (§ 48), its forms of the negative participle are *e. g.* ಉಣ್ಣದೆ (of ಉಣ್ಣು), ಎನ್ನದೆ (of ಎನ್ನು), ಗೆಲ್ಲದೆ (of ಗೆಲ್ಲು). *Cf.* § 215, 7, *f.*

The themes ತರ್ and ಬರ್ generally appear as ತಾರ್ and ಬಾರ್ in forming their negative participle, which is ತಾರದೆ and ಬಾರದೆ; only in the mediæval and modern dialect also ತರದೆ and ಬರದೆ occasionally occur. (*Cf.* §§ 184. 210.)

In repetition (see § 165, letter *b*, and *cf.* §§ 209. 211) the first verb drops the suffix ಅದೆ, *e. g.* ಬಿಡ ಬಿಡದೆ. (*Cf.* §§ 211, 4. 339.)

171. It becomes evident from the formation of the so-called negative participle given in § 170 that its primitive meaning was not that of direct negation, but that of futurity, *i. e.* the state of being yet to come or of once having been yet to come, or, in other words, the state of not being or of not having been. ಅದೆ is ಅದು, the remote demonstrative pronoun (*cf.* the ದು and ತು of § 169, and the ಉತ್ತೆ, etc. of § 173), in combination with ಎ, the particle of emphasis (*cf.* § 215, 6, remark 1). The form under consideration, therefore, is so to say a pronominal noun, and the first meaning of the above-mentioned ಇರ ಅದೆ or ಇರದೆ is 'yet to be or stay-even-it', 'not yet being or staying-even-it', or 'the state or condition of not actually being or staying', 'not actually being or staying'.

or, according to circumstances, 'not having actually been or stayed'. Thus also *e. g.* ಮಾಡದೆ, 'yet to make-even-it', 'having been yet to make-even-it': 'not actually making', 'not actually having made'.

172. In § 154 it has been stated that **the second form** of the Kannaḍa verb that has been called a verbal participle or gerund by Europeans, **is the present verbal participle** (vartamânakriyĕ, vartamânakâlakriyĕ; see § 362).

It is formed by adding to the verbal theme one of the following ten suffixes:— ಉತುಂ (in the ancient and mediæval dialect), ಉತೆ (in the ancient and mediæval one), ಉತ್ತುಂ (in the ancient one), ಉತ್ತೆ (in the ancient one), ಉತಂ (in the mediæval one), ಉತ (in the mediæval and modern one)., ಉತ್ತಂ (in the mediæval and, occasionally, ancient one), ಉತ್ತ (in the mediæval and modern one), ಉತಾ, ಉತ್ತಾ (in the modern one).

The final ಉ of a theme **disappears** (according to the rule of sandhi, § 213 *seq.*) when any of the terminations is annexed; **if a theme ends in** ಇ, ಎ, ಆ, ಈ, ಏ, or ಓ, a **euphonic** ಯ್, **or occasionally** (in the mediæval dialect) ವ್, is put between the vowel and termination; after ಓ, to love, the insertion of ವ್ is always required.

Instances are ಅೞುತುಂ (of ಅೞ್), weeping, ಗೆಯ್ಯುತ್ತುಂ or ಗೆಯ್ಯುತ್ತುಂ (of ಗೆಯ್; *cf.* § 215, 7, *e*), doing, ಎನುತುಂ (of ಎನ್), saying, ನಗುತುಂ (of ನಗು), laughing, ನೋಡುತುಂ (of ನೋಡು), seeing, ಇೞಿಯುತುಂ (of ಇೞಿ), descending, ಕರೆಯುತುಂ (of ಕರೆ), calling, ಕಾಯುತುಂ (of ಕಾ), guarding, ಈಯುತುಂ (of ಈ), giving, ಬೇಯುತುಂ (of ಬೇ), burning;— ಇಸುತೆ (of ಇಸು), throwing, ಎನುತೆ (of ಎನ್), saying, ಬೞಲುತೆ (of ಬೞಲ್), becoming weary;— ಕಾದುತ್ತುಂ (of ಕಾದು), fighting, ಜಡಿಯುತ್ತುಂ (of ಜಡಿ), threatening;— ಕೆತ್ತುತ್ತೆ (of ಕೆತ್ತು), quivering;— ಎನುತಂ (of ಎನ್), ಕೊಳುತಂ (of ಕೊಳ್);— ಆಳುತ (of ಆಳ್ or ಆಳು), ಎನುತ (of ಎನ್), ಅನುತ (of ಅನು), ಮಾಡುತ (of ಮಾಡು), ನುಡಿಯುತ (of ನುಡಿ);— ಉಣುತ್ತಂ (of ಉಣ್), ಬರುತ್ತಂ (of ಬರ್), ಕಾಣುತ್ತಂ (of ಕಾಣ್);— ಅೞುತ್ತ (of ಅೞ್ or ಅೞು), ಎನುತ್ತ (of ಎನ್), ಅನ್ನುತ್ತ (of ಅನ್ನು), ಮಾಡುತ್ತ (of ಮಾಡು), ನಡೆಯುತ್ತ (of ನಡೆ), ಬೇಯುತ್ತ (of ಬೇ), ನೋಯುತ್ತ (of ನೋ);— ಕೇಳುತ್ತಾ (of ಕೇಳು), ಕೊಳ್ಳುತ್ತಾ (of ಕೊಳ್ಳು), ಹೋಗುತ್ತಾ (of ಹೋಗು), ಹೊಡೆಯುತ್ತಾ (of ಹೊಡೆ);— ಕರೆವುತೆ (of ಕರೆ), ನಡೆವುತೆ (of ನಡೆ), ಸುಯ್ವುತೆ (of ಸುಯ್); ಈವುತ್ತೆ (of ಈ), ಓವುತ್ತೆ (of ಓ); ಮುಳಿವುತಂ (of ಮುಳಿ), ನೆನೆವುತಂ (of ನೆನೆ); ಬಯ್ವುತ (of ಬಯ್), ಪಿಡಿವುತ (of ಪಿಡಿ), ಸುರಿವುತ (of ಸುರಿ), ಕರೆವುತ (of ಕರೆ), ಕೞಿವುತ (of ಕೞಿ), ಕೆರೆವುತ (of ಕೆರೆ), ಈವುತ (of ಈ); ಬಳೆವುತ್ತಂ (of ಬಳೆ); ಸುಯ್ವುತ್ತ (of ಸುಯ್),

ನಡೆವುತ್ತ (of ನಡೆ), ಬಳೆವುತ್ತ (of ಬಳೆ). (The Basavapurâṇa has once, 22, 29, ಕೊಲುವುತ್ತ, treating the final ಉ as radical).

Before the euphonic ವ್ the vowel ಎ of the theme may be dropped, *e. g.* ನಡವುತಂ (of ನಡೆ), ಬರವುತಂ (of ಬರೆ); ಕಡವುತ (of ಕಡೆ), ತೆಗವುತ (of ತೆಗೆ), ಮಲವುತ (of ಮಲೆ), ಹೊಳವುತ (of ಹೊಳೆ). *Cf.* § 151, letters *a*, 4 and *b*, 2; etc. Instances regarding the present verbal participle see in § 362.

From ಕೊಳ್ಳು exceptionally ಕೋತ, a contraction of ಕೊಳುತ, is formed in the modern dialect.

Further, in the modern dialect there are the puzzling forms ಅನ್ತ and ಎನ್ತ used, like the past participles ಅನ್ದು and ಎನ್ದು (§ 155), to introduce words and sentences (see § 332). They are likely to be forms corrupted from the present participles ಅನುತ or ಅನುತ್ತ, ಎನುತ or ಎನುತ್ತ, saying (*cf.* the rustic form of the present tense in § 196, remark 3, and also the explanation of ಅನ್ತೆ, ibid., remark 4). ಅನ್ತಾ and ಎನ್ತಾ which may take the place of ಅನ್ತ and ಎನ್ತ, would be equal to ಅನುತಾ or ಅನುತ್ತಾ and ಎನುತಾ or ಎನುತ್ತಾ. Another explanation will be offered in § 198, 7, remark 1.

In repetition the ಉತ್ತಾ of the first verb may be dropped (see § 339, 6).

173. Considering the origin of the suffixes of the present participle adduced in § 172 **we take ಉತು to be their primitive form.** ಉತು is known to be another form of ಉದು, the intermediate demonstrative pronoun neuter (Šabdmaṇidarpaṇa sûtra 148; § 122; § 272, 2), from which ಉದು, analogously to the formation of ಅತ್ತು from ಅದು and ಇತ್ತು from ಇದು, ಉತ್ತು may be formed.

These pronominal suffixes ಉತು and ಉತ್ತು we believe to be attached to verbal nouns to form the present participle correspondingly to the formation of the past one which suffixes the pronouns ದು and ತು to verbal nouns (§ 169) and to the present-past negative one which suffixes the pronoun ಅದೆ (*i. e.* ಅದು + the emphatic ಎ) to the short infinitive (§ 171) which will finally prove to be also a verbal noun (§ 188). Let us take, for instance, the verbal noun ಓದು, reading; when to this ಉತು or ಉತ್ತು is added, it would have the form of ಓದುತು or ಓದುತ್ತು and mean 'a reading-this'. (*Cf.* the bhâvavačanas or verbal nouns of §§ 198. 200).

The final ಉಂ in ಉತುಂ, ಉತ್ತುಂ is still to be explained. It is the conjunction ಉಂ, further, denoting progression or continuity, which conveys the specific idea of the present participle, as ಓದುತುಂ or ಓದುತ್ತುಂ, standing before a conjugated verb, *e. g.* before 'he was' (ಇರ್ದಂ, literally

'a reading-this-further' he. was), expresses that the reading was a progressing or continuing action. The final conjunction ಅಂ has the same meaning.

The final ಎ in ಉತೆ, ಉತ್ತೆ (put to ಉತು and ಉತ್ತು like the ಎ of ಅದೆ in § 171) is emphatical, the idea of the ಉಂ or ಅಂ disappearing (*cf.* § 196, remark 3)[1]. **In the final** ಅ of ಉತ, ಉತ್ತ the sonnĕ has been dropped, or perhaps ಅ stands for ಎ (*cf. e. g.* the past participles before the ದು or ತು of which the ಎ of the verbal themes becomes ಅ, § 157), and in ಉತಾ, ಉತ್ತಾ the ಅ has then been changed into ಆ for the sake of euphony.

The use of the intermediate pronouns (ಉತು, ಉತ್ತು) may denote that the action is neither past nor future.

174. There are two forms of the Kannaḍa verb that have been called **relative participles.** This name has been given to them by Europeans, because they regarded them as including the relative pronouns within themselves. But the Kannaḍa language has no relative pronouns whatever; its pronouns ಆವ (ಯಾವ), ಆವುದು (ಯಾವದು), ಆವಂ (ಯಾವನು), ಆವಳ್ (ಯಾವಳು), ಏನ್ (ಏನು) are not relative, but interrogative (§ 102, 8, letter *b,* remark), and the relative pronouns' place is somehow supplied by the so-called relative participles. (*Cf.* § 267 regarding the interrogatives.)

The first is **the preterite or past relative participle** (bhûtavatikṛit, §§ 175-179), **the second comprises the present and future relative participles** (bhavishyantikṛit, §§ 180-186) which have the same form.

175. The past relative participle (bhûtavatikṛit) **is formed**

1, **by removing the final** ಉ **of the past participle** (§§ 155-164) or **changing it into** ಅ, *e.g.* ಪೂಣ್ದ (of ಪೂಣ್ದು), ಎನ್ದ (of ಎನ್ದು), ಅಮರ್ದ or ಅಮರ್ದ್ದ (of ಅಮರ್ದು, ಅಮರ್ದ್ದು), ಒಸರ್ದ or ಒಸರ್ದ್ದ (of ಒಸರ್ದು, ಒಸರ್ದ್ದು), ಸೋರ್ದ or ಸೋರ್ದ್ದ (of ಸೋರ್ದು, ಸೋರ್ದ್ದು), ತಿಳಿದ (of ತಿಳಿದು), ಕಲ್ತ (of ಕಲ್ತು), ಕೆಯ್ದ (of ಕೆಯ್ದು), ಮೊಳೆತ (of ಮೊಳೆತು), ಆನ್ತ (of ಆನ್ತು), ನೇಲ್ತ (of ನೇಲ್ತು), ಎಱಿಸಿದ (of ಎಱಿಸಿದು), ಕಡದ (of ಕಡದು), ಒದ್ದ (of ಒದ್ದು), ತೆತ್ತ, ಬೆನ್ದ, ಸತ್ತ, ಉಣ್ಡ, ಕಣ್ಡ, ಕೊಣ್ಡ, ಅಟ್ಟ, ಕೊಟ್ಟ, ಬಿಟ್ಟ, ಇರ್ದ or ಇದ್ದ, ನಕ್ಕ, ಪೊಕ್ಕ; *cf.* § 189;

2, **by adding** ದ **to the short past participle ending in** ಇ (§§ 166-168), *e.g.* ಅಳ್ಕಿದ (of ಅಳ್ಕಿ), ಒಗ್ಗಿದ (of ಒಗ್ಗಿ), ನಚ್ಚಿದ, ಮುಚ್ಚಿದ, ಕುಟ್ಟಿದ, ಮುಟ್ಟಿದ, ಒಡ್ಡಿದ, ಪಾಡಿದ, ಮಾಡಿದ, ಅಲರ್ಚಿದ, ಓಸರಿಸಿದ, ರಾಗಿಸಿದ; *cf.* § 189;

---

[1] **The** ಎ **might, however, in this case, be merely formative like the** ಎ **in** ಸವತೆ, ನಿಬತೆ, ಕೆಡೆ, ಮನೆ **and other nouns.**

3, by changing the final ಎ of the negative participle (§§ 170. 171) into ಅ, *e. g.* ಇರದ (of ಇರದೆ), ಇಲ್ಲದ (of ಇಲ್ಲದೆ), ಅಲ್ಲದ (of ಅಲ್ಲದೆ), ಅಂಜದ, ಕಟ್ಟದ, ಉಡದ, ಕಿಡದ, ಆಗದ, ತೀರದ, ಬೇಡದ, ಮಾಡದ, ಒಡಮ್ಬಡದ, ಇಱಿಯದ, ಉಱಿಯದ, ಕುಡಿಯದ, ಉಣ್ಣದ, ಎನ್ನದ, ತಾರದ.

Regarding the meaning see § 179 and regarding the use § 363.

176. The formation of the past relative participle of ಆಗು, ಪೋಗು, ಹೋಗು is irregular, for, instead of ಆಗಿದ, ಪೋಗಿದ, ಹೋಗಿದ, they have ಆದ, ಪೋದ, ಹೋದ, formed from the irregular past participles ಆಯ್, ಪೋಯ್, ಹೋಯ್ (§ 166) by means of syncope, the original forms being ಆಯ್ದ, ಪೋಯ್ದ, ಹೋಯ್ದ. ಆದ occasionally takes also the forms ಆನ (§ 292), or ಆಣ or ಅಣ (§ 293, Tamil = ಆನ, Tĕlugu ಅಯಿನ, the consonants ನ್, ಣ್ being used for ದ್; *cf.* the remark concerning ನ್, ಣ್ and ದ್ in § 141 under dative singular) and probably also that of ಅನ too (see § 278, 2, the explanation of ಅನೆ; *cf.* § 212, remark 2). The original form of ಆದ, *viz.* ಆಯ್ದ, appears still as ಅಯ್ದ, and, by syncope, as ಅದ, in the old rustic forms ಅಯ್ದಾನೆ, etc. and ಅದಾನೆ, etc., used for the third person present still in the modern dialect (§ 196, *cf.* ಅದೇನು, § 195). In the same dialect there is also the old rustic form ಅಯ್ತು, used for the third person neuter singular of the present tense (as to form originally of the past or preterite tense) which is ಅಯ್ (the irregular past participle, § 166) and ತು (§ 193) in combination with the ಉ of emphasis. Regarding the form ಅಗು (= ಆಗು) see also the ಅಗೆ in § 212, remark 2, the ಅಪ್ಪ, ಅಪ, ಅಹ in §§ 183, 7, remark; § 184, the ಅಕ್ಕುಂ in § 203, and the ಅಕ್ಕೆ in § 205.

177. The grammarian Kêšava calls the past relative participle in combination with any one of the terminations ಅಂ (ಅ), he, ಅಳ್, she, ಉದು, it, and their plurals ಅರ್, they (men or women), ಉವು, they (children, things, etc., see *e. g.* § 254) a ಭೂತವತಿಕೃತ್ or ಕೃಲ್ಲಿಂಗ (§ 68, 1), also ಎವಾ ಚ್ಯಲಿಂಗ, ವಿಶೇಷ್ಯಾಧೀನಲಿಂಗ (§ 102, 8, *e*), *e. g.* ಮಾಡಿದಂ (of ಮಾಡಿದ), ಮಾಡಿದಳ್, ಮಾಡಿದುದು, ಮಾಡಿದರ್, ಮಾಡಿದುದು, the genitive singular, for instance, becoming ಮಾಡಿದನ, ಮಾಡಿದಳ, ಮಾಡಿದುದಱ, and the genitive plural ಮಾಡಿದರ, ಮಾಡಿದುವಱ. Further instances are ಅಲ್ಲದಂ (of ಅಲ್ಲದ), ಇಲ್ಲದಂ, ಉಣ್ಣದಂ. (*Cf. e. g.* §§ 180. 185. 193. 198 under 3. 254.) [Observe that bhûtavatikṛit may mean either the past relative participle or the noun formed from it.]

The terminations ಅಂ and ಅಳ್ appear also as ಒಂ and ಒಳ್; we find *e. g.* ಸನ್ದೊಂ (in a šâsana of 707 A. D.), ಆೞಿದೊಂ (in a šâsana of 866 A. D. and in one of 887 A. D.), and ಇೞಿದ್ದೊಳ್, ಕೊಟ್ಟೊಳ್ (in a šâsana of about

778 A. D.). For ಉದು there occurs also ಒದು, as there is *e. g.* twice ಇತ್ತೊದು (in a śâsana between 597 and 608 A. D.); for the plural ಅರ್ we have also ಒರ್ according to § 185, *q. v.*

Instead of the above-mentioned terminations which, except the pronouns ಉದು and ಉವು, are pronominal forms, also **demonstrative pronouns themselves** are very frequently used in the mediæval dialect; in the modern one only pronouns are in use. Two additional pronominal forms of the mediæval dialect are ಅನು and ಅ (for ಅಂ).

The demonstrative pronouns used for krilliṅgas in the mediæval dialect are ಅವಂ, ಅವನು, ಅವ, ಆತಂ, ಆತನು, ಆತ, ಅವಳ್, ಅವಳು, ಆಕೆ, ಉದು, ಅದು, ಅವರ್, ಅವರು, ಉವು, ಅವು, and those in the modern one ಅವನು, ಅವ, ಆತನು, ಆತ, ಅವಳು, ಆಕೆ, ಅದು, ಅವರು, ಅವು (see §§ 117. 119. 121. 122. 134. 136). ಆತಂ and ಆಕೆ are met with as suffixes for krilliṅgas also in the ancient dialect. See § 254.

But not only pronominal forms and pronouns are suffixed to the past relative participles, but nearly every declinable base (see § 67 *seq.*) is used after them, *e. g.* ಅಡಿದ ಪೊಲ, ಪೂಸಿದ ಭಸ್ಮರಾಗ, ಕೊಟ್ಟ ವಸ್ತು, ಮೊಳೆತ ಪುಲ್, ಕಲ್ತ ಪಾಠ, ಪೊಯ್ದ ಬಟಿ, ಆದ ಏಷ್ಣು, ಮಾಡದ ಕೆಯ್, ಅಲ್ಲದ ಕಾರ್ಯ, ಕಿಡದ ಪಕ್ಷ, ಆಗದ ಕಾರ್ಯ. See § 282 regarding declinable and other adverbs used after them, and § 363 the translation of the above instances. Further instances see in § 254.

Kêśava terms the instances in which a relative past participle is followed by a declinable base (noun), **consecutive compounds** (gamakasamâsa see § 253, 2, *d* and *cf.* § 185).

178. The author of the present grammar considers **the past relative participle** to be **the genitive singular** of the so-called past participle formed by means of the pronominal suffixes ದು and ತು (§ 169), in which case ಅ, the primitive termination of the genitive (§ 141), would have been employed without the usual augment ಅಜ್ (§ 124).

With regard to ಅದೆ (§ 171) it is to be remarked that ಎ, the particle of emphasis, was removed in order to form the genitive ending in ಅ, *viz.* ಅದ (ಅದು + ಅ).

Compare the explanation of the relative present-future participle in § 185.

179. Now turning back to § 175 *seq.* we translate *e. g.* ಪೂಣ್ದ (ಪೂಣ್ದು + ಅ) 'of the having promised', ಎನ್ದ 'of the having said', ಅಮರ್ದ 'of the having closely united', ಅಳ್ಕಿದ 'of the having feared', ಪೋದ

'of the having gone'; ಇರದ 'of the not being' or 'of the not having been', ಅಂಜದ 'of the not fearing' or 'of the not having feared'.

ಪಾಡಿದಂ (ಪಾಡಿದ+ಅಂ) means 'a man of the having sung', *i. e.* a man who has sung or sang; ಪಾಡಿದಳ್ (ಪಾಡಿದ+ಅಳ್), 'a woman of the having sung', *i. e.* a woman who has sung or sang; ಪಾಡಿದುದು (ಪಾಡಿದ+ಉದು), 'a child of the having sung', *i. e.* a child which has sung or sang; ಆಡಿದ ಪೊಲಂ, 'a place of the having played', *i. e.* a place where (somebody) has played or played; ಪೂಸಿದ ಭಸ್ಮರಾಗಂ, 'a colour of ashes of the having smeared with', *i. e.* a colour of ashes with which (somebody) has smeared or smeared (*e. g.* the body); ಅಲ್ಲದಂ (ಅಲ್ಲದ+ಅಂ), 'a man of the not being proper', *i. e.* a man who is not proper; ಇಲ್ಲದಂ (ಇಲ್ಲದ+ಅಂ), 'a man of the (something) not being', *i. e.* a man who lacks (something); ಉಣ್ಣದಂ (ಉಣ್ಣದ+ಅಂ), 'a man of the not eating' or 'of the not having eaten', *i. e.* a man who does not eat or has not eaten; ಮಾಡದ ಕೆಯ್, 'a field of the not cultivating', *i. e.* a field which (anybody) does not cultivate, or has not cultivated, or did not cultivate, *i. e.* a field which nobody cultivates, etc.; ಆಗದ ಕಾರ್ಯಂ 'an affair of the not being possible', *i. e.* an affair which is impossible.

Regarding the use of the present time in translating the so-called relative past participle see §§ 169. 170.

Note.

In the modern dialect a change of ಅವ into ಓ is occasionally met with (*cf.* § 181, note *a*), *e. g.* ಅಟ್ಟೋಳು stands for ಅಟ್ಟವಳು (ಅಟ್ಟ+ಅವಳು), 'a woman of the having cooked', *i. e.* a woman who has cooked; ಕೊಡೋರಿಗೆ (*i. e.* ಕೊಡುವರಿಗೆ) ಕೊಟ್ಟೋರಿಗೆ (*i. e.* ಕೊಟ್ಟವರಿಗೆ) ಕೋಟಿ ಲಾಭವನ್ನುತ್ತೆ, they say "there (is) much more gain for them who give than for them who take".

180. The present and future relative participles (bhavishyantikṛit, § 174) that are identical as to shape and receive their respective meaning only from the context, are formed by means of the suffixes ವ, ಬ, ಪ and ಹ. Regarding their meaning see §§ 185. 186. See § 364.

Instances of the present-future relative participle formed by means of ವ·

1, such as regard verbal themes ending in consonants in which the suffix is added directly to the theme, in the ancient and mediæval dialect, are ಅಳ್ವ (of ಅಳ್), ಉಟ್ವ (of ಉಟ್), ಊಳ್ವ (of ಊಳ್), ಕೊಳ್ವ, ಬಾಟ್ವ, ಪೇಟ್ವ, ಪೇಟ್ವ, ಪಣ್ವ, ಸೀಳ್ವ, ಬಯ್ವ, ಪೊಯ್ವ, ಕೊಲ್ವ, ಗೆಲ್ವ, ಅಲರ್ವ (of ಅಲರ್), ಕಲಿಲ್ವ,

ನುಸುಳ್ವ, ಆರ್ವ (of ಆರ್), ಸಾರ್ವ, ಪೀರ್ವ. *Cf.* § 183, 2. 4. 10; about themes with final ಱ್ see § 183, 3.

Themes ending in ರ್ optionally double the ವ by ವ್, *e. g.* ಅಲರ್ವ್ವ, ಕುಳಿರ್ವ್ವ, ಕೊನರ್ವ್ವ, ತಳಿರ್ವ್ವ, ತಿಮಿರ್ವ್ವ, ಪೊಣರ್ವ್ವ. See § 371, 3.

Remark.

About ಸಾವ for ಸಾಯ್ವ see § 163, remark.

2, such as regard **monosyllabic verbal themes that end in a vowel or are a vowel,** in which the suffix is added directly to the theme, in the ancient and mediæval dialect, are ಕಾವ (of ಕಾ), ವಿಾವ, ಬೇವ, ಮೇವ, ನೋವ, ಈವ, ಓವ.

ಓವ occurs only in the mediæval dialect, the ancient form being ಓಪ (see 183, 6); instead of ವಿಾವ the mediæval dialect has also ವಿಾಪ.

3, such as regard **verbal themes that also in the ancient dialect end in** ಉ, in which the suffix is added directly to the theme, in the three dialects, are ಉಡುವ (of ಉಡು), ಕುಡುವ (of ಕುಡು), ನಡುವ, ಎತ್ತುವ, ಆಗುವ, ತೂಗುವ, ಪೂಸುವ, ಪೊಣ್ಮುವ, ಮುಚ್ಚುವ, ಪಾಡುವ, ನೋಡುವ, ಮಾಡುವ, ಬೇಡುವ, ತೂಱುವ, ತೋಱುವ, ನಾಱುವ, ಪಾಱುವ, ಬೀಱುವ, ಮಾಱುವ, ಬೀಸುವ, ಬಿಸುಡುವ, ಧರಿಸುವ. See No. 6 and § 183, 2. 4. 7. 8.

4, such as regard **verbal themes ending in** ಇ or ಎ in which the suffix is added directly to the theme, in the ancient and mediæval dialect, are ಅಱಿವ (of ಅಱಿ), ಇಱಿವ, ಇಱಿನ, ಕಡಿವ, ತಿಳಿವ, ಪಿಡಿವ, ಬಿರಿವ; ಎಱೆವ (of ಎಱೆ), ಎಸೆವ, ಕಡೆವ, ನಡೆವ, ಪಡೆವ, ಪೊಡೆವ.

5, such as regard **verbal themes with final** ಎ **which drop this vowel** before the suffix, in the mediæval dialect and occasionally also in the ancient one, are ಅಡವ (of ಅಡೆ), ಅರವ (of ಅರೆ), ಅಳವ (of ಅಳೆ), ಎರವ, ಎಱವ, ಒದವ, ಕಡವ, ಕಱವ, ತೊಳವ, ಬೆಳವ, ಹೊಸವ, ಹೊಳವ; ನಡವ (of ನಡೆ, in a śâsana of 1019 A. D.). *Cf.* § 157.

6, such as regard **verbal themes that may change their final** ಱು **into** ಱ್ before the suffix, in the mediæval dialect, are ಗಜರ್ವ (of ಗಜಱ್ = ಗಜಱು), ಬೆದರ್ವ, ಚೀರ್ವ, ತೂರ್ವ, ನಾರ್ವ, ಪಾರ್ವ, ಬೀರ್ವ, ಮಾರ್ವ. *Cf.* No. 3 and § 183, 2.

Remark.

The present participle of the verb ಉಳ್ is anomalously formed, it being not ಉಳ್ವ, but ಉಳ್ಳ in the three dialects. *Cf.* § 243, *B*, 20; § 194, remark 1.

181. In § 180 we have found only one form of the present-future participle with ವ in the modern dialect, *viz.* that of No. 3, in which the suffix is added directly to themes that end in ಉ also in the ancient dialect; let us now give the other forms:—

1, That of No. 1 in § 180 it forms by attaching a euphonic ಉ to the themes with final consonants (*cf.* §§ 48. 166) and then suffixing the ವ, a formation which occasionally occurs also in the mediæval dialect.

Instances belonging to both dialects are ಆಳುವ (of ಆಳು = ಆಳ್), ಉಗುೞುವ (of ಉಗುೞು = ಉಗುೞ್), ಉರುಳುವ, ಏೞುವ, ಕೀೞುವ, ಕೇಳುವ, ಜೋಲುವ, ನೋನುವ, ಬಾೞುವ, ಸೀಳುವ, ಹೇೞುವ, ತೊೞಲುವ, ನಿಗರುವ.

Instances belonging to the mediæval one alone are ಅಲರುವ, ಈಸುವ, ಕೊಲುವ, ಕೊಳುವ, ಪೇೞುವ, ಮಾಣುವ, ಪೊಗೞುವ.

Instances belonging to the modern one alone are ಇರುವ, ಉಣ್ಣುವ, ಎನುವ or ಎನ್ನುವ, ಕಾಣುವ, ಕೊಯುವ or ಕೊಯ್ಯುವ, ಕೊಲ್ಲುವ, ಕೊಳ್ಳುವ, ತರುವ, ತಿನುವ or ತಿನ್ನುವ, ಬರುವ, ಬೀೞುವ, ಸಾಯುವ, ಹೊಯ್ಯುವ. (*Cf.* § 182.)

2, That of No. 2 in § 180 it forms from originally monosyllabic themes to which a euphonic ಉ (by means of ಯ್ as a help to enunciation) has been added, suffixing the ವ to the ಉ, *e.g.* ಈಯುವ (of ಈಯು, to bring forth), ಕಾಯುವ (of ಕಾಯು), ಗೇಯುವ (of ಗೇಯು), ನೇಯುವ (of ನೇಯು), ನೋಯುವ (of ನೋಯು), ಬೇಯುವ (of ಬೇಯು), ಮಾಯುವ (of ಮಾಯು), ಮೇಯುವ (of ಮೇಯು).

3, That of No. 4 in § 180 it forms by adding a euphonic ಉ (by means of ಯ್ as a help to enunciation) and then suffixing the ವ, *e.g.* ಅಱಿಯುವ (of ಅಱಿ), ತಿಳಿಯುವ (of ತಿಳಿ), ನುಡಿಯುವ, ಸುರಿಯುವ; ಕಡೆಯುವ (of ಕಡೆ), ಕೞೆಯುವ (of ಕೞೆ), ಕೆರೆಯುವ, ನಡೆಯುವ.

Notes.

a) In the mediæval and modern dialect the final ಉ of the verbal theme and the suffix ವ are pretty often changed into ಒ or ಓ, *e.g.* ಅಡರೊ (= ಅಡರುವ), ಉರುಳೊ (= ಉರುಳುವ), ಒಸರೊ, ತೆರಳೊ, ಪೊಗೞೊ (ಹೊಗೞೊ); ಆಗೋ (= ಆಗುವ), ಊಡೋ, ಕಾಯೋ, ಕೊಯ್ಯೋ, ಪಡೋ, ಬೀೞೋ, ಬಡಿಯೋ, ನಡೆಯೋ. (*Cf.* §§ 179, note; 202. 205, 3, first pers. plural.)

b) In the mediæval and occasionally in the modern dialect the final ಉ of the verbal theme and the suffix ವ may be changed into ಊ, *e.g.* ಇರೂ (= ಇರುವ), ಎೞಗೂ (= ಎೞಗುವ), ಪಾಱೂ (= ಪಾಱುವ), ಸುತ್ತೂ (= ಸುತ್ತುವ). (*Cf.* §§ 202. 205, 3, first pers. plural.) ಬರು ಹೋಗುವ ಪಾನ್ಥಸ್ತರು (that is found in the modern dialect) may be ಬರೂ ಹೋಗುವ ಪಾನ್ಥಸ್ತರು.

c) Some vulgar forms in which the participle ends in ಅ, that are found in a South-Mahratta school-book, *e. g.* ಕೇಳ (in ಕೇಳವನು), ಮಾಡ (in ಮಾಡವನು)

and ಮುಕ್ಕ (in ಮುಕ್ಕವನು), are. to be explained by the change of the ಉ of No. *a* into ಅ, so that ಕೇಳ, ಮಾಡ and ಮುಕ್ಕ stand for ಕೇಳೊ, ಮಾಡೊ and ಮುಕ್ಕೊ (ಕೇಳೊವನು, etc.). (*Cf.* the remark in § 187, under 2). *Cf.* § 211, 5.

182. The second suffix for the present-future participle is ಬ, which is added to four of the monosyllabic themes that end in ಣ್ (ṇânta) and to four of them that end in ನ್ (nânta), *viz.* ಉಣ್ಬ (of ಉಣ್), ಕಾಣ್ಬ (of ಕಾಣ್), ಪೂಣ್ಬ (of ಪೂಣ್), ಮಾಣ್ಬ (of ಮಾಣ್); ಎನ್ಬ (of ಎನ್), ತಿನ್ಬ, ನಾನ್ಬ, ಬಾನ್ಬ. *Cf.* § 183, 5.

ಉಣ್ಬ becomes also ಉಮ್ಬ in the mediæval dialect, and always so in the modern one; ಕಾಣ್ಬ becomes ಕಾಮ್ಬ in the modern one; ಎನ್ಬ and ತಿನ್ಬ appear also as ಎಮ್ಬ and ತಿಮ್ಬ in the ancient dialect, and always so in the mediæval and modern one; the ancient ಬಾನ್ಬ gets also the form of ಬಾಮ್ಬ.

The present-future participle of the themes ಕೂನ್ and ಪೇನ್ the author of the present grammar has not yet met with. Regarding the other modern form of the participle of ಉಣ್, ಕಾಣ್, ಎನ್ and ತಿನ್ see § 181, 1.

The present-future participle of ಕೊಳ್ (ಕೊಳು, ಕೊಳ್ಳು) which in the ancient dialect is ಕೊಳ್ವ (180, 1) appears therein also as ಕೊಮ್ಬ, is frequently ಕೊಮ್ಬ in the mediæval dialect, and occurs in this form also in the modern one. Its other modern form is ಕೊಳ್ಳುವ (181, 1).

183. The third suffix for the present-future participle is ಪ. It is used:—

1, In some themes ending in ರ್ (rêpha), *viz.* ಇರ್ಪ (of ಇರ್), ತರ್ಪ (of ತರ್), ಬರ್ಪ (of ಬರ್), ಕೂರ್ಪ (of ಕೂರ್), ಗೋರ್ಪ (of ಗೋರ್), and ನೇರ್ಪ (of ನೇರ್) of the ancient dialect (*cf.* No. 10 of this paragraph). The ಪ may be doubled by a ಪ್ after the ರ್, *e.g.* ಇರ್ಪ್ಪ, ತರ್ಪ್ಪ. *Cf.* No. 10, and see § 371, 3.

In the mediæval dialect ಇರ್ಪ, ತರ್ಪ, ಬರ್ಪ and ಕೂರ್ಪ generally appear as ಇಪ್ಪ, ತಪ್ಪ, ಬಪ್ಪ and ಕೂಪ (for ಕೂಪ್ಪ). *Cf.* § 184. Regarding the modern dialect see § 181, 1.

2, In some themes ending in ಱ್ (ṟakâra) with a preceding long vowel, *viz.* ಆರ್ಪ (of ಆಱ್), ತೋರ್ಪ (of ತೋಱ್), ನಾರ್ಪ (of ನಾಱ್), and ಮಾರ್ಪ (of ಮಾಱ್) of the ancient dialect. ಆರ್ಪ and ತೋರ್ಪ are found also in the mediæval one. The ಪ may be doubled, *e.g.* ಆರ್ಪ್ಪ, ತೋರ್ಪ್ಪ (see § 371, 3).

ಆಪರ್ is ಆಪ in the modern dialect, and not unfrequently also in the mediæval one.

ಮೂಱ್, ನಾಱ್, etc. occasionally form their participle by means of ವ in the mediæval dialect, e. g. ನಾವರ್, ಮೂವರ್ (see § 180, 6). When ತೋಱ್, ನಾಱ್, ಮಾಱ್, etc. are used with the final ಉ, their participles are ತೋಱುವ, ನಾಱುವ, ಮಾಱುವ, etc. in the three dialects (see § 180, 3).

3, In themes ending in ೞ್ (ḻakâra, according to Kêšava), *viz.* ಅಗೞ್ಪ, ಕೀೞ್ಪ of the ancient dialect. The present-future participle of ಕೀೞ್ appears twice as ಕೀೞ್ವ in the Šabdânušâsana. The use of ಪ in themes with final ೞ್ was perhaps to some extent optional. See § 180, 1.

4, In themes ending in ೞ್ (ḻakâra) when it is a substitute (âdêša) of ಡ್ (ḍakâra), *viz.* ನೋೞ್ಪ (of ನೋಡು), ಬಿಸುೞ್ಪ (of ಬಿಸುಡು), ಬೆಗೞ್ಪ (of ಬೆಗಡು), ಬೇೞ್ಪ (of ಬೇಡು), ಮಾೞ್ಪ (of ಮಾಡು), ಸೂೞ್ಪ (of ಸೂಡು) of the ancient dialect. ನೋೞ್ಪ, ಬೇೞ್ಪ and ಮಾೞ್ಪ occur also in the mediæval one. *Cf.* § 234.

ನೋಡು, ಬಿಸುಡು, etc. form their participle also by means of ವ, *viz.* ನೋಡುವ, ಬಿಸುಡುವ, etc. in the three dialects. *Cf.* 180, 3.

5, In four themes ending in ನ್ (nakâra, *cf.* § 182), *viz.* ಅನ್ಪ (of ಅನ್), ಈನ್ಪ (of ಈನ್), ನೋನ್ಪ, ಸೀನ್ಪ of the ancient dialect.

6, In the themes ಓ and ಪೂ, *viz.* ಓಪ (*cf.* § 180, 2), ಪೂಪ.

7, In themes with final ಗು (gânta), in which case the ಗು suffers elision (lôpa, *cf.* § 165, *b*, 3; 211, 7. 10), *viz.* ತಾಪ (of ತಾಗು), ತೂಪ (of ತೂಗು), ಪೋಪ (of ಪೋಗು), ತೊಳಪ (of ತೊಳಗು), ಬೆಳಪ (of ಬೆಳಗು), ಮಿನುಪ (of ಮಿನುಗು), ಮಿಱುಪ (of ಮಿಱುಗು), ಮಿಸುಪ (of ಮಿಸುಗು) of the ancient dialect. These participial forms are occasionally found likewise in the mediæval one, once ಹೋಪ for ಪೋಪ. The ಪ of the themes with a short initial may be doubled, *e. g.* ತೊಳಪ್ಪ, ಬೆಳಪ್ಪ (see § 371, 3). *Cf.* ಆಪ್ಪಾರ್ in the remark.

All themes ending in ಗು form their participle also by means of ವ, *e. g.* ಆಗುವ, ತಾಗುವ, ತೊಳಗುವ, etc. in the three dialects (*cf.* § 180, 3).

Remark.

The present-future participle of ಆಗು (*i. e.* ಆಗುವ) often appears as ಅಪ್ಪ, ಅಪ or ಅಹ (§§ 176. 184) in the ancient and mediæval dialect. The Šabdânušâsana (sûtras 496. 502) teaches that its participle becomes also ಆಪ (or ಆಪ್ಪ); we can substantiate its statement only by one instance which belongs to the ancient dialect, *viz.* by ಆಪ್ಪಾರ್ (for ಅಪ್ಪರ್, in a šâsana between 680 and 696 A. D.), the third person plural of the future of ಆಗು (see § 201, 1). The occasionally used

ಆಹ in § 184 might be adduced also in support of the Śabdânuśâsana's ಆಪ. ಆಪ (of ಆಱ್) appears in the paragraph under No. 1.

8, In themes that have been formed by means of the suffixes ಇಸು or ಸು (sânta) whether they be causative, transitive or intransitive (§§ 148. 151), in which case the final ಸು suffers elision. Kannaḍa instances are ಅಗುರ್ವಿಪ (of ಅಗುರ್ವಿಸು), ಅಗ್ಗಲಿಪ (of ಅಗ್ಗಲಿಸು), ಅಲಪ (of ಅಲಸು), ಇರಿಪ (of ಇರಿಸು), ಉಗಿಪ (of ಉಗಿಸು), ಎನಿಪ, ಏೞಿಪ, ಏೞ್ಚಿಪ, ಕಾಪ (of ಕಾಸು), ಕಿನಿಪ, ತರಿಪ, ತೂಂಕಡಿ, ದಾಣ್ಟಿಪ, ನಡಯಿಪ, ಪತ್ತಿಪ, ಪಾೞಿಪ, ಬರಿಪ, ಮಾಡಿಪ, ಸುತ್ತಿಪ;— instances of themes formed from Saṁskṛita are ಅಂಗೀಕರಿಪ (of ಅಂಗೀಕರಿಸು), ಅವಧರಿಪ, ಆಕಾಂಕ್ಷಿಪ, ಆಚರಿಪ, ಉದಯಿಪ, ಉದ್ಭಾವಿಪ, ಉಪ್ಪರಿಪ, ಚಿತ್ರಿಪ, ನರ್ತಿಪ, ನಿರವಿಪ, ಪರಿಹರಿಪ, ಪೂಜಿಪ, ಬೆಸಪ (of ಬೆಸಸು), ರಕ್ಷಿಪ, ವರಿಪ, ಸನ್ನಿಪ. The instances are found in the ancient and mediæval dialect. The ಪ may be doubled, *e. g.* ಎನಿಪ್ಪ, ತರಿಪ್ಪ, ಬರಿಪ್ಪ, ಮಾಡಿಪ್ಪ; ಉದಯಿಪ್ಪ, ಬೆಸಪ್ಪ (see § 371, 3).

All themes with final ಇಸು and ಸು form their participle also by means of ವ (§ 180, 3), *e. g.* ಅಲಸುವ, ಏೞಿಸುವ, ಕಿನಿಸುವ, ಬೆಸಸುವ, ವರಿಸುವ, in the three dialects.

9, In the themes ಅವು and ತವು, these changing their final ಉ into ಇ before ಪ, *viz.* ಅವಿಪ, ತವಿಪ (Śabdânuśâsana sûtras 473. 480. 513). This rule is not in the Śabdamaṇidarpaṇa, in which the verb ಅವು does not occur at all. ಅವಿಪ, ತವಿಪ would, according to No. 8, be regular forms of ಅವಿಸು, ತವಿಸು.

10, Optionally in eleven of the themes ending in ರ್ (*cf.* No. 1 of this paragraph), *viz.* ಅಡರ್ಪ (of ಅಡರ್), ಅದಿರ್ಪ (of ಅದಿರ್), ಉದಿರ್ಪ, ಉಸಿರ್ಪ, ಕಸರ್ಪ, ತೊಡರ್ಪ, ಪಸರ್ಪ, ಪೊಡರ್ಪ, ಬಿದಿರ್ಪ, ಬೆಳರ್ಪ, ಮಿಳಿರ್ಪ (Śabdânuśâsana sûtra 511) in the ancient dialect. ಒಡರ್ಪ appears in the Jaimini bhârata. The ಪ may be doubled after the ರ್, *e. g.* ಅಡರ್ಪ್ಪ, ಉದಿರ್ಪ್ಪ (§ 371, 3).

Their usual forms with ವ are ಅಡರ್ವ or ಅಡರ್ವ್ವ, ಅದಿರ್ವ or ಅದಿರ್ವ್ವ, ಉದಿರ್ವ or ಉದಿರ್ವ್ವ, etc. (§ 180, 1; § 371, 3).

184. The fourth suffix of the present-future participle is **ಹ**. Originally it may have had the form of ಹ್ಹ too, as it first appears as a substitute of ಪ್ಪ in ಅಪ್ಪ (of ಆಗು), ಇಪ್ಪ (of ಇರ್), ತಪ್ಪ (of ತರ್), ಬಪ್ಪ (of ಬರ್, see § 183, 1. 7, remark). ಅಪ್ಪ (or ಅಪ, see § 189) optionally appears as **ಅಹ** in the ancient and mediæval dialect (*cf.* § 223). **ಇಹ** (for ಇಪ್ಪ), ತಹ (for ತಪ್ಪ), ಬಹ (for ಬಪ್ಪ) occur only in the mediæval one, in which there are likewise **ಬೇಹ** (for ಬೇೞ್ಪ) and **ಹೋಹ** (for ಪೋಪ, ಹೋಗುವ). The mediæval dialect occasionally shows the forms **ಆಹ** (for ಅಪ್ಪ, ಆಗುವ,

cf. the remark about ಅಪ in § 183, 7) and ಬಾಹ (for ಬಪ್ಪ or a ಬಾರ್ಪ; about theme ಬಾರ್ see §§ 52. 170. 210).

185. The simplest and, as it would appear, true **explanation of the so-called present-future participle** is to take it to be the genitive of verbal nouns, an explanation which is analogous to that given in § 178 regarding the so-called past participle (see also § 169) and well suits to its use. There are numerous verbal nouns in Kannaḍa formed by suffixing ಪು, ವು and ಹು to verbal themes (see § 243); such nouns allow the formation of the genitive singular by means of its primitive termination ಅ (§ 141, 1). The circumstance that many of the verbal nouns used to form the present-future participle do not exist nowadays apart from that use, constitutes no valid objection to the offered explanation.

A number of verbal nouns ending in ವು of which the genitive with final ಅ would exactly form the present-future participle, are ಅಱಿವು (knowing, genitive ಅಱಿವ), ಅೞಿವು (perishing, genitive ಅೞಿವ), ಇಱಿವು (stabbing), ಉೞಿವು (remaining), ಎರವು (begging), ಒಲವು (being pleased), ಕಳೆವು, ಕೞಿವು, ತಿಳಿವು, ತೆಱಿವು, ನಲಿವು, ನಿಲುವು, ಸೆನವು, ನೆರೆವು, ನೋವು, ಪಡುವು, ಪೞಿವು, ಮಱಿವು, ಮುರಿವು, ಮೇವು, ಸಾವು, ಹರೆವು, ಹಸಿವು; ತೊಳಪು, ಮಿಱುಪು, ತೋರ್ಪು, ಮಾರ್ಪು would be such as end in ಪು. See § 243, *A*, 18 *a*. 24.

What the grammarian Kêšava states regarding the past relative participle that in combination with suffixes it forms a kṛit or kṛilliṅga and vâčyaliṅga or višêshyâdhînaliṅga, in other words a declinable verbal base (see § 177. 200), he does state likewise regarding the present-future participle in combination with suffixes, it forming the bhavishyantikṛit or kṛilliṅga (*cf.* § 174 and see § 177).

The pronominal forms and pronouns mentioned in § 177 (*cf.* 193. 200) are the suffixes also for this participle, and besides nearly every declinable base is used after it. If it is followed by a noun, a consecutive compound is formed (*cf.* § 177 and see § 253, 2, *d*). About its combination with adverbs see § 282. See further §§ 254. 282. 298, 5. 316, 1. (330). 364.

The suffixes ಅಂ and ಅಳ್ appear, as in § 177, also as ಒಂ and ಒಳ್; thus we find ಅೞಿವೊಂ, ಕೆಯ್ವೊಂ, ಸಲ್ವೊಂ (in a šâsana between 680 and 696 A. D.), ಕಿಡಿಪೊಂ (in a šâsana of 707 A. D.), and ಎಮ್ಬೊಳ್ (in one of about 778 A. D.). The plural ಅರ್ has also the form of ಒರ್ in ಅಪ್ಪೊರ್, ಉಳ್ವೊರ್ (in a šâsana between 750 and 814 A. D.).

186. The **primitive meaning** of the so-called present-future participle (*cf.* § 179), if derived from the genitive singular of verbal nouns, will appear from the following instances, *viz.* ಅಱಿವಂ (ಅಱಿವ+ಅಂ), he or a man of knowing (either now or in future), *i. e.* he who knows or will know; ಅಱಿವಳ್ (ಅಱಿವ+ಅಳ್), she or a woman of knowing, *i. e.* she who knows or will know; ಅಱಿವುದು (ಅಱಿವ+ಉದು), it or a child, etc. of knowing, *i. e.* it which knows or will know; ಅಱಿವರ್ (ಅಱಿವ+ಅರ್), they or people (male or female) of knowing, *i. e.* they who know or will know; ಅಱಿವುವು (ಅಱಿವ+ಉವು), they or children, etc. of knowing, *i. e.* they which know or will know; ಕನ್ನಡವನ್ ಅಱಿವಂ, he of knowing Kannaḍa, *i. e.* he (or one) who knows Kannaḍa; ಮೇವ ಪುಲ್, grass of eating, *i. e.* grass which (an animal) eats or will eat; ತಿಳಿವ ನೀರ್, water of clearing, *i. e.* water that becomes clear or will become clear; ತೊಳಪ ಕನ್ನವುರಂ, an ear-ornament of shining, *i. e.* an ear-ornament which shines or will shine; ತೋರ್ಪ ಅಕ್ಕರಂ, a letter of appearing, *i. e.* a letter which appears or will appear.

In the above instances actually existing nouns appear the genitive of which presents the participle; in the now following instances nouns are to be assumed to exist:— ಉಳ್ಳಂ (of an ಉಳ್ಳವು), he of being (or having); ಉಳ್ಳಳ್, she of being (or having); ಉಳ್ಳುದು, it of being (or having); ಧನಮ್ ಉಳ್ಳಂ, riches of being he, *i. e.* he who has riches; ಎಳೆದು ಅಪ್ಪ (of an ಅಪ್ಪುವು) ಪಶು, an animal of being young, *i. e.* an animal which is young; ಪಾಡುವ (of a ಪಾಡುವು) ತುಮ್ಬಿ, a black bee of humming, *i. e.* a black bee which hums or will hum; ಬರ್ಪ (of a ಬರ್ಪು) ಕಾಲಂ, time of coming, *i. e.* time which comes; ಮಾಡುವ (of a ಮಾಡುವು) ಕಾರ್ಯಂ, a business of making, *i. e.* a business which (somebody) makes or will make; ಬೀಸುವ (of a ಬೀಸುವು) ಚಾಮರಂ, a chowrie of waving, *i. e.* a chowrie which (somebody) waves or will wave; ಮಾಟ್ಪರ್ (of a ಮಾಟ್ಪು), they of making, *i. e.* they who make or will make; ಹೋಗುವವನು (of a ಹೋಗುವು), he of going, *i. e.* he who goes or will go; ಹೋಗುವವಳು, she of going, *i. e.* she who goes or will go; ಹೋಗುವದು, it of going, *i. e.* it which goes or will go.

187. What Europeans call the infinitive of a verb Kannaḍa grammarians call ಕ್ರಿಯಾರ್ಥ, *i. e.* the meaning of a verb, and then the object, purpose or scope of (a verb's) action, ಕ್ರಿಯಾಪ್ರಯೋಜನ. Regarding the explanation of the infinitive see § 188.

There are four kinds of the infinitive, *viz.*

1, The first infinitive is formed by suffixing ಅಲ್ to the verbal theme, in which case, by euphonic junction (§ 213 *seq.*), a theme's final ಉ disappears, *e.g.* ಇರಲ್ (of ಇರ್), ಉಣಲ್ (of ಉಣ್), ಕಳಲ್ (of ಕಳ್), ಕೊಲಲ್,

ಕೊಳಲ್, ಗೆಲಲ್, ತರಲ್, ತಿನಲ್, ಪೇೞಿಲ್, ಮೆಲಲ್, ಪೊಗೞಿಲ್, ಬೇಡಲ್ (of ಬೇಡು), ಮಾಡಲ್ (of ಮಾಡು), ಮುತ್ತಲ್ (of ಮುತ್ತು), ಬಿತ್ತರಿಸಲ್ (of ಬಿತ್ತರಿಸು).

When the theme ends in ಇ or ಎ, ಅಲ್ may be suffixed immediately, as in ಕರೆ ಅಲ್ (a form that was occasionally used in the ancient dialect, § 215, 5, letter *a*), but generally an enunciative ಯ್ is used between, in in the three dialects, *e. g.* ಅಱಿಯಲ್ (of ಅಱಿ), ತಱಿಯಲ್, ನುಡಿಯಲ್, ಎಱಿಯಲ್ (of ಎಱಿ), ಕರೆಯಲ್, ಮಱೆಯಲ್. *Cf.* § 215, 2, letters *f. i.*

Infinitives with ಅಲ್ of monosyllabic themes that are a vowel or end in a vowel, are ಈಯಲ್ (of ಈ), ಕಾಯಲ್ (of ಕಾ), ತೇಯಲ್ (of ತೇ), ತೋಯಲ್ (of ತೋ), ನೋಯಲ್ (of ನೋ), ಬೇಯಲ್ (of ಬೇ), ವಿಶಾಯಲ್ (of ವಿಶಾ). *Cf.* § 215, 2, letters *d. g. k. m.*

Some monosyllabic themes ending in ಯ್ optionally double (dvitvavikalpa) the ಯ್ before ಅಲ್, *e. g.* ಪೊಯಲ್ or ಪೊಯ್ಯಲ್ (of ಪೊಯ್), ಕೊಯಲ್ or ಕೊಯ್ಯಲ್ (of ಕೊಯ್), ಗೆಯಲ್ or ಗೆಯ್ಯಲ್ (of ಗೆಯ್); the ಯ್ of the four themes ಉಯ್, ನೆಯ್, ಬಯ್ and ಸುಯ್ is always doubled (nityadvitva) before it, *viz.* ಉಯ್ಯಲ್, ನೆಯ್ಯಲ್, ಬಯ್ಯಲ್ and ಸುಯ್ಯಲ್. The dissyllabic theme ಅರಯ್ optionally doubles its ಯ್, *viz.* ಅರಯಲ್ or ಅರಯ್ಯಲ್. *Cf.* § 215, 7, *e.*

Nâgavarma (sûtra 234) suffixes ಅಲ್ to the lengthened theme of ತರ್ and ಬರ್, *viz.* ತಾರಲ್, ಬಾರಲ್ (*cf.* ತಾರೆ under No. 4 of this paragraph). *Cf.* § 210.

In the modern dialect ಅಲ್ is used only in the so-called passive (see § 315); in all other cases it uses ಅಲು, *i. e.* ಅಲ್ with a euphonic ಉ, a form that is not unfrequently found in the mediæval one too, *e. g.* ಅಲುಗಲು, ಇರಲು, ಗೆಲಲು, ತರಲು, ನಾಚಿಸಲ್ಲು, ಭಕ್ಷಿಸಲು, and occasionally also in the later ancient one, *e. g.* ಅಳಿಯಲು, ರಕ್ಷಿಸಲು, ಭಾವಿಸಲು, ಅಗಲು, ಇರಲು (in a šâsana of 1123 A. D.), ನಿರೀಕ್ಷಿಸಲು, ಎಱಗಲು (in a šâsana of 1182 A. D.). *Cf.* § 96, remark; see § 121, *a.*

In the ancient and mediæval dialect a **dative is formed from the infinitive with** ಅಲ್ **by means of** ಕೆ (see § 120, letters *a. b*), *e. g.* ಅಗಲ್ಕೆ, ಎನಲ್ಕೆ, ಪೇೞಿಲ್ಕೆ, ನುಡಿಯಲ್ಕೆ, ಮಱೆಯಲ್ಕೆ, ಪೊಗೞಿಲ್ಕೆ, ಬಿತ್ತರಿಸಲ್ಕೆ. **The dative of the infinitive with** ಅಲು **is formed by means of** ಇಕೆ **or** ಇಕ್ಕೆ in the modern dialect (see § 121, letter *c*), *e. g.* ತಿನ್ನಲಿಕೆ or ತಿನ್ನಲಿಕ್ಕೆ, ಬರೆಯಲಿಕೆ or ಬರೆಯಲಿಕ್ಕೆ. In the later ancient dialect we meet with the curious forms ಪೊಗಳಲುಕೆ (= ಪೊಗೞಿಲ್ಕೆ), ಅಗಲುಕೆ (= ಅಗಲ್ಕೆ, in a šâsana of 1123 A. D.; see § 121, *a.* Dat.).

About ಅಲ್ § 208 is to be compared.

2, The second infinitive ends in the vowel ಅ. The grammarian Kêšava states that this ಅ has originated by the elision (lôpa) of the final ಲ್ of ಅಲ್. This statement is only in so far of value, as it makes any rule about the way of suffixing the ಅ unnecessary, because it is identical with that of ಅಲ್.

This infinitive is used in the three dialects. Instances are ಕೊಯು or ಕೊಯ್ಯ್ಯ, ಗೆಯು or ಗೆಯ್ಯ್ಯ, ತರ, ಬರ, ಉಡ, ಮಾಡ, ಹೋಗ, ಎಸಗ, ಪ್ರಯೋಗಿಸ, ಕಡಿಯು, ನಡೆಯು, ಕರೆಯು, ಈಯು, ಕಾಯು, ತೇಯು.

In the infinitive formed by ಅ from themes with final ಇ and ಎ a sort of lengthening is allowed in the modern dialect, in which the ಅ disappears (*cf.* the accusative and genitive under letter *c* in § 130), *e. g.* ಇಟೀ may be used for ಇಟಿಯು, ಕರೇ for ಕರೆಯು.

An abnormal infinitive of ಕೊಳ್ (ಕೊಳ್ಳು) is ಕೋ, often used in the modern dialect. *Cf.* ಕೋತ in § 172; ಕೋ in § 206.

Remark.

The author once entertained the opinion (see Dictionary under ಅ 4) that the infinitive (or verbal noun, see § 188) ending in ಅ had a dative in the South-Mahratta country, *e. g.* ಮಾಡಕೆ or ಮಾಡಕ್ಕೆ, ಬರಕೆ or ಬರಕ್ಕೆ, and with the lengthening of ಅ, ನೋಡಾಕ (for ನೋಡಾಕೆ), ತಿಮ್ಬಾಕ (for ತಿಮ್ಬಾಕೆ, Nuḍigaṭṭu, page 36). Such dative forms are in common use there; but, instead from the infinitive (or verbal noun) with final ಅ, we now derive them from a verbal noun formed by means of the suffix ವ (for ಹ, see § 243, *A*, 20. 27), *i. e.* in the present instances from ಮಾಡುವ (= ಮಾಡುಹ), ಬರುವ, ನೋಡುವ, ತಿಮ್ಬುವ, the ಉವ being changed into ಒ and ಓ, *viz.* ಮಾಡೊ, ಬರೊ, ನೋಡೋ, ತಿಮ್ಬೋ, and then again into ಅ and ಆ, *viz.* ಮಾಡ, ಬರ, ನೋಡಾ, ತಿಮ್ಬಾ (*cf.* § 181, note *c*, and see ಓಕೆ in Dictionary; concerning the change of ಅ into ಒ see § 117, *a*, Nom. and Acc.; §§ 177. 185. 193). An instance with ಓ is: ಮಾತು ಅನ್ನೋಕೆ ಮಾಡಿ ಅದೆ, ಬೋನ ಉಣ್ಣೋಕೆ ಮಾಡಿ ಅದೆ, a word (or words) is (or are) made for saying, boiled rice is made for eating.

3, The third infinitive is represented by the verbal theme itself, and is occasionally found in the three dialects. It always immediately precedes a verb, ಇಟಿ ಬಿಡು (= ಇಟಿಯ ಬಿಡು), ಇಟಿವಾಯ್ತು (= ಇಟಿಯ ಹಾಯ್ತು), ಇಟಿಸು ನೂಂಕು (= ಇಟಿಸ ನೂಂಕು), ಕರೆ ಕಳಿಸು (= ಕರೆಯು-), ಕೆಡೆ ನೂಂಕು (= ಕೆಡೆಯು-), ಕೆಡೆ ಬಡಿ (= ಕೆಡೆಯು-), ತಿಳಿ ಹೇಟಿಬಿ (= ತಿಳಿಯು-), ತೂಗು ಹಾಕು (= ತೂಗ-), ತೆಗೆ ನೆಟಿ (= ತೆಗೆಯು-), ನೆನೆ ಹಾಕು (= ನೆನೆಯು-), ಪರೆಗಡಿ (= ಪರೆಯು ಕಡಿ), ಪರೆ ಮಾಡು (= ಪರೆಯು-), ಸದೆ ಬಡಿ (= ಸದೆಯು-).

4. The fourth infinitive consists of the theme with the suffix ಎ. The way of annexing the ಎ to verbal themes is identical with that of ಅಲ್ and ಅ. This infinitive of which the meaning and use is nearly the same as that of No. 1, belongs to the ancient and mediæval dialect; occasionally it is found also in modern poetry (§§ 365. 366, remark *a*).

Instances are ಎನೆ, ಕೊಲೆ, ಕೊಳೆ, ಉಣೆ, ತಿನೆ, ಬರೆ, ಮೆಲೆ, ಪೇೞೆ; ಕೊಯೆ or ಕೊಯ್ಯೆ, ಪೊಯೆ or ಪೊಯ್ಯೆ; ಆರಯೆ or ಆರಯ್ಯೆ; ಉಯ್ಯೆ, ನೆಯ್ಯೆ, ಬಯ್ಯೆ, ಸುಯ್ಯೆ; ಈಯೆ; ನುಡಿಯೆ, ನಡೆಯೆ; ಪಾಡೆ, ಪೊರ್ದೆ, ಪೋಗೆ; ಅಡರೆ, ಅದಿರೆ, ಬೆದಱೆ. *Cf.* § 215, 7, *e*.

The Basavapurâṇa suffixes the ಎ once to the long base of ತರ್, as it has ತಾರೆ (12, 43; *cf.* Nâgavarma's ತಾರಲ್ under No. 1; see § 210).

The grammarian Kêšava calls the infinitive with ಎ, from a meaning it not unfrequently has, **the locative state or condition (satisaptami or sati**, see §§ 188, remark; 286. 365).

188. **The force of the so-called infinitive** in Kannaḍa may be expressed by the following particles: — **to, in its prepositional meaning,** as ready to go, fit to eat; **to, denoting purpose, end, and futurity; so as to, so that; at the time that, when, while,** *e. g.* ತರಲ್, ತರ, to bring; ಮಾಡಲ್, ಮಾಡ, to make; ನಡೆಯಲ್, ನಡೆಯ, to walk; ಕೆಡಲ್, ಕೆಡ, so as to perish, so that (somebody or something) perishes or perished; ಕೆಡೆಯಲ್, ಕೆಡೆಯ, ಕೆಡೆ, ಕೆಡೆಯೆ, so as to fall down, so that (somebody or something) falls or fell down; ಪಾಡೆ, ಪಾಡಲ್, when (somebody or something) sings or sang; ಬರೆ, ಬರಲ್, while (something or somebody) comes or came. *Cf.* the use of the short infinitive with ಅ in §§ 170. 171. 210.

But these special significations are not primitive; they are derived somehow from the verbal noun which the infinitive originally was and very often still is. *Cf.* the verbal noun in § 100, and its use in §§ 165. 169. 173. 205, and also in the so-called passive (§ 315).

That **the infinitive ending in ಅಲ್** (ಅಲು, expressing 'being', 'condition') **is a verbal noun,** is an indisputable fact, because *e. g.* ಅೞಲ್ means 'grieving' and 'to grieve, etc.', ಉೞಲ್, 'ploughing' and 'to plough, etc.', ಊದಲ್, 'swelling' and 'to swell, etc.', ಒಕ್ಕಲ್, 'thrashing' and 'to thrash, etc.', ಕೂಡಲ್, 'joining' and 'to join, etc.', ಪಡಲ್, 'lying down' and 'to lie down, etc.', and because this infinitive is declinable, as it has a dative (see § 187, 1).

The character of being originally **a verbal noun** can **also** be attributed to the second infinitive, *viz.* **that with final** ಅ, as *e.g.* ಅಡ means 'cooking' and 'to cook, etc.', ಅಡಕ, 'compressing' and 'to compress, etc.', ಎತ್ತ, 'lifting up' and 'to lift up, etc.', ಗೆಲ, 'gaining' and 'to gain, etc.', ತೀರ, 'ending' and 'to end, etc.', ತೊಡ, 'putting on' and 'to put on, etc.', ಬರ, 'coming' and 'to come, etc.', ಸೋಲ, 'losing' and 'to lose, etc.'. *Cf.* § 205, 1, *b*, singular.—Verbal nouns, however, corresponding to the infinitive formed by ಅ and the insertion of ಯ್ between it and themes ending in ಇ and ಎ (as to form *e. g.* ಕಡಿಯ, ನಡೆಯ), are nowadays scarcely met with in Kannaḍa, although a few nouns end in ಯ, *e. g.* ಕೊಣ್ಡೆಯ, ಚಳೆಯ, ಚೊಲ್ಲೆಯ, ಪೊಲ್ಲೆಯ, ಬಱಿಯ, ಹೊಲ್ಲೆಯ. We think that ಯ has been superseded by ಹ or ವ in verbal nouns. There are numerous verbal nouns that end in ಹ (see § 243, *A*, 27) and some that end in ವ (see § 243, *A*, 20), and, besides, of the above nouns, ಚೊಲ್ಲೆಯ appears also as ಚೊಲ್ಲೆಹ, and ಹೊಲ್ಲೆಯ as ಹೊಲ್ಲೆಹ. Remember that in the present verbal participle (§ 172) ವ್ is not unfrequently used instead of ಯ್. At the same time we may conjecture that for verbal nouns, instead of themes with the formative ಯ, the simple theme ending in ಇ and ಎ was preferred (*cf.* §§ 100. 187, 3).

The third infinitive, being nothing else but **the verbal theme** itself which is **very often used as a noun,** requires no special remark.

Some verbal nouns which are equal in form to the fourth **infinitive** *i. e.* that with **final** ಎ, are ಉೞ್ಗೆ, 'loving' and 'to love, etc.', ಕಟ್ಟೆ, 'a structure' and 'to construct, etc.', ಕೆಡೆ, 'throwing down' and 'to throw down, etc.', ಕೆತ್ತೆ, 'a chip' and 'to chip, etc.', ಕೊಲೆ, 'killing' and 'to kill, etc.', ನಗೆ, 'laughing' and 'to laugh, etc.', ಪೊರೆ, 'joining' and 'to join, etc.', ಪೊಱೆ (or ಹೊಱೆ), 'a load for the head' and 'to carry on the head, etc.', ಬಾೞೆ, 'cultivating' and 'to cultivate, etc.'.—Verbal nouns which correspond to the infinitive with ಎ suffixed by means of the euphonic ಯ್ (*e. g.* ಕೆಡೆಯೆ, ನುಡಿಯೆ, ನಡೆಯೆ), we have not found in Kannaḍa; it may be that in such nouns ಯ್ was, for the sake of euphony, changed into ಗ್ (*cf.* ನಡಿಗೆ, ನಿಱಿಗೆ, ಮುರಿಗೆ, ಮುಱಿಗೆ) or ವ್ (*cf.* ತೆಱವೆ, ಮಱವೆ).

That the infinitive with ಎ was considered to be a verbal noun in ancient times seems to be corroborated by the following two sentences quoted by Kêšava (under sûtra 134, from Sujanôttaṁsa Hampa râja?):—ನಿಶ್ಶಂಕೆಯಿಂ ನೃಪನ ಪೇೞೆ, and ಚಿತ್ತಭವಗ್ರಹದ ಸೊಂಕೆ, literally 'an ordering of the king without fear' and 'a touching of the pudendum muliebre', *i. e.*

'when the king ordered fearlessly', and 'when the p. m. touched', in which the genitive stands before that infinitive as before a noun. *Cf.* 352, 1*a*.

Let us show by some further instances how the meaning of the infinitive was attached to the verbal noun by Kannaḍa people in their own peculiar way:—ತೊೞ್ತು ಗೆಲಸವಂ ಗೆಯ್ಯಲ್ ಅನುವಾದಂ, literally 'a female servant's work a doing he became ready', *i. e.* he became ready to do a female servant's work; ನೀರಂ ತರವೇೞ್ದಂ, lit. 'he ordered a bringing water', *i. e.* he ordered to bring water; ತಿನಲ್ ಕೊನ್ದಂ, lit. 'an eating he killed', *i. e.* he killed to eat; ತಿಳಿ ಹೇೞು, lit. 'an understanding tell!', *i. e.* tell (it) so that (I) understand!; ಮಾಡ ಹೋದನು, lit. 'a making he went', *i. e.* he went to make; ಕೆಡೆ ನೂಂಕಿದಂ, lit. 'a falling down he pushed', *i. e.* he pushed so that (it) fell down; ವನ್ದಿ ಪೊಗೞೆ, lit. 'the bard a praising', *i. e.* when the bard praises or praised; ಆನೆ ಬರೆ, lit. 'the elephant a coming', *i. e.* when the elephant comes or came; ನೇಸಱ್ ಮೂಡಲ್, lit. 'the sun a rising', *i. e.* when the sun rises or rose.

Regarding instances etc. see § 365.

Remark.

The specific meaning of 'at the time that', 'when', 'while' of the suffix ಅಲ್ or ಅಲು, which, like the suffix ಎ (§ 187, 4), it often has in the infinitive, can so to say be accounted for by the meaning of ಅಲ್, ಅಲು in § 109, letters *a* and *b*, locative. The suffix ಎ, expressing ಸತಿಸಪ್ತಮಿ, reminds one of the ಇ of the locative in § 109, letters *a*, *b*, *c*, as a final ಇ is occasionally used for ಎ; compare *e. g.* that the ancient form ಎ of the instrumental is ಇ in § 109, letters *b* and *c*.

189. The grammarian Kêšava observes "the verbal action (kriyĕ) changes according to the three times or tenses (kâlatrayapariṇâmi), and "the three (forms of) the conjugated verb (kriyâpada) tell the three times or tenses".

The three tenses (§§ 144. 145) are formed by suffixes (âgama) which are called "the indicators of the three tenses (kâlatrayasûčaka)".

The names of the suffixes are ದ, ತ; ದಪ, ದಪ್ಪ, ತಪ, ತಪ್ಪ, ದಹ; ವ, ಬ, ಪ, ಪ್ಪ, ಹ. Of these ದ, ತ are used for the past tense, ದಪ, ದಪ್ಪ, ತಪ, ತಪ್ಪ, ದಹ for the present tense, and ವ, ಬ, ಪ, ಪ್ಪ, ಹ for the future one.

It will be observed that ದ and ತ are the forms of the past relative participle (see § 175, 1. 2; § 176), and ವ, ಬ, ಪ, ಪ್ಪ and ಹ those of the (present-) future one (§§ 180-184).

ದಪ, ದಪ್ಪ, ತಪ, ತಪ್ಪ and ದಹ, the tense-suffixes of the present, are the past relative participle with final ದ and ತ to which ಅಪ, ಅಪ್ಪ and ಅಹ

are annexed. ಅಪ್ಪ and ಅಹ we have met with as substitutes of ಆಗುವ, the present-future relative participle of ಆಗು (see § 183, 7, remark; § 184); ಅಪ is another form of ಅಪ್ಪ and ಅಹ.

ದಹ is found only in the mediæval dialect wherein ಹ very frequently takes the place of ಪ.

190. Of the tense-suffixes mentioned in § 189 the **modern** dialect uses ದ and ತ for the past tense, and ವ (exceptionally also ಬ and ಹ, see § 182 and § 195 *seq.*) for the present-future one. **Its suffixes for indicating the present tense are,** as a rule, peculiar, **being** ಉತ and ಉತ್ತಂ, *i. e.* two of the terminations of the present verbal participle (see § 172).

191. It is necessary to remark that ದ and ತ are but two representatives of the finals of the variously formed past relative participle; they are to indicate that all the forms of the past relative participle as based on the past participle (see §§ 155-164; §§ 175, 1. 2, and 176) are meant.

The rules given regarding the formation of the (present-) future relative participle (§ 180 *seq.*) hold good also when it is used as the theme of the future tense.

192. In conjugation (âkhyâtamârga) **personal terminations** (vibhakti, pratyaya, âkhyâtavibhakti, kriyâvibhakti) are used. They are suffixed to the participial forms that indicate the tenses (§§ 189-191). When a verb ends in such a termination, it is a conjugated verb (pada, âkhyâtapada, kriyâpada; see §§ 69. 144).

By means of the personal terminations **the three persons** (purusha, § 147) in the singular and plural are formed.

It is the custom of Kannaḍa grammarians to speak of only six (ಆರು) personal terminations (though there are actually ten), adducing those for the first person (prathamapurusha) feminine singular (and plural) and those for the third person (uttamapurusha) neuter singular and plural separately; we shall exhibit them all at one view in the next paragraph.

193. In presenting the personal terminations let us use the European way of placing and naming the persons, *viz.* **first person** (**uttamapurusha**), **second person** (**madhyamapurusha**), and **third person** (**prathamapurusha**).

1, The following are **the personal terminations** of **the present, past and future tense in the ancient dialect:**

	Singular.	*Plural.*
1st pers.	ಎಂ, (before vowels) ಎನ್.	ಎಂ (if not followed by a vowel); ಎವು (*cf.* § 137, *a*, nominative plural).
2nd pers.	ಅಯ್.	ಇರ್.
3rd pers.		
masc.	ಅಂ, (before vowels) ಅನ್; ಒಂ.	ಅರ್; ಒರ್ (§ 198, 3, **remark**; § 200, 1); ಆರ್ (§ 198, 3, **remark**; § 201, 1); ಅರು (198, 3, remark).
fem.	ಅಳ್; ಒಳ್; ಆಳ್ (§ 198, 3, remark).	ಅರ್; (ಒರ್).
neut.	ಉದು; ಇತು, ಇತ್ತು; ಅತ್ತು; ತು.	ಉವು; exceptionally ಅವು (§ 194, remark 1; § 198, 1).

About ಅದು and ಅವು of the negative see §§ 209. 210.

The personal terminations ಅಂ, ಒಂ, ಅಳ್, ಒಳ್, ಉದು, ಅರ್, and ಉವು are also the suffixes for the kṛilliṅgas in §§ 177. 179. 185. 186. 198, remark 1. 253.

2, The following are the corresponding personal terminations of the mediæval dialect:

	Singular.	*Plural.*
1st pers.	ಎಂ, (before vowels) ಎನ್; ಎನು; ಎ.	ಎವು.
2nd pers.	ಎ.	(ಇರ್); ಇರಿ.
3rd pers.		
masc.	ಅಂ, (before vowels) ಅನ್; ಅನು; ಅ.	(ಅರ್); ಅರು.
fem.	(ಅಳ್); ಅಳು.	(ಅರ್); ಅರು.
neut.	ಉದು; ಇತು, ಇತ್ತು; ಅತ್ತು; ತು.	ಅವು.

An occasional ಅದು for ಉದು in MSS. for the third person singular neuter is perhaps a mistake of the copyist.

3, The following are the corresponding personal terminations of the modern dialect:

	Singular.	*Plural.*
1st pers.	ಎನು; ಎ.	ಎವು; ಇವಿ.
2nd pers.	ಎ; ಇ.	ಇರಿ.
3rd pers.		
masc.	ಅನು; ಅ.	ಅರು.
fem.	ಅಳು.	ಅರು.
neut.	ಅದು; ಇತು; ತು.	ಅವು.

Remarks.

From a comparison of the forms of the terminations in the three dialects it follows that the sŏnnĕ in ಎಂ, the sŏnnĕ in ಅಂ, and the ನು (*i. e.* the sŏnnĕ and a euphonic ಉ) in ಅನು and ಎನು are not radical.

The sŏnnĕ or its substitute ವು in the first person plural reminds one of the plural of the neuter pronouns (§ 136) and of the sŏnnĕ and its substitutes ವ್ and ವು of that of the personal ones (§ 137).

ಅದು, ಉದು, ಇತು (for ಇದು), ಅತ್ತು (for ಅದು), ತು (for ಅದು or ಇದು or ಉದು, *cf.* §§ 116. 122. 138, *d*, 3. 173. 265), are the demonstrative neuter pronouns singular ಅದು, ಉದು, ಇದು (§§ 90. 102, 8, letter *b*) and the corresponding pronominal forms; ಅವು, ಉವು are the plural of ಅದು, ಉದು (§ 136).

ಅಂ, ಅನು and (the crude form) ಅ mean 'he' (see § 115; § 138, *d*, 3 and remark; § 177), ಅಳ್ and ಅಳು (*i. e.* ಅಳ್ with a euphonic ಉ), 'she' (*cf.* §§ 177. 185. 186). In ಓಂ and ಓಳ್, ಅ has taken the form of ಓ (*cf.* § 117, *a*). The ಆ in ಆಳ್ is either simply euphonically lengthened, or ಆಳ್ stands for the pronoun ಅವಳ್.

ಅರ್ and ಅರು (*i. e.* ಅರ್ with a euphonic ಉ) are the plural of ಅಂ, ಅನು, ಅ, ಅಳ್ and ಅಳು (*cf.* §§ 119, *a*; 134. 177). In ಓರ್, ಅ has taken the form of ಓ. The ಆ in ಆರ್ is either euphonically lengthened or stands for the pronoun ಅವರ್.

ಇ, ಎ and ಅಯ್ are connected with the ಇ, ಈ of the pronoun of the second person (§ 138); their plural ಇರ್ has taken the plural sign ರ್ (for ಅರ್, etc.; *cf.* § 119); ಇರಿ is ಇರ್ and an honorific ಇ, ಇರಿ often being an honorific plural (*cf.* § 205, 2. 3, plural). The ಎ in ಎ, ಎಂ, ಎನು, and ಎವು is connected with the ಎ of the pronoun of the first person (§ 138).

By the way it may be stated that from ಅಂ, ಅನು, ಅ, ಅಳ್, ಅಳು the remote, intermediate and proximate demonstrative pronouns are formed by prefixing ಅ, ಉ and ಇ by means of a euphonic ವ್, *viz.* ಅವಂ (ಅ+ ವ್ +ಅಂ), lit. 'that-he', ಅವನು, ಅವ; ಅವಳ್, lit. 'that-she', ಅವಳು; ಉವಂ, lit. 'this intermediate-he'; ಉವಳ್; ಇವಂ, lit. 'this-he', ಇವನು, ಇವ; ಇವಳ್, ಇವಳು, ಅ, ಉ and ಇ being other forms of ಆ, ಊ and ಈ (see § 265). *Cf.* § 122 about ತ್, ತ್ತು, ದ್.

194. The personal terminations of the preceding paragraph are, as remarked (§ 192), suffixed to the participial forms that indicate the tenses which in the case of the present tense are ದ+ಅಪ, ದ+ಅಪ್ಪ, ತ+ಅಪ, ತ+ಅಪ್ಪ in the ancient dialect, and generally ದ+ಅಹ in the mediæval one.

Let us take as an illustration the verb ಕೇಳ್, to hear, the relative past participle of which is ಕೇಳ್ದ (ಕೇಳ್+ದ), meaning 'of the having heard' (see § 179); to this *e. g.* ಅಪ, meaning 'of the being' (§§ 186. 201), is added, and then *e. g.* the personal termination of the first person singular

ಎಂ, meaning 'I'. So the literal translation would be 'of the having heard-of the being-I', *i. e.* I who is one who has heard, or I hear. The present tense is therefore a sort of compound tense (see § 313). To comprehend that its meaning can be expressed by Kannaḍa people in the above manner, it is necessary to know that they, in order to show their ready attention or obedience, not unfrequently use the past tense for the present or future one. For instance, if you say to some one, Come!, the reply is, I came, *i. e.* my coming is an accomplished fact. See § 366, remark *b*.

The present tense in the ancient dialect of the verb ಕೇಳ್ accordingly is as follows:

	Singular.	*Plural.*
1st pers.	ಕೇಳ್ದಪೆಂ (ಕೇಳ್ದ+ಅಪ+ಎಂ) or ಕೇಳ್ದಪ್ಪೆಂ (ಕೇಳ್ದ+ಅಪ್ಪ+ಎಂ), I hear.	ಕೇಳ್ದಪೆಂ (ಕೇಳ್ದ+ಅಪ+ಎಂ) or ಕೇಳ್ದಪ್ಪೆಂ (ಕೇಳ್ದ+ಅಪ್ಪ+ಎಂ), and ಕೇಳ್ದಪೆವು (ಕೇಳ್ದ+ಅಪ+ಎವು) or ಕೇಳ್ದಪ್ಪೆವು (ಕೇಳ್ದ+ಅಪ್ಪ+ಎವು), we hear.
2nd pers.	ಕೇಳ್ದಪಯ್ (ಕೇಳ್ದ+ಅಪ+ಅಯ್) or ಕೇಳ್ದಪ್ಪಯ್ (ಕೇಳ್ದ+ಅಪ್ಪ+ಅಯ್), thou hearest.	ಕೇಳ್ದಪಿರ್ (ಕೇಳ್ದ+ಅಪ+ಇರ್) or ಕೇಳ್ದಪ್ಪಿರ್ (ಕೇಳ್ದ+ಅಪ್ಪ+ಇರ್), you hear.
3rd pers.		
masc.	ಕೇಳ್ದಪಂ (ಕೇಳ್ದ+ಅಪ+ಅಂ) or ಕೇಳ್ದಪ್ಪಂ (ಕೇಳ್ದ+ಅಪ್ಪ+ಅಂ), he hears.	ಕೇಳ್ದಪರ್ (ಕೇಳ್ದ+ಅಪ+ಅರ್) or ಕೇಳ್ದಪ್ಪರ್ (ಕೇಳ್ದ+ಅಪ್ಪ+ಅರ್), they hear.
fem.	ಕೇಳ್ದಪಳ್ (ಕೇಳ್ದ+ಅಪ+ಅಳ್) or ಕೇಳ್ದಪ್ಪಳ್ (ಕೇಳ್ದ+ಅಪ್ಪ+ಅಳ್), she hears.	ಕೇಳ್ದಪರ್ (ಕೇಳ್ದ+ಅಪ+ಅರ್) or ಕೇಳ್ದಪ್ಪರ್ (ಕೇಳ್ದ+ಅಪ್ಪ+ಅರ್), they hear.
neut.	ಕೇಳ್ದಪುದು (ಕೇಳ್ದ+ಅಪ+ಉದು) or ಕೇಳ್ದಪ್ಪುದು (ಕೇಳ್ದ+ಅಪ್ಪ+ಉದು) it hears.	ಕೇಳ್ದಪುವು (ಕೇಳ್ದ+ಅಪ+ಉವು) or ಕೇಳ್ದಪ್ಪುವು (ಕೇಳ್ದ+ಅಪ್ಪ+ಉವು), they hear.

Other instances in the first person singular are ಕುಡಿದಪೆಂ (ಕುಡಿದ+ಅಪ+ಎಂ) or ಕುಡಿದಪ್ಪೆಂ (ಕುಡಿದ+ಅಪ್ಪ+ಎಂ, of ಕುಡಿ, to drink), ನಾಣ್ಚಿದಪೆಂ (ನಾಣ್ಚಿದ+ಅಪ+ಎಂ) or ನಾಣ್ಚಿದಪ್ಪೆಂ (ನಾಣ್ಚಿದ+ಅಪ್ಪ+ಎಂ, of ನಾಣ್ಚು, to become abashed), ಕಲ್ತಪೆಂ (ಕಲ್ತ+ಅಪ+ಎಂ) or ಕಲ್ತಪ್ಪೆಂ (ಕಲ್ತ+ಅಪ್ಪ+ಎಂ, of ಕಲ್, to learn), ತನ್ದಪೆಂ (ತನ್ದ+ಅಪ+ಎಂ) or ತನ್ದಪ್ಪೆಂ (ತನ್ದ+ಅಪ್ಪ+ಎಂ, of ತರ್, to bring), ಕೊಟ್ಟಪೆಂ (ಕೊಟ್ಟ+ಅಪ+ಎಂ) or ಕೊಟ್ಟಪ್ಪೆಂ (ಕೊಟ್ಟ+ಅಪ್ಪ+ಎಂ, of ಕುಡು, to give), ಇತ್ತಪೆಂ (ಇತ್ತ+ಅಪ+ಎಂ) or ಇತ್ತಪ್ಪೆಂ (ಇತ್ತ+ಅಪ್ಪ+ಎಂ, of ಈ, to give). See § 366.

The present tense of ಕೇಳ್ or ಕೇಳು (see § 166), in the mediæval dialect, in which ಅಹ, 'of the being', is nearly constantly used instead of ಅಪ or ಅಪ್ಪ, is as follows:

	Singular.	*Plural.*
1st pers.	ಕೇಳ್ದಹೆಂ (occasionally ಕೇಳ್ದಪೆಂ), ಕೇಳ್ದಹೆನು, ಕೇಳ್ದಹೆ, or ಕೇಳಿದಹೆಂ (occasionally ಕೇಳಿದಪೆಂ), ಕೇಳಿದಹೆನು, ಕೇಳಿದಹೆ.	ಕೇಳ್ದಹೆವು.
2nd pers.	ಕೇಳ್ದಹೆ (or ಕೇಳಿದಹೆ).	ಕೇಳ್ದಹಿರಿ.
3rd pers.		
masc.	ಕೇಳ್ದಹಂ, ಕೇಳ್ದಹನು (or ಕೇಳಿದಹಂ, etc.).	(ಕೇಳ್ದಹರ್), ಕೇಳ್ದಹರು.
fem.	(ಕೇಳ್ದಹಳ್), ಕೇಳ್ದಹಳು (or ಕೇಳಿದಹಳ್, etc.).	(ಕೇಳ್ದಹರ್), ಕೇಳ್ದಹರು.
neut.	ಕೇಳ್ದಹುದು (or ಕೇಳಿದಹುದು).	ಕೇಳ್ದಹವು.

Other instances in the first person singular are ಇರ್ದಹೆಂ (of ಇರ್, to be), ಎನ್ದಹೆಂ (of ಎನ್, to say), ಕವಿದಹೆಂ (of ಕವಿ, to rush upon), ಕೆಡೆದಹೆಂ or ಕೆಡದಹೆಂ (of ಕೆಡೆ, to fall down), ಕೊಟ್ಟಹೆಂ (of ಕುಡು or ಕೊಡು, to give), ಕೊಣ್ಡಹೆಂ (of ಕೊಳ್, to take), ಸತ್ತಹೆಂ (of ಸಾಯ್, to die), ಆದಹೆಂ (of ಆಗು, to become), ಹೋದಹೆಂ (of ಹೋಗು, to go), ಹೇೞ್ದಪೆಂ (or ಹೇೞ್ದಹೆಂ, of ಹೇೞು, to tell). Regarding ಅಹೆಂ, etc. see § 201, 2.

Remarks.

1, **There is one irregularly formed present in the ancient language, namely that of ಉಳ್, to be, which changes its vowel ಉ into ಒ in that tense (except in the 3rd person singular neuter, *cf.* also § 180, remark after 6) and receives no participial form to indicate the tense. As ಒಳ್ is also a verbal noun, the personal terminations (§ 193) appear to have been attached to the genitive of this ಒಳ್, *i. e.* ಒಳ, ಒಳೆಂ (ಒಳ + ಎಂ), *e. g.* meaning 'of the being-I', *i. e.* I am. A peculiarity is that it uses the suffix ಅವು (for ಉವು) in the 3rd person plural neuter. Its paradigm is:**

	Singular.	*Plural.*
1st pers.	ಒಳೆಂ.	ಒಳೆವು.
2nd pers.	ಒಳಯ್.	ಒಳಿರ್.
3rd pers.		
masc.	ಒಳಂ.	ಒಳರ್.
fem.	ಒಳಳ್.	ಒಳರ್.
neut.	ಉಣ್ಟು.	ಒಳವು.

ಉಣ್ಟು, originally ಉಳ್ತು (*i. e.* ಉಳ್ + ತು, § 122), is a verbal noun (bhâvavačana) meaning literally 'a being-it', and as such is used for the 3rd person masculine, feminine and neuter, singular and plural in the mediæval and modern dialect. About bhâvavačanas see the paragraphs quoted in § 243.

2, The author of the Šabdânušâsana, against Kêšava's sûtra 73, makes the 3rd person singular of the present tense a kṛit or kṛilliṅga and declines it, *e. g.* ನೋಡಿದಪನಂ, ಮಾಡಿದಪಂಗೆ, in his sûtras 447. 448; Kêšava calls only the past relative participle and the present-future relative participle a declinable kṛit; see §§ 177. 185.

195. In § 190 it has been stated that **modern Kannaḍa has a peculiar present tense.** It has, however, not abandoned the use of the grammatical structure of the present tense as it appears in § 194, but has changed the form of the tense-suffix ಅಹ, 'of the being', combined with the personal terminations (see § 201, 2), and **given a different meaning to the tense.**

Its forms of ಅಹ combined with the personal terminations are as follows:

	Singular.	*Plural.*
1st pers.	ಹೇನು (ಏನು) for ಅಹೆನು (ಅಹ+ಎನು).	ಹೇವು (ಏವು) for ಅಹೆವು (ಅಹ+ಎವು).
2nd pers.	ಹೀ (ಈ) for ಅಹಿ (ಅಹ+ಇ).	ಹೀರಿ (ಈರಿ) for ಅಹಿರಿ (ಅಹ+ಇರಿ).
3rd pers.		
masc.	ಹಾನು (ಆನು) for ಅಹನು (ಅಹ + ಅನು).	ಹಾರು (ಆರು) for ಅಹರು (ಅಹ+ಅರು).
fem.	ಹಾಳು (ಆಳು) for ಅಹಳು (ಅಹ + ಅಳು).	ಹಾರು (ಆರು) for ಅಹರು (ಅಹ+ಅರು).
neut.	ಹೀತು (ಈತು) for an ಅಹಿತು (ಅಹ + ಇತು, which must have been another form of ಅಹುದು).	ಹಾವು (ಆವು) for ಅಹವು (ಅಹ+ಅವು).

The initial ಹ್ of the forms of ಹೇನು, ಹೀ, ಹಾನು, ಹಾಳು, ಹೀತು, etc., which have been formed by metathesis and lengthening the vowels (see the frequently used ಹೌದು for ಅಹುದು in § 201, 2, and compare the noun ಸೂಲು for ಉಸುಲು, and the adverbs ಹೀಗೆ, ಹಾಗೆ for ಇಹಗೆ, ಅಹಗೆ in § 212, 4), is commonly left out, so that the forms in parenthesis ಏನು, ಈ, ಆನು, ಆಳು, ಈತು, etc. are in general use, whereas those with ಹ್ are at present only occasionally still employed for the verb ಇರು (ಇರ್), to be, especially when the ಏ of emphasis is added (see § 196).

Let us give a paradigm of the present tense of ಇರು (ಇರ್), the past relative participle of which is ಇದ್ದ (=ಇದ್ರ, see §§ 160, 7; 175, 1), 'of the having been'.

	Singular.	*Plural.*
1st pers.	ಇದ್ಧೇನು (ಇದ್ದ + ಹೇನು), or ಇದ್ದೇನು (ಇದ್ದ+ ಏನು), literally 'of the having been-of the being-I' (see § 194).	ಇದ್ಧೇವು, or ಇದ್ದೇವು.
2nd pers.	ಇದ್ಧೀ, or ಇದ್ದೀ.	ಇದ್ಧೀರಿ, or ಇದ್ದೀರಿ.
3rd pers.		
masc.	ಇದ್ಧಾನು, or ಇದ್ದಾನು.	ಇದ್ಧಾರು, or ಇದ್ದಾರು.
fem.	ಇದ್ಧಾಳು, or ಇದ್ದಾಳು.	ಇದ್ಧಾರು, or ಇದ್ದಾರು.
neut.	ಇದ್ಧೀತು, or ಇದ್ದೀತು.	ಇದ್ಧಾವು, or ಇದ್ದಾವು.

Other instances of the first person singular are ಬನ್ದೇನು (originally ಬನ್ಧೇನು, of ಬರು, to come), ನುಡಿದೇನು (orig. ನುಡಿಧೇನು, of ನುಡಿ, to speak), ಆದೇನು (orig. ಆಧೇನು, of ಆಗು, to become, to be). For ಆದೇನು the rustic dialect occasionally uses ಅದೇನು in the sense of ಇದ್ದೇನು (ಅದ being used for ಆದ, see §§ 176. 196).

A peculiarity is that in the formation of the present tense under consideration the suffix ದ is not added to the ಇ of the past participle of themes ending in ಉ in the three dialects (see §§ 166. 168), ಏನು, ಈ, ಆನು, etc. being annexed directly to ಇ, in which case ಇ occasionally disappears before them (see § 215). Thus ಮಾಡು, to make, forms this tense in the following manner:

	Singular.	*Plural.*
1st pers.	ಮಾಡ್ಯೇನು (ಮಾಡಿ + ಎನು for ಮಾಡಿದ+ಎನು), or ಮಾಡೇನು.	ಮಾಡ್ಯೇವು, or ಮಾಡೇವು.
2nd pers.	ಮಾಡೀ (ಮಾಡಿ + ಈ for ಮಾಡಿದ + ಈ).	ಮಾಡೀರಿ.
3rd pers.		
masc.	ಮಾಡ್ಯಾನು, or ಮಾಡಿಯಾನು.	ಮಾಡ್ಯಾರು, or ಮಾಡಿಯಾರು.
fem.	ಮಾಡ್ಯಾಳು, or ಮಾಡಿಯಾಳು.	ಮಾಡ್ಯಾರು, or ಮಾಡಿಯಾರು.
neut.	ಮಾಡೀತು.	ಮಾಡ್ಯಾವು, or ಮಾಡಿಯಾವು.

There can be no doubt whatever that we have here the ancient present tense in a somewhat altered form, although the meaning has undergone an essential change; for this form of the present tense is nowadays used to convey the idea of uncertainty or possibility, and may be called the

contingent present-future tense, as *e. g.* ಇದ್ದೇನು or ಇದ್ದೇನು means 'I may be' or 'I shall perhaps be'; ಬನ್ದೇನು, 'I may come' or 'I shall perhaps come'; ಮಾಡ್ಯೇನು, 'I may make' or 'I shall perhaps make'.

In the mediæval dialect the author has met with only one clear instance of this present, *viz.* ನಡೆದಾನು (see under ಅವಸೊಬ್ಬು in the Dictionary, which however stands for ನಡೆದಹನು without the meaning of contingency. ಬನ್ದೀತು (in Basavapurâṇa 16, 28) may be a mistake for ಬನ್ದಿತ್ತು.

The idea of uncertainty or possibility was, as it would appear, not attached to the present tense of this paragraph before the introduction of the present tense of § 196 into the modern Kannaḍa dialect.

About instances see § 366, remark *a*.

196. The modern dialect having given a different meaning to the present tense of the ancient and mediæval one, **formed a present tense of its own.**

1, For this purpose, **in the first instance,** it suffixed **the letter** ಎ **of emphasis** to the personal **terminations** ending in ಉ combined with ಅಹ (§ 195) in order to express the idea of certainty or to distinctly denote the present, leaving however the second person singular and plural as it was, but allowing to shorten the ಹೀ or ಈ of the second person singular.

For the third person singular neuter it introduced the forms ಅಯ್ತೆ (*i. e.* ಅಯ್ತು+ಎ, see § 199), ಅದೆ (*i. e.* ಅದು+ಎ) and ಇದೆ (*i. e.* ಇದು+ಎ); and for the third person plural neuter it introduced, as optional forms, ಅವೆ (*i. e.* ಅವು+ಎ) and ಇವೆ (*i. e.* ಇವು+ಎ).

ಅದೆ, ಇದೆ, ಅವೆ, ಇವೆ probably are the demonstrative pronouns of that shape (§§ 102, 8, *b*; 122. 136)+ಎ, 'even that', 'even this', 'even those', 'even these'.

The verbs concerned here are two, *viz.* ಆಗು, to be (to become), of which the relative past participles are ಅಯ್ದು, ಆದ (see §§ 166. 176. 199; *cf.* ಆದೇನು in § 195), and ಇರು (ಇರ್), to be.

The personal terminations combined with ಅಹ to which the ಎ of emphasis is suffixed, and the additional forms are the following:

	Singular.	*Plural.*
1st pers.	ಹೇನೆ, ಏನೆ (for ಹೇನು, ಏನು of § 195).	ಹೇವೆ, ಏವೆ (for ಹೇವು, ಏವು).
2nd pers.	ಹೀ, ಈ, or ಹಿ, ಇ.	ಹೀರಿ, ಈರಿ.

3rd pers.	*Singular.*	*Plural.*
masc.	ಹಾನೆ, ಆನೆ (for ಹಾನು, ಆನು of § 195).	ಹಾರೆ, ಆರೆ (for ಹಾರು, ಆರು).
fem.	ಹಾಳೆ, ಆಳೆ (for ಹಾಳು, ಆಳು of § 195).	ಹಾರೆ, ಆರೆ (for ಹಾರು, ಆರು).
neut.	ಅಯ್ತೆ, ಅದೆ, (ಇದೆ).	ಹಾವೆ, ಆವೆ (for ಹಾವು, ಆವು), ಅವೆ, (ಇವೆ).

Compare the forms of the Perfect ಬಿಟ್ಟಾನೆ, ಕೂತಾರೆ in § 313, 4.

The verb ಅಗು, to be, is conjugated in this present tense as follows:

	Singular.	*Plural.*
1st pers.	ಅಯ್ದೇನೆ (ಅಯ್ದ + ಏನೆ) or ಅದೇನೆ (ಅದ + ಏನೆ), literally 'of the having been-of the being-I-indeed', *i. e.* I am indeed, I am.	ಅಯ್ದೇವೆ, ಅದೇವೆ.
2nd pers.	ಅಯ್ದಿ, ಅದಿ, or ಅಯಿದ್ದಿ, ಅದೀ.	ಅಯಿದ್ದಿರಿ, ಅದೀರಿ.
3rd pers.		
masc.	ಅಯ್ದಾನೆ, ಅದಾನೆ.	ಅಯ್ದಾರೆ, ಅದಾರೆ.
fem.	ಅಯ್ದಾಳೆ, ಅದಾಳೆ.	ಅಯ್ದಾರೆ, ಅದಾರೆ.
neut.	ಅಯ್ತೆ, or ಅದೆ; ಇದೆ.	ಅಯ್ದಾವೆ, ಅದಾವೆ, or ಅವೆ; ಇವೆ.

The verb ಇರು (ಇರ್), to be, a paradigm of the contingent present tense of which has been given in § 195, is conjugated in this present tense as follows:

	Singular.	*Plural*
1st pers.	ಇದ್ಧೇನೆ (ಇದ್ದ + ಹೇನೆ), literally 'of the having been-of the being-I-indeed', *i. e.* I am indeed, I am.	ಇದ್ಧೇವೆ.
2nd pers.	ಇದ್ಧೀ, or ಇದ್ಧಿ.	ಇದ್ಧೀರಿ.
3rd pers.		
masc.	ಇದ್ಧಾನೆ.	ಇದ್ಧಾರೆ.
fem.	ಇದ್ಧಾಳೆ.	ಇದ್ಧಾರೆ.
neut.	ಅಯ್ತೆ, or ಅದೆ; ಇದೆ.	ಇದ್ಧಾವೆ, or ಅವೆ; ಇವೆ.

In the Southern Mahratta country there exist also the forms ಇದ್ದೇನೆ, ಇದ್ದೀ, etc., the initial ಹ್ of ಹೇನೆ, ಹೀ, etc. being omitted.

2, But this way of conjugation is restricted to the present of ಆಗು and ಇರು; for, as stated in § 190, ಉತ and ಉತ್ತ, two pronominal forms (see § 173), are the tense-suffixes to which, in all other cases, the modern dialect attaches ಏನೆ, ಈ or ಇ, ಆನೆ, etc.

The present tense of ಇರು, to be, formed according to this method, is as follows:

	Singular.	*Plural.*
1st pers.	ಇರುತೇನೆ (ಇರು + ಉತ + ಏನೆ) or ಇರುತ್ತೇನೆ (ಇರು + ಉತ್ತ + ಏನೆ), literally 'a being-this-I am indeed', *i. e.* being I am indeed, I am.	ಇರುತೇವೆ or ಇರುತ್ತೇವೆ.
2nd pers.	ಇರುತೀ or ಇರುತ್ತೀ, ಇರುತಿ or ಇರುತ್ತಿ.	ಇರುತೀರಿ or ಇರುತ್ತೀರಿ.
3rd pers.		
masc.	ಇರುತಾನೆ or ಇರುತ್ತಾನೆ.	ಇರುತಾರೆ or ಇರುತ್ತಾರೆ.
fem.	ಇರುತಾಳೆ or ಇರುತ್ತಾಳೆ.	ಇರುತಾರೆ or ಇರುತ್ತಾರೆ.
neut.	ಇರುತಯ್ತೆ, ಇರುತದೆ, or ಇರುತ್ತಯ್ತೆ, ಇರುತ್ತದೆ.	ಇರುತಾವೆ, ಇರುತವೆ, or ಇರುತ್ತಾವೆ, ಇರುತ್ತವೆ.

Other instances in the first person singular are ಬರುತೇನೆ or ಬರುತ್ತೇನೆ (of ಬರು, to come, literally 'a coming-this-I am indeed', I come), ಹೋಗುತೇನೆ or ಹೋಗುತ್ತೇನೆ (of ಹೋಗು, to go), ಕೇಳುತೇನೆ or ಕೇಳುತ್ತೇನೆ (of ಕೇಳು, to hear), ಇೞಿಯುತೇನೆ or ಇೞಿಯುತ್ತೇನೆ (of ಇೞಿ, to descend), ನಡೆಯುತೇನೆ or ನಡೆಯುತ್ತೇನೆ (of ನಡೆ, to walk).

Remarks.

1, ಅದೆ, (ಅವೆ), ಇದೆ, ಇವೆ are employed also in the mediæval dialect, either by themselves or in union with ಉತ, ಉತ್ತ, to form the third person singular and plural of the present tense, *e. g.* ತುಪ್ಪವ್ ಅದೆ ನೆಲುಹಿನ ಗಡಿಗೆಯಲಿ; ಧನ(ಂ) ಸಿಂಹಾಸನದ ಕೆಳಗೆ ಇದೆ; ಕಱೆವುತದೆ; ಮೂಡುತ್ತಿದೆ; ಹೇಱುತಿವೆ.

2, In the rustic modern dialect the present tense of the verb ಅನ್ (ಅನು, ಅನ್ನು), to say, is as follows:

	Singular.	*Plural.*
1st pers.	ಅನ್ತೇನೆ (for ಅನುತೇನೆ, ಅನುತ್ತೇನೆ).	ಅನ್ತೇವೆ.
2nd pers.	ಅನ್ತೀ or ಅನ್ತಿ.	ಅನ್ತೀರಿ.
3rd pers.		
masc.	ಅನ್ತಾನೆ.	ಅನ್ತಾರೆ.
fem.	ಅನ್ತಾಳೆ.	ಅನ್ತಾರೆ.
neut.	ಅನ್ತಯ್ತೆ or ಅನ್ತದೆ.	ಅನ್ತಾವೆ, ಅನ್ತವೆ.

3, In the modern dialect there is a form used for the third person singular neuter of the present tense which in reality is nothing but the present participle (with the emphatical or perhaps formative ಎ) bearing its original meaning, *viz.* that of a verbal noun (see § 173), *e.g.* ಆಗುತ್ತೆ, it becomes, that literally means 'a becoming-this-indeed', if the ಎ be emphatical. Other instances are ಇರುತ್ತೆ, it is, ಪಡುತ್ತೆ, it experiences, ಬರುತ್ತೆ, it comes. *Cf.* No. 4.

4, Again in the modern dialect the form ಅನ್ತೆ of the verb ಅನ್ (ಅನು, ಅನ್ನು), to say, expresses 'it (rumour) says', 'they say', '*on dit*' (see § 336). It is possible that this ಅನ್ತೆ is corrupted from ಅನುತೆ or ಅನುತ್ತೆ, the present participle of ಅನ್, used in its primitive sense of 'a saying-this-indeed', if the ಎ be emphatical. Another possibility see in § 198, 7, remark 2.

197. In § 153 appellative verbs or conjugated appellatives have been mentioned. They have a present tense for words of the masculine and feminine gender singular and plural, but, as it would appear, without a third person singular feminine. The personal terminations are those of the ancient dialect (§ 193).

When they are suffixed to form the first person singular of Kannaḍa nouns, Saṁskṛita compound bases and Saṁskṛita adjectives ending in ಅ, the sŏnnĕ (ಂ, the sign of the nominative singular, § 117, *cf.* § 114) is put between, *e. g.* ಮಗಳ ಮಗನೆಂ, I (am) the son of the daughter, ದೌಹಿತ್ರನೆಂ, ಮಲ್ಲಿಕಾರ್ಜುನಸುತನೆಂ, ಕವಿಕೇಶವನೆಂ, ಕಲಾಪಣ್ಡಿತನೆಂ, ಕೃತಿಲಕ್ಷಣಾವದಾನನೆಂ, ಉದ್ಧತನೆಂ, ಅತಿಚದುರನೆಂ; this seems to be the rule also, if a Kannaḍa attributive noun ends in ಯ (*i. e.* euphonic ಯ್ + ಅ + ಅ, § 115), as the only instances given by the grammarian Kêšava are ಅಸಿಯನೆಂ, I (am) a weak person, ಪಿರಿಯನೆಂ, (although he adduces for the plural both ಪಿರಿಯೆವು and ಪಿರಿಯರೆವು). Other Kannaḍa attributive nouns and Kannaḍa appellative nouns of number (§ 90) ending in ಅ may insert the sŏnnĕ or may not, *e. g.* ಒಳ್ಳಿದೆಂ or ಒಳ್ಳಿದನೆಂ, I (am) a good person, ಒವರ್ೆಂ or ಒರ್ವನೆಂ. The adverb ಸುತ್ತ forms ಸುತ್ತೆಂ, I (am) a bewildered person.

Kannaḍa nouns and Saṁskṛita compound bases ending in ಇ add ಎಂ preceded by a euphonic ಯ್ for the first person singular, *e. g.* ಪೆಣ್ಡತಿಯೆಂ, I (am) a or the wife, ಕೇಶಿರಾಜಕವಿಯೆಂ.

For the formation of the first and second person plural Saṁskṛita words suffix ಅರ್ (the sign of the nominative plural, §§ 119. 132) before the personal terminations, *e. g.* ಉದ್ಧತರೆವು, ನಯವಿದರೆವು; ಉದ್ಧತರಿರ್, ವೃದ್ಧರಿರ್, ಅಪ್ರರಿರ್, ಅತಿಬಲರಿರ್; with regard to all Kannaḍa words the insertion of ಅರ್ is optional, *e. g.* ಪಿರಿಯೆವು or ಪಿರಿಯರೆವು, ಒಳ್ಳಿದೆವು or ಒಳ್ಳಿದರೆವು, ಪೆಱಿತೆವು

or ಪೆಱಿರೆವು, ಒರ್ವೆವು or ಒರ್ವರೆವು; ಒಳ್ಳಿದಿರ್ or ಒಳ್ಳಿದರಿರ್, ಕೂರಿದಿರ್ or ಕೂರಿದರಿರ್, ನೇರಿದಿರ್ or ನೇರಿದರಿರ್, ಪೆಱಿರ್ or ಪೆಱರಿರ್, ಒರ್ವಿರ್ or ಒರ್ವರಿರ್.

In the second person singular and the third person singular and plural the personal terminations are attached immediately to the declinable bases, *e.g.* ಉದ್ಧತಯ್, ಉದ್ಧತಂ, ಉದ್ಧತರ್; ಒಳ್ಳಿದಯ್, ಒಳ್ಳಿದಂ, ಒಳ್ಳಿದರ್.

Paradigms given in Kêšava's grammar are:

	Singular.	*Plural.*
	1, of ಉದ್ಧತ.	
1st pers.	ಉದ್ಧತನೆಂ, I (am) an elate person.	ಉದ್ಧತರೆವು.
2nd pers.	ಉದ್ಧತಯ್.	ಉದ್ಧತರಿರ್.
3rd pers.	ಉದ್ಧತಂ.	ಉದ್ಧತರ್.
	2, of ಒಳ್ಳಿದ.	
1st pers.	ಒಳ್ಳಿದೆಂ or ಒಳ್ಳಿದನೆಂ, I (am) a good person.	ಒಳ್ಳಿದೆವು or ಒಳ್ಳಿದರೆವು.
2nd pers.	ಒಳ್ಳಿದಯ್.	ಒಳ್ಳಿದಿರ್ or ಒಳ್ಳಿದರಿರ್.
3rd pers.	ಒಳ್ಳಿದಂ.	ಒಳ್ಳಿದರ್.
	3, of ಪೆಱ.	
1st pers.	ಪೆಱೆಂ or ಪೆಱನೆಂ, I (am) a stranger.	ಪೆಱೆವು or ಪೆಱರೆವು.
2nd pers.	ಪೆಱಯ್.	ಪೆಱಿರ್ or ಪೆಱರಿರ್.
3rd pers.	ಪೆಱಂ.	ಪೆಱರ್.
	4, of ಒರ್ವ.	
1st pers.	ಒರ್ವೆಂ or ಒರ್ವನೆಂ, I (am) a single person.	ಒರ್ವೆವು or ಒರ್ವರೆವು.
2nd pers.	ಒರ್ವಯ್.	ಒರ್ವಿರ್ or ಒರ್ವರಿರ್.
3rd pers.	ಒರ್ವಂ.	ಒರ್ವರ್.

An exceptional form is ಭ್ರಾನ್ತೆಂ (for ಭ್ರಾನ್ತನೆಂ).

198. The past or preterite tense (imperfect, perfect, aorist) is generally formed by suffixing the personal terminations (§ 193) to any form of the relative past participle (§§ 175. 176).

The exceptions relate only to the third person neuter singular, and are chiefly the following:— in the ancient and mediæval dialect it is optional to suffix the two terminations ಇತು and ಇತ್ತು directly to the short past participle ending in ಇ (§§ 166. 168); and in the modern dialect it is necessary to suffix the termination ಇತು not only directly to that participle, but also by means of a euphonic ಯ್ to the short participle ending in ಇ and ಉ (§ 165, *a*, 2; § 165, *b*, 1) which is identical with the theme, and then to all the relative forms of the past participle formed by the removal of its final ಉ (§ 175, 1) which are treated of in §§ 158-164 (as far as they concern the modern dialect).

1, A paradigm of the past tense of ಕೇಳ್, to hear, in the ancient dialect, is:

	Singular.	Plural.
1st pers.	ಕೇಳ್ದೆಂ (*i. e.* ಕೇಳ್ದ+ಎಂ), literally 'of the having heard-I' (see §§ 169. 179. 194), I have heard, I heard.	ಕೇಳ್ದೆಂ or ಕೇಳ್ದೆವು.
2nd pers.	ಕೇಳ್ದಯ್.	ಕೇಳ್ದಿರ್.
3rd pers.		
masc.	ಕೇಳ್ದಂ or ಕೇಳ್ದೊಂ.	ಕೇಳ್ದರ್ or ಕೇಳ್ದೊರ್.
fem.	ಕೇಳ್ದಳ್ or ಕೇಳ್ದೊಳ್.	ಕೇಳ್ದರ್ or ಕೇಳ್ದೊರ್.
neut.	ಕೇಳ್ದುದು or ಕೇಳ್ದತ್ತು.	ಕೇಳ್ದುವು.

If the relative past participle is formed by ತ, the termination ಅತ್ತು, it would seem, is avoided; thus we find ಮುಗುಳ್ತುದು, but not ಮುಗುಳ್ತತ್ತು; ತಳಿರ್ತುದು, but not ತಳಿರ್ತತ್ತು; ಸತ್ತುದು, but not ಸತ್ತತ್ತು. ಮುಗುಳ್ದತ್ತು, ತಳಿರ್ದತ್ತು are allowable forms. In ಬೆರಣ್ಟಾವು (§ 164, 6), the third person neuter plural of ಬೆರಣ್ಟು, to scratch, we have exceptionally ಅವು instead of ಉವು.

2, A paradigm of the past tense of ನುಡಿ, to speak, in the ancient dialect, is:

	Singular.	Plural.
1st pers.	ನುಡಿದೆಂ (*i. e.* ನುಡಿದ+ಎಂ), literally 'of the having spoken-I', I have spoken, I spoke.	ನುಡಿದೆಂ or ನುಡಿದೆವು.
2nd pers.	ನುಡಿದಯ್.	ನುಡಿದಿರ್.
3rd pers.		
masc.	ನುಡಿದಂ or ನುಡಿದೊಂ.	ನುಡಿದರ್ or ನುಡಿದೊರ್.
fem.	ನುಡಿದಳ್ or ನುಡಿದೊಳ್.	ನುಡಿದರ್ or ನುಡಿದೊರ್.
neut.	ನುಡಿದುದು or ನುಡಿದತ್ತು.	ನುಡಿದುವು.

3, A paradigm of the past tense of ಪಾಡು, to sing, in the ancient dialect, is:

	Singular.	Plural.
1st pers.	ಪಾಡಿದೆಂ (*i. e.* ಪಾಡಿದ+ಎಂ).	ಪಾಡಿದೆಂ or ಪಾಡಿದೆವು.
2nd pers.	ಪಾಡಿದಯ್.	ಪಾಡಿದಿರ್.
3rd pers.		
masc.	ಪಾಡಿದಂ or ಪಾಡಿದೊಂ.	ಪಾಡಿದರ್ or ಪಾಡಿದೊರ್.
fem.	ಪಾಡಿದಳ್ or ಪಾಡಿದೊಳ್.	ಪಾಡಿದರ್ or ಪಾಡಿದೊರ್.
neut.	ಪಾಡಿದುದು, or ಪಾಡಿದತ್ತು, or ಪಾಡಿತು (*i. e.* ಪಾಡಿ + ಇತು), or ಪಾಡಿತ್ತು (*i. e.* ಪಾಡಿ + ಇತ್ತು).	ಪಾಡಿದುವು.

Other instances of the third person neuter in its four forms are ಓದಿದುದು, ಓದಿದತ್ತು, ಓದಿತು, ಓದಿತ್ತು (of ಓದು, to read); ಬೆಳಗಿದುದು, ಬೆಳಗಿದತ್ತು, ಬೆಳಗಿತು, ಬೆಳಗಿತ್ತು (of ಬೆಳಗು, to shine); ಪಸರಿಸಿದುದು, ಪಸರಿಸಿದತ್ತು, ಪಸರಿಸಿತು, ಪಸರಿಸಿತ್ತು (of ಪಸರಿಸು, to spread). That of ಇರ್ (or ಇರು, to be) is ಇರ್ದುದು, ಇರ್ದತ್ತು in the ancient dialect, and ಇತ್ತು in the modern one (see under No. 7). See instances in § 366.

The third person singular and plural, excepting its forms with ಅತ್ತು, ಇತ್ತು and ಇತು, is used also as a declinable kṛilliṅga (§ 102, 8, e; § 177). The third person neuter singular ending in ಉದು is a bhâvavačana expressing the action or state of the verb in the past (cf. 200, 1; see § 254, remark 2). ಇರ್ದುದು means either 'that which has been' and 'that which is', or 'a having been', 'the having been' and 'a being', 'the being' (see e. g. § 313, under 4).

Remarks.

ಬಿಟ್ಟೊಂ is found in a šâsana of 866 A. D., ಬಿಡಿಸಿದೊಂ in one of 916 A. D., ಬರೆದೊಂ in one of 929 A. D.; ಇತ್ತೊರ್ in one of about 750 A. D., ಕೊಟ್ಟೊರ್ in one of 929 A. D.;—the termination ಒಂ occurs also in the Šabdamaṇidarpaṇa; ಒಳ್ is found in sûtras 179 and 183 of the Šabdânušâsana.

Further, ಕೊಟ್ಟಾಳ್ occurs in a šâsana of about 778 A. D.; ಕೆಯ್ದಾರ್ is found in one between 680 and 696 A. D., ಕೊಟ್ಟಾರ್ is in one of 707 A. D. and in one of 887 A. D., ಬಿಟ್ಟಾರ್ in one of 807 A. D., and ಪಡೆದಾರ್ in one of about 750 A. D.

In the later ancient dialect we meet with ಬಿಟ್ಟರು in a šâsana of 1123 A. D., ಕೊಟ್ಟರು, ಬಿಟ್ಟರು, ಇಕ್ಕಿದರು in one of 1182 A. D., and ಮಾಡಿದರು in one of 1187 A. D.

4, A paradigm of the past tense of ಕೇಳ್, to hear, in the mediæval dialect in which it optionally takes the final ಉ, i. e. becomes ಕೇಳು (see § 166), is:

	Singular.	*Plural.*
1st pers.	ಕೇಳ್ದೆಂ (ಕೇಳ್ದ+ಎಂ), or ಕೇಳ್ದೆನು, or ಕೇಳ್ದೆ; ಕೇಳಿದೆಂ (ಕೇಳಿದ+ಎಂ), or ಕೇಳಿದೆನು, or ಕೇಳಿದೆ.	ಕೇಳ್ದೆವು or ಕೇಳಿದೆವು.
2nd pers.	ಕೇಳ್ದೆ or ಕೇಳಿದೆ.	ಕೇಳ್ದಿರಿ or ಕೇಳಿದಿರಿ.
3rd pers. masc.	ಕೇಳ್ದಂ or ಕೇಳಿದಂ, ಕೇಳ್ದನು or ಕೇಳಿದನು, ಕೇಳ್ದ or ಕೇಳಿದ.	(ಕೇಳ್ದರ್ or) ಕೇಳ್ದರು, or ಕೇಳಿದರು.

	Singular.	*Plural.*
3rd pers.		
fem.	(ಕೇಳ್ದಳ್ or) ಕೇಳ್ದಳು, or ಕೇಳಿದಳು.	(ಕೇಳ್ದರ್ or) ಕೇಳ್ದರು, or ಕೇಳಿದರು.
neut.	ಕೇಳ್ದುದು or ಕೇಳಿದುದು, ಕೇಳ್ದತ್ತು or ಕೇಳಿದತ್ತು; ಕೇಳಿತು (*i. e.* ಕೇಳ್ + ಇತು), or ಕೇಳಿತ್ತು (*i. e.* ಕೇಳ್ + ಇತ್ತು).	ಕೇಳ್ದವು or ಕೇಳಿದವು.

5, A paradigm of the past tense of ಕೇಳು, to hear, in the modern dialect in which it always has the final ಉ (see § 166), is:

	Singular.	*Plural.*
1st pers.	ಕೇಳಿದೆನು (ಕೇಳಿದ + ಎನು) or ಕೇಳಿದೆ.	ಕೇಳಿದೆವು or ಕೇಳಿದಿವಿ.
2nd pers.	ಕೇಳಿದೆ or ಕೇಳಿದಿ.	ಕೇಳಿದಿರಿ.
3rd pers.		
masc.	ಕೇಳಿದನು or ಕೇಳಿದ.	ಕೇಳಿದರು.
fem.	ಕೇಳಿದಳು.	ಕೇಳಿದರು.
neut.	ಕೇಳಿತು (ಕೇಳ್ + ಇತು).	ಕೇಳಿದವು.

Other verbal themes with final ಉ are *e. g.* ಸೀಳು, ಹೇಱು, ಓದು, ಮಾಡು, ಹಾಡು.

6, A paradigm of the past tense of the theme **ಹಿಡಿ**, to seize, (the short past participle of which is identical with the theme), in the modern dialect, is:

	Singular.	*Plural.*
1st pers.	ಹಿಡಿದೆನು or ಹಿಡಿದೆ.	ಹಿಡಿದೆವು or ಹಿಡಿದಿವಿ.
2nd pers.	ಹಿಡಿದೆ or ಹಿಡಿದಿ.	ಹಿಡಿದಿರಿ.
3rd pers.		
masc.	ಹಿಡಿದನು or ಹಿಡಿದ.	ಹಿಡಿದರು.
fem.	ಹಿಡಿದಳು.	ಹಿಡಿದರು.
neut.	ಹಿಡಿಯಿತು (*i. e.* ಹಿಡಿ, the short past participle that is identical with the theme, + ಯ್ + ಇತು).	ಹಿಡಿದವು.

Other verbal themes with final ಇ are *e. g.* ಉಱಿ, ನುಡಿ, ಬಡಿ, ಮುಗಿ, and ಹಱಿ. Themes with final ಎ, *e. g.* ಕಡೆ, ನಡೆ and ಹೊಳೆ, form the past tense in the same way, the third person neuter singular being ಕಡೆಯಿತು, ನಡೆಯಿತು, ಹೊಳೆಯಿತು.

In the third person neuter singular of themes with final ಇ a contraction of vowels often takes place in the modern dialect, when, *e. g.* ಉಟಿಾಯಿತು, ನುಡಿಯಿತು, ಬಡಿಯಿತು, ಮುಗಿಯಿತು and ಹಟಿಾಯಿತು appear as ಉಟೀತು, ನುಡೀತು, ಬಡೀತು, ಮುಗೀತು and ಹಟೀತು (*cf.* § 205, 3, second pers. plural; § 130, *c*).

7, A paradigm of the past tense of ಅನ್ನು (ಅನು), to say, the relative past participiple of which is ಅನ್ದ, in the modern dialect, is:

	Singular.	*Plural.*
1st pers.	ಅನ್ದೆನು or ಅನ್ದೆ.	ಅನ್ದೆವು or ಅನ್ದಿವಿ.
2nd pers.	ಅನ್ದೆ or ಅನ್ದಿ.	ಅನ್ದಿರಿ.
3rd pers.		
masc.	ಅನ್ದನು or ಅನ್ದ.	ಅನ್ದರು.
fem.	ಅನ್ದಳು.	ಅನ್ದರು.
neut.	ಅನ್ದಿತು (*i. e.* ಅನ್ದ + ಇತು).	ಅನ್ದವು.

In the same manner the past tense of the relative past participles ಅಟ್ಟ, ಉಣ್ಡ, ಉತ್ತ, ಎನ್ದ, ಕಣ್ಡ, ಕೆಟ್ಟ, ತನ್ದ, ತಿತ್ತ, ನಿನ್ತ, ಬನ್ದ, ಸತ್ತ, ಸನ್ದ, ಸುಟ್ಟ, ಹೊತ್ತ, etc. is formed in the modern dialect. Also in the mediæval dialect there are, as occasional forms of the third person neuter singular, *e. g.* ನಿನ್ತಿತು (ನಿನ್ತ+ಇತು), ಬನ್ದಿತು (ಬನ್ದ+ಇತು), ಸನ್ದಿತು (ಸನ್ದ+ಇತು), and ಸನ್ದಿತ್ತು (ಸನ್ದ+ಇತ್ತು).

From the full forms ಅನ್ದಿತು, ಎನ್ದಿತು, ತನ್ದಿತು, ತಿನ್ದಿತು, ಬನ್ದಿತು and ಸನ್ದಿತು of the third person neuter singular, by means of syncope, ಅನ್ತು, ಎನ್ತು, ತನ್ತು, ತಿನ್ತು, ಬನ್ತು and ಸನ್ತು are often formed and used in the modern dialect.

The third person neuter singular of ಇದ್ದೆನು (of ಇರು), I was, is always ಇತ್ತು in the modern dialect, and that of ಬಿದ್ದೆನು (of ಬೀಳು), I fell, always ಬಿತ್ತು.

Instead of ಬೆನ್ದಿತು (of ಬೇ, to burn) the form ಬೇಯಿತು (ಬೆ+ಯ್+ಇತು), and instead of ಮೇದಿತು (of ಮೇ, to graze) the form ಮೇಯಿತು (ಮೆ+ಯ್+ಇತು) may be used in the modern dialect. In the mediæval one we find, as an occasional form, ಬೇಯಿತ್ತು (=ಬೇಯಿತು).

Remarks.

1, In § 172 it has been said that an explanation of ಅನ್ತ and ಎನ್ತ different from that given there, would be offered here. For this purpose it is required to consider the third person neuter singular of the past tense to be a kṛilliṅga or declinable base (§ 102, 8, letter *e*; § 177), as it in reality is; for like the kṛilliṅgas ಎನ್ನುದು (ಎನ್ದ + ಉಧು, of the ancient and mediæval dialect) and ಎನ್ದದು or ಅನ್ದದು (ಎನ್ದ + ಅದು or ಅನ್ದ + ಅದು, of the modern one) ಅನ್ದಿತು and ಎನ್ದಿತು are kṛilliṅgas composed of the relative past participle ಅನ್ದ or ಎನ್ದ and ಇತು (another form of ಇದು, § 193, remarks), literally meaning 'of the having said-this', 'a having said-this', from which ಅನ್ತು and ಎನ್ತು are formed by syncope. The final ಅ in ಅನ್ತ and ಎನ್ತ would be the sign of the accusative of bases with final ಉ (see § 121, letters *b* and *c*; § 122, letters *b* and *c*) governed by a following ಹೇಳು or ಅನು (ಅನ್ನು), ಎನು (ಎನ್ನು); see §§ 331. 332, and some instances in § 286. ಅನ್ತಾ and ಎನ್ತಾ would be lengthened forms of the accusative (see § 121, letter *c*; 122, letter *c*).

2, In remark 4 of § 196 the opinion has been expressed that it is not impossible that ಅನ್ತೆ, '*on dit*', is a form of the present participle. Another explanation is that it is the kṛilliṅga ಅನ್ತು (*i. e.* ಅನ್ದಿತು, by syncope) with the ಎ of emphasis, originally meaning 'of the having said-this-indeed', 'a having said-this-indeed'. (In Tēlugu ಅನ್ತೆ appears as ಅಣ್ಟೆ or ಅಟೆ, probably other forms of ಅನುಟೆ, 'a saying', the verbal noun of ಅನು, to say).

199. In § 166 there are adduced the irregular past participles ಅಯ್, ಪೋಯ್, ಹೋಯ್ of ಆಗು, ಪೋಗು, ಹೋಗು, which stand instead of the regular ಆಗಿ, ಪೋಗಿ, ಹೋಗಿ, and in § 176 appear the irregular relative past participles ಆದ, ಪೋದ, ಹೋದ, which stand for ಆಗಿದ, ಪೋಗಿದ, ಹೋಗಿದ, or ಅಯ್ದ, ಪೋಯ್ದ, ಹೋಯ್ದ. From these irregular past and relative past participles the third person neuter singular is formed, *viz.* in the ancient dialect either ಆದುದು and ಆದತ್ತು, ಪೋದುದು and ಪೋದತ್ತು, or ಆಯ್ತು, ಪೋಯ್ತು; in the mediæval one either ಆದುದು and ಆದತ್ತು, ಪೋದುದು and ಪೋದತ್ತು, or ಆಯ್ತು, ಆಯಿತು, ಆಯಿತ್ತು, ಪೋಯ್ತು, ಹೋಯ್ತು, ಹೋಯಿತು, ಹೋಯಿತ್ತು; and in the modern one only ಆಯ್ತು, ಆಯಿತು, ಹೋಯ್ತು, ಹೋಯಿತು.

In § 166 it will be seen that there exists also the irregular past participle ಅಯ್ (for ಆಯ್), used in the formation of the third person neuter singular ಅಯ್ತು (§ 196, regarding the past meaning of which used for the present see § 194), and in § 176 that the irregular relative past participles are also ಅಯ್ದ and ಅದ, used in ಅಯ್ದೇನೆ, etc. and ಅದೇನೆ, etc. (§ 196; *cf.* ಅದೇನು in § 195).

200. The future tense is formed by suffixing the personal terminations (§ 193) to the variously formed relative (present-) future participles (§§ 180-184. 191). (Remember the contingent present-future tense of § 195.)

1, A paradigm of the future tense of ಕುಡು, to give, in the ancient dialect, is as follows:

	Singular.	Plural.
1st pers.	ಕುಡುವೆಂ (*i. e.* ಕುಡುವ + ಎಂ), literally 'of giving-I' (see §§ 185. 186), I shall give (see § 316, 3).	ಕುಡುವೆಂ or ಕುಡುವೆವು, we shall give.
2nd pers.	ಕುಡುವಯ್, thou wilt give (see § 316, 12).	ಕುಡುವಿರ್, you will give.
3rd pers.		
masc.	ಕುಡುವಂ or ಕುಡುವೊಂ, he will give (see § 316, 12).	ಕುಡುವರ್ or ಕುಡುವೊರ್, they will give.
fem.	ಕುಡುವಳ್ or ಕುಡುವೊಳ್.	ಕುಡುವರ್ (or ಕುಡುವೊರ್).
neut.	ಕುಡುವುದು.	ಕುಡುವುವು.

The whole third person (singular and plural) is a declinable kṛilliṅga (§ 185. 186). Its neuter singular, in the present case ಕುಡುವುದು, lit. 'of giving-it', is also used to express the notion (bhâva) of the verb (here its action) in the present, and is therefore a bhâvavačana (*cf.* § 100; the §§ quoted in 243; § 254, remark 1) meaning 'giving'. Other instances are ಈವುದು, giving, ಕೂರ್ಪುದು, loving, ಇರ್ಪುದು, being, ಎನ್ಬುದು, saying, ಮಾೞ್ಪುದು, making. Such bhâvavačanas are used in the three dialects. Their use in the imperative appears in § 205.

Other instances of the first person singular of the future tense in the ancient dialect are: ಆಳ್ವೆಂ (of ಆಳ್), ಪೇೞ್ವೆಂ (of ಪೇೞ್), ಕೊಲ್ವೆಂ (of ಕೊಲ್), ಪೊಣ್ಮುವೆಂ (of ಪೊಣ್ಮು), ಅಱಿವೆಂ (of ಅಱಿ), ನಡೆವೆಂ (of ನಡೆ), ಉಣ್ಬೆಂ (of ಉಣ್), ತಿನ್ಬೆಂ (of ತಿನ್), ತರ್ಪೆಂ or ತರ್ಪ್ಪೆಂ (of ತರ್), ತೋರ್ಪೆಂ or ತೋರ್ಪ್ಪೆಂ (of ತೋಱ್), ನೋೞ್ಪೆಂ or ನೋಡುವೆಂ (of ನೋಡು), ಮಾೞ್ಪೆಂ or ಮಾಡುವೆಂ (of ಮಾಡು), ಅಪ್ಪೆಂ, ಅಪೆಂ or ಆಗುವೆಂ (of ಆಗು), ಪೋಪೆಂ or ಪೋಗುವೆಂ (of ಪೋಗು), ಇರಿಪೆಂ or ಇರಿಪ್ಪೆಂ (of ಇರಿಸು), ಎನಿಪೆಂ or ಎನಿಪ್ಪೆಂ (of ಎನಿಸು). See instances in § 366.

For the third person masculine singular ಅದಾಪೊಂ is found in a šâsana between 597 and 608 A. D., and for the third person masculine plural ಕಿಡಿಪ್ಪೊರ್ (of ಕಿಡಿಸು), ಸಲಿಪ್ಪೊರ್ (of ಸಲಿಸು) occur in a šâsana of about 750 A. D.

2, A paradigm of the future tense of ಕೊಡು (or occasionally also ಕುಡು), to give, in the mediæval dialect, is:

	Singular.	Plural.
1st pers.	ಕೊಡುವೆಂ (ಕೊಡುವ + ಎಂ), ಕೊಡುವೆನು, ಕೊಡುವೆ.	ಕೊಡುವೆವು.
2nd pers.	ಕೊಡುವೆ.	ಕೊಡುವಿರಿ.

	Singular.	Plural.
3rd pers.		
masc.	ಕೊಡುವಂ, ಕೊಡುವನು, ಕೊಡುವ.	(ಕೊಡುವರ್), ಕೊಡುವರು.
fem.	(ಕೊಡುವಳ್), ಕೊಡುವಳು.	(ಕೊಡುವರ್), ಕೊಡುವರು.
neut.	ಕೊಡುವುದು, (ಕೊಡುವದು).	ಕೊಡುವವು.

Another instance of the first person singular in the mediæval dialect is ಪೇೞ್ವೆಂ, ಪೇೞ್ವೆನು, ಪೇೞ್ವೆ, or ಪೇೞುವೆಂ, ಪೇೞುವೆನು, ಪೇೞುವೆ, or ಹೇೞುವೆಂ, ಹೇೞುವೆನು, ಹೇೞುವೆ (of ಪೇೞ್, ಪೇೞು, ಹೇೞು, to say).

3, A paradigm of the future tense of ಕೊಡು, to give, in the modern dialect, is:

	Singular.	Plural.
1st pers.	ಕೊಡುವೆನು (ಕೊಡುವ + ಎನು), ಕೊಡವೆ.	ಕೊಡುವೆವು.
2nd pers.	ಕೊಡುವೆ, ಕೊಡುವಿ.	ಕೊಡುವಿರಿ.
3rd pers.		
masc.	ಕೊಡುವನು, ಕೊಡುವ.	ಕೊಡುವರು.
fem.	ಕೊಡುವಳು.	ಕೊಡುವರು.
neut.	ಕೊಡುವದು.	ಕೊಡುವವು.

Other instances of the first person singular in the modern dialect are ಹೇೞುವೆನು, ಹೇೞುವೆ (of ಹೇೞು, to say), ನುಡಿಯುವೆನು, ನುಡಿಯುವೆ (of ನುಡಿ, to speak), ನಡೆಯುವೆನು, ನಡೆಯುವೆ (of ನಡೆ, to walk). The forms ಕೊಡುವದು, ಹೇೞುವದು, ನುಡಿಯುವದು, ನಡೆಯುವದು are bhâvavačanas; see under No. 1; § 209, 3.

201. In § 184 there appears ಹ as a substitute of ಪ in the relative present-future participle, *viz.* in ಅಹ of the ancient and mediæval dialect, and in ಇಹ, ತಹ, ಬಹ, ಆಹ, ಬಾಹ, ಬೇಹ, ಹೋಹ of the mediæval one. In § 183, 7, remark, we have ಅಪ್ಪು; and in §§ 189. 194 we find ಅಪ, ಅಪ್ಪ and ಅಹ as constituents of the present tense. In § 195 we have the conjugated form of ಅಹ, *viz.* ಅಹೆನು, etc. changed, by metathesis and lengthening of the vowels, into ಹೇನು, etc. Here follow the paradigms of the conjugation of ಅಪ or ಅಪ್ಪ, (ಆಪ್ಪ), ಅಹ, ಇಹ, and some other conjugated forms.

1, A paradigm of the conjugation of ಅಪ or ಅಪ್ಪ, (ಆಪ್ಪ) in the grammatical ancient dialect, is:

	Singular.	Plural.
1st pers.	ಅಪೆಂ (see § 194) or ಅಪ್ಪೆಂ, literally 'of the becoming or being-I' (see § 186), I shall become, I shall be, (I am).	ಅಪೆಂ or ಅಪ್ಪೆಂ, ಅಪೆವು or ಅಪ್ಪೆವು.
2nd pers.	ಅಪಯ್ or ಅಪ್ಪಯ್.	ಅಪಿರ್ or ಅಪ್ಪಿರ್.
3rd pers.		
masc.	ಅಪಂ or ಅಪ್ಪಂ, ಅಪೊಂ or ಅಪ್ಪೊಂ.	ಅಪರ್ or ಅಪ್ಪರ್, ಅಪೊರ್ or ಅಪ್ಪೊರ್, ಅಪ್ಪಾರ್.
fem.	ಅಪಳ್ or ಅಪ್ಪಳ್, ಅಪೊಳ್ or ಅಪ್ಪೊಳ್.	ಅಪರ್ or ಅಪ್ಪರ್, (ಅಪೊರ್ or ಅಪ್ಪೊರ್), ಅಪ್ಪಾರ್.
neut.	ಅಪುದು or ಅಪ್ಪುದು.	ಅಪುವು or ಅಪ್ಪುವು.

2, A paradigm of the conjugation of **ಅಹ**, in the **mediæval** dialect, is:

	Singular.	Plural.
1st pers.	ಅಹೆಂ, ಅಹೆನು, ಅಹೆ, literally 'of the becoming or being-I', I shall become, I shall be.	ಅಹೆವು.
2nd pers.	ಅಹೆ.	ಅಹಿರಿ.
3rd pers.		
masc.	ಅಹಂ, ಅಹನು, (ಅಹ).	(ಅಹರ್), ಅಹರು.
fem.	(ಅಹಳ್), ಅಹಳು.	(ಅಹರ್), ಅಹರು.
neut.	ಅಹುದು.	ಅಹವು.

Of the above forms we have met with ಅಹಂ, ಅಹಳ್ and ಅಹುದು also in the ancient dialect.

ಅಹುದು in the form of ಹೌದು has remained in the modern dialect (*cf.* § 195); ಹೇನು, etc. and ಏನು, etc., other forms of ಅಹೆನು, etc. in this dialect, appear, as has been stated, in its conjugation of the contingent present-future tense (§ 195); compare the modern present in § 196.

3, A paradigm of the conjugation of **ಇಹ**, in the **mediæval** dialect, is:

	Singular.	Plural.
1st pers.	ಇಹೆಂ, ಇಹೆನು, ಇಹೆ, literally 'of the being-I', I shall be, (I am).	ಇಹೆವು.
2nd pers.	ಇಹೆ.	ಇಹಿರಿ.

	Singular.	*Plural.*
3rd pers.		
masc.	ಇಹಂ, ಇಹನು, (ಇಹ).	(ಇಹರ್), ಇಹರು.
fem.	(ಇಹಳ್), ಇಹಳು.	(ಇಹರ್), ಇಹರು.
neut.	ಇಹುದು.	ಇಹವು.

Other instances of the first person singular of the future tense formed from relative participles with final ಅ in the mediæval dialect are ತಹೆಂ, 'of the bringing-I', I shall bring, ಬಹೆಂ, 'of the coming-I', I shall come, ಬಾಹೆಂ, 'of the coming-I', I shall come.

The only form of these left in the modern dialect is the third person neuter singular of ಬಹೆಂ, *viz.* ಬಹುದು, it will come, it comes.

202. According to note *a* of § 181 the third person singular and the third person masculine and feminine plural of the future tense occur also with ಒ and ಓ in the **mediæval** and **modern** dialect, *e. g.* ತಿರಗೊನು (for ತಿರಗುವನು), ತಿರಗೊಳು (for ತಿರಗುವಳು), ತಿರಗೊದು (for ತಿರಗುವುದು or ತಿರಗುವದು); ಹೋಗೋದು (for ಹೋಗುವುದು or ಹೋಗುವದು), ಹೋಗೋರು (for ಹೋಗುವರು);—and according to note *b* of the same paragraph the third person neuter singular of the future tense occurs also with ಊ in those two dialects, *e. g.* ಮಾಡೂದು (for ಮಾಡುವುದು or ಮಾಡುವದು).

203. A particular third person is formed by the terminations ಗುಂ, ಕುಂ, ಕ್ಕುಂ, and ಕು, ಗು. It is used for the present, future and past tense (*cf.* § 169) without regard to number and gender.

ಗುಂ is suffixed to most verbal themes ending in consonants and vowels, *e. g.* ಅಳ್ಗುಂ, ಗೆಲ್ಗುಂ, ಒಲ್ಗುಂ, ಕಾಣ್ಗುಂ, ತೀರ್ಗುಂ, ಪೋೞ್ಗುಂ, ಮಾಣ್ಗುಂ, ಸುಯ್ಗುಂ, ಸೋರ್ಗುಂ, ಅಮರ್ಗುಂ, ನಿಮಿರ್ಗುಂ, ನುಸುಳ್ಗುಂ, ಮುಸುಳ್ಗುಂ, ನೆಗೞ್ಗುಂ, ಪೊಗೞ್ಗುಂ, ಉಲಿಗುಂ, ನುಡಿಗುಂ, ನಡೆಗುಂ, ಪಡೆಗುಂ, ನೋಡುಗುಂ, ಪಾಡುಗುಂ, ಪುಟ್ಟುಗುಂ, ಬೀಸುಗುಂ, ಮಾಡುಗುಂ, ಎಱಗುಗುಂ, ಪೊಗಿಸುಗುಂ, ಮಾಡಿಸುಗುಂ, ರಾಗಿಸುಗುಂ, ಸೂಚಿಸುಗುಂ. According to the Šabdânušâsana also ಆಗುಗುಂ, ಪೋಗುಗುಂ, (see remark), ತೋರ್ಗುಂ (for ತೋಱುಗುಂ, and ತೋರ್ಕುಂ, see ಕುಂ), ಕೊೞ್ಗುಂ (for ಕೊಡುಗುಂ), ನೋೞ್ಗುಂ (for ನೋಡುಗುಂ), ಮೂೞ್ಗುಂ (for ಮೂಡುಗುಂ) are in use.

ಕುಂ, according to instances from the Šabdamaṇidarpaṇa, is suffixed to ಬೇೞ್ (of ಬೇಡು), ಮಾೞ್ (of ಮಾಡು), ತೋಱ್, ಇರ್, ತರ್, ನಿಲ್ and ಬರ್, and the forms are ಬೇೞ್ಕುಂ, ಮಾೞ್ಕುಂ, ತೋರ್ಕುಂ, ಇರ್ಕುಂ, ತರ್ಕುಂ, ನಿಲ್ಕುಂ and ಬರ್ಕುಂ; according to the Šabdânušâsana it is optional to use ತೋ

ರ್ಕುಂ or ತೋರ್ಗುಂ, ನಿಲ್ಕುಂ or ನಿಲ್ಗುಂ, ನೋನ್ಕುಂ or ನೋನ್ಗುಂ, ಬಾೞ್ಕುಂ or ಬಾೞ್ಗುಂ, ಮಾಣ್ಕುಂ or ಮಾಣ್ಗುಂ, ಮಾೞ್ಕುಂ or ಮಾೞ್ಗುಂ, ಬೆದರ್ಕುಂ or ಬೆದರ್ಗುಂ, ಸೋರ್ಕುಂ or ಸೋರ್ಗುಂ.

From ಪೋಗು ಪೋಕುಂ is formed, and from ಆಗು ಅಕುಂ (this form in a šâsana between 597 and 608 A. D.), generally ಅಕ್ಕುಂ (*cf.* § 176).

Verbs formed by means of the suffix ಇಸು (see § 149 *seq.*) may use ಕುಂ, in which case they drop their final ಸು, *e. g.* ಎನಿಕುಂ (of ಎನಿಸು), ಪುರುಡಿಕುಂ (of ಪುರುಡಿಸು), ಪೊಗೞಿಕುಂ, ಮಾಡಿಕುಂ, ಮಾಣಿಕುಂ, ಸಮನಿಕುಂ; ಕೇಳಿಕುಂ (of ಕೇಳಿಸು, to play), ಪರಿಹರಿಕುಂ, ಪಾಳಿಕುಂ, ಪೂಜಿಕುಂ, ಭಾವಿಕುಂ, ರಕ್ಷಿಕುಂ, ರಂಜಿಕುಂ, ರಾಗಿಕುಂ, ಸೂಚಿಕುಂ.

The forms with ಗುಂ and ಕುಂ are used in the ancient and mediæval dialect.

ಕ್ಕುಂ, in the ancient dialect, is an optional termination for ಕುಂ, the doubling of the consonant being euphonic, *e. g.* ಪುರುಡಿಕ್ಕುಂ, ಪೊಗೞಿಕ್ಕುಂ; ಪಾಳಿಕ್ಕುಂ, ಪೂಜಿಕ್ಕುಂ, ರಕ್ಷಿಕ್ಕುಂ, ರಂಜಿಕ್ಕುಂ. It is beautiful (manôhara) especially in verbs that come from Saṁskṛita.

If a form is produced that is disagreeable to the ear (ašrâvya), ಕ್ಕುಂ is not used in Kannaḍa verbs, so that it is improper to use *e. g.* ಕಿಡಿಕ್ಕುಂ, ಬಿಡಿಕ್ಕು, ಸೊಪ್ಪಿಕ್ಕುಂ; (and ಕಿಡಿಕುಂ, ಬಿಡಿಕುಂ, ಸೊಪ್ಪಿಕುಂ or ಕಿಡಿಸುಗುಂ, ಬಿಡಿಸುಗುಂ, ಸೊಪ್ಪಿಸುಗುಂ would be right).

ಕು (*i. e.* ಕುಂ without the sŏnnĕ) of the ancient dialect is formed in ಅಕ್ಕು (in a šâsana of 1084 A. D.) and ಸೊಗಯಿಕ್ಕು (in a šâsana of 1123 A. D.); in the mediæval dialect it is in common use, and we meet therein *e. g.* with ಅಕ್ಕು, ತೋರ್ಕು, ಬೇೞ್ಕು. In the modern dialect two forms with ಕು, found also in the mediæval one, have remained, *viz.* ಬೇಕು (for ಬೇೞ್ಕು, § 316, 4) and ಸಾಕು (for ಸಾಲ್ಕು).

ಗು (*i. e.* ಗುಂ without the sŏnnĕ) is a mediæval suffix which we see *e. g.* in ಎನಿಸುಗು, ಎಸೆಗು, ಒರೆಗು, ದೊರಕುಗು, ನೆಗೞ್ಗು, ಪೇೞ್ಗು, ವರ್ತಿಸುಗು, ವರ್ಧಿಸುಗು, ಸಲ್ಗು, ಸಾರ್ಗು, ಸಿದ್ಧಿಗು.

Instances see in § 366.

Remark.

According to sûtra 464 of the Šabdânušâsana (*cf.* §§ 472. 498) some savants (âčâryas) have employed an additional ಗುಂ after the regular terminations ಗುಂ and ಕುಂ, dropping their final sŏnnĕ, *e. g.* ಆಗುಗುಗುಂ (for ಆಗುಗುಂ), ಓದುಗುಗುಂ, ಕುಣಿಗುಗುಂ, ನಿಲ್ಗುಗುಂ, ನೊಡೆಗುಗುಂ, ನೋನ್ಗುಗುಂ, ಪಾಡುಗುಗುಂ, ಪೋಗುಗುಗುಂ, ಬಾೞ್ಗುಗುಂ, ಬೆದರ್ಗುಗುಂ, ಮಾಡಿಸು ಗುಗುಂ, ಮಾಣ್ಗುಗುಂ, ರಾಗಿಸುಗುಗುಂ, ಸೋರ್ಗುಗುಂ; ಅಕ್ಕುಗುಂ, ಪೋಕುಗುಂ, ಮಾಡಿಕುಗುಂ,

ತೋಱುರ್ಗುಂ, etc. It will be observed that these savants knew the forms ಗು and ಕು without the sŏnnĕ, to which they suffixed their ಗುಂ.

204. With regard to the terminations of § 203 the question arises, which of them are radical, ಗುಂ, ಕುಂ or ಗು, ಕು?

From etymological reasons we are inclined to consider ಗು and ಕು to be original, as they appear to be nominal suffixes ಗು (=ಗೆ) occurring *e. g.* in ಉರುಗು (of ಉರಿ) and ಸೆಱಗು (of ಕಿಱ್ = a ಚಿಱ್, see ಕಿಱ್ and ಕಿಱಿ in Dictionary), and ಕು (=ಕೆ) *e. g.* in ಉಱುಕು (of ಉಱು), ಒಡಕು (of ಒಡೆ), ಹಱಿಕು (of ಹಱಿ). According to this our opinion that the verbal forms with ಗು and ಕು are nouns (bhâvavačanas), *e. g.* ಎಸೆಗು would originally mean 'a shining', ಒರೆಗು, 'an uttering', ಪೇೞ್ಗು, 'a saying', ಅಕ್ಕು, 'a becoming', ತೋಱ್ಕುರ್, 'an appearing', ಬೇೞ್ಕು, 'a requiring'.

This explanation at once makes it clear, why the forms by themselves have no reference whatever to tense, number and gender. Compare in this respect the verbal nouns (bhâvavačanas) ಉಣ್ಬು in § 194, remark 1, and ಕುಡುವುದು in § 200, 1, those ending in ಉದು and ಅದು in § 205, and those ending in ಗೆ and ಕೆ in the same paragraph.

But why have ancient grammarians added the sŏnnĕ? If we take the forms with ಗು and ಕು to be nouns, we most probably have to regard the sŏnnĕ as a conventional sign of the nominative singular (*cf.* § 114). Thus ಅಕ್ಕುಂ, etc. would be the nominative with the suffix ಂ.

205. The forms of the imperative (vidhi, etc., § 146) **are based partly on the relative present-future participle, partly on verbal nouns,** as will be seen from **the** paradigms.

1, Paradigm of the forms of the imperative in the ancient dialect:

	Singular.	*Plural.*
1st pers.	(The first person singular of the future tense ending in ಎಂ, see § 200, 1, according to the Šabdânušâsana's sûtra 491, *i. e.* ಮಾಳ್ಪೆಂ or ಮಾಡುವೆಂ, I shall do, *i. e.* let me do! ಪೂಜಿಸುವೆಂ, let me worship!— This rule is not in the Šabdamaṇidarpaṇa.)	ಅಂ (a short form of ಆಂ, we; see §§ 137. 138) suffixed to the relative present-future participle, *e. g.* ತಾಗುವಂ (ತಾಗುವ + ಅಂ) or ತಾಪಂ (ತಾಪ + ಅಂ), literally 'of attacking-we!', let us attack! ಇಱಿರ್ಗಂ! ಗೆಲ್ವಂ! ಮಾಡುವಂ or ಮಾಳ್ಪಂ!
2nd pers.	*a*) the verbal theme, which in this case is a verbal noun (bhâva-	*a*) ಇಂ (another form of ನೀಂ or ಈಂ, you; see §§ 137. 138),

Singular.

vaċana, see § 100) used with emphasis or the sense of a sign of exclamation, *e.g.* ಆಗು, (thy) becoming (is required or requested)! *i.e.* become (thou)! ಊದು, (thy) blowing (is required or requested)! blow (thou)! ನೋಡು! ಮೆಟ್ಟು! ನುಡಿ! ನಡೆ! ಅಡಂಗು! ಬಗ್ಗಿಸು! ಪೂಜಿಸು! ಕೇಳ್! ಗೆಯ್! ನಿಲ್! ಇರ್ or ಇರು!

Plural.

suffixed to the verbal theme considered as a verbal noun, *e.g.* ಅರಯಿಂ or ಅರಯ್ಯಿಂ (ಅರಯ್ + ಇಂ), literally 'searching-ye!' search ye! ಇರಿಸಿಂ! ಗೆಯಿಂ or ಗೆಯ್ಯಿಂ! ತರಿಸಿಂ! ಪುಗಿಂ! ಪೇಳಿಂ! ಬೆಸಸಿಂ! ಮಾಡಿಂ! ಸಮಕಟ್ಟಿಂ!

b) the theme with final ಅ (ಧಾತುವಿನ ಅತ್ವಂ), most probably a verbal noun (see § 188), *e.g.* ಕುಡ, (thy) giving (is required or requested)! *i.e.* give (thou)! ಕೇಳ! ಇರ! ಗೆಯ or ಗೆಯ್ಯ! ನೋಡ! ಮಾಡ! ಅರಯ or ಅರಯ್ಯ! ಬಾರ! (for ಬರ, see §§ 206. 210).

c) the third person neuter singular of the present-future tense with ಉದು, it being a verbal noun (kṛilliṅga and bhâvavaċana, see § 200, 1), *e.g.* ಈವುದು, (thy) giving (is required or requested)! *i.e.* give (thou)! mayest (thou) give! ಬೆಸಸುವುದು! ಮಾಡುವುದು or ಮಾಳ್ಪುದು! ಅವಧರಿಪುದು! ರಕ್ಷಿಪುದು!

b) the third person neuter singular of the present-future tense with ಉದು, *e.g.* ಈವುದು, (your) giving (is required or requested)! *i.e.* give (ye)! may (you) give!

3rd pers.

a) ಗೆ, ಕೆ or optionally ಕ್ಕೆ, suffixed in the very same manner as the terminations ಗುಂ, ಕುಂ, ಕ್ಕುಂ, etc. (see §§ 203. 204. The forms thus produced are in reality verbal nouns like ಉಡುಗೆ, ಏಳ್ಗೆ, ಪಸುಗೆ, ಪೊಳ್ಗೆ, etc.; ಕಾಣ್ಕೆ, ತೆರಳ್ಕೆ, ಮಡಿಕೆ, ಹಡಿಕೆ, etc.; see § 243, *A*, 10. 12), *e.g.* ಗೆಯ್ಗೆ (ಗೆಯ್ + ಗೆ), (his, her, its) doing (is required or requested)!

a) ಗೆ, ಕೆ or ಕ್ಕೆ, the forms being the same as those of the singular, *e.g.* ಗೆಯ್ಗೆ, (their) doing (is required or requested)! *i.e.* (they) shall do! let (them) do! may (they) do!

Singular.

i. e. (he, she, it) shall do! let (him, her, it) do! may (he, she, it) do! ಗೆಲ್ಗೆ! ಬಾೞ್ಗೆ (or ಬಾೞ್ಕೆ)! ಅದಿರ್ಗೆ! ತೆಗೞ್ಗೆ! ತೊಡರ್ಗೆ! ನುಸುಳ್ಗೆ! ಅಱುಗೆ! ನುಡಿಗೆ! ಪಡೆಗೆ! ಓದುಗೆ! ಕುಡುಗೆ! ನಮ್ಬುಗೆ! ಮಾಡುಗೆ! ಓದಿಸುಗೆ! ಮಾಡಿಸುಗೆ! ಆಚರಿಸುಗೆ! ಪೂಜಿಸುಗೆ! ರಕ್ಷಿಸುಗೆ!; — ಇರ್ಕೆ! ತರ್ಕೆ! ತೋರ್ಕೆ! ಸೋರ್ಕೆ (or ಸೋರ್ಗೆ)! ನಿಲ್ಕೆ (or ನಿಲ್ಗೆ)! ಬರ್ಕೆ! ಮಾೞ್ಕೆ (or ಮಾೞ್ಗೆ)!; — ಅಕ್ಕೆ! ಪೋಕೆ!; — ಪೆರ್ಚಿಕೆ (of ಪೆರ್ಚಿಸು)! ಮಾಡಿಕೆ (of ಮಾಡಿಸು)! ಪರಿಪಾಳಿಕೆ! ಪೂಜಿಕೆ! ರಕ್ಷಿಕೆ!; — ಪೆರ್ಚಿಕ್ಕೆ! ಪೂಜಿಕ್ಕೆ! ರಕ್ಷಿಕ್ಕೆ!

Plural.

Singular: *b*) the third person neuter singular of the present-future tense with ಉದು, *e. g.* ಈವುದು, (his, her or its) giving (is required or requested)! *i. e.* (he, she or it) shall give! let (him, her or it) give! may (he, she, it) give!

Plural: *b*) the third person neuter singular of the present-future tense with ಉದು, *e. g.* ಈವುದು, (their) giving (is required or requested)! *i. e.* (they) shall give! let (them) give! may (they) give!

Further instances see in § 367.

2, Paradigm of the forms of the imperative in the mediæval dialect:

Singular.

1st pers. (The first person singular of the future tense ending in ಎಂ, ಎನು and ಎ, see § 200, 2, *e. g.* ಕೊಡುವೆಂ, ಕೊಡುವೆನು, ಕೊಡುವೆ.)

Plural.

(ಅಂ), ಅ (*i. e.* ಅಂ without the euphonic sŏnnĕ, see §§ 137. 138), *e. g.* ಉಸುರುವ, let us utter!

2nd pers.

Singular: *a*) the verbal theme, *e. g.* ಏೞ್ or ಏೞು, rise (thou)! ನುಡಿ! ಪೊರೆ! ಇರ್ or ಇರು! ಆಗು! ರಕ್ಷಿಸು!, in which case also themes like ಕಾಯಿ, guard (thou)! (for ಕಾ) appear (see 3, 2nd person in this paragraph).

Plural: *a*) (ಇಂ), ಇ (*i. e.* ಇಂ without the euphonic sŏnnĕ, see §§ 137. 138), ಇರಿ (*i. e.* ಇರ್ + the honorific ಇ, see § 193, remarks), *e. g.* ಇರಿ, be ye! ಎನ್ನಿ! ಏೞಿ! ಕೇಳಿ! ಕೊಳ್ಳಿ! ನೋಡಿ! — ಕುಳ್ಳಿರಿ! ತೊಲಗಿರಿ! ಹೇೞಿರಿ! ಹೋಗಿರಿ!

Singular: *b*) the theme with final ಅ, *e. g.* ಹೇೞ, speak (thou)! ಬಾರ!

Singular. | *Plural.*

c) the third person neuter singular of the present-future tense with ಉದು, *e.g.* ನೋಡುವುದು, see (thou)!

b) the third person neuter singular of the present-future tense with ಉದು, *e. g.* ಬೇಡುವುದು, solicit (ye)!

3rd pers.

Singular:

a) ಗೆ, ಕೆ, *e.g.* ಈಗೆ, let (him, her or it) give! ಉದ್ಧರಿಸುಗೆ!— ಮಾಳ್ಕೆ! (In mediæval-modern works, *e.g.* in the the Râmâyaṇa, we find also forms like ನಲುಗೆ, Râm. 1, 6, for ನಲ್ಗೆ.)

b) the third person neuter singular of the present-future tense with ಉದು, *e.g.* ಉಮ್ಬುದು, let (him, her or it) eat!

c) ಅಲಿ, for which see § 207, 2, *a*.

Plural:

a) ಗೆ, ಕೆ (as in the singular), *e. g.* ಪಾಲಿಸುಗೆ, let (them) guard!

b) the third person neuter singular of the present-future tense with ಉದು, *e. g.* ನಡೆವುದು, let (them) walk!

c) ಅಲಿ (§ 207, 2, *a*).

3, Paradigm of the forms of the imperative in the modern dialect:

1st pers.

Singular.

a) (The first person singular of the future tense ending in ಎ and ಎನು, *e. g.* ಮಾಡುವೆ, ಮಾಡುವೆನು; ನುಡಿಯುವೆ, ನುಡಿಯುವೆನು.)

Plural.

a) ಅ, ಆ, (*i. e.* ಅಂ without the euphonic sŏnnĕ, see §§ 137. 138), ಅನು (*i. e.* ಅಂ with a euphonic ಉ), ಅನ (*i. e.* ಅನು + ಅ), ಅಣ (a form in which the dental ನ್ has been changed into the cerebral ಣ್), *e. g.* ಕೇಳುವ, let us hear! ಹೋಗುವ! ನಡೆಯುವ!—ಶಿಳಿಸುವಾ! ನೋಡುವಾ! ಮಾಡುವಾ! ನುಡಿಯುವಾ!—ಮಾಡೂನು! ಹೋಗೂನು! (see § 202)—ಹೋಗುವನ! ಮಾಡೂನ! ಹೋಗೂನ!—ಹೋಗುವಣ! ಹೋಗೋಣ! ಇರೋಣ! ಓಡೋಣ! ಮಾಡೋಣ! (see § 181, note *a*; § 202). (The forms ಹೋಗೋಣ, etc. are used also as verbal nouns; see § 315, 2, *f*; § 316, 10.)

Singular.	*Plural.*
b) ಅಲಿ, for which see § 207, 2, *b*.	*b*) ಅಲಿ (§ 207, 2, *b*).
2nd pers.	
a) the verbal theme, *e. g.* ನೋಡು, see (thou)! ಕೇಳು! ಬಾಳು! ನುಡಿ! ನಡೆ!, in which case also the lengthened themes ತಾಯಿ! (for ತಾ), ಒಯ್ಯಿ! (for ಒಯ್), ಕೊಯಿ! (for ಕೊಯ್), ಸಾಯಿ! (for ಸಾಯ್), ಹೊಯ್ಯಿ! (for ಹೊಯ್) appear (*cf.* §§ 48. 54. 92. 93).	*a*) ಇ, ಇರಿ, ಅರಿ (vulgarly for ಇರಿ), *e. g.* ಇರಿ, be ye! ಮಾಡಿ!—ನೋಡಿರಿ! ಮಾಡಿರಿ! ಹೋಗಿರಿ! ಕಡಿಯಿರಿ! ನಡಿಯಿರಿ or ನಡೆಯಿರಿ! ಹೊಡಿಯಿರಿ or ಹೊಡೆಯಿರಿ! or, by contraction, ಕಡೀರಿ! ನಡೀರಿ! ಹೊಡೀರಿ! (*cf.* § 198, 6)—ಕೇಳರಿ! ನೋಡರಿ! ಹಾಕರಿ!
b) the theme with final ಅ (see Nuḍigaṭṭu page 78 *seq.*), *e. g.* ನೋಡ, see (thou)! ಬಾಳ! ಮಾಡ! ನುಡಿಯ! ಕರೆಯ!	
c) the third person neuter singular of the present-future tense with ಅದು, *e. g.* ನೋಡುವದು, see (thou)! ತಿಳಿಯುವದು! ಕರೆಯುವದು!	*b*) the third person neuter singular of the present-future tense with ಅದು, *e. g.* ನೋಡುವದು, see (ye)!
3rd pers.	
a) the third person neuter singular of the present-future tense with ಅದು, *e. g.* ಹೋಗುವದು, let (him, her or it) go!	*a*) the third person neuter singular of the present-future tense with ಅದು, *e. g.* ನಡೆಯುವದು, let (them) walk!
b) ಅಲಿ, for which see § 207, 2, *b*.	*b*) ಅಲಿ, (§ 207, 2, *b*).

206. An alphabetical list of irregular forms of the imperative is as follows:

ಇರ್ರಿ (for ಇರಿ of ಇರು, the doubling of the ರ್ being euphonic), be ye!, in the modern dialect.

ಕೋ (for ಕೊಳ್ or ಕೊಳ್ಳು, take (thou)!, in the mediæval and modern dialect (*cf.* the ಕೋ in § 187 under 2).

ಜೋ (for ಜೋಲು), swing (thou)!, in the modern dialect (Nuḍigaṭṭu, page 86).

ತನ್ನಿ (*i. e.* ತನ್+ಇ, =ತನ್ನಿಂ, *q. v.*), bring ye!, in the mediæval and modern dialect.

ತನ್ನಿಂ (*i. e.* ತನ್+ಇಂ, for ತರಿಂ of ತರ್, the ನ್ having arisen of the past participle ತನ್ದು and being euphonically doubled), bring ye! (not in the text of the Šabdamaṇidarpaṇa, but) according to the Šabdânušâsana (sûtras 492. 520 and Čandraprabhapurâṇa 3, 46) in the ancient dialect.

ತನ್ನಿರಿ (*i. e.* ತನ್+ಇರಿ), bring ye!, in the (mediæval and) modern dialect (*cf.* ಬನ್ನಿರಿ).

ತರ್ರಿ (for ತರಿ of ತರು, the doubling of the ರ್ being euphonic), bring ye!, in the modern dialect.

ತಾ (for ತರ of ತರ್ or ತರು), bring (thou)!, in the mediæval and modern dialect, and, according to the Šabdânušâsana (sûtras 519. 520), also in the ancient one.

ತಾರ್, ತಾರು (for ತರ್ or ತರು), bring (thou)!, in the mediæval and modern dialect. (It is, however, probable that the instances require ತಾರ for ತಾರ್ or ತಾರು; *cf.* ಬಾರ್.)

ತಾರ (for ತರ of ತರ್ or ತರು), bring (thou)!, in the mediæval and modern dialect.

ಬನ್ನಿ (*i. e.* ಬನ್ + ಇ, = ಬನ್ನಿಂ, *q. v.*), come ye!, in the mediæval and modern dialect.

ಬನ್ನಿಂ (*i. e.* ಬನ್ + ಇಂ, the ನ್ having arisen of the past participle ಬನ್ದು and being euphonically doubled), come ye!, in the ancient dialect according to the Šabdânušâsana (sûtras 470. 492).

ಬನ್ನಿರಿ (*i. e.* ಬನ್ + ಇರಿ), come ye!, in the mediæval and modern dialect.

ಬರ್ರಿ (for ಬರಿ of ಬರು, the doubling of the ರ್ being euphonic), come ye!, in the modern dialect.

ಬಾ (for ಬರ of ಬರ್ or ಬರು), come (thou)!, in the mediæval and modern dialect, and, according to an instance in Nâgavarma's Karṇâṭaka-bhâshâbhûshaṇa (under sûtra 27) and according to the Šabdânušâsana (sûtras 41. 385. 400. 519. 520), also in the ancient one.

ಬಾರ್, ಬಾರು (for ಬರ್ or ಬರು), come (thou)!, in the mediæval and modern dialect. (It is, however, probable that the instances require ಬಾರ for ಬಾರ್ and ಬಾರು; *cf.* ತಾರ್.)

ಬಾರ (for ಬರ of ಬರ್), come (thou)!, in the ancient, mediæval (and modern) dialect.

207. There are three forms connected with the imperative still to be adduced. They are produced by means of the suffixes ಅಲಿಂ, ಅಲಿ and ಅಲ್.

1, According to one translation of a rule in Kêšava's Šabdamaṇidarpaṇa (sûtra 234, prayôga) which has been adopted by the author of the Šabdânušâsana (see further on under No. 1), ಅಲಿಂ is used "when (the action of) the second person of the negative (see § 209) gets the sense of the imperative" (madhyamapurushapratishêdhada vidhiyôḷ or madhyamapurushapratishêdhada kriyĕ vidhyartham âdalli). The ಇಂ in ಅಲಿಂ (ಅಲ್ + ಇಂ) indicates that the second person plural is to be understood (see § 205, 1, plural, *a*). Let us take *e. g.* the verbal theme ಸಾರ್, to approach. Of this the second person plural of the negative is ಸಾರಿರ್,

you do not approach, and ಸಾರಲಿಂ would mean 'you shall not or must not approach!' (*Cf.* the use of ಅಲ್ under No. 3 of this paragraph.)

But when considering the meaning of ಅಲಿ under No. 2, *a* and *b*, the mediæval and modern form of ಅಲಿಂ, it might appear as if Kêšava's rule required another translation, *viz.* ಅಲಿಂ is used "when a prohibition (pratishêdha, given) concerning (the action of) the second person (plural, *e.g.* ನೀಂ ಸಾರ ಬೇಡ, you must not approach!) becomes an order or permission (vidhi)" in an indirect form, so that ಸಾರಲಿಂ means 'they may approach!' 'let them approach!', the ಇಂ of the second person plural in ಸಾರಲ್ (the meaning of which see in § 208, 2) being retained in an honorific sense (*cf.* the honorific German '*Sie*', they, used for English 'you') in order to show that now kind feelings prevail where previously more or less aversion had obtained; compare with regard to ಇಂ the free use made of the honorific ಇರಿ of the modern dialect (see the Dictionary). In order to make Kêšava's rule in this form fully correspond to No. 2, *a* and *b*, we must, by implication, take for granted that not only the second person of the plural is to be understood, but also that of the singular, and that ಇಂ in this case too is honorific, so that ಸಾರಲಿಂ signifies also 'he, she or it may approach'.

Kêšava's instances, as they are taken and adduced by him out of the context, mostly allow the meaning of both translations; they are (sûtra 234 of the Šabdamaṇidarpaṇa) — ಉಸುರಲಿಂ! — ಸಾರಲಿಂ! ಬಲ್ಲೆಱಿಯನ್ ಎನ್ದುದೆ ಮಾತು. — ಮೀಱಲಿಂ! — ಏಳಿದಂ ಗೆಯ್ಯಲಿಮ್ ಈಗಳ್ ಎಮ್ಮೊಳ್! — ಆರಯ್ದಾರುಂ ಸಾರಲಿಂ! — ಆಂ ಪೆಱಿನೆನ್ ಎನ್ದು, ಬಗೆಯಲಿಮ್ ಈಗಳ್! (page 258); but his instance ಓಹೋ, ಇರಲಿಂ ಪೆಱವಱ ಮಾಹಾತ್ಮ್ಯಮುಂ! (page 68, which occurs in the Šabdânušâsana under its sûtra 44 that treats of nipâtas, as ಆಹೋ, ಇರಲಿಂ ಪೆಱವಱ ಮಾಹಾತ್ಮ್ಯಂ!) seems to show clearly the meaning of the second translation, *i.e.* "oho, may also the greatness of other things remain!"

The Šabdânušâsana (sûtra 529), however, plainly and exclusively teaches the meaning of the first translation; it says ಪೆಣ್ಡಿರಂ ನಮ್ಬಲಿಂ! means "you must not trust women!" "do not you (in any way) trust women (sarvatrâpi strîyô mâ šraddhata)!", and ಅಕಾರ್ಯಮಂ ಮಾಡಲಿಂ! "you must not commit an improper act!" "do not commit an improper act (akâryaṁ mâ kurudhvaṁ)!"

2, *a)* In the mediæval (and mediæval-modern) dialect the form of ಅಲಿಂ is ಅಲಿ (*i.e.* ಅಲ್ + ಇ, see § 205, 2 and 3, 2nd pers. plural, *a*), or occasionally ಅಲೀ, and is used only in the meaning of the second translation of **Kêśava's rule** (or in the imperative, § 205, 2. 3), **expressing request, permission, allowance, concession, and wish regarding a third person or thing, singular and plural**, *e. g.* ಒಡೆಯರಿರ, ನಿಮ್ಮಡಿಗಳ್ ಎನ್ನಂ ಬಿಡದೆ ಸಲಹಲಿ! sir, may your feet continually preserve me! (Basavapurâṇa 27, 72); — ಅಧಮನ್ ಅವನು; ಇರಲಿ! he is a vile person; (but what is that to us?) let him be! (39, 47); — ನಿಮ್ಮ ಹಿರಿಯತನಂಗಳ್ ಆಗಳು ನಿಮ್ಮೊಳ್ ಇರಲೀ! ನಮಗೇತಕೆ? let your excellencies always be among you! why should they concern us? (46, 15); — ಯುಧಿಷ್ಠಿರ ಜನಪನ್ ಆಗಲಿ! let Yudhishṭhira become king (Bhârata 1, 8, 5); — ಪಂಪಾವಿರೂಪಾಕ್ಷಸೂರ್ಯನ್ ಆನನ್ದಮಂ ನಮಗೀಯಲಿ! may the sun of Pampâ's Virûpâksha give us joy! (Čannabasavapurâṇa 1, 2); — ಪರಬಲವನು ಭಂಗ ಮಾಡಲಿ! ಎನ್ದು, ಜೋದರು ಮಾಡುವ ಸಿಂಹನಾದವು, a war-cry used by elephant-drivers with the object 'may it discomfit the hostile army!' (Nâčirâjîya); — ಮೆಯ್ಯ ಹೂಸಲಿ! ಎನ್ದು, ಮಾಡಿದ ಗುಳಿಗೆ, (a pill or) an ointment made with the object '(people) may smear the body (with it)!' (Nâčirâjîya).

b) In the modern dialect ಅಲಿಂ has the same forms and meaning as in the mediæval one, with the only difference that ಅಲಿ, ಅಲೀ are used also interrogatively for the first person, *e. g.* ಅವನು ಬರೆಯಲಿ! let him write! (or he may write). ಅವಳು ಬರೆಯಲಿ! let her write! ಅದು ಬರೆಯಲಿ! let it (the child) write! ಅವರು ಬರೆಯಲಿ! let them (the men or women) write! ಅವು ಬರೆಯಲಿ! let them (the children) write! ಕರು ತಾಯಿ ಮೊಲೆ ಉಣ್ಣಲಿ! let the calf suck (its) mother's breast! ಬೇಕಾದವರು ಈ ಹಣ್ಣುಗಳನ್ನು ತಕ್ಕೊಳ್ಳಲಿ! let those who want (them) take these ripe fruits! ದೇವರು ನಿಮ್ಮ ಮಕ್ಕಳಿಗೆ ಕಲ್ಯಾಣ ಮಾಡಲಿ! may God grant welfare to your children! ಈ ಮಾತು ನೆನಪು ಇರಲಿ! let (him, her, it or them) hold this word in mind! ಧೈರ್ಯ ಮಾತ್ರ ಇರಲಿ! let only (thy, your or their) courage remain! ಓಹೋ, ಚನ್ದವೆಷ್ಟೆನ್ತ, ಹೇಳಲಿ? o, how shall I (or we) tell how great the beauty is? ಅವನ ಫಜೀತಿ, ಎಷ್ಟೆನ್ತ, ಹೇಳಲಿ? how shall I (or we) tell how great his annoyance is? ನಾಲ್ಕು ಆಣೆ ರೊಕ್ಕಾ ಎಲ್ಲಿನ್ದ ತರಲಿ? whence shall I (or we) bring four annas? ರೊಟ್ಟಿಯನ್ನು ತನ್ದು, ಆಕಳಿಗೆ ಹಾಕಲೀ? shall I (or we) bring the bread and give (it) to the cow? ನಾನು ಹೋಗಲ್ಯಾ (*i. e.* ಹೋಗಲಿ + ಆ)? shall I go? ಇದನ್ನು ನಾನು ಮಾಡಲಿ? shall (or may) I do this?

ಆಗಲಿ! means 'let (him, her, it or them) become!', and then also 'let it be, be it!', and when repeated it gets the meaning of the English 'either — or' (see § 317).

See § 316, 14.

Note.

Tho Šabdânušâsana (sûtras 524. 525. 526. 527. 529) toachos another use of the ancient ಅಲಿಂ, saying that it may stand for the ಅಲ್ and ಅ of the infinitive (see § 187) before ಬೇಡ or ಬೇಡಂ, it is not requested, it must not, etc. (see § 209, note 1). Its instances (under sûtra 529) show that it wants to express the second person plural by the ಇಂ in ಅಲಿಂ, for it translates ಪೆಣ್ಡಿರಂ ನಮ್ಬಲಿಂ ಬೇಡ or ಪೆಣ್ಡಿರಂ ನಮ್ಬಲಿಂ ಬೇಡಂ, "you must not (in any way) trust women" (sarvatrâpi strîyô mâ śraddhata).

3, Instead of the ಅಲಿಂ of No. 1 of this paragraph Kêšava's sûtra and vṛitti (234) have the form of ಅಲ್, that of ಅಲಿಂ appearing only and alone in the prayôga, *i. e.* in his first instances, quoted under No. 1. He, no doubt, accepted ಅಲ್ to be the leading form to which ಇಂ was to be suffixed. But as to the second instances in the prayôga under his vṛitti he introduces ಅಲ್ again, saying "when there does not occur the sense of permission (vidhyartha) in the action of the negative (pratishêdhakriyĕ)", *i. e.* when a prohibition is not changed into a permission or when there is a direct prohibition or interdiction, "ಅಲ್ is used" (vidhyartham allada pratishêdhakriyĕyoḷ al akkuṁ). His two instances with ಅಲ್ are: — ಪೆಱಿತೊನ್ದನ್ ಆಣಂ ಬಗೆಯಲ್! ಗಡ, ನಿನಗೆ ಸುಮತಿ ಬೇಱೊಂ ಬೇಱೆ, do not (thou) consider any other thing! verily, thy good disposition is different, (and so) am I different, (but the good disposition of both of us is beyond doubt). ಬನದಲ್ಲಿ ಪುಗಲ್ ಪುಗಲ್! ಎಮ್ಬ ಗಣ್ಡುಗೋಗಿಲೆ, the male cuckoo which said (or says) 'do not enter, do not enter the wood!'. A similar instance is in the Ċandraprabhapurâṇa (2, after 93), *viz.* ತಳಿರ್ಗೊಮ್ಬುಗಳೊಳಿರ್ದ್ದ, ಮುನ್ನಿನನ್ದದಿನ್ದಿನ್ದು ಪೊಕ್ಕಡೆ ಪೊಲ್ಲದಕ್ಕುಮ್ ಎನ್ದು, ಕನ್ದರ್ಪಂಗೆ ಪುಗಲ್ ಪುಗಲ್! ಎಮ್ಬನ್ದದಿಂ ಸರಂಗೆಯ್ವ ಗಣ್ಡುಗೋಗಿಲೆಯ ದನಿಗಳ್, the sounds of the male cuckoo which was in the branches with young leaves, said 'if he as before enters to-day, it will be improper', and cried out to Kandarpa as it were 'do not enter, do not enter (the wood)!' (*cf.* the use made of ಅಲಿಂ according to the first translation of Kêšava's rule under No. 1).

The Šabdânušâsana (sûtra 528) has the following instances: — ನೀವ್ ಈ ಬನಮಂ ಪುಗಲ್! do not enter this wood! (yûyam êtad vanaṁ mâ pravišata). ನೀವ್ ಈ ಮನೆಯಂ ನೋಡಲ್! do not look at this house! (yûyam êtad gṛihaṁ mâ pašyata). ಯತಿಗಳ್, ನೀವ್ ಅಂಗಜನ ಆಟಕ್ಕೆ ಸಲಲ್! devotees, do not you engage in Aṅgaja's sport! (bhô yatayô bhavantô madanakriyâyâṁ mâ pravartadhvaṁ).

208. How are we to explain the possibility of the use made in § 207 of ಅಲಿಂ, ಅಲಿ and ಅಲ್?

It rests on the meaning of the infinitive (see §§ 170. 171. 187. 188. 210) which in the present case ends in ಅಲ್.

1, In the instance ಸಾರಲಿಂ (ಸಾರಲ್+ಇಂ), you shall not or must not approach!, ಸಾರಲ್ means 'to approach, yet to approach', *i. e.* approaching has not yet taken place (and shall not do so), and ಇಂ means 'you'. The primitive sense of ಸಾರಲಿಂ, therefore, is 'you are yet to approach', *i. e.* you have not approached yet (and shall not do so).

2, When ಸಾರಲಿಂ (ಸಾರಲ್+ಇಂ) or ಸಾರಲಿ (ಸಾರಲ್+ಇ) means 'they may approach!' 'let him, her or it approach!' the meaning of the infinitive ಸಾರಲ್ is that of a verbal noun, *viz.* approaching, combined with the sense of a sign of exclamation and with the honorific ಇಂ or ಇ: 'approaching!' '(his, her, its, or their) approach may take place!'

3, When the infinitive with ಅಲ್, without the honorific ಇಂ and ಇ, is used prohibitively, as in ಪುಗಲ್, do not enter!, the primitive meaning is (analogously to that of ಸಾರಲ್+ಇಂ under No. 1) 'yet to enter', *i. e.* entering has not yet happened (and shall not do so).

209. The conjugated negative (pratishêdha, § 146) of the verb is formed by suffixing the personal terminations of § 193 to the infinitive ending in ಅ (see §§ 170. 187, 2, and note 2 of this paragraph), with the exception of the terminations ಇತು, ಇತ್ತು, ಅತ್ತು, ತು.

A difference, however, regarding those terminations in the conjugated negative is that, instead of ಉದು and ಉವು of the neuter singular and plural of the ancient dialect, ಅದು and ಅವು are used; ಉದು, the neuter singular in the mediæval dialect, becomes ಅದು; (in the modern dialect both ಅದು and ಅವು remain).

What has been stated in § 170 about the doubling of final consonants in the formation of the negative participle remains in effect also in the present case. *Cf.* 215, 7, *f.*

In the three dialects the themes ತರ್, to bring, and ಬರ್, to come, always lengthen their ಅ, changing it into ಆ, in the conjugated negative.

The conjugated negative is used for the present, past, and future tense, according to circumstances (*cf.* § 170).

Concerning its original meaning see § 210.

1, Paradigms of the negative in the **ancient** dialect:

one of ನೋಡು, **to see.**

	Singular.	*Plural.*
1st pers.	ನೋಡೆಂ (*i. e.* ನೋಡ + ಎಂ), I do not see, I did not see, I have not seen), I shall not see.	ನೋಡೆವು.
2nd pers.	ನೋಡಯ್.	ನೋಡಿರ್.
3rd pers.		
masc.	ನೋಡಂ.	ನೋಡರ್.
fem.	ನೋಡಳ್.	ನೋಡರ್.
neut.	ನೋಡದು.	ನೋಡವು.

one of ಉೞಿ, **to remain.**

	Singular.	*Plural.*
1st pers.	ಉೞಿಯೆಂ (*i. e.* ಉೞಿಯ + ಎಂ), I do not remain, I did not remain, (I have not remained), I shall not remain.	ಉೞಿಯೆವು.
2nd pers.	ಉೞಿಯಯ್.	ಉೞಿಯಿರ್.
3rd pers.		
masc.	ಉೞಿಯಂ.	ಉೞಿಯರ್.
fem.	ಉೞಿಯಳ್.	ಉೞಿಯರ್.
neut.	ಉೞಿಯದು.	ಉೞಿಯವು.

one of ನಿಲ್, **to stand.**

	Singular.	*Plural.*
1st pers.	ನಿಲ್ಲೆಂ (*i. e.* ನಿಲ್ಲ for ನಿಲ + ಎಂ), I do not stand, I did not stand, (I have not stood), I shall not stand.	ನಿಲ್ಲೆವು.
2nd pers.	ನಿಲ್ಲಯ್.	ನಿಲ್ಲಿರ್.
3rd pers.		
masc.	ನಿಲ್ಲಂ.	ನಿಲ್ಲರ್.
fem.	ನಿಲ್ಲಳ್.	ನಿಲ್ಲರ್.
neut.	ನಿಲ್ಲದು.	ನಿಲ್ಲವು.

one of ತರ್, **to bring.**

	Singular.	*Plural.*
1st pers.	ತಾರೆಂ (ತಾರ for ತರ + ಎಂ), I do not bring, I did not bring, (I have not brought), I shall not bring.	ತಾರೆವು.
2nd pers.	ತಾರಯ್.	ತಾರಿರ್.
3rd pers.		
masc.	ತಾರಂ.	ತಾರರ್.
fem.	ತಾರಳ್.	ತಾರರ್.
neut.	ತಾರದು.	ತಾರವು.

2, A paradigm of the negative of **ನೋಡು, to see,** in the **mediæval** dialect:

	Singular.	*Plural.*
1st pers.	ನೋಡೆಂ, ನೋಡೆನು, ನೋಡೆ, I do not see, etc., etc.	ನೋಡೆವು.
2nd pers.	ನೋಡೆ.	ನೋಡಿರಿ (*i. e.* ನೋಡ+ಇರಿ).
3rd pers.		
masc.	ನೋಡಂ, ನೋಡನು, (ನೋಡ).	(ನೋಡರ್), ನೋಡರು.
fem.	(ನೋಡಳ್), ನೋಡಳು.	(ನೋಡರ್), ನೋಡರು.
neut.	ನೋಡದು.	ನೋಡವು.

Other instances in the first person singular are *e.g.* ಉೞಿಯೆಂ, ಉೞಿಯೆನು, ಉೞಿಯೆ (of ಉೞಿ); ಕಡೆಯೆಂ, ಕಡೆಯೆನು, ಕಡೆಯೆ (of ಕಡೆ); ಗೆಲ್ಲೆಂ, ಗೆಲ್ಲೆನು, ಗೆಲ್ಲೆ or ಗೆಲೆಂ, ಗೆಲೆನು, ಗೆಲೆ (of ಗೆಲ್); ಬಾರೆಂ, ಬಾರೆನು, ಬಾರೆ (of ಬರ್).

3, A paradigm of the negative of **ನೋಡು, to see,** in the **modern** dialect:

	Singular.	*Plural.*
1st pers.	ನೋಡೆನು, ನೋಡೆ, I do not see, etc., etc.	ನೋಡೆವು.
2nd pers.	ನೋಡೆ.	ನೋಡರಿ (*i. e.* ನೋಡ+ಅರಿ, see Nuḍigaṭṭu page 78).
3rd pers.		
masc.	ನೋಡನು, ನೋಡ.	ನೋಡರು.
fem.	ನೋಡಳು.	ನೋಡರು.
neut.	ನೋಡದು.	ನೋಡವು.

Other instances in the first person singular are *e.g.* ಅೞಿಯೆನು, ಅೞಿಯೆ (of ಅೞಿ); ನಡೆಯೆನು, ನಡೆಯೆ (of ನಡೆ); ತಾರೆನು, ತಾರೆ (of ತರ್).

The conjugated negative is somewhat seldom used in the modern colloquial dialect (except in proverbs and in the verb ಒಲ್, see § 316, 12), and its second person plural ನೋಡರಿ is anomalous, its termination ಅರಿ standing for ಇರಿ. The same dialect generally uses the third person neuter singular of the (present-)future tense which is a bhâvavačana (§ 200, 1. 3), and the infinitive with ಅಲು (ಅಲ್) which too is a bhâvavačana or verbal noun (§ 188), followed by ಇಲ್ಲ (see note 1), *e.g.* ಕೊಡುವದಿಲ್ಲ, ಕೊಡಲಿಲ್ಲ, the first form for the present and future (I, etc. do not give, I, etc. shall not give), and the second one for the past (I, etc. did not give). See §§ 298, 3; 299, 1. 2; 316, 1. 2; 368.

When in the ancient dialect repetition of the conjugated negative (§ 211, 6) is used, the first verb may drop its personal termination and the ಅ of the infinitive, *e.g.* ಬಾರ್, ಬಾರೆಂ (for ಬಾರೆಂ ಬಾರೆಂ, Šabdânušâsana sûtra 398). *Cf.* ಬಿಡ ಬಡದೆ in § 170.

Notes.

1, It is a peculiarity of the only two defective verbs ಅಲ್, to be fit, and ಇಲ್ (another form of ಇರ್), to be, that in the three dialects they have the forms ಅಲ್ಲ and ಇಲ್ಲ for all persons in the singular and plural of the conjugated negative. The formation is the following: the infinitives are ಅಲ and ಇಲ, to which ಅ is added with the regular doubling of the final ಲ್ of the theme, this ಅ representing all the personal terminations (*cf.* the suffix ಇಲ in § 243, and see their use in §§ 298; 316, 1. 9). The meaning of ಅಲ್ಲ and ಇಲ್ಲ depends on their nominative or subject which is either expressly put or is to be supplied (see § 210). Occasionally a euphonic sŏnnĕ may be added to ಅಲ್ಲ and ಇಲ್ಲ, so that we get ಅಲ್ಲಂ, ಇಲ್ಲಂ (see *e.g.* Šabdânušâsana sûtra 523; § 298, 4; § 300), which (sŏnnĕ) may change into ಮ್ or ವ್ when it meets with a following vowel. The same holds good with regard to ಬೇಡ of ಬೇಡು, to be required, and, with the sŏnnĕ, ಬೇಡಂ (see *e.g.* Šabdânušâsana sûtra 524 *seq.*; §§ 207, note; 316, 5). In the modern dialect ಸಲ್ಲ of ಸಲ್ (§ 316, 15), to be proper, is another instance of this kind. The Šabdânušâsana (sûtras 19. 584) introduces also ಆಗ or ಆಗಾ, for ಆಗದು.

The grammarian Kêšava calls ಇಲ್ಲ a particle (avyaya) that partakes of the nature of a verb (kriyâtmaka); see § 212, 7; 298.

2, When the author has stated at the beginning of this paragraph that in the conjugation of the negative the personal terminations are attached to the infinitive with ಅ, he seems to be at variance with what Kêšava in and under his sûtra 216 writes, *viz.* that a verb's theme (dhâtu, according to his instances a theme ending in ಉ) appears when one removes the termination (vibhakti) ಅಂ of the conjugated negative (pratishêdhakriyĕ), so that *e. g.* the themes ನೋಡು, ಮಾಡು, ಕೊಡು are formed from ನೋಡಂ, ಮಾಡಂ, ಕೊಡಂ; but because his rule is superficial (see § 143) and therefore seems to give only a certain practical hint to students, we must not lay too much stress on its wording, and not conclude that ನೋಡು+ಅಂ, ಮಾಡು+ಅಂ, ಕೊಡು+ಅಂ showed the exact final rule for the formation of the negative; we have to take the infinitive with final ಅ and the termination ಅಂ, *i. e.* ನೋಡ+ಅಂ, ಮಾಡ+ಅಂ, ಕೊಡ+ಅಂ in order to get ನೋಡಂ, ಮಾಡಂ, ಕೊಡಂ, and find the theme by removing the termination and by adding ಉ in the instances given by Kêšava.

210. In examining the origin of the conjugated negative we have to reject the thought, as if the change of the suffixes ಉದು and ಉವು into

ಅದು and ಅವು could help us to find it, for already in the ancient dialect we have, side by side with ಉದು, ಅತ್ತು (that is another form of ಅದು, § 193 under remarks) as a termination of the past tense, and the positive forms ಒಳವು, they are (§ 194, remark 1) and ಬೆರಣ್ಚವು they scratched (§ 198, 1); then in the mediæval one ಅವು in the third person neuter plural of the present, past and future tense (§§ 194; 198, 4; 200, 2; 201, 2. 3), and in the modern one ಅದು in the third person neuter singular of the future tense (§ 200, 3) and ಅವು in the third person neuter plural of the past and future tense (§§ 198, 5; 200, 3). Also the change of the vowel ಅ into ಆ in ತರ್ and ಬರ್ (§ 209) cannot assist us to do so, as some other monosyllabic verbs appear in their positive forms with long and short vowels (see §§ 52. 53), as we have the positive forms ತಾರಲ್, ಬಾರಲ್ for ತರಲ್, ಬರಲ್ (§ 187, 1), ತಾರೆ for ತರೆ (§ 187, 4), ತಾರ, ಬಾರ, ತಾ, ಬಾ for ತರ, ಬರ, ತರ್, ಬರ್ (§§ 205. 1, 2nd pers., *b;* 205, 2, 2nd pers., *b;* 206), ಬಾಹ for ಬಹ (§ 184), and the negative forms ತರದೆ, ಬರದೆ for ತಾರದೆ, ಬಾರದೆ (§ 170).

There can be no doubt that the origin of the conjugated negative is based, as has been stated in § 209, on the so-called infinitive ending in ಅ (§ 187) in the same manner as that of the negative participle is (see § 170). That infinitive originally was a verbal noun and only in course of time came to get its specific meanings (§ 188). Thus *e. g.* ನೋಡ at first meant 'seeing', 'a seeing', and thereupon 'to see', 'about to see', 'yet to see'. ನೋಡೆಂ (ನೋಡ+ಎಂ), therefore, signifies 'a yet to see-I', *i. e.* my seeing (is or was) yet to be or (will be) yet be, or my seeing (is) not actually existing, (was) not so, or (will) not be so, whence we arrive at the meaning 'I do not see', 'I did not see', '(I have not seen)', 'I shall not see'.—Regarding the meaning of ಅಲ್ಲ, ಇಲ್ಲ, ಬೇಡ and ಸಲ್ಲ it has been stated in note 1 of § 209 that their meaning depends on their nominative or subject which is either expressly put or is to be supplied. Originally they denote 'a yet to be fit—', 'a yet to be—', 'a yet to be required—', 'a yet to be proper—', (the dashes denoting the ಅ of § 209, note 1), *i. e.* fitting (is, was or will be) yet to be, being (is, was or will be) yet to be, requiring (is, was or will be) yet to be, being proper (is, was or will be) yet to be, or being fit (is or was) not really existing or (will) not be so, being (is or was) not really existing or (will) not be so, requiring (is or was) not really existing or (will) not be so, etc. Now if for instance ಅವಂ (ಅವನು), he, becomes the subject, the translation is 'he is not fit, he was not fit, he will not be fit', 'he is not, he was not, he will not be', 'he is not required, he was not required, he will not be required', etc. *Cf.* the prohibitive forms of the infinitive with ಅಲ್ in § 208.

That ಅದು and ಅವು are suffixed for ಉದು and ಉವು is very probably done to show off the use of the infinitive with ಅ in the formation of the tense.

211. In § 152 (*cf.* § 165, *b*, 1-3; § 170) there is the statement that **frequentative or iterative action of the verb is expressed by simple or triple repetition.** Without respect to the various meanings created by that process (see § 339) we give here a number of instances as they occur in the three dialects:—

1, regarding doubling the verb without any alteration (in the present, future, past, imperative, infinitive, participle, and conjugated negative) ಉಣ್ಬುಣ್ಬು (ಉಣ್ಬು ಉಣ್ಬು); ಅಪ್ಪುದಪ್ಪುದು (ಅಪ್ಪುದು ಅಪ್ಪುದು), ತೋರ್ಪುದು ತೋರ್ಪುದು, ಪೋಪೆಂ ಪೋಪೆಂ, ಅಕ್ಕಕ್ಕು (ಅಕ್ಕು ಅಕ್ಕು), ಸಾಕು ಸಾಕು, ಅಹುದಹುದು (ಅಹುದು ಅಹುದು), ಹೌದು ಹೌದು; ಆದುದಾದುದು (ಆದುದು ಆದುದು), ಕಣ್ಡಂ ಕಣ್ಡಂ, ಪೋದಂ ಪೋದಂ, ಬನ್ದಯ್ ಬನ್ದಯ್; ಒಪ್ಪಿಸೊಪ್ಪಿಸು (ಒಪ್ಪಿಸು ಒಪ್ಪಿಸು), ಕೊಯ್ ಕೊಯ್, ಬಾ ಬಾ, ನುತಿಸು ನುತಿಸು, ಕುಡಿ ಕುಡಿ, ಪಿಡಿ ಪಿಡಿ, ನಿಲ್ ನಿಲ್, ಹೇೞು ಹೇೞು, ಕೋ ಕೋ, ಆಗಲಾಗಲಿ (ಆಗಲಿ ಆಗಲಿ); ಕೂಡೆ ಕೂಡೆ, ಪುಗೆ ಪುಗೆ, ಬರೆವರೆ (for ಬರೆ ಬರೆ); ಆಗುತ್ತಾಗುತ್ತಾ (ಆಗುತ್ತಾ ಆಗುತ್ತಾ), ಆಡಿಯಾಡಿ (ಆಡಿ ಆಡಿ), ಮಾಡಿ ಮಾಡಿ, ಅತ್ತತ್ತು (ಅತ್ತು ಅತ್ತು), ಉಣ್ಡುಣ್ಡು (ಉಣ್ಡು ಉಣ್ಡು), ಬನ್ದು ಬನ್ದು, ಆದ ಆದ, ಬನ್ದ ಬನ್ದ; ಬಾರೆಂ ಬಾರೆಂ, ಬೇಡ ಬೇಡ;

2, regarding tripling the verb without any alteration (in the imperative, past, and past participle) ಒಡ್ಡೊಡ್ಡೊಡ್ಡು (ಒಡ್ಡು ಒಡ್ಡು ಒಡ್ಡು), ಒಪ್ಪಿಸೊಪ್ಪಿಸೊಪ್ಪಿಸು (ಒಪ್ಪಿಸು ಒಪ್ಪಿಸು ಒಪ್ಪಿಸು), ಕುಡು ಕುಡು ಕುಡು, ನೋಡು ನೋಡು ನೋಡು, ಬಾ ಬಾ ಬಾ; ಬನ್ದಂ ಬನ್ದಂ ಬನ್ದಂ; ಉಣ್ಡುಣ್ಡುಣ್ಡು (ಉಣ್ಡು ಉಣ್ಡು ಉಣ್ಡು);

3, regarding doubling the verb, dropping ಅಲು (or also ಅಲು+ಎ *i. e.* ಅಲೆ) of the first one (in the infinitive) ಹೋಗ ಹೋಗಲು, ಬರ ಬರಲು, ಕೂಡ ಕೂಡಲೆ;

4, regarding doubling the verb, dropping the termination of the past participle of the first one, *e. g.* ಕಡಿ ಕಡಿದು, ಕುಡಿ ಕುಡಿದು, ಕಾಯ್ ಕಾಯ್ದು, ಸೆಳೆ ಸೆಳೆದು (see § 165, *b*, 1), and also its vowel, *e. g.* ಕಳ ಕಳೆದು, ತೆಗ ತೆಗೆದು (see § 165, *b*, 2), to which class may likewise be referred the doubled negative participle dropping its ಅದೆ, *viz.* ತಪ್ಪ ತಪ್ಪದೆ, ನಿಲ್ಲ ನಿಲ್ಲದೆ, ಬಿಡ ಬಿಡದೆ (§ 170);

5, regarding doubling the verb, dropping the termination of the relative present participle or that of the present participle of the first one, *e. g.* ನೋಡ ನೋಡುವ, ಮಾಡ ಮಾಡುವ;[1] ಇರ ಇರುತ್ತ, ಬರ ಬರುತ್ತ, ಹೋಗ ಹೋಗುತ್ತ;

6, regarding doubling the verb, dropping the personal termination of the first one, *e. g.* ಪೋಪ ಪೋಪೆಂ, ಪೋದ ಪೋದಂ, ಬನ್ದ ಬನ್ದಯ್, ಬಾರ್ ಬಾರೆಂ (for ಬಾರೆಂ ಬಾರೆಂ or ಬಾರ ಬಾರೆಂ, see § 209);

7, regarding doubling the verb, dropping the final syllable of the first one, *e. g.* ತಿರ ತಿರಗು, ತೊಲ ತೊಲಗು, ಮುಱು ಮುಱುಗು, ಮೊಗ ಮೊಗಸು, ಸೊಗ ಸೊಗಸು (see § 165, *b*, 3, and *cf.* § 183, 7 and remark 1 and 2 of this paragraph; *cf.* also § 253, 3; § 243, *A*, 16);

8, regarding tripling the verb, dropping the termination of the past participle of the two first ones, *e. g.* ಬಡ ಬಡ ಬಡೆದು (§ 165, *b*, 2, remark, where ಬಡ ಬಡ ಕೊಳ್ is adduced as a peculiar form);

9, regarding tripling the verb, dropping the personal termination of the two first ones, *e. g.* ಅಪ್ಪಪ್ಪಪ್ಪೆಂ (ಅಪ್ಪ ಅಪ್ಪ ಅಪ್ಪೆಂ), ಬನ್ದ ಬನ್ದ ಬನ್ದಂ;

10, regarding tripling the verb, dropping the last syllable of the two first ones, *e. g.* ತೊಳ ತೊಳ ತೊಳಗು, ಬೆಳ ಬೆಳ ಬೆಳಗು (see § 165, *b*, 3, remark). *Cf.* also ನಡ ನಡ ನಡುಗು.

11, Observe also the curious repetition of verbs wherein the initial of the second one is changed, *e. g.* ಕೊಡು ಗಿಡುವುದು, ತನ್ದರೆ ಗಿನ್ದರೆ. *Cf.* § 303, 1, after *e*. Observe also the colloquial expression ನೀರ ತ ತಾ (for ತಾ ತಾ).

Remarks.

1, Also by setting a sort of adverb which is of the same root as the verb, before the verb and occasionally doubling it repetition is expressed, *e. g.* ಚಿಮಿ ಚಿಮಿಸು; ನಡ ನಡಗು, ನಡ ನಡುಗು; ಮಲ ಮಱುಗು; ಮಿಡು ಮಿಡುಕು; ಮಿನು ಮಿನಿಸು, ಮಿನು ಮಿನುಗು;— ಚಿಟ್ ಚಿಟ್ ಚೀಱು; ಚಿಟ್ಟ ಚಿಟ್ಟನೆ ಚೀಱು; ನಡ ನಡ ನಡುಗು; ನಡ ನಡನೆ ನಡುಗು; ಮಱ ಮಱ ಮಱುಗು; ಮಱ ಮಱನೆ ಮಱುಗು; ಮಲ ಮಲನೆ ಮಱುಗು; ಮಿಡ ಮಿಡನೆ ಮಿಡುಕು, ಮಿಡು ಮಿಡನೆ ಮಿಡುಕು; ಮಿಣ ಮಿಣನೆ ಮಿಂಚು; ಮಿಱು ಮಿಱನೆ ಮಿಂಚು.

It is possible that some of the instances are connected with No. 7 above.

2, Of double nouns not seldom verbs are formed by means of ಇಸು (§ 149 *seq.*) which may be regarded as frequentative ones, *e. g.* ಅಟ ಮಟಿಸು (of ಅಟ ಮಟ), ಅಡ ಬಡಿಸು, ಅಡ ಹಡಿಸು, ಕದ ಕದಿಸು, ಕರ ಕರಿಸು, ಕಳ ಕಳಿಸು, ಕಳ ವಳಿಸು, ಕಱ ಕಱುಸು, ಗಡ ಬಡಿಸು, ಗದ ಗದಿಸು, ಗಲ ಗಲಿಸು, ಗುಡಿ ಗುಡಿಸು, ಗುಡು ಗುಡಿಸು, ಗುಱು ಗುಱುಸು, ತಡ ಬಡಿಸು, ತಳ ತಳಿಸು, ತಳ ತಳಾಯಿಸು, ತಳ ದಳಿಸು, ದಳ ದಳಿಸು, ಮಗ ಮಗಿಸು, ಮಱ ಮಱುಸು, ಸರ ಸರಿಸು.

---

[1] ನೋಡ and ಮಾಡ might however be ನೋಡೊ and ಮಾಡೊ (see § 181, note *c*) so that there would be no dropping.

VI. On adverbs, etc. (See § 281 *seq.*)

212. In the present paragraph a class of words is introduced which are called **indeclinables** (avyaya) by Kannaḍa grammarians; some of the words they term also **particles** (nipâta, see remark 1). Many of the words would be called **adverbs** by Europeans.

The expression of 'indeclinables' is not quite exact, as some admit of being declined, to which the letter *d* (declinable) in parenthesis will be added in the **alphabetical** lists given below.

These alphabetical lists are composed of the adverbs, etc. found in the Šabdamaṇidarpaṇa and Šabdânušâsana. The adverbs, etc. contained in these two works belong to the ancient dialect and are left unmarked; if they occur also in the mediæval one, they are marked with med. (mediæval) in parenthesis; and if they are used also in the modern one, with mod. (modern) in the same parenthesis; the additional words in brackets have not been met with in the ancient one. Slight differences of form in the three dialects have not been regarded. A few words and peculiar meanings rest on the Šabdânušâsana.

1, Numeral adverbs

(exceptionally arranged according to their natural order).

ಒರ್ಮೆ, once (med.); ಇರ್ಮೆ, twice; ಮೂರ್ಮೆ, thrice; ಕೆಲರ್ಮೆ, sometimes; ಪಲರ್ಮೆ, several times; ಸಾಸಿರ್ಮೆ, a thousand times. [ಒಮ್ಮೆ, once, ಇಮ್ಮೆ, twice, ಮೂಮ್ಮೆ, thrice, are other forms in the mediæval dialect; ಒಮ್ಮೆ occurs also in the mod. one.] See § 279.

2, Adverbs of place.

ಅತ್ತ, ಅತ್ತಲ್, that direction; in that direction (*d*; med., mod.); ಅನ್ತಱಿಂ, after, afterwards; ಅಲ್ಲಿ, there (*d*; med., mod.); ಇತ್ತ, ಇತ್ತಲ್, this direction; in this direction (*d*; med., mod.); ಇದಿರ್, the front; in the front (*d*; med., mod.; mod. also ಎದಿರು, ಎದುರು); ಇಲ್ಲಿ, here (*d*; med., mod.); ಉತ್ತ, ಉತ್ತಲ್, in this intermediate direction; ಉಲ್ಲಿ, in this intermediate place; ಎತ್ತ, ಎತ್ತಲ್, what direction? (*d*; med., mod.); ಎಲ್ಲಿ, where? (*d*; med., mod.); ಒಡನೆ, together with (med., mod.); ಒಳಗೆ, in, within, into (med., mod.); ಕೂಡೆ, together (med., mod.); ಕೆಳಗೆ, below (med., mod.); ತೆಂಕ, ತೆಂಕಲ್, the south; in the south (*d*; med., mod.); ನಡುವೆ, in the middle (med., mod.); ಪಡುವ, ಪಡುವಲ್, the west; in the west (*d*; med., mod.); ಪಿನ್ದೆ, behind (mod.); ಪೆಱಗೆ, behind; ಪೊಱಗೆ, outside (med., mod. ಹೊಱಗೆ); ಬಡಗ, ಬಡಗಲ್, the north; in the north (*d*; med., mod.); ಬೇಱೆ, ಬೇಱೆ ಬೇಱೆ, separately, apart (med., mod.); ಮುನ್ದೆ, in front; forward (med., mod.); ಮೂಡ, ಮೂಡಲ್, the east; in the east (*d*; med., mod.); ಮೇಲ್, above (*d*; med., mod.); ಮೇಲೆ, above (med., mod.); ಸುತ್ತು, around; that surrounds (*d*; med., mod.). [ಆಚೆ, that side; on that side (*d*), ಈಚೆ this side; on this side (*d*),

ಮುಂಚೆ, in advance, first, occur in the med. and mod. dialect;—ಹತ್ತಿರ, ಹತ್ತಿರು, nearness; near, close by (*d*) belong to the med. one, and appear as ಹತ್ತರ, ಹತ್ತ in the mod. one.]

3, Adverbs of time.

ಅನ್ದು, that time; then (*d*; med., mod.); ಅನ್ನಂ, at the time that, when; (so that); ಅನ್ನೆಗಂ=ಅನ್ನಂ (see § 365; until, in med.); ಅನ್ನೆವರಂ, ಅನ್ನೆವರೆಗಂ, until that time, so long as; ಅಲೊಡಂ, ಅಲೊಡನೆ=ಅನ್ನಂ (§ 365; ಅಲೊಡನೆ, med.); ಆಗಡು, that time; then (*d*); ಆಗಳ್, that time; then (*d*; mod.); ಅವಗಂ, continually (med.); ಇಂ, ಇನ್, from that time, afterwards (med.); ಇನಂ=ಅನ್ನಂ (§ 365); ಇನೆಗಂ=ಅನ್ನಂ (§ 365); ಇನ್ದು, this time; to-day (*d*; med., mod.); ಇನ್ನೆಗಂ, up to this time (in med.); ಇನ್ನೆವರಂ, ಇನ್ನೆವರೆಗಂ, until this day; ಈಗಡು, this moment; now (*d*.); ಈಗಳ್, this time; now (*d*; med.); ಈವಜು, a little while ago (*d*); ಉನ್ದು, at this intermediate time; ಉನ್ನೆವರಂ, ಉನ್ನೆವರೆಗಂ, up to this intermediate time; ಎನ್ದು, when? (*d*; med., mod.); ಎನ್ನೆಗಂ, ಎನ್ನೆವರಂ, ಎನ್ನೆವರೆಗಂ, till what time?; ಒಡನೆ, forthwith (med.); ತಱುವಾಯ್, subsequent time; subsequently, afterwards (*d*; med., mod.); ತಳಿಸಲ್, at dawn; ನಾಡಿದು, the day after to-morrow; on the day after to-morrow (*d*; med., mod.); ನಾಳೆ, to-morrow (*d*; med., mod.); ನಿನ್ನೆ, yesterday (*d*; med., mod.); ಪೊಱ್ತಡೆ (ಪೊಱ್ತಱ್, ಪೊಱ್ತಟ್, ಪೊತ್ತಱ್, ಪೊತ್ತಱು), daybreak; at dawn (*d*); ಬೞ (*d*), ಬೞಕಂ, ಬೞಕೆ, ಬೞಕ್ಕಂ, ಬೞಕ್ಕೆ, ಬೞಯಂ, afterwards (ಬೞ, ಬೞಕ, med., mod.; ಬೞಕಂ, ಬೞಕ್ಕ, ಬೞಕ್ಕಂ, med.); ಮಗುೞ್, again (med.); ಮುನ್, that is before; before (*d*; med., mod.); ಮೂನೆಯೇಡು, ಮೊನೆಯಿಾಡು, some time ago (*d*); ಮೊನ್ನೆ, the day before yesterday; on the day before yesterday (*d*; med., mod.); ಸವಳದೆ, at daybreak; ಸವಳ್ತಡೆ, daybreak; at daybreak (*d*). [ಆಗ, that time; then (*d*); ಈಗ, this time; now (*d*); ಈಚೆ, after this, afterwards, are med. and mod.; ಪೊಱ್ತಡೆ appears as ಹೊತ್ತಱು and ಹೊತ್ತಱು (*d*) in the med. dialect, and as ಹೊತ್ತಾರೆ (*d*) in the mod. one; ಕೂಡಲೆ, forthwith, and ಬೆಳಿಗ್ಗ, at dawn, are mod. words; ಹೊತ್ತುಗ್ಗಲೆ, ಹೊತ್ತುಟ್ಟ (*i. e.* ಹೊತ್ತು ಹೊಱಡುತ್ತಲೆ), at daybreak, early (mod.); regarding ಇನ್ನು, still, etc. see Dictionary.]

4, Adverbs of circumstance and manner.

(The meanings given are to be somewhat modified according to circumstances.)

ಅಗುನ್ದಲೆ, abundantly, exceedingly; ಅಣಂ, soever: whatsoever; ಅಣಿಯರಂ, abundantly, exceedingly; ಅನ್ತಿರೆ, ಅನ್ತಿರೆವೊಲ್, ಅನ್ತಿರೆವೋಲ್=ಅನ್ತು, etc. ಅನ್ತು, ಅನ್ತುಟು (ತಥಾ Śabdânuśâsana), ಅನ್ತೆ, ಅನ್ತೆವೊಲ್, ಅನ್ತೆವೋಲ್, in that manner, in like manner; like; similar to; in the manner in which (ಅನ್ತು, ಅನ್ತೆ, med., mod.; ಅನ್ತುಟು med.); ಅಯ್ದೆ, excessively, exceedingly (mod.); ಅರವೆ, ಅರೆ, ಅರೆ ಉಱ, a little, to some extent (ಅರೆ mod.); ಅಲ್ಲವೞ್, causelessly; ಅಹಗೆ=ಅನ್ತು, etc. (med.); ಆಣಂ, soever: whatsoever; ಆದಂ, further; ಆಯ್ಕಗೆ, ಆಯ್ಕನೆ, vehemently, quickly; ಆರ್ಪಿನಂ, excessively, exceedingly; ಇನ್ತು, ಇನ್ತುಟು (ಇತ್ಥಂ Śabdânuśâsana), ಇನ್ತೆ, in this manner (ಇನ್ತು, med., mod.; ಇನ್ತುಟು, med., also ಇನಿತುಟು); ಇಮ್ಮನೆ, in a proper manner; ಇಹಗೆ, in this manner (med.); ಉಣ್ಣವಳಿಯದು, greatly, much; ಉನ್ತು, ಉನ್ತೆ, in this intermediate manner; how (ಕಥಂ Śabdânuśâsana); ಉನ್ತುಟು, how? (ಕಥಂ Śabdânuśâsana); ಉನ್ತೆ, silently (ತೂಷ್ಣೀಂ

Sabdânuśâsana); ಉರ್ವಿನಂ,. excessively, exceedingly; ಉಸಿಕಂ, ಉಸಿಕನೆ, silently (ಉಸಿಕನೆ, med.); ಎಕ್ಕೆಕ್ಕೆ, by degrees, slowly, irresolutely; ಎಡೆ, spaciously, extensively; ಎನ್ತು, ಎನ್ತೆ, how? (ಎನ್ತ, med., mod.); ಎನ್ತುಟು, how? (ಕಥಂ Šabdânušâsana; med.); ಎಹಗೆ, how? (med.); ಏಗಂ, most certainly; ಒಡಂ, certainly (ನಿಶ್ಚಯಾರ್ಥಂ Šabdânušâsana); ಒಯ್ಯನೆ, clearly, evidently; ಕಡು, excessively; swiftly (med.); ಕಮ್ಮಗೆ, ಕಮ್ಮನೆ, fragrantly, deliciously (med., mod.); ಕರಂ, excessively, greatly (med.); ಕಟ್ಕನೆ, suddenly; ಕಿಱಮ (o. r. ಕೀಱದು), closely, densely; ಕೆಚ್ಚನೆ, redly (med., mod.); ಕೆನ್ನಂ, excessively, exceedingly; ಖಣಿಲನೆ, ಖಣಾಲನೆ, ಖಣಾಲೆ, in a shrill, piercing, rough manner; ಗಡ, ಗಳ, certainly (ಗಡ, med., ಗಡಾ is used in emotion and command); ಗಬಗಬನೆ, quickly (med.; ಗಳಗಳ, mod.); ಗಿಜ್ಜಗೆ, ಗಿಜ್ಜನೆ, spinningly, round and round (med.); ಗುಬುಗುಮ್ಮಗೆ, inactively, silently; ಘಣಾಲನೆ, quickly; ಚಕ್ಕನೆ, quickly (med.); ಚಡುಪುಡನೆ quickly (see § 307, *a*); ಚಿಕ್ಕನೆ, quickly; ಚೆಚ್ಚರಂ, quickly; ಚೆಚ್ಚರಂ, manifestly, clearly, certainly; ತಡಬಡ, with embarrassment (in speaking, med., mod.); ತಣ್ಣಗೆ, ತಣ್ಣನೆ, coolly, refreshingly (med., mod.); ತಳಮಳಂ, decisively (ನಿರ್ಣಯವಾಚಿ Śabdânuśâsana); ತಳತಳನೆ, ತಟತಟನೆ, glitteringly (med.); ತಿಟ್ಟಗೆ, ತಿಟ್ಟನೆ, ತಿಬ್ಬಗೆ, ತಿಬ್ಬನೆ, whirlingly, round and round (ತಿಬ್ಬನೆ, med.); (ತೆಪ್ಪನೆ, see § 307, *a*); ತೆಳ್ಳನೆ, thinly (med., mod.); ತೇನಂ, not firmly, irresolutely (ಅದೃಢಾರ್ಥಂ Śabdânuśâsana); ತೇನತೇನಂ, by degrees, slowly, irresolutely; ತೊಟ್ಟಗೆ, ತೊಟ್ಟನೆ, vehemently (med.); (ತೊಪ್ಪನೆ, see § 307, *a*); ದಣ್ಣನೆ, wearisomely (med., mod.); ದಲ್, certainly (med.); ಧಿಗಿಲನೆ, with consternation (med., mod.); ನಾಡೆ, excessively, greatly, further (med.); ನಿಕ್ಕುವಂ, certainly; ನಿರ್ನರ್, ನಿರ್ನರಂ, causelessly; ನೀಡು, ನೀಡುಂ, extensively, excessively; ನುಣ್ಣಗೆ, ನುಣ್ಣನೆ, softly (med., mod.); ನೂಳದು, much, exceedingly; ನೆಟ್ಟಗೆ, ನೆಟ್ಟನೆ, clearly, distinctly, nicely (med., mod.); ನೆಟ್ಟಗೆ, ನೆಟ್ಟನೆ, vehemently (ನಿರ್ಭರಾರ್ಥಂ Šabdânuśâna); ನೆಱ್, exceedingly; much (med.); (ನೊಪ್ಪನೆ, see § 307, *a*); ಪಕ್ಕಗೆ, ಪಕ್ಕನೆ, suddenly (med., mod.); ಪಚ್ಚನೆ, greenly (med.); ಪಯ್ಯನೆ, quickly; ಪಿರಿದು, ಪಿರಿದುಂ, extensively, greatly, further (med.); ಪೀನಂ, profusely, much, further; ಪೌವಗೆ, ಪೌವನೆ (ಪವ್ವಗೆ, ಪವ್ವನೆ), suddenly; ಬಯ್ಯನೆ, quickly; ಬಱಿದೆ, in vain (med., mod.); ಬಾಡಂ, much, further; ಬಿನ್ನಗೆ, ಬಿನ್ನನೆ, silently. inactively; ಬಿಮ್ಮಗೆ, ಬಿಮ್ಮನೆ, silently; ಬಿಬ್ಬನೆ, firmly, tightly; ಬೆಚ್ಚನೆ, hotly, warmly (med., mod.); ಬೆಚ್ಚರಂ, quickly; ಬೆಚ್ಚರಂ, clearly (ವ್ಯಕ್ತಾರ್ಥಂ Šabdânušâsana); ಬೆಳ್ಪಡಂ, ಬೆಳ್ಪಳಂ, timidly, tremblingly; ಭೋಂಕನೆ, swiftly, quickly (med.); ಭೋಂಕಲ್, swiftly, quickly, without restraint; ಭೋರನೆ, swiftly, quickly; ಮತ್ತಿನ, other, different; ಮಿಗೆ, excessively, much (med.); ಮೆಲ್ಲಗೆ, ಮೆಲ್ಲನೆ, slowly (med., mod.); ವರಂ, ವಲಂ, ವಲ್ಲಂ, ವೇಱಂ, most certainly; clearly; (ಸಪ್ಪನೆ, see § 307, *a*); ಸಲೆ, perpetually, constantly (med.); ಸಿಯ್ಯನೆ, sweetly; ಸುಮ್ಮಗೆ, ಸುಮ್ಮನೆ, silently, inactively (med., mod.); ಸೋಡಂ, ಸೋಡಂ ಬಾಡಂ, much, more, further; ಸೋಡಂ ಬಾಡಂ, causelessly; ಹುಂ, how? ಹೌವನೆ (ಹವ್ವನೆ), suddenly (med., mod.). [ಅಹಗೆ, ಇಹಗೆ appear also as ಹಾಗೆ, ಹಾಂಗೆ, ಹೀಗೆ, ಹೀಂಗೆ in the med. dialect, and always so in the mod. one; ಎಹಗೆ is also ಹ್ಯೇಗೆ, ಹ್ಯೇಂಗೆ, ಹೆಂಗೆ in the med. dialect, and always ಹ್ಯಾಗೆ, ಹ್ಯಾಂಗೆ in the modern one.] Regarding ಎಹಗೆ—ಅಹಗೆ, ಹೆಂಗೆ—ಹಾಗೆ, ಹ್ಯಾಗೆ—ಹಾಗೆ, ಎನ್ತು—ಅನ್ತೆ see § 327. (ಮೇರೆ, a tadbhava of ಮರ್ಯೆ, may be adduced here too, *e. g.* ಈ ಮೇರೆ or ಈ ಮೇರೆಗೆ, in this manner, thus; ಅವನ ಅಪ್ಪಣೆಯ ಮೇರೆಗೆ, according to his command. Saṁskṛita ಪ್ರಕಾರ is similarly used, *e. g.* ಈ ಪ್ರಕಾರ

in this manner; ಅದಱ ಪ್ರಕಾರ, according to that; ವಿವಿಧ ಪ್ರಕಾರದಿನ್ದ, in various ways. Likewise ಕ್ರಮ, ತರ, ರೀತಿ, ವಿಧ aro used. *Cf.* also ತಱುವಾಯ್, ಬಿರಿಪಿಡಿ.)

5, Conjunctions.

ಅಂ, ಉಂ, and (med.); ಬಳ್ಕೆ, again, furthor, and; ಬೞಿ, again, furthor; ಮತ್ತಂ, ಮತ್ತೆ, again, furthor, and (med.; ಮತ್ತೆ, mod.; also tho form ಮತ್ತು is used in tho mod. dialect); ಮೇಣ್, furthor, and, or (mod.). [ಉಂ appears also as ಉ, ಊ in the mediæval dialect, and generally as ಊ, exceptionally as ಉ in tho modern one.] Soo §§ 284 *seq.*; 297.

6, Postpositions.

Several of the above-mentioned adverbs of place and time and of the conjunctions are used also as postpositions; they are adduced under this heading again, but without their meaning.

Postpositions, *i. e.* words and letters (particles) placed after, or at the end of, nouns, pronouns, participles, etc. (see § 282), are:

ಅ, a particlo of emphasis; a vocative particle; ಅಂ; ಅತ್ತ (ಅತ್ತಣಿಂ, etc., see § 109, *a*, 5); ಅತ್ತಲ್; ಅನ್ತಿರೆ; ಅನ್ತಿರೆವೊಲ್; ಅನ್ತೆ; ಅನ್ತೆವೊಲ್; ಅನ್ದು; ಅನ್ನಂ; ಅನ್ನೆಗಂ; ಅಲ್, in; to; at the time that, when, whilst (med., mod.; see §§ 109, *a*, 5. 187, 1); ಅಲ್ಲಿ (med., mod.; seo §§ 109. 117 *seq.*); ಅಹಗೆ; ಆ, a particlo of emphasis; a vocative particle (med., mod.); ಇ, there (med., mod.); ಇಂ, from that place or time; thence (med.; soe *e. g.* §§ 109. 120, *a*, 3); ಇದಿರ್; ಇನಂ; ಇನೆಗಂ; ಉ; ಉಂ; ಉದುಂ, at the time that, when (§ 286); ಊ; ಎ, by means of, from (see § 109, *a*, 3); ಎ, at the time that, when; so that (med.; soo § 187, 4); ಎ, ಏ, particles of emphasis; vocative particles; particles of intorrogation (med., mod.); ಒ, ಓ, vocativo particles; particles of interrogation (med., mod.); ಒಡನೆ, togethor with, along with (med., mod.); ಒಡೆ, if (mod.); ಒಳ್, (ಉಳ್), in, within; into (mod.; seo *e. g.* § 109); ಒಳಗೆ; ಕೆಳಗೆ; ಪಿನ್ದೆ; ಪೊಱಗೆ; ಬೞಿಕಂ, ಬೞಿಕೆ, ಬೞಿಕ್ಕಂ, ಬೞಿಕ್ಕೆ, ಬೞಿಯುಂ; ಮುಟ್ಟೆ, as far as; till (mod., mod.); ಮುನ್ದೆ; ಮೇಲೆ; ವರಂ, ವರೆಗಂ, until; ವೊಲ್, ವೋಲ್, liko; as; in tho manner in which; so that (mod.; see § 242). [ಅಡೆ, if, another form of ಒಡೆ, appears in a šâsana of 1076 A. D. (ಇದ್ದಡೆ), in ono of 1123 A. D. (ಎನ್ದಡೆ, ಆದಡೆ), in one of 1181 A. D. (ಪೇಳ್ದಡೆ = ಪೇೞ್ದಡೆ), and in ono of 1182 A. D. (ನಡೆವಡೆ); ಒಡೆ occasionally has the form of ಅಡೆ and ಅರೆ in the mod. dialect, and always that of ಅರೆ in tho med. ono;—ಅನಕ, till (med., mod.); ಆಗ, at tho time that, when (med., mod.); ಅರೆ (seo sub ಅಡೆ), ಆಚೆ; ಈಚೆ; ಒನ್ದಿಗೆ, togethor with (mod.); ಓಸುಗ, ಓಸುಗರ, ಓಸ್ಕರ, on account of (med.; ಓಸ್ಕರ also mod.); ತನಕ, till, until; as far as (med., mod.); ತುಸುಕ, for, on account of, in ordor to (mod.); ಬಗ್ಗೆ, ಬಗ್ಗೆ, on account of; concerning; for, in ordor to (mod.); ಮುಂಚೆ, previously, boforo; ಮುನ್ದೆ; ಹಾಗೆ; ಹೊರ್ತು, oxcept (mod.).]

7, Some verbal forms, etc.

which are classed under tho avyayas by tho Śabdânušâsana, but of which only one, *viz.* ಇಲ್ಲ (seo § 209, noto 1), is called an avyaya by tho Śabdamaṇidarpaṇa.

They are:

ಅಲ್ತು (=an ಅಲ್ಲತು § 122 or ಅಲ್ಲದುದು, of ಅಲ್, § 209, note 1), a bhâvavačana or verbal noun, (literally 'a yet to be fit-it', 'a not actually being fit-it', used for all persons singular and plural, expressly put or not, in the three tenses, *viz.*) I am not fit or meant, thou art not fit or meant, he, she or it is not fit or meant; we, you or they are not fit or meant; I was not fit or meant, etc., etc. (see §§ 301. 338); ಅಲ್ತೆ (*i. e.* ಅಲ್ತು+ಎ) am I not fit or meant? etc.; I am indeed not fit or meant, etc. (§§ 301. 338); ಅಲ್ಲ (or ಅಲ್ಲಂ; see § 209, note 1; § 210; med., mod.; § 300); ಅಲ್ಲದೆ, except (see §§ 170. 171; med., mod.; §§ 301. 338); ಆನುಂ — ಆನುಂ, either — or, § 293; ಇಲ್ಲ (or ಇಲ್ಲಂ; see § 209, note 1; § 210; med., mod.; mod. also ಇಲ್ಲವು; see § 298, 1-4; § 316, 1. 2); ಇಲ್ಲದೆ, in absence of, without (see §§ 170. 171; med., mod.; § 338); ಎಲ್ಲಂ, wholly (§ 301); ಏಗುವೆಂ, what shall I do? (med.; § 301); ಏನ್, what? how? why? (med., mod.; § 301); ಏವೆಂ, what shall I do? (§ 301); ಬೇಡ (or ಬೇಡಂ; see § 209, note 1; § 210; med., mod.; §§ 301. 318, 5).

8, Interjections.

ಅಃ, ah! (in admiration); alas! (in affliction or grief); ಅಕ್ಕಟ, ಅಕ್ಕಟಾ, alas! (in affliction or grief, med., mod.); ah! (in wonder or surprise, med.); [ಅಮ, ha! ah!, in surprise and in grief, med., mod.]; ಅಯ್ಯೋ, alas! (in affliction or grief, med., mod.); ah! (in pity, med., mod.); ಅಹಹ, alas! (in grief); aha! ah! (in surprise, med., mod.); ಅಹಹಂ, oh! alas! (in pain); ಅಹೋ, oh! (in pain); ho! stop!; ಆ, alas! (in affliction or grief); ಆಃ, ah! (in surprise, med., mod.); alas! (in affliction or grief, med., mod.); ಇಶ್ಶಿ, fie! (med., mod.); ಉ, fie!; ಉಃ, ah! ha! (in pleasure); fie!; alas! (in pain or sorrow); ಊ, fie!; ಊಃ, alas! (in pain or sorrow); ಎಮ, well, all right! certainly!; ಎಲವೊ, ಎಲವೋ, ಎಲೆ, ಎಲೆಲೆ, ಎಲೇ, ah! oh! (in recollection); let us see! (in deliberation or investigation); ho! halloo! (in calling, med., mod.); ಓಹೋ, ho! stop! (med.); o! alas! (in pain); ಛಃ, fie! (med., mod.); ಛೇಃ, fie!; ಹವ್ವನೆ, oh! woe to me!; ಹೋ, ಹೋ ಹೋ, ho! stop! (med., mod.); o! alas! (in pain, med.). *Cf.* § 308.

9, Imitative sounds.

Imitative sounds (anukaraṇa, anukaraṇapada, anukṛiti), *i. e.* sounds used in imitation of the effects of the operations of nature (as the rolling of thunder, agitations of water, pattering of hail-stones, voices of birds, bodily functions, falling, breaking and the like) are very frequent in Kannaḍa and essential parts of the language; in fact there is scarcely any sound in nature that has not been imitated in it. Such sounds are often idiomatical and therefore strange to the ear of foreigners. For the vast number of imitative sounds the Dictionary is to be consulted.

Those mentioned in the Śabdamaṇidarpaṇa and Śabdânuśâsana are ಕವಕವ, the sound of kavakava (a particular sound of the cuckoo); ಖಱಿಲನೆ with the sound of khaḷil (in speaking); ಗಹಗಹಂ, the sound of gahagahaṁ (in laughing); ಗಳಗಳ, the sound of gaḷagaḷa (in running water); ಗುಲ್ಗುಲ್, the sound of gulgul (*e.g.* in the clanging of bracelets); ಗುಳುಗುಳು, ಗುಱುಗುಱು, the sound of guḷuguḷu or guḷuguḷu (in the gurgling of water, etc., med., mod.); ಛಟಛಟಂ, the sound of čhaṭačhaṭaṁ (in breaking); ಛಱಿಲನೆ, with the sound of čhaḷil; ಝುಮ್ಮನೆ, with the sound of jhum (in oozing); ಡರ್ರನೆ, with the sound of ḍarr (in belching, med., mod.); ಢಮ್ಮನೆ, with the sound of ḍhamm (in banging, mod.); ತಳತಳ, ತಱತಱ, ತಳ್ತಳ, the sound of taḷataḷa or taḷataḷa or taḷtaḷa (in boiling with a briskly bubbling noise, med., mod.); ದುಢುಮ್ಮನೆ, with the sound of duḍhumm (in plumping or plunging into water, mod.); ಢಱಮ್ಮನೆ, with the sound of dhaḷamm (*e.g.* of a kettle-drum when beaten, med.); ಧುಮ್ಮನೆ, with the sound of dhumm (in jumping down suddenly from above, med., mod.); ನೆಱಿಲನೆ, with the sound of nĕḷil (in breaking); ನೆಳ್ಕನೆ, with the sound of nĕḷk (in breaking); ಪಠಿಲ್ಲನೆ, with the sound of paṭhill (in banging or slapping, mod.); ಪಱಪಱನೆ, ಪಳ್ಪಱನೆ, with the sound of paḷapaḷa or paḷpaḷa (*e.g.* in the pattering of hail-stones, mod.); ಭುಗಿಲ್, the sound of bhugil (*e.g.* in the blazing of flames, med., mod.); ಭೋರ್; the sound of bhôr (*e.g.* in the running of streams, med., mod.); ಸಿಗ್ಗನೆ, with the sound of sigg (in splitting); ಸುರ್ರನೆ, with the sound of surr (*e.g.* in flowing or showering); ಹಿಳ್ಳನೆ, with the sound of hiḷḷ (in cracking). *Cf.* § 309.

Remarks.

1, The Śabdamaṇidarpaṇa expressly calls only ಅರಮ, ಅರೆ, ಎ, ಎಲೆ, ಎಲೇ, ಏ, ಒ, ಓ and ಓಹೋ nipâtas, to which the Śabdânuśâsana adds ಅ, ಅಃ, ಅಕ್ಕಟಾ, ಅಯ್ಯೋ, ಅರೆ ಉಚ್, ಅಲ್ತೆ ಅಲ್ತೆ, ಅಹೋ, ಆ, ಆಃ, ಉ, ಊ, ಊಃ, ಎಡೆ, ಎಮ, ಎಲಮ, ಕಡು, ಗಡಾ (ಗಡ + ಆ), ಗಳಾ (ಗಳ + ಆ), ಚೀ, ಚೀಃ, ನಾಡೆ, ನಿನ್ನೆ, ನೆಱ, ಮಿಗೆ, ಮೊನ್ನೆ, ಹೋ, ಹೋ ಹೋ. Nâgavarma's Karṇâṭakabhâshâbhûshaṇa has the following nipâtas: — ಅಂ (used in bhêda and vismaya), ಅಃ, ಅಯ್ಯೊ, ಅಯ್ಯೋ, ಅರಮ, ಅರೆ, ಅಲ್ತೆ, ಅಹ, ಎ, ಎಲೆ, ಎಲೇ, ಏ, ಓಹೋ.

2, Regarding the formation of adverbs, etc. it may be stated that not unfrequently ಅಗೆ or ಅನೆ appears at their end, *e.g.* ಕಮ್ಮಗೆ, ನೆಟ್ಟಗೆ, ಬಿನ್ನಗೆ, ಸುಮ್ಮಗೆ: ಕಮ್ಮನೆ, ನೆಟ್ಟನೆ, ಬಿನ್ನನೆ, ಸುಮ್ಮನೆ. ಅಗೆ may be the same as ಆಗೆ, 'so that it becomes' (both ಅಗು and ಆಗು appearing as Kannaḍa verbal themes, § 176); ಅನೆ may be another form of ಅಗೆ (§ 176), or belong (especially in anukaraṇas which not unfrequently are written either with final ಅನೆ or ಎನೆ, *e.g.* ಛಱಿಲನೆ or ಛಱಿಲೆನೆ) to ಅನ್ and ಎನ್, to say, and mean 'so that it says'. *Cf.* § 275; § 281 note below the text.

3, Some of the adverbs of circumstance and some imitative sounds exhibit consonants with strong aspiration or aspirates (mahâprâṇa, § 29), *e.g.* ಖಱಿಲನೆ, ಧಿಗಿಲನೆ, ಭೋಂಕನೆ, ಝುಮ್ಮನೆ, ಪಠಿಲ್ಲನೆ, ಮಢುಮ್ಮನೆ (see § 218).

4, There are no prepositions in true Kannaḍa.

VII. Euphonic junction of letters.

213. **Euphonic junction of letters** (sandhi, saṁhitĕ) has not unfrequently been referred to in the preceding paragraphs. It occurs in the ancient, mediæval and modern dialect, especially in poetry. The colloquial dialect and modern prose writings often disregard it. We in the main follow the Šabdamaṇidarpaṇa in describing it.

Generally speaking it takes place when a consonant with a final vowel (svarayuktavyañjana) is followed by a vowel, *e.g.* ಕೂರ್ತು ಈವಂ becomes ಕೂರ್ತೀವಂ, ಎನ್ನ ಅರಸಂ ಎನ್ನರಸಂ, ಮುನ್ನೆ ಇರ್ದವಂ ಮುನ್ನಿರ್ದವಂ; and when a consonant without a final vowel (svararahitavyañjana) is followed by a vowel or consonant, *e.g.* ಜಾಣ್ ಉಣ್ಬ್ಟ becomes ಜಾಣುಣ್ಬ್ಟ, ಕುರುಳ್ ಕೊಂಕು ಆಯ್ತು ಕುರುಳ್ಕೊಂಕಾಯ್ತು.

It would, therefore, be wrong to use *e.g.* ಅಸಿಯ ಒಳ್ಪು (for ಅಸಿಯೊಳ್ಪು), ಮಿಸುಗುವ ಅಱಿಂ (for ಮಿಸುಗುವಱಿಂ), ಪೊನ್ನ ಅನ್ದಳಂ (for ಪೊನ್ನನ್ದಳಂ).

214. **According to the place** where euphonic junction of letters takes place, it is stated to be of two kinds, *viz.*

a) the junction in the middle of words (padamadhyasandhi), *i. e.* either the junction of a declinable word and a case-termination (nâmavibhakti), or that of a verbal theme and a personal termination (kriyâvibhakti), *e.g.* ಮಾತು+ಅಂ becomes ಮಾತಂ, ಮಾತು+ಇಂ ಮಾತಿಂ, ಮಾತು+ಇಂಗೆ ಮಾತಿಂಗೆ, ಮಾತು+ಇನ ಮಾತಿನ, ಮಾತಿನ+ಅತ್ತಣಿಂ ಮಾತಿನತ್ತಣಿಂ, ಮಾತಿನ+ಒಳ್ ಮಾತಿನೊಳ್ (see § 122); ನುಡಿದ+ಅಂ becomes ನುಡಿದಂ, ನುಡಿದ+ಅರ್ ನುಡಿದರ್, ನುಡಿದ+ಆಯ್ ನುಡಿದಯ್, ನುಡಿದ+ಇರ್ ನುಡಿದಿರ್, ನುಡಿದ+ಎಂ ನುಡಿದೆಂ, ನುಡಿದ+ಎವು ನುಡಿದೆವು (see § 198, 2);

b) the junction at the end of words (padântyasandhi), *i. e.* either the junction of a declinable word (nâmapada) and another declinable word, or that of a conjugated verb (kriyâpada) and a declinable word, *e.g.* ಅವನ ಅಳ್ತನಂ becomes ಅವನಾಳ್ತನಂ, ಕಾಮನ ಅಣ್ಡಲೆ ಕಾಮನಣ್ಡಲೆ; ನುಡಿದರ್ ಅವರ್ becomes ನುಡಿದರವರ್, ಬೆಸಸಿದೆವು ಒಳ್ಪಂ ಬೆಸಸಿದೆವೊಳ್ಪಂ.

215. Euphonic junction takes place by elision (lôpa), the insertion of ಯ್ and ವ್, the permutation of consonants (učitâksharâgama), and the doubling of final consonants.

Sometimes it is optional whether elision happens or ಯ್ and ವ್ are inserted, sometimes euphonic junction itself is optional, sometimes also euphonic junction is forbidden, sometimes the permutation of consonants and sometimes their doubling are necessary, and sometimes do not take place.

1, Euphonic junction by elision.

a) When the final vowel of a case-termination (vibhaktisvara), either of a Saṁskṛita declinable base (saṁskṛitaprakṛiti) or of a Kannaḍa (or Tadbhava) one (karṇâṭakaprakṛiti), is followed by a vowel, it suffers elision, *e. g.* ಕ್ರಮದೆ ಆಯಿತು becomes ಕ್ರಮದಾಯಿತು, ಇನ್ದ್ರಂಗೆ ಐರಾವತಂ ಇನ್ದ್ರಂಗೈರಾವತಂ, ಗಿರಿಯತ್ತಣಿನ್ದೆ ಇೞಿದಂ ಗಿರಿಯತ್ತಣಿನ್ದಿೞಿದಂ, ಗೃಹದಲ್ಲಿ ಇರ್ದಂ ಗೃಹದಲ್ಲಿರ್ದಂ, ಈಶ್ವರನ ಒಲವು ಈಶ್ವರನೊಲವು; ನೆಲದಿನ್ದೆ ಉಣ್ಡಂ becomes ನೆಲದಿನ್ದುಣ್ಡಂ, ಲೇಸಿಂಗೆ ಒಡೆಯಂ ಲೇಸಿಂಗೊಡೆಯಂ, ಮರದತ್ತಣಿನ್ದೆ ಇೞಿದಂ ಮರದತ್ತಣಿನ್ದಿೞಿದಂ, ಜಲದ ಆಣ್ಮಂ ಜಲದಾಣ್ಮಂ, ಪೊಲದಲ್ಲಿ ಇರ್ದಂ ಪೊಲದಲ್ಲಿರ್ದಂ, ಪೊಲದೆ ಎೞ್ತಿನ್ದಂ ಪೊಲದೆೞ್ತಿನ್ದಂ.

b) The same happens when a case-termination, or a conjugated verb, or the formative ಇಸು (§§ 150. 151, remarks) is suffixed to a Saṁskṛita word ending in the vowel ಅ, *e. g.* ಬುಧ+ಅರ್ becomes ಬುಧರ್, ಉದ್ಧತ+ಅರ್ ಉದ್ಧತರ್; ದೇವ ಎಮ್ಬರ್ ದೇವೆಮ್ಬರ್; ರಾಗ+ಇಸು ರಾಗಿಸು, ಭಂಗ+ಇಸು ಭಂಗಿಸು, ಭಾವ+ಇಸು ಭಾವಿಸು (*cf.* 2, *c*).

c) Likewise a final ಅ, ಇ, ಎ, or a euphonic ಉ (§§ 96. 98) suffers elision when it is followed by a vowel, *e. g*, ಅರಸ ಆಳ್ becomes ಅರಸಾಳ್, ಅಜ್ಜ ಆನೆ ಅಜ್ಜಾನೆ, ಜಿಯ ಎಮ್ಬಂ ಜಿಯೆಮ್ಬಂ, ಬಡಬಡ ಆದಂ ಬಡಬಡಾದಂ, ಸಾವನ್ತ ಓಲಗಂ ಸಾವನ್ತೋಲಗಂ, ನೋಡಿದ+ಅಂ ನೋಡಿದಂ, ಮಾಡಿದ+ಅಂ ಮಾಡಿದಂ, ಕೂಡಿದ +ಅಂ ಕೂಡಿದಂ;—ದಾೞಿ ಇಟ್ಟಂ ದಾೞಿಟ್ಟಂ, ಹನ್ದಿ ಇಟ್ಟಂ ಹನ್ದಿಟ್ಟಂ, ಸವಡಿ ಇಟ್ಟಂ ಸವಡಿಟ್ಟಂ (*cf.* 4);—ಸೇಸೆ ಇಕ್ಕಿದಂ ಸೇಸಿಕ್ಕಿದಂ, ಮುಡಿಗೆ ಇಕ್ಕಿದಂ ಮುಡಿಗಿಕ್ಕಿದಂ, ಮತ್ತೆ ಎಲ್ಲಂ ಮತ್ತೆಲ್ಲಂ, ಮುನ್ನೆ ಇೞಿವಂ ಮುನ್ನಿೞಿವಂ (*cf.* 2, *f. i.*);—ಸುತ್ತು ಓಲೆ ಸುತ್ತೋಲೆ, ಹತ್ತು ಎಣ್ಬು ಹತ್ತೆಣ್ಬು, ಲೇಸು ಎಲ್ಲಂ ಲೇಸೆಲ್ಲಂ, ಸೊವಡು ಒನ್ದು ಸೊವಡೊನ್ದು (*cf.* 4). *Cf.* §§ 213. 214.

d) Also when the final vowel is that of a personal termination (§ 198) or of the participial suffixes ಇ, ತು and ದು (§§ 155. 156. 166), elision happens, *e. g.* ಮಾಡಿದೆವು ಒಳ್ಪಂ becomes ಮಾಡಿದೆವೊಳ್ಪಂ; ಕೂಡಿ ಇರ್ದಂ ಕೂಡಿರ್ದಂ; ಕೂರ್ತು ಈವಂ ಕೂರ್ತೀವಂ, ಪಸಿದು ಉಣ್ಡಂ ಪಸಿದುಣ್ಡಂ.

2, Euphonic junction by the insertion of ಯ್.

a) If the ಅ of the genitive is followed by the ಎ of emphasis, ಯ್ generally comes between (*cf.* 6, *g.*), *e. g* ಆತನ+ಎ becomes ಆತನಯೆ, ಅವಳ+ಎ ಅವಳಯೆ, ಅದಱ+ಎ ಅದಱಯೆ, when, as the Šabdânušâsana states (sûtra 45), for ತನ್ನಯೆ, ನಿನ್ನಯೆ and ಎನ್ನಯೆ ತನ್ನಯ, ನಿನ್ನಯ and ಎನ್ನಯ may be put.

b) If the final ಅ of imitative sounds (§ 212, 9) is followed by a vowel, ಯ್ is generally put between, *e. g.* ಪಟಿಪಟಿ ಎನ್ದು becomes ಪಟಿಪಟಿಯೆನ್ದು, ಗಟಿಗಟಿ ಎನ್ದು ಗಟಿಗಟಿಯೆನ್ದು (*cf.* 5, *d*).

c) If to a class of Saṁskṛita and Kannaḍa themes with final ಅ the formative ಇಸು is suffixed (*cf.* 1, *b* and 3, *a*), ಯ್ comes between, *e. g.* ಶುದ್ಧ+ ಇಸು becomes ಶುದ್ಧಯಿಸು, ತಾರ+ ಇಸು ತಾರಯಿಸು, ಪೂರ+ ಇಸು ಪೂರಯಿಸು, ಮೇಳ+ ಇಸು ಮೇಳಯಿಸು, ತೀರ+ ಇಸು ತೀರಯಿಸು, ತೆಲ್ಲ+ ಇಸು ತೆಲ್ಲಯಿಸು, ಸೊಗ+ ಇಸು ಸೊಗಯಿಸು. *Cf.* § 151, remarks.

d) If the letter ಆ is followed by a vowel, ಯ್ is often inserted (*cf.* 3, *b* and 6, *h*), *e. g.* ಆ ಇರ್ದ ಮಾಟಿಕ್ಕೆ becomes ಆಯಿರ್ದ ಮಾಟಿಕ್ಕೆ, ಆ ಇರವು ಆಯಿರವು, ಆ ಎಡೆ ಆಯೆಡೆ, ಕಾ+ ಅಲ್ ಕಾಯಲ್ (§ 187, 1), ಜ್ಯಾ+ ಒಳ್ ಜಾಯೊಳ್.

e) If the letter ಇ of a declinable base is followed by a cases termination beginning with a vowel, ಯ್ always comes between (§ 130), *e. g.* ಬಲಿ+ ಅಂ becomes ಬಲಿಯಂ, ಗಿರಿ+ ಅತ್ತಣಿನ್ದೆ ಗಿರಿಯತ್ತಣಿನ್ದೆ.

f) If the letter ಇ of a declinable base is followed by a vowel that is not the initial of a case-termination (*cf.* 1, *c*), or if a verb with final ಇ is followed by a vowel, ಯ್ is generally put between, *e. g.* ಕವಿ ಆರ್ becomes ಕವಿಯಾರ್, ನಿಪ್ಪಾಕ್ಕಾಮಿ ಆವಳ್ ನಿಪ್ಪಾಕ್ಕಾಮಿಯಾವಳ್, ಮುನಿ ಈತಂ ಮುನಿಯೀತಂ, ನದಿ ಎಲ್ಲಂ ನದಿಯೆಲ್ಲಂ, ದಧಿ ಇಲ್ಲದುಣಿಸು ದಧಿಯಿಲ್ಲದುಣಿಸು, ಕುಱಿ ಇದು ಕುಱಿಯಿದು, ಜತಿ ಇತ್ತಂ ಜತಿಯಿತ್ತಂ; ನುಡಿ ಎನ್ದು ನುಡಿಯೆನ್ದು, ಅಱಿ+ ಅಲ್ ಅಱಿಯಲ್ (§ 187, 1).

g) If the letter ಈ is followed by a vowel, ಯ್ is mostly inserted (*cf.* 3, *c*), *e. g.* ಶ್ರೀ ಎಡೆ becomes ಶ್ರೀಯೆಡೆ, ಶ್ರೀ+ ಅಂ ಶ್ರೀಯಂ, ಸ್ತ್ರೀ+ ಅಂ ಸ್ತ್ರೀಯಂ (§ 130), ಸ್ತ್ರೀ ಎಮ್ಬ ಸ್ತ್ರೀಯೆಮ್ಬ; ಮೀ+ ಇಸು ಮೀಯಿಸು (§ 151, *a*, 5), ಈ+ ಅಲ್ ಈಯಲ್ (§ 187, 1).

h) If the letter ಎ of a declinable base is followed by a case-termination beginning with a vowel, ಯ್ is always put between (§ 130), *e. g.* ತೊಱೆ+ ಅಂ becomes ತೊಱೆಯಂ, ಕೆಱೆ+ ಅ ಕೆಱೆಯ.

i) If the letter ಎ of a declinable base is followed by a vowel that is not the initial of a case-termination (*cf.* 1, *c*), or if a verb with final ಎ is followed by a vowel, ಯ್ is mostly put between, *e. g.* ಪಡೆ ಇದು becomes ಪಡೆಯಿದು, ಆಸೆ ಒಡ್ಡು ಆಸೆಯೊಡ್ಡು, ಕದುರೆ ಅಕ್ಕುಂ ಕುದುರೆಯಕ್ಕುಂ, ಪಸೆ ಇರ್ದಂ ಪಸೆಯಿರ್ದಂ; ನಡೆ ಎನ್ದು ನಡೆಯೆನ್ದು, ಮಱೆ+ ಅಲ್ ಮಱೆಯಲ್ (§ 187, 1).

k) If the letter ಏ is followed by a vowel, ಯ್ comes between, *e. g.* ತೇ+ ಇಸು becomes ತೇಯಿಸು, ಮೇ+ ಇಸು ಮೇಯಿಸು (§ 151 *a*, 5), ಏ ಎನ್ದು ಏಯೆನ್ದು, ಉಘೇ ಎನ್ದು ಉಘೇಯೆನ್ದು, ತೇ+ ಅಲ್ ತೇಯಲ್ (§ 187, 1).

l) If the letter ಐ is followed by a vowel, ಯ್ is inserted, *e.g.* ರೈ ಒದವಿತ್ತು becomes ರೈಯೊದವಿತ್ತು, ದೈ ಎಸ್ದಂ ದೈಯೆಸ್ದಂ, ಛೈ ಎಚ್ಚಿಸಂ ಛೈಯೆಚ್ಚಿಸಂ.

m) If the letter ಓ is followed by a vowel, ಯ್ is often put between (*cf.* 3, *g*; 6, *a-d*), *e.g.* ಸೋ+ಇಸು becomes ಸೋಯಿಸು (§ 151, *a*, 5), ತೋ+ ಅಲ್ ತೋಯಲ್ (§ 187, 1), ಭೋ ಎನ್ದು ಭೋಯೆನ್ದು, ಅವಿಧೋ ಎನಲ್ ಅವಿಧೋ ಯೆನಲ್.

3, Euphonic junction by the insertion of ವ್.

a) If to the class of Saṁskṛita and Kannaḍa themes with final ಅ mentioned under 2, *c*, the formative ಇಸು is suffixed, ವ್ comes frequently between, *e.g.* ತಾರವಿಸು, ಪೂರವಿಸು, ಬಿನ್ನವಿಸು, ಮೇಳವಿಸು, ಹಾರವಿಸು. See § 151, remarks.

b) If ಅ is followed by a vowel, ವ್ does not unfrequently come between (*cf.* 2, *d*; 6, *h*), *e.g.* ಅ ಉದಕಂ becomes ಅವುದಕಂ, ಅ ಊಟಂ ಅವೂಟಂ, ಅ ಊರ್ ಅವೂರ್, ಅ ಒಳೆ ಅವೊಳೆ, ಅ ಓಲೆ ಅವೋಲೆ.

c) If ಈ, which stands for ಇದು and ಇವು, is followed by a vowel, ವ್ comes between (*cf.* 2, *g*), *e.g.* ಈ ಉದ್ಯಾನಂ becomes ಈವುದ್ಯಾನಂ, ಈ ಇದು ಗ್ರನ್ಥಂ ಈವಿದು ಗ್ರನ್ಥಂ, ಈ ಇವು ಗ್ರನ್ಥಂಗಳ್ ಈವಿವು ಗ್ರನ್ಥಂಗಳ್, in which case the ಈ may be shortened, *e.g.* ಈ ಇದು may become ಇವಿದು.

d) If a radical ಉ (see §§ 97. 128) or radically used ಉ is followed by a vowel, ವ್ always comes between, *e.g.* ಪಟು ಏಕವಾಕ್ಯಂ becomes ಪಟು ವೇಕವಾಕ್ಯಂ, ವಿಧು ಇದು ವಿಧುವಿದು, ವಿಧು ಇಲ್ಲದ ವಿಧುವಿಲ್ಲದ, ನೆಗಟ್ದಿನಾ ವಿಭು ಇಳೆ ಯೊಳ್ ನೆಗಟ್ದಿನಾ ವಿಭುವಿಳೆಯೊಳ್, ಸುರಸಿನ್ಧು+ಎ ಸುರಸಿನ್ಧುವೆ, ಗುರು+ಇನ ಗುರುವಿನ, ಮನು+ಇನ ಮನುವಿನ, ಕುಡು ಇಲ್ಲ ಕುಡುವಿಲ್ಲ, ಮಡು ಇದು ಮಡುವಿದು, ಮಡು+ಇಂ ಮಡುವಿಂ; ಕುಡು+ಉದು ಕುಡುವುದು.

e) If ಊ is followed by a vowel, ವ್ is always inserted, *e.g.* ಭ್ರೂ ಇದು becomes ಭ್ರೂವಿದು, ಪೂ+ಇನ ಪೂವಿನ (§ 129).

f) If ಋ and ೠ are followed by a vowel, ವ್ is always put between, *e.g.* ಕರ್ತೃ ಆದಂ becomes ಕರ್ತೃವಾದಂ, ಹೋತೃ+ಎ ಹೋತೃವೆ, ಪಿತೃ+ಇಂ ಪಿತೃವಿಂ (§ 129); ೠ ಎನ್ದಂ ೠವೆನ್ದಂ, ೠ ಇತ್ತಂ ೠವಿತ್ತಂ, ೠ+ಇನ ೠವಿನ (§ 129).

g) If the final ಓ of a declinable base is followed by a vowel, ವ್ always comes between, *e.g.* ಗೋ+ಅಂ becomes ಗೋವಂ, ಗೋ+ಇನ ಗೋ ವಿನ, ಗೋ+ಇನ್ದಂ ಗೋವಿನ್ದಂ (§ 129).

h) If ಔ is followed by a vowel, ವ್ always comes between, *e.g.* ನೌ+ಅಂ becomes ನಾವಂ, ಗ್ಲೌ+ಅಂ ಗ್ಲಾವಂ, ಗ್ಲೌ+ಇನ ಗ್ಲಾವಿನ (§ 129).

4, Cases wherein **euphonic elision is optional.**

If Kannaḍa words end in (ಇ), ಎ, or a euphonically used ಉ, elision is sometimes optional (*cf.* 1, *c*), *i. e.* in its stead ಯ್ or ವ್ may be inserted, *e. g.* ಒತ್ತೆ ಇಟ್ಟಂ may become ಒತ್ತಿಟ್ಟಂ or ಒತ್ತೆಯಿಟ್ಟಂ, ತಗವೆ ಅಪ್ಪೊಡೆ ತಗವಪ್ಪೊಡೆ or ತಗವೆಯಪ್ಪೊಡೆ, ಮಾತು ಎಲ್ಲಂ ಮಾತೆಲ್ಲಂ or ಮಾತುವೆಲ್ಲಂ, ಸೊವಡು ಒನ್ದು ಸೊವಡೊನ್ದು or ಸೊವಡುವೊನ್ದು (*cf.* § 97 and remark thereon), (ಅದು+ಎ) ಅದುವೆ or ಅದೆ, (ಇದು+ಎ) ಇದುವೆ or ಇದೆ, (ಅದು+ಎಮ್ಬ) ಅದುವೆಮ್ಬ or ಅದೆಮ್ಬ.

5, Cases in which **euphonic junction itself is optional.**

a) If ಅಲ್ is added to ಕರೆ (§ 187, 1) and ಅದೆ to ಇರ್ (§ 170), euphonic junction is optional, *viz.* ಕರೆ ಅಲ್ or ಕರೆಯಲಾ, ಇರ ಅದೆ or ಇರದೆ.

b) At the end of a half (kanda) verse (padyârdha) euphonic junction is optional, *e. g.*

either

ಅಲ್ಲಿ ಯಿದುಕ್ಕೆಮ್ಬರ್ಥದೊ
ಳೆಲ್ಲಿಯುಮುಳ್ಳೊಡೆಯುವನ್ತ ಶಬ್ದಮುಮಕ್ಕುಂ ।
ಎಲ್ಲನ್ದದೊಳಂ ಪೋಲಿಸು
ವಲ್ಲಿ ಗುಣಾಧಿಕರೊಳನ್ತೆ ಪೋಲೆನಲಕ್ಕುಂ ॥ in the sense 'there is this' there occur everywhere the words ಉಳ್ಳ, ಒಡೆಯ, ವನ್ತ (§ 243, *B*, 20. 23. 36); where comparison in any way takes place among excellent persons, ಅನ್ತೆ, ಪೋಲ್ are used;

or

ಬನದೊಳಗೆ ಪೋಗಿ ಪೊಸ ಪೂ
ವಿನ ಗೊಂಚಲನಕ್ಕ ನಿನಗೆ ತನ್ದಪ್ಪೆಂ ನೀ ।
ನಿನಿತೊನ್ದು ಬೇಗದಿಂ ನಿ
ನ್ನಿನಿಯನ ಪಟ್ಟೆಯೊಳಿರೆನ್ದು ಸಖಿ ತೊಲಗುವುದುಂ ॥ when the female friend said "Sister, I will go into the garden and bring thee a bunch of nice flowers; (go) thou a little quick (and) remain in the dormitory of thy beloved one", and went away.

c) In a quotation from Saṁskṛita (vâkyavêshṭana) euphonic junction is optional, *e. g.*

either

ಕಃ ಕೇನಾರ್ಥೀ ಕೋ ದರಿದ್ರ ಎನಿತುಮನಿತುಮಂ ಧರ್ಮಜಂ ಸೂಜೆಗೊಟ್ಟಂ,

or

ಕಃ ಕೇನಾರ್ಥೀ ಕೋ ದರಿದ್ರಃ ಎನಿತುಮನಿತುಮಂ ಧರ್ಮಜಂ ಸೂಜೆಗೊಟ್ಟ, "who? why a petitioner? who? a poor man": how much soever, Dharmaja gave (it) all away;

either

ವರ್ಣಾನಾಂ ಬ್ರಾಹ್ಮಣೋ ಗುರು ಎಮ್ಬ ವಚನಂ,

or

ವರ್ಣಾನಾಂ ಬ್ರಾಹ್ಮಣೋ ಗುರುಃ ಎಮ್ಬ ವಚನಂ.

d) If a Kannada imitative sound (§ 212, 9) is followed by a vowel, euphonic junction is occasionally optional (*cf.* 2, *b*), *e. g.*

either

ಕವಕ್ಕವ ಎಲೆ ಎಲೆ ಉ ಊ ಘುಗಲ್ ಘುಗಲ್ ಎನ್ದೆೞ್ಚತ ಊಳ್ವ ಕೋಗಿಲೆಯುಂ;

or

ಛಟಛಟೆಮ್ಮು, ಛಮೆಮ್ಮು, ಛುಮ್ಮೆಮ್ಮು.

But if the imitative sound is from Saṁskṛita, it has always to retain its original form, *e. g.* ಧಗಧಗ never becomes ಧಗಧಗವ್ before a vowel.

e) If ಋ is preceded by a sŏnnĕ or a vowel, euphonic junction is optional, *e. g.*

either

ಎಸೆಗುಂ ಋಜ್ವಾಗತಂ, ಕಣ್ಗೊಳಿಸುಗುಮಳವಟ್ಟಿರ್ದ ಋಜ್ವಾಗತಂ; ಆಯನದ ಋತು; ಸ್ತ್ರೀ ಋತುಮತಿ; ಕ್ರತು ಋತ್ವಿಜರ್ಗೆ;

or

ಸರಸಮೃಜುವೀರನೆನ್ದು ತರುಣಿಯನೊಸೆದಿತ್ತಂ.

6, Cases in which **euphonic junction is forbidden.**

a) If the nipâtas ending in ಎ, ಏ, ಒ and ಓ (§ 212, remark 1) are followed by a vowel, they do not form junction with it, *e. g.* ಅರಮೆ ಅರಲ್ದ ಬಯಲ್ದಾವರೆಗಳ್; ಅರೆ ಎಡೆ ಹಸ್ತಿಶಿಕ್ಷಣವಿಚಕ್ಷಣರ್; ಅರೆ ಎಡೆಯೊಳ್; ಎಲೆ ಅಭಿಮನ್ಯು!; ಎಲೇ ಇದಲ್ತೆ ತುಹಿನಕ್ಷೋಣೀಧ್ರದುತ್ತುಂಗಸಾನುಗಳ್? ಓಹೊ (or ಓಹೋ) ಇರಲಿಂ ಪೆಱ ವಱ ಮಾಹಾತ್ಮ್ಯಂ! *Cf.* remark 1.

b) If the vowels ಎ, ಏ, ಒ and ಓ are used as nipâtas, ಎ, ಏ expressing emphasis (avadhâraṇa) or doubt (viśaṅkĕ, or also simple question) and ಒ, ಓ, doubt, and are followed by a vowel, there is no euphonic junction, *e. g.* ಇನ್ದ್ರನಾತನೆ ಗುಣೋನ್ನತನಾತನೆ ಅಮ್ಬುಜೋದರಂ!;

ನುಡಿದನೆ ಕಾವುದನೇ ಎರ್ದೆ
ಗಿಡದಿರ್ ಜವನಿಟ್ಟುರಕ್ಕೆ ನಿನಗೀವುದನೇ |
ನುಡಿದನೆ ಅದು ಕಯ್ಯೆದು ಮೇಣ್
ನುಡಿದುದು ತಪ್ಪುಗುಮೆ ಗಂಗಚೂಡಾಮಣಿಯಾ ||

did he say he would certainly protect? Let not thy courage fail on account of Yama's gruffness! Did he say he would certainly give? That seems to be scarcely possible. But will what he said fail to occur, o best of the Gaṅgas?; ಈತನೇ ಈವಂ; ಕೂರ್ಪನೇ ಆಪ್ತಂ; ಪೊರವನೇ ಆಳ್ವಂ;—ಇನಿಯನೆ ಬೆಲ್ಲದಿನ್ದಿನಿಯನೀವನೆ ಅಃ ಪಿರಿದೀವನಿತ್ತುದಂ ನೆನೆವನೆ ಛಿಃ ಅದಂ ನೆನೆಯಂ; ಗುರುವಿಲ್ಲ ಕರ್ಣನಿಲ್ಲ ಗುರುವಿನ ಮಗನಿಲ್ಲ ಎನ್ನಿರೆ ಎನ್ನನಿನಿಯುಂ ಕವಿರಾಜಕುಂಜರಂ; ಅಕ್ಕುಮೇ ಆಗದು;—ಆನೆಯೊ ಅದ್ರಿಯೊ?; ರಜ್ಜುವೋ ಅಹಿಯೋ?; ನಿಜಮನಃಪ್ರಿಯನಪ್ಪಿವನೋ ಅಗಲ್ದನೋ?

c) If ಓ is used in approval (mĕčču) or abuse (âkshêpa) and followed by a vowel, there is no euphonic junction, *e. g.* ಎನ್ತೆನ್ತೋ ಆಃ ಕಬ್ಬವೊಳ್ಳಿತ್ತಾಯಿತು! ಏನೇನೋ ಓದಿನ ಪರಿ ಲೇಸು!;—ಎಡಱಿದನೋ ಅವನ ನೊಸಲಕ್ಕರವಂ ತೊಡೆದುದಕ್ಕುಂ; ಮುತ್ತಿದನೋ ಇಸ್ದೆ ಕೋಣ್ಟೆ ಧೂಳಿಪಟಂ.

d) If ಅಯ್ಯೋ and ಅಕ್ಕಟಾ express 'sorrow, grief' (khêda) and are followed by a vowel, there is no euphonic junction, *e. g.* ಅಯ್ಯೋ ಅಕ್ಕಟಾ ಇನ್ದ್ರಂಗೆ ಕೊಡಾಯಿತೆ?

e) If ಎಮ (§ 212, 8) is used in the sense of 'certainly, well' (angîkâra; *cf.* another ಎಮ in 137, *a,* plural) and followed by a vowel, no euphonic junction takes place, *e. g.* ನಿಮಗಕ್ಕೆಮ ಅಬ್ಜಗರ್ಭನಾಯುಂ ಶ್ರೀಯುಂ!; ಸಿಂಗಮಕ್ಕೆಮ ಅಂಜೆಂ!

f) If ಆ is used in the sense of 'indeed' (gaḍa; § 212, 4. 6) and followed by a vowel, there is no euphonic junction, *e.g.* ಪಾಲಾ ಅಮರ್ದಾ ಇನಿದು ಗಡಾ!; ಆನಾ ಇರ್ಮಡಿಯಾ ಎರೞ್ಕದುರೆಯಾ ಇರ್ವಗೇಱೞ್ಕಿಯುದ್ದವಾ!

g) If the ಅ of the genitive or its lengthened form ಆ is followed by the vowel of a nipâta, the Šabdânušâsana says (sûtra 45), there is exceptionally no euphonic junction (*cf.* 2, *a*), *e. g.* ಆತನ ಎ ತೋರದೊಡೆಗಳ್; ಕಸ್ತುವ ಆಃ ಕಬ್ಬುವಿಲ್ಲನೀತಂ ಮುಱಿದಂ; ಎನ್ನಾ ಉಃ ಪಾಪಫಲಂ.

h) If ಆ is followed by ಅ and ಆ, there is not unfrequently no euphonic junction (*cf.* 2, *d;* 3, *b*), and if followed by ಐ and ಔ, there is always none, the Šabdânušâsana says (sûtra 43), *e. g.* ಆ ಅರಸಂ, ಆ ಅಂಜೆ, ಮೃಡನಾ ಅರ್ಧೇನ್ದು, ಸತಿಯಾ ಆಯಲ್ಲಕಂ;—ಆ ಐಶ್ವರ್ಯಂ, ಆ ಐಲವಿಲಂ, ಆ ಔನ್ನತ್ಯಂ, ಆ ಔಷಂ.

i) If ಪೊಱ, ಒಳ, ಪೊಸ, ಪಱ and ಎಳ are followed by a vowel, there is no euphonic junction, *e.g.* ಪೊಱ ಅಡಿ, ಒಳ ಅಟ್ಟಂ, ಪೊಸ ಅಡಿಕೆ, ಪಱ ಅಲಗು, ಎಳ ಅಂಜೆ. *Cf.* § 246, *b;* § 247, *d,* 5.

k) If a protracted vowel (pluta, § 20) is followed by a vowel, no euphonic junction takes place, *e.g.* ಕು ಕೂ ಕೂೞ ಎನ್ದು, ಕೋೞಿ ಕೂಗಿತ್ತಾಗಳ್; ಹಾ ರಾಮಾೞ ಎನ್ದು, ಸೀತೆ ಬಾಯಱಿದಟ್ಟಿಳ್; ಎಲೇ ಅಣ್ಣಾೞ, ಇತ್ತ ಬಾ!; ಅಕ್ಕಾೞ ಇಲ್ಲಿ ಬಾ!

Remarks.

1, With regard to 6, *a* and *b* it is to be observed that when the ಎ of emphasis loses its exact meaning, *e. g.* in ಅಲ್ಲದೆ (§§ 170. 171), or when the nipâta ಅರೆ (§ 212, 4; 212, remark 1) gets the meaning of 'half a thing', there is euphonic junction, *e. g.* ಮಾಮರನಲ್ಲದೆ ಇಲ್ಲ becomes ಮಾಮರನಲ್ಲದಿಲ್ಲ, ತನಿಗಮ್ಪಿನ ಮಲ್ಲಿಗೆಯಲ್ಲದೆ ಇಲ್ಲ ತನಿಗಮ್ಪಿನ ಮಲ್ಲಿಗೆಯಲ್ಲದಿಲ್ಲ (see § 338 under ಅಲ್ಲದೆ); —ಕುರುಪತಿಯುಂ ವಿಷ್ಣು ಬೇಡಿದಂ ಧರೆಯರೆಯುಂ.

2, If two rêphas come together or in any other way cacophony (śrutikashṭa) happens, it is wrong to form sandhi, *e.g.* ಬನ್ದರ್ರಾಮರ್; ದೇವರ್ರಕ್ಷಿಸುಗೆ; — ವಿದ್ವಿಟ್ಸ್ತ್ರೀಯರ್.

3, If a bad notion (dushpratîti) is likely to be produced, sandhi is to be avoided, as *e.g.* ಪೂಱವಕೆಯನ್ತರವೇೞನೇ (does he not tell to bring a bodice with flowers?) may be read ಪೂಱವ ಕೇ ಅನ್ತರವೇೞನೇ; ಪೊಸ ತುಲ್ಲಾರಂ ಪೊಸ ತುಲ್ಲ ಆರಂ; ಮೆಚ್ಚುತುಣ್ಣೆ ಮೆಚ್ಚು ತುಣ್ಣೆ. (*Cf.* § 241.)

7, **Euphonic junction of consonants: their permutation in the formation** of compounds (samâsa, see §§ 244. 246. 247. 248. 249. 251. 252) and in **their doubling** when final.

a) As a general rule it may be stated that the hard letters ಕ, ತ, ಪ become the soft ones ಗ, ದ, ಬ (see § 28), *e.g.* ಪಱಿ ಕನ್ನಡಂ becomes ಪಱಿಗನ್ನಡಂ, ಗಱಿ ಕೂಸು ಗಱಿಗೂಸು, ಪಣೆ ಕಟ್ಟು ಪಣೆಗಟ್ಟು, ಅಱಿ ಕುಲಿ ಅಱಿಗುಲಿ, ಮೀನ್ ಕುಲಿ ಮೀನಂಗುಲಿ; ಕಣ್ ತೆಱೆ ಕಣ್ದೆಱೆ, ಮೇಲ್ ತುಡುಗೆ ಮೇಲ್ದುಡುಗೆ, ಉಡಿ ತೊವಲ್ ಉಡಿದೊವಲ್, ನಿಱಿ ತಲೆ ನಿಱಿದಲೆ, ಬಳೆ ತುಡು ಬಳೆದುಡು; ಕಣ್ ಪನಿ ಕಣ್ಬನಿ, ತಣ್ ಪುೞಿಲ್ ತಣ್ಬುೞಿಲ್, ಕಣ್ ಪೊಲಂ ಕಣ್ಬೊಲಂ; ಬೆಳರ್ ಕೆಮ್ಪು ಬೆಳರ್ಗೆಮ್ಪು; ಅಲರ್ ತೋರಣಂ ಅಲರ್ದೋರಣಂ; ಮುಗುಳ್ ಕಾಯ್ ಮುಗುಳ್ಗಾಯ್; ಅಮಳ್ ತೊಂಗಲ್ ಅಮಳ್ದೊಂಗಲ್; ಎತ್ತುಂ ಕೋಲ್ ಎತ್ತುಂಗೋಲ್; ತೂಗುಂ ತೊಟ್ಟಿಲ್ ತೂಗುನ್ದೊಟ್ಟಿಲ್; ಆಡುಂ ಪೊಲಂ ಆಡುಮ್ಬೊಲಂ; ಸಿಡಿಯುಂ ತಲೆ ಸಿಡಿಯುನ್ದಲೆ. See § 243, *B*, 26.

Exceptions are *e.g.* ತಲೆಕಟ್ಟು, ಬೆಸೆಕೋಲ್, ಒಳಕೆಯ್, ಎದುಪನ್ದಿ, ಬಿಣ್ಪೊಱೆ.

Further specific exceptions are that after ಒರ್ (ಒಱ್), one, and ಇರ್ (ಇಱ್), two, after a rêpha (ಱ್) that is a substitute (âdêśa) of ೞ್, and after a ಱ್ that is a substitute of ಡ್ or ಳ್, the letters ಕ, ತ, ಪ retain their shape, *e.g.* ಒಱ್ಕೆಯ್ಯು, ಒಱ್ತುತ್ತು, ಒಱ್ಪಿಡಿ; ಇಱ್ಕೋಡಿ, ಇಱ್ತಲೆ; ಮಾಱ್ಕೊರಲ್ ಮಾಱ್ಕಟ್ಟಳೆ, ಮಾಱ್ತಲೆ, ಬೇಱ್ಪಡು, ಏಱ್ಪೆಱು; ಎರಱ್ಕುದುರೆ, ಕಾಱ್ಕಿಚ್ಚು, ಕೋಱ್ಕಟ್ಟು, ನಾಱ್ತುಡುಗುಣೆ, ನಾಱ್ಪಿಗರಣಂ, ನಾಱ್ಪೊರಂ; ಕೀಱ್ಪಡೆ, ಕೀಱ್ಕೆಱೆ (see under letter *b*). *Cf.* § 234.

ಚ and ಟ always remain as they are, *e.g.* ಕಡುಚಾಗಿ, ಕಣ್ಚಲ್ಲಂ, ಚಿಕ್ಕಚೋಜಿಗಂ; ಕಡುಟಕ್ಕು, ಪೊಸಟೊಪ್ಪಿಗೆ, ಕಳ್ಳಟಪ್ಪಣಂ.

b) After vowels and radical consonants (sahajavyañjana) ಪ, ಬ and ಮ are generally changed into ವ, *e.g.* ಎಳ ಪೆಱೆ becomes ಎಳವೆಱೆ, ಬೆಳೆ ಪೊಲಂ ಬೆಳೆವೊಲಂ, ಕಡು ಬೆಳ್ಪು ಕಡುವೆಳ್ಪು, ಮರ ಮಣೆ ಮರವಣೆ, ಪಲ ಪಣ್ ಪಲವಣ್; ನೀರ್ ಪೊನಲ್ ನೀರ್ವೊನಲ್, ಬಾಱ್ ಪೆಣಂ ಬಾಱ್ವೆಣಂ; ಮೆಯ್ ಬಸಂ ಮೆಯ್ವಸಂ, ಗೇಣ್ ಬಾಯ್ ಗೇಣ್ವಾಯ್, ಆಳ್ ಬಲ್ಮೆ ಆಳ್ವಲ್ಮೆ, ತೋಳ್ ಬಲ್ಮೆ ತೋಳ್ವಲ್ಮೆ, ಬೇರ್ ಬೆರಸು ಬೇರ್ವೆರಸು; ಮೆಲ್ ಮಾತು ಮೆಲ್ವಾತು; ಪೊಗರ್ ಬಟ್ಟೆ ಪೊಗರ್ವಟ್ಟೆ; ಎಸಳ್ ಬಱಿ ಎಸಳ್ವಱಿ (*cf.* ಮೂವತ್ತು, ಅಱುವತ್ತು, etc. see § 278, 1, ಮೂವಡಿ, etc. in § 280).

This rule holds good also in sentences (vâkya, *i. e.* cases of nouns or the infinitive of verbs to which a relative participle or a conjugated verb is suffixed), *e. g.* ತಮರೂರ್ಗೆವೋಪ (- ಪೋಪ) ಕುಲಜಾಂಗನೆಯರ್; ದಿವದಿಂ ಕೆಲಸಕ್ಕೆ ವರ್ಪ (- ಬರ್ಪ) ದೇವಾಂಗನೆಯರ್; ಬೆಂಗೆವಸ್ದಂ (- ಬಸ್ದಂ); ನೆಲೆಗೆವಸ್ದಂ (- ಬಸ್ದಂ); ತರ ವೇೞ್ದಿಂ (- ಪೇೞ್ದಿಂ).

Exceptions are *e. g.* ಕೆಯ್ಪಿಡಿ, ಪೂಪುಣಮ್ಪು, ಪಲ್ಪಿಡಿ; ಕಣ್ಬೇಟಂ, ಸುಡುಬಾಡು; ಬಾಳ್ಕೊನೆ, ಪಾಟ್ಮಿನೆ, ಕತ್ತುರಿಮಿಗಂ, ಬಿಡುಮುಡಿ, ಬೆಳ್ಮುಗಿಲ್.

Further specific exceptions are that after ಇರ್, two, the substitute of ಎರಡು, and after ಕಿಱ್, the substitute of ಕೆಳಗು, the letters ಪ, ಬ and ಮ remain unchanged, *e. g.* ಇರ್ಬಾಳ್; ಇರ್ಮಡಿ; ಕಿಱ್ಪೆಡೆ (see sub letter *a*).

c) After final consonants the letter ಸ generally becomes ಚ and ಜ, and when the numeral ಸಾಸಿರಂ is concerned, ಛ, *e. g.* ನುಣ್ ಸರಂ becomes ನುಣ್ಚರಂ, ಇನ್ ಸರಂ ಇಂಚರಂ; ಪೊನ್ ಸುರಿಗೆ ಪೊಂಜುರಿಗೆ, ಮುನ್ ಸೂರ್ ಮುಂಜೂರ್, ಮುನ್ ಸೆಱಂಗು ಮುಂಜೆಱಂಗು, ತಣ್ ಸೊಡರ್ ತಂಜೊಡರ್; ಇರ್ ಸಾಸಿರಂ ಇರ್ಛಾಸಿರಂ (§ 278, 1), ನೂಱ್ ಸಾಸಿರಂ ನೂರ್ಛಾಸಿರಂ (§ 278, 1), ಪದಿನೆಣ್ ಸಾಸಿರಂ ಪದಿನೆಣ್ಛಾಸಿರಂ (see § 218); further remark ಕಟ್ಟು+ಂ+ಸುರಿಗೆ ಕಟ್ಟುಂಜುರಿಗೆ, ತೂಗು+ಂ+ಸೊಡರ್ ತೂಗುಂಜೊಡರ್.

Exceptions are ಕಣ್ಸೋಲಂ, ಬೆಳ್ಸರಿ, ಕಳ್ಸವಿ.

Further specific exceptions are that after ಯ್ and ಲ್ the letter ಸ retains its shape, *e. g.* ಬಾಯ್ಸವಿ, ಮೆಯ್ಸೊಬಗು, ಕೆಯ್ಸುರಿಗೆ; ಬಲ್ಸೋನೆ, ಕಲ್ಸೆಱೆ, ಮೆಲ್ಸರಂ.

Another rule is that ಸ after a short vowel sometimes becomes double ಚ (*i. e.* ಚ್ಚ) or ಜ, *e. g.* ಮು ಸೆರೆ becomes ಮುಚ್ಚೆರೆ, ಮು ಸಾಲ್ ಮುಚ್ಚಾಲ್, ಮು ಸವಡಿ ಮುಚ್ಚವಡಿ, ಮು ಸೋಟು ಮುಚ್ಚೋಟು; ತುಡು ಸೊಡರ್ ತುಡುಜೊಡರ್. *Cf.* ಮುಚ್ಛಾಸಿರ in § 278, 1.

d) When the vowel of monosyllabic declinable bases ending in ನ್, ಣ್, ಲ್, ಯ್ and ಳ್ is short, and such bases are followed by a vowel, their final consonant is doubled, *e. g.* ಬಿಡುಮುಡಿ ಬೆನ್ ಅಪ್ಪಳಿಸೆ becomes ಬಿಡುಮುಡಿ ಬೆನ್ನಪ್ಪಳಿಸೆ, ಪೊನ್+ಇಂ ಪೊನ್ನಿಂ, ಪೊನ್+ಉಳ್ಳವನೆ ಪೊನ್ನುಳ್ಳವನೆ, ಪನ್+ಒನ್ದು ಪನ್ನೊನ್ದು; ಕಣ್+ಅಂ ಕಣ್ಣಂ, ಪೆಣ್+ಅಂ ಪೆಣ್ಣಂ, ಪಣ್+ಅಂ ಪಣ್ಣಂ, ಪುಣ್+ಏಂ ಪುಣ್ಣೇಂ; ಕಲ್+ಅ ಕಲ್ಲ, ಕಲ್+ಎಲ್ಲಂ ಕಲ್ಲೆಲ್ಲಂ, ಪುಲ್+ಉಂ ಪುಲ್ಲುಂ, ನೆಲ್+ಉಂ ನೆಲ್ಲುಂ; ಮೆಯ್+ಅಂ ಮೆಯ್ಯಂ, ಕೆಯ್+ಅಂ ಕೆಯ್ಯಂ; ಮುಳ್+ಅಂ ಮುಳ್ಳಂ, ಕಳ್+ಆಟಂ ಕಳ್ಳಾಟಂ, ಒಳ್+ಆಳ್ ಒಳ್ಳಾಳ್, ಎಳ್+ಅಂ ಎಳ್ಳಂ. (*Cf.* §§ 120, *a*; 247, *d*, II.)

But if their vowel is long, that doubling does not take place, *e. g.* ಏನಾನಾಗಿಯುಮೆಸಡಿಯಾಗಿಯುಮೇನಾಗಿಯುಂ ತಾನೆಲ್ಲಂ, ಬಾನುದ್ದಂ, ಏನಾಯ್ತು;

ಜಾಣಂ, ನಾಣಂ, ಏಣುಣ್ಣು; ಕೀಲಂ, ಕೇಲಂ, ಕೋಲಂ, ನೂಲಂ; ತಾಯೊರ್ವಳ್, ಬಾಯಾರ್ವಳ್; ಆಳ್ಗೋಳಿ, ತೋಳ್ಗಾಟಂ, ಬಾಳೊಪ್ಪಂ; nor if the declinable base is polysyllabic (anêkâkshara), *e.g.* ಸರಣಾರ್, ಪರಲೆಲ್ಲಂ, ತೊಡಳುಣ್ಬೆ, ಪವಣಿಲ್ಲ; nor if the final consonant of a monosyllabic avyaya having a short vowel meets with a vowel, *e. g.* ಕಲಿ ದಲಿವಂ (see § 212, 4).

e) When to monosyllabic verbal themes with a short vowel ending in ನ್, ಣ್, ಲ್ and ಳ್ the formatives ಅಲ್, ಅಲೊಡಂ (ಅಲ್+ಒಡಂ) and ಎ are suffixed (*cf.* § 187, 1 and 4), there is no doubling, *e.g.* ತಿನಲ್ಕೊನ್ದಂ, ಉಣಲ್ಬನ್ದಂ, ಮೆಲಲ್ಪೋದಂ, ಕೊಲಲ್ಬಗೆದಂ, ಕೊಳಲ್ಸಾರ್ದಂ, ಕಳಲ್ನೋಡಿದಂ; ಉಣಲೊಡಂ, ಕಳಲೊಡಂ; ಎನೆ, ಕೊಲೆ, ಉಣೆ; when such verbal themes end in ಯ್, the doubling is optional, *e, g.* ಪೊಯಲುಂ (ಪೊಯ್+ಅಲ್+ಉಂ) or ಪೊಯ್ಯಲುಂ, ಕೊಯಲುಂ or ಕೊಯ್ಯಲುಂ, ಗೆಯಲುಂ or ಗೆಯ್ಯಲುಂ; — the verbal themes ಉಯ್, ನೆಯ್, ಸುಯ್ and ಬಯ್, however, always double their final consonant, *e. g.* ಉಯ್ಯಲುಂ, ನೆಯ್ಯಲುಂ.

ಆರಯ್, which has a long initial and is dissyllabic, may or may not double the final consonant before ಅಲ್, ಅಲೊಡಂ, ಎ, and before a personal termination, *e. g.* ಆರಯಲುಂ or ಆರಯ್ಯಲುಂ; ಆರಯೆ or ಆರಯ್ಯೆ; ಆರಯಿಂ or ಆರಯ್ಯಿಂ.

f) In the negative form of the verb, either the conjugation (§ 209) or the participle (§ 170), monosyllabic themes with a short vowel ending in ನ್, ಣ್, ಲ್, ಯ್ and ಳ್ always double their final, *e. g.* ಎನ್ನಂ, ಎನ್ನರ್; ಉಣ್ಣಂ, ಉಣ್ಣರ್; ಉಯ್ಯಂ, ಉಯ್ಯರ್; ನೆಯ್ಯಂ, ನೆಯ್ಯರ್; ಮೆಲ್ಲಯ್, ಮೆಲ್ಲಿರ್; ಸುಯ್ಯಯ್, ಸುಯ್ಯಿರ್; ಬಯ್ಯೆನ್, ಬಯ್ಯೆವು; ಕೊಳ್ಳೆನ್, ಕೊಳ್ಳೆವು; ಬಯ್ಯದು, ಬಯ್ಯವು; ಎನ್ನದೆ, ತಿನ್ನದೆ, ಉಣ್ಣದೆ, ಒಲ್ಲದೆ, ಬಯ್ಯದೆ, ಕೊಳ್ಳದೆ.

The only exception forms ಕಳ್, *e. g.* ಕಳದೆ ಬನ್ದಂ.

Remark.

When, in samâsa, ಣ್ is followed by ನ್, this ನ್ may take the form of ಣ್, *e. g.* ತಣ್ ನೆಬಲ್ may become ತಣ್ಣೆಬಲ್, ಕಣ್ ನೀರ್ ಕಣ್ಣೀರ್, ಕಣ್ ನೋಟಂ ಕಣ್ಣೋಟಂ. *Cf.* § 222.

8, Rules concerning the final sŏnnĕ (ಂ) are the following:—If the sŏnnĕ precedes a consonant, it may change into ನ್ (in the singular), into ಮ್ (in the plural) or retain its form, *e. g.* ಅನ್ ವಾದಿ or ಅಂ ವಾದಿ, ನೀನ್ ಶುಚಿ or ನೀಂ ಶುಚಿ, ತಾನ್ ಸುಜನಂ or ತಾಂ ಸುಜನಂ; ನೀಮ್ ಯೋಗ್ಯರ್ or ನೀಂ ಯೋಗ್ಯರ್, ಆಮ್ ಸುಖಿಗಳ್ or ಆಂ ಸುಖಿಗಳ್, ತಾಮ್ ಸೇವ್ಯರ್ or ತಾಂ ಸೇವ್ಯರ್; —

concerning the ವರ್ಗಪಂಚಮ see § 220;—when the sŏnnĕ of the nominative singular of Kannaḍa neuter nouns ending in ಅ (§ 109) meets with a vowel, it often changes into ನ್, *e. g.* ಮರಂ ಇರ್ದುದು becomes ಮರನಿರ್ದುದು, ನೆಲಂ ಇದು ನೆಲನಿದು, ಪೊಲಂ ಇದು ಪೊಲನಿದು, ನೆಲಂ ಒಳ್ಳಿತ್ತು ನೆಲನೊಳ್ಳಿತ್ತು, but may also become ಮ್, *e. g.* ಮರಮಿದು, ನೆಲಮಿದು, ಪೊಲಮಿದು, ನೆಲಮೊಳ್ಳಿತು; in Saṁskṛita and Tadbhava nouns (which are neuter in Kannaḍa) it uses to change into ಮ್ or ವ್, *e. g.* ವೃಕ್ಷಮಿದು, ಪ್ಲಕ್ಷಮಿದು; ಕಬ್ಬಮೊಳ್ಳಿತ್ತು, ನಿರ್ದಾಣಮೆಸೆದುದು, ದೋಷವಿದು, ನಾಸಿಕವಡ್ಡಂ;—when the sŏnnĕ of the nominative singular of masculines and feminines ending in ಅ (§ 117) is followed by a vowel, it becomes ನ್, *e. g.* ಜಿನನೀತಂ, ಅವನೊಳ್ಳಿದಂ, ಅರಸನಾಳ್ದಪಂ, ಅಕ್ಕನಿವಳ್, ಅಮ್ಮನಿವಳ್;—when the sŏnnĕ of the pronouns ಆಂ, ನೀಂ and ತಾಂ (§ 137) is followed by a vowel, it becomes ನ್ in the singular, *e. g.* ಆನಱಿವೆಂ, ನೀನರಸಂ, ತಾನೆಚ್ಚಂ, and ಮ್ in the plural, *e. g.* ಆಮಱಿವೊಡಂ, ನೀಮಿರೆ, ತಾಮೊಳ್ಳಿದರ್;—when the sŏnnĕ of the accusative singular and plural is followed by a vowel, it changes into ನ್, *e. g.* ಕೊಪ್ಪನೊದೆದು, ವರಮನರಸಂಗಿತ್ತರ್, ಎಡಱಿದರನಟ್ಟಿ, ಅರಸುಗಳನನಿಬರುಮಂ ಗೆಲ್ದಂ, ಗಂಗೆಯ ಮಡುಗಳನಡಹಡಿಸಿ ಪುಗುವಿನಂ;—when the sŏnnĕ of the third person singular meets with a vowel, it becomes ನ್, *e. g.* ಗೆಲ್ದನೊರ್ವನೆ ಪಾರ್ಥಂ, ಗೆಲ್ದನಾ ವಿಭು;—when ಗುಂ and ಕುಂ (§ 203) precede a vowel, their sŏnnĕ becomes ಮ್, *e. g.* ಬರ್ಕುಮೆ (ಬರ್ಕುಂ+ಎ), ಸೊಗಯಿಸುಗುಮೆ, ಪೋಕುಮವಳ್;—when the ಇಂ and ಅಲಿಂ of the imperative (§§ 205. 207), the adverbs of time and postpositions ಬಱಿಕಂ, ಬಱಿಕ್ಕಂ, ಬಱಿಯಂ, the postpositions ಅನ್ನಂ, ಅನ್ನೆಗಂ, ಇಸಂ, ಇನೆಗಂ, ಇನ್ನೆಗಂ, ಉದುಂ, etc., the copulative conjunctions ಅಂ, ಉಂ, and the ಒಡಂ in ಅಲೊಡಂ are followed by a vowel, their sŏnnĕ becomes ಮ್, *e. g.* ಶಿವಸುಖಮಂ ಮಾಡಿಮೆಮಗೆ ಪರಮಜಿನೇಶ್ವರರ್, ಬಗೆಯಲಿಮೀಗಳ್, ಬಱಿಕ್ಕಮಾತಂ, ವರಮ್ಮಡೆವನ್ನಮಾರಾಧಿಸಿದಂ, ಈವನ್ನೆಗಮಿರ್ದಂ, ಓಲಗಂ ಪರೆವುದುಮಾಲೋಚನೆಗೆ ಪೊಕ್ಕಂ, ಎಲ್ಲೆಡೆಯೊಳಮೆಲ್ಲ ತೆಱದೊಳಂ, ಅರ್ಗಮಧಿಕಂ, ಎಲ್ಲರುಮಾ ಕರ್ಣನನ್ತಿರೇನ್ ಚಾಗಿಗಳ್, ಶರಣಾರುಮೊಳರೆ, ಗಾಳಿ ಬೀಸಲೊಡಮೆಲೆ ಕಱಿಲ್ದುವು, ಗುಣಮಾಣಮಿಲ್ಲೆನಲೊಡಮೇನುಮಿಲ್ಲೆಮ್ಮರ್ಥಂ.—ಛಟಛಟಮೆಮ್ಬ may become ಛಟಛಟೆಮ್ಬ (see § 215, 5, *d*).

216. In §§ 213-215 Kannaḍa euphonic junction of letters has been introduced. Now as many Saṁskṛita compounds, joined together according to the rules of Saṁskṛita grammar, have been borrowed by Kannaḍa scholars and used in their writings, it becomes necessary to point out also some of the principal ways of Saṁskṛita euphonic junction of letters. Because there are no Saṁskṛita rules of sandhi in the Śabdamaṇidarpaṇa, etc., we make the following alphabetical selection ourselves.

1, Junction of vowels (svarasandhi)).

ಅ + ಅ = ಆ, *e. g.* ಪಟ್ಟ + ಅಭಿಷೇಕ = ಪಟ್ಟಾಭಿಷೇಕ.

ಅ + ಆ = ಆ, *e. g.* ದೇವ + ಆಲಯ = ದೇವಾಲಯ.

ಅ + ಇ = ಏ, *e. g.* ಕಾಮ್ಯ + ಇಷ್ಟಿ = ಕಾಮ್ಯೇಷ್ಟಿ.

ಅ + ಈ = ಏ, *e. g.* ಗಣ + ಈಶ = ಗಣೇಶ.

ಅ + ಉ = ಓ, *e. g.* ಸೂರ್ಯ + ಉದಯ = ಸೂರ್ಯೋದಯ.

ಅ + ಊ = ಓ, *e. g.* ಗುಣ + ಊರ್ಜಿತ = ಗುಣೋರ್ಜಿತ.

ಅ + ಋ = ಅರ್, *e. g.* ದೇವ + ಋಷಿ = ದೇವರ್ಷಿ.

ಅ + ಏ = ಐ, *e. g.* ಪುಣ್ಯ + ಏಕಕರ್ಮ = ಪುಣ್ಯೈಕಕರ್ಮ.

ಅ + ಐ = ಐ, *e. g.* ರಾಮ + ಐಶ್ವರ್ಯ = ರಾಮೈಶ್ವರ್ಯ.

ಅ + ಓ = ಔ, *e. g.* ಸರ್ವ + ಓಘ = ಸರ್ವೌಘ.

(The ಅ + ಓ in ಅಧರ + ಓಷ್ಠ, ಬಿಮ್ಬ + ಓಷ್ಠ, and ಸ್ಥೂಲ + ಓತು may become either ಓ or ಔ.)

ಅ + ಔ = ಔ, *e. g.* ದಿವ್ಯ + ಔಷಧ = ದಿವ್ಯೌಷಧ.

ಆ + ಅ = ಆ, *e. g.* ವಿದ್ಯಾ + ಅಭ್ಯಾಸ = ವಿದ್ಯಾಭ್ಯಾಸ.

ಆ + ಆ = ಆ, *e. g.* ವಿದ್ಯಾ + ಆಲಯ = ವಿದ್ಯಾಲಯ.

ಆ + ಇ = ಏ, *e. g.* ಮಹಾ + ಇನ್ದ್ರ = ಮಹೇನ್ದ್ರ.

ಆ + ಈ = ಏ, *e. g.* ಇಲಾ + ಈಶ = ಇಲೇಶ.

ಆ + ಉ = ಓ, *e. g.* ಮಹಾ + ಉತ್ಪಲ = ಮಹೋತ್ಪಲ.

ಆ + ಊ = ಓ, *e. g.* ಮಹಾ + ಊರು = ಮಹೋರು.

ಆ + ಋ = ಅರ್, *e. g.* ಮಹಾ + ಋಷಿ = ಮಹರ್ಷಿ.

ಆ + ಏ = ಐ, *e. g.* ಪ್ರಥಮಾ + ಏಕವಚನ = ಪ್ರಥಮೈಕವಚನ.

ಆ + ಐ = ಐ, *e. g.* ಮಹಾ + ಐಶ್ವರ್ಯ = ಮಹೈಶ್ವರ್ಯ.

ಆ + ಓ = ಔ, *e. g.* ಮಹಾ + ಓಜಸ್ = ಮಹೌಜಸ್.

ಆ + ಔ = ಔ, *e. g.* ಮಹಾ + ಔನ್ನತ್ಯ = ಮಹೌನ್ನತ್ಯ.

ಇ + ಅ = ಯ, *e. g.* ಅತಿ + ಅಲ್ಪ = ಅತ್ಯಲ್ಪ.

ಇ + ಆ = ಯಾ, *e. g.* ಅತಿ + ಆಶೆ = ಅತ್ಯಾಶೆ.

ಇ + ಇ = ಈ, *e. g.* ಕವಿ + ಇನ್ದ್ರ = ಕವೀನ್ದ್ರ.

ಇ + ಈ = ಈ, *e. g.* ಮುನಿ + ಈಶ್ವರ = ಮುನೀಶ್ವರ.

ಇ + ಉ = ಯು, *e. g.* ಅತಿ + ಉತ್ತಮ = ಅತ್ಯುತ್ತಮ.

ಇ + ಊ = ಯೂ, *e. g.* ಅತಿ + ಊರ್ಧ್ವ = ಅತ್ಯೂರ್ಧ್ವ.

ಇ + ಏ = ಯೇ, *e. g.* ಪ್ರತಿ + ಏಕ = ಪ್ರತ್ಯೇಕ.

ಇ + ಓ = ಯೋ, *e. g.* ಶಾಲಿ + ಓದನ = ಶಾಲ್ಯೋದನ.

ಇ + ಔ = ಯೌ, *e. g.* ಮನ್ತ್ರಿ + ಔದಾರ್ಯ = ಮನ್ತ್ರ್ಯೌದಾರ್ಯ.

ಈ + ಇ = ಈ, *e. g.* ನದೀ + ಇನ = ನದೀನ.

ಈ + ಈ = ಈ, *e. g.* ಮಹೀ + ಈಶ = ಮಹೀಶ.

ಉ + ಅ = ವ, *e. g.* ಗುರು + ಅಕ್ಷರ = ಗುರ್ವಕ್ಷರ.

ಉ + ಆ = ವಾ, *e. g.* ಮಧು + ಆಸವ = ಮಧ್ವಾಸವ.

ಉ + ಇ = ವಿ, *e. g.* ಮಧು + ಇವ = ಮಧ್ವಿವ.

ಉ + ಉ = ಊ, *e. g.* ಮೃದು + ಉಕ್ತಿ = ಮೃದೂಕ್ತಿ.

ಉ + ಊ = ಊ. *e. g.* ಸಿನ್ಧು + ಊರ್ಮಿ = ಸಿನ್ಧೂರ್ಮಿ.

ಉ + ಐ = ವೈ, *e. g.* ಗುರು + ಐಶ್ವರ್ಯ = ಗುರ್ವೈಶ್ವರ್ಯ.
ಊ + ಉ = ಊ, *e. g.* ಭೂ + ಉತ್ತಮ = ಭೂತ್ತಮ.
ಋ + ಅ = ರ, *e. g.* ಪಿತೃ + ಅರ್ಜಿತ = ಪಿತ್ರರ್ಜಿತ.
ಋ + ಆ = ರಾ, *e. g.* ಮಾತೃ + ಆದರ = ಮಾತ್ರಾದರ.
ಋ + ಋ = ೠ, *e. g.* ಪಿತೃ + ಋಣ = ಪಿತೃಣ.

2, Junction of consonants (vyañjanasandhi).

ಕ್ arises from ಚ್ and ಶ್, *e. g.* ಋಕ್ = ಋಚ್, ತಿರ್ಯಕ್ = ತಿರ್ಯಚ್, ತ್ವಕ್ = ತ್ವಚ್, ವಾಕ್ = ವಾಚ್, ದಿಕ್ = ದಿಶ್, and remains unaltered when no special rule is given.

ಕ್ before a vowel becomes ಗ್, *e. g.* ತಿರ್ಯಕ್ + ಈಕ್ಷ = ತಿರ್ಯಗೀಕ್ಷ, ತ್ವಕ್ + ಅಂಕುರ = ತ್ವಗಂಕುರ, ವಾಕ್ + ಈಶ = ವಾಗೀಶ, ದಿಕ್ + ಇಭ = ದಿಗಿಭ.

ಕ್ before the consonants ಗ, ಜ, ದ, ಧ, (ನ), ಬ, ಭ, (ಮ), ಯ, ರ, ಲ, ವ becomes ಗ್, *e. g.* ಋಕ್ + ಗಾಥೆ = ಋಗ್ಗಾಥೆ, ದಿಕ್ + ಗಜ = ದಿಗ್ಗಜ, ತಿರ್ಯಕ್ + ಗ್ರಾಸ = ತಿರ್ಯಗ್ಗ್ರಾಸ, ದಿಕ್ + ಜಯ = ದಿಗ್ಜಯ, ತಿರ್ಯಕ್ + ಜೀವ = ತಿರ್ಯಗ್ಜೀವ, ದಿಕ್ + ದನ್ತಿ = ದಿಗ್ದನ್ತಿ, ತಿರ್ಯಕ್ + ಧಾರ = ತಿರ್ಯಗ್ಧಾರ, (ದಿಕ್ + ನಾಗ = ದಿಗ್ನಾಗ), ದಿಕ್ + ಬಲಿ = ದಿಗ್ಬಲಿ, ದಿಕ್ + ಭ್ರಮಣ = ದಿಗ್ಭ್ರಮಣ, (ದಿಕ್ + ಮಣ್ಡಲ = ದಿಗ್ಮಣ್ಡಲ), ಋಕ್ + ಯಜುಸ್ = ಋಗ್ಯಜುಸ್, ವಾಕ್ + ರೋಧ = ವಾಗ್ರೋಧ, ದಿಕ್ + ಲಾಭ = ದಿಗ್ಲಾಭ, ಋಕ್ + ವೇದ = ಋಗ್ವೇದ, ವಾಕ್ + ವಿಭವ = ವಾಗ್ವಿಭವ, ದಿಕ್ + ವಿಜಯ = ದಿಗ್ವಿಜಯ.

ಕ್ before the consonants ನ and ಮ becomes also ಙ್, *e. g.* ತಿರ್ಯಕ್ + ನಾಸ = ತಿರ್ಯಙ್ನಾಸ (or ತಿರ್ಯಗ್ನಾಸ), ದಿಕ್ + ನಾಗ = ದಿಙ್ನಾಗ (or ದಿಗ್ನಾಗ), ದಿಕ್ + ಮಣ್ಡಲ = ದಿಙ್ಮಣ್ಡಲ (or ದಿಗ್ಮಣ್ಡಲ), ವಾಕ್ + ಮಯ = ವಾಙ್ಮಯ (or ವಾಗ್ಮಯ).

ಛ್ after the vowels ಅ, ಇ and ಉ becomes ಚ್ಛ್, *e. g.* ಅಕ್ಷರ + ಛನ್ದಸ್ = ಅಕ್ಷರಚ್ಛನ್ದಸ್, ಗೃಹ + ಛಿದ್ರ = ಗೃಹಚ್ಛಿದ್ರ, ಪದ + ಛೇದ = ಪದಚ್ಛೇದ, ಶ್ವೇತ + ಛತ್ರ = ಶ್ವೇತಚ್ಛತ್ರ, ಪ್ರತಿ + ಛನ್ನ = ಪ್ರತಿಚ್ಛನ್ನ, ತನು + ಛದ = ತನುಚ್ಛದ, ತನು + ಚ್ಛಾಯೆ = ತನುಚ್ಛಾಯೆ, ಬಹು + ಛದ = ಬಹುಚ್ಛದ, ಬಹು + ಛಿನ್ನೆ = ಬಹುಚ್ಛಿನ್ನೆ, ಮಧು + ಛನ್ದಸ್ = ಮಧುಚ್ಛನ್ದಸ್.

ಟ್ arises from ಷ್ in ಷಷ್ = ಷಟ್, and remains unaltered when no special rule is given.

ಟ್ before a vowel becomes ಡ್, *e. g.* ಷಟ್ + ಅಂಗ = ಷಡಂಗ, ಷಟ್ + ಋತು = ಷಡೃತು.

ಟ್ before the consonants ಗ, ಜ, ದ, ಧ, ಭ, ರ, ವ becomes ಡ್, *e. g.* ಷಟ್ + ಗುಣ = ಷಡ್ಗುಣ, ಷಟ್ + ಜ = ಷಡ್ಜ, ಷಟ್ + ದರ್ಶನ = ಷಡ್ದರ್ಶನ, ಷಟ್ + ಧಾ = ಷಡ್ಧಾ, ಷಟ್ + ಭಾಗ = ಷಡ್ಭಾಗ, ಷಟ್ + ರಸ = ಷಡ್ರಸ, ಷಟ್ + ವರ್ಗ = ಷಡ್ವರ್ಗ.

ಟ್ before the consonants ನ and ಮ becomes ಣ್, *e. g.* ಷಟ್ + ನವತಿ = ಷಣ್ಣವತಿ (ನ becoming ಣ), ಷಟ್ + ಮುಖ = ಷಣ್ಮುಖ.

ತ್ before a vowel becomes ದ್, *e. g.* ಜಗತ್ + ಅಮ್ಬೆ = ಜಗದಮ್ಬೆ, ಬೃಹತ್ + ಆರಣ್ಯಕ = ಬೃಹದಾರಣ್ಯಕ, ಜಗತ್ + ಈಶ = ಜಗದೀಶ.

ತ್ before the consonants ಗ, ದ, ಧ, ಬ, ಭ, ಯ, ರ, ವ becomes ದ್, *e. g.* ಜಗತ್ + ಗುರು + ಜಗದ್ಗುರು, ಜಗತ್ + ದರ್ಪಣ = ಜಗದ್ದರ್ಪಣ, ಜಗತ್ + ಧಾತ್ರಿ = ಜಗದ್ಧಾತ್ರಿ, ಜಗತ್ + ಬಲ = ಜಗದ್ಬಲ, ಜಗತ್ + ಭಾರ = ಜಗದ್ಭಾರ, ಜಗತ್ + ಯೋನಿ = ಜಗದ್ಯೋನಿ, ಬೃಹತ್ + ರಥ = ಬೃಹದ್ರಥ, ಲಸತ್ + ವಚನ = ಲಸದ್ವಚನ.

ತ್ before ಚ becomes ಚ್, *e. g.* ಜಗತ್ + ಚಕ್ಷುಸ್ = ಜಗಚ್ಚಕ್ಷುಸ್, ವಿಯತ್ + ಚರ = ವಿಯಚ್ಚರ, ಸತ್ + ಚರಿತ = ಸಚ್ಚರಿತ.

ತ್ before ಜ becomes ಜ್ *e. g.* ಜಗತ್ + ಜೀವ = ಜಗಜ್ಜೀವ, ವಿದ್ಯುತ್ + ಜಿಹ್ವ = ವಿದ್ಯುಜ್ಜಿಹ್ವ, ಸರಿತ್ + ಜಲ = ಸರಿಜ್ಜಲ.

ತ್ before ಡ becomes ಡ್, *e. g.* ರಟತ್ + ಡಮರು = ರಟಡ್ಡಮರು.

ತ್ before ನ and ಮ becomes ನ್, *e. g.* ಜಗತ್ + ನಾಥ = ಜಗನ್ನಾಥ, ಝಣತ್ + ನೂಪುರ = ಝಣನ್ನೂಪುರ, ಚಿತ್ + ಮಯ = ಚಿನ್ಮಯ, ಜಗತ್ = ಮಯ = ಜಗನ್ಮಯ, ಭವತ್ + ಮತ = ಭವನ್ಮತ, ಸತ್ + ಮಾರ್ಗ = ಸನ್ಮಾರ್ಗ.

ತ್ before ಲ becomes ಲ್, *e. g.* ಬೃಹತ್ + ಲಲಾಟ = ಬೃಹಲ್ಲಲಾಟ, ವಿದ್ಯುತ್ + ಲತೆ = ವಿದ್ಯುಲ್ಲತೆ.

ತ್ before ಶ becomes ಚ್, *e. g.* ಚಿತ್ + ಶಕ್ತಿ = ಚಿಚ್ಛಕ್ತಿ (ಶ becoming ಛ), ಮಹತ್ + ಶಬ್ದ = ಮಹಚ್ಛಬ್ದ, ಸತ್ + ಶೀಲ = ಸಚ್ಛೀಲ.

ದ್ before the consonants ಕ, ತ, ಪ, ಫ, ಸ becomes ತ್, *e. g.* ತದ್ + ಕಾಲ = ತತ್ಕಾಲ, ವಿಪದ್ + ಕಾಲ = ವಿಪತ್ಕಾಲ, ತದ್ + ತೀರ್ಥ = ತತ್ತೀರ್ಥ, ತದ್ + ಪರ = ತತ್ಪರ, ತದ್ + ಫಲ = ತತ್ಫಲ, ತದ್ + ಸಮ = ತತ್ಸಮ, ವಿಪದ್ + ಸಾಗರ = ವಿಪತ್ಸಾಗರ.

ದ್ before ಚ becomes ಚ್, *e. g.* ತದ್ + ಚಾತುರ್ಯ = ತಚ್ಚಾತುರ್ಯ.

ದ್ before ಜ becomes ಜ್, *e. g.* ತದ್ + ಜಯ = ತಜ್ಜಯ, ತದ್ + ಜ್ಞ = ತಜ್ಜ್ಞ.

ದ್ before ಟ becomes ಟ್, *e. g.* ತದ್ + ಟೀಕೆ = ತಟ್ಟೀಕೆ.

ದ್ before ನ and ಮ becomes ನ್, *e. g.* ತದ್ + ನಾಶ = ತನ್ನಾಶ, ತದ್ + ಮಾತ್ರ = ತನ್ಮಾತ್ರ.

ದ್ before ಶ becomes ಚ್, *e. g.* ತದ್ + ಶೀಲ = ತಚ್ಛೀಲ (ಶ becoming ಛ), ತದ್ + ಶಾಸ್ತ್ರ = ತಚ್ಛಾಸ್ತ್ರ.

ಸ್ (preceded by ಇ and ಉ) before a vowel becomes ರ್, *e. g.* ಬಹಿಸ್ + ಅಂಗ = ಬಹಿರಂಗ, ಹವಿಸ್ + ಅಶನ = ಹವಿರಶನ, ಜ್ಯೋತಿಸ್ + ಇಂಗ = ಜ್ಯೋತಿರಿಂಗ, ಚಕ್ಷುಸ್ + ಇನ್ದ್ರಿಯ = ಚಕ್ಷುರಿನ್ದ್ರಿಯ, ಧನುಸ್ + ಆಕಾರ = ಧನುರಾಕಾರ.

ಸ್ before the vowel ಅ becomes ಓ, *e. g.* ಅಯಸ್ + ಅಸ್ತ್ರ = ಅಯೋಸ್ತ್ರ, ಶಿರಸ್ + ಅಹ್ಯ = ಶಿರೋಹ್ಯ, ತಪಸ್ + ಅನುಭಾವ = ತಪೋನುಭಾವ, ತಮಸ್ + ಅಪಹ = ತಮೋಪಹ, ಮನಸ್ + ಅಧಿನಾಥ = ಮನೋಧಿನಾಥ, ಮನಸ್ + ಅನುಗ = ಮನೋನುಗ, ಮನಸ್ + ಅಪಹಾರಿ = ಮನೋಪಹಾರಿ, ಮನಸ್ + ಅಮ್ಬುಜ = ಮನೋಮ್ಬುಜ, ಶಿರಸ್ + ಅಸ್ಥಿ = ಶಿರೋಸ್ಥಿ.

ಸ್ before the consonants ಗ, ಜ, ದ, ಧ, ನ, ಬ, ಭ, ಮ, ಯ, ರ, ಲ, ವ, ಹ becomes ಓ, *e. g.* ತಮಸ್ + ಗುಣ = ತಮೋಗುಣ, ಮನಸ್ + ಗತ = ಮನೋಗತ, ಮನಸ್ + ಜ = ಮನೋಜ, ಮನಸ್ + ದಣ್ಡ = ಮನೋದಣ್ಡ, ತಪಸ್ + ಧನ = ತಪೋಧನ, ಶಿರಸ್ + ಧರೆ = ಶಿರೋಧರೆ, ಮನಸ್ + ನಿಗ್ರಹ = ಮನೋನಿಗ್ರಹ, ತಪಸ್ + ಬಲ = ತಪೋಬಲ, ಮನಸ್ + ಭವ = ಮನೋಭವ, ಶಿರಸ್ + ಮಣಿ = ಶಿರೋಮಣಿ, ಮನಸ್ + ಯೋಗ = ಮನೋಯೋಗ, ಮನಸ್ + ರಥ = ಮನೋರಥ, ಮನಸ್ + ಲಯ = ಮನೋಲಯ, ಮನಸ್ + ವಿಕಾರ = ಮನೋವಿಕಾರ, ಮನಸ್ + ಹರ = ಮನೋಹರ.

ಸ್ before the consonants ಕ, ಖ, ಪ, ಫ, ಶ, ಸ becomes ಃ, *e. g.* ತಪಸ್ + ಕ್ಲೇಶ = ತಪಃಕ್ಲೇಶ, ಧನುಸ್ + ಖಣ್ಡ = ಧನುಃಖಣ್ಡ, ಚಕ್ಷುಸ್ + ಪಥ = ಚಕ್ಷುಃಪಥ, ತಪಸ್ + ಪ್ರಭವ = ತಪಃಪ್ರಭವ, ತಪಸ್, + ಫಲ = ತಪಃಫಲ, ಆಯುಸ್ + ಶೇಷ = ಆಯುಃಶೇಷ, ತಪಸ್ + ಶೀಲ = ತಪಃಶೀಲ (or ತಪಶೀಲ), ಮನಸ್ + ಶಾನ್ತಿ = ಮನಃಶಾನ್ತಿ (or ಮನಶ್ಶಾನ್ತಿ), ಹವಿಸ್ + ಶೇಷ = ಹವಿಃಶೇಷ, ಚಕ್ಷುಸ್ ಶ್ರವಸ್ = ಚಕ್ಷುಃಶ್ರವಸ್, ತಪಸ್ + ಸಾಧ್ಯ = ತಪಃಸಾಧ್ಯ, ಮನಸ್ + ಸಾಕ್ಷಿ = ಮನಃಸಾಕ್ಷಿ (or ಮನಸ್ಸಾಕ್ಷಿ), ಬಹಿಸ್ + ಸಂಸ್ಥ = ಬಹಿಃಸಂಸ್ಥ.

ಸ್ (preceded by ಇ, ಉ, ಓ) before the consonants ಗ, ಜ, ದ, ಧ, ನ, ಬ, ಭ, ಮ, ಯ, ಲ, ವ, ಹ becomes ರ್, *e. g.* ಬಹಿಸ್ + ನಿರ್ಗಮನ = ಬಹಿರ್ನಿರ್ಗಮನ, ಜ್ಯೋತಿಸ್ + ಮಯ = ಜ್ಯೋತಿರ್ಮಯ, ಬಹಿಸ್ + ವೇದಿ = ಬಹಿರ್ವೇದಿ, ಧನುಸ್ + ಗುಣ = ಧನುರ್ಗುಣ, ಧನುಸ್ + ಜ್ಯಾ = ಧನುರ್ಜ್ಯಾ, ಧನುಸ್ + ದಣ್ಡ = ಧನುರ್ದಣ್ಡ,

ಧನುಸ್ + ಧರ = ಧನುರ್ಧರ, ಧನುಸ್ + ಬಲ = ಧನುರ್ಬಲ, ಬಹಿಸ್ + ಭಾಗ = ಬಹಿರ್ಭಾಗ, ಧನುಸ್ + ಮಧ್ಯ = ಧನುರ್ಮಧ್ಯ, ಧನುಸ್ + ಯಾಸ = ಧನುರ್ಯಾಸ, ಯಜುಸ್ + ಲಕ್ಷ್ಮಿ = ಯಜುರ್ಲಕ್ಷ್ಮಿ, ಆಯುಸ್ + ವೇದ = ಆಯುರ್ವೇದ, ಧನುಸ್ + ಹಸ್ತ = ಧನುರ್ಹಸ್ತ, ದೋಸ್ + ದಣ್ಡ = ದೋರ್ದಣ್ಡ, ದೋಸ್ + ಬಲ = ದೋರ್ಬಲ.

ಸ್ before ಚ and ಛ becomes ಶ್, *e. g.* ತಪಸ್ + ಚರಣ = ತಪಶ್ಚರಣ, ಪಯಸ್ + ಚಯ = ಪಯಶ್ಚಯ, ಉರಸ್ + ಛದ = ಉರಶ್ಛದ, ಶಿರಸ್ + ಛೇದ = ಶಿರಶ್ಛೇದ.

ಸ್ (preceded by ಇ and ಉ) before the consonants ಕ, ಪ, ಮ often becomes ಷ್, *e. g.* ಬಹಿಸ್ + ಕೃತ = ಬಹಿಷ್ಕೃತ, ಸರ್ಪಿಸ್ + ಕುಣ್ಡಿಕೆ = ಸರ್ಪಿಷ್ಕುಣ್ಡಿಕೆ, ಆಯುಸ್ + ಕಾಮ = ಆಯುಷ್ಕಾಮ, ಧನುಸ್ + ಕೋಟಿ = ಧನುಷ್ಕೋಟಿ (or ಧನುಃಕೋಟಿ), ಧನುಸ್ + ಪಟ = ಧನುಷ್ಪಟ (or ಧನುಃಪಟ), ಚಕ್ಷುಸ್ + ಪತಿ = ಚಕ್ಷುಷ್ಪತಿ, ಸರ್ಪಿಸ್ + ಮತ್ = ಸರ್ಪಿಷ್ಮತ್, ಧನುಸ್ + ಮತ್ = ಧನುಷ್ಮತ್.

VIII. Particulars of some letters, also in prosody.

217. That the vowels ಎ, ಐ, ಒ and ಔ are no real diphthongs, *i. e.* compound vowels, in true Kannaḍa has been stated in § 21. Kannaḍa ಎ does never arise of ಇ preceded by ಅ, nor its ಒ of ಉ preceded by ಅ, *i. e.* they are never formed by Saṁskṛita guṇa (§ 22); likewise its ಐ does never arise of ಇ, ಈ and ಎ, nor its ಔ of ಉ, ಊ and ಒ, *i. e.* they are never formed by Saṁskṛita vṛiddhi (§ 22). ಎ, ಐ, ಒ, ಔ are innate (sahaja) in Kannaḍa or exist therein by nature (svabhâva). Kêšava states that an ಅಯ್ or ಅಯಿ may optionally be written ಐ, *e. g.* ಕಯ್ವಾರಂ may be written ಕೈವಾರಂ, ಕೋರಯಿಸಿದಂ ಕೋರೈಸಿದಂ, ತೇರಯಿಸಿದಂ ತೇರೈಸಿದಂ, ತೆಲ್ಲಯಿಸಿದಂ ತೆಲ್ಲೈಸಿದಂ, ಹೊಲ್ಲಯಿಸಿದಂ ಹೊಲ್ಲೈಸಿದಂ (see § 151, under remarks); and an ಅವು ಔ, *e. g.* ಕವುಂಗು may be written ಕೌಂಗು, ಕವುಂಕುಳ್ ಕೌಂಕುಳ್, ಅವುಂಕಿದಂ ಔಂಕಿದಂ, ಅವುಣ್ಡು ಔಣ್ಡು, ಕವುಣ್ಡೆ ಕೌಣ್ಡೆ, ತವುಂಕಲ್ ತೌಂಕಲ್. It is also customary to write ಅವ for ಔ, as ಕವರು for ಕೌರು, ಸವಳು for ಸೌಳು (see § 21).

218. In § 29 letters with strong aspiration or aspirates have been mentioned, in § 212, remark 3 it has been stated that some Kannaḍa adverbs of circumstance and some imitative sounds exhibit aspirates;

and in § 215, 7, *c* the aspirate ಛ್ has been introduced, for which there is the instance ಪದಿನೆಣ್ಛಾಸಿರಂ ಲೋಹಪಕ್ಕರೆಯ ಜಾತ್ಯಶ್ವಂಗಳಿಛ್ಛಾಸಿರಂ ಮದಮಂ ಮುಕ್ಕುಳಿಸಿರ್ದ ದನ್ತಿಘಟೆಗಳ್, ನೂಛ್ಛಾಸಿರಂಗಳ ವ್ರೋಲಾಯ್ತು ರಥಕಡುವೇಗದಿಂ.

Aspirates, however, are rare in pure Kannaḍa. The grammarian Kêšava adduces the following probably for the greatest part uncommon Tadbhava terms (regarding the form of which MSS. disagree; *cf.* § 370) in which aspirates are used — ವಕ್ಖಾಣ (o. r. ವಖ್ಖಾಣ), ದೆಖ್ಖಾಣ (o. r. ದೆಖ್ಖಾಳ), ಪಖ್ಖಾಳ (§ 370), ಅಖ್ಖಣ್ಡ (o. r. ಅಖ್ಖಡ), ಖೊಪ್ಪರ, ಖಾಣ, ಖಾರಿಗೆ (§ 370), ಛಲ್ಲ (o. r. ಛಲ್ಲಿ), ಛರ್ಪಿಸು (o. r. ಛಪ್ಪಿಸು), ಎಕ್ಕಛಾಯ (o. r. ಎಕ್ಕಥಾಯ), ಠಾವು, ಠಾಣ, ತಕ್ಕಿಸು (o. r. ಠೆಕ್ಕಿಸು), ಠಾಣಿಸು, ಥಟ್ಟು, ಥಾಪಣೆ (§ 370), ಸುತ್ಥಣೆ (o. rs. ಸುತ್ಥಣೆಯಂ, ಸತ್ಥಣೆ), ಮತ್ಥವಟ್ಟಿಗೆ (?), ಕಥಾಯ (o. r. ಕಥ್ಥಾಯಿ), ಫಳೆಯಕಾಱಿ, ಫೆಳಾವುಗ, ಫೆಳಿ (probably ಫೇಳಿ), ಅಫಳಿಯ (o. r. ಅಪ್ಫಳೆಯ), ಫಱಿಯ, ಫಾಱಿಗೆ (o. r. ಫಾರಿಗೆ), ಫೋಱಿಗೆ (§ 370), ಘೋಸ, ಘಾಸಿ (o. r. ಘಾಸೆ), ಘಾಸರ, ಝುಳ (§ 370), ಝುಳಕ (o. r. ಝುಱಿಕ; § 370), ಝುಲ್ಲಱಿ (§ 370), ಝೂಳಿಸು, ಝುಱಿಸು (?), ಝುಳಪಿಸು (o. r. ಝುಱಿಪಿಸು), ಝುಲ್ಲಿ, ಝುಂಕೆ, ಢೊಂಕಣಿ, ಢೆಂಕಣಿ, ಢೊಕ್ಕರ, ಢೆಂಕೆ, ಢಾಳ, ಅಢಾಳ (?), ವೇಢೆಯ, ಧಱಿ, ಧಾಳಿ (§ 370), ಧೂಳಿ (?, § 370), ಧಾರಿ (?), ಧವಳ (ಧವಡ), ಧನಿ (§ 370), ಭಂಗಾರ, ಭಣ್ಡಾರ, ಭರಿಕೆಯ್, ಭಲ್ಲೆಯ, ಭಾವ; ಕವ್ಭ or ಕಮ್ಬ, ಭಾಸೆ or ಬಾಸೆ (§ 370).

The true place of aspirates is in some Kannaḍa adverbs of circumstance (§ 212, 4 and remark 3, that originally were imitative sounds), *e. g.* ಖಣಿಲನೆ, ಖಱಿಲನೆ, ಖಱಿಲೆ, ಘಱಿಲನೆ, ಧಿಗಿಲನೆ, ಭೋಂಕನೆ, ಭೋಂಕಲ್, ಭೋರನೆ; **and in some imitative sounds** (§ 212, 9), *e. g.* ಛಟಛಟಂ, ಝುಮ್ಮನೆ, ಢಮ್ಮನೆ, ದುಢುಮ್ಮನೆ, ಧಱಿಮ್ಮನೆ, ಧುಮ್ಮನೆ, ಘುಱಿಮ್ಮನೆ (o. r. ಘುಱುಮ್ಮನೆ), ಛಱಿಲನೆ, ಫಱಿಲನೆ, ಪಠಿಲ್ಲನೆ, ಭುಗಿಲ್, ಭೋರ್, ಛಲಲಲೆ, ಛಮ್ಮನೆ, ಧಣಮ್ಮನೆ, ಝುಲುಮ್ಮನೆ, ಝುಲ್ಲನೆ, ಝುಳಮ್ಮನೆ, ಥೊಪ್ಪನೆ, ಧೊಪ್ಪನೆ, ಫ್ರೊಟ್ಟನೆ (the form of a few of which is doubtful).

219. In § 33 it has been stated that **the letters** ಯ, ಲ, ವ **are not nasal and sometimes nasal.** Such is the case in some Kannaḍa and Tadbhava (§ 370) words. According to Kêšava ಯ is not nasal in ಬಯಕೆ, ಬಿಯದ, ಬಿಯಳ, ದಯಕಾಱಿ, ದಾಯಿಗ, ವಾಯ, ಬಯಲ್, and nasal in ಮೇಯಿಸಿದಂ, ಸೋಯಿಸಿದಂ, ಮಯಣ, ನಯಣ, ಮಾಯ; ಲ is not nasal in ಹಾಲಿಗೆ, ಹಲಸಿಗ, ಹಲಗೆ, ನೆಲಕಲ, and nasal in ಕೊಲ್ಲಣಿಗೆ, ಅಲ್ಲಣಿಗೆ, ಹಲ್ಲಣ, ಇಲ್ಲಣ; ವ is not nasal in ಕವಳ, ಹವಳ, ತಿವಳಿ, ತವಕ, and nasal in ಸೇವ, ಸೋವೆ, ಸಾವೆ, ಜಾವ, ಪಾವ, ಮಾವನ್ತ, ಕೋವಣ, ಕಾವಣ, ಸೇವಗೆ, ಸೋವಿ.

220. In § 39 it has been shown **how the upper nasals without a** vowel may take the form of the circlet called sŏnnĕ, and in § 40 how they also in connection with a vowel may take that form. We give here an ancient Kanda verse quoted by Kêšava in which not the sŏnnĕ, but **the vargapañčama letters** (§ 28) themselves have been used:

ಬಿಙ್ಕಮ್ಬೆತ್ತೆಸೆವಞ್ಚೆಯ
ಸಙ್ಕುಳಮುಂ ತೊಣ್ಡುಗೆಡೆವ ಶುಕಸಾರಿಕೆಯುಂ ।
ಸೊಙ್ಕಿ, ಬಲವನ್ದು ತೀಡುವ
ತೆಙ್ಕಣ ಗಾಳಿಯುಮದೇಮ್ಮನಙ್ಗಳಿಸುದುವೋ? ॥

His further instances refer to final ೦ or sŏnnĕ (see § 215, 8) which may likewise take the form of the vargapañčama letters without and within compounds, *e. g.* ಅವಂ ಕಡುಗಲಿ may be written ಅವಙ್ಕಡುಗಲಿ, ಅವಂ ಚಲವಾದಿ ಅವಞ್ಚಲವಾದಿ, ಕರಂ ಟಕ್ಕಂ ಕರಣ್ಟಕ್ಕಂ; ಕೆಂದಳಿರ್ ಕೆನ್ದಳಿರ್, ಕೆಂಮಣ್ ಕೆಮ್ಮಣ್, ಹೊಂಬಣ್ಣಂ ಹೊಮ್ಬಣ್ಣಂ, ಪೊಂಮದಿಲ್ ಪೊಮ್ಮದಿಲ್.

221. There are **several words that** in the ancient dialect **always have the sŏnnĕ or bindu** (§ 34) or are nityabindugaḷ, *e. g.* ಬೆಡಂಗು, ಕಡಂಗು, ಅಡಂಗು, ತೊಡಂಬೆ (ತೊಡಮ್ಬೆ), ತೊಡಂಕು, ಕೊಡಂತಿ (ಕೊಡನ್ತಿ), etc. (see Šabdamaṇidarpaṇa p. 48; Šabdânušâsana p. 69). In the mediæval and modern dialect this rule is not found; there is rather the tendency of leaving out the sŏnnĕ, especially in the modern one wherein scarcely once the sŏnnĕ is employed.

Other words of the ancient dialect **optionally appear with the bindu and without** it or are sabinduka and abinduka words, *e. g.* ಕದಂಪು (ಕದಮ್ಪು), ಕದಪು; ಕೊಡಂಕೆ, ಕೊಡಕೆ; ಇಱಿಂಪೆ (ಇಱಿಮ್ಪೆ), ಇಱಿಪೆ; ನೊರಂಜು, ನೊರಜು.

Others of the same dialect **appear always with double letters** or are nityadvitvaṅgaḷ, *e. g.* ಪಪ್ಪುಕ, ಬಿಪ್ಪಣ್ಡ, ತಿಪ್ಪುೞ್, ಬಗ್ಗ, ಮೊಗ್ಗರ, ಕೊಬ್ಬು, ಕಱ್ತೆ, ತೊಱ್ತು, etc. This rule holds good also in the other dialects and regarding the same words as far as they occur in them.

222. It has been remarked in § 215 (7, remark after *f*) that in samâsas or compounds ನ್ **preceded by** ಣ್ **may become** ಣ್. Such is also the case in the ancient dialect when there is no composition of words (asamâsa, bhinnapada), *e. g.* ಕಣ್ ನೊನ್ದಪುದು may become ಕಣ್ಣೊನ್ದಪುದು, ಪುಣ್ ನಾಳಿವೋದಪುದು ಪುಣ್ಣಾಳಿವೋದಪುದು, ಜಾಣ್ ನೆರೆದಪುದು ಜಾಣ್ಣೆರೆದಪ್ಪುದು.

223. **The change of the letter** ಪ **into** ಹ has been referred to in §§ 64 and 184. Kêšava teaches that in Kannaḍa and Tadbhava words an initial ಪ may optionally be changed into ಹ, *e. g.* ಪನ್ದರ್ may become ಹನ್ದರ್,

ಪನಿ ಹನ್ದಿ, ಪುಲಿ ಹುಲಿ, ಪಲಗೆ, ಹಲಗೆ, ಪಲಸು ಹಲಸು (see § 370), and says that this change is (especially) beautiful (sundara, čelvu) in a provincial or native dialect (dêŝi).

But the change is bad (dushkara) and as a rule does not occur, if ಪ is not initial and is a double letter (dvitva), *e. g.* ಉಪ್ಪರಂ, ಕಪ್ಪುರಂ, ಟಿಪ್ಪಣಂ, ತಪ್ಪು, ಬಿಪ್ಪಣ್ಣಂ, ಮುಪ್ಪು, ಮುಪ್ಪುರಿ, ಸೊಪ್ಪು, ಹೆಪ್ಪು.

Howbeit, as we have learned already from § 184 (*cf.* § 194), the present-future participle **ಅಪ್ಪ** exceptionally becomes **ಅಹ**, also when it stands at the end of ಅನ್ತು, ಇನ್ತು, ಉನ್ತು, ಎನ್ತು, *viz.* ಅನ್ತಹ, being such as that, ಇನ್ತಹ, being such as this, ಉನ್ತಹ, being such as this intermediate one, ಎನ್ತಹ, being like what?, which forms occur as well in the mediæval dialect (except ಉನ್ತಹ) as in the ancient one.

Besides, the mediæval dialect has changed ಅನ್ತಹ, ಇನ್ತಹ and ಎನ್ತಹ into ಅನ್ಥ, ಇನ್ಥ and ಎನ್ಥ, and, with a euphonic ಅ into ಅನ್ಥಾ, ಇನ್ಥಾ and ಎನ್ಥಾ, which forms exist also in the modern one; at the same time the modern one has also the mutilated forms ಅನ್ತ, ಇನ್ತ, ಎನ್ತ; ಅನ್ತಾ, ಇನ್ತಾ, ಎನ್ತಾ. See § 224.

224. Kêŝava says that ಅನ್ತಹ, ಇನ್ತಹ, ಉನ್ತಹ, ಎನ್ತಹ (§ 223) in the ancient dialect become ಅನ್ನ, ಇನ್ನ, ಉನ್ನ, ಎನ್ನ (*cf.* § 275), and, with the addition of ಅ, he, and ಂ, the sign of the nominative (§ 115), ಅನ್ನಂ, such a man as that, ಇನ್ನಂ, such a man as this, ಉನ್ನಂ, such a man as this intermediate one, ಎನ್ನಂ, what kind of man?

He gives the following instances in which **the genitive precedes** ಅನ್ನಂ, etc.

*ಸಿಡಿಲನ್ನಂ ಸಿಂಗದನ್ನಂ ಪುರಹರನುರಿಗಣ್ಣನ್ನನೀ ನಾರಸಿಂಹಂ । Nârasiṁha is a man like a thunder-bolt, one like a lion, one like the flaming eye of Ŝiva.

ಮನಸಿಜನೆನ್ನನಿನ್ನನರುಣಪ್ರಿಯಸನ್ನನನೆನ್ನನಿನ್ನನಾ ದಿನಕರನೆನ್ನನಿನ್ನಂ । what kind of person Kâma is, such a one is this man; what kind of being the beloved son of Aruṇa (Jaṭâyu) is, such a one is this man; what kind of being the sun is, such a one is this man.

The feminine of ಅನ್ನಂ is **ಅನ್ನಳ್** (ಅನ್ನ+ಅಳ್, she, § 193 under remarks), *e. g.* ಮನದನ್ನಳ್, such a woman as (is agreeable to) the heart, a dear woman, which takes also the form of **ಅನ್ನೆ**, *e. g.* ಮನದನ್ನೆ.

The neuter is **ಅನ್ನದು** (ಅನ್ನ+ಅದು), such a child, etc. as that.

With reference to the terms ಅನ್ಥ, ಇನ್ಥ and ಎನ್ಥ, etc. in § 223 it is to be stated that the masculine forms are ಅನ್ಥವನು (ಅನ್ಥವಂ, *i. e.* ಅನ್ಥ+ಅವನು,

ಅಸ್ಥ+ಅವಂ), such a man as that, ಇಸ್ಥವನು (ಇಸ್ಥವಂ), such a man as this, ಎಸ್ಥವನು (ಎಸ್ಥವಂ), what kind of man?, the feminine ಅಸ್ಥವಳು (ಅಸ್ಥವಳ್), ಇಸ್ಥವಳು (ಇಸ್ಥವಳ್), ಎಸ್ಥವಳು (ಎಸ್ಥವಳ್), and the neuter ones ಅಸ್ಥದು, ಇಸ್ಥದು, ಎಸ್ಥದು.

If ಅಸ್ಥವನು, ಅಸ್ಥವಳು, ಅಸ್ಥದು are added to another word, this is put in the genitive, *e. g.* ನಿನ್ನಸ್ಥವನು, such a man as thou, ತಾಯಿಯಸ್ಥವಳು, such a woman as a mother, ಸಕ್ಕರೆಯಸ್ಥದು, such a thing as sugar, (or also ನಿನ್ನಸ್ಥಾವನು, ತಾಯಿಯಸ್ಥಾವಳು, ಸಕ್ಕರೆಯಸ್ಥಾದು, *cf.* § 223).

225. The letter ಮ appears also as ವ, as for ತಾಮರೆ there is likewise ತಾವರೆ, for ಸಾಮನ್ತಂ ಸಾವನ್ತಂ, for ತಿಮಿರ್ ತಿವಿರ್, for ತೆಮರ್ ತೆವರ್, and for ಸಾಮಿ ಸಾವಿ. See the datives plural ಎಮಗೆ and ಎವಗೆ, ತಮಗೆ and ತವಗೆ in § 137, *b;* § 304.

226. Regarding the lengthening of the letter ಅ into ಆ in the accusative and genitive singular (see § 141) Kêśava quotes the following instances:

ಎನಿತ್ತೆನಿತ್ತಮ್ಬುಜಪತ್ರನೇತ್ರೆಯಾ
ಘನಸ್ತನಂಗಳ್ ಒಳಿಗುಂ ಕಿರಾತೆಯಾ, ।
ಅನಿತ್ತನಿತ್ತಂ ವನದೊಳ್ ವನೇಚರಂ
ತನತ್ತು ಬಿಲ್ಲಾನದನಸ್ತೆ ಕೀಸುಗುಂ. ॥ (see § 303, 2, *a*).
ಈದ ಪುಲಿಯಾ ಪೋಲಿರ್ದಳ್ ।

and adds that such a lengthening occurs optionally within some words, as one may use ಇನ್ದೊಳ or ಇನ್ದೋಳ (Tadbhava of ಹಿನ್ದೋಲ), ಆರೊಗಿಸಿದಂ or ಆರೋಗಿಸಿದಂ, ಎಣೆಗೊಣಂ or ಎಣೆಗೋಣಂ, ಗೇಯಂಗಂ or ಗೇಯಾಂಗಂ.

227. In §§ 15. 17 (under ಳ) and 31 the so-called ಕ್ಷಳ (a grammatical invention) has been introduced. A few instances showing how it may be optionally used for Saṁskṛita ಲ, are the following: ಜಳ or ಜಲ, ತಿಳ or ತಿಲ, ಫಳ or ಫಲ, ಬಳ or ಬಲ, ಖಿಳ or ಖಿಲ, ಕಮಳ or ಕಮಲ, ಕುಳ or ಕುಲ, ಅಳಿ or ಅಲಿ, ಸಳಿಲ or ಸಲಿಲ, ಮಳ or ಮಲ, ಮರಾಳ or ಮರಾಲ. *Cf.* § 231, also §§ 239. 370.

228. The so-called ಕುಳ or the Kannaḍa ಳ (that in fact is not different in form and sound from the so-called ಕ್ಷಳ of § 227) has been mentioned in §§ 15. 17 (under ಳ) and 31. Kêśava adduces a few of the words in which it has to occur, *viz.* ಇಳಿದಳಿಯು, ಎಳಿದ, ಸೂಕುಳಿ, ಓಕುಳಿ, ಕಳಲಿು, ಪೆಳಲಿು, ಮದುಕುಳಿ, ಅಳಿಯ, ಕುಳಿಯ, ಪೊಳಿಗೆ, ಜಾಳಿಗೆ, ತಳಿಗೆ, ಬಳಿಲ್,

ಬಳಸು, ಬಳಸಿಗ, ಮೊಳೆ, ಆಳಿಸಿದ, ಪೇಳಿಸಿದ, ಕೇಳ, ಜೂದಾಳಿ, ಅಳಿಲೆ, ಕಳವಳ, ಮೆಯ್ಮೇಳ, ಮಾಳ, ತಾಳಿಗೆ, ಈಳಿಗೆ, ಇಱುಕುಳಿ[1].

Rustics use ಳ erroneously (according to Kêšava) in the Kannaḍa words ಬೆರಲ್, ಎರಲ್, ಒರಲ್, ಕೊರಲ್, ಸರಲ್, ಅರಲ್, ಪರಲ್, ಮರಲ್, ನರಲ್, pronouncing them ಬೆರಳ್ (ಬೆರಳು), ಎರಳ್ (ಎರಳು), ಒರಳ್ (ಒರಳು), ಕೊರಳ್, ಸರಳ್, ಅರಳ್, ಪರಳ್, ಮರಳ್, ನರಳ್. ಎರಳೆ often stands for ಎರಲೆ.

Occasionally ಳ is also **represented by** ಣ, *e. g.* ಅಳಿಲೆ or ಅಣಿಲೆ, ಓಳಿ or ಓಣಿ, ಕೊಳ or ಕೊಣ, ಕೊಳಗು or ಕೊಣಗು, ಗಂಜಳಿ or ಗಂಜಣಿ, ಗಿಣಿ or ಗಿಳಿ, ನೊಳ or ನೊಣ, ಮಳಲ್ or ಮಣಲ್, ಗಳೆ (the ancient ಗಱೆ) or ಗಣೆ, ಕೊತ್ತಳಿ (the ancient ಕೊತ್ತಱಿ) or ಕೊತ್ತಣಿ, ತಲ್ಲಳ (the ancient ತಲ್ಲಱ) or ತಲ್ಲಣ, ಸೆಳಸು or ಸೆಣಸು. *Cf.* § 235.

ಳ is frequently employed **for the ancient** ಱ in the mediæval and modern dialect (see § 32) in which *e. g.* ಅಱ್ appears as ಅಳ್ (ಅಳು), ಅಱೆ as ಅಳೆ, ಇಱೆ as ಇಳೆ, ಉಱ್ as ಉಳು, ಕಱೆ as ಕಳೆ, ಪೊಱೆ as ಪೊಳೆ or ಹೊಳೆ, which peculiarity partly dates back about as far as 900 A. D. (see § 32, note). As stated in the same paragraph, the letter ಱ has has been retained in the present grammar.

About **the change of** ಟ **into** ಳ see § 229, and about that of ಡ into ಳ § 230. For words in which ಳ or ಱ may occur see § 232.

229. Letter ಟ is **changed into** ಳ in the following words when they are in the apabhraṁša state or are tadbhavas *i. e.* words corrupted from Saṁskṛita — ಸ್ಫಟಿಕ, ಪೇಟಿಕೆ, ವೀಟಿಕೆ, ಘುಟಿಕೆ, ವರಾಟ, ರಘಟೆ, ಸ್ಫುಟ, ಸ್ಫೋಟಕ, ಲಮ್ಪಟ, in which case their forms are ಪಳಿಕ, ಪೇಳಿಗೆ, ವೀಳಿಗೆ, ಗುಳಿಗೆ, ಪರಾಳ, ರಗಳೆ, ಪುಳ, ಹೋಳಿಗೆ, ಲಮ್ಪಳ. ಸ್ಫೋಟಕ and ಲಮ್ಪಟ may once appear as ಹೋಱಿಗೆ and ಲಮ್ಪಱ. See § 370.

230. When the words ದಾಡಿಮ, ಕೂಷ್ಮಾಣ್ಡ, ಗೌಡ, ಗುಡ, ಝುಗಡೆ, ವಿಡಂಗ, and ಏಡಕ are in the apabhraṁša state or are tadbhavas *i. e.* words corrupted from Saṁskṛita, their ಡ is usually **converted into** ಳ, and they appear as ದಾಳಿಮ್ಬ, ಕುಮ್ಬಳ, ಗೌಳ, ಗುಳ, ಝುಗಳೆ (ಜಗಳೆ), ವಿಳಂಗ, and ಏಳಗ. See § 370. (The change of ಡ into ಳ takes place also in Saṁskṛita itself; *cf.* § 15.)

---

[1] As there evidently are a few Tadbhavas (regarding which see § 370) among the words, it seems as if, at least in this case, such words on account of their ಳ (that was taken for the ಕುಳ) were considered to have become true Kannaḍa words, losing their Tadbhava character.

231. In the apabhraṁśa or tadbhava state the letters ಟ, ಠ, ತ, ರ, and the ಕ್ಷಳ (see § 227) of the words ಘಟಿಕೆ, ಘೋಟಿಕೆ, ಧಾಟಿ, ಲಾಟ, ಲಾಟಭಾಷಿಕ, ಘೋಟಾರೂಢ, ಕುಕ್ಕುಟ, ಮಠಿಕೆ, ಪೀಠಿಕೆ, ಪ್ರತಿಹಸ್ತ, ಪ್ರತಿಪಾದುಕ, ಕ್ರೂರ, ಝುಲ್ಲರಿ, ತಾಳ (ತಾಲ), ಪುಳಿನ (ಪುಲಿನ), ಕಳಮ (ಕಲಮ), ಅರ್ಗಳ (ಅರ್ಗಲ), ಮನ್ಯಾಳಿ (ಮನ್ಯಾಲಿ, o. r. ಮಾನ್ಯಾಳಿ), and ಅಳಿಕಾಬದ್ಧ (ಅಲಿಕಾಬದ್ಧ) become ಱ according to Kêśava, in which case the words appear as ಗಱಿಗೆ, ಗೋಱಿಗೆ, ದಾಱಿ, ಲಾಱಿ, ಲಾಱಬಾಸೆಗ, ಗೋಱಾಯಿಲ, ಕೋೞಿ, ಮಱಿಗೆ, ಪೀಱಿಗ, ಪಱಿಹತ್ತ, ಪಱಿವಾವುಗೆ, ಕೂಱ್, ಝುಲ್ಲಱಿ, ತಾಱ್, ಪುೞಿಲ್, ಕಱವೆ, ಅಗುೞಿ, ಮನ್ನಱಿ, and ಅಱಿಗೆವದ್ದ. See § 370.

The Śabdânuśâsana (under its sûtra 140) adds ಪರ್ಪಟ=ಹಪ್ಪಱ, ಆಕ್ಷೋಟ=ಅಕ್ಷೋಱ, ಮಾತರ=ಮಾಱಲ, ಪಾಠೀನ=ಪಾಱಿಲ್, ಅತಿಪಾತ=ಅಱಿವಾದ, ಮರಿಚ=ಮೆಱಸು (see § 370), ವಾಗುರಾ=ಬಾಗುೞಿ, ಭೃಂಗಾರಿ=ಬಿಂಗಱಿ, ಅಂಗಾರ=ಇಂಗಱ, ವಾಹ್ಯಾಳಿ=ವಯ್ಯಾೞಿ.

232. There are twelve words regarding which it is to be remarked that it is somewhat **doubtful** whether they ought to be written with ಳ or ಱ; they are ಝುಳಕ or ಝುಱಕ (§ 370), ಝುಳಿಪಿಸು or ಝುೞಿಪಿಸು, ಜೊಂಗುಳಿ or ಜೊಂಗುೞಿ, ಬೊಮ್ಮುಳಿ or ಬೊಮ್ಮುೞಿ, ಅಳಮಾಳ or ಅಱಮಾಱ, ತಮಾಳ or ತಮಾಱ, ಪಳಿಗೆ or ಪೞಿಗೆ (§ 370), ಒಸ್ದುಳಿ or ಒಸ್ದುೞಿ, ಜಂಗುಳಿ or ಜಂಗುೞಿ, ಪುತ್ತಳಿ or ಪುತ್ತೞಿ (§ 370), ಗೋಳಿ or ಗೋೞಿ, ಪೇಳಿ or ಪೇೞಿ (o. r. ಫೇಳಿ or ಫೇೞಿ; § 370). *Cf.* ಸ್ಫೋಟಕ and ಲಮ್ಪಟ in § 229.

233. Kêśava saw the following **words with** ಱ in the works of the first great poets:—

ಅಗಱ್ತೆ, ಅಗುೞ್, ಅಗ್ಗಱಿಕೆ (o. r. ಅರ್ಗಱಿಕೆ), ಅದವಱಲ್, ಅವಗಱಿಯ, ಅಸಕಱಿ, ಅಱ್, ಅಱಿ, ಅಱಿವು, (ಅಱ್ಕಜ), ಅಱ್ಕಿಮೆ, ಅಱ್ಕಿಱ್, ಅಱ್ಕೆ, ಅಱ್ತಿ, ಅಱ್ದು, ಆಱ್, ಆಱಾಱಿಗ, ಆಱಿ, ಇಕ್ಕುಱ್, ಇೞಿ, ಈಱ್, (ಉಗುೞಿ), ಉಣ್ಬಱಿ (o. r. ಉಮ್ಬಱಿ), ಉಱ್, ಉಱಿ, ಉಱಿಕು, ಉಱಿಗ, ಉಱಿವು, ಉಱುಗು (o. r. ಉಱಿಗು), ಉಱ್ಕೆ, ಎಸಱ್, ಎಱ್, ಎಱಲ್, ಎಱವು, ಎಱೆ, ಎಱ್ಚಿಱ್, ಎಱ್ತು, ಎಱ್ಬಿಸು, ಏಱ್, ಒಱ್ಕು, ಒಱ್ಗು, ಕಜ್ಜಱಿ, ಕಱಕಱಿಸು, ಕಱಕುಱ, ಕಱಲ್, ಕಱಲೆ, ಕಱಿ, ಕಱಿಲೆ, ಕಱಿವು, (ಕಱು), ಕಱ್ಕನೆ, (ಕಱ್ಗು), ಕಱ್ತಲೆ, ಕಱ್ತೆ, ಕಿಮುಱ್ಚು, ಕಿಮುಱ್ದುಱಿ, ಕಿಱ್, ಕಿಱ್ಗು, ಕೀಱ್, ಕುಱ, ಕುಱ್, (ಕುಱ್ಗು), ಕೂಱ, ಕೆಱಿವ (o. r. ಕೆಱವ), ಕೇೞಿ, ಕೊಂಕುಱ್ (o. r. ಕವುಂಕುಱ್), ಕೊತ್ತಱಿ, ಕೊಱಲ್, ಕೊಱೆ, ಖಱಿಲ್, ಗಱಗಱ, ಗಱಗಱನೆ, ಗಱಪ, ಗಱಿಯಿಸು (see ಘಱಿಯಿಸು), ಗಱೆ, ಗೀಱಿಡು, ಗುಱ, ಗುಱುಗುಱು, ಗೆಱಸು, ಗೋೞಿಡು, ಘಱಿಯ, ಘಱಿಯಿಸು (o. r. ಗಱಿಯಿಸು), ಘಱಿಲ್,

ಘುೞಿಂ, ಘುೞುಂ, ಚಕ್ಕೞಿ, ಚಾೞ್, ಛೞಿಲ್, ಜಗುೞ್, ಜೀಕೊರ್ೞಿವಿ, ತಲ್ಲೞಿ, ತೞ ತೞಿ, ತೞತೞನೆ, ತೞಿಲ್, ತೞಿ, ತೞೆ, ತೞ್ಕಿಯಪ್ಪು, ತೞ್ಗು, ತೞ್ತೞಿ, ತಾೞ್, ತಿಪ್ಪೞ್, ತುಪ್ಪೞ್, (ತುಮುೞ್), ತುೞಿ, ತುೞಿಕಲ್, ತುೞಿಲ್, ತೆಗೞ್, ತೇೞ್, ತೊೞಿಲ್, ತೊೞ್ತು, ತೊೞ್ತುೞಿ, ದಣ್ಡೞಿಗ, ದೞಿ, ದೞಿದುೞಿ (o. r. ದೞಿವೃೞಿ), ದೞ್ದೞಿ, ಧೞಿಂ, ನಾೞ, ನಾೞವಾಸಗೆ, (ನುೞ್ಗು), ನೆಗೞ್, ನೆಗೞ್ತೆ, ನೇೞಿಲ್, ನೆೞಿಲ್, ನೆೞ್ಕಿಸೆ, ಪೞಿಗ, ಪೞದು, ಪೞಪೞನೆ, ಪೞಿಪು, ಪೞಯಿಗೆ, (ಪೞಿಸು), ಪೞಹ, ಪೞಿ, ಪೞಿವು, ಪೞ್ಕೆ, ಪೞ್ತೆ, ಪೞ್ಪೞನೆ, ಪಾೞ್, ಪಾೞಿ, ಪುಚ್ಚೞಿ, ಪುೞು, ಪುೞ್ಗು, ಪೆೞಕು, ಪೆೞವ, ಪೇೞ್, ಪೊಕ್ಕೞ್, ಪೊಗೞ್ತೆ, (ಪೊದೞ್ or ಪೊದಳ್), ಪೊಮ್ಪೞಿ, ಪೊೞಕು, ಪೊೞಲ್, ಪೊೞೆ, ಪೊೞ್ತಿಡೆ, ಪೊೞ್ತು, ಪೋೞ್, ಪೋೞಲ್, ಫೞಿಲ್, ಬೞ್, ಬೞಿ, ಬೞಿಕಂ, ಬೞಿಕೆ, ಬೞಿಕ್ಕಂ, ಬೞಿಕ್ಕೆ, ಬೞಿಯಂ, ಬೞಿಲ್ (o. r. ಬೞಲ್), ಬೞಿವೞಿ (o. r. ಬೞುವೞಿ), ಬುೞ್ದಂಕು, ಬಾೞ್, ಬಾೞಕ, ಬಾಸುೞ್, ಬಾೞ್ತೆ, ಬಿೞ್, ಬೀೞ್ಕೆ, ಬೀೞ್, ಬೀೞಿಲ್ (o. rs. ಬೞಿಲ್, ಬೞಲ್), ಬೆಮ್ಬೞಿ, ಬೆೞಲ್, ಬೋೞ್, ಬೋೞ, ಬೋೞತರ, ಬೋೞೆ, (ಮಗುೞ್), ಮಣ್ಮೞಿ, ಮಲ್ಲೞಿ, ಮೞಮೞಿಸು, ಮೞಲ್, ಮೞೆ, ಮೞ್ತೆ, (ಮಿೞ್ತು), (ಮುಮ್ಮೞಿ), (ಮುೞುಂಗು), ಮುೞ್ಗು, ಮುೞ್ತಿಗ, ಮೂೞಿ, ಮೊೞ, ಮೊೞಕಾಲ್, ಮೊೞಗು, ಸಾೞಿಗೆ (o. r. ಜಾೞಿಗೆ), ಸುೞಿ, ಸೂೞ್, ಸೂೞಾಯ್ತು, ಸೂೞ್ಗರೆ, (ಸೊಮ್ಪುೞಿ), ಹೞ್ಗು, ಹಾೞ್ಮನೆಹಾೞ, ಹಿೞಿ.

To these are to be added the tadbhava words of § 231, as far as they are not repeated here, and under circumstances the words of § 232. In § 32, note 1 there are in the šâsanas also ಇೞ್ (to be), ಕೆೞಗೆ, ಗೞ್ದೆ, ಗೆೞ್ದು, ಪೞ್ದಲ್, ೞೋಕ (for ಳೋಕ, ಲೋಕ). See also § 234; Kêšava's Dhâtupâṭha (Šabdamaṇidarpaṇa pp. 330. 331); and regarding the meaning of the terms with ೞ the Dictionary.

Concerning the anukaraṇa words that have no aspirate (§§ 29. 218) at the beginning, Kêšava observes that they may appear either with ೞ or ಳ.

The Šabdânušâsana (under sûtra 140) adduces nearly the same terms in which ೞ has to be used, as the Šabdamaṇidarpaṇa. Besides, it adds a small number of others; but as their meaning is not given (the work does not give the meaning of any term with ೞ there) and thus the possibility of explaining them becomes difficult, as the reading of at least a few may be doubtful, and as the use of ೞ in a few of them was seemingly wrong at Kêšava's time, we mention them with diffidence. They are the following:—

ಅೞ್ತು (the act of weeping?), ಆೞ್ತು (the act of diving?), ಉೞುಕಲ್ (?), ಉೞುಕಟ (?), ಉೞಿಲ (?), ಉೞ್ಕು (= ಉಳ್ಕು?), ಎೞದು (= ಎಳದು?), ಎೞ್ಕೆ (the act of rising?), ಎೞ್ಗು (?), ಎೞ್ತು (= ಎೞ್ಕೆ?), ಕಮ್ಪೞಿ (= ಕಮ್ಪಳಿ), ಕೞ್ಕೆ (?), ಕೞ್ತು (?), ಕುೞು (= ಕುಳ?), ಕೆೞೆ (= ಕೆಳೆ?), ಕೇೞ (= ಕೇಳ?), ಕೊಲ್ಲೞ (?), ಗಿೞಿ (= ಗಿಳಿ?), ಗುೞುಕಲ್ (?), ಗೊೞಸು (= ಗೊಣಸು?), ಚಪ್ಪೞಿ (= ಚಪ್ಪಳಿ?), ಚೞಿ (= ಚಳಿ?), ಜೆೞೆ (?), ಜೋೞಿಗೆ (= ಜೋಳಿಗೆ?), ತಮುೞ್ (?), ತೞ (= ತಳ?), ತೆಮುೞ್ (= ತೆವೞ್), ತೊೞಿಕಲ್ (= ತೊೞಲಿಕಲ್?), ತೊೞೆ (= ತೊಳೆ?), ತೋೞ್ (= ತೋಳ್?), ಥಟ್ಟುೞ್, (?), ನಾೞಲ್ (?), ನೆಮುೞ್ (?), ನೆೞ್ಕೞ (?), ನೊೞವು (= ನೊಳವು?), ಪಸೞ್ (?), ಪೆೞವು (= ಪೆಳವು?), ಪೆೞ್ಗು (? not in

Mr. Rice's Index), ಪೊಱವು (= ಪೊಳವು?), ಬಱ್ತು (the act of living?), ಬಱ್ತಲೆ (= ಬತ್ತಲೆ?), ಬಿಱ್ಕ (?), ಬೆಱಗು (= ಬೆಳಗು; the Index has ಬೆಱವು), ಬೆಱ್ (= ಬೆಳೆ?), ಮಱ್ಗ (?), ಮುಗುಱ್ (= ಮುಗುಳ್), ಮುಱ್ತು (= ಮುಳ್ತು, the state of being irritated?), ಮೆಱ್ (= ಮೆಳೆ?), ಮೊಱ್ (= ಮೊಳೆ?), ರಾಱ್ಕಱ್ (?), ಸೆಱವು (= ಸೆಳವು?), ಸೆಱಸು (= ಸೆಳಸು?).

234. It is a rule of the ancient dialect (and to some extent of the mediæval one too, but which uses ಳ್ instead of ೞ್) that a **final ಡು** becomes ೞ್ when it euphonically joins a following consonant (see § 215, 7, under *a*), *e. g.* ಕಡುಕಿಚ್ಚು becomes ಕಾೞ್ಕಿಚ್ಚು, ಕಾಡುಪುರ ಕಾೞ್ಪುರ, ಕಾಡುತುಱು ಕಾೞ್ತುಱು, ಕಿವುಡು ಕೇಳ್ವಂ ಕಿವುೞ್ಕೇಳ್ವಂ, ಕೋಡು ಕುಟ್ಟು ಕೋೞ್ಕುಟ್ಟು, ಕೋಡು ಮೊನೆ ಕೋೞ್ಮೊನೆ, ನಾಡುಕಡೆ ನಾೞ್ಕಡೆ, ನಾಡುತುಡುಗುಣಿ ನಾೞ್ತುಡುಗುಣಿ, ನಾಡು ತೊಲೆ ನಾೞ್ತೊಲೆ, ನಾಡುಪಗರಣ ನಾೞ್ಪಗರಣ, ನೀಡುಕರಿಸು ನೀೞ್ಕರಿಸು, ಮುದುಡು ಗಣ್ಬು ಮುದುೞ್ಗಣ್ಬು, ಬೀಡು ಕೊಳ್ ಬೀೞ್ಕೊಳ್, ಬೀಡುತಾಣ ಬೀೞ್ತಾಣ, ಸೆಡು ಪಡು ಸೆೞ್ಪಡು, ಎರಡುಕಡಿ ಎರೞ್ಕಡಿ, ಎರಡುತರ ಎರೞ್ತರ, ಎರಡುಮಾತು ಎರೞ್ಮಾತು, ಎರಡು ಮೂಱು ಎರೞ್ಮೂಱು. *Cf.* § 58.

In the formation of the present-future participle a similar rule exists, *e. g.* ಮಾಡುವ may become ಮಾೞ್ಪ, ನೋಡುವ ನೋೞ್ಪ, ಬೇಡುವ ಬೇೞ್ಪ, ಬಿಸುಡುವ ಬಿಸುೞ್ಪ, ಬೆಗಡುವ ಬೆಗೞ್ಪ (§§ 58. 183, 4).

A similar change of ಡ into ೞ್ we find also in ತಡ ಕೆಯ್ಸು = ತೞ್ಕೆಯ್ಸು, ನೀರಡಿಕೆ = ನೀರೞ್ಕೆ, ನಾಡಿಕಾ = ನಾೞಿಗೆ, ಎಸಡಿಗೆ (dative of ಎಸಡಿ) = ಎಸೞ್ಗೆ.

235. The middle ರ in the Kannaḍa words ಮರಲ್, ಅರಲ್ (*cf.* § 228) and ಎರಲ್ may become ಲ, *viz.* ಮಲಲ್, ಅಲಲ್, ಎಲಲ್, in which case the final ಲ್ may be changed into ರ್, *viz.* ಮಲರ್, ಅಲರ್, (ಎಲರ್). ಮಲಲ್ appears also as ಮಣಲ್, and in the mediæval and modern dialect as ಮಳಲ್ or ಮಳಲು.

236. Words in which it was customary at Kêšava's time to use a **half rêpha** (ಱ್), are *e. g.* ಉದುಱ್, ಬಿದುಱ್, ಗದೆಱ್ (= ಗೞ್ದೆ, *cf.* § 32 and § 233), etc.; ನುಗುಱ್ (ನುೞ್ಗು), ತಗುಱ್ (= ತೞ್ಗು), ಕಿಗುಱ್ (= ಕಿೞ್ಗು), ಕುಗುಱ್ (= ಕುೞ್ಗು), etc.; ಇರ್ಪುಱ್, ಕೆರ್ಪುಱ್, ಕೂರ್ಪುಱ್, etc.; ಅರ್ದಱಂ, ಸಾರ್ದಱಂ, ಪೋರ್ದಱಂ, etc.; ಊರ್ಗಱಳ್, ಕೇರ್ಗಱಳ್, ಬೇರ್ಗಱಳ್, etc.

It will be observed that in some words ೞ್ had been given up in the common language of that time and ಱ್ had taken its place, which peculiarity we found also in the participles ಎರ್ದುಱ್, ಬಿರ್ದುಱ್, ಅರ್ದುಱ್ (§ 160, 1; see also § 32, note; § 239 regarding a kind of prâsa). The remaining words (ಇರ್ಪುಱ್, etc.) present no irregularities.

237. It is a peculiarity of the modern dialect that it changes a middle ರ before a ಳ into ಳ್, *e.g.* ಅರಳು may become ಅಳ್ಳು, ಅರಳೆ ಅಳ್ಳೆ, ಉರಳಿ ಉಳ್ಳಿ, ಉರುಳು ಉಳ್ಳು, ಒರಳು ಒಳ್ಳು, ಕರುಳು ಕಳ್ಳು, ಕುರುಳು ಕುಳ್ಳು, ಕೊರಳು ಕೊಳ್ಳು, ಗುರುಳೆ ಗುಳ್ಳೆ, ತಿರುಳು ತಿಳ್ಳು, ನೆರಳು ನೆಳ್ಳು, ಮರುಳು ಮಳ್ಳು, ಹರಳು ಹಳ್ಳು, ಹೊರಳು ಹೊಳ್ಳು.

238. In § 33 it has been stated that when two consonants are produced in (about) the same place or by (about) the same organs, they are called **êkasthâni** in grammar. The êkasthâni letters are ರ and ಱ, ಡ and ೞ, ಲ and ಳ (see § 239).

239. Grammars of the Kannaḍa language are **based chiefly on poetical standard works,** because almost every thing of its literature was composed in verse in the three periods; it is, therefore, to be expected that they contain some terms connected with prosody (čhandas) and the way of poetical composition (kâvyamârga).

Such terms employed by Kêšava are ಪ್ರಾಸ (called also ನಿಯಾಮ or ನಿಯಮ by him), ವರ್ಣಾವೃತ್ತಿ, ಯಮಕ, and ರೂಪಕ.

ಪ್ರಾಸ in Kannaḍa is an alliteration in which the second letter (generally a consonant with or without a vowel) of the first line of a stanza is set in the same place in every other line.

ವರ್ಣಾವೃತ್ತಿ is an additional alliteration in which the prâsa letter or a cognate one is set also in other places in the course of a stanza.

ಯಮಕ is the repeating or setting in opposition alliteratively in the same stanza of words or syllables different in meaning but similar in sound (paronomasia).

ರೂಪಕ is metaphorical diction.

Kêšava, when introducing the first three terms, does so in order to show the proper use of the êkasthâni letters ಡ and ೞ, ಲ and ಳ, ರ and ಱ (§ 238) in them, presupposing that ಡ and ಡ, ೞ and ೞ, ಲ and ಲ, ಳ and ಳ, ರ and ರ, ಱ and ಱ form regular prâsas, etc.

He states that ಕುಳ and ಕ್ಷಳ (§§ 227. 228) **form a right prâsa,** *e.g.*

ಕಿಳಿಱಿ ಹಯಂಗಳ್, ಗರ್ಜಿಸೆ
ಜಳದನಿಭಂಗಳ್ ಗಜಂಗಳ್ |

but that ಲ and ಕ್ಷಳ **cannot form a right one,** *e.g.*

ಓಲಗದೊಳೊರ್ಮೆ ನತನರ
ಪಾಳಕಚೂಡಾಮಣಿದ್ಯುತಿಪ್ರುತಚರಣಂ |

as also ಲ and ಕುಳ cannot do, *e. g.*

ನೆಲದೊಳ್ ಪಗೆ ಪುಗೆ ಫಣಿಯ ವೊ
ಲೊಳ ಪೊಕ್ಕಳಱಿಸಿದಂ | .

Further ರ and ಱ are wrong in prâsa, *e. g.*

ಧುರದೊಳ್ ಪಱಿಮಱಿಯಾಡುವ
ತೆಱದಿನ್ದುಱದಿಱಿದಂ |

as also ಡ and ಱ are wrong, *e. g.*

ಕೋಡದಿಱಿದಿನ್ದ್ರರಾದ
ನಾರ್ಱಿಗೆಯೊಳ್ ವೀರರ್ |

Regarding varṇâvṛitti Kêšava says that it is properly formed by ರ and ಱ, *e. g.*

ಸುರಗಿಱಿದೊಱಗಿದ ಬಿರುದರ
ಕರುಳಂ ಕೊಱೆಕೊಱೆದು ಮರುಳರುಳ್ತಿಮ್ಬಡೆಯೊಳ್ |

and by ಡ and ಱ, *e. g.*

ಖಱಿಲೆ ನುಡಿದಱಿಲೆ ಬಗ್ಗಿಸಿ,
ಫಱಿಲನೆ ನಡೆಯೆನ್ದು, ಜಡಿದು ಸಾರಥಿಯಂ |

and also by ಲ and ಳ (the kuḷa), *e. g.*

ದೆಸೆಗಳನಳುರ್ದುದು; ಮಿಳಿ
ರ್ದು, ಸುಲಿದು, ಬಲಿದುದು, ಕೆಳರ್ದು ಪೋಯಿತ್ತಾಗಳ್ | . (This half Kanda verse bears various shapes in the MSS.; its purpose, however, appears clearly in the present reading.)

Concerning the vamaka Kêšava says that the employment of ಡ and ಱ, ಲ and ಳ (the kuḷa), and ರ and ಱ as letters of alliteration is wrong in it (as in the prâsa), and in order to show this brings forward only the following anomalous instance:

ಕರೆಯುಂ ನೆರವಂ, ವಂಶಂ
ಕಱೆಯುಂ ಪೊತ್ತಪ್ಪುದೆನ್ದು ಸಂಗರಮುಖದೊಳ್ | , remarking "herein the application of words is spoiled, and if for ಕಱೆಯುಂ ಕರೆಯುಂ be read, no meaning is brought about; therefore there is not the characteristic (lakshaṇa) of the yamaka".

With regard to the prâsa with ಱ it is to be added (according to Kêšava) that a double consonant formed by means of a half rêpha may be substituted for ಱ (*cf.* § 236), *e. g.*

ಬಱ್ದಿದು ಬಳ್ಳವಾಡಿ, ನೆಱೆ ನ
ೞ್ಬಿದುರ್ದಾರುಹತಂ, ಜಿನೇನ್ದ್ರನ
ನ್ತಿರ್ದ ಮಹಾನುಭಾವರ್ |
and
ಜುರ್ಚಿದ ಪ್ರೋಲ್ ಬಿಸಿಲಳುರೆ ಕಿ
ಮುಱ್ಚಿದ ತಳಿರನ್ತೆ ನೊನ್ದು ಗುಣನನ್ದಿ |
and
ಒಕ್ಕುಡಿತೆನೀರ್ಗೆ, ಪಱಿ ಪ
ಟ್ಟಿರ್ಕೆಯ ಪಣ್ಣೆಲೆಯ ಮುಱಿಗೆ ದೇಸಿಗರಂ ದೇ |
ವರ್ಕಳ್ಗೊಡೆಯರ್ ಮಾಱ್ಪರೆ?
ನೀಱ್ಕಿರಿಸದೆ, ನಿಮ್ಮ ದೊರೆಗೆ ಬೋಱಿಯರೊಳರೇ? ||

The Šabdânušasana remarks that also ಱ and ೞ may be used as letters of alliteration in the prâsa.

Rûpaka has been mentioned in § 104 with regard to nouns, *e. g.* ನೆಲ, which are of neuter gender, but receive another gender when they are used metaphorically. There is the following quotation concerning ನೆಲ in the Šabdamaṇidarpaṇa.

ಉದಯಾಸ್ತೋನ್ನತಶೈಲಸೇತುಹಿಮವತ್ಕುತ್ಕೀಲಪರ್ಯನ್ತಸ
ಮ್ಪದೆಯಂ ವಾರ್ಧಿತರತ್ತರಂಗನಿನದತ್ಕಾಂಚೀಕಲಾಪಾಂಚಿತಾ |
ಸ್ಪದೆಯಂ ಸಾಧಿಸಿ ಕಬ್ಬಿಗಂಗೆ ನೆಲನಂ ನಿರ್ವ್ಯಾಜದಿನ್ದಂ ನಿಮಿ
ರ್ಚಿದಗೆಲ್ಲಂ ಭುವನೈಕರಾಮಮಹಿಪಂಗಕ್ಕುಂ. ಪೆಱರ್ಗಕ್ಕುಮೇ? || ;

and concerning ಜಗದ್ದರ್ಪಣ there are the instances ಆತಂ ಜಗದ್ದರ್ಪಣಂ, ಆ ಪೆಣ್ ಜಗದ್ದರ್ಪಣಂ, ಅದು ಜಗದ್ದರ್ಪಣಂ.

240. Double consonants (§§ 20. 38) **in prosody are sometimes "slack"** (šithila), *i. e.* they have not the power of lengthening a preceding syllable. Such double consonants appear

1, in the nominative plural and dative singular of nouns ending in ಱ್, ೞ್, ರ್, and ಱ್, *e. g.* ಅಗಱ್ಗಳ್, ಉಗುಱ್ಗಳ್, ಎಸಱ್ಗಳ್, ನೆಗಱ್ಗಳ್; ಅಗಱ್ಗೆ, ಉಗುಱ್ಗೆ, ಎಸಱ್ಗೆ, ನೆಗಱ್ಗೆ; — ಆಮೞ್ಗಳ್, ಎಸೞ್ಗಳ್, ಪುಗುೞ್ಗಳ್, ಮುಗುೞ್ಗಳ್; ಆಮೞ್ಗೆ, ಎಸೞ್ಗೆ, ಪುಗುೞ್ಗೆ, ಮುಗುೞ್ಗೆ; — ಅಲರ್ಗಳ್, ಉಗುರ್ಗಳ್, ಉಸುರ್ಗಳ್, ಎಲರ್ಗಳ್, ಎಸರ್ಗಳ್, ಒಗರ್ಗಳ್, ಒಸರ್ಗಳ್, ಕದಿರ್ಗಳ್, ಕಸರ್ಗಳ್, ಕುದಿರ್ಗಳ್, ಕುಳಿರ್ಗಳ್, ಕೊನರ್ಗಳ್, ಚಿಗುರ್ಗಳ್, ತಳಿರ್ಗಳ್, ತಿಮಿರ್ಗಳ್, ತೆಮರ್ಗಳ್, ನವಿರ್ಗಳ್, ಪಸಿರ್ಗಳ್, ಬಿದಿರ್ಗಳ್, ಬೆಮರ್ಗಳ್; ಅಲರ್ಗೆ, etc.; — ಎಡರ್ಗಳ್ (ಎಡಱ್ಗಳ್), ಕೆಸರ್ಗಳ್ (ಕೆಸಱ್ಗಳ್), ಪೆಸರ್ಗಳ್, ಬಸಿರ್ಗಳ್, ಹಗರ್ಗಳ್; ಎಡರ್ಗೆ, etc.

Exceptions are formed by words with a long initial, *e. g.* ಬಾಸುೞ್, ಇಕ್ಕುೞ್ ಪೊಕ್ಕುೞ್, and by some words with final ಳ್, *e. g.* ಕುರುಳ್, ಪುರುಳ್, ಮುರುಳ್. ಕಾದಲರ್ಗಳ್, though its initial is long, generally has a slack double consonant.

2, in the conjugation of verbs ending in ೞ್, ಳ್, ರ್, and ಱ್, *e. g.* ಅಗುೞ್ದಂ, ಜಗುೞ್ದಂ, ತಗುೞ್ದಂ, ತುಮುೞ್ದಂ, ತೆಗೞ್ದಂ, ನೆಗೞ್ದಂ, ಮಗುೞ್ದಂ; ಜಗುೞ್ದಪಂ; ಜಗುೞ್ವಂ; ತೆಗೞ್ಗೆ, ನೆಗೞ್ಗೆ, ಪೊಗೞ್ಗೆ; ಜಗುೞ್ಗುಂ, ತೆಗೞ್ಗುಂ, ನೆಗೞ್ಗುಂ, ಪೊಗೞ್ಗುಂ;— ನುಗುಳ್ದಂ, ನುಸುಳ್ದಂ, ಮುಸುಳ್ದಂ; ಮುಸುಳ್ದಪಂ; ಮುಸುಳ್ವಂ; ನುಗುಳ್ಗೆ, ನುಸುಳ್ಗೆ, ಮುಸುಳ್ಗೆ; ನುಸುಳ್ಗುಂ, ಮುಸುಳ್ಗುಂ;— ಅದಿರ್ದಂ, ತಳರ್ದಂ, ತಿಮಿರ್ದಂ, ನಿಮಿರ್ದಂ, ಬಿದಿರ್ದಂ; ನಿಮಿರ್ದಪಂ; ನಿಮಿರ್ವಂ; ಅದಿರ್ಗೆ, ತೊಡರ್ಗೆ; ಅಮರ್ಗುಂ, ನಿಮಿರ್ಗುಂ;— ಎಡಱ್ದಂ (ಎಡೞ್ದಂ), ಅಳಱ್ದಂ; ಎಡಱ್ಗೆ, ಅಳಱ್ಗೆ.

Exceptions are formed by verbs with a long intial, *e. g.* ಆರ್, ನೇರ್, ಸೋರ್; and by some verbs with final ಳ್, *e. g.* ತೆರಳ್, ಪೊರಳ್, in which the use of slackness is optional.

3, in words ending in ರ್ and ಳ್ the first syllable of which is short and which form the first member of a compound (samâsa), *e. g.* ಬೆಳರ್ಗೆಮ್ಮು, ಅಲರ್ದೋರಣಂ, ಬಿದಿರ್ದಟ್ಟಿ, ಪೊಗರ್ವಟ್ಟೆ, ಬೆಮರ್ವನಿ, ಅಲರ್ಜೊಮ್ಪಂ, ಕದಿರ್ಜೊನ್ನಂ; ಮುಗುಳ್ಗಾಯ್, ಅಮುಳ್ದೊಂಗಲ್, ಎಸಳ್ವಸೆ, ಅಮಳ್ಜನ್ತ್ರಂ. *Cf.* § 246, *a.*

4, in some words in which it is inherent (sahaja). They are ಅದಿರ್ಮುತ್ತೆ, ಅಮರ್ದು, ಎರ್ದೆ, ಗರ್ದುಗು, ಬರ್ದಿಲಂ. (ಅದಿರ್ಮುತ್ತೆ seems to belong to No. 3.)

5, optionally in the dative plural of Saṁskṛita and Kannaḍa terms that are masculine or feminine, *e. g.* ಬಾನ್ಧವರ್ಗೆ, ಬುಧರ್ಗೆ; ಕಾನ್ತೆಯರ್ಗೆ, ಸ್ತ್ರೀಯರ್ಗೆ; ಎರೆವರ್ಗೆ; ಸೂಳೆಯರ್ಗೆ.

When, however, in their dative plural no "slackness" (śithilatva) is to occur, it is customarily indicated by doubling the ಗ of the dative in the ancient dialect, *viz.* ಬಾನ್ಧವರ್ಗ್ಗೆ, ಬುಧರ್ಗ್ಗೆ; ಕಾನ್ತೆಯರ್ಗ್ಗೆ, ಸ್ತ್ರೀಯರ್ಗ್ಗೆ; ಎರೆವರ್ಗ್ಗೆ; ಸೂಳೆಯರ್ಗ್ಗೆ (see § 119, *a,* under dative). *Cf.* § 371, 1.

Remark.

Some people have thought that in the elaborate prose composition called ಗದ್ಯ which belongs to prosody (čhandas) and frequently is found in poetry, it is allowed to treat a double letter with rêpha, *e. g.* ಕ್ರಿ, ಪ್ರ, ಪ್ರಿ, as "slack" *i. e.* as not lengthening a preceding short syllable; but this their thought is quite wrong according to Kêśava. *Cf.* § 241.

241. In writing stanzas (pada) it is bad to leave no space between the different words unless they fall under the rules of sandhi (§ 213 *seq.*). Thus one has to write:

ಬನ್ನಿಯ ತರು ಡಕ್ಕೆಗೆ ಸುರ
ಹೊನ್ನೆಯ ತರು ಡಮರುಗಕ್ಕೆ ಕರುವಿಡಿದಿರ್ಪಾರ್ ।
ಚೆನ್ನಂಗಿಯ ತರು ಡಾಣೆಗೆ
ಹೊನ್ನಂ ಕುಡುವೆಡೆಗೆ ಕಲ್ಪತರು ಡಾಕರಸಾ ॥

and not ಬನ್ನಿಯತರುಡಕ್ಕೆಸುರ etc., in this case especially also because the obscene word ತರುಡು might be thought of in four places (*cf.* § 215, 6, remark 3).

Likewise one has to write:

ಬರಿಸಿ ಪ್ರಧಾನರಂ ಕು
ಳ್ಳಿರಿಸಿ ಪ್ರಿಯಕುಶಲವಾರ್ತೆಯಂ ನೆಱೆ ಕೇಳ್ದು ।
ಸ್ಥಿರಮಿರ್ದು ಪ್ರಭು ನುಡಿಯೆ
ಪ್ರರೂಢಮುದನಾದನಾತನ್ . . . ॥

and not ಬರಿಸಿಪ್ರಧಾನರಂಕುಳ್ಳಿರಿಸಿಪ್ರಿಯ etc., as the prosodical length of the short-vowelled syllables ಸಿ, ಳ್ದು and ಯೆ results at once from the following double letters ಪ್ರ, ಪ್ರಿ and ಸ್ಥಿ (see § 20) to an observing eye. Some use to write ಪ್ತ್ರ, ಪ್ತ್ರಿ, ಸ್ಥ್ಥಿ, which is unnecessary. *Cf.* § 240, remark.

IX. On primitive nominal bases.

242. Nominal bases (nâmaliṅgas) or crude nouns in general have been mentioned in § 68, 4. As slightly indicated there under No. *b* by Kêšava's introducing the compounds (samâsas) ದಯಾಪರ, ಹೆಱೆಗಾಲ, etc., they finally include also all the other true declinable bases, *viz.* taddhita, samâsa, sarvanâma, guṇavačana, saṅkhyĕ and kṛit, which in fact are nothing but nominal bases or nouns in their crude state.

In § 100 a number of crude nouns has been given that are identical with verbal themes (nijadhâtu). Such are, therefore, primitive nominal bases without any suffixes (taddhitas or taddhitapratyayas) and also the simplest bhâvavačanas or verbal nouns (*cf.* § 243).

Another primitive nominal base, that is a mere verbal theme, is still to be adduced, *viz.* the ancient ಪೋಲ್, which has also the forms ಪೊಲ್, ಬೋಲ್, ಬೊಲ್, 'likeness', 'equivalence'. In the mediæval dialect its forms are ಪೋಲ್, ಪೊಲ್, ಪೊಲು, ಓಲ್, ಒಲ್, ಒಲು; in the modern one it has remained as ಒಲು, 'equivalence': 'bail', etc. Its original form was ಪೋಲ್ (ಹೋಲ್, ಹೋಲು); the change of ಪ into ವ or ಬ was done, because it was originally mostly used as the second member of a compound (see § 215, 7, *a. b*); for the omission of ವ see Dictionary under ಒ 1 and ಓ 1. In rendering it into English its meaning often becomes 'like', 'as', etc. In the ancient dialect ವೋಲ್ or ವೊಲ್ is frequently preceded by ಅನ್ತೆ which is nearly identical in meaning, so that the forms become ಅನ್ತೆವೋಲ್, ಅನ್ತೆವೊಲ್, "without the fault of tautology" (punarukti) according to Kêšava, its meaning remaining the same, *viz.* 'as', 'like', etc. ಬೋಲ್, ಬೊಲ್ are used only in compounds, when they are always preceded by a euphonic sŏnnĕ.

Kêšava quotes the following instances to elucidate the use of ವೋಲ್, etc.

ಜಲನಿಧಿಯ ವೋಲ್ ಗಭೀರಂ,
ಬಲವೈರಿಯ ವೋಲ್ ಸಮುಗ್ರವಿಭವಸನಾಥಂ, ।
ಕುಲಗಿರಿವೋಲ್ ನಿಷ್ಕಮ್ಪಂ,
ಬಲಿಯನ್ತೆವೊಲಧಿಕದಾನಿ ದಾನವಿನೋದಂ ॥ .

ರವಿಸುತನನ್ತೆವೋಲಧಿಕದಾನಿ, ಪರಾಕ್ರಮಿ ಸಿಂಗದನ್ತೆವೋಲ್ । .

ಆ ಮುನೀಶ್ವರಂ ಶಾನ್ತರಸದ ಕಡಲ ವೋಲಿರ್ದಂ । .

ನಿಜತೇಜಂ ನೀಳ್ದ ಕರ್ನೆಯ್ದಿಲ ವೊಲಿರೆ । .

ಇನ್ದ್ರಂಬೋಲ್ ವಿಭವಯುತಂ,
ಚನ್ದ್ರಂಬೋಲ್ ಕಾನ್ತಿವನ್ತನಾದಿತ್ಯಂಬೋಲ್ ।
ಸಾನ್ದ್ರಪರಿಪೂರ್ಣತೇಜನು
ಪೇನ್ದ್ರಂಬೋಲ್ ನೀತಿನಿಪುಣನಾ ನರನಾಥಂ ॥ .

The Šabdânušâsana has the following additional instances:

ಹರಿವೊಲ್, ಹರಿವೋಲ್; ಗಿರಿವೊಲ್, ಗಿರಿವೋಲ್; ವಿಧುವೊಲ್, ವಿಧುವೋಲ್; ಪಿತೃವೋಲ್, ಪಿತೃವೊಲ್; ಮಾತಂಗದ ವೋಲ್; ರಾಜ್ಯದ ವೋಲ್; ವೃತ್ತದ ವೋಲ್; ಧರ್ಮದ ವೋಲ್;— ಅಣ್ಣಂಬೋಲ್, ಸೋಮಂಬೋಲ್;— ಇನ್ದ್ರನ ವೋಲ್, ಇನ್ದ್ರನ ವೊಲ್; ಹರಿಯ ವೋಲ್, ಹರಿಯ ವೊಲ್; ವಿಧುವ ವೋಲ್, ವಿಧುವ ವೊಲ್; ಪಿತೃವ ವೋಲ್, ಪಿತೃವ ವೊಲ್.

Other bhâvavačanas or verbal nouns formed, without taddhita suffixes (§ 243), by a mere change in the verbal theme are ಆಟ, ಪಾಟ, ನೋಟ, ತೀಟ, ಕೂಟ, ಬೇಟ, ಮಾಟ, etc. (of ಆಡು, ಪಾಡು, etc.; see § 58), ಈಡು, ಬೀಡು, ಸೂಡು (of ಇಡು, etc.; see § 101), ಕೇಡು, ಏಸು (of ಕಿಡು, etc.; see § 101).

ಕೋಡು, ತೋಡು (of ಕುಡು, etc.; see § 101). These may perhaps be classed with the primitive nominal bases; but others are apparently not found in Kannaḍa.

X. On secondary nominal bases.

243. Taddhitaliṅgas or taddhitas have been referred to in § 68, 2; 99. 100. 102, 8, *f*. They are **secondary nominal bases or nouns,** as they are formed by means of suffixes (taddhita, taddhitapratyaya) from nouns and verbs.

When neuters and derived from verbs, they express the abstract notion (bhâva) of a verb either as to state or action, *i. e.* are bhâvavačanas or verbal nouns; when neuters and formed from nouns, they have a similar character. [About bhâvavačanas in general see §§ 100 (ಅಟ್ಟು, etc.); 188 (ಅರಿಲ್, ಅಱಿಲು, etc.); 194, remark (ಉಣ್ಬು); 198 (ಓದಿದುದು, etc.); 200 1. 3 (ಕುಡುವುದು, ಹೇೞುವದು, etc.); 203. 204 (ಆಳ್ಗಂ, ಬೇೞ್ಕಂ, etc.); 205, 1, *c* (ಈವುದು, etc.); 205, 1, *d* (ಗೆಯ್ಗ, etc.); 242; 254, remarks 1 and 2 (ಮಾಡುವುದು, ಮಾಡದದು, etc.); 298, 3 (ಆದುದಿಲ್ಲ, ಇರುವದಿಲ್ಲ, etc.); *cf.* 316, 2.]

A. **The chief suffixes for forming neuters are:**

1, ಅ, *e. g.* ಅಱ, ಗೆಲ, ನೀೞ, ಸಾಲ, ಸೋಲ (of the verbs ಅಱ್, etc.; see § 100).

2, ಎ, *e. g.* ಕಟ್ಟೆ, ಕೊಲೆ, ನಗೆ (of the verbs ಕಟ್ಟು, ಕೊಲ್, ನಗು; see § 100), and (by altering the vowel of the theme) ಕೆಱೆ, ತೆಱೆ, ನೆಲೆ, ಬೆಲೆ (of the verbs ಕಿಱ್, etc.; see § 101).

3, ಅಮೆ, *e. g.* ಅಬ್ಬಮೆ, ತೀರಮೆ (of the verbs ಅಬ್ಬು, ತೀರ್).

4, ಅವು, *e. g.* ಇರವು, ಒಲವು, ಕಳವು, ಗೆಲವು, ನಿಲವು, ಬರವು, ಬಲವು, ಸಲವು (of the verbs ಇರ್, ಒಲ್, ಕಳ್, etc.).

5, ಇಕೆ, *e. g.* ಆಯುತಿಕೆ, ಉದ್ಧತಿಕೆ, ಪನ್ನತಿಕೆ, ಬಲ್ಗಣ್ತಿಕೆ, ಮಾನಸಿಕೆ (of the nouns ಆಯತ, etc.). The Šabdânušâsana has ಅಲಸಿಕೆ, ಗರುವಿಕೆ, ಚಮರಿಕೆ, ಚೆಲ್ವಿಕೆ, ಜಾಣಿಕೆ (of ಅಲಸ, etc.), ಆಟಕಾಱಕೆ, ಓಲೆಕಾಱಕೆ, ಕಂಚುಗಾಱಕೆ, ಬಳೆಗಾಱಕೆ (of ಆಟಕಾಱ, etc.). In another place it adduces ಅಂಜಿಕೆ, ಒಪ್ಪಿಕೆ, ಕಪ್ಪಿಕೆ, ನಪ್ಪಿಕೆ, ಪೊಣ್ಣಿಕೆ (of the verbs ಅಂಜು, etc.), ಅವುಡಿಕೆ, ಓದಿಕೆ, ಕದಡಿಕೆ, ಕವಡಿಕೆ, ಮುದುಡಿಕೆ, ಮೋಡಿಕೆ, ಸುಪ್ಪಿಕೆ, ಸೇಪ್ಪಿಕೆ, ಹರಡಿಕೆ (of the verbs ಅವುಡು, etc.), ಆಡಿಕೆ, ಚಿವುಡಿಕೆ, ತಲೆವಡಿಕೆ, ಪೊತಮುಡಿಕೆ, ಬಿಡಿಕೆ (of the verbs ಆಡು, etc.).

Kêšava says that ಕಾಣಿಕೆ (of verb ಕಾಣ್), ಪೂಣಿಕೆ (of ಪೂಣ್), ತೆರಳಿಕೆ (of ತೆರಳ್) in which ಇಕೆ has been suffixed to verbs ending in consonants, are wrong (dôsha; see under ಕೆ); consequently the Šabdânušâsana's ಕಲಿಕೆ (of ಕಲ್, under sûtra 568) would also be wrong according to him.

Instead of ಇಕೆ also ಇಕ್ಕೆ occurs, *e. g.* in ಉನ್ನತಿಕ್ಕೆ, ಉದ್ಧತಿಕ್ಕೆ.

6, ಇಗೆ, *e.g.* ತಾೞಿಗೆ, ಪಾಡಿಗೆ, ಬೇಡಿಗೆ, ಮಾಱಿಗೆ, ಮೂಡಿಗೆ (of the verbs ತಾೞು, etc.), and ಪೊಲಿಗೆ (of the verb ಪೊಲ್). This is only in Šabdânušâsana, sûtra 565.

7, ಇಸು, *e.g.* ಉಣಿಸು, ತಿನಿಸು (of the verbs ಉಣ್, etc.; Šabdânušâsana, sûtra 578).

8, ಉವೆ, *e.g.* ತಕ್ಕುವೆ (of the noun ತಕ್ಕ). The Šabdânušâsana's sûtra 572 seems to refer to this suffix when it teaches that ತರ್ಕುವೆ and ಬರ್ಕುವೆ are derived from the verbs ತರ್ and ಬರ್ by means of ಉವೆ and the insertion of ಕು. This sûtra might have taken notice of ತರ್ಕು, ಬರ್ಕು, verbal nouns which are used for the third person (§§ 203. 204), to which the suffix ಉವೆ would have been added.

9, ಕ, *e.g.* ಉಡುಕ (of the verb ಉಡು), ನಡುಕ (from the verb ನಡುಗು, the final ಗು having been dropped; *cf.* No. 16).

10, ಕೆ, *e.g.* ಕಾಣ್ಕೆ, ಪೂಣ್ಕೆ, ತೋರ್ಕೆ, ತೆರಳ್ಕೆ (of the verbs ಕಾಣ್, etc.), ಮಡಿಕೆ, ಹಡಿಕೆ (of the verbs ಮಡಿ, ಹಡಿ). The Šabdânušâsana has no ಮಡಿಕೆ, ಹಡಿಕೆ, but adds ಆಯ್ಕೆ, ಆರಯ್ಕೆ (of the verbs ಆಯ್, etc.), ಆನ್ಕೆ, ಕೊನ್ಕೆ, ಪೇನ್ಕೆ, ಬಾನ್ಕೆ, ಸೀನ್ಕೆ (of ಆನ್, etc.), ನೇಲ್ಕೆ, ಪೋಲ್ಕೆ, ಸೋಲ್ಕೆ, ಕವಲ್ಕೆ, ಮಡಲ್ಕೆ (of ನೇಲ್, etc.), ಅದಿರ್ಕೆ, ಪೊಣರ್ಕೆ, ಬಿದಿರ್ಕೆ, ಸಾರ್ಕೆ (of ಅದಿರ್, etc.), ಉಣ್ಕೆ, ಪಣ್ಕೆ, ಮಾಣ್ಕೆ (of ಉಣ್, etc.), ಕಿೞುಕೆ (of ಕಿೞು = ಕಿೞ್), ತಿೞುಕೆ (of ತಿೞು = ತಿೞ್), ಪೊೞುಕೆ (of ಪೊೞು = ಪೊೞ್), ಅೞ್ಕೆ, ಉೞ್ಕೆ (of ಅೞ್, etc.), ಆಳ್ಕೆ, ಊಳ್ಕೆ (of ಆಳ್, etc.), ಬಾೞ್ಕೆ ಮಾೞ್ಕೆ (of ಬಾೞ್, etc.).

Compare the termination ಕೆ of the imperative in § 205.

11, ಗುಳ್, *e.g.* ಪೊಯ್ಗುಳ್ (beating, of the verb ಪೊಯ್) ಬಯ್ಗುಳ್ (of ಬಯ್). This suffix is given only in the Šabdânušâsana.

12, ಗೆ, *e.g.* ಉಡುಗೆ, ಪಣ್ಣುಗೆ, ಪತ್ತುಗೆ, ಪಸುಗೆ, ಬಿಸುಗೆ (of the verbs ಉಡು, etc.), ಪೊಲ್ಗೆ (of ಪೊಲ್), to which the Šabdânušâsana adds ಆಡುಗೆ, ಅರ್ದುಗೆ (for ಅಬ್ಬುಗೆ), ಅಬುಗೆ, ತಾಳ್ದುಗೆ, ತುಡುಗೆ, ತುಮ್ಬುಗೆ, ತೆಮಳ್ದುಗೆ, ನಮ್ಬುಗೆ (of ಅಡು, etc.), ಏೞ್ಗೆ, ಬೀಳ್ಗೆ, ಸಲ್ಗೆ (of ಏೞ್, etc.).

Compare the termination ಗೆ of the imperative in § 205.

13, ತ, *e.g.* ಅೞಿತ, ಉೞಿತ, ಕಡಿತ (of the verbs ಅೞಿ, etc.), ಎರ್ತ (of ಎೞ್ = ಎೞು), ಪೊರ್ತ (of ಪೊೞ್ = ಪೊೞು), ಏತ (= ಏೞುತ of ಏೞು), ಓತ (= ಓದುತ of ಓದು), to which the Šabdânušâsana adds ಈತ, ಈನ್ತ, ಕಾಯ್ತ, ಕೆಯ್ತ, ಗೆಯ್ತ, ತೊಯ್ತ, ಪಾಯ್ತ, ಸುಯ್ತ (of ಈ, ಈನ್, etc.), ಅಗಿತ, ಇೞಿತ, ಕುಣಿತ, ತಿರಿತ, ಬಿಗಿತ, ಮಣಿತ, ಮುಗಿತ, ಮುೞಿತ, ಸುಗಿತ, ಓತ (the act of loving, of ಓ, which is different from Kêšava's ಓತ).

14, ತನ, *e.g.* ಆಳ್ತನ (of the verb or noun ಆಳ್), ಎಗ್ಗತನ, ಕಲಿತನ, ಪೆಣ್ತನ, ಮರುಳ್ತನ (of the nouns ಎಗ್ಗ, etc.). The Šabdânušâsana adduces ಕೆಳೆಯತನ, ಚೆಲ್ವತನ, ಬಲ್ಲತನ (of the nouns ಕೆಳೆಯ, etc.), ಗರತಿತನ, ಸೂಳೆತನ (of the tadbhavas ಗರತಿ, etc.). Kêšava adds that ತನ is not suffixed to Saṁskṛita nouns, and *e.g.* ಆರೋಹಕತನ is wrong (ಅಬದ್ಧ); the Šabdânušâsana (sûtras 430 *seq.*), however, expressly teaches how to form ಪುರುಷತನ, ವೀರತನ, ಶೂರತನ, ಉನ್ನತತನ, ಪನ್ನತತನ, ಸುಖತನ.

15, ತೆ, *e.g.* ಅಗೞ್ತೆ, ನೆಗೞ್ತೆ, ಪೊಗೞ್ತೆ, ಮುಗುಳ್ತೆ (of the verbs ಅಗೞ್, etc.), ಉಗುತೆ, ಪುಗುತೆ, ಮಿಗುತೆ (of ಉಗು, etc.), (ನಿೞುತೆ, of the verb ನಿೞ್).

16, ಪ, *e. g.* ತೆಗೆಪ, ತಗೆಪ, ತೊಡೆಪ, ನಡೆಪ, ನೊಗೆಪ, ತಡೆಪ, ಅಡೆಪ, ಪೊಸೆಪ, ನನೆಪ, ತೊನೆಪ, ಅಲೆಪ, ಬರೆಪ, ಒರೆಪ (of the verbs ತೆಗೆ, etc.), ಕುದಿಪ, ಮಿದಿಪ, ತಳಿಪ (of the verbs ಕುದಿ, etc.), ತೊಳಪ (of the verb ತೊಳೆ). This suffix and the instances (except ಬರೆಪ which is used also in the Šabdamaṇidarpaṇa) are mentioned only in the Šabdânušâsana. We adduce still (from the Dictionary) ಬರಪ, ಬಱಪ (of ಬರೆ, ಬಱ³) in which the final ಎ of the verbal theme has been dropped (*cf.* § 60 and the ತೊಳಪ above), and ತಳಪ (of ತಳಗು = ತೊಳಗು), ತಿರಪ (of ತಿರಗು) in which the final ಗು is dropped (*cf.* § 211, 7; see under No. 18, *a*).

Compare the suffix ಹ.

17, ಪಿ, *e. g.* ಕಲ್ಪಿ, ನೋನ್ಪಿ (of the verbs ಕಲ್, ನೋನ್).

18*a*, ಪು, *e. g.* ಪಡೆಪು (of the verb ಪಡೆ), ತೋರ್ಪು, ಮಾರ್ಪು (of the verbs ತೋಱ್, ಮಾಱ್), ನಡಪು (of the verb ನಡೆ), ಕಡುಪು (of the noun ಕಡು), ತಣ್ಪು, ನುಣ್ಪು, ಬಲ್ಪು, ಮೆಲ್ಪು (of the nouns ತಣ್, etc.), ಕರ್ಪು, ಕೆಮ್ಪು (of the nouns ಕರ್, ಕೆಮ್), ಕೂರ್ಪು, ನೇರ್ಪು (of the nouns ಕೂರ್, ನೇರ್), ಒಳ್ಪು, ತೆಳ್ಪು (of the nouns ಒಳ್, ತೆಳ್), ಬಿಳ್ಪು (of the noun ಬಿಳ್ = ಬೆಳ್), ಪಸುರ್ಪು (of the verb ಪಸುರ್⁵), ಬಿಸುಪು (of the noun ಬಿಸು), ಓಪು, ಕಾಪು, ಮೇಪು (of the verbs ಓ, etc.). ಪೆಮ್ಪು comes from the noun ಪಿರಿ. The Šabdânušâsana adds that ಪೊಳಪು is to be derived from the verb ಪೊಳಗು; likewise there are ತೊಳಪು, ಮಿಱುಪು (of the verbs ತೊಳಗು, ಮಿಱುಗು, see under No. 16). *Cf.* § 185. Could ಸೊಮ್ಪು be a formation of ಸೊಬಗು, the ಗು being dropped?

Compare the suffix ಹು.

18*b*, (ಮು, *e. g.* ಪೊರಮು, of the verb ಪೊರೆ).

18*c*, (ಮು, *e. g.* ಅಣ್ಮು of a verb ಅಣ್?; ಇಮ್ಮು of the noun ಇಮ್⁵).

19, ಮೆ, *e. g.* ಒಲ್ಮೆ, ನಲ್ಮೆ, ಬಲ್ಮೆ (of the verbs ಒಲ್, etc.), ಕೂರ್ಮೆ (of the verb ಕೂರ್⁵), ಪೆರ್ಮೆ (of the noun ಪೆರ್), ಕಡುಮೆ, ಮೆಯ್ಮೆ (of the nouns ಕಡು, etc.), ಜಾಣ್ಮೆ (of the noun ಜಾಣ್).

Compare the use of this suffix for the numerals in § 279.

The curious form ಅಱಿಯಮೆ is found *e. g.* in Čandraprabha 4, 2; Abhinava-pampa 7, after 11; 8, 45; 11, 54. It is quite possible that its meaning is 'the not knowing', 'absence of knowledge'. If thus, it would have been formed from ಅಱಿಯ, yet to know, *i. e.* not to know (see *e. g.* §§ 170. 171) and ಮೆ, so that it would be a negative noun. *Cf.* the noun ಇಲ್ಲವೆ under No. 25. The meaning given to ಅಱಿಯಮೆ in the Dictionary is possibly wrong.

20, (ವ, *e. g.* ಇಕ್ಕುವ, ಹಣ್ಣುವ, ಹಳಿದಿಸುವ; of the verbs ಇಕ್ಕು, etc.; *cf.* ಹ).

21, (ವಣಿಗೆ, *e. g.* ನೆಱವಣಿಗೆ, Šabdamaṇidarpaṇa pp. 219. 387, ಮೆಱವಣಿಗೆ, mediæval and modern dialect, of the verbs ನೆಱ³ and ಮೆಱ³. Regarding the dropping of the ಎ see under ವಿ. *Cf.* ವಣಿಗ and ಅಣಿಗ under *B*).

22, ವಳಿ, *e. g.* ಸಲ್ವಳಿ (of the verb ಸಲ್), ನಡೆವಳಿ, ನುಡಿವಳಿ (of ನಡೆ, etc.).

23, ವಿ, *e. g.* ತೊಱವಿ, ಬಳವಿ (of the verbs ತೊಱೆ, ಬಳೆ), ಅಳವಿ. Observe that in ತೊಱವಿ, ಬಳವಿ the final ಎ of the verbal theme is dropped; *cf.* § 60.

24, ವು, *e. g.* ಅಱವು, ಅೞವು, ಉೞವು, ತಿಳಿವು, ಪಱವು, ಬಸಿವು, ಪೞವು, ಸುೞವು (of the verbs ಅಱ್, etc.); — ಎರವು, ಕಱವು, ತೆಱವು, ನೆಱವು, ಮೆಱವು, ಸೆಳವು (of the verbs ಎರೆ, etc.); — ಕೆಳವು (?), ಪೆಳವು (or ಪೆಱವು? see § 233); — ಕೀವು, ನೋವು, ಸಾವು (of the verbs ಕೀ, etc.). Observe that in ಎರವು, ಕಱವು, etc. the ಎ of the verbal theme has been dropped; *cf.* § 60. See § 185.

A few nouns ending either in ವು or ಅ are given in § 96.

25, ವೆ, *e. g.* ತೆಱವೆ, ಮಱವೆ (of the verbs ತೆಱ್, etc.), ಪಳವೆ (?), ಎಳವೆ (? o. r. ಎಡವೆ). Observe that in ತೆಱವೆ, ಮಱವೆ the final ಎ of the verbal theme has been dropped; *cf.* § 60.

ಇಲ್ಲವೆ, the state of being not, may be compared with ಅಱಯುವೆ under No. 19.

26, ಸು, *e. g.* ಮುನಿಸು, ಮುಳಿಸು (of the verbs ಮುನಿ, etc.); ಕಿನಿಸು, ಬೆಳಸು; ಪೊಲಸು (of the noun ಪೊಲ್). Observe that in ಬೆಳಸು (of the verb ಬೆಳೆ) the final ಎ of the verbal theme has been dropped; *cf.* § 60.

27, ಹ (*cf.* ವ), *e. g.* ವಿಸಾಹ, ಇಕ್ಕ್ಯಹ, ನಡಹ, ಬರಹ (of the verbs ವಿಸಾ, ಇಕ್ಕ್ಯ, ನಡೆ, ಬರೆ). Observe that in ನಡಹ, ಬರಹ the ಎ of the verbal theme has been dropped; *cf.* § 60.

Compare the suffix ಪ.

28, ಹು, *e. g.* ಕಾಹು, ಬಾಹು, ಮೇಹು (of the verbs ಕಾ, etc.).

Compare the suffix ಪು.

These and others are the suffixes for forming neuter nouns (Kêšava says).

Remarks.

a) Kêšava states that some taddhitaliṅgas end also in ಉ, and gives the instances ಉಗ್ಗು, ಸಿಗ್ಗು, ಎಗ್ಗು, ಕಿವುಡು, ಕೆಂಚು, ಗುಜ್ಜು. Their suffixes (taddhitas) are not adduced by him. ಉಗ್ಗು may belong to the primitive nominal bases (§ 242); ಸಿಗ್ಗು may be connected with ಸಿಡಿ, perplexity; ಎಗ್ಗು seems to be another form of ಎಱಗು, the quality of a simpleton; ಕಿವುಡು may be ಕಿವಿ and ಉಡು (= ಉಡಿ), 'ear-breakage'; ಕೆಂಚು is ಕೆಂ and ಚು (= ಸು); ಗುಜ್ಜು is ಗುಜ್ (= ಕುಱು) and ಜು.

b) Other taddhita nouns are ಪಿನ್ದು (ಪಿನ್ + ದು) or ಹಿನ್ದು and ಮುನ್ದು (ಮುನ್ + ದು). They optionally take the form of ಪಿನ್ತು (ಪಿನ್ + ತು) and ಮುನ್ತು (ಮುನ್ + ತು, see § 122). Their final ಉ may become ಎ, in which case they appear as ಪಿನ್ದೆ (ಹಿನ್ದೆ), ಮುನ್ದೆ, ಪಿನ್ತೆ, ಮುನ್ತೆ.

The same change of final ಉ into ಎ may take place also in the taddhita nouns ಒಳಗು (ಒಳ + ಗು), ಕೆಳಗು (ಕೆಳ + ಗು), ಪೆಱಗು (ಪೆಱ + ಗು), ಪೊಱಗು (ಪೊಱ + ಗು), ಮೇಗು (ಮೇ + ಗು), in which case they become ಒಳಗೆ, ಕೆಳಗೆ, ಪೆಱಗೆ, ಪೊಱಗೆ, ಮೇಗೆ.

B. The chief suffixes for forming masculines, feminines, (epicenes and neuters) are

1, ಆಟಿಗ (ಆಟ + ಇಗ, a player, a man who busies himself with, one who is occupied with), *e. g.* ಕೊಲ್ಲಟಿಗ, ಏವಟಿಗ, ಮಾವಟಿಗ.

2, ಅಡಿಗ (ಅಡ + ಇಗ, = ಆಟಿಗ), *e. g.* ದೇವಡಿಗ, ಪಾವಡಿಗ (o. r. ಹಾವಡಿಗ), ಪೂವಡಿಗ.

3, ಅಣಿಗ (ಅಣ + ಇಗ, = ಅಡಿಗ), *e. g.* ಎರವಣಿಗ, ಪೂವಣಿಗ.

4, ಅಯಿಲ (=ಆಯಿಲ), *e. g.* ಘೋಡಯಿಲ, ಸಜ್ಜೆಯಿಲ, ಪದಯಿಲ. This is only in the Šabdânušâsana. See ಘೋಡಯಿಲ in Dictionary.

5, ಆಯ್ತ, *e. g.* ಅಚ್ಚುಳಾಯ್ತ, ಕಡಂಗಾಯ್ತ, ಕಲ್ಲಾಯ್ತ, ಝುಳಮ್ಬಾಯ್ತ, ಸೂಱಾಯ್ತ. It occurs also as ಆಯತ, ಆಯಿತ; see Dictionary. The Šabdânušâsana adds ಬಾಗಿಲಾಯ್ತ, ಅವಸರಾಯ್ತ, and says that the suffix means 'superintendent', 'controller' (adhikṛita).

6, ಆಯಿಲ (=ಅಯಿಲ), *e. g.* ಅಡ್ಡಾಯಿಲ, ಓಜಾಯಿಲ, ಘೋಡಾಯಿಲ, ಪುಗರ್ಾಯಿಲ (o. r. ಪುಗ್ಗಾಯಿಲ), ರೇಖಾಯಿಲ. It has also the form of ಆಯ್ಲ (see Dictionary), and is used for Kannaḍa and Saṁskṛita nouns. In the Šabdamaṇidarpaṇa p. 30 ಘೋಡಾಯಿಲ appears as tadbhava of ಘೋಟಾರೂಢ.

7, ಆಳಿ (another form of ಆಡಿ, 'that moves, plays, performs', etc.; see Dictionary), *e. g.* ಏಱಾಳಿ, ಓದಾಳಿ, ಕೇಡಾಳಿ, ಜೂದಾಳಿ, ಪಡಪಾಳಿ, (o. r. ಹಡಪಾಳಿ), ಮಾತಾಳಿ, ಮಾಱಾಳಿ, ಸಿಗ್ಗಳಿ. It forms epicene nouns which occasionally are used also as neuters, *e. g.* ಓದಾಳಿ ಇವಂ, ಓದಾಳಿ ಇವಳ್, ಓದಾಳಿ ಇದು.

8, ಇ (a feminine suffix added to ಉಗ, etc.), *e. g.* ತಾಳುಗಿ (ತಾಱುಗಿ), ನಾರುಗಿ, ಬೂತುಗಿ, ಬೇರುಗಿ, ಮಾತುಗಿ (*cf.* Nos. 16. 17. 28); ನಿಡುಗಣ್ಣಿ, ನಿಡುವೆರಲಿ, ಸುರ್ಕುಂಗುರುಳಿ; ಕರಿಕಿ, ಬಿಳಿಕಿ, ಮುದುಕಿ; ಸೂಳಾಯ್ತಿ, ಅವಸರಾಯ್ತಿ; ಅರಸಿ;—(a masculine and neuter suffix) *e. g.* ಆಱುಗುಲಿ, ಆನೆಗುಲಿ, ಇಲಿಗುಲಿ, ಪಾವುಗುಲಿ (see No. 26 *b*);—(an epicene suffix) *e. g.* ಕಡುಗೆಲಸಿ, ಕಡುಚಾಗಿ, ಚಲವಾದಿ, ನಿಡುಮೂಗಿ.

9, ಇಕ, *e. g.* ಅಸಿಕ, ಕರಿಕ, ದಸಿಕ (o. r. ಹಿಸಿಕ), ಬಾರಿಕ. The Šabdânušâsana has ಕುಸಿಕ, ಸಸಿಕ, ಬಾರಿಕ. It refers ಕರಿಕ to suffix ಕ, teaching that it is formed of ಕರಿದು which drops its final syllable; see No. 24.

10, ಇಗ, *e. g.* ಕಬ್ಬಿಗ, ತೋಣ್ಟಿಗ, ಸರವಣ್ಣಿಗ, ಸಿಂಗರಿಗ, ಪಟ್ಟಸಾಲಿಗ, ಮನ್ದುರಿಗ, ಬಾಣಸಿಗ;—ಗನ್ದಿಗ, ಮೂಸಿಗ, ತಮ್ಬುಲಿಗ;—ಅಡಪಿಗ, ಚಾಮರಿಗ, ಕರಹಟ್ಟಿಗ (o. r. ಕರಹಟಿಗ);—ಆಟಮಟಿಗ, ಮಾಳಿಗ (*o. r.* ಮಾಲಿಗ), ಪುಸಿಗ;—ಜೋಯಿಸಿಗ, ಲೆಕ್ಕಿಗ, ಪೊಲಮ್ಬಿಗ;—ಸಾಲಿಗ, ಹಂಗಿಗ;—ದೇಗುಲಿಗ, ಅಕ್ಕರಿಗ, ಭಾಣ್ಡಸಿಗ;—ಚಿಪ್ಪಿಗ;—ಮೂಲಿಗ.

The Šabdânušâsana has the following series:—ತಮ್ಬುಲಿಗ, ದವಸಿಗ, ದೂಸಿಗ, ಕಾಯಿಗ, ಪಣ್ಣಿಗ;—ಮದ್ದಳಿಗ, ಸರವಣ್ಣಿಗ, ಬೀಣೆಗ, ಗಾಣಿಗ, ಕೇಣಿಗ;—ಷಡಿಸಣಿಗ, ಆಟಮಟಿಗ, ಪುಸಿಗ, ಉಪವಾಸಿಗ, ನಿಯಮಿಗ, ವ್ರತಿಗ;—ಜೋಯಿಸಿಗ, ಗಣಿದಿಗ, ಸಿದ್ಧಾನ್ತಿಗ, ಲೆಕ್ಕಿಗ, ಶಾಸ್ತ್ರಿಗ, ಬಾಗರಣಿಗ;—ಗನ್ದಿಗ, ಮೆಣಸಿಗ, ಪಿಪ್ಪಲಿಗ;—ದೇವಿಗ, ಪಾಕಿಗ, ಅಡುಗಗ, ಕಬ್ಬಿಗ, ಚೌಪದಿಗ;—ಕಮ್ಮಿಗ, ಕುಮ್ಬಿಗ, ಅಕ್ಕರಿಗ, ಮದನವತಿಗ; ಸುಂಕಿಗ, ಬಾಗಿಲಿಗ, ದ್ವಾರಿಗ, ಭಣ್ಡಾರಿಗ;—ಕಾಲೂರಿಗ, ಕರಹಾಡಿಗ, ಒಳ್ಳೂರಿಗ, ಬಾನಿಗ, ಪಟ್ಟಣಿಗ, ಕನ್ನಡಿಗ.

11, ಇಚ, *e. g.* ಆಲರಿಚ, ಪೊಱಲಿಚ. The Šabdânušâsana has ಕನ್ನಡಿಚ. In some instances a preceding vowel is shortened, *e. g.* ಕಾಲುರಿಚ (for ಕಾಲೂರಿಚ). The Šabdânušâsana adduces also ಒಳ್ಳುರಿಚ (for ಒಳ್ಳೂರಿಚ), ಮೆಲುರಿಚ (for ಮೇಲೂರಿಚ), ಬನಿಚ (for ಬಾನಿಚ), ಕಲಿಚ (for ಕಾಲಿಚ), ಕರಹಡಿಚ (for ಕರಹಾಡಿಚ).

12, ಇತಿ (a feminine suffix added to ಇಗ, etc.), *e. g.* ಚಾಮರಿಗಿತಿ, ಮದ್ದಳಿಗಿತಿ, ಆವುಜಿಗಿತಿ, ಕನ್ನಡಿಗಿತಿ, ದೇಸಿಗಿತಿ, ಲೇಪಾಳಿಗಿತಿ, ಪಂಚಮಿಗಿತಿ, ತೆಲ್ಲಿಗಿತಿ, ಚಿಪ್ಪಿಗಿತಿ, ಒಕ್ಕಲಿಗಿತಿ, ಹಾದರಿಗಿತಿ. The Šabdânušâsana has also ಗಾಣಿಗಿತಿ, ಅಗಸಿಗಿತಿ, ಕೊಂಕಣಿಗಿತಿ, ಸುಂಕಿಗಿತಿ, ತೋಣ್ಟಿಗಿತಿ, ಪಾವಡಿಗಿತಿ, ಮಾಲೆವಡಿಗಿತಿ, ಸರವಣ್ಣಿಗಿತಿ, ಪಟ್ಟಸಾಲಿಗಿತಿ, ಗನ್ದಿಗಿತಿ;—ದೇವುಳಿಗಿತಿ, ಪಾಕುಳಿಗಿತಿ, ಕೆಯ್ದುಳಿಗಿತಿ;—ಮಾತುಗಿತಿ, ಬೂತುಗಿತಿ, ನಾರುಗಿತಿ, ಬೇರುಗಿತಿ, ತಾಳುಗಿತಿ (ತಾಱುಗಿತಿ);—ಲಂಚಗಿತಿ.

Occasionally ಇತಿ is suffixed to simple Kannaḍa nouns, *e. g.* ಒಕ್ಕಲಿತಿ, ಕುಱುಮ್ಬಿತಿ, ತೆಲುಂಗಿತಿ, ಪಾರ್ವಿತಿ, or to tadbhavas, *e. g.* ಅಕ್ಕಸಾಲಿತಿ, ಅರಸಿತಿ, ಜೋಗಿತಿ, ತಳವರಿತಿ, ನಾವಿದಿತಿ,

ಪಟ್ಟಸಾಲಿತಿ, or to secondary forms of tadbhavas, *e.g.* ಕಮ್ಮಱಿತಿ, ಕುಮ್ಬಱಿತಿ, or also to Saṁskṛita nouns, *e. g.* ಕ್ಷತ್ರಿಯಿತಿ, ಪ್ರಧಾನಿತಿ, ಬ್ರಾಹ್ಮಣಿತಿ.

13 *a*, ಇಲ, *e. g.* ಪಚ್ಚೆಯಿಲ, ಘಳಯಿಲ (?), ಪಡೆಯಿಲ, ಗಾವಿಲ, ಸಾವಿಲ. (*Cf.* ಅಯಿಲ ಆಯಿಲ?).

13 *b*, ಇಲ (a negative form of ಇಲ್), *e. g.* ಬರ್ದಿಲ. *Cf.* § 209, note 1, and No. 14.

14, ಇಲಿ (a negative form of ಇಲ್, used for masculines, feminines and neuters), *e. g.* ಅಗಿಲಿಲಿ, ಕಣ್ಣಿಲಿ, ಕೂರಿಲಿ, ನಾಣಿಲಿ, ಬೆಳಗಿಲಿ.

15, ಉಕ, *e. g.* ಅಣ್ಣುಕ, ಕಟ್ಟುಕ, ಕಾರುಕ, ತಟ್ಟುಕ, ದಿಣ್ಣುಕ, ಬೊನ್ನುಕ, ಸಣ್ಣುಕ. The Śabdânuśâsana has also ಚಟ್ಟುಕ, ಪಟ್ಟುಕ, ಸಣುಕ (= ಸಣ್ಣುಕ).

16, ಉಗ, *e. g.* ಊರುಗ, ಕಾೞುಗ (ಕಾಳುಗ), ನಾರುಗ, ನೇಱುಗ, ಬೇರುಗ, ಮಣ್ಣುಗ, ಹೆಣ್ಣುಗ. The Śabdânuśâsana has also ಕಲ್ಲುಗ, ಅಚ್ಚುಳುಗ, ತಾಳುಗ (ತಾೞುಗ), ಪರಳುಗ, ಪಾಲುಗ, ಪೊನ್ನುಗ, ಸೂೞುಗ. *Cf.* No. 8.

17, ಉಗಿ (a feminine suffix), *e. g.* ತಾಳುಗಿ (ತಾೞುಗಿ), ನಾರುಗಿ, ಬೂತುಗಿ, ಬೇರುಗಿ, ಮಾತುಗಿ. This is only in the Śabdânuśâsana. *Cf.* No. 8.

18, ಉಣಿ (of verb ಉಣ್, a masculine, feminine and neuter suffix), *e. g.* ಅಮರ್ದುಣಿ, ಕಳ್ಳುಣಿ, ತುಡುಗುಣಿ. The Śabdânuśâsana adds ಅರಲುಣಿ, ಅಲರುಣಿ, ಎರಲುಣಿ, ಎಲರುಣಿ, ಕಮ್ಬುಣಿ, ಪಾವುಣಿ, ಬಣ್ಣುಣಿ.

19, ಉಳಿಗ (= ಉೞಿಗ), *e. g.* ದೇವುಳಿಗ, ಮಣ್ಣುಳಿಗ. The Śabdânuśâsana has also ಅಡುಗುಳಿಗ, ಕಬ್ಬುಳಿಗ, ಚೌಪದುಳಿಗ, ಪಾಕುಳಿಗ.

20, ಉಳ್ಳ, which is the present participle of ಉಳ್ (see § 180, remark after 6; § 215, 5, *b*), and by adding the suffixes ಅಂ, ಅಳ್, ಉದು, (ಅವನು, ಅವಳು, ಅದು) may be used to form masculines, feminines and neuters (see §§ 185. 186). Kêśava's instances are all of the masculine gender, *viz.* ಧನಮುಳ್ಳಂ (ಧನಂ+ ಉಳ್ಳಂ), ಧಾನ್ಯಮುಳ್ಳಂ, ಗುಣಮುಳ್ಳಂ, ಓದುಳ್ಳಂ, ತೇಜಮುಳ್ಳಂ. See § 273.

21, ಉೞಿಗ (= ಉಳಿಗ; *cf.* ಊಳಿಗ in Dictionary?), *e. g.* ದಣ್ಣುೞಿಗ.

22, ಎ (a feminine suffix; *cf.* § 74), *e. g.* ಚದುರೆ, ಜೋಡೆ, ಪಾಪ್ಪೆ, ಸಿತಗೆ. The Śabdânuśâsana adds ಎಗ್ಗೆ, ಕಳ್ಳೆ, ಕೆಪ್ಪೆ, ತುಪ್ಪೆ, ತೇಪೆ, ಬಡ್ಡೆ, ಬೆಳ್ಳೆ, ಬೊಳ್ಳೆ, ಮುಣ್ಡೆ, ರುಂಡೆ, ಲಡ್ಡೆ, ಹೆಡ್ಡೆ;—ಸೂಱಾಯ್ತೆ, ಅವಸರಾಯ್ತೆ;—ಕಾಲುರಿಚೆ, ಕರಹಡಿಚೆ;—ಲಂಚವಣಿಗೆ, ಊಟವಣಿಗೆ;—ಸಿರಿವನ್ತೆ, ಗುಣವನ್ತೆ.

23, ಒಡೆಯ (a noun of the masculine gender preceded by the genitive), *e. g.* ಕೊಡೆಯೊಡೆಯ, ಜಗದೊಡೆಯ, ಜಾಣೊಡೆಯ, ನೆಲದೊಡೆಯ (Mdb. ನೆಲನೊಡೆಯ), ಪೆರ್ಮೆಯೊಡೆಯ. See § 215, 5, *b*. Its feminine is ಒಡತಿ.

24, ಕ, *e. g.* ಅಱಿಕ, ಒಣಕ, ಕಿಡುಕ, ಕೊಳಕ (ಕೊೞಕ?), ತೊಳಕ, ನಡುಕ, ಬಡಕ, ಬಣುಕ, ಬೆಳುಕ (o. r. ಬಳಕ). The Śabdânuśâsana has ಕರಿಕ (see under ಇಕ), ಕಡಿಕ, ತೋರಿಕ, ಬಿಳಿಕ.

25, ಕಾೞಿ, *e. g.* ಇಚ್ಚೆಕಾೞಿ, ಕೆಯ್ದುಕಾೞಿ, ಗೆಱೆಕಾೞಿ, ಪಗೆಕಾೞಿ, ಪಾಱೆಕಾೞಿ, ಬಗೆಕಾೞಿ, ಬನ್ನಿಕಾೞಿ, ಬೇಟಕಾೞಿ, ಬೇಹುಕಾೞಿ, ಒಳ್ನುಡಿಕಾೞಿ, ನಗೆವಳಿಕಾೞಿ (o. r. ನಗೆವಡಿಕಾೞಿ). The Śabdânuśâsana has ಆಟಕಾೞಿ, ನಗೆಕಾೞಿ, ನುಡಿಕಾೞಿ, ಮುಣ್ಡುಕಾೞಿ, ಮೋಸಕಾೞಿ. *Cf.* No. 29.

26 *a*, ಕುಟಿಗ, *e. g.* ಕಲ್ಕುಟಿಗ, ಕಟ್ಟಿಕುಟಿಗ, ನೀರ್ಕುಟಿಗ, ಮರಕುಟಿಗ. The Śabdânuśâsana makes it ಗುಟಿಗ (according to the sandhi rule in § 215, 7, *a*) in the following words:—ಕೆಯ್ಗುಟಿಗ, ಗಱಿಗುಟಿಗ, ದಾರಿಗುಟಿಗ.

26*b*, ಕುಳಿ. It is used with the application of the sandhi rule in § 215, 7, *a*. See No. 8.

27, ಕುಳಿ (= ಗುಳಿ, a masculine, feminine and neuter suffix; probably of ಕುಳ್ = ಕೊಳ್, to seize, etc.), *e. g.* ಓಡುಕುಳಿ, ಆಯ್ಕುಳಿ, ಪೇಂಕುಳಿ, ಪೋರ್ಕುಳಿ, ಮಱುಕುಳಿ. The Šabdânušâsana has also ಅಡುಕುಳಿ, ಅಬ್ಕುಳಿ, ಮಾಬ್ಕುಳಿ (see § 58), ಸಾಲ್ಕುಳಿ.

28, ಗ, *e. g.* ಎಡೆಗ, ಕನ್ತೆಗ, ನವಸಿಗ, ಬಿದಿಗ, ಬೂತುಗ, ಬೊನ್ತೆಗ, ಮಾತುಗ, ಸಟೆಗ. See under No. 8. The Šabdânušâsana adduces also ಊಟಗ, ಜೂದುಗ, ಪೞಿಗ, ಪಾಡುಗ, ಮಾರಿಗ, ಲಂಚಗ.

29, ಗಾಱಿ (= ಕಾಱ, with the application of the sandhi rule in § 215, 7, *a*), *e. g.* ಒಱೆಗಾಱ, ಗೆಜ್ಜೆಗಾಱ, ಬಳೆಗಾಱ, ಮಣಿಗಾಱ, ಮಾಲೆಗಾಱ.

When ಗಾಱ is preceded by ಉ, a euphonic sŏnnĕ is put after the ಉ, *e. g.* ಅಲಸುಂಗಾಱ, ಓದುಂಗಾಱ, ಜೂದುಂಗಾಱ, ಪಾಡುಂಗಾಱ, or the ಉ may be dropped, *e. g.* ಕಂಚ ಗಾಱ (for ಕಂಚುಗಾಱ).

ಕಮ್ಮ and ಕುಮ್ಮ drop the ಗಾ of ಗಾಱ, so that they become ಕಮ್ಮಱ, ಕುಮ್ಮಱ.

30, ಗುಳಿ (= ಕುಳಿ, with the application of the sandhi rule in § 215, 7, *a*, preceded by a euphonic sŏnnĕ), *e. g.* ಆಟಂಗುಳಿ, ಕುತ್ತಂಗುಳಿ (o. r. ಕುತ್ತುಂಗುಳಿ), ಪಣಂಗುಳಿ, ಲಂಚಂಗುಳಿ, ಸಾಲಂಗುಳಿ. The Šabdânušâsana has also ಕಾಯ್ಗುಳಿ, ಪಣ್ಗುಳಿ.

31, ತಿ (a feminine suffix), *e. g.* ಎಡತಿ, ಎಱತಿ, ಗೆಣತಿ, ನರತಿ, ಪೊಲತಿ (with the elision of final ಎ); ಪೆಣ್ತಿ, ಕಣಿತಿ, ಪಾರ್ವತಿ, ಸೆಟ್ಟಿತಿ; ಕಮ್ಮಱತಿ, ಕುಮ್ಮಱತಿ (see under No. 29); ಆಟಕಾತಿರ್, ಗಾಡಿಕಾತಿರ್, ನಗೆಕಾತಿರ್, ನುಡಿಕಾತಿರ್, ಬಗೆಕಾತಿರ್, ಬೇಟಕಾತಿರ್ (of ಆಟಕಾಱ, etc., with the elision of final ಅ); ಒಱೆಗಾತಿರ್, ಕಂಚಗಾತಿರ್, ಜಾಲಗಾತಿರ್, ಜೂಜುಗಾತಿರ್, ಬಳೆಗಾತಿರ್, ಮಣಿಗಾತಿರ್, ಮಾಲೆಗಾತಿರ್, ಸಂಚಗಾತಿರ್ (of ಒಱೆಗಾಱ, etc., with the elision of final ಅ); ಅಡಪವಳ್ತಿ, ಘಟ್ಟಿವಳ್ತಿ, ಪಡೆವಳ್ತಿ, ಮುಡಿವಳ್ತಿ, ಸೆಜ್ಜೆವಳ್ತಿ (of ಅಡಪವಳ, etc., with the elision of final ಅ).

32, (ದಿ, = ತಿ, *e. g.* ಕೆಳದಿ, ಪೊಲದಿ, with the dropping of final ಎ).

33, ವಟಿಗ, *e. g.* ಗರವಟಿಗ, ಗಱಿವಟಿಗ, ನೀರ್ವಟಿಗ. This suffix is only in the Šabdânušâsana. (Regarding ಗರವಟಿಗ it says — ಗರ ಇತಿ ಜಲಯನ್ತ್ರವಿಶೇಷಃ । ತತ್ರ ನಿಯುಕ್ತಃ ॥ ಅಥವಾ ಗರವಟ ಇತಿ ದುರ್ಗಾದೌ ಪ್ರಹರೇ ಪರ್ಯಟನಾದಿನಾ ಕ್ರಿಯಮಾಣೋ ರಕ್ಷಾವಿಶೇಷಃ । ತತ್ರ ನಿಯುಕ್ತೋ ವಾ ॥.)

34, ವಡಿಗ, *e. g.* ಕುಂಚವಡಿಗ, ಪುಲ್ಲವಡಿಗ. The Šabdânušâsana has ಕಂಚುವಡಿಗ, ಮಾಲೆವಡಿಗ.

35, ವಣಿಗ, *e. g.* ಕೂಲ್ವಣಿಗ, ಊಟವಣಿಗ, ಲಂಚವಣಿಗ, ಸಾಲವಣಿಗ.

36, ವನ್ತ, *e. g.* ಜಸವನ್ತ (o. r. ಜಯುವನ್ತ), ಸಿರಿವನ್ತ, ಹೊನ್ನವನ್ತ (o. r. ಪೊಣ್ಣವನ್ತ). See § 215, 5, *b*.

37, ವಳ, *e. g.* ಅಡಪವಳ, ಅಡುವಳ, ಪಡೆವಳ, ಮುಡಿವಳ, ಮಾಸವಳ, ಸೆಜ್ಜೆವಳ, (ಸೇನೆವಳ).

38, ವಳ್ಳ (= ವಳ), *e. g.* ಅಡಪವಳ್ಳ, ಅಡುವಳ್ಳ, etc.

These and others are the suffixes for forming masculine, feminine (and neuter) nouns (Kêšava says).

The taddhita nouns mentioned under letters *A* and *B* are more or less used in the three dialects.

Remark.

According to § 115 (*cf.* § 249) masculine nominal bases are frequently formed by the addition of the suffixes ಅ, he, and ಂ, the grammatical sign of the nominative, to the genitive. Kêšava adduces the following additional instances:— ಬಲದಂ (ಬಲದ+ಅ+ಂ), a man of the right, ತೆಂಕಣಂ (ತೆಂಕಣ+ಅ+ಂ), a man of the south, ಬಡಗಣಂ, ಪಡುವಣಂ, ಮೇಗಣಂ, ಕೆಳಗಣಂ, ನಡುವಣಂ, ಒಳಗಣಂ, ಪೊಱಗಣಂ, ಅಲ್ಲಿಯಣಂ (ಅಲ್ಲಿಯಣ+ಅ+ಂ, see § 139), ಇಲ್ಲಿಯಣಂ, ಎಲ್ಲಿಯಣಂ, ಕಡೆಯಣಂ (see § 139), ಮುನ್ತಣಂ (ಮುನ್ತಣ+ಅ+ಂ), ಪಿನ್ತಣಂ, ಅತ್ತಣಂ, ಇತ್ತಣಂ.

The feminine forms in the ancient dialect are ತೆಂಕಣಳ್ (ತೆಂಕಣ+ಅಳ್), a woman of the south, ಬಡಗಣಳ್, ನಡುವಣಳ್, ಕಡೆಯಣಳ್. In the modern dialect ಅವ (ಅವನು) and ಅವಳು are added to the genitive, *e. g.* ತೆಂಕಣವ (ತೆಂಕಣವನು), a man of the south, ಕಡೆಯುವ, ಒಳಗಿನವ, ಮುನ್ದಿನವ, ಅಲ್ಲಿಯುವ; ಕಡೆಯುವಳು, a woman of the side, etc.

A strange form, however, appears, when in the ancient dialect ದ and ಂ are suffixed to ಅಲ್ಲಿ, ಇಲ್ಲಿ, ಉಲ್ಲಿ, and ಎಲ್ಲಿ, *viz.* ಅಲ್ಲಿದಂ, a man of that place, ಇಲ್ಲಿದಂ, a man of this place, ಉಲ್ಲಿದಂ, a man of this intermediate place, ಎಲ್ಲಿದಂ, a man of what place, *e. g.*

ಕೆಲದನಲ್ಲಿದನಿಲ್ಲಿದನೀಗಳೆಯ್ದಿನಂ ಮುತ್ತಿದನೊಡ್ಡೆ ತೇಱೊಳಮರೇನ್ದ್ರಸುತಂ |.
ವಿನೋ
ದದ ಮೊದಲೆಲ್ಲಿದಂ ಸೊಬಗಿನಾಗರಮೆಲ್ಲಿದನಿಚ್ಛೆಯುಣ್ಮನೆ
ಲ್ಲಿದನೆರ್ದೆಗಾಣ್ಮನೆನ್ನರಸನೆಲ್ಲಿದನೋ ಲಲಿತಾಂಗಿವಲ್ಲಭಂ? ||.

A ದ and ಂ are found in the attributive nouns ಒಳ್ಳಿದಂ, ಕಮ್ಮಿದಂ, ಕೂರಿದಂ, ತೆಳ್ಳಿದಂ, ತೋಱಿದಂ, ನೇಱಿಪಂ, ಬಲ್ಲಿದಂ, ಬಿಟ್ಟಿದಂ, ಮೆಲ್ಲಿದಂ (§§ 273. 274. 276).

How is the ದಂ in ಅಲ್ಲಿದಂ, etc. to be explained? Let us take the corresponding modern form ಅಲ್ಲಿಯವನು, a man of that place, as our guide. It is composed of ಅಲ್ಲಿ, that place, ಯ್, a euphonic letter to connect the ಅ of the genitive with the crude base of the noun (§§ 109 under genitive; 130; 141, remark under dative), ಅ, the termination of the genitive, ಅವ, he, and ನು, the grammatical sign of the nominative (§ 114). It is evident that the ದ್ in ಅಲ್ಲಿದಂ is a substitute for the euphonic ಯ್ in ಅಲ್ಲಿಯವನು, which connects the ಅ of the genitive with ಅಲ್ಲಿ, so that ಅಲ್ಲಿದ (for ಅಲ್ಲಿಯ) is obtained, to which ಅ, he, and ಂ, the grammatical sign of the nominative, are suffixed. (See under ಒಳ್ಳಿದಂ in § 276.)

The feminine forms of ಅಲ್ಲಿದಂ, etc. are ಅಲ್ಲಿದಳ್, ಇಲ್ಲಿದಳ್, ಉಲ್ಲಿವಳ್, ಎಲ್ಲಿದಳ್.

XI. On compound bases.

244. Compound bases (samâsaliṅgas) have been mentioned in § 68, 3; 102. 8, *d;* 215, 7, *a seq.* "When (two or more) nominal bases (etc.) seek for a meaning (directly, without intermediate augments and terminations) as a calf does for the close union of its mother, a compound is produced", Kêšava says. In such a case intervening augments (âgamas) and terminations (vibhaktis) are elided, *e. g.* ತೊಱೆಯ (*i. e.* ತೊಱೆ+ಯ್+ಅ) ಮಾವು becomes ತೊಱೆಮಾವು, ತೊಡೆಯ ಸೆಕ್ಕೆ ತೊಡೆಸೆಕ್ಕೆ, ಎಡೆಯ ನುಡಿ ಎಡೆನುಡಿ, ಮಾತಿನ ಬಲ್ಲಹಂ ಮಾತುಬಲ್ಲಹಂ, ನೂಱಿಱ ಪತ್ತು ನೂಱುಪತ್ತು (§ 278, 1), ತೆಂಕಣ ಪಕ್ಕಂ ತೆಂಕವಕ್ಕಂ (*cf.* § 215, 7, *b*), and also substitutes (âdêśas) are introduced, *e. g.* ಮೆಲ್ಲಿತು ಅಡಿ becomes ಮೆಲ್ಲಡಿ (§ 247, 11), ಕೆಳಗಿನ ಕೊವ್ವು ಕಿಱುಕ್ಕೊವ್ವು (§ 246, *b*), ಕಿಱಿದು ಅಡಿ ಕುತ್ತಡಿ (§ 247, 13), ಒನ್ದು ಮೊದಲ್ ಒರ್ಮೊದಲ್ (§ 248, 1), ಎರಡು ಮೆಯ್ ಇರ್ಮೆಯ್ (§ 248, 2).

Compounds are used more or less in the three dialects; about the extent of their use in each dialect the Dictionary is to be consulted.

The rules about euphonic junction (sandhi) in § 215, 7,*a seq.* are to be remembered.

245. First there are **six compounds in Kannaḍa which are also in Saṁskṛita,** *viz.* ತತ್ಪುರುಷ, ಕರ್ಮಧಾರಯ, ದ್ವಿಗು, ಬಹುವ್ರೀಹಿ, ದ್ವನ್ದ್ವ, and ಅವ್ಯಯೀಭಾವ. **About three other Kannaḍa compounds see § 253.**

246. The first Kannaḍa compound is **ತತ್ಪುರುಷ.** It is called so, because the leading instance of this class in Saṁskṛita is tatpurusha, 'the servant of him', indicating that the last word 'purusha' governs the preceding one 'tat', requiring in this case (and in Kannaḍa, it may be said, generally) the genitive. *Cf.* § 253, 2.

a) **Instances in which the first member of the compound is unaltered,** are:—ತೊಱೆಮಾವು, a mango of a river (*i. e.* a mango grown near a river), ಎಡೆನುಡಿ, a word of inferiority, ಮಾಮರಂ, a tree of the mango, ಮಲ್ಲಿಗೆಸಸೆ, ಮಾಣಿಕಗೆಮ್ಪು, ಅಲರ್ವಕ್ಕಿ, ಕನ್ನಡವಕ್ಕಿ, ಕಡೆಸೆಱಂಗು, ಉಡೆನೂಲ್, ಕುಳಿರ್ಗಾಳಿ, ಬೆಳಗೆಮ್ಪು, ಅಲದೋಟಂ, ಅಲದೋರಣಂ, ತಳಿದೋರಣಂ, ಬಿದಿರ್ವಟ್ಟೆ, ಪೊಗರ್ವಟ್ಟೆ, ಬೆಮರ್ವನಿ, ಅಲಜೊಮ್ಪಂ, ಕೆಸರ್ಮಲ್ಲಿಗೆ, ನೇಸರ್ಮಯಣಂ, ಬೇಸರ್ನುಡಿ, ಕದಿರ್ಜೊನ್ನಂ, ಮುಗುಳ್ನಾಯ್, ಎಸಳ್ವಸೆ, ಅಮಳ್ದಿಂಗಲ್, ತನಿಗಮ್ಪು, ಕಣ್ಣೀರ್, ಕಣ್ಣೋಟಂ, ಗಱಿಗೂಸು, ಉಡಿದೊವಲ್, ಪಣೆಗಟ್ಟು, ಕಣ್ಬೊಲಂ, ತಲೆಕಟ್ಟು, ಬೆಸೆಕೋಲ್, ಕಣ್ಣಲ್ಲಂ, ಅಲದೊಂಗಲ್, ಬೆಳೆವೊಲಂ, ಮರವಣಿ, ಎಳನೀರ್ವೊನಲ್, ಆಳ್ವಲ್ಮೆ, ತೋಳ್ವಲ್ಮೆ, ಬಾಳ್ಮೊನೆ, ಪೂಪುಣಮ್ಪು, ಕಣ್ಬೇಟಂ, ಪೊಂಜುರಿಗೆ, ಕಣ್ಸೋಲಂ, ಕಳ್ಸವಿಗೆ, ಬಾಯ್ಸವಿಗೆ, ಮೆಯ್ಸೊಬಗು, ಕೆಯ್ಸುರಿಗೆ, ಕಲ್ಸರಿ, ಕಳ್ಕಾಟಂ, ತೋಳಾಟಂ, ಬಾಳೊಪ್ಪಂ.

In such compounds a double letter may appear after a rêpha (ರ್), *e. g.* ನೀರ್ಗ್ಗಿಚ್ಚು (for ನೀರ್ಗಿಚ್ಚು), ಊರ್ವ್ವೇಲಿ, ನೀರ್ವ್ವಾವಸೆ, ಕಾರ್ಗ್ಗಾಲ್. See § 371, 4.

Also where there is no compound such a doubling happens, *e. g.* ಬೇರ್ಪ್ಪಱಿದುದು, ತೇರ್ಪ್ಪರಿದುದು, ನೀರ್ತ್ತಿಳಿದುದು, ಕೇರ್ಕ್ಕಡೆದುದು (*cf.* § 119, *a*, dative). See § 371, 4.

b) Instances in which the first member loses its last syllable, or a homogeneous letter (uċitâkshara) together with elision is introduced, or a homogeneous letter without elision comes in, are—ಒಳಕೋಣ್ಟೆ (=ಒಳಗು or ಒಳಗಣ ಕೋಣ್ಟೆ), ಒಳಕೆಯ್, ಒಳವಾಲಂ, ಪೊಱಕೋಣ್ಟೆ (=ಪೊಱಗು or ಪೊಱಗಣ—), ಪೊಱಕಟ್ಟು, ಒಳತೋಟಂ, ಜೇನೆಯ್ (=ಜೇನ್ or ಜೇನ—), ತೆಂಗಾಳಿ (=ತೆಂಕ or ತೆಂಕಣ—), ಅರಮನೆ (=ಅರಸು or ಅರಸಿನ—);—ತೆಮ್ಬೆಲರ್ (*i. e.* ತೆಂ+ಬ+ಎಲರ್=ತೆಂಕ or ತೆಂಕಣ ಎಲರ್), ದಾಂಗುಡಿ (=ದಾಣ್ಬು or ದಾಣ್ಬಿನ ಕುಡಿ), ಮಾಂಗಾಯ್ (=ಮಾವು or ಮಾವಿನ ಕಾಯ್), ಅಂಗೊಳಗು (=ಅವು or ಅವಿನ ಕೊಳಗು), ಕಮ್ಮಂಗಣೆ (=ಕಮ್ಪು or ಕಮ್ಪಿನ ಕಣೆ), ಕಿಱುಕೊಮ್ಬು (=ಕೆಳಗು or ಕೆಳಗಣ—), ಕಿಱ್ಕಿವಲ್, ಕಿಱ್ಕಿಣೆ, ಕಿಱ್ಕಿಟ್ಟು, ಕಿಱ್ಕಿಡಲ್, ಕಿನ್ನೀರ್ (=ಕೆಳಗು or ಕೆಳಗಣ—), ಕಿನ್ನೆಲಂ;—ಬಾನಂಗುಳಿಗೆ (*i. e.* ಬಾನ್ +ಅಂ=ಬಾನಿನ—), ಮೀನಮ್ಬುಱು (*i. e.* ಮೀನ್+ಅಂ=ಮೀನಿನ ಪುಱು), ಕಣ್ಣನ್ದೊಱಿಲಿ (*i. e.* ಕಣ್+ಅಂ=ಕಣ್ಣಿನ ತೊಱಿಲಿ), ಜಕ್ಕನ್ದೊಱಿಲಿ (*i. e* ಜಕ್ಕ+ಂ=ಜಕ್ಕದ ತೊಱಿಲಿ), ನಟ್ಟೆಗೊಮ್ಬು (*i. e.* ನಟ್ಟ+ಎ-ಕೊಮ್ಬು, which finally is=ನಡುವಿನ ಕೊಮ್ಬು), ನಟ್ಟೆವನೆ, ನಟ್ಟೆವನಿ, ನಟ್ಟೆವಾನ್, ಕಾಱ್ಕಿಚ್ಚು (=ಕಾಡು or ಕಾಡಿನ ಕಿಚ್ಚು), ನಾಱ್ಕಿಡೆ, ಕಾಱ್ತಿಱು, ಕಾಱ್ಪಿರಂ, ನಾಱ್ತಿಡುಗುಣೆ, ನಾಱ್ಪಿಗರಣಂ (see § 234).

Observe that there is no sandhi when ಒಳ and ಪೊಱ are followed by a vowel, *e. g.* ಒಳ ಅಟ್ಟಂ, ಪೊಱ ಅಡಿ; see § 215, 6, *i*.

247. The second compound is **ಕರ್ಮಧಾರಯ**. Kêśava says that "when the (two members of a) tatpurusha are in the same relationship (êkâśraya), it is a karmadhâraya". That is to say, in a karmadhâraya the component words stand in the same case (as two nouns in apposition), the first word being but the predicate of the second one or expressing a peculiar quality of it. Kêśava elucidates this by saying that ಅಲರ್ಗಣ್ means ಅಲರನ್ತಪ್ಪ ಕಣ್, an eye that is like a flower. *Cf.* § 253, 2.

a) Instances in which **the first word remains unaltered**, are:—ಸುಡುಗಾಡು, a burning-wild (a wild where corpses are burnt), ಅಡುಗೂೞ್, boiling-rice (rice that has been boiled), ಬಿಡುಗಣ್, an opening-eye (an eye that is opened), ಬಿಡುಮುಡಿ, ಬಿಡುಮುತ್ತು, ಬಿಡುವಾಯ್, ಇಡುಗಿಚ್ಚು, ಉಡುಗೊಱೆ, ಮಾಱುದಾಣ್ಬು, ತುಡುಜೊಡರ್, ಅಱುಗೆಱೆ, ತಡಗಾಲ್, ಅಲರ್ಗಣ್, ಪೆಱೆನೊಸಲ್, ತುಮ್ಬಿಗುರುಳ್, ತೊಂಗಲ್ಗುರುಳ್, ಉರ್ಕಾಳ್, ಕಡುಟಕ್ಕು, ಕಡುವೆಳ್ಪು, ಗೇಣ್ಬಾಯ್, ಕಳ್ಳಟಿಪ್ಪಣಂ, ನಿಱಿದಲೆ, ನಗೆಗಣ್, ಬಾಱ್ವಣಂ, ಸುಡುಬಾಡು.

b) Instances in which **a euphonic sônnĕ is inserted after the first word**, are:—ಎತ್ತುಂಗೋಲ್, ಕುತ್ತುಂಗಱೆ, ಪೊತ್ತುಂಗೊಱಡು, ಪುಟ್ಟುಂಗುರುಡಂ, ಸುರ್ಕುಂಗುರುಳ್, ಕರ್ಚುಂಗಲ್ಲಂ, ಇಡುಕುಂಗಬ್ಬಂ, ಕಡುಕುನ್ದಱೆ, ಉರ್ಕುನ್ದೊಱೆ, ತೂಗುನ್ದೊಟ್ಟಿಲ್,

ಆಡುನೊದ್ದಲೆ, ತೂಗುನೊದ್ದಲೆ, ಬತ್ತುಮ್ಬಯಂ, ಬತ್ತುಮ್ಬೞಿ, ಅಟ್ಟುಮ್ಬರಿ, ಆಡುಮ್ಬೊಲಂ, ಮಿಂಚುಮ್ಬುೞಿ, ಪೆರ್ಚುಮ್ಬುರುಳ್, ತೋಱುಮ್ಬೊಣೆ, ಪಾಱುಮ್ಬಳೆ, ತೂಗುಂಜೊಡರ್, ಅಟ್ಟುಂಜಗಳಂ, ಕಟ್ಟುಂಜುರಿಗೆ, ಕಟ್ಟುಂಜೋಳಂ, ಏಱುಂಜವ್ವನಂ, ಬೆಟ್ಟುಮ್ಬೊೞೆ (here: a hill-like load), ದಕ್ಕುನ್ದಲೆ, ತಾಱುಮ್ಬೞಿ, ಬಕ್ಕಮ್ಬಯಲ್, ಕಳ್ಳಂಗಡಲೆ, ತಡಂಗಾಲ್.

c) Instances in which an ಉ is put before that sŏnnĕ, are: ಸಿಡಿಯುನ್ದಲೆ (ಸಿಡಿ+ಉ+ಂ—), ಇೞಿಯುಮ್ಬೊೞ್ತು. *Cf.* ಬೆಳ್ಳುಮ್ಬಟ್ಟೆ under *d*, No. 23.

d) Instances in which substitutes (*cf.* §§ 273. 277) are used. In them

1, ಪೆಱಗು becomes ಪೆಡ or ಪೆಡಂ, *e. g.* ಪೆಡಗೆಯ್ or ಪೆಡಂಗೆಯ್, ಪೆಡದಲೆ or ಪೆಡನ್ದಲೆ (*cf.* § 251);

2, ಎಲ್ಲ retains its form or becomes ಎಲ್ಲಾ (*cf.* § 266), *e. g.* ಎಲ್ಲಕಾರ್ಯಂ or ಎಲ್ಲಾ ಕಾರ್ಯಂ, ಎಲ್ಲರತ್ನಂ or ಎಲ್ಲಾರತ್ನಂ, ಎಲ್ಲಧನಂ or ಎಲ್ಲಾಧನಂ, ಎಲ್ಲಪುರುಷರ್ or ಎಲ್ಲಾಪುರುಷರ್, ಎಲ್ಲಕಾನ್ತೆಯರ್ or ಎಲ್ಲಾಕಾನ್ತೆಯರ್;

3, ಮಹತ್ becomes ಮಾ, *e. g.* ಮಾದೇವಂ, ಮಾಕಾಳಿ, ಮಾದಾನಿ, ಮಾಶೌರ್ಯಂ, ಮಾಸಾವನ್ತಂ, ಮಾಲಕುಮಿ, ಮಾಸಾಮಿ;

4, ಬಡವು becomes ಬಡ, *e. g.* ಬಡನಡು; ಅರಸು ಅರ, *e. g.* ಅರನೇಱಲ್, a kingly *Eugenia jambolana* tree (*cf.* § 246 under *b* about ಅರಮನೆ);

5, ಪೊಲ್ಲದು appears as ಪೊಲ್ಲ, ಪೞದು as ಪೞ, ಪೊಸತು as ಪೊಸ, ಎಳದು as ಎಳ, *e. g.* ಪೊಲ್ಲಮೊಗಂ, ಪೞಗನ್ನಡಂ, ಪೊಸಪೂ, ಎಳವೆಱ್; (if ಪೊಸ, ಪೞ and ಎಳ are followed by a vowel, there is no sandhi; see § 215, 6, *i*);

6, ಬಟ್ಟಿತು appears as ಬಟ್ಟ, ಬೆಟ್ಟಿತು as ಬೆಟ್ಟ (*cf.* No. 21), ದಟ್ಟಿತು as ದಟ್ಟ, *e. g.* ಬಟ್ಟದೊಡೆ, ಬೆಟ್ಟವೆಸಗೆ, ದಟ್ಟವಳ್ಳಿ;

7, ತೆಳ್ಳಿತು appears as ತೆಳ್, ಒಳಿತು as ಒಳ್, ಬಲ್ಲಿತು as ಬಲ್, ಮೆಲ್ಲಿತು as ಮೆಲ್, *e. g.* ತೆಳ್ಗದಮ್ಪು, ತೆಳ್ವಸಿಱ್, ಒಳ್ಗನ್ನಡಂ, ಒಳ್ನುಡಿ, ಬಲ್ಮುಗುಳ್, ಬಲ್ಸೋನೆ, ಮೆಲ್ಲರಂ, ಮೆಲ್ನುಡಿ, ಮೆಲ್ಮಾತು (*cf.* No. 11);

8, ಬಿಣ್ಣಿತು appears as ಬಿಣ್, ತಣ್ಣಿತು as ತಣ್, ನುಣ್ಣಿತು as ನುಣ್, ಇನಿದು as ಇನ್ (ಇಮ್, etc.), *e. g.* ಬಿಣ್ಗೊನೆ, ಬಿಣ್ಪೊಱೆ, ತಣ್ಬೞಲ್, ತಣ್ಜೊಡರ್, ನುಣ್ದನಿ, ನುಣ್ಚರಂ, ಇಮ್ಬುಳಿ, ಇಮ್ಮಾವು, ಇಂಗಡಲ್, ಇಂಚರಂ (*cf.* No. 10. 11);

9, ಪಿರಿದು, before consonants, appears as ಪೆರ್, ಬಿಳಿದು as ಬೆಳ್ (*cf.* Nos. 10. 11), *e. g.* ಪೆರ್ವೊಗಲೆ, ಪೆರ್ಮರಂ, ಪೆರ್ಮಾತು, ಬೆಳ್ದಿಂಗಳ್, ಬೆಳ್ಮುಗಿಲ್, ಬೆಳ್ವಲ್, ಬೆಳ್ವಯಲ್, ಬೆಳ್ಸರಿ;

10, ಪಿರಿದು, before vowels, appears as ಪೇರ್, *e. g.* ಪೇರಾನೆ, ಪೇರಡವಿ, ಪೇರೊಕ್ಕಲ್, ಪೇರಡಿ, ಪೇರೊಡಲ್; (regarding ಇನ್ of ಇನಿದು, see No. 8, it is to be remarked that before consonants it may appear also as ಈನ್, *e. g.* ಈಂಚರಂ, ಈಮ್ಬುಳಿ, ಈಂಗಡಲ್, ಈನ್ದುಟಿ);

11, ಇನ್, ಒಳ್, ತಣ್, (ತೆಳ್, see No. 23), ನುಣ್, ಬಲ್, ಬೆಳ್, ಮೆಲ್ (see Nos. 7. 8. 9) and ಅಳ್, ಪೆಣ್ take dvirbhâva, *i. e.* double their final before a vowel, *e. g.* ಇನ್ನುಣಿಸು, ಒಳ್ಳಾಳ್, ಒಳ್ಳುಣಿಸು, ತಣ್ಣೆಲರ್, ನುಣ್ಣುರಿಸಿನಂ, ಬಲ್ಲೞಯಂ, ಬೆಳ್ಳಾನೆ, ಮೆಲ್ಲಡಿ, ಅಳ್ಳೆಱು, ಪೆಣ್ಣುಡೆ;

12, ಕಿಱಿದು, before vowels, appears as ಕಿಟ್, ನಿಡಿದು as ನಿಟ್, ನಡುವು as ನಟ್, the final ಟ್ being doubled, *e. g.* ಕಿಟ್ಟಳ್ಕೆ, ಕಿಟ್ಟಾಯಂ, ಕಿಟ್ಟಾಳ್, ಕಿಟ್ಟುಬ್ಬಟ್ಟೆ, ಕಿಟ್ಟುಬ್ಬಸಂ, ನಿಟ್ಟಡಕಿಲ್, ನಿಟ್ಟೆಯ್ದು, ನಿಟ್ಟೆಱ್ಕೆ, ನಿಟ್ಟೆಸಳ್, ನಟ್ಟಡವಿ, ನಟ್ಟಾಳಂ, ನಟ್ಟಿರುಳ್;

13, ಕಿಱಿದು, before vowels, appears as ಕಿಱ್ and ಕುಱ್ (*cf.* § 151, *b*, 2; No. 14), the final ಱ್ being doubled, *e. g.* ಕಿಱ್ಱಡಿ, ಕಿಱ್ಱಿಳಿ, ಕಿಱ್ಱೆಸಳ್, ಕುಱ್ಱಡಿ, ಕುಱ್ಱೆಸಳ್, ಕುಱ್ಱಿವಂ;

14, ಕಡಿದು, before consonants, appears as ಕಡು, ನಿಡಿದು as ನಿಡು, ನಡುವು as ನಡು, ಕಿಱಿದು as ಕಿಱು and ಕುಱು, *e. g.* ಕಡುಗುದುರೆ, ಕಡುಗಾಳಿ, ನಿಡುದೋಳ್, ನಡುವಯಣಂ, ನಡುಮಾಳಂ (o. r. ನಡುವಮಾಳಂ), ನಡುಸೆಱಂಗು, ಕಿಱುಗೂಸು, ಕಿಱುನೆಲ್ಲಿ, ಕಿಱುವಿದಿರ್, ಕಿಱುವಲೆ, ಕಿಱುನಾಯ್, ಕುಱುಪಡಿ, ಕುಱುಗಿಡಂ, ಕುಱುಗಡ್ಡಂ, ಕುಱುಗಣ್ಬು, ಕುಱುಗೆಯ್; ನಿಡಿದು appears also as ನಿಡಿ, *e. g.* ನಿಡಿದೋಳ್, ನಿಡಿಯಲರ್ಗಣೆ;

15, ಪಚ್ಚನೆ, ಕೆಚ್ಚನೆ, ಬೆಚ್ಚನೆ appear as ಪಂ, ಕೆಂ, ಬೆಂ (*cf.* § 251), *e. g.* ಪಸ್ಸೊವಲ್, ಪನ್ನಲೆ, ಪನ್ನಳಿರ್. ಕೆಂಗಱು, ಕೆಂಗಣ್, ಕೆಂಗುಡಿ, ಕೆಂಗೊಡೆ, ಕೆಂಜೆಡೆ, ಕೆನ್ನಳಿರ್, ಕೆಮ್ಮುಟ್ಟೆ, ಕೆಮ್ಮಿಸಿಲ್, ಬೆಂಗಲ್, ಬೆನ್ನೀರ್;

16, ಕೆಚ್ಚನೆ appears also as ಚೆಂ, *e. g.* ಚೆಂಗಣಿಗಿಲ್, ಚೆಂಗೊರಲ್, ಚೆನ್ನುಡಿ, ಚೆನ್ದಂಗು, ಚೆನ್ನೆಯ್ದಿಲ್, ಚೆಮ್ಬೋತಂ, ಚೆಮ್ಬೊನ್;

17, ಕೆಚ್ಚನೆ, before vowels, appears as ಕೇಸು (ಕೇಸ್), *e. g.* ಕೇಸಕ್ಕಿ, ಕೇಸಡಿ, ಕೇಸುರಿ;

18, ಕೆಚ್ಚನೆ, ಬೆಚ್ಚನೆ appear also as ಕಿಸು, ಬಿಸು, *e. g.* ಕಿಸುಗಣಿಗಿಲ್, ಕಿಸುಗಲ್, ಕಿಸುಗಟ್ಟು, ಕಿಸುವೊನ್, ಕಿಸುಸಂಜೆ, ಬಿಸುಗದಿರ್, ಬಿಸುನೆತ್ತರ್, ಬಿಸುನೀರ್, ಬಿಸುಗಾಳಿ;

19, ಪಚ್ಚನೆ, before vowels, appears also as ಪಚ್ಚು (ಪಚ್ಚ್), *e. g.* ಪಚ್ಚೋಲೆ, ಪಚ್ಚಡಕೆ, ಪಚ್ಚೆಲೆ;

20, ಪಚ್ಚನೆ appears also as ಪಸು followed by a euphonic sŏnnĕ, *e. g.* ಪಸುಂಗಱು;

21, ಬೆಟ್ಟಿತು (see No. 6) appears also as ಬಿಱು, *e. g.* ಬಿಱುವೊಯ್ಲು, ಬಿಱುವಡೆ, ಬಿಱುಗಾಳಿ;

22, ಕೊಂಕು appears as ಕುಡು, *e. g.* ಕುಡುವುರ್ವು, ಕುಡುಗೋಲ್, ಕುಡುವೆಱ್, ಕುಡುದಾಡೆ, ಕುಡುಮಿಂಚು;

23, ಬೆಳ್, ತೆಳ್ (see No. 11) may be followed by a euphonic ಉಂ, *e. g.* ಬೆಳ್ಳುಮ್ಬಟ್ಟೆ, ತೆಳ್ಳುಮ್ಬುಸುಱ್.

248. The third compound is ದ್ವಿಗು, *i. e.* (worth) two cows, this word being in Saṁskṛita an example after which this whole class of compounds is called. Kēšava says that "when (the last word of) a tatpurusha is saṅkhyāpûrvaka, *i. e.* preceded by a numeral, it becomes a dvigu". The numeral is the predicate of the noun which follows. Also ಕೆಲವು and ಪಲವು are reckoned among the numerals (*cf.* § 90; § 278, 4).

Substitutive forms are often employed in dvigus, especially in the ancient dialect:—

1, ಒನ್ದು often appears as ಒರ್, *e. g.* ಒರ್ನುಡಿ (for ಒನ್ದು ನುಡಿ), ಒರ್ತಲೆ (for ಒನ್ದು ತಲೆ), ಒರ್ಪೆಸರ್, ಒರ್ವೊಡಲ್, ಒರ್ಪಿಡಿ, ಒರ್ಸೂತ್ತು, and as ಓರ್ before vowels, *e. g.* ಓರೆಂಜಲ್, ಓರೊನ್ದು. See § 278, 1 and Dictionary under ಒಱ್ 1.

2, ಎರಡು often appears as ಎರಟ್ (*cf.* §§ 215, 7, *a*; 234), *e. g.* ಎರಟ್ಟುದುರೆ, ಎರಟ್ಮಾತು, ಎರಟ್ಪಡಿ, ಎರಟ್ಕಡಿ, ಎರಟ್ತರಂ, ಎರಟ್ಮಾಱು, or as ಇರ್, *e. g.* ಇರ್ಬೇನೆ, ಇರ್ತೆರೆ, ಇರ್ಕಟ್ಟು, ಇರ್ತಡಿ, ಇರ್ಕೋಡಿ, ಇರ್ತಲೆ, ಇರ್ಮೆಯ್, ಇರ್ಬಾಳ್, ಇರ್ನುಡಿ, ಇರ್ಭಾಸಿರಂ, ಇರ್ಪಣ್ದಿರ್, ಇರ್ಪತ್ತು, or as ಈರ್ before vowels, *e. g.* ಈರಯ್ದು, ಈರೊತ್ತೆ. See § 278, 1 and Dictionary under ಇಱ್.

3, ಮೂಱು often appears as ಮೂ, *e. g.* ಮೂಗೊಂಕು, ಮೂವಳಸು, ಮೂನೂಱು, ಮೂದೆಱಂ, ಮೂಲೋಕಂ, ಮೂದಲೆ, ಮೂವಾಟ್, ಮೂವಡಿ, ಮೂಗೇಣ್, ಮೂಗಾವುದಂ, ಮೂಗೋಱು, ಮೂಗೆಯ್,

or sometimes as ಮು after which the consonants ಕ್, ಗ್, ನ್, ಪ್, ಮ್ are doubled, *e. g.* ಮುಕ್ಕುಪ್ಪೆ, ಮುಕ್ಕೊಡೆ, ಮುಗ್ಗುಡ್ಡೆ, ಮುನ್ನೀರ್, ಮುಪ್ಪೊಡಲ್, ಮುಪ್ಪುರಿ, ಮುಮ್ಮಾಱು, or sometimes before ಸ್ which then becomes ಚ್ and is doubled, *e. g.* ಮುಚ್ಚೋಟು, ಮುಚ್ಚವಡಿ, ಮುಚ್ಚಿರೆ, ಮುಚ್ಚಾಲ್, or before vowels, when it gets an ಯ್ between which is doubled, *e. g.* ಮುಯ್ಯಿರ್, ಮುಯ್ಯಡಿ, ಮುಯ್ಯೆಲ್, ಮುಯ್ಯಾನೆ. See § 278, 1 and Dictionary under ಮು, and *cf.* ಮುವ್ವತ್ತು in § 278.

4, ನಾಲ್ಕು often appears as ನಾಲ್, *e. g.* ನಾಲ್ವತ್ತು, ನಾಲ್ವಡಿ, ನಾಲ್ವೆರಲ್. See § 278, 1 and Dictionary under ನಾ 2.

5, ಅಯ್ದು often appears as ಅಯ್, *e. g.* ಅಯ್ವಡಿ, ಅಯ್ಗಣ್ಣುಗಂ, ಅಯ್ಸಾಸಿರಂ, ಅಯ್ವಾಯ್. See § 278, 1 and Dictionary under ಅಯ್ 5.

6, ಆಱು often appears as ಅಱು, *e. g.* ಅಱುವತ್ತು, ಅಱುವಡಿ, ಅಱುನೂಱು, ಅಱುದಿಂಗಳ್. See § 278, 1 and Dictionary under ಅಱು 3.

7, ಏೞು often appears as ಎೞ್, *e. g.* ಎೞ್ಪತ್ತು, ಎೞ್ಕಡಲ್, ಎೞ್ಕೋಟೆ, ಎೞ್ಪೊರೆ, ಎೞ್ಕುರಿ. See § 278, 1 and Dictionary under ಎೞ್ 4.

8, ಎಣ್ಟು often appears as ಎಣ್, *e. g.* ಎಣ್ಪತ್ತು, ಎಣ್ಛಾಸಿರಂ, ಎಣ್ದೆಸೆ. See § 278, 1 and Dictionary under ಎಮ್ 2.

9, ಒಮ್ಬತ್ತು appears as ತೊಮ್ before ಪತ್ತು, *viz.* ತೊಮ್ಬತ್ತು, and as ಒಮ್ಬಯ್ before ನೂಱು and ಸಾಸಿರ (ಸಾಯಿರ, ಸಾವಿರ), *viz.* ಒಮ್ಬಯ್ನೂಱು, ಒಮ್ಬಯ್ಸಾಸಿರಂ. See § 278, 1 and Dictionary under ಒಮ್.

10, ಪತ್ತು appears as ಪಯಿನ್ before ಸಾಸಿರ, *viz.* ಪಯಿಂಛಾಸಿರಂ, as ಪನ್ (ಪನ್ನ್, ಹನ್, ಹನ್ನ್) before ಒನ್ದು and ಎರಡು, *viz.* ಪನ್ನೊನ್ದು, ಪನ್ನೆರಡು, as ಪದಿ (ಹದಿ) before ಮೂಱು and ನಾಲ್ಕು, *viz.* ಪದಿಮೂಱು, ಪದಿನಾಲ್ಕು, and as ಪದಿನ್ (ಹದಿನ್) before ಅಯ್ದು, ಆಱು, ಏೞು, ಎಣ್ಟು, *viz.* ಪದಿನಯ್ದು, ಪದಿನಾಱು, ಪದಿನೇೞು, ಪದಿನೆಣ್ಟು. See § 278, 1.

11, ನೂಱು and ಸಾಸಿರ appear also as ನೂಱ್ (ನೂರ್) and ಸಾಸಿರ್, *e. g.* ನೂರ್ಮಡಿ, ನೂರ್ಮಾತು, ನೂರ್ಛಾಸಿರಂ, ಸಾಸಿರ್ಮಡಿ, ಸಾಸಿರ್ದಲೆಯಂ, ಸಾಸಿರ್ದೋಳಂ, ಸಾಸಿರ್ವರ್. See § 278, 1.

12, ಕೆಲವು and ಪಲವು appear also as ಕೆಲ and ಪಲ, *e. g.* ಕೆಲದೆವಸಂ, ಪಲದೆವಸಂ, ಪಲಗಣ್, ಪಲವಣ್.

249. The fourth compound is ಬಹುವ್ರೀಹಿ. It is a predicate referring to some subject or other, or serves to qualify or define another word, sometimes being so to say an adjective (see § 102, 8, *d*). The word bahuvrîhi, 'possessing much rice' is, in Saṁskṛita, the instance after which this class of compounds has been named.

Bahuvrîhi compounds terminate in ಅ (ಅಂ) and ಇ.

Instances are: (ಅವಂ) ವಿಮಲಮತಿ, (ಅವಳ್) ವಿಮಲಮತಿ, (ಅದು) ವಿಮಲಮತಿ, (ಅವಂ) ಕುಸಿಗೊರಲಂ, (ಅವಳ್) ಕುಸಿಗೊರಲಿ, (ಅವಂ) ಹೆಱೆಗಾಲಂ, (ಆವಳ್) ಹೆಱೆಗಾಲಿ, ಕಡುಚಾಗಿ, ಚಲವಾದಿ, ಮೆಲ್ವಿನ್ನಣಿ, ಕಡುಗೇಡಿ, ಕಡುಗೆಲಸಿ, ನಿಡುಮೊಗಂ, ನಿಡುಮೂಗಿ, ನಿಡುಗಣ್ಣಿ, ನಿಡುವೆರಲಿ, ಸುರ್ಕುಂಗುರುಳಿ (*cf.* § 243, *B*, 8), ಸವಟೆವಾಯಂ, ಗುಳ್ಳಿಗಣ್ಣಂ, ಹಱಿದಲೆಯಂ, ಅಲರ್ಗಣ್ಣಂ, ಬಟ್ಟದೊಡೆಯಂ, ಕೇಸಡಿಯಂ, ಕುಡುವಿಲ್ಲಂ,

ನಾಲ್ದೋಳಂ, ನಿಡುಗಾಳಂ, ನಿಡುವಣೆಯಂ, ಬಲ್ದಲೆಯಂ, ಅಗಲ್ದುರದಂ, ಪೆಱಸೊಸಲಂ, ಕಲ್ಲೆರ್ದೆಯಂ, ಪಲಗೆರ್ದೆಯಂ, ಸುಣ್ಣೊಡೆಯಂ (*cf.* § 115; § 243, *B*, remark), ಕರ್ಬೇಡಂ, ಪಱಿವಾನಿಸಂ, ಅಱೆಗವಿ, ಪುಸಿಬಾದಿ, ಬಲ್ಲುಜ್ಜುಗಿ, ಪಲ್ಲಿಲಿ (ವಾಯ್), ಅಗಿಲಿಲಿ (ಗನ್ಧಂ), ಕೂರಿಲಿ (ಕುಡುಗೋಲ್), ಬೆಳಗಿಲಿ (ಗಣ್), ನಾಣಿಲಿ (ಪೆಣ್, *cf.* § 243, *B*, 14), ಮೀಂಗುಲಿ, ಅಱಿಗುಲಿ (*cf.* § 243, *B*, 8), to which the Šabdânušâsana adds ಆನೆಗುಲಿ, ಇಲಿಗುಲಿ, ಪಾವುಗುಲಿ. Feminines with ಅಳ್ are *e. g.* ಬಟ್ಟಮೊಲೆಯಳ್, ನಿಡುಜಡೆಯಳ್, ಪೆಱೆವಣೆಯಳ್.

In mutually fighting with swords, fists, etc. a kind of bahuvrîhi is formed in which the same word occurs twice, the final one taking the suffix i and the preceding one taking the suffix â, *e. g.* ಖಾಡಾಖಾಡಿ, ಮುಟ್ಟಾಮುಟ್ಟಿ, ಹೆಲ್ಲಾಹೆಲ್ಲಿ, ದಾಱಾದಾಱಿ, ದೆಬ್ಬಾದೆಬ್ಬಿ (o. r. ದಬ್ಬಾದಬ್ಬಿ), ಹಾಣಾಹಾಣಿ (o. r. ಹಣಾಹಣಿ), ಘಟ್ಟಾಘಟ್ಟಿ, ಮಲ್ಲಾಮಲ್ಲಿ. The Šabdânušâsana has ಕಲ್ಲಾಕಲ್ಲಿ, ಕೋಲಾಕೋಲಿ, ಡಾಣಾಡಾಣಿ.

250. The fifth compound is ದ್ವನ್ದ್ವ. It unites two or more words which, if uncompounded, would be in the same case and connected by the conjunction ಉಂ (ಊ) 'and' the last word frequently taking the terminations of the plural, *e. g.* ಅಳಿಗಿಳಿಗಳ್, ಕರಿತುರಗಂಗಳ್, ತನ್ದೆತಾಯ್ಗಳ್, ಮರಗಿಡುಗಳ್, ರಾಮಲಕ್ಷ್ಮಣರ್, ಮರಗಿಡುಬಳ್ಳಿಪುಲ್ಪೊದಱುಪಕ್ಕಿಮಿಗಂಗಳ್, ಆಟಪಾಟಕೂಟಂಗಳ್, but being also in the singular, *e. g.* ಮರಗಿಡು, ಕಾವಚನ್ದಿರಂ, ಅಳಿಗಿಳಿ ಪುಲ್ಪೊದಱು. See § 354, II, 4.

When ತಮ್ಮ and ತಮ್ಮ are joined, the first ತಮ್ಮ may drop its last syllable, *e. g.* ತಮ್ತಮ್ಮ ರಾಜ್ಯಂ, ತಮ್ತಮ್ಮ ವಿಭೂತಿ, ತಮ್ತಮ್ಮ ಬಲಂ, ತಮ್ತಮ್ಮ ಸಿರಿ. *Cf.* § 137, *a*, genitive plural; § 304, *a. b.*

251. The sixth compound is ಅವ್ಯಯೀಭಾವ. In Saṁskṛita this compound is formed by joining an indeclinable particle with another word, the resulting compound, in which the indeclinable particle forms always the first element, is again indeclinable. In Kannaḍa the first is a substituted form of a noun, which form by itself is indeclinable; but the compound is declinable, and may be said to be identical in quality with a tatpurusha (*cf.* Kêšavâ's ಕಿಱುತ್ತೊಮ್ಬು, etc. in § 246).

The substituted form of ಅಡಿ is ಅಂ, of ಮೇಗು ಮೇಂ, of ಮುನ್ದು ಮುಂ, of ಪಿನ್ದು ಪಿಂ, of ಕೆಳಗು ಕಿಱು, of ಪೆಱಗು ಪಿನ್ತು, of ಬಿಸು ಬೆಂ (*cf.* § 247, *d*, 15. 18), *e. g.* ಅಂಗೆಯ್, ಅಂಗಾಲ್, ಮೇಂಗೆಯ್, ಮೇಂಗಾಲ್, ಮುಂಗೆಯ್, ಮುಂಗಾಲ್, ಮುಂಜೂರ್, ಮುಂಜೆಱಿಂಗು, ಮುಮ್ಬಗಲ್, ಮುಮ್ಮಾಗಿ, ಪಿಂಗಾಲ್ (o. r. ಹಿಂಗಾಲ್),

ಪಿಪ್ಪೆದೆ, ಪಿಮ್ಮೊಟ್ಟು, ಕಿಟ್ಟಿರೆ, ಕಿಱುಕ್ಕೆಱಿ, ಕಿಱುಪ್ಪೊಡೆ, ಪಿನ್ನಿಲ್, ಪಿನ್ನೊಲೆ, ಬೆಂಗಾಲ್, ಬೆಪ್ಪುಸಿಲ್. *Cf.* also the substitute ಪೆಡ or ಪೆಡಂ of ಪೆಱಗು in § 247, *d*, 1.

252. After the six compounds that occur in Kannaḍa as well as in Saṁskṛita, have been treated of, it remains to draw attention towards the rules which exist in Kannaḍa as to choosing words for them which are congruous.

1, The general rule is that Kannaḍa words may form compounds with Kannaḍa words, as will appear from §§ 240-251.

2, Another general rule is that Samasaṁskṛita words (§ 70) are not to be compounded with Kannaḍa words (see the few exceptions under No. 11, *a*). It is therefore wrong to say ಕಣ್ಕಮಲಂ, ಮುಖತಾವರೆ, and to use such compounds as appear in the following part of a verse:

> ಅರಸುಕುಮಾರನ್ ಅನಾಯತ
> ತರಗಡೆಗಣ್ಣಿನ್ದೆ ನೋಡಿ, ಕೆಳದಿಸಮೇತಂ ।
> ಪರಿಗತನಗೆಯಿನ್ದಿರ್ದಂ. (Regarding ಅರಸುಕುಮಾರಂ see under No. 7.)

In such cases there occurs what is called an arisamâsa or viruddhasamâsa, *i. e.* unsuitable, incongruous compound (*cf.* No. 11).

3, The Tatsamas mentioned in § 71 may be compounded with Tatsama, Samasaṁskṛita, Tadbhava (No. 4), and Kannaḍa words, *e. g.* ಅಂಕವಡಿ, ಅಂಕಮಾತು, ಕಟ್ಟಂಕಂ, ಮಾಱಂಕಂ, ಮೃಗಾಂಕಂ, ವೃಷಾಂಕಂ;—ಅಂಗಣವಲಯಂ, ಅಂಗಣವಾವಿ, ಅಂಗಣವೆಟ್ಟಿ, ಗೃಹಾಂಗಣಂ, ರಾಜಾಂಗಣಂ;—ಅಟ್ಟಗವಲ್, ಅಟ್ಟವಡಿ, ಅಟ್ಟಹಾಸಂ;—ಗುಬ್ಬಿಗಂಕಣಂ, ಮಣಿಗಂಕಣಂ, ಹಸ್ತಕಂಕಣಂ, ಹಿಣ್ಡುಗಂಕಣಂ;—ತಱುಗೋಟ್ಟೆ, ಧೂಳಿಗೋಟ್ಟೆ, ರಾಯಗೋಟ್ಟೆ, ಹತ್ತುಗೋಟ್ಟೆ, ಹೆಡಗೆಗೋಟ್ಟೆ;—ಗಣ್ಡಗರ್ವಂ, ಗಣ್ಡಗಲಿ, ಗಣ್ಡಗುಣಂ, ಗಣ್ಡಪೆಣ್ಡಿರ್, ಗಣ್ಡವರಿಜು, ಗಣ್ಡವಸದನ;—ಗಲ್ಲಗಿವಿ, ಗಲ್ಲಗುಗ್ಗುರಿ, ಗಲ್ಲಮುಗ್ಗುರಿ, ಗಲ್ಲಸ್ಥಲಂ, ತೆಳ್ಗಲ್ಲಂ;—ಎಡೆಗಾಳಂ, ಗಳಗಾಳಂ, ಸಣ್ಣಗಾಳಂ;—ಕಿಱುಗೋಣಿ, ಗೋಣಿಕಾಪುತ್ರಂ, ಪೆಗೋರ್ಣಿ;—ಕರತಳಂ, ಕೆನ್ದಳಂ, ತಟ್ಟತಳಂ, ತಳಹಗ್ಗಂ, ಧರಣೀತಳಂ;—ಕಾಂಸ್ಯತೋರಣಂ, ತಳಿದೋರ್ರಣಂ, ಪಚ್ಚೆದೋರಣಂ, ಮಕರತೋರಣಂ;—ಚೌವಟ್ಟಂ, ದಾರವಟ್ಟಂ, ಪಟ್ಟಗದುರ್ಗೆ, ಪಟ್ಟಗೊಟಿ, ಪಟ್ಟಮಹಿಷಿ, ಪಟ್ಟವಣಿ, ಪಟ್ಟವರ್ಧನಂ, ಪಟ್ಟಶರಂ, ಪಟ್ಟಸಾಲೆ, ಪಾಯವಟ್ಟಂ;—ಬನ್ದಿಗ್ರಹಣಂ, ಬನ್ದಿವಿಡಿ (ಬನ್ದಿವಿಡಿದಂ ಬಿಮ್ಬಾಧರಸ್ಥಾನಮಂ), ಬಲ್ಬನ್ದಿಕಾಱಂ;—ಆಳ್ವಲಂ, ಇರ್ಬಲಂ, ತೋಳ್ವಲಂ, ನೆಲವಲಂ, ಪೆರ್ವಲಂ (or ಪೆರ್ಬಲಂ), ಭುಜಬಲಂ, ಭೂಬಲಂ, ಮಾರ್ವಲಂ (or ಮಾರ್ಬಲಂ);—ಪೆರ್ಬಿಲಂ, ಬಿಲದ್ವಾರಂ, ಬಿಲಸಗ್ಗಂ;—ಕಾಂಚನಮಂಚಂ, ತೂಗುಮಂಚಂ, ರತ್ನಮಂಚಂ, ಸೆಳೆಮಂಚಂ;—ಉಡೆವಣಿ, ಕೆಲವಣಿ, ದಿನಮಣಿ, ಮಕುಟಮಣಿ, ರನ್ನಮಣಿ;—ಮಲ್ಲಗಾಳಗಂ, ಮಲಮುರಾನ್ತಕಂ, ಮಲ್ಲವಾತು;—ಅಕ್ಕರಮಾಲೆ, ಕಣ್ಮಾಲೆ, ಪಚ್ಚೆಮಾಲೆ, ಪೂಮಾಲೆ, ಮಾಲೆದೋರಣ, ವನಮಾಲೆ;—ಎಳಲತೆ, ನವಲತೆ, ಲತೆವನೆ, ಲತೆವಳ್ಳಿ;—ಸಬಳಗದ್ಯಾಣಂ, ಸಬಳತ್ರಿಣೇತ್ರಂ, ಸಬಳವಿನ್ನಣಿ, ಸಬಳಸಹಸ್ರಬಾಹು.

4, Two Tadbhavas (§ 370) may be compounded, *e. g.* ಅಂಕುಸಸಾರಣಿ, ಅಚ್ಚವಳಿಕು, ಅನ್ದಳಸತ್ತಿಗೆ, ಅವಣಜವಣಂ, ಅಱುಗೆವನ್ದಂ, ಎಕ್ಕತಳಂ, ಎಕ್ಕವತ್ತಿ, ಕಕ್ಕಸಜವ್ವನಂ, ಕಣ್ಟೆಯಬಾರಂ, ಕಣ್ಡಪಡಂ, ಕನ್ನವುರಂ, ಕಪ್ಪುರಗರಡಗೆ, ಕರಸಾಣೆ, ಕಾಗೆದೊಣ್ಣೆ, ಕಾಸಿಗಪ್ಪಡಂ, ಕೂವಕಮ್ಬಂ, ಕೂಟ್ಟಮಿಮ್ರ, ಕೈರದಮ್ಮುಲಂ, ಕೊಟ್ಟಾರಂ, ಚಕ್ಕವಕ್ಕಿ, ಚಟ್ಟಿಗರಣಂ, ಚಿತ್ತಾಗಾರಂ, ಚಿಪ್ಪಿಗಬಿಜ್ಜ, ಚೌಕಣ್ಡಂ, ಚೌಗಾವೆ, ಚೌಜನ್ತಂ, ಚೌವಟಂ, ಜಗವತ್ತಿ, ಜವಹುರಂ, ಜವಳಿವದ್ದಳೆ, ಜೊನ್ನವಕ್ಕಿ, ಜೋಗವಾವುಗೆ, ತಾಣದೀವಿಗೆ, ತಾಣಬಟ್ಟಂ, ತಿವದಿ, ತಿವಡೆ, ತಿವಳಿ, ತಿಸರಂ, ತಿಸುಳಂ, ತಿಹುರಾನ್ತಕಂ, ದಸಸಿರಂ, ದಿಟ್ಟಬಿಸಂ, ದುವಟ್ಟಿಗೆ, ದುಸರಂ, ದುಹತ್ತಂ,

ಪೂವಟ್ಟಿಗೆ, ಪೂಹತ್ತಂ, ಪಡಿಚನ್ದಂ, ಪೞಮಾವುಗೆ, ಪೞಹತ್ತಂ, ಪಾಣಿಯಬಾರಂ, ಬಣ್ಣಪುರಂ, ಬಣ್ಣಸರಂ, ಬಳ್ಳಿಮಾಡಂ, ಬೀರಸಿರಿ, ಮಾನಸಗಬ್ಬಂ, ಮಾನಸಪೊತ್ತಗೆ, ಮಾಪತಂ, ಮಾಲಕುಮಿ, ಮಾಸಾವನ್ತಂ, ರಕ್ಕಸಂಕಲೆ, ರಕ್ಕಸವಗರಣಂ, ರನ್ನಗಮ್ಬಳಿ, ರನ್ನವಟ್ಟಿಗೆ, ರಾಯಗೋಟೆ, ವಂಕದರಂ, ವಂಕದಾರಂ, ವಂಕಬಾರಂ, ಸಂಕರಪಸಾಯಿತಂ, ಸಂಗಡವೆಕ್ಕಣಂ, ಸನ್ತೆವಟ್ಟಣಂ, ಸಬ್ಬಲಕ್ಕಣಂ, ಸಬ್ಬಸನ್ನಣಂ, ಸಮ್ಬರಗವಳಂ, ಸರವನ್ದಂ, ಸವಗಸನ್ನಣಂ, ಸಿರಿಕಣ್ಠಂ, ಸಿರಿಯವರಂ, ಸಿರಿಯದಾರಂ, ಸಿರಿಯಬಾರಂ. ಹಂಜರವಕ್ಕಿ.

5, **The first word may be a Samasaṁskṛita** (§ 70) **and the second one a Tadbhava,** *e. g.* ಉತ್ತರದೇಸಂ, ಕರಣಸಾಲೆ, ಗೋಹುರಂ, ದಾನಸಾಲೆ, ದೇವವಾಸಸಂ, ಪಂಚಸರಂ, ಪತಬೊಮ್ಮಂ, ಪರಮಸಿರಿ, ಪಾದರಕ್ಕೆ, ಪಾದವಾಸಂ, ಪಾದಸಂಕಲೆ, ಬಾಹುಬಳಿ, ಮಂಗಳವಸವಸಂ, ಮಂಗಳಾರತಿ, ವಿಜಯಸೇಸಿ, ಸುರಹೊನ್ನೆ.

6, **The first word may be a Tadbhava and the second one a Samasaṁskṛita,** *e. g.* ಅನ್ತಪುರಂ, ಅರಸುಗುಣಂ, ಎಕ್ಕಸರಂ, ಕಣ್ಣಪಟಂ, ಗಾವರಸಂ, ಗುಜ್ಜರಪಟ್ಟಿ, ಚನ್ದಪುರಂ, ಚಾಪದಂ, ಚಾವೇದಿ, ಜವದಣ್ಡಂ, ತಿಗುಣಂ, ತಿಪುರಾನ್ತಕಂ, ತಿವಳಿ, ದುಗುಣಂ, ದೂಹಸ್ತಿ, ದೆಸೆಬಲಿ, ದೆಸೆವಲಿ, ಪಯಗತಿ, ಪಸುಪತಿ, ಬೊಮ್ಮಣ್ಡಂ, ಮಾಕಾಳಿ, ಮಾಜನಂ, ಮಾದಾನಿ, ಮಾದೇವಂ, ಮಾಪಾತಕಂ, ಮಾಪುರುಷಂ, ಮಾಕಾರ್ಯಧನಂ, ಮೊಗರಾಗಂ, ಸಂಗಡದಾಳಂ, ಸಣಿವಾರಂ, ಸನ್ದವಾತಂ, ಸರಕರಣಂ, ಸರವಾದಿ, ಸಾದೇವಂ, ಸಾಮವಣ್ಣಂ, ಸಾವಾಸಿ, ಸಿರಿರಾಮಂ, ಸೂಳಪಾಣಿ.

7, **A Samasaṁskṛita term of which a Tadbhava exists should not be combined with a Tadbhava term,** *e. g.* the poet Harirâja's ತರವೇಱ್ ಮಾಣಿಕ್ಯಭಣ್ಡಾರದ ಪುಟಿಕೆಗಳಂ should be ತರವೇಱ್ ಮಾಣಿಕಭಣ್ಡಾರದ ಪುಟಿಕೆಗಳಂ. ಅರಸುಕುಮಾರಂ (under No. 2) ought to be ಅರಸುಗುವರಂ.

Remark by the author of the present grammar:—It seems that Kêśava means a generally known and as such used Tadbhava, not one which is less known and seldom used, as ಪಾಯ, for he himself (under No. 5) uses ಪಾದರಕ್ಕೆ, ಪಾದವಾಸಂ, and ಪಾದಸಂಕಲೆ instead of ಪಾಯರಕ್ಕೆ, ಪಾಯವಾಸಂ, and ಪಾಯಸಂಕಲೆ (ಪಾಯ being a Tadbhava of ಪಾದ).

8, It is allowed to compound a **Tadbhava** and a **Kannaḍa** (dêśîya) **term,** *e.g.* ಅರಗಿಳಿ, ಅರಮನೆ, ಪಡಿವಾನಿಸಂ, ಪೊನ್ನನ್ದಳಂ, ಸೆಜ್ಜೆವನೆ, ಸಿಂಗವೇಣ್ಟೆ, ಸಸಿದೋಣ್ಬಂ.

9, It is allowed to add a **Kannaḍa** term to a **Tadbhava compound,** *e. g.* ಜವಳಿಮದ್ದಳೆದೊಂಗಲ್, ಜೊನ್ನವಕ್ಕಿಗಣ್ಗಳ್, ತಾಣದೀವಿಗೆವೆಳಗು.

10, It is allowed to add a **Kannaḍa term to a Tatsama compound** (see No. 3), *e. g.* ಕಟ್ಟಂಕದಲ್ಲಣಂ, ಪೂಮಾಲೆದುಱುಮ್ಬು, ಸಬಳಗದ್ಯಾಣದೆಱ್.

11, **Of old a number of incongruous compounds** (arisamâsas, see under No. 2) **were in use and may still be used,** *viz.:*

a) eight compounds of Kannaḍa and Samasaṁskṛita words:—ಅಱುಕೆನಾಯಕಂ, ಅಱುಜನಂ (o. r. ಅಱುಜನಂ), ಕಟ್ಟೇಕಾನ್ತಂ, ಕಡುದರ್ಪಂ (o. r. ಕಡುತಪಂ), ಕೂರಸಿ, ಗುಣಕರು, ತುರಗದಱಂ, ಮಂಗಳವಱ್; and

b) titles (birudu) or a string of titles (birudâvaḷi), *e. g.* ಕಲಿವೇಣ್ಟೆಗಾಱಂ, ಗಜಮುಱ, ಗಜಪಾಱು, ಗುಣಕ್ಕೆನಲ್ಲಗಣೇಶಂ, ಗೇಣಂಕಚಕ್ರೇಶ್ವರಂ, ದಱಮುಖಧವಳಂ, ದಱಮುಱಾದಿತ್ಯಂ, ಮಾಸವಳಮದನಮಹೇಶಂ, ನರಲೋಕವಲ್ಲಣಂ, etc. In such titles or string of titles incongruous compounds may be used at pleasure (ಮೆಚ್ಚಿದನ್ತೆ).

In the compounds under numbers 3. 4. 5. 6. 8. 9. 10 and 11 a change of an initial consonant of a compound member may occur according to § 215, 7, *a. b.*

253. As stated in § 245, there are **three other samâsas** in Kannaḍa, *viz.* ಕ್ರಿಯಾಸಮಾಸಂಗಳ್, ಗಮಕಸಮಾಸಂಗಳ್, and ವೀಪ್ಸಾಸಮಾಸಂಗಳ್. They are found more or less in the three dialects.

1, **The kriyâsamâsa or verbal compound** is formed "when as the compound's first member a noun that has a certain relation to the verb (kâraka, § 344) and a verb are placed together (sannida), *i. e.* compounded, so as to give a distinct meaning (arthavyakti).

In forming such verbal compounds a sŏnnĕ must be added to Saṁskṛita nouns ending in ಅ, whereas concerning such Kannaḍa (or tadbhava) nouns this is optional; Kannaḍa and Saṁskṛita nouns ending in ಉ optionally insert a sŏnnĕ; in some cases the final syllable of the first member is elided. See the sandhi rules in § 215, 7, *a. b.*

a) Instances wherein **the Kannaḍa** (or tadbhava) **noun** (ending either in ಎ, ಇ, consonants, ಅ, or ಉ) **has the meaning of the accusative,** are *e. g.* ಬೞಿದೊಟ್ಟಂ (*i. e.* ಬೞಿಯಂ ತೊಟ್ಟಂ), ಕೆೞಿಗೊಣ್ಡಂ (*i. e.* ಕೆೞಿಯಂ ಕೊಣ್ಡಂ), ತೆಱದೆತ್ತಂ (*i. e.* ತೆಱೆಯಂ ತೆತ್ತಂ), ಮಱೆವೊಕ್ಕಂ (*i. e.* ಮಱೆಯಂ ಪೊಕ್ಕಂ), ಪಲ್ಪಱೆಗುಟ್ಟಿದಂ, ಎರ್ದೆಗೊಳಿಸಗುಂ;—ನುಡಿಗಲ್ತಳ್, ಪರಿವೆತ್ತುದು;—ನೀರ್ಗುಡಿದಂ (*i. e.* ನೀರಂ ಕುಡಿದಂ), ಪಾಲ್ಗುಡಿದೆಂ, ಕಾಲ್ವಿಡಿದಪೆಂ, ಕಣ್ಬಿಟ್ಟಂ, ಕಣ್ದೆಱೆದಂ, ಪಲ್ಗಿರಿದಂ, ಬಾಯ್ಬಿಟ್ಟಂ;—ಮರವಾಯ್ದಂ (*i. e.* ಮರನಂ ಪಾಯ್ದಂ), ಮರಗಡಿದಂ, ಬೞವಿಡಿದಂ, ನೆಲವಿಡಿದಂ, ಕಡಂಗೊಣ್ಡಂ or ಕಡಗೊಣ್ಡಂ, ಕೆಯ್ವೊಲಂಗಾದಂ or ಕೆಯ್ವೊಲಗಾವಂ, ಪದಂಗೊಟ್ಟಂ or ಪದಗೊಟ್ಟಂ, ಮೊಗಂನೋಡಿದಂ or ಮೊಗನೋಡಿದಂ, ಬೆಸಮ್ಬಡೆದಂ or ಬೆಸವಡೆದಂ, ಮನಂಸನ್ದಂ or ಮನಸನ್ದಂ;—ಪುದುಂಗೊಳಿಸಿದಂ or ಪುದುಗೊಳಿಸಿದಂ, ಮಾತುಂಗುಟ್ಟಿದಂ or ಮಾತುಗುಟ್ಟಿದಂ, ಕಾಡುಂಗಣ್ಡಂ or ಕಾಡುಗಣ್ಡಂ, ಗಿಡುಂಗಡಿದಂ or ಗಿಡುಗಡಿದಂ, ಬೀಡುಮ್ಬೊಕ್ಕಂ or ಬೀಡುವೊಕ್ಕಂ, ಅಸುಂಗೊಣ್ಡಂ or ಅಸುಗೊಣ್ಡಂ, ವಿಧುಂಗಣ್ಡಂ or ವಿಧುಗಣ್ಡಂ; ಪಿರಿದೀವಂ (ಪಿರಿದು ಈವಂ) is an instance in which the initial of the verb is a vowel (in which caso the accusative is generally used; see § 346).

If, however, distinctness of meaning (arthavyakti) is injured, the insertion of the sŏnnĕ after nouns with final ಅ is requisite (Kêśava says), *e. g.* ಪಯಣಮ್ಬೋದಂ, ಪಸರಮ್ಬಡೆದಂ, ಗಡಣಂಗೊಣ್ಡಂ, ಬಿಯಂಗೆಯ್ದಂ, ಕೆಲಸಮ್ಬೊಕ್ಕಂ, ಕರಗಮ್ಬೊತ್ತಂ.

As remarked above, Saṁskṛita nouns with final ಅ always require the insertion of the sŏnnĕ, *e. g.* ಗುಣಂಗೊಣ್ಡಂ, ಪ್ರಿಯಂನುಡಿದಂ, ಧನಮ್ಬಡೆದಂ, ರಂಗಮ್ಬೊಕ್ಕಂ, ಭಯಂಗೊಳಿಸಿದಂ, ಚಕ್ರಂಗೊಣ್ಡಂ, ವಜ್ರಂಗೊಣ್ಡಂ, ಖಡ್ಗಮ್ಬಿಡಿದಂ, ದಣ್ಡಂಗೊಣ್ಡಂ.

b) Instances in which **the noun has the meaning of the instrumental,** aro *e. g.* ನೀರ್ದೊಳೆದಂ, ಕಣ್ಗಣ್ಡಂ, ಕುಡುಗೋಲ್ಗೊಯ್ದಂ, ಮನಗಣ್ಡಂ, ಕೋಲ್ಬುಟ್ಟಿದುದು, ಬೇಗಬನ್ದಂ, ತಿಬ್ಬನುಡಿದಂ; an instance in which **the noun has the meaning of the dative,** is ಪುಯಲ್ಬೋದಂ (= ಪುಯಲ್ಗೆ ಪೋದಂ); and an instance in which **the noun has the meaning of the locative,** is ಮಡುಂಬಿದ್ದಂ or ಮಡುವಿದ್ದಂ.

In tho kriyâsamâsa, as tho instances show, an **arisamâsa** (§ 252) is faultless (nirdôsha). Kêśava's special instanco is:

ಸವಣಂ ಬಳಸಂಗೊಳೆ, ಗಾ
ಣ್ಡಿವಿ ಬಿಲ್ಗೊಳೆ, ಬಲವಿರೋಧಿ ವಜ್ರಂಗೊಳೆ, ದಾ |
ನವರಿಪು ಚಕ್ರಂಗೊಳೆ, ಕಾ
ರವಾರಿ ಗದೆಗೊಳೆ, ಪೊಣರ್ಕೆಗಾವಂ ನಿಲ್ವಂ? ॥ (see § 271).

c) Instances in which **the final syllable of the first word is elided,** are *e. g.* ಪೋತನ್ದಂ (for ಪೋಗು ತನ್ದಂ), ಅಯ್ತನ್ದಂ (for ಅಯ್ದು ತನ್ದಂ), ಕೆಳಸಾರ್ದಂ (for ಕೆಳಗು ಸಾರ್ದಂ), ಕಳಸುತ್ತಿದಂ (for ಕಳವಂ ಸುತ್ತಿದಂ), ಏವೇೞ್ದಂ (for ಏನಂ or ಏನ ಪೇೞ್ದಂ), ಏವನ್ದಂ (for ಏತರ್ಕೆ ಬನ್ದಂ); ಏಪೋದಂ (for ಏತರ್ಕೆ ಪೋದಂ).

2, "**When a noun with the notion of a case** (kâraka, *i. e.* the kartṛi) **is preceded by a numeral** (saṅkhyâ), **or a pronoun** (sarvanâma), **or an attributive noun** (so-called adjectives, guṇavačana), **or a kṛit** (§§ 68; 177 *seq.*; 185. 186), **a gamakasamâsa** is formed", Kêšava says. Gamakasamâsa may be translated **'consecutive compound',** having this name probably because its members succeed one another without alteration. Consecutive compounds "may be", Kêšava says, "a class of karmadhârayas, and occasionally may be tatpurushas"; he does, however, not state which belong to which.

a) **Instances regarding numerals** (*cf.* §§ 244. 248. 278, 1) **are:** — ಇರ್ಪತ್ತಯ್ದು, ನೂಱುಪತ್ತು, ಮೂವತ್ತಾಱು (ಅಯ್ದು, ಪತ್ತು, ಆಱು being the kâraka nouns). We may perhaps say that such instances are tatpurushas, the first word expressing the connection which it has with the second one, *i. e.* the connection of the genitive (§ 246), *e. g.* ಇರ್ಪತ್ತಯ್ದು (ಇಪ್ಪತ್ತು + ಅಯ್ದು), of (*i. e.* above) twenty (there are) five, *i. e.* twenty-five. (Would such compounds not be rather dvandvas? See § 250.)

b) **Instances regarding pronouns** *viz.* ಆವ, (ಯಾವ), ಆ, ಈ, ಊ (see §§ 264. 265) **are:** — ಆವಮಾತು ಆವಕಾರ್ಯಂ, ಆವಕಾನ್ತೆ. ಆವರಾವುತರ್ ಆವವಾಜಿಗಳ್ ಆವುವಾನೆಗಳ್ (ಆವುವು ಆನೆಗಳ್), ಆವನಾಳ್ (ಆವನ ಆಳ್) ಒಳವು ಆವನಾಯಕರುಮ್ ನಿಮ್ಮ ಪ್ಯಾಹಮೊಳ್? ಆಬನಮ್ ಈಬನಮ್ ಊಬನಮ್ ಎನ್ನದೆ, ತೊಡಲ್ದು, ಪೂಗೊಯ್ದರ್ ಅವರ್. Here, we may say, the two words are in the same relationship (êkâšraya) and form karmadhârayas (§ 247).

c) **Instances regarding artributive nouns** are: — ಅಸಿಯುನಡು, ಪಸಿಯುಬಣ್ಣಂ, ಬಿಳಿಯುಕರ್ಪೂರ, ನಿಡಿಯುನಾಲಿಗೆ, ಪಿರಿಯುಮುಗಂ. If we consider these instances to be compounds, they are karmadhârayas; but they are in reality no compounds, and ought not to be written as such (*cf.* § 241). They are genitives combined with nominatives, *e. g.* ಅಸಿಯ is the genitive of ಅಸಿ (*cf.* § 273).

d) **Instances regarding verbal declinable bases** (kṛilliṅgas) are: — ಪಾಡುವತುಮ್ಬಿ, ಕೊಡುವಪುಲ್, ತೂಗುವಸೊಡರ್, ಪೊಯ್ವಮುಬ್, ಬೀಸುವಚಾಮರಂ, ಪೊಡೆವಭೇರಿ, ಪೂರಯ್ಸುವಶಂಖಂ, ಪಿಡಿವಕಹಳೆ, ಪೊಣ್ಮುವಘರ್ಮಜಲಂಗಳ್ (see § 364); ಆಡಿದಪೊಲಂ, ಬಿಗಿದಮಿಳಿ, ಬೇಡಿದದಾನಂ, ಆದವಿಪ್ಲು (see § 363); ಆಗದಕಾರ್ಯಂ, ಮಾಡದಕೆಯ್ (see § 179). If we consider these instances of compounds, they are karmadhârayas; but, as stated by us in §§ 178.

179. 185. 186, their first words are very probably genitives of the so-called present-future and past participles combined with nominatives. See § 254.

As will be learned from the instances, an **arisamása** is faultless in consecutive compounds.

Remark.

Such instances as are adduced under number 2 letters *b*, *c*, and *d* are commonly, and we think quite justly, not considered to be compounds.

3, **The vipsâsamâsa** or **repetition-compound** (which has various meanings, *vide* §§ 303. 307. 308. 309) is formed by repeating adverbs, interjections, imitative sounds, and nouns, the final syllable of the first word being often dropped or also changed, *e. g.* ಕಪ್ಪಕಪ್ಪನೆ (=ಕಪ್ಪನೆ ಕಪ್ಪನೆ), ಕಮ್ಮಕಮ್ಮನೆ (=ಕಮ್ಮನೆ ಕಮ್ಮನೆ), ತಣ್ಣತಣ್ಣನೆ, ಮೆಲ್ಲಮೆಲ್ಲನೆ, ಸಪ್ಪಸಪ್ಪನೆ, ನೊಪ್ಪನೊಪ್ಪನೆ (?), ತೆಪ್ಪತೆಪ್ಪನೆ, ತಟಿತಟಿನೆ, ಚಳಚಳನೆ; — ಅಕಟಕಟ; — ಚಿಂವ್ಚಿಂವ್; — ಕಟ್ಟಕಡೆ (=ಕಡೆ ಕಡೆ), ನಟ್ಟನಡು (=ನಡು ನಡು), ತುತ್ತತುದಿ (=ತುದಿ ತುದಿ), ಮೊತ್ತಮೊದಲ್ (=ಮೊದಲ್ ಮೊದಲ್); — ಕೆಳಕೆಳಗೆ (=ಕೆಳಗೆ ಕೆಳಗೆ), ಮೇಮೇಗೆ, ಮೊದಮೊದಲ್ (=ಮೊದಲ್ ಮೊದಲ್), ತಪ್ಪತಪ್ಪಲ್ (=ತಪ್ಪಲ್ ತಪ್ಪಲ್). Regarding the repetition of verbs see §§ 211. 339.

XII. On verbal declinable bases (*cf.* §§ 363. 364).

254. **Verbal declinable bases** (kṛits, kṛilliṅgas, §§ 68, 1; 102, 8, *e*), as we have seen, are formed from the so-called past relative participle positive and negative (bhûtavatikṛit, §§ 175-179) and from the so-called present-future relative participle (bhavishyantikṛit, §§ 180-186) by suffixing the pronominal forms and pronouns ಅಂ, ಒಂ, (ಅವಂ), ಆತಂ, ಅಳ್, ಒಳ್, (ಅವಳ್), ಆಕೆ, ಉದು, ಒದು, ಅರ್, ಒರ್, ಉವು (*cf.* § 193) in the ancient dialect, or ಅನು, ಅ, ಅವಂ, ಅವನು, ಅವ, ಆತಂ, ಆತನು, ಆತ, ಅವಳ್, ಅವಳು, ಆಕೆ, ಉದು, ಅದು, ಅವರ್, ಅವರು, ಉವು, ಅವು in the mediæval one, or ಅವನು, ಅವ, ಆತನು, ಆತ, ಅವಳು, ಆಕೆ, ಅದು, ಅವರು, ಅವು in the modern one (see §§ 198 under 3; 200, 1; 267; 273; 316, 1; 330).

Similarly any nouns (§§ 253, 2, *d;* 363; 364) and certain adverbs (postpositions) are suffixed to both kinds of participles.

Instances are: — ಪಾಡಿದಂ, ಸನ್ದೊಂ, ಬಗೆದಾತಂ, ಪಾಡಿದಳ್, ಕೊಟ್ಟೊಳ್, ಸೋವಾಕೆ, ಪಾಡಿದುದು, ಇತ್ತೊದು, ಮಾಡಿದರ್, ಕೊಟ್ಟೊರ್, ಪಾಡಿದುವು; ತಿಮ್ಬನು, ಉಮ್ಬ, ಉಮ್ಬವಂ, ಉಳ್ಳವನು, ಉಳ್ಳವ, ಸಯ್ರಿಸುವಾತಂ, ಉಳ್ಳುದು, ಉಳ್ಳಾತನು, ಎಱುವಾತ, ಹೋಹಳ್, ಸುಡುವಳು, ಬಪ್ಪಾಕೆ, ಬಪ್ಪುದು, ಉಳ್ಳದು (=ಉಳ್ಳುದು), ಎಬ್ಬವರ್, ಬದುಕುವವರು, ಕೆಡುವುವು, ಹೋಹವು; ನುಡಿಯುವಂ, ಬಾರದುದು, ಮಗುಳದವರು; ಬೆಳೆವ ತೆನೆ, ಪರಿವ ತೊಱೆ; ತೀರದ ಕಜ್ಜಂ; ಬರ್ಪನ್ನೆಬರ, ಹೋದ ಮೇಲೆ.

An explanation of the structure of verbal declinable bases has been given in §§ 178. 179. 185. 186.

1, If the participles are combined with **pronominal forms or pronouns,**

a) the declinable bases may **stand by themselves** without reference to something or somebody, *e. g.* ಆಡಿದಂ, he that played, ಪಾಡಿದಂ, he that sang, ಆಡಿದಳ್, she that sang, ಆಡಿದುದು, it that played, ಪಾಡಿದುದು, it that sang; ನೋಡಿದದು (or generally ನೋಡಿದ್ದು, see remark 3), it that saw, ತನ್ದದು (or generally ತನ್ದದ್ದು), it that brought; ಪೊರೆವಂ, he that nourishes or will nourish, ಪೊರೆವರ್, they that nourish or will nourish, ಉಳ್ಳುದು, that which is; ನಿಲ್ಲದಂ, he that does not or did not stand, ಅಂಜದವಳು, she who is not or was not afraid, ಅೞಿಯದುದು, that which does not or did not perish, ಬಾರದುವು, they that do not or did not come, ಮಾಡದದು (or generally ಮಾಡದ್ದು, see remark 3), that which does not or did not make, ಇಲ್ಲದದು (or generally ಇಲ್ಲದ್ದು), that which does not or did not exist;

b) they may be **preceded by a nominative,** *e. g.* ಕುತ್ತಮ್ ಓಸರಿಸಿದಂ, he whose affliction was removed, ಗಣ್ಡನು ಸತ್ತವಳು, she whose husband died, ದೇವನ್ ಒಲಿದಾತನು, he whom God was or is pleased with; ಮಕ್ಕಳು ಬಾೞುವವಳು, she whose children are alive, ದೃಢಬುದ್ಧಿ ಹಿಂಗುವವನು, he whose firm mind fails, ಧನಮ್ ಉಳ್ಳಂ, he to whom wealth belongs (*i. e.* he who possesses wealth), ನುಣ್ಪುಳ್ಳಂ, he to whom neatness belongs (*i. e.* he who is neat), ಬತ್ತಲೆಯಿಹವನು, he to whom nakedness belongs (*i. e.* he who is naked), ಪೊನ್ನುಳ್ಳವಂ, he to whom gold belongs (*i. e.* he who possesses gold); ಕಾಲ್ ಇಲ್ಲದವಂ, he to whom feet do not belong (*i. e.* he who is without feet or a cripple), ಭಕ್ತನ್ ಅಲ್ಲದವಂ, he that is not or was not a devotee, ಪುತ್ರನು ಹುಟ್ಟದವರು, they to whom a son is not or was not born, ಮಕ್ಕಳು ಬಾೞದವಳು, she who loses or lost her children by death, ದಿಕ್ಕಿಲ್ಲದದು (or generally ದಿಕ್ಕಿಲ್ಲದ್ದು, see remark 3), it for which there is no refuge;

c) they may **govern the accusative,** as the verbs do from which they are formed, *e. g.* ಎರಡಂ ಬಗೆದಾತಂ, he who intended two things, ದಾನಮಂ ಬೇಡಿದಂ, he that asked a boon, ಶತ್ರುಗಳನು ಕೊನ್ದವನು, he that killed enemies; ಕೂೞನ್ ಉಮ್ಬ, he that eats boiled rice, ಮಾಂಸವ ತಿಮ್ಬುವ, he that eats flesh, ಎಲ್ಲವಂ ತಿಮ್ಬುವಂ, he that eats all kinds of food, ಆನೆಯನ್ ಏಱುವಾತ, he who mounts an elephant, ತಪದ ಬಾಧೆಯಂ ಸಯ್ರಿಸುವಾತಂ, he that patiently endures the pain of austerities, ಗಿಳಿ ಸೋವಾಕೆಗಳ್, females that scare away parrots, ಗರ್ವವನ್ ಉಳ್ಳವ, he that possesses pride, ನುಣ್ಪನ್ ಉಳ್ಳಂ, he that possesses neatness, ಸೂಕ್ಷ್ಮಬುದ್ಧಿಯನ್ ಉಳ್ಳವನು, he that possesses acute discernment (regarding the accusative see § 316, 1); ಭಕ್ತಿಮಾರ್ಗವನ್ ಅಱಿಯದವನು, he that does not or did not know devotedness, ದುರ್ಜನರನ್ನು ಸೇರದವ, he that does not or did not join bad men;

d) they may be **joined also to other cases** just as the verbs from which they are formed, *e. g.* ಪೊಲದಲ್ಲಿರ್ದಂ, he that was in the field, ಹಳ್ಳಿಗೆ ಹೋದವರು, they that went to the hamlet, ತಾವರೆಗೆ or ತಾವರೆಯೊಳ್ ಪುಟ್ಟಿದಂ, he that sprang from a lotus, ತೊತ್ತಿಂಗೆ ಪುಟ್ಟಿದಂ, he that was born of a female servant, ಕುತ್ತದಿನ್ದ ಕೊರಗಿದವನು, he that is emaciated by sickness, ತನಗೆ ತಾನೆ ಹುಟ್ಟುವುದು, that which grows by its own force (*i. e.* spontaneously), ಊರಿನ್ದ ಬನ್ದವನು, he that came from the village, ಸದ್ವಂಶದತ್ತಣಿಂ ಪುಟ್ಟಿದಂ, he that sprang from a good family; ತಾಯ್ಯ ಮೇಲೆ ಪ್ರೀತಿ ಮಾಡುವವನು, he that loves (his) mother; ಕಾಳೆಗದತ್ತಣಿನ್ದ ಮುಗುಚದವರು, they that do not or did not recede from a fight, ಮರಣಕ್ಕಂಜದವರು, they that are not afraid of death, ಕೆಲಸಕ್ಕೆ ಬಾರದವನು, he that is not serviceable.

e) they may be preceded by an infinitive, *e. g.* ಹೋಗ ಬಾರದುದು, that which cannot be gone to (or reached), ಅಱಿಯ ಬನ್ದುದು, that which came to one's knowledge.

2, If the participles are combined with nouns, the rules regarding the thus formed declinable bases are similar to those of number 1, *a. b.*

a) ಅಟ್ಟ ಕೂಳ್, rice that was or is boiled, ಕೆಟ್ಟ ತಪಸ್ಸು, penance that was or is bad, ತೀಡಿದ ಅನಿಲಂ, wind that blew; (ತೋಟದಲ್ಲಿ) ಇರುವ ಬಾವಿ, a well that is (in the garden), ಕುಳ್ಳಿಹಾಸನಂ, a chair on which one sits, ಹರಿವ ತೊಱೆ, a stream that runs, ಹೊಡೆವ ಗಾಳಿ, wind that is violent; ಸೇರದ ಗಣ್ಡನು, a husband that is not or was not in harmony (with his wife). Observe also ಮಿಾವುದು (for ಮಿಾವ) ಗೃಹಂ. a room in which (one) bathes, and ನಡೆವಲ್ಲಿ, in the place where (one) walks (or in walking), ಪೋಲಿಸುವಲ್ಲಿ, in the place where (one) compares (or in comparing), ಬಿದ್ದಲ್ಲಿಗೆ, to the place where (one) has fallen, ಬೀೞ್ವಲ್ಲಿಗೆ, to the place where (one) falls (or to his falling). Regarding the 'one' in parenthesis see § 358.

b) ಕೊಮ್ಬು ಮುರಿದೆತ್ತು, an ox whose horns were or are broken, ಬೇಗೆ ಹತ್ತಿದ ಕಾಡು, a jungle in which wild fire broke out, ತನ್ದೆ ಬನ್ದ ಮನೆ, a house to which the father came, or a house from which the father came, ತಾಂ ಬನ್ದ ಕಾರ್ಯಂ, the business for which he came, ಅವನು ಹೋದ ಕಾರಣ, the reason for which he went; ತಾಯ್ ಸಾಕುವ ಕೂಸು, a child which the mother brings up, ಕೆಸಱುಳ್ಳೆಡೆ, a place where there is mud; ಕೋಗಿಲೆ ಕೂಗದ ತೋಟ, a garden in which the cuckoo does not or did not cry, ಹಣ್ಣುಗಳಾಗದೂರು, a village in which ripe fruits do not grow, ನಾಮರೂಢಿಯಱಿಯದ ಪಕ್ಷಂ, a case in which the conventional meaning of a word is not or was not damaged, ದೊರೆಯಿಲ್ಲದ ಬಂಗಾರಂ, gold that is not of use (*i. e.* is valueless), ಜನರು ಪೊಗದ ಹಱುವು, a jungle which people do not or did not enter, ಒಕ್ಕಲಿಲ್ಲದೂರು, a village in which there are no tenants.

It is to be remarked that if a nominative (a subject) does not precede the kṛilliṅga and the verb used in its formation is transitive, the subject is somehow to be supplied mentally (*cf.* § 315, 2, *k*), *e. g.* ಕಟ್ಟಿದ ಹೋರಿ, the young bull that (people) tied, ಪೊಯ್ದ ಬಱಿ, the place that (somebody) struck, ಪೊಡೆದ ಭೇರಿ, the kettle-drum that (warriors) struck, ಕೊಯ್ದ ಕಾಲು, the foot that (somebody) cut off, ಹೆತ್ತ ಮನೆ, the room in which (a woman) has given birth to (a child); ಕುಡುವೆಡೆ, a place where (somebody) gives; ಮಾಡದ ಕೆಯ್ಯ್, a piece of land that (people) do not or did not cultivate. See § 358.

c) ಕುದುರೆಯನ್ ಏಱಿದ ರಾವುತಂ, a horseman that mounted a horse; ಅಶ್ವಾದಿಗಳ ಹೊಡೆವ ಸಜ್ಜಳ, a whip with which (people) beat horses etc., ಮದ್ಯವ ಕುಡಿವ ಬಟ್ಟಲು.

a cup from which (people) drink spirituous liquor; ತಾಯು ಬಟಯನ್ ಉಬಯದ ಕರು, a calf that does not or did not leave (its) mother's place.

d) ತನ್ನಿಚ್ಛೆಗೆ ಬಾರದ ಕಾರ್ಯ, an affair that does not suit to one's wish, ನರೆಗಿಕ್ಕುವ ಕರ್ಪು, a black colour that (people) apply to grey hair, ನರಕದಲ್ಲಿ ಬೀಳುವ ಪಾಪಿ, a sinner that falls into hell, ಮರದೊಳ್ ಸಮೆದ ಅಂಕವಣೆ, a decorated seat that was made of wood, ಬನಂಗಳಿಂ ಬಳಸಿದೂರ್ಗಳ್, villages that are surrounded by gardens, ಬೆಟ್ಟದತ್ತಣಿನ್ದ ಉರುಳ್ವ ಕಲ್ಲುಗಳ್, stones that roll down from a mountain.

3, Regarding kṛilliṅgas formed by suffixing declinable postpositions the following instances may be adduced:—ರಾಜನು ಬರುವನ್ನು (ರಾಜನು ಬರುವನ್ನಿನಿನ್ನ), ತನ್ದೆ ಬಂದ ಮೇಲೆ (ತನ್ದೆ ಬನ್ದ ಮೇಲಿನ ದಿನ), ಅವನು ಬಾರದ ಮುಂಚೆ (ಅವನು ಬಾರದ ಮುಂಚಿನ ಸಮಯ). Concerning the general use of postpositions after kṛits see § 282, *i*.

Remarks.

1, As seen from the remark in § 200 under 1 the verbal declinable base (kṛilliṅga) formed from the so-called present-future relative participle is **used also as the third person singular neuter of the future tense and as a bhâvavaĉana** (§ 243). Thus ಮಾಳ್ಪುದು, ಮಾಡುವುದು, ಮಾಡುವದು means 'that which makes or will make'; 'it will make'; and 'a making', 'the making', 'the act of making', 'to make'.

Regarding its use **as a bhâvavaĉana** we adduce the following instances:— ಲೇಸು ಮಾಳ್ಪುದು, the making or to make beautiful, ವಶಂ ಮಾಡುವುದು, the act of making subject, ಕಿಱಿದಂ ಪಿರಿದು ಮಾಡುವುದು, to make large what is small, ಅತಿಥಿಯಂ ಪೂಜೆ ಮಾಡುವದು, to honour a guest, ಚನ್ದನಾದಿಗಳಿನ್ದ ಶರೀರಮಂ ಚೊಕ್ಕಟ ಮಾಡುವದು, to embellish the body by means of sandal etc., ನಿದ್ರೆ ಮಾಡುವದು, to sleep, ಮೋಸ ಮಾಡುವದು ಅನ್ಯಾಯ, to deceive is injustice, ಈವುದು ಕರ್ಣಂಗೆ ಸಹಜಂ, giving (was) an innate quality of Karṇa, ಇಷ್ಟಮಂ ಸಲಿಪುದು ಕರ್ಣಂಗೆ ಜನ್ಮವ್ರತಂ, to grant the wish (of another) was Karṇa's vowed observance from birth, ಒನ್ದ ಕೊಟ್ಟು ಒನ್ದ ಕೊಮ್ಬುದು, to give one thing and take another thing (in its stead), ಪಿನ್ದೆ ಬರ್ಪುದು, to come after (*i. e.* to follow), ನಾವು ಹೋಗುವದು, our going, ನೀವು ಕೊಡುವದು, your giving, ಅವರು ಬರುವದು, their coming, ಬಿಡದೆ ಆಡುವದು, to play incessantly, ಅಂಜದೆ ಇರುವದು, to be fearless.

The bhâvavaĉana may be declined, *e. g.* ನಾವೆಯಂ ನಿಲ್ಲಿಸುವುದಕ್ಕುಪಾಯಮಂ ಮಾಡಿಂ, contrive ye a means to stop the boat, ನಿಮ್ಮನ್ನು ನೋಡುವದಕ್ಕೆ ಬನ್ದಿದ್ದೇನೆ, I am come to see you, ಅವರು ನನಗೆ ಸಹಾಯ ಮಾಡುವದಱಿನ್ದ ಕೆಲಸ ಸಾಗುತ್ತದೆ, because they assist me, the business advances, ನಾನು ಬರುವದಱೊಳಗೆ ಅಡಿಗೆಯಾಗಿರಲಿ, let dinner be ready within (the time of) my coming.

2, Likewise **the third person neuter singular of the past tense** in the ancient and mediæval dialect ending in ಉದು (see § 198 under 3), the **kṛilliṅgas** formed from the relative past participle by means of the suffix ಅದು in the modern dialect, and the kṛilliṅgas formed from the relative negative participle when used for the past (§ 209) by means of the suffix ಉದು in the ancient and mediæval dialect and ಅದು in the modern one, have been used as **bhâvavačanas** expressing the action or state of the verb in the past. *E. g.* ಚಾಗಿಯಿತ್ತುದು, lit. a liberal person a having given-it (*i. e.* a liberal person's gift), ರಾಜರು ಹೋದದು, lit. the king a having gone-it (*i. e.* the king's departure), ನೀವು ಬನ್ದದು, your having come (*i. e.* your arrival), ತಾಯಿ ಸತ್ತದು, the mother's having died (*i. e.* the mother's death), ಕೂಸು ಮೊಲೆಯುಣ್ಡದು, the child's having drunk milk, ಅವರು ನೋಡಿದದು, their having seen; ಅವರ್ ಕಾಣದುದು, their having not seen, ಅವರು ಬಾರದದು, their having not come, ಅವರು ಮಾಡದದು, their having not done. See ನಿಕ್ಷೇಪಿಸಿದದು in the portion of a verse in § 258.

Also this kind of bhâvavačana is declined, *e. g.* ತಾಯಿ ಸತ್ತದದಿನ್ದ ಮಕ್ಕಳಿಗೆ ಬಹಳ ದುಃಖವಾಯಿತು, because (their) mother died, the children grieved very much; ತನ್ದೆ ಯೆರಡು ಮಾವಿನ ಹಣ್ಣು ಕೊಟ್ಟದಕ್ಕೆ ಮಗುವು ಹಿಗ್ಗಿತು, because the father gave (him) two ripe mangoes, (his) little boy rejoiced; ಹುಡುಗರು ತಮ್ಮ ಪಾಠ ಕಲಿಯದದದಿನ್ದ ಪನ್ತೋಜಿ ಸಿಟ್ಟು ಮಾಡಿದನು, because the boys had not learned or did not learn their lesson, the schoolmaster became angry; ನನ್ನ ಪುಸ್ತಕದ ಮೇಲೆ ಮಸಿ ಬಿದ್ದದ್ದನ್ನು ಕಣ್ಡು ಅಯ್ಯನವರು ನನಗೆ ಸಿಟ್ಟು ಮಾಡಿದರು, the schoolmaster saw the having fallen of ink (*i. e.* that ink had fallen) on my book and became angry with me.

3, **It is a peculiarity of the modern dialect to double,** almost generally, the ದು in ಅದು, when it is the suffix of a bhâvavačana of the past, *e. g.* ಬನ್ದದ್ದು (for ಬನ್ದದು), ಹೋದದ್ದು (for ಹೋದದು), ಸತ್ತದ್ದು, ಉಣ್ಡದ್ದು, ಕೊಟ್ಟದ್ದು, ಆದದ್ದು; if such a bhâvavačana is formed from verbal themes with final ಇ (§§ 166. 175, 2) or from the so-called negative (§ 175, 3), the suffix ಅದು almost generally becomes ದು (*cf.* § 122), *e. g.* ಮಾಡಿದ್ದು (for ಮಾಡಿದದು), ಬೇಡಿದ್ದು, ಬಿತ್ತಿದ್ದು, ಮಾಡದ್ದು (for ಮಾಡದದು), ಬಾರದ್ದು, ನುಡಿಯದ್ದು; also forms like ತಿಳಿದ್ದು (for ತಿಳಿದದು or ತಿಳಿದದ್ದು), ನಡೆದ್ದು (for ನಡೆದದು), ಆದ್ದು (for ಆದದು), ಹೋದ್ದು (for ಹೋದದು) are used. This peculiarity holds good, of course, also with regard to the similarly formed kṛilliṅgas, *e. g.* in No. 1, *a. b.*

It may be remarked here too that in adding ಅದು to the genitive of neuter nouns ending in ಅ, its initial ಅ is generally elided, *e. g.* ಕೆಲಸದ್ದು (for ಕೆಲಸದದು), ಮರದ್ದು, ಶಾಸ್ತ್ರದ್ದು.

XIII. On pronouns.

255. The pronouns are declinable bases (§ 90). ಆಂ, ಆನು, ನಾಂ, ನಾನು, ನಾ, ನೀಂ, ನೀನು, ನೀ are called (by Europeans) **personal pronouns**, and ತಾಂ, ತಾನು, ತಾ is called (by them) the **reflexive** (reciprocal) **pronoun** (see § 102, 8, *a*).

ಅದು, ಇದು, ಉದು (see § 122; ಅತು, ಅತ್ತು, ಉತು § 272), ಪೆಱತು, ಪೆಱದು, ಎಲ್ಲದು; ಅವಂ, ಇವಂ, ಉವಂ, ಅವನು, ಇವನು, ಅವ, ಇವ, ಪೆಱಂ; ಅವಳ್, ಇವಳ್, ಉವಳ್, ಅವಳು, ಇವಳು, ಪೆಱಳ್; ಆತಂ, ಈತಂ, ಊತಂ, ಆತನು, ಈತನು, ಆತ, ಈತ (§ 265); ಆಕೆ, ಈಕೆ, ಊಕೆ are **demonstrative pronouns**; and ಅವುದು (§§ 265.

269), ಯಾವದು, ದಾವದು; ಆವಂ, ಆವೆ, ಯಾವನು, ದಾವನು; ಆವಳ್, ಯಾವಳು, ದಾವಳು; ಏನ್, ಏನು are **interrogative pronouns** (see § 102, 8, *b*). The initials ಯಾ and ದಾ are dialectical forms of later time; ಅವನು, ಇವನು, ಅವಳು, ಇವಳು, ಆತನು, ಈತನು, ಯಾವನು, ದಾವನು, ಯಾವಳು, ದಾವಳು, ಏನು are modern forms with a euphonic final ಉ (§ 112); ಅವಳು, ಇವಳು appear also in the mediæval dialect.

256. The declension of the personal pronouns ಆಂ, ನಾಂ, ನಾನು, ನಾ, I, ನೀಂ, ನೀನು, ನೀ, thou, and of the reflexive pronoun ತಾಂ, ತಾನು, ತಾ, he, he himself, she, she herself, it, it itself, is given in § 137, and their probable origin appears in § 138.

In § 138, remark, their connection with the personal terminations of the verb is alluded to (*cf.* § 193 and remarks thereon). They express, Kêšava says, the meaning of the three persons of the verb (§ 193), *e. g.* ಆನ್ ಅಱಿವೆಂ. ಆಮ್ ಅಱಿವೊಡಮ್ ಉಸಿರಲಮ್ಮೆವಾಳ್ದನ ಗತಿಯಂ, though we know, we cannot tell the state of the king.—ರಣಕ್ಕೆನ್ನಿನ್ದೆ ನೀಂ (or ನೀನ್) ಮುಂಚಿದಯ್, thou wentst before me to the battle. ನೀಂ (or ನೀಮ್) ಪೇೞ್ವಿರ್.—ತಾನ್ ಎಚ್ಚಂ ಪೊಚ್ಚಮಲ್ಲದರಿವಾಹಿನಿಯಂ, he threw arrows at the enemy's army (or river) which was no river. ತಾಂ (or ತಾಮ್) ಸವ್ಯಸಾಚಿಯೊಳೆ ತೊಡರ್ದಿಱಿಯರ್, they met even Arjuna, (but) did not pierce.—ಆನ್ ಕೇಳ್ದೆಂ, ಆಂ ಕೇಳ್ದೆವು; ನೀನ್ ಕಣ್ಡಯ್, ನೀಂ ಕಣ್ಡಿರ್; ತಾನ್ ಇರ್ದಂ, ತಾಮ್ ಇರ್ದರ್ (*cf.* the remarks on the final sŏnnĕ in § 215, 8).

Their gender is shown in § 102, 7. 8 to be depending on that of the noun to which they refer, *i. e.* višêshyâdhîna, *e. g.* ಆಂ (or ಆನ್) ಶಿವಂ, ಆಂ ಗೌರಿ, ಆಂ ನನ್ದಿ; ನೀಂ (or ನೀನ್) ಕಾಮಂ, ನೀಂ ರತಿ, ನೀಂ ಗಿಳಿ; ತಾನ್ ಅವಂ, ತಾನ್ ಅವಳ್, ತಾನ್ ಅದು, ತಾನ್ ಅವಂ ಚದುರಂ, ತಾನ್ ಅವಳ್ ಚದುರೆ, ತಾನ್ ಅದು ಪಿರಿದು (see § 357, 3); ಆಂ (or ಆಮ್) ರಾಜಪುತ್ರರ್, ನೀಂ ಶ್ರೀಮನ್ತರ್, ತಾಂ ಸೇವಕರ್; ಆಂ ಗೋಪಿಗಳ್, ನೀಂ ಪೆಣ್ಗಳ್, ತಾಂ ಬಾಲೆಯರ್; ಆಮ್ ಎರಲೆಗಳ್, ನೀಂ ಕುದುರೆಗಳ್, ತಾಮ್ ಇಲಿಗಳ್.

257. ನಾವು (the plural) is generally used for ನಾನು (the singular) in modern Kannada when people of some standing speak of themselves, *e. g.* ನಾವಿಲ್ಲದೆ ಏನು ಮಾಡುವಿರಿ, what will you do without me? This way of expression occasionally appears also in the mediæval dialect, *e. g.* ನಾವೀತನಂ ಮರ್ತ್ಯಕ್ಕೆ ಕಳುಪುವೆವು, I will send this one to the world of mortals. Also in the oblique cases this holds good in the modern dialect, *e. g.* ನಮ್ಮ ಮನೆಗೆ ಬನ್ನಿ, come to my house!, and in the mediæval one wherein *e. g.* a girl says: ಗುರುಮಠದೊಳ್ ಎಮ್ಮಯ್ಯಗಳ್, and: ಇವೆಲ್ಲವನು (*i. e.* ಈ ಚಲೋ ವಸ್ತುವೆಲ್ಲವನು) ತನ್ದು ಕೊಡುವರು ನಾಳೆಯೆಮ್ಮಯ ತನ್ದೆ ತಾಯಿಗಳ್ ಎನಗೆ, and: ಎಮ್ಮವರು (ಎಮ್ಮ ಅವರು, lit. 'of us they', *i. e.* our people, my parents) ಎನ್ನನಾಗಳೆ ಬೀಱಿ ಸದೆದಸುವಂ ಕಳೆವರು. In the last three sentences the girl intends to honour her master and parents by using the plural of the pronoun (*i. e.* ಎಮ್ಮ for ಎನ್ನ) before them, a practice that obtains also in the modern dialect, *e. g.* ನಮ್ಮ ತಾಯಿಯನ್ನು ಕೇಳು, ask my mother! (Is § 354, II, 1 to be compared?).

In the Southern Mahratta country ನಮ್ಮವರು (ನಮ್ಮ ಅವರು,=ಎಮ್ಮವರು, our people, he that is mine) is often used by native women when speaking of their husbands, while the husband when speaking of his wife says ನಮ್ಮಾಕೆ (ನಮ್ಮ ಆಕೆ, of us she, she that is mine).

258. In the ancient dialect ನೀಂ, thou, is used, without the least savour of disrespect, in addressing a person of respectability, *e. g.* ನೀನರಸಂ; ನೀನರಸಿ; ನೀನಾರ ಮಗಳ್?

ನೀನುಳ್ಳೊಡುಣ್ಬು ರಾಜ್ಯಂ;
ನೀನುಳ್ಳೊಡೆ ಪಟ್ಟವುಣ್ಟು, ಸೇೞಿಗೆಯುಣ್ಟು;
ನೀನುಳ್ಳೊಡುಣ್ಬು ಬೆಳ್ಗೊಡೆ;
ನೀನಿಲ್ಲದಿವೆಲ್ಲಮ್ ಒಳವೆ, ಭಾನುತನೂಜಾ? ‖ (See translation in § 360)

and

ಕೂರ್ಮೆಯಿನಾ ಮುನಿಯಂ ಕ
ಣ್ಡಾರ್ಮಂ ನೀನಲ್ಲದಿಲ್ಲ ಪೆಱತೆನ್ದರಸಂ ।
ಮೂರ್ಮೆ ಬಲವನ್ದು, ನುತಿಸಿ, ಪ
ಲರ್ಮೆ ತುಱುಗ್ಗೆಯ್ದು, ಭಕ್ತಿಯಿಂ ಬೆಸಗೊಣ್ಡಂ. ‖ the king having seen that Muni and said "A venerable man (?) thou art, nothing else!", lovingly moved three times round (him) with the right side turned towards (him), praised (him), bowed several times, and worshipped (him) with devotion.

Regarding ನೀಂ, thou, such is often the case also in the mediæval dialect, *e. g.*

ಅರಸ ಕೇಳ್!
ನಿನ್ನ ಚಾಳೋಕ್ಯಾನ್ವಯದವರು
ಮುನ್ನ ನಿಕ್ಷೇಪಿಸಿದದೆಪ್ಪತ್ತೆಣ್ಟುಕೋಟಿಧನಾ: ।
ನಿನ್ನ ಸಿಂಹಾಸನದ ಕೆಳಗಿದೆ.

and

ಬಸವರಾಜಾ! ನಿನ್ನನೆಲ್ಲಾ
ದೆಸೆಗೆ ನಮ್ಬಿದೆಂ.

and

ಕಾರುಣ್ಯಾತ್ಮಕಣ್ಣಪ್ಪಾ!
ಇನ್ನು ನೀನೇ ಶಿವನಲಾ!

But the mediæval dialect, in accosting a single person, uses also the plural ನೀವು, *e.g.* ನೀವೆ ಬಿಜಯಂಗೆಯ್ದು, even thou having gone.

In the modern colloquial dialect the following distinction is made between ನೀನು and ನೀವು:—when addressing a person of some respectability, the plural ನೀವು (also in its oblique cases) is always used, followed by a verb in the plural (*cf.* ತಾವು in § 261); and when addressing a person of low rank, or a child, the singular ನೀನು is always used.

Further, in the modern dialect of conversation it is considered uncivil to say even to a little child *e. g.* ನಿನ್ನ ಅಕ್ಕ, ನಿನ್ನ ಅಪ್ಪ, ನಿನ್ನ ಅವ್ವ, and it is expected to say ನಿಮ್ಮ ಅಕ್ಕ, ನಿಮ್ಮ ಅಪ್ಪ, ನಿಮ್ಮ ಅವ್ವ, etc., because the elder sister, the father, the mother, etc. require to be honoured by the pronoun in the plural; it becomes particularly uncivil, even abusive, if one says to another ನಿನ್ನ ಹೆಣ್ಡತಿ, instead of ನಿಮ್ಮ ಹೆಂಡತಿ. It is not unfrequent in such polite language to add ಅವರು to the words ಅಪ್ಪ, ಅವ್ವ, ತಾಯಿ, ಅಣ್ಣ, ತಂಗಿ, etc. (see §§ 119, *c*, 1; 131, *c*, 1), *e. g.* ನಿಮ್ಮ ಅಪ್ಪನವ್ರು, ನಿಮ್ಮ ತಾಯಿಯವರು, etc. (Plurals that are formed with ಅವರು are in themselves honorific, *e. g.* ಅಯ್ಯನವರು. Similar plural forms are met with also in the ancient dialect, *e. g.* ಬಿಟ್ಟೀಱವರ್, he of the spear, literally 'they of the spear'.)

When addressing a deity (or God) in prayer, the singular ನೀಂ, ನೀನು, ನೀ, or one of its oblique cases **is always used in the three dialects,** *e. g.* ಎಲೆ, ಸರ್ವೇಶ, ನಿನ್ನ ನಿಜಮಂ ತೋಱು!— ಎಲೆ, ಮಹಾದೇವಾ, ಮುನ್ನ ನೀ ಪಾಲನೀಣ್ಬು!— ಕಾಯಜನ ಪಿತನೆ (Vishṇu), ನೀ ಸಲಹು ಎನ್ನ!— ದಯೆ ಗೆಯ್ ನೀನ್ ಎಮಗೆ ಸೌಖ್ಯಮಂ, ಜಿನರಾಜಾ!— **The pronoun may also be omitted,** *e. g.* ಎಲೆ, ದೇವ, ರಕ್ಷಿಸು!— ಮನದೊಲವಿಂ ಮಾಡು ಸಮ್ಪುದಂಗಳನ್, ಅರುಹಾ! *Cf.* § 355, I, 1, where ದೇವರು has its verb in the singular.

259. In the three dialects ತಾಂ, ತಾನು, ತಾ, he, he himself, etc., and their plural ತಾಂ (ತಾಮ್), ತಾವು, they, they themselves, are used

1, **when they, in the nominative, refer to the subject mentioned in a sentence,** *e. g.* ಮನುವುಂ ತಾನುಂ ಸಚ್ಚರಿತರ್ ಎನಿಪನ್ ಉದಯಾದಿತ್ಯಂ, of Udayāditya it is said "Manu and he (are) virtuous people".— ಒರ್ವಂ ಶಿವಾರ್ಚಕಂ ಶಿವದೇವನೆಮ್ಬಾತ ನಾರಿಯುಂ ತಾನುಂ ಕಪಿಲಕ್ಷೀರವೊಬ್ಬಳವಂ ಶಿವಂಗವಧಾರೆನ್ನುತರ್ಪಿಸಿ.-- ಜ್ಞಾನವಿಲ್ಲದ ಮನುಜ ತಾನಿದ್ದು, ಫಲವೇನು?

2, **when they, in the nominative, refer to a noun that is not mentioned in a sentence, but understood to be the subject,** *e. g.* ತಾನ್ ಎಚ್ಚಂ.— ತಾನು ಹಗೆಯ ಮೇಲೆ (ದಣ್ಡನ್ನು) ಎತ್ತಿ ಹೋಹಲ್ಲಿ ಹಿನ್ದೆ ರಾಜ್ಯವನ್ ಉಪದ್ರವ ಮಾಡುವವನು.—

ತಾನೊನ್ದು ಎಣಿಸಿದರೆ ದೈವವೊನ್ದು ಎಣಿಸಿತು.— ತಾ ಕಳ್ಳನಾದರೆ ಪರರಿಗೆ ನವ್ಬ.— ನಾ ಬಲ್ಲಿದ, ತಾ ಬಲ್ಲಿದನೆನ್ದು, ಒಬ್ಬರಿಗೊಬ್ಬರಹಂಕರಿಸುಹಂ.— ತಾಮ್ ಇರ್ದರ್.— ತಾವು ಮಾಡುವದು ಗನ್ಧರ್ವರು ಮಾಡಿದರು.— ತಾವು ಮೂವರು ಸಕಲಭಕ್ತಗಣಾವಳಿಗೆ ಸೆಯ್ಗೆ ಡೆಯಲು.

3, **when they, in the nominative, accompany the subject of a sentence and may occasionally be translated 'indeed', 'in fact', etc.,** *e. g.* ಬಹುಲತೆ ಯತ್ವ ವತ್ವದೊಳ್ ಸಂಸ್ಕೃತಕ್ಕೆ ತಾನ್ ಇಲ್ಲ, for Saṁskṛita (words used in Kannaḍa) there is with regard to (the euphonic insertion of) ಯ್ and ವ್ in fact no muchness (*i. e.* ಯ್ and ವ್ are always inserted, ತಾನ್ referring to ಬಹುಲತೆ).— ಕಾವ್ಯಮಾರ್ಗದೊಳ್ ಲಕ್ಷ್ಯಮ್ ಉಣ್ಟು ತಾನ್ ಈ ತೆಱದಿಂ (ತಾನ್ referring to ಲಕ್ಷ್ಯಂ).— ದೇವಾರ್ಚನಕ್ಕಿದು ತಾನ್ ಅವಸರಂ.— ಸತ್ಯಮ್ ಇದು ತಾಂ.— ನರವುಂ ನೆರವುಂ . . . ತಾಮ್ ಅರೆಬರ ಮತದಿನ್ದನ್ಯಲೋಪಮನ್ ಆಳ್ಗುಂ.— ಭಕ್ತರು ತಾವು ಸರ್ವರು ಸನ್ದಣಿಸಿ, ನೋಡಲ್ಕೆ.

4, **Instances by which the use of ತಾಂ, etc. is shown when these are in oblique cases,** are:— ಅವನು ತನ್ನ ಆಕಳನ್ನು ಹೊಡೆಯುತ್ತಾನೆ, he beats his cow.— ಪಕ್ಷಿಗಳು ತಮ್ಮ ಗೂಡುಗಳನ್ನು ಕಟ್ಟುತ್ತವೆ, birds build their nests.— ತನ್ನ ಸುಖವೇ ಲೋಕದ ಸುಖ, ತನ್ನ ಕಷ್ಟವೇ ಲೋಕದ ಕಷ್ಟ, his own joy (is) the world's joy, his own trouble (is) the world's trouble.— ಕರ್ಣನೊಳ್ನುಡಿ ತನಗದು ನಿಜಮಾಗೆ ನೆಗೞ್ದಿನ್ ಆ ವಿಭುವಿಳೆಯೊಳ್, that ruler became famous on earth, when that true speech of Karṇa became his (ತನಗೆ) property.— ತನಗಿಲ್ಲದವನು ಪರರಿಗೇನು ಕೊಟ್ಟಾನು, who has nothing himself, what should he give to others?— ಪರರಿಗೆ ಕೇಡು ಮಾಡಿ ತನಗೆ ಲೇಸು ಮಾಡಿ ಕೊಳುಹ, to cause evil to others and to cause welfare to himself.— ತಮ್ಮ ಕಲಹಕೆ ತಾವು ಅಯ್ವರು, ಪರರ ಕಲಹಕೆ ನೂಱ ಅಯ್ವರು, for their own quarrel (there are) they five, for the quarrel of others (there are) one hundred and five.— ತನ್ನ ದನ್ತಾ ತಾನು ಮುಱಿ ಕೊಣ್ಡು, ಅನ್ಯನ ಮೇಲೆ ದೂಱು ಹೇಱಿದ, he broke his tooth himself, and blamed another person (for it).— ತನ್ನ ಒಡಲ ಹೊರೆವಾತನು, he who nourishes (only) his own belly.— ತನ್ನ ಮಗಳ ಪತಿ, one's daughter's husband.— ತನ್ನಯ ವಧುವಿಲ್ಲದ ಲೀಲೆ, play at which one's own wife is not present.— ತನ್ನ ಸ್ತ್ರೀ, one's own wife.— ತನ್ನ ಇಚ್ಛೆ, one's own will.— ತನ್ನ ಇಚ್ಛೆಕಾಱ, he who follows his own likings.— ತನ್ನಿರವು, one's state.— ತನ್ನಿನ್ದ, of one's own accord.— ತನ್ನಿನ್ದ ಹಿರಿಯಳು, a (sister) older than one's self.— ತನ್ನವರಿನ್ದಲೇ ತನಗೆ ಉಣ್ಟಾಗುವ ಭೀತಿ, fear that arises in himself (ತನಗೆ) even from his very own people.— ಕನ್ನಡದ ನುಡಿ ಯಲಿ ತಿಳಿದು, ತನ್ನೊಳು ತನ್ನ ಮೋಕ್ಷವ ಗಳಿಸಿ ಕೊಣ್ಡರೆ ಸಾಲದೇ, is it not enough, if one learns (the way to beatitude) in the Kannaḍa language, and (thereby) acquires his beatitude in himself?— ತನ್ನ ತಾನ್ ಅಱಿತರೆ ಸುಜ್ಞಾನಿ,

if one knows himself, he (is) a wise person.— ತನ್ನ ತಾನು ಅಱಿತರೆ ತಾನಾದಾನು, ತನ್ನ ತಾನು ಮಱೆತರೆ ತಾನು ಹೋದಾನು, if one knows himself, he is likely to succeed; if one forgets himself, he is likely to go (without gain). ತಾನು ಪರರಿಗೆ ಹಿತ ಮಾಡಿದರೆ ನಿಶ್ಚಯವಾಗಿ ದೇವರು ತನಗೆ ಹಿತ ಮಾಡುವನು, (he ought to know that) if he bestows benefits on others, God will certainly bestow benefits on him.

260. To ಆಂ, ನಾಂ, ನಾನು, ನೀಂ, ನೀನು, ತಾಂ, ತಾನು and their plural the particles ಎ or ಏ (§ 212, 6) are often added in order to give them either the meaning of emphasis or also to express the 'self' quite distinctly (*cf.* § 282).
Instances of the first kind are *e.g.* ಊರೊಡೆಯಂ ನಾನೆ, I (am) the ruler of the town!— ನೀನೇ ಶಿವನಲಾ, verily, thou (art) Śiva!— ಈ ಕೆಲಸ ನೀನೇ ಮಾಡಿದಿ, it is thou who hast done this business!— ತಾನೆ ಲೋಕದೊಳ್ ಲಾಕ್ಷಣಿಕಂ, he (is) a distinguished teacher in the world!— ನಾವೇ ಇದ್ದೆವೇ, it is we!— ಶಂಕರನು ನೀವೇ, thou (art) Śaṅkara!— ತನ್ದೆ ತಾಯಿಯು ನೀನೆ! ಬನ್ಧು ಬಳಗವು ನೀನೆ!
Instances of the second kind are *e.g.* ನಾನೇ ಪತ್ರವನ್ನೋದುತ್ತೇನೆ, I shall read the letter myself. ನಾನೇ ಮಾಡಿದೆನು, I made (it) myself. ಈ ಕೆಲಸ ನಾನೇ ನೋಡುತ್ತೇನೆ, I shall see to this business myself. ಅಣ್ಣಾ, ನೀನೇ ನೋಡು, brother, see thou thyself. ತನ್ನ ಮಕ್ಕಳಿಗೆ ಕೊಡದೆ ತಾನೇ ಉಣ್ಡಳು, she ate (it) herself without giving (anything) to her children. ತಾನೆ ಮೇಲೆಮ್ಬುದು, to say that one's self (is) superior (to others). ತನ್ನ ನೆೞಲಿಗೆ ತಾನೆ ಮುನಿವುತ, ತನ್ನ ತಾನ್ ಅಱಿಯದೆ, he (the mad elephant) being angry himself at his (own) shadow, (and) not knowing himself (any longer). ತನ್ನ ಕಾಲಿಗೆ ತಾನೇ ಸರಣು ಮಾಡಿ ಹರಿಸಿ ಕೊಣ್ಡ ಹಾಗೆ, (it is) as if one himself gave protection to his own feet and blessed himself (this 'himself' being expressed somehow by the verb ಕೊಳ್, see § 341). ಅಯ್ಗಳೇ, ಅಯ್ಗಳೇ, ಅಯ್ದಱಿಂಕೆ ನೀವೇ (you yourself) ಬರೆದರೆ ಚನ್ದ.
Occasionally ತಾನೆ or ತಾನೇ denotes also 'of itself', 'spontaneously', and ತಾವೆ or ತಾವೇ, 'of themselves', 'spontaneously', *e.g.* ಯಾವ ಪದಾರ್ಥವಾದರೂ ತಾನೇ ಆಗದು, no thing whatsoever comes of itself into existence. ಫಲವಾಗಿ ಬಲಿಯಲೊಡನೆ ತಾವೆ ಕೆಡುವ ಧಾನ್ಯಂಗಳು, plants which die of themselves after they have had fruit and have become ripe (ಓಷಧಿಗಳು).

The same meaning is not unfrequently expressed *e.g.* by ತನ್ನ ತಾನೆ, ತನಗೆ ತಾನೆ, ತನ್ನಿಷ್ಟ ತಾನೇ, ತಮ್ಮಿಷ್ಟ ತಾವೇ, ತಮ್ಮಷ್ಟಕ್ಕೆ ತಾವೇ, as shown by the following instances:— ತತ್ತನಯರೊಳ್ ತನ್ನ ತಾನೆ ದೊರೆ ಕೊಣ್ಡವಂ ತತ್ತನಸ್ದನನ್ ಇವಂ ತನಗೆಸ್ದವಂ ಮುದದೊಳ್ ಎತ್ತಿ ಕೊಣ್ಡು, saying: "of those (ten) sons one who has of himself (*i. e.* accidentally) been found, a genuine son (is) this one to me (ತನಗೆ)", he lifted (him) up with joy. ತನಗೆ ತಾನೆ ಹುಟ್ಟುವುದು, that which grows of itself. ಈ ಸೃಷ್ಟಿ ತನ್ನಿನ್ದ ತಾನೇ ಆದದ್ದಲ್ಲ, this creation is not something that has come into existence of itself. ಆ ತತ್ತಿಗಳು ಬಿಸಲಿನ ಕಾವಿಗೆ ತಮ್ಮಿನ್ದ ತಾವೇ ಒಡೆದು, those eggs having opened of themselves (*i. e.* having been hatched) by the heat of the sun. ನಿಮ್ಮ ಮನೆಯೊಳಗೆ ತಪೇಲಿ ಮಣಿ ಮುನ್ತಾದ ಒಡವೆಗಳು ಉಣ್ಟು; ಅವೆಲ್ಲ ತಮ್ಮಿನ್ದ ತಾವೇ ಆಗಿವೆಯೋ? in your house there are cooking vessels, stools and other things; have they all come into existence of themselves? ಕುದುರೆಗಳು ತಮ್ಮಷ್ಟಕ್ಕೆ ತಾವೇ ನಿಲ್ಲುವವು, the horses will stop of themselves.

Further, by suffixing ಆಗಿ (§ 166), 'having become', to ತಾನ್, ತಾನು, ತಾವು, they express 'of one's own accord', 'of their own accord', 'spontaneously', *e. g.* ತಾನಾಗಿ (of his own accord) ಬನ್ದನು.—ತಾನಾಗಿ ಬನ್ದ ಅತಿಥಿ.—ತಾನೆ ತಾನಾಗಿ ಯೊಡನೆ ಗುರುದಕ್ಷಿಣೆಯನ್ ಒನ್ದಂ ಕೊಡುವೊಡೆ, when he himself of his own accord at once gave a fee to (his) guru.—ಕಾಡಿನಲ್ಲಿ ಯಾರಿನ್ದಲೂ ಬಿತ್ತಲ್ ಪಡದೆ ತಾನಾಗಿ (of itself, spontaneously) ಬೆಳೆಯುವ ಯಜ್ಞಭತ್ತ.—ತಾನಾಗಿ (of her own accord) ಓಡಿ ಹೋದಳು.—ತಾನಾಗಿ ಬೀಳುವ ಮರಕ್ಕೆ ಕೊಡಲೀ ಹಾಕಿದ ಹಾಗೆ.— ಆನೆಗಳು ತಾವಾಗಿ (of their own accord) ಯಾರಿಗೂ ಉಪದ್ರವ ಕೊಡುವದಿಲ್ಲ.— ಮನುಷ್ಯರು ತಾವಾಗಿ ತಮ್ಮ ಮೇಲೆ ಗಣ್ಡಾನ್ತರ ತನ್ದು ಕೊಳ್ಳ ಬಾರದು.

261. **In the modern dialect,** when speaking to a superior, ತಾವು and its oblique cases are often used as a **term of great respect** (*cf.* ನೀವು in § 258) being equivalent to 'your honour', 'your lordship', etc., *e. g.* ಅಯ್ಯಾ, ತಾವು ಮಹಾ ಪರಾಕ್ರಮಿಗಳು. ಸ್ವಾಮಿಾ, ತಾವು ಆಡಿದ ಮಾತು ತಿಳಿಯಿತು. ತಾವು ಯಾವಾಗ ದಯ ಮಾಡಿದಿರಿ? (*i. e.* when did your honour come?). ಒಡೆಯಾ, ಈಗ ನಾನು ಕೇಳುವ ಮಾತಿಗೆ ದಯ ಮಾಡಿ ತಮ್ಮಿನ್ದ ಉತ್ತರ ದೊರೆಯ ಬೇಕು. ಸ್ವಾಮಿಾ, ಎಲ್ಲಿಯಾದರೂ ತಮ್ಮನ್ಥವರಲ್ಲಿ ಬೇಡಿ ಕೊಣ್ಡು, ಹೊಟ್ಟೇ ತುಮ್ಬಿ ಕೊಳ್ಳುತ್ತೇನೆ. ತಮ್ಮ ಕಟಾಕ್ಷದಿನ್ದ ಬದುಕುತ್ತೇನೆ. ತಾವು ಹೋಗಿರಿ! ತಾವು ತಕ್ಕೊಳ್ಳಿರಿ!

262. The declension of the singular of the masculine demonstrative pronouns ending in ಅ appears in § 117, and that of their plural in § 119. The declension of the singular of the feminine demonstrative pronouns ending in ಅಳ್ and ಅಳು appears in §§ 120. 121, and that of their plural in § 134; the singular of ಆಕೆ, ಈಕೆ, ಊಕೆ is declined in § 130, and their plural in §§ 131. 132. The declension of the singular of the neuter demonstrative pronouns is given in § 122, and that of their plural in § 136.

The declension of the singular of the masculine interrogative pronouns with final ಅ is given in § 117, that of the singular of their feminines in §§ 120, 121, and that of the plural of both masculines and feminines in § 135; the declension of the singular of the neuter interrogative pronouns appears in § 122, and that of their plural in § 136. ಏನ್ (ಏನು) is declined in § 125. [Regarding ಏನ್ the Šabdamaṇidarpaṇa (s. sûtra 112) says that its nominative is also ಏತಱ್ *(sic!)*, and gives a dubious instance.]

The gender of the demonstrative and interrogative pronouns is visêshyâdhîna (§ 102, 8) with the exception of ಏನ್ when it is not declined, which in that case is added to masculines, feminines and neuters in the singular and plural, *e. g.* ಅವನೇನ್, ಅವಳೇನ್, ಅದೇನ್, ತತ್ಪರಿಜನಾಲಾಪಂಗಳೇನ್ (§ 271).

In the following verse

ಏನ್ ಎಮ್ಬ ಪೆರ್ಮೆ ! ಮನುವುಂ
ತಾನುಂ ಸಚ್ಚರಿತರ್, ಅಮರಕುಜಮುಂ ತಾನುಂ ।
ದಾನಿಗಳ್, ಅಮ್ಭೋನಿಧಿಯುಂ
ತಾನುಂ ಗಮ್ಭೀರರ್ ಎನಿಪನ್ ಉದಯಾದಿತ್ಯಂ. ॥

according to Kêšava ಏನ್ means ಎನ್ತಹವರ್ಗಳ್ (ಎನ್ತು ಅಹ ಅವರ್ಗಳ್), what persons! A translation, therefore, would be:—A greatness which speaks of what persons! Manu and he (are) virtous men, the celestial tree and he (are) donors, the ocean and he (are) deep. (Thus) Udayâditya causes himself to be called (*i. e.* such is Udayâditya's fame).

263. The demonstrative pronouns are remote, intermediate, and proximate, *viz.* ಅವಂ (ಅವನು, ಅವ), that man, he; ಉವಂ, this intermediate man, he; ಇವಂ (ಇವನು, ಇವ), this man, he;—ಅವಳ್ (ಅವಳು), that woman, she; ಉವಳ್, this intermediate woman, she; ಇವಳ್ (ಇವಳು), this woman, she;—ಆತಂ (ಆತನು, ಆತ), that man, he; ಊತಂ, this intermediate man, he; ಈತಂ (ಈತನು, ಈತ), this man, he;—ಆಕೆ, that woman, she; ಊಕೆ, this intermediate woman, she; ಈಕೆ, this woman, she;—ಅವರ್ (ಅವರು), those men or women; ಉವರ್, these intermediate men or women; ಇವರ್ (ಇವರು), these men or women;—the neuters ಅದು, that, it; ಉದು, this intermediate; ಇದು, this;—and their plurals ಅವು, ಉವು, ಇವು. *Cf.* § 262.

The intermediate forms have mostly disappeared in the mediæval dialect except ಉದು for the third person singular of the verb (see § 193); the modern one has abandoned them altogether, if one does not consider its ಹೌದು, which stands for ಅಹುದು (§ 201).

Remark.

Regarding the occasional forms ಅತು, ಅತ್ತು, ತು, ತ್ತು, ದು, ಉತು etc. see §§ 122. 272, 2, remark.

264. When ಅದು, ಇದು, ಉದು become demonstrative adjective pronouns, their forms (without the final ದು and with the demonstrative vowels lengthened) are ಆ, ಈ, ಊ (this in the ancient dialect). Such adjective vowel-pronouns are used before masculine, feminine and neuter nouns in the singular and plural. The following are some instances:— ಆ ತನ್ದೆ, ಈ ತನ್ದೆ, ಊ ತನ್ದೆ, ಊ ಮಾನಿಸಂ; ಆ ಮಗಳ್, ಈ ಮಗಳ್, ಊ ಮಗಳ್; ಆಯೆರಲೆ, ಈ ಪುಲ್ಲೆ, ಆ ಬನಂ, ಈ ಬನಂ, ಊ ಬನಂ; ಆ ಪೊಟಿಲಿಜರ್, ಈ ಕವಿಗಳ್, ಈ ಗ್ರನ್ಥಂಗಳ್, ಆ ಕಲ್ಲುಗಳು, ಈ ಕೋಣಗಳು, ಆ ಹೆಂಗಸರು (see § 253, 2, *b*).

265. Kêšava says that the demostrative pronouns ಅವಂ, ಇವಂ, ಉವಂ, ಅವಳ್, ಇವಳ್, ಉವಳ್, ಅವರ್, ಇವರ್, ಉವರ್, ಆತಂ, ಈತಂ, ಊತಂ, ಆಕೆ, ಈಕೆ, ಊಕೆ (see § 263) and the interrogative pronouns ಆವಂ (ಆವೆ), ಆವಳ್, ಆರ್ (*cf.* §§ 270. 271) come from ಅದು, ಇದು, ಉದು, ಆವುದು.

This statement is rather unsatisfactory. Let it be said that the pronominal forms ಅಂ, he, ಅಳ್, she, ಅರ್, they, which especially in the ancient dialect were used in kṛilliṅgas (§§ 177. 185. 254) and only in course of time were superseded by the demonstrative pronouns (ಅವಂ, etc.) and which appear as the personal terminations of the verb (§ 193), are, together with the demonstrative vowels ಅ, ಇ, ಉ and their lengthened forms ಆ, ಈ, ಊ, the elements of the remote, proximate and intermediate pronouns. Thus ಅವಂ is ಅ+ euphonic ವ್+ಅಂ, ಅವಳ್ ಅ+ವ್+ಅಳ್, ಇವಂ ಇ+ವ್+ಅಂ, ಇವಳ್ ಇ+ವ್+ಅಳ್, ಉವಂ ಉ+ವ್+ಅಂ, ಉವಳ್ ಉ+ವ್+ಅಳ್, ಅವರ್ ಅ+ವ್+ಅರ್, ಇವರ್ ಇ+ವ್+ಅರ್, ಉವರ್ ಉ+ವ್+ಅರ್.

ಅದು is ಅ+ದ್ (the primitive sign which in a general way points to an object, see § 122) + euphonic ಉ, ಇದು ಇ+ದ್+ಉ, ಉದು ಉ+ದ್+ಉ, ಅವು ಅ+ವ್+ಉ (see § 137, *a* under nominative plural), ಇವು ಇ+ವ್+ಉ, ಉವು ಉ+ವ್+ಉ.

ಆತಂ is ಆ+ತು (or ತ್+ euphonic ಉ)+ಅಂ (see § 122; § 136, *d*, 3), ಈತಂ ಈ+ತು+ಅಂ, ಊತಂ ಊ+ತು+ಅಂ.

Regarding ಆಕೆ, ಈಕೆ, ಊಕೆ so much may be stated that they are ಆ, ಈ, ಊ either with the suffix ಕೆ mentioned in § 109, *a*, 4, or perhaps with the suffix ಕೆ in § 243, *A*,. No. 10.

The interrogative pronouns ಆವಂ (ಯಾವನು, ದಾವನು), ಆವಳ್ (ಯಾವಳು, ದಾವಳು), ಆವುದು (ಯಾವದು, ದಾವದು), ಆರ್ (ಯಾರು, ದಾರು), ಆವುವು (ಯಾವವು, ದಾವವು) rest on the interrogative ಏ, that becomes ಯಾ in the oblique cases of the mediæval and modern dialect, which is another form of ಆ (see §§ 41. 125. 138. 269). Thus ಆವಂ is ಏ+ euphonic ವ್+ಅಂ, ಯಾವನು ಏ+ವ್+ಅನು, ಆವಳ್ ಏ+ವ್+ಅಳ್, ಯಾವಳು ಏ+ವ್+ಅಳು, ಆವುದು ಏ+ವ್+ ಉದು, ಯಾವದು ಏ+ವ್+ಅದು, ಆರ್ ಏ+ಅರ್, ಯಾರು ಏ+ಅರು, ಆವುವು ಏ+ವ್+ ಉವು, ಯಾವವು ಏ+ವ್+ಅವು. The modern forms with initial ದಾ are in so far interesting as they show that initial ಯ್ may become ದ್ in Kannaḍa (as in Tuḷu, wherein ಯೇನು occurs as ದಾನೆ, and also as ಜಾನೆ, initial ಯ್ having become ಜ್; *cf. e. g.* the Kannaḍa tadbhava terms ದವಸ=ಯವಸ, ಜೋಗಿ=ಯೋಗಿ, and see § 141, 1, remark under dative). The remark may be made that in ಎಲ್ಲಿ, where? which comes from ಏ+ಅಲ್ಲಿ, the ಏ has become short (*cf.* § 138, *c*); ಎಲ್ಲಿ appears also as ಆವಲ್ಲಿ in the ancient and mediæval dialect.

The forms ಆವ, ಯಾವ, ದಾವ which appear in the so-called gamaka compounds (§ 253, 2, *b,* only before consonants in the ancient dialect, as it would seem according to the instances given there), are nothing but a substitute of ಏ (§ 269). Some additional instances are:— ಆವ ಜಗಮಂ ಸಾಧಿಸಲ್ ಪೋದಯ್?— ಆವ ದೇಶ ನಿಮ್ಮದು? ಇನ್ನಾವ ಶಾಸ್ತ್ರ ಬಲ್ಲಿರ್? ಆವ ವಿದ್ಯೆ ಬರ್ಕುಗುಂ (see § 203, remark)? ನೀವು ಪೇೞಿ ಬೇಗದಿಂ!— ಯಾವ ಕಾಲ ತಪ್ಪಿದರೂ ಸಾಯುವ ಕಾಲ ತಪ್ಪದು.— ನೀವು ಯಾವ ಊರಿನವರು?— ಯಾವ ಊರಿನಿನ್ದ ಬನ್ದಿರಿ?— ಇದು ಯಾವ ಊರು?— ಇದು ಯಾವ (ಅಥವಾ ಎನ್ಥ) ಕಾವ್ಯವು?— ಯಾವ ಹುಡುಗರು ಇವರು?— ಸಿನ್ಧುನದಿಯ ಆಚೆಗೆ ಯಾವ ಜನರು ವಾಸ ಮಾಡುತ್ತಾರೆ?— ನಿನ್ನೆ ಯಾವ ವಾರ? ಸೋಮವಾರು.— ಯಾವ ಸಾಲೆಗೆ ಹೋಗುತ್ತಿ? ಕನ್ನಡಸಾಲೆಗೆ.— ಯಾವ ಸ್ತ್ರೀ?— ಆವ ದೊರೆ?— ಆವ ಜನರು?— ಆಚಾರ್ಯರೇ, ದಾವ ಊರು? ಅನ್ದರೆ ದಾವಳಿ ಮೂಱು ಹಣ! ಅನ್ದ ಹಾಗೆ.— (ಇವುಗಳಲ್ಲಿ) ಯಾವ ಕುದುರೆ ಚಲೋದು?— (ಇವರಲ್ಲಿ) ಯಾವ ಸ್ತ್ರೀ ಸುನ್ದರಿ? Regarding the meaning see § 271.

266. In §§ 102, 8, *b;* 255 it has been stated that ಪೆಱಂ, ಪೆಱಳ್, ಪೆಱಿತು, ಪೆಱದು and ಎಲ್ಲದು are classed with the (demonstrative) pronouns by the grammarians Kêšava and Nâgavarma.

ಪೆಱಂ is ಪೆಱ (the being on the outer side or foreign) + ಅಂ, another he or another man, ಪೆಱಳ್ ಪೆಱ+ಅಳ್, another she or another woman, ಪೆಱಿತು ಪೆಱ+ಅತು (see remark under § 263) or ಪೆಱದು ಪೆಱ+ಅದು, another it or another thing, ಪೆಱರ್ ಪೆಱ+ಅರ್, other men or women, ಪೆಱವು ಪೆಱ+

ಅವು, other things, *e. g.* ನರನೆಮ್ಬಾತಂ ಪೆಱನ್ ಅಲ್ಲೀತನ್ ಆಗಲ್ವೇೞ್ಕುಂ, he who is called Arjuna, is no stranger; he (lit. this man) must become (the leader?). ಆತಂ ಪೆಱಳೆಳ್ಗೀತಂ, that man (is) one who is attached to a foreign (or another) woman. ಭುವನೈಕರಾಮಮಹಿಪಂಗಕ್ಕುಂ, ಪೆಱರ್ಗಕ್ಕುಮೆ, it (the victory?) will be Râma's who has no equal in the world; will it be other persons'? ಪೆಱವಱ ಧರ್ಮಂಗಳನೆ ತೆಱದಿನ್ದಂ ತನ್ದು, having mannerly introduced even laws of other things.— ಪೆಱಂ (with an initial ಪ್) is ancient; the same form and ಹೆಱಂ occur in the mediæval dialect; ಹೆಱಂ is the only modern form.

ಎಲ್ಲದು (which is classed also with the nouns that express indefinite quantity, §§ 90. 278, 3. 4) is ಎಲ್ಲ+ಅದು, it all, ಎಲ್ಲರ್ ಎಲ್ಲ+ಅರ್, they all (men or women), ಎಲ್ಲವು ಎಲ್ಲ+ಅವು, all the things, etc. In ಎಲ್ಲವರ್ (=ಎಲ್ಲರ್) of the ancient dialect the ವ್ is euphonic like the ಬ್ in ಕೆಲಬರ್, etc. (see § 278, 4). ಎಲ್ಲಂ (nominative of ಎಲ್ಲ) is used also adverbially (see § 212, 7).

ಎಲ್ಲ, all (here without suffixes, see it with suffixes at the close of the present paragraph when it stands at the end of nouns), is used in karmadhâraya compounds wherein it may take also the form ಎಲ್ಲಾ (§ 247, *d*, 2)[1], *e. g.* ಎಲ್ಲಕಾರ್ಯಂ; ಎಲ್ಲಪುರುಷರ್; ಎಲ್ಲಕಾನ್ತೆಯರ್. ಎಲ್ಲಂಗಮ್ (*i. e.* ಎಲ್ಲ ಅಂಗಮ್, in all ways) ಎಲ್ಲಧನಮುಮನ್ ಎಲ್ಲೆಡೆಯೊಳಮ್ ಎಲ್ಲತೆಱದೊಳಂ ಕುಡುಗೆಮು! ಎಲ್ಲ ಜನರು. ಎಲ್ಲ ಮನೆ ಮಾಱುಗಳು. ಎಲ್ಲ ನಾಡುಗಳು. ಎಲ್ಲ ದೇಶಗಳು.— ಎಲ್ಲಾ ಕಾರ್ಯಂ. ಎಲ್ಲಾ ಧಾನ್ಯ ಬೆಳೆವ ಭೂಮಿ. ಎಲ್ಲಾ ರತ್ನಮುಂ ವಸುಮಣಿಯೆಮ್ಬುದು. ಎಲ್ಲಾ ವೇದಮನ್ ಓದಿದಾತನು. ಎಲ್ಲಾ ದೋಷ ಬೆಲ್ಲದಲ್ಲಿ ಪರಿಹಾರ. ಎಲ್ಲಾ ಬಣ್ಣಾ ಮಸಿ ನುಂಗಿತು. ಎಲ್ಲಾ ರಸಗಳ ಮೇಲಣ ಉದಕವು.—The modern dialect uses also ಎಲ್ಲಾದು and ಎಲ್ಲಾರು for ಎಲ್ಲದು and ಎಲ್ಲರು.

In the modern dialect ಎಲ್ಲಾ by itself is used for the nominative and accusative, and then, at least often, conveys an emphatical meaning, *e. g.* ಎಲ್ಲಾ (*i. e.* the whole earth) ದೇವರ ಜಗಲಿಯಾದರೆ ನಿಲ್ಲೋ (=ನಿಲ್ಲುವ) ಸ್ಥಳವೆಲ್ಲಿ?. ಎಲ್ಲಾ ಬಿಟ್ಟು ಬಂಗಿ ನಟ್ಟ. ಎಲ್ಲಾ (the whole body) ಹೊಕ್ಕಿತು, ಬಾಲ ಮಾತ್ರ ಉಳಿಯಿತು. ಹೇಳಿದ್ದೆಲ್ಲಾ ಸರಿ. ಇವೆಲ್ಲಾ ಕರೇ ಬಣ್ಣದವು. ನನ್ನದೆಲ್ಲಾ ನಿನ್ನದೇ.— ಎಲ್ಲಾನು, as accusative of ಎಲ್ಲಾ, occurs also in that dialect.

Concerning the use of ಎಲ್ಲ, ಎಲ್ಲಾ, etc. at the end of nouns observe the following instances:— ದವಸವನ್ ಎಲ್ಲವಂ. ಪೂಜೆಯನ್ ಎಲ್ಲವಂ. ಎಮ್ಮನ್

[1] The compound-rule regarding ಎಲ್ಲ and ಎಲ್ಲಾ has been retained only in Kêśava's instances.

ಎಲ್ಲರಂ. ಪರದೇಶಿಗಳಿಗೆಲ್ಲರಿಗೆಜಿಿದು.— ಅವರನ್ ಎಲ್ಲಂ. ಕುಟುಂಬರಿಗೆಲ್ಲಂ ಕೇಳಿಸುವನ್ತೆ. ಭೂಮಿಗೆಲ್ಲಾ ಒಬ್ಬನೇ ಅರಸಾಗಿ.— ಅವರೆಲ್ಲರನ್ನು ಕರೆ! ಜೀವಿಗಳೆಲ್ಲರಿಗೆ ಕೊಟ್ಟಂ ಸುಗತಿಯು. ಅವಯವಗಳೆಲ್ಲಕ್ಕೆ (see § 124 after No. 6). ವಿಶ್ವವೆಲ್ಲಕ್ಕೆ. ಪಾಳಿಕ್ಕುಂ ಜಗವೆಲ್ಲಮಂ ಕಮಲಭವಂ.— ಐಶ್ವರ್ಯಮ್ ಎಲ್ಲಮ್ ಅಧ್ರುವಂ. ಭುವನಂಗಳೆಲ್ಲಂ. ಪೊರೆಯು ಶಬರಿಯರೆಲ್ಲ (ತಮ್ಮ) ಕರವೆತ್ತಿ ಪೊಗಟ್ಟಿರ್ ಅವನ. ನರರೆಲ್ಲಂ ಜನ್ಮಸಾರೂಪ್ಯಮನೇ ಪಡೆದರ್. ಮನುಜರೆಲ್ಲರು. ಜನಂಗಳೆಲ್ಲರು. ಶಿಷ್ಯರುಗಳೆಲ್ಲರು. ನೀವೆಲ್ಲರು. ನೋಡುವರೆಲ್ಲಾ. The Nuḍigaṭṭu has: ಜನರೆಲ್ಲ, ಜನರನ್ನೆಲ್ಲ, ಜನರಿನ್ದೆಲ್ಲ, ಜನರಿಗೆಲ್ಲ; ಜನರೆಲ್ಲರು, ಜನರೆಲ್ಲರನ್ನು, ಜನರೆಲ್ಲರಿನ್ದ, ಜನರೆಲ್ಲರಿಗೆ.

267. In § 174 it has been stated that there are no relative pronouns in Kannaḍa, and their place is somehow supplied by the so-called relative participles; from the translation of the instances concerning these in §§ 179, 186 and 254 this peculiarity has already become evident. Occasionally, however, there occur sentences in the three dialects which might suggest the thought as if the interrogative pronouns were used as relative ones, *e. g.* ಆವನ್ ಅಧಿಕ ಪುಣ್ಯನ್ ಅವನೆ ಸೇವ್ಯಂ, who (is) a very righteous man, he indeed (is) venerable. But this translation is misleading; the correct literal translation is 'who (is) a very righteous man? he indeed is venerable'.

That the meaning of the above and similar sentences is thus to be explained by the interrogative pronoun followed by a demonstrative one becomes plainer in instances taken from the modern dialect, in which dialect the vowel ಓ of questioning (§ 212, 6) is often used, *e. g.* ಆನೆಯ ಮುಮ್ಭಾಗ ಯಾವದೋ? ಅದು ದನ್ತಭಾಗ, what (is) the fore-part of an elephant('s head)? it (is) the dantabhâga. ಯಾವವನು (*i. e.* ಯಾವ ಅವನು) ಹಗೆಯುವನನ್ನು ಗೆಲ್ಲುವದಕ್ಕಾಗಿಯೇ ಬಹಳವಾಗಿ ಹೊರಡುತ್ತಾನೋ? ಅನ್ಥವನು ಅಭ್ಯಮಿತ್ರ್ಯ, who does often march out with the very object of vanquishing an enemy? such a one (is) an abhyamitrya. ಯಾವನು ಕೆಲಸ ಮಾಡುವನೋ? ಅವನು ಉಣ್ಣುವನು, who does work? he shall have a dinner. ನೀನು ನಮ್ಬಲಿಕ್ಕೆ ಯಾರು ತಕ್ಕವರೋ? ಅನ್ಥವರನ್ನು ನಿನ್ನ ಸ್ನೇಹಿತರಾಗಿ ಆರಿಸು, who (are) the people whom thou canst trust? such people choose for thy friends! ತಮ್ಮನ್ನು ಎರಡನೆಯವರು ಯಾವ ರೀತಿಯಲ್ಲಿ ನಡಿಸಿ ಕೊಳ್ಳ ಬೇಕೆನ್ದು ತಮ್ಮ ಅಪೇಕ್ಷೆ ಇರುತ್ತದೋ? ಅದೇ ರೀತಿಯಲ್ಲಿ ತಾವು ಎರಡನೆಯವರನ್ನು ನಡಿಸಿ ಕೊಳ್ಳಲಿಕ್ಕೆ ಬೇಕು, in what manner do they wish that other people should treat them? in that very manner they should treat other people. *Cf.* § 271 (ಅವು ಪಿರಿಯುವು etc.).

In § 330 this paragraph will be adverted to again.

268. **In the present dialect of the Southern Mahratta country the singular of ಅವನು, ಇವನು, ಅವಳು, ಇವಳು is not used in speaking of grown up persons whom one considers respectable;** the plural of the pronouns (ಅವರು, ಇವರು with the verb in the plural) or the singular of ಆತನು, ಈತನು, ಆಕೆ, ಈಕೆ being used instead (*cf.* § 354, II, and about ನೀನು § 258). In writing about such persons this custom is generally observed only (as it would appear), if they are still alive at the writer's time (see *e. g.* Bombay Fourth Book, Mangalore, Basel Mission Press, 1884, lessons 2. 4. 36. 38. 105).

In the modern dialect of the Mysore country (according to the Rev. Th. Hodson's Grammar § 209) "the singular ಅವನು, ಅವಳು is used when speaking of an equal or an inferior. The plural ಅವರು is used as an honorific singular when speaking of a superior. ಆತನು, ಆಕೆ, ಈತನು, ಈಕೆ are used of an equal or superior when respect is intended".

In the ancient dialect the use of the singular of the pronouns ಅವಂ, ಇವಂ, ಉವಂ, ಅವಳ್, ಇವಳ್, ಉವಳ್ was apparently not connected in any way with disrespect, *e. g.* ಅವಂ ವಿಮಲಮತಿ, ಅವಂ ಹಿರಿಯಂ, ಅವನ್ ಒಳ್ಳಿದಂ, ಅವಳ್ ವಿಮಲಮತಿ, ಅವಳ್ ಸಜ್ಜನವೆಣ್, ಅವಳ್ ಚದುರೆ; ಓದಾಳಿಯಿವಂ, ದೇವನ್ ಇವಂ, ಓದಾಳಿಯಿವಳ್, ಇವಳ್ ದೇವರ ತೊೞ್ತು. Regarding a rather disrespectful use of ಆತಂ observe the sentence ಎರಡಂ ಬಗೆದಾತನುಂ ನರಕದೊಳ್ ಬೀೞ್ವಲ್ಲಿಗೇಂ ಸನ್ದಯಂ?

The mediæval dialect does not seem to differ in this respect from the ancient one (see *e. g.* the use of ಇವಂ in Basavapurâṇa 47, 33 and that of ಅವಳ್ in Jaimini 30, 1); ಆತಂ, ಈತಂ may be used therein also with a certain degree of disrespect, *e. g.* ಪೆಱರ ಕಾಡುವಾತಂ. ಏಡಿಸುವಾತನು. ತನ್ನ ಒಡಲ ಹೊರೆವಾತನು. ಅವನೊಬ್ಬನು ಗುಱಿಯನೆಚ್ಚು ತಪ್ಪಿದವನುಣ್ಟು? ಈತನು ಅಪರಾದ್ಧ ಪೃಷತ್ಕನು. Likewise ಆಕೆ, ಅವಳು are found promiscuously in passages that smell of dishonour, *e. g.* ರಕ್ಕಸರ ವೃನ್ದಮುಂ ಪಡದಾಕೆ. ಅಸುರರ ಪಡೆದಾಕೆ. ಇನ್ದ್ರಾರಿಯುಂ ಪಡದವಳು. ಉರಗಸನ್ದೋಹಮುಂ ಪಡದವಳು. When in Basavapurâṇa 5, 48-50 women speak to one another of Basava and use, six times, ಈತನೆ (for ಇವನೆ) regarding him, they may or may not do so on account of respect; they perhaps thought the term to be more expressive on account of the fullness of its sound.

269. In § 265 it has been stated that the origin of ಅವುದು is ಏ+ವ್+ಉದು. Concerning this we remark that the Šabdânušâsana says that ಅವುದರ್ಕೆ optionally appears as ಏಕೆ and ಏತರ್ಕೆ and ಅವುದು as ಏನ್ (sûtras 177. 178); (the Šabdamaṇidarpaṇa derives ಏಕೆ, ಏತರ್ಕೆ or

ಏತಕೆ directly from ಏನ್, sûtras 112. 114). ಏ is used ಆವ, e. g. ಏ ತೆಱ ದಿಂ for ಆವ ತೆಱದಿಂ (Śabdamaṇidarpaṇa); ಏ ಮಾತು for ಆವ ಮಾತು (Nâgavarma's Chandas); ಏವುದು for ಆವುದು (Abhinavapampa); ಏ ಪರಿಯೊಳ್ for ಆವ ಪರಿಯೊಳ್ (see Dictionary). The accusative ಏ is used for ಆವುದಂ or ಏನಂ, e. g. ಏವೇೞ್ವೆಂ for ಆವುದಂ or ಏನಂ ಪೇೞ್ವೆಂ; the dative ಏ for ಆವುದರ್ಕೆ, ಏತರ್ಕೆ or ಏಕೆ, e. g. ಏವನ್ದಂ for ಆವುದರ್ಕೆ, ಏತರ್ಕೆ or ಏಕೆ ಬನ್ದಂ. About the meaning of ಏನ್ see § 271.

270. **The interrogative pronoun ಆರ್ (ಆರು, ಯಾರು)**, the plural of ಆವಂ, ಆವಳ್ (ಯಾವನು, ಯಾವಳು), has been mentioned in § 265 wherein Kêśava derives it from ಆವುದು, as does also Bhaṭṭâkalaṅka; we have stated there that ಆರ್ is ಏ+ವ್+ಅರ್. (*Cf.* § 272 under No. ೨).

It is used for the masculine and feminine gender singular and plural, e. g. ಕವಿಯಾರ್, who is a poet? ಇವನ್ ಆರ್, who (is) this man?

ನಾಳೆಯೊ ನಾಡಿದೊ ಕಾಲನ
ದಾಟಿಯವಂ ನುಂಗಿ ನೊಣೆಗುಗುಂ (§ 203) ಶರಣ್ ಆರ್ ಏ ।
ನ್ದಾಳೋಚಂಗೆಯ್ಯದೆ ದಿಟ
ಬಾಟಿನ್ನುಱಿ ಬೆಱತು ಬೀಗುವಗೇನಗೆಯ್ವೆಂ ॥ what shall I do

to people who do not reflect "will he of the inroad of Kâla swallow and devour (us) to-morrow or the day after to-morrow? who (will be our) preserver?", say "destined life (there is for us)", and are conceited and elated? ಇದನ್ ಆರ್ ತನ್ದರ್, who brought this? ತಾಯ್ ಆರ್ ನಿನಗೆ, who is thy mother? ನೀನ್ ಆರ್? ನಿನಗೆ ವಲ್ಲಭನ್ ಆರ್, who (art) thou? who (is) thy husband? ಈಶಾಜ್ಞೆಯನ್ ಬಲ್ಲನ್ ಆರ್, who knows Śiva's command? ನೀನ್ ಆರ ತನೂಭವೆ, whose daughter (art) thou? ಆತೀ ತುರಂಗಂ (=ಆರದೀ ತುರಂಗಂ), of whom (is) this horse (*i. e.* whose horse is this)? ಅಯ್ಯನ್ ಆರ್ ಎನಗೆ? ಅವ್ವೆಯಾರ್? ಪಿರಿಯಯ್ಯನ್ ಆರ್, who (is) my father? who (my) mother? who (my) grandfather? ಮಗನೇ, ನಾನು ಯಾರು, (my) son, who (am) I? ಎಲೋ, ನೀನು ಯಾರು, O, who (art) thou? ನೀನು ಯಾರ ಮಗನು, whose son (art) thou? ಇವರು ಯಾರು, who (are) these men (or women)? ಈ ಚೂರಿ ಬಹು ಚನ್ದವದೆ; ನಿನಗೆ ಅದನ್ನು ಯಾರು ಕೊಟ್ಟರು, this knife is very nice, who gave it to you? ಒಬ್ಬನು ಆ ಹಾರುವನ ಎದುರಿಗೆ ಬನ್ದು, ನೀನು ಯಾರಯ್ಯ? ಎನ್ದು, ಕೇಳಿದನು, somebody met the Brâhmaṇa and asked "who (art) thou, sir?" ಸೂರ್ಯನನ್ನು ಮಾಡಿದವರು ಯಾರು, who made the sun? ಅಲ್ಲಿ ಯಾರು ಹೋಗು ತ್ತಾರೆ, who goes there? ಅವು ಯಾರ ತೋಟಗಳಲ್ಲಿ ಹುಟ್ಟುತ್ತವೆ, in whose (in what people's) gardens do they (the mangoes) grow? ಆ ಮನೆ ಯಾರದು, of whom (is) that house (*i. e.* whose house is that)? ಈ ಮನುಷ್ಯನು ಯಾರು, who (is) this man? ಆರು ಹಿತವರು ನಿನಗೆ ಮೂಱು ಮನ್ದಿಗಳೊಳಗೆ? ನಾರಿಯೋ? ಧಾರುಣಿಯೊ? ಬಲುಧನದ ಸಿರಿಯೋ, which of (these) three people (is) thy friend (ಹಿತವರು, honorific plural)? (is it) woman? (or) land? (or) the beauty of great riches? ಎಲ್ಲರಿಗಿನ್ತ ಬೇಗ ಯಾರು ಹೋಗುವರು, which (what one) will go faster than all? ಈ ಹುಡುಗರಲ್ಲಿ ಯಾರು ಯಾರು ಈಸುತ್ತಿದ್ದರು, which of these boys were swimming? ಪ್ರಮಥರ್ ಆರೋ? ಇವರೊಳಗೆ ಮದ್ರಮಣನ್ ಆವನೊ, which (are) Śiva's attendants? (and) which of these (is) my lover?

From the instances given above it will be seen that **the interrogative pronoun ಆರ್ (ಆರು, ಯಾರು) means 'who' and occasionally 'which'.**

In a note under No. 8, *b* of § 102 it has been stated that the demonstrative pronoun ಅದು is occasionally used in combination with masculine terms. This occurs when **ಅದು pleonastically precedes the interrogatives ಆವಂ and ಆರ್** (ಆರು), *e. g.* ಅದಾವನ್ ಇಲ್ಲಿಗೆ ಬನ್ದಂ? — ದೀರ್ಘಾಯುವಂ ಕೊಡುವವನ್ ಅದಾವಂ? — ಇತ್ತಲ್ ಅದಾರು ಹೋದವರ್? — ನಿನ್ನ ಕೋಮಲ ತನುವನು ಪೊಯ್ದವರ್ ಅದಾರ್? In the modern dialect the question ಅದು ಯಾರು, who is that? (who is there?) is now and then heard. The Nuḍigaṭṭu has: ಪತಿಯನ್ನು ಬಿಟ್ಟರೆ ಹೆಣ್ಣಿಗೆ ಅದಾರು ಗತಿ? ದೇವರಿಗಿನ್ತ ಹೆಚ್ಚಿನ ಸರ್ವಜ್ಞನು ಅದಾವನು?

271. Regarding the interrogatives ಆವ, ಯಾವ, ದಾವ in the so-called gamaka compounds some instances have been adduced in §§ 253, 2, *b*; 265. From those instances it appears that **their meaning is 'what', 'what kind', and 'which'** according to circumstances.

The use of ಆವಂ, ಆವಳ್, ಆವುದು; ಯಾವನು, ದಾವನು, ಯಾವಳು (ಯಾವಾಕೆ, ದಾವಳು), ಯಾವದು, ದಾವದು; ಆವುವು, ಯಾವವು (ದಾವವು) has been alluded to in § 267 where instances are given that might be supposed to be relative ones. Here follows a number of various instances:— ಆವಂ ಮುರನಂ ಕೊನ್ದಂ? ಆವಂ ಬಕಕಂಸಕೇಶಿಗಳನ್ ಅದಟಲೆದಂ, who killed Mura? who overwhelmed and disgraced Baka, Kaṁsa, (and) Kēśi? ನೀನಲ್ಲದಾವನ್ ಅಧಿಕನ್ ಇಳೆಯೊಳ್, ಜಿನಪಾ, except thee, Arhat, who (is) excellent on earth?

ಸವಣಂ ಬಳಪಂಗೊಳೆ, ಗಾ
ಣ್ಡಿವಿ ಬಿಲ್ಗೊಳೆ, ಬಲಬಿರೋಧಿ ವಜ್ರಂಗೊಳೆ, ದಾ |
ನವರಿಪು ಚಕ್ರಂಗೊಳೆ, ಕಾ
ರವಾರಿ ಗದೆಗೊಳೆ ಪೊಣರ್ಕೆಗಾವಂ ನಿಲ್ವಂ? || when a Jaina

seizes (his) pot-stone pencil, when Arjuna seizes (his) bow, when Indra seizes (his) thunderbolt, when Krishṇa seizes (his) discus, when Bhîma seizes (his) club, who will stand to fight? ನಿಷ್ಕಾಮಿಯಾವಳ್, what woman (is) free from desire? ಇವರೊಳ್ ಮದ್ರಮಣನ್ ಆವನೊ, which of these (is) my lover? ಪಾಪ ಪುಣ್ಯಮ್ ಎಮ್ಬೆರಡರ ಬಣ್ಣಮ್ ಆವುದು? ಅದಂ ಬಲ್ಲವರಾರ್, what (is) the colour of sin (and) virtue? who know it? ಬನ್ದ ಕಾರ್ಯಮ್ ಆವುದು, what (is) the business (you) have come (for)? ನಿಮ್ಮ ಗುಣಸಾರಮುಮ್ ಆವುದು, what (is) the substance of your qualities? ಅವನ ಉದ್ಯೋಗ ಯಾವದು, what (is) his profession? ಆವುದು ಸಂಕಟಂ ನಿನಗೆ, what (is) thy distress?

ಅವು ಪಿರಿಯವು, ಭಾವಿಪೊಡಿ
ನ್ತಿವು ಕಿಱಿಯವೆನಿಪ್ಪುದಿದುವೆ ಭೇದಂ. ನಿಮಗಾ |
ವುವು ಮನಕೇಱುವುವಟ್ಟಿಱಿನ್
ಅವನ್ ಆಯ್ಕುಳಿಗೊಳ್ಳಿಮ್ ಎನ್ದು, ನವರತ್ನಮುಮಂ || "if (one) considers, those (pearls are) large and these make themselves to be called (*i. e.* are) small; even this (is) the difference. Which do suit you? them choose with pleasure", (thus) saying (he exhibited) all the nine precious gems. ನಿಮ್ಮಲ್ಲಿ ಯಾವನು ಹೋಗುತ್ತಾನೆ, which of you goes? ಇವರಲ್ಲಿ ಯಾವಾಕೆ (or ಯಾವಳು) ನಿಮ್ಮಕ್ಕ, which of these (is) your elder sister? ಇವರೊಳಗೆ ಯಾವನ ಮೇಲೆ ಕಣ್ಣಿಟ್ಟೆ, on which (person) of these didst thou fix (thine) eye? ಈ ಮನುಷ್ಯರಲ್ಲಿ ಯಾವನು, which of these men? ಈ ಪುಸ್ತಕಗಳಲ್ಲಿ ಯಾವದು ನಿನ್ನ ಮನಸ್ಸಿಗೆ ಬರುತ್ತದೆ, which of these books doest thou like? ನಿನಗೆ, ಅರಮನೆ ಯಾವದು? ಧರ್ಮಶಾಲೆ ಯಾವದು? ಎಮ್ಬುವದಿಷ್ಟು ಸಹ ತಿಳಿಯುವದಿಲ್ಲವೋ, doest thou even not know which (is) the palace (and) which (is) the building erected for the accommodation of travellers? ನಿನ್ನ ಎಡಗೆಯು ಯಾವದು? ಬಲಗೆಯ್ ಯಾವದು, which (is) thy left hand? (and) which (is thy) right hand? ಈ ಜೋಡುಗಳಲ್ಲಿ ನಿನ್ನದು ಯಾವದು, which of these pairs of shoes (is) thine? ಈ ಮನೆಗಳಲ್ಲಿ ನಿನ್ನ ಮನೆ ಯಾವದು, which of these houses (is) thy house? ಸೃಷ್ಟಪದಾರ್ಥಗಳಲ್ಲಿ ಮುಖ್ಯ ಮೂಱು ಕೋಟಿಗಳು ಯಾವವು? ಪ್ರಾಣಿಕೋಟಿ, ಉದ್ಭಿಜ್ಜಕೋಟಿ, ಖನಿಜಕೋಟಿ, which (are) the three principal branches of created things? the animal branch, the vegetable branch (and) the mineral branch. ಉತ್ತರಹಿನ್ದುಸ್ಥಾನದಲ್ಲಿ ಆಱು ವಿಭಾಗಗಳು, ಅವು ಯಾವವು, in North India (there are) six divisions; what (are) they? ನಾಮಪದದ ಬಹುವಚನ ಮಾಡುವ ಬಗ್ಗೆ ಮುಖ್ಯವಾದ ನಿಯಮಗಳು ಯಾವವು, what (are) the chief rules for forming the plural of nouns?—From the instances quoted above it will be seen that the meaning of ಆವಂ, etc.

is **'who', 'what person', 'which person',** and that of ಅವುದು, etc. **'what', 'which'.** About ಅರ್, etc., the plural of ಅವಂ, etc., see § 270.

(ಏ, § 269), ಏಂ, ಏನು **mean 'what', 'what kind or manner of'; 'why', 'how',** when they might be taken also as exclamatory words (*cf.* § 262). ಏಂ ಸನ್ದಯಂ, what doubt (is there)? ತಡೆದನ್ತೇಂ ಕಾರಣಂ, what (is) the reason so that (thou) delayest (*i. e.* of thy delay). ಅದೇಂ, what (is) that? ಆತಂ ಮಾಡಿದ ದೋಷಮ್ ಏಂ, what (is) the fault he has done? ತಪಮ್ ಏಂ ಕಾರಣಂ, (your) religious austerity (for) what reason (*i. e.* why are you ascetics)? ಅವನೇಂ, what manner of man (is) he? ಅವಳೇಂ, what manner of woman (is) she? ತತ್ಪರಿಜನಾಲಾಪಂಗಳೇಂ, what (do) the discourses of those attendants (mean)? ಎಲ್ಲರುಮ್ ಆ ಕರ್ಣನನ್ತಿರೇಂ ಚಾಗಿಗಳ್, how (could) all (be) liberal persons like Karṇa? ನೀಹಾರಮಯೂಖಮಣ್ಡಲಮ್ ಅದೇನ್ ಎಸೆದಿರ್ದುದೊ ಪಶ್ಚಿಮಾದ್ರಿಯೊಳ್, O, how that mass of bright fog shines on the western mountain! ಏಂ ತುಱುಗಿರ್ದುವೊ ತುದಿಗೊಂಬೊಳ್ ವಿಹಂಗಳ್, O, how the birds crowd on the highest branch! ಹಲವು ಮಾತೇಂ, why many words? ಇದಱ ಅರ್ಥವೇನು, what (is) the meaning of this? ಆ ಊರಿನ ಹೆಸರೇನು, what (is) the name of that town? ನೀನು ಏನು ಮಾಡುತ್ತೀ, what doest thou make? ನಿನಗೆ ಏನು ಬೇಕು, what doest thou want? ಅವನು ಏನು ಕೇಳುತ್ತಾನೆ, what does he ask? ಅವನಿಗೆ ತಿಂಗಳಿಗೆ ಸಮ್ಬಳವೇನು, what (is) his monthly pay? ಅಲ್ಲಿ ಅವನಿಗೆ ಏನು ಸಿಕ್ಕಿತು, what did he find there? ಅವನು ನಿನಗೆ ಏನು ಉತ್ತರ ಕೊಡುತ್ತಾನೆ, what answer does he give thee?—**The genitive of** ಏಂ, ಏನು (ಏತಱ, ಯಾತಱ) **is frequently used in the sense of 'of what', 'of what kind', 'of what substance, caste, etc.', 'what kind', 'what',** *e. g.* ಏತಱ ಮಾತೋ ಭೂತಳದೊಳ್, what kind of word on earth! ಏತಱಾತನೇ, of what caste (is) he? ಎಲವೊ, ನೀನ್ ಏತರ ಭುಜಂಗನೊ, O, what kind of paramour thou art! ಅದೇತಱ ಭಕ್ತಿಗುಣಂ, what quality of devotion (is) that? ಉಱೆ ಮೃಗಂಗಳನ್ ಅಸುಗಳೆವುದೇತಱ ಘನಂ, what greatness (is) the excessive killing of beasts? ಏತಱ ಸೀಮೆ, what kind of country? ಏತಱ ಮಾತು, what kind of word? ಈ ಕೊಡ ಯಾತಱದು, of what (is) this pitcher (made)? ಇದು ಯಾತಱ ಹಾವು, what kind of snake (is) this? ಇವನು ಯಾತಱವನು, of what caste (or profession is) he?—**The dative** (ಏತರ್ಕೆ, ಏತಕ್ಕೆ, ಏತಕೆ, ಏಕೆ; ಯಾತಕ್ಕೆ, ಯಾತಕೆ, ಯಾಕೆ) **means 'for what', 'wherefore', 'why',** *e. g.* ಏತರ್ಕೆ ಮುನಿಸು, why passion? ಏಕೆನ್ದಱೆಯೆಂ, I do not know why. ಏತಕ್ಕೆ ಹೊಯ್ದಪಿರ್ ಎನ್ನಂ, why do you beat me? ಪದವಿಗಳ್ ಗಿದವಿಗಳ್ ಇವೇತಕೆ, wherefore these various (high) ranks? ಇವನ ದುರ್ಗದೊಳ್ ಇರಲದೇಕೆ, for what (is) the staying in this man's fort? ಈ ನುಡಿ ಯಾಕೆ, why this word (or speech)? ಇದು ಯಾತಕ್ಕೆ ಬೇಕು, why (or for what) is this required? ಯಾಕೆ ಬನ್ದಿರಿ, why did you come?

272. In § 102, 8, *b*, remark possessive pronouns have been mentioned. There are no distinct possessive pronouns in Kannaḍa, but their place is supplied 1, by the genitive case of the personal pronouns, of the reflexive pronoun and of the demonstrative pronouns, and 2, by the addition of the demonstrative pronouns to the genitive case of the mentioned ones.

The first class corresponds to the English possessive pronominal adjectives — my, thy, his, her, its, our, your, their; the second one represents the English possessive pronouns — mine, thine, his, hers, its, ours, yours, theirs.

1, The possessive pronominal adjectives are formed by the genitives.

ಎನ, ಎನ್ನ, ನನ, ನನ್ನ, ಎಮ, ಎಮ್ಮ, ನಮ, ನಮ್ಮ, and a following noun, *e.g.* ಎನ ಮನೆ, ಎನ್ನ ಮನೆ, ನನ ಮನೆ, ನನ್ನ ಮನೆ, the house of me, *i.e.* my house; ಎಮ ಕುದುರೆ, ಎಮ್ಮ ಕುದುರೆ, ನಮ ಕುದುರೆ, ನಮ್ಮ ಕುದುರೆ, the horse of us, *i.e.* our horse;

ನಿನ, ನಿನ್ನ, ನಿಮ, ನಿಮ್ಮ, and a following noun, *e.g.* ನಿನ ಮನೆ, ನಿನ್ನ ಮನೆ, thy house; ನಿಮ ಕುದುರೆ, ನಿಮ್ಮ ಕುದುರೆ, your horse;

ತನ, ತನ್ನ, ತಮ, ತಮ್ಮ (reflexive) and a following noun, *e.g.* ತನ ಮನೆ, ತನ್ನ ಮನೆ, his house; ತಮ ಕುದುರೆ, ತಮ್ಮ ಕುದುರೆ, their horse;

ಅವನ, ಆತನ, ಇವನ, ಈತನ, ಉವನ, ಊತನ, ಅವರ, ಆತಂಗಳ, ಇವರ, ಈತಂಗಳ, ಉವರ, ಊತಂಗಳ (demonstrative masculine) and a following noun, *e.g.* ಅವನ ಮನೆ, ಆತನ ಮನೆ, ಇವನ ಮನೆ, ಈತನ ಮನೆ, ಉವನ ಮನೆ, ಊತನ ಮನೆ, his house; ಅವರ ಕುದುರೆ, ಆತಂಗಳ ಕುದುರೆ, ಇವರ ಕುದುರೆ, ಈತಂಗಳ ಕುದುರೆ, ಉವರ ಕುದುರೆ, ಊತಂಗಳ ಕುದುರೆ, their horse;

ಅವಳ, ಆಕೆಯ, ಇವಳ, ಈಕೆಯ, ಉವಳ, ಊಕೆಯ, ಅವರ, ಆಕೆವಿರ, ಇವರ, ಈಕೆವಿರ, ಉವರ, ಉವಳ್ದಿರ (demonstrative feminine) and a following noun, *e.g.* ಅವಳ ಮನೆ, ಆಕೆಯ ಮನೆ, ಇವಳ ಮನೆ, ಈಕೆಯ ಮನೆ, ಉವಳ ಮನೆ, ಊಕೆಯ ಮನೆ, her house; ಅವರ ಕುದುರೆ, etc., their horse;

ಅದಱ, ಇದಱ, ಉದಱ, ಅವಱ, ಇವಱ, ಉವಱ, ಅವುಗಳ, ಇವುಗಳ (demonstrative neuter) and a following noun, *e.g.* ಅದಱ ಮನೆ, etc., its house; ಅವಱ ಕುದುರೆ, etc., their horse.

Remark.

Occasionally a possessive pronoun of the second class (*i.e.* one of No. 2) is used for the first class, *e.g.* in the following instance of the ancient dialect:— ವನೇಚರಂ ತನತ್ತು (his) ಬಿಲ್ಲಾನ್ ಅದನ್ ಅನ್ತೆ ಕೆಱಸುಗುಂ, the forester thus scraped his bow (*cf.* No. 2).

2, **The possessive pronouns** are formed by the genitives adduced above under No. 1 and a following demonstrative pronoun, *e. g.* ಎನ್ನದು (ಎನ್ನ+ಅದು), ನನ್ನದು (ನನ್ನ+ಅದು), of me it, *i. e.* mine (referring to a neuter singular), ಎನ್ನವಂ (ಎನ್ನ+ಅವಂ), ನನ್ನವಂ (ನನ್ನ+ಅವಂ), ನನ್ನವನು (ನನ್ನ+ಅವನು), of me he, *i. e.* mine (referring to a masculine singular), ಎನ್ನವಳ್ (ಎನ್ನ+ಅವಳ್), ನನ್ನವಳ್ (ನನ್ನ+ಅವಳ್), ನನ್ನವಳು (ನನ್ನ+ಅವಳು), of me she, *i. e.* mine (referring to a feminine singular); ಎನ್ನವು (ಎನ್ನ+ಅವು), ನನ್ನವು (ನನ್ನ+ಅವು), ನನ್ನವುಗಳು (ನನ್ನ+ಅವುಗಳು), of me they, *i. e.* mine (referring to a neuter plural), ಎನ್ನವರ್ (ಎನ್ನ+ಅವರ್), ನನ್ನವರ್ (ನನ್ನ+ಅವರ್), ನನ್ನವರು (ನನ್ನ+ಅವರು), mine (referring to a masculine or feminine plural), etc., etc. The following instances may show the use:— ಈ ಮನೆಯೆನ್ನದು, ಈ ಮನೆ ನನ್ನದು, this house (is) mine; ಈ ಮಗನೆನ್ನವಂ, ಈ ಮಗಂ ನನ್ನವಂ, ಈ ಮಗನು ನನ್ನವನು, this son is mine; ಆ ಮಗಳ್ ಎನ್ನವಳ್, ಆ ಮಗಳ್ ನನ್ನವಳ್, ಆ ಮಗಳು ನನ್ನವಳು, this daughter (is) mine; ಆ ಪುತ್ರರ್ ಎನ್ನವರ್, ಆ ಪುತ್ರರ್ ನನ್ನವರ್, ಆ ಪುತ್ರರು ನನ್ನವರು, those sons (are) mine; ಈಯಾಳ್ಗಳ್ ಎಮ್ಮವರ್, ಈಯಾಳ್ಗಳ್ ನಮ್ಮವರ್, ಈ ಆಳು ಗಳು ನಮ್ಮವರು, these servants (are) mine; ಈಯೆತ್ತುಗಳ್ ತನ್ನವು (reflexive), ಈ ಎತ್ತುಗಳು ತನ್ನವುಗಳು, these oxen (are) his; ಆ ಕುದುರೆಗಳ್ ಅವರವು, ಆ ಕುದು ರೆಗಳು ಅವರವುಗಳು, those horses (are) theirs. ಆವೊಡವೆಯವಳದು, ಆವೊಡವೆ ಯುವಳದು, that ornament (is) hers. ಇವರೊಳ್ ಈತನ್ ಎಮ್ಮಾತಂ, of these men this man (is) ours. ನನ್ನದೆಲ್ಲಾ ನಿನ್ನದೇ, all mine (*i. e.* all that is mine, is) thine indeed.

The possessive pronouns ಎನ್ನದು, ನನ್ನದು, mine, ನಿನ್ನದು, thine, ತನ್ನದು, his, appear, in the ancient dialect, also as ಎನತು (ಎನ+ಅತು), ನನತು (ನನ+ಅತು), ನಿನತು (ನಿನ+ಅತು), ತನತು (ತನ+ಅತು), or as ಎನತ್ತು (ಎನ+ಅತ್ತು), ನನತ್ತು (ನನ+ಅತ್ತು), ನಿನತ್ತು (ನಿನ+ಅತ್ತು), ತನತ್ತು (ತನ+ಅತ್ತು), *e. g.*

ನಿನತು ಚಲಮ್, ಎನತು ಶೌರ್ಯಂ,
ತನತು ಮಹಾಧೈರ್ಯಮ್ ಅವನಿಪತಿಗೆನೆ । when (he) said

"Firmness of character (is) thine, valour (is) mine, to the king (belongs) his great courage" (*cf.* No. 1, remark),

or

ಮುನಿಸಿದು ನಿನತ್ತು, ಸೈರ್ಪಣೆಯೆನತ್ತು, ಕೆಳದಿಗೆ ತನತ್ತು ಸನ್ನಿಸುವೆಸಕಂ,

passion (is) thine, patience (is) mine, to the female companion (belongs) her conciliatory appearance.

Also ಎನ್ತು (ಎನ್+ತು, see § 122), mine, ನಿನ್ತು (ನಿನ್+ತು), thine, ತನ್ತು (ತನ್+ತು), his, are occasional, though undesirable, forms in that dialect, as in the modern one ನನದು may appear as ನನ್ದು, ನಿನದು as ನಿನ್ದು, ತನದು as ತನ್ದು. The plural of ಎನತು, ನನತು, ನಿನತು, ತನತು is ಎಮ್ಮತು, ನಮ್ಮತು, ನಿಮ್ಮತು, ತಮ್ಮತು or ಎಮ್ಮತ್ತು, ನಮ್ಮತ್ತು, ನಿಮ್ಮತ್ತು, ತಮ್ಮತ್ತು.

There is, however, the rule in the ancient dialect that ಎಮ್ಮತು, ನಮ್ಮತು, ನಿಮ್ಮತು, ತಮ್ಮತು may take the forms of ಎಮ್ಮುತು (ಎಮ್ಮ+ಉತು), ನಮ್ಮುತು, ನಿಮ್ಮುತು and ತಮ್ಮುತು before the appellative nouns of number (see § 278, 4, except, of course, ಒಬಱಂ, etc.) and before the numerals from two to nine, e. g. ಎಮ್ಮುತಯ್ವರ್ (ಎಮ್ಮುತು+ಅಯ್ವರ್), ಎಮ್ಮುತೇೞ್ವರ್, ಎಮ್ಮುತೆಣ್ಬರ್, ಎಮ್ಮುತೊಮ್ಬದಿಮ್ಬರ್, ನಿಮ್ಮುತಿರ್ವರ್, ನಿಮ್ಮುತೆಣ್ಬರ್, ತಮ್ಮುತಯ್ದರ್, ತಮ್ಮುತಮೂವರ್, and ಎಮ್ಮುತೆಣ್ಬು ಮಕ್ಕಳ್, ನಿಮ್ಮುತಾಱು ಗಿರಿಗಳ್, ತಮ್ಮುತಯ್ದು ಮನೆಗಳ್. The affix ಉತು is the intermediate demonstrative pronoun used for ಉದು (cf. § 173). The meaning of the instances is 'we five (persons)', 'we seven (persons)', etc., and 'us eight children', etc. The same meaning may be expressed by the genitive, e. g. ಎಮ್ಮಯ್ವರ್ (ಎಮ್ಮ+ಅಯ್ವರ್) ಬನ್ದೆವು, we five came, ನಿಮ್ಮಯ್ವರ್ ಪೋದಿರ್, you five went, or by the nominative, e. g. ಆಮ್ ಅಯ್ವರ್ ಬನ್ದೆವು, ನೀಮ್ ಅಯ್ವರ್ ಪೋದಿರ್.

Instances with the suffixes ಅತು and ಉತು do not seem to occur in the mediæval dialect in which the forms with the genitive and nominative prevail, e. g. ನಾವಿಬ್ಬರ್ (ನಾವು+ಇಬ್ಬರ್), ತಾವಿಬ್ಬರ್, ತಾವು ಮೂವರ್, ನಮ್ಮ ನೂರ್ವರು. Regarding the declension we find therein e. g. ಎಮ್ಮನ್ ಇರ್ಬರನು, ನಿಮ್ಮನ್ ಇಬ್ಬರಂ, ತಮ್ಮನ್ ಇಬ್ಬರಂ, ಎಮ್ಮಗಿಬ್ಬರಿಗೆ. In the modern dialect we have e. g. ನಾವಿಬ್ಬರು, ನಮ್ಮಿಬ್ಬರು, ನೀವಿಬ್ಬರು, ನಿಮ್ಮಿಬ್ಬರು.

It may be remarked that regarding the appellative nouns of indefinite quantity ಅನಿಬರ್, ಇನಿಬರ್ (§ 278, 4) a similar practice is observed; we find e. g. in the mediæval dialect ನೀವನಿಬರುಂ (ನೀವು+ಅನಿಬರುಂ); ನಿಮ್ಮನಿಬರ್ (ನಿಮ್ಮ+ಇನಿಬರ್); ನಿಮ್ಮನಿಬರಂ, ನಿಮ್ಮನ್ ಇನಿಬರನು.

'Whose', in questions like 'whose horse is this', 'whose ripe fruits are those', is expressed by ಆರದು (ಆರ+ಅದು), ಯಾರದು, ಆರವು (ಆರ+ಅವು), ಯಾರವುಗಳು, e. g. ಈ ಕುದುರೆಯಾರದು, ಈ ಕುದುರೆ ಯಾರದು? ಆ ಪಣ್ಗಳ್ ಆರವು, ಆ ಹಣ್ಣುಗಳು ಯಾರವುಗಳು? In the ancient dialect ಆರದು becomes also ಆರ್ತು (ಆರ್+ತು), e. g. ಆರ್ತೀ ತುರಂಗಂ? (See § 270.)

Remark with regard to ತು (see § 263, remark):—

'Of what, or in what, direction (is) it?' 'where (is) it?' may be rendered by ಎತ್ತಣದು (ಎತ್ತಣ+ಅದು), which appears also as ಎತ್ತಣ್ತು (ಎತ್ತಣ್+ತು), e. g. ದೆಸೆಯೆತ್ತಣ್ತಾಗಸಮ್ ಎತ್ತಣ್ತೆತ್ತಣ್ತುರ್ವಿಯೆನಿಸಿ, ಪರ್ವದುದು ತಮಂ, "in what direction (are) the points of the compass? where (is) the sky? where (is) the earth?" (thus) making (people) say (*i. e.* in such a manner that people uttered the above questions) darkness spread about. ಎತ್ತಣ is the genitive of ಎತ್ತ, a declinable adverb of place (§ 212, 2; § 123).

XIV. On adjectives.

273. In § 90 adjectives or attributive nouns (guṇavačanas) are introduced as declinable bases, and their gender has been stated, in § 102, 8, *c*, to be vâčya or visêshyâdhîna, in which place it has also been remarked that they are formed from nouns by means of pronominal suffixes (see § 276).

In ancient Kannaḍa and other books **thirty-three** attributive nouns are usually employed; they are, in their singular neuter forms, the following:—

ಅಗಲಿತು or ಅಗಲಿತ್ತು, ಉದ್ದಿತು or ಉದ್ದಿತ್ತು, ಒಳ್ಳಿತು or ಒಳ್ಳಿತ್ತು, ಕಮ್ಮಿತು or ಕಮ್ಮಿತ್ತು, ಕೂರಿತು or ಕೂರಿತ್ತು, ಗುಣ್ಡಿತು or ಗುಣ್ಡಿತ್ತು, ತಣ್ಣಿತು or ತಣ್ಣಿತ್ತು, ತೆಳ್ಳಿತು or ತೆಳ್ಳಿತ್ತು, ತೋರಿತು or ತೋರಿತ್ತು, ದಟ್ಟಿತು or ದಟ್ಟಿತ್ತು, ದೊಡ್ಡಿತು or ದೊಡ್ಡಿತ್ತು, ನುಣ್ಣಿತು or ನುಣ್ಣಿತ್ತು, ನೇರಿತು or ನೇರಿತ್ತು, ಬಟ್ಟಿತು or ಬಟ್ಟಿತ್ತು, ಬಲ್ಲಿತು or ಬಲ್ಲಿತ್ತು, ಬಿಣ್ಣಿತು or ಬಿಣ್ಣಿತ್ತು, ಬೆಟ್ಟಿತು or ಬೆಟ್ಟಿತ್ತು, ಮೆಲ್ಲಿತು or ಮೆಲ್ಲಿತ್ತು, ಸಣ್ಣಿತು or ಸಣ್ಣಿತ್ತು (see their declension in § 122);—ಅಸಿದು, ಇನಿದು, (ಇಮ್ಮಿದು), ಎಳದು (ಎಳೆದು), ಕಡಿದು, ಕರಿದು, ಕಿಱಿದು, ನಿಡಿದು, ಪಱದು (ಪಱಿದು), ಪಿರಿದು (ಹಿರಿದು), ಪೊಸದು (ಪೊಸತು), ಬಱಿದು, ಬಸಿದು, ಬಿಳಿದು (see their declension in § 122), of which four are tadbhavas (§ 370), *viz.* ಉದ್ದಿತು, ಬಟ್ಟಿತು, ಮೆಲ್ಲಿತು, ಸಣ್ಣಿತು.

As will be seen, they form two classes according to their finals.

The neuter plural of the first class is *e. g.* ಒಳ್ಳಿದುವು, ಕೂರಿದುವು, ತೆಳ್ಳಿದುವು, ತೋರಿದುವು, ದಟ್ಟಿದುವು, ನೇರಿದುವು, ಬಟ್ಟಿದುವು, ಬೆಟ್ಟಿದುವು, ಮೆಲ್ಲಿದುವು (see § 136); that of the second class is *e. g.* ಅಸಿಯವು, ಇನಿಯವು, ಕಡಿಯವು, ಕರಿಯವು, ಕಿಱಿಯವು, ನಿಡಿಯವು, ಬಸಿಯವು, ಬಿಳಿಯವು (see § 136).

The masculine singular of the first class is *e. g.* ಒಳ್ಳಿದಂ, ಕಮ್ಮಿದಂ, ಕೂರಿದಂ, ತೆಳ್ಳಿದಂ, ತೋರಿದಂ, ನೇರಿದಂ, ಬಲ್ಲಿದಂ, ಬೆಟ್ಟಿದಂ, ಮೆಲ್ಲಿದಂ (see § 117); that of the second class *e. g.* ಅಸಿಯಂ, ಇನಿಯಂ, ಎಳೆಯಂ, ಕಡಿಯಂ, ಕರಿಯಂ, ಕಿಱಿಯಂ, ನಿಡಿಯಂ, ಪಱಿಯಂ, ಪಿರಿಯಂ, ಪೊಸಪ್ಪಂ (*cf.* the formation of the appellative nouns of number in § 278, 4 and the modern ಹಱಿಬ), ಬಱಿಯಂ or ಬಱುವಂ, ಬಸಿಯಂ, ಬಿಳಿಯಂ (see § 117).

The feminine singular of the first class is *e. g.* ಒಳ್ಳಿದಳ್, ಕಮ್ಮಿದಳ್, ಕೂರಿದಳ್, ನೇರಿದಳ್, ಬೆಟ್ಟಿದಳ್, ಮೆಲ್ಲಿದಳ್ (see § 120); that of the second class *e. g.* ಅಸಿಯಳ್, ಇನಿಯಳ್, (ಇವ್ಮಿದಳ್), ಎಳೆಯಳ್, ಕರಿಯಳ್, ಕಿಱಿಯಳ್, ನಿಡಿಯಳ್, ಪೞೆಯಳ್, ಪಿರಿಯಳ್, ಪೊಸವ್ಬಳ್, ಬಱುವಳ್, ಬಿಳಿಯಳ್ (see § 120).

The epicene plural of the first class is *e. g.* ಒಳ್ಳಿದರ್, ನೇರಿದರ್, ಬಲ್ಲಿದರ್ (see § 119); that of the second class *e. g.* ಇನಿಯರ್, ಎಳೆಯರ್, ಕಿಱಿಯರ್, ಪಿರಿಯರ್, ಪೊಸವ್ಬರ್, ಬಱುವರ್, ಬಳಿಯಳ್ದರ್ (see §§ 119. 134).

Some instances regarding their use in the ancient and mediæval dialect are the following (*cf.* § 276):—

ಬೆಟ್ಟಿತಂಗುಳಿ (ಬೆಟ್ಟಿತು ಅಂಗುಳಿ), a severe disease of the uvula. ಬಟ್ಟಿದುವು ಮೊಲೆ (for ಮೊಲೆಗಳ್, see § 354, I, 3, *b*), round breasts. ಇನಿದು ಪಾಲ್, sweet milk. ಕರಿದು ಕತ್ತುರಿ, black musk. ಬಿಳಿದು ಮುತ್ತು, a white pearl. ಪಿರಿದಾಸೆ, great desire. ಪಿರಿದು ಚಾಗಂ, great liberality. ಪಿರಿದುರಿ, a large flame. ಕಿಱಿದು ಕೂಟಂ, a small quantity. ಹಿರಿದು ಸತ್ವಂ, great vigour. ತೋರಿದುವು ಜಘನಂ (for ಜಘನಂಗಳ್), big buttocks. ನೇರಿದುವು ಬೆರಲ್ (for ಬೆರಲ್ಗಳ್), straight fingers. ಇನಿಯಳ್ ಕಾದಲೆ, a sweet paramour. ಇನಿಯವು ವಿಷಯ ಸುಖಂ (for ವಿಷಯಸುಖಂಗಳ್) ನಂಜಿನ ಸವಿವೋಲ್, the sweet pleasures of the objects of sense (are) like the sweetness of poison.

But though such instances in which the so-called adjectives are immediately connected with nouns, not unfrequently occur in the mentioned two dialects, there is also another more common way of doing so, *viz.* by putting ಅಪ್ಪ, ಅಹ, ಅಹ and ಆದ between them. ಅಪ್ಪ, ಅಹ, ಅಹ are the present relative participles of ಆಗು (§§ 183, remark after No. 7. 184. 223), 'becoming', 'being' (literally 'of the becoming or being', § 186), and ಆದ is the past relative participle of ಆಗು (§ 176), 'having become', 'being' (literally 'of the having become or being'; about the possibility of ಆದ being used also for the present tense see § 169). The translation of the participles into English is, according to circumstances, 'that is', 'who is', 'which are', 'who are', instead of which (the so-called Kannaḍa) adjectives alone may be used in rendering.

Instances in the ancient and mediæval dialect are:—ಬೆಟ್ಟಿತಪ್ಪ ಧ್ವನಿ, a sound that is harsh or a harsh sound. ಮೆಲ್ಲಿದುವಪ್ಪ ಕಾಲ ತಳಮುಂ ಕಡು ವೆಟ್ಟಿದುವಪ್ಪ ಹಸ್ತಮುಂ, soft soles of the feet and very rough hands. ಇನಿದಪ್ಪ ಧ್ವನಿ, a melodious tone. ಎಳೆದಪ್ಪ ಪಶು, a young cow. ಹಿರಿದಪ್ಪ ಹೆಮ್ಮೆ, great supremacy. ಹಿರಿಯುವಪ್ಪ ಮೀನ್, large fishes. ಎಳೆಯಳಪ್ಪ ಕುವರಿ, a young daughter. ಬಲ್ಲಿದಂಪ್ಪ ರಕ್ಕಸರ್, powerful demons. ಒಳ್ಳಿತಹ ರತ್ನಂ, a precious pearl. ಒಳ್ಳಿತಹ ಹಸು, a good cow. ಪಿರಿದಹ ಇಚ್ಛೆ, great desire. ಸಣ್ಣಿತ್ತುಂ ಕೂರಿತ್ತುಮ್ ಅಹ ಧಾನ್ಯದ ತುದಿ, the small and sharp point of corn. ಪಿರಿದಾಹ ದಾನ, an excellent gift. ಕೂರಿತ್ತಾದ ಗನ್ಧಂ, a sharp smell. ಕಡಿದಾದಾಶ್ಚರ್ಯ್ಯಂ, extreme astonishment. ಸಮಾಸಂ ಪಿರಿದಾದ ಹಲವು ಪದಗಳು, various verses in which compounds are extensive.

It is to be remarked that also words which do not belong to the above-mentioned thirty-three so-called adjectives (as Saṁskṛita adjectives, etc.), may be made such in Kannaḍa by the addition of ಅಪ್ಪ, ಅಹ, ಆದ, *e. g.* ನಿರ್ಮ್ಮಲಮಪ್ಪ ವಸ್ತು, ಅವ್ಯಕ್ತಮಪ್ಪ ಕಹಿನಸೆ, ಪ್ರಿಯವಪ್ಪ ನುಡಿ, ಅತಿಶಯಮಪ್ಪ ಪರಾಕ್ರಮಂ, ಲೇಸಪ್ಪ ಮನದವಂ, ಅಳಕಮಹ ಮೊಸರು, ಹ್ರಸ್ವಮಾದ ಎ ಒ, ದೀರ್ಘ ಮಾದ ಪಕ್ಷಂ.

Instead of ಅಪ್ಪ, ಅಹ and ಆದ also ಆಗಿ, **'having become', together with a form of ಇರ್, to be,** is used, *e. g.* ನಸುಗೆಮ್ಪಾಗಿರ್ದುದು (*i. e.* ನಸುಗೆಮ್ಪು ಆಗಿ ಇರ್ದುದು), that is brown; ಲೇಸಾಗಿರ್ಪ್ಪುದು, that is excellent; ವಿದಗ್ಧೆಯುಂ ಮುಗ್ಧೆಯುಮ್ ಆಗಿರ್ಪವಳು, she who is shrewd and clever; ದೂರವಾಗಿಹ ಹಾಳು ಬಟ್ಟೆ, a long desolate road. ವಿಖ್ಯಾತಮ್ ಆಗಿಹ ರಾಜಧಾನಿಕುನ್ತಲಂ, the celebrated capital of Kuntala. ದಟ್ಟವಾಗಿ ನಯಮಾಗಿ ಇದ್ದಾತನು, he who is stout and fine.

Also ಉಳ್ಳ, **'being', 'possessing'** (literally 'of the being', etc., § 186), the present relative participle of ಉಳ್ (§ 180, remark after No. 6), which has been mentioned as one of the taddhita suffixes (§ 243, *B,* No. 20), may be introduced here again, as similar adjectives or attributive nouns are formed by means of it, in which it signifies 'who has', etc., *e. g.* ಧನಮುಳ್ಳಂ, a man who has riches or a rich man; ಓದುಳ್ಳಂ, a studying man; ಗುಣಮುಳ್ಳಂ, a man endowed with good qualities; ಧಾನ್ಯಮುಳ್ಳಂ, a man well supplied with grain; ಸೊಬಗುಳ್ಳವಳ್, a charming woman; ಅಱಿವುಳ್ಳರ್, wise men (see § 316 under 1; ಉಳ್ಳ in combination with the accusative see ibid.). The contrary may be expressed by ಇಲ್ಲದ, **'not being'** (§ 175, 3), **'not having'**, *e. g.* ಓದಿಲ್ಲದಂ, a man in whom there is no studying, *i. e.* a not-studying man; ಜ್ಞಾನವಿಲ್ಲದಂ, a stupid man; ಕೆಯ್ಯಿಲ್ಲದವನು, a crook-armed man; ದೊರೆಯಿಲ್ಲದ ಭಂಗಾರಂ, worthless gold. ವಿಭಕ್ತಿಯನ್ ಇಲ್ಲದುದು, that which has no terminations (see § 316 under 1). ಒಕ್ಕಲಿಲ್ಲದ ಊರು ಮಕ್ಕಳಿಲ್ಲದ ಮನೆಯು ಅಕ್ಕಱಿಲ್ಲದ ತವುರು ಇದ್ದು ಫಲವೇನು, though there be a village in which there are no tenants, a house in which there are no children, one's own people who have no love, what (is their) worth? (see § 275).

Prominently in the mediæval dialect ಇಹ, 'being', present relative participle of ಇರ್ (§ 184), is used like ಉಳ್ಳ, when it is suffixed to one of the original forms of the thirty-three attributive nouns which will be adduced presently, *e. g.* ದೊಡ್ಡಿಹ ಎತ್ತು, a large ox; ದೊಡ್ಡಿಹ ಕಲ್ಲುಗಳು large stones; ಒಳ್ಳಿಹ ನುಡಿ, good speech; ತೋರಿಹ ಕೆಚ್ಚಲ್, swelling udders; ಬಟ್ಟಿಹ ತೊನ್ನು, round leprosy.

It remains to be stated that the above-mentioned thirty-three adjectives or attributive nouns possess what we may call **original forms. Those of the first class are**

ಅಗಲ (for ಅಗಲಿತು), ಉದ್ದ (for ಉದ್ದಿತು), ಒಳ್ (for ಒಳ್ಳಿತು), ಕಮ್ಮ (for ಕಮ್ಮಿತು; *cf.* § 102, 9), ಕೂರ್ (for ಕೂರಿತು), (ಗುಣ್ಪು, for ಗುಣ್ಡಿತು), ತಣ್ (for ತಣ್ಣಿತು), ತೆಳ್ (for ತೆಳ್ಳಿತು), ತೋರ (for ತೋರಿತು), ದಟ್ಟ (for ದಟ್ಟಿತು), ದೊಡ್ಡ (for ದೊಡ್ಡಿತು), ನುಣ್ (for ನುಣ್ಣಿತು), ನೇರ್ (for ನೇರಿತು), ಬಟ್ಟ (for ಬಟ್ಟಿತು), ಬಲ್ (for ಬಲ್ಲಿತು), ಬಿಣ್ (for ಬಿಣ್ಣಿತು), ಬಿಱು (for ಬೆಟ್ಟಿತು), ಮೆಲ್ (for ಮೆಲ್ಲಿತು), ಸಣ್ಣ (for ಸಣ್ಣಿತು). (ಚಿಕ್ಕ is also ancient, though it would seem, as if its longer form did no longer exist.)

Those of the second class are

ಅಸಿ (for ಅಸಿದು), ಇನ್, ಇನಿ (for ಇನಿದು), ಇಮ್ (ಇನ್, for ಇಮ್ಮಿದು), ಎಳ್, ಎಳ (for ಎಳದು), ಕಟ್ಟು, ಕಡು (for ಕಡಿದು), ಕರ್ (for ಕರಿದು), ಕಿಱಿ, ಕಿಱು, ಕಿತ್, ಕುತ್, etc. (for ಕಿಱಿದು), ನಿಟ್ಟು, ನಿಡಿ, ನಿಡು (for ನಿಡಿದು), ಪಱಿ (for ಪಱಿದು), ಪಿರಿ, ಪೆರ್, ಪೇರ್ (for ಪಿರಿದು), ಪೊಸ (for ಪೊಸದು), ಬಱಿ, ಬಱು (for ಬಱಿದು), ಬಸಿ (for ಬಸಿದು), ಬಿಳಿ, ಬೆಳ್ (for ಬಿಳಿದು).

We have already met with these original forms in karmadhâraya compounds, in § 247, *d*, 5 *seq.*, where they are regarded as substitutes by native grammarians. *Cf.* also § 244 (ಮೆಲ್, ಕುತ್).

Regarding ಅಸಿ, ನಿಡಿ, ಪಿರಿ, ಬಿಳಿ there is the ancient rule (§ 253, 2, *c*) that where they form so-called consecutive compounds (gamakasamâsas) they insert ಯು, *viz.* ಅಸಿಯುನಡು, ನಿಡಿಯುನಾಲಗೆ, ಪಿರಿಯುಮುಗಂ (o. r. ಕಿಱಿಯುಮುಗಂ), ಬಿಳಿಯುಕರ್ಪೂರ, to which Kêšava adds also ಪಸಿಯುಬಣ್ಣಂ, though there is apparently no ಪಸಿದು (but ಪಸು). It has been remarked already in § 253 that this ಯು is ಯ್ + ಉ, *i. e.* the genitive. Instead of ಅಸಿಯುನಡು the Jaimini Bhârata and the modern dialect have ಅಸಿನಡು; the Jaimini Bhârata has also ಅಸಿಪೆರಲ್ for ಅಸಿಯು ಬೆರಲ್. The same Bhârata uses ನಿಡಿಗುರುಳ್ for ನಿಡಿಯು ಕುರುಳ್, and ಪಸಿದೊವಲ್ for ಪಸಿಯು ತೊವಲ್. For ಪಿರಿಯುಮುಗಂ the modern dialect uses ಪಿರಿಮಗ, and for ಬಿಳಿಯುಕರ್ಪೂರ it has ಬಿಳಿ

ಕಬ್ಬು or ಬಿಳಿಗಬ್ಬು. ಅಸಿನಡು, ಅಸಿವೆರಲ್, ನಿಡಿಗುರುಳ್, ಪಸಿದೊವಲ್, ಬಿಳಿಗಬ್ಬು would be regular karmadhâraya compounds like the ancient ತಿಳಿಗೊಳ, ತಿಳಿನೀರ್; *cf.* ಕಹಿನನೆ in the Nâčirâjîa.

ಎಳೆ, ಒಳ್ಳೆ (both mediæval and modern) and ಹಟಿ (ancient?, mediæval and modern) often follow the ancient rule regarding ಅಸಿ, etc., that is to say suffix the ಅ of the genitive by means of a euphonic ಯ್ (§ 130, *b*, *c*), *e. g.* ಎಳೆಯ (or ಎಳೇ) ಪಿಡಿಯಾನೆ, a young she-elephant; ಒಳ್ಳೆಯ (or ಒಳ್ಳೇ) ಕೆಲಸ, a good business; ಹಟಿಯ (or ಹಟೀ) ಸೀರೆ, the old garment of a female.

274. If attributive nouns do not precede the nouns or pronouns with which they are connected, but follow them, they appear *e. g.* as follows: ಕಬ್ಬಮ್ ಒಳ್ಳಿತಾಯ್ತು, the poetry became good. ಅವನ್ ಒಳ್ಳಿದಂ, he (is a) good (man). ಅವಳ್ ಒಳ್ಳಿದಳ್, she (is a) good (woman). ಅವು ಪಿರಿಯುವು, they (the pearls are) large. ಅವರ್ ಬಲ್ಲಿದರ್, they (are) able (persons).

It will be observed that in such a case the attributive noun agrees in gender with the nominative to which it is added.

Saṁskṛita adjectives are used similarly, *e. g.* ಕಬ್ಬಂ ಶ್ರೇಷ್ಠಂ, ಅವನ್ ಉತ್ತಮಂ, ಇವಳ್ ದೀನೆ, ಅವು ರಮ್ಯಂ, ಅವರ್ ಉತ್ತಮರ್, ಆ ಸ್ತ್ರೀಯರ್ ಐಶ್ವರ್ಯವನ್ತರ್.

275. Grammars and other books of the modern dialect adduce various adjectives or attributive nouns, *e. g.* ಅಂಜುಬುರುಕ, ಉದ್ದ, ಎತ್ತರ, ಎಳೆ, ಒಳ್ಳೆ, ಕಹಿ, ಕಿವಡ, ಕುಣ್ಣ, ಕುರುಡ, ಚನ್ದ, ಚಿಕ್ಕ, ಚೆಲುವ (ಚೆಲೋ), ಜಾಣ, ತಮ್ಮು, ದಡ್ಡ, ದಿಟ್ಟ, ದೊಡ್ಡ, ಪುಟ್ಟ, ಬಡ, ಬುದ್ಧಿವನ್ತ, ಮುದುಕ, ಮೂಕ, ಸಣ್ಣ, ಸೀ, ಹಟಿ, ಹುಚ್ಚು, etc. (Nuḍigaṭṭu p. 58; Anglo-Kanarese Translation Series I, pp. 39. 41. 42: etc.), of which several are known to be ordinary nouns (*cf.* § 277).

Their use may be learned from the following instances (*cf.* § 316, 2):—

ದೊಡ್ಡದೊನ್ದು (ದೊಡ್ಡದು ಒನ್ದು) ಗುದಿ, a large bunch. ದೊಡ್ಡದೊನ್ದು ನೆಲ ಮನೆ.—ಉದ್ದ ಕೂದಲು. ಎತ್ತರ ಗದ್ದೆ. ಕಹಿ ಹಣ್ಣುಗಳು. ಚಲೋ ಮಾವಿನ ಹಣ್ಣುಗಳು. ಚಳಿ ನಾಡುಗಳು. ಚಿಕ್ಕ ಊರು. ಚಿಕ್ಕಪ್ಪ. ಚೆಲುವ ಮೋಟಿ. ತಮ್ಪು ನಾಡು. ದಡ್ಡ ಮಗ. ದಿಟ್ಟ ಪುರುಷನು. ದುಣ್ಣ ಪದಾರ್ಥವು. ದೊಡ್ಡ ಮನೆತನದವರು. ದೊಡ್ಡ ಪೆಟ್ಟಿಗೆಗಳು. ಪುಟ್ಟ ಮಗು. ಬಡ ಎತ್ತು. ಬಿಳಿ ಜಾಲಿ. ಸಣ್ಣ ಗೆರೆಗಳು. ಹುಚ್ಚು ಕುಟಿಮಟಿ. ಹುಚ್ಚು ಹುಡುಗನು. (The instances are taken from South-Mahratta school-books that were composed by natives.)

ಅದು ಅವಶಕವದೆ, that is necessary. ಆ ಮನುಷ್ಯನು ಎತ್ತರ ಇದ್ದನು. ಆ ಕುದುರೆಗಳು ಏಟು ಗೇಣು ಎತ್ತರ. ನೀಲಿಯ ಗಿಡವು ಸಾಧಾರಣವಾಗಿ ಎರಡು ಎರಡುವರೆ ಮೊಟಿ ಎತ್ತರವಿರುತ್ತದೆ. ಕತ್ತೆಯ ಧ್ವನಿ ಕರ್ಕಶ. ಆನೆಗಳು ಕಪ್ಪು ಇರುತ್ತವೆ. ಕೆಲವು

ಹಣ್ಣುಗಳು ಕಸಕು ಇದ್ದವು. ಹಣ್ಣುಗಳು ಕಹಿ ಇದ್ದವು. ಒನ್ದು ಕಣ್ಣು ಕುರುಡ. ಹಡಗ ಗಳು ಗಟ್ಟಿ ಅವೆ. ಎತ್ತುಗಳ ಕೋಡುಗಳು ಗಟ್ಟಿ ಇರುತ್ತವೆ. ಪೃಥ್ವಿಯು ಗೋಲಾಕಾರವದೆ. ಹುಡುಗನು ಚೆಲುವನಿದ್ದನು. ಹುಡುಗಿಯರು ಚಲುವೆಯರು ಇದ್ದಾರೆ. ಚಾಕು ಚಲೋದು ಅದೆ, ಆ ಪಾತಗಳು ಚಲೋ ಅವೆ. ಅವನು ಚಲೋ ಹುಡುಗನು. ಅವನು ಚಿಕ್ಕವನು. ಆ ಮನುಷ್ಯನು ದಯೆಯುಳ್ಳವನಿದ್ದಾನೆ. ಆ ಸ್ತ್ರೀಯರು ಚಿಕ್ಕವರಿದ್ದಾರೆ. ಕಬ್ಬು ಡೊಂಕಾ ದರೆ ಸವಿ ಡೊಂಕೇ? ಕಾಗದವು ದಪ್ಪ ಅದೆ. ಹುಡುಗರು ದಿಟ್ಟರಿದ್ದಾರೆ. ದೇವರು ದೊಡ್ಡವ ನಿದ್ದಾನೆ. ಅವನ ಮನೆ ದೊಡ್ಡದು ಅದೆ. ಕತ್ತಿಗಳು ದೊಡ್ಡವು. ಆ ಹುಲಿಯ ಕಣ್ಣು ದೊಡ್ಡವು ಇದ್ದವು. ಗಿಣೀ ಬಣ್ಣವೂ ಹಸೀ ಹುಲ್ಲಿನ ಬಣ್ಣವೂ ಹಸರು. ಗಿಳಿಗಳಲ್ಲಿ ಕೆಲವು ದೊಡ್ಡವು, ಕೆಲವು ಸಣ್ಣವು ಇರುತ್ತವೆ. ಆಕಾಶವು ನಿರಭ್ರ (cloudless) ಅದೆ. ನಾನು ಬಡವನಿದ್ದೇನೆ. ಅವನು ಬಹಳ ಬಡವನಿದ್ದಾನೆ. ಅವನ ತನ್ದೆ ತಾಯಿಗಳು ಬಡವರಿದ್ದರು. ಕುದುರೆ ಬಿಳೀದು ಅದೆ. ಆ ಕಲ್ಲುಗಳು ಬಹಳ ಮಿದುವು. ಅರಬಿಸ್ಥಾನದ ಕುದುರೆಗಳು ಮೇಲು. ಅವನ ತುಬಾಕಿ ಸಣ್ಣದು. ತೆಂಗಿನ ಎಳೆಗಾಯೊಳಗಿನ ನೀರು ಬಹಳ ಸವಿ ಇರು ತ್ತವೆ (see § 355, 8). ಹೂಗಳು ಹಸರು ಅವೆ. ತೋಟೆ ಹುರುಬರುಕು ಇರುವದು. ಹಣ್ಣು ಹುಳಿಯದೆ. (Instances from S.-Mhr. school-books. It is to be remarked that there are instances among them in which other authors would perhaps prefer to use ಆಗಿ and a form of ಇರು, instead of ಇರು alone, after the attributive nouns, *e. g.* ಆಕಾಶವು ನಿರಭ್ರವಾಗಿದೆ; see further on in this paragraph, and *cf.* the forms with ಇಹ suffixed to the original forms of attributive nouns in § 273. In the mediæval Basavapurâṇa there occurs once ಬಢವರಿರ್ದಪೆವು, 29, 28.)

ಅಗಲವಾದ ಗೋಡೆಗಳು, broad walls. ಅಗ್ಗವಾದ ಪದಾರ್ಥಗಳು. ಅವಶ್ಯಕವಾದ ಮಾತು. ಆಜ್ಞಾಧಾರಕನಾದ ಸೇವಕನು. ಆಟಿವಾದ ಬಾವಿ. ಇಮ್ಪಾದ ರಾಗ. ಉತ್ಕೃಷ್ಟ ವಾದ ಸಕ್ಕರೆ. ಎತ್ತರವಾದ ಗಿಡಗಳು. ಎತ್ತರವಾದ ಸ್ಥಳ. ಕಿವಡಿಯಾದ ತಾಯಿ. ಗಟ್ಟಿ ಯಾದ ಬಾಗಿಲುಗಳು. ಒನ್ದು ಚನ್ದವಾದ ತೋಟವು. ತುಣ್ಟನಾದವನು. ದುಷ್ಟನಾದ ವಿದ್ವಾಂಸನು. ಧೀರನಾದ ಮನುಷ್ಯನು. ಪರೋಪಕಾರಿಯಾದ ಹುಡುಗನು. ಭದ್ರವಾದ ಕೋಟೆಗಳು. ಮನೋಹರವಾದ ಗ್ರನ್ಥಗಳು. ಮಿಕ್ಕಾದ ಇಲಿಗಳು. ಮುಖ್ಯವಾದದೊನ್ದು ಕುದುರೆ. ಮೂರ್ಖರಾದವರು. ಮೇಲಾದ ಚಿತ್ರಗಾರನು. ಜ್ಞಾನವು ಮೇಲಾದ ವಸ್ತುವು. ಸುನ್ದರವಾದ ಪಕ್ಷಿ. ಸ್ವಚ್ಛವಾದವುಗಳು. ಬೆಕ್ಕಿಗೆ ಹದನಾದ ಉಗುರುಗಳು. ಹದನಾದ ಕತ್ತಿ. ಹಿರಿಯನಾದ ರಾಮನು. ಹೆಚ್ಚಾದ ಹಣವು. (Instances from S.-Mhr. school-books.)

ಕಪಟವುಳ್ಳ ಸ್ನೇಹಿತನು, a false friend. ದೈವವುಳ್ಳ ಗೃಹಸ್ಥನು. ಧೈರ್ಯವುಳ್ಳ ಗೃಹಸ್ಥನು. ಸಿಂಹದ ಹಲ್ಲು ಬಲವುಳ್ಳವು ಇರುತ್ತವೆ. ಬುದ್ಧಿಯುಳ್ಳ ಹುಡುಗ. ಬೆಲೆ ಯುಳ್ಳ ಧಾತುಗಳು. ಹಟವುಳ್ಳವು. ಹಣವುಳ್ಳ ಒಕ್ಕಲಿಗನು.— ಗಿಡಗಳಿಲ್ಲದ ಅಡಿವೆಗಳು,

treeless deserts. ಫಲವಿಲ್ಲದ ಮರಗಳು. ಬುದ್ಧಿ ಇಲ್ಲದವ. ಬಾಯು ಸವಿಯಿಲ್ಲದ ರಸಾಯನ. (Instances from the same.)

Instead of ಆದ also ಆಗಿ, 'having become', together with a relative participle of ಇರು, to be, is used, *e.g.* ಬಹಳ ಅಧಿಕವಾಗಿರುವದು (for ಅಧಿಕವಾದದು), (it is) excessive. ಆಭರಣವಾಗಿರುವ ಭಂಗಾರ, ornamental gold. ಶ್ರೀಮನ್ತರಾಗಿರುವವರು, illustrious persons. (Instances from the same and from a Mysore book.)

With reference to the remark made above in this paragraph that some authors would perhaps prefer to use ಆಗಿ and a form of ಇರು, instead of ಇರು alone, after attributive nouns, the following instances, taken from S.-Mhr. school-books, may be given:—ಇನ್ಥ ದುರ್ಘಟ ರೋಗದಿನ್ದ ಮಕ್ಕಳು ಮಱಿಗಳನ್ನು ಉಱಿಸಿ ಕೊಳ್ಳುವದು ಎಲ್ಲರಿಗೂ ಅವಶ್ಯಕವಾಗಿದೆ. ಆತನು ಆಡುವ ಮಾತು ವಿಪರೀತವಾಗಿದೆ. ಹಾವಿನ ಮೆಯ್ ಉದ್ದವಾಗಿರುವದು. ಆಕೆಯ ತಲೆ ಬುಟ್ಟಿಯಾಗಿದೆ. ಕೆಲವು ಹುಡುಗರು ದನಗಳೊಳಗೆ ಎಣಿಸಲಿಕ್ಕೆ ತಕ್ಕವರಾಗಿದ್ದಾರೆ. ಪವಿತ್ರವಾದ ಜನರು ಬಹಳ ನಮ್ರವಾಗಿರುತ್ತಾರೆ. ಒಬ್ಬ ಅರಬನು ಬಹಳ ಬಡವನಾಗಿದ್ದನು. ಉಪ್ಪು ಬಹು ಶುದ್ಧವೂ ರುಚಿಕರವೂ ಆಗಿರುವದು. ನಾನು ಸಿದ್ಧನಾಗಿರುವೆನು. ಕಪ್ಪುರದ ಕಟ್ಟಿಗೆ ಹಗುರಾಗಿಯೂ ನುಣುಪಾಗಿಯೂ ಇರುವದು. ಗಿಳಿಯ ಮೂಗು ಬಹಳ ಹದನಾಗಿರುವದು.

Occasionally ಅನ್ಥ (*i. e.* ಅನ್ತು + ಅಹ, § 223) is suffixed to ಆದ and ಉಳ್ಳ, *e. g.* ಸುನ್ದರವಾದನ್ಥ (beautiful) ತೇಜವುಳ್ಳನ್ಥ ಒಡವೆಗಳು. (Instance from a S.-Mhr. school-book.)

Frequently this ಅನ್ಥ appears as ಅನ್ನ (*cf.* §§ 223. 224) and ಅನ without ಆದ or ಉಳ್ಳ in the formation of so-called adjectives, *e. g.* ಉದ್ದನ್ನ ಕೂದಲು, long hair, ತಣ್ಣನ್ನ ಉಸುಬು, ತೆಳ್ಳನ್ನ ತಗಡು, ದಟ್ಟನ್ನ ಹವೆ, ದಪ್ಪನ್ನ ಅಱಿವೆ, ಬೆಳ್ಳನ್ನ ಹೊಗೆ, ಮೆತ್ತನ್ನ ತುಪ್ಪಟಿ; or ಉದ್ದನ ಕೂದಲು, etc. (Instances from S.-Mhr. school-books.) ಅನ occurs also as ಅನೆ, *e. g.* ದಪ್ಪನೆ ಬಟ್ಟೆ, and ಆನೆ, *e. g.* ದುಣ್ಣಾನೆ ಪದಾರ್ಥ.

Lastly also forms with ಅಗೆ (§ 212, remark ೨) have been used as so-called adjectives, *e. g.* ಕಲ್ಲಿದ್ದಲಿಗಳು ಕಱ್ಱಗೆ ಇರುತ್ತವೆ, mineral coals are black. ಆ ಹೆಂಗಸಿನ ಕೂದಲು ಕಱ್ಱಗದೆ. ಪೃಥ್ವಿಯು ದುಣ್ಡಗದೆ. ಕಪ್ಪುರಗಿಡದ ಎಲೆಗಳು ದುಣ್ಡಗವೆ. ಬೆಳ್ಳಿಯು ಬೆಳ್ಳಗಿರುತ್ತದೆ. ಪಕ್ಷಿಗಳ ಱೆಕ್ಕೆಗಳು ಮೆತ್ತಗಿರುತ್ತವೆ. ಹುಲ್ಲು ಹಚ್ಚಗಿರುತ್ತದೆ. ಗಿಳಿಗಳು ಬಹು ತರವಾಗಿ ಹಚ್ಚಗೆ ಇರುತ್ತವೆ. (Instances from S.-Mhr. school-books.)

Also so-called relative participles have been called adjectives in modern grammars, *e. g.* ಹೊಳೆಯುವ ನಕ್ಷತ್ರಗಳು, bright stars, ಕೆಟ್ಟ ಸೇವಕರು.

bad servants (Anglo-Kanarese Translation Series, Book I, pp. 39. 40), and even plain genitives, as ಸಿಟ್ಟಿನ, ಸೊಕ್ಕಿನ, ಹೆಮ್ಮೆಯ (Nuḍigaṭṭu, p. 58).

To express 'very' before an adjective, ಅತಿ, ಬಲು, ಬಹಳ and ಬಹು may be used, *e. g.* ಅತಿ ದಪ್ಪ, very thick; ಬಲು ಜಾಣ, very clever; ಬಹಳ ದೊಡ್ಡ, very great; ಬಹು ಶುದ್ಧ, very clean. About another way of rendering 'very' see § 305, *a.* In the case of inferiority also ತೀರ is used for 'very', *e.g.* ತೀರ ಸಣ್ಣ, very small, which ತೀರ is employed also to express 'quite', 'wholly', *e. g.* ಮಂಗಗಳು ತೀರಾ ಮನುಷ್ಯನ ಹಾಗೆ ಕಾಣುತ್ತವೆ, monkeys appear quite like men.

On comparison see §§ 343. 348, 7. 349, 8.

276. Looking back at § 273 we find that the so-called adjectives in the ancient and mediæval dialect consist of original forms (as ಒಳ್, ಕೂರ್, etc., ಅಸಿ, ನಿಡಿ, etc.) combined with certain suffixes. What are these?

They are the pronominal forms ತು, ತ್ತು, ದು of the neuter singular introduced in § 122, so that *e. g.* ಒಳ್ಳಿತು or ಒಳ್ಳಿತ್ತು would be the original form ಒಳ್+ಇ+ತು or ತ್ತು, the ಇ being a euphonic addition (*cf.* § 168), and the primitive form being ಒಳ್ತು. To assume that the ಇ is not euphonic, and ಇತು, ಇತ್ತು (for ಇದು) are the suffixes added to ಒಳ್, seems to be excluded on account of the absence of analogy, as ಅತು, ಅತ್ತು would have been the proper suffixes, and the neuter plural ಒಳ್ಳಿದುವು and the masculine singular ಒಳ್ಳಿದಂ would raise insuperable difficulties.

In ಅಸಿದು, ಇನಿದು, etc. there is no euphonic letter, but the pronominal suffix ದು is immediately joined to the original forms ಅಸಿ, ಇನಿ, etc.

In the masculine form ಒಳ್ಳಿದಂ (originally, we believe, ಒಳ್ದಂ) the ಇ and ದ್ are euphonic (about the euphonic ದ್ see § 119, *a,* §§ 132. 134. 136, and *cf.* ಒಳ್ಳಿದುವು further on in the present paragraph); ಒಳ್ಳಿದಂ, therefore, is ಒಳ್+ಇ+ದ್+ಅಂ (or ಅ), the ಅಂ (or ಅ) meaning 'he' (see §§ 115. 177. 193, under remarks). The feminine form ಒಳ್ಳಿದಳ್ is ಒಳ್+ಇ+ದ್+ಅಳ್, the ಅಳ್ meaning 'she' (see *e. g.* § 177). (ಅಲ್ಲಿದಂ in § 243 might be explained similarly as ಅಲ್ಲಿ+ಇ+ದ್+ಅಂ, but the given explanation seems to recommend itself.)

In the masculines ಅಸಿಯಂ, ಇನಿಯಂ, etc. the neuter suffix ದು has been dropped, and ಅಂ has been joined, by means of the genitive (see § 130), to the original forms ಅಸಿ, ಇನಿ, etc. (see § 115). The feminine forms ಅಸಿಯಳ್, etc. are ಅಸಿಯ+ಅಳ್, etc.

The neuter plural *e. g.* of ಒಳ್ಳಿತು or ಒಳ್ಳಿತ್ತು is ಒಳ್ಳಿದುವು, and this consists of ಒಳ್+euphonic ಇ+euphonic ದ್+ಉವು (see § 136, *a*); the neuter plural *e. g.* of ಅಸಿದು is ಅಸಿಯುವು, *i. e.* ಅಸಿಯ (the genitive of ಅಸಿ)+ಅವು (see ibid.), ಅವು having taken the place of ಉವು (*cf.* ಉವು and ಅವು in §§ 209. 210).

The epicene plural is *e. g.* ಒಳ್ಳಿದರ್, *i. e.* ಒಳ್+ಇ+ದ್+ಅರ್ and ಇನಿಯರ್, *i. e.* ಇನಿಯ (the genitive of ಇನಿ)+ಅರ್, the ಅರ್ meaning 'they' (see *e. g.* § 177).

Thus the pronominal suffixes of the mentioned so-called adjectives in the ancient and partly in the mediæval dialect are ತು, ತ್ತು, ದು, ಅಂ, ಅಳ್, ಉವು, ಅವು, ಅರ್.

In the modern dialect the suffixes are partly the pronouns ಅದು, ಅವನು, ಅವಳು, ಅವು (or ಅವುಗಳು), ಅವರು, *e. g.* ದೊಡ್ಡದು (ದೊಡ್ಡ+ಅದು), ದೊಡ್ಡವನು, ದೊಡ್ಡವಳು, ದೊಡ್ಡವು (or ದೊಡ್ಡವುಗಳು), ದೊಡ್ಡವರು; ಸಣ್ಣದು (ಸಣ್ಣ+ಅದು), etc.; ಚಿಕ್ಕದು (ಚಿಕ್ಕ+ಅದು), etc. (see § 124, 4), the pronouns being added to the short original forms (see § 273); partly the pronominal forms ದು, ಅನು (=ಅಂ), ಅಳು (=ಅಳ್), ಅರು (=ಅರ್), *e. g.* ಕಿಱಿದು, ಕಿಱಿಯನು, ಕಿಱಿಯಳು, ಕಿಱಿಯರು.

277. The so-called adjectives or attributive nouns in Kannaḍa are **partly ordinary nouns and partly pronominal nouns.**

The first are represented by their short original forms (§ 273), *e. g.* ಅಗಲ; ಅಸಿ. At least some of the forms of the first class mentioned in § 273 are declined, *e. g.* ಅಗಲಕೆ, ಅಗಲದ, ಅಗಲದಲ್ಲಿ; ಉದ್ದಕ್ಕೆ, ಉದ್ದದ, ಉದ್ದದಲ್ಲಿ; ತೋರದ, ತೋರದೊಳ್; ನೇರ್ಗಳ್; and some of the second class too, for instance ಅಸಿಯ, ಕಿಱಿಯ, ನಿಡಿಯ, ಬಿಳಿಯ.

The pronominal nouns are represented by the forms composed of the short original forms and the suffixes ತು, ತ್ತು, etc. They are used also just like ordinary nouns, as will be seen from the following instances:— ಕಿಱಿದಱೊಳೆ ಪಿರಿದುವರ್ಥಮನ್ (for ಪಿರಿದುವರ್ಥಂಗಳನ್) ಅಱಿಪಲ್ ನೆಱೆವಾತನ್ ಆತನಿಂ ಜಾಣಂ, he who brings about to make known great things even in short (ಕಿಱಿದಱೊಳೆ, *i. e.* in a few words, is) wiser than that man. ನೇರಿತ್ತಂ ಮಾಡುವುದು, to make right. ಒಳ್ಳಿತಂ ಮಾಡ್ಪಿವಂ, a man who causes welfare. ಇನಿದಂ ನುಡಿವವ, a man who utters pleasantness (*i. e.* pleasing words). ಒಳ್ಳೇದು ಕೆಡಕು good (and) bad. ಪಿರಿಯಂ, a Brâhmaṇa. ಜಡೆಯುಳ್ಳ ಹಿರಿಯರು, eminent persons who have (or wear) the jaṭĕ. ಹಿರಿಯರಿಗೆ ಇದಿರಾಗಿ ಏಱುವುದು, rising (from a sitting posture) before elders. ಕಿಱಿದಂ ಪಿರಿದು ಮಾಡುವುದು, to make a small thing an extensive one. ಇನಿಯನೆ ಬೆಲ್ಲದಿನ್ದಿನಿಯಂ,

a paramour (is) indeed a man sweeter than jaggory. ಎನಗೆ ಬಲ್ಲಿದರ್ ಆಗ ಲಾರ್ಪರೆ ಗಾವಿಲರ್, can rustics become persons of (greater) ability than I?

Such compounds as ಒಳ್ಳುಣಿಸು, ಇನ್ನುಣಿಸು (§ 247, *d*, 11), ಬಿಙ್ಗೊನೆ, ಇಂಗ ಡಲ್ (ibid. 8) are, therefore, to be translated literally:—a goodness-food (*i. e.* a good food), a sweetness-meal (*i. e.* a sweet meal), a largeness-bunch (*i. e.* a large bunch), the sweetness-sea (*i. e.* the sweet or milk sea); and such as ಬೆಟ್ಟಿತಂಗುಳಿ, ಪಿರಿದಾಸೆ, ತೋರಿದುವು ಜಘನಂ (§ 273), a severity-it-disease (*i. e.* a severe disease) of the eyes, a greatness-it-desire (*i. e.* a great desire), bigness-they-buttocks (*i. e.* big buttocks). All these instances bear the character of karmadhâraya compounds, as do also the compounds of the three dialects: ಚಿಕ್ಕಚೋಜಿಗ, ದೊಡ್ಡಾನೆ, ಸಣ್ಣಗಾಳ, a littleness-wonder, a greatness-elephant, a smallness-fishing hook.

In § 275 it has been remarked that modern Kannaḍa grammars and other books adduce and use several ordinary nouns as adjectives, *e. g.* ಅಂಜುಬುರುಕ, timid, ಎತ್ತರ, ಕಹಿ, ಕಿವಡ, ಚೆಲುವ, ತಮ್ಪು, ಮುದುಕ, ಸೀ, ಹುಚ್ಚು.

Occasionally a so-called adjective in its neutral form is used as an adverb, *e. g.* ಪಿರಿದುರಿ, to burn greatly; ಹಿರಿದು ಚಿನ್ತಿಸು, to be greatly disturbed in thought.

XV. On numerals.

278. Numerals are declinable bases, and comprise also appellative nouns of number and words that express indefinite quantity (§ 90). Their declension is given in §§ 122. 131 (*cf.* § 354, I, 5), their gender is indicated in § 102, 8, *g*, and their figures appear in § 44.

1, **The not compounded cardinal numbers up to ten** are:—ಒನ್ದು 1, ಎರಡು 2, ಮೂಱು 3, ನಾಲ್ಕು 4, ಅಯ್ದು (ಅಯಿದು, also mediæval) 5[1], ಆಱು 6, ಏೞು 7, ಎಣ್ಟು 8, ಪತ್ತು (ಹತ್ತು, also mediæval) 10. ಒಮ್ಬತ್ತು 9, is a compounded cardinal number, consisting of ಒಮ್ (another form of ಒನ್ದು) and ಪತ್ತು or ಹತ್ತು (see further on in the present paragraph).

When, up to nineteen, the mentioned cardinal numbers are compounded with a preceding ಪತ್ತು or ಹತ್ತು 10, this ಪತ್ತು or ಹತ್ತು takes the forms ಪನ್ or ಹನ್, ಪದಿ or ಹದಿ, ಪದಿನ್ or ಹದಿನ್ (§ 248, 10), except before ಒಮ್ಬತ್ತು. Thus we get ಪನ್ನೊನ್ದು (*cf.* § 215, 7, *d*; ಹನ್ನೊನ್ದು, also mediæval) 11, ಪನ್ನೆರಡು (ಹನ್ನೆರಡು, also mediæval) 12, ಪದಿಮೂಱು (ಹದಿಮೂಱು) 13, ಪದಿನಾಲ್ಕು

[1] The numbers in parenthesis are such as occur, partly as additional forms, in the modern dialect alone, if 'also mediæval' is not added.

(ಹದಿನಾಲ್ಕು) 14, ಪದಿನಯ್ದು (ಹದಿನಯ್ದು, also mediæval) 15, ಪದಿನಾಱು (ಹದಿನಾಱು; also mediæval) 16, ಪದಿನೇೞು (ಹದಿನೇೞು, also mediæval) 17, ಪದಿನೆಣ್ಟು (ಹದಿನೆಣ್ಟು, also mediæval) 18, ಪತ್ತೊಮ್ಬತ್ತು (ಹತ್ತೊಮ್ಬತ್ತು) 19.

From twenty up to twenty-nine the compounds (a kind of gamaka compounds or tatpurushas, § 253, 2, *a*) have as their first member ಇರ್ (§ 248, 2) or ಇಪ್, which are other forms of ಎರಡು. Thus: ಇರ್ಪತ್ತು (ಇಪ್ಪತ್ತು, also mediæval) 20, ಇರ್ಪತ್ತೊನ್ದು (ಇಪ್ಪತ್ತೊನ್ದು) 21, ಇರ್ಪತ್ತೆರಡು (ಇಪ್ಪತ್ತೆರಡು) 22, ಇರ್ಪತ್ತುಮೂಱು (ಇಪ್ಪತ್ತುಮೂಱು, ಇಪ್ಪತ್ಮೂಱು, occasionally ಇಪ್ಪತ್ತಮೂಱು) 23, ಇರ್ಪತ್ತುನಾಲ್ಕು (ಇಪ್ಪತ್ತುನಾಲ್ಕು, ಇಪ್ಪತ್ನಾಲ್ಕು, ಇಪ್ಪತ್ತನಾಲ್ಕು) 24, ಇರ್ಪತ್ತಯ್ದು (ಇಪ್ಪತ್ತಯ್ದು) 25, ಇರ್ಪತ್ತಾಱು (ಇಪ್ಪತ್ತಾಱು) 26, ಇರ್ಪತ್ತೇೞು, ಇರ್ಪತ್ತೇೞ್ (ಇಪ್ಪತ್ತೇೞು) 27, ಇರ್ಪತ್ತೆಣ್ಟು (ಇಪ್ಪತ್ತೆಣ್ಟು) 28, ಇರ್ಪತ್ತೊಮ್ಬತ್ತು (ಇಪ್ಪತ್ತೊಮ್ಬತ್ತು; South-Mahratta also ಇಪ್ಪತ್ತೊಮ್ಬತ್ತು, ಇಪ್ಪತಱೊಮ್ಬತ್ತು) 29.

From thirty up to ninety-nine the compounds have as their first members ಮೂ (§ 248, 3), ಮು (*cf.* 248, 3, other forms of ಮೂಱು), ನಾಲ್ (§ 248, 4), ನಲು (other forms of ನಾಲ್ಕು), ಅಯ್ (§ 248, 5), ಅಯಿ (other forms of ಅಯ್ದು), ಅಱು (§ 248, 6), ಅಱಿ, ಅಱ್ (other forms of ಆಱು), ಏೞ್ (§ 248, 7), ಎೞ್, ಎಪ್ (other forms of ಏೞು), ಎಣ್ (§ 248, 8), ಎಮ್ (other forms of ಎಣ್ಟು), and ತೊಮ್ (§ 248, 9, about which see further on); their second member is ಪತ್ತು or ಹತ್ತು, joined according to the rules of euphony (see § 215, 7, *a. b*). The forms produced are the following:— ಮೂವತ್ತು (ಮುವ್ವತ್ತು) 30, ನಾಲ್ವತ್ತು (ನಲುವತ್ತು) 40, ಅಯ್ವತ್ತು (ಅಯಿವತ್ತು, also mediæval) 50, ಅಱುವತ್ತು (ಅಱಿವತ್ತು, also mediæval, ಅರ್ಪತ್ತು) 60, ಏೞ್ಪತ್ತು, ಎೞ್ಪತ್ತು (ಎಪ್ಪತ್ತು) 70, ಎಣ್ಪತ್ತು (ಎಮ್ಬತ್ತು, also mediæval) 80, ತೊಮ್ಬತ್ತು 90, to which the cardinal numbers from one to nine are added in the same way as to ಇರ್ಪತ್ತು, ಇಪ್ಪತ್ತು, *e. g.* ಮೂವತ್ತೊನ್ದು 31, ಮೂವತ್ತೊಮ್ಬತ್ತು (ಮೂವತ್ತೊಮ್ಬತ್ತು) 39, ತೊಮ್ಬತ್ತೊಮ್ಬತ್ತು (ತೊಮ್ಬತ್ತೊಮ್ಬತ್ತು, ತೊಮ್ಬತ್ತಱೊಮ್ಬತ್ತು, the ತೊಮ್ಬತ್ತಱ being the genitive, see further on under ನೂಱು) 99.

100 is ನೂಱು, to which the other cardinal numbers are suffixed in the manner indicated above, *e. g.* ನೂಱೊನ್ದು 101, ನೂಱೆರಡು 102, ನೂಱುಪತ್ತು 110, ನೂಱಯ್ವತ್ತು 150; but this manner has been generally given up in the modern dialect, wherein ನೂಱು becomes ನೂಱಾ (the short genitive of ನೂಱು, § 120, *a*, 6, instead of ನೂಱಱ+ಅ), *e. g.* ನೂಱಾ ಒನ್ದು 101, ನೂಱಾ ನಾಲ್ಕು 104, ನೂಱಾ ಹನ್ನೊನ್ದು 111, ನೂಱಾ ಇಪ್ಪತ್ತು 120,

ನೂಱಿಽಾ ಮೂವತ್ನಾಲ್ಕು 134, ನೂಱಿಽಾ ಅಯ್ವತ್ತು 150, ನೂಱಿಽಾ ತೊಮ್ಬತ್ತೊಮ್ಬತ್ತು or ನೂಱಿಽಾ ತೊಮ್ಬತ್ತಱೊಮ್ಬತ್ತು 190.

If ನೂಱು is preceded by not compounded numbers, these numbers for the greatest part appear in another form. The other forms are ಎರಟ್ (§ 248, 2), ಇನ್ (for ಎರಡು), ಮೂ (§ 248, 3), ಮುನ್ (for ಮೂಱು), ನಾಲ್ (§ 248, 4), ನಾ (for ನಾಲ್ಕು), ಅಯ್ (for ಅಯ್ದು, § 248, 5), ಅಱು (248, 6), ಅಱ್ (for ಆಱು), ಏೞ್ (for ಏೞು, § 248, 7), ಒಮ್ಬಯ್ (§ 248, 9), ಒಮ್ಬಯಿ (for ಒಮ್ಬತ್ತು), *e. g.* ಒನ್ದು ನೂಱು, one 100, ಎರಟ್ನೂಱು (ಇನ್ನೂಱು) 200, ಮೂನೂಱು (ಮುನ್ನೂಱು, also mediæval) 300, ನಾಲ್ಕುನೂಱು (ನಾಲ್ನೂಱು, ನಾನೂಱು) 400, ಅಯ್ನೂಱು 500, ಆಱುನೂಱು (ಅರ್ನೂಱು) 600, ಏೞ್ನೂಱು (ಏೞುನೂಱು, also mediæval) 700, ಎಣ್ಟುನೂಱು 800, ಒಮ್ಬಯ್ನೂಱು (ಒಮ್ಬಯಿ ನೂಱು) 900, ಪತ್ತುನೂಱು 10,00. Observe also *e. g.* ಇನ್ನೂಱಿಽಾ ನಾಲ್ವತ್ತೆಣ್ಟು 248, ಮುನ್ನೂಱ (for ಮುನ್ನೂಱಿಽಾ, Basavapurâṇa) ಅಱುವತ್ತು 360, ಅಯ್ನೂಱಿಽಾ ಅಱುವತ್ತು 560.

The Kannaḍa language has no own **special word for 1,000**; the ancient dialect uses ಸಾಸಿರ and ಸಾಯಿರ, the mediæval one ಸಾಸಿರ and ಸಾವಿರ, and the modern one ಸಾವಿರ, ಸಾವರ and ಸಾವಿರು. All these terms are corrupted from Saṁskṛita ಸಹಸ್ರ. When not compounded numbers precede it, these numbers (mostly) change their form in the ancient dialect, *viz.* ಒರ್ (for ಒನ್ದು), ಎರಟ್, ಇರ್ (for ಎರಡು), ಮು (for ಮೂಱು, see § 248, 3), ನಾಲ್ (for ನಾಲ್ಕು), ಅಯ್ (for ಅಯ್ದು), (ಆಱ್, only mediæval), ಏೞ್ (for ಏೞು), ಎಣ್ (for ಎಣ್ಟು), ಒಮ್ಬಯ್ (for ಒಮ್ಬತ್ತು), ಪಯಿನ್ (for ಪತ್ತು), ನೂಱ್ (for ನೂಱು, § 248, 11). Thus we have, together with the (mediæval and) modern forms, the following:— ಒರ್ಛಾಸಿರ (see § 215, 7, *c*), (ಒನ್ದು ಸಾವಿರ) one 1000, ಇರ್ಛಾಸಿರ (§ 215, 7, *c*), ಎರಟ್ಸಾಸಿರ (ಎರಡುಸಾವಿರ, also mediæval) 2000, ಮುಚ್ಚಾಸಿರ (*cf.* § 215, 7, *c*; ಮೂಱುಸಾವಿರ) 3,000, ನಾಲ್ಸಾಸಿರ (ನಾಲ್ಕುಸಾವಿರ) 4,000, ಅಯ್ಸಾಸಿರ (ಅಯ್ದುಸಾವಿರ) 5,000, (ಆರ್ಸಾವಿರ, mediæval, ಆಱುಸಾವಿರ) 6,000, ಏೞ್ಸಾಸಿರ (ಏಳುಸಾವಿರ) 7,000, ಎಣ್ಚಾಸಿರ (§ 215, 7, *c*; ಎಣ್ಟುಸಾವಿರ) 8,000, ಒಮ್ಬಯ್ಸಾಸಿರ (ಒಮ್ಬತ್ತುಸಾವಿರ, also mediæval) 9,000, ಪಯಿಂಛಾಸಿರ (ಹತ್ತುಸಾವಿರ) 10,000, (ತೊಮ್ಬತ್ತುಸಾವಿರ, also mediæval) 90,000, ನೂರ್ಛಾಸಿರ (§ 215, 7, *c*; ನೂಱುಸಾವಿರ) 100,000. Some instances of the modern dialect regarding the use of the genitive of ಸಾವಿರ will prove useful:— ಒನ್ದು ಸಾವಿರದ ಒನ್ದು 1,001; ಒನ್ದು ಸಾವಿರದ ಒನ್ದುನೂಱಿಽಾ ಹನ್ನೊನ್ದು 1,111; ಮೂಱುಸಾವಿರದಾ ಎರಡುನೂಱಿಽಾ ಮೂವತ್ನಾಲ್ಕು 3,234; ನಾಲ್ವತ್ತೆರಡು ಸಾವಿರದಾ ಅಯ್ನೂಱಿಽಾ ನಾಲ್ವತ್ತೆಣ್ಟು 42,548.

100,000 is very frequently expressed in Kannaḍa by Saṁskṛita ಲಕ್ಷ, *e.g.* ಏೞುಲಕ್ಷದ ಅಯ್ದು ಸಾವಿರದಾ ಮೂವತ್ತಾಱು 7,05,036, or by its tadbhava ಲಕ್ಕ, *e.g.* ನಾಲ್ಕುಲಕ್ಕದ ಮೇಲೆ ತೊಮ್ಬತ್ತಾಱುಸಾವಿರ ಗೀತಂಗಳ್, 4,96,000 songs; ಲಕ್ಕಮುಂ ತೊಮ್ಬತ್ತುಸಾವಿರದಚಲಶಿವಲಿಂಗಂಗಳ್, 4,90,000 immoveable šivalingas.

As shown above, the short forms for ಒನ್ದು, ಎರಡು, ಮೂಱು, ನಾಲ್ಕು, ಅಯ್ದು, ಆಱು, ಏೞು, ಎಣ್ಟು, ಪತ್ತು (ಹತ್ತು) and ನೂಱು are ಒಮ್, ಒರ್; ಇನ್, ಇಪ್, ಇರ್, ಎರಡ್; ಮು, ಮುಚ್, ಮುನ್, ಮೂ; ನಾ, ನಾಲ್; ಅಯ್, ಅಯಿ; ಅಱ್, ಅಱ, ಅಱು, ಆಱ್; ಎೞ್, ಎೞ್, ಏೞ್; ಎಣ್, ಎಮ್; ಪದಿ (ಹದಿ), ಪದಿನ್ (ಹದಿನ್), ಪನ್ (ಹನ್), ಪಯ್, ಪಯಿನ್.

ಒರ್ **before a vowel gets its vowel lengthened,** *e. g.* ಓರೊನ್ದು, each, ಓರೊರ್ವಂ, each man, **as does** ಇರ್, *e. g.* ಈರಯ್ದು 10, ಈರಾಱು 12, ಈರೇೞು 14, ಈರೆಣ್ಟು 16; ಮೂಱು **before a vowel becomes** ಮುಯ್, *e. g.* ಮುಯ್ಯಿರ್, ಮುಯ್ಯೆರಡು, 6, ಮುಯ್ಯೇೞ್ 21 (see § 248, 1. 2. 3). Such compounds do not occur in the modern dialect.

ಒಮ್ಬತ್ತು, 9, literally means 'one-ten', *i. e.* one to ten or one before ten. Regarding **ತೊಮ್ಬತ್ತು** ancient grammars state that **ತೊಮ್** is a substitute (âdêša) of ಒಮ್ (Šabdmaṇidarpaṇa sûtra 190; Šabdânušâsana sûtras 90. 361; Nâgavarma sûtra 166, formed in order to distinguish 90 from 9; see § 248, 9); according to them ತೊಮ್ probably signifies 'the ninth', and ತೊಮ್ಬತ್ತು 'the ninth ten'. But one may think that ತೊಮ್ is another form of ತುದಿ or ತುತ್ತ (§ 253, 3, which appears also as ತೊಚ್), meaning 'point', 'upper', 'first', 'prior', so that ತೊಮ್ಬತ್ತು would signify 'the upper ten', or 'the ten that is foregoing' (one hundred).

The compounded numbers from 11 to 19, having ಪತ್ತು (ಹತ್ತು) at their beginning, might be called dvandva compounds (§ 250), as they are formed by means of addition, requiring an 'and' between; but Kêšava terms them dvigu compounds (§ 248, 10). In those from 20 to 100,000 the first member of the compounds denotes that the second member is to be added to itself as many times as it (the first member) indicates. This too is a sort of addition which in course of time was called multiplication. Kêšava classes the numerals from 20 to 100,000 also with the dvigu compounds.

The mentioned **multiplication** is used likewise *e.g.* in ಎರಡೆರಡು 4, ಎರಡಯ್ದು (=ಈರಯ್ದು) 10, ಮೂಱೆರಡು 6, ಅಯ್ದೆರಡು 10, ಒಮ್ಬತ್ತು ನಾಲ್ಕು 36 (see ಈರಯ್ದು, etc. above); ಎರಡಯ್ದು, however, in an additional way, means also 7 (2+5) and ಅಯ್ದಾಱು 11 (5+6). Further when the meaning of 'or' is expressed, ಎರಡುಮೂಱು denotes also 2 or 3, ಎರಡಯ್ದು 2 or 5, ನಾಲ್ಕೆಣ್ಟು 4 or 8, ಆಱೇೞು 6 or 7; ಪತ್ತೆಣ್ಟು 10 or 8. Besides, compounds like ಒನ್ದೊನ್ದು, ಎರಡೆರಡು, ಮೂಱುಮೂಱು, ಹತ್ತುಹತ್ತು mean also 'one and one' 'two and two', 'three and three', 'ten and ten' **in a distributive sense**: each one, etc. (§ 306 *a; cf.* § 303, 8).

If a number is added to ನೂಱು, it may be done by means of the genitive in the ancient dialect too, as would appear from Kēšava's instance ನೂಱಱ ಪತ್ತು (110) that forms the compound ನೂಱುಪತ್ತು (§ 244), a gamakasamâsa (§ 253, 2, *a*); instead of this full form of the genitive its abbreviated form ನೂಱಾ (*i. e.* ನೂಱ+ಅ) came into use, as we have seen above under ನೂಱು. The genitive ಸಾವಿರದ or ಸಾವಿರದಾ of ಸಾವಿರ is similarly used; see above under ಸಾವಿರ. That the genitive may be used also when a number is added to ಪತ್ತು (ಹತ್ತು) follows from the instances of the modern dialect quoted above:—ಇಪ್ಪತ್ತರೊಮ್ಬತ್ತು, ಇಪ್ಪತ್ತೊಮ್ಬತ್ತು, 29, ತೊಮ್ಬತ್ತರೊಮ್ಬತ್ತು, ತೊಮ್ಬತ್ತೊಮ್ಬತ್ತು, 99.

That cardinal numbers were optionally used in the singular and plural (§ 131) in the ancient dialect appears from the following instances:—ಒನ್ದುನಾಲ್ಕು or ಒನ್ದುನಾಲ್ಕುಗಳ್, ಎರಡಯ್ದು or ಎರಡಯ್ದುಗಳ್, ಪತ್ತು ನೂಱು or ಪತ್ತುನೂಱುಗಳ್.

In connection with nouns of any gender the cardinal numbers remain unchanged, *e. g.* ಸಾಯಿರ ಗಣ್ಡರ್, ಸಾಯಿರ ಪೆಣ್ಡಿರ್, ಸಾಯಿರ ಮನೆಗಳ್; ಎರಡು ಬಗೆ; ಎರಡುಸಾವಿರ ಬೌದ್ಧರ್; ಮೂಱು ಲೋಕಂ, ನಾಲ್ಕು ಯುಗಂ, ಎರಡು ಸಾವಿರ ಯುಗಂಗಳು (*cf.* § 102, 8, *g*).

Concerning the occasional place of cardinal numbers observe *e. g.* ದಿನವೊನ್ದಕ್ಕೆ, for one day, (daily, *cf.* § 303, 1, *a*, foot-note), ದಿನವೊನ್ದಱಲ್ಲಿ, in one day, ವರುಷ ನೂಱು, a hundred years.

The modes of expressing 'times' in the multiplication-table (ಮೊಗ್ಗಿಗಳ ಕೋಷ್ಟಕ, ಮಗ್ಗಿಗಳ ಕೋಷ್ಟಕ) nowadays are two. The **first mode**, used in Mysore, is done by putting the multiplicand in the nominative and the multiplier in the locative formed from the short genitive (without the augment ಅಱ) by means of ಅಲು (see *e. g.* § 109, *a*, 7), for instance:

ಎರಡೊನ್ದಲು	ಎರಡು,	$2 \times 1 = 2$
ಎರಡೆರಡಲು	ನಾಲ್ಕು,	$2 \times 2 = 4$
ಎರಡು ನಾಲ್ಕಲು	ಎಣ್ಟು,	$2 \times 4 = 8$
ಆಱು ಏೞಲು	ನಾಲ್ವತ್ತೆರಡು,	$6 \times 7 = 42$.

The **second mode**, used in South-Mahratta, is done by giving a final ಅ (*i. e.* the form of the short genitive instead of ಅಱ) to the multiplicand and putting the multiplier in the locative formed by ಅಲೆ or ಲೆ, *i. e.* ಅಲು+ಎ, ಲು+ಎ, exceptionally in its fuller form of ಅಱಿಲೆ, *i. e.* ಅಱಿಲ+ಎ. For instance:

ಎರಡೊನ್ದಱಲೆ	ಎರಡು
ಎರಡೆರಡ್ಲೆ	ನಾಲ್ಕು
ಎರಡ ಮೂಱ್ಲೆ	ಆಱು
ಎರಡ ನಾಲ್ಕಲೆ	ಎಣ್ಟು
ಎರಡ ಹತ್ತಲೆ	ಇಪ್ಪತ್ತು
ಮೂಱೊನ್ದಲೆ	ಮೂಱು
ಮೂಱೆರಡ್ಲೆ	ಆಱು
ಮೂಱ ಮೂಱ್ಲೆ	ಒಮ್ಬತ್ತು
ಮೂಱ ಆಱ್ಲೆ	ಹದಿನೆಣ್ಟು
ನಾಲ್ಕೆರಡ್ಲೆ	ಎಣ್ಟು
ಆಱ ಅಯ್ದ್ಲೆ	ಮೂವತ್ತು
ಏೞ ಏೞ್ಲೆ	ನಾಲ್ವತ್ತೊಮ್ಬತ್ತು
ಎಣ್ಟ ಅಯ್ದ್ಲೆ	ನಾಲ್ವತ್ತು
ಒಮ್ಬತ್ತ ಅಯ್ದ್ಲೆ	ನಾಲ್ವತ್ತಯ್ದು.

It is to be remarked that in South-Mahratta also such forms as ಮೂಱ್ರಾ ಎರಡ್ಲೆ, ನಾಲ್ಕಾ ಎರಡ್ಲೆ, ನಾಲ್ಕಾ ಎರಡಲೆ, ಆಯ್ದಾ ನಾಲ್ಕು, ಆಯ್ದಾ ನಾಕಲು, ಆಯ್ದಾ ನಾಕ್ಲ are used.

2, **The ordinal numbers are formed by suffixing** ಅನೆಯ to the cardinal numbers in the three dialects, *e. g.* ಒನ್ದನೆಯ, first, ಎರಡನೆಯ, second, ಮೂಱನೆಯ, third, ನಾಲ್ಕನೆಯ, ಪದಿನಾಱನೆಯ (ಹದಿನಾಱನೆಯ), ನೂಱನೆಯ, ಆಯ್ನೂಱನೆಯ. In the modern dialect ಮೊದಲನೆಯ, of the noun ಮೊದಲು, is frequently used instead of ಒನ್ದನೆಯ. Instances are:—ನಾಲ್ಕನೆಯಕ್ಕರಂ, ನಾಲ್ಕನೆಯ ವರ್ಣಂ, ಎಣ್ಟನೆಯ ವರ್ಷಂ, ಪತ್ತನೆಯ ಮನೆ (ಹತ್ತನೆಯ ಮನೆ), ಮೊದಲ ನೆಯ ಭಾಗ.

In the ancient dialect 'he', 'she', 'it', 'they', expressed by suffixing ಅಂ (ಅ+ಂ, *e. g.* § 115), ಅಳ್ (*e. g.* § 177), ಅದು (*e. g.* § 122), ಅರ್ (*e. g.* § 177), ಅಳ್ದಿರ್ (§ 134), ಅವು (§ 136), *e. g.* ಒನ್ದನೆಯಂ, the first man, ಎರಡನೆಯಂ, the second man; ಒನ್ದನೆಯಳ್, the first woman, ಎರಡನೆಯಳ್ the second woman, ಮೂಱನೆಯಳ್, ಪತ್ತನೆಯಳ್; ಒನ್ದನೆಯದು, the first thing, etc., ಎರಡನೆಯದು; ಎರಡನೆಯರ್, the second persons, ಪತ್ತನೆಯರ್; ಎರಡನೆಯಳ್ದಿರ್, the second women, ಮೂಱನೆಯಳ್ದಿರ್, ಪತ್ತನೆಯಳ್ದಿರ್; ಒನ್ದನೆಯವು, the first things, etc.

In the (mediæval and) modern dialect the pronouns ಅವ, ಅವನು, ಅವಳು, ಆಕೆ, ಅದು, ಅವರು, ಅವು are used as suffixes, *e. g.* ಮೂಱನೆಯುವ, ಮೂಱನೆಯವನು, the third man; ಮೂಱನೆಯುವಳು, ಮೂಱನೆಯಾಕೆ; ಮೂಱನೆಯುದು; ಮೂಱನೆಯುವರು; ಮೂಱನೆಯುವು (ಮೂಱನೆಯುವುಗಳು).

The modern dialect often changes the suffix ಅನೆಯ into ಅನೇ (*cf.* § 130, *c*, genitive), *e. g.* ಒನ್ದನೇ ಮನೆ, ಮೊದಲನೇ ಪುಸ್ತಕ, ಎರಡನೇ ಪುಸ್ತಕ, ಮೂಱನೇದು, ಅಯ್ದನೇದು, ಆಱನೇದು.

Examining the meaning of ಅನೆಯ we come to the conclusion that the original form was ಅನೆ, *i. e.* ಅನ (of ಆಗು § 176) and the formative taddhita syllable ಎ (§ 243, A, 2), originally meaning 'a state of having become or being', to which ಅ, the sign of the genitive (§ 130), was suffixed.

3, The declension, in the singular, of the nouns ಅನಿತು, ಇನಿತು, ಉನಿತು, ಎನಿತು which express indefinite quantity or are ಪರಿಣಾಮ ಪೇೞ್ವ ನಿರ್ವಿಶೇಷಶಬ್ದಂಗಳ್ (to which ಎಲ್ಲದು also belongs, see §§ 90. 266), appears in § 122. See the epicene plural of the appellative nouns of indefinite quantity derived from them, under No. 4.

ಅನಿತು, that much, so much as that (ತಾವತ್), ಇನಿತು, this much, so much as this (ಇಯತ್), ಉನಿತು, so much as this (in an intermediate sense, ಏತಾವತ್), ಎನಿತು, how much (ಕಿಯತ್) occur in the ancient and mediæval dialect; in the mediæval one ಅಷ್ಟು, ಇಷ್ಟು, ಎಷ್ಟು are often substituted for them, as is generally done in the modern one (§ 122, *b, c*). The substitutional forms ಅಯ್ಸು, ಆಸು; ಈಸು; ಏಸು are also frequently used in the two last mentioned dialects. In the modern one there are likewise ಅಟೆ, ಅಟು, ಅಟ್ಟು, ಅಟು; ಇಸ, ಈಟು; ಏಟು. The Šabdânušâsana introduces (under its sûtras 238. 441) ಅಷ್ಟು, ಇಷ್ಟು, ಉಷ್ಟು, ಎಷ್ಟು; ಅಯ್ಸು, ಈಸು, ಊಸು, ಏಸು as belonging to the ancient dialect. Some instances are:—ಅನಿತು ಕಾಲಂ, so much time as that; ಎನಿತು ಮಹಿ, how much land; ಇಷ್ಟು ಹೊತ್ತು, so much time as this; ಅಷ್ಟು ಶಬ್ದಂಗಳ್, so many terms as those; ಎಷ್ಟು ಮನೆ or ಎಷ್ಟು ಮನೆಗಳು, how many houses.

ಅನಿತು, ಇನಿತು, etc., like the cardinal numbers (see No. 2), also suffix ಅನೆಯ, *e. g.* ಅನಿತನೆಯ, ಇನಿತನೆಯ, ಎನಿತನೆಯ, ಅಷ್ಟನೆಯ, and to this (besides any noun) the same pronominal forms and pronouns in the singular and plural, *e. g.* ಅನಿತನೆಯಂ, a man of that or such a place, or state, or degree; ಇನಿತನೆಯಂ, a man of this or such a place, or state, or degree; ಉನಿತನೆಯಂ, a man of this intermediate place, etc.; ಎನಿತನೆಯಂ, a man of what place, or state, or degree; ಅನಿತನೆಯಳ್; ಅನಿತನೆಯರ್; ಅಷ್ಟನೆಯವನು,

ಇಷ್ಟನೆಯವನು, ಎಷ್ಟನೆಯವನು; ಎಷ್ಟನೆಯವಳು; ಎಷ್ಟನೆಯದು or ಎಷ್ಟನೇದು; ಅಷ್ಟನೆಯವರು.

4, Ancient appellative nouns of number of which a few instances in their epicene nominative plural have been given in § 119, are *e. g.* ಒರ್ಬಂ or ಒರ್ವಂ, one man; ಒರ್ಬಳ್ or ಒರ್ವಳ್, one woman; ಇರ್ಬರ್ or ಇರ್ವರ್, two men or women; ಮೂವರ್ or ಮೂವರ್ಕಳ್, three men or women; ನಾಲ್ವರ್ or ನಾಲ್ವರ್ಕಳ್, four men or women; ಅಯ್ವರ್, five men or women; ಅಱುವರ್, six men or women; ಏೞ್ಬರ್ or ಏೞ್ವರ್, seven men or women; ಎಣ್ಬರ್; ಒಮ್ಬದಿಮ್ಬರ್; ಪದಿಮ್ಬರ್ or ಪಯಿಮ್ಬರ್; ನೂರ್ವರ್; ಸಾಸಿರ್ವರ್; — ಮೂವತ್ತಿರ್ವರ್, ಮೂವತ್ತುಮೂವರ್, ಅಱುವತ್ತುಮೂವರ್ (*cf.* § 272, 2).

The mediæval dialect uses *e. g.* ಒರ್ಬಂ, ಒರ್ಬಳ್, and also ಒಬ್ಬಂ, ಒಬ್ಬಳ್; ಇರ್ಬರ್ and ಇಬ್ಬರ್; ಮೂವರ್; ನಾಲ್ವರ್; ಅಯ್ವರ್; ಅಱುವರ್; ಏೞ್ವರ್; ಪದಿನೆಣ್ಬರ್. The modern dialect has ಒಬ್ಬನು, ಒಬ್ಬಳು, ಇಬ್ಬರು, ಮೂವರು or ಮುವ್ವರು, ನಾಲ್ವರು, ಅಯ್ವರು or ಅಯ್ಬರು, ಅಱುವರು or ಅರ್ವರು, ಏೞ್ವರು. See also §§ 310, 1; 311, remark.

Frequently the modern dialect, and occasionally also the mediæval one, express such appellative nouns of number by adding ಮನ್ದಿ (or ಜನರು), persons, to cardinal numbers, *e. g.* ಮೂಱು ಮನ್ದಿ, three persons ನಾಲ್ಕು ಮನ್ದಿ, ಅಯ್ದು ಮನ್ದಿ, (ಎಣ್ಟು ಜನರು).

Other ancient appellative nouns of number are ಕೆಲಬರ್, ಕೆಲಮ್ಬರ್, ಕೆಲರ್ (of ಕೆಲವು), some men or women; ಪಲಬರ್, ಪಲಮ್ಬರ್, ಪಲರ್ (of ಪಲವು, *cf.* § 90; § 248, 12, and as to form ಪೊಸಮ್ಬರ್ in § 273), many or several men or women. In the mediæval dialect they are ಕೆಲಬರ್, ಕೆಲಮ್ಬರ್, ಕೆಲರ್; ಪಲಬರ್, ಪಲರ್, ಹಲಬರ್, ಹಲರ್, and in the modern one ಕೆಲವರು; ಹಲಬರು, ಹಲವರು. In the modern dialect ಕೆಲವು ಮನ್ದಿ or ಕೆಲವು ಜನರು, ಹಲವು ಮನ್ದಿ or ಹಲವು ಜನರು may be used instead of ಕೆಲವರು, etc.

The ancient appellative nouns of indefinite quantity in their epicene plural, derived from ಅನಿತು, ಇನಿತು, ಉನಿತು, ಎನಿತು, ಎಲ್ಲದು (see under No. 3), are ಅನಿಬರ್, so many men or women as those, ಇನಿಬರ್, so many men or women as these, (ಉನಿಬರ್), ಎನಿಬರ್, how many men or women, ಎಲ್ಲವರ್ (the ವ್ being euphonic, see § 266), ಎಲ್ಲರ್, all men or women, all of which are found also in the mediæval dialect with the exception of ಎಲ್ಲವರ್ (*cf.* § 272 under No. 2). Only ಎಲ್ಲರ್, in the forms of ಎಲ್ಲರು and ಎಲ್ಲಾರು, appears in the modern one.

The epicene nominative plural of ಅಷ್ಟು and ಇಷ್ಟು (see above under No. 3) in the modern dialect is ಅಷ್ಟರು, so many men or women as those, and ಇಷ್ಟರು, so many men or women as these. Instead of ಎಷ್ಟರು, how many persons, ಎಷ್ಟು ಮನ್ದಿ or ಎಷ್ಟು ಜನರು is used.

279. By suffixing ಮೆ to the short form of a cardinal number (§ 278, 1) words are formed in the ancient dialect that express 'time' or 'times', *e. g.* ಒರ್ಮೆ, one time or turn, once; ಇರ್ಮೆ, two times, twice; ಮೂರ್ಮೆ, ಮೂವೆ, ಮುಮ್ಮೆ, ಮುಯ್ಮೆ, three times, thrice; ನಾಲ್ಮೆ; ಅಯ್ಮೆ; ಅಱುವೆ; ಏೞ್ಮೆ; ಎಣ್ಮೆ; ಒಮ್ಬಯ್ಮೆ; ಪಯ್ಯಿಮ್ಮೆ; ನೂರ್ಮೆ; ಸಾಸಿರ್ಮೆ. For instance ಮಕಾರಕ್ಕೊರ್ಮೆ ವಕಾರಮಕ್ಕುಂ, for the letter ಮ once the letter ವ is used.

In the mediæval dialect we find ಒರ್ಮೆ, ಒಮ್ಮೆ (for ಒರ್ಮೆ) and ಇಮೆ (for ಇರ್ಮೆ), and in the modern one ಒಮ್ಮೆ. (See § 212, 1; *cf.* § 306, *b.*)

In the ancient dialect there are formed also ಕೆಲರ್ಮೆ (from ಕೆಲರ್ of ಕೆಲವು, see 278, 4), some times, and ಪಲರ್ಮೆ (from ಪಲರ್ of ಪಲವು), many or several times, *e. g.*

ಕೂರ್ಮೆಯಿನ್ ಆ ಮುನಿಯಿಂ ಕ
ಣ್ಡಾರ್ಮಂ ನೀನಲ್ಲದಿಲ್ಲ ಪೆಱತೆನ್ದರಸಂ ।
ನೂರ್ಮೆ ಬಲವನ್ದು, ನುತಿಸಿ, ಪ
ಲರ್ಮೆ ತುಱುಗಲ್ಗೆಯ್ದು, ಭಕ್ತಿಯಿಂ ಬೆಸಗೊಣ್ಡಂ ॥ (See translation in § 258.)

The ಮೆ is one of the taddhita suffixes (§ 243, *A,* 19), and only in course of time got the meaning of time or turn.

In the ancient and mediæval dialect 'time' or 'times' used to be expressed also by ಸೂೞ್ (ಸೂೞು) or ಬಾರಿ, *e. g.* ಒನ್ದು ಸೂೞ್, ಎರಡು ಸೂೞ್, ಒನ್ದು ಬಾರಿ, ಎರಡು ಬಾರಿ; in the modern one the terms used are ಆವರ್ತಿ, ಬಾರಿ, ಸರತಿ, ಸರದಿ, ಸರ್ತಿ, ಸಲ, ಸಾರಿ, ಸಾರೆ, etc., *e. g.* ಒನ್ದಾವರ್ತಿ, ಎರಡು ಸರ್ತಿ.

280. To form words expressing 'fold' the ancient dialect frequently used ಮಡಿ, a fold, suffixed to the short forms of cardinal numbers (§ 278, 1), *e. g.* ಇರ್ಮಡಿ, two-fold, twice as much, ಮೂರ್ಮಡಿ or ಮೂವಡಿ (*i. e.* ಮೂ+ಮಡಿ), three-fold, three times as much, ನಾಲ್ವಡಿ (*i. e.* ನಾಲ್+ಮಡಿ), ಅಯ್ವಡಿ (*i. e.* ಅಯ್+ಮಡಿ), ಅಱುವಡಿ (*i. e.* ಅಱು+ಮಡಿ, § 215, 7, *b*), ನೂರ್ಮಡಿ, ಸಾಸಿರ್ಮಡಿ.

Instances are:—

ಧರೆಯೊಳ್ ಬೀರದ ಪೆಮ್ಪಿನ
ನರನಿನ್ದಿರ್ಮಡಿ, ಬಕಾರಿಯಿಂ ಮೂವಡಿ, ಭಾ ।
ಸ್ಕರಸುತನಿಂ ನಾಲ್ವಡಿ, ಮುರ
ಹರನಿನ್ದಯ್ವಡಿ ನೆಗೞ್ತೆಯದಟರ ಭೀಮಂ ॥ a terrible man of the heroes

of famo on earth (ho was): twice as much as Arjuna of eminent valour, thrice as much as Bhîma, four times as much as Karṇa, five times as much as Kṛishṇa. (*Cf.* § 343, 3.)

ಇರ್ಮಡಿ ಬಲಿಗೆ, ದಧೀಚಿಗೆ
ಮೂರ್ಮಡಿ, ಜೀಮೂತವಾಹನಂಗಂ, ಬಗೆಯಲ್, |
ನೂರ್ಮಡಿ, ಶಿಬಿಗಂ ದಿಟ ಸಾ
ಸಿರ್ಮಡಿ ಮಿಗಿಲ್ ಇಳೆಗೆ ಚಾಗದೊಳ್ ನೃಪತುಂಗಂ || Nṛipatuṅga (was) in liberality on earth surpassing Bali two times, Dadhîči three times, also Indra, if one considers, a hundred times, (and) indeed also Šibi a thousand times. (*Cf.* § 343, 1.)

In the mediæval and modern dialect we find ಇಮ್ಮಡಿ (for ಇರ್ಮಡಿ), ಮುಮ್ಮಡಿ (for ಮೂರ್ಮಡಿ), in the mediæval one ನೂರ್ಮಡಿ, ನೂಱುಮಡಿ, ಎಣ್ಬುಮಡಿ, and in the modern one ಹತ್ತುಮಡಿ.

To form **multiplication numbers** in the modern dialect ಅಷ್ಟು and ಇಷ್ಟು (§ 278, 3) are frequently used, *e.g.* ಮತ್ತಷ್ಟು (ಮತ್ತು+ಅಷ್ಟು), again so much as that, ಮತ್ತಿಷ್ಟು, again so much as this, or ಇನ್ನಷ್ಟು (ಇನ್ನು+ಅಷ್ಟು), ಇನ್ನಿಷ್ಟು; ಎರಡಷ್ಟು (ಎರಡು+ಅಷ್ಟು), twice as much as that, ನಾಲ್ಕಷ್ಟು, four times as much as that; *e.g.* ಮತ್ತಷ್ಟು ಅಗಲ or ಇನ್ನಷ್ಟು ಅಗಲ, as broad again, ಮೂಱಿಷ್ಟು ಉದ್ದ, thrice as long (*cf.* § 310, 1).

XVI. On adverbs.

281. In § 212 lists of adverbs (particles, avyaya and nipâta) have been given, and in § 102, 9 their so-called gender has been adverted to. Kêšava calls such as are particularly used to modify the action of a verb 'kriyâvišêshaṇas', and gives the instance ತಿಬ್ಬಂ ಮಾಡಿದಂ, explaining it by ತಿಬ್ಬಮೆಹಗಹುದು ಅಹಗೆ ಮಾಡಿದಂ. In § 277 it has been remarked that some adjectives or attributive nouns in their neuter forms are used as adverbs.

It remains to be stated that in the ancient, mediæval and modern dialect **adverbs** are frequently formed by adding ಆಗಿ, 'having become'[1], *e.g.* ಅಮಲಿನವಾಗಿ or ನಿರ್ದೋಷವಾಗಿ, faultlessly; ಸ್ಥಿರವಾಗಿ ಸ್ನೇಹ ಮಾಡ್ಪಿ

---

[1] The author thinks that this ಆಗಿ originally was, at least often, ಆಗೆ, 'so that it becomes or became or is' (*cf.* § 212, remark 2). This, certainly, is the case in our present Šabdamaṇidarpaṇa's ಚಿಕ್ಕಣವಾಗಿ ಮಾಡಿದಂ, he made (a thing) level (by crushing), and ಸಣ್ಣವಾಗಿ ತುಳಿದಂ, he trampled (a thing) into a mass of small particles, wherein the forms ಚಿಕ್ಕಣವಾಗೆ and ಸಣ್ಣವಾಗೆ only give the required meaning. Observe also the modern instance ಪುಸ್ತಕ ಅಱುವೆಗಳನ್ನು ಬಹು ಸ್ವಚ್ಛವಾಗಿ ಇಟ್ಟು ಕೊಳ್ಳ ಬೇಕು, in which only ಸ್ವಚ್ಛವಾಗೆ can give the meaning intended, *viz.* it is proper to keep the books and clothes so that they be (or remain) very clean.

ವನು, one who loves constantly; ವ್ಯಕ್ತವಾಗಿ ನುಡಿಯಲಱಿಯದಾತ, one who cannot speak distinctly; ಹಿರಿದಾಗಿ ಪೀಡಿಸುವುದು, to distress greatly; ಗಿಡಗಳು ಚನ್ನಾಗಿ ಫಲಿಸುತ್ತವೆ, the trees bear fruit abundantly; ನಮ್ಮ ಒಡೆಯನು ನಮ್ಮನ್ನು ಬಹಳ ಚನ್ನಾಗಿ ಸಾಕುತ್ತಾನೆ, our master fosters us very well; ಒಳಿತಾಗಿ ಮಾತಾಡುವದು, to speak properly; ಅವನನ್ನು ಒಳಿತಾಗಿ ತಳಿಸಿದನು, he beat him soundly; ಗಟ್ಟಿಯಾಗಿ ಕೂಗಿದನು, he cried out loudly; ನೀನು ತೀವ್ರವಾಗಿ ನಡೆಯುತ್ತೀ, thou walkest quickly; ನಿಮ್ಮ ಹುಡುಗನು ಶುದ್ಧವಾಗಿ ಬರೆಯುತ್ತಾನೆ, your boy writes correctly; ಸ್ಪಷ್ಟವಾಗಿ ಓದ ಬೇಕು, (you) must read distinctly; ಯೋಗ್ಯವಾಗಿ ನಡೆದಳು, she walked becomingly. Others are ಮಱೆಯಾಗಿ, covertly; ಮುಖ್ಯವಾಗಿ, chiefly; ವೆಗ್ಗಳವಾಗಿ, exceedingly; ಸಾಧಾರಣವಾಗಿ, generally; ಹೇರಳವಾಗಿ, abundantly; etc.

From the foot-note of § 166 it appears that in the ancient dialect ಅಯ್ (=ಆಗಿ) and ಆಯ್ (=ಆಗಿ) were once suffixed to nouns of direction, *e. g.* ತೆಂಕು and ಮೂಡು, in order to make them adverbs, became ತೆಂಕಯ್, ತೆಂಕಾಯ್, meaning 'southward, toward the south', and ಮೂಡಯ್, ಮೂಡಾಯ್, 'eastward, toward the east'.

Adverbs are expressed in the three dialects also by the instrumental, *e. g.* ಐಕಲ್ಪದಿಂ, optionally; ಸನ್ತಸದಿಂ, ಸನ್ತೋಷದಿನ್ದ, gladly, willingly; ಬೇಗದಿಂ, quickly; ಉಲ್ಲಾಸದಿನ್ದ, merrily; ಮೂಢತನದಿನ್ದ, foolishly; ಸುಖದಿನ್ದ, happily.

To express 'very', 'in a high degree' before adverbs ಅತಿ, ಬಲು, ಬಹಳ, ಬಹು may be used (*cf.* § 275), *e. g.* ಅತಿ ದೂರವಾಗಿ, very far; ಬಲು ಭಯಂಕರವಾಗಿ, in a very formidable manner; ಬಹಳ ಕ್ರೂರವಾಗಿ, very cruelly; ಬಹು ಸುಲಭವಾಗಿ, very nimbly. About the use of repetition of adverbs to express 'very' see § 307, *a.*

Kešava calls adverbs also avyayaliṅgas (§ 90, likewise avyayapadas), adverbial declinable bases, his reason for doing so being the circumstance that in a few instances adverbs show case-terminations, as ಮತ್ತಿನ (genitive of ಮತ್ತೆ), ಅನ್ನಱಿಂ (ablative of ಅನ್ತಱ್).

When adverbs are in connection with verbs, they generally precede the verb immediately or the subject and its predicate, undergoing no change of gender and number, *e. g.* ತಿಬ್ಬಂ ಮಾಡಿದಂ; ದೋಷರಹಿತಂ ಪೇಟ್ದಿಂ (see § 327); ನಿರ್ನೆರಂ ಬನ್ದಂ; ಚೆಚ್ಚರಂ ನುಡಿದಂ; ಮಿಗೆ ಬೞಿಲ್ದಂ, ಮಿಗೆ ಬೞಿಲ್ದಳ್, ಮಿಗೆ ಬೞಿಲ್ದುದು; ಮತ್ತೆ ನೋಡಿದಂ, ಮತ್ತೆ ನೋಡಿದಳ್, ಮತ್ತೆ ನೋಡಿದುದು; ಭೋಂಕನೊರ್ವಂ ಬನ್ದಂ; ಮೆಲ್ಲನಿರ್ವರ್ ನುಡಿದರ್; ನೆಟ್ಟಗೆಲ್ಲರುಂ ಪೋದರ್. If something is put between the subject and predicate, it is to be done so that the adverb stands where it clearly modifies the sense of the predicate, as in the following instance:—

ಭೋಂಕನೆ ದೇವಸ್ತ್ರೀಯರ್ ಅನ್ದಾರತಿಯನ್, ಉಘೇ ಎನ್ದು, ತನ್ದೆತ್ತುತ್ತಿರ್ದರ್. In a stanza, however, the position may be sometimes chosen at the convenience of its author, as ತಗುಳ್ಗಂ ಸಮಸನ್ದಾ ಯುಗಂಗಳೊಳ್ ಅಮಲಿನಮ್ ಆಗೆಲ್ಲಿಯುಂ ಸವರ್ಣ ವಿಧಾನಂ, homogeneousness takes place faultlessly everywhere in those well-known couples (of vowels, *e. g.* ಅ ಅ). ಸನ್ದ ಪಕಾರಕ್ಕೆ ಹಕಾರಂ ದೊರೆಕೊಳ್ಗಂ ವಿಕಲ್ಪದಿಂ, instead of the generally known letter ಪ the letter ಹ may be optionally used.

282. Regarding the adverbs which have been called postpositions by us and regarding **the adverbs of place and time** (§ 212, 2. 8. 6) the following instances may be given **in which they govern the genitive**:— ಮರದತ್ತಣಿಂ (ಮರದ ಅತ್ತಣಿಂ), from the tree; ತಮ್ಮತ್ತಲ್ (ತಮ್ಮ ಅತ್ತಲ್), to their side; ಕರ್ಣನನ್ತಿರೆ (ಕರ್ಣನ ಅನ್ತಿರೆ), like Karṇa; ಗಿರಿಯನ್ತೆ (ಗಿರಿಯ ಅನ್ತೆ), like a hill; ತಳಿರನ್ತೆ (ತಳಿರ ಅನ್ತೆ), like young shoots; ನನ್ನನ್ತೆ, like me; ಬಲಿಯನ್ತೆವೊಲ್, like Bali; ಅರ್ಥದಲ್, in the meaning; ಮರದಲ್ಲಿ, in the tree; ಅವನಲ್ಲಿ, in him; ನುಡಿಗಳಹಗೆ, like (one's) words; ಊರಿಂ (ಊರ ಇಂ), from the village; ತನ್ನೆದುರಿಗೆ, in front of him; ಭಯದೆ (ಭಯದ ಎ), from fear; ಗಿಳಿಯೊಡನೆ, with a parrot; ನಿನ್ನೊಡನೆ, with thee; ಮನೆಯೊಳ್, in the house; ನೀರೊಳಗೆ, in the water; ಪೇರಾಲದ ಕೆಳಗೆ, under a large banyan tree; ಅವನ ಪಿನ್ದೆ, after him; ಊರ ಹೊರಗೆ, outside the village; ಅರಮನೆಯ ಮುನ್ದೆ, before the palace; ಆನೆಯ ಮೇಲೆ, on an elephant; ಜಲನಿಧಿಯ ವೋಲ್, like the ocean; ಅವನ ಹಾಗೆ, like him; ತೊಱೆಯಾಚೆ, on the other side of a stream; ಹಣ್ಣಿನ ಸುತ್ತು, round a ripe fruit; ಕೆಲವು ವರುಷಗಳ ಮುಂಚೆ, some years ago; ಸೈನ್ಯದೊನ್ದಿಗೆ, with the army; ಅದಱ ತುಸುಕ, on account of that; ಅವನ ಕೂಡ, with him; ತನ್ದೆಯ ಸಂಗಡ, with the father; ದೇವರ ಬಗ್ಯೆ, concerning God; ಇದಱ ಹೊರ್ತು, except this; ನನ್ನ ಹತ್ತರ, near me, about me; ಬಾಗಿಲ ಹತ್ತರ, near the door; ಕಾನ್ತನ ಹತ್ತಿರ, near a lover; ಇನ್ದಿನ ವರೆಗೆ, till to-day; ಇನ್ದಿನ ತನಕ, till to-day; ಕೆಲವು ದಿವಸಗಳ ತರುವಾಯ, after some days.

Instances in which some of them govern **the dative**, are:— ಬಿನ್ದುವಿಂಗಿದಿರ್, in front of a bindu; ಹಿರಿಯರಿಗೆ ಇದಿರಾಗಿ, before elder people; ತನ್ನ ದೇಶಕ್ಕೆ ಆಚೆಯ ದೇಶ, the country beyond his country; ಪ್ರತಿಷೇಧದ ಧಾತುಗೆ ಮುನ್ದೆ, in front of the theme of the negative; ಕೆಲವು ವರುಷಗಳಿಗೆ ಮುಂಚೆ, some years ago; ಈಯುವದಕ್ಕೆ ಮುಂಚೆ, before bringing forth; ಪಾದಪ್ರಕ್ಷಾಲನೆಗೋಸುಗ, on account of washing the feet; ಕಾಳೆಗಕ್ಕೋಸ್ಕರ, on account of battle; ಅದಕ್ಕೋಸುಗರ, on account of that; ಪರ್ವತಕ್ಕೆ ಹತ್ತರ, near the mountain.

Instances in which some of them govern the **instrumental** (*i. e.* **ablative**), are:— ಮಿತ್ರಮಣ್ಡಲದಿಸ್ದೆ ಅಜೆಯ ಮಣ್ಡಲಂ, a province beyond the province of an ally; ಉಡಿಯಿನ್ದ ಕೆಳಗೆ, below the waist; ಅದಱಿನ್ದ ಮುನ್ದೆ, from that (time), more remote than that; ಅದಱಿಂ ಮುನ್ನ, from that (time); ಅತ್ತಲಿಂ ಮುನ್ನ, before that time; ನಾಮಾಖ್ಯಾತವಿಭಕ್ತಿಗಳಿಂ ಪಿನ್ದೆ, behind the noun- and verb-suffixes. See § 352, 4 *a*.

Instances in which one of them is used with the **dative of verbal nouns combined with** ಇನ್ತ (another form of ಇನ್ದ, the termination of the instrumental *i. e.* ablative; *cf.* 343, 2), are:— ಅವನು ಬರುವದಕ್ಕಿನ್ತ ಮುಂಚೆ, (lit. he of the coming-to it-from before), before he comes. ತಾನು ಹಾಱು ವದಕ್ಕಿನ್ತ ಮುಂಚೆ, (lit. he of the jumping-to it-from before), before he jumps. ಯಾರೂ ತಿಳಿದದಕ್ಕಿನ್ತ ಮುಂಚೆ, (lit. any one of the having known or knowing-to it-from before), before anybody knew or knows. ಅವನು ಬಾರದ್ದಕ್ಕಿನ್ತ ಮುಂಚೆ, (lit. he of the not having come or not coming-to it-from before), as long as he did not or does not come.

Instances in which they are used **immediately in connection with nouns, pronouns, so-called adjectives, adverbs, inflected forms of the verb, imperatives, infinitives** (§§ 187. 188), **past participles** (§ 154 *seq.*), and the so-called **relative participles** (§§ 175-186), are:—

a) ಇನ್ದ್ರಮ್ನೋಲ್, like Indra. ಇನ್ನೆವರಂ, up to this time. ಮೂಱುದಿನ ತನಕ, for three days. ವಾರ್ಧಿಮುಟ್ಟ, as far as the sea. ದೆಸೆಗಳಿರ, O directions of the compass! ರಾಮಾ, O Ráma! ಪಿರಿದೊ, grandeur indeed! ಆನೆಯೊ, (is it) an elephant? ಆ ಪ್ರಕಾರವೇ, even that manner. See § 287, 3 regarding numerals.

b) ಆತನೆ, even he. ನೀವೇ, even you! ಆತನಯೆ, even of him. ಅದೇ, that very thing. ಇದೇನೋ, what (could) this (be)? ಚಿನ್ತೆ ಯಾತಕೋ, why sorrowful thoughts? *Cf.* §§ 260. 283. 312. About ಅಂ, ಉಂ, ಉ, ಊ see §§ 284. 285.

c) ಕಪ್ಪೊ, (is it) black? ಬಿಳಿದೆ, (it is) even white! ಕಠಿಣವೇ, difficult indeed! ಉಚಿತವೇ, (could it be) proper?

d) ಹಾಗೇ, just so; (or could it be) thus? ಹೀಗೆಯೇ, in this very manner; (or could it be) thus? ಅನ್ತೇ = ಹಾಗೇ. ಕೆಟ್ಟೆನಲ್ಲೊ, am not I ruined? *Cf.* § 299, 1. 2. 3; § 300, 3. 4.

e) ನಿಮಗೀಯೆಡಱಾಯಿತೆ, could this poverty have befallen you? ಕೇಳಿರೆ, do you not ask? ಎಡಱಿದನೊ, did he behave dishonestly? ಬಿದ್ದನೋ, did he fall? ಹೊಡೆದೆನೋ, did I beat? ಬನ್ದಿರಾ, have you come (in questioning politely)? ಹೋಗುತ್ತೀರಾ, do you go? ಮಥನಕಾಲದಲ್ಲಿ ಕಥೆ ಕೇಳುವದುಣ್ಟೆ, would (one) ask for a tale at the time of churning? ಮೂಢ ಬಲ್ಲನೆ ಜ್ಞಾನದೃಢ ಭಕ್ತಿಯ, does a fool know the firm devotion of wisdom? ದಡ್ಡಿಗೆ ಹೋದೇನೆ? ಅದು ದೂರ ಉಳಿಯಿತು, should I go to the fold? that remained far behind.

f) ನೋಡ ಬನ್ನಿರೊ, come to see! ಹೇಳಿಲೋ, shall I say? ಪಾಲಿಸೊ, ಜಗದೀಶ, protect, lord of the universe! ಕೇಳೊ, ಕೇಳೊ, ಮನುಜನೇ, hear, hear, O man! ಅಕ್ಕಾ, ತಟಕುಜೇನುತುಪ್ಪಾ ಕೊಡೇ, O elder sister, give me a drop of honey (the ಏ being here used in addressing a female, *cf.* 283). ತಂಗೀ, ಇಲ್ಲಿ ಬಾರೇ, O younger sister, come here!

g) ಪಾಡೆ (ಪಾಡು+ಎ), when (he, she, it) sings or sang, when (they) sing or sang. ನುಡಿಯೆ, when (he, she, it) speaks or spoke, when (they) speak or spoke. ಉಣಲ್ (ಉಣ್+ಅಲ್), when (he, she, it) eats or ate, when (they) eat or ate. ಆಡಲೇ ಬಾರದು, it is not allowed to speak at all. ಕಿಡಲೊಡಂ, when (it) was destroyed; ನುಡಿಯಲೊಡಂ, when (he) spoke; ಬರಲೊಡನೆ, directly when (he) came (see § 365).

h) ನಮ್ಬಿಸಿಯೆ, having even caused to confide. ಆಗಿಯೇ, having indeed become. ನಿಲ್ಲದೇ, not standing (or waiting) at all. ನೋಡದಲೇ, not seeing at all (about the ಅಲ್ see the end of this paragraph). About ಉಂ and ಊ see §§ 286. 287, 5.

i) ಮುತ್ತುಂ ಮೆಣಸುಂಗೋದನ್ತಿರೆ, (lit. pearls and pepper corns of the having been threaded thus) as if pearls and pepper corns were threaded (together). ಗೆಲ್ದ ಬೞಿಕ, (lit. of the having won or of the winning after), after having won or after winning. ಅರ್ಚಿಸಿದಿಂ (ಅರ್ಚಿಸಿದ+ಇಂ) ಬೞಿಕ, (lit. of the having worshipped-from after), after (he, etc.) had worshipped. ಮನಸಿಗೆ ಬನ್ದ ಹಾಗೆ, (lit. of the having been or of the being fit thus), as was or is fit (about ಹಾಗೆ, *cf.* §§ 298, 5; 300, 2). ಬನ್ದ ಮೇಲೆ, (lit. of the having come or of the coming after), after coming. ಹೋದ ಮೇಲೆ, after going; ಕಣ್ಡಾಗ, (lit. of the having seen then), when (he, etc.) saw. ಆದನ್ದು, (lit. of the having become or of the coming then), when (he, etc.) became or when (he, etc.) becomes. ಮಾಡಿದ ಪೋಲ್, as if (he, etc.) made or makes. ಪರೆವುದುಂ, when (it, etc.) dispersed (see § 365). ಪುಗುವಿನಂ, when (he, etc.) enters or when (we, you, they) enter (see § 365). ಈವನ್ನೆಗಂ, till (or so that he, etc.) might give (see § 365). ಮುಗಿಯುವಾಗ, when (it) is finished. ಬರ್ಪನ್ದು=ಬರುವಾಗ. ಬರುವಾಗ, when (he, etc.) comes or when (we, you, they) come. ಕೆಟ್ಟು ಹೋಗುವ ಹಾಗೆ ಇರುತ್ತಾನೆ, he is likely to be ruined. ಮನಮ್ಪುಗುವನ್ತೆ, so that (it) enters the mind. ಪಡೆವನಕ, till (he, she, it) obtains or till (we, you, they) obtain. ಆಗುವ

ತನಕ, till (he, etc.) becomes or till (we, etc.) become. ಕುಡಿಯುವ ಬಗ್ಗೆ; in order to drink. ಲಾಲಿಸುವ ಪ್ರೋಲ್, so that (he, etc.) listens or so that (they) listen. ಸಿಕ್ಕದ ಹಾಗೆ, (lit. of the not having found or of the not finding thus), so that (he, etc.) was not found or so that (we, etc.) were not found. ನೋಯಿಸದನ್ತೆ, so that (it) did not or does not pain. ಅಜ ಹರಿ ಜನಿಸದತ್ತ, at the time that Aja and Hari had not been born. ಬಾರದ ಮುಂಚೆ, as long as (he, etc.) does not come or (we, etc.) do not come or as long as (he, etc., we, etc.) did not come. ಉಳ್ಳೊಡೆ, if (he, etc.) is (or be), if (we, etc.) are (or be). ಅಳದರೆ, if (he, etc.) measures (or measure), if (we, etc.) measure. ಬೇಡಿದ ಹೊರ್ತು, unless (he, etc.) prays (or pray), unless (we, etc.) pray. ಮಾಡದ ಹೊರ್ತು, unless (he, etc.) does or makes (or do or make), unless (we, etc.) do or make. *Cf.* §§ 363. 364. Regarding the subjunctive see §§ 287, 5; 314.

About the different meanings of the adverbs of question as specified in ancient grammars see Dictionary, and also § 283.

Occasionally a euphonic ಲ್ is used in the mediæval and modern dialect to suffix the ಎ or ಏ of emphasis, *e. g.* ಬಱಿಕಲೆ, ಸಹಿತಲೆ, ಅಕ್ಷತೆಯಿನ್ದಲೆ, ಎನುತಲೆ, ಕೂಡಲೆ, ಕೂಡಲೇ (*cf.* the ಲ್ before ಉ in §§ 285. 286). In the negative participle of the modern dialect this ಲ್ appears also as ಅಲ್, *e. g.* ನೋಡದಲೆ (*i. e.* ನೊಡದ+ಅಲೆ), ಕೂಡದಲೇ (*i. e.* ಕೂಡದ+ಅಲೇ). The ಎ of emphasis in combination with euphonic ಅಲ್ may take the form of ಇ in modern poetry, *e. g.* ಬುದ್ಧಿಯಿನ್ದಲಿ, ಒಡಮ್ಬಡುತಲಿ (*cf.* § 109, *b, c,* instr.; § 362, after *c*).

283. Some peculiar instances of the modern dialect regarding the use of the adverbial suffixes ಏ and ಓ, added to the interrogative pronouns ಏನು, ಯಾವದು, ಯಾವನು, ಯಾವಳು and the interrogative noun of indefinite quantity ಎಷ್ಟು (§ 278, 3), are:—ಏನೇ, what? eh? (used in calling to a female or asking a female, *e. g.* ಏನೇ, ಅವ್ವಾ? ಏನೇ, ತಂಗೀ? *cf.* § 282, *f*); what, eh? *i. e.* whatsoever (*e. g.* ಮಾವಾ, ಏನೇ ಇರಲಿ);

ಏನೋ, what? (used in asking males contemptuously); O! (used in addressing males, *e. g.* ಏನೋ, ಗೋವಿನ್ದ?); O what? what could it be? (*e. g.* ಒನ್ದು ದೊಡ್ಡ ಹಱಿವೋ? ಏನೋ? ಅನ್ನುವ ಹಾಗೆ ಆ ಆಲದ ಮರವು ಕಾಣಿಸುತ್ತದೆ); O what? I do not know (*e. g.* question: ಹೇೞಿದ ಕೆಲಸವಾಯಿತೋ? answer: ಏನೋ? or question: ಕೂಸಿಗೆ ಏನಾಯಿತೋ? answer: ಏನೋ?); O what? one does not know what? *i. e.* something one does not know (*e. g.* ಏನೋ ಆಗಿ ಸತ್ತನು; ಆ ಮೂಕಿ ಮನಸ್ಸಿನೊಳಗೆ ಏನೋ ಯೋಚಿಸಿ ಕೊಣ್ಡು; ಏನೋ ಒನ್ದು ಕಾರಣದ ಸಲುವಾಗಿ);

ಯಾವದೋ, O what? *i.e.* something one does not know, a certain (object, with or without ಒನ್ದು, *e.g.* ಯಾವದೋ ಆಟ, a certain play; ಯಾವದೋ ಒನ್ದು ದೇವಾಲಯು); ಯಾವನೋ, ಯಾವಳೋ, O who? *i. e.* a certain man, a certain woman (generally with ಒಬ್ಬನು, ಒಬ್ಬಳು, *e.g.* ಯಾವನೋ ಒಬ್ಬನು, ಯಾವಳೋ ಒಬ್ಬಳು; see remark under § 292);

ಯಾರೋ, O who? *i.e.* a certain person, somebody (with or without ಒಬ್ಬರು, *e.g.* ಆ ಮಾಂಸವನ್ನು ಯಾರೋ ಕದ್ದುಕೊಣ್ಡನು. ಯಾರೋ ಅತ್ತ ಹಾಗೆ. ಯಾರೋ ಒಬ್ಬರು ಅವನಿಗೆ ಒನ್ದು ಸಣ್ಣ ಕೊಡ್ಲಿಯನ್ನು ಕೊಟ್ಟರು);

ಎಷ್ಟೋ, O how many? how very many! very many! (*e.g.* ಕೆಲವು ಮಂಗಗಳು ಮನುಷ್ಯರ ಹಾಗೆ ಎಷ್ಟೋ ಕೆಲಸಗಳನ್ನು ಮಾಡುತ್ತವೆ. ಆ ಹುತ್ತಿನೊಳಗೆ ಎಷ್ಟೋ ಇಱುವೆಗಳು ಇರುತ್ತಿದ್ದವು. ಗುಡ್ಡದ ಮೇಲೆ ಎಷ್ಟೋ ಜನರು ಆಡ್ಡಾಡುತ್ತಾರೆ); O how much or many! one does not know how much or many (*e.g.* ಆ ವರ್ತಕನಿಗೆ ಎಷ್ಟೋ ದಿವಸ ಮಕ್ಕಳಿದ್ದಿಲ್ಲ. ಕೂೞು ದೊರೆಯದಾಗ ಕಾಡ ನಾಯಿಗಳು ಹಾಗೆ ಎಷ್ಟೋ ದಿವಸ ಉಪವಾಸವಿರುತ್ತವೆ).

Concerning questions in general in the same dialect it may be stated here that in such questions as ಇದು ನಿನ್ನದೋ, is this thine? ಇದು ನಿನ್ನದೇನು may be used. The suffixed ಏನು may also become ಏನೋ, *e. g.* ನಾಲ್ಕಾಣೆ ಕೊಟ್ಟನೇನೋ, did he give four Annas? ಬೆಳಿಗ್ಗೆ ಎದ್ದಳೇನೋ, did she rise early in the morning? At the same time, in common conversation, the sign of question is sometimes entirely omitted and the question shown by the tone of the voice, *e. g.* ತೋಟಕ್ಕೆ ಹೋಗುತ್ತಾನೆ, does he go to the garden? ಹಣ ಕೊಡುತ್ತಾರೆ, does he give the (promised) money? ನಾಳೆ ಬರುವರು, will they come to-morrow? If there is an interrogative in the question, the question simply is *e.g.* ಹುಚ್ಚಾ, ನಿನ್ನ ಮನಸಿಗೆ ಯಾವ ಆಟ ಬರುತ್ತದೆ, O Huččā, what play do you like? See ಎಲ್ಲಿದಂ in § 243, remark; regarding ಆವ, ಯಾವ, etc. §§ 265. 271; regarding questions in general § 356, II, 12.

284. Of the conjunctions mentioned in § 212, 5, four, *viz.* ಅಂ, ಉಂ, ಉ, ಊ, are postpositions (§ 212, 6).

First they serve to unite words, which uniting is called samuččaya. The way of doing so is called also umuvidhi (*i. e.* uṁ + vidhi, the u after uṁ being euphonic), 'the copulative method or rule'.

In this respect ಅಂ and ಉಂ are suffixed to case-terminations of words except in the genitive (see § 351, remark). In the nominative and instrumental ಉಂ alone is used; and again ಉಂ alone is suffixed to the accusative, in which case it is inserted before the case-termination. In the locative ಅಂ is generally preferred to ಉಂ. These rules about ಅಂ and ಉಂ apply to the ancient and mediæval dialect.

ಅಂ and ಉಂ express 'and', the first ಅಂ or ಉಂ being not translated into English.

Instances regarding the nominative are:—ನರನುಂ ನರನನ್ದನನುಂ ಗುರುವುಂ, Arjuna and Abhimanyu and Drôṇa. ಹರಿಯುಂ ಹರನುಂ, Hari and Hara. ಜಿನೇನ್ದ್ರರುಂ ಗಣೇನ್ದ್ರರುಂ, Jinêndras and Gaṇêndras. ಕೇವಲಿಗಳುಂ ಶ್ರುತಕೇವಲಿಗಳುಂ, Kêvalis and Śrutakêvalis. ಅದುಮ್ ಇದುಂ, that and this. ಅರಸರುಮ್ ಅರಸಿಯರುಂ ಕೂಡಿ ಇಹ ಬನಂ, a pleasure ground where king and queen are together. ಆಲಿವರಲ್ಗಳುಮ್ ಇನ್ದ್ರಗೋಪಮುಂ ಸೂಸಿದವಭ್ರದಿಂ, hail-stones and fire-flies showered from the sky. ಮೇಲೆಯುಂ ಕೆಳಗೆಯುಂ, above and below. ಆನೆಯ ಮೇಲೆಯುಮ್ ಆಳ ಮೇಲೆಯುಂ ಕುದುರೆಯ ಮೇಲೆಯುಂ ಪರಿದುದೊನ್ದೆ ಗಜಂ ಭುವನೈಕರಾಮನಾ, on the elephants and on the soldiers and on the horses rushed the one elephant of Bhuvanaikarâma.

Instances regarding the accusative are:—ಒನ್ದೆಡೆಯೊಳ್ ಕಟ್ಟುವುದೆ ಪಿರಿಯ ಪುಲಿಯುಮಂ ಕವಿಲೆಯುಮಂ, must one tie a large tiger and a brown cow in the same place? ಅವನುಮಮ್ ಆಕೆಯುಮಂ, him and her. ಫಲಮುಮಂ ಪುಷ್ಪಮುಮಂ, fruit and flower. ಅವರುಮಮ್ ಆಕೆಗಳುಮಂ, them (the males) and them (the females). Occasionally the first ಅಂ is omitted, as in ಜಲನಿಧಿ ಜಲಚಯಮಂ ರತ್ನಚಯಮುಮಂ ಧರಿಸುವ ವೋಲ್, like the ocean containing a mass of water and a mass of pearls.

Instances regarding the instrumental are:—ಕಾಲಿನ್ದೆಯುಂ ಕೆಯ್ಯಿನ್ದೆಯುಂ ಘಟ್ಟಿಸಿದಂ, he struck with his feet and hands. ಫಲದಿನ್ದಮುಂ ಪುಷ್ಪದಿನ್ದಮುಂ ಪೂಜಿಸಿದಂ, he worshipped with fruits and flowers.

Instances regarding the dative are:—ದ್ರೋಣಂಗಂ ನಿನಗಂ ಬಿಲ್ಜಾಣಿಕೆ ಸಕ್ಕಸಮನೆ, are Drôṇa and you quite equal in the skill of archery? (*cf.* § 321). ವಂಚಿಸುವುದವಂಗೆಯುಂ ನಿನಗೆಯುಂ ಸಹಜಂ, cheating naturally belongs to him and you. ಆತಂಗಮ್ ಅರಸಿಗಂ ವಿಖ್ಯಾತಿಯಶಂ ಪುಟ್ಟಿದಂ ಕುಲಕಂ ಚಲಕ್ಕಂ ಭೂತಲದೊಳ್ ಆರ್ಗಮ್ ಅಧಿಕಂ, Vikhyâtiyaśa was born to him and the queen, superior to all in the world as to family and firmness of character (*cf.* § 343, 1, *b*). ಕನ್ನಡಕ್ಕಂ ಸಂಸ್ಕೃತಕ್ಕಂ ಸಮಾಸಮಿಲ್ಲ, (generally there) is no composition for (*i. e.* of) Kannaḍa and Saṁskṛita words.

An instance regarding the ablative is:—ಜಾದಿಯತ್ತಣಿನ್ದೆಯುಂ ಕೇದಗೆಯತ್ತಣಿನ್ದೆಯುಂ ಕಮ್ಪು ಬನ್ದುದು, fragrance proceeded from the great-flowered jasmine and the screw-pine.

Instances regarding the locative are:—ಚಲದೊಳಮ್ ಆಚಾರದೊಳಂ ಕಲಿತನದೊಳಂ, in firmness of character, and in good behaviour, and in valour. ಎಲ್ಲಂಗಮ್ ಎಲ್ಲ ಧನಮುಮನ್ ಎಲ್ಲೆಡೆಯೊಳವ್ ಎಲ್ಲ ತೆಱದೊಳಂ ಕುಡುಗೆಮ, O, in every wise may he give (us) all kinds of riches in all places and every manner. To ಅಲ್ಲಿ (also when case-termination in the locative), ಇಲ್ಲಿ, ಎಲ್ಲಿ ಉಂ uses to be suffixed, as ಅಲ್ಲಿಯುಂ, ಇಲ್ಲಿಯುಂ, ಎಲ್ಲಿಯುಂ. The Śabdânuśâsana has ಅವನೊಳುಂ and ಅವನೊಳಂ.

ಉಂ is sometimes omitted in the nominative of the ancient dialect (see §§ 348, 8; 354, II, 4 foot-note; 357, 2, *d*) and in its instrumental or ablative (see the verse quoted in § 352, 4, *a* ಮತ್ತಹಸ್ತಿಗಳ etc.); and (according to Nuḍigaṭṭu, p. 185) likewise ಊ in the locative of the modern dialect, *e.g* ಎಚ್ಚರಿದಲ್ಲಿ ಕನಸಿನಲ್ಲಿ ಗಾಢನಿದ್ರೆಯಲ್ಲಿ ನನ್ನನ್ನು ದೇವರು ಕಾಯುತ್ತಾನೆ, (according to the same), at the end of past participles, *e. g.* ಶುದ್ಧವಾಗಿ ಸ್ಪಷ್ಟವಾಗಿ ಕೇಳಿಸುವನ್ತೆ ಓದು (*cf.* § 286), and in the nominative, when a series of nouns is introduced, which last practice appears also in the other two dialects (see § 354, II, remarks *a. b*).

285. ಅಂ and ಉಂ appear, as stated in § 284, only in the ancient and mediæval dialect.

In addition to them the mediæval dialect uses ಉ and ಊ, *e. g.* ಲಜ್ಜೆಯುಂ ನಾಚಿಕೆಯು ಮೊಳೆವುತಿರೆ, when embarrassment and shame were arising. ಉಣಲುಡಲು ತಮಗಿಲ್ಲ, they have nothing to eat and to put on. ಸಾಲವ ಕೊಡುವವನೂ ಸಾಲವ ಕೊಮ್ಬುವನೂ, a lender of money and a borrower of money. See the close of this paragraph.

In the modern dialect ಊ **alone is generally used.** As the two other dialects it does not suffix it to the genitive; to the other cases it immediately (sometimes with the application of euphonic elision, § 215) adds it, except to the instrumental and ablative in which it puts a euphonic ಲ್ between (*cf.* the close of § 282, and ಎನ್ತಲೂ in § 286). Instances are:— ರಾಮನೂ ಕೃಷ್ಣನೂ ಬರುತ್ತಾರೆ, Râma and Kṛishṇa come. ವಿದ್ಯೆ ಕಲಿಸುವವನೂ ಅನ್ನ ಕೊಡುವವನೂ ಕಷ್ಟದೊಳಗಿನ್ದ ಕಾಯುವವನೂ, he who teaches knowledge, and he who gives food, and he who saves from trouble. ಹೋಗುವದೂ ಬರುವದೂ, going and coming. ಆಡಿನ ಮಱಿಗಳಿಗೆ ಮನಸ್ಸಿಗೆ ಬನ್ದನ್ತೆ ತಿರಿಗಾಡುವದೂ ಹಾಱಾಡುವದೂ ಬೇಕು, to walk and jump about at pleasure is the desire of young goats. ದೊಡ್ಡದೂ ಕಸವುಳ್ಳದೂ, that (is) large and powerful. ಹಗಲೂ ಇರುಳೂ, day and night. ಅನ್ತೂ ಇನ್ತೂ ಕುನ್ತೀ ಮಕ್ಕಳಿಗೆ ರಾಜ್ಯವಿಲ್ಲ, in that way and in this way the children of Kunti do not get a kingdom. ದನಕ್ಕೆ ಹೊಡೆದದೂ ತಿಳಿಯುತ್ತದೆ, ಪ್ರೀತಿ ಮಾಡಿದ್ದೂ ತಿಳಿಯುತ್ತದೆ, cattle know when they are beaten and know when they are treated kindly. ತಾಯಿ ತನ್ದೆಗಳ ಮೇಲೆಯೂ ಬನ್ಧುವಿನ ಮೇಲೆಯೂ ನನ್ನ ಪ್ರೇಮ ಬಹಳ, on (my) parents and relatives my love (is) abundant (*i. e.* I love them abundantly).—ಹೆಱರ ಮೇಲೆ ಪ್ರೀತಿಯನ್ನೂ ಉಪಕಾರವನ್ನೂ ಮಾಡ ಬೇಕು, (we) must show love and kindness to others. ತೋೞಗಳು ಹನ್ದಿಗಳನ್ನೂ ನಾಯಿ ಗಳನ್ನೂ ಒಯ್ಯುವವು, wolves use to carry off pigs and dogs.—ಪ್ರೀತಿಯಿನ್ದಲೂ ಭಕ್ತಿಯಿನ್ದಲೂ ದೇವರನ್ನು ಸೇವಿಸು, serve God with love and devotion. ಹಳ್ಳಿ ಗಳಿನ್ದಲೂ ಊರುಗಳಿನ್ದಲೂ ಜನರು ಬನ್ದರು, (there) came people from villages and towns.—ಹಿನ್ದುಸ್ಥಾನಕ್ಕೂ ಆ ದ್ವೀಪಕ್ಕೂ ನಡುವೆ, between Hindusthân and that island. ನಿಂಗಪ್ಪನಿಗೂ ಅವನ ಮಕ್ಕಳಿಗೂ ಭೋಜನ ಮಾಡಿಸಿದನು, he gave Niṅgappa and his children to eat. ಒಡೆಯನ ಮೋಱೆಯ ಕಡೆಗೂ ಮಾತಿನ ಕಡೆಗೂ ನಾಯಿಗಳ ಲಕ್ಷ್ಯವಿರುತ್ತದೆ, the attention of dogs is (directed) towards the face and towards the words of (their) master. ಮನೆಗಳೊಳಗೆ ಬರಲಿಕ್ಕೂ ಹೊಱಗೆ ಹೋಗಲಿಕ್ಕೂ ಬಾಗಿಲುಗಳನ್ನು ಹಚ್ಚುವರು, doors are put for coming into a house and for going out.—ಎಚ್ಚಱದಲ್ಲಿಯೂ ಗಾಢನಿದ್ರೆಯಲ್ಲಿಯೂ ದೇವರು ನಿನ್ನ ಕಾಯುತ್ತಾನೆ, God preserves thee in waking and deep sleep. ದನ್ತದಲ್ಲೂ (=ದನ್ತದಲ್ಲಿಯೂ) ಓಷ್ಠದಲ್ಲೂ, in the teeth and lips. ಔಷಧಗಳೊಳಗೂ ಪಕ್ವಾನ್ನ ಗಳೊಳಗೂ ಬಹುತರವಾಗಿ ಸಕ್ಕರೆ ಹಾಕುತ್ತಾರೆ, they frequently put sugar into medicines and dishes.

Instances of the conjunction ಉ being exceptionally used also in the modern dialect will be drawn attention to in § 295.

286. ಉಂ and ಊ are in a copulative sense suffixed, also to past participles, the first 'and' disappearing in an English translation, *e. g.* ಮೀನಾಗಿಯುಮ್ ಎಸಡಿಯಾಗಿಯುಮ್ ಏನಾಗಿಯುಂ ತಾನೆಲ್ಲಂ, he is a fish and a crab and all (whatever it may be). ತಱುವಾಯಿಂ ಸನ್ಧಿಯೆನ್ದುಂ ನಾಮಮ್ ಎನ್ದುಂ ಸಮಾಸಮ್ ಎನ್ದುಂ ತದ್ಧಿತಮ್ ಎನ್ದುಮ್ ಆಖ್ಯಾತಮ್ ಎನ್ದುಂ ಧಾತುವೆನ್ದುಮ್ ಅಪಭ್ರಂಶಮ್ ಎನ್ದುಮ್ ಅವ್ಯಯಮ್ ಎನ್ದುಮ್ ಈ ಶಬ್ದಮಣಿದರ್ಪಣದೊಳ್ ಪ್ರಕರಣಮ್ ಎಣ್ಟಕ್ಕುಂ, in successive order there are eight topics in the Šabdamaṇidarpaṇa (*viz.*) sandhi (literally 'and sandhi a having said'), and nâma (lit. 'and nâma a having said'), and samâsa, and taddhita, and âkhyâta, and dhâtu and apabhraṁśa, and avyaya. ಸಂಸ್ಕೃತದ ವ್ಯಂಜನಾನ್ತಲಿಂಗಂಗಳ್ ಅತ್ವಮಂ ಪಡೆದುಂ ದ್ವಿತಂ ಬೆರಸಿದುತ್ವಮಂ ಪಡೆದುಮ್ ಅನ್ತ್ಯಲೋಪಮಂ ಮೇಣ್ ಬಡೆದುಂ ಲಿಂಗಮ್ ಅಕ್ಕುಂ, Saṁskṛita nominal themes ending in consonants become declinable bases (in Kannaḍa) when they receive an ಅ, and when they receive an ಉ

with doubling of the final consonant, and, further, when they receive end-dropping (*i. e.* when their final is dropped). ರಥರ ಕಾವಲವನ್ದಿರ ಹೆಸರು ಸವ್ಯೇಷ್ಠ ಎನ್ದೂ ದಕ್ಷಿಣಸ್ಥ ಎಂದೂ ಉಣ್ಟು, the names of the guards of champions are savyêshṭha and dakshiṇastha. ಅನ್ತುಮ್ ಅಲ್ಲದೆಯೂ, thus and further. ಶುದ್ಧವಾಗಿಯೂ ಸ್ಪಷ್ಟವಾಗಿಯೂ ಕೇಳಿಸುವನ್ತೆ ಓದು, read so that thou canst be heard in a pure manner and in an intelligible manner. ಆ ಕಾಗದ ದಪ್ಪಾಗಿಯೂ ಹುರುಬರಕಾಗಿಯೂ ಇರುತ್ತದೆ, that paper is thick and rough. ನೀನು ಬಹಳ ಚಿಕ್ಕವನಾಗಿಯೂ ತಿಳಿಗೇಡಿಯಾಗಿಯೂ ಇದ್ದೀ, thou art very little and stupid. ಗಾಳಿಯ ಸಲುವಾಗಿಯೂ ಬೆಳಕಿನ ಸಲುವಾಗಿಯೂ ಮನೆಗೆ ಕಿಡಿಕಿಗಳನ್ನು ಹಚ್ಚುವರು, they use to furnish a house with windows on account of air and on account of light. ಈ ಹಡಗುಗಳಲ್ಲಿ ಗಾಳಿಯಿನ್ದ ಸಾಗುವ ಹಡಗು ಎನ್ತಲೂ ಉಗಿಯಿನ್ದ ಸಾಗುವ ಹಡಗು ಎನ್ತಲೂ (in the modern dialect ಊ is suffixed to ಎನ್ತ by means of a euphonic ಲ್, *cf.* the ಲ್ of the instrumental and ablative in § 285 and the ಲ್ in § 362 after *c*; about ಎನ್ತ see § 198, remark 1) ಎರಡು ತರಗಳುಣ್ಟು, of these vessels there are two kinds (*viz.*) vessels that move forwards by wind and vessels that move forwards by steam. ಕೆಲವರು ಆ ಹುಡುಗನನ್ನು ಊರ ಬಿಡಿಸಿ ಹೊರಗೆ ಹಾಕ ಬೇಕೆನ್ತಲೂ ಕೆಲವರು ಅವನನ್ನು ಸೆರೆಯೊಳಗೆ ಇಟ್ಟರೆ ಒಳ್ಳೇದೆನ್ತಲೂ ಹೇಳಿದರು, some said "it is necessary to remove the boy from the village and cast (him) out", and some "it is good, if one puts him into prison". ಹೆಣ್ಣುಬೆಕ್ಕಿಗೆ ಕಾಮಿ ಎನ್ದೂ ಗಣ್ಡಿಗೆ ಬಾವುಗ ಎನ್ದೂ ಅನ್ನುತ್ತಾರೆ, they call a female cat kâmi and a male one bâvuga.

In the ancient dialect this copulative sense holds good also when ಉಂ is **added to the infinitive with final** ಎ (§ 187, 4), *e. g.* ಪ್ರಥಮಾರ್ಥಂ ತೋಱೆಯುಂ ದ್ವಿತೀಯಾರ್ಥಂ ತೋಱೆಯುಮ್ ಅಲ್ಲಿ ಷಷ್ಠಿ ದೊರೆ ಕೊಣ್ಡು ಇರ್ಕುಂ, when the sense of the nominative appears and when the sense of the accusative appears, the genitive may be used there (instead; see § 352, 1 *a.* 1 *b*). ಕ್ರಮಗಣನವ್ ಇರೆಯುಮ್ ಒಲ್ದನ್ತೆ ಇರೆಯುಂ ಯುಗಪದುಕ್ತಿಗೆ ಉತ್ತಮಪುರುಷಂ ಪರಂ, when (in a sentence) they (the three pronouns) are enumerated together in their order (as ಅತಂ, ನೀಂ, ಆಂ) and when they are (enumerated together) ad libitum (as ನೀಂ, ಅತಂ, ಆಂ), the first person follows (them, see § 355, II, 1).

The same meaning obtains also **when ಅಂ is suffixed to the postposition** ಒಡೆ, 'if', this being at the end of a relative participle, *e. g.* ಪೂರ್ವದೀರ್ಘಮ್ ಆದೊಡಮ್ ಅವ್ಯಯಮ್ ಆದೊಡಮ್ ಅನೇಕಾಕ್ಷರಮ್ ಆದೊಡಂ ದ್ವಿತ್ವಮ್ ಇಲ್ಲ, if there is a preceding long (letter), and if the word is an avyaya, and if it is polysyllabic, there is no doubling (of the final consonant). ಪ್ರತಿ

ಷೇಧದರ್ಥದೊಳೆ ಧಾತುವಿಂಗೆ ವಿಭಕ್ತಿ ಪರಮ್ ಆದೊಡಂ ಭೂತಕಾಲಕ್ರಿಯೆಯೊಳ್ ಪ್ರತಿಷೇಧಮನ್ ಉಸಿರ್ವ ಅದೆಯೆಮ್ಬುದು ಪರಮ್ ಆದೊಡಂ ನ ಣ ಲ ಯ ೞಂಗಳಿಗೆ ದ್ವಿತ್ವವೃತ್ತಿ ನಿತ್ಯಂ, if in the very sense of the negative a personal termination follows the verbal theme, and if ಅದೆ which in the past participle expresses negation, follows, (the letters) ನ ಣ ಲ ಯು ೞ are always doubled. A similar way of expression we meet with in the modern dialect when ಊ is suffixed to ಅರೆ (= ಒಡೆ, ಅಡೆ) and this stands at the end of a relative participle, *e. g.* ನಾಯಿಯು ಮನುಷ್ಯನಿಗೆ ನಮ್ಬಿಗೆಯ ಸೇವಕನೆನ್ದರೂ ಜೀವದ ಗೆಳೆಯನೆನ್ದರೂ ಸಲ್ಲುವದು, dogs are well known as faithful servants and as true friends of man.

It may be remarked here that if ಉಂ in the last-mentioned connection occurs but once, it may occasionally be translated 'furthermore', 'and', *e. g.* ದೋಷಮ್ ಇದಱೊಳ್ ಏನಾನುಮ್ ಉಳ್ಳೊಡಂ ಪ್ರಿಯದಿಂ ತಿರ್ದುವುದು, furthermore if (there) is any mistake in this (Śabdamaṇidarpaṇa), correct (it) with friendly disposition. The same takes place sometimes when in the modern dialect ಅರೂ (ಅರೆ+ಊ) is added to a relative participle and occurs but once, the meaning being 'and', 'also', *e. g.* ಬೇಡುವದೇ ಕಷ್ಟ, ಬೇಡಿದರೂ ಇಲ್ಲವೆನ್ನುವದು ಅತಿಕಷ್ಟ, begging (is) affliction indeed; and if (somebody) begs, to say "no (I do or can not give you anything" is) an excessive affliction. ನನಗಾದರೂ ಅದೇ ಬೇಕು, also I want the very same thing. ಅರಳೆ ಹಾಲು ಇವಾದರೂ ಬಿಳೇ ಬಣ್ಣದವು, cotton (and) milk also these (are) of a white colour. ಈ ನಾಡೊಳಗಾದರೂ ಬಲ್ಲನ್ಥ ತೋಟಿಗರು ಮರದ ಬುಡಕ್ಕೆ ಮಣ್ಣು ಏಱಿಸಿ ಮಸಾಲೇ ಹಾಕುತ್ತಾರೆ, also in this district intelligent gardeners lift up the soil at the bottom of mango trees and put seasoning drugs. ಕುದುರೆಗಳನ್ತೆ ಕತ್ತೆಗಳಾದರೂ ತುಸು ನಿದ್ರೆ ಮಾಡುತ್ತವೆ, like horses also donkeys sleep (but) little. (About the general meaning of ಒಡಂ and ಅರೂ in the mentioned combination see § 287, 5, *b*; *cf.* also § 287, 6. 7. 8).

Also when in such a case ಉಂ is suffixed to ಒಡೆ by the insertion of ಅಲ್ (ಅಲ್+ಒಡಂ) to the verbal theme, the meaning of 'and' seems to remain in force, *e. g.* ಪಾವಸೆ ಕಿಡಲೊಡಂ ನೀರ್ ತಿಳಿವುದು (o. r. ತಿಳಿದುದು), and if the duck-weed is destroyed (lit. and if the duck-weed a being destroyed), the water becomes clear, though Kêšava says that ಅಲೊಡಂ is a substitute of the ಎ of satisaptami and means 'when' (§§ 187, 4; 188; see § 365).

The conjunction ಉದುಂ which Kêšava adduces as a suffix with the meaning of the above ಅಲೊಡಂ, 'at the time that', is in fact the personal termination of the present-future in the neuter singular and ಉಂ, 'and'.

This third person neuter singular, as we have seen in § 200, 1, is used as a krillinga or bhâvavaĉana. Kêŝava's instances are the following (see § 365):—ಬರವೇೞ್ ಎಮ್ಬುದುಮ್ ಅಂಜನಾಚಲದ ವೊಲ್ ಕಣ್ಗೊಪ್ಪಿ ಬರ್ಪಮ್ಬುಜೋದರನಂ, and a saying (*i. e.* and when he said) "tell Vishnu to come (him) who appears and is coming (there) like the Añjanâĉala!" ಓಲಗಂ ಪರೆವುದುಮ್ ಆಲೋಚನಕ್ಕೆ ಪೊಕ್ಕಂ, and the assembly a dispersing (*i. e.* and when the assembly dispersed), he began to consider. ನಿನ್ನಿನಿಯನ ಪೞ್ಕೆಯೊಳ್ ಇರು! ಎನ್ದು ಸಖಿ ತೊಲಗುವುದುಂ, and the female companion a going away (*i. e.* and when the female companion went away) having said "remain near thy sweatheart". Similar instances are frequently met with in ancient narration.

287. If ಅಂ, ಉಂ, ಉ and ಊ do not join two or more words, they have the following meanings:—

1, **'also', 'likewise', 'too', 'and'**, *e. g.* ಅವರುಮನ್ ಅನ್ತಕನ್ ಒರ್ಮೆಯೆ ಸವಿ ನೋಡಲ್, when Yama all at once tasted also them. ಸ್ತ್ರೀಲಿಂಗದೊಳಂ ಪುಲ್ಲಿಂಗದಹಗೆ ಸಪ್ತವಿಭಕ್ತಿಗಳೆಲ್ಲಂ ಪತ್ತುಗುಂ, all the seven case-terminations are joined also in the feminine gender in the same manner as in the masculine gender. ಗಣ್ಡಾದ ನಪುಂಸಕಲಿಂಗದಲ್ಲಿಯುಂ ಸಪ್ತವಿಭಕ್ತಿಗಳೆಲ್ಲಂ ಪುದಿಗುಂ, also in (originally) neuter terms when they are used as masculines, all the seven case-terminations join (in the same manner as in the masculine gender). ರೇಖೆ ರಾಜಿ ಎನ್ದೊಡೆ ವೃಕ್ಷಾದಿಗಳ ಸಾಲಿನ ಮಧ್ಯವೆನ್ದೂ ಎಮ್ಬರು, rêkhĕ and râji denote likewise the middle of a row of trees and other things. ಅವನೂ ಬನ್ದನು, also he came. ಅದೂ ನನಗೆ ಬೇಕು, I want that too. ನೀನೂ ಹೋಗ ತಕ್ಕವನೋ, are you also fit to go? ತನ್ದೆ ತಾಯಿಗಳ ಮಾತು ಮೀಱಿ ಬಾರದೆನ್ತಲೂ ಅದಱಲ್ಲಿ ಬರೆದದೆ, it is also written therein (in the book) "one must not transgress the words of one's parents". ಗುರುಗಳೂ ಪಾಪಕ್ಕಂಜದಿದ್ದರೆ ಶಿಷ್ಯರು ಹ್ಯಾಗೆ ಅಂಜುವರು, if religious teachers too do not fear sin, how shall (their) disciples fear it? ಎರಡನೆಯವರು ನಮಗೆ ಸೇರದಿದ್ದರೆ ನಾವೂ ಎರಡನೆಯವರಿಗೆ ಸೇರುವದಿಲ್ಲ, if others are not agreeable to us, we too are not agreeable to others. ಎಲ್ಲರೂ ನಕ್ಕರೆ ಹುಚ್ಚ ತಾನೂ ನಕ್ಕ, when all without exception laughed, the fool too laughed. ಜಾತಿಯಲ್ಲದಲ್ಲಿಯುಂ, also where (there) are no collective nouns. ಪ್ರತಿಷೇಧಮಲ್ಲದಲ್ಲಿಯುಂ, also where (there) is no negative sense. ಅನ್ತುಂ, and thus. ಇನ್ತುಮ್ ಅಲ್ಲದೆ, in this manner and further. ಅನ್ತಲ್ಲದೆಯುಂ, thus and further. ಮತ್ತೂ, and besides, *e. g.* ಮತ್ತೂ ಯಾರ ಯಾರ ಅಪ್ಪಣೆ ಪಾಲಿಸ ಬೇಕು, and besides whose commands have (we) to obey? ಮತ್ತೂ, also other, *e. g.* ಯಾವದಾದರೊನ್ದು ಪದಾರ್ಥವು ಒನ್ದು ಇಱಿವಿಗೆ ಬಾರದ

ಹಾಗೆ ಇದ್ದರೆ ಮತ್ತೂ ಕೆಲವು ಇಱುವೆಗಳು ಕೂಡಿ ಅದನ್ನು ಎೞೆ ಕೊಣ್ಡು, if anything becomes too much for one ant, also some other ants join, drag it, etc. ಮತ್ತೂ, and still, *e. g.* ಎತ್ತೂ ಮಾಱಿ, ಮತ್ತೂ ಗಂಜಿ, he sold even (his) oxen, and still (there was only) rice gruel. ಹಾಗೂ, and likewise. ಇನ್ನುಂ, also up to the present time, *e. g.* ಅವರೊಳ್ ಇನ್ನುಂ ಕಾದುತ್ತಿರ್ಪ್ಪಂ, he is fighting with them also up to the present time. ಅವರು ಇನ್ನೂ ಬರಲಿಲ್ಲ, they did not come also up to the present time. ನಾನು ಅವನಿಗೆ ಎರಡು ಪತ್ರಗಳನ್ನು ಕಳುಹಿಸಿದೆನು, ಆದರೆ ಇನ್ನೂ ನನಗೆ ಉತ್ತರವೇ ಬರಲಿಲ್ಲ, I sent him two letters, but up to the present time indeed no answer was received by me. ಇನ್ನೂ, and yet, *e. g.* ಇನ್ನೂ ನೆಟ್ಟಗೆ ಆಗಿದ್ದಿಲ್ಲ, (they had made various endeavours), and yet he had not become better. Occasionally the meaning of 'and' disappears, and ಇನ್ನೂ may be translated 'still', *e. g.* ಅವನು ಹೇೞಿದ್ದಕ್ಕಿನ್ತ ಅವನಿಗೆ ಇನ್ನೂ ಹೆಚ್ಚಿಗೆ ಗೊತ್ತಿತ್ತು, he knew still more than what he said. ಅವನು ಬರಲಿಕ್ಕೆ ಇನ್ನೂ ಗೞಿಗೆ ಎರಡು ಗೞಿಗೆ ಅವಕಾಶವದೆ, there is still (one) gaḻigĕ, or two gaḻigĕs, of time till he comes. ನೀನು ಇನ್ನೂ ಸಂಸಾರವೆಮ್ಬ ಮಹಾಸಾಗರದೊಳಗಿನ್ದ ದಾಟಿ ಹೋಗ ತಕ್ಕವನು, thou hast still to get over the ocean of mundane affairs. ಯಾವತ್ತು ಪ್ರಮಾಣಗಳು ಇಷ್ಟೇನೋ? ಅಲ್ಲ, ಇನ್ನೂ ಕೆಲವು ಉಣ್ಟು, are these all the arguments? No, there are still some (or some more).

2, **'even', 'indeed'**, *e. g.* ಮೊದಲೆರಡು ವಿಭಕ್ತಿಯೊಳಂ ಪೊದಱ್ಗುಮ್ ಅಲ್, even in the two first cases ಅಲ್ is used (ಮೂಡಲ್, etc.). ಈ ಎರಡು ಸಮಾಸ ಪದಕ್ಕಮ್ ವಿಕಲ್ಪಮ್ ಇಲ್ಲ, even regarding these two compound words (*i. e.* ಪಾಣೆಯುಬಾರಂ and ಕಣ್ಬೆಯುಬಾರಂ, there) is no option (allowed). ಸಂಸ್ಕೃತ ಕರ್ಣಾಟಕಮ್ ಎರಡಱೊಳಂ ಸ್ವರಮ್ ಇದಿರೊಳ್ ಇರೆ ವಿಭಕ್ತಿಸ್ವರಕ್ಕಂ ಪ್ರಕೃತಿಸ್ವರಕ್ಕಂ ಲೋಪಮ್ ಅಕ್ಕುಂ, when even in both, Saṁskṛita and Karṇâṭaka, a vowel follows, elision takes place regarding the vowels of the case-terminations and regarding the vowels of uninflected words. ಈ ಪೇೞ್ದೆಣ್ಟುಮ್ ಅಕ್ಕರಮ್ ಉದಯಿಪ ತಾಣಮ್ ಆದುವು, (the throat, the palate, etc., § 33) even these mentioned eight are the places where the letters originate. ಒಮ್ಬತ್ತುಮ್ ಅವರ್ಗಂ, even nine (letters are) not classified. ಅದು ನಾಲ್ಕುಂ ಭೇದವನ್ ಆಳ್ಕುರ್ಗಂ, it (the karma or objective noun) is (first) even of four kinds (see § 346). ತೋಳ್ ನಾಲ್ಕುಂ ಕರಮ್ ಎಸೆದಿರ್ಕುಂ ಪದೋದರಂಗೆ, even four arms appear nicely on Vishṇu. ಅಮ್ ಉಮ್ ಎಮ್ಬಿವೆರಡುಮ್ ಅಮರ್ಗುಂ ಸಮುಚ್ಚಯಾರ್ಥದೊಳ್, ಅಂ ಉಂ, even these two are used in the sense of conjunction. ಪಾದ ದೇವ ಭಟ್ಟಾರಕ ಈ ಮೂಱುಂ ಪೆಸರ ಕಡೆಯೊಳು ಪೂಜಾವಚನಂ, pâda, dêva, bhaṭṭâraka, even these three, are titles of respect at the end of names. ಅರಸೂೞಿಗವುಂ (=ಅರಸೂೞಿಗಮುಂ, mediæval) ಭಕ್ತಿಯುಮ್ ಇನ್ತೆರಡುಮಂ ಕೂಡಿ ನಡೆಸುವುದೆನ್ತಹುದು, how is it possible to perform together a king's service and devotion (to a deity), thus even two? ಎರಡುಮನ್ ಈಸಿಕೊಣ್ಡು, having taken even the two (cadjan leaves). ಪರವನಿತೆಯರನ್ ಒಮ್ಮೆಯು (=ಒಮ್ಮೆಯುಂ, mediæval) ನೀ ನೋಡದಿರು, do not even once look on the wife of another. ಕುತರ್ಕದಿಂ ಮಚ್ಚರಿಪ ಪರವಾದಿಗಳನ್ ಒಮ್ಮೆಯು ಸೋಲಿಸುವ ಭಾಷೆ, the oath of even at once defeating controversialists who show (their) enmity by sophistry. ಎತ್ತೂ ಮಾಱಿ, ಮತ್ತೂ ಗಂಜಿ, he sold even (his) oxen, and still (there was only) rice gruel. ಚತುರ್ವರ್ಗವೆನ್ದು ಮೋಕ್ಷದೊಡಗೂಡಿದ ಧರ್ಮ ಕಾಮ ಅರ್ಥಗಳು ನಾಲ್ಕಕ್ಕೂ ಒನ್ದೇ ಹೆಸರು, čaturvarga is the one name for môksha, dharma, kâma and artha, even (these) four. ಬಲನಾರಾಯಣರಿರ್ವರುಂ, Bala (and) Nârâyaṇa, even both. ಪೋಲಿಸುವೊಡಿರ್ವರುಂ ತಕ್ಕರ್, if (one) compares (them), even both (are) good men. ಅವರಿಬ್ಬರೂ, even both of them. ಅವರಿಬ್ಬರಿಗೂ, even to both of them. ನಾವಿಬ್ಬರೂ, even both of us. ನೀವಿಬ್ಬರೂ, even both of you. ಒಮ್ಮೊಮ್ಮೆ ಮನುಷ್ಯರೂ ತೋಳಗಳ ಕೈಯ್ಯೊಳಗೆ ಸಿಗುವದುಣ್ಟು, sometimes it happens that even men get into the power of wolves. ಕಡೆಗೂ, to the very end. ಕೊಣ್ಡಾಡಿ ಬೇಡಿದರೆ ಕೊಡರೊನ್ದು ರುವ್ವಿಯನ್ನು, if (one) praises and solicits (them), they do not give even one ruvvi. ದೇವರು ತಿಳಿಯದ್ದು ಒನ್ದೂ ಇಲ್ಲ, (there) is not even one thing that God does not know. ನಾನು ಮನೆಯೊಳಗೆ ಹೊಕ್ಕೆನು, ಆದರೆ ಅಲ್ಲಿ ಒಬ್ಬರೂ ಇದ್ದಿಲ್ಲ, I entered the house, but (there) was not even one person inside. ನಮ್ಮಿಬ್ಬರಲ್ಲಿ ಒಬ್ಬನೂ ಮಾತಾಡಲಿಲ್ಲ, not even one of us two spoke.

3, the meaning of a peculiar emphasis, namely emphasis to express that the whole of a definite number of things which either naturally belong together or are considered to belong together, is understood, *e. g.* ಹಸ್ತಂಗಳೆರಡುಂ, both arms, the two arms (that a person has; if we say ಹಸ್ತಂಗಳೆರಡು, it means 'two arms', 'two of the arms', for instance of Čaturbhuja or Vishṇu who is considered to have four arms). ಎರಡುಂ ಕಣ್ಗಳ್, both eyes, the two eyes (that a man or animal has; if we say ಎರಡು ಕಣ್ಗಳ್, it means 'two eyes', for instance of Čaturânana or Brahmâ who is considered to have eight eyes). ಅಡಿಗಳೆರಡುಮಂ ಕಡಿ ಕಡಿದು, having cut off the two feet (he had). ಹತ್ತನೆಯ ತಲೆಯುಮಂ ನೇದಾರ್ಗಳ್, when (he) cut off the tenth head (of Dašašira or Râvaṇa, who is considered to have had ten heads). ಇವಱುದಾಹರಣೆಗಳಂ ಸೊಲ್ಲಿಸುವೆನ್ ಎರಡು ಮೆಯ್ಗಂ, I shall utter instances of them (of tadbhavas and their compounds) with regard to the two forms (Saṁskṛita and Kannaḍa). ಮೂಱು ವೇದಂಗಳುಂ, the three vêdas (omitting the atharva vêda). ಮೂಱುಂ ಲೋಕಂಗಳ್, the three worlds (heaven, earth and the lower region). ಆಱುಂ ಋತುಗಳ್, the six seasons (which Hindus accept). ಎಣ್ಟು ದೆಸೆಗಳ್ ಒಡೆಯರು, the guardians for the eight cardinal points of the compass. ಎರಡು ಕೆಯ್ (for ಎರಡೂ ಕೆಯ್, mediæval), the two hands (he had). ಆ ಟೊಂಗಿಯನ್ನು ಎರಡೂ ಕೆಯ್ಲಿ ಗಟ್ಟಿಯಾಗಿ ಹಿಡು ಕೊಣ್ಡು, having firmly seized the branch with both (his) hands. ಎರಡೂ ಎತ್ತು ತಾ, bring the two oxen (which are in the shed, etc.; ಎರಡು ಎತ್ತುಗಳನ್ನು ತಾ would mean 'bring two oxen'). ನಾಲ್ಕೂ ಕಡೆ, the four directions (north, south, east, west) or the four sides (of a thing). ನಾಲ್ಕು ಕಡೆಗೂ, to or on the four sides (of a country, etc.).

4, **'together', 'without exception', 'in concert'**, *e.g.* ಎನಿತುಮ್ ಅನಿತುಮಂ ಧರ್ಮಜಂ ಸೂಱೆಗೊಟ್ಟಂ, how much soever, Dharmaja gave (it) altogether away (*cf.* § 321). ಕೊಪ್ಪರಿಗೆಗಳನ್ ಅನಿತುಮಂ ತರ ಹೇೞು, tell to bring all the boilers without exception. ಸಂಸ್ಕೃತದ ಭಾವವಚನಂಗಳನ್ ಆಯ್ದನಿತರ್ಕಮ್ ಇಸು ಪ್ರತ್ಯಯಮನೆ ಪತ್ತಿಸಿ, having chosen Saṁskṛita abstract verbal nouns (*e. g.* ಭಾವ, ಭಂಗ, ಭಾಗ) and having added even the suffix ಇಸು to all (of them) without exception. ಗೌಳ ತಪಸಿಗಳು ಅನಿತು (for ಅನಿತುಂ, mediæval) ಗುಗ್ಗುಳವಂ ಮಡಗಲೊಡನೆ, when the Gauḷa religious mendicants put away all the frankincense without exception. ಅನಿಬರುಮ್ ಒನ್ದಾಗಿ ತಾಗುವಂ ಫಲ್ಗುನನೊಳ್, let us altogether in union attack Phalguna! ನೀವನಿಬರುಂ ಹೇೞುವುದು, all of you without exception tell! ನೆರೆದರಸುಗಳನಿಬರುಮಂ ಕಾದಿ ಗೆಲ್ದನ್ ಒರ್ಬನೆ ಪಾರ್ಥಂ, Arjuna overcame alone all the gathered kings w. e. in fight. ಆರ್ದಂ ಸಾರ್ದಂ ಪೋರ್ದಂ . . . ಎನ್ದೊಡಂ ತಾವಿನಿತುಂ ಗುರೂಪಧೆ, furthermore ಆರ್ದಂ ಸಾರ್ದಂ ಪೋರ್ದಂ . . . all these w. e. have a long penultimate. ಇನಿಬರುಂ ನೀವು, all you here w. e. ಅಷ್ಟರ್ಕೆಯುಂ, to all (of the abstract verbal nouns) without exception. ಜೇನುತುಪ್ಪ ಅಷ್ಟೂ ಸವಿ ಅದೆ, all honey w. e. is sweet. ಅದು ಅಷ್ಟೂ ಬೇಕು, all that w. e. is wanted. ಅಷ್ಟರೂ ಬನ್ದರು, they came all w. e. ಅರಣ್ಯಮ್ ಎಲ್ಲಮುಂ ನೆಲಸರಿಯಪ್ಪಿನಂ, till the whole forest together became level with the ground. ತುಪ್ಪ ಮೊಸರು ಮೊದಲಾದವೆಲ್ಲವೂ, ghee, curds, and all the other things (made of milk) w. e. ಎಲ್ಲಾ ಸೇನೆಯುಂ ತೆರಳುವುದು, a moving forward of the whole army together. ಎಲ್ಲರುಂ ಪೋದರ್, all of them w. e. went. ಎಲ್ಲರುಮ್ ಆ ಕರ್ಣನನ್ನಿರೇಂ ಚಾಗಿಗಳ್, are all w. e. liberal persons like that Karṇa? ಎಲ್ಲರೂ ಪಾಲಕೀಲಿ ಕೂತರೆ ಹೊಱೋರು ಯಾರು, if all w. e. sit in a palanquin, who will be the bearers? ನೀವೆಲ್ಲರೂ, all of you w. e. ಪಾಪಕ್ಕೆ ಅಂಜದವರು ಎಲ್ಲರಿಗೂ ಅಂಜುತ್ತಾರೆ, who are not afraid of sin (*i. e.* to commit sin) are afraid of all persons w. e. ಅರೋ

ಗ್ಯವೇ ಎಲ್ಲಕ್ಕೂ ಹೆಚ್ಚಿನ ಸೌಖ್ಯವು, health indeed (is) happiness that exceeds all w. e. ಎಲ್ಲ ಕಡೆಗಳಲ್ಲಿಯೂ, on all sides w. e.

5, **'though', 'although'** (§ 314), when they are suffixed

a, to past participles, *e.g.* ಅಪತ್ಯಕಲತ್ರಶಬ್ದಂಗಳ್ ಸ್ತ್ರೀವಾಚಕಮ್ ಆಗಿಯುಂ ಜನಶಬ್ದಲೋಕಶಬ್ದಂಗಳ್ ಪುರುಷವಾಚಕಂಗಳಾಗಿಯುಂ ನಪುಂಸಕಂ, though the terms ಅಪತ್ಯ, ಕಲತ್ರ are feminine nouns (and) the terms ಜನ, ಲೋಕ are masculine nouns, (they are used as) neuters. ಪಳಿಕಂ ಪೇಳಿಗೆ . . . ಟಕಾರಕ್ಕೆ ಪುಟ್ಟಿಯುಂ ಕುಳಂಗಳ್ ಅದುವು, though ಪಳಿಕಂ, ಪೇಳಿಗೆ . . . have arisen of the letter ಟ, they are terms with the ಕುಳ (§§ 15, 229). ಕಾದಲರ್ಗಳೆಮ್ಬ ಪದನಾದಿ ದೀರ್ಘಮ್ ಆಗಿಯುಂ ಶಿಥಿಲಮ್ ಆಯಿತು, though the initial of the term ಕಾದಲರ್ಗಳ್ is long, 'slackness' occurs (§ 240, 1). ಎನಿತುಂ ಕಾಯ್ದುಂ ಬೆನ್ನೀರ್ ಮನೆ ಸುಡದು, though hot water gets however so hot, a house does not take fire (on account of it). ನೃಪಂ ಬೆಮ್ಬಿಟ್ಟುಂ ದೂದಟ್ಟಿಯುಂ ಬಾರಂ, although the king followed and the female messenger pursued, he did not come. ಕಚ್ಚುವನ್ ಅಱಿಸಿಯು (=ಅಱಿಸಿಯುಂ, mediæval) ಕಾಣದೆ, not seeing the tuck, though he sought (it). ಶರೀರದಲ್ಲಿ ಆರೋಗ್ಯವಿಲ್ಲದಿದ್ದರೆ ಇತರ ಸೌಖ್ಯಗಳು ಇದ್ದೂ ಇಲ್ಲದ ಹಾಗೆ ಸರಿ, if (there) is no health in the body, though (there) are other comforts, it is in fact so as if they did not exist.

b, to relative past participles in connection with ಒಡೆ, ಅಡೆ and ಅರೆ, *e.g.* ಅನ್ತೆ ವೋಲ್ ಎಮ್ಬೆರಡುಮನ್ ಒನ್ದು ಮಾಡಿ ಪೇೞ್ದೊಡಂ ಪುನರುಕ್ತದೋಷಮ್ ಇಲ್ಲ, though the very two (words) ಅನ್ತೆ (and) ವೋಲ್ are uttered together, (there) is not the fault of tautology. ಮಧುವನ್ ಎಱಿದೆಱಿದೊಡಂ ಬೇವಿನೊಳ ನಾರು ಕಡೆಗೆ ತಾನ್ ಇನಿದಹುದೆ, though (one) repeatedly drops (or drop) honey (thereon), could the fibres in the neem become sweet at last? ಧನವನಿತ್ತಾದೊಡೆಯು (=ಇತ್ತಾದೊಡೆಯೂ, mediæval) ಸಹಭೋಜನವನುಣ್ಡಾದೊಡೆಯು, though (he) gives (or gave) riches and eats (or ate) together (with you). ಕರಗಸದ ನಡು ಬಡವಾದರೆಯು (=ಆದರೆಯೂ, mediæval) ಕೊಯ್ದಿಕ್ಕದೇ ತರುವ, though the middle of a saw is weak, does it not cut a tree? ಕಾಗೆ ಕೋಗಿಲೆಯ ಹಾಗಿದ್ದರೂ ರಾಗದಲ್ಲಿ ಭೇದವಿಲ್ಲವೇ, though the crow is like the cuckoo, is there no difference in (their) sound? ನಮ್ಮನ್ನು ಮನುಷ್ಯರು ನೋಡದಿದ್ದರೂ ದೇವರು ನಮ್ಮನ್ನು ಯಾವಾಗಲೂ ನೋಡುತ್ತಿರುತ್ತಾನೆ, though men do not see us, God sees us always. ವೇದಾ ತಿಳಿದವನಾದರೂ ವೇದನೆ ಬಿಟ್ಟೇತೇ, though he knows the vêdas, does pain leave him? ಹಾಱುವನ ಮೋಱೆಯಾದರೂ ನೀರಿನಿನ್ದ ತೊಳೆಯದಿದ್ದರೆ ನಾಱದೇ ಇದ್ದೀತೇ, though it is (or be) a Brâhmaṇa's face, does it not stink, if it is not washed with water. ನೀರಾದರೂ ಮಜ್ಜಿಗೆ, ಮರು

ಳಾದರೂ ತಾಯಿ, though diluted, (it is) buttermilk, though stupid, (it is) the mother. ಹೆಣ ಸುಟ್ಟರೂ ರುಣ ಸುಡಲಿಲ್ಲ, though the corpse is burned, debts are not burned.

Regarding the meaning of 'furthermore', 'and', 'also' which ಅಂ, ಉಂ, ಊ may have in the same combination, see § 286.

6, **'at least', 'at any rate'** in combination with ಒಡೆ, ಅಡೆ and ಅರೆ added to a relative past participle, *e. g.* ಒನ್ದು ತೆಱಿನ ಮಗನಾದೊಡಂ ಬೇಕು, (of the ten kinds of sons) at least a son of one kind is required. ನಮಗಾದರೆಯು (= ಆದರೆಯೂ, mediæval) ಕಣ್ಡುದ ನುಡಿಯು ಬೇಕು, at least us (you) must tell what you have seen (*i. e.* the truth). ಇನ್ನಾದಡೆಯು (= ಇನ್ನಾದಡೆಯೂ, mediæval) ಬಿಡು ಚಲವ, hence at any rate give up (your) obstinacy. ಅ ಆ ಬಾರದಿದ್ದರೆ ಅಮರವಾದರೂ ಹೇೞೆಮ್ಬನ್ತೆ, it is as if (somebody) said to one who does not know a â (the first letters of the alphabet), "repeat at least the Amarakôsa" (as you certainly know still more). ನೀನಾದರೂ ಕೃಪೆಯನಿಡು ಬೇಗ, ಹರಿಯೇ, thou at least be merciful quickly, O Hari!

7, **'even', 'so much as', 'as was not to be expected'** in connection with ಒಡೆ, ಅಡೆ, ಅರೆ suffixed to a relative past participle, *e. g.* ಬಸವನೆನ್ದುಸುರಿದಡೆ ಸಾಲದೆ? ಪಸುವಿಗಾದಡು (= ಆದಡೂ, mediæval) ಭಕ್ತಿ ದೊರಕುಗು, is it not enough if one utters "Basava"? even a beast will (thereby) obtain devotion. ಭಾವಿಯೆನಿಸಿರ್ದುದು ಪರಿಭಾವಿಸಿ ಕಳೆಯಲ್ಕೆ ಸಾಧ್ಯಮ್ ಆಗದು ಜಗದೊಳ್ ದೇವಂಗಾದೊಡಂ, it is impossible in the world to remove by scorn what is called predestination, even for a king (or a god). ಉದ್ಭಿಜ್ಜಗಳ ಹಾಗೆ ಅವಾದರೂ ಹಲವು ರೀತಿಯಿನ್ದ ಪ್ರಾಣಿಗಳ ಉಪಯೋಗಕ್ಕೆ ಬೀಳುತ್ತವೆ, like plants even they (stones, earth, water, etc.) are useful in various ways to living beings. ಆಗಾದರೂ ಈಗಿನನ್ತೆಯೇ ನಾವಿನೊಳಗೆ ಕೂತು ಕೊಣ್ಡು ಹೊೞೆಯನ್ನು ದಾಟ ಬೇಕಾಗುತ್ತಿತ್ತು, even at that time, just as nowadays, it was necessary to cross the river in a boat. ಅವನು ನನಗೆ ಒನ್ದು ಕಾಸಾದರೂ ಕೊಡಲಿಲ್ಲ, he did not give me even one farthing (see remark under No. 8).

8, **'whether—or'** in combination with ಒಡೆ, ಅಡೆ, ಅರೆ suffixed to a relative past participle, *e. g.* ಆ ಪತ್ತಕ್ಕರಂಗಳೊಳ್ ಎರಡೆರಡಕ್ಕರಂ ತಮ್ಮೊಳ್ ಅನುಲೋಮದೊಳ್ ಇರ್ದೊಡಂ ವಿಲೋಮದೊಳ್ ಇರ್ದೊಡಂ ಸವರ್ಣಸಂಜ್ಞೆಯಂ ಪಡೆಗುಂ, those ten letters (ಅ ಆ ಇ ಈ ಉ ಊ ಋ ೠ ಌ ೡ), whether they two by two among themselves are in regular order or out of the usual order, bear the sign of the same class (§ 21). ಅಣ್ಣಪ್ಪ ಊರಿನಲ್ಲಿ ಇದ್ದರೂ ಸರಿ, ದಣ್ಡಿನಲ್ಲಿ ಇದ್ದರೂ ಸರಿ, (it is) the same whether a useless man is in a town or in an army. ಕಬ್ಬು ಕೊನೆಯಿನ್ದ ಮೆದ್ದರೂ ಬುಡದಿನ್ದ ಮೆದ್ದರೂ ಸವಿ ಒನ್ದೇ, whether (one) eats sugar-cane from the top or eats (it) from the bottom, (its) sweetness is the very same. ಮಾಡುವದಾದರೂ ಸರಿಯೇ, ಬಿಡುವದಾದರೂ ಸರಿಯೇ, (it will) be right whether you do it or let it alone (Hodson). *Cf.* § 319.

Remark.

It seems to be a grammatical anomaly, if ಆದೊಡಂ, ಆವಡಂ, ಆದಡೆಯುಂ, ಆವಡು, ಆದರೂ, literally 'a having become or a being if and', are combined with the accusative; but there are sentences like the following:— ಕುಡುವುದು ಕೂರ್ಮೆಯಲ್ಲಿ ಕಲೆಯಿಲ್ಲದೆ ಮನ್ನಿಪ ಪೆಣ್ಗೇನನ್ ಆದೊಡಂ, (one) has to give whatsover to a woman whom (one) respects deceitlessly (Śabdamaṇidarpaṇa Mḍb. Ms.). ಹಾಗವನ್ ಆವಡಂ ಕಳದು ಕೊಳ್ಳದೆ, (he) taking not even a hâga (from the devotees; in a śâsana of about A. D. 1200). ಏನನಾದಡೆಯು (= ಏನನಾದಡೆಯೂ) ಮುನ್ತೆ ಕೊಡುವೆವು, ಬೇಡು, hereafter we shall give (thee) whatsoever; pray! (Basavapurâṇa). ಎನ್ನನ್ ಅಲ್ಲದೆ ಸತತಂ, ಬಱಿಕೆನ್ನ ಪದವಿಯನ್ ಆದೊಡಾತಂ ತನ್ನ ಮನದೊಳು ನೆನೆವುದಿಲ್ಲ, except always upon me, he does not think even upon (my) high rank (Bp.). ನಾನು ಪುಣೆಯನ್ನಾದರೂ ಸುಟ್ಟು ಬಿಡ ಬೇಕು, I must burn up even Poona (South-Mahratta schoolbook). ನಾನು ವೇದವನ್ನಾದರೂ ಪುರಾಣವನ್ನಾದರೂ ಓದಲಿಲ್ಲ, I have not read either Vêda or Purâṇa (Hodson's Grammar; about either—or see § 292. 317). (A similar seeming anomaly is found in the use of ಅಲ್ಲ, § 300, 1, remark *b,* in that of ಆಗಲಿ, § 317, and in that of ಅಲ್ಲದೆ, § 338 under ಅಲ್ಲದೆ).

In No. 7 of the present paragraph there is, however, the instance ಅವನು ನನಗೆ ಒನ್ದು ಕಾಸಾದರೂ ಕೊಡಲಿಲ್ಲ, he did not give me even one farthing, and a similar instance is:— ಒನ್ದು ವೇಳೆ ಏನಾದರೂ ತಿನ್ನುವ ಅಪೇಕ್ಷೆಯಾದರೂ ದೇವರು ನನಗೆ ಅಡವಿಯ ಮೂಲಿಕೆಗಳನ್ನೂ ಫಲಗಳನ್ನೂ ಎಲೆಗಳನ್ನೂ ಸಮೃದ್ಧಿಯಾಗಿ ಕೊಟ್ಟಿದ್ದಾನೆ, though at times the desire arises to eat whatsoever, God has abundantly given me roots and fruits and leaves of the jungle. The first instance no doubt requires the accusative, which may be ಕಾಸು or ಕಾಸ (see § 122, *c*); the second instance one might translate 'though at times the desire arises to eat — whatsoever it may —, God etc., the 'whatsoever it may be' being not governed by 'to eat', but being an insertion standing by itself. But ಏನಾದರೂ may be, and most probably is, ಏನು or ಏನ (accusative, see § 125, *c*) + ಆದರೂ.

One is, therefore, constrained to think that when ಆದೊಡಂ, etc. are preceded by an accusative, they have lost their original meaning and become mere adverbs.

288. When in the modern dialect ಆಗ್ಯೆ, then, receives the suffix ಊ and is added to a relative past participle, it gets the meaning of 'though', 'although', *e. g.* ಒಬ್ಬೊಬ್ಬರು ತಮ್ಮ ಮೊಣಕಾಲು ಹಚ್ಚಿ ಕಸುವಿನಿನ್ದ ಯತ್ನ ಮಾಡಿದಾಗ್ಯೂ ಆ ಹೊಱೆ ಮುಱಿಯಲಿಲ್ಲ, though they one by one put their knee to (the bundle of sticks) and with (all their) strength made effort, that bundle did not break. ಹಾವಿನ ಹೆಡೆಯಲ್ಲಿ ರತ್ನವಿದ್ದಾಗ್ಯೂ ಸಮೀಪಕ್ಕೆ ಯಾರೂ

ಹೋಗರು, though there be a pearl in the hood of the cobra, nobody goes near. ನಾಮವಿದ್ದಾಗ್ಯೂ ನಮ್ಬಿಗೆಯಿರ ಬೇಕು, though the sectarian (Vaishṇava) mark be (put to the forehead), faithfulness is necessary (*i. e.* is not to be put away by the bearer). *Cf.* § 314.

289. If **ಆದಾಗ್ಯೂ and ಆದರೂ** are used by themselves **at the beginning of a sentence, they mean 'however', 'but', 'notwithstanding', 'yet',** *e. g.* ಆಕಳ ಹಯ್ನು ತುಸು, ಆದಾಗ್ಯೂ ಬಹು ಆರೋಗ್ಯವು, the milk of cows is little, but very wholesome. ಮನುಷ್ಯನು ತರತರದ ಪದಾರ್ಥಗಳನ್ನೂ ಚಿತ್ರಗಳನ್ನೂ ಮಾಡ ಬಲ್ಲನು, ಆದರೂ ಅವುಗಳಿಗೆ ಜೀವಕಳೆಯನ್ನು ಹಾಕ ತಕ್ಕನ್ಥ ಶಕ್ತಿಯು ಅವನಿಗಿಲ್ಲ, man can make various things and (draw various) pictures, but he has not the power of giving them life. ಅವನು ನನಗಿನ್ತ ಮೂಱು ನಾಲ್ಕು ವರ್ಷಕ್ಕೆ ಚಿಕ್ಕವನು ಇದ್ದಾನೆ, ಆದರೂ ಅವನು ಬಹಳ ಒಳ್ಳೆಯವನು, he is three or four years younger than I, notwithstanding he is very good. ಆ ಹುಡುಗನು ಈ ಎರಡು ವರುಷದಿನ್ದ ಇಂಗ್ಲಿಷ ಕಲಿಯುತ್ತಾ ಇದ್ದಾನೆ, ಆದರೂ ಅವನಿಗೆ ಇನ್ನೂ v ಮತ್ತು w ಇವುಗಳನ್ನು ಚನ್ನಾಗಿ ಉಚ್ಚರಿಸಲಿಕ್ಕೆ ಬರುವದಿಲ್ಲ, that boy is learning English these two years, yet he cannot pronounce v and w well. *Cf.* §§ 296. 314.

290. **ಅಂ, ಉಂ, ಊ and ಉ, when suffixed to the interrogatives** 'who', 'what', 'where', 'whither', 'when', 'how', express **'soever', and are used so to say to form also indefinite pronouns** (see § 102, s, *b*, remark).

The translation into English of such pronouns, etc. in the instances of this paragraph and the next four paragraphs is quite literal, but the student will be able to turn it into proper English for himself. The instances of this paragraph are:—

ಬಡವಾದಿರ್, ಅರಸ? ಕಾಲೊಳ್ ನಡೆದಪಿರ್, ಒಡನಾರುಮ್ ಇಲ್ಲ, have you become poor, O king? you walk on foot, whosoever is not with you (*i. e.* none is with you). ಆರುಮಂ ಪುಗಲ್ ಈಯದೆ ರಾಣಿವಾಸಮ್ ಇಹುದಕ್ಕೆ ಯೋಗ್ಯ ಮಾದೊಡೆ ವನವೆ ಪ್ರಮದವನಮ್ ಎನಿಸುಗು, if it does not allow whomsoever to enter and is fit to be the gynecæum, that garden is called pramadavana. ಭೂತಲದೊಳ್ ಆರ್ಗಮ್ ಅಧಿಕಂ, (he is) superior to whomsoever in the world. ಯಾರೂ ಇಲ್ಲದ ಊರಿಗೆ ಅಗಸರ ಮಾಳೆಯೇ ಮುತ್ತಯ್ದೆ, for a village in which whosoever is not (*i. e.* nobody is), the washermen's Māḷe is the respectable woman. ಇದನ್ನು ಯಾರೂ ಅಱಿಯರು, whosoever does not know this. ಕೋಣೆಯೊಳಗೆ ಯಾರು ಇದ್ದಾರೆ? ಯಾರೂ ಇಲ್ಲ, who is in the room? (there) is not whosoever (*i. e.* none at all). ನಾನು ಯಾರನ್ನೂ ನೋಡಲಿಲ್ಲ, I have not seen whomsoever (*i. e.* I have seen nobody). ಯಾರಿಗೂ ಕೇಡು ಬಯಸ

ಬೇಡಿರಿ, do not entertain malice against whomsoever. ಭೂಪತೀಶ್ವರ, ನಿಮ್ಮರಸಿಯರು ದೋಷವೇನುಮನ್ ಇಲ್ಲಿ ಮಾಡಿದುದಿಲ್ಲ, O king, your queen has committed here no fault whatsoever. ಏನೂ ಅಱಿಯದವನು, one who does not know whatsoever. ಅವನಿಗೆ ಅದಱ ವಿಷಯಕ್ಕೆ ಏನೂ ಗೊತ್ತಿಲ್ಲ, he has no knowledge whatsoever regarding that. ಈ ಕೊಡೆಯು ಏನೂ ಕೆಲಸದ್ದಲ್ಲ, this umbrella is of no use whatsoever. ಅವನಿಗೆ ಈ ಹೊತ್ತು ಏನೂ ಗುಣವಿಲ್ಲ, in his health there is to-day no improvement whatever. ಕೂಸು ಈ ಹೊತ್ತು ಏನೂ ತಿನ್ನಲೊಲ್ಲದು, the child will not eat whatsoever to-day. ಊಟಕ್ಕಿಲ್ಲದ ಉಪ್ಪಿನಕಾಯಿ ಯಾತಕ್ಕೂ ಬೇಡ, pickles absent at dinner are not good for whatsoever. ಹಣ್ಣಿನ ಗಿಡಗಳೊಳಗೆ ಇಷ್ಟು ಬೇಗ ಫಲ ಬರುವವು ಮತ್ತು ಯಾವವೂ ಇಲ್ಲ, among fruit-trees there are none whatsoever which bear fruits so quickly (as plantain trees). ಏನೂ ಇಲ್ಲದವ ಯವದಕ್ಕೂ ಹೇಸ, he who has nothing whatsoever, does not feel aversion to whatsoever.

ಎನಿತುಂ ಕಾಯ್ದುಂ ಬೆನ್ನೀರ್ ಮನೆ ಸುಡದು, though hot water gets hot how much soever, a house does not take fire (on account of it). ಕವಿಗೆ ಕೇಡಿಲ್ಲೆನ್ನುಂ, there is no disaster in what manner soever to a poet. ಎನ್ದುಂ ಕಾಣೆವೀ ಚೋದ್ಯವಂ, we have not seen whensoever such a wonderful thing. ಎನ್ದೂ ಗೆಯ್ಯದ ಭೂಮಿ, a piece of land that is not cultivated at what time soever. ಎನ್ದೂ ಏಱಿದ ರಾವುತ ಕುದುರೇ ಹಿನ್ದು ಮುನ್ದಾಗಿ ಏಱಿದ, a horseman who did not mount (a horse) at what time soever, mounted the horse in a reversed way. ಎನ್ದಿಗೂ ತನ್ದೆ ತಾಯಿಗಳ ಮಾತು ಮಿಾಱಬಾರದು, one must not transgress the word of (one's) parents at what time soever. ಆವಗಂ ಗೆಯ್ಮೆಯಿಲ್ಲದ ಇಳೆ, a piece of land that is not cultivated at what time soever. ಆವಾಗಳುಂ, whensoever. ವಿದ್ಯೆ ಕಲಿತ ಹೆಂಗಸು ತನ್ನ ಗಣ್ಡನನ್ನೂ ಮಕ್ಕಳನ್ನೂ ಯಾವಾಗಲೂ ಸನ್ತೋಷ ಪಡಿಸುವಳು, a female who has learned science, will at what time soever make her husband and children happy. ಜೀನನ ಮನಸ್ಸು ಯಾವಾಗಲೂ ಹೀನವೇ, a miser's mind is whensoever base. ಹ್ಯಾಗೂ ಹಬ್ಬದೊಳಗೆ ಅಯ್ದು ದಿವಸ ಸಾಳೆ ಇರುವದಿಲ್ಲ, howsoever on the feast there will be no school for five days. ಆವಳೊರ್ವಳು (*i. e.* ಅವಳ್+ಉ mediæval+ಒರ್ವಳು) ಒಪ್ಪಚ್ಚಿ ಮುದುಕಿಯಾಗಿ ಕಾವಿಯ ಸೀರೆಯನ್ ಉಟ್ಟವಳು ಕಾತ್ಯಾಯನಿ ಎನಿಸುಗು, whatsoever a female is somewhat old and has put on a cloth dyed with red ochre, is called kâtyâyani. ಅಲ್ಲಿಯುಮ್ ಇಲ್ಲಿಯುಮ್ ಎಲ್ಲಿಯುಂ ನರಂ, there and here (and) wheresoever (is) Arjuna. ಆದೆಲ್ಲಿಯು (=ಎಲ್ಲಿಯೂ, mediæval) ನಿಲ್ಲದು, it does not stand wheresoever. ನಿನ್ನ ಸಮಾನ ಸುನ್ದರವಾದ ಪಕ್ಷಿಯನ್ನು ನಾನು ಇನ್ದಿನ ವರೆಗೂ ಎಲ್ಲಿಯೂ ಕಾಣಲಿಲ್ಲ, wheresoever I have not seen such a beautiful bird as thee up to this very time. ಎತ್ತಿದ ಕೆಯ್ಯೊಳ್ ಮುತ್ತಿದನ್,

ಅತ್ತಿತ್ತುತ್ತಿತ್ತಂ ಸಾರ್ವರ್ ಇನ್ನಹಿತರ್ಕಳ್, with lifted hands he attacked, there (and) here (and) in the intermediate places wheresoever the enemies not waiting approached.

291. 'Soever' is likewise expressed by suffixing ಅಂ and ಊ to the past relative participle ಆದ (of ಆಗು) combined with ಒಡೆ and ಅರೆ, and adding the thus obtained forms ಆದೊಡಂ and ಆದರೂ to interrogatives, *e. g.* ಆರಾದೊಡಂ, whosoever. ಎನ್ತಾದೊಡಂ, in what manner soever. ಹ್ಯಾಗೆಯಾದೊಡಂ, howsoever. ಆರಿಗಾದರೂ ಪೂರ್ವಕರ್ಮ ಬಿಡದು, actions done in a former state of existence do not leave whomsoever (Dâsapada). ಯಾರಾದರೂ, whosoever. ಯಾರಿಗಾದರೂ, to whomsoever. ಯಾವನಾದರೂ, whosoever, whichsoever. ಯಾವದಾದರೂ, whatsoever, whichsoever. ಏನಾದರೂ, whatsoever. ಎಷ್ಟಾದರೂ, however so much. ಎನ್ದಾದರೂ, whensoever. ಎನ್ತಿಗಾದರೂ, up to what time soever, at what time soever. ಯಾವಾಗಲಾದರೂ, whensoever. ಹ್ಯಾಗಾದರೂ, howsoever. ಎಲ್ಲಿಯಾದರೂ, ಎಲ್ಲಾದರೂ, wheresoever. ಎಲ್ಲಿಗಾದರೂ, whithersoever. ಎಲ್ಲಿನ್ದಾದರೂ, whencesoever. ಎಷ್ಟುಮಾತ್ರವಾದರೂ, whatsoever, or to whatsoever, extent. ಯಾವ ರೀತಿಯಿನ್ದಾದರೂ, in whatsoever manner.

The same meaning is obtained also by adding any past relative participle combined with ಅರೆ and ಊ (*i. e.* ಅರೂ), ಒಡೆ and ಅಂ (*i. e.* ಒಡಂ), ಅಡೆ and ಅಂ (*i. e.* ಅಡಂ), ಅಡೆ and ಊ or ಉ (*i. e.* ಅಡೂ or ಅಡು), to interrogatives, *e. g.* ಕಾಡ ನಾಯಿಗಳು ಬಹು ತೀವ್ರವಾಗಿ ಓಡುವವು, ಏನು ಮಾಡಿದರೂ ಕೆಯ್ಗೆ ಸಿಗ್ಗುವದಿಲ್ಲ, jungle dogs run very fast; whatsoever one does, they cannot be caught. ಎಷ್ಟು ಮಾಡಿದರೂ ನಷ್ಟವಾಗದೇ ಬಿಡದು, how much soever (he) does, loss will never fail. ಎಲ್ಲಿ ನೋಡಿದರೂ ಕಾಡು, wheresoever one sees, (is) a wilderness. ಎತ್ತ ಹೋದರೂ ಮೃತ್ಯು ಬಿಡದು, whithersoever (he) goes, death does not leave (him). ಏನು ಮಾಡಿದರೂ ಮಗ ಹರಿಯೆಮ್ಬುವದನ್ನು ಬಿಡ, whatsoever (they) may do, (their) son does not leave to say 'Hari'. ಏನ್ ಎನ್ದಡು (mediæval) ಎಷ್ಟಾದಡಂ ಬಿಡ ತನ್ನನ್ದವ ನೀಚ ತಾಂ, whatsoever one says (and) however so much, a vile man does not give up his ways. ಎನ್ತೋದಿದೊಡಂ, howsoever one reads.[1)]

[1)] Instances in which the conjunction ಅಂ is not suffixed in such a case, occur in the following verse of the Jaimini Bhârata (16, 43):—

ಎಲ್ಲಿ ನೋಡಿದೊಡೆ ಗಂಗಾಪ್ರವಾಹದ ಸಲಿಲಮ್,
ಎಲ್ಲಿ ನೋಡಿದೊಡೆ ಪುಣ್ಯಾಶ್ರಮಕುಟೀರಂಗಳ್,
ಎಲ್ಲಿ ನೋಡಿದೊಡೆ ನಿಬಿಡದ್ರುಮಚ್ಛಾಯೆಗಳ್ ಕುಸುಮಫಲಮೂಲಂಗಳು, |
ಎಲ್ಲಿ ನೋಡಿದೊಡೆ ಶುಕಪಿಕಮಯೂರಧ್ವನಿಗಳ್,
ಎಲ್ಲಿ ನೋಡಿದೊಡೆ ಸಾತ್ವಿಕಮ್ ಆದ ಮೃಗನಿಕರಮ್,
ಎಲ್ಲಿ ನೋಡಿದೊಡೆ ಸಂಚರಿಪ ತಾಪಸವಟುಗಳ್ ಎನೆಪವರ್ಜುನನ ಕಣ್ಗೆ. ||

Also if ಉಂ is suffixed to the infinitive with ಎ and this form is added to an interrogative, the meaning of 'soever' is produced, *e. g.* ಇದಿರೊಳ್ ಸ್ವರಂಗಳ್ ಆವುವು ನಿಲೆಯುಂ, when whatsoever vowels stand in front.

292. Another way of expressing 'soever' is to suffix **ಆನುಂ** or **ಆನು** to interrogatives. This suffix is composed of ಆನ (see § 176) and ಉಂ, ಉ (=ಉಂ), and literally means 'having become though', 'though having become'. *E. g.* ಆರಾನುಂ, whosoever. ಏನಾನುಂ, whatsoever. ಏನಾನುಮೊನ್ದು ಭಾವಂ, whatsoever a state. ಏನಾನು (=ಏನಾನುಂ, mediæval), whatsoever. ಎತ್ತಾನುಂ, in what place soever, occasionally. ಎನ್ತಾನುಂ, howsoever. ಎನ್ದಾನುಂ, whensoever. ಎಲ್ಲಿಯಾನುಂ, wheresoever. ಆವುದಾನು, whatsoever, *e. g.* ಆವುದಾನೊನ್ದರಿಂ ತೊಲಗುವುದು, the removal from whatsoever a thing; ಆವುದಾನೊನ್ದು ಮರದ ಮೇಲೆ, on whatsoever a (piece of) wood. ಆವನಾನು, whosoever, *e. g.* ಆವನಾನೊಬ್ಬನು, whosoever a man.

When ಆನುಂ, ಆನು are not suffixed to interrogatives, they signify 'a little', 'moderate', *e. g.* ಇನಿಸಾನುಂ ಬೇಗದೊಳ್, in this much little or moderate haste; — or 'a certain', *e. g.* ಒಬ್ಬಾನು, a certain one, in ಒಬ್ಬಾನೊಬ್ಬನು, a certain one man (*i. e.* some one man, some man); ಒಬ್ಬಾನೊಬ್ಬಳು, a certain woman; ಒಬ್ಬಾನೊಬ್ಬ ಒಕ್ಕಲಿಗನು, a certain husbandman; ಒನ್ದಾನು, a certain one (neuter), in ಒನ್ದಾನೊನ್ದು ವೇಳೆಯಲ್ಲಿ, at a certain one time (*i. e.* at some time or other); — in repetition 'either—or' (*cf.* § 317), *e. g.* ಮೂಡಲಾನುಂ ಬಡಗಲಾನುಂ, either east or north; ಅಲ್ಲಿಯಾನುಮ್ ಇಲ್ಲಿಯಾನುಂ, either there or here; ಅನ್ದಾನುಮ್ ಇನ್ದಾನುಂ, either then or now; ಒನ್ದಾನುಮ್ ಎರಡಾನುಂ, either one or two; ಪತ್ತಾನುಂ ನೂಱಾನುಂ, either ten or hundred; — 'about' in ಎಣ್ಟಾನೆಣ್ಟು (ಎಣ್ಟಾನು+ ಎಣ್ಟು), about eight.

Remark.

In the modern dialect 'a certain' is expressed also by the interrogative suffix ಓ (see § 283), *e. g.* ಆಕೆ ಯಾವನೋ ಒಬ್ಬ ಅಮ್ಬಿಗನ ಹೆಣ್ಡತಿ, she (is) the wife of a certain boatman. *Cf.* also § 310, 2 at the end.

293. The ಆನುಂ of § 292 appears also as **ಆಣಂ**, *i. e.* ಆಣ (for ಆನ)+ಅಂ and this ಆಣಂ again appears with a short ಅ (see § 176) as **ಅಣಂ**, *i. e.* ಅಣ (for ಅನ) + ಅಂ. ಆಣಂ, ಅಣಂ mean 'soever', 'whatsoever', elliptically for ಏನಾಣಂ, ಏನಣಂ, *e. g.* ಗುಣಮ್ ಆಣಮ್ ಇಲ್ಲ, (there) is no merit whatsoever. ಕಾರ್ಯಮ್ ಅಣಮ್ ಇಲ್ಲ, (there) is no business whatsoever. ಸನ್ದಯಮ್ ಅಣಂ ತಾನಿಲ್ಲ, (there) is no doubt whatsoever.

294. If the interrogatives ಆವ, ಯಾವ, ಎಷ್ಟು, etc. are connected with a following noun, ಉಂ, ಊ are suffixed to this noun in order to express 'soever', *e. g.* ಆವ ದೆಸೆಯಲ್ಲಿಯುಂ, in whatsoever direction. ಮೇಜಿನ ಮೇಲೆ ಯಾವ ಪುಸ್ತಕವೂ ಇಲ್ಲ, (there) is not whatsoever book (*i. e.* there is no book at all) on the table. ನೀನು ಯಾವ ಅಡಚಣೆಯನ್ನೂ ಸಹಿಸ ಬೇಕಾಗಲಿಕ್ಕಿಲ್ಲ, you will not have to suffer whatsoever distress. ತಿಳಿಗೇಡಿಹುಡುಗರು ಯಾವ ಕೆಲಸಕ್ಕೂ ಬರುವದಿಲ್ಲ, foolish boys are not good for whatsoever business. ಯಾವ ಪ್ರಕಾರದಿನ್ದಲೂ ಅಲ್ಲ, not in whatsoever manner (*i. e.* in no way). ಎಷ್ಟು ಮಾತ್ರಕ್ಕೂ, to whatsoever extent. Also if the genitive ಯಾರ (ಆರ) stands before a noun, ಊ (ಉಂ) is suffixed to this noun in the same sense, *e. g.* ನಿಮ್ಮ ಮೇಲೆ ಯಾರ ಕಾಟವೂ ಸಾಗದು, annoyance of whomsoever will not come upon you. ಇದನ್ನು ಮಾಡುವದು ಯಾರ ಮನಸಿಗೂ ಬರಲಿಕ್ಕಿಲ್ಲ, to do this will not suit the mind of whomsoever. (About ಇಲ್ಲ see § 298, about ಅಲ್ಲ § 300).

If ಏನು is used instead of ಯಾವ, the ಊ is commonly suffixed to ಏನು, *e. g.* ಈ ಕೊಡೆಯು ಏನೂ ಕೆಲಸದ್ದಲ್ಲ, this umbrella is of no use whatsoever. ಅವನ ಹತ್ತರ ಏನೂ ಹಣವಿದ್ದಿಲ್ಲ, (there) was no money whatsoever about him. ನನಗೆ ಏನೂ ಉಪದ್ರವ ಮಾಡಲಿಲ್ಲ. ತಾನು ಏನೂ ತಪ್ಪು ಮಾಡಲಿಲ್ಲ. ನೀನೇನೂ ಅಪರಾಧ ಮಾಡಿಲ್ಲ. ಏನೇನೂ ಸಂಶಯ ಉಳಿಯಲಿಲ್ಲ. ಆ ನಡತೆಗಳಲ್ಲಿ ಏನೇನೂ ದೋಷವಿಲ್ಲ. But on the other hand there is *e. g.* ನಿಮ್ಮರಸಿಯರು ದೋಸವೇನುಮನ್ ಇಲ್ಲಿ ಮಾಡಿದುದಿಲ್ಲ, your queen has committed here no fault whatsoever. ಇದಕ್ಕೆ ಸಂಶಯವೇನೂ ಇಲ್ಲ, about this there is no doubt whatsoever.

295. In § 285 it has been stated that besides in the mediæval dialect also in the modern one ಉ is used instead of ಊ. Thus we find *e. g.* ಏನಾದರು (for ಏನಾದರೂ), ಯಾರಾದರು (for ಯಾರಾದರೂ), ಎನ್ತಾದರು (for ಎನ್ತಾದರೂ), ಯಾರಿಗಾದರು (for ಯಾರಿಗಾದರೂ), ಯಾವದಾದರು (for ಯಾವದಾದರೂ), ಎಷ್ಟಾದರು (for ಎಷ್ಟಾದರೂ), ಎಲ್ಲಿಯಾದರು (for ಎಲ್ಲಿಯಾದರೂ), ಯಾವಾಗಲು (for ಯಾವಾಗಲೂ), ಯಾವದಾದರೊನ್ದು (for ಯಾವದಾದರೂ ಒನ್ದು), ಏನಿಲ್ಲ (for ಏನೂ ಇಲ್ಲ).

296. In § 289 ಆದರೂ (*i. e.* ಆದ+ಅರೆ+ಊ) appears in the meaning of 'but'. It may get also that of 'also', *e. g.* ಸ್ವಲ್ಪ ವಿಚಾರ ಮಾಡಿ ನೋಡಿದರೆ ನಿನಗಾದರೂ ಹಾಗೆಯೇ ತೋಟಿಯೀತು, if (thou) reflectest a little, it is likely to appear also to thee in that very manner. ನಾನಾದರೂ ಇನ್ದಿನ ವರೆಗೆ ಅವನು ಮಾಡಿದ ತಪ್ಪುಗಳನ್ನು ಕ್ಷಮಿಸಿದೆನು, till now also I put up with the faults committed by him.

A remark is here to be made regarding **ಆದರೆ** (*i. e.* ಆದ + ಅರೆ), which literally means 'if becomes or is', 'if become or are', *e. g.* ಸತಿಯು ಆದರೆ ಚಿನ್ತೆ, ಸತಿಯು ಇಲ್ಲದಿರೆ ಚಿನ್ತೆ, if (there is) a wife, (there is) sorrowful thought; when (there is) no wife, (there is) sorrowful thought. ಬೆಳ್ಳಿಯು ಆದರೆ ಕಳ್ಳಗೆ ಆಗದೇ, if it is silver, is it not agreeable to the thief? ಮಕ್ಕಳಾದರೆ ಕಷ್ಟ, ಮಕ್ಕಳಿಲ್ಲದಿರೆ ಕಷ್ಟ, if (there) are children, (it is) trouble; when (there) are no children, (it is) trouble. ಆಕಳು ಕಪ್ಪಾದರೆ ಹಾಲು ಕಪ್ಪೇ, if the cow is black, (is its) milk black? ಹಾಗಾದರೆ, if (it) is so. ಬೇಕಾದರೆ, if (it) is required.

ಆದರೆ, however, is often used somewhat like ಆದರೂ, 'but', if it stands at the head of a sentence, *e. g.* ನೀವೆಲ್ಲರೂ ಪಡಸಾಲೆಯೊಳಗೆ ಹೋಗಿರಿ, ಆದರೆ ಅಲ್ಲಿ ಏನೂ ಗದ್ದಲ ಮಾಡ ಬೇಡಿರಿ, go all of you into the veranda, but you must not make any noise there. ಕೆಲವು ಗಿಡಗಳು ಕೈಯ್ ಚಾಚಿದ ಕೂಡಲೆ ಮುಚ್ಚಿಕೊಳ್ಳುತ್ತವೆ, ಆದರೆ ಅವುಗಳಿಗೆ ಪ್ರಾಣಿಗಳನ್ತೆ ಆನನ್ದ ದುಃಖಗಳು ಆಗುವದಿಲ್ಲ, some plants, as soon as they are touched, close, but do not experience joy and sorrow like living beings. ಈ ದೇಶದಲ್ಲಿ ಕೆಲವು ಸ್ಥಳಗಳಲ್ಲಿ ಜಾಜಿಕಾಯಿ ಗಿಡಗಳುಣ್ಟು, ಆದರೆ ಅಲ್ಲಿಯ ಹಾಗೆ ಕಾಯಿ ಆಗುವದಿಲ್ಲ, in this country there are in some places nutmeg trees, but (their) nuts do not become like (those) of that place. *Cf.* § 314 and see the use of ಆದರೆ in § 334.

297. The conjunctions **ಬಲ್ಲೆ, ಬಱಿ**, (ಬಱಿಕಂ, etc. § 212, 3), **ಮತ್ತಂ, ಮತ್ತೆ, ಮೇಣ್**, again, further, and, are used in adducing something additional, *e. g.* ಮತ್ತೆ (ಏನ್ ಎಮ್ಬುದು) ಕೃತಿಪದ್ಧತಿಯೊಳ್ ಪೀನಂ ಬಹುವಚನಾರ್ಥಮನ್ ಆನಲ್ ಸಾಲ್ದತ್ತು. ಮತ್ತೆ ಕೆಲವಱೊಳ್ ಅರುವಿನ (*i. e.* ಅರಾಗಮದ) ಮೇಲೆ ಕಳಾಗಮಮುಕ್ಕುಂ. ಕಸೀ ಮಾಡಿದ ಮರವು ಚಿಗಿತು, ಮತ್ತೆ ಬೆಳೆದು, ದೊಡ್ಡ ಮರವಾಗುವದಿಲ್ಲವೋ? — ಮತ್ತಂ is composed of ಮತ್ತೆ + ಅಂ, so that it originally means 'and further' like ಮತ್ತೆಯುಂ.

> ಇವು ಜಮ್ಬೂಫಲಮಂಜರಿ
> ಯಿವು ಫಲನೀಫಲಗುಲುಚ್ಛಮ್, ಇವು ಚೂತಫಲ ।
> ಸ್ತವಕಂಗಳೆನ್ದು, ತೋಱುವನ್
> ಅವನೀಪಾಲಂಗೆ ಲೀಲೆಯಿಂ ವನಪಾಲಂ ॥

ಮತ್ತಂ

> ಇವು ಕಂಕೇಲ್ಲಿದಲಪ್ರಸೂನಮ್, ಇವು ಮಲ್ಲಿಸ್ಮೇರಪಲ್ಲವಂ, etc.

> ತರಿಸಿ ಕೊಳ್ಪಿಡಿದ ಹಯಮಂ, ಸುವೇಗನ ವಶದೊ
> ಳಿರಿಸಿ, ಭದ್ರಾವತಿಗೆ ಬರಲಾ ನೃಪಂ ಪೊಬಲ ಸಿಂಗರಿಸಿ, ಮೇಣ್ ಅವರನೂ ।
> ಅರಸಿಯರ ಗಡಣದೊಳದಿರ್ಗೊಣ್ಡು, ಮನೆಯೊಳಾ
> ದರಿಸಿ, etc.

An instance in which ಮೇಣ್ means 'or' is the following:— ಎರಡಕ್ಕರಂ ಮೇಣ್ ಪಲವಕ್ಕರಂ ತಮ್ಮೊಳ್ ಅನ್ಯೋನ್ಯವಾಗಿ ಕೂಡುವುದು ಸನ್ಧಿಯೆನಿಸುಗುಂ.

In the modern dialect ಮತ್ತು (which we met with already in multiplicative and additional numbers at the close of § 280) is used like ಮತ್ತಂ, ಮತ್ತೆ (*cf.* § 310), *e. g.* ನಮ್ಮ ಹಿನ್ದುಸ್ಥಾನದಲ್ಲಿ ಹತ್ತಿ ಹುಟ್ಟುತ್ತದೆ; ಆದರೆ ನಮ್ಮ ಹತ್ತರ ತಕ್ಕ ಯನ್ತ್ರಗಳು ಇಲ್ಲ, ಮತ್ತು ನಾವು ಒಳ್ಳೇ ಜಾಣರೂ ಅಲ್ಲ. ನಮ್ಮ ದೇಶದ ಒಕ್ಕಲಿಗರು ಯುರೋಪದ ಸುಧಾರಿಸಿದ ರೀತಿಯನ್ನೆ ಹತ್ತಿ ಬೆಳ ಕೊಳ್ಳಲಿಕ್ಕೆ ಅರಿಯರು, ಮತ್ತು ಉತ್ತಮ ಜಾತಿಯ ಹತ್ತಿಯೊಳಗೆ ಕೀಳುಹತ್ತಿಯನ್ನು ಬೆರಿಸುತ್ತಾರೆ. See an instance in § 289 (v ಮತ್ತು w).

In the same dialect ಹಾಗೂ (ಹಾಂಗೂ), so also, likewise also, has been used in the sense of 'and', *e. g.* ಇದು (ಕೇಸರವು) ಬಹಳ ಬೆಳೆಯುವದಿಲ್ಲ, ಹಾಗೂ ಬಹಳ ಸ್ಥಳಗಳಲ್ಲಿ ಬೆಳೆಯುವದಿಲ್ಲ.

298. The Šabdamaṇidarpaṇa states that ಇಲ್ಲ (of ಇಲ್ = ಇರ್) is a kriyâtmakâvyaya, *i. e.* a particle (avyaya) that partakes of the nature of a verb. Its formation has been shown in § 209, note 1 (see also § 210). ಇಲ್ಲ appears also with a final euphonic sŏnnĕ as ಇಲ್ಲಂ, *e. g.* ದೇವದತ್ತ, ನಿನಗೇನುಮ್ ಇಲ್ಲಂ, and in the modern dialect with a euphonic ವು (*i. e.* ಂ+ಉ) as ಇಲ್ಲವು (§ 209, note 1; § 212, 7).

When followed by a vowel, the final letter of ಇಲ್ಲ either disappears, *e. g.* ಇಲ್ಲಾಗು, ಇಲ್ಲೆನ್ (*cf.* § 215, 1), or a euphonic ವ್ is inserted, *e. g.* ಇಲ್ಲವಾಗು, ಇಲ್ಲವೆನ್ (*cf.* § 215, 3).

ಇಲ್ಲ is used either by itself, or in combination with nouns, pronouns, etc. In combination with bhâvavačanas, *i. e.* verbal nouns ending *e. g.* in ಉದು and ಅದು (§ 200, 1. 3, once also in ತು, see § 194, remark 1) or in ಅಲು (§§ 187, 1; 188. 209, 3), it forms so to say a third person in the conjugation of the negative.

In the modern dialect bhâvavačanas with ಅಲು (the nominative) and ಇಲ್ಲ conventionally convey the meaning of the past (§ 209, 3). If ಅಲು is changed into the dative (ಅಲಿಕ್ಕೆ, ಅಲಿಕೆ) and ಇಲ್ಲ is suffixed, the meaning of the past disappears.

In the same dialect ಇಲ್ಲ is joined also to past participles.

1, ಇಲ್ಲ by itself.

ನೀಲಗ್ರೀವರುಮ್ ಅರ್ತರ್? ಇಲ್ಲ, and is (king) Nilagrîva able (to gain the victory)? (No), he is not. ನೀನು ಎನ್ದಾದರೂ ಕಲ್ಲಂಗಡೀ ಹಣ್ಣು ನೋಡಿದ್ಧಿಯಾ? ಇಲ್ಲ, ever having seen a ripe water-molon art thou? I am not (*i. e.* hast thou ever seen a ripe water-melon? No, I have not). ಅವೆಲ್ಲ ತಮ್ಮಿನ್ದ ತಾವೇ ಆಗಿವೆಯೋ? ಇಲ್ಲ, having become (*i. e.* have become and) are all those (things in the house) of themselves? (No), they are not. ಅವನಿಗೆ ನೀನು ಏನಾದರೂ ಕೆಟ್ಟ ಮಾತು ಆಡಿದ್ದೀ? ಇಲ್ಲ, ಸ್ವಾಮಿ, having spoken whatever bad words to him wast thou? I was not, sir (*i. e.* hadst thou abused him in any way? No, I had not, sir). ಜೇನುನೊಣಗಳು ಮೆಯ್ಗೆ ಎಲ್ಲಾದರೂ ಕಡಿದವೇನು? ಇಲ್ಲ, did the bees sting (you) anywhere on the body? They were not (*i. e.* no, they did not). ತೆಂಗಿನ ಮರದ ಮೇಲೆ ಹುಲ್ಲು ಇರುತ್ತದೇನೋ? ಎನ್ದು, ತೋಟಿಗನು ಕೇಳಿದನು. ಇಲ್ಲವೆನ್ತಲೇ ಇಳಿದು ಬರುತ್ತೇನೆನ್ದನು, "is (there) grass upon the cocoa-nut tree?" asked the gardener. "(There) is not, (thus) saying indeed (to myself), I come down", replied he (*i. e.* no, there is not; and for that very reason I come down, replied he).

2, **ಇಲ್ಲ in combination with nouns and pronouns** (*cf.* § 316, 1).

ಕನ್ನಡಕ್ಕಂ ಸಂಸ್ಕೃತಕ್ಕಂ ಸಮಾಸಮಿಲ್ಲ, (generally there) is not a composition (*i. e.* generally there is no composition) of Kannaḍa and Saṁskṛita words. ಸಂಸ್ಕೃತಪದಂ ಪರಕ್ಕೊದವಲೊಡಂ ದೋಷಮಿಲ್ಲ, also if a Saṁskṛita word follows (the terms ಎಲ್ಲ and ಮಾ), a fault it is not (*i. e.* it is no fault). ಆಃ, ಸನ್ದಯಮಿಲ್ಲ, O, doubt (there) is not (*i. e.* O, there is no doubt). ಗುರುವಿಲ್ಲ ಕರ್ಣನಿಲ್ಲ ಗುರುವಿನ ಮಗನಿಲ್ಲ, Drôṇa is not (present), Karṇa is not (present), the son of Drôṇa is not (present). ಒಡನಾರುಮಿಲ್ಲ, (there) is not whosoever with (you, *i. e.* nobody is with you). ಘಟಮಿಲ್ಲ, (there) is not a pot (*i. e.* there is no pot). ಉಣಲುಡಲು ತಮಗಿಲ್ಲ, an eating and a putting on (there) is not for them (*i. e.* they have nothing to eat and to put on). ಎನಗೆ ಪಿರಿದಾಯಸಮ್ ಇನ್ನಿಲ್ಲ, for me great trouble still (there) is not (*i. e.* there is no longer great trouble for me). ಮದನನ ಮೇಲೆ ತಪ್ಪಿಲ್ಲ, (there) is not a fault on Madana (*i. e.* there is no fault on Madana). ಅನ್ತಕನ ದೂತರಿಗೆ ಕಿಂಚಿತ್ತು ದಯವಿಲ್ಲ, in Yama's messengers whatever mercy (there) is not (*i. e.* Yama's messengers have no mercy at all). ಕಟ್ಟೆ ತುಮ್ಬಿದ ಮೇಲೆ ಚಣಮಾತ್ರ ಇರವಿಲ್ಲ, after the period (of life) has expired, for a moment a stay (there) is not (*i. e.*—there is no stay for a moment). ನನ್ನ ಹತ್ತರ ಯಾವ ಪುಸ್ತಕವೂ ಇಲ್ಲ, near me whatsoever book (there) is not (*i. e.* I have no book at all with me). ಈ ಹೊತ್ತು ಆದಿತ್ಯವಾರ, ಸಾಲೆ ಇಲ್ಲ, to-day (is) Sunday, school (there) is not (*i. e.* — there is no school). ಮತಿ ಇಲ್ಲದವರಿಗೆ ಗತಿ ಇಲ್ಲ, for those who have no understanding, fortune (there) is not (*i. e.* — there is no fortune). ನನಗೆ ದಣುವೇ ಇಲ್ಲ, for me (the sun, there) is not fatigue indeed (*i. e.* I never suffer fatigue). ಅದು ನನಗೆ ಗೊತ್ತು ಇಲ್ಲ, that to me knowledge is not (*i. e.* I do not know that). ನೀನು ಏನೂ ಹೇಳುವ ಕೆಲಸವಿಲ್ಲ, thou whatever saying a business (there) is not (*i. e.* thou doest not want to say anything). ತಾಯಿಗಿನ್ನ ಹಿತವರಿಲ್ಲ, ಸಕ್ಕರೆಗಿನ್ನ ಸವಿಯಿಲ್ಲ, greater than a mother benefactors (there) are not, greater than sugar sweetness (there) is not (*i. e.* there are no greater benefactors than a mother, there is no greater sweetness than that of sugar). ಪುತ್ತಳಿಗಿನ್ನ ಮೇಲು ಬಂಗಾರವಿಲ್ಲ, ಮಕ್ಕಳಿಗಿನ್ನ ಮೇಲು ತೊದಲಿಲ್ಲ, better than pure gold (there) is not, better than children lisping (there) is not (*i. e.* there is no gold better than pure gold, there is no lisping better than that of children). ಇನ್ದಿಲ್ಲ, ನಾಳೆ ಯಾದರೂ ಆ ಕೆಲಸವು ಕೆಯ್ಗೂಡಿ ಬರುವದು, to-day it is not, but to-morrow that work will be accomplished (*i. e.* to-day it is not likely to be accomplished, but to-morrow that work will be accomplished). ನಿನಗೆ ತನ್ದೆ ತಾಯಿಗಳುಣ್ಟೋ? ಯಾರೂ ಇಲ್ಲ, to thee father and mother are (there)? Whosoever (there) are not (*i. e.* hast thou still thy parents? No, I have nobody). ನಿನಗೆ ಈ ಚೂರಿಯನ್ನು ಯಾರು ಕೊಟ್ಟರು? ಯಾರೂ ಇಲ್ಲ; ನಾನು ಇದನ್ನು ನಾರಾಯಣನ ಗಣ್ಟು ಬಿಚ್ಚಿ ತೆಕೊಣ್ಡೆನು, who gave thee this knife? Whosoever not (*i. e.* nobody); having opened the bundle of Nârâyaṇa I took it to myself. ನಿಮ್ಮ ಹತ್ತರ ತುಪ್ಪವದೆ? ಏನೂ ಇಲ್ಲ, is (there) ghee near you (*i. e.* have you some ghee)? (there) is not any (*i. e.* I have none).

3, **ಇಲ್ಲ in combination with verbal nouns** (*cf.* § 316, 2. 12) **and past participles (which are finally also verbal nouns, see § 169).**

ಇನ್ನೆವರಂ ಗುಱಿಯಾದುದಿಲ್ಲ ಕಾಮಕರವಿಮುಕ್ತಬಾಣಹತಿಗೆ, till now (he) is not a having become an object of aim to a stroke of an arrow discharged by the hand of Kâma (*i. e.* till now he has not become an object etc.).

ಕೋಗಿಲೆವಱಿ ಮಾಮರದೊಳ್
ಕಾಗೆಯ ಕೊತ್ತಱಿಯೊಳ್ ಎರ್ದು ಪೋಗಲುಮ್ ಇರುಳುಂ |
ಕೂಗಲುಮ್ ಎವೆದೆಱೆದಿಕ್ಕಲುಮ್
ಏಗೆಯ್ಯಲುಮ್ ಆರ್ತುದಿಲ್ಲ ಬನದೊಳ್ ಪೆಳಱಿಂ || the young cuckoo in a mango tree among a flock of crows in the wood a having been able not (*i. e.* was not able) to rise and go away, and also at night to cry, and to open and shut (its) eyelids, (in short) to do anything on account of fear.

ಮುಸುಱಿದ ಕುಳಿಱಿೊಳ್ ದೆಸೆಯಾ
ಗಸಮ್ ಇಳೆ ಬಿಟ್ಟಡವಿಯೆಮ್ಬಿವೆತ್ತಾನುಂ ಕಾ |

ಣಿಸಲಾರ್ತುದಿಲ್ಲಮೆನೆ ಮಾ

ಮಸಗಿರ್ದುದು ಮಾಗೆ ಮಾಗೆ ಸೆಕ್ಕೆವೆಸರಿಳೆಯೊಳ್ || the month Mâgĕ grandly made its appearance so that in the covering cold the points of the compass, the sky, the earth, mountains (and) forests, howsoever, a having been able not to be seen (*i. e.* could not be seen) on the earth which is known for (its) misty heat when fruits are growing fully ripe.

ಅರಸಿಯರು ದೋಸವೇನುವನ್ ಇಲ್ಲಿ ಮಾಡಿದುದಿಲ್ಲ, the queen a having made not any fault here (*i. e.* the queen has not committed any fault here).— ಕೆಲವು ಮಂಗಗಳಿಗೆ ಬಾಲವು ಇರುವದಿಲ್ಲ, to some monkeys a tail a being (there) is not (*i. e.* some monkeys have no tail). ಜ್ಞಾನವಿಲ್ಲದಿದ್ದರೆ ಮಾನ ಬರುವದಿಲ್ಲ, if (there) is no knowledge, honour a coming (there) is not (*i. e.*—honour is not obtained). ತಿಳಿಗೇಡಿಹುಡುಗರು ಯಾವ ಕೆಲಸಕ್ಕೂ ಬರುವದಿಲ್ಲ, stupid boys a coming (there) is not for whatsoever work (*i. e.* stupid boys are good for nothing). ಎಲ್ಲಿ ಇದ್ದಾಳೋ? ಕಾಣುವದಿಲ್ಲ, where is she? (she) an appearing is not (*i. e.* she does not appear). ಇನ್ಥಾ ಹಣ್ಣು ಹಮ್ಪಲ ಗಳನ್ನು ಒಬ್ಬನೇ ಕೂತು ತಿನ್ನುವ ಹಾಗೆ ನನಗೆ ಆಗುವದಿಲ್ಲ, so that (I) having sat down eat such (good) ripe fruits alone is not a being pleasant to me (*i. e.* to sit down and eat such good ripe fruits alone is not pleasant to me).— ಕಪಟ ಕಲ್ಮಷ ಕಳೆಯಲಿಲ್ಲ, ಕಾಮಿತಾರ್ಥ ಪಡೆಯಲಿಲ್ಲ, (he) a having abandoned not deceit (and other) sin, (and) a having obtained not the desired object (*i. e.* he has not abandoned deceit and other sin, and has not obtained the desired object). ಆತನ ತಾಯಿ ಬೇಕಾದಷ್ಟು ತಿಳಿಸಿ ಹೇಳಿದರೂ ಕೇಳಲಿಲ್ಲ, though his mother having made clear (and) told (him) so much as was necessary, (he) a hearing was not (*i. e.* though his mother clearly told him all that was necessary, he did not hear). ಕಲ್ಲು ಮುಳ್ಳುಗ ಳನ್ನು ತುಳಿದು ಬೇಸತ್ತನು, ಆದರೂ ದಾರಿ ಸಿಗಲಿಲ್ಲ, he having trodden on stones (and) thorns grew fatigued, but the way a being found was not (*i. e.* he trod on stones and thorns and grew fatigued, but the way was not found).—ಅವನು ಹೋಗಲಿಕ್ಕಿಲ್ಲ, he to a going is not (*i. e.* he does not intend to go or probably will not go). ಹೀಗೆ ಮಾಡಿದರೆ ಅವನ ಸಿಟ್ಟು ಇಳಿಯುವದು, ನಿನಗೂ ಲತ್ತೆ ಬೀಳಲಿಕ್ಕಿಲ್ಲ, if (you) do so, his anger will be assuaged, and blows to a falling on thee are not (*i. e.*—and blows will not fall on thee). ನಿನ್ನನ್ನು ಯಾರೂ ಹತ್ತರ ಬರಗೊಡಲಿಕ್ಕಿಲ್ಲ, whosoever are not to an allowing thee to come near (*i. e.* nobody will allow thee to come near).— ಇನ್ನೂ ನಿನ್ನ ಹಲಿಗೇ ಮೇಲಿನ ಬರಹ ತೀರಿಲ್ಲವೋ, yet writing on thy board a having been finished (see §§ 168. 169) is not?

(*i. e.* has writing on thy board not yet been finished?). ಸೂರ್ಯನನ್ನು ಮನುಷ್ಯರು ಮಾಡಿಲ್ಲ, men a having made the sun are not (*i. e.* man has not made the sun). ದೇವರನ್ನು ಯಾರೂ ನೋಡಿಲ್ಲ, whosoever a having seen God is not (*i. e.* nobody has seen God). ಈ ದ್ರಾಕ್ಷೆಯ ಹಣ್ಣುಗಳು ಹುಳಿ ಅವೆ, ಅದಱಿಂದ ಇವು ನನಗೆ ಬೇಕಾಗಿಲ್ಲ, these grapes are sour, therefore these a requiring for me having become are not (*i. e.*—therefore these are not required for me, that is to say: I do not want these). ಆಗ ಗುರುಪಾದಗೆ ಬಡತ ಬಿದ್ದವು. ಅದು ಯಾಕೆ? ಅವನ ದವತಿಯೊಳಗೆ ಮಸಿ ಇದ್ದಿಲ್ಲ, ಗಣ್ಟಿನೊಳಗೆ ಲೆಕ್ಕಣಿಕೆಯೂ ಕಾಗದವೂ ಇದ್ದಿಲ್ಲ, then Gurupâda was beaten (by his schoolmaster). Why? In his inkstand ink a having been was not (*i. e.*—there was no ink—), (and) in his bundle a pen and paper a having been were not (*i. e.*—there was not a pen or paper).

4, about ಇಲ್ಲವು.

ಮುನ್ದಾಗೊ ಗತಿಗೆ ಸಾಧನವಿಲ್ಲವು, a means (there) is not for (obtaining) future happiness (*i. e.* there is no means for obtaining future happiness). ಎಷ್ಟು ಜಿಗಿದಾಗ್ಯೂ ಬಾಯಿಗೆ ನಿಲುಕಲಿಕ್ಕಿಲ್ಲವು, however so much (the fox) jumped (the bunches of grapes) a coming in reach for (his) mouth were not (*i. e.*—could not be reached with his mouth). See also Dâsapadas 23, 1; 48, 2; 148, 7.

5, about the combination of ಇಲ್ಲ with ಹಾಗೆ.

ಅವ್ವಾ, ಅವ್ವಾ, ಒನ್ದು ಬಟ್ಟಲ ಬೇಕು; ಲಗು ಕೊಡು! ಇಷ್ಟು ಅವಸರವು ಯಾಕೋ, ರಾಮು? ಮುಂಚೆ ಬಟ್ಟಲಾ ಕೊಡು! ಮಾತಾಡುತ್ತ ನಿಲ್ಲುವ ಹಾಗಿಲ್ಲ, mother, mother, a basin is required; give (it) quickly! Why so much hurry, Râma? (Mother) give (me) first a basin! a staying thus (quite literally: of the staying in this wise, see § 186) talking (there) is not (*i. e.* there is no time for me to stay and talk now). ಕಣಿಕೆ ನನ್ನ ಕೆಯ್ಗೆ ನಿಲುಕುವ ಹಾಗಿಲ್ಲ, the millet-stalks a reaching thus for my hands (there) is not (*i. e.* the millet-stalks cannot be reached with my hands). ನನ್ನ ವಯಸ್ಸಾದರೂ ಮೀಱಿ ಹೋಯಿತೆನ್ನುವ ಹಾಗೆ ಇಲ್ಲ, "also my prime of life has passed" a saying thus (there) is not (*i. e.* you cannot say that also my prime of life has passed).

299. About the combination of ಎ, ಏ, ಒ, ಓ with ಇಲ್ಲ.

1, ಇಲ್ಲವೆ or ಇಲ್ಲವೇ.

In these two forms ಇಲ್ಲ is combined with ಎ and ಏ, two particles of interrogation (§ 212, 6), suffixed by means of a euphonic ವ್. The meaning of ಇಲ್ಲವೆ and ಇಲ್ಲವೇ is first "is (there) not?" "are (there) not?", *e.g.* ಎಳ್ಳಿನೊಳಗೆಣ್ಣೆಯಿಲ್ಲವೇ, is there no oil in the gingely-oil seed? (answer: yes, there is). ಪುಷ್ಪವೊನ್ದು ಬಟಿಲಲ್ ಭೃಂಗಕ್ಕೆ ಪೂವಿಲ್ಲವೆ, if one flower fades, are there no flowers for the black humble bee? (answer: yes, there are).

This meaning, however, often changes into 'or', literally "is it not (this)?", *i. e.* if this is not the case, then it may be also this, *e.g.* ನಿನಗೆ ಏನಾದರೂ ನೋವು ಆದಾಗ ಇಲ್ಲವೆ ಬೇನೆ ಬನ್ದಾಗ ತಾಯಿ ತನ್ದೆಗಳು ಕ್ಲೇಶ ಪಡುವರು, when thou getst any pain, is it not (this? is it not pain? then also *i. e.* or) when sickness happens (to thee), thy parents will grieve. ಮನುಷ್ಯನ ಮನಸ್ಸು ಅವನ ನುಡಿಯಿನ್ದ ಇಲ್ಲವೆ ನಡೆಯಿನ್ದ ತಿಳಿಯುತ್ತದೆ, man's mind is known by his words, is it not (this? is it not by his words? then also *i. e.* or) by (his) conduct. ಗಾಯದೊಳಗಿನ ನೆತ್ತರಾ ತೆಗದರೆ ವಿಷವು ಏಱುವದಿಲ್ಲ, ಇಲ್ಲವೇ ಆ ಗಾಯುವನ್ನು ಕೊಳ್ಳಿಯಿನ್ದ ಸುಟ್ಟರೆ ವಿಷವು ಏಱುವದಿಲ್ಲ, if (one) removes the blood out of the wound (made by the teeth of a snake), the poison will take no effect, is it not (this? is it not the removal of the blood? then also *i. e.* or) if that wound is cauterised, the poison will take no effect.

2, ಇಲ್ಲವೊ or ಇಲ್ಲವೋ.

When the interrogative particles ಒ and ಓ (§ 212, 6) are suffixed to ಇಲ್ಲ by means of a euphonic ವ್, it conveys **first** the meaning of a question, occasionally one of more or less displeasure, *e.g.* ನಿನಗೆ ಮಜ್ಜಿಗೆ ಸೇರುವದಿಲ್ಲವೋ, does buttermilk not agree with thee? ಅವನ ಬಱಿಯಲ್ಲಿ ಚೀಲವಿಲ್ಲವೋ, is there no sack near him? ಆ ಹಾಲು ಆಱಿಲ್ಲವೋ, has that milk not got cool? ಅವನು ಬರಲಿಕ್ಕಿಲ್ಲವೋ, will he not come? ಇನ್ನೂ ನಿನ್ನ ಹಲಿಗೇ ಮೇಲಿನ ಬರಹ ತೀರಿಲ್ಲವೋ, has writing on thy board not been finished yet (*i. e.* doest thou still write on thy board)? ಅವನು ಇನ್ನೂ ಹೋಗಲಿಲ್ಲವೋ, has he not yet gone? ನೀನು ಬರುವದಿಲ್ಲವೋ, wilt thou not come?

But then ಇಲ್ಲವೊ, ಇಲ್ಲವೋ frequently mean 'is it not?', 'will it not be?', 'was it not?', *i.e.* 'or not?', *e.g.* ಶಿವನ ಅಗ್ಗವಣಿಯಂ ಶೋಧಿಸಿದುದಿಲ್ಲವೊ, a having strained the water of Śiva, or not? (*i. e.* Śiva's water was strained, or not?). ಕಸೀ ಮಾಡಿದ ಮರವು ಚಿಗಿತು, ಮತ್ತೆ ಬೆಳೆದು, ದೊಡ್ಡ ಮರವಾಗುವದಿಲ್ಲವೋ? ಅಮಾಸಿಯಲ್ಲಿ ಕಳೆಗುನ್ದಿದ ಚನ್ದ್ರನು ಹುಣ್ಣಿವೆಗೆ ಪೂರ್ಣನಾಗುವದಿಲ್ಲವೋ, a pruned tree will sprout and grow, (and) become a large tree, or not? The moon that lost its splendour on the day of new moon, will become full on the day of full moon, or not? ತನ್ನ ಹೊಸ ಕೊಡ್ಲಿಯು ಹದನವದೆಯೋ? ಇಲ್ಲವೋ? ನೋಡ ಬೇಕೆನ್ದು, ಕಣ್ಣಿ ಕಣ್ಡದನೆಲ್ಲ ಕಡಿಯ ಹತ್ತಿದನು, he (the boy) said, "is my (literally: his) new axe sharp? or not? let (me) see", and began to cut down all he saw.

To ಇಲ್ಲ the ಓ may also be added without a euphonic ಓ, and then its form is ಇಲ್ಲೋ.

3, ಇಲ್ಲವೇ ಇಲ್ಲ or ಇಲ್ಲೇ ಇಲ್ಲ.

In ಇಲ್ಲವೇ ಇಲ್ಲ an ಏ of emphasis has been suffixed to ಇಲ್ಲ by means of a euphonic ವ್, and ಇಲ್ಲ has been repeated; its literal meaning is 'certainly it is not, it is not' (or 'certainly it will not be, it will not be', or 'certainly it was not, it was not'), by which 'not at all' is expressed.

In ಇಲ್ಲೇ ಇಲ್ಲ the ಏ of emphasis has been joined to the first ಇಲ್ಲ without a euphonic ವ್, *e. g.* ದಣಿದು ಇದ್ದಿಯಾ? ಇಲ್ಲೇ ಇಲ್ಲ, art thou tired? Not at all. ಸೃಷ್ಟಿಯಲ್ಲಿ ಅಯೋಗ್ಯವಾದವುಗಳು ಇಲ್ಲೇ ಇಲ್ಲ, in the universe there are unsuitable things not at all (*i. e.* in the universe there are no unsuitable things, none at all).

300. In § 212, 7 ಅಲ್ಲ is introduced as an avyaya. In § 209, note 1 and in § 210 we have seen that it is a form of the negative of the verbal theme ಅಲ್, meaning 'fits not', 'is not fit', 'are not fit', 'was not fit', etc., 'is not corresponding to', 'is not becoming', 'does not answer to', 'is not equivalent', 'is not according to facts', 'is opposite to', etc. It takes also the form of ಅಲ್ಲಂ (*cf.* ಇಲ್ಲಂ in § 298), *e. g.* ಬನ್ದನೀಗಳ್ ಪೆಱನಲ್ಲಂ ದುರ್ಜಯಂ ಕೌರವಕುಳನಳಿನೀಕುಂಜರಂ ಭೀಮಸೇನಂ, now came Bhîmasêna, a stranger he did not answer to (*i. e.* he was no stranger), invincible, pre-eminent in the lotus-pond of the Kaurava race. (ಇದು) ನೀತಿಯಲ್ಲಂ, (this) does not correspond to justice (*i. e.* this is no justice). (ಇದು) ಪಟಮ್ ಅಲ್ಲಂ, (this) does not answer to silk (*i. e.* this is no silk).

For the existence of ಅಲ್ಲವು in the modern dialect (*cf.* ಇಲ್ಲವು in § 298, 4) the author is unable to cite an instance.

When followed immediately by a vowel, the final of ಅಲ್ಲ either disappears, *e. g.* ಅಲ್ಲೆನ್, or a euphonic ವ್ is put after it, *e. g.* ಅಲ್ಲವಾಗು.

Instances are:

1, regarding ಅಲ್ಲ.

ನರನೆಮ್ಬಾತಂ ಪೆಱನಲ್ಲೀತನಾಗಲ್ವೇೞ್ಕುಂ, Arjuna a stranger does not answer to (*i. e.* Arjuna is no stranger), he to become is required (*i. e.* he must become . . .). (ಇದು) ಘಟಮಲ್ಲ, (this) does not correspond to a pot (*i. e.* this is no pot). (ಇದು) ಊರಲ್ಲ, ಅಡವಿಯಹುದು, (this) does not correspond to a town (*i. e.* is no town), it is a wild. ಧರ್ಮವಲ್ಲವಿದು, this is opposite to virtue (*i. e.* this is no virtue). ಓಜನೊಕ್ಕಲಲ್ಲ, ಹೂಜಿ ಭಾಣ್ಡದೊಳಗಲ್ಲ, ಗಾಜೊನ್ದು ಲೋಹದೊಳಗಲ್ಲ, ಅಮ್ಬಲಿ ಭೋಜನವೆ ಅಲ್ಲ, a teacher is not corresponding to a farmer (*i. e.* is no farmer), a goglet is not fit (to be ranked) in the class of pots (*i. e.* is no pot), glass is not fit amongst metals (*i. e.* is no metal), indeed porridge is not fit (for) a dinner (*i. e.* certainly is no proper dinner). ಒಕ್ಕಲಿಗನೋದಲ್ಲ, ಬೆಕ್ಕು ಹೆಬ್ಬುಲಿಯಲ್ಲ, ಎಕ್ಕೆಯ ಗಿಡವು ಬನವಲ್ಲ; ಇವು ಮೂಱು ಲೆಕ್ಕದೊಳಗಲ್ಲ, a peasant's reading is not proper, a cat is not corresponding to a royal tiger (*i. e.* is no royal tiger), a swallow-wort shrub is not corresponding to a garden (*i. e.* is no garden); these three are not fit in account (*i. e.* are unworthy of much notice). ಹಕ್ಕಿಯಿಲ್ಲದ್ದು ತೋಟವಲ್ಲ; ಮಕ್ಕಳಿಲ್ಲದ್ದು ಮನೆಯಲ್ಲ, wherein there are no birds, is not answering to a garden; wherein there are no children, is not answering to a house (*i. e.* a garden wherein there are no birds, is no garden; a house wherein there are no children, is no house). ಗುರುವಿಲ್ಲದ ಮಠವಲ್ಲ, ಹಿರಿಯರಿಲ್ಲದ ಮನೆಯಲ್ಲ, wherein there is no guru, is not answering to a maṭha; wherein there are no elders, is not answering to a house (*i. e.* a maṭha without a guru is no maṭha, a house without elders is no house). ಸನ್ತೆಯೊಳಗೆಲ್ಲಿಟ್ಟು ಮಾಱುವದಲ್ಲ . . . . ವಿಠಲನ ನಾಮವು, Viṭhala's name . . . . in a fair wheresover a putting and selling is not equal to (*i. e.* Viṭhala's name is not such a thing as is put and sold somewhere in a fair). ತನು ತನ್ನದಲ್ಲ, (man's) body his is not according to facts (*i. e.* man's body is not his own). ಇವನಲ್ಲ, ಅವನು ಬೇಕು, this man is not fit (*i. e.* not this man, but) that man is wanted. ಹಳದೀ ಬಣ್ಣದ್ದು ಹೊಳೆಯುವದೆಲ್ಲ ಬಂಗಾರವಲ್ಲ, all that shines (with) yellow colour gold does not answer to (*i. e.* is not gold). ಇದನ್ನೇನು ತುಡುಗು ಮಾಡಿದಿಯೋ? ತುಡುಗು? ಅಲ್ಲಾ, hast thou perhaps stolen this? Stolen property? certainly it is not answering to (*i. e.* certainly it is not). ಎಮ್ಮೆಯ ಹಾಲು ಆಕಳ ಹಾಲಿನಷ್ಟು ಆರೋಗ್ಯವಲ್ಲ, buffalo's milk so much wholesome as cow's milk is not fit (*i. e.* buffalo's milk is not so wholesome as cow's milk). ರಾಜಾಪುರ ಪಟ್ಟಣ ಮುನ್ತಾದ ಸ್ಥಳಗಳಲ್ಲಿ ಸಕ್ಕರೆಯನ್ನು ಮಾಡುತ್ತಾರೆ, ಆದರೆ ಅದು ಬಹಳ ಚೆಲೋದಲ್ಲ, they manufacture sugar (also) at Râjâpura, Paṭṭaṇa and other places, but its great goodness is not according to facts (*i. e.* but it is not very good). ಅಫುವಿನ ವ್ಯಸನವು ಬಹಳ ಕೆಟ್ಟದು; ಅದಱಿ ಸಲುವಾಗಿ ಸಮ್ಪತ್ತಿಗಿಷ್ಟೇ ಅಲ್ಲ, ಪ್ರಾಣಕ್ಕೆ ಸಹ ಎರವಾಗುತ್ತಾರೆ, addiction to opium is a very bad thing; on account of it they do harm to (their) property, this much is not corresponding (*i. e.* not only this, but) also to (their) life. ಇಷ್ಟೇ ಅಲ್ಲ, this much is not corresponding to facts (*i. e.* this is not all). ಯಾವತ್ತು ಪ್ರಮಾಣಗಳು ಇಷ್ಟೇಯೋ? ಅಲ್ಲ, ಇನ್ನು ಕೆಲವು ಉಣ್ಟು, are these all the arguments? (this much) is not fit (*i. e.* no, it is not so), there are still some others. ಇದು ಧರ್ಮಶಾಲೆಯಲ್ಲ, ಅರಮನೆಯು, this a poor-asylum is not corresponding to facts (*i. e.* this is not a poor-asylum, but) a palace. ಈ ಗುಡ್ಡದಲ್ಲಿ ಒನ್ದಲ್ಲ, ಎರಡಲ್ಲ, ಮುನ್ನೂರು ಕಣಿಗಳನ್ನು ಅಗಿದಿರುತ್ತಾರೆ, one is not fit, two are not fit (*i. e.* not only one, not only two, but) three hundred mines they have dug in this hill. ನೀನು ಹೀಗೆ ಮಾಡುವದು ತಕ್ಕದಲ್ಲ, thou in this way a making a proper thing it is not corresponding to (*i. e.* it is not right for thee to do so; *cf.* § 316, 9). ಈ ಕೊಡೆಯು ಏನೂ ಕೆಲಸದ್ದಲ್ಲ, (is) this umbrella of any use (see remark *b*)? it is not fit (*i. e.* this umbrella is good for nothing). ಯಾವ ಪ್ರಕಾರದಿನ್ದಲೂ ಅಲ್ಲ, in whatever manner it is not fit (*i. e.* in no way). Other instances are:— ಇದು ಮಂಜಲ್ಲ, ಬೆಳದಿಂಗಳು. ಇವನು ಮನುಷ್ಯನಲ್ಲ, ರಕ್ಕಸನು. ಇವಳು ಹೆಣ್ಡತಿಯಲ್ಲ, ಮಾರಿಯು. ಇವರು ಆಪ್ತರಲ್ಲ, ವೈರಿಗಳು.

Remarks.

a) Regarding the practical difference in the use of ಇಲ್ಲ (§ 298) and ಅಲ್ಲ it may be said that ಇಲ್ಲ expresses positive non-existence and positive denial, and ಅಲ್ಲ relative negation and negation of quality, nature or character.

b) It is not impossible that ಅಲ್ಲ when following a noun, etc., originally formed an answer to a question. Let us take a few of the above-mentioned instances to show this. ನರನೆಮ್ವಾತಂ ಪೆಱನಲ್ಲ might be translated '(is) Arjuna a stranger? No (he is not)'. Likewise (ಇದು) ಘಟಮಲ್ಲ '(is this) a pot? No (it is not)'. (ಇದು) ಊರಲ್ಲ, ಅಡವಿಯಹುದು '(is this) a town? No, it is a wilderness'.

To give this meaning to ಅಲ್ಲ would recommend itself, when ಅಲ್ಲ is sometimes put after an accusative, *e. g.* ನನ್ನನ್ನು ಅಲ್ಲ, ನಮ್ಮ ತಮ್ಮನನ್ನು ಹೊಡೆದೆನು (Bombay school-book 3, 6), 'me (*i. e.* did I beat me)? No, I beat my younger brother'. ಇವನನ್ನಲ್ಲ, ಅವನನ್ನು ಕರೆ (Rev. F. Ziegler in his Practical Key, page 27), '(shall I call) this man? No, call that man'. *Cf.* the accusative after ಅಲ್ಲದೆ in § 338, and see § 287, remark.

Sûtra 47 of the Šabdamaṇidarpaṇa teaches that ಅಲ್ಲದೆ, when it denotes emphasis (nirdhâraṇârtha, and is composed of ಅಲ್ಲದು, = ಅಲ್ತು, + ಎ, or is the so-called negative participle, see § 171 and ಅಲ್ಲದೆ in § 338), occasionally drops its ದೆ, and gives the instance ಗೊರವನಲ್ಲ ಪೊಗೞೆಂ which stands for ಗೊರವನಲ್ಲದೆ ಪೊಗೞೆಂ. A translation would be 'Gŏrava a being not fit indeed (or a being not meant indeed) I do not praise (*i. e.* I do not praise anybody but Gŏrava)'. Thus the instance appears in Liṅgâyta manuscripts; a Jaina manuscript of Mûḍabidaru has ದೇವರಲ್ಲ ಪೊಗೞೆಂ which stands for ದೇವರನಲ್ಲದೆ ಪೊಗೞೆಂ, putting the accusative ದೇವರಂ before ಅಲ್ಲದೆ, but ದೇವರ್, the nominative, before ಅಲ್ಲ. The Mûḍabidaru

MS.'s writing in this case may be wrong, or may be not, so far as the accusative is concerned.

2, regarding ಅಲ್ಲ in combination with ಹಾಗೆ (or ಅನ್ತೆ).

ಹಾಗಲ್ಲ, thus (as you think) it is not fit (*i. e.* thus it is not). ಆಕಳ ಕೊಳಗು ಕುದುರೆಯ ಕೊಳಗಿನ ಹಾಗಲ್ಲ, ಸೀಳಿರುತ್ತದೆ, the hoof of cows so as the hoof of horses is not corresponding to facts (*i. e.* the hoof of cows is unlike the hoof of horses), it is split. ಪಶುಗಳೊಳಗೆ ಕುದುರೆಯ ಹಾಗೆ ಚನ್ದವೂ ಗಟ್ಟಿಯೂ ಅಲ್ಲ, amongst beasts like the horse beautiful and strong (any) are not fit (*i. e.* amongst beasts there are none so beautiful and strong as the horse). ಮೀನುಗಳು ನೀರ ಬಿಟ್ಟು ಹ್ಯಾಗೆ ಬದುಕಲಾರಿವೋ, ಹಾಗೇನು ಇವು (ಕಪ್ಪೆಗಳು) ಅಲ್ಲ, as fishes cannot leave water and live, so anyhow these (frogs) are not according to facts (*i. e.* — so these frogs are in no way).

3, regarding ಅಲ್ಲವೆ, ಅಲ್ಲವೇ or ಅಲ್ಲೇ.

These forms bear the suffixes of question ಎ and ಏ, expecting an answer in the affirmative; the first two insert a euphonic ವ್, the last one adds ಏ immediately to ಅಲ್ಲ. *E. g.* ಏರಾಗಮ ಏರಾಗಮಂಗಳ್ಗೆ ಗಳಾಗಮಂ ವಿಕಲ್ಪದಿನ್ದೆ ಆಗುವುದು, ಅಲ್ಲವೆ, instead of the augments 'ದಿರ್ and ಏರ್ the augment ಗಳ್ is used ad libitum, is it not fit? (*i. e.*—is it not so? or not?). ಸ್ಥಿರಮಿದಲ್ಲವೆಮ್ಬ ಜೀವಿ ಜ್ಞಾನಿಯಲ್ಲವೆ? ನರಕಭಯವ ಮಱೆವ ಜಡನಜ್ಞಾನಿಯಲ್ಲವೆ? a living being that says "this (life) is unstable", (is) a wise person, or not? an apathetic man that forgets the fear of hell, (is) an unwise person, or not? ಇನ್ದಿಗೆ ಆಱು ದಿವಸ ದೀವಳಿಗೇ ಹಬ್ಬ, ಅಲ್ಲವೇ? to-day six days (or six days hence is) the illumination-festival, or not? ನಿನ್ನದೂ ಅದೇ ಹಾದಿ, ಅಲ್ಲವೇ? and thine (is) the same road, or not? ಅದು ಗುಬ್ಬಿ, ಅಲ್ಲೇ, that (is) a sparrow, or not?

4, regarding ಅಲ್ಲವೊ, ಅಲ್ಲವೋ, or ಅಲ್ಲೋ.

In these three forms the suffixes of question ಒ, ಓ appear, the answer being in the affirmative; in ಅಲ್ಲೋ the ಓ is joined immediately to ಅಲ್ಲ. *E. g.* ವ್ಯೋಮ ಚಾರುಚರಿತ್ರನಲ್ಲವೊ? Vyôma (is) a well-behaved man, is it not fit? (*i. e.*—is it not so? or not?). ನಾವು ಮರಣಾಧೀನರಲ್ಲವೋ? we are mortals, or not? ವ್ಯೋಮ ಸಜ್ಜನಮಿತ್ರನಲ್ಲೋ?— ಅಯ್ಯೋ, ನನ್ನ ಮಗನೇ, ಮರದ ಮೇಲಿನ್ದ ಬಿದ್ದಿದ್ದರೆ ಸತ್ತು ಹೋಗುತ್ತಿದಿ, ಅಲ್ಲೋ?

301. ಅಲ್ಲು, ಅಲ್ತೆ, ಅಲ್ಲದೆ, ಇಲ್ಲದೆ and ಬೇಡ which are classed under the avyayas by the Śabdânuśâsana (§ 212, 7), will be treated of in another place (§§ 338. 316, 5).

In the Śabdânuśâsana's ಎಲ್ಲಂ (§ 212, 7) the nominative of ಎಲ್ಲ (§ 266) has been used adverbially (see the verse quoted under No. 17 in § 348); in its ಏನ್ the same has happened regarding this interrogative pronoun (§ 255). Its ಏಗುವೆಂ and ಏವೆಂ are compounds of ಏ, what? (the accusative, see § 125) and curtailed ಗೆಯ್ವೆಂ, I shall do.

302. Here follow some peculiarities (chiefly) of the modern dialect regarding the way of expressing certain English adverbs:—

1, **Since** (with regard to time).

This is expressed by means of the instrumental (*i. e.* ablative, § 352, 4 *a*), *e. g.* ಈ ಶಿವನ್ ಏಸು ದಿನದಿನ್ದುಣ್ಣದಿರ್ದಹನೋ, since how many days has this Śiva not dined? ಒನ್ದು ನರಿಯ ಮನಸಿನೊಳಗೆ ಹುಲಿಗೆ ಸರಿಯಾಗ ಬೇಕೆಮ್ಬ ಹೆಮ್ಮೆ ಬಹು ದಿವಸದಿನ್ದ ಇತ್ತು, since many days there existed in the mind of a fox the haughty desire to become like a tiger. ಅಱುವತ್ತು ವರ್ಷದಿನ್ದ, since sixty years. ಸೋಮವಾರದಿನ್ದ ನಾನು ನನ್ನ ತಮ್ಮನನ್ನು ನೋಡಿಲ್ಲ, I have not seen my brother since Monday. ಅನ್ದಿನಿನ್ದ ಅವರು ಒಬ್ಬರ ಮೇಲೊಬ್ಬರು ಪ್ರೀತಿ ಮಾಡ ಹತ್ತಿದರು, since (or from) that time they began to love each other. ಚಿಕ್ಕನ್ದಿನಿನ್ದ, since (my or thy or his or her or its or their) youth (or from my, etc. youth).

But there is another way of expressing 'since' (in the modern dialect), namely by means of the verb ಆಗು in combination with a so-called past participle, *e. g.* ಈ ಊರಿಗೆ ದೊರೆಗಳು ಬನ್ದು ಎಷ್ಟು ದಿವಸ ಆಯಿತು, literally: to this town the gentleman a having come (§ 169) how many days have passed, *i. e.* how many days is it since the gentleman came to this town? ಇವನು ಸತ್ತು ಇಪ್ಪತ್ತು ವರುಷವಾಯಿತು, it is twenty years since he died (or he died twenty years ago). ನೀನು ಸಾಲೆಗೆ ಹೋಗಲಿಕ್ಕೆ ಹತ್ತಿ ಎಷ್ಟು ತಿಂಗಳಾಯಿತು, how many months is it since you began to go to school? ಪುಸ್ತಕಗಳನ್ನು ಅಚ್ಚು ಹಾಕುವ ಯುಕ್ತಿ ಗೊತ್ತಾಗಿ ಈಗ ಸುಮಾರು ನಾಲ್ನೂಱು ವರುಷಗಳಾದವು, it is now about 400 years since the art of printing became known. ಅವನು ಎದ್ದು ಬಹಳ ಹೊತ್ತಾಯಿತು, much time has passed since he got up (or he got up long ago).

Also the past participle of ಮೊದಲುಗೊಳ್ಳು may be used in a similar manner, *e. g.* ಅನ್ದಿನ ದಿವಸ ಮೊದಲುಗೊಂಡು, since that day.

The Saṁskṛita ಆರಭ್ಯ is used so too, *e. g.* ಅನ್ದಿನ ಆರಭ್ಯ, since that time.

2, **Hence** (with regard to time).

This may be rendered in the following manner: ಇನ್ದಿಗೆ ಆಱು ದಿವಸ ದೀವಳಿಗೇ ಹಬ್ಬ, to-day six days (will be) the illumination festival, or six days hence (will be) the illumination festival. ಈ ತಿಂಗಳಿಗೆ ಆಱು ತಿಂಗಳು, six months this month. *Cf.* § 348, 29.

3, **Before** (previous to).

In § 282, as will be seen, some instances in which this adverb is expressed by ಮುಂಚೆ, have been given. It is to be remarked here that it is rendered also by ಮೊದಲು, *e.g.* ತಮಗಿನ್ತ ಮೊದಲು ಇಲ್ಲಿ ಯಾರು ಇರುತ್ತಿದ್ದರು, before you who were living here? ಅದಕ್ಕಿನ್ತ ಮೊದಲು, prior to that. ಮನೆ ಕಟ್ಟುವದಕ್ಕಿನ್ತ ಮೊದಲು ಚನ್ನಾಗಿ ತಳಾ ಸೋಸ ಬೇಕಾಗುತ್ತದೆ, before building a house it is necessary to clear the foundation properly.

Thus also: ಮಾತಿಗೆ ಮೊದಲು ಗಾದೆ, ಊಟಕ್ಕೆ ಮೊದಲು ಉಪ್ಪಿನಕಾಯಿ, previous to words a proverb (is fit), previous to dinner pickles (are fit).

In connection with ಮುನ್ನಂ, ಮುನ್ನ, before, previous to, the negative participle is also used, *e.g.* ಕಿಳಿರ್ವ ಗೋಱಿಯ ದನಿ ಕಿವಿಗೊಗದ ಮುನ್ನಂ, before the neighing sound of the mares entered the ear; ನಿನ್ನ ಕೊರಳಿಗೆ ಕಪ್ಪು ಬಾರದ ಮುನ್ನ, before the black colour came to thy throat. The same is done in connection with ಮುಂಚೆ, *e.g.* ಅವರು ಬಾರದ ಮುಂಚೆ, before they came (*cf.* ಅವನು ಬಾರದ್ದಕ್ಕಿನ್ತ ಮುಂಚೆ, etc. in § 282).

4, **As.**

'**As usual**', '**as on previous occasions**' may be expressed by ದಿನದನ್ತೆ or ದಿನದ ಹಾಗೆ, *e.g.* ಶಾಮನು ದಿನದನ್ತೆ ನಿನ್ನದೇನಾದರೂ ಕುಚೇಷ್ಟೆ ಮಾಡಿರ ಬಹುದು, as usual Śâma may have annoyed thee somehow. ದಿನದ ಹಾಗೆ ಊಟದ ಹೊತ್ತು ಆಗಲು ಚಾಕರನು ಬನ್ದನು, as usual the servant came at dinner-time. Also: ಮೊದಲಿನನ್ತೆ, as before; and in the mediæval dialect: ಎನ್ದಿನನ್ತೆ, ಎನ್ದಿನ ವೊಲ್, ಎನ್ದಿನಹಗೆ, ಎನ್ದಿನ ಹಾಗೆ.

'**As to**', '**as for**' may be rendered by means of ಆದರೆ, if becomes, if become, *e.g.* ನಾವಾದರೆ ಮಾಡ ಕೂಡದು (Hodson's grammar), as for us we cannot do (so). ಅವನಾದರೆ ಹೋಗುತ್ತಾನೆ (Ziegler's Practical Key), as to him he will go;—or, as in the South-Mahratta country, by means of ಅನ್ನೂ (ಅನ್ನು), *e.g.* ಆಟದ ಒಡವೆಗಳು ಅನ್ನೂ ನನಗೆ ಬೇಡ, as for toys they are not required for me;—or by means of Saṁskṛita ವಿಷಯ, regard, concern, *e.g.* ತುಪ್ಪದ ವಿಷಯಕ್ಕೆ ಧಾರಣೆ ಇನ್ನೂ ಎಷ್ಟು ಏಱೀತೆವ್ಬುವದು ಹೇಳಿ ಕೂಡದು, as to ghee it is impossible to say how much it will still rise in price. ಮೋಕ್ಷದ ವಿಷಯಕ್ಕೆ ಚಿನ್ತಿಸುತ್ತಾನೆ, he is anxious concerning (his) môksha. ಅವನ ವಿಷಯದಲ್ಲಿ, as to him. ಅದಱ ವಿಷಯವಾಗಿ, as for that. (*Cf.* § 348, 17).

'As if' is rendered by means of the relative past participle with ಹಾಗೆ (or ಅನ್ತೆ), *e. g.* ಸಾಲೆಗೆ ಹೋಗದೆ, ಆಡುವದಕ್ಕೆ ನಿನ್ತು, ಮಱುದಿನ ಗುರುಗಳು ಕೇಳಿದಾಗ, ನಿನ್ನೆ ಜ್ವರ ಬನ್ದಿದ್ದವೆನ್ದು ಹೇೞಿದರೆ ಸುಳ್ಳು ಹೇೞಿದ ಹಾಗಾಯಿತು; ಹೆಱವರ ಪುಸ್ತಕ ಮುನ್ತಾದವುಗಳನ್ನು ಕದ್ದು ಕೊಣ್ಡರೆ ಅಸತ್ಯದಿನ್ದ ನಡೆದ ಹಾಗಾಯಿತು, if (we) do not go to school, stay (at home) to play, and when on the next day the teacher asks (the reason), say that a fever had befallen (us), it is as if (we) had told a lie; if (we) steal the books etc. of others, it is (the same) as if (we) acted feloniously.

'As long as' is expressed in the ancient dialect as follows: ಎನ್ನೆವರಂ ಸಿರಿ ತಮಗುಣ್ಟನ್ನೆವರಂ ಸೇವ್ಯರಲ್ತೆ ಬಳರುಂ, as long as they possess riches, will not also scoundrels be honourable persons?

'As soon as' is rendered by means of the relative participle combined with an adverb of time to which the ಏ or ಎ of emphasis is joined, *e. g.* ಅವನು ಬನ್ದನ್ದೆ or ಅವನು ಬನ್ದಾಗಲೇ ಅಪ್ಪನ ತನ್ದೆ ಹೊಱಟನು, as soon as he had come, his father started. ಗುರುಗಳು ಒಳಗೆ ಬರುವನ್ದೆ or ಬರುವಾಗಲೇ ಎಲ್ಲರೂ ಇದಿರೆದ್ದರು, as soon as the guru came inside, all rose. See also the close of § 349.

5, **At least** (with regard to a sum),

This is expressed by ಏನಿಲ್ಲೆನ್ದರೂ, if (one) says it is nothing, *e. g.* ಅವೆಲ್ಲಾ ಕಣಿಗಳೊಳಗಿನ್ದ ಪ್ರತಿವಾರಕ್ಕೆ ಏನಿಲ್ಲೆನ್ದರೂ ಒನ್ದು ಲಕ್ಷ ರೂಪಾಯಿಗಳ ಬೆಳ್ಳಿ ಹೊಱಡುತ್ತದೆ, out of all those mines silver is put at least to the amount of one lac of rupees a week. ನಾನು ಈ ಪೆಟ್ಟಿಗೆಗೆ ಏನಿಲ್ಲೆನ್ದರೂ ಐದು ರೂಪಾಯಿ ತಕ್ಕೊಳ್ಳುವೆನು, I shall get at least five rupees for this box.

6, **Just, precisely, exactly** (as to a standard or fact).

These terms may occasionally be rendered by ಇದ್ದಕ್ಕಿದ್ದ ಹಾಗೆ (*i. e.* ಇದ್ದದಕ್ಕೆ ಇದ್ದ ಹಾಗೆ), to (*i. e.* corresponding to) its being being thus, *e. g.* ಇದ್ದಕ್ಕಿದ್ದ ಹಾಗೆ ಆತನ ವರ್ಣನೆ ಮಾಡಿದಿರಿ, you have described him exactly.

7, **For.**

If a person wants to adduce the reason (or cause) of something he writes or speaks about, 'for', 'because' are expressed by ಯಾಕನ್ದರೆ, if I say (or if one says) why? *e.g.* ನಾವು ಈ ಗಿಡದ ಕೆಲವು ಮಾವಿನ ಹಣ್ಣುಗಳನ್ನು ಕೊಯ್ಯೋಣೇನು? ಬೇಡ! ಯಾಕನ್ದರೆ ಅವು ನಮ್ಮವಲ್ಲ, shall we cut some (of the) ripe mangoes of this tree? It is not fit, for they are not ours. ಮೋಸಗಾಱರಿಗೆ ಯಾವದೊನ್ದು ಕೆಲಸದಲ್ಲಿ ಬಹಳ ಬುದ್ಧಿ ಬೇಕಾಗುತ್ತದೆ, ಯಾಕನ್ದರೆ ಪ್ರಾಣಿಗಳೆಲ್ಲ ತಮಗೆ ಮೋಸವಾಗ ಬಾರದೆನ್ದು ಬಹಳ ಎಚ್ಚಱಿದಿನ್ದ ಇರುತ್ತಾರೆ, deceitful men must use much shrewdness in any affair, for all beings are watchful, lest they be deceived. ನಾವು ಕಳವು ಮಾಡ ಬಾರದು, ಯಾಕನ್ದರೆ ಒನ್ದು ವೇಳೆ ನಮ್ಮನ್ನು ಮನುಷ್ಯರು ನೋಡದಿದ್ದರೂ ದೇವರು ನಮ್ಮನ್ನು ಯಾವಾಗಲೂ ನೋಡುತ್ತಿರುತ್ತಾನೆ, we must not (or should not) steal, for though men do perhaps not see us, God sees us always. *Cf.* § 322, and see further *e. g.* Bombay school-books, 2, 1. 10. 48; 3, 58. 105; 4, 10. 16. 20. 52. 98. 111. 141.

'For', 'on account', 'because of'. In § 282 we have ಓಸುಗ, ಓಸುಗರ, ಓಸ್ಕರ with the genitive to express these adverbs; similarly are used also ಸಲವಾಗಿ, lit. the reason a becoming or a having become, *e.g.* ಅದರ ಸಲವಾಗಿ, on that account; ತುಸುಕ, (reason?), *e. g.* ಅದರ ತುಸುಕ, on that account; and ದೆಸೆಯಿನ್ದ, lit. from the side, *e. g.* ಅವನ ದೆಸೆಯಿನ್ದ, on account of him.

The same is expressed **also simply by the dative,** *e. g.* ಅದಕ್ಕೆ, on that account; ಕೆಲಸಕೆ, on account of (a) work or (a) business; ಹಬ್ಬಕ್ಕೆ, because of the feast; ಬೇಡುವದಕ್ಕೆ, for requesting or begging; ಓದುವದಕ್ಕೆ, for reading; ಕೊಳ್ಳಲಿಕ್ಕೆ, for buying; — **or by adding** ಆಗಿ, **a having become, to the dative,** *e. g.* ನಿನಗಾಗಿ, lit. for thee a having become, *i. e.* on thy account; ಬೇಟೆಯ ಶೋಧಕ್ಕಾಗಿ, for search (or in search) of game; ತನ್ದೆಯ ಮಾತಿಗಾಗಿ, on account of the father's word; ಆ ಕೆಲಸಕ್ಕಾಗಿ, for that business; ಕೊಳ್ಳುವದಕ್ಕಾಗಿ, in order to buy. (Regarding the use of the dative see § 348.)

'For', 'therefore', 'on account' are frequently **to be rendered by the instrumental** (*i. e.* ablative § 352, 4 *a*) of ಅದು, *e. g.* ಮಂಗಗಳು ನಮ್ಮ ಹಾಗೆ ಎರಡೇ ಕಾಲಿನಿನ್ದ ನಡಿಯುತ್ತವೆ; ಅದರಿನ್ದ ಅವು ತೀರ ಮನುಷ್ಯನ ಹಾಗೆ ಕಾಣುತ್ತವೆ, monkeys walk like us even on two feet; therefore they appear quite like man. ನೀನು ನಿನ್ನ ತಾಯಿ ತನ್ದೆಗಳಿಗೆ ಸನ್ಮಾನ ಮಾಡು; ಅದರಿನ್ದ ನಿನಗೆ ಅವರ ಆಶೀರ್ವಾದ ಉಣ್ಟಾಗುವದು, honour thy mother and father; for it (on its account) their blessing will come upon you. 'Therefore' is often rendered also by ಆದದರಿನ್ದ (ಆದ+ಅದರಿನ್ದ), and sometimes also by Saṁskṛita ಉದ್ದಿಶ್ಯ (with the genitive), ನಿಮಿತ್ತ (with the genitive), ಕಾರಣ, ಅದು ಕಾರಣ, ಅದು (or ಆ) ಕಾರಣದಿನ್ದ, ಆದ ಕಾರಣ. (*Cf.* § 322.)

'For', 'in order', 'for the purpose'. Above it has been stated that these adverbs are partly expressed by the dative or by the dative with ಆಗು; but there is still **another way to express them,** namely **first by adding** ಎನ್ದು, a having said, **to the dative** (see § 332), *e. g.* ಕಾಳೆಗಕ್ಕೆನ್ದು ಸನ್ನದ್ಧಮಹ ಚತುರಂಗಬಲವನ್ನು ತಕ್ಕೆಡೆಯಲ್ಲಿ ಇರಿಸುಹವು, to place the army that is ready for battle, in the proper place; ಯಾಗಕ್ಕೆನ್ದು ಮಾಡಿದ ಜಗಲಿ, an altar prepared for sacrifice; ವಧಿಸಲ್ಕೆನ್ದು ಕುರಿಯಂ ಬಿಲಿತು ಕೊಣ್ಡು, having bought a sheep for the purpose of **killing**; ದೇವತೆಗೆನ್ದು ನೀಂ ಬಿಲಿತು ತನ್ದ ಕುಱಿ, the sheep which you have bought and brought for the deity; ಅವನಲ್ಲಿ ಓದಲಿಕ್ಕೆನ್ದು ಒಬ್ಬ ಶಿಷ್ಯನಿದ್ದನು, there was a pupil with him for reading; — **and secondly by adding** ಎನ್ದು **to the infinitive ending in** ಅಲ್ (§§ 187. 188), *e. g.* ಅರಸಿಯುಂ ಸನ್ತಯಿಸಲೆನ್ದಿನ್ತೆನ್ದಂ, in order to comfort the queen he spoke in this manner (Cpr. 3, after 63); ಸತ್ತವನ ಸುಡಲೆನ್ದು ಒಟ್ಟಿದ ಕಟ್ಟಿಗೆ, wood piled up in order to burn a dead man; ಪಶುವ ಕಟ್ಟಲೆನ್ದು ಕಳದಲ್ಲಿ ನಟ್ಟ ಗುಣ್ಟವು, a post fixed in a threshing-floor for the purpose of binding cattle to; ನೀರೊಳಗೆ ಮುೞುಂಕಿ, ಸರ್ವಪಾಪಕ್ಷಯವಾಗಲೆನ್ದು, ಮಾಡುವ ಜಪವು, a prayer muttered for the removal of all sins when one has immersed himself into water.

'For' (with regard to exchange or price), *e. g.* ಹತ್ತು ರೂಪಾಯಿಗೆ ಇದನ್ನು ಕೊಣ್ಡೆನು, I bought this for ten rupees (see § 348, 19).

'For', 'instead of'. These adverbs used to be rendered, in the ancient dialect, by the dative, *e. g.* ದಿರಾಗಮ ವಿರಾಗಮಂಗಳ್ಗೆ ಗಳಾಗಮಂ ವಿಕಲ್ಪದಿನ್ದೆ ಆಗುವುದು, instead of the augments ದಿರ್ and ವಿರ್ the augment ಗಳ್ is used ad libitum. (See § 348, 15.)

In the modern dialect the Hindusthâni ಬದಲ್ (ಬದಲು), change, with ಆಗಿ is very frequently used, *e. g.* ಅವನ ಹೞೇ ಪುಸ್ತಕದ ಬದಲಾಗಿ ನಾನು ಅವನಿಗೆ ಒನ್ದು ಹೊಸ ಪುಸ್ತಕವನ್ನು ಕೊಟ್ಟೆನು, instead of his old book I gave him a new book; ಅದಕ್ಕೆ ಬದಲಾಗಿ, instead of that (in its stead); ಬರೆಯುವದಕ್ಕೆ ಬದಲಾಗಿ, instead of writing. The Saṁskṛita ಪ್ರತಿ (Tadbhava ಪಡಿ, ಪಱಿ), in the place of, in combination with ಆಗಿ is used in the same manner.

'For', expressing time, *e. g.* ಎರಡು ವರ್ಷಕ್ಕೆ, for two years. *Cf.* § 348, 29.

'For', when it denotes privilege, duty or assigning, may be rendered as follows: — ಮೇಲುಪಂಕ್ತಿಯಲ್ಲಿ ಕುಳ್ಳಿರ್ಪುದು ಕವಿಯದು (or ಕವಿಗೆ ತಕ್ಕದು), it is for the poet to sit in the principal row. ಅವನು ಆ ಕೆಲಸ ಮಾಡ ಬೇಕು, it is for him to do that work. ಈ ಮಾವಿನ ಹಣ್ಣು ರಾಮನದು, this mango (is) for Râma.

'For', denoting that in view of which anything is done, *e. g.* ಭೂಮಿಯನ್ ಉಮ್ಬಳಿಯಾಗಿ ಕೊಟ್ಟಂ, he gave a plot of ground for a rent-free grant. ಇನಾಮಾಗಿ ಕೊಟ್ಟನು, he gave for (or as) a present.

'For' when it expresses that in the character of which anything is regarded, *e. g.* ಅವನು ರಾಮನೆನ್ದು ತಿಳಿದೆನು, I took him for Râma.

8, **Enough,** *e. g.*

ಈ ಮನೆಯು ಬೇಕಾದಷ್ಟು (*i. e.* ಬೇಕು ಆದ ಅಷ್ಟು) ದೊಡ್ಡದದೆ, this house is large enough. ನಮಗೆ ಬೇಕಾದಷ್ಟು ರೊಟ್ಟಿ ಅದೆ, we have bread enough. ನನ್ನಲ್ಲಿ

ಬೇಕಾದಷ್ಟು ಹಣ ಅದೆ, I have money enough. See Dictionary under ಸಾಕು 3 and ಬೇಕು.

XVII. On the repetition of nouns, pronouns, adjectives, numerals, adverbs, interjections, and imitative sounds

(*cf.* § 253, 3).

303. In §§ 152 and 211 it has been stated that repetition of verbs is used in Kannaḍa (see § 339); such a **repetition** (vîpsâ) obtains in the three dialects also

1, **regarding common nouns when it is intended**

a) **to express simple regular succession** (vîpsâ, ânupûrvya), **'one after the other'**, that occasionally signifies totality, **'all'**, **'every'**, *e. g.* ಕೇರಿ ಕೇರಿಯೊಳ್ ಮೆಱೆದಂ, he appeared with pomp in street after street (or in every street); ಮನೆ ಮನೆಗಳ್ ಒಪ್ಪಿದುವು, house after house shone; ಊರೂರೊಳ್ ಅತಿಶುಭಕರಮೆನಲು, so that one could say (there was) auspiciousness in town after town; ಕರಿಕಾಲಚೋೞನು ಮನೆ ಮನೆಗೂರೂರಿಗೆ ಎಲ್ಲಾ ಜನಕೆ ಬಿಟ್ಟಿಯನ್ ಒರೆವ ಕೆಲಸಕೆ ಪೋಪ ಸಮಯದಲಿ, when Karikâlacôḷa went from house to house, from village to village for the purpose of ordering all people to perform press-service; ಹೊನ್ನನ್ ಈಗಳೆ ಬಿತ್ತಿಸುವೆನ್ ಈ ಬೀದಿ ಬೀದಿಯಲಿ, I will just now sow gold coins in all these streets; ದೆಸೆ ದೆಸೆಗೆ ಪದ್ಮಂಗಳ್ ಅರಳಿದವು, in direction after direction (*i. e.* in all directions) lotuses began to flower; ದೆಸೆ ದೆಸೆಗಳನ್ ಈಕ್ಷಿಸುತ, looking at one point of the compass after the other (*i. e.* at all points of the compass); ಅವನ ಕೀರ್ತಿ ದೆಸೆ ದೆಸೆಗಳಂ ಮುಸುಕೆ, when his renown covered region after region; ಕಾಲಮೇಘಂ . . . ಕೆರಳ್ದು, ಕಿಡಿ ಕಿಡಿವೋಗೆ ನೋಡಿ, Kâlamêgha . . . began to rage, and whilst spark after spark (of anger) was emitted (from his eyes), looked.

ತಪ್ಪ ತಪ್ಪಲೊಳ್ ಅಲ್ಲಿಗಲ್ಲಿ ಮಂಜುಗಳೆಸೆವ
ಕಪ್ಪ ಕಪ್ಪನೆಯ ಗಿರಿಗಳ ಪರ್ಬುಗೆಗಳನ್ತೆ
ಬಪ್ಪ ಬಪ್ಪೆಳೆನಾಯ್ಗಳಂ ಹಾಸೊಳಾನ್ತು ಬನ್ದುದು ಶಬರಸೇನೆ; ಬೞಿಕ |
ಸೊಪ್ಪ ಸೊಪ್ಪುಗಳ ಮೆಳೆ ಮೆಳೆಗಳಂ ಸೋವುತ್ತ
ತಪ್ಪ ತಪ್ಪದೆ ಶರ ಶರಂಗಳಂ ತೆಗೆದೆಚ್ಚು
ತೊಪ್ಪ ತೊಪ್ಪನೆ ಮೃಗ ಮೃಗಂಗಳಂ ಕೆದಹಿದರ್ ಕಾನನದೊಳ್. ಏವೇೞ್ವೆನು? ||,

on table-land after table-land (as to the Kannaḍa form see § 253, 3) there and there (*i. e.* everywhere) the host of Šabaras came like a spreading out of very black hills on which fog appeared, holding the accompanying and accompanying (*i. e.* the many accompanying) dogs by the collars; then beating bush after bush of abundant foliage they discharged, never failing to hit, arrow after arrow, and with the repeated sound of falling blows felled all sorts of game in the wood. What shall I say? ಕಲ್ ಕಲ್ಗೆಱಗಿದಂ, he made obeisance to stone after stone (*i. e.* to every stone); ತುತ್ತು ತುತ್ತಿಗೆ ಸವಿದು, having eaten mouthful after mouthful; ಪೊೞೆ ಪೊೞೆಗಳ ಚೆಲ್ವು, the beauty of river after river (*i. e.* of all rivers or of every river); ಅಜ್ಜಜ್ಜರಂ (ಅಜ್ಜ ಅಜ್ಜರಂ) ವನ್ದಿಸು, greet elder after elder (*i. e.* every elder)! ಕಿಱಿಯ ಕಿಱಿಯರಂ ಬೆಸಗೊಳ್, ask young man after young man (*i. e.* all young men or every young man)! ಅಲ್ಲಿಗಲ್ಲಿ, there and there (here and there or everywhere, also ಅಲ್ಲಲ್ಲಿ); ಅಡಿಗಡಿಗೆ, step after step (*i. e.* repeatedly or again and again); ನುಡಿ ನುಡಿಗೊರ್ಮೊರ್ಮೆ ತೆಗೆದು ಮುದ್ದಾಡುತ್ತುಂ, once and once (*i. e.* once) at every word taking (his son to his breast) and caressing (him); ಮೊದ ಮೊದಲೊಳ್ (as to form see § 253, 3) ದೊಡ್ಡಿತ್ತು, ತುದಿ ತುದಿಯೊಳ್ ಸಣ್ಣಂ, in every one of (its) roots (the tree is) stout, in every one of (its) tops (it is) small; ದಿಣ್ಡಿನ ಸುತ್ತಲೆ ಮಾರು ಮಾರುದ್ದ ಎಲೆಗಳು ಜೋತಾಡುತ್ತಿರುತ್ತವೆ, all around the stem (of the plantain tree there) wave leaves every one of which (is) a fathom long; ದಿನಾಲು ಹೊತ್ತು ಹೊತ್ತಿಗೆ (ಸಾಲೆಗೆ) ಹೋಗುತ್ತಿರ ಬೇಕು, (you) must go (to school) daily time after time (*i. e.* at all the definite points of time); ಆಕಳು ಬಹು ಸಭ್ಯವಾಗಿ ಹೊತ್ತು ಹೊತ್ತಿಗೆ ಹಾಲು ಕೊಡುತ್ತಿತ್ತು, the cow was very mild in disposition, and used to give milk at the proper times; ತೆಂಗಿನ ಮರಗಳಿಗೆ ತಿಂಗ ತಿಂಗಳಿಗೆ (as to form see § 253, 3) ಹೊಸ ಹೂವು ಬಿಡುತ್ತವೆ, cocoa-nut trees get new flowers month after month (*i. e.* every month, monthly); ತಿಂಗ ತಿಂಗಳಿಗೆ ಹೊಱಡುವ ಸಮಾಚಾರಪುಸ್ತಕ, a magazine that is published every month (*i. e.* a monthly magazine); ತಾಸು ತಾಸಿಗೆ, hour after hour, hourly; ದಿನ ದಿನ or ದಿನ ದಿನಕ್ಕೆ, ದಿವಸ ದಿವಸ or ದಿವಸ ದಿವಸಕ್ಕೆ, day by day, every day, daily; ವರುಷ ವರುಷ or ವರುಷ ವರುಷಕ್ಕೆ, year by year, every year, yearly; ಬಾರಿ ಬಾರಿ or ಬಾರಿ ಬಾರಿಗೆ, repeatedly; ಆಗಾಗ, that time-that time, *e. g.* repeatedly[1]; (also with regard to the interrogative ಎನ್ದು, as ಎನ್ದೆನ್ದು, what time-what time-soever, *i. e.* at all times, ever, continually);

Remark.

[1] As to the repetition of nouns of time it is to be observed that the intended meaning is somehow also obtained in the following way:—ಅವನಿಗೆ ತಿಂಗಳಿಗೆ ಸಮ್ಬಳವೇನು, what is his monthly pay? ಚಣ್ಡಿಕೆಯ ಕೂದಲನ್ ಆಱು ತಿಂಗಳಿಗೊಮ್ಮೆ ಕತ್ತರಿಸಿದಂ, he cut the hair of the tuft once in six months. ಕೆಲವು ಗಡಿಯಾರಗಳಿಗೆ ದಿನಕ್ಕೊಮ್ಮೆ, ಕೆಲವುಗಳಿಗೆ ವಾರಕ್ಕೊಮ್ಮೆ, ಕೆಲವುಗಳಿಗೆ ತಿಂಗಳಿಗೊಮ್ಮೆ

b) **to express a distributive sense** (pratyêkârtha), *e. g.* ಈ ಜಾಳಿಗೆಯೊಳ್ ಇವರ್ಗೆ ಪೊನ್ನಂ ಪೊನ್ನಂ ಕುಡು, ಈ ಗಂಟಿನೊಳ್ ಇವರ್ಗೆ ಪೊನ್ನಂ ಪೊನ್ನಂ ಕುಡು, give each of these persons a gold coin out of this purse! give each of these persons a gold coin out of this bag!;

which takes place with regard to ಕೆಳಗು and ಮೇಗು also in close proximity (sâmîpya, pratyâsatti; as to form *cf.* § 253, 3), *e. g.* ಕೆಳ ಕೆಳಗೆ ನರಕಬಿಲಂಗಳ್, the pits of hell (are) lower and lower, *i. e.* each at a small distance below the other; ಮೇ ಮೇಗೆ ಸ್ವರ್ಗಪಟಲಂಗಳ್, the (various) regions of heaven (are) higher and higher, *i. e.* each at a small distance above the other; ಕೆಳ ಕೆಳಗೆ ದುರ್ಭಿಕ್ಷಂ, times of famine (were) preceding and preceding, *i. e.* preceded each other at small intervals; ಮೇ ಮೇಗೆ ಸುಭಿಕ್ಷಂ, times of plenty (were) following and following, *i. e.* followed each other at small intervals;

c) **to express previousness** (anyatôtiśaya), *e. g.* ಬಸನ್ತದೊಳ್ ಅಸುಗೆ ಮೊದ ಮೊದಲೊಳ್ (as to form *cf.* § 253, 3) ಪೂತುದು, the Aśôka tree flowered first of all; ಧುರದೊಳ್ ಇವರ್ ಮೊದ ಮೊದಲೊಳ್ ಎಚ್ಚರ್, these shot first of all in the battle;

d) **to express high degree, excellence, intensity or emphasis** (atiśaya, viśêsha, âdhikya, prakarsha), *e. g.* ತುಱಿಲ್ ತುಱಿಲ್, great valour; ಲೇಸು ಲೇಸು, excessive pleasantness, etc.; ಒಳ್ಳಿದಳ್ ಒಳ್ಳಿದಳ್, a very good woman; (ಮಗನಂ) ತನ್ನೊಳಗೊಳಗು ಮಾಡಿ ಕೊಳುತ, taking (his son) completely inside into himself (from love); ಒಳಗೊಳಗೆ ನೆಲನ್ ಉರಿವುತಿರೆ, when the soil burnt deeply inside; ಅದನ್ನು ನೋಡಲಿಕ್ಕೆ ಜನರು ಹಿಂಡಿಗೆ ಹಿಂಡು ನೆರೆದರು, in order to see that people assembled in large crowds; ಮಜ್ಜಿಗೆಯ ರುಚಿ ಹ್ಯಾಗೆ? ಅವು ಹುಳಿ ಹುಳಿ ಇರುತ್ತವೆ, what is the taste of buttermilk? it (the buttermilk) is very sour; ಸೀಗೆ ಮುಳ್ಳು ಮುಳ್ಳಾಗಿದೆ, the sîgĕ is full of thorns; (ಕಪ್ಪುರದ) ಸತ್ವವು ಬೆಳ್ಳಗೆ ಕಾಱು ಕಾಱಾಗಿರುವದು, the elementary substance (of camphor) is white and consists of many small grains; ಸುತ್ತಿಗೆಯಿನ್ದ ಹೊಡೆದರೆ ಕಲ್ಲುಗಳು ಒಡೆದು ಚೂರು ಚೂರಾಗುತ್ತವೆ, if (one) beats (them) with a hammer, stones break and become bits and pieces; ಮೊದಲು ಮೊದಲು ಪತ್ರ ಮುಟ್ಟ ತಕ್ಕ ಅನ್ತರದ ಮಾನದಿನ್ದ ಹಾಸಿಲು ಕೊಡ ಬೇಕಾಗುತ್ತಿತ್ತು, at the very first it used to be

---

ಕ್ಕೊಮ್ಮೆ ತಿರುವ ಬೇಕಾಗುತ್ತದೆ, some clocks are to be wound up every day, some once a week, some once a month. ತಾಸಿಗೊನ್ದು ಕೂಸು ಹೆತ್ತರೆ ಈಸೀಸು ಮುತ್ತು, if she bears a child every hour, (there is) the same amount of kisses. ದಿನವೊನ್ದಕ್ಕೆ ಹತ್ತತ್ತು (instead of ಹತ್ತು ಹತ್ತು) ಇಪ್ಪಿಪ್ಪತ್ತು ಸಾವಿರ ಕಾಗದಗಳನ್ನು ಮುದ್ರಿಸುತ್ತಾರೆ, every day they print from ten to twenty thousand papers.

ದಿನ ದಿನಕ್ಕೆ is expressed also by ದಿನಾಲು, a contraction of ದಿನವಾಗಲು, 'when a day becomes', *i. e.* every day.

necessary to pay postage according to the measured distance of the place to which letters had to go; ನಡು ನಡುವೆ, in the very middle; ತುಣ್ಡು ತುಣ್ಡಾಗಿ ಕತ್ತರಿಸಿ, having cut (the sugar-cane) into very small bits; ಹೆಚ್ಚು ಹೆಚ್ಚಿಗೆ, more and more, excessively;—

ಕೆಳ ಕೆಳಗೆ (as to form see § 253, 3) ಪೋದಂ, he went down and down; ಸೆರ ಸೆರಗು, great calamity or sin; ಬೆಳ ಬೆಳಗು, excessive lustre; ತಳ ತಳಕು, great shine; ಮೇ ಮೇಗು, (as to form see § 251 and § 253, 3), up and up; ಮೂ ಮೂಗು, great dumbness; ಹೀಗೆ ಮಾಡುವದರಿನ್ದ ಮೊದ ಮೊದಲು ಕೆಲವು ದಿವಸ ಹಳೇ ಜನರ ಕೂಡ ವಿರೋಧವುಣ್ಟಾಗ ಬಹುದು, by doing so at the very first, for a while, quarrels with old people may arise;—

ಕಟ್ಟ ಕಡೆ (as to form see § 253, 3) ಪೆರ್ಬಟ್ಟೆ ಕರಂಗೊಣ್ಡು, even at last having taken the high-road; ಒನ್ದು ಶಬ್ದದ ಕಟ್ಟಕಡೆಯ ಅಕ್ಷರವು, the very last letter of a word; ಕಟ್ಟ ಕಡೆಗೆ, at the very end, at last; ಮಹಿಮೆಗಳ ನಟ್ಟ ನಡುಗಳು, the very centre of energies; ನಟ್ಟ ನಡುವೆ, in the very middle; ನೆಗೆದಯ್ ಲೋಕದ ನೀಳ್ದ ತುತ್ತ ತುದಿಯಂ, thou rosest to the world's far-stretched very point; ಆ ಸೀತಾನದಿಯ ದಕ್ಷಿಣತೀರಾಸ್ಪದಂಗಳಪ್ಪೆಣ್ಬು ಜನಪದಂಗಳ್ಗೆ ತಾನೆ ಮೊದಲೆಮ್ಬನ್ತೆ ಮೊತ್ತ ಮೊದಲ್ ಆವಗಮೊಪ್ಪುಗುಂ. . . ಲೀಲಾವತಿ, there always shone Lîlâvati at the very first, as the chief (town) for the inhabited countries that were situated on the south bank of the Sîtâ river[1];

e) to express variety, *e.g.* ತರ ತರದ ಬಣ್ಣದ ಬೆಕ್ಕುಗಳು ಇರುತ್ತವೆ, there are cats of various colour; ಎಲೆಗಳು ತರ ತರದ ಆಕಾರದವು ಇರುವವು, leaves are of various form; ಕೆಟ್ಟ ಕೆಲಸಗಳಿನ್ದ ಬಗೆ ಬಗೆಯ ಕೇಡುಗಳು ಒದಗುತ್ತವೆ, by bad deeds various evils are produced; ತೋಟದೊಳಗೆ ಬಗೆ ಬಗೆಯ ಬಳ್ಳಿಗಳನ್ನು ನೋಡಿದರು, they saw various creepers in the garden; ಮೃಗ ಮೃಗಂಗಳಂ ಕೆದಹಿದರ್, they felled all sorts of game; ದೇಶ ದೇಶದ ಹಲವು ತರದ ಒಡವೆಗಳು, many kinds of things of various countries; ತುಣ್ಡು ತುಣ್ಡು ದೊರೆಗಳು ಕೂಡಿ ಹಿಣ್ಡು ಹಿಣ್ಡು ಸೈನ್ಯ ಕೂಡಿಸಿದರು, the various petty chieftains came together and assembled an army that formed a miscellaneous mass; ಹೊಲ ಕಾಯುವವರು

---

[1] A curious way of expressing No. *d* is found in the following instances of the modern dialect in which the action of the verb is intensified by the repetition of nouns, viz. ಎಮ್ಮೆ ಸತ್ತದರಿನ್ದ ಆ ಗವಳಿಗನು ಎದೆ ಎದೆ ಬಡ ಕೊಣ್ಡನು, because the buffalo died, the cowherd repeatedly (or vehemently) beat (his) breast; ಅವನ ತಾಯಿ, ಮಗ ಸಾಯುತ್ತಾನೆನ್ದು, ಎದೆ ಎದೆ ಬಡ ಕೊಳ್ಳ ಹತ್ತಿದಳು, his mother saying "my son dies", began repeatedly (or vehemently) to beat (her) breast; ತಾಯಿ, ಸರ್ಪಳಿ ತನ್ದು ಕೊಟ್ಟಾಗಲೇ ನೀನು ನನ್ನ ಮೋಟಿ ಮೋಟಿ ಬಡಿದಿದ್ದರೆ ಈ ಗತಿಗೆ ನಾನು ಯಾಕೆ ಬರುತ್ತಿದ್ದೆನು, O mother, if thou hadst repeatedly (or soundly) beat my head at the very time when I brought and gave (thee) the chain (that had been stolen by me), why should I have got into this (miserable) lot?

. . . ಈ ಅವನ್ನು ಹಿಡಿದು, ಬಡಿ ಬಡಿಗೆಯಿನ್ದ ಬಡಿದರು, they who watched the corn-land . . . seized this cow, and beat (it) with various clubs; ಸವಿ ಸವಿ ಪದಾರ್ಥಗಳು, things of various sweetness (*i. e.* various sweet things).

In addressing a person repetition of nouns may convey the following meanings:—

1. envy (asûyĕ), *e. g.* ದೇವದತ್ತ, ದೇವದತ್ತ, ನಿನಗೇನುಮ್ ಇಲ್ಲ ;
2. approval (sammati), *e. g.* ಮಗನೆ, ಮಗನೆ, ನೀನ್ ಒಳ್ಳಿತು ಗೆಯ್ದ ಯ್!
3. anger (kôpa), *e. g.* ಬಾಣಸಿಗ, ಬಾಣಸಿಗ, ನೀನ್ ಇರ್ದಪಯೋ? ಸತ್ತಯೋ?
4. reproach (kutsana, nindĕ), *e. g.* ಸತಿಯೆ, ಸತಿಯೆ, ನಿನ್ನ ಪೆಣ್ತನಮಂ ಸುಡುಗೆ!
5. menace (bhartsana), *e. g.* ದುರುಳ, ದುರುಳ, ನಿನ್ನ ಕೊನ್ದಪೆಂ! ಕಡಿದಪೆಂ!

Instead of repeating the same noun for the sake of intensity, variety, and comprehensiveness **also duplication** and **reiteration are used** more or less in the three dialects.

1. **Duplication** denotes the use of a couple of nouns that are not the same as to form and often also as to meaning, *e.g.* ಅಕಳ ಚಕಳ, excessive tickling; ಅಱುವೆ ಅಂಚಡಿ, all sorts of cloth; ಆಸಱು ಬೇಸಱು, great weariness; ಒಗ್ಗುಮಿಗೆ, abundance; ಕಾಕ ಪೋಕ, a very profligate fellow ಕಾಯಿ ಪಲ್ಯ, pod and leaf vegetable; ಗಿಡಗಣ್ಟೆ (-ಕಣ್ಟಿ), all kinds of small trees and thorny shrubs; ದನ ಕಱು, cattle and calves; ನುಚ್ಚು ನುಱು, fragments and bits; ಬನ್ಧು ಬಳಗ, all sorts of kinsmen; ಮಕ್ಕಳು ಮಱುಗಳು, children and grandchildren; ಮಾತು ಕಥೆ, words and speech; ಸನ್ದಿ ಗೊನ್ದಿ, narrow ways and nooks; ಸುತ್ತು ಮುತ್ತು, the state of being all around (roundabout).

2. **Reiteration** denotes the use of a couple of nouns

a) the first of which is meaningless by itself, forming a sort of alliteration, *e.g.* ಅಕ್ಕಡಿ ತಕ್ಕಡಿ, fraud in weighing; ಅನ್ದಾ ದುನ್ದಿ, prodigality; ಅಱು ದಾಱು, great tumult; ಏರು ಪೇರು, considerable unevenness in scales; ತಟವಟ (-ಮಟ), great fraud;

b) the second of which is meaningless by itself, being a mere alliterative formation, *e.g.* ಅಡ್ಡಿ ಸಡ್ಡಿ, opposition; ಒಕ್ಕಲು ದಕ್ಕಲು, tenants; ಕೆಲಸ ಬೊಗಸಿ, all sorts of work; ಡೊಂಕು ಡೊಸಕು, great crookedness; ದೇವರು ದಿಣ್ಡರು, all kinds of deities (or idols); ದೊಡ್ಡೆ ಬಿಡ್ಡೆ, inarticulate, stammering speech; ಬೇಪಾರ ಸಾಪಾರ, trade of different kinds; ವೆಚ್ಚ ಸಚ್ಚ, various expense; ಹಣ್ಣು ಹಮ್ಪಲು, all sorts of fruits.—In this second kind of reiteration the syllables ಗಿ and ಪ are often used, being put instead of the first syllable of the first noun, *e.g.* ಆಳು ಗೀಳು, ರವಿ ಗಿವಿ, ಶಿಬಿ ಗಿಬಿ; ಒಕ್ಕಲು ಪಕ್ಕಲು, ತೊಳ್ಳೆ ಪಳ್ಳೆ, ಲೆಕ್ಕ ಪಕ್ಕ, ಚೂರು ಪಾರು.

2, **regarding nouns of indefinite quantity** (§ 278, 3) **when it is intended**

a) **to express intensity or abundance,** *e.g.* ಎನಿತ್ತೆನಿತ್ತಪ್ಪುಬ್ಬಜನೇತ್ರೆಯಾ ಘನ ಸ್ತನಂಗಳ್ ಬಳೆಗುಂ ಕಿರಾತೆಯಾ, ಅನಿತ್ತನಿತ್ತಂ ವನದೊಳ್ ವನೇಚರಂ ತನತ್ತು ಬಿಲ್ಲಾನ್ ಅದನ್ ಅನ್ತೆ ಕೀಸುಗುಂ, how much, how much (*i.e.* the more) the plump breasts of the lotus-eyed Kirâta woman increased, so much, so much (*i.e.* the more) the forester in the wood thus scraped that his bow; ಇನಿತಿನಿತಾಗಲಿಕ್ಷುವ ಕಡಿದಡೆ ಅಗ್ಗದ ಮಧುರವಾಗದೆ, if (one) cuts sugar-cane be it (ever) so much, so much, is it not very sweet? ಈಸೀಸು ಅಗಲ ದೋಸೆ, ಎಸೇಸು ಮೆದ್ದೀ, so large, so large (are) the cakes; how many, how many canst thou eat?

b) **to express a not specially mentioned amount,** *e.g.* ಇನ್ಥ ಇನ್ಥ ಹೊತ್ತಿಗೆ ಇಷ್ಟಿಷ್ಟು ಕೆಲಸಗಳನ್ನು ಮಾಡ ಬೇಕೆಮ್ಬುದಾಗಿ ಗೊತ್ತು ಮಾಡಿದ ಮೇರೆಗೆ ಆ ಕೆಲಸಗಳನ್ನು ಕಡೆಗಾಣಿಸುವದಕ್ಕೆ ಗಡಿಯಾರವು ಬಹಳ ಉಪಯೋಗವಾದದ್ದು, when it has been fixed that in such and such a time so and so many (various) works are to be done, a watch is of great use to finish those (various) works within that limit.—This ಇಷ್ಟಿಷ್ಟು is similarly rendered by ಇನ್ನಿಷ್ಟು, *e.g.* ತೋಳಗಳ ನ್ನು ಕೊಲ್ಲಿಸ ಬೇಕೆನ್ದು, ಅಲ್ಲಿಯ ಒಬ್ಬ ಅರಸನು, ಇನ್ನಿಷ್ಟು ತೋಳಗಳ ತಲೆಗಳನ್ನು ತನ್ದು ಕೊಟ್ಟವರು ಇನ್ನಿಷ್ಟು ಭೂಮಿಯನ್ನು ಸಾಗು ಮಾಡಿ ಕೊಳ್ಳ ಬೇಕೆನ್ತಲೂ, ಇನ್ಥ ಇನ್ಥ ತಪ್ಪು ಮಾಡಿದವರು ಇನ್ನಿಷ್ಟು ತೋಳಗಳ ತಲೆಗಳನ್ನು ತನ್ದು ಕೊಟ್ಟರೆ ಬಿಡುಗಡೆಯಾಗುವರೆನ್ತಲೂ, ಕಟ್ಟಳೆ ಮಾಡಿದನು.

3, **regarding appellative nouns of number** (§ 278, 4) **when it is intended to express a distributive sense as to persons: 'each', 'every', 'each severally', 'one by one',** etc., *e.g.* ಓರೊರ್ವರಿಗೆ ಕಾಮ್ಯಾರ್ಥತತಿಯನ್ ಅಪೂರ್ವಭಕ್ತಿಯೊಳ್ ಬಸವಂ ಕೊಡುತಿರಲು, when Basava with unparalleled affection granted every one numbers of things desired; ಒಬ್ಬೊಬ್ಬ ಹುಡುಗನು ಒನ್ದೊನ್ದು ಶಬ್ದವನ್ನು ಓದಿ ಅದರ ಅರ್ಥವನ್ನು ಹೇಳುತ್ತಾ ಹೋಗ ಬೇಕು, each boy must read every term and tell its meaning; ಶಿಕ್ಷಕನು ಒಬ್ಬೊಬ್ಬ ಹುಡುಗನಿಗೆ ಈ ಪ್ರಶ್ನೆಗಳನ್ನು ಕೇಳ ಬೇಕು, the teacher must put these questions to each boy; ಒಬ್ಬೊಬ್ಬ ದೊರೆಸಾನಿಯ ಹತ್ತಿರ ಒಬ್ಬೊಬ್ಬ ದಾಸಿ, near each lady (there is) a servant-maid; ಬೇಡರು ಗಡಬಡಿಸುತೊಬ್ಬೊಬ್ಬರೆದ್ದವಗಡಿಸಿ ನುಡಿಯಲು, when each (or every one) of the Bêḍas rose with commotion and spoke arrogantly; ಧಾರುಣೀತಳಕೆ ಪೊಡೆಗೆಡೆದರ್ ... ಒಬ್ಬೊಬ್ಬರೊನ್ದು ಕಡೆಗೆ, they (two) fell headlong on the ground ... each one to a side; ಒಬ್ಬೊಬ್ಬನು ತನ್ನ ತನ್ನಷ್ಟಕ್ಕೆ ತಾನೇ ಇರುತ್ತಾನೆ, each one remains for himself; ಒಬ್ಬೊಬ್ಬರಿಗೆ ಎರಡೆರಡು ರೂಪಾಯಿ ಕೊಡುತ್ತೇನೆ, I shall give them two Rupees each; — ಒಬ್ಬೊಬ್ಬರು, one by one, by ones; ಇಬ್ಬಿಬ್ಬರು, two and two, two by two, by twos; ಮುವ್ವ ಮುವ್ವರು, three and three, three by three, by threes; ಅವನು ಅವರನ್ನು ಇಬ್ಬಿಬ್ಬರಾಗಿ ಕಳುಹಿಸಿ ಬಿಟ್ಟನು, he sent them away two by two; ನಾವು ಅವನ ಬಳಿಗೆ ಒಬ್ಬೊಬ್ಬರು ಇಬ್ಬಿಬ್ಬರು ಮುವ್ವ ಮುವ್ವರು ಈ ಪ್ರಕಾರ ಹೋಗ ತಕ್ಕದು, we are to go to him by ones, by twos, (and) by threes, in this manner; — ಕೆಲ ಕೆಲಬರು means 'some here and there'.

Remarks on No. 3.

a) **Saṁskṛita** ಪ್ರತಿ is also used to express distributiveness, *e. g.* ಪ್ರತಿ ಒಬ್ಬ ಹುಡುಗನು ತನ್ನ ಸ್ವಂತ ಪುಸ್ತಕವನ್ನು ತರ ಬೇಕು, each boy must bring his own book; ಪ್ರತಿ ಒಬ್ಬ ಮನುಷ್ಯನಲ್ಲಿ ಏನಾದರೂ ಕೊಂಕು ಇರುತ್ತದೆ, every man has his failings.

b) '**One another**', '**each other**' in a reciprocal relation is rendered by the declension of ಓರೊರ್ವ, ಒರ್ವ, ಒಬ್ಬ, or ಒಬ್ಬ in the plural, *e. g.* (ಅಬಲೆಯರ್) ತಮ ತಮಗೆ ಕಟುಂ ಕೊಣ್ಡು ವಿವಿಧಗನ್ಧಜಲಂಗಳಿನ್ ಓರೊರ್ವರ್ ಓರೊರ್ವರ್ ಮೇಲೆ ಸಿವ್ಸಿಸುವಾಗಳ್, when (the females) went to some distance from one another, and besprinkled one another with various kinds of scented water; ಒರ್ವ ಒರ್ವಗೆ ಮುಂಚುವುದು, (to try) to surpass one another; ಅವರು ಒಬ್ಬರ ಮೇಲೊಬ್ಬರು ಪ್ರೀತಿ ಮಾಡುತ್ತಾರೆ, they love one another (or each other); ಅವರು ಒಬ್ಬರಿಗೊಬ್ಬರು ಸೇರುವದಿಲ್ಲ, they are not in peace with one another; ಒಬ್ಬರನ್ನೊಬ್ಬರು ಅಗಲಿದರು, they left one another; ಒಬ್ಬರ ಕೂಡ ಒಬ್ಬರು ಪ್ರೀತಿಯಿನ್ದ ಇರ ಬೇಕು, (they) must be on friendly terms with one another.

The nominative plural ಒಬ್ಬರೊಬ್ಬರು, ಒಬ್ಬರೊಬ್ಬರು expresses 'these and the others', *i. e.* all, *e. g.* ನೆರೆದ ಜಂಗಮರ್ ಒಬ್ಬರೊಬ್ಬರು ಕೆಯ್ಯೊಯಿದು ನಗಲು, when the assembled Jaṅgamas all clapped (their) hands and laughed; ಒಬ್ಬರೊಬ್ಬರು ಬನ್ದು ಕುಳ್ಳಿರಿ ನೀವು, come you all and sit down!

c) ಒಬ್ಬ in connection with ಇಬ್ಬರು, *i. e.* ಒಬ್ಬಿಬ್ಬರು, denotes 'one or two', *e. g.* ಒಬ್ಬಿಬ್ಬರು ಹೆಂಗಸರು, one or two women; ಇನ್ನೂ ಒಬ್ಬಿಬ್ಬರಿಗೆ ಹೇಳ ಬೇಕು, one or two are still to be invited. *Cf.* § 278, 1 (ಎರಡ್ಮೂರು, etc.).

d) ಒಬ್ಬಾನೊಬ್ಬನು, ಒಬ್ಬಾನೊಬ್ಬಳು, as we have seen in § 292, mean 'a certain man', 'a certain woman'. About another way to express the indeterminate 'certain' see § 283.

304. Repetition of pronouns is used in the three dialects

a) **to express** '**respective**', '**several**', *e. g.* ಜನರು ತಮ್ಮ ತಮ್ಮ ಗುಡಾರಗಳಲ್ಲಿ ಮಲಗಿ ಕೊಣ್ಡಿದ್ದರು, the people were sleeping in their several tents; ಅವರಿಬ್ಬರೂ ಎದ್ದು, ತಮ್ಮ ತಮ್ಮ ಕೋಣೆಗಳೊಳಗೆ ಹೋದರು, even they two rose, and went into their respective rooms; ಆಯ್ದಿದರ್ ತಮ ತಮ್ಮ ಮನೆಗಳಿಗೆ, they went to their several houses; ತಮ್ ತಮ್ಮ (a dvandva compound, § 250) ರಾಜ್ಯಂ, their respective kingdom; ತಮ್ ತಮ್ಮ ಮನೆಯ ಹಾದೀ ಹಿಡಿಯುತ್ತಾರೆ, they take the way to their several houses; ಆವಾ (or ಆಯಾ) ಇನ್ದ್ರಿಯದ ವಿಷಯಮಂ ಶ್ರೋತ್ರದೊಳ್ ಶಬ್ದದಿನ್ ಉದ್ಭಾವಿಪ ಶ್ರೀವಾಗ್ದೇವಿ, the excellent goddess Speech who originates the respective objects of sense in the ear by words; ಆಯಾ ಸಮಯಕ್ಕೆ ಆಯಾ ಕೆಲಸವನ್ನು ಮಾಡುತ್ತ ಹೋಗ ಬೇಕು, (one) must do every work at (its) respective time; ಒಟ್ಟಿದ ನಿರ್ಜರಬಲದೊಳ್ ಕಟ್ಟಿದಿರಾಗಿರ್ದು ನಿನ್ದರಾರಾರ್, in the assembled mass of deities who are those each severally by themselves that stand just opposite? ಯಾರ ಯಾರ ಅಪ್ಪಣೆ ಪಾಲಿಸ ಬೇಕು, of whom when severally mentioned have (I) to obey the command? ತವ ತವಗೆ (§ 225) ಜಯ ಜಯಯೆನಿಪ ರವನಿವಹವಾಗೂರ್ಮಿಸಲ್, when they respectively raised the loud cry 'the victory (is) theirs (*i. e.* ours), the victory (is) theirs (*i. e.* ours)'; ಎಲ್ಲರಿಗೂ ತಮ್ಮ ತಮ್ಮ ನಡತೆ ಚಲೋದು ಕಾಣುತ್ತದೆ, even to all their respective behaviour appears to be nice;

b) to express reciprocality, *e. g.* ತಮ ತಮಗೆ ಕಬಿದು ಕೊಣ್ಡು, having gone to some distance from one another; ತಾವು ತಮ ತಮಗೆಲ್ಲರುಂ ಮನವೋಲಿ, all of them having taken pleasure in one another; ಪುರಜನವೆಲ್ಲರುಂ ತಮ ತಮಗೆ ಬೆಱಗಾಗಿ, all the towns-people looking astonished at one another; ದಿನಾಲು ತಮ್ಮ ತಮ್ಮೊಳಗೆ ಜಗಳಾಡುತ್ತಿದ್ದರು, daily they used to fight with each other; ಅವರು ತಮ್ಮ ತಮ್ಮೊಳಗೆ ಪ್ರೀತಿಯಿನ್ದ ಇದ್ದಾರೆ, they love one another;

c) to express emphasis, *e. g.* ಆರ್ತಸ್ವರಮ್ ಇದೇನೇನ್, what does this cry of pain mean? ಏನೇನೋ, ಓದಿನ ಪರಿ ಲೇಸು ಲೇಸು, O what! the way of reciting is very excellent! ಏನೇನೂ ಉದ್ಯೋಗ ಮಾಡುವದಿಲ್ಲ, (they) do not perform the least work; ನನದು ಏನೇನೂ ಅಡ್ಡಿ ಇಲ್ಲ, as for me there is not the least hinderance (or objection).

305. Repetition of so-called adjectives (§ 273) takes place in the three dialects

a) to express excess, intensity or emphasis (âdhikya), *e. g.* ತೋರ ತೋರ ಮುತ್ತುಗಳ್, very large pearls; ಬಟ್ಟ ಬಟ್ಟ (see § 247, *d*, 6) ಮೊಲೆಗಳ್, very round female breasts; ಬಿಳಿಯ ಬಿಳಿಯಂಚೆಗಳ್, very white swans; ದೊಡ್ಡ ದೊಡ್ಡ ಆನೆಗಳ್, very big elephants (these four instances according to sûtra 391 of the Šabdânušâsana); ತೋರ ತೋರದ ತುತ್ತುಗಳ್, very large morsels (in which ತೋರ appears as a noun); ಪಿರಿ ಪಿರಿದು, that is very large; ದೊಡ್ಡ ದೊಡ್ಡ ಬಯ್ಲುಗಳು, very extensive plains; ದೊಡ್ಡ ದೊಡ್ಡ ಪಟ್ಣಗಳು, very large towns; ಚಿಕ್ಕ ಚಿಕ್ಕ ಹಡಗು, a very small vessel (a boat); ಅರಿದರಿದು, that is very wonderful (also thrice repeated: ಅರಿದರಿದರಿದು); ದೊರೆ ದೊರೆಗಳು ನಿಡು ನಿಡು

ಸರಳ್ ನಾಣ್ಟೆ ಮೂರ್ಛೆವಡದಿರ್ಪುದಂ . . . ನೋಡಿ, seeing that chiefs after chiefs had fainted pierced by many long arrows; ದೂರ ದೂರ, very far; ಚಲೋ ಚಲೋ, very fine; ಬಡ ಬಡ, very poor or feeble; ಸಣ್ಣ ಸಣ್ಣ, very small;

b) **to express variety,** *e. g.* ಅದನ್ನು (ಸಕ್ಕರೆಯನ್ನು) ಮಾರಾಟದ ಸಲುವಾಗಿ ದೂರ ದೂರ ದೇಶಕ್ಕೆ ಕಳಿಸುತ್ತಾರೆ, they send that (sugar) to various distant countries in order to sell (it); ದೂರ ದೂರ ಸ್ಥಳಗಳಿಗೆ ಪತ್ರ ಕಳುಹಿಸ ಬೇಕಾದರೆ ಅರ್ಧ ರೂಪಾಯಿ, ಮುಕ್ಕಾಲು ರೂಪಾಯಿ, ಒನ್ದು ರೂಪಾಯಿ ತನಕ ಬೀಳುವದು, if (in by-gone times one) had to send letters to various distant places, the postage was half a rupee, three-fourth of a rupee, up to one rupee; ಮೊದಲು ಜನರು ಸಣ್ಣ ಸಣ್ಣ ತಪ್ಪುಗಳನ್ನು ಮಾಡುತ್ತಾರೆ, at first (before they commit great crimes) people use to commit various small faults; ಅವನಿಗೆ ಆರು ಮನ್ದಿ ಸಣ್ಣ ಸಣ್ಣ ಮಕ್ಕಳು, he has six little children of various size; ಸಮುದ್ರದಲ್ಲಿ ಎಷ್ಟೋ ಸಣ್ಣ ಸಣ್ಣ ನಡುಗಡ್ಡೆಗಳೂ ಉಸುಬಿನ ದಿನ್ನೆಗಳೂ ಅವೆ, how many small islands and sandbanks of various size there are in the sea! (but also *e. g.* ಖಣ್ಡದೊಳಗೆ ಅನೇಕ ಸಣ್ಣ ದೊಡ್ಡ ದೇಶಗಳು ಸೇರಿರುತ್ತವೆ, to a division of the terrestrial globe belong many small and large countries); ದಣ್ಡಿನ ಮುಖ್ಯ ಮುಖ್ಯ ಸರದಾರರು, the various chief officers of the army; ಅಮೃತರಾವ, ಗೋವಿನ್ದರಾವಕಾಳೆ ಮುನ್ತಾದವರನ್ನು ದೊಡ್ಡ ದೊಡ್ಡ ಉದ್ಯೋಗಸ್ಥರನ್ನು ಮಾಡಿ, having made Amṛitarâva, Gôvindarâvakâḷĕ and others various eminent officials. (All the instances under letter *b* are from South-Mahratta school-books.)

c) **to express separateness, otherness,** *e. g.* ಬೇರೆ ಬೇರೆ, separate, different, several; ಹುಲಿಯ ಕಿವಿಗಳು ಕಿರಿದಾಗಿ ದೂರ ದೂರ ಇರುವವು, the tiger's ears are small and far from one another; ಹೊತ್ತು ಬನ್ದ ಹಾಗೆ ಹೊಸ ಹೊಸ ಯುಕ್ತಿಯಿನ್ದ ನಾನು ಜಾರಿ ಕೊಣ್ಡು ಹೋಗುತ್ತೇನೆನ್ದು, ನರಿ ಹೇಳಿತು, "according to each occasion I steal away by another trick", said the fox; ನಾವು ದಿನಾಲು ಹೊಸ ಹೊಸ ಸೋಜಿಗಗಳನ್ನು ನೋಡುತ್ತೇವೆ, daily we see new strange things.

Remarks.

1, The meaning of 'very' (âdhikya) may likewise be expressed by ಬಹಳ, etc., as shown in § 275.

2, Also reiteration (§ 303, 1, after *e*, 2, *b*) of so-called adjectives takes place, *e. g.* ಬಡ ಬಗ್ಗ, (a) very poor (male person).

306. Repetition of numerals takes place in the three dialects

a) **in a distributive sense, 'each', 'every', 'each severally'** (*cf.* § 278, 1), *e. g.* ಶಾಕಂಗಳೊಳಗಱಿಸುತ್ತೊನ್ದನೊನ್ದಂ ವಿವರಿಸುತ್ತ, searching the vegetables (and) separating each one; ಬಸದಿಯೊನ್ದೊನ್ದಕ್ಕೆ ಒನ್ದೊನ್ದು ಮೇಲೆನಿಪ ಲಿಂಗಂಗಳಂ

ತನ್ದಂ, he brought one excellent liṅga to every basti; ಬೇಱೆ ಬೇಱವರವರ್ಗೆ ಪ್ರತ್ಯೇಕಮ್ ಒನ್ದೊನ್ದು ಬಳ್ಳ ಮುಕ್ತಾಫಲವಂ ಕೊಟ್ಟಂ, he gave one baḷḷa of pearls to each of the different persons separately; ಹತ್ತು ಮನ್ದಿ ಪ್ರಸಿದ್ಧಪ್ರಧಾನಿಗಳ್ ಆಗ ಹತ್ತು ಹತ್ತಮ್ಬುಗಳನ್ ಒರ್ವರೊರ್ವರ್ ಎಚ್ಚರ್, then the ten renowned chief officers discharged each ten arrows; ದಿನವೊನ್ದಕ್ಕೆ ಹತ್ತತ್ತು (*i. e.* ಹತ್ತು ಹತ್ತು) ಇಪ್ಪಿಪ್ಪತ್ತು (*i. e.* ಇಪ್ಪತ್ತು ಇಪ್ಪತ್ತು) ಸಾವಿರ ಕಾಗದಗಳನ್ನು ಮುದ್ರಿಸುತ್ತಾರೆ, every day they print from ten to twenty thousand papers; ತೊಗಲಬಾವುಲಿಗಳ ಒನ್ದೊನ್ದು ಱೆಕ್ಕೆಗಳು ನಾಲ್ಕು ಗೇಣು ಉದ್ದ ಇರುತ್ತವೆ, each wing of the flying fox is four spans long; ಆ ಹೊಱೆಯ ಬಿಚ್ಚಿಸಿ ಅದಱೊಳಗಿನ ಒನ್ದೊನ್ದು ಕಟ್ಟಿಗೆಯನ್ನು ಬೇಱೆ ಬೇಱೆ ಮಾಡಿ ಮುಱಿಯ ಹೇಳಿದನು, he made (them) untie that bundle, and told (them) to make each (piece of) wood separate and break (it); ಬಾೞೆಯ ಒನ್ದೊನ್ದು ಗೊನೆಯೊಳಗೆ ಹತ್ತು ಹದಿನಯ್ದು ಹಣಿಗೆಗಳು ಇರುವವು, ಒನ್ದೊನ್ದು ಹಣಿಗೆಗೆ ಹತ್ತು ಹನ್ನೆರಡು ಕಾಯಿಗಳು ಇರುತ್ತವೆ, on each bunch of the plantain there are from ten to fifteen clusters, each cluster has from ten to twelve fruits; ಹಲಿಗೆಯ ಮೇಲೆ ಒನ್ದೊನ್ದು ಅಕ್ಷರವನ್ನೂ ಬರೆ, write even each letter on (thy) board; ಅವನವನಿಗೆ ಒನ್ದೊನ್ದು ರೂಪಾಯಿ ಕೊಡು, give a rupee to each; ಅಯ್ದಯ್ದು ವರ್ಣಂಗಳ್ ಒನ್ದೊನ್ದು ವರ್ಗಮಾಗೆ ವರ್ಗಮ್ ಅಯ್ದಕ್ಕುಂ, as five letters each form a class, there are five classes; ಎರಡೆರಡು ಮಾಸಂ ಕೂಡಿದೊಡೆ ವಸನ್ತ ಗ್ರೀಷ್ಮ ವರ್ಷ ಶರದ್ ಹೇಮನ್ತ ಶಿಶಿರ ಎನ್ದು, ಆಱುಂ ಋತುಗಳ್ ಅಕ್ಕುಂ, if two and two months are taken together, the six seasons, namely vasanta, grîshma, varsha, šarad, hêmanta, (and) šišira are formed; ಬೆಕ್ಕುಗಳ ಕಾಲಿಗೆ ಅಯ್ದಯ್ದು ಉಗುರು ಇರುವವು, there are five claws on each foot of the cat; ದೇವರು ಎಲ್ಲರಿಗೂ ಎರಡೆರಡು ಕಣ್ಣುಗಳನ್ನು ಕೊಟ್ಟಿದ್ದಾನೆ, God has given two eyes to every man; ಕೇಸರದ ಗಡ್ಡೆಗಳನ್ನು ಎರಡೆರಡು ಮೊೞದ ಅನ್ತರದ ಮೇಲೆ ಸಾಲ ಹಿಡಿದು ಹಚ್ಚುತ್ತಾರೆ, they plant the bulbs of saffron in rows at the distance of two cubits each; ಒನ್ದೊನ್ದಾಗಿ, each separately; (ಸುತನಂ) ನುಡಿ ನುಡಿಗೊಮ್ಮೊರ್ಮೆ (§ 279) ತೆಗೆದು ಮುದ್ದಾಡುತ್ತುಂ, once at every word taking (his son to his breast) and caressing (him); ಅಡಿಗಡಿಗೆಯೊನ್ದೊನ್ದು ಗೞಿಗೆಗೆ ತಡೆಯ ದಿನ್ದೊಮ್ಮೊಮ್ಮೆ ಬಲು. ದನಿಗೊಡುವ ಗಿರಿಗಳ್, mountains which thus without ceasing again and again once at each gaḻige sounded loudly;

b) **in indicating a thing, etc. as not known more specifically, 'some', 'certain',** *e. g.* ರತ್ವಕ್ಕಂ ಲಳಮುಮ್ ಅಕ್ಕುಂ ಒರೊನ್ದೆಡೆಯೊಳ್ (Commentator: ಒನ್ದೊನ್ದು ತಾವಿನಲ್ಲಿ; see § 248, 1), and ರ becomes ಲ or ಳ in some places; ಅಮಾತ್ಯರ್ ಒನ್ದೊನ್ದಿಭೇನ್ದ್ರಂಗಳನ್ ಆರ್ಪಿನ್ದೇಱೆ ಪಿನ್ತಯ್ತರೆ, when the minister valiantly mounted some excellent elephant and followed; ಒನ್ದೊನ್ದು ನಾಗರ ಹಾವಿನ

ಮೆಯ್ಮೇಲೆ ಕೂದಲು ಬನ್ದಿರುತ್ತವೆ, on the body of certain cobras hair has grown; ಒನ್ದೊನ್ದು ಕಪ್ಪೆಗಳು ಇಡೀ ಕೋೞಿ ಮಱಿಗಳನ್ನು ನುಂಗುತ್ತವನ್ತೆ, some frogs are said to swallow whole chickens; ಒನ್ದೊನ್ದು ವೇಳೆ, at some time, at times, occasionally; ಕೆಲ ಕೆಲವು (*cf.* § 248, 12) ವಿಕಲ್ಪಾರ್ಥಬಿನ್ದುಗಳ್, diverse (Kannaḍa words) have an optional bindu; ಇನ್ನು ಕೆಲ ಕೆಲ ದಿನಕೆ, some few days hence; ಕೆಲ ಕೆಲವು ಸ್ಥಳಗಳಲ್ಲಿ ಜನರು ಯಾಲಕ್ಕಿಗಳ ಸಸಿಗಳನ್ನು ಹಚ್ಚುತ್ತಾರೆ, in one place or other (or somewhere) people plant seedlings of cardamom; ಕೆಲ ಕೆಲವು ಹಣ್ಣುಪರಿದು ಸೊಮ್ಪಾಗಿ ತೋಱುತ್ತಿದ್ದವು, some few fruits had become ripe and looked fine; ಓರೊರ್ಮೆ (§ 279), sometimes; ಒಮ್ಮೊಮ್ಮೆ, sometimes; also ಒರ್ಮೆಗೊರ್ಮೆ, occasionally. Compare the instance (ಸುತನಂ) ನುಡಿ ನುಡಿಗೊರ್ಮೆರ್ಮೆ etc. above under *a*;

c) in multiplication, *e. g.* ಎರಡೆರಡು, four (§ 278, 1).

Remarks.

1, Distributiveness is also expressed by **Saṁskṛita** ಪ್ರತಿ, *e. g.* ಪ್ರತಿಯೊನ್ದು ಊರು, each village; ಪ್ರತಿಯೊನ್ದು ನಾಡಿನ ಜನರು, the people of each country.

2, **reciprocal relation** is expressed by **declension**, *e. g.* ಚೀರಿಲ್ಲಿ ತಿಮಿ ತಿಮಿಂಗಿಲ ತಿಮಿಂಗಿಲಗಿಲ ಈ ನಾಲ್ಕು ಒನ್ದೊನ್ದಕ್ಕೆ ಹಿರಿಯವಪ್ಪ ಮೀನು, ćīrilli, timi, timiṅgila, timiṅgilagila these four are fishes of which the one is larger than the other; ಆ ಖಣ್ಡಗಳೆಲ್ಲಾ ಒನ್ದಕ್ಕೊನ್ದು ಹೊನ್ದಿರುತ್ತವೆ, those divisions of the terrestrial globe join one another; ಒನ್ದಕ್ಕೊನ್ದು ಹತ್ತರವಾದ ಮನೆಗಳು, houses that are near each other; ಆ (ಬಾೞೆ) ಎಲೆಗಳ ನಡುವೆ ಗಿಡದೊಳಗಿನ್ದ ಒನ್ದರ ಹಿನ್ದೊನ್ದು ಹೊಸ ಸುಱು ಏಱುತ್ತವೆ, between those (plantain) leaves (there) rise still folded leaves one after the other out of the tree.

There is the following curious instance in the Śabdamaṇidarpaṇa, called an instance of itarêtara or anyônya: ಓರೊನ್ದರ ಕ್ರಿಯೆಯನ್ ಓರೊನ್ದು ಕೆಯ್ಕೊಣ್ಡು ಮಾಡುವೆಡೆಯೊಳ್, where one (party) takes up and performs the same action of another (party, in mutual fighting).

3, Also ಒನ್ದಾನೊನ್ದು uses to express **'a certain'**, as ಒನ್ದಾನೊನ್ದು ವೇಳೆ, a certain time, at some time or other; ಒನ್ದಾನೊನ್ದು ದೇಶ, a certain country (see § 292 and *cf.* § 283).

307. **Repetition of adverbs** (§§ 212. 253, 8. 281) in the three dialects expresses

a) 'very' (atiśayatara), *e. g.* ಕಪ್ಪ ಕಪ್ಪನೆ, very blackly; ಕಮ್ಮನೆ ಕಮ್ಮನೆ or ಕಮ್ಮ ಕಮ್ಮನೆ, very fragrantly; ತಣ್ಣನೆ ತಣ್ಣನೆ or ತಣ್ಣ ತಣ್ಣನೆ, very coolly; ಮೆಲ್ಲನೆ ಮೆಲ್ಲನೆ or ಮೆಲ್ಲ ಮೆಲ್ಲನೆ, very gently, etc.; ಸಪ್ಪ ಸಪ್ಪನೆ, very insipidly, etc.; ತೞ ತೞನೆ, brightly, etc.; ಜಳ ಜಳನೆ, dazzlingly; ತೆಪ್ಪ ತೆಪ್ಪನೆ, very quickly; ಗಿಟ್ಟ ತಿಟ್ಟನೆ, very quickly; ಜಡು ಪುಡನೆ, rapidly; ತಕ ಪಕನೆ, vehemently (as to form *cf.* § 303, 1, *e*, reiteration); ಮಿಗೆ ಮಿಗೆ, very abundantly; ಲಗು ಲಗು, very quickly;

b) **variousness,** *e. g.* ಇನ್ತಿನ್ತು ನೋಡುತಂ ಬರೆ, when (he) was seeing thus-thus (*i. e.* these various objects);

c) **mental excitement,** *e. g.* ಎನ್ತೆನ್ತೆಲವೊ, ಮಗುೞ್ದು ಪೇೞ್, how-how (*i. e.* how is that? how is that?); Oh, tell (it) again!

308. **Repetition of interjections** (see § 212, 8) happens in intensity in the three dialects, *e. g.* ಅಕಟಕಟ, ಅಮಮ, ಎಲವೆಲವೊ, ಎಲೆ ಎಲೆ, ಎಲೆಲೆ, ಛಿಃ ಛಿಃ.

309. **Repetition of imitative sounds** (§§ 212, 9; 253, 3) takes place in the three dialects, **when the sounds occur more than once or repeatedly at short intervals, or also continually,** *e. g.* ಗುಬ್ಬಿ ಚಿಂವ್ ಚಿಂವ್ ಅನ್ನುತ್ತವೆ; ಬೆಕ್ಕು ಮ್ಯಾಂವು ಮ್ಯಾಂವು ಅನ್ನುತ್ತದೆ; ಗೆಜ್ಜೆ ಗಿಲ್ ಗಿಲ್ ಅನ್ನುತ್ತವೆ; ಗಱಿ ಗಱಿನೆ ಗುಱಿ ಗುಱಿವೆಸುತುಂ ಪರಿವವೊನಲ್ ಸೊಗಯಿಸುಗುಂ; ತೊಪ್ಪ ತೊಪ್ಪನೆ (with the repeated sound of falling blows). Such a repetition may be used also thrice, *e. g.* ಬಳೆಗಳ್ ಗುಲ್ ಗುಲ್ ಗುಲ್ಲೆನೆ.

XVIII. On the expression of 'other', on the article, and on the expression of 'only', 'alone'.

310. The pronoun ಪೆಱ (ಹೆಱ), other, in its masculine, feminine and neuter forms, has been introduced in § 266; another way of expressing the English 'other' we find in the reciprocal use of appellative nouns of number (§ 303, 3, remark *b*), of reflexive pronouns (§ 304, *b*), and of numerals (§ 306, remark 2). *Cf.* also § 305, *c*.

It is necessary to bring in the manner of rendering 'other' here again, *viz.* 1, **in the sense of 'additional',** and 2, **in that of 'different'.** As in English 'other' is used in both of the said senses, so also the Kannaḍa words to be given below admit both of them, according as the circumstances require, in the three dialects.

1, The meaning of **'additional'** is expressed by prefixing the adverbs ಇನ್ನು (ಇನ್), afterwards, further, ಬೇಱೆ^{3}, separate, and ಮತ್ತೆ (ಮತ್ತು, § 297), again, to appellative nouns of number (§ 278, 4) and to the numeral ಒನ್ದು, one, *e. g.* ಇನ್ನೊರ್ವಂ, (lit. afterwards-a-man), another man; ಇನ್ನೊಬ್ಬಂ, another man; ಇನ್ನೊಬ್ಬಳು, another woman; ಇನ್ನೊಬ್ಬ ಕಳ್ಳನು, another thief; ಇನ್ನೊನ್ದು, another thing; ಇನ್ನೊನ್ದು ಕೆಲಸ, another business;—ಬೇಱೊಬ್ಬನು^{3},

(lit. separate-a-man), another man; ಬೇಱೊಬ್ಬಳು, another woman; ಬೇಱೊನ್ದು, another thing; ಬೇಱೊನ್ದೆಡೆ, another place; ಬೇಱೊನ್ದು ದಿನ, another day; ಬೇಱೊನ್ದು ನಾಯಿ, another dog; ಬೇಱೆ ಹಲವರು, some other persons;— ಮತ್ತೊರ್ವ, (lit. again-a-man), another man; ಮತ್ತೊರ್ವಳ್, another woman; ಮತ್ತೊನ್ದು, another thing; ಮತ್ತೊನ್ದೆಡೆ, another place; ಮತ್ತೊನ್ದು ಪರಿ, another manner; ಮತ್ತೊನ್ದು ವಸ್ತು, another thing, a substitute; ಮತ್ತೊನ್ದು ದೇಶ, another country; ಮತ್ತೊನ್ದು ಕೆಯ್, another (or the other) hand; ಮತ್ತೆ ಕೆಲರ್, some other persons. (About ಮತ್ತು *cf.* § 280.)

The same is expressed (especially in South-Mahratta) by ಎರಡನೆಯ (ಎರಡನೇ), second (§ 278, 2), *e.g.* ಎರಡನೆಯವನು, another man; ಎರಡನೆಯಾಕೆ, another woman; ಎರಡನೆಯವರು, other people; ಎರಡನೆಯದು, another thing; ಎರಡನೇ ಸ್ಥಲ, another place.

2, The meaning of 'different' is, as remarked above, also expressed by prefixing the same adverbs to the same appellative nouns of number and to ಒನ್ದು. ಬೇಱೆ, separate, different, may be prefixed immediately to a following noun, *e.g.* ಬೇಱೂರ್, another or a different village; ಬೇಱೆ ಕೆಲಸ, different work.

Both numbers, 1 and 2, are expressed also without the mentioned prefixes, *e.g.* ಒನ್ದ ಕೊಟ್ಟು ಒನ್ದ ಕೊಮ್ಬುದು, to give one thing and take another (*i. e.* bartering). ಒಬ್ಬ ಗೃಹಸ್ಥನಿಗೆ ಎರಡು ಮಕ್ಕಳು ಇದ್ದವು, ಒನ್ದು ಹೆಣ್ಣು, ಒನ್ದು ಗಣ್ಡು, a gentleman had two children, the one (was) a girl (and) the other a boy. ಅವರು ನಮ್ಮಿಬ್ಬರ ಮೇಲೆಯೂ ಸರಿಯಾಗಿ ಮಮತೆಯನ್ನು ಮಾಡದೆ, ಒಬ್ಬವನಿಗೊನ್ದು ಒಬ್ಬವನಿಗೊನ್ದು ಮಾಡುತ್ತಾರೆ, they (the parents) do not equally love us two, (but do one thing to the one and another thing to the other. ಒಬ್ಬ ಭೋಗಿ ಆದರೆ ಒಬ್ಬ ಜೋಗಿ, if one (is) a sensualist, the other (is) an ascetic. ಒನ್ದು ಅತ್ತೇ ಕಾಲ, ಒನ್ದು ಸೊಸೇ ಕಾಲ, the mother-in-law's time (is) one, and the daughter-in-law's time (is) another (*i. e.* different). ಇದು ಒನ್ದು ಕೆಲಸ, ಅದು ಒನ್ದು ಕೆಲಸ, this (is) one business, (and) that (is) another one (*i. e.* a different one).

To this belongs also the expression ಒನ್ದಿಲ್ಲೊನ್ದು (ಒನ್ದು ಇಲ್ಲ ಒನ್ದು), lit. one it is not, one, *i. e.* if it is not this, it is another, **some or other,** *e. g.* ಬಹಳ ಮಾತಾಡುವದಱಿನ್ದ ಒನ್ದಿಲ್ಲೊನ್ದು ತರದ ಅಪರಾಧವಾಗದೆ ಎನ್ದೂ ಇರದು, by talking much some kind of offence or other always happens. ಹುಟ್ಟಿದ ಪ್ರಾಣಿಯು ಒನ್ದಿಲ್ಲೊನ್ದು ದಿನ ಸಾಯಲಿಕ್ಕೇ ಬೇಕು, a born living being must die some day or other.

311. There are no articles in Kannaḍa that are perceivable by the ear and eye; both the English definite article 'the' and the English indefinite article 'a' ('an') are mentally to be supplied, *e. g.*

ಕರ್ಣನೊಳ್ನುಡಿ, the sensible speech of Karṇa. ತಱಿ ತಱಿನೆ ನೇಸಱ್ ಮೂಡಿದುದು, the sun rose brightly. ಬನದೊಳಗೆ ಪೋಗಿ, having gone into the garden. ಕಬ್ಬಮೊಳ್ಳಿತ್ತಾಯಿತು, the poetry has become good. ಮರದತ್ತಣಿನ್ನಿೞಿದಂ, he descended from the tree. ಮಲ್ಲಿಕಾರ್ಜುನಸುತನೆಂ, I am the son of Mallikârjuna. ಹುಡುಗನು ಓದುತ್ತಾನೆ, the boy reads. ಅವನು ಎತ್ತನ್ನು ಬಡಿಯುತ್ತಾನೆ, he beats the ox. ಶಿಕ್ಷಕನು ಹುಡುಗನಿಗೆ ಕಲಿಸುತ್ತಾನೆ, the teacher teaches the boy. ಅವರು ಸಿಂಹಕ್ಕೆ ಅಂಜುತ್ತಾರೆ, they fear the lion. ಪಕ್ಷಿಯ ಗೂಡು, the bird's nest. ತಲೆಯ ಕೂದಲು, the hair of the head. ಕುದುರೆಯು ಬಿಳೀದದೆ, the horse is white. ಕೂಸು ಅೞುತ್ತಾ ಅದೆ, the child is weeping. ಕೂಸು ತಾಯಿಯ ತೊಡೆಯ ಮೇಲೆ ಕೂಡ್ರುತ್ತದೆ, the child sits on the lap of the (or its) mother. ನಾನು ಹಾದೀ ತೋಱಿಸುತ್ತಿದ್ದೇನೆ, I am showing the way. ತೋಟಿಗನ ಮಗಳು ಹೂ ಕೊಯ್ಯುತ್ತಿದ್ದಳು, the daughter of the gardener was gathering flowers. ನಾಯಿಯೂ ನರಿಯೂ ಒನ್ದೇ ವರ್ಗದವು, the dog and the fox are of one genus. ನೀನು ಆಡಿದ ಮಾತು, the word you spoke. ಕನ್ನಡ ಭಾಷೆ, the Kannaḍa language. ಹಿನ್ದುಜನರು, the Hindus. ಪರೋಪಕಾರಿಯಾದ ಕರ್ಣನು, the philanthropic Karṇa. ಪ್ರಖ್ಯಾತಸಿಕನ್ದರನು, Alexander the great. ಶ್ರೀಮನ್ತರು, the rich. ಗಂಗಾನದಿ, the river Ganges. ಅಗಸವಣಿ, the gem of the sky (*i. e.* the sun).—

ತಲೆಕಟ್ಟು, a head-tie. ತಳಿಗೋಣ್ಟೆ, a fort with a choultry. ಊರೊಡೆಯಂ, a village-chief. ಓದಾಳಿಯಿವಂ, this (is) a learned man. ಅವಳ್ ಸಜ್ಜನವೆಣ್, that (is) a respectable woman. ಊರಿಂಗೆ ದೂರದೊಳ್ ಇರ್ದ ವನಂ, a garden that is at a distance from a town. ಅವನ ಹತ್ತರ ಲೆಕ್ಕಣಿಕೆಯುಣ್ಟು, he has a pen. ನಿನ್ನ ಹತ್ತರ ದೌತಿಯುಣ್ಟು, you have an inkstand. ಸಣ್ಣ ಮನೆ, a small house. ಹುಡುಗನು ಪುಸ್ತಕವನ್ನು ಓದುತ್ತಾನೆ, the boy reads a book. ನಾನು ಸಪ್ಪಳ ಕೇಳುತ್ತೇನೆ, I hear a noise. ಯಜಮಾನನು ಸೇವಕನನ್ನು ಕಳಿಸುತ್ತಾನೆ, the master sends a servant. ನಾವು ಹಡಗವನ್ನು ನೋಡುತ್ತೇವೆ, we see a ship. ಹೊಸ ಪುಸ್ತಕ, a new book. ಒಳ್ಳೇ ಕೂಸು, a good child. ದೊಡ್ಡ ಪೆಟ್ಟಿಗೆ, a big box. ಕೆಟ್ಟ ಹುಡುಗನು, a bad boy. ಎನ್ಥಾ ದೊಡ್ಡ ಬಿಱುಗಾಳಿ, what a great storm! ಎಷ್ಟು ಉಪಯೋಗವುಳ್ಳ ಆಯುಧವು, how useful an instrument! ಇನ್ಥಾ ಆನೆ, such an elephant.

Remark.

The appellative nouns of number ಒರ್ವ, ಒರ್ಬ, ಒಬ್ಬ (§ 278, 4) and the numeral ಒನ್ದು (§ 278, 1) in its different forms (ಒಕ್, ಒಟ್, ಒತ್, ಒನ್, ಒಪ್, ಒಬ್, ಒಮ್, ಒರ್, ಓರ್) when used so to say as adjectives, cannot be used as articles; they denote 'a certain', 'a particular kind', 'single', 'one' (nearly equivalent to the indefinite article 'a' or 'an') ಒರ್ಬನರಸಂ, a certain king. ಸತ್ಕವಿಗೊರ್ವ ಗರ್ವವಿಭು ತಾನುಂ ಲೋಭಿಯಾಗಲ್ ನಿಜಂ ಧರೆಯೊಳ್ ದಾತರು ಪುಟ್ಟರೇ, and when one proud king treats an excellent poet stingily, will not continually liberal persons be born on earth? ಶಿವು ಎಮ್ಬವನು ಒಬ್ಬ ಅಯ್ದು ವರುಷದ ಹುಡುಗನಿದ್ದನು, (there) was a certain boy of five years called Šivu. ದುಷ್ಟನಾದ ಒಬ್ಬ ವಿದ್ವಾಂಸನು ಒಬ್ಬ ಅರಸನ ಬಳಿಗೆ ಹೋಗಿ, a certain bad scholar having gone to a certain king. ಮುಳ್ತಗವೆಮ್ಬುದು ಒನ್ದು ಮರಂ, mul̤taga is a certain tree. ಒನ್ದು ಕಾಗೆ, a certain crow. ಒನ್ದು ದಿವಸಂ, one day, on a certain day. ಒನ್ದು ರಾತ್ರಿ, one night, in a certain night. ಒನ್ದು ದಿನ ಒಬ್ಬ ಮನುಷ್ಯನು ಬೇರೂರಿಗೆ ಹೋಗುವಾಗ ಅಡವಿಯೊಳಗೆ ಒನ್ದು ಮರದ ಕೆಳಗೆ ಒನ್ದು ಹುಲೀ ಮರಿಯು ಮಲಗಿತ್ತು, when one day a certain man went to a foreign town, there was the young of a certain tiger lying under a certain tree. ಅವರಿಗೆ ಒಬ್ಬ ಮಗನು ಉಣ್ಟು, they had one boy. ಒಬ್ಬ ಬ್ರಾಹ್ಮಣನ ಮನೆಯಲ್ಲಿ ಒನ್ದು ಆಕಳು ಇತ್ತು, in the house of a certain Brâhmaṇa there was one cow. ಅಲ್ಲಿ ಒನ್ದು ಮರ ಕಾಣಿಸುತ್ತದೆ, there a single tree appears. ಒನ್ದು ದಿವಸದೊಳ್ ಬನ್ದಂ, he came in one day. ಒನ್ದು ವರ್ಷವಿರ್ದಂ, he stayed one year. ಒಬ್ಬ ಗೃಹಸ್ಥನಿಗೆ ಚನ್ದ್ರನಾಥನೆಮ್ಬ ಒಬ್ಬ ಮಗನೂ ಸುಭದ್ರಾ ಎಮ್ಬ ಒಬ್ಬ ಮಗಳೂ ಇದ್ದರು, a certain gentleman had a certain son called Čandranâtha, and a certain daughter called Subhadrâ.

312. 'Only', 'alone' are expressed by suffixing the postpositions ಎ or ಏ to ಒರ್ವ, ಒರ್ಬ, ಒಬ್ಬ, ಒನ್ದು, *e.g.* ಒರ್ವನೆ ಗಣ್ಡನಲ್ತೆ ಜಗತೀತಲದೊಳ್, is he not the only powerful man in the world? ಒರ್ಬನೆ ಸುತನಲಾ ತನಗೆನ್ನದೆ, "O, is he not my only son?" (thus he, the father) not saying. ಒಬ್ಬನೇ ಕೂತನು, he sat down alone. ಒಬ್ಬನೇ ಮನೆಯಲ್ಲಿ ಬಿದ್ದು ಕೊಣ್ಡನು, he lay down alone in the house. ನನಗೆ ಒಬ್ಬನಿಗೇ ಆ ಕುದುರೆ ಆಸ ಕೊಳ್ಳಲಿಕ್ಕಿಲ್ಲ, I alone cannot manage that horse. ಅವರೊಬ್ಬರೇ ಬನ್ದರು, they came alone. ಅರಸನು ಒಬ್ಬನೇ ಇದ್ದದನ್ನು ಕಣ್ಡೆನು, I saw the king was alone. ಅವನು ತಾನೊಬ್ಬನೇ ಮನೆ ಕಟ್ಟ ಬೇಕಾದರೆ ಬಹಳ ಶ್ರಮ ಬೀಳುವದು, if he alone has to build the house, great toil will come to pass. ನಾನು ಹೇಳಿದ ಬುದ್ಧೀ ಮಾತು ಅವನೊಬ್ಬನೇ ಕೇಳಿದನು, he alone took to heart the advice I gave. ತಾಯೊರ್ವಳೆ, the mother alone. ಅವಳೊಬ್ಬಳೆ, she alone. ಇದೊನ್ದೇ ಮಾರ್ಗ, this is the only way. ಅವನಿಗೆ ಇವನೊಬ್ಬನೇ ಮಗನು, this is his only son. ಒನ್ದೇ ಪಟ್ಣ, a single town. (See § 212, c, and *cf.* § 282.)

XIX. On additional tense-forms of the verb.

313. Ancient Kannaḍa grammarians enumerate three tenses (kâlatraya, § 145): the present (§ 194), the future (§ 200), and the past (§ 198). We have seen that both the two forms of the present tense of the

modern dialect differ from the form of the ancient one (§ 196). Besides, the contingent present-future of the modern dialect has been introduced (§ 195).

On examination it will be found that the ancient form of the present is a compound-tense, and that the two forms of the present and the form of the contingent present-future of the modern dialect are also compound-tenses.

Analogously also other compound-tenses are formed in Kannaḍa (*cf.* § 362), although they are not specified in ancient grammars, viz.

1, A sort of continuative Present, *e. g.* ಬರೆಯುತ್ತಾ ಇದ್ದೇನೆ, writing I am, *i. e.* I am writing (see §§ 172; 196, 1), or ಬರೆಯುತ್ತಾ ಇರುತ್ತೇನೆ (§ 196, 2). ಆಕೆ ಆಲೋಚಿಸುತ್ತಾ ಇದ್ದಾಳೆ. ಅವನು ಹಾಲು ಕುಡಿಯುತ್ತಿದ್ದಾನೆ. ದೇವರು ನಮ್ಮನ್ನು ಯಾವಾಗಲೂ ನೋಡುತ್ತಿರುತ್ತಾನೆ. ನಾವು ಎಲ್ಲರಿಗೂ ಒಳಿತು ಮಾಡುತ್ತಿರ ಬೇಕು. ಮಱಿ ಮಾಡುವದಕ್ಕೋಸ್ಕರ ಹೆಣ್ಣುಗುಬ್ಬಿಯಾಗಲಿ ಗಂಡು ಗುಬ್ಬಿಯಾಗಲಿ ತತ್ತಿಯ ಮೇಲೆ ಕೂಡ್ರುತ್ತಿರುತ್ತವೆ. ಸೂಜಿಗಳು ಸಿದ್ಧವಾಗಿ ಮಾಱಾಟಕ್ಕೆ ಬರುವ ವರೆಗೆ ಅವುಗಳನ್ನು ಮಾಡುವ ಕೆಲಸಕ್ಕೆ ಬೇಕಾಗುವಷ್ಟು ಮನ್ದಿ ಇನ್ನೊನ್ದು ಯಾವ ಕೆಲಸಕ್ಕೂ ಬೇಕಾಗುತ್ತಿರ ಲಿಕ್ಕಿಲ್ಲ, till needles become ready and can be sold, (there) being are not, *i. e.* (there) are not, required for any other work so many persons as are required for the work of making them.

It is to be remarked that this continuation is also used, when the present participle is combined with the infinitive or with the imperative, *e. g.* ನಿಪಾತವಿಷಯದೊಳ್ ಅಲ್ಪಾರ್ಥಮನ್ ಅರ್ಧರೆ, ವಸ್ತುವಿನರ್ಧಮನ್ ಉಸಿರುತ್ತಿರೆ ತಗುಳ್ದುವುದು ಸಂಹಿತೆಯಂ, when ಅರೆ which as a particle (or adverb) has the meaning of 'a little', expressing is, *i. e.* expresses, 'the half of a thing', it partakes of (the rules regarding) euphonic combination (see § 215, 6, remark 1). ನಗುತಿರ ಬೇಡ, (you) must not (continually) laugh. ಮಗಳೇ, ಅತ್ತೆ ಮಾವನ್ದಿರನ್ನು ಸೇವಿಸುತ್ತಿರು, O daughter, (continually) serve (your) mother-in-law and (your) mother's brother. ನಾವು ತೋಟದಲ್ಲಿ ಆಡುತ್ತಿರೋಣ, let us play in the garden.

A sort of contingent present is likewise formed, *e. g.* ಅವನು ಈಗ ಬರೆಯುತ್ತಿದ್ದಾನು, writing he may be now, *i. e.* he may be writing now.

2, The continuative Imperfect, *e. g.* ಪುಗುತುಮಿರ್ದಂ, entering he was, *i. e.* he was entering. ಕಪಿಧ್ವಜಂ ನಿಳ್ಕಿ ನಿವರ್ತಿಸುತ್ತುಮಿರೆ, when the monkey-banner rose to its full height and repelling was, *i. e.* was repelling, (the foe, the idea of the past arising from the past participle ನಿಳ್ಕಿ). ನುರ್ಗುತಿರೆ, whilst he crush d (them, see § 362, 2, *b*). ಭೋಂಕನೆ ದೇವಸ್ತ್ರೀಯರ್ ಅನ್ದಾರತಿಯನ್ ಉಘೆಯುಘೆಯೆನ್ದು ತನ್ದೆತ್ತುತ್ತಿರ್ದರ್, then the Apsaras, saying "huzza,

huzza", quickly brought waving-platters and holding (them) up were, *i. e.* were holding (them) up. ಅಗಸನು ಅಱುವೆಗಳನ್ನು ಒಗೆಯುತ್ತಿದ್ದನು, the washerman washing was, *i. e.* was washing, clothes. ನೀನು ಅೞುವಾಗ ತನ್ದೆ ತನ್ನ ಕೆಲಸಗಳನ್ನು ಒತ್ತಟ್ಟಿಗೆ ಇಟ್ಟು ನಿನ್ನ ಸಮಾಧಾನ ಮಾಡುತ್ತಿದ್ದನು, when thou (as a little child) weptest, (thy) father laid his work aside, and comforting was, *i. e.* was comforting (or used to comfort) thee. ನಾನು ಹೋದಾಗ ಅವನು ಉಣ್ಣುತ್ತಿದ್ದನು, when I went, dining he was, *i. e.* he was dining. ಮೊದಲನೇ ಪುಸ್ತಕ ಓದುವಾಗ ಅಕ್ಷರಗಳು ಸೆಟ್ಟಗೆ ತಿಳಿಯುತ್ತಿದ್ದಿಲ್ಲ; ಅದಱಿನ್ದ ಒನ್ದೊನ್ದೇ ಅಕ್ಷರ ಓದುತ್ತಿದ್ದಿ, when reading the first book, the letters being known well were not, *i. e.* were not known (to thee) well; therefore reading thou wast, *i. e.* thou wast reading (or usedst to read), even each letter separately. ಅನ್ದಾದರೂ ಈಗಿನನ್ತೆಯೇ ನಾವಿನೊಳಗೆ ಕೂತು ಕೊಣ್ಡು ಹೊೞೆಯನ್ನು ದಾಟ ಬೇಕಾಗುತ್ತಿತ್ತು, also then just as now becoming it was, *i. e.* it became (or used to become) necessary to sit in a boat and cross the river.

3, **The continuative (or habitual) Future,** *e. g.* ಪ್ರಯೋಗಿಸುತಿರ್ಪರ್ (Šabdamaṇidarpaṇa sûtra 14), employing they will be, *i. e.* they will employ (or use to employ;" vṛitti ಪ್ರಯೋಗಿಸುವರ್). ಸಂಹಿತೆಯೊಳ್ ಸ್ವರರಹಿತ ವ್ಯಂಜನಮ್ ಅವು ಪರವರ್ಣಮನ್ ಅಯ್ದುತಿರ್ಪುವು (Šmd. s. 59), in euphonic combination of letters consonants without a vowel uniting will be with, *i. e.* will unite with (or use to unite with), a following letter (vṛitti ಅಯ್ದುವುವು). ನೀನು ಅಯ್ದು ಗಣ್ಟೆಗೆ ಬನ್ದರೆ ನಾನು ಆಗ ಬಹುತರವಾಗಿ ಪತ್ರಾ ಬರೆಯುತ್ತಿರುವೆನು, if thou comest at five o'clock, most probably writing I shall be, *i. e.* I shall most probably be writing, a letter. ಹೆಂಗಸರು ಆಭರಣಗಳನ್ನು ಬೇಡುತ್ತಿರುವರು, women asking for will be, *i. e.* use to ask for, ornaments. *Cf.* § 366, *c.*

4, **The Perfect,** *e. g.* ಅರ್ಕೇನ್ದುಗಳಂ ತವೆ ನುಂಗಿರ್ಪುದಂ ಕತ್ತಲೆ, darkness having quite swallowed is (see § 203), *i. e.* has quite swallowed, sun and moon. ವರ್ಗದನ್ತ್ಯಂಗಳನ್ ಅಱಿ; ಅನುನಾಸಿಕಾಖ್ಯೆಯಂ ತಳೆದಿರ್ಪುದಂ, know the last letters of the (five) classes; having got they are, *i. e.* they have got, the name of nasals. ಕುಳಿನ್ದಂಗೆ ಸೂನು ಜನಿಸಿರ್ದಪನೆ, having been born is a son, *i. e.* has a son been born, to Kuḷinda. ಕಾಲಿದಾಸನು ಸರಸಕಾವ್ಯಗಳನ್ನು ರಚಿಸಿರುತ್ತಾನೆ, Kâlidâsa having composed is, *i. e.* has composed, charming poetry. ಹುಡುಗರು ಸಾಲೆಗೆ ಹೋಗಿದ್ದಾರೋ, having gone are the boys, *i. e.* have the boys gone, to school? ಗೌರಿ ಆಡಲಿಕ್ಕೆ ಯಾಕೆ ಬರಲಿಲ್ಲ? ಆಕೆ ನನ್ನ ಸಹೋದರಮಾವನ ಮನೆಗೆ ನಿನ್ನೆ ಹೋಗಿದ್ದಾಳೆ.— ಆಕೆ ನನಗೆ ಒನ್ದು ಕೆಮ್ಪು ಜರದ ಮದರೀ ರುಮಾಲ ತನ್ದಿದ್ದಾಳೆ.— ಸೋಮಾ, ನೀನು ಎನ್ದಾದರೂ ಕಲ್ಲಂಗಡೀ ಹಣ್ಣು ನೋಡಿ

ದ್ದೀಯಾ? — ಅವನು ಸಾಲೆಯನ್ನು ಬಿಟ್ಟಾನೆ (*i. e.* ಬಿಟ್ಟು ಆನೆ, see § 196). — ಅವರು ಊಟಕ್ಕೆ ಕೂತಾರೆ (*i. e.* ಕೂತು ಆರೆ). *Cf.* § 315, 2, *l.*

In the ancient dialect this so-called Perfect may convey the meaning of the present, *e. g.* ತೋಳ್ ನಾಲ್ಕುಂ ಕರಮ್ ಎಸೆದಿರ್ಕುಂ ಪದ್ಮೋದರಂಗೆ, four arms having nicely appeared are, *i. e.* nicely appear, on Vishṇu. Also when the common future of ಇರ್ is used (like ಇರ್ಕುಂ), this meaning holds good, *e. g.* ಅಣಿಯರಮ್ ಎಸೆದೊಪ್ಪಿರ್ಪುವು ಮಣಿಗಾಱಿರ. . . . ಗಣನಾತೀತಂಗಳ್ ಆಪಣಂಗಳ್, nicely having appeared and having shone will be, *i. e.* nicely appear and shine, even the numberless shops of jewellers, etc. ಇರ್ದುದನ್ ಅೞಿದಿರ್ಪುದರಿಯು ವೋಲ್ ಆದೇಶಂ, a substitute having destroyed will be, *i. e.* destroys, like a foe, that which is (§ 198 under 3). If the final verb is in the infinitive, the meaning of the imperfect too is produced, *e. g.* ಕನ್ನವುರಂ ಚೆಲ್ವೆಸೆದಿರೆ, when the ear-ornament having shone beautifully was, *i. e.* when the ear-ornament shone beautifully.

If this Perfect is formed by the combination of the past participle and a verbal noun of the past, again the present may be represented (see § 169 and § 198 under 3), *e. g.* ಪ್ರಕೃತಿ ಪ್ರತ್ಯಯಮ್ ಒದವಿದ ಪದಯುಗದ ಬೆರಕೆ ಬೇಡಿರ್ದುದಱಿಂ ಪದಮಧ್ಯಂ ಪದದನ್ತ್ಯಂ ವಿದಗ್ಧರಿಂ ಸನ್ಧಿವಿಷಯಮ್ ಎರಡಕ್ಕುಂ, a union of two words which consist of a base (and) a suffix, having desired by having been (or by being), *i. e.* when a union of two words which consist of a base and a suffix, is desired (or is to take place), two euphonic combinations are formed by the learned, (*viz.*) the internal (and) final one (§ 214). ಭಾವಿಯೆನಿಸಿರ್ದುದು ಪರಿಭಾವಿಸಿ ಕಳೆಯಲ್ಕೆ ಸಾಧ್ಯಮ್ ಆಗದು ಜಗದೊಳ್ ದೇವಂಗಾದೊಡಂ, it is impossible also for a king to remove by slight what having been called has been, *i. e.* what is called, destiny.

It may still be mentioned that this kind of Perfect may be used in the imperative, *e. g.* ನಾನು ಬಱುವದಱೊಳಗೆ ಅಡಿಗೆ ಆಗಿರಲಿ, dinner having become be, *i. e.* dinner be ready, within my arrival! ಗುರುಗಳು ಬರುವದ ಱೊಳಗೆ ನಾವು ಹೋಗಿರೋಣ, having gone let us be, *i. e.* let us be gone, within the guru's arrival.

It is scarcely necessary to state that this Perfect is used also when the participle is a negative one, *e. g.* ಈ ಶಿವನ್ ಎಸು ದಿವಸದಿನ್ದುಣ್ಣದಿರ್ದಹನೋ, since how many days has this Śiva not dined?

5, **The future Perfect,** *e. g.* ನಾನು ನಿನ್ನ ಕಡೆಗೆ ಬನ್ದಾಗ ನೀನು ಎಷ್ಟು ಪತ್ರಗಳನ್ನು ಬರೆದಿರುವಿ, when I come to thee how many letters having written thou shalt be, *i. e.* how many letters shalt thou have written? ಅಯ್ದು ಬಡಿದ ಮೇಲೆ

ನಾನು ಹೊಱಗೆ ಹೋಗಿರುವೆನು, when it has struck five o'clock, having gone out I shall be, *i. e.* I shall have gone out. ನಿನ್ನ ದೇವತಾರ್ಚನೆ ಆಗುವದಱೊಳಗೆ ನನ್ನ ಅಡಿಗೆ ಆಗಿರುವದು, whilst thy worship of the gods takes place, my cooking having become will be, *i. e.* will have been done.

6, **The contingent future Perfect,** *e. g.* ನೀನು ಬನ್ದಾಗ ನನ್ನ ಕೆಲಸವು ಮುಗಿದಿದ್ದೀತು, when thou comest, my work having been finished may be, *i. e.* may have been finished. ಯಾರು ಈ ಪತ್ರ ಬರೆದಿದ್ದಾರು, who having written this letter may be, *i. e.* who can have written this letter? ಅಷ್ಟು ಹೊತ್ತಿಗೆ ಅಡಿಗೆ ಆಗಿದ್ದೀತು, at that time dinner having become may be, *i. e.* may have become ready.

7, **The Pluperfect,** *e. g.* ಅವನು ಬರುವದಕ್ಕಿನ್ತ ಮುಂಚೆ ನಾನು ಪತ್ರಾ ಬರೆದಿದ್ದೆನು, having written I was, *i. e.* I had written, the letter, before he came. ಹತ್ತು ಗಂಟೆಗಿನ್ತ ಮುಂಚೆ ಅವನು ಮನೆ ಬಿಟ್ಟಿದ್ದನು, having left he was, *i. e.* he had left, the house before ten o'clock. ಅವನು ಭರುವದಕ್ಕಿನ್ತ ಮುಂಚೆ ನಾನು ಪತ್ರಗಳನ್ನು ಬರೆಯುತ್ತ ಕೂತಿದ್ದೆನು, having sat writing letters I was, *i. e.* I had been writing letters, before he came. ನಾನು ಅವನ ಮನೆಗೆ ಹೋಗಿದ್ದೆನು, ಆದರೆ ಅವನು ಮನೆಯೊಳಗಿದ್ದಿಲ್ಲ, having gone I was, *i. e.* I had gone (or went), to his house, but he was not at home. ಮೊನ್ನೆ ನೀನು ಸಾಲೆಗೆ ಯಾಕೆ ಬನ್ದಿದ್ದಿಲ್ಲ, why having come thou wast not, *i. e.* why hadst thou not come (or didst thou not come), to school the day before yesterday? ಈ ಮುದುಕನ ಮನೆಗೆ ಎನ್ದಾದರೂ ಹೋಗಿದ್ದಿಯೋ? ಮೊನ್ನೆ ಹೋಗಿದ್ದೆನು, having gone thou wast ever, *i. e.* didst thou ever go, to the house of this old man? Having gone I was, *i. e.* I did go, the day before yesterday. ಒನ್ದು ಮರದ ಕೆಳಗೆ ಒನ್ದು ಹುಲೀಮಱಿ ಮಲಗಿತ್ತು, under a certain tree a certain tiger-cub having lain down was, *i. e.* had lain down. ಹದ್ದಿನ ಕಾಲಿಗೆ ಒನ್ದು ಹಾವು ಸುತ್ತು ಹಾಕಿತ್ತು, a certain snake having coiled itself was, *i. e.* had coiled itself, round the foot of a kite. ತತ್ತಿಗಳ ಮೇಲೆ ಹೆಣ್ಣುಗುಬ್ಬಿ ಕೂತಿತ್ತು, the female sparrow having sat was, *i. e.* sat, on the eggs. ಅಚ್ಯುತರಾಯನು ಕೃಷ್ಣರಾಯನಿಗಿನ್ತ ಮುಂಚೆ ಮರಣ ಹೊನ್ದಿದ್ದನು, king Aćyuta having died was, *i. e.* had died, before king Kṛishṇa. ಓದುವ ಪುಸ್ತಕದೊಳಗಿನದೊನ್ದು ಪುಟ ಹಱಿದಿತ್ತು, one leaf within the reading book having been torn was, *i. e.* had been torn. ಈ ರೂಪಾಯಿ ಎಲ್ಲಿ ಕಣ್ಡು ಕೊಣ್ಡೆ? ನನ್ನ ಮನೆಯಲ್ಲಿ ಬಿದ್ದಿತ್ತು, where did you find this rupee? Having fallen it was, *i. e.* it had fallen (or was lying) in my house. ಅವ್ವಾ, ನಮ್ಮ ಹಿತ್ತಲೊಳಗಿನ ಮಾವಿನ ಮರದ ಮೇಲೆ ಜೇನು ಇಟ್ಟಿತ್ತು, O mother, in our back-yard on the mango tree (bees) honey having put was, *i. e.* honey had been put (by bees). ಒಬ್ಬ ಸಿಪಾಯಿಯು ಕಾಳಗಕ್ಕೆ ಹೋಗ

ಬೇಕೆನ್ದು ಒನ್ದು ಬಹು ಹದನಾದ ಕತ್ತಿಯನ್ನು ಮಾಡಿಸಿದ್ದನು, a native soldier having caused was, *i. e.* had caused, a certain very sharp sword for going to war. ಅವನು ನನ್ನ ಭೆಟ್ಟಿಗೆ ಬನ್ದಾಗ ನಾನು ಉಣ್ಡಿದ್ದಿಲ್ಲ, when he came to see me, having dined I was not, *i. e.* I had not dined.

Already from the instances quoted above it will appear that this kind of Pluperfect, though in form a pluperfect, does not always clearly express the meaning of it. Thus in the **ancient dialect** it may simply denote the **aorist**, *e.g.* ಮಾ ಮುಸಗಿದ್ರ್ದುದು ಮಾಗೆ, the mouth Mâgĕ grandly made its appearance (see § 298 under ౩), or **the present** in the instance ನೀಹಾರಮಣ್ಡಲಮ್ ಆದೇನ್ ಎಸೆದಿರ್ದುದೊ ಪಶ್ಚಿಮಾದ್ರಿಯೊಳ್? and in the instance ಏಂ ತುಱುಗಿದ್ರ್ದುವೊ ತುದಿಗೋಡೊಳ್ ವಿಹಂಗಂ? (see § 271 under ೨೦). Compare § 315, ೨, *l* (about the passive).

Remark.

Also **relative compound-participles** may be formed, *e. g.* the continuative present one:— ಅವನು ಬರೆಯುತ್ತಿರುವ ಹೊತ್ತು; the continuative imperfect one:— ನಾನು ಅವನನ್ನು ನೋಡುತ್ತಿದ್ದಾಗ ಯಾವನೋ ಒಬ್ಬನು ಸಮೀಪಕ್ಕೆ ಬನ್ದನು; the perfect one:— ಕರುವಿಡಿ ದಿರ್ಪಾ ಚೆನ್ನಂಗಿಯು ತರು ದಾಣೆಗೆ, (let the wood of) that čennaṅgi tree ornamented with bosses (be taken) for a club (§ 241); ಗುಬ್ಬಿ ಹಿತ್ತಲೊಳಗೆ ಬಿದ್ದಿರುವ ಕಾಬು ಕಡಿಗಳನ್ನು ಆರಿಸಿ ಕೊಣ್ಡು ತಿನ್ನುತ್ತದೆ.

314. Here may also be introduced, especially if the compound-forms of the modern dialect given in the remark on this paragraph are considered, what is called **the Conditional or Subjunctive** by Europeans. Does it exist in Kannaḍa?

There is no subjunctive mode (mood) or particular form of the verb in Kannaḍa, which is used to express condition, hypothesis and contingency; the Kannaḍa conditional is formed simply by certain suffixes added to such parts of the verb in its indicative tense (see § 144) as we do already know, *i. e.* to the present-future relative participle (§ 180 *seq.*) and past relative participle (§ 175 *seq.*) in the ancient and mediæval dialect, and to the latter participle in the modern dialect.

The suffixes or postpositions for expressing 'if' (§ 212, ೬) are ಒಡೆ (in the ancient and mediæval dialect), ಅಡೆ (in the mediæval one), and ಅರೆ (in the mediæval and modern one), ಒಡೆ being the original form.

ಒಡೆ very probably is ಒಡ್ (which we believe to be another form of ಒಳ್, ಉಳ್, to be, see § 194, remark ೧) and the ಎ of the infinitive (§§ 187, ೪; 188, which ಎ means 'at the time that', 'when'), *e.g.* ಪೋದೊಡೆ, at the time that, or when, (I) go (= the English 'if I go').

About ಒಡೆ (= ಅಡೆ, ಅರೆ) the grammarian Kêšava says the following:—

"The word ಒಡೆ which expresses a case (or supposition, paksha) and ends in (the vowel) ಎ, is added to the end of verbs (dhâtu), it being connected with the three genders, the three numbers (and) the three persons", *e. g.* ನೋೞ್ಪೊಡವಳ್ ಕಿಱಿಯಳ್, if (she) sees (or inquires, *i. e.* for inquiring), she (is) the junior; ಸಮಂ ನುಡಿವೊಡವಂ ಪಿರಿಯಂ, if (he) speaks properly (*i. e.* for, or in, speaking properly), he (is) the senior; ತೀಡುವೊಡಲ್ಲಿ ಕಮ್ಮೆಲರೆ ತೀಡುಗುಂ, if (it) blows, a fragrant breeze blows there;— ಕಾದುವೊಡೊರ್ವನೆ ಬಲ್ಲಿದಂ, if (he) fights (*i. e.* in fighting), he alone (is) one who possesses skill; ಪೋಲಿಸುವೊಡಿರ್ವರುಂ ತಕ್ಕರ್, if (they) compare (*i. e.* for comparing), even both (are) fit persons; ನುಡಿವೊಡೆಲ್ಲರುಂ ಮಾತಱಿಯರ್, if (they) speak, all of them do not know (proper) words;— ಪೊರ್ದುವೊಡವನೊಳ್ಳಿದಂ, if he approaches, he (is) a good one; ತಿರ್ದುವೊಡವರೊಳ್ಳಿದರ್, if (they) correct, they (are) good ones; ಬೇಡಿಪ್ಪೊಡೆ ನೀನ್ ಒಳ್ಳಿದಯ್, if (thou) solicitest, thou (art) a good one; ಈವೊಡೆ ನೀಮ್ ಒಳ್ಳಿದಿರ್, if (you) give, you are good ones; ಭಾವಿಪೊಡಾನ್ ಒಳ್ಳಿದೆಂ, if (I) consider, I am a good one; ಸೇವಿಪೋಡಾಮ್ ಒಳ್ಳಿದೆವು, if (we) serve, we are good ones. (It will be observed that ಒಡೆ may sometimes be translated into English by 'for', 'to', 'in', as also ಅಡೆ, ಅರೆ may get that meaning in the mediæval dialect.)

"Also for the three tenses ಒಡೆ is used", Kêšava adds, *e. g.* ಪುಸಿದೊಡೆ ಬಿಟ್ಟಂ, if (he) lied, he ceased; ಪಳಂಚಿದಪೊಡೆ ಕೊಂದಪಂ, if (he) opposes, he kills; ಚಿತ್ರಿಪೊಡೆ ತೂಳಿಕೆಯಂ ತರಿಸುವಂ, if (he) will paint, he will have a brush brought.

Another instance of Kêšava's is the following verse:—

ನೀನುಳ್ಳೊಡುಣ್ಟು ರಾಜ್ಯಂ;
ನೀನುಳ್ಳೊಡೆ ಪಟ್ಟಮುಣ್ಟು, ಪೇಳಿಗೆಯುಣ್ಟು; ।
ನೀನುಳ್ಳೊಡುಣ್ಟು ಬೆಳ್ಗೊಡೆ;
ನೀನಿಲ್ಲದಿವೆಲ್ಲಮೊಳವೆ, ಭಾನುತನೂಜಾ? ‖ (See its translation in § 360.)

Instances from other sources:— ಜಿನನ ವಿಧಿಗಳ ಕೋಟಲೆಯನ್ ಎಣಿಸುವೊಡೆ ತಾಂ ಫಣಿಪತಿಗೆ ಹವಣಲ್ಲ.— ಕಾವೊಡಂ (if he protects and) ಕೊಲುವೊಡೆ (if he kills, *i. e.* for protecting and killing) ಸಮಸ್ತಕೆ ದೇವನೊಬ್ಬನೆ ಕರ್ತನಲ್ಲದೆ ಕಾವೊಡಂ ಕೊಲುವೊಡೆಯಿದಕೆ ನೀಂ ಕರ್ತನೇ?— ಅಡಿಯಿಡುವೊಡಸದಳಮೆಮ್ಮ ಕರ್ಕಶದ ಮಾರ್ಗಂ.— ಕೊಡುವಡೆಯೆಮಗಿಲ್ಲ (if we shall give, *i. e.* to give etc.).— ತಪ್ಪುಳ್ಳೊಡೊಪ್ಪಂ ಗೆಯ್ವುದು[1].

[1] It may be remarked that the Tulu ಡ in the so-called subjunctive, *e. g.* in ಮಾಳ್ಪುವೆ-ಡ, if I make, seems to have originated from ಅಡ (= ಅಡೆ) by the euphonic elision of initial ಅ after a preceding vowel.

ನಿರಪರಾಧಿಯನ್ ಇನ್ನು ಕೊಲುವರೆ ಪರಮಪಾತಕಮ್ ಆಗದೇ? — ಜನಪರ್ ಉಣ್ಬ ಓಲಯ್ಸಿ ಕೊವ್ಸರೆ. — ಹೆಬ್ಬೊಟ್ಟು ಸುಟ್ಟುವೆಬ್ಬ ಕೂಡಿ ಅಳದರೆ ಪ್ರಾದೇಶ ಎನಿಸುಗು. — ಕೆಯ್ಲಿ ಇದ್ದರೆ ಅರ್ಥ, ಹತ್ತರ ಇದ್ದರೆ ಹೆಣ್ಡತಿ.

ಒಡೆ and ಅಡೆ are suffixed also immediately to the negative relative participle (§ 175), *e.g.* ಕೆಯ್ಸಾರದೊಡೆ, ಅಲ್ಲದೊಡೆ, ಇಲ್ಲದೊಡೆ, ಇಲ್ಲದಡೆ, ಅಱಿದಡೆ; but they are chiefly suffixed to a following ಇರ್ದ, as ಇರ್ದೊಡೆ and ಇರ್ದಡೆ, these being joined to a preceding so-called negative gerund ending in ಅದೆ (§ 170), *e.g.* ಅಲ್ಲದಿರ್ದೊಡೆ (ಅಲ್ಲದೆ+ಇರ್ದೊಡೆ), ಇಲ್ಲದಿರ್ದೊಡೆ (ಇಲ್ಲದೆ+ಇರ್ದೊಡೆ), ಕತ್ತರಿಸದಿರ್ದೊಡೆ, ತೆಱೆಯದಿರ್ದೊಡೆ, ಕೊಡದಿರ್ದೊಡೆ. In the modern dialect wherein ಅರೆ is employed and ಇದ್ದ takes the place of ಇರ್ದ, there are *e.g.* ಅಲ್ಲದಿದ್ದರೆ, ಇಲ್ಲದಿದ್ದರೆ, ನಡೆಯದಿದ್ದರೆ, ಮಾಡದಿದ್ದರೆ; instead of ಇದ್ದರೆ it uses also ಹೋದರೆ (ಹೋದ+ಅರೆ), *e.g.* ಮಾಡದೆ ಹೋದರೆ, ಹೇಳದೆ ಹೋದರೆ.

Also Saṁskṛita ಪಕ್ಷ has been used by Kêśava in the so-called conditional instead of ಒಡೆ, (ಅಡೆ and ಅರೆ), his three instances referring to the negative relative participle, viz. ನಾಮರೂಢಿಯುಱಿಯದ ಪಕ್ಷಂ, if the conventional meaning of a word is not destroyed. ನಾಮಪ್ರಸಿದ್ಧಿ ಕಿಡದ ಪಕ್ಷಂ, if the well-known meaning of a word is not destroyed (ನಾಮಪ್ರಸಿದ್ಧಿಯು ಕೆಡದ ಪಕ್ಷದಲ್ಲಿ, commentator). ಆ ಪ್ರತಿಷೇಧವಿಧಿಯುಮ್ ಒದವದ ಪಕ್ಷಂ (sûtra 235).

In § 287, 5, *a. b* it has been seen that 'though', 'although' are expressed by ಒಡೆ, ಅಡೆ and ಅರೆ in connection with ಅಂ, ಉಂ, ಊ joined to the past relative participle, and without those postpositions by ಉಂ, ಊ joined to the so-called gerund (§ 154 *seq.*), and in § 288 by ಆಗ್ಯೂ joined to the past relative participle.

According to § 287, 8 ಒಡೆ, ಅಡೆ and ಅರೆ in connection with ಅಂ, ಊ added to past relative participles express 'whether — or'. In § 286 we see that ಒಡೆ and ಅರೆ in connection with ಅಂ, ಊ are used also in a copulative sense. According to § 287, 6. 7 ಒಡೆ, ಅಡೆ and ಅರೆ in connection with ಅಂ, ಉಂ are used to express 'at least', 'at any rate', 'even', etc. According to § 289 ಆದರೂ or ಆದಾಗ್ಯೂ express 'however', 'but', etc. According to § 291 ಒಡೆ and ಅರೆ in connection with ಅಂ, ಊ mean 'soever'; and in § 296 it is stated that ಅರೆ joined to the past relative participle ಆದ, expresses 'but'. In § 338 it will be stated that ಒಡೆ, etc., when added to a past participle and followed by ಅಲ್ಲದೆ, get the meaning of 'except'.

In the modern dialect 'unless', 'except' are frequently expressed by ಹೊರ್ತು (ಹೊಱತು) following a relative past participle (§ 282, *i*), *e. g.*

ದೀಕ್ಷೆ ಮಾಡಿದ ಹೊರ್ತು ಮೋಕ್ಷ ಬರಲಿಕ್ಕಿಲ್ಲ, unless (the guru) initiates, final beatitude does not come. ನಾವು ಹೆಱವರನ್ನು ಲಕ್ಷಿಸಿದ ಹೊರ್ತು ಹೆಱವರು ನಮ್ಮನ್ನು ನಿಶ್ಚಯವಾಗಿ ಲಕ್ಷಿಸರು, unless (you) take notice of other persons, other persons certainly do not take notice of you. ಫಿರ್ಯಾದಿ ಮಾಡದ ಹೊರ್ತು ದಾಯಾದಿ ಕೇಳ, except (one) makes a legal complaint, the kinsman does not hear.

'Lest' is to be expressed in a particular way, viz. by ಹಾಗೆ (or ಅನ್ತೆ) in connection with the relative negative participle, *e.g.* ನಿಮ್ಮ ಕಾಲಿಗೆ ಕುಡುಗೋಲು ತಾಕದ ಹಾಗೆ ಜೋಕೆಯಾಗಿರ್ರಿ, take care lest your foot is (or be) hit by the sickle. ನಿಮಗೆ ಹೊಟ್ಟೆನೋವು ಆಗದ ಹಾಗೆ ಬಹಳ ಕಾರ ತಿನ್ನ ಬಾರದು, do not eat many pungent substances lest your stomach pains (or pain). ಮೋಸಗಾಱರಿಗೆ ಯಾವದೊನ್ದು ಕೆಲಸದಲ್ಲಿ ಬಹಳ ಬುದ್ಧಿ ಬೇಕಾಗುತ್ತದೆ, ಯಾಕನ್ದರೆ ಪ್ರಾಣಿಗಳೆಲ್ಲ ತಮಗೆ ಮೋಸವಾಗ ಬಾರದೆನ್ದು ಬಹಳ ಎಚ್ಚಱದಿನ್ದ ಇರುತ್ತಾರೆ, deceitful men must use much shrewdness in any affair, for all beings are watchful lest they be deceived.

Remark.

Some pertinent instances from the modern dialect of South-Mahratta (S.-Mhr. school-books) with regard to the use of ಅರೆ in the so-called conditional are the following:—ನನಗೆ ಬರೆಯಲಿಕ್ಕೆ ಬರುತ್ತಿದ್ದರೆ ನಾನು ನಿನ್ನ ಕೂಡ ಬರೆಯುತ್ತಿದ್ದೆನು, (literally) coming if it was (or is) to me to write, writing I was in company with thee, *i. e.* if I could write, I should write (here) in company with thee. ನನ್ನದು ಅದೇ ಹಾದಿ, ಅಲ್ಲವೇ? ಬರುತ್ತಿದ್ದರೆ ನಾಳೇ ಬಾ! ಕೂಡಿ ಹೋಗುವಾ, is mine not the same road (to school)? Coming if (you) are (*i. e.* if you come), come even to-morrow! Let us go together. ಸೂರ್ಯನು ಇಲ್ಲದಿದ್ದರೆ ಎಲ್ಲಾ ಕಡೆಯಲ್ಲಿಯೂ ಚಳಿ ಬೀಳುತ್ತಿತ್ತು, ಕತ್ತಲು ಕವಿಯುತ್ತಿತ್ತು, ಗಿಡ ಬಳ್ಳಿಗಳು ಏನೂ ಹುಟ್ಟುತ್ತಿದ್ದಿಲ್ಲ, ನಾವೂ ಬದುಕುತ್ತಿದ್ದಿಲ್ಲ, the sun not being if was (*i. e.* if there were not the sun), on all sides coldness falling was (*i. e.* it would be cold everywhere), darkness would cover, trees and creepers would not grow at all, and we should not live. ಹಡಗುಗಳು ಇಲ್ಲದಿದ್ದರೆ ಸಮುದ್ರದೊಳಗಿನ್ದ ಒನ್ದು ದೇಶದಿನ್ದ ಮತ್ತೊನ್ದು ದೇಶಕ್ಕೆ ಹೋಗಲಿಕ್ಕೂ ಬರಲಿಕ್ಕೂ ಜನರಿಗೆ ಬರುತ್ತಿದ್ದಿಲ್ಲ, ships not being if were (*i. e.* if ships had not existed), coming not was to men (*i. e.* it would have been impossible for men) to go to and to come from one country to another country. ನನ್ನ ತಾಯಿಯ ಮಾತು ಕೇಳಿದ್ದರೆ ಈ ಅರಿಷ್ಟವು ನನಗೆ ಯಾಕೆ ಬರುತ್ತಿತ್ತು, my mother's word having heard if (I) was (*i. e.* if I had listened to my mother's word), this misfortune why befalling me was (*i. e.* why should this misfortune have befallen me)? ನನ್ನ ಮಗನೇ, ಮರದ ಮೇಲಿನ್ದ ಬಿದ್ದಿದ್ದರೆ ಸತ್ತು ಹೋಗುತ್ತಿದ್ದಿ, my son, from the tree having fallen if (thou) wast, having died going thou wast, (*i. e.* my son, if thou hadst fallen from the tree, thou wouldst have died). ಅಯ್ವತ್ತು ರೂಪಾಯಿ ಕೊಟ್ಟಿದ್ದರೂ ಈ ಗಿಡವನ್ನು ನಾನು ಯಾರಿಗೂ ಕೊಡುತ್ತಿದ್ದಿಲ್ಲ, fifty rupees (one) having given was though (*i. e.* though one had given fifty rupees), this tree to whomsoever giving I was not (*i. e.* I should not have given this tree to anybody). ಆ ಮರಿಯು ತನ್ನ ತಾಯಿಯ ಮಾತು ಕೇಳಿದ್ದರೆ ಅದಕ್ಕೆ ಕೇಡು ಆಗುತ್ತಿದ್ದಿಲ್ಲ, the young one its mother's word having heard if was (*i. e.* if the young one had listened to its mother's word), to it disaster becoming was not (*i. e.* no disaster would have happened to it). Regarding ಇದ್ದಿಲ್ಲ see § 316, 2.

The author of the present grammar has not met with similar instances in the ancient and mediæval dialect. The Rev. Mr. Hodson writes in his elementary grammar of the Kannaḍa language (second edition, Bangalore, 1864):—

" ನೀನು ಮೊನ್ನೆ ಹೇಳಿದರೆ ನಿನ್ನೆ ಬರುವೆನು, if you had told me the day before yesterday, I should have come yesterday."

"This sentence may with equal propriety be expressed by: ನೀನು ಮೊನ್ನೆ ಹೇಳಿದ್ದರೆ ನಿನ್ನೆ ಬನ್ದಿದ್ದೆನು, or ನೀನು ಮೊನ್ನೆ ಹೇಳಿದ್ದರೆ ನಿನ್ನೆ ಬನ್ದಿರುವೆನು, or ನೀನು ಮೊನ್ನೆ ಹೇಳಿದ್ದರೆ ನಿನ್ನೆ ಬರುತ್ತಿದ್ದೆನು, or ನೀನು ಮೊನ್ನೆ ಹೇಳಿದ್ದರೆ ನಿನ್ನೆ ಬರುತ್ತಿರುವೆನು."

"The negative is similarly expressed by the use of the negative mood, as: ನೀನು ಇಲ್ಲಿ ಇದ್ದರೆ ನನ್ನ ಸಹೋದರನು ಸಾಯನು, or ನೀನು ಇಲ್ಲಿ ಇರುತ್ತಿದ್ದರೆ ನನ್ನ ಸಹೋದರನು ಸಾಯನು, or ನೀನು ಇಲ್ಲಿ ಇದ್ದರೆ ನನ್ನ ಸಹೋದರನು ಸಾಯುತ್ತಿದ್ದಿಲ್ಲ, or ನೀನು ಇಲ್ಲಿ ಇದ್ದರೆ ನನ್ನ ಸಹೋದರನು ಸಾಯದೆ ಇರುವನು, if thou hadst been here, my brother would not have died."

315. Also what has been called the **Passive** (§ 148), named **karmaṇivâċya** in Saṁskṛita, **may be classed with the compound verbal forms** of Kannaḍa.

1, The term of karmaṇiprayôga, or the use of the passive voice, was distinctly used in Kannaḍa grammar **first by Bhaṭṭâkalaṅka** in the year 1604 A. D. (§ 8, note); long before his time both Nâgavarma and Kêšava had not yet given that name to the peculiar compound-verbal form and its use which he designated by that term. Sûtra 251 *b* about karmaṇiprayôga that has got into Kêšava's Šabdamaṇidarpaṇa, is not found in our best MSS., and in those wherein it is found, it is called an anuktasûtra or interpolation; it is based on Bhaṭṭâkalaṅka's Šabdânušâsana.

Bhaṭṭâkalaṅka's instances regarding the karmaṇiprayôga under his sûtras 443 *seq.* are the following:—

ತಾನ್ ಇರಲ್ ಪಟ್ಟಂ, ತಾಮ್ ಇರಲ್ ಪಟ್ಟರ್; ನೀನ್ ಇರಲ್ ಪಟ್ಟಯ್, ನೀಮ್ ಇರಲ್ ಪಟ್ಟಿರ್; ಆನ್ ಇರಲ್ ಪಟ್ಟೆಂ, ಆಮ್ ಇರಲ್ ಪಟ್ಟೆವು;— ಪಾರ್ವನಿನ್ ಅರಸಂ

ಗ್ರಾಮಮಂ ಬೇಡಲ್ ಪಟ್ಟಂ; ಗೋವಳನಿನ್ದೆಮ್ಮೆ (=ಎಮ್ಮೆ) ಪಾಲಂ ಕಱೆಯಲ್ ಪಟ್ಟುದು; ಉಪಾಧ್ಯಾಯಂ ಶಿಷ್ಯರಿಂ ತತ್ವಮಂ ಬೆಸಗೊಳಲ್ ಪಟ್ಟಂ; ಬೇಹುಕಾಱಿನ್ ಅರಸನಿಂ ಸುದ್ದಿಯಂ ಕೇಳಲ್ ಪಟ್ಟಂ;—ತುಱುಗಳ್ ಊರನ್ ಅಯ್ದಿಸಲ್ ಪಟ್ಟುವು ಗೋವಳನಿಂ; ಗುರುಗಳಿನ್ ಅರಸಂ ಧರ್ಮಮನ್ ಅಱಿಯಿಸಲ್ ಪಟ್ಟಂ; ಅರಸನಿನ್ ಅಂ ಪೆರ್ಚಿಸಲ್ ಪಟ್ಟಂ;— under his sûtra 530:—ಮಾಡಲ್ ಪಟ್ಟುದು ಘಟಂ ಕುಮ್ಬಾರನಿಂ; ನೋಡಲ್ ಪಟ್ಟನ್ ಅರಸನ್ ಅಂಗನೆಯಿಂ; ಬಯಸಲ್ ಪಟ್ಟಳ್ ತರುಣಿ ರಮಣನಿಂ; ಮಾಡಲ್ ಪಡುಗೆಮಗೆ ಸಮ್ಪದಂ ಜಿನಪತಿಯಿಂ; ಕಿಡಿಸಲ್ ಪಡುಗೆಮ್ಮ ದುಃಖಸನ್ತತಿ ಜಿನನಿಂ;—under his sûtra 532:—ಮಾಡೆ ಪಟ್ಟಂ or ಮಾಡಲ್ ಪಟ್ಟಂ; ನೋಡೆ ಪಟ್ಟಂ or ನೋಡಲ್ ಪಟ್ಟಂ; ಕಿಡಿಸೆ ಪಟ್ಟುದು or ಕಿಡಿಸಲ್ ಪಟ್ಟುದು;—and under his šûtra 209:—ಅಕ್ಕಸಾಲೆಯಿಂ ಪದಕಂ ಗೆಯ್ಯಲ್ ಪಟ್ಟುದು; ಅರಸನಿಂ ಬಾಣಸಿಗನಿನ್ ಅನ್ನಂ ಮಾಡಿಸಲ್ ಪಟ್ಟುದು; ಹರಿಯಿನ್ದರ್ಜುನನಿಂ ಕರ್ಣಂ ಕೊಲ್ಲಿಸಲ್ ಪಟ್ಟಂ.

Now let us see how Nâgavarma and Kêšava introduced the form of the verb which Bhaṭṭâkalaṅka says that it belongs to the karmaṇiprayôga or the use of the passive.

Nâgavarma introduces it under his sûtra 80 when he writes, the agent (kartṛi) may be expressed by the instrumental (tṛitîyĕ), *e.g.* ದೇವದತ್ತನಿಂ ಮಾಡಲ್ ಪಟ್ಟುದು; ಯಜ್ಞದತ್ತನಿಂ ಪೇೞಲ್ ಪಟ್ಟುದು.

Kêšava introduces it under his sûtras 126 and 128 saying: also when the agent has the meaning of the instrumental (*cf.* § 347, 9) the nominative (prathamĕ) occurs, *e. g.* for ಅವನಿಂ ಮಾಡೆ (o. r. ಮಾಡಲ್) ಪಟ್ಟುದು there may be used ಅವಂ ಮಾಡಿದಂ; ಪದಕಮ್ ಅಕ್ಕಸಾಲೆಯಿಂ ಮಾಡಲ್ (o. rs. ಮಾಡೆ and ಮಾಡ) ಪಟ್ಟುದು; ಕಾವ್ಯಮ್ ಎನ್ನಿಂ ಪೇೞೆ ಪಟ್ಟುದು.

In other places of the Šabdamaṇidarpaṇa we find: ಪೇೞಲ್ ಪಡೆಗುಂ (sûtras 51 and 128, where the commentator has ಪೇೞಲ್ ಪಡೆವುವು, ಹೇೞಲ್ ಪಟ್ಟುವು); ಆಯ್ದಲ್ ಪಡೆವುದು (vṛitti to sûtra 127); ಈ ಪೇೞಲ್ ಪಡೆದ ಶಬ್ದಂಗಳ್ (vṛitti to sûtra 272); and ಪ್ರಯೋಗಿಸ ಪಡೆಗುಂ (sûtra 110, commentator ಪ್ರಯೋಗಿಸಲ್ ಪಡುವುದು).

From the above instances it is learned that what is termed karmaṇiprayôga by Bhaṭṭâkalaṅka, is the use of the infinitive ending in ಅಲ್, ಎ and ಅ (§ 187) followed by the verbs ಪಡು or ಪಡೆ. Instead of ಅಲ್ the **mediæval dialect** frequently has ಅಲು (see Dictionary *sub* ಪಡು 1), *e. g.* ಅಲುಗಲು ಪಟ್ಟುದು. The initial ಪ of ಪಡು may be changed into ಬ, *e. g.* ಉಣಲ್ ಬಟ್ಟುದು (*cf.* § 215, 7, *a*). According to § 188 the said infinitives are verbal nouns.

Both ಪಡು and ಪಡೆ mean 'to experience', 'to suffer'; 'to acquire', 'to get or obtain'; Nâgavarma's instances under his sûtra 80 (see above) are therefore to be translated literally: by Dêvadatta a making it experienced (*i. e.* it was made by Dêvadatta); by Yajñadatta a saying it experienced (*i. e.* it was said by Yajñadatta);—and Kêśava's instances under his sûtras 126 and 128: by him a making it experienced (*i. e.* it was made by him); a padaka by the goldsmith a making experienced (*i. e.* a padaka was made by the goldsmith); a poem by me a saying experienced (*i. e.* a poem was said or told by me).

Let also some of Bhaṭṭâkalaṅka's above instances be translated literally: by a Brâhmaṇa the king a village a begging (the begging of a village) experienced (*i. e.* the king was asked for a village by a Brâhmaṇa); by the cowherd a buffalo milk a milking (the milking of milk) experienced (*i. e.* a buffalo was milked by the cowherd);—by the king by the cook food a causing to prepare experienced (*i. e.* food was ordered by the king to be prepared by the cook); by Hari by Arjuna Karṇa a causing to kill experienced (*i. e.* Karṇa was ordered by Hari to be killed by Arjuna).

The so-called passive, especially in the instances of Bhaṭṭâkalaṅka, is rather queer and clumsy in character to a European's idea; but as stated, it was used in the literature of the ancient and mediæval period. That it has been used also in the modern written dialect will appear *e. g.* from the following instance met with in a South-Mahratta school-book: ಶರೀರದಲ್ಲಿ ಯಾವದೊನ್ದು ಬಗೆಯ ರೋಗವಿಲ್ಲದಿದ್ದರೆ, ಅದು ಆರೋಗ್ಯವಾದದ್ದೆನ್ದು, ಹೇಳಲ್ ಪಡುತ್ತದೆ, if (there) is no sickness of any kind in the body, that a saying experiences (*i. e.* that is called) health;—but it is rare in modern literature, and in colloquial language it is avoided, and if used, is generally not understood by the populace.

A peculiar way of expression is found in Bhaṭṭâkalaṅka's first instances ತಾನ್ ಇರಲ್ ಪಟ್ಟಂ, ತಾವ್ ಇರಲ್ ಪಟ್ಟರ್, etc., which are to be translated 'he a being experienced' (*i. e.* he was), 'they a being experienced' (*i. e.* they were), etc. This may be called periphrastic, as in the present case the simple verb ಇರ್, to be, is expressed by ಇರ್ and ಪಡು. A similar expression presents itself in the following instance from an ancient classical work:—ಮನ್ಮಥಂ ಮತಿಗಿಡುವಂ ಗೆಲಲ್ ಪಡೆಯದಾ ನಯಕೀರ್ತಿ ಮುಮುಕ್ಷುಮುಖ್ಯಂ, Cupido will lose his wits, not an overcoming obtaining (*i. e.* not overcoming) that Nayakîrti, the chief of those who strive after mukti.

2, **Other modes of expressing the idea or force of the passive in** Kannaḍa are the following: —

a) the mode of **joining the verbs ಪಡು or ಪಡೆ to nouns,** *e. g.* ಅಚ್ಚರಿವಡು (-ಪಡು), lit. to get surprise, *i. e.* to be surprised; ಅಳವಡು (-ಪಡು), lit. to get a fit state, *i. e.* to be made ready; ಕಟ್ಟು ಪಡು, to be bound; ಪ್ರೀತಿವಡು (-ಪಡು), to be loved; ನಾಚಿಕೆ ಪಡು, to be ashamed; ಶ್ರಮ ಪಡು, to be wearied; ಕಡಿವಡೆ (-ಪಡೆ), to be cut off; ಪುಡಿವಡೆ (-ಪಡೆ), to be powdered; ಬಡಿವಡೆ (-ಪಡೆ), to be struck; ಮುಱಿವಡೆ (-ಪಡೆ), to be broken or defeated. *Cf.* letter *n.*

b) that of **joining the verb** ಪೆಱ್ (ಪೆಱು), to get, to receive, **to nouns;** in the ancient and mediæval dialect, *e. g.* ಏಪೆಱ್, lit. to get a wound or wounds, *i. e.* to be wounded; ಓಜೆವೆಱ್ (-ಪೆಱ್), to be arranged in proper order; ಕಡಿವೆಱ್ (-ಪೆಱ್), to be cut. *Cf.* letter *n.*

c) that of **joining the verb ಪೋಗು to nouns,** *e. g.* ಕಡಿವೋಗು (-ಪೋಗು), lit. to go a cutting off, *i. e.* to be cut off. *Cf.* letter *o.*

d) that of **joining ಹೋಗು to the past participle** or gerund of verbs that are commonly used as transitives, *e. g.* ಕಳದು ಹೋದದು, that is past, that is lost; ಅವನ ಎರಡೂ ಕಾಲುಗಳು ಕಡಿದು ಹೋದವು, his two legs were cut off. ಬೆಣ್ಣು ಬತ್ತಾಸು ಕೊಣ್ಡರೆ ತಿನ್ದು ಹೋಗುತ್ತವೆ, if (I) buy sweetmeats, they will be eaten.

e) that of **using the causative verb** ಎನಿಸು (ಅನಿಸು), to make say or call, to cause (one's self) to be called (see Dictionary *sub voce*), very frequently in the three dialects, *e. g.* ಆದಿಯ ಪತ್ತಕ್ಕರಮುಂ ಸಮಾನಮ್ ಎನಿಸುಗುಂ, and the first ten letters are called monophthongs; ದಾನವರ ತಾಯಿ ದನುವೆನಿಕುಂ, the mother of the Dânavas is called Danu; ಅರ್ಧದೇಹಮ್ ಎನಿಸುವ ಸತಿಯು, the wife that is called the half body (of her husband). ಮನುವುಂ ತಾನುಂ ಸಚ್ಚರಿತರ್ ಎನಿಪನ್ ಉದಯಾದಿತ್ಯಂ, of Udayâditya it is said "Manu and he (are) virtuous people".

In the ancient, and especially in the mediæval and modern dialect, **any causative verb in the past participle followed by the verb** ಕೊಳ್ (ಕೊಳು, ಕೊಳ್ಳು) **also expresses the force of the passive,** *e. g.* ಸಮ್ಪ್ರದಾನವೆನ್ದಾವುದಾನೊನ್ದು ವಸ್ತುವೆನಿಸಿ ಕೊಮ್ಬ ಪಾತ್ರಂ, any object which is called a recipient, (is) a saying sampradâna (*i. e.* is what one calls sampradâna); ತಲೆಯನ್ ಅರಿಸಿ ಕೊಳಲ್ ತಕ್ಕವನು, one who is fit (or deserves) to be beheaded; ಕಟ್ಟಿಸಿ ಕೊಣ್ಡವನು, one who is fettered; ನೂಕಿಸಿ ಕೊಣ್ಡವನು, one who is pushed away; ಬಯ್ಸಿ ಕೊಣ್ಡವನು, one who is calumniated; ಚಮ್ಮಟಿಗೆಯಿನ್ದ ಹೊಡಸಿ ಕೊಳಲ್ ತಕ್ಕವನು, one who is fit (or deserves) to be whipped; ಶಾಸ್ತ್ರಕ್ರಮದಿನ್ದ ಅಭಿವಾದನಂ

ಮಾಡಿಸಿ ಕೊಳುವಾತನು, one who is respectfully saluted according to the manner of the śâstras; ಬಯಕೆ ಕೊಟ್ಟರೂ ಬಯ್ಸಿ ಕೊವ್ಪುದು ತಪ್ಪಲಿಲ್ಲ, though (one) gives the desired object, (one) does not go without being abused; ಸಾಕಿದವನು ಎಷ್ಟು ಹೊಡಿದರೂ ಸುಮ್ಮನೇ ಹೊಡಿಸಿ ಕೊಣ್ತು ಮನಸ್ಸಿನೊಳಗೆ ಸಿಟ್ಟು ಸಹ ಹಿಡಿಯುವದಿಲ್ಲ, however so much (one) beats (the dog) one has reared, it quietly allows itself to be beaten and does also not become inwardly angry. *Cf.* § 341.

f) that of adding the verb ಆಗು to a verbal noun used more or less in all dialects, *e. g.* ಪ್ರಯೋಗಿಸುವದಹುದು, lit. it becomes a using, *i. e.* it is used; ಪೋಲಿಸುವಲ್ಲಿ... ಅನ್ತೆ ಪೋಲ್ ಎನಲಕ್ಕುಂ, lit. where comparison takes place... a saying ಅನ್ತೆ (and) ಪೋಲ್ becomes, *i. e.* ಅನ್ತೆ and ಪೋಲ್ are said (or used); ಒನ್ದು ತಾಸಿನೊಳಗೆ ನಾಲ್ಕು ಸಾವಿರ ತಾವು ಮುದ್ರಿಸೋಣವಾಗುತ್ತದೆ, in one hour four thousand sheets (of paper) a printing it becomes, *i. e.* are printed; ಅವನಿನ್ದ ಇಷ್ಟು ಭಾರವ ಹೊಱೋಣವಾಗದು, lit. by him a carrying such a burden it does not become, *i. e.* by him no such burden can be carried; ಪುಸ್ತಕಗಳನ್ನು ತರೋಣವಾಗಿದೆ, lit. a bringing the books having become it is, *i. e.* the books have been brought; ಕೆಟ್ಟ ಸ್ಥಲದಲ್ಲಿ ಮಾಡುವ ಒಳ್ಳೇ ಕೆಲಸಗಳು ಸಹ ಕೆಟ್ಟ ಕೆಲಸಗಳೇ ಎಣಿಸಲಾಗುವವು, also good deeds one performs in an improper place, a considering bad deeds it becomes, *i. e.* are considered bad deeds; ಅದು ಹೇೞೋಣವಾಯಿತು or ಅದನ್ನು ಹೇೞೋಣವಾಯಿತು, that was said; ಕಾಲಿದಾಸನಿನ್ದ ಶಾಕುನ್ತಲಾನಾಟಕವು ರಚಿಸಲಾಯಿತು, the drama Śâkuntalâ was composed by Kâlidâsa. (About verbal nouns see § 243; about verbal nouns like ಮುದ್ರಿಸೋಣ, etc. see § 205, 3, 1 pers. plural.)

In the ancient dialect there is found the following sentence in which the infinitive or verbal noun ending in ಅಲ್ stands in the dative:— ಎತ್ತಣದೆಮ್ಬಾ ಶಬ್ದಮಮ್ ಎತ್ತಣ್ತೆನ್ದು ಕೂಡಿ ನುಡಿಯಲ್ಕಕ್ಕುಂ, the term ಎತ್ತಣದು is (or may be) contracted, and uttered ಎತ್ತಣ್ಣು;—and in the same dialect ಆಗು is joined to a verbal noun in the past, *e. g.* ಅವನ ನೊಸಲಕ್ಕರಂ ತೊಡೆದುದಕ್ಕುಂ, the writing on his forehead will be wiped out.

g) that of using the verb ತಿನ್ (ತಿನ್ನು) with the noun ಪೆಟ್ಟು, *e. g.* ಅವನು ಪೆಟ್ಟು ತಿನ್ದ, he was beaten, lit. he ate blows; or the verb ಬೀೞ್ (ಬೀೞು) with the noun ಬಡತ (or ಲತ್ತೆ), *e. g.* ಗುರುಪಾದಗೆ ಬಡತ (or ಲತ್ತೆ) ಬಿದ್ದವು, Gurupâda was beaten, lit. to (or on) Gurupâda blows fell.

h) that of using such transitive verbs as are more or less commonly also intransitives, in the three dialects, *e. g.* ಒಡೆದುದು, that is broken;

ವೃಷಭನಿನ್ದ ಕಟ್ಟಿದ ಆಕಳು, a cow that has been covered by the bull; ತೆಱೆದ ಕಿಟಕಿ, a window that is opened; ಕಟ್ಟುಗಳು ಪಱಿದುವು, the ties were torn; ಗವುಡನ ಮನೆ ಸುಟ್ಟಿತು, the Gauḍa's house was burnt.

i) that of **using such transitive verbs as do commonly not allow an intransitive sense**, *e. g.* ಇನ್ತಿದಱೊಳ್ ಸಾಕಲ್ಯಸಂಜ್ಞೆ ಪೇೞಿವೆನಲ್ ಬೇಡ, (you) must not say that thus in this (section) all signs (or letters) are not mentioned (Šabdamaṇidarpaṇa sûtra 51); ಪ್ರಥಮೆ ಚತರ್ಥಿಗಳ್ ಸೂತ್ರದೊಳ್ ಪೇೞ್ದುವು, the nominative and dative are mentioned in the rule (s. 140, vṛitti); ಚಿತ್ರಮಯುವಾಗಿ ಕಟ್ಟಿತು ಪರ್ಣಶಾಲೆ, the arbour was built in a wonderful manner.

k) that of **using transitive verbs which are not accompanied by an agent, but to which the agent has to be supplied mentally** (*cf.* § 254, 2, under *b*), very frequently used in the three dialects, *e. g.* ಪೇೞ್ದ ವಿಭಕ್ತಿಗಳ್, the mentioned terminations, lit. the terminations which (I) have mentioned (see another ancient instance in § 351, remark); ಶಿವನಗ್ಗವಣಿಯಂ ಶೋಧಿಸಿದುದಿಲ್ಲವೊ, was Šiva's offering of water not filtered? lit. Šiva's offering of water (I) a having filtered was it not? ತಿದ್ದಿ ಬೆಳಿಸಿದ ಎರಡನೆಯ ಆವೃತ್ತಿ, a revised and enlarged second edition, lit. a second edition which (the author) has revised and enlarged; ಸಿದ್ಧ ಮಾಡಿದ ರಸವು, a prepared fluid, lit. a fluid that (people) have prepared; ಹೊಯಿದ ಮೊಳೆಗಳು, cast types, lit. types that (workmen) have cast; ಅಚ್ಚು ಹಾಕಿದ ಪುಸ್ತಕಗಳು, printed books, lit. books that (people) have printed; ಬರೆದ ಪುಸ್ತಕ, a written book, lit. a book that (somebody) has written; ಹೇೞಿದ್ದು ಸಾಕು, what was (or has been) said is sufficient, lit. what (the man) said is sufficient; ಇಟ್ಟಿಗೆ ಮೊದಲಾದುದಱಿಂ ಮಾಡಿದ ಅರಮನೆ, a palace made (or built) of bricks and other things, lit. a palace which (they) have made of bricks etc.; ಒನಕೆಯಿಂ ಕೊಲಲ್ ತಕ್ಕವನು, one who deserves to be killed with a club, lit. one who deserves (people) killing (him) with a club; ಸಾಯ ಕೊಲ್ಲ ತಕ್ಕವನು, one who deserves to be slain so that (he) dies, lit. one who deserves (people) slaying (him) etc. *Cf.* § 358.

Very often the present-future relative participle of ಎನ್ (ಎನ್ನು), **to say, to call, is met with as an instance of this rule**, *e. g.* ಕಾನ್ತಿಯೆಂಬ ಗುಣ ದೊಳ್ ಅನ್ವಿತೆಯಪ್ಪ ವಾಕ್ಕೆನ್ಬ ದೇವಿ, the goddess who is called speech and is endowed with the quality which is called splendour, lit. the goddess whom (people) call speech etc.; ಅ ಇ ಉ ಋ ಌ ಎನ್ಬುವು, these (vowels) called a i u ṛi lṛi, lit. these (vowels) which (they) call a, etc.; ಕುಲಿನ್ದಕನ್ ಎನ್ಬ ದೊರೆ, the chief called Kulindaka, lit. the chief whom (they) call Kulindaka;

ಗೃಹಸ್ಥನು ಸ್ನಾತಕನ್ ಎಮ್ಬುದು, a gṛihasta is called a snâtaka, lit. a gṛihasta (they) a calling it (*i. e.* they call) a snâtaka; ಸಾಕೆಮ್ಬುದು, what is called 'enough', lit. what (they) call 'enough'; ಎರಡುಂ ವ್ಯಂಜನಮನ್ ಉಚ್ಚರಿಸುವನಿತು ಕಾಲಮಂ ಮಾತ್ರೆಯೆಮ್ಬುದು, a mâtrĕ is called that length of time in which (one) pronounces even two consonants, lit. a mâtrĕ (they) a calling it (*i. e.* they call) etc.; ದೊಡ್ಡಪ್ಪ ಚಿಕ್ಕಪ್ಪ ಎಮ್ಬ ಇಬ್ಬರು ಮಕ್ಕಳು, two children called, lit. whom (they) call, Dŏḍḍappa (and) Cikkappa. See § 332.

l) that of **using the compound perfect** (*cf.* § 313, 4), **the agent being mentally supplied** to the participle, as under letter *k*, *e. g.* ಗೂಡುಗಳು ಕೂದಲುಣ್ಣೆಯೆಚಿರೆ ಹಲ್ಲುಗಳಿನ್ದ ಚಮತ್ಕಾರವಾಗಿ ಹೆಣೆದಿರುತ್ತವೆ, lit. nests (birds) having skilfully knit (them) with hair, wool, threads and grass are, *i. e.* nests are skilfully knit etc.; ಬಾಗಿಲ ಮಾಡಕ್ಕೆ ಕೀಲಿ ಹಾಕಿದೆ (-ಇದೆ), lit. to the upstair house the key (the owner) having put (it) is, *i. e.* the upstair house is locked; ಹಾಲು ತನ್ದದೆ, lit. milk (people) having brought (it) is, *i. e.* milk has been brought; ಈ ಪುಸ್ತಕದಲ್ಲಿ ಎಷ್ಟೋ ಸೋಜಿಗದ ಸಂಗತಿಗಳು ಬರೆದಿರುತ್ತವೆ, lit. how many wonderful things (somebody) having written in this book are, *i. e.* how many wonderful things are written in this book; ಭೀಮನ ಮಗಳನ್ನು ರಾಮನ ಮಗನಿಗೆ ಕೊಟ್ಟದೆ, lit. (they) having given Bhîma's daughter to Râma's son it is, *i. e.* Bhîma's daughter has been given to Râma's son; ಪುಸ್ತಕಗಳನ್ನು ತನ್ದದೆ, lit. (somebody) having brought the books it is, *i. e.* the books have been brought;—or **also the compound pluperfect** (*cf.* § 313, 7), *e. g.* ಗೂಡಿನಲ್ಲಿ ಮೂಱು ತತ್ತಿಗಳು ಹಾಕಿದ್ದವು, in the nest three eggs (a bird) having laid (them) were, *i. e.* three eggs had been laid in the nest (by a bird); ಸೀತೆಯನ್ನು ರಾಮನಿಗೆ ಕೊಟ್ಟಿತ್ತು, lit. (they) having given Sîtĕ to Râma it was, *i. e.* Sîtĕ had been given to Râma.

m) a curious way in which **the verb** ಬೇಡು **with an infinitive** is used to express a sort of passive in the ancient and mediæval dialect, may also be mentioned here, *e. g.* ಆವುದು ಮಾಡಲ್ ಬೇಡಿದುದು, ಅದುವೆ ಕರ್ಮಂ, that toward which an activity is directed, is the object (of a transitive verb), lit. that which desires a doing (concerning itself) is the object; ಮಾಱಲ್ ಬೇಡಿ ಅಂಗಡಿಯಲ್ಲಿ ಪಸರಿಸಿದ ದ್ರವ್ಯವು, a substance that is to be sold (lit. that wants a selling) and is spread out in a shop; ಆಗಲು ಬೇಡಿದುದು, what will happen, what is about to be, lit. what begs to become.

n) then **the frequent use** (in the three dialects) of **the verb** ಕೊಳ್ (ಕೊಳ್ಳು), **to take, to get, in combination with nouns** is also to be adduced (*cf.* letters *a* and *b*), *e. g.* ಭಯಂಗೊಳ್ (-ಕೊಳ್), to become or be alarmed, lit. to get alarm; ಆಶ್ಚರ್ಯಗೊಳ್ಳು, to become surprised, to begin to be surprised, lit. to get surprise; ತೊಂದರೆಗೊಳ್ಳು, to get or become embarrassed; ಬೇಸರಿಗೊಳ್ಳು, to get or become wearied.

o) lastly the verb ಪೋಗು (*cf.* letter *c*) in the sense of 'to become' remains to be mentioned, *e. g.* ಈಚುವೋದ (-ಪೋದ) ಕಾವು, a stalk that has become dry.

All the modes of expressing, somehow, the force of the passive, mentioned under Nos. 1 and 2, go to show that the Kannaḍa language is destitute of a passive which as to form and idea corresponds to the Saṁskṛita and English one.

XX. On so-called auxiliary verbs.

316. In English there are some verbs that are called **auxiliaries**, as have, be, shall, will; such, in a strict sense of the word, are not in Kannaḍa. It is, however, not only instructive, but necessary to learn how Kannaḍa does express them.

1, The English auxiliary verb '**have**', *e. g.* in 'I have seen', is **expressed by the aorist** (imperfect, perfect), *e. g.* ಕೇಳ್ದಂ (ಕೇಳಿದಂ, ಕೇಳಿದೆನು, § 198, 1 *seq.*), I have heard (I heard), or **by the compound perfect**, *e. g.* ಹೋಗಿದ್ದಾನೆ, he has (or is) gone (§ 313, 4; *cf.* § 315, 2, *l*), –and '**had**' **by the compound pluperfect**, *e. g.* ಅಚ್ಯುತರಾಯನು ಮರಣ ಹೊಂದಿದ್ದನು, king Aćyuta had died (§ 313, 7; *cf.* § 315, 2, *l*). *Cf.* also § 314, remark; and § 155 *seq.* about the past participles.

The English verb 'to **have**', 'to **possess**' is expressed by the **verbs** ಉಳ್ (§ 194, remark 1), to be, or ಇರ್ (ಇರು), to be, or ಅದೆ, is, ಅವೆ, are (§ 196) **preceded by the dative case**, etc., *e. g.* ಜಸಮ್ ಉಣ್ಟೀತಂಗೆ, lit. renown is to him, *i. e.* he has or possesses renown. ಅಲರ್ಗಣ್ಣುಣ್ಟೀತಂಗೆ, lit. flower-like eyes are to him, *i. e.* he has flower-like eyes. ಆತಂಗೆ ಕುದುರೆಗಳ್ ಒಳವು, lit. to him horses are, *i. e.* he possesses horses. ಅವನಿಗೆ ಹಣ ಉಣ್ಟು, he has money. ಅವನಲ್ಲಿ ಐಯ್ದು ಆಕಳುಣ್ಟು, lit. with him five cows are, *i. e.* he has five cows. ಅವನ ಹತ್ತರ ದೌತಿ ಉಣ್ಟು, lit. near him an inkstand is, *i. e.* he has (or has got) an inkstand. ನನ್ನ ಬಳಿಯಲ್ಲಿ ಕಾಳಿರುಣ್ಟು, lit. in my vicinity corn is, *i. e.* I have (or have got) corn. ಆತನಿಗೆ ಇಬ್ಬರು ಮಕ್ಕಳಿದ್ದರು, he had two sons. ಒಬ್ಬ ಗೃಹಸ್ಥನಿಗೆ ಇಬ್ಬರು ಮಕ್ಕಳಿದ್ದವು, a certain gentleman had two children. ಒಬ್ಬ ಗವಳಿಗನ ಬಳಿಯಲ್ಲಿ ಒನ್ದು ಎಮ್ಮೆ ಇತ್ತು, a certain cowherd had one she-buffalo. ಹಾವುಗಳಿಗೆ ಎರಡು ಸೀಳಿದ ಪೊಳ್ಳು

ಹಲ್ಲುಗಳು ಇರುತ್ತವೆ, snakes have two pointed hollow teeth. ನನ್ನ ಹತ್ತರ ಚಲೋ ಕಾಗದ ಅದೆ, I have fine paper. ಅವಳಿಗೆ ತಲೆನೋವು ಅದೆ, she has a headache. ನನಗೆ ನೀರಡಿಕೆ ಆಗಿದೆ, I have got thirst. ನಿನ್ನ ಹತ್ತರ ಎಣ್ಟು ಹಣ್ಣು ಅವೆ, thou hast eight ripe fruits. Also: ನನ್ನ ಹತ್ತರ ಹಣ ಅದೆ, I have money by (or about) me. ಅವನ ಬಱಿಯಲ್ಲಿ ಗಡಿಯಾರ ಉಣ್ಟು, he has a watch with him. *Cf.* § 360.

Regarding the so-called relative participles (§§ 175 *seq.*; 180 *seq.*; 253, 2, *d*; 254. 267. 273. 330. 364) the following instances may be given:— ಧನಮ್ ಉಳ್ಳಂ, he who has riches. ಪೊನ್ನುಳ್ಳವಂ, he who possesses gold. ಸೊಬಗುಳ್ಳವಳ್, she who has beauty. ಅರ್ಥಮ್ ಉಳ್ಳುದು, that has meaning. ಅಱಿವುಳ್ಳರ್, they who have knowledge. ಹಣವುಳ್ಳವನು, he who has money. ಮಮತೆಯುಳ್ಳವಳು, she who has love. ಅಧಿಕಾರವುಳ್ಳ ಮನುಷ್ಯನು, a man who has authority. ಱೆಕ್ಕೆಯುಳ್ಳ ಹುೞು, an insect that has wings. ಬತ್ತಲೆ ಇಹವನು, lit. he who has nakedness, *i. e.* he who is naked.

If the negative is to be expressed, ಇಲ್ಲ, ಇಲ್ಲಂ (§ 209, note 1; § 298) or ಇರುವದಿಲ್ಲ or ಇರಲಿಲ್ಲ (§ 209, under No. 3) are used, *e. g.* ದೇವದತ್ತ, ನಿನಗೇನುಮ್ ಇಲ್ಲಂ, Dêvadatta, thou possessest nothing. ಆ ಗಿಡಕ್ಕೆ ಎಲೆಗಳಿಲ್ಲ, that tree has no leaves. ಅವಳ ಹತ್ತರ ಸೂಜಿಗಳಿಲ್ಲ, she has no needles. ಅವನ ಬಱಿಯಲ್ಲಿ ಚೀಲವಿಲ್ಲ, he has no sack. ಆಕಳಿಗೆ ಇಣೆ ಇರುವದಿಲ್ಲ, cows have no hump. ಅನ್ದು ಆತನಿಗೆ ಹಣವಿರಲಿಲ್ಲ, at that time he had no money.

As to so-called **negative relative participles** the following are instances (*cf.* § 273):—ಜ್ಞಾನವಿಲ್ಲದಂ, he who has no knowledge. ಕಾಲಿಲ್ಲದವಂ, he who has no feet. ಕುತ್ತವಿಲ್ಲದವನು, he who has no sickness. ಇಲ್ಲದವಳು, she who has nothing. ನೀರಿಲ್ಲದ ಭೂಮಿ, soil destitute of water. ಮತಿ ಇಲ್ಲದವರಿಗೆ ಗತಿ ಇಲ್ಲ, those who have no understanding, have no happiness.

It is a very curious fact that, in the ancient and mediæval dialect, ಉಳ್ಳ, the present participle of ಉಳ್ (§ 180, remark), **may be used transitive,** *e. g.* ನುಣ್ಪನ್ ಉಳ್ಳಂ, he who possesses gentleness (instead of ನುಣ್ಪುಳ್ಳಂ). ತೋರಿಹ ಕೆಚ್ಚಲನ್ ಉಳ್ಳ ಆಕಳು, a cow which has swelling udders (instead of ತೋರಿಹ ಕೆಚ್ಚಲುಳ್ಳ ಆಕಳು). There is also ವಿಭಕ್ತಿಯನ್ ಇಲ್ಲದುದು, that which has no terminations (Šabdamaṇidarpaṇa sûtra 72 and vṛitti; see § 338 under ಇಲ್ಲದೆ).

For 'to have' followed by an infinitive, *e. g.* he has to learn, see under No. 4 of this paragraph.

2, The English verb 'to be' is auxiliary in the passive, the way of expressing it therein in Kannaḍa has been treated of in § 315.

When 'to be' is no auxiliary, it is ಉಳ್ (ಒಳ್) and ಇರ್ (ಇರು) (ಇರ್, in the negative, frequently forms ಇಲ್) in Kannaḍa; ಅದೆ (ಅಯ್ತು), ಇದೆ, is, and ಅವೆ, ಇವೆ, are, being also used (§ 196), *e.g.* ನುಂಗುವ್ರವುಮ್ ಒಳವುದಧಿಯೊಳ್ ಮಹಾಮತ್ಸ್ಯಗಳ್, (there) are also swallowing fishes in the ocean. ಶರಣ್ ಆರುಮ್ ಒಳರೆ ಖಲಸಂಸರಣದೊಳ್, are (there) any protectors in the base world? ಆತನ್ ಒಳಂ, he is (present or he exists). ಆತನ್ ಇರ್ದಂ, he was (present or he existed). See some sentences in § 275, and regarding ಇರ್ (ಇರು) being omitted when a mere copula see § 359.

If ಉಳ್, etc. are connected with a dative, etc., they express the English 'to have', 'to possess'; see No. 1 of this paragraph.

About the negative ಇಲ್ಲ, (I) am not, (thou) art not, (he, she, it) is not etc. (of ಇಲ್ = ಇರ್) see §§ 209, note 1; 298. It has been stated in § 298 that it is used by itself, in connection with nouns and pronouns, and in combination with verbal nouns (see § 243) with which also the so-called past participles or gerunds are classed by the author of the present grammar (§§ 154 *seq.;* 169). In paragraph 298, 3 there are given as instances the forms ಅದುದಿಲ್ಲ, ಆರ್ತುದಿಲ್ಲ, ಮಾಡಿದುದಿಲ್ಲ; ಇರುವದಿಲ್ಲ, ಬರುವದಿಲ್ಲ, ಕಾಣುವದಿಲ್ಲ, ಆಗುವದಿಲ್ಲ; ಕಳೆಯಲಿಲ್ಲ, ಪಡೆಯಲಿಲ್ಲ, ಕೇಳಲಿಲ್ಲ, ಸಿಗಲಿಲ್ಲ; ಹೋಗಲಿಕ್ಕಿಲ್ಲ, ಬೀಳಲಿಕ್ಕಿಲ್ಲ, ಕೊಡಲಿಕ್ಕಿಲ್ಲ; ತೀರಿಲ್ಲ, ಮಾಡಿಲ್ಲ, ನೋಡಿಲ್ಲ, ಆಗಿಲ್ಲ, ಇದ್ದಿಲ್ಲ.

Forms like ಅದುದಿಲ್ಲ, ಆರ್ತುದಿಲ್ಲ, ಮಾಡಿದುದಿಲ್ಲ, in the ancient and mediæval dialect, stand for the simple form of the negative (§ 209) to express the past tense of the negative in a clear manner (though there occur rare exceptions, as ನಾನ್ ಅಱಿದುದಿಲ್ಲ, I did not know, has been once used for 'I do not know'). Forms like ಇರುವದಿಲ್ಲ, ಬರುವದಿಲ್ಲ, ಕಾಣುವದಿಲ್ಲ, ಆಗುವದಿಲ್ಲ, in the modern dialect, take the place of the simple negative to express the present tense of the negative in a clear way; ಕಳೆಯಲಿಲ್ಲ, ಪಡೆಯಲಿಲ್ಲ, ಕೇಳಲಿಲ್ಲ, ಸಿಗಲಿಲ್ಲ are used in the modern dialect to express clearly the past tense of the simple negative, which use however is conventional (see § 298 just before No. 1), because verbal nouns ending in ಅಲು originally rather denote the present tense, as ಕಳೆಯಲು, an abandoning, ಪಡೆಯಲು, an obtaining. This their primitive meaning appears in their dative, when *e.g.* it is, as in the instances quoted in § 298, 3 (*cf.* No. 12 in the present §), followed by ಇಲ್ಲ.

Forms like ತೀರಿಲ್ಲ, ಮಾಡಿಲ್ಲ, ನೋಡಿಲ್ಲ, ಆಗಿಲ್ಲ, ಇದ್ದಿಲ್ಲ of the modern dialect are such in which ಇಲ್ಲ has been suffixed to short past participles which we know also to be verbal nouns from §§ (168). 169, in the present case ತೀರಿ, ಮಾಡಿ, ನೋಡಿ, ಆಗಿ. **By their use it is intended to express the past tense of the negative in a very conspicuous manner.** Other instances are:— ಇದನ್ನು ನಾನು ಬರೆದಿಲ್ಲ, I have not written (or did not write) this. ಇನ್ನೂ ಅವನು ಉಣ್ಡಿಲ್ಲ, he has not yet eaten (or did not eat yet). ಅವನ ಮುಣ್ಡಾಸು ಹಸರುಬಣ್ಣದ್ದು ಇದ್ದಿಲ್ಲವೋ, was not his turban of a green colour? ಅವನು ಸೌಖ್ಯದಿನ್ದಿದ್ದಿಲ್ಲ, he was not happy. See the instances quoted in §§ 298, 8; 313, 7; 314, remark.

3, The English auxiliary verb **'shall'**, when it implies a simple futurity, as in **'I shall give'**, is expressed by the future tense in Kannaḍa, *e. g.* ಕುಡುವೆಂ or ಕೊಡುವೆನು, I shall give (§ 200; *cf.* No. 12 of this §). **'Shall not'**, as in the future 'I shall not give', is expressed by the negative, *e. g.* ಕುಡೆಂ or ಕೊಡೆನು, I shall not give (§ 209), or by a verbal noun to which ಇಲ್ಲ is added, *e. g.* ನಾನು ಕೊಡುವದಿಲ್ಲ, I shall not give (see also under No. 2 of this §).

When **'shall' indicates a duty or necessity**, as in 'he shall go', 'you shall go', it may be expressed by (ಬೇೞ್ಕುಂ, ಬೇೞ್ಕು), ಬೇಕು, *e. g.* ಅವನು ಹೋಗ ಬೇಕು; ನೀವು ಹೋಗ ಬೇಕು. *Cf.* No. 4.

In a question 'shall' is expressed by the suffix ಅಲಿ or ಅಲೀ (§ 207, 2, *a. b; cf.* No. 10), *e. g.* ನಾನೇನು ಮಾಡಲಿ? ಹೋಗಲಿಯಾ? what shall I do? Shall I go? ಹೆಚ್ಚಿಗಿನ್ನೇನು ಹೇೞಲಿ, what shall I say more? ನೀನು ನನಗೆ ಇನ್ತಾ ಕೆಟ್ಟ ಬುದ್ಧೀ ಹೇೞುತ್ತೀಯಾ? ತಾಯಿಗೆ ತಿಳಿಸದೆ ನಾನು ಆಕೆಯ ರೊಕ್ಕಾ ಹಿಡಿಯಲೀ? ಇದು ತುಡುಗು ಮಾಡಿದ ಹಾಗೆ ಆಗುವದಿಲ್ಲವೋ? doest thou give me such a bad advice? Shall I take away the money of (my) mother without her knowledge? Would this not be the same as stealing?;—**or also by a verbal noun**, *e. g.* ನಾನು ನಿಲ್ಲುವದೋ? ಹೋಗುವದೋ? shall I stand? (or) go?

The way of expressing **'should'**, the imperfect of 'shall', by (ಬೇೞ್ಕುಂ, ಬೇೞ್ಕು), ಬೇಕು will be seen from the following instances; ನೋಡಿ ಓದ ಬೇಕು, you should read carefully. ನೀನು ಈ ಹಣವನ್ನು ಕೂಡಲೆ ಕೊಡ ಬೇಕು, you should pay this money immediately. ನಾವು ಏನು ಮಾಡ ಬೇಕು, what should we do? ನೆರೆಯುವರ ಮೇಲೆ ಪ್ರೀತಿ ಮಾಡ ಬೇಕು, (we) should love (our) neighbours. See Nos. 4. 9; § 314, remark.

About **'should not'** see Nos. 5. 6. 8. 9.

4, The English auxiliary **'must'** ('is solicited', 'is desired', 'is required', 'is necessary', 'ought', 'should', 'is probable or evident') is expressed by ಬೇೞ್ಕುಂ, ಬೇೞ್ಕು, ಬೇಕು (§ 203), *e. g.* ಸಸ್ಯಾದಿ ತರುಲತಾವಳಿಯ

ಪೆರ್ಚುಗೆಯುಂ ಪೇೞ್ವಿ ಧಾತುವಿನೊಳ್ ಬೆಳೆಯೆನಲ್ವೇೞ್ಕುಂ (-ಬೇೞ್ಕುಂ), in (*i. e.* for) the verb which expresses the growing of corn etc. and that of trees and creepers, ಬೆಳೆ (and not ಬಳೆ) must (or is to be) uttered. ಈ ತಪ್ಪಂ ಕ್ಷಮಿಸಲ್ವೇೞ್ಕು, you must (or please) put up with this mistake. ಅವನು ವ್ಯಾಕರಣವ ಕಲಿಯ ಬೇಕು, he must (or has to) learn grammar. ಬಿಸಿಯಾದ್ದು ಆಱಿಸ ಬೇಕು, you should make cool what is hot. ನಾವು ಊರಿಗೆ ಹೋಗ ಬೇಕು, we must go to town (or abroad), ನಾನು ಯಾವಾಗ ಬರ ಬೇಕು, when must I (or am I to) come? ಅವನು ಹೋಗಿರ ಬೇಕು, he must have gone. ಈಗ ಪುಣೆಯಲ್ಲಿ ಬಹಳ ಚಳಿ ಬಿದ್ದಿರ ಬೇಕು, it must be very cold now at (the town of) Puṇĕ. ಯಾರಾದರೂ ಅವನಿಗೆ ಈ ವಿಷಯದಲ್ಲಿ ವರ್ತಮಾನ ತಿಳಿಸಿರ ಬೇಕು, somebody must have communicated these tidings to him.

It will be seen from the above instances that infinitives ending in ಅಲ್ or ಅ are used before ಬೇೞ್ಕುಂ, ಬೇೞ್ಕು and ಬೇಕು; the infinitive ending in ಅಲು and its dative may also precede ಬೇಕು, *e. g.* ಇವನನ್ ಅಱಿಯಲು ಬೇಕು, I must learn to know this man. ಹಸಿದು ಬನ್ದವರಿಂಗೆ ಅಶನವೀಯಲು ಬೇಕು. ನಾಳೆ ಮಾಡೊ ಧರ್ಮ ಇನ್ದೆ ಗೆಯ್ಯಲು ಬೇಕು. ಸಚೇಲಸ್ನಾನವ ಮಾಡಲಿಕೆ ಬೇಕು. ನಿಮ್ಮೊಳಗಿನ ಪ್ರತಿಯೊಬ್ಬನು ಸಾಲೆಗೆ ತನ್ನ ಪುಸ್ತಕವನ್ನು ತರಲಿಕ್ಕೆ ಬೇಕು. ಗೋವೂ, ನೀನು ಸಂಜೇ ತನಕ ನಮ್ಮ ಮನೆಯಲ್ಲಿಯೇ ಇರಲಿಕ್ಕೆ ಬೇಕು. ನಾನು ಹೋಗಲಿಕ್ಕೇ ಬೇಕು. ನಾನು ಹೀಗೆ ಮಾಡಲಿಕ್ಕೇ ಬೇಕು.

'Must' is also expressed by ಬೇೞ್ಪುದು, a verbal noun of ಬೇಡು, *e. g.* ಸಂಜಾತವಸ್ತುಗಳ ಸಿದ್ಧಾಯಮಂ ಕೊಡವೇೞ್ಪುದರಸಂಗೆ ನಾವು.

'Must', when denoting obligation, has been expressed in the modern dialect also by the infinitive ending in ಅಲ್, ಅಲು, followed by ಉಳ್ಳ, being (§ 180, remark), and a demonstrative pronoun, *e. g.* ನಾನು ಕೊಡಲುಳ್ಳವನು (*cf.* ಕೊಡಲಿಕ್ಕೆ ಇರುವವನು), I must give, lit. I to give a being-he. Forms as ಕೊಳ್ಳಲುಳ್ಳ, ನಿಯಮಿಸಲುಳ್ಳ occur also occasionally in the mediæval dialect (*e. g.* of the Vivêkačintâmaṇi), and may denote the simple relative present-future participle, as they do likewise in the modern dialect, *e. g.* ರಕ್ತವನ್ನು ನೋಯಿಸನ್ತೆ ಹೀರಿಕೊಳ್ಳಲುಳ್ಳ ಜನ್ತು, a worm that sucks (or abstracts) blood without causing pain. ಚನ್ನಾಗಿ ಹೊಱಲುಳ್ಳ ಕುದುರೆ, a horse which carries nicely.

To ಬೇಕು the verb ಆಗು, to become, is frequently added, (when ಬೇಕು is considered a verbal noun, see § 204), *e. g.* ಹತ್ತೀ ಕಾಯಿಗಳು ಬಲಿತು ಹಣ್ಣಾಗಲಿಕ್ಕೆ ಹೆಚ್ಚುಕಡಿಮೆ ಎರಡು ತಿಂಗಳು ಬೇಕಾಗುತ್ತದೆ, about two months are required for cotton pods to become full-grown and ripe. ನೀವು ಇನ್ನು ಮುನ್ದೆ ಹೆಚ್ಚು

ಶ್ರಮ ತಕ್ಕೊಂಡು ಕಲಿಯ ಬೇಕಾಗುವದು, it is necessary for you henceforth to exert yourself to learn. ನೀನು ಸುಳ್ಳು ಮಾತಾಡ ಬೇಡ, ಮಾತಾಡಿದರೆ, ನಾನು ನಿನ್ನನ್ನು ಶಿಕ್ಷಿಸ ಬೇಕಾಗುವದು, thou must not (or shalt not) utter falsehood, if thou utterest, I shall be obliged to punish thee. ರಾಮನು ಎಲ್ಲರಿಗೂ ಬೇಕಾದನು, Râma was (or is) wanted by all. ಅಣ್ಣಾ, ಕರುವಿಗೆ ತುಸ ಹುಲ್ಲು ಬೇಕಾಗಿತ್ತು, brother, a little grass was required for the calf. ಮೊದಲು ಮೊದಲು ಪತ್ರ ಮುಟ್ಟ ತಕ್ಕ ಸ್ಥಳದ ಅಂತರದ ಮಾನದಿಂದ ಹಾಸಿಲು ಕೊಡ ಬೇಕಾಗುತ್ತಿತ್ತು, at the very first it was (or used to be) necessary to pay postage according to the measured distance of the place to which letters had to go. ನೀನು ಆರು ತಿಂಗಳುಗಳ ಕೆಳಗೆ ಕೊಡ ಬೇಕಾಗಿತ್ತು, you ought to have given (it) six months ago. ಹ್ಯಾಗೆ ಬರೆಯ ಬೇಕಾಗಿತ್ತು, how was it to be written? ಅವನು ಹೋಗ ಬೇಕಾಯಿತು, he had to go. ಬೇಕಾದುದು, that is needed. ಬೇಕಾದನಿತು ವಿತ್ತವನ್ ಇತ್ತಂ, he gave as much money as was desired. ಬೇಕಾದಷ್ಟು, as much as is needed or required. ನಾನು ಮುಮ್ಬಯಿಗೆ ಹೋಗ ಬೇಕಾಗಿದೆ, I must go to Bombay. ಈ ಹಣ್ಣುಗಳು ಹುಳಿಯುವೆ, ಅದರಿಂದ ಇವು ನನಗೆ ಬೇಕಾಗಿಲ್ಲ, these fruits are sour, therefore these have not become desired (by me), *i. e.* therefore I do not want these. ಅನ್ನ ಬೇಕೋ? ಬೇಕಾಗಿಲ್ಲ, do you want (some) rice? It has not become wanted, *i. e.* I do not want (any). ನೀವು ಬರಲಿಕ್ಕೇ ಬೇಕಾಗುವದಿಲ್ಲ, you need not come. *Cf.* No. 5.

5, **'Must not'** ('is not fit', 'shall not', 'should not', 'is not desired or wanted', *cf.* ಬೇಕಾಗುವದಿಲ್ಲ, etc. under No. 4) **is commonly expressed by ಬೇಡ** (§§ 209, note 1; 212, 7; 301; and *cf.* No. 6), *e. g.* ಬಿಡಿಕ್ಕುಂ ಕಿಡಿಕ್ಕುಂ ಸೊಪ್ಪಿಕ್ಕುಮ್ ಎನವೇಡ (-ಬೇಡ), one must not (or should not) say ಬಿಡಿಕ್ಕುಂ ಕಿಡಿಕ್ಕುಂ ಸೊಪ್ಪಿಕ್ಕುಂ (§ 203). ಇತ್ತ ಬರ ಬೇಡ! ಎಲವೋ, ಹೋಗು, (thou) must not (or do not (*cf.* No. 13) come this side! O, go away! ಕೆಟ್ಟ ಮಾತುಗಳನ್ನು ಆಡ ಬೇಡ, (thou) must not (or shalt not) use bad words. ನೀನು ಸುಳ್ಳು ಮಾತಾಡ ಬೇಡ, thou must not (or shalt not) lie. ಸುಳ್ಳು ಹೇಳ ಬೇಡರಿ, you must not (or should not) utter falsehood. ಕಾಕು ಮಾತು ಆಡ ಬೇಡ, ಪೋಕವಿದ್ಯೆಗೆ ಹೋಗ ಬೇಡ, (thou) shalt not utter perverse words, (and) shalt not learn from rogues. ಟವುಳಿಗಾರನಾಗಿ ತಿರುಗ ಬೇಡ, (thou) shalt not wander about as a deceiver. ಕುದುರೇ ಹಿನ್ದೆ ಇರ ಬೇಡ, ಅರಮನೆಯ ಮುನ್ದಿರ ಬೇಡ, (you) should not be behind a horse (and) should not be before a royal mansion. ಇದು ನನಗೆ ಬೇಡ, I do not want this. ಏನೂ ಬೇಡ, (I) do not want anything. ನಾವು ಈ ಗಿಡದ ಕೆಲವು ಮಾವಿನ ಹಣ್ಣುಗಳನ್ನು ಕೊಯ್ಯೋಣೇನು? ಬೇಡ! ಯಾಕನ್ದರೆ ಅವು ನಮ್ಮವಲ್ಲ, shall we cut some (of the) ripe mango fruits? (No) it is not right, for they are not ours.

ಬೇಡ is also preceded by the infinitive with final ಅಲ್ or ಅಲು, *e.g.* ಎನಲ್ ಬೇಡ. ಕಳ್ಳತನಗಳ ಮಾಡಿ ಒಡಲ ಹೊರೆಯಲು ಬೇಡ. ಒಳ್ಳೆಯವನೆನ್ದು ಉಬ್ಬಲು ಬೇಡ. ದೊರೆತನವು ಬನ್ದಾಗ ಕೆಟ್ಟು ನುಡಿಯಲು ಬೇಡ.

The idea of **ಬೇಡ can also be expressed by the negative participle and the verb** ಇರು, to be, *e.g.* ಕೋಪವನ್ನು ಮಾಡದಿರು, ಪಾಪಕ್ಕೆ ಗುಱಿಯಾಗದಿರು. See under No. 6 and 13.

As frequently to ಬೇಕು (No. 4) so also occasionally **to ಬೇಡ the verb ಆಗು is added,** *e.g.* ಮೂರ್ಖನು ಊರಿಗೆ ಬೇಡಾಗುತ್ತಾನೆ. ಲೋಕಾಪವಾದದಿನ್ದ ಜನರಿಗೆ ಬೇಡಾದವನು. ಬೇಡವಾದದು ಕೂಡಿಸಿದರೆ ಆದೀತೇ?

6, The English auxiliary **'ought not'** ('is not becoming', 'must not', **'should not', etc.;** *cf.* Nos. 5. 7. 8. 9. 11) **is expressed by** ಬಾರದು (the negative of ಬರ್, ಬರು), *e.g.* ಇವಂ (ಬೆರಲ್, ಕೊರಲ್) ಬೆರಳು, ಕೊರಳೆಮ್ಬನ್ತೆ ಉಚ್ಚರಿಸ ಬಾರದು, (one) ought not to pronounce (or should not pronounce) these (ಬೆರಲ್, ಕೊರಲ್) ಬೆರಳು, ಕೊರಳು. ದೊಡ್ಡವರು ಸಣ್ಣ ಮಾತುಗಳನ್ನು ಕೇಳ ಬಾರದು, eminent persons ought not to listen to insignificant words. ಮಾಡ ಬಾರದ ಕೆಲಸ, a business that (one) ought not to do. ಕದ್ದು ಕೊಣ್ಡು ತಿನ್ನ ಬಾರದು, (one) should not steal and (thus) eat. ಮಟ್ಟು ತಿಳಿಯದೆ ಮಾತಾಡ ಬಾರದು, without knowing propriety (one) ought not to speak. ತನ್ದೆ ತಾಯಿಗಳ ಮಾತು ಮೀಱಿ ಬಾರದು, (one) ought not to (or should not) transgress the word of (one's) parents. ತುಡುಗು ಮಾಡ ಬಾರದು, (you) ought not to (or should not) commit theft. ಸಣ್ಣ ಪ್ರಾಣಿಗಳನ್ನು ಪೀಡಿಸ ಬಾರದು, (one) ought not to (or should not) torment little creatures. ನೀನು ಅಲ್ಲಿಗೆ ಹೋಗ ಬಾರದು, thou shouldst not go there. ನೀವು ಬರ ಬಾರದು, you are not permitted to come. ಇಲ್ಲಿರ ಬಾರದು, (you) must not remain here. ನಾವು ಕಳವು ಮಾಡ ಬಾರದು, we must not (or should not) steal. ಧ್ವನಿ ತೆಗೆದು ಓದ ಬಾರದು, ಓದುವಾಗ ಅವಸರ ಮಾಡ ಬಾರದು, ಬಹಳ ಗಟ್ಟಿಯಾಗಿ ಓದ ಬಾರದು, ಬಹಳ ಮೆಲ್ಲೆ ಓದ ಬಾರದು, (you) must not drawl in reading, when reading (you) should not hurry, (you) must not read too loud, (you) must not read too low. ಕೆಟ್ಟ ಕೆಲಸಗಳನ್ನು ಮಾಡ ಬಾರದು, (you) ought not to do evil deeds. ಕೆಲಸ ಮಾಡದವರು ಉಣ್ಣ ಬಾರದು, those that will not work (or have not worked) shall not eat. ಧರಣಿಯ ಕಲ್ಲಿಗೆ ಶರಣೆನ್ದು ಪೂಜೆಯ ಮಾಡ ಬಾರದು; ಪಾಪಿಗಳಿದ್ದಲ್ಲಿ ರೂಪುಳ್ಳ ವಸ್ತುವ ತೋಱಿ ಬಾರದು; ಬಹು ಕೋಪಿಗಳಿದ್ದಲ್ಲಿ ಅನುಭವಗೋಷ್ಠಿ ಮಾಡ ಬಾರದು; ಬಡತನ ಬನ್ದಾಗ ನೆಣ್ಟರ ಬಾಗಿಲ ಸೇರ ಬಾರದು. ಸಂರಕ್ಷಿಸಿದ ತಾಯಿ ತನ್ದೆಗಳ ಉಪಕಾರವನ್ನು ಮಱೆಯ ಬಾರದು. ಆತನನ್ನು (ಅನ್ದರೆ ದೇವರನ್ನು) ನಾವೆಲ್ಲರೂ ಎನ್ದಿಗೂ ಮಱೆಯ ಬಾರದು. ಸುಮ್ಮ ಸುಮ್ಮನೆ ದನಾ ಬಡಿಯ ಬಾರದು.

The idea of ಬಾರದು may also be expressed by the negative participle and the verb ಇರು, to be, *e.g.* ತಾವು ಇನ್ಥ ಮಾತುಗಳನ್ನು ಆಡದಿರ್ರಿ, you ought not to speak such words. See under Nos. 5 and 13.

7, The English auxiliary 'must not' ('ought not', 'is not fit') further is sometimes expressed by ಕೂಡದು, *e.g.* ಅದನ್ನು ಕೊಲ್ಲ ಕೂಡದು, (one) must not kill that. ನೀನು ಹೋಗ ಕೂಡದು, you must not go. ನಾನು ನಿನ್ನ ಆಟದ ಗೆಳೆಯರ ಕೂಡ ನಿನಗೆ ಆಡ ಹೋಗಗೊಡುವೆನು, ಆದರೆ ನೀನು ರಾತ್ರಿ ತಡ ಮಾಡಿ ಬರ ಕೂಡದು, I shall allow thee to go to play with thy play-fellows, but thou must not loiter and come at night.

8, The English auxiliary 'must not' ('ought not', 'is unfit', 'improper or forbidden') is not unfrequently expressed by ಆಗದು, *e.g.* ಪೊನ್ನ ಅನ್ದಳಮ್ ಎನ್ದಿನ್ನು ಸನ್ಧಿಯಂ ಕಿಡಿಸಲಾಗದು, (one) must not spoil euphonic combination (for instance) by using ಪೊನ್ನ ಅನ್ದಳಂ (for ಪೊನ್ನನ್ದಳಂ). ನುಡಿಯಲಾಗದ ನುಡಿ, a word that is unfit to be uttered. ಹಗೆಯ ಪೆಣ್ಗಳನ್ ಅರಮನೆಗಳೊಳು ಪೊಗಿಸ ಲಾಗದು, (one) must not allow inimical women to enter palaces. ಕೊಲಲಾ ಗದಕಟಾ, alas, (you) ought not to kill (it). ನೀನು ಹೋಗಲಿಕ್ಕೆ ಆಗದು, you must not go. ಯಾರೂ ಇಲ್ಲಿ ಬರಲಾಗದು, nobody must come here. (*Cf.* No. 11.)

9, The English auxiliary 'ought' ('should'; *cf.* Nos. 3. 4) is also expressed by ತಕ್ಕದು (ತಕ್ಕುದು, fit, etc.), *e.g.* ನೀನು ಹೀಗೆ ಮಾಡ ತಕ್ಕದು, thou ought to do so. ಅವರು ಇಲ್ಲಿಗೆ ಬರ ತಕ್ಕದು, they should come here. ಆ ಬೀಜ ಗಳನ್ನು ಈ ದೇಶದಲ್ಲಿ ಬಿತ್ತಿ ಪರೀಕ್ಷಿಸ ತಕ್ಕವರಿದ್ದಾರೆ, they should sow and try those seeds in this country. ಅಣ್ಣ ತಮ್ಮನ್ದಿರು ಒಬ್ಬರ ಮೇಲೊಬ್ಬರು ಪ್ರೀತಿ ಮಾಡ ತಕ್ಕದು, brothers ought to love each other. ಅವನು ಹೋಗ ತಕ್ಕದಿತ್ತು, he should have gone. ನೀವು ಅವನಿಗೆ ಹೀಗೆ ಹೇಳಿ ತಕ್ಕದಿತ್ತು, you ought to have told him so. ನೀನು ಆ ಪುಸ್ತಕವನ್ನು ಅನ್ದೇ ತಿರಿಗಿ ಕೊಡ ತಕ್ಕದಿತ್ತು, thou shouldst have returned that book to him long ago.

'Ought not' ('should not') is, in this case, expressed by suffixing ಇಲ್ಲ or ಅಲ್ಲ, *e.g.* ತಂಗೀ, ನೀನು ಹಾಗೆ ಮಾಡ ತಕ್ಕದಿದ್ದಿಲ್ಲ, sister, thou shouldst not have done so (see § 298, 3 about ಇಲ್ಲ, and No. 2 of this §). ಇಷ್ಟು ಬಾರೀ ಕ್ರಯಕ್ಕೆ ಈ ಕಪಾಟವನ್ನು ನೀವು ಕೊಣ್ಡು ಕೊಳ್ಳ ತಕ್ಕದಿದ್ದಿಲ್ಲ, you ought not to have bought this almira at so high a price.—ನೀನು ಹೋಗ ತಕ್ಕದಲ್ಲ, thou ought not to go (see § 300, 1 about ಅಲ್ಲ). See Nos. 5. 6. 7. 8. 15 (ಸಲ್ಲ).

10, The English auxiliary 'may' ('is allowed', 'is possible', 'is fit', etc.) is expressed by ಬಹುದು (of ಬರ್), to come, *e.g.* ನೀವು ಒಳಗೆ ಬರ ಬಹುದು, you may (or are allowed to) come in. ನೀನು ಹೋಗ ಬಹುದು, thou mayest (or art allowed to) go. ನಮ್ಮಲ್ಲಿರ ಬಹುದು, you may stay with us. ಹೀಗಿರ ಬಹುದು, it may be so. ಅವನು ನಿನ್ನ ಜೀವದ ಗೆಳೆಯ ಇರ ಬಹುದು, he may be thy true friend. ಅವನ ವೃತ್ತಾನ್ತವು ಎಲ್ಲರಿಗೂ ಗೊತ್ತಿರ ಬಹುದು, his tale may (more or less) be known to all. ತಾವು ಇಲ್ಲಿ ಕುಳ್ಳಿರ ಬಹುದು, you may sit here. ಅವನು ಇದನ್ನು ಬರೆದಿರ ಬಹುದು, he may have written this. ಇದಕ್ಕಿನ್ತ ಹೆಚ್ಚು ಕೊಡ ಬಹುದಿತ್ತು, you might have given more than this. ಅವರು ಹೋದ ವರುಷದಲ್ಲಿ ಬರ ಬಹುದಾಗಿತ್ತು, they might have come last year.

Another way of expressing 'may' (in desire, wish, permission, expectation, or possibility) **is by using the imperative** (§ 205, 1; *cf.* No. 14; § 367), *e.g.* ವೇದದೊಳ್ ಒನ್ದಿದಾಯು ನಿನಗಕ್ಕೆ, may the age which prevails in the vêda (*i.e.* one hundred years), become thine! ಅವಂ ಕುಡುಗೆ, may he give! ಅವರ್ ಮಾಳ್ಕೆ, may they make! ಆತಂ ಮಾಡುವುದು or ಆತಂ ಮಾಳ್ಪುದು, may he make!—**or by using the suffix** ಅಲಿ (§ 207, 2, *a. b*), *e.g.* ನಿಮಗೆ ಕಲ್ಯಾಣವಾಗಲಿ, may you become happy! ಆ ವರ್ತಮಾನವು ಸತ್ಯವಾಗಲಿ, may that news prove true! ಅವನು ಬರಲಿ, may he come! ಸ್ವಾಮಿಾ, ನಾನು ಹೋಗಲಿಯಾ, may I go, sir? ನಾನು ಅವನಿಗೆ ಹೀಗೆ ಹೇಳಲಿಯಾ, may I tell him so? ಹಾಗೇ ಆಗಲಿ, may (it) become so (*i.e.* so be it, very well)! ಆಗಲಿ, may (it) become (*i.e.* be it, very well)! ಇರಲಿ, may it be (be it, very well)!—**or by using the contingent present-future tense** (§ 195), *e.g.* ಈಗ ಬನ್ದಾಳು, she may (*i.e.* is likely to) come now. ಇದು ತಿಳಿದರೆ ಅಪ್ಪ ಬಡಿದಾನು, if (he) learned to know this, father might beat (us). ಸಾಯಂಕಾಲಕ್ಕೆ ಮಳೆ ಬನ್ದೀತು, it may rain this evening. ನಾನು ಬನ್ದರೆ ಬನ್ದೇನು, if I come, I may come, *i.e.* I may come (perhaps I come).

'May' in a question has also been expressed by a verbal noun, *e. g.* ಈ ಹೊಲದೊಳಗಿನ್ದ ನಾವು ಹೋಗೋಣೇನು, may we (*i. e.* are we allowed to) cross this field? (regarding the form ಹೋಗೋಣ see § 205, 3).

11, The English auxiliary 'can' is expressed by ಬಹುದು, ಬರುತ್ತದೆ **and other forms of the verb** ಬರ್ (ಬರು, *cf.* No. 10), to come, preceded by the infinitive ending in ಅ or ಅಲು, this last termination being put in the dative (ಅಲಿಕ್ಕೆ), *e. g.* ಕಾಣ ಬಹುದು, what can be seen. ಅಂಗಾಲಿಗೆ ತ್ರಾಣವಿದ್ದರೆ ಬಂಗಾಳಕ್ಕೆ ಹೋಗ ಬಹುದು, if (there) is power in (one's) sole of the foot, (one) can go to Bengal. ಮೊರದಿನ್ದ ಕತ್ತಲೆಯನ್ನು ಹೊರ ಹಾಕ ಬಹುದೇ, can (one) throw out darkness with the bamboo fan? ಅವನು ಕೆಲಸವ ಮಾಡ ಬಹುದು, he can do work. ಇದನ್ನು ಯಾರು ಮಾಡಿರ ಬಹುದು, who can have done this? ನನಗೆ ಓದಲಿಕ್ಕೆ ಬರುತ್ತದೆ, I can read. ನನಗೆ ಈಸಲಿಕ್ಕೆ ಬರುತ್ತದೆ, I can swim. ಅವನಿಗೆ ಬರೆಯ ಬರುವದು, he can write. ಹನುಮಂತನಿಗೆ ಹಾರಲಿಕ್ಕೆ ಬರುತ್ತಿತ್ತು, Hanumanta could jump. ಈ ಹೊಲದೊಳಗಿನ್ದ ನಮಗೆ ಹೋಗಲಿಕ್ಕೆ ಬನ್ದೀತೇ, can we cross this field (*i. e.* is there a road for us to cross this field)? ಇದನ್ನು ಬರೆಯಲಿಕ್ಕೆ ಯಾರಿಗೆ ಬನ್ದಿದ್ದೀತು, who can have written this?

'Can' is also expressed by the verb ಆಗು, *e. g.* ಈ ಕೆಲಸ ಅವನಿನ್ದ ಆಗುತ್ತದೆ, he can do this work. ನಿನ್ನಿನ್ದ ಆಗುತ್ತದೋ, canst thou do it? ನಾವು ಹೆರರನ್ನು ಕೆಯ್ಲಾದ ಮಟ್ಟಿಗೆ ಸನ್ತೋಷ ಪಡಿಸ ಬೇಕು, we should make happy others as much as we can.

'Cannot' is expressed by the negative of ಬರ್ (ಬರು), *e. g.* ಆ ಹುಡುಗನಿಗೆ ಬರೆಯಲಿಕ್ಕೆ ಬಾರದು (or ಬರುವದಿಲ್ಲ), that boy cannot write. ಉಚ್ಚರಿಸಲ್ ಬಾರದುವು ಅಕ್ಕರವ್ ಅಲ್ತು, such as cannot be uttered, are no letters. ಲೆಕ್ಕಿಸ ಬಾರದುದು, that cannot be counted. (*Cf.* No. 6.)

'Cannot' is expressed also by the negative of ಆಗು, *e. g.* ಈ ಕೆಲಸವು ನನ್ನಿನ್ದಾಗದು, I cannot do this work. ಇದು ಅವನ ಕೆಯ್ಯಲಿ ಆಗದು, he cannot do this. ಆಗದು, ಅಯ್ಯೋ, ತಮ್ಮ ಕೆಯ್ಯಲಿ, alas, you cannot do it. ಇನ್ಥ ಬಿಸಿಲಿನಲ್ಲಿ ನನ್ನಿನ್ದ ಹೋಗುವದು (or ಹೋಗೋಣವು) ಆಗದು, I cannot go in such a heat of the sun (see also § 315, 2, *f*). ನಿನ್ನಿನ್ದ ನಿಲ್ಲೋಣವಾಗದು, thou canst not stay (or stand). ವಜ್ರವನ್ನು ಯಾತರಿನ್ದಲೂ ಕೊಯ್ಯಲಾಗದು, (one) cannot cut a diamond with anything. ಅವನ ಸನ್ತೋಷವನ್ನು ಹೇಳಲಾಗದು, (one) cannot tell his joy. ಅವನಿನ್ದ ಈ ಕೆಲಸ ಆಗುವದಿಲ್ಲ (or ಆಗದು), he cannot do this work. ಆಗದ ಕಾರ್ಯವು, a business that cannot be effected. ದೇವರಿಗೆ ತಿಳಿಯದ ಹಾಗೆ ಮಾಡುವದು ಎನ್ದಿಗೂ ನಮ್ಮಿನ್ದಾಗದು, without the knowledge of God we can never do (anything). (*Cf.* No. 8.)

'Cannot' may further be expressed by ಕೂಡದು (*cf.* No. 7), *e. g.* ಬಣ್ಡೆಯೊಡೆಯ ಬಹುದು, ರಣ್ಡೇ ಮನಸೊಡೆಯ ಕೂಡದು, (one) can break a rock, (but) cannot break the mind of a whore. ಬಳಿಕೆಯಿದ್ದಲ್ಲಿ ಬಾಳ ಬಹುದು, ಚಳೀ ಕಾಟ ಸಯ್ರಿಸ ಕೂಡದು, (one) can live where familiar intercourse is, (but) cannot stand the trouble of cold. ಹೇಳ ಕೂಡದಷ್ಟು ಕ್ಲೇಶವಾಗಿದೆ, so much pain as cannot be told has befallen (me).

For 'cannot' ಅಸು (see Dictionary) **in combination with** ಅಲ್ಲ **is also occasionally used,** *e. g.* ಆ ಮೂವರ ಗೋಳಾಟ ಹೇಳಲಾಸಲ್ಲ, (one) cannot tell the lamentation of those three.

There are some special terms in Kannaḍa which directly denote 'to can', *viz.*

a) ಅಱ್, *e. g.* ನುಡಿಯಲ್ ಅಱಿಯದೆ ಕೇಳಲ್ ಅಱಿಯದೆ ಇರ್ದಡೆ ಎಡಮೂಕನೆನಿಸುಗು, if (a man) cannot speak (and) cannot hear, he is called dumb and deaf. ಮೂರ್ಖರು ಕೀರ್ತಿಯನ್ನು ಗಳಿಸಲ್ ಆಱಿಯರು, fools cannot gain fame.

b) ಆಱ್, *e. g.* ಎನಗೆ ಬಲ್ಲಿದರ್ ಆಗಲ್ ಆರ್ಪರೆ ಗಾವಿಲರ್, can rustics become abler than I? ಹುಡುಗರು ಅರ್ಥವನ್ನು ಗ್ರಹಿಸಲ್ ಆಱರು, the boys cannot understand the meaning. ಹೊನ್ನು ಹಣವುಣ್ಟು ಎನಗೆ, ಸಾಯಲ್ ಆಱೆನು, I have gold (and other) property, I cannot die. ನಾನು ಹೋಗಲಾಱೆನು, I cannot go. ಅದಱ ವಿಷಯಕ್ಕೆ ನಾನು ನಿಮಗೆ ಹೆಚ್ಚು ಹೇೞಲಾಱೆನು, I cannot tell you more about it. ತೆಱಲ್ ಆಪರೆ (=ಆರ್ಪರೆ) ಹೊಣೆಯಾಗು, if (thou) canst pay, become a surety. ಶೂರನು ಕಾಳಗವ ಮಾಡಲಾಪನು, a valiant man can fight. ದೇವರಿನ್ದ ನಾವು ಏನೇನೂ ಬಚ್ಚಲಾಱೆವು, we cannot hide anything from God. ಬರೆಯಲಾಱದವ ಕುಱಿ ಕಾಯುವವನಿಗಿನ್ತ ಕಡೆ, he who cannot write is inferior to one who feeds sheep.

c) ಬಲ್ಲ, *e. g.* ಕೋಣ ಬಲ್ಲುದೆ ವೇದವನೋದಿ ಪಠಿಸಲಕೆ, can the male buffalo recite the vêdas? ನಾನು ಈಸ ಬಲ್ಲೆನು, I can swim. ಅವನು ಬರೆಯ ಬಲ್ಲನು, he can write. ಕವಿಗಳು ವಸ್ತುಗಳನ್ನು ವರ್ಣಿಸ ಬಲ್ಲರು, poets can depict objects.

12, The English auxiliary verb 'will' when it implies a simple futurity (*cf.* No 3), is expressed by the future tense in Kaṇnaḍa, *e. g.* ಕುಡುವಂ or ಕೊಡುವನು, he will give. ಕುಡುವಿರ್ or ಕೊಡುವಿರಿ, you will give. ಅಕ್ಕುಂ or ಅಕ್ಕು or ಆಗುವದು, it will become (§§ 200. 203). The future 'will not' is expressed by the negative, *e.g.* ಕುಡಂ or ಕೊಡನು, he will not give;—or by a verbal noun to which ಇಲ್ಲ is suffixed, *e. g.* ನೀವು ಕೊಡುವದಿಲ್ಲ, you will not give (§§ 209. 298, 3).

Regarding the suffix ಇಲ್ಲ in its connection with the dative of a verbal noun ending in ಅಲು (ಅಲ್, § 298) it is to be remarked that South-Mahratta people, at least sometimes, attach the idea of doubt (saṁśaya, Nuḍigaṭṭu p. 135) to it, *e.g.* ಅವನು ನನ್ನ ಕರೆಯಲಿಕ್ಕಿಲ್ಲ, he is not to invite me (to dinner), *i. e.* he will (probably) not invite me. ಆಕೆ ಉಣ್ಣಲಿಕ್ಕಿಲ್ಲ, she is not to eat, *i. e.* she will (probably) not eat. Other instances chosen at random from S.-Mhr. shool-books, may, or may not, express doubt:—ಅವನು ಬರಲಿಕ್ಕಿಲ್ಲ. ಅವರು ಜಗಳಾಡಲಿಕ್ಕಿಲ್ಲ. ಆಕಳ ಕೋಡುಗಳು ಕಱುವನ್ನು ನೋಯಿಸಲಿಕ್ಕಿಲ್ಲ. ಅವನು ಕೆಲಸ ಮಾಡಲಿಕ್ಕಿಲ್ಲ. ನಾನು ಆ ಪುಸ್ತಕವನ್ನು ಕಳ ಕೊಳ್ಳಲಿಕ್ಕಿಲ್ಲ. ನೀನು ದುಃಖದಲ್ಲಿ ರಲಿಕ್ಕಿಲ್ಲ. ನನಗೆ ಈ ಗುಡ್ಡದೊಳಗೆ ದಾರಿ ಸಿಗಲಿಕ್ಕಿಲ್ಲ. See also some instances in § 298, 3, and *cf.* No. 2 in the present paragraph.

The English verb 'to will', 'to be pleased', 'to desire' is expressed by ಒಲ್, of which (ಒಲ್ಲೆಂ), ಒಲ್ಲೆನು, ಒಲ್ಲೆ, vulgarly ವಲ್ಲೆ, I will not, and other persons of the negative are in every body's mouth, *e. g.* ಉಣ್ಣಲೊಲ್ಲೆನು or

ಉಣ್ಣ ವಲ್ಲೆ, I will not eat. ಕೊಡಲೊಲ್ಲನು or ಕೊಡ ವಲ್ಲ, he will not give. ಕೇಳಲೊಲ್ಲರು or ಕೇಳ ವಲ್ಲರು, they will not hear.

13, The English auxiliary verbal forms **'does not'**, **'do not'**, **'did not'** are expressed by the negative or a verbal noun with ಇಲ್ಲ, *e. g.* ಬರೆಯೆಂ, I do (or did) not write. ಅನ್ ಅಱಿಯೆಂ, I do (or did) not know. ಅವಂ ಮಾಡಂ, he does (or did) not make. ಸೋಮು ಬರುವದಿಲ್ಲ, Sôma does not come. ಬಾಚಯ್ಯನಿಲ್ಲಿಗೇತಕ್ಕೆ ಬಾರಂ, why does Bâčayya not come here? ಹುಡುಗರು ಆಡಲಿಕ್ಕೆ ಯಾಕೆ ಬರಲಿಲ್ಲ, why did the boys not come to play? ಅೞ ಬೇಡ, do not cry (*cf.* No. 5).—Also the following way of expression (see under Nos. 5 and 6) is to be paid attention to: ಬಱಿದೆ ಹೊತ್ತು ಕಳೆಯದಿರು; ಉನ್ನತಾಶೆ ಮಾಡದಿರು, do not spend (your) time idly! do not desire great things!

The English **'does'**, **'do'**, **'did' in questions** is expressed as follows:— ಎಡಱಿದನೋ? ಅವನ ನೊಸಲಕ್ಕರಂ ತೊಡೆದುಡಕ್ಕುಂ, did he become dishonest? The writ on his forehead will be wiped out. ಅವನು ಬರುತ್ತಾನೋ, does he come? ಅವನು ಬನ್ದನೋ, did he come? ಅವನು ಊರಿಗೆ ಹೋಗುತ್ತಾನೇಸು, does he go abroad? ಕನ್ನಡಿ ಒಡಿದಿಯಾ, ಅಣ್ಣಾ, O brother, didst thou break the looking-glass? ಏತರ್ಕೆ ಪೋದಂ, why did he go? ಅಕ್ಕಟಾ, ಮರುಳ್ದುಮ್ಬಿಗಳ್ ಸಮ್ಪಗೆಗಳೊಳ್ ಏಕೆ ಪಗೆಗೊಣ್ಡವೊ ನಿರ್ನಿಮಿತ್ತದಿಂ, alas, why did the mad black bees become inimical to čampaka trees? ಯಾಕೆ ಬನ್ದರು, why did they come? ಯಾಕೆ ಹೋಗುತ್ತೀರಪ್ಪ, father, why do you go? ಸೀತೆ, ಯಾಕೆ ಅೞುತ್ತೀ? ಯಾರಾರೂ ಒಡಿದರೋ, Sîtĕ, why doest thou weep? Did somebody beat thee? ಎಲ್ಲಿನ್ದ ಬನ್ದಂ, whence did he come? ಆವಂ ಮುರನಂ ಕೊನ್ದಂ, who did kill Mura? ಆ ಗುಬ್ಬಿಯನ್ನು ನೀನು ಯಾವಾಗ ನೋಡಿದಿ, when did you see that sparrow? ಅವನು ಹೋಗುವದು ಎಲ್ಲಿಗೆ, whither does he go? ನೀವು ಬನ್ದದು ಯಾಕೆ, why did you come? ನೀವು ಬನ್ದ ಕಾರಣವೇನು, why did you come?

The English **'do' in connection with the imperative**, as 'do write!', may be expressed in Kannada by the simple imperative or by its repetition, *e. g.* ಬರೆ! or ಬರೆ ಬರೆ!, ಬರೆಯಿರಿ! or ಬರೆಯಿರಿ ಬರೆಯಿರಿ!

14, When the English **'let'** is used as an auxiliary in the imperative, **denoting 'exhortation'**, etc., it **is expressed** simply **by the imperative** (§ 205; *cf.* No. 10; see § 367), *e. g.* ಗೆಯ್ಗೆ, let (him) do! ಪೋಕೆ, let (him) go! ತಾಗುವಂ, let us attack! ಉಸುರುವ, let us utter! ನಡೆಯುವ, let us walk! ಹೋಗೋಣ, let us go!

Compare also the forms with ಅಲಿ of the mediæval and modern dialect in § 207, ೭, *a. b.*

The English verb 'to let', *i. e.* 'to allow', 'to permit', is expressed by the verbs ಈ, to give, etc.; ಕೊಡು, to give, etc.; and by their causatives (§ 151) ಈಸು and ಕೊಡಿಸು. The first syllable of ಈಸು is exceptionally shortened by some writers so that it becomes ಇಸು (in imitation of Tĕlugu ఇచ్చు, to permit, of its ఈ, to give; *cf.* § 151, *b,* ३).

The mediæval dialect has, *e. g.* ನೀರ ಹರಿಯಲ್ ಈಯದೆ ಕಟ್ಟಿದ ಕಟ್ಟೆ ಆಧಾರ ಎನಿಸುಗು, a structure which does not allow water to flow, is called âdhâra (dam); and ತರುಗಳ್ ಅಲ್ಲಿ ಪಣ್ಗಾಯ್ಗಳಂ ಬೀಯಲ್ ಈಸದು, the trees there do not let (their) ripe fruits and nuts fail. ಈಸು occasionally occurs also in the modern dialect, *e. g.* ಸುಲಭವಾಗಿ ಹಾಲು ಕರೆಯಲೀಸುವ ಆಕಳು, a cow that allows itself to be milked with ease. ಅವನು ನನ್ನನ್ನು ಬರಲೀಸನು, he does not allow me to come. Thus also does ಇಸು, *e. g.* ಅವನನ್ನು ಸೇರಲಿಸನು, he does not let him enter.

The modern dialect generally uses ಕೊಡು and ಕೊಡಿಸು, *e. g.* ಅವನನ್ನು ಹೋಗಗೊಡು (-ಕೊಡು), let him go (or allow him to go)! ಅವನು ನನ್ನ ಬರಗೊಡನು, he does not let me come. ನನ್ನನ್ನು ಇಲ್ಲಿ ನಿಲ್ಲಗೊಡಿಸು, let me stay here! ಆ ಕುದುರೆ ಯಾರನ್ನೂ ತನ್ನ ಹತ್ತಿರ ಬರಗೊಡಿಸುವದಿಲ್ಲ (or ಬರಗೊಡುವದಿಲ್ಲ), that horse lets no one come near it. ಅಂಗಳದಲ್ಲಾಗಲಿ ಹಿತ್ತಲಲ್ಲಾಗಲಿ ಹೊಲಸು ಇರಗೊಡ ಬಾರದು, one ought not to let filth lie either in front of a house or in (its) back-yard. See an instance under No. ೭.

Also the verb ಬಿಡು, to let loose, has been used in the mediæval and modern dialect for 'to let' in instances like the following:—ಪಶುಗಳಂ ಹೋಗ ಬಿಡಿ, let the cattle go! ನನ್ನನ್ನು ಹೋಗ ಬಿಡು, let me go! ತಾನೂ ಕುಡಿಯ, ಕುಡಿಯುವವನಿಗೂ ಬಿಡ, he neither drinks himself nor lets him who will drink (do so).

15, It is still to be mentioned that the English 'ought not' ('is improper', *cf.* ತಕ್ಕದಲ್ಲ under No. ೯) is also expressed by ಸಲ್ಲ (§ 209, note ೧) preceded by an infinitive generally ending in ಅ, *e. g.* ಗುರು ಹಿರಿಯರಾದವರ ಜರಿಯ ಸಲ್ಲ; ಕಡುಚೆಲ್ವೆ ಕುರುಡನಿಗೆ ಮಡದಿಯಾಗ ಸಲ್ಲ; ಹಗೆಯೊಡನೆ ಸ್ನೇಹವನು ಮಾಡ ಸಲ್ಲ (Dâsapada 157), (one) ought not to abuse those that are (one's) guru and elders; a very handsome woman ought not to become the wife of a blind man; (one) ought not to court the friendship of enemies.

XXI.

On either — or (§ 317); **neither — nor** (§ 318); **whether — or** (§ 319); **the — the** (§ 320); **as — as** (§ 321); **for** (§ 322); **namely, as follows** (§ 323); **what is that?** (§ 324); **what happened?** (§ 325); **in this manner** (§ 326); **as — so** (§ 327); **how much — so much, how many — so many** (§ 328); **when?** (§ 329); **who — he, etc.** (§ 330).

317. In the ancient dialect 'either — or' is expressed by ಅಕ್ಕೆ — ಅಕ್ಕೆ, lit. be it — be it (§ 205, 1; *cf.* § 316, Nos. 10. 14), *e. g.* ಪೆಱಗಣ ಮೊಯ್ಸ್ಯಳ್ ಲಘು ಮೊದಲಾಗಿರ್ದ ೞಳಕುಳರೇಫಾನ್ತ್ಯಗಳಪ್ಪ ಅಂಗಂಗಳಿರೆ — ಮುನ್ನೆ ಗಳ್ ಅಕ್ಕೆ, ಮೇಣ್ ಚತುರ್ಥಿಗಾದ ಗೆಕಾರಮ್ ಅಕ್ಕೆ — ಶಿಥಿಲಮ್ ಅಕ್ಕುಂ, when (there) are nominal themes that end in ḻ, ḷ, r or ṟ and have their first (syllable) short in the back part (*i. e.* in the beginning), slackness (§ 240) takes place either before ಗಳ್ or further before the ಗೆ of the dative; — or also by ಆನುಂ — ಆನುಂ, as appears in § 292.

As has been remarked in § 207, 2, *b*, the modern dialect uses ಆಗಲಿ — ಆಗಲಿ, lit. be it — be it, to express 'either — or', *e. g.* ಇದನ್ನು ನೀನಾಗಲಿ ಅವನಾಗಲಿ ಮಾಡ ಬೇಕು, either thou or he must do this. ಶುಕ್ರವಾರ ಆಗಲಿ ಶನಿವಾರ ಆಗಲಿ ಹೊಱಟಾರು, they may start either on Friday or Saturday. ಒಳಿತಾಗಲಿ ಕೆಡಕಾಗಲಿ ನನಗೆ ನಿಮ್ಮ ಅಪ್ಪಣೆಯೇ ಮಾನ್ಯವು, either good or bad your command is agreeable to me. ಕಾಗದವಾಗಲಿ ನಿನಗೆ ಬೇಕಾದದು ಮತ್ತೇನಾದರೂ ಆಗಲಿ ಕೊಂಡು ಕೋ, buy either paper or whatever thou wantest. ಇರುಳು ಬೆಕ್ಕುಗಳಾಗಲಿ ಬೆಕ್ಕಿನ ಮಱಿಗಳಾಗಲಿ ಸಿಕ್ಕಿದರೆ ಗೂಗೆಗಳು ಕಣ್ಣು ಕುಕ್ಕಿ ಅವುಗಳನ್ನು ಕೊಲ್ಲುವದುಂಟು, if at night either cats or the young of cats are met (by them), owls will peck (their) eyes and kill them. ವಾಂತಿಗಾಗಲಿ ಪಿತ್ತಕ್ಕಾಗಲಿ ದಾಲ್ಚಿನ್ನಿಯ ಕಷಾಯ ಕುಡಿಯುತ್ತಾರೆ, either for vomiting or for bile they drink a decoction of cinnamon. ಉತ್ತಮರೀತಿಯಿಂದ ಸೇವೆ ಮಾಡಿದ್ದಱಿಂದಾಗಲಿ ಪರರ ಮೇಲೆ ಉಪಕಾರ ಮಾಡಿದ್ದಱಿಂದಾಗಲಿ ದೊರಕಿದ ಇನಾಮು, a present got either by having done service in an excellent manner or by having afforded friendly aid to others. ಕಾಲ ನಡಿಗೆಯಿಂದಾಗಲಿ ಕುದುರೆಯ ಮೇಲಿಂದಾಗಲಿ ಇಲ್ಲವೆ ಬಣ್ಡಿಯ ಮೇಲಿಂದಾಗಲಿ ಪ್ರವಾಸ ಮಾಡುತ್ತಿದ್ದರು, they used to travel abroad either on foot or on horseback or also by means of carriages. ಇನ್ಥವರು ನೆಣ್ಟರ ಮನೆಯಲ್ಲಿ ಸೇರಿ ಕೊಣ್ಡಾಗಲಿ (*i. e.* ಕೊಂಡು ಆಗಲಿ) ಹಿರಿಯರ ಗಳಿಕೆಯಿಂದಾಗಲಿ ಉದರನಿರ್ವಾಹ ಸಾಗಿಸುವರು, such people will subsist either having entered the house (*i. e.* by living in the house) of relations or by what has been acquired by (their) fathers. ಗಿಳಿಗಳು ಮರಗಳ ಹೊದರುಗಳಲ್ಲಾಗಲಿ ಹಾಳು ಗೋಡೆಯ ಬಿರುಕುಗಳಲ್ಲಾಗಲಿ ಗೂಡು ಕಟ್ಟಿ ಕೊಂಡು ಇರುತ್ತವೆ, parrots build their nests and live either in tufts of trees or fissures of dilapidated walls. ಬಳಿಕ ಸಕ್ಕರೆಯನ್ನು ಸನ್ದುಕಗಳೊಳಗಾಗಲಿ ಚೀಲಗಳೊಳಗಾಗಲಿ ತುಮ್ಬುತ್ತಾರೆ, then they fill the sugar either into boxes or sacks. ಯುದ್ಧ ಮಾಡುವದಕ್ಕಾಗಿ ಮಣ್ಟಪದ ಮೇಲ್ಗಡೆಯಾಗಲಿ ಕೋಟೆಕೊತ್ತಳದ ಮೇಲ್ಗಡೆಯಾಗಲಿ ಉಪ್ಪರಿಗೆಯ ಹಿನ್ದಗಡೆಯಾಗಲಿ ಕಟ್ಟಿರುವ ಮನೆ, a building that has been erected either on an open hall or on a bastion of a fort or behind a palace for the purpose of warring. ಉಣ್ಣುವದಕ್ಕೆ ಮುಂಚೆಯಾಗಲಿ ಉಣ್ಡ ಮೇಲಾಗಲಿ ದೇವರನ್ನು ಸ್ತುತಿಸು, praise God either before (thou) eatest or after (thou) hast eaten.

As will be learned from the instance quoted above (ಕಾಗದವಾಗಲಿ ನಿನಗೆ ಬೇಕಾದದು ಮತ್ತೇನಾದರೂ ಆಗಲಿ ಕೊಣ್ಡು ಕೋ) ಆಗಲಿ—ಆಗಲಿ (be it—be it) is constructed, as might appear, with the nominative after a transitive verb; but sentences in which the accusative occurs in such a case, are not rare, *e. g.* ಒಮ್ಮೊಮ್ಮೆ ಹೆಬ್ಬಾವುಗಳು ಅಡವಿಯಲ್ಲಿ ಮಲಗಿದ ಮನುಷ್ಯರನ್ನಾಗಲಿ ಕರುಗಳನ್ನಾಗಲಿ ನುಂಗುವವು, occasionally boas will swallow either people that have reclined in the jungle or calves. ನಾನು ನಿನಗೆ ಹೇಳದೆ ನಿನ್ನ ಪುಸ್ತಕವನ್ನಾಗಲಿ ಕಾಗದವನ್ನಾಗಲಿ ತಕ್ಕೊಣ್ಡರೆ ನೀನು ಸುಮ್ಮನೆ ಇರುವಿಯೋ, if I, without telling thee, take away either thy book or paper, shalt thou remain quiet? Regarding this see what has been stated in § 287, remark.

The Rev. Mr. Hodson, according to § 287, remark, has used ಆದರೂ—ಆದರೂ also in the sense of 'either—or'. He has the following additional sentence: ಈ ಸ್ಥಳಕ್ಕಾದರೂ ಆ ಸ್ಥಳಕ್ಕಾದರೂ ಹೋಗ ಬೇಡ, do not go to either this place or that.

318. The English **'neither—nor'** may be expressed by the copulatives ಉಂ, ಅಂ and ಊ (§ 284 *seq.*) followed by a negative, *e. g.* ಪೂಜೆಗೆ ಫಲಮುಂ ಪುಷ್ಪಮುಮ್ ಇಲ್ಲ, for the worship of idols (there) is neither fruit nor flower. ಅವರುಮಮ್ ಇವರುಮಂ ಪರಿಭವಿಸನು, he disrespects neither those nor these persons. ಆಕೆಗೆ ಲಜ್ಜೆಯುಂ ನಾಚಿಕೆಯುಮ್ ಇಲ್ಲ, she has neither a sense of shame nor modesty. ಅವನ ಗಣ್ಟಿನೊಳಗೆ ಲೆಕ್ಕಣಿಕೆಯೂ ಕಾಗದವೂ ಇದ್ದಿಲ್ಲ, in his bundle (there) was neither pen nor paper. ಅನ್ತೂ ಇನ್ತೂ ಕುನ್ತೀ ಮಕ್ಕಳಿಗೆ ರಾಜ್ಯವಿಲ್ಲ, neither in that nor in this manner (there) is a kingdom for the children of Kunti. ತಾನೂ ಕುಡಿಯ, ಕುಡಿಯುವವನಿಗೂ ಬಿಡ, he neither drinks himself nor lets him who will drink (do so). ಅವನು ಹುಲಿಗೂ ಹೆದರಿನು, ಹಾವಿಗೂ ಹೆದರಿನು, he fears neither tigers nor snakes. ಅವನು ಇದನ್ನೂ

ಮಾಡುವದಿಲ್ಲ, ಅದನ್ನೂ ಮಾಡುವದಿಲ್ಲ, he will do neither this nor that (Hodson).

ಬೆಟ್ಟವುಮ್ ಅಲ್ಲ, ರಕ್ಕಸನ ರುಣ್ಡಮುಮ್ ಅಲ್ಲ, ಆನೆಯೇ, it is neither a hill nor the headless body of a demon, (but) an elephant. ಹಗ್ಗವೂ ಅಲ್ಲ, ಹಾವೂ ಅಲ್ಲ, ಬಟ್ಟೆಯ ಪಟ್ಟಿಯೇ, it is neither a rope nor a snake, (but) a long piece of cloth. ಇದು ಸಮುದ್ರವೂ ಅಲ್ಲ, ನದಿಯೂ ಅಲ್ಲ, ಕೆಱೆಯೇ, this is neither a sea nor a river, (but) a lake (Hodson). ಇವು ಬೆಳುಸಕ್ಕರೆಗೋಲಿಯಲ್ಲ, ಉದರ್‌ದ ಹಲ್ಲಲ್ಲ, ಆಲಿಕಲ್ಲೇ, these are neither balls of white sugar nor fallen out teeth, (but) hail-stones.

319. The English **'whether — or' may be expressed** by ಒಡೆ, ಅಡೆ and ಅರೆ, 'if', in combination with the copulatives ಅಂ and ಉ, for which see the instances in § 287, 8.

In the verse quoted below the five times repeated ಆದೊಡೆಯು (=ಆದೊಡೆಯೂ, ಆದರೂ) may be translated 'though' (see § 287, 6, *b*), but 'whether — or' would also not be wrong:

ಧನವನಿತ್ತಾದೊಡೆಯು ಸಹಭೋ
ಜನವನುಣ್ಡಾದೊಡೆಯು ಮೇಣ್ ನಿಜ
ತನುಜೆಯರನಿತ್ತಾದೊಡೆಯು ಬೞಿ ಸನ್ದು ಬೇಸಱದೇ ।
ತನುವ ಬೆರಸಿದ್ದಾದೊಡೆಯು ನೂ
ತನಗುಣವ ನುಡಿದಾದೊಡೆಯು ರಿಪು
ಜನಪತಿಯ ವಶ ಮಾಟ್ಪುದುಚಿತವೆಂದೆನ್ದನಾ ಶಕುನೀ ॥

"whether he gives (you) riches, or eats together (with you), or also gives his own daughters, or follows and joins (you) without weariness, or utters novel wisdom, it is proper to keep down a hostile king" said that Šakuni. *Cf.* § 334.

Another way of rendering 'whether — or' occurs in the following modern sentence wherein ಇರಲಿ — ಇರಲಿ, be it — be it, is used: — ನಾನು ತಪ್ಪು ಮಾಡಿರಲಿ ಮಾಡದಿರಲಿ ಬಾದಶಹನ ಅಪ್ಪಣೆಯನ್ನು ಮನ್ನಿಸಲಿಕ್ಕೆ ಬೇಕು, whether I have committed, or have not committed, a fault, I have to honour the command of Bâdašaha.

320. The English **'the — the' before comparatives** can be expressed only by paraphrasing, see *e. g.* the ancient instance quoted in § 303, 2, *a*. South-Mahratta school-book instances are *e. g.* the following: — ನೀವು ಅಭ್ಯಾಸ ಮಾಡುತ್ತಾ ಹೋದ ಹೋದ ಹಾಗೆ ಹೆಚ್ಚೆಚ್ಚು (*i. e.* ಹೆಚ್ಚು ಹೆಚ್ಚು) ಕಲಿಯುವಿರಿ, the more you study, the more you will learn. ಪಾಕದೊಳಗಿನ ಕಸರು ತೆಗ ತೆಗದ ಹಾಗೆ

ಸಕ್ಕರೆ ಹೆಚ್ಚು ಬೆಳಗಾಗುವದು, the more (they) remove the impurities of the syrup, the whiter the sugar will become. ಹಡಗವು ತೆಂಕಣಕ್ಕೆ ಬನ್ದ ಬನ್ದ ಹಾಗೆ ಧ್ರುವನಕ್ಷತ್ರವು ಕೆಳಗೆ ಇೞಿದನ್ತೆ ಕಾಣುತ್ತದೆ, the more a ship approaches the south, the more the polar star seems to go down.

321. The English **'as — as'** may be expressed as follows:— ಅತಂಗೀತಂ ತಕ್ಕಂ, this man (is) as deserving as that man (§ 348, 14). ದ್ರೋಣಂಗಂ ನಿನಗಂ ಬಿಲ್ಜಾಣಿಕೆಯದು ಸಕ್ಕಸಮನೆ, doest thou know archery as well as Drôṇa? (*cf.* § 284 under dative). ಎನಿತುಮ್ ಅನಿತುಮಂ ಧರ್ಮಜಂ ಸೂಱೆಗೊಟ್ಟಂ, Yudhishṭhira lavished as much as he had. ವೀಳೆಯವನ್ ಅಪನಿತನ್ ಇತ್ತು, having given betel as much as possible. ಬೊಟ್ಟಿನನಿತು ಭಸಿತವುಂ ಪೂಸಿ, having applied as much ashes as a (forehead) circlet. ನಿನ್ನುದ್ದಕ್ಕೆ ಹೊನ್ನಂ ಸುರಿಯೆನೆ, do I not pour out gold as high as thou art?— ಅಫಿನ ಕಾಯಿ ಬರ ಬರುತ್ತಾ ಚಣ್ಡಿನಷ್ಟು ದೊಡ್ಡದಾಗುವವು, poppy pods become, by degrees, as large as balls. ಕೊಹಿನೂರ ಎಮ್ಬ ವಜ್ರವು ಕೋೞೀ ತತ್ತಿಯ ಅರ್ಧದಷ್ಟು ಅದೆ, the diamond called Cohinor is as large as the half of a hen's egg. ಪೊರ್ತುಗಾಲ ದೇಶದ ಅರಸನಲ್ಲಿ ಒನ್ದು ದೊಡ್ಡ ವಜ್ರವದೆ, ಅದಱಿಷ್ಟು ದೊಡ್ಡ ವಜ್ರವು ಪೃಥ್ವಿಯ ಮೇಲೆ ಎಲ್ಲಿಯೂ ಇಲ್ಲೆನ್ದು ಹೇೞುತ್ತಾರೆ, with the king of Portugal there is a large diamond; people say there is no diamond on the whole earth as large as that. ಅವನು ನನ್ನಷ್ಟು ಬಡವನು, he (is) as poor as I. ಈ ಮಾವಿನ ಹಣ್ಣು ಸಕ್ಕರೆಯಷ್ಟು ಸವಿ, this ripe mango is as sweet as sugar.— ಇಲ್ಲಿತನಕ, as far as this place. ನಿಮ್ಮ ಮನೇ ತನಕ ಬರುತ್ತೇನೆ, I come as far as your house.— ವಾರ್ಧಿ ಮುಟ್ಟಿ, as far as the ocean. ಮನೆ ಮುಟ್ಟ ಬನ್ದನು, he came as far as the house.— ಕೆಯ್ಲಾದ ಮಟ್ಟಿಗೆ, as much as possible. ನಾನು ಬಾೞಿರುವ ಮಟ್ಟಿಗೆ, as long as I live.— ತುದಿವರಂ, as far as the end.— ಕಿವಿವರೆಗೆ, as far as the ear.— ಅರಸು ಬನ್ದಾಗಲೇ ಹೊಱಟರು, as soon as the king came, they started. ಆ ಸುದ್ದಿ ಮುಟ್ಟುತ್ತಲೆ, as soon as that news arrived. ಅದು ಅವನನ್ನು ಕಣ್ಡು ಕೂಡಲೆ, as soon as it saw him.— ಗಿರಿಯನ್ತೆ ಬಿಣ್ಪಿದಂ ಸುರಕರಿಯನ್ತೆ ಬಲಾಢ್ಯನ್ ಅಬ್ಧಿಯನ್ತೆ ಗಭೀರಂ, (he is) as big as a hill, as strong as an elephant of the gods, as deep as the ocean. ಬಲಿಯನ್ತೆವೋಲ್ ಅಧಿಕದಾನಿ, he (is) as liberal as Bali.— ಮನೆಯೊಳಗೆ ಇರುವಷ್ಟರು, as many persons as are in the house. ಮಱಾಟಕ್ಕೆ ತನ್ದ ಕಾಱಿಷ್ಟನ್ನು ಕೊಣ್ಡು ಕೊಣ್ಡನು, he bought as much grain as was brought for sale. ಅವನು ಎಷ್ಟು ವಿದ್ವಾಂಸನಿದ್ದಾನೋ, ಅಷ್ಟು ಸದ್ಗುಣಗಳುಳ್ಳವನಿದ್ದಾನೆ, he is as virtuous as he is learned. See an instance in § 327 (ದೊಡ್ಡ ಬೆಂಕಿಯಿನ್ದೊನ್ದು *etc.*).

'Such — as' is expressed as follows:— ಗಣ್ಡನು ಬಯಸುವನ್ತಪ್ಪಳು, such a wife as a husband desires. ಮಾರ್ಗ ಬಲ್ಲಂತಹವರುಗಳು, such as know the (proper) way. ನಿನ್ನಂಥ ತಾಯಿ, such a mother as thou.

'Not so — as' is expressed by adding the negative ಅಲ್ಲ (see § 300, 1), *e. g.* ಅವನು ನನ್ನಷ್ಟು ಬಡವನಲ್ಲ, he (is) not so poor as I. ಅವನು ಮಾರ್ಗ ಬಲ್ಲಂತಹವನಲ್ಲ, he (is) not such a one as knows the (proper) way. ಅಣ್ಣನು ತಮ್ಮನನ್ಥಾ ಜಾಣನಲ್ಲ, the elder brother (is) not so clever as (his) younger brother.

322. In § 302, 7 ಯಾಕನ್ದರೆ, why if I say, *i. e.* for, because, has been introduced. It may be added that ಕಾರಣವೇನನ್ದರೆ, the reason (or cause) what, if I say (or one says), and ಕಾರಣವೇನಾಯಿತನ್ದರೆ, the reason (or cause) what has it become (or what is it), if I say (or one says), are similarly used, *e. g.* ತಾಯಿ ತನ್ದೆಗಳು ತಮ್ಮ ಮಕ್ಕಳಿಗೆ ಚಿಕ್ಕನ್ದಿನಿನ್ದ ಒಳ್ಳೇ ನಡತೆಯನ್ನು ಕಲಿಸ ಬೇಕು, ಕಾರಣವೇನನ್ದರೆ, parents must teach good conduct to their children from (their) youth, for—. ಮಾನವಿಲ್ಲದ ಬಾಳ್ವಿಕೆಗಿನ್ತ ಸಾವು ಲೇಸೆನ್ದು ತೋಱುವದು, ಕಾರಣವೇನನ್ದರೆ, death appears preferable to a life without honour, for—. ತುಳಾಪುರವೆನ್ದರೆ ತೂಕದ ಊರು; ಈ ಹೆಸರು ಬೀಟಿಲಿಕ್ಕೆ ಕಾರಣವೇನಾಯಿತನ್ದರೆ, Tuḷâpura means the town of weight [lit. Tuḷâpura, if (one) says, is town of weight]; what was the cause that it got this name? (or why did it get this name?)—. Regarding the verbs ಅನ್ and ಎನ್ see § 331 *seq.*

323. If a writer or speaker wants to adduce something that is or was said or that happens or happened, the English 'namely', 'as follows' are expressed by adding ಏನೆನ್ದೊಡೆ, ಏನನ್ದರೆ, if I say (or one says) what, to the pronoun ಅದು, or to a conjugated verb, or to a verbal noun, *e. g.* ಅದೇನೆನ್ದೊಡೆ or ಅದೇನನ್ದರೆ, that is to say. ಹುಡುಗನು ನುಡಿಯುತ್ತಾನೆ, ಏನನ್ದರೆ, the boy speaks as follows—. ಗುರುಗಳು ನನಗೆ ಅಪ್ಪಣೆ ಮಾಡಿದ್ದಾರೆ, ಏನನ್ದರೆ, the guru has given me the following command—. ಒಬ್ಬ ಸ್ನೇಹಿತನು ಅವನಿಗೆ ಧೈರ್ಯ ಹೇೞಿದನು, ಏನನ್ದರೆ, a certain friend gave (lit. told) him courage with the following words—. ಆ ಅರಸುಮಗನು ಹೇೞಿದ್ದೇನನ್ದರೆ, what that prince said was this (or that prince spoke as follows)—. ದ್ವಾರನಾಥಭಟ್ಟನು ಅನ್ದದ್ದೇನನ್ದರೆ, Mr. Dvâranâtha spoke as follows—. ಗುರುವು ಅವನಿಗೆ ಉಪದೇಶ ಮಾಡಿದ್ದೇನನ್ದರೆ, the guru instructed him as follows—. ಫಕೀರನು ನ್ಯಾಯಾಧೀಶನಿಗೆ ಬಿನ್ನೈಸಿದ್ದೇನನ್ದರೆ, what the mendicant represented respectfully to the judge was this—. ಅದಱಿನ್ದ ಆಗುವದೇನನ್ದರೆ, thereby happens the following—. ತಱುವಾಯ ಆದದೇನನ್ದರೆ, afterwards (there) happened the following—. *Cf.* § 325.

To this class belong also ಯಾವದನ್ನರೆ, which (thing, etc.) if I say (or one says)—. ಅವುವೆನ್ನೊಡೆ, which (things, *etc.*) if I say—. ಯಾವಳನ್ನರೆ, which woman if I say—. ಆರೆನ್ನೊಡೆ or ಯಾರನ್ನರೆ, who if I say—. ದಶರಥನಿಗೆ ಹೆಣ್ಣು ಗಣ್ಡು ಕೂಡಿ ಅಯ್ದು ಮಕ್ಕಳಿದ್ದರು, ಅವರು ಯಾರನ್ನರೆ, Daśaratha had five children including females and males, they are the following—.

324. 'What is that?' may be expressed by ಅನ್ನರೇನು, if I say (or one says) what, *e.g.* ತಮ್ಮಾ, ನಿನಗೆ ದನ ಅನ್ನರೇನು ಗೊತ್ತದೆಯೋ, brother, do you know what cattle are? ಅವು ಆಣೇ ಕಲ್ಲು. ಅನ್ನರೇನು, ಅಪ್ಪಾ, they (are) hail-stones (the father says). What is that, father? ಗೋಪುರ ಅನ್ನರೇನು, what is a gôpura?

325. 'What happened?' (*cf.* § 323), **if followed by an answer of the writer or speaker himself, may be expressed by** ಏನಾಯಿತಂದರೆ, if I say (or one says) what happened, *e.g.* ದುರ್ದೈವದಿನ್ದ ಏನಾಯಿತನ್ನರೆ, what happened through bad luck?—. ಅಷ್ಟರೊಳಗೇನಾಯಿತನ್ನರೆ, what happened meanwhile?—.

326. If a writer or speaker wants to tell the manner in which something is or was done or how something is or was, the English **'in this manner', 'in the following manner' is expressed by ಎನ್ತೆನ್ನೊಡೆ, ಹೇಗನ್ನರೆ, ಹ್ಯಾಗನ್ನರೆ,** how if I say (or one says), *e.g.* ವಿವೇಕಚಿನ್ತಾಮಣಿಯೆಮ್ಬ ಪ್ರಕರಣಮಂ ಪೇೞ್ದಿನ್ ಅದೆನ್ತೆನ್ನೊಡೆ, he told (*i.e.* wrote) the treatise called Vivêkačintâmaṇi in the following manner—. ಸೂಜಿಗಳನ್ನು ಮಾಡುವದು ಹ್ಯಾಗನ್ನರೆ, needles are made in this manner—. ನಾವು ಬನ್ದದ್ದು ಹ್ಯಾಗನ್ನರೆ, we came in this manner—. ಬೆಕ್ಕುಗಳು ನಿತ್ಯದಲ್ಲಿ ಹಾಲು ಮೊಸರುಗಳಿನ್ದ ಬದುಕುತ್ತವೆ ಹೇಗೆನ್ನರೆ, cats live continually (by stealth) on milk and curds in this manner—. ಚಿನ್ನ ಶೋಧಿಸುವ ಹದ ಹ್ಯಾಗನ್ನರೆ, the way of refining gold is the following—. ಇಕ್ಕಟ್ಟಿನೊಳಗಿನ್ದ ಪಾರಾದರು ಹ್ಯಾಗನ್ನರೆ, they got out of (their) strait in this manner—. ಈ ವಿಷಯದಲ್ಲಿ ಒನ್ದು ಕಥೆಯುಣ್ಟು ಹ್ಯಾಗನ್ನರೆ, regarding this (there) is a story (I shall tell) in the following manner—.

Instead of suffixing ಒಡೆ, if, to ಎನ್ತು, how, the ancient and mediæval dialect frequently suffixes ಎನೆ, when I say (one says), to it, *e.g.* ಆ ಕಥೆಯೆನ್ತೆನೆ, that story (is told) in the following manner—. ಅದೆನ್ತೆನೆ, it is thus—. ಆ ಸಿದ್ಧಾನ್ತಮ್ ಎನ್ತೆನೆ, that dogma is as follows—.

327. The English **'as—so' is expressed** in Kannaḍa **by an interrogative of manner followed by a demonstrative of manner,** *e.g.* ತಿಬ್ಬಮ್ ಎಹಗಹುದಹಗೆ ಮಾಡಿದಂ, as (lit. how) is rash, so he made (= ತಿಬ್ಬಂ ಮಾಡಿದಂ). ದೋಷರಹಿತಮ್ ಎಹಗಹುದಹಗೆ ಪೇೞ್ದಿಂ, as is faultless, so he spoke (= ದೋಷರಹಿತಂ

ಪೇೞ್ದಿಂ). ಯುಕ್ತಿಗೆಹಂಗಹುದಹಂಗೆ, as is according to fitness, so (=ಯಥೇಷ್ಟಂ). ಹೆಂಗೆ ಅಹುದು ಹಾಂಗೆ, as is fit, so (=ಯಥಾಸ್ವಂ). ನೆನವು ತಾನ್ ಎಹಗೆಹಗೆ, as the remembrance (is), so. ಎಹಗೆ ಭಕ್ತಂ ಭಾವಿಸುತ್ತಿಹನ್, ಅಹಗೆ ಶಿವನ್ ಆ ರೂಪು ಗೊಣ್ಡೊಳಿದಿಹುದು ಚೋದ್ಯಮೆ, is it a wonder that as the devotee thinks, so Śiva will graciously assume that form (*i. e.* such a form Śiva will graciously assume)? ನಿನ್ನ ಸಂಗಡ ಅನ್ಯರು ಹೇಗೆ ವರ್ತಿಸ ಬೇಕೋ, ಹಾಗೆ ಅನ್ಯರ ಸಂಗಡ ನೀನು ನಡ ಕೋ, as thou wouldst that others should behave towards thee, so behave thou towards others. ಸುಮ್ಮ ಸುಮ್ಮಗೆ ಬಡಿದರೆ ನಿನಗೆ ಹ್ಯಾಗೆ ಸಿಟ್ಟು ಬರುವದೋ, ಹಾಗೆ ಆಕಳಿಗೂ ಬರುತ್ತದೆ, as thou becomest angry, if (one) beats thee quite causelessly, so does a cow too. ನಿನಗೆ ಹ್ಯಾಗೆ ನೋವು ಆಗುವದೋ, ಹಾಗೆ ಈ ನೊಣಕ್ಕೂ ಆಗುತ್ತದೆ, as thou feelest pain, so does this fly too. ಮೀನುಗಳು ನೀರ ಬಿಟ್ಟು ಹ್ಯಾಗೆ ಬದುಕಲಾರಿವೋ, ಹಾಗೇನು ಕಪ್ಪೆಗಳು ಅಲ್ಲ, as fishes cannot leave the water and live, so are frogs not at all. ಘಟಕ್ಕೆ ಮೃತ್ತಿಕೆ ಯೆನ್ತನ್ತೆ ಅಕ್ಷರಾತ್ಮಕವಾದ ಶಬ್ದಂಗಳ್ ಪುಟ್ಟುವುದರ್ಕೆ ಉಪಾದಾನಕಾರಣವಾದ ವಸ್ತುವೆನ್ದಱಿವುದು, as clay (is the material cause) for a pot, so (one) must consider (it) to be a substance which is the material cause for the origin of sounds as represented by letters.

ಬೆಂಕಿಯಿನ್ದೊನ್ದು ಕಿಡಿ ಹಾರಿ ಬಿದ್ದರೆ ದೊಡ್ಡ ಗುಡ್ಡದ ಹಾಗೆ ಒಟ್ಟಿದ ಬಣಿವೆಯು ಒನ್ದು ಅರಕ್ಷಣದೊಳಗೆ ಹ್ಯಾಗೆ ಸುಟ್ಟು ಬೂದಿಯಾಗುವದೋ, ಹಾಗೆಯೇ ಸಿಟ್ಟಿನ ಭರದಲ್ಲಿ ಮಾಡಿದ ಜಿನ್ದು ಸಣ್ಣ ಕೆಲಸದಿನ್ದ ಜನ್ಮದ ಸೌಖ್ಯವೆಲ್ಲ ನಾಶವಾಗುವದು, as a stack that is piled up as high as a big hill, if one spark flies from a fire and falls (upon it), burns and is reduced to ashes in half a moment, even so all happiness of (one's) life is destroyed by a small act done (lit. that one does) in violent passion. ಕಿತ್ತಳೇ ಹಣ್ಣಿನ ಮೇಲೆ ತಿರುಗಾಡುತ್ತಿರುವ ಇರುವೆಯು ಮೇಲಿನ್ದ ಕೆಳಗೆ ಬನ್ದರೂ ಹ್ಯಾಗೆ ಉರುಳಿ ಬೀಳುವದಿಲ್ಲವೋ, ಹಾಗೆಯೇ ಪೃಥ್ವಿಯ ಮೇಲಿನ ಮನುಷ್ಯರೂ ಉರುಳಿ ಬೀಳುವದಿಲ್ಲ, as an ant that walks about on an orange, though it comes from above to the bottom, does not roll down (from it), even so does also a man on the earth not roll down.

328. The English **'how much — so much', 'how many — so many' is expressed by an interrogative noun of indefinite quantity (§ 278, 3) followed by such a demonstrative noun,** *e.g.* ಸುರರ ಪಡೆ ನೆರವಿಯೊಳ್ ಕರಿಗಳೆನಿತನಿತಱೊಳೆ, elephants how many, even in so many (places there occurs) a number of suras in union (*i. e.* seven times ⏑⏑⏑; Chandas under kusumaśara). ಎಸು ಭಟರ್ ಅಮ್ಬುಗಳನ್ ಎಸುವರ್, ಅಯ್ಸು ಅಮ್ಬುಗಳನ್ ಆ ಸುಭಟರಂಗದೊಳ್ ಕಾಣಿಸಿದನ್; ಆ ಬಲದೊಳ್ ಎಸು ಕೆಯ್ದುಗಳ್ ಒಳೊದಗಿದವಯ್ಸು ಕೆಯ್ದುಗಳೆಲ್ಲಮಂ ತಡೆಗಡಿದನು; ಎಸಾನೆ

ಕುದುರೆಗಳ್ ಕವಿಯಲ್ ಆಯ್ಸಂ ಸೀಳ್ದನ್; ಏಸು ತೇರ್ ಉರವಣಿಸಲ್ ಆಯ್ಸುಱಿದಟಂ ಮುಱಿದನ್; ಏಸು ಮನ್ದಿಗಳ್ ಉಱುಬಿತಯ್ಸನುಂ ಕೊನ್ದಂ, how many arrows the warriors shot, so many arrows he caused to appear in the body of those valiant men; how many weapons entered that force, so many weapons he stopped altogether by cutting (them down); how many elephants (and) horses attacked, so many he split; how many chariots came on with impetuosity, the vehemence of so many he broke; how many people rushed on, even so many he killed. ಏಸು ಹರಿಗಳ್ ಬೇಕು, ನಿನಗಯ್ಸನ್ ಈವೆಂ, how many horses (thou) wantest, so many I shall give thee. ಚನ್ದನಮನ್ ಅರ್ಪಿಸುತಿರಲು ತನ್ನ ಮೂಲಧನವೇಸುಣ್ಟಾವೆಲ್ಲವುಮೋಳಿಯಲ್ಲಿ ಚನ್ದನಕೆ ಸವೆಯಲು, when he was offering sandalwood, (and) his capital how much it was, (so much, ಆಸು, which is to be supplied) was spent all in succession for the sandalwood. ಒನ್ದು ದಿನದಲ್ಲಿ ಕುದುರೆ ಎಷ್ಟು ದೂರ ದಾರಿಯನ್ನು ನಡೆಯಲ್ ಆವುದೋ, ಅಷ್ಟು ದೂರದ ದಾರಿ, how much far (*i. e.* how far) a horse can journey in a day, so much (*i. e.* so) distant a road (= ಆಶ್ತೀನ). ಮನೆಯಲ್ಲಿ ನಾಯಿ ಸತ್ತರೆ ಇಜಿಪ್ತದ ಜನರು ಮೈಯೆಲ್ಲ ಬೋೞಿಸಿ ಕೊಳ್ಳುವ ನಡತೆಗೆ ನಾವು ಎಷ್ಟು ನಗುತ್ತೇವೋ, ಅಷ್ಟೇ ನಮ್ಮ ದೇಶದಲ್ಲಿ ಗಣ್ಡ ಸತ್ತ ಹೆಂಗಸರು ತಲೆ ಬೋೞಿಸಿ ಕೊಳ್ಳುವದನ್ನು ನೋಡಿ ಪರದೇಶಸ್ಥರು ನಗುತ್ತಾರೆ, how much we laugh at the custom of the Egyptians to have (their) whole body shaved, if a dog dies in the house, even so much foreigners laugh when they see that in our country a woman whose husband has died, has (her) head shaved. ನಮ್ಮಲ್ಲಿ ಎಷ್ಟು ರೊಕ್ಕ ಉಣ್ಟೋ, ನಮ್ಮಲ್ಲಿ ಅಷ್ಟು ಲೆಕ್ಕ ಉಣ್ಟು, how much money we have, so much calculation we have.

329. Where a relative participle with a demonstrative adverb of time, as ಬರುವಾಗ (ಬರುವ+ಆಗ), when I come, when thou comest, when he, she, it comes, when we, you, they come (§ 282, *i*), is commonly used, **the 'when' is occasionally expressed by an interrogative adverb of time followed by a demonstrative one,** *e. g.* ನೀವು ಯಾವಾಗ ಪುಣೆಯಿನ್ದ ತಿರಿಗಿ ಬರುವಿರೋ, ಆಗ ಅವರ ಭೆಟ್ಟಿ ತಕ್ಕೊಳ್ಳಿರಿ, when you come back from Puṇě, visit him. ನಿನ್ನ ಪಾಠವು ಯಾವಾಗ ಮುಗಿದಿರುವದೋ, ಆಗ ತಿರುಗಾಡಲಿಕ್ಕೆ ಹೋಗ ಬಹುದು, when thou hast prepared thy lesson, thou mayest go out for a walk. This is, so to say, an imitation of Saṁskṛita ಯದಾ, when, and its correlative ತದಾ, then. *Cf.* the close of § 330.

330. Regarding the translation into English of the relative past participle followed by nouns and demonstrative pronouns see §§ 179. 254, and regarding that of the relative present-future participle followed by such terms §§ 186. 254. *Cf.* §§ 363. 364. In § 282 the use of those participles in connection with adverbs has been adduced.

It remains to refer to § 267 in which it has been stated that it might appear, as if there existed relative pronouns and their correlatives in Kannaḍa (just as in Saṁskṛita). **That such an appearance is not based upon idiom, has been indicated in that place,** though in English the instances given there, would naturally suggest the existence of relatives and their correlatives, *e.g.* 'who—he', 'who—she', etc. However the pronouns resembling relative ones are interrogatives, and the correlatives are demonstratives, and therefore the instances quoted in § 267 and some additional ones in this paragraph are literally to be translated as follows:—ಧನಮುಳ್ಳನ್ ಆವನ್? ಅವನೆ ಇನ್ದ್ರಂ, who (is) a rich man? he indeed (is) a prince (in English: who is a rich man, he indeed is a prince, or a rich man is a prince indeed). ಕೊಂಕಿದ ಬಿಲ್ಲ್ ಆವಂಗಾತಂ ಕುಡುವಿಲ್ಲಂ, who has an (always) bent bow? he (is) Kâma. ಬಸವನೆನ್ಬಕ್ಷರತ್ರಯವನ್ ಒಸೆದು ಚಿತ್ತದೊಳ್ ಒರ್ಮೆಯುಂ ಧ್ಯಾನಿಸುವನ್ ಆವನ್? ಅವನ ವದನಸಾರಸವೆ ನೆಲೆಯಾಗಿರ್ಪುದು, who (is) the man that only once contemplates joyfully in (his) mind the three syllables Ba-sa-va? the lotus of his countenance indeed will remain steady. ಎದೆಯೊಳ್ ಆವನು ನೆನೆವನ್ ಎಮ್ಮುವನ್? ಅದುವೆ ತಾಂ ಬಸವಾಂಶಂ, who does think of us in his heart? (Šiva asks) that one (or he) even is a part of Basava. ಆವಳ್ ಪತಿವ್ರತೆಯವಳೆ ಮಾನ್ಯೆ, who is a wife faithful to her husband? she indeed is a venerable woman. ಯಾವನು ಕೆಲಸ ಮಾಡುವನೋ? ಅವನು ಉಣ್ಣುವನು, who does work? he shall have a dinner. ಯಾವನು ಸತ್ಕಾರ್ಯಗಳನ್ನು ಮಾಡುವನೋ? ಅವನು ಸುಖ ಪಡುತ್ತಾನೆ, who does perform virtuous actions? he is happy. ಯಾವ ಮನುಷ್ಯನು ತನಗೆ ಕಲ್ಯಾಣವಾಗ ಬೇಕೆನ್ದು ಬಯಿಸುತ್ತಾನೋ? ಅವನು ಕೆಯ್ಲಾದ ಮಟ್ಟಿಗೆ ಯಾವತ್ತೂ ಜನರ ಮೇಲೆ ಉಪಕಾರ ಮಾಡ ಬೇಕು, what man does desire welfare? he must be kind to all men as much as possible. ಯಾವವನು ಹಗೆಯವರನ್ನು ಗೆಲ್ಲುವದಕ್ಕಾಗಿಯೇ ಬಹಳವಾಗಿ ಹೊಱಡುತ್ತಾನೋ? ಅನ್ಥವನು ಅಭ್ಯಮಿತ್ರ್ಯ, who does frequently march out with the very purpose of overcoming an enemy? such a one is an abhyamitrya.

ಆವುದು ಮಾಡಲ್ ಬೇಡಿದುದದುವೆ ಕರ್ಮಂ, what is that towards which an activity is directed? even that is the object (see § 315, 2, *m*). ಆವುದು ರೂಢಿಯನುಳ್ಳುದು? ಅದುವೆ ಲೇಸು, what is in customary usage? even that is fit. ಆವುದು ಚೆಲ್ವಾದುದು? ಅದು ದರ್ಶನೀಯಂ, what is beautiful? that is worthy of being seen. ಆಧಾರಂ ತಾನ್ ಆವುದು? ಅದು ಅಧಿಕರಣಂ, what is location? that (forms) the sense of the locative case. ಇತರೇತರಕ್ರಿಯಾಸಂಹತಮ್ ಅದು ತಾನ್

ಅವುದಲ್ಲಿ ಮತ್ತೆ ಬಹುವ್ರೀಹಿ ತಗುಳ್ಗುಂ, what is a combination of mutual action? there also a bahuvrîhi compound (§ 249) is formed. ಆನೆಯ ಮುಪ್ಪಾಗವು ಯಾವದೋ? ಅದು ದನ್ತಭಾಗ, what is an elephant's forepart? that (is) the dantabhâga. ಯಾವ ದೇಶದಲ್ಲಿ ಜನರು ವಿದ್ಯೆ ಕಲಿಯುವದಿಲ್ಲವೋ? ಆ ದೇಶದಲ್ಲಿ ಸೌಖ್ಯ ವಿರುವದಿಲ್ಲ, in what country do people not study science? in that country (there) is no happy state. ತಮ್ಮನ್ನು ಎರಡನೆಯವರು ಯಾವ ರೀತಿಯಲ್ಲಿ ನಡಿಸಿ ಕೊಳ್ಳ ಬೇಕೆನ್ದು ತಮ್ಮ ಅಪೇಕ್ಷೆ ಇರುತ್ತದೆಯೋ? ಅದೇ ರೀತಿಯಲ್ಲಿ ತಾವು ಎರಡನೆಯವರನ್ನು ನಡಿಸಿ ಕೊಳ್ಳಲಿಕ್ಕೆ ಬೇಕು, in what manner do they desire that others should treat them? in that very manner they should treat others.

ಮದವನಿಗನ ಆರು ಕೆಲಮ್ಬರು ಸ್ನೇಹಿತರುಣ್ಟು? ಅವರು ಜನ್ಯರು ಎನಿಸುವುದು, who are some friends of the bridegroom? they are called janyas. ನೀನು ನಮ್ಬಲಿಕ್ಕೆ ಯಾರು ತಕ್ಕವರೋ? ಅನ್ಥವರನ್ನು ನಿನ್ನ ಸ್ನೇಹಿತರಾಗಿ ಆರಿಸು, who (are) fit for thee to trust? such people choose for thy friends!

ನಿಮಗಾವುವು ಮನಕೇಱುವುವು? ಅಱ್ಕಿಱಿನ್ ಅವನ್ ಆಯ್ದುಕೊಳ್ಗೊಳ್ಳಿಂ, which (pearls) do suit you? them choose with pleasure! (See § 271.)

Such sentences appear to have originally been formed in imitation of Saṁskṛita ones with the relatives ಯದ್, ಯಾವದ್, ಯಥಾ and their correlatives ತದ್, ತಾವದ್, ತಥಾ (*cf.* § 329). Their translation, as given above, can be easily changed into proper English.

XXII. On the verbs ಎನ್ and ಅನ್.

331. In §§ 302, 7; 322. 323. 324. 325. 326 the peculiar use of the verbs ಎನ್ (ಎನು, ಎನ್ನು), ಅನ್ (ಅನು, ಅನ್ನು), to say, when their past relative participle (in the sense of the present) is in combination with ಒಡೆ, (ಅಡೆ), and ಅರೆ and an interrogative (ಯಾಕನ್ದರೆ, ಕಾರಣವೇನನ್ದರೆ, ಏನೆನ್ದೊಡೆ, ಏನನ್ದರೆ, ಆರೆನ್ದೊಡೆ, etc.; ಅನ್ದರೇನು; ಏನಾಯಿತನ್ದರೆ; ಎನ್ತೆನ್ದೊಡೆ, ಹೇಗೆನ್ದರೆ, ಹ್ಯಾಗನ್ದರೆ), has been introduced.

It appears from those paragraphs that if a person wants to state the reason (or cause) of something he writes or speaks about, if a writer or speaker adduces something that is or was said or that happens or happened, if a writer or speaker is going to answer a question put by himself, and if a speaker or writer wants to tell the manner in which something is or was done or how something is or was, those verbs in the mentioned combination are employed.

332. Before expatiating on the other use made of the verbs ಎನ್ and ಅನ್ we have to give their past participles ಎನ್ದು, ಅನ್ದು (§ 155) and their substitutes ಎನ್ತ and ಅನ್ತ (§ 172 and § 198, 7, remark 1), as the said verbs are often followed by ಎನ್, ಅನ್, ಉಸಿರ್ (ಉಸುರ್), ನುಡಿ, ಪೇೞ್ or ಹೇೞ್, (occasionally also ಒರೆ) combined with their past participles, for we may say either ಕೊಟ್ಟೆನೆನ್ದಂ, ಕೊಟ್ಟೆನೆನ್ದನು, ಕೊಟ್ಟೆನನ್ದನು; or also ಕೊಟ್ಟೆನೆನ್ದು ಎನ್ದಂ, ಕೊಟ್ಟೆನೆನ್ದು ಅನ್ದನು; ಕೊಟ್ಟೆನೆನ್ದು ಉಸಿರ್ದಂ; ಕೊಟ್ಟೆನೆನ್ದು ನುಡಿದಂ; ಕೊಟ್ಟೆನೆನ್ದು ಪೇೞ್ದಂ, ಕೊಟ್ಟೆನೆನ್ದು ಹೇೞಿದನು, ಕೊಟ್ಟೆನೆನ್ತ ಹೇೞಿದನು, ಕೊಟ್ಟೆನನ್ತ ಹೇೞಿದನು, all meaning 'he said I gave' or 'he said I will give'.

It may be said about the use of ಎನ್ and ಅನ್ in their simple and combined form that they generally introduce a statement by words or on paper (or on cadjan leaves, copper plates and stone tablets), this being either a statement made by somebody regarding himself or another, or one of what another has said or written, or one of command, or one of message, when it may be said to answer to the English conjunction 'that' or the quotation marks in English, *e.g.* ಪೂಗಳಂ ತನ್ದಪೆನ್ ಎನ್ದಳ್, she said "I bring flowers". ಆನ್ ಇದಂ ಮಾೞ್ಪೆನ್ ಎನ್ದಂ, he said "I shall do this". ಈವೊಡೆ ನೀಮ್ ಒಳ್ಳಿದಿರ್ ಎನ್ದರ್, they said "if (you) give, you (are) good ones". ಅಯ್ಯಾ, ತಾವು ಪರಾಕ್ರಮಿಗಳು, ಯಾರಿಗೂ ಅಂಜದವರು ಎನ್ದು, ಆತನನ್ನು ಹೊಗೞಿದನು, he said "sir, you (are) a great hero and fear nobody", and (thus) praised him. ಆಗ ಸಿಂಹವು — ಇದು ನನ್ನ ಪಾಲು, ನನಗೆ ಮುಟ್ಟಿತು ಅನ್ದಿತು, then the lion said "this (is) my share, it fell to me". ಮುನ್ದೆ ನನ್ನ ಗತಿ ಹೀಗಾದೀತೆನ್ದು, ಆಗ ನನ್ನ ಧ್ಯಾನದಲ್ಲಿ ಬರಲಿಲ್ಲ, it did not come to my mind at that time that hereafter my fate would become thus. ನಾನು ಆ ಊರಿಗೆ ಹೋಗಿ ಬರುತ್ತೇನೆನ್ತ, ಹೊಱಟನು, he said "I go to that town and return", and started. ಅಕ್ಕಾ, ದಯ ಮಾಡಿ ಒನ್ದು ತಟಕು ಜೇನುತುಪ್ಪಾ ಕೊಡೇ! ದೇವರು ನಿನಗೆ ಕಲ್ಯಾಣ ಮಾಡ್ಯಾನು ಎನ್ದು, ಬೇಡಿ ಕೊಣ್ಡಿತು, "elder sister," prayed she, "kindly give me a drop of honey! God will make thee happy". ಪರರ ಮೇಲೆ ಮಾಡಿದ ಉಪಕಾರವು ಎನ್ದಿಗೂ ವ್ಯರ್ಥವಾಗಿ ಹೋಗುವದಿಲ್ಲೆನ್ದು, ಮನಸ್ಸಿನೊಳಗೆ ನಿಶ್ಚಯ ಮಾಡಿ ಕೊಣ್ಡನು, he arrived at the certain decision that help afforded to others would never be in vain. ಅವನು — ಇದೇನೆಲೇ, ಇಲ್ಲಿಯ ಸೊಪ್ಪಿಯ ಮಱೆಗೆ ಸಾರಂಗವಿದ್ದನ್ತೆ ತೋಱುತ್ತದೆ ಎನ್ದು, ಕೂಗಿದನು, "ha, what is this?" cried he, "in this straw there appears a deer to be hidden". ಮಾನವಿಲ್ಲದ ಬಾೞ್ಕೆಗಿನ್ತ ಸಾವು ಲೇಸೆನ್ದು, ತೋಱುವದು, it appears that death is preferable to a dishonorable life. ಪೂವಡಿಗಂ ಹರನ ಪೂಜಾರ್ಥದ ಕುಸುಮಮಂ ಪರಿಮಳವನ್ ಈಣ್ಟಿದಳ್ ಎನುತ್ತೀಯರಸಿಯರ ಮೂಗಂ ಕಡಿದನ್ ಆ ಕ್ಷಣದೊಳ್ ಎನ್ದೆನಲು, when they told (the king) that the florist, saying "she tasted the flower (and) fragrance with which Hara should be worshipped", cut off the nose of this queen at that moment. ನಿನ್ನ ಮಾತಿನ

ಆಶಯವು ನನಗೆ ಪೂರಾ ತಿಳಿಯಿತು ಎನ್ನು, ಬಲುಬಗೆಬಗೆಯಿನ್ದ ಅನ್ದನು, he said hastily "the meaning of your word is perfectly known to me". ಈ ಭವಹರಚರಿತಂ ಪುಣ್ಯಶ್ರವಕಾರಣಮೆನ್ದೆ, ಪೇೞಲ್ ಉದ್ಯತನಾದೆಂ, having said even "this worldly existence-removing-story (shall become) a cause of pleasure for the ear", I endeavoured to tell (it). ಎಲ್ಲ ಹಣವನ್ನು ಇಸ ಕೊಣ್ಡು ಹೋದನೆನ್ದು ಹೇೞಿದಳು, she said "he took all the money and went away". ನೀನು ಮಾಡಿದ ತೀರ್ಪು ಸಮವಲ್ಲ ಎನ್ದು ನನಗೆ ಹೇೞಿದರು, they told me that the decision thou madest, was not proper. ಎತ್ತು, ಅವನ ಕೆಯ್ಯೊಳಗಿನ್ದ ನೀನು ಪಾರಾಗಿ ಹೋಗಲಾಱೆ ಎನ್ದು, ಹೇೞಿತು, the ox said "thou canst not be saved from his hand". ಕೊಟ್ಟೆಂ ಕೊಟ್ಟೆನೆನ್ದು, ಸಿಂಹಳೇನ್ದ್ರಂ ನುಡಿದಂ, "I shall certainly give" king Siṁhaḷa said. ಮಾವಾ, ನೀನು ನನ್ನ ಕರೆದಿ ಎನ್ತ, ಫಕೀರನು ಹೇೞಿದನು, Phakîra said "uncle, thou didst call me". ಆ ಕೂಸುಗಳ ಚಿನ್ತೆ ಬಿಡಿರಿ! ನಾನು ಇವುಗಳನ್ನು ಜತನದಿನ್ದ ಕಾಯುತ್ತ ಹತ್ತರ ಕುಳಿತಿರುತ್ತೇನೆ ಅನ್ನಲು, when it (the wolf) said (to the wild hog) "give up anxious thought as to those (your) little ones! I shall sit near (them) guarding them with care". ತಾನು ಮಾಡುತ್ತೇನೆನ್ತ ಹೇೞಿದನು, he said "I will do it".

ತನ್ದೆ, ಶಿಕ್ಷಿಸುವದಕ್ಕಿನ್ತ ಕ್ಷಮಿಸುವದು ಬಹುಯೋಗ್ಯವು ಎನ್ದು, ತನಗೆ ಬುದ್ಧೀ ಹೇೞಿದ ಮಾತನ್ನು ಮಗನು ಮನಸ್ಸಿಗೆ ತನ್ದು, ಆ ಹುಡುಗನನ್ನು ಕ್ಷಮಿಸಿ ಬಿಟ್ಟನು, the son took to heart that (his) father had given him the advice that it was much fitter to bear with than to punish, and pardoned the boy. ಎನ್ದಿಗೂ ತಾಯಿ ತನ್ದೆಗಳ ಮಾತು ಮೀಱಿ ಬಾರದು ಎನ್ತಲೂ ಮನುಷ್ಯ ಪಶು ಪಕ್ಷಿ ಗಿಡ ಭೂಮಿ ಆಕಾಶ ಸೂರ್ಯ ಚನ್ದ್ರ ಮುನ್ತಾದವುಗಳನ್ನೆಲ್ಲ ದೇವರು ಹುಟ್ಟಿಸಿದನೆನ್ತಲೂ ಅದಱಲ್ಲಿ ಬರೆದದೆ, it is written in it (viz. in the old or former book) that (you) should never transgress the word of (your) parents and that God created man, beasts, birds, trees, the earth, the sky, the sun, the moon, and all the other things.

ನಾಯಿಗಳನ್ನು ಒನ್ದು ಗಿಡಕ್ಕೆ ಕಟ್ಟಿ ಹಾಕಿ ಹೋಗಿರಿ ಎನ್ದು ಅನ್ದನು, he said "tie the dogs to a tree and go!". ಬಯ್ದಾಡುವ ನಡತೆ ಬಹಳ ಕೆಟ್ಟದು, ಇದನ್ನು ಚನ್ನಾಗಿ ನೆನಪಿನಲ್ಲಿಡು ಎನ್ದು, ಬುದ್ಧೀ ಹೇೞಿದನು, he exhorted him "the habit of using improper language (is) very bad; remember this well!". ಅಸೂಯೆಗೀಡಾಗ ಬೇಡೆನ್ದು, ನಿಜಸನ್ದನಂಗಾ ಕುಳಿನ್ದಂ ಪೇೞ್ದಂ, that Kuḷinda told his son "do not become subject to envy!". ಚಕ್ರವರ್ತಿ, ತನ್ನ ದಣ್ಡಿನವರನ್ನೆಲ್ಲಾ ಮೊದಲು ದಾಟಿಸ ಬೇಕೆನ್ದು, ಅಮ್ಬಿಗರಿಗೆ ಅಪ್ಪಣೇ ಮಾಡಿದನು, the king commanded the boatmen that they should first transport all his soldiers over (the river). ಆತನು ನೋಡುವ ಎನಲು, when he said "let us see!". ನೋಡೋಣ, ಬಾ ಎನ್ದನು, he said "let us see, come!".

ಅವನಿಗೇನೆನ್ತ ಹೇೞಲಿ? ನಮ್ಮಲ್ಲಿಗೆ ಬರ ಬೇಕೆನ್ತ ಹೇೞಿರಿ, what am I to tell him?

Tell (him) he must come to me. ಹೋಗಿ, ಸಾಯಂಕಾಲದಲ್ಲಿ ಅವರ ಮನೆಗೆ ಊಟಕ್ಕೆ ಬರುತ್ತೇನೆನ್ದು ಹೇೞು, go, and tell (him) that I will come to his house to dinner this evening. ದೊರೆ, ಸಾಯಂಕಾಲದಲ್ಲಿ ತಮ್ಮ ಮನೆಗೆ ಊಟಕ್ಕೆ ಬರುತ್ತೇನೆನ್ದು, ಹೇೞಲಿಕ್ಕೆ ನನ್ನನ್ನು ಕಳುಹಿಸಿದರು, the gentleman sent me to say that he would come to your house to dinner this evening. ದೂತರು ಚಕ್ರವರ್ತಿಯ ಬೞಿಗೆ ಬನ್ದು, ಎಲೇ ಮಹಾರಾಜನೇ, ನಮ್ಮೊಡೆಯನು ಇವುಗಳನ್ನು ತಮಗೆ ಕಾಣಿಕೆಯಾಗಿ ಕಳುಹಿಸಿರುತ್ತಾರೆನ್ದನು, the messenger went to the ruler and said "O king, my master has sent you these things as a present".

The verbs **ಎನ್ and ಅನ್** are also **used in questions,** *e. g.* ಯಾಕೆ ಮರದ ಮೇಲೆ ಏಱಿದ್ದಿ ಎನ್ದನು, he said "why hast thou ascended the tree?". ಆ ಕುಣ್ಟನು, ನಿನ್ನ ಸಹಾಯಕ್ಕೆ ಹ್ಯಾಗೆ ಬರಲಿ ಎನ್ದು, ಚಿನ್ತಿಸುತ್ತಿರಲು, when the cripple said "how shall I come to thy help?" and was sorrowful. ಯಾವ ಆಟ ಆಡಬೇಕು ಅನ್ನುತ್ತೀ, what doest thou say that (we) shall play? ಈ ಮರವನ್ನು ಈ ಹಾಡು ಮಾಡಿದವರು ಯಾರು ಎನ್ದು, ತೋಟದೊಳಗಿನ ಆಳುಗಳನ್ನು ಕರೆದು ಕೇಳಿದನು, he called the servants that were in the garden and asked "who are they who have treated this tree in this manner?". ನಿಮಗೆ ಹ್ಯಾಗೆ ತಿಳಿಯಿತು ಎನ್ದು, ಕೇಳಿದರು, they asked "how did you know (that)?". ಯಾವಾಗ ತರುವಿ ಎನ್ದು, ಕೇಳಿದನು, he asked "when wilt thou bring (it)?". ನೀನು ಯಾಕೆ ಅೞುತ್ತಿದ್ದಿ ಎನ್ದು, ರಾಮಚನ್ದ್ರನನ್ನು ಕೇಳಿದನು, he asked Râmačandra "why doest thou weep?".

Further the said verbs are used **to express 'for the purpose'**, regarding which some instances have been given in § 302 under No. 7.

Then the said verbs are also used **to give an explanation of nouns, verbs or adverbs,** *e. g.* ಕೞ್ತೆಯೆನ್ದು ಗರ್ದಭಂ, kaḻtĕ means an ass [lit. kaḻtĕ (people) having said (is) an ass]. ಮುೞ್ತಗವ್ ಎನ್ದೊಡನ್ದು ಮರಂ, muḻtaga means a certain tree. ಕೂೞನೆನ್ದುಗ್ರಂ, kûḻa means a rude man. ತೆಗೞ್ದನೆನ್ದು ಪೞಿದಂ, tĕgaḻdan means 'he reviled'. ಅಗುೞ್ದನೆನ್ದು ನೀರ್ನೆಲೆದಪ್ಪಿದಂ, aguḻdan means 'he sank in water'. ಕೞ್ಕನೆಯೆನ್ದು ಆಕಸ್ಮಿಕಂ, kaḻkanĕ means suddenly. ಗೞಗೞನೆಯೆನ್ದು ಬೇಗಂ, gaḻagaḻanĕ means quickly. — **Also when a series of nouns is given ಎನ್ or ಅನ್ is used,** *e. g.* ನಾಗರ ಹಾವು, ಕೇರೀ ಹಾವು, ಮಣ್ಣುಕ್ಕಹಾವು, ಚಿಣಿಗೀ ಹಾವು, ಬಳೆಗಡಕಹಾವು, ಹೆಬ್ಬಾವು ಎನ್ದು, ಹಲವು ತರದ ಹಾವುಗಳುಣ್ಟು.

Also when imitative sounds, feeling, etc. are to be expressed, the said verbs are used, *e. g.* ಪೞಿಪೞಿ ಪೞ್ಪೞಿಯೆನ್ದಾಲಿಕಲ್ಗಳ್ ಉದಿರ್ದುವು ನಭದಿಂ, hailstones fell down from the sky with the sound of paḻapaḻa paḻpaḻa. ನೊಣವು ಗುಂಯಿ ಗುಂಯಿ ಎನ್ದು, ಹಾಡುತ್ತದೆ, the fly sings gumyi gumyi. ನನ್ನ

ಅಂಗೆಯ್ ಜುಮ್ ಅನ್ನುತ್ತದೆ, the palm of my hand has the sensation of jum (from cold).

The relative participles of the said verbs are used similarly (*cf.* the use of ಎಮ್ಬ in the passive, § 315, 2, *k*). Regarding ಎಮ್ಬ when forming a verbal noun in combination with ಉದು or ಅದು, the following instances may be given:—ವಿರಸವೆನಗಿದು ಮುಂಜಿಯೆಮ್ಬುದನ್ ಒರೆಯದಿರು, do not say "this investiture with the sacred thread is sapless to me". ಕೊತ್ತಿ ಬಲ್ಲುದೆ ಹಾಲು ವಿಾಸಲ್ ಎಮ್ಬುದನು, does the cat know (the difference between common) milk (and) that which is vowed? ತಾನು ಈ ಹೊತ್ತು ಹೊಸವಾಗಿ ಎಷ್ಟು ಕಲಿತೆನೆಮ್ಬುದನ್ನು ಪ್ರತಿದಿನ ನೋಡುತ್ತಿರ ಬೇಕು, he must daily examine "how much more have I learned to-day?". ಮಕ್ಕಳಿರಾ, ಯಾವದೊನ್ದು ಕೆಲಸಕ್ಕೆ ಕೆಯ್ ಹಾಕುವದಕ್ಕಿನ್ತ ಮುಂಚಿತವಾಗಿ ಅದನ್ನು ಮಾಡುವದಱಿನ್ದ ನಿಮಗೇನಾದರೂ ಉಪಯೋಗವದೆಯೋ ಇಲ್ಲವೋ ಎಮ್ಬುದನ್ನು ಪೂರ್ಣವಾಗಿ ವಿಚಾರ ಮಾಡಿ ನೋಡಿರಿ, children, before you apply (your) hand to anything, examine thoroughly whether it is in any way useful to you or not. ನಾವು ಸುಮ್ಮನೆ ಬಾಯಿಗೆ ಬನ್ದ ಹಾಗೆ ಮಾತಾಡ ಬಾರದೆಮ್ಬುವದಕ್ಕೆ ಒನ್ದು ದೊಡ್ಡ ಕಾರಣವುಣ್ಟು, there is an eminent reason, why we should not vainly (and) inconsiderately speak. ಆ ಪುಸ್ತಕದಲ್ಲಿ ನೀತಿಯ ಪಾಠಗಳುಣ್ಟು; ಅವುಗಳನ್ನು ಚನ್ನಾಗಿ ಓದಿ ನೆನಪಿಟ್ಟು ಕೊಣ್ಡು ಅದಱಿನ್ತೆ ನಡ ಕೊಳ್ಳ ಬೇಕೆಮ್ಬದಾಗಿ (ಎಮ್ಬುದು + ಆಗಿ) ಬರೆದದೆ, in that book there are ethic rules; it is written (therein) that you should read and remember them carefully and walk accordingly. ಭೃತ್ಯನನ್ನು ಕರೆದು ಹೀಗೆ ಮಾಡೆಮ್ಬದಾಗಿ ಆಜ್ಞಾಪಿಸುವದು, calling (one's) servant and ordering "do thus". ನರಿಯು, ಅಣ್ಣಾ, ಹೋಗಿ ಬರುತ್ತೇನೆ, ಲೋಭವಿರಲಿ ಎನ್ದು, ಅನ್ದದ್ದೇ (past relative participle) ಹೊಱಟಿತು, the fox said with emphasis (to the fowl) "elder brother, I go (now) and shall return. (Your) favour remain (on me)!", and started.

333. **ಎನ್ದರೆ or ಅನ್ದರೆ are frequently used after a conjugated verb to express the meaning which that verb would give, if its relative participle in combination with ಅರೆ were used,** *e. g.* ಇನಿನಿನ್ದ ನೀನು ನಮ್ಮ ಸಾಲೆಗೆ ದಿನಾ ಬರುತ್ತ ಬಾ ಅನ್ದರೆ ಒನ್ದೆರಡು ತಿಂಗಳೊಳಗೇ ನಿನಗೆ ನನ್ನನ್ತೆ ಬರೆಯಲಿಕ್ಕೆ ಬನ್ದೀತು, if hence thou daily come [lit. "daily come" if (one) says] to our school, you will probably become able to write like me even in one or two months. ದೊರೆ ಬನ್ದರನ್ದರೆ, if master has come [lit. if (one) says "master has come"]. ಗುಬ್ಬಿಯು ಆ ತತ್ತಿಯ ಮೇಲೆ ಕೂತಿತೆನ್ದರೆ ಅದಱ ಮೆಯ್ಕಾವಿನಿಂದ ಮಱಿಯಾಗುತ್ತದೆ, if the sparrow sits on that egg [lit. "sat" if (one) says], a young will be born by the warmth of its body. ತಮ್ಮ ಕೆಯ್ಲ್ಲಿ ಆದಷ್ಟು ಬಡವರ ಪರಾಮರಿಕೆ ಮಾಡ ಬೇಕು ಅನ್ದರೆ

ದೇವರು ತಮಗೆ ದಯ ಮಾಡುವನು, if you take care of the poor [(lit. "you must take care of the poor" if (one) says] as much as you can, God will be kind towards you. ಕಾಯಿಗಳು ಹಣ್ಣಾದವೆನ್ದರೆ ಬಿಸಲಿಗೂ ಗಾಳಿಗೂ ಅರಳಿ ಒಳಗಿನ ಹತ್ತಿ ಹೊರಗೆ ಬರುತ್ತದೆ, if the pods are ripe, they will open by the effect of sunshine and wind, and the cotton that is inside, will come out. ರಾಮಪುರವೆಮ್ಬ ಊರಿಗೆ ಹೋಗು ಅನ್ದರೆ ನಿನಗೆ ಎರಡು ದುಡ್ಡಿಗೊನ್ದು ತೆಂಗಿನ ಕಾಯಿ ದೊರೆಯುವದು, if thou goest to the town called Râmapura, thou wilt get a cocoa-nut for two duddus. ಇಲ್ಲಿ ಕತ್ತಲಾಯಿತನ್ದರೆ ನನಗೆ ಈ ಗುಡ್ಡದೊಳಗೆ ದಾರಿ ಸಿಗಲಿಕ್ಕಿಲ್ಲ, if darkness sets in here, I shall not find the way in this hilly country. ಈ ಕಠಾಣಿಯನ್ನು ನಾವಿಬ್ಬರೂ ಹಂಚಿ ಕೊಣ್ಡು ಬಿಡುವಾ ಅನ್ದರೆ ಜನ್ಮದ ದರಿದ್ರ ವಿಚ್ಛಿನ್ನವಾಗುವದು, if we two divide this costly pearl among us, (our) poverty of birth will cease. Observe also the following instance — ದೊರೆಗಳು ಶನಿವಾರ ಬನ್ದರು; ಈ ಶನಿವಾರತನಕ ಅನ್ದರೆ ಒನ್ದು ವಾರ ಆಯಿತು, the gentleman came last Saturday; (from that time) till this Saturday, if one says, it is a week.

It is to be remarked here that ಎನ್ದರೆ or ಅನ್ದರೆ is also used to express the English 'that is to say', *e. g.* ಸನ್ನ ೧೪೯೦ನೇ ಇಸವಿಯಿನ್ದ ೧೬೮೭ನೇ ಇಸವಿಯ ತನಕ ಅನ್ದರೆ ಸುಮಾರು ಇನ್ನೂರು ವರ್ಷಗಳ ವರೆಗೆ, from A. D. 1490 till A. D. 1687, that is to say for about 200 years. ಗ್ರೇಟ್ ಬ್ರಿಟನ ಸಂಯುಕ್ತರಾಜ್ಯದ ಕ್ಷೇತ್ರಫಲವು ತುಸು ಹೆಚ್ಚುಕಡಿಮೆ ಸಿಂಹಲದ್ವೀಪದಷ್ಟು ಅನ್ದರೆ ೨೫ ಸಾವಿರ ಚಚ್ಚೌಕಮೈಲು ಉಣ್ಟು, the area of the united kingdom of Great Britain is about as great as that of Ceylon, that is to say 25000 square miles. ಈ ಮೀನು ತಿರಿಗಾಡಿದರೆ ಕಡಲುಕ್ಕಿ ನೀರು ಹೆಚ್ಚುವದು ಅನ್ದರೆ ಅಷ್ಟು ದೊಡ್ಡ ಮೀನು, if this fish moves about, the sea swells and increases, that is to say such a big fish.

334. **With regard to the use of ಎನ್ದರೆ or ಅನ್ದರೆ after a conjugated verb** adduced in § 333 the remark is to be made that ಆದೊಡೆ, ಆದಡೆ or ಆದರೆ (*cf.* the verse in § 319) **are similarly used,** *e. g.* ಶೂಲಿಮನ್ತ್ರವನ್ ಅಱಿದೆಯಾದೊಡೆ, if thou knowest Śiva's mantra. ನಿಮ್ಮೋಲಗವ ತಪ್ಪಿಸಿದನಾದೊಡೆ, if he left your service undone. ಹೋರಿ ಬಿದ್ದರಾದೊಡೆ, if they escaped. ಸನ್ನಿಸಿದರಾದಡೆ, if they touch. Also ನೀನು ನಾಳೆ ಪುಣೆಗೆ ಹೋಗುವದಾದರೆ, if to-morrow thou goest to Puṇĕ. *Cf.* § 296.

335. In the modern dialect **'intentionally'** is expressed by ಬೇಕೆನ್ತ, (lit. having said "it must"), *e. g.* ನಾನು ಬೇಕೆನ್ತ ಕನ್ನಡಿಯನ್ನು ಒಡಿಯಲಿಲ್ಲ, I have not broken the looking-glass intentionally; (and 'unintentionally' may be translated ಸಾಕೆನ್ತ or ಬೇಡೆನ್ತ).

336. In the same dialect **'they say'**, *'on dit'* **is expressed by adding** ಅನ್ತೆ (§ 196, remark 4; § 198, 7, remark 2) **to a sentence,** *e. g.* ಬ್ರಾಹ್ಮಣನು ಆ ಚಿನಿವಾರನ ಬಳಿಗೆ ಹೋಗಿ, ಅನ್ದದ್ದು (see § 337) — ನಾಯಕರೇ, ತಮ್ಮಲ್ಲೀನೋ ನೀರು ತುಮ್ಬುವದೊನ್ದು ದೊಡ್ಡ ಹಣ್ಡೆ ಅದೆಯನ್ತೆ, the Brâhmaṇa went to that money-changer and said "sir, they (people) say you have a certain large metal vessel into which water uses to be filled". ಒನ್ದು ಜಾತಿಯ ಕಪ್ಪೆಗಳು ಇಡೀ ಕೋಳೀ ಮರಿಯನ್ನು ನುಂಗುತ್ತವನ್ತೆ, they say that a sort of frogs swallows a whole chicken. ಬರುತ್ತಾರನ್ತೆ, "they are coming" they say (or I am told). ಬನ್ದರನ್ತೆ, "they are come", I am told.

337. From the instances in § 332 it appears that ಎನ್ or ಅನ್ are **generally placed at the end of a statement, etc.; it is, however, allowed to put them also before it in order to introduce it,** *e. g.* ತನ್ದೆಯು ಇಬ್ಬರನ್ನು ಕರೆದು ತನ್ನೆದುರಿಗೆ ನಿಲ್ಲ ಹೇಳಿ, ಅನ್ದದ್ದು — ಮಕ್ಕಳಿರಾ, ನೀವಿಬ್ಬರೂ ದಿನಾಲು ಕನ್ನಡೀ ನೋಡುತ್ತಾ ಇರ್ರಿ, etc., the father called both (his children), told them to stand before him, and said (lit. a having said) "children, daily look on the looking-glass". ಒನ್ದು ದಿನ ಒಬ್ಬ ಮುದುಕನು ಕೆಲವು ಹುಡುಗರಿಗೆ ಅನ್ದದ್ದು — ಮಕ್ಕಳಿರಾ, ನಾನು ನಿಮಗೆ ಹಿತವಾಗ ಬೇಕೆನ್ದು, ಅಪೇಕ್ಷಿಸುತ್ತೇನೆ, on a certain day an old man said to some boys "children, I desire your welfare". ದೇವನೆನ್ದನು ನಮ್ಬಿಯಣ್ಣಂಗೆ — ಆವಗಂ ಬಹುವೇದವೇ ದಾರಿ, the god said to Nambiyaṇṇa — "always (are) even the manifold vêdas the road". ಸತಿಯೆನ್ದಳ್ ಇನೆಯಂಗೆ — ಅರಿಯೆ ನರಿಯೆನು ಭಕ್ತಿಯಂ, the wife told the beloved one "I do not know, I do not know devotion".

In such a case ಎನ್ **or** ಅನ್ **may be preceded by** ಇನ್ತು (*cf.* § 326 ಅದೆ ನ್ತೆನ್ದೊಡೆ), *e. g.* ಬಳಿಯಮ್ ಅರಸಿಯಂ ಸನ್ತಯ್ಸಲೆನ್ದಿನ್ತೆನ್ದಂ, thereupon, in order to appease the queen, he spoke thus —. ಮತ್ತಮ್ ಅರಸನ್ ಇನ್ತೆನ್ದಂ, again the king spoke thus —. ಮತ್ತಮ್ ಇನ್ತೆನ್ದಳ್, again she spoke thus —. ಅವಳ್ ಇನ್ತೆನ್ದಳ್, she spoke thus —. ಅವರ್ ಇನ್ತೆನ್ದರ್, they spoke thus —. ತನ್ದೆಗಿನ್ತೆನ್ದಂ, he spoke thus to (his) father —. ನರೇನ್ದ್ರನನ್ದನಂಗೆ ಪತಿಮೋಹಿನನ್ದನನ್ ಇನ್ತೆನ್ದಂ, to the son of the king the son of Patimôhi spoke thus —. Also: ಇನ್ತೆನ್ದೊರೆದು, having spoken thus (with reference to preceding words).

Or ಇದಂ, this, may be put **after** ಎನ್, *e. g.* ಅವನ್ ಎನ್ದನ್ ಇದಂ, he spoke this —.

There is still to be mentioned the use **of a relative participle in the form of a verbal noun** to introduce a statement, etc., **without** ಎನ್ **or** ಅನ್, *e. g.* ಅವನು ಆಲೋಚಿಸಿದ್ದು — ಈಕೆಯು, ಕರೀ ಬೀಜದ ಚೀಲವೆನ್ನು, ಹೇಳುವದು ಮದ್ದಿನ

ಚೀಲವು, he reflected "what she says is a bag of black seed, (is) the bag of gunpowder". ಸಿಂಹವು ಹೇಳಿದ್ದು — ನೀವೆಲ್ಲರೂ ತಿಳಿದವರೇ ಇದ್ದೀರಿ, the lion said "all of you certainly know". In such a case ಏನಂದರೆ is to be supplied, for which see § 323.

XXIII. On ಇಲ್ಲದೆ, ಅಲ್ಲದೆ, ಅಲ್ತು.

338. In § 212, No. 7 ಇಲ್ಲದೆ, ಅಲ್ಲದೆ (*cf.* §§ 170. 361) and ಅಲ್ತು appear as classed with the adverbs by the Šabdânušâsna.

ಇಲ್ಲದೆ.

In that case ಇಲ್ಲದೆ has the meaning of 'in absence of', 'without' (vinârthaṁ), *e. g.* ಅಕ್ಕರಮ್ ಇಲ್ಲದೆ ತಕ್ಕರ್ ಅಕ್ಕುಮೆ, do distinguished people originate without letters (*i. e.* without the knowledge of letters or science)? ನೀನ್ ಇಲ್ಲದಿವೆಲ್ಲಮ್ ಒಳವೆ, ಭಾನುತನುಜಾ, without thee are all these (valuable things) in existence (for me), O Karṇa? ಭಕ್ತಿಯಿಲ್ಲದೆ ಕೆಟ್ಟು ಹೋದೆ, without devotion thou wilt be ruined. ತಳುವಿಲ್ಲದೇ ಬಪ್ಪೆನೆ, shall I not come even without delay? ತೆರಹಿಲ್ಲದೇ, even without intermission. ಅನೇಕಜನರಿಗೆ ಕಷ್ಟವಿಲ್ಲದೆ ಇರುವದು ಬೇಕು, many men like to live without labour.

But originally ಇಲ್ಲದೆ is the negative participle of ಇಲ್, not being present or not having been present, not being, not having been (see § 170; *cf.* ಇಲ್ಲ § 298), *e. g.* ಇನಿತಿಲ್ಲದಿಹ ರಾಜ್ಯಂ ದುರ್ಬಲಮ್ ಎನಿಕ್ಕುಂ, a kingdom in which so much (*viz.* a strong king, etc.) is not existing, is called weak. ಔರಸ ಪುತ್ರನ್ ಉತ್ತಮಂ, ಮೇಣ್ ಅವನ್ ಇಲ್ಲದೊಡೆ, a son generated by one's self (is) the best; and if not being he is (*i. e.* if he did not exist). ಇಲ್ಲಿ ಭಕ್ಷಿಸಲ್ ಒನ್ದುವುಂ ಮುನ್ನಿಲ್ಲದಿರ್ದೊಡೆ, thereafter not being anything to eat here if is (*i. e.* if thereafter there were nothing to eat here). ಬುದ್ಧಿ ಇಲ್ಲದಿದ್ದರೆ ನೀತಿ ಇರುವದಿಲ್ಲ, if (there) is no understanding, (there) is no right behaviour. ಪ್ರಯೋಜನಕ್ಕಿಲ್ಲದೇ ವ್ರಯವಾಗಿ ಹೋಗುವಿಕೆ ವ್ಯಯವೆನ್ದೆನಿಸುವದು, to a useful purpose even not being a spending a going (*i. e.* spending even for no use or without use) is called vyaya.

ಇಲ್ಲದೆ being thus originally a negative participle or gerund, forms also the relative participle ಇಲ್ಲದ (see § 273), *e. g.* ದುಃಖವಿಲ್ಲದರ್, those who have no sorrow. ಎಡೆದೆರಹು ಇಲ್ಲದ ಸಾಲು, a line that has no break. ಕೊಮ್ಬಿಲ್ಲದ ಎತ್ತು, an ox that has no horns. ಬುದ್ಧಿ ಇಲ್ಲದವನು, a man who has no understanding. ಇಲ್ಲದುದು, that is not existing. — It is to be remarked that ಇಲ್ಲದ, like ಉಳ್ಳ, may govern also the accusative, *e.g.* ವಿಭಕ್ತಿಯನಿಲ್ಲದುದು (see § 316 under No. 1).

ಅಲ್ಲದೆ (*cf.* § 300, 1, remark *a*).

ಅಲ್ಲದೆ when considered as an adverb (§ 212, 7) means **'excepting'**, **'except'** (vinârtham̐, Šabdânušâsana), and occasionally 'but', *e.g.* ಜಿನನ್ ಅಲ್ಲದೆ ದೇವರ್ ಒಳರೇ, are (there any) gods except Jina? ನೀನ್ ಅಲ್ಲದಾವನ್ ಅಧಿಕನ್ ಇಳೆಯೊಳ್ ಜಿನಪಾ, except thee, Jinapa, who is an excellent person on earth? ಖದ್ಯೋತಂಗಳ್ಗಿರುಳಲ್ಲದರ್ಕಮ್ ಇದಿರೊಳ್ ಮೆಯ್ದೋರ್ಕೆಯೇನ್ ಆರ್ಕುಮೆ, except at night fire-flies (have not the ability to shine); let the sun shine in front, what ability (to shine) have they? ಕುಸುಮಾಯುಧ, ನಿನ್ನ ಬಲ್ಪು ಪೆಣ್ಮಕ್ಕಳೊಳ್ ಅಲ್ಲದಿಲ್ಲ, Kâma, except among females, thou hast no power. ಕುಳದ ನಿಯಾಮದೊಳ್ ಎನ್ದುಂ ಕ್ಷಳಕ್ಕೆ ಲಾಕ್ಷರವಿಕಲ್ಪಮ್ ಇಲ್ಲ; .ವಿಕಲ್ಪಂ ಕ್ಷಳನ್ ಅಲ್ಲದಿಲ್ಲ, in an alliteration wherein the kuḷa (the Kannaḍa ಳ್) is, the optional use of the letter ಲ್ for the kshaḷa (the Sam̐skṛita ಳ್) does never occur; an optional use, excepting (that of) the kshaḷa, is not to occur (in such a case). ಉಯ್ ನೆಯ್ ಸುಯ್ ಒಯ್ ಧಾತುಗಳೊಳ್ ದ್ವಿತ್ವಮ್ ಅಲ್ಲದಿಲ್ಲ ವಿಕಲ್ಪಂ, in the verbal themes uy nĕy suy ŏy (there) is no other use except the doubling (of their final letter when ಅಲ್ is suffixed). ಅಕಾರಾನ್ತಮ್ ಅಲ್ಲದುಬಿದ ಸ್ವರವ್ಯಂಜನಾನ್ತಂಗಳ್ಗೆ ಪರಮಾದ ಚತುರ್ಥಿಗೆ ಗೆಯೆನ್ದಕ್ಕುಂ, excepting the terms that end in ಅ, (there) is (the suffix) ಗೆ for the dative when it (*i. e.* its suffix) follows the rest (*viz.*) those that end in (other) vowels and in consonants. ಧನವನ್ ಈಯಲು ಬರ್ಪುದಲ್ಲದೆ ತನುವನ್ ಈಯಲ್ ಅದೆನ್ತು ಬರ್ಪುದು, it is possible to offer (one's) riches, but how will it be possible to offer (one's) body? ಆದಿಶಿವಭಕ್ತಂಗೆ ಮದುವೆಯನ್ ಆದರದಿ ನಾ ಮಾಟ್ಟಿನ್ ಅಲ್ಲದೇ ದುಹಿತೆಯಂ ಭವಿಗೆ ಕೊಡೆಂ, except I reverently marry (her) to a devotee of Âdišiva, I do not give this (my) daughter to a worldling. ದೇವರ ಕೃಪೆಯಿನ್ದಲ್ಲದೆ ಪಾಪಕ್ಕೆ ಪರಿಹಾರವಿಲ್ಲ, except through the grace of God (there) is no forgiveness for (*i. e.* of) sin. ಹಾಲು ಮೊಸರಾಗುವದಲ್ಲದೆ ಮೊಸರು ಹಾಲಾದೀತೇ, except that milk becomes curds, could curds become milk?

Occasionally ಒಡೆ or ಅಡೆ (or ಅರೆ) **may precede ಅಲ್ಲದೆ**, *e.g.* ನಿಮ್ಮ ಕೆಯ್ಯಲಿ ಮಡಿದೊಡಲ್ಲದೆಯೆಮ್ಮ ಶಾಪವಿಮೋಕ್ಷವಾಗದು, except he die by your hand, I shall get no deliverance from my curse. ಎಮ್ಮಮಂ ಪೂಜಿಸಿದಡಲ್ಲದೆ ಭಕ್ತಿ ದೊರೆಯದು, except one adores me, devotion will not be obtained.

ಅಲ್ಲದೆ sometimes loses so much of its originally verbal character that it is **added to a relative past participle** (unless the rule in § 167 be applied), *e.g.* ನಿನ್ನಂ ನೋಡಿದಲ್ಲದೆ (=ನೋಡಿದ ಅಲ್ಲದೆ, or perhaps ನೋಡಿದು ಅಲ್ಲದೆ), except I see thee. ಬೆಳಗಿದಲ್ಲದೆ, except it become bright. ಶತ್ರ್ಯಂತನ್ತ್ಯಂ ಸಂಸ್ಕೃತದೊಳ್ ಪದವಿಧಿಯಂ ನೆಱೆ ತಳೆದಲ್ಲದೆ (Commentary: ಧರಿಸಿದಲ್ಲದೆ) ಕನ್ನಡದಲ್ಲಿ ಲಿಂಗವಾಗದು ನಿಜದಿಂ, a term with final ಅತ್ may well form a word in a Saṁskṛita compound, but in (true) Kannaḍa does not become a nominal theme by itself. ಊರಿಗೆ ಬನ್ದ ಮಾರಿ ಉಣ್ಣಲ್ಲದೇ ಹೋಗದು, Mâri that has come to a town, does never go away except she eats.—On the other hand we have also: ತಲೆ ತಾಗಿಸಿದ್ದಲ್ಲದೆ (=ತಾಗಿಸಿದ್ದು ಅಲ್ಲದೆ) ಬುದ್ಧಿ ಬಾರದು, except he knock (his) head (against something), understanding will not be obtained (by him).

Likewise this disappearance of its original character seems to occur when ಅಲ್ಲದೆ is followed by an accusative (see § 300, 1, remark *b*), *e. g.* ಮೃಡನ ಭಕ್ತರನ್ ಅಲ್ಲದಾರುವನ್ ಅಱಿಯೆವರ್ತಿಸೆವು, except devotees of Śiva we know and love nobody. ಎನ್ನನ್ ಅಲ್ಲದೆ ಸತತಂ, ಬಱಿಕೆನ್ನ ಪದವಿಯನ್ ಆದೊಡಾತಂ (see § 287, remark) ತನ್ನ ಮನದೊಳು ನೆನೆವುದಿಲ್ಲ, except always upon me, he does not think even upon my (high) rank.

ಅಲ್ಲದೆ may also get the meaning of 'besides' (ಮೇಣ್, ಮತ್ತೆ), *e.g.* ಅದಲ್ಲದೆ, besides that. ಇದಲ್ಲದೆ, besides this. ಅವನಲ್ಲದೆ ಮತ್ತೆ ಕೆಲವರು ಬನ್ದರು, besides him some others came. ನೊಣಗಳು ಸೊಗಸಿನ್ದ ಹಾಱಾಡುತ್ತ ಹೊತ್ತುಗಳೆಯುತ್ತಿದ್ದವಲ್ಲದೆ ತಮ್ಮ ಹಿತದ ಕೆಲಸವನ್ನೇನೂ ಮಾಡಿ ಕೊಳ್ಳುತ್ತಿದ್ದಿಲ್ಲ, the flies spent (their) time by joyfully flying about, besides (that) they did not do any work useful to themselves. ದೇವರಾಜನು ದಕ್ಷಿಣಕ್ಕೆ ತನ್ನ ರಾಜ್ಯವನ್ನು ಬೆಳಿಸಿದ್ದಲ್ಲದೆ ಉತ್ತರದಲ್ಲಿ ವಿಜಾಪುರದವರ ಹೊಸಕೋಟೆಯ ಪರಗಣೆಯನ್ನು ತಕ್ಕೊಣ್ಡನು, Dêvarâja, besides enlarging his kingdom much towards the south, took, in the north, the district of Hŏsakôṭĕ of the Vijâpura people. ಅವನು ಹಣಗಾಱನಲ್ಲದೆ ಧರ್ಮಿಷ್ಠನಾಗಿದ್ದಾನೆ, besides a rich man he is a very liberal man.

The original verbal character of ಅಲ್ಲದೆ as a gerund (*cf.* § 300) appears still in the following instances:—ಸ್ಥಿರಮ್ ಅಲ್ಲದೆ ಸ್ನೇಹ ಮಾಳ್ಪವನು, a man who, (his love) not being steady, loves (*i. e.* a man unsteady in his affection). ಮಾಮರನ್ ಅಲ್ಲದಿಲ್ಲ, a mango tree not being it is not (*i. e.* it certainly is a mango tree). ತನಿಗಮ್ಪಿನ ಮಲ್ಲಿಗೆಯುಲ್ಲದಿಲ್ಲ, a jasmine of rich fragrance not being it is not (*i. e.* it certainly is a jasmine of rich fragrance). ಪ್ರಯತ್ನಮಲ್ಲದಿರ್ಪ ಗುರುತ್ವದೊಳ್, in respectability that requires no (particular) effort (to acknowledge).

The relative participle of ಅಲ್ಲದೆ is ಅಲ್ಲದ, *e.g.* ಅದಲ್ಲದೊಡೆ, if it be not that (or thus). ಅಲ್ಲದುದು, that is improper. ತಾನ್ ಅಲ್ಲದನ್ಯಂ, another who is not he. ಸ್ಪಷ್ಟಮಲ್ಲದ ನುಡಿ, speech that is not distinct. ಅಲ್ಲದ ಕಾರ್ಯಂಗಳ್, acts that are not proper. ಬಿನ್ದುವಿಂಗೆ ಬನ್ದುದಲ್ಲದ ನಿಜವಹನ್ನ ಮಕಾರಂ, such an ಮ್ as does not stand for the bindu. ಪ್ರತಿಷೇಧಮ್ ಅಲ್ಲದಲ್ಲಿಯುಂ, also where there is no negative sense.

ಅಲ್ತು.

In § 212, 7 ಅಲ್ತು is classed with the adverbs that are verbal forms; it is a bhâvavačana of the verb ಅಲ್ and another form of ಅಲ್ಲದುದು. It is used, like ಅಲ್ಲ (which see in § 300), in **pratishêdha, negativing,** etc., *e. g.* ಬರೆಪವೊಬ್ಬಿಕ್ಕ ಉಚ್ಚರಿಸಲ್ ಬಾರ್ಧದುವು ಅಕ್ಕರಮ್ ಅಲ್ತು, (sounds) that are written (but) cannot be read (except in an inarticulate manner, as sounds for thunder, etc.), are no letters (lit. letters a being not). ಅವನಲ್ತು, not he! ಅವಳಲ್ತು, not she! ಅದಲ್ತು, not that! ತಕ್ಕದಲ್ತು, it is not fit. ಮುಳಿಸಲ್ತೆಮಗಾತನೊಳ್, we have no (such a thing as can be called) anger against him. ದೇವಾ, ಸಿಂಹಳೇನ್ದ್ರನ್ ಎನ್ದುಂ ಕಪ್ಪಮ್ ಇತ್ತನ್ ಅಲ್ತು, O king, Simhaḷêndra is one who has never paid tribute.

ಅಲ್ತೆ, *i. e.* ಅಲ್ತು to which the ಎ of inferential interrogation (§ 212, 6) is suffixed, is used as follows: — ಎಲೇ, ಇದಲ್ತೆ ತುಹಿನಕ್ಷ್ಮೋಣೀಧ್ರದುತ್ತುಂಗಸಾನುಗಳೊಳ್ ಭೋರನೆ ಬನ್ದು ಪಾಯ್ದುದು ನೋಡಾಕಾಶಗಂಗಾಜಲಂ, O look, is not this the water of the celestial Ganges that runs swiftly down on the table-lands of the snowy mountain? ಪೊನ್ನಿಂ ಸಮನಿಸುಗುಮ್ ಅಲ್ತೆ ಹೆಣ್ಣುಂ ಮಣ್ಣುಂ, are not women and lands acquired by means of gold? (*Cf.* ಅಲ್ಲವೆ § 300, 3).

XXIV. On the repetition of verbs, and on the combination of certain verbs.

339. The repetition of nouns, pronouns, adjectives, numerals, adverbs, interjections and imitative sounds has been treated of in §§ 303—309.

In § 152 it has been stated that there are no true frequentative or iterative verbs in Kannaḍa, but that a kind of iterative verbs may be formed by simple repetition (yugaḷôččaraṇa, dviḥprayôga) or triple repetition (triprayôga).

Instances of such iterative verbs elucidating their forms are given in § 165, *b*, 1—4, where short participles are concerned, and in § 211, 1—11, where all the various repetitions are given, but without the respective various meanings conveyed by them. (*Cf.* § 361.)

In the present paragraph the meanings are adduced. They are the following:—

1, directing the attention of others to a distant object or affair (dûra, Šabdamaṇidarpaṇa), *e. g.* ಆ ತೋರ್ಪುದಾ ತೋರ್ಪುದು ಬಾನೋಳ್ ಧ್ವಜಪಟಂ, there in the sky (lit. in that — that sky) appears, appears the banner!

2, directing the attention of others to a near object or affair (samîpa, Šmd.), *e. g.* ಇದೆ ಇದೆ ಸಾರ್ಕೆ ಸಾರ್ಕೆ ಗಣಕಾವಳಿ ಪೇಟ್ದ ಮುಹೂರ್ತಂ, lo, lo! let (them) approach, let (them) approach! (it is) the time told by the assemblage of astrologers.

3, repeatedly directing one's own face or attention towards an object or affair (abhîkshaṇa, abhîkshṇa, pratimukhâvalôkana, Šmd.), a person's own repetition of action or experiencing (abhîkshaṇya, Šabdânušâsana), *e. g.*

ಗಿಳಿಯೊಡನೋದಿಯೋದಿ ನುಡಿಗಲ್ತು, ಮದಾಲಸರಾಜಹಂಸಮ
ಣ್ಡಳಿಯೊಡನಾಡಿಯಾಡಿ ನಡೆಗಲ್ತು, ಕಲಾಪಿಗಳಾಟಮಂ ಮನಂ |
ಗೊಳೆ ನಡೆ ನೋಡಿ ನೋಡಿ ಕುಣಿಯಲ್ ನೆಱೆ ಕಲ್ತು, ಕಲಾಗುಣಂ ಪೊದ
ಟ್ದಿಳವಡೆ ಬಾಲಭಾವದೊಳೆ ಭಾವಕಿಯರ್ ಬಳೆವರ್ ನಿರನ್ತರಂ || having

read and read (*i. e.* having repeatedly read) with parrots and (thus) learned speech, having played and played with the assemblage of flamingoes languid with passion and (thus) learned walking, having inquisitively and carefully seen and seen the dance of peacocks and (thus) having learned to dance well, the females with (their innate) taste for the beautiful continually grew up to the development of the excellence of fine arts (Šmd.).— ಅಟ್ಟಟ್ಟಿಱುಪಿದಂ, he lowered (the pot) after continual boiling (its contents). ಉಣ್ಡುಣ್ಡು ಪೋದಂ, he repeatedly ate and (then) went. ನೋಡಿ ನೋಡಿ ನಕ್ಕಂ, he looked on and looked on and (then) laughed (Šabdânušâsana). ಉಸಿಕನಿದ್ದಿದ್ದೆಂ ಕಾರಣಂ, he was and was (*i. e.* continued to be) silent; what (is) the cause? (Basavapurâṇa). ಓದೋದಿ ಬೇಸತ್ತನು, he read and read, and became tired. ಆಡಾಡಿ ಕೆಟ್ಟನು, he played and played, and (at last) was ruined (Nuḍigaṭṭu). ಒನ್ದೇ ಕಡೆಯಲ್ಲಿ ಕುಳಿತು ಕುಳಿತು ನಿಮಗೆ ಬಹಳ ಬೇಸಱಿ ಬನ್ದಿದ್ದೀತು, having sat and sat in one place you will be much wearied. ಬಿದ್ದು ಬಿದ್ದು ನಕ್ಕನು, he fell and fell and laughed (*i. e.* he rolled with laughter). ಆ ಬೇನೆಯಿನ್ದ ಸತ್ತು ಸತ್ತು ಉಳಿದನು, of that disease he died and died (*i. e.* was on the brink of death) and (still) remained alive.

4, enjoining on others the repetition of an act in order to encourage or incite them (Kriyâsamabhihâra, Šmd.), *e. g.* ನಡೆ ನಡೆಯೆನ್ದು ನುಡಿದರ್,

"walk, walk!" they said. ಇದಿರ್ಚಿದಿರ್ಚೆನೆ ಜಟಾಯು, when Jaṭâyu said "withstand, withstand!"

5, ordering with agitation, or hurrying an action; expressing anxiety, (čapalatĕ, Šmd.; sambhrama, Šabdânušâsana), *e. g.* ಒಪ್ಪಿಸೊಪ್ಪಿಸು ಸುದತಿಯಂ, deliver, deliver the woman with handsome teeth! ಅಣ್ಮಣ್ಮು, be manly, be manly! (Šmd.). ಹೋಗು ಹೋಗಯ್ಯ, go, go, sir! ಬಿಡು ಬಿಡಾ ಸನ್ದೇಹವ, give up, give up (your) doubt! ಎಲೆ ಬಸವ, ಕೊಡು ಕೊಡು ಪೆಟ್ಟಿಗೆಯ ಹೊನ್ನೆಲ್ಲವ, O Basava, give, give all the gold of the box! (Basavapurâṇa). ಒಡ್ಡೊಡ್ಡೊಡ್ಡೆನು ತೊಡ್ಡಿ ಮೇಳದವಳ್ ಕುಂಕುಮವಾರಿ ಕುಪ್ಪಳಿಸಿ ಪೊಯ್ದಳ್, the female buffoon saying "resist, resist, resist!" resisted, gathered saffron water and threw (it, Šmd.). ಇತ್ತ ಬಾ, ಇತ್ತ ಬಾ, ಇತ್ತ ಬಾ, come this way, come this way, come this way! ಆನೆ ಬನ್ದುದಾನೆ ಬನ್ದುದಾನೆ ಬನ್ದುದು, an elephant has come! an elephant has come! an elephant has come! ದಣ್ಡು ಬನ್ದುದೇಳಿ, ದಣ್ಡು ಬನ್ದುದೇಳಿ, ದಣ್ಡು ಬನ್ದುದೇಳಿ, the army has come, arise! the army has come, arise! the army has come, arise! (Šabdânušâsana).

6, continuous, unceasing action (sâtatya, Šabdânušâsana), *e. g.* ಬನ್ದಂ ಬನ್ದಂ, he came and came. ಪೋದಂ ಪೋದಂ, he went and went. ಕಣ್ಡಂ ಕಣ್ಡಂ, he saw and saw. ಬರೆವರೆ (-ಬರೆ), when (it) came and came (Ršv.). ಬರುತ್ತ ಹೋಗುತ್ತ, ಬರುತ್ತ ಹೋಗುತ್ತ ಇದ್ದಾನೆ, he is coming and going, coming and going (Nuḍigaṭṭu). ಬರುತ್ತಾ ಬರುತ್ತಾ ರಾಯನ ಕುದುರೆ ಕತ್ತೆ ಆಯಿತು, the king's horse coming and coming (nearer) was (but) a donkey. ಆ ಚಕ್ರವರ್ತಿ ಶತ್ರುಗಳನ್ನು ಅಟ್ಟಿ ಕೊಣ್ಡು ಹೋಗುತ್ತಾ ಹೋಗುತ್ತಾ ಅವರ ದೇಶದ ಮಧ್ಯಭಾಗದಲ್ಲಿ ಹೋಗಿ ತಲಪಿದನು, that emperor pursued the foes, and going and going (*i. e.* marching on) arrived in the midst of their country. ಕುರಿಬರೆಲ್ಲ ಓಡುತ್ತೋಡುತ್ತ ಅಲ್ಲಿ ಬನ್ದು ನೋಡಿದರೆ ತೋಳ ಇಲ್ಲ, when all the shepherds running and running came there and looked, (there) was no wolf. ಅಡವಿಕುರಿಗಳು ಮನುಷ್ಯರಿಗೆ ಮೊದಲು ಹೆದರಿದಾಗ್ಯೂ ಬರ ಬರುತ್ತಾ (see § 172) ಈಲಾಗುತ್ತವೆ, though the ribfaced deer at first are afraid of men, coming and coming (*i. e.* in course of time) become attached (to them). ಅಫಿನ ಕಾಯಿ ಬರ ಬರುತ್ತಾ ಚಣ್ಡಿನಷ್ಟು ದೊಡ್ಡದಾಗುವದು, the pods of opium become in course of time as big as balls. ಹೋಗ ಹೋಗುತ್ತಾ ದಾರಿಯೊಳಗೆ ಅವರಿಬ್ಬರೂ ಆಲೋಚಿಸಿದ್ದೇನಂದರೆ, proceeding and proceeding on the road both of them reflected as follows.

7, completeness of an action (kriyâsâkalya, Šabdânušâsana), *e. g.* ಕೊಯ್ ಕೊಯ್ಯ್ಯ ಎನ್ದು ಕೊಯ್ದಂ, he said (to himself and another) "reap,

reap!" and (thus) reaped (the whole harvest). ಪೊಯ್ ಪೊಯ್ಯ್ಯ ಎನುತ್ತೆ ಪೊಯ್ದಂ, saying (to himself and another) "beat, beat!" he (thus) beat (consummately). ಬಾ ಬಾಯೆನುತ್ತೆ ಬನ್ದಂ, saying (to himself) "come, come!" and (thus) came. The Nuḍigaṭṭu has the following instances:—ಸವರು ಸವರೆನ್ದು ಸವರಿದನು. ಕುಡಿ ಕುಡಿಯೆನ್ದು ಕುಡಿದನು. ಎಣಿಸೆಣಿಸೆನ್ದು ಎಣಿಸಿದನು.

8, intensity, emphasis, high degree (âdhikya, Śabdânuśâsana), *e. g.* ಆದುದಾದುದಂ, it has been done, it has been done! ಎಮಗಪ್ಪುದೆಮಗಪ್ಪುದು, it must become ours, it must become ours! ತೊಳ ತೊಳಗಿದುದು, it shone very much. ಬೆಳ ಬೆಳಗಿದುದು, it became very bright. ಮುೞು ಮುೞುಗಿದುದು, it sank rapidly. ಮೊೞ ಮೊೞಗಿದುದು, it roared very much (Śabdânuśâsana). ಅಹುದಹುದು, it will become, it will become! ಅಸಮನೇತ್ರನು ವಿಷವನ್ ಆರೋಗಿಸಿದುದುಣ್ಬುಣ್ಬು, Śiva drank poison, it is (so), it is (so)! ಅಭವನ್ ಈ ಘಟದೊಳ್ ಉಣ್ಬುಣ್ಟೆನಿತು ಸನ್ದೇಹವಿಲ್ಲ, the unborn one (Rudra) is, is in this earthen vessel! (there) is not the least doubt. ಆಗಲಾಗಲಿ, may it become (so, or let it be so), may it become (so)! ಪರಸುಖಾಮ್ಭೋರಾಶಿಯೊಳು ನೆಱೆ ತೋದು ನೆಱೆ ತೋದು, having dipped well, having dipped well in the ocean of excellent joy (Basavapurâṇa). ಇಱುವೆಗಳು ಹಗಲೆಲ್ಲ ದುಡಿದು ದುಡಿದು ಕಷ್ಟ ಪಡುತ್ತವೆ, ants work and work and exert themselves the whole day. ಬೇಟೆಯಾಡುವ ಕೆಲಸಕ್ಕೆ ನಾಯಿಗಳು ಬೇಕೇ ಬೇಕು, dogs are absolutely required for the chase. ಕೆನ್ನೆಯ್ದಿಲೆ ಸಿಕ್ಕೇ ಸಿಗುತ್ತದೆ, a red water-lily will certainly be found. ಜ್ಞಾನಿಗಳು ವಿಷಯಸುಖವನ್ನು ಬಿಟ್ಟೇ ಬಿಡುತ್ತಾರೆ, the wise will decidedly abandon sensual enjoyment. ಇದ್ದೇ ಇರುತ್ತದೆ, it certainly is. ಇದನ್ನು ಮಾಡೇ ಮಾಡುವಿರಿ, you will certainly do this.

ಪಥಮ್ ಇದಲ್ಲಲ್ಲ, this is not, is not the proper way. ಬೇಡ ಬೇಡ, it is not required, it is not required. ಬೇಡ ಬೇಡೆನ್ದು ಬಿಡಿಸಿದಂ, he said "it is not fit, it is not fit!" and loosened (him). ಅನ್ಯಾಯದ ಹಣವು ನಮಗೆ ಬೇಡೇ ಬೇಡ, we absolutely do not want money of (*i. e.* acquired by) injustice. ಒಲ್ಲೆನೊಲ್ಲೆನು, I will not, I will not. ಸಾಕು ಸಾಕು, enough, enough! ಸೃಷ್ಟಿಯಲ್ಲಿ ಅಯೋಗ್ಯವಾದವುಗಳು ಇಲ್ಲೇ ಇಲ್ಲ, certainly (there) are no useless things in creation.

ತಪ್ಪ ತಪ್ಪದೆ ಶರ ಶರಂಗಳಂ ತೆಗೆದೆಚ್ಚುತ, taking arrow after arrow and shooting without ever failing. ನಿಲ್ಲ ನಿಲ್ಲದೆ, without waiting in the least. ಬಿಡ ಬಿಡದೆ ನಡೆ ತಪ್ಪ ವೀಚೆಗಳು, waves that came incessantly.

In intensity, etc. triple repetition also occurs, *e. g.* ಬನ್ದ ಬನ್ದ ಬನ್ದಂ, he came, he came, he came. ಉಣ್ಡುಣ್ಡುಣ್ಡು ಪೋದಂ, he ate and ate and ate, and (then) went. ತೊಳ ತೊಳ ತೊಳಗಿತ್ತು, it shone excessively. ಬೆಳ ಬೆಳ ಬೆಳಗಿತ್ತು, it became excessively bright (Šabdânušâsana). (ನಡ ನಡ ನಡುಗುತ್ತ, trembling excessively.)

9, pain or trouble (âbâdha, pîḍĕ, Šabdânušâsana), *e.g.* ಪೋದ ಪೋದಂ, alas, he went. ಬನ್ದ ಬನ್ದಯ್, alas, thou hast come. ಬಾರ್ ಬಾರೆಂ, oh, I do not come. ಪೋಪ ಪೋಪೆಂ, oh, I shall go.

10, succession (one after the other): totality, *e.g.* ಶಿಶುವಂ ಕಣ್ಡ ಕಣ್ಡ ಬಲೆಯರ್ ಕರೆ ಕರೆದರ್, the women who one after the other happened to see the child, called (it near). ಕಣ್ಡ ಕಣ್ಡವರಿಗೆಲ್ಲಾ ಹಲ್ಲು ಕಿರಿದರೂ ಗಣ್ಡ ಸತ್ತ ಮುಣ್ಡೆಗೆ ಬೋಳಿಸದೇ ಬಿಡರು, though the widow whose husband has died, grins at all she sees, they do not let her be unshaved. ಬನ್ದ ಬನ್ದವರು ನಿನ್ದಿಸಿದರೆ ಗಣ್ಡ ಸತ್ತ ದುಃಖ ಬಿಟ್ಟು ಹೋದೀತೇ, if all who come revile (her), will the grief caused by (her) husband's death leave (her)? ಕಣ್ಡ ಕಣ್ಡವರನ್ನೆಲ್ಲ ಸಮಾಧಾನ ಮಾಡುವದಕ್ಕಾಗಿ ಆ ಮುದುಕನು ಮಾಡಿದ ಯತ್ನವು ಕೆಯ್ಗೂಡಲಿಲ್ಲ, the endeavour made by the old man to please all he saw, was unsuccessful. ಕಣ್ಡ ಕಣ್ಡದನ್ನೆಲ್ಲ ಕಡಿಯುತ್ತಿದ್ದನು, he was cutting down every thing he saw. ಆಗ ಅವರು ಆ ಕಟ್ಟಿಗೆಗಳನ್ನು ನೋಡ (see § 181, note *c;* § 211, ೩, foot-note) ನೋಡುವಷ್ಟರಲ್ಲಿ ಮುರಿದು ಹಾಕಿದರು, then (after the bundle of sticks had been untied) they broke the sticks one after the other as they saw them.

11, variety, *e.g.* (ಶ್ರೀಮನ್ತರು) ತಾವು ಹೋದ ಹೋದಲ್ಲಿ ಜನರು ರಾಜನಿಷ್ಠೆಯಿನ್ದ ಮಾಡಿದ ಆದರಾತಿಥ್ಯಕ್ಕೆ ಬಹಳ ಮೆಚ್ಚಿದರು, he (the Prince of Wales) was much pleased with the courteous hospitality which the people, from attachment to the ruler, showed in the various places to which he went. ಅವನು (ರಾಮರಾಜನು) ಹೋದ ಹೋದಲ್ಲಿ ಮಸೀದಿಗಳನ್ನು ಕೆಡಿಸಿದನು, he (Râmarâja) destroyed the mosques in the various places to which he went. ಒಳ್ಳೇ ನಡತೆಯ ಮನುಷ್ಯನು ಎಲ್ಲರಿಗೂ ಬೇಕಾದವನು; ಹೋದ ಹೋದಲ್ಲಿ ಬಹುಮಾನ ಹೊನ್ದುವನು, a man of good conduct is welcome to all; in the various places to which he goes, he is respected.

ಆ ಹಾಳೆಯನ್ನು ಬೇಕು ಬೇಕಾದ ಹಾಗೆ ಕೊರೆದು ಕಿಡಿಕೀ ಕನ್ನಡಿ ಮುನ್ತಾದವುಗಳನ್ನು ಮಾಡುವರು, that sheet of glass they cut according to the various requirements, and make window-panes, etc. (of it). ಬಡಿಗೆಯವನು ಕಟ್ಟಿಗೆಗಳನ್ನು ಕೊರೆದು ಕೆತ್ತಿ ಬೇಕು ಬೇಕಾದ ಹಾಗೆ ಜೋಡಿಸಿ ಕೊಳ್ಳ ಬೇಕು, the carpenter has to cut the pieces of wood, to plane (them) and to join (them) according to the various requirements. ಕರಾಚೀ ಹತ್ತರದ ಹಳ್ಳಿಯವರು ಮೊಸಳೆಗಳನ್ನು ಪೂಜಿಸುತ್ತಿದ್ದರು; ಅವುಗಳಿಗೆ ಬೇಕು ಬೇಕಾದನ್ಥ ಸವಿ ಸವಿ ಆಹಾರಗಳನ್ನು ಒಯಿದು ನೈವೇದ್ಯ

ಕೊಡುತ್ತಿದ್ದರು, the villagers near Karâči used to worship alligators; they took, according to the various circumstances, different sweet eatables to them and presented them as offerings.

340. Certain verbs are often (especially in the colloquial dialect) combined with others, being placed after their past participle (gerund). They are principally the following: —

1, ಆಡು, to play, which gives the preceding verb the meaning of

a) playful motion or action, *e. g.* ಹುಡುಗರು ಕುಣಿದಾಡುತ್ತಾರೆ, ಒದಱಾಡುತ್ತಾರೆ, ಚೀ ಆಡುತ್ತಾರೆ, boys dance, cry and scream. ಒಣಗಿದ ಎಲೆ ಉದುರುವಾಗ್ಯೆ ಹಸಿಯೆಲೆ ನಗಾಡುತ್ತದೆ, when the dry leaves drop, the green leaves laugh. ಸರೋವರದೊಳ್ ಅಬಲೆಯರ್ ನಲವಿನ್ದೆ ಮುೞುಕಾಡಿದರ್, the women joyfully immersed themselves in the pond. ಕತ್ತೆ ಹೊರಳಾಡುತ್ತದೆ, the ass wallows.

b) moving here and there or about, *e. g.* ಹಾವು ಹರಿದಾಡುತ್ತದೆ, the serpent creeps about. ನಾಯಿಯ ಕುನ್ನಿಗಳು ಒನ್ದೆರಡು ತಿಂಗಳಿಗೆ ಚನ್ನಾಗಿ ಓಡಾಡ ಹತ್ತುತ್ತವೆ, young dogs begin to run about well in one or two months. ಆ ಜನರು ತಿರಿಗಾಡುತ್ತಾರೆ, those people wander (or walk) about. ಕಳ್ಳರು ಸುೞಿದಾಡುತ್ತಾರೆ, thieves roam about. ಹಕ್ಕಿ ಹಾಱಾಡುತ್ತವೆ, birds fly about.

c) moving backward and forward, moving to and fro as a body suspended, oscillation, waving, *e. g.* ಜೋಕಾಲೆ ತೂಗಾಡುತ್ತದೆ, the swing moves to and fro. ತೆನೆಗಳು ಒಲೆದಾಡುತ್ತವೆ, the ears of corn move. ತೂಕವಿದ್ದದ್ದು ತೂಗ್ಯಾಡೀತೇ, does that which is poised, oscillate? ಕೊರಳಲ್ಲಿ ನೇತಾಡುವ ಒಡವೆ, a pendulous ornament depending from the neck.

d) reciprocal motion done by one (or each) to the other: mutuality, *e. g.* ಚೂಣಿಯೊಳ್ ಬೆರಸಿ ಪೊಯ್ದಾಡಿದರ್, they met in the van and beat each other. ರಾಮ ರಾವಣರು ಹೊಡೆದಾಡುತ್ತಾರೆ, Râma and Râvaṇa beat one another. ಅವರಿಬ್ಬರು ಬಯ್ದಾಡುತ್ತಾರೆ, they revile each other. (Peculiar is ಮಾಱಾಡು, to exchange one thing for another; to sell).

It may be remarked here that ಆಡು is also suffixed to the infinitive ending in ಅಲ್ and ಅ, *e. g.* ನಳನು ಜೂಜಿನಿನ್ದ ರಾಜ್ಯವನ್ನು ಹೋಗಲಾಡಿದನು, Naḷa made (his) kingdom to go (*i. e.* lost his kingdom) by gambling. ರಥಗಳು ತಾಕಲಾಡಿದವು, the chariots struck one against the other. ಮಾನವಂ ಹೋಗಾಡಿದಂ, he made to go (*i. e.* lost his) honour.

2, ಇಡು, to put, which makes the idea of the preceding verb, so to say, complete, *e. g.* ಅಜ್ಞಾನಿಗಳು ವಿದ್ಯೆಯನ್ನು ಮುಚ್ಚಿಡುತ್ತಾರೆ, stupid persons completely hide learning from sight. ಲುಬ್ಧರು ಹಣವನ್ನು ಹೂೞಿಡುತ್ತಾರೆ, greedy persons bury (their) money. ತಾನು ಕಣ್ಡದನ್ನೂ ಕೇಳಿದ್ದನ್ನೂ ವಿಚಾರದಿನ್ದ ಬರೆದಿಟ್ಟನು, he wrote down with deliberation what he saw and heard.

3, **ಕುಡು, ಕೊಡು**, to give, which occasionally, to some extent, complete the idea of the preceding verb, *e.g.* ಪದದೊಳ್ ಇರ್ದರ್ಥಮಂ ತಮ್ಮತಮ್ಮರ್ಥಾನುಗುಣಮಾಗೆ ವಿಭಾಗಿಸಿ ಕುಡುವದಱಿಂ ವಿಭಕ್ತಿಗಳೆನಿಸುಗುಂ, from separating the meaning which is in a word, into species according to their various purposes, the vibhaktis (inflections) have got their name (Šabdamaṇi-darpaṇa, vṛitti to sûtra 35; in this case ಕುಡು is superfluous, as is shown by Kêšava's sûtra which has only ಪದಾರ್ಥಮಂ ವಿಭಾಗಿಸುವದಱಿನ್ದೆ ವಿಭಕ್ತಿ). ನೀನ್ ಎನಗೆ ವಸನ್ತನಾಗಮನವಂ ನೆಱೆ ಸೂಚಿಸಿ ಕೊಟ್ಟಯ್, thou indicatedst the arrival of spring to me very nicely. ರಾಮನು ಕೃಷ್ಣನಿಗೆ ಲೆಕ್ಕವ ತಿಳಿಸಿ ಕೊಟ್ಟನು, Râma ṃade known arithmetic to Kṛishṇa. ಅವನು ನಿನಗೆ ಹೇೞಿ ಕೊಡುತ್ತಾನೆ, he tells thee. ಕುದುರೆಯು ಕಣ್ಬಲೆಯನ್ನು ಒಕ್ಕೊಟ್ಟಿತು (for ಒಗೆದು ಕೊಟ್ಟಿತು), the horse threw the double bag off (from its back). ಅದು (ಆ ಬೆಲ್ಲ) ತುಸು ಎನ್ದು ತಿಳಿದು, ಅದನ್ನು ಚೆಲ್ಲಿ ಕೊಟ್ಟನು, he thought that it (the piece of jaggory was) small, and threw it away.

4, **ಬರು** (ಬರ್), to come, which sometimes is used to complete the idea of the preceding verb, *e. g.* ಜವೆ ಅಱುವತ್ತು ದಿನಕ್ಕೆ ಬೆಳೆದು ಬಹ ಭೂಮಿ, a soil in which barley ripens in sixty days. ಮಹಾಸಾಗರದ ಆೞವು ಕೆಲವು ಕಡೆಯಲ್ಲಿ ಒಮ್ಬತ್ತು ಮೆಯ್ಲು ಇದ್ದನ್ತೆ ಕಣ್ಡು ಬನ್ದಿರುತ್ತದೆ, it has appeared that the depth of the ocean in some places is nine miles. ಮಹಾಸಾಗರದಲ್ಲಿಯು ಬೆಟ್ಟಗಳ ಶಿರೋಭಾಗಗಳು ಬಹಳ ಸ್ಥಳದಲ್ಲಿ ನೀರ ಮೇಲೆ ಕಣ್ಡು ಬರುತ್ತವೆ, the tops of mountains in the ocean in many places appear above the water.

It may be remarked that to say *e. g.* ಅಮ್ಮಾ, ಹೋಗುತ್ತೇನೆ, is unidiomatic in colloquial language, it is to be ಅಮ್ಮಾ, ಹೋಗಿ ಬರುತ್ತೇನೆ, mother, I go and come (back).

5, **ಬಿಡು**, to leave, which also makes the idea of the preceding verb somehow complete, *e. g.* ಅವನು ಹೆಣ್ಡತಿಯನ್ನು ಬಿಟ್ಟು ಬಿಟ್ಟನು, he left (his) wife. ರಾಮನು ವ್ಯಾಕರಣವನ್ನು ಕಲಿತು ಬಿಟ್ಟನು, Râma learned grammar. ಅದನ್ನು ಕೊನ್ದು ಬಿಡುತ್ತೇನೆ, I shall kill it. ಅವನು ಹೋಗಿ ಬಿಟ್ಟನು, he went away. ಕುದುರೆಯನ್ನು ಮಾಱಿ ಬಿಟ್ಟನು, he sold the horse.

6, **ಹಾಕು**, to put, to throw, which also makes the idea of the preceding verb somehow complete, *e. g.* ಇವನನ್ನು ವರ್ಗದೊಳಗಿನ್ದ ತೆಗೆದು ಹಾಕಿದರು, they removed him out of the class. ಬಾಯ್ಬಡಕರು ಅನ್ಯರ ವಸ್ತುಗಳನ್ನು

ಎತ್ತಿ ಹಾಕುತ್ತಾರೆ, great talkers remove the things of others by stealing. ಭೀಮನು ಕೌರವರನ್ನು ಕೊನ್ದು ಹಾಕಿದನು, Bhîma killed the Kauravas. ಕಟ್ಟಿಗೆಗಳನ್ನು ಮುಱಿದು ಹಾಕಿದರು, they broke the pieces of wood. ನಾಯಿಗಳನ್ನು ಒನ್ದು ಗಿಡಕ್ಕೆ ಕಟ್ಟಿ ಹಾಕಿದರು, they tied the dogs to a tree.

7, ಹೋಗು, to go, which likewise makes the idea of the preceding verb somehow complete, *e. g.* ಲೆಕ್ಕವು ತಪ್ಪಿ ಹೋಯಿತು, the account is wrong. ದುಷ್ಟರು ಹಾೞಾಗಿ ಹೋಗುತ್ತಾರೆ, bad people will be ruined. ಕಿಸೆಯ ಒನ್ದು ತೂತಿನೊಳಗಿನ್ದ ದುಡ್ಡು ಬಿದ್ದು ಹೋದವು, the duḍḍus fell out of a hole in (his) pocket. ಕುದುರೆ ಕನ್ದಕದೊಳಗೆ ಬಿದ್ದು ಸತ್ತು ಹೋಯಿತು, the horse fell into a ditch and died. ಮಾತು ಬನ್ದಾಗ ಸೋತು ಹೋಗುವವನೇ ಜಾಣ, when a dispute comes on, even he is a wise man who submits. ಕೆಟ್ಟು ಹೋಗುವ ಹಾಗಿದ್ದಾನೆ, he is likely to be ruined.

341. In order to form what may be called **a sort of reflexive verb,** ಕೊಳ್ (ಕೊಳ್ಳು), to take, **is added to the past participle of a preceding verb** (to that of ಕೊಳ್ itself too), **also if this participle is a short one** (see § 165, *a*, 1—7, and *cf.* § 169). We have already met with this kind of formation in the passive (see § 315, 2, *e*; *cf.* also § 260). This so-called reflexive verb is used to denote that the action takes place in behalf of the subject (agent), regarding the subject's good or damage, and so on as circumstances require; it will be seen that 'to take', the original meaning of ಕೊಳ್, will not unfrequently offer a sufficiently clear explanation of its meaning.

The following instances taken from the three dialects will elucidate its use:—

ಈ ಕ್ರಮದಿನ್ ಅಱಿದು ಕೊಳ್ಗೆ, in this order one may learn to know (the terminations of the instrumental).—ಕಮಲಮುಖೀ, ತಿಳಿದು ಕೊಳ್ವುದೆನ್ನಯ ಮತದಿಂ, O wife, understand (the daṇḍaka metre) even through my rule. ಮೂಕರು ಮೋಸಗಾಱರಿರುತ್ತಾರೆನ್ದು ಹೆಡ್ಡರು ತಿಳಿಯುತ್ತಾರೆ; ಅದಱನ್ತೆಯೇ ಈ ತೊತ್ತು ಆದರೂ ತಿಳು ಕೊಣ್ಡಳು, foolish people think that the dumb are tricksters; thus also this maid-servant thought. ಗೂಗೆಗಳು ಕೂಗಿದರೆ ಕೇಡಾಗುವದೆನ್ದು ಬುದ್ಧಿಹೀನರು ತಿಳ ಕೊಣ್ಡು ಹೆದಱುತ್ತಾರೆ, foolish persons think that if owls cry, evil will happen, and are afraid. ಬಿಸಲೊಳಗೆ ದಾರಿ ನಡೆದು, ದಣಿದು, ನೀರಡಿಸಿ, ಒಬ್ಬ ಬ್ರಾಹ್ಮಣನು ಒನ್ದು ಈಚಲ ಮರದ ನೆರಳಿಗೆ ಹೋಗಿ, ಕುಳಿತು ಕೊಣ್ಡು, ತಮ್ಬಿಗೆಯೊಳಗಿನ ಹಾಲು ಕುಡಿಯ ಹತ್ತಿದನು; ಅದನ್ನು ಎರಡನೇ ದಾರಿಕಾಱರು ನೋಡಿ, ಈ ಹಾರುವನು ಹೆಣ್ಡ ಕುಡಿಯುತ್ತಾನೆನ್ದು ತಿಳು ಕೊಣ್ಡು, ಊರೊಳಗೆ ಸುದ್ದೀ ಬೀಱಿದರು, a Brâhmaṇa who had travelled in the hot sun, felt fatigued and had become thirsty, went to the shade of a wild date tree, sat down and began to drink the milk that was in (his) copper vessel; other travellers saw it, thought "this Brâhmaṇa drinks toddy", and spread the news in the town.—ತಾವೆ ಕೃಪಾಶೂನ್ಯರೆನ್ದು ನಿನ್ದಿಸಿ ಕೊಣ್ಡರ್, even they blamed themselves that they (were) destitute of pity.—ಪರರಿಗೆ ಕೇಡ ಮಾಡಿ ತನಗೆ ಲೇಸು ಮಾಡಿ ಕೊಳ್ಳುಹ, causing damage to others and causing welfare to one's self. ಮಾಡಿ ಕೊಣ್ಡ ನಣ್ಬನು, a friend that one has acquired. ಒನ್ದು ಕತ್ತಿ ಮಾಡಿ ಕೊಣ್ಡನು, he made himself a knife. ಅವನು ತನಗೆ ತಾನೇ ನೋವು ಮಾಡಿ ಕೊಳ್ಳುತ್ತಿದ್ಧಾನೆ, he is hurting even himself. ರಾಮಾ, ನಿನ್ನ ಕಾಲಿಗೆ ಏನು ಮಾಡಿ ಕೊಣ್ಡೆ, Râma, what hast thou done to thy foot? ಇವನು ರಾಜಕನ್ನಿಕೆಯನ್ನು ಮದುವೆ ಮಾಡಿ ಕೊಣ್ಡನು, he married a king's daughter. ಆ ಗುಬ್ಬಿ ಎಲ್ಲಿ ಮನೆ ಮಾಡಿ ಕೊಣ್ಡು ಇರುತ್ತದೆ? ನಮ್ಮ ಮನೆಯ ಮಾಳಿಗೆಯ ಕುಮ್ಬೇ ಮೇಲೆ ಗೂಡು ಕಟ್ಟಿ ಕೊಣ್ಡು ಇರುತ್ತದೆ, where has that sparrow made (its) house? it has built (its) nest on the balustrade of the flat roof of our house. ಒಡವೆಗಳನ್ನು ಮಾರಿ ಹಣ ಮಾಡಿ ಕೊಣ್ಡನು, he sold (his) jewels and (thus) made money. ಈ ಹುಡುಗನು ಕಣ್ಡ ಹುಡುಗರನ್ನೆಲ್ಲ ಗೆಳೆಯರನ್ನು ಮಾಡಿ ಕೊಳ್ಳ ಬೇಕೆನ್ದು ಬಹು ಆತುರ ಪಡುತ್ತಿದ್ದನು, this boy felt great desire to make all the boys he saw his friends.—ವಸಿಷ್ಠ ಪುತ್ರ ಶೋಕದಿನ್ದ ಕೊರಳಲ್ಲಿ ಕಲ್ಲ ಕಟ್ಟಿ ಕೊಣ್ಡು ಬಿದ್ದರೆ ನೂಱು ತೆಱನಾದ ನದಿ, the river which became a hundred branches when the son of Vasishṭha, from sorrow, tied a stone to (his) neck and fell (into it). ಸಪ್ತದ್ವೀಪಗಳಂ ಕಟ್ಟಿ ಕೊಣ್ಡು, having made the seven divisions of the terrestrial world his own.—ಮುಸುಡನ್ ಎತ್ತಿ ಕೊಣ್ಡು ಇರ್ಪ ವನು, he who has lifted up (his) face.—ಕೞದು ಕೊಳುಹ, grasping (for one's self). ಒಬ್ಬ ಸಾವಕಾರನು ವ್ಯಾಪಾರದೊಳಗೆ ಎಲ್ಲ ಹಣ ಕಳ ಕೊಣ್ಡನು, a certain merchant lost all (his) money in trade. ನೀವು ಒನ್ದು ಒಣ್ಟೆಯನ್ನು ಕಳ ಕೊಣ್ಡನ್ತೆ ತೋಱುತ್ತದೆ, it seems as if you had lost a camel.—ಪರರರ್ಥವ ಸೆಳೆದು ಕೊಮ್ಬ ಪಾತಕತನಂ, the sin of robbing the things of others.—ತನ್ನ ಸೋಲವ ನುಡಿದು ಕೊಮ್ಬಂ, he who confesses his being overcome.—ರಾಮನು ಪುಸ್ತಕವನ್ನು ಓದಿ ಕೊಳ್ಳುತ್ತಾನೆ, Râma reads a book (for his own benefit).—ನಾನು ಈ ಚೂರಿಯ ನ್ನ ನಾರಾಯಣನ ಗಣ್ಟು ಬಿಚ್ಚಿ ತೆಕ್ಕೊಣ್ಡೆನು, I opened the bundle of Nârâyaṇa and took his knife (to myself).—ಆ ಹಾಲು ಮಾಱಿ ಕೊಣ್ಡು ಅವನು ಹೊಟ್ಟೆ ತುಮ್ಬಿ ಕೊಣ್ಡನು, he sold that milk and (thus) satisfied the wants of (his) stomach.—ಕಟ್ಟ ಕಡೆಯಲ್ಲಿ ಅವನು ತನ್ನನ್ನೇ ಮಾಱಿ ಕೊಣ್ಡನು, at last he sold even himself.—ಪುಸ್ತಕ ಕೊಣ್ಡು ಬರುವೆನು, I shall buy a book (for myself) and return.—ರೊಕ್ಕಾ ಕೊಟ್ಟು ಕೊಣ್ಡು ಹೀಗೆ ಕೆಡಿಸಿದರೆ ನಮಗೇ ಕೇಡು, if you thus wastefully spend money (in your own behalf), it will be even our ruin.—

ಸಿಪಾಯಿಯ ಮಗನು ತನ್ದೆಯ ಹದನಾದ ಕತ್ತಿಯನ್ನು ತಕ್ಕೊಣ್ಡು, ಪಲ್ಲೆ ಹೆಚ್ಚಲಿಕ್ಕೆ ಹೋಗಿ, ತನ್ನ ಬೊಟ್ಟು ಕೊಯಿದು ಕೊಣ್ಡನು, the native soldier's son took the sharp sword of his father, went to mince vegetables (with it) and (in doing so) cut off one of his fingers.— ನೀನು ಎದೆ ಬಡ ಕೊಣ್ಡು ಚಿನ್ತೆ ಮಾಡ ಬೇಡ, you must not (thus) beat your chest and grieve.— ಬೆಳಿಗ್ಗೆ ಕುಱಿಗಳನ್ನು ಹೊಡ ಕೊಣ್ಡು ಹೋಗಿ ಅಡವಿಯೊಳಗಿನ ಗಿಡ ಗಣ್ಟೆಗಳನ್ನು ಮೇಯಿಸಿದನು, at dawn he drove (his) sheep to the jungle and made them eat the shrubs therein.— ಸಿಂಹಗಳೂ ಹುಲಿಗಳೂ ನನ್ನನ್ನು ಕಣ್ಡು ತಮ್ಮ ತಮ್ಮ ಗವಿಗಳೊಳಗೆ ಹಗಲೆಲ್ಲ ಮಲಗಿ ಕೊಳ್ಳುತ್ತವೆ, when lions and tigers see me (the sun), they lie down the whole day in their respective dens. ಪೂರ್ವರಾತ್ರೆಯಲ್ಲಿ ಬೇಗ ಮಲಗಿ ಕೊಣ್ಡು ಬೆಳಗ್ಗೆ ಬೇಗ ಏೞುವದು ಬಹಳ ಹಿತವು, it is very salutary to lie down (to sleep) quickly (early) in the first part of the night and to rise quickly (early) at dawn.— ಹೊದ್ದು ಕೊಮ್ಬ ಸೀರೆ, a garment that is wrapped round one's self. ಅವನಿಗೆ ಹೊದ್ದು ಕೊಳ್ಳಲಿಕ್ಕೆ ಅಱುವೆ ಅಂಚಡಿ ಇದ್ದಿಲ್ಲ, he had no cloth whatever to cover himself with.— ಯಜಮಾನನು ಕೆಯ್ ಕಾಲು ತೊಳ ಕೊಳ್ಳಲಿಕ್ಕೆ ಎದ್ದನು, the master stood up to wash (his) hands and feet.— ಆಕಳು ಮೆಯ್ ಮೇಲೆ ಆಗಾಗ್ಗೆ ಬಾಲಾ ಯಾಕೆ ಬಡ ಕೊಳ್ಳುತ್ತದೆ? ನೊಣಾ ಜಾಡಿಸಿ ಕೊಳ್ಳುತ್ತದೆ, why does the cow now and then beat (with its) tail on (its) body? It drives the flies away.— ಮಱಿದುಮ್ಬಿಗಳ ವೃನ್ದಮಂ ಕೂಡಿ ಕೊಣ್ಡೆಳೆವೆಲರ್ ಬನ್ದುದು, the breeze joined a flock of young black bees and came along (with them).— ಕಾಲಿಗೆ ನೋವು ಆದದಱಿನ್ದ ಎಣ್ಟು ದಿವಸ ನಾನು ಸಾಲೆಗೆ ಹೋಗಲಾಱದೆ ಮನೆಯಲ್ಲಿಯೇ ನಿನ್ತು ಕೊಣ್ಡೆನು, because I had got pain in (my) feet, I could not go to school for eight days and remained at home.— ಅದು ಪಾನ್ಥಸ್ಥರು ಇೞಿ ಕೊಳ್ಳುವದಕ್ಕಾಗಿ ಕಟ್ಟಿದ ಧರ್ಮಛತ್ರವು, that is a house built with the object that travellers may alight (or lodge therein).— ಗಣ್ಡಾನ್ತರ ಬನ್ದಾಗ ಉೞಿ ಕೊಳ್ಳುವ ಹಂಚಿಕೆಗಳು ಏನಾದರೂ ನಿನಗೆ ಗೊತ್ತು? do you know any means by which one may escape when danger approaches.— ರಾಯನು ಒನ್ದು ಆನೇ ಮೇಲೆ ಕುಳಿತು ಕೊಣ್ಡು ವಿಜಯನಗರಕ್ಕೆ ಬನ್ದನು, the king took a seat on an elephant and came to Vijayanagara. ಮರದ ನೆರಳಿಗೆ ಹೋಗಿ ಕೂತು ಕೊಣ್ಡನು, he went to the shadow of a tree and sat down.— ಬೇನೆಯಿನ್ದ ದಣು ಕೊಣ್ಡವ, he who is exhausted by sickness.— ಒನ್ದು ಕತ್ತಿ ಮಾಡಿಸಿ ಕೊಣ್ಡನು, he had a knife made (for himself).— ತನ್ನನ್ನು ತಾನೇ ಕೆಡಿಸಿ ಕೊಣ್ಡನು, he ruined himself.— ಬೆಸನ ಹೇೞಿಸಿ ಕೊಳುಹ, obtaining permission. ಸಾಕ್ಷಿ ಹೇೞಿಸಿ ಕೊಣ್ಡನು, he got evidence (in his own interest).— ಒನ್ದು ಜಾತಿಯ ಚಿರ್ಚ ಸಮುದ್ರದ ದಣ್ಡೆಯಲ್ಲಿದ್ದು ಕೊಣ್ಡು, ಕೊಳಿಕ ಮಾಂಸ ಮುನ್ತಾದ್ದನ್ನು ತಿನ್ನುತ್ತವೆ, a kind of leopard lives on the sea-coast, and eats decayed flesh and other things.— ನಾಲ್ಕು ಮನ್ದಿ ಕಳ್ಳರು ಕೂಡಿ, ಪಟ್ಟಣಸೆಟ್ಟೀ ಮನೆಯ ಕನ್ನಾ ಕೊಱೆದು, ಇದ್ದ ವಸ್ತು ಒಡವೆಗಳನ್ನೆಲ್ಲ ಕದ್ದು ಕೊಣ್ಡು, ಹಂಚಿ ಕೊಳ್ಳುವದಕ್ಕೆ ಅಡವಿಯೊಳಗಿನದೊನ್ದು ಹಾೞು ದೇಗುಲದ ಹಾದೀ ಹಿಡಿದರು, four thieves united, made a hole (in the wall) of the house of the chief merchant, stole all the valuable things that were (there), and took the road to a dilapidated temple in the jungle in order to divide (them among themselves).— ದನ ಕಱು ಮುನ್ತಾದವುಗಳನ್ನು ಸರಿಯಾಗಿ ಮೂಱು ಪಾಲು ಮಾಡಿ ಹಂಚಿ ಕೊಳ್ಳಿರೆನ್ದು ವರ್ತಕನು ತನ್ನ ಮೂಱು ಮನ್ದಿ ಮಕ್ಕಳಿಗೆ ಹೇೞಿ, ಸತ್ತು ಹೋದನು, the merchant told his three children to make three equal parts of the cattle etc. and divide them (among themselves), and died.— ಆ ಹೆಂಗಸು ತಲೆಯ ಮೇಲೆ ಏನು ಹೊತ್ತು ಕೊಣ್ಡು ಬರುತ್ತಾಳೆ, what does that woman carry on (her) head and comes (here)?— ಹೆಣ್ಡತಿಯನ್ನು ಕರೆದು ಕೊಣ್ಡು, ಊರಿಗೆ ಹೊಱಟು ಹೋದನು, he called (his) wife and went abroad (with her).— ಕುದುರೆ ಕಣ್ಡು ಕೊಣ್ಡರೋ, did they find the horse?— ಅದನ್ನೆಲ್ಲಿ ಇಟ್ಟು ಕೊಣ್ಡಳು, where did she hoard it? ಈ ಕುದುರೆ ಇಟ್ಟು ಕೊಳ್ಳುತ್ತೀರೇನು, are you going to keep this horse?— ದೊಡ್ಡ ಹುಡುಗನು ತೊಟ್ಟು ಕೊಂಡ ಅಂಗಿ, the jacket which the big boy had put on.— ನೀವು ಯಾರಯ್ಯಾ? ಹುಚ್ಚು ನಾಯಿಗಳನ್ನು ಹಿಡ ಕೊಣ್ಡು ಎಲ್ಲಿಗೆ ಹೋಗುತ್ತೀರಿ? who are you, sir? where do you go having seized (*i. e.* with) the mad dogs? ಕೊಡ್ಲೀ ಹಿಡ ಕೊಣ್ಡು, ತೋಟಕ್ಕೆ ಬನ್ದನು, he seized the axe, and went to the garden. ಹಿಡು ಕೊಳ್ಳುವದು, seizing (laying hold of).— ಸಾಲೆಯಲ್ಲಿ ಅಯ್ಯನವರ ಅಪ್ಪಣೆಯನ್ತೆ ನಡ ಕೊಳ್ಳ ಬೇಕು, at school (one) must conduct one's self according to the command of the master. ನಾವು ತಾಯಿ ತನ್ದೆ ಅಕ್ಕ ತಂಗಿ ಅಣ್ಣ ತಮ್ಮನ್ದಿರ ಕೂಡ ಪ್ರೀತಿಯಿನ್ದ ನಡ ಕೊಳ್ಳ ಬೇಕು, we must converse in love with (our) parents, sisters and brothers. ಅವರೆಲ್ಲರ ಮೇಲೆ ಒಬ್ಬನೇ ಅರಸು ಆಳುತ್ತಿರುತ್ತಾನೆ; ಅವನಿಗೂ ಅವನು ನೇಮಿಸಿದ ಅಧಿಕಾರಿಗಳಿಗೂ ಅವರು ಭಯ ಭಕ್ತಿಯಿನ್ದ ನಡ ಕೊಳ್ಳ ಬೇಕು, over them all rules one king; they must obey him and the officers appointed by him with fear and devotion. ಮುಖ್ಯವಾದದೊನ್ದು ಕುದುರೆ ಹಿಣ್ಡಿನ ಮುನ್ದೆ ಇರುತ್ತದೆ, ಅದಱ ಸೂಚನೆಯನ್ತೆ ಎಲ್ಲ ಕುದುರೆಗಳು ನಡ ಕೊಳ್ಳುವವು, a chief horse is in front of the herd, all the horses follow its guidance.— ನಿಂಗಪ್ಪನು ಒಬ್ಬ ವೈದ್ಯನ ಮನೆಗೆ ಹೋಗಿ, ಅವನ ಕೆಯ್ ಕಾಲು ಬಿದ್ದು— ಸ್ವಾಮಿಾ, ನನ್ನ ಮಗನೊಬ್ಬನು ಮನೆಯಲ್ಲಿ ಬೇನೆಯಿನ್ದ ಮಲಗಿದ್ದಾನೆ; ಅದಕ್ಕೆ ದಯ ಮಾಡಿ ಮನೆತನಕ ಬನ್ದು, ಅವನನ್ನು ನೋಡಿ, ಔಷಧ ಕೊಟ್ಟರೆ ನಾನು ಬಾೞುರುವ ಮಟ್ಟಿಗೆ ತಮ್ಮ ಉಪಕಾರ ಮಱೆಯಲಿಕ್ಕಿಲ್ಲ ಎನ್ದು, ಹೇೞಿ ಕೊಣ್ಡನು, Niṅgappa went to the house of a physician, fell at his hands and feet, and spoke "sir, a son of mine lies prostrate in the house from sickness; if therefore you please to come to (my) house, examine him and give (him) medicine,

I shall not forget your kindness as long as I live". ಹೊನ್ನನು — ವೈದ್ಯನೇ, ಸುಮ್ಮನೇ ಔಷಧಗಳನ್ನು ಯಾಕೆ ತರಿಸುತ್ತೀರಿ? ನಾನು ಅವನ್ನು ಎನ್ದಿಗೂ ತಕ್ಕೊಳ್ಳುವದಿಲ್ಲ ಎನ್ದು, ಏಚ್ಛಿನ್ನವಾಗಿ ಹೇೞಿದನು. ಆಗ ವೈದ್ಯನು ಯಾಕೆ ತಕ್ಕೊಳ್ಳುವದಿಲ್ಲ ಎನ್ದು ಕೇಳಲು— ದಯ ಮಾಡಿ ಆ ಮಾತು ಕೇಳ ಬೇಡರಿ! ನಾನು ಹೇೞಿಲಾಱೆನು ಎನ್ದು, ಸುಮ್ಮನಾದನು. ಅದಕ್ಕೆ ವೈದ್ಯನು — ಏನಯ್ಯಾ? ಹೇೞುವದಕ್ಕೆ ಅಡ್ಡಿಯೇನು? ನೀನು ಒಳ್ಳೇ ಹಟಮಾರಿ ಕಾಣುತ್ತೀ ಅನ್ನಲು, ಹೊನ್ನನು — ಸ್ವಾಮಿಾ, ದಯ ಮಾಡಿ ಹಾಗೆ ಮಾತ್ರ ತಿಳಿಯ ಬೇಡರಿ! ಎನ್ದು, ವಿನಯದಿನ್ದ ಹೇೞಿ ಕೊಣ್ಡನು, "doctor", Hŏnna (Niṅgappa's son who was not sick, but nearly starved, as he refused to take any food himself in order that his poor father, brothers and sisters might have something to eat) said positively, "why do you send for medicines (on my account)? I shall never take them". Then the physician asked "why will you not take (them)?" Hŏnna answered "please, do not ask so. I cannot tell (you)", and became silent. Thereupon the physician said "sir, what obstacle is there to telling (me)? You seem to be a perfect obstinate fellow". Then Hŏnna entreated (him) with humility, saying "O sir, please, only do not think so!" ಅವರಿಗೆ ಹೇೞಿ ಕೊಳ್ಳ ಬೇಕು, you should speak to him. ಹೇೞಿ ಕೊಳ್ಳಲಿಕ್ಕೆ ಮಾತದೆ, I have something to say (to you).— ಬೇಡಿ ಕೊಣ್ಡು ತಿನ್ನ ಬಹುದು, ಕದ್ದು ಕೊಣ್ಡು ತಿನ್ನ ಬಾರದು, one may solicit (and receive alms) and (thus) eat, (but) by stealing one should not eat.— ನಾನು ತಲೆಯ ಮೇಲೆ ಕಿರೀಟ ಹಾಕಿ ಕೊಣ್ಡು, (the sun says) "I having put a diadem on (my) head". ದಯ ಮಾಡಿ ಇದೊನ್ದು ಸಾರಿ ಆತನ ತಪ್ಪು ಹೊಟ್ಟೆಯೊಳಗೆ ಹಾಕಿ ಕೋ, please, put his fault in your belly (*i. e.* conceal and forgive it) this one time.— ಆ ಆನೆಯನ್ನು ಆತನು ಹತ್ತಿ ಕೊಣ್ಡು, ತಿರಿಗಿ ಆನೆಗುನ್ದಿಗೆ ಹೋದನು, he mounted that elephant and returned to Ânĕgundi.— ಮೋಡವೆಮ್ಬ ಶೆಲ್ಲೆಯನ್ನು ತಲೆಗೆ ಸುತ್ತಿ ಕೊಳ್ಳುತ್ತೇನೆ, (the sun says) "I put a muslin cloth, that is to say clouds, round (my) head".

For comparison's sake the following instances which contain verbs without ಕೊಳ್ (and of which some show at first sight a not easily perceivable difference in meaning from the above-given ones) may here be introduced:—

ರೂಢಾನ್ವರ್ಥಾಂಕಿತಮ್ ಎನ್ದು ನಾಮಂ ಮೂಱೆಱಮ್, ಅಱಿಗೆ (commentator ತಿಳಿಗೆ), those ready nouns are of three kinds, *viz.* rûḍha, anvartha, aṅkita; know!—ನಲ್ಲಳೆ, ನಿನ್ನ ಕಾಲ್ವಿಡಿದಪೆಂ, ತಿಳಿ, O beloved woman, I seize thy feet; know! ತಂಗಿಗೆ ತಕ್ಕ ವರನ್ ಈತನೆನ್ದು, ಮದನಂ ತಿಳಿದಂ, Madana perceived that this man (was) a suitable husband for (his) younger sister. ತರಲಾಕ್ಷಿಯದಕ್ಕೆ ಮತ್ತೊನ್ದಭಿಪ್ರಾಯಮಂ ತಿಳಿದಳ್, the woman with tremulous eyes understood it differently. ಅತಿಜೀವಮ್ ಇರಲು ಮೋಕ್ಷದ ಗೊತ್ತು ತಿಳಿ, whilst yet living learn the marked peculiarities of final liberation!— ಮನೆಯಂ

ಮಾಡಿದಂ, he made a house. ಆವ್ ಎಲ್ಲರ್ ಈಗಳ್ ಅಶ್ವಮೇಧವಂ ಮಾಡುವಂ, let all of us now make a horse-sacrifice! ಸ್ನಾನ ಮಾಡಿರೊ ಜ್ಞಾನತೀರ್ಥದಲಿ, bathe in the sacred water of knowledge! ಮನೆ ಕಟ್ಟಿ ನೋಡು, ಮದುವೆ ಮಾಡಿ ನೋಡು, build a house and (then) see, marry (*i. e.* unite in wedlock) and (then) see! ಒನ್ದೆಡೆಯೊಳ್ ಕಟ್ಟುವುದೆ ಪಿರಿಯ ಪುಲಿಯುಮಂ ಕವಿಲೆಯುಮಂ, must (one) tie a royal tiger and a brown cow in one place? ಆಳು ಕಟ್ಟಿದವನೇ ಅರಸು, ಕೂೞು ಇಕ್ಕಿದವನೇ ದಾತ, one who has enlisted soldiers (is) a king, one who has distributed boiled rice (is) a donor.— ಮಾವನ ಮನೆಯೊಳ್ ಆಂ ತಲೆಯೆತ್ತಿ ನಡೆಯೆಂ, I shall not lift up (my) head and walk in my uncle's house.— ತಕ್ಕ ಔಷಧ ಕೊಡಿಸಿ, ಪಥ್ಯ ಮಾಡಿಸಿ, ಬೇಗ ಅವರ ಬೇನೆಯನ್ನು ಕಳೆಯುವರು, they will have proper medicine given, have diet prescribed, and quickly remove their sickness.— ಬಾಣಮಂ ಸೆಳೆದಂ, having pulled an arrow (out of his quiver).—ಸತ್ಯಮಂ ನುಡಿ, speak the truth! ಸೋಲೆ ನುಡಿವವನು, he who acknowledges that (he) has been overcome.— ವೇದವನ್ ಓದಿದಾತನು, he who has read the vêdas. — ತೆಗೆದಯ್ ಮೋಕ್ಷದ ಬಟ್ಟೆಯಂ, thou tookest the road of final liberation.— ಹೆಣನೊಳ್ ಪ್ರಾಣಮಂ ತುಮ್ಬುವ ಸಮರ್ಥಿಕೆ, power which fills life into a corpse.— ಕಳ್ಳ ಮಾಱುವ ಗೃಹ, a house in which toddy is sold. ಈ ಆನೆಗಳನ್ನು ಯಾರಿಗೂ ಮಾಱ ಬೇಡಿರಿ, you should not sell these elephants to anybody.— ಸಾಲವ ಕೊಮ್ಬುವನು, he who borrows. ಮದ್ಯವ ಕೊಮ್ಬ ಠಾವು, a place where spirits are bought. ನಾನು ಒನ್ದು ಕುದುರೆ ಕೊಳ್ಳ ಬೇಕು, I must buy a horse. ಎರಡು ದುಡ್ಡಿನ ಹಾಲು ಕೊಣ್ಡನು, he bought milk for two duḍḍus. — ಕಾಮವಸ್ತುಗಳಂ ಕುಡುವುದು, granting the things desired. ಕೊಟ್ಟು ಕೆಟ್ಟವನಿಲ್ಲ, ತಿರಿದು ಬದುಕಿದವನಿಲ್ಲ, (there) is none who has given (alms, etc.) and (thus) been ruined, (there) is none who has (idly) roamed about (in quest of alms) and (thus) lived (happily). — ಕೊಯ್ದ ಕಾಲನ್ನು ನಾಯಿ ತಿನ್ದರೇನು? ನರಿ ತಿನ್ದರೇನು? what does it matter whether a dog eats the leg that has been cut off, or whether a jackal eats (it)? ಮೂಗು ಕೊಯಿದರೂ ಮೂಗಿನ ಸೊಳ್ಳೆ ಉಣ್ಟಲ್ಲ? ಅನ್ದ ಹಾಗೆ, as if (one) said "though (one's) nose be cut off, do not the nostrils remain?"— ಒಬ್ಬ ಕೂಲಿಕಾಱನು ತನ್ನ ಹೆಣ್ಡತಿಯನ್ನು ಆಗಾಗ್ಗೆ ಬಡಿಯುವನು, a day-labourer used to beat his (quarrelsome) wife repeatedly. — ಬೆತ್ತದ ಪೆಟ್ಟು ಹೆತ್ತವರು ಹೊಡೆದರೆ ನೋಯದೇ, if (one's) parents apply the blows with a cane, do they not pain? — ಕುಳ್ಳಿರಲಱಿಯದೆ ಮೇಲು ಮೊಗವಾಗಿ ಮಲಗಿಹ ಮಗವು, an infant that cannot (yet) sit up and lies with (its) face turned upwards. ಅಡವಿಯೊಳಗೆ ಒನ್ದು ಮರದ ಕೆಳಗೆ ಒನ್ದು ಹುಲೀ ಮಱಿಯು ಮಲಗಿತ್ತು, a young tiger lay in the jungle under a tree.— ಅಂಗಡೀ ಮಾಱಿ, ಗೊಂಗಡೀ ಹೊದ್ದ, he sold (his) shop and put on a blanket.— ಅವನ ತನ್ದೆಯು ಅವನಿಗೆ ಏನಾದರೂ ಕೊಣ್ಡು ತಿನ್ನು ಎನ್ದು ನಾಲ್ಕು ದುಡ್ಡು ಕೊಟ್ಟನು, his father gave him six duḍḍus, saying "buy something to eat!"— ಚನ್ದ್ರಹಾಸಂ ನಿದ್ರೆಯಂ ತ್ಯಜಿಸಿ, ಮೊಗದೊಳೆದು, ಮುಕ್ಕುಳಿಸಿದಂ, Čandrahâsa quitted sleep, washed (his) face, and rinsed his mouth. — ಆತನ ತಲೇ ಹುೞುಗಳನ್ನು ಜಾಡಿಸಿದೆನು, I dusted away the insects of his head (*i. e.* I beat him soundly). — ಬೆಳುದಿಂಗಳೊಡನೆ ಕೂಡಿದ ಇರುಳು, a night united with moonlight. ದಕಾರದೊಳ್ ಕೂಡಿದ ಯಕಾರಕ್ಕಂ ದ್ವಿತ್ವದ ಜಕಾರಮ್ ಅಕ್ಕುಂ, and the letter ಯ್ combined with ದ್ becomes ಜ್ಜ. — ನಿನ್ದು ಇರ್ದವ, a man who stands. ನಿನ್ದಂ, a man who stands. — ಮರದತ್ತಣಿನ್ದಿೞಿದಂ, he came down from the tree. ದಣ್ಡು ಇೞಿದಿದ್ದ ಸ್ಥಳ, a place where an army is encamped. — ಕಱು ತಾಯ ಬೞಿಯನ್ ಉೞಿಯದು, a calf does not leave the company of (its) mother. ಹುಟ್ಟೂರಿಂಗೆ ಉೞಿದವನೇ

ಗವುಡ, even he who has remained alive, is the chief officer of the ruined village.— ಪಱುಗೋಲೊಳ್ ಕುಳ್ಳಿರ್ದಂ, he sat down in the basket-boat. ಈ ಕಾನ್ತೆ ಚಿನ್ತೆಯಾಗುತ ಕುಸ್ತು, ನೋಮ್ಪಿಗಳಂ ಪಲವನ್ ಉಡ್ ನೋನ್ತು, ಬೇಸತ್ತಳ್, the wife sat in distress, performed several meritorious acts of devotion, and became dispirited (as these proved useless). ಈಚಲ ಮರದ ಕೆಳಗೆ ಕೂತು ಅಳೆ ಕುಡಿದ ಹಾಗೆ, as if (one) sits under a wild date tree and drinks buttermilk. ಗಣ್ಡಸು ಕೂತು ಕೆಟ್ಟನು, ಹೆಂಗಸು ತಿರುಗಿ ಕೆಟ್ಟಳು, the male sat (idly) and (thus) was ruined, the female roamed about and (thus) was ruined. ಈ ಬದುಕು ತಾವಿಬ್ಬರೇ ತಕ್ಕೊಳ್ಳ ಬೇಕೆನ್ದು ಹವಣಿಸಿ ಕೊಣ್ದು ಕುಳಿತಿದ್ದರು, they thought that even both of them should take this property to themselves, and sat (there in the jungle).— ಓಡಿ ಓಡಿ ಹುಡುಗ ದಣಿದರೂ ತನ್ದೆಗೆ ಎಚ್ಚರವೇ ಇಲ್ಲ, though the boy ran and ran and became tired, (his) father did not care at all.— ಒಬ್ಬ ಸಿಪಾಯಿಯು ಕಾಳಗಕ್ಕೆ ಹೋಗ ಬೇಕೆನ್ದು ಒನ್ದು ಬಹು ಹದನಾದ ಕತ್ತಿ ಮಾಡಿಸಿದ್ದನು, a native soldier having said "I must go to war", had had a very sharp sword made.— ಅವನು ಹೋದ ಹೋದಲ್ಲಿ ಮಸೀದಿಗಳನ್ನು ಕೆಡಿಸಿದನು, wherever he went, he destroyed the mosques. ತನ್ನ ಕೆಡಿಸಿದಂಗೆ ಕೇಡ ಮಾಡುಹ, (one) causing ruin to the man who has ruined him.— ಕವಿತೆಯಂ ಪೇೞಿಸಿದಂ, he had a poetic composition told.— ಬತ್ತಲೆಯಿರ್ದವಳು, she who is naked. ಇದ್ದ ತಂಗಳು ನನಗೆ ಇಕ್ಕು, give me the stale-food (thou) hast.— ಕದ್ದ ಕಳ್ಳನ ಮಾತು ಬದ್ದಮ್ ಆದರೆ ಏನು, what is it, if a thief's word (once) become true?— ಅಣ್ಣ ತಮ್ಮನ್ದಿರಾದರೂ ಹಣ್ಣು ಹಂಚಿ ಉಣ್ಣುತ್ತಾರೆ, even brothers divide a ripe fruit and eat.— ಹೊಱೆಯ ಹೊತ್ತು ಬದುಕುವವನು, a man who lives by carrying loads. ಕತ್ತೆ ಬಲ್ಲುದೆ ಹೊತ್ತ ಕಸ್ತೂರಿಯ ಪರಿಮಳವ, does a donkey know the fragrance of the musk it carries?— ಕರೆದರೆ ಉಣ್ಣು, if (one) invites (thee), eat. ಉಣ್ಣಲಿಕ್ಕೆ ಮನ್ದೀ ಕರೆಯ ಬೇಕು, (you) should invite people to dinner. ತನ್ನ ಆಳು ಕರೆದು, ಒನ್ದು ತಮ್ಬಿಗೆಯೊಳಗೆ ನೀರು ತುಮ್ಬಿ ಕೊಣ್ದು ಬಾ ಎನ್ದು, ಹೇೞಿದಳು, she called her servant and said "fill water into a brass vessel and bring (it)".— ಭಾನುವಂ ಕೌಶಿಕವು ಕಾಣ್ಬುದೇ, does an owl see the sun?— ಚಿತ್ತವಿಟ್ಟು ಕೇಳುವದು, to apply the mind to and listen. ಕಾಲ್ಚಕಪ್ಪಸವುನ್ ಇಟ್ಟು, ಸೀಸಕವುಂ ಸಿಂಗರಿಸಿ, having put on trowsers and embellished (their) helmets.— ಕನತ್ಕನಕಕವಚಮುಂ ತೊಟ್ಟು, ಕಾಲ್ಚಕಪ್ಪಸವುನ್ ಇಟ್ಟು, having invested themselves with shining golden coats of mail and put on trowsers. ತುಡಿಗೆಯುಂ ತೊಟ್ಟಂ, he put on (his) ornaments. ಪಸುರಂಗಿಯುಂ ತೊಟ್ಟನು, he put on a green coat.— ಮೃಗಂಗಳಂ ಹಿಡಿವ ಬಲೆ, a net with which wild animals are caught.— ಮೂಗಾವುದವುಂ ನಡೆದಂ, he walked three leagues. ಮನುಷ್ಯನು ಬದುಕಿ ಇರುವ ಮಟ್ಟಿಗೂ ಒಳ್ಳೇ ನಡತೆಯಿನ್ದ ನಡೆಯ ಬೇಕು, a person should walk very properly as long as he lives. ವಿದ್ಯೆ ಕಲಿತರೆ ಅವರು ನೀತಿಯಿನ್ದ ನಡೆಯುವರು, if (they) learn knowledge, they will walk properly. See an instance in this paragraph under 'to fear'.— ಮಣಿಯಗಾಱನಿಗೆ ದುಃಖ ಸುಖ ಹೇೞಿದರೆ ಮಣುವಿನ ಲೆಕ್ಕ ಬಿಟ್ಟಾನೇ, if (he) tells the maṇiyagâṟa (his) bad and good circumstances, will he not count the mounds? ತಾಯಿಯೆ, ನೀನಾದರೂ ಒನ್ದು ಹಂಚಿಕೆ ಹೇೞು ಎನ್ದು, ಬೇಡಿ ಕೊಣ್ಡಳು, she requested "mother, tell even you a means (to me)!"— ಕುರುಪತಿಯುಂ ವಿಷ್ಣು ಬೇಡಿದಂ ಧರೆಯರೆಯುಂ, Vishṇu asked the half of the land of the lord of the Kurus. ಈ ಮುದುಕ ಬಿಕ್ಕೆ ಬೇಡಿ ಕಾೞು ತರುತ್ತಾನೆ, this old man solicits alms and (thus) brings grain (to his house).— ಕಿಸೆಯೊಳಗೆ ಕೈಯ್ ಹಾಕಿ ನೋಡಲು ರೊಕ್ಕವಿದ್ದಿಲ್ಲ, when (he) put (his) hand into (his) pocket and examined, (there) was no money.— ಕಾಳಗದ ಬಣ್ಣಿಯುಂ

ಹತ್ತಿ ಪೊಡಹಂ, he who mounts a war-chariot and drives. ಕೋಟೆಯುಂ ಪತ್ತುವೆಂ, I shall ascend the fort. ತೆಂಗಿನ ಮರ ಯಾಕೆ ಹತ್ತುತ್ತಿ, why doest thou ascend the cocoa-nut tree? ಕುದುರೆಯನ್ನು ಹತ್ತುವ ಸವಾರ, a horseman who mounts a horse. — ಅಲ್ಲಿಯ ಪೆಣ್ಡಿರನ್ ಅಗ್ನಿ ಸುತ್ತಿದಂ, Agni surrounded the women of that place.

The terms that express 'to fear' generally appear without ಕೊಳ್, *e. g.* ಪಾಪಕ್ಕಂಜುಗುಂ ತಕ್ಕಂ, a worthy person fears sin. ಆ ಹುಡುಗನು ಅಂಜಿ, ತೋಳ ಬನ್ತಲೆ ತೋಳ ಬನ್ತು ಎನ್ದು, ಒದರಿದನು, the boy feared, and cried "the wolf has come, O the wolf has come!" ಕುದುರೆ ಕಡಿವಾಣಕ್ಕೆ ಅಳುಕುತ್ತದೆ, the horse is afraid of the bridle. ಆ ತೊತ್ತು ಹೆದರಿದಳು, that servant-maid was afraid. On the other hand there are also instances like the following one: — ದೇವರಿಗೆ ಅಂಜಿ ಕೊಣ್ಡು ಯಾವಾಗಲೂ ಒಳ್ಳೇ ರೀತಿಯಿನ್ದ ನಡೆದರೆ ಆತನು ನಮಗೆ ಸಹಾಯ ಮಾಡುವನು, if (we) fear God and always behave properly, He will help us. *Cf.* § 348, 6.

342. For the sake of emphasis ಉಣ್ಟು, is, is occasionally added to the end of a verb which appears in the form of a verbal noun, *e. g.* ಕೆಲವು ಗಿಡಗಳ ತೋಟೆಗಳಿನ್ದ ಸಹ ಕಾಗದ ಮಾಡುವದುಣ್ಟು, also of the bark of some trees (they) make paper. ಇರುಳು ಬೆಕ್ಕುಗಳಾಗಲಿ ಬೆಕ್ಕಿನ ಮರಿಗಳಾಗಲಿ ಸಿಕ್ಕಿದರೆ ಗೂಗೆಗಳು ಕಣ್ಣು ಕುಕ್ಕಿ ಅವುಗಳನ್ನು ಕೊಲ್ಲುವದುಣ್ಟು, if at night cats or young cats are met (by them), owls will peck (their) eyes and kill them. ಗುರುವಿನನ್ತೆ ಶಿಷ್ಯ ಎನ್ತ ಅನ್ನುವದುಣ್ಟು, (they) use to say "the pupil (is) like (his) spiritual teacher". ಹಿಂದುಸ್ಥಾನಕ್ಕೆ ಪರದೇಶಗಳಿನ್ದ ತರ ತರದ ಸರಕುಗಳು ಬರುವದುಣ್ಟು, various objects of commerce come from foreign countries to India. ಹಣ್ಡೆ ಈಯಿತೆಮ್ಬ ಮಾತು ಎನ್ನಾದರೂ ಸಮ್ಭವಿಸುವದುಂಟೊ, does it ever happen that a metal pot brings forth young? ಬ್ರಹ್ಮನು ಫಣೆಯಲ್ಲಿ ಬರದ ಬರಹ ತಪ್ಪುವದುಣ್ಟೇ, will the writing that Brahmâ has written on the forehead, fail?

XXV. On comparison.

343. In Kannaḍa **the comparative and superlative degrees** are expressed in the following way:—

1, **by the simple dative** (*cf.* § 348, 7), *e. g.*

a) ಲೋಕಕೀತನ್ ಅಧಿಕಂ, this man (is) excellent to the world, *i. e.* this man (is) most excellent in the world. ತಿಮಿಂಗಿಲಾದಿಗಳ್ ಅದೊನ್ದಕ್ಕೊನ್ದು ಪಿರಿದಪ್ಪ ಮೀನು, the timingila and so on are fishes of which the one is large to the one, *i. e.* of which one is larger than the other. ಒನ್ದಕ್ಕೊನ್ದು ಪಿರಿಯವಪ್ಪ ಮೀನು, fishes of which one is larger than the other.

b) ಮೇರುವೆಂಗೀತನ್ ಅಗ್ಗಳಂ, this man (is) great (or high) to Mêru, *i. e.* higher than Mêru. ಕುಲಕಂ ಚಲಕಂ ಭೂತಳದೊಳ್ ಅಗ್ಗಮ್ ಅಧಿಕಂ, superior to all in the world as to family and firmness of character (see § 284). ಸೊಲ್ಲಿಸಿ ಭೇದವನ್ ಅಱಿದೊಡೆ ಕಿಱಿಯು ತಾನ್ ಎಲ್ಲರಿಗೆ ಹಿರಿಯು, the small one, if (he) speaks discriminately, (is) great to all, *i. e.* (is) greater than all (or the greatest of all). ಕಾಗೆಗೆ ನೇರಿಲ ಹಣ್ಣು ಕಪ್ಪು, the ripe fruit of the *Eugenia jambolana* (is) black to, *i. e.* blacker than, the crow. ನನ್ನ ಕುದುರೆಗೆ ನಿನ್ನ ಕುದುರೆ ದೊಡ್ಡದು, thy horse (is) larger than mine. (*Cf.* the second verse in § 280.)

c) ತನಗೆ ಇದಕ್ಕೂ ಬಹಳ ಬೆಲ್ಲ ಬೇಕೆನ್ದನು, he said he wanted much more jaggory than even this. ನಾಗರ ಹಾವಿನ ವಿಷವು ಎಲ್ಲಕ್ಕೂ ಕೆಟ್ಟದು, the poison of the cobra (is) the worst of all. ಗೋಧೀ ರೊಟ್ಟಿ ಎಲ್ಲಕ್ಕೂ ಮೇಲಾದದು, wheaten bread (is) the best of all.

2, **by the dative combined with** ಇನ್ದೆ, (ಇನ್ದ or) ಇನ್ತ (ಇನ್ತಾ), 'from' (ಇನ್ತ being another form of ಇನ್ದ, *cf.* § 282), suffixes of the ablative (or instrumental, see §§ 109 *seq.*; 352, 4, *a*), *e. g.*

a) ಕಱುಬರ್ ಇರ್ದೂರ್ಗಿನ್ದೆ ಕಾಡೊಳ್ಳಿತು, a jungle (is) good to-from a town in which (there) are envious people, *i. e.* a jungle (is) better than a town in which envious people are.

b) ಆಕಾಶಕ್ಕಿನ್ತ ಎತ್ತರವಿಲ್ಲ, ಭೂಮಿಗಿನ್ತ ಅಗಲವಿಲ್ಲ, (there) is no height to-from the sky, (there) is no breadth to-from the earth, *i. e.* (there) is nothing higher than the sky, (there) is nothing broader than the earth. ವಿದ್ಯಕ್ಕಿನ್ತ ಬುದ್ಧಿ ಶ್ರೇಷ್ಠ, ಬುದ್ಧಿಗಿನ್ತ ಅನ್ನ ಶ್ರೇಷ್ಠ, intellect (is) far better than science, food (is) far better than intellect. ವಿದ್ಯೆಯು ದ್ರವ್ಯಕ್ಕಿನ್ತ ದೊಡ್ಡದು, knowledge (is) greater than wealth. ತಾಮ್ರಕ್ಕಿನ್ತ ಬಂಗಾರವು ತುಟ್ಟಿ ಇರುತ್ತದೆ, gold is dearer than copper. ಸಿಂಹಕ್ಕಿನ್ತ ಹುಲಿಯು ಬಹಳ ಕ್ರೂರವು, the tiger (is) much fiercer than the lion. ಇದಕ್ಕಿನ್ತ ಅದು ರಮಣೀಯವಾದದ್ದು, that (is) more beautiful than this. ಏನು ಅಱಿಯದವ ಶ್ವಾನಕ್ಕಿನ್ತ ಕಡೆ, he who knows nothing (is) viler than a dog. ಇದಕ್ಕಿನ್ತ ಅದು ದೊಡ್ಡದು, that (is) larger than this. ಜ್ಞಾನಕ್ಕಿನ್ತ ಹೆಚ್ಚು ಇಷ್ಟವಾದದು ಯಾವದು, what (is) more dear than knowledge?

c) ತಾಯಿಗಿನ್ತ ಹಿತವರಿಲ್ಲ, ಸಕ್ಕರೆಗಿನ್ತ ಸವಿ ಇಲ್ಲ, (there) are none more beneficial than a mother, (there) is nothing sweeter than sugar. ಮಾನವಿಲ್ಲದ ಬಾಳ್ವಿಕೆಗಿನ್ತ ಸಾವು ಲೇಸು, death (is) better than a life without honour. ಕತ್ತೆಯ ಕಿವಿ ಕುದುರೆಯ ಕಿವಿಗಿನ್ತ ಉದ್ದು, the ears of the donkey (are) longer than the ears of the horse. ಬಿಳೀ ಕರಡಿಗಳು ಊದೀ ಬಣ್ಣದ ಕರಡಿಗಳಿಗಿನ್ತ ದೊಡ್ಡ

ವಿರುತ್ತವೆ, white bears are bigger than bears of brown colour. ಅವನು ನನಗಿನ್ತ ನಾಲ್ಕು ವರ್ಷ ಚಿಕ್ಕವನು, he (is) four years younger than I. ಆ ಬಾವಿಗಿನ್ತ ಈ ಬಾವಿಯು ಆಳವಾಗಿರುತ್ತದೆ, this well is deeper than that well. ಆ ಹುಡಿಗಗಿನ್ತ ನಿಮ್ಮ ಹುಡಿಗಿಯು ಜಾಣೆ, your girl (is) more clever than that girl. ಕಬ್ಬಿಣವು ಮಿಕ್ಕ ಧಾತುಗಳಿಗಿನ್ತ ಬಹಳ ಉಪಯೋಗವುಳ್ಳದು, iron (is) much more useful than the other metals. ಆಲದ ಬೀಜವು ಕಸಕಸೀ ಕಾಳಿಗಿನ್ತ ಬಹು ಸಣ್ಣದು, the seed of the Banian tree (is) much smaller than poppy-seed. ಹೆಬ್ಬಾವುಗಳು ಉಳಿದ ಹಾವುಗಳಿಗಿನ್ತ ಬಹಳ ದೊಡ್ಡವು, boas (are) much larger than the other snakes. ಕೆಟ್ಟ ಹಾವಿಗಿನ್ತ ನಾಗರ ಹಾವಿಗೆ ಸಿಟ್ಟು ಬಹಳ, cobras have more wrath than the (so-called) vicious snakes. ನಾಯಿಗಳಿಗಿನ್ತ ತೋಳಗಳು ತುಸು ದೊಡ್ಡವು, wolves (are) a little larger than dogs. ಕುರಿಯ ಹಾಲಿಗಿನ್ತಲೂ ಆಕಳ ಹಾಲಿಗಿನ್ತಲೂ ಆಡಿನ ಹಾಲು ಮನ್ದವಾಗಿ ಸವಿ ಇರುತ್ತದೆ, the milk of goats is thicker and sweeter than the milk of sheep and the milk of cows. ಪುತ್ತಳಿಗಿನ್ತ ಮೇಲುಬಂಗಾರವಿಲ್ಲ, ಮಕ್ಕಳಿಗಿನ್ತ ಮೇಲುತೊದಲಿಲ್ಲ, (there) is no gold better than pure gold, (there) is no lisping nicer than (that of) children. ಭೂಮಿಯ ಮೇಲಿನ ಎಲ್ಲ ಸುನ್ದರವಾದನ್ಥ ತೇಜವುಳ್ಳನ್ಥ ಒಡವೆಗಳಿಗಿನ್ತ ಮೇಲಾದ ಸುನ್ದರನೂ ತೇಜವುಳ್ಳವನೂ (ಸೂರ್ಯನಾದ) ನಾನೇ, of all the beautiful and brilliant things on earth even I (the sun, am) the most beautiful and brilliant. ತಮಗಿನ್ತ ಮೇಲಾದವರನ್ನು ಸರಿಗಟ್ಟಿ ಕೊಳ್ಳ ಬೇಕೆಮ್ಬ ಒಣಹೆಮ್ಮೆ, the vain pride that wants to make equal to one's self those who are greater than one's self. ಕೆಲವು ಪಶುಗಳಿಗೆ ಇತರ ಪಶುಗಳಿಗಿನ್ತ ಹೆಚ್ಚು ಬುದ್ಧಿ ಇರುತ್ತದೆ, some animals have more understanding than other animals. ಮೂರು ತಾಸುಗಳಿಗಿನ್ತ ಹೆಚ್ಚು, more than three hours. ನೂರು ರೂಪಾಯಿಗಿನ್ತ ಕಡಿಮೆ, less than a hundred rupees. ಸಿಂಹಲದ್ವೀಪದಲ್ಲಿ ಮಳೆಗಾಲ ನಮ್ಮಲ್ಲಿಗಿನ್ತ ಹೆಚ್ಚು, the rainy season (is) more (abundant) in Ceylon than with us. ಗುಡ್ಡದೊಳಗಿನ್ದಲೂ ಕಲ್ಲ ದಾರಿಯಿನ್ದಲೂ ಒಜ್ಜೆ ಹೊತ್ತು ಕೊಣ್ಡು ಹೋಗ ಬೇಕಾದರೆ ಕುದುರೆಗಳಿಗಿನ್ತ ಕತ್ತೆಗಳೇ ಬೇಕು, if (it) is necessary to carry burdens over mountains and stony roads, donkeys are more desirable (or useful) than horses.

d) ಬಂಗಾರಕ್ಕಿನ್ತಲೂ ಜ್ಞಾನವು ಹೆಚ್ಚಿನದು, knowledge (is) something greater than even gold. ಎಲ್ಲರಿಗಿನ್ತಲೂ ದೇವರು ದೊಡ್ಡವನು, God (is) greater than all.[1]

3, **by the ablative and its substitute the instrumental** (§ 352, 4, *a*), *e. g.*

a) ಕೃಷ್ಣನತ್ತಣಿಂ ಬಲಭದ್ರಂ ಪಿರಿಯಂ, Balabhadra (is) old from Kṛishṇa,

---

[1] It is to be remarked that uneducated people occasionally use such sentences as ವಾಲೀ ನಾಗೆ ಬಲವನ್ತನಿಲ್ಲ, ಹಾಲಿನಕ್ಕಿನ್ತ ಸವಿ ಇಲ್ಲ. ಮುಂಚಿನಕ್ಕಿನ್ತ ಚನ್ನಾಗಿ. ಅಯ್ವತ್ತು ರೂಪಾಯಿಗಳಕ್ಕಿನ್ತ ಕಡಿಮೆ. ಕತ್ತೆಗಳು ದೊಡ್ಡ ಹೋತಿನಕಿನ್ತ ಸ್ವಲ್ಪ ಉದ್ದ ಇರುತ್ತವೆ. They evidently think that ಅಕ್ಕಿನ್ತ or ಅಕಿನ್ತ are separate suffixes which require the genitive case.

i. e. older than Krishṇa. ನಕುಲನತ್ತಣಿಂ ಸಹದೇವಂ ಕಿಱಿಯಂ, Sahadêva (is) younger than Nakula. ಅರ್ಜುನನತ್ತಣಿಂ ವಾಸುದೇವನ್ ಅಧಿಕಂ, Vâsudêva (is) more excellent than Arjuna. ಆತನತ್ತಣಿನ್ದೀತಂ ಪಟು, this man (is) more clever than that man. See § 349, 8.

b) ಕೃಷ್ಣನಿಂ ಪಿರಿಯಂ ಬಲಭದ್ರಂ, Balabhadra (is) old from Krishṇa, *i. e.* older than Krishṇa. ದುರ್ಯೋಧನನಿಂ ಕಿಱಿಯಳ್ ದುಶ್ಶಲೆ, Duššalê (is) younger than Duryôdhana. ಜ್ಞಾನವಿಲ್ಲದ ಕಾಯವು ಹಾಟಿಊರ ಸ್ಥಾನದಿಂ ಕಡೆಯೆ, a body without knowledge (is) even worse than a village in ruins. (*Cf.* the first verse in § 280.)

c) ಇನಿಯನೆ ಬೆಲ್ಲದಿನ್ದಿನಿಯಂ (— ಬೆಲ್ಲದಿನ್ದೆ ಇನಿಯಂ), a (or my) paramour (is) indeed a man sweet from jaggory, *i. e.* sweeter than jaggory. ರಣಕ್ಕೆನ್ನಿನ್ದೆ ನೀಂ ಮುಂಚಿದಯ್, thou art more excelling than I in respect of war (*i. e.* thou excellest me in war).

d) ಎಮ್ಮಿನ್ದಮ್ ಇಳೆಯೊಳು ನೀವು ಹೀನಮೆ, you (are) mean from us indeed, *i. e.* indeed meaner than we, on earth.

e) ಪೆಱರಿನ್ದ ಮೇಲೆಮ್ಬಂ, a man who says "I am better from others" *i. e.* "better than others". ದಾರಿದ್ರ್ಯದಿನ್ದ ಮರಣ ಒಳ್ಳೇದು, death (is) better than poverty. ಕಾಗೆಯಿನ್ದ ನೀಱಲ ಹಣ್ಣು ಕಪ್ಪು, the ripe fruit of the *Eugenia jambolana* (is) blacker than the crow. ತುಚ್ಛಮಾತು ಆಡುವವನು ಹುಚ್ಚನಿನ್ದ ಕಡೆ, a man who utters low words (is) worse than a fool.

f) ತನ್ನಿನ್ದವೂ ಹಿರಿಯನು, a male older from him, *i. e.* older than him (or an elder brother). ತನ್ನಿನ್ದಲೂ ಹಿರಿಯಳು, a female older than her (or an elder sister). (In these two instances the ವೂ and ಲೂ, 'also', 'even', appear to be redundant.)

4, by the locative (*cf.* § 350, 2), *e. g.*

a) ತನುಜರೊಳ್ ಚಿಕ್ಕವಂ, in (or among) sons the young one, *i. e.* the youngest son. ದೇವರೊಳ್ ನಿರ್ದೋಷಿಯಾಪ್ತಂ, the fit one among princes (is) the guiltless one, *i. e.* the guiltless one (is) the fittest of princes. ರತ್ನಂಗಳೊಳ್ ಮಾಣಿಕ್ಯಮ್ ಉತ್ತಮಂ, the ruby (is) the best of precious stones. ತುಱುಗಳೊಳ್ ಕಾರಾಕಳ್ ಪಾಲುಳ್ಳುದು, of cows the black cow has most milk. ವಸ್ತ್ರದೊಳ್ ಬೆಳ್ಪಟ್ಟೆಯೊಳ್ಳಿತ್ತು, white cloth (is) the best cloth. ಅವರೊಳ್ ಓಡುವಂ ಕಾಲ್ವೇಗಿ, he who runs (is) the quickest of them.

b) ಎಲ್ಲ ನಾಡುಗಳ ಕುದುರೆಗಳೊಳಗೆ ಅರಬಿಸ್ಥಾನದ ಕುದುರೆಗಳು ಮೇಲು, Arabian horses (are) the best horses of all countries.

c) ಆವುಗಳಲ್ಲಿ ಕಪಿಲೆ ಉತ್ತಮ, the brown cow (is) the best of cows. ಹುಡು

ಗರಲ್ಲಿ ರಾಮನು ಜಾಣನು, Râma (is) the most clever of the boys. ವಜ್ರವು ರತ್ನಗಳಲ್ಲಿ ಶ್ರೇಷ್ಠವಾದದ್ದು, the diamond (is) the most excellent of precious stones. ಸಿಂಹವು ಎಲ್ಲ ಶ್ವಾಪದಗಳಲ್ಲಿ ಬಲು ಭಯಂಕರವು ಇರುತ್ತದೆ, the lion (is) by far the most formidable of all wild beasts. ಎಲ್ಲ ವಸ್ತುಗಳಲ್ಲಿ ವಜ್ರವು ಕಠಿಣವಾದದ್ದು, the diamond (is) the hardest of all things. ಆ ಮನೆಯು ಎಲ್ಲ ಮನೆಗಳಲ್ಲಿ ಹಳೇದು, that house (is) the oldest of all houses.

5, **by the genitive** as a substitute of the locative (see § 352, 1, *c*), *e. g.* ಚಾಗಿಗಳ ಬಲ್ಲಹಂ, the best of liberal persons. ಈವರ ದೇವಂ, the most eminent of donors. ರಸಿಕರ ಚಕ್ರವರ್ತಿ, the most splendid of the witty.

XXVI. On Syntax.

344. The ancient Kannaḍa grammars which the author of the present grammar has consulted, do not use a particular word to express **syntax** or **the construction of sentences**; however the Saṁskṛita term vâkyavinyâsa which expresses it, may be adopted.

Regarding the construction of a sentence (vâkya) **kâraka**, *i. e.* the relation of the noun to the verb, is to be considered. Kêšava says that kâraka is on account of the verb (kriyânimitta), and that the case terminations (nâmavibhaktis) are suffixed by the power of kâraka (kârakavašadiṁ). (Regarding kâraka see §§ 253, 2; 357, 1. 2, *a*). *Cf.* also § 354, 3, *a*.

There are six such kârakas or relations, *viz.*

1, **kartṛi**, the doer of an action, the active noun, the agent (*cf.* § 150), used in connection with a transitive or active verb (sakarmaka) or if expressing the agent's circumstances or state, in connection with an intransitive (akarmaka, see § 148). It stands in **the nominative** case and is the subject of the verb (*cf.* §§ 347, 9; 357, 2).

2, **karma**, the object on which the action of the kartṛi falls, *i. e.* the idea expressed by **the accusative** case.

3, **karaṇa**, the instrument, *i. e.* the idea expressed by **the instrumental** case.

4, **sampradâna**, the recipient of the object of giving or of the gift, *i. e.* the idea expressed by **the dative** case.

5, **apâdâna**, ablation, *i. e.* departure or removal from a fixed point, coming from, *i. e.* the idea expressed by **the ablative** case.

6, **adhikaraṇa,** location, place of the **action** or state of the agent, *i. e.* the idea expressed by **the** locative case.

The idea of **the genitive case is not considered a kâraka,** because it expresses the relation of two nouns to each other (sambandhârtha), but not the relation of a noun and verb (§ 351).

345. **The nominative** (*cf.* 352, 6, *a*. 6, *b*) **considered by itself** expresses

1, liṅga, *i. e.* specification, *e. g.* ಚನ್ದ್ರಂ, ಇನ್ದ್ರಂ, ಮನುಷ್ಯಂ, ಗೋಮಿನಿ, ಕಾಮಿನಿ, ಆನೆ, ಕುದುರೆ, ಮರಂ, ಗಿಡು, ಪಕ್ಕಿ, ಮಿಗಂ;

2, artha, bhâva, *i. e.* sort or kind, state of being, *e. g.* ನಿಡಿಯಂ, ಗುಜ್ಜಂ, ಕೆಂಚಂ, ಕರಿಯಂ, ಅಸಿಯಂ, ಇನಿಯಂ;

3, vačana, vačanamâtra, gaṇanĕ, *i. e.* (mere grammatical) number, numeration, *e. g.* ಒನ್ದು, ಎರಡು, ಮೂಱು, ಒರ್ವಂ, ಇರ್ವರ್, ಮೂವರ್;

4, sambôdhanĕ, abhimukhîkaraṇa, *i. e.* addressing (see § 140), *e. g.* ದೇವ! ಸರ್ವೇಶ! ಚಕ್ರವರ್ತಿ!

When it becomes the agent or subject (kartṛi), **simple sentences formed** by it are *e. g.* the following:— ದೇವನ್ ಒಳ್ಳಿದಂ, the king (is) good. ಪಾಲ್ ಬಿಳಿದು, milk (is) white. ಅವಂ ವಿಮಲಮತಿ, he (is) pure-minded. ನೀಂ ಕಾಮಂ, thou (art) Kâma. ಆಂ ನನ್ದಿ, I (am) Nandi. ತಾನ್ ಅವಂ, it (is) he. ಇವರ್ ಪುರುಷರ್, these (are) males. ಅವರ್ ಪೆಣ್ಡಿರ್, those (are) females. ನೇಸಱ್ ಮೂಡಿದುದು, the sun rose. ಒರ್ವಂ ಬನ್ದಂ, one man came. ಇರ್ವರ್ ನುಡಿದರ್, two persons spoke. ದೇವಂ ಮೆಚ್ಚಿದಂ, the king was pleased. ಅವಂ ಕೊನ್ದಂ, he killed. ಅವರ್ ಮಾಟ್ಟಿ, let them make! ಸರ್ವೇಶ, ಕೇಳ್, hear, O paramount lord!

It is to be remarked that when the subject is a personal pronoun, it is often omitted, as it is contained in the personal terminations of the verb (see § 193 *seq.*), *e. g.* ಇರ್ದಪೆಂ, ಇದ್ದೇನೆ, ಇರುತ್ತೇನೆ, I am; ಬನ್ದಪಂ, ಬರುತ್ತಾನೆ, he comes; ಪೋದಯ್, ಹೋದೆ, ಹೋದಿ, thou wentest; ನುಡಿದಳ್, ನುಡಿದಳು, she uttered; ನಡೆದರ್, ನಡೆದರು, they walked.

346. **In sentences in which the accusative or object** (karma, *cf.* § 352, 2, *a seq.*; 5, *b*. 6, *b*), *i. e.* the case of things (vastu), etc. on which the action of the verb falls, **occurs, the things, etc. may be said to be:—**

1, ishṭa, *i. e.* wished for, *e. g.* ಸೇವಳಮಂ ತೆಗೆದಂ, he took the necklace; ತುಡಿಗೆಯಂ ತೊಟ್ಟಂ, he put on the ornament; ಪೂವಂ ಮುಡಿದಂ, he set flowers in the hair.

In such a case also a **double accusative** (dvikarma) uses to take place, *e. g.* ಗುರುವಂ ಜ್ಞಾನಮಂ ಬೆಸಗೊಣ್ಡಂ, he asked wisdom of the guru; ದಾನಿಯುಂ ದಾನಮಂ ಬೇಡಿದಂ, he begged a gift of the liberal man; ಕುರುಪತಿಯಂ ವಿಷ್ಣು ಬೇಡಿದಂ ಧರೆಯುರೆಯುಂ, Vishṇu asked the king of the Kurus for the half of (his) land; ಪಶುವಂ ಪಾಲಂ ಕಱೆದಂ, he extracted milk from the cow; ಅವರ್ಗಳಂ ಭಕ್ತರಂ ಮಾಡಿದಂ, he made them devotees.

Regarding a **double accusative with causal verbs** the following sentences may be adduced:— ಅರಸಂ ಭೃತ್ಯನನ್ ಊರನ್ ಅಯ್ದಿಸಿದಂ, the king caused (his) servant to go to the town; ಗೋವಳಂ ತುಱುಗಳಂ ಮನೆಯಂ ಪುಗಿಸಿದಂ, the cowherd caused the cows to enter the house; ಜೋದನ್ ಅರಸನನ್ ಆನೆಯನ್ ಏಱಿಸಿದಂ, the driver caused the king to mount the elephant; ಗುರು ಶಿಷ್ಯನಂ ವ್ಯಾಕರಣಮನ್ ಓದಿಸಿದಂ, the teacher caused (his) disciple to read the grammar (see § 149 *seq.*).

2, anishṭa, *i. e.* not wished for, *e. g.* ಪಾವಂ ದಾಣ್ಟಿದಂ, he crossed a snake.

3, nivartya, *i. e.* to be produced (as something new), *e. g.* ಮನೆಯಂ ಮಾಡಿದಂ, he built a house; ಕಾವ್ಯಮಂ ಪೇೞ್ದಂ, he told a poem.

4, vikârya, *i. e.* to be transformed, *e. g.* ಪೞುವಂ ಕಡಿದಂ, he cut down the forest; ಕಾಯಂ ಪೋೞ್ದಂ, he split the fruit.

5, prâpya, *i. e.* to be reached or arrived at, *e. g.* ಊರನ್ ಅಯ್ದಿದಂ, he reached the town; ಮರನಂ ಸಾರ್ದಂ, he approached the tree.

6, vaishayika, *i. e.* to be observed by the senses, *e. g.* ನೇಸಱಿಂ ನೋಡಿದಂ, he saw the sun; ಗೀತಮಂ ಕೇಳ್ದಂ, he heard a song; ಪೂವಂ ಮೂಸಿದಂ, he smelt a flower; ಅವನಂ ನೋಡಿದಂ, he saw him.

7, kâla, *i. e.* relating to time (*cf.* § 348, 29), *e. g.* ಆಱುದಿಂಗಳಂ ತಳ್ವಿದಂ, he lingered six months; ತ್ರಿರಾತ್ರಮನ್ ಇರ್ದಂ, he remained three nights; ಜಾವಮಂ ತೊೞಲ್ದಂ, he wandered about a night-watch; ಮಾಸಮಂ (ವ್ಯಾಕರಣಮನ್) ಓದಿದಂ, he studied (grammar) for a month.

8, adhva, *i. e.* relating to space, *e. g.* ಅರೆಗಾವುದಮಂ ಪರಿದಂ, he ran half a league; ಮೂಗಾವುದಮಂ ನಡೆದಂ, he walked three leagues.

347. In sentences in which the instrumental case (karaṇa, *cf.* § 352, 2, *b.* 3. 4, *a.* 4, *b*) is used, the following specific meanings are considered to be expressed by it:—

1, karaṇa, *i. e.* an instrument, *e. g.* ಕೊಡಲಿಯಿಂ ಕಡಿದಂ, he cut with an axe; ಗದೆಯಿಂ ಮೋದಿದಂ, he struck with a club; ಕಣ್ಣಿಂ ನೋಡಿದಂ, he saw with (his) eyes; ಕುಡುಗೋಲಿಂ ಕೊಯ್ದಂ, the cut off with a sickle.

2, hêtu, *i. e.* cause, instrumentality, means, *e. g.* ಓಲಗದಿಂ ಪಡೆದಂ, he obtained through service; ತಗಹಿಂ ಸಿಲ್ಕಿದಂ, he was impeded by an obstacle; ದೈವದಿಂ ಬಾಳ್ದಿಂ, he lived by fate; ಧನದಿಂ ಕುಲಂ, by wealth high station (is acquired); ಬಿಜ್ಜೆಯಿಂ ಜಸಂ, by learning fame (is acquired); ತತ್ವಜ್ಞಾನದಿಂ ಮೋಕ್ಷಂ, by the knowledge of truth final liberation (is obtained).

To this class of sentences may be added the following instances with causative verbs taken from the Šabdânušâsana:—ಪುರೋಹಿತನ್ ಅರಸನಿಂ ದಾನಮಂ ಕುಡಿಸಿದಂ, the domestic priest had a gift given by the king; ಅರಸಂ ಗವುಡನಿಂ ಪೊಲನನ್ ಉೞಿಸಿದಂ, the king had the field ploughed by the gavuḍa; ಗುರು ಶಿಷ್ಯನಿಂ ವ್ಯಾಕರಣಮನ್ ಓದಿಸಿದಂ, the teacher had the grammar read by (his) pupil.

3, saṁyôga, *i. e.* association, *e. g.* ಸಂಗಡದಿಂ ಬನ್ದಂ, he came in company (Šabdamaṇidarpaṇa); ಮಗನಿಂ ಕೂಡಿ ಬನ್ದಂ, he came accompanied by (his) son; ಲಕ್ಷ್ಮಿಯಿಂ ಬೆರಸಿ ಹರಿಯೊಪ್ಪಿದನು, Hari shone joined by Lakshmî; ಉಮೆಯಿಂ ಸಂಗಡಿಸಿ ಮೆೞಿದಂ ಪೆೞಿದಲೆಯುಂ, he on whose forehead is a crescent (*i. e.* Šiva) assumed an ostentatious appearance accompanied by Umĕ (Šabdânušâsana).

4, upâdâna, *i. e.* material cause (*cf.* § 350, ೨), *e. g.* ಮರದಿಂ ಮಾಡಾನೆಯುಂ, make an elephant of wood!

5, siddhi, *i. e.* accomplishment (within a time, within a distance), *e. g.* ಮಾಸದಿಂ ವ್ಯಾಕರಣಂ ಪೂರ್ಣಮಾಯಿತು, the grammar became complete within a month; ಬರಿಸದಿಂ ಶಾಸ್ತ್ರಂ ಮುಗಿದುದು, the treaty was finished in the rainy season; ಕ್ರೋಶದಿಂ ವೇದವನ್ ಓದಿದಂ, he read the vêda within a cos; ಗಾವುದದಿಂ ಶಾಸ್ತ್ರಮಂ ಪಠಿಸಿದಂ, he recited the treatise in the course of a league (Šabdânušâsana).

6, bhêda, prakâra, *i. e.* speciality, particular sign or mark, *e. g.* ಕಣ್ಣಿಂ ಕುರುಡಂ, he (is) blind of (both his) eyes; ಕಾಲಿಂ ಕುಣ್ಟಂ, he (is) lame in (his) legs; ಕೆಯ್ಯಿಂ ಮೋಟಂ, he (is) deprived of a forearm; ಜಾತಿಯಿಂ ಪಾರ್ವಂ, he (is) a Brâhmaṇa as to (his) caste; ಪ್ರಕೃತಿಯಿನ್ ಒಳ್ಳಿದಂ, he (is) good as to (his) nature (Šabdânušâsana).

7, (vidhi, *i. e.* manner, *e. g.* ತ್ವರೆಯಿನ್ದ ನಡೆದನು, he walked in a quick manner; ಚನ್ದದಿನ್ದ ಓದಿದನು, he read in a beautiful manner; ಜಾಣ್ಮೆಯಿನ್ದ ಮಾ

ತಾಡಿದನು, he spoke in a clever manner). *Cf.* adverbs expressed by the instrumental in § 281.

8, itthambhûtalakshaṇa, a so circumstanced characteristic mark, characterised in such manner, characterised by, *e.g.* ಕಮಣ್ಡಲುವಿಂ ಛಾತ್ರನಂ ಕಣ್ಡಂ, he discerned the pupil by the (characteristic) water-pot; ಜೆಣ್ಡಿಕೆಯಿಂ ವಟುವನ್ ಅಱಿದಂ, he knew the boy by the tuft of hair (Šabdânušâsana).

9, kartri (*cf.* § 344), *i.e.* the efficient cause of a thing (in the so-called passive, § 315), *e.g.* ಪದಕಮ್ ಅಕ್ಕಸಾಲೆಯಿಂ ಮಾಡೆ ಪಟ್ಟುದು, the breast-ornament was made by the goldsmith; ಕಾವ್ಯಮ್ ಎನ್ನಿಂ ಪೇೞೆ ಪಟ್ಟುದು, the poem was told by me.

In such a case also **instances with a double instrumental case** occur, *e.g.* ಅರಸನಿಂ ಬಾಣಸಿಗನಿನ್ ಅನ್ನಂ ಮಾಡಿಸಲ್ ಪಟ್ಟುದು, by the king rice was caused to be made by the cook; ಹರಿಯಿನ್ದರ್ಜುನನಿಂ ಕರ್ಣಂ ಕೊಲ್ಲಿಸಲ್ ಪಟ್ಟಂ, by Hari Karṇa was caused to be killed by Arjuna.

348. In sentences in which the dative case (sampradâna, *cf.* § 352, 2 *c.* 5, *a.* 5, *b.* 5, *c*) **is used, the following specific meanings are considered to be expressed by it:—**

1, sampradâna, *i.e.* (simple) bestowing, *e.g.* ಬ್ರಾಹ್ಮಣಂಗೆ ಗೋವಂ ಕೊಟ್ಟಂ, he gave a cow to the Brâhmaṇa; ಯತಿಗೆ ಭಿಕ್ಷಮನ್ ಇಕ್ಕಿದಂ, he gave alms to the religious mendicant; ಬಸದಿಗೆ ಪೂಮಾಲೆಯನ್ ಇತ್ತಂ, he gave a garland of flowers to the temple.

2, ruči, *i.e.* being pleasurable or palatable, *e.g.* ಕೂಸಿಂಗೆ ಲಡ್ಡುಗೆಯಿನಿಯವು, sweet-meat balls (are) agreeable to the taste of a child; ಬೆನಕಂಗುಣ್ಡಲಿಗೆ ಯಿನಿಯವು, rice-cakes (are) agreeable to the taste of Gaṇêša. ಧಾರ್ಮಿಕಂಗೆ ಧರ್ಮಂ ರುಚಿಯಕ್ಕುಂ, alms-giving is a pleasure to the pious man.

3, îrshĕ, *i.e.* jealousy, *e.g.* ಕವಿಗೆ ಕವಿ ಮುನಿವಂ, a poet uses to be displeased with a poet; ಕುಜನಂ ಸುಜನಂಗೆ ಸಯ್ರಿಸಂ, a bad man cannot bear a good man.

4, matsara, *i.e.* envy, *e.g.* ಸವತಿಗೆ ಸವತಿ ಪುರುಡಿಪಳ್, a rival wife uses to envy a rival wife; ಬಿರುದರ್ಗೆ ಬಿರುದರ್ ಸೆಣೆಸುವರ್, men of distinction use to envy men of distinction.

5, hita, *i.e.* suitableness, etc. (the Šabdânušâsana has ishṭa, *i.e.* desirableness), *e.g.* ಪಶುವಿಂಗೆ ತೃಣಂ ಹಿತಂ, grass (is) good for cows; ರೋಗಿಗಾಪಧಂ ಹಿತಂ, medicine (is) fit for a sick person; ಯಾಜ್ಞಿಕಂಗೆ ಸ್ವರ್ಗಮ್ ಇಷ್ಟಂ, heaven (is) an object of desire for the sacrificer.

6, bhîti, *i. e.* fear (*cf.* § 349, 2), *e. g.* ಪಾಪಕ್ಕಂಜುಗುಂ ತಕ್ಕಂ, a good person fears sin; ಪುಲಿಗಳ್ಗುಗುಂ ಪಿಡಿ, a female elephant fears tigers.

7, unnati, âdhikya, (gurutva), *i. e.* greatness, superiority (age, in comparison, *cf.* §§ 343, 1. 2; 349, 8; 352, 2, *c*), *e. g.* ಲೋಕಕ್ಕೀತನ್ ಅಧಿಕಂ, this man (is) greater than all (or the greatest of all); ಮೇರುವಿಂಗೀತನ್ ಅಗ್ಗಳಂ, this man (is) higher than Mêru; ಹರಿಗೆ ಹರನ್ ಅಧಿಕಂ, Hara (is) greater than Hari; [ಒನ್ದಕ್ಕೊನ್ದು ಹಿರಿಯವಪ್ಪ ಮೀನು, (various) fishes of which one is larger than the other; ಶೂದ್ರರಿಗೆ ಬ್ರಾಹ್ಮಣರು ಪೂಜ್ಯರು, Brâhmaṇas (are) more respectable than Śûdras; ಕಾಗೆಗೆ ನೇರಿಲ ಹಣ್ಣು ಕಪ್ಪು, the ripe fruit of *Eugenia jambolana* (is) blacker than a crow; ರಾಮನಿಗೆ ಕೃಷ್ಣನು ಕಿರಿಯನು, Kṛishṇa (is) younger than Râma].

8, svasti, *i. e.* well-wish, *e. g.* ಸಮನಿಸುಗೆ ಜಗಕ್ಕೆಲ್ಲಿಯುಮಭೀಷ್ಟಂ, ಕ್ಷೇಮವೃತ್ತಿ, ಕುಶಲಂ, ಭಾವುಕಂ (Ngv. ಭವ್ಯಂ), ಶ್ರೇಯಂ, ಶಿವಂ, ಶುಭಂ, ಸ್ವಸ್ತಿ, ಮಂಗಳಂ, ಕಲ್ಯಾಣಂ (a quotation of Kêśava from Nâgavarma's nighaṇṭu, our MS. p. 105), may everywhere accrue to the world desired objects, a state of well-being, happiness, prosperity, bliss, luck, joy, auspiciousness (and) good fortune.

9, svabhâva, *i. e.* natural disposition, nature, *e. g.* ಸಿಂಹಕ್ಕೆ ಶೌರ್ಯಂ, to the lion (is) valour (*i. e.* the lion possesses valour); ಕಪಿಗೆ ಚಪಲತೆ, the monkey possesses agility.

10, hêtu, *i. e.* cause (*cf.* § 349, 6), *e. g.* ಸಿರಿಗುದ್ಯೋಗಂ, by wealth offices (are obtained); ಮಳೆಗೆ ಮುಗಿಲ್, clouds (are the cause) of rain.

11, namaskâra, *i. e.* obeisance, *e. g.* ದೇವರ್ಗೆ ಪೊಡಮಟ್ಟಂ, he made obeisance to the king; ಗುರುವಿಂಗೆಱಗಿದಂ, he made obeisance to the guru; ಜಿನಂಗೆ ನಮಸ್ಕರಿಸಿದಂ, he made obeisance to the Jina.

12, prâṇyanâdarasmaraṇa, *i. e.* contemptuous thought concerning, or contemptuous mentioning of, beings, *e. g.* ಮಾನಸರಂ ಪುಲ್ಗೆ ಕಷ್ಟಮಾಗೆ ನೆನೆವಂ, when misery happens (to him), he will count men (but) straw; ಸಿರಿಗೆ ಕಷ್ಟಮಾಗೆ ನುಡಿವಂ, when misery happens (to him), he will speak against the goddess of fortune (Śabdamaṇidarpaṇa); ಅವನನ್ ಆತಂ ತೃಣಕ್ಕೆ ಬಗೆದಂ, he counted him (but) straw; ಖಲನಂ ಸೌಮಿತ್ರಿ ಪುೞಿತ ಕವಡೆಗೆ ಬಗೆದಂ, Saumitri (*i. e.* Lakshmaṇa) counted the rogue (but) a worm-eaten cowrie; ನೀನ್ ಆತನನ್ ಒನ್ದಡಕೆಗೆ ಬಗೆದಯ್, thou countedst him (but) an areca nut (Śabdânuśâsana).

In such sentences also a double accusative may be used, *e. g.* ಅವನನ್

ಆತಂ ತೃಣಮುಂ ಬಗೆದಂ, he counted him (but) straw; ಅವನಂ ಪುಲ್ಲಂ ತಿಳಿದಂ, he regarded him as (mere) straw.

13, anishṭa, *i. e.* hatred, dislike, undesirableness, *e. g.* ಆತಂಗೆ ವಿಷಮನ್ ಇಕ್ಕಿದಂ, he poisoned him; ಆತಂಗೆ ಕತ್ತಿಯಂ ಮಸೆದಂ, he whetted (his) sword against him; ಮಲ್ಲಂಗೆ ಬಳ್ಳಿತಲ್ತು ವಜ್ರಮುಷ್ಟಿ, the vajramushṭi-weapon (is) noxious to wrestlers; ಲೋಕಕ್ಕನಿಷ್ಟಂ ಬರಿಂ, famine (is) disagreeable to the world.

14, sâdriśya, *i. e.* similarity, *e. g.* ಆತಂಗೀತಂ ತಕ್ಕಂ, this man (is) as deserving as that man; ಐರಾವತಕ್ಕೆ ಸುಪ್ರತೀಕನ್ ಓರಗೆ, the (elephant) Supratîka (is) equal to the (elephant) Airâvata; ಗೋವಿಂಗೆ ಗವಯಂ ಸದೃಶಂ, the (ox) Gayal likens a cow; ಚನ್ದ್ರಂಗೆ ಸಮಾನಂ ಮುಖಂ, a face (is) like the moon.

15, pratinidhi, *i. e.* substitution, the being put or coming in the place of another, *e. g.* ಜೇನ ತುಪ್ಪಕ್ಕೆ ಸಕ್ಕರೆ ಸಲ್ವುದು, for honey sugar may be used; ಆ ಕಬ್ಬಕ್ಕೀ ಕಬ್ಬಮ್ ಆಯಿತು, for that poetical composition this poetical composition has been substituted; ಪುಷ್ಕರಕ್ಕೇರಣ್ಡಮ್ ಅಕ್ಕುಂ, costus is used instead of Ricinus.

16, ishṭa, *i. e.* love, *e. g.* ಭಕ್ತಂಗೆ ವರಮನ್ ಇತ್ತಂ, he gave a boon to the devotee; ಕೆಳೆಯಂಗೆ ಸನ್ತಸಮಂ ಮಾಡಿದಂ, he made (his) friend glad.

17, prati, *i. e.* regard, with regard to, as to, *e. g.*

ಸುಡಿಗೆಲ್ಲಂ ಸಲ್ಲದ ಕ
ನ್ನಡದೊಳ್ ಜತ್ತಾಣಮುಂ ಬೆದಣ್ಡೆಯುಮ್ ಎನ್ದೀ ।
ಗಡಿನ ನೆಗಜ್ತೆಯ ಕಬ್ಬದೊಳ್
ಒಡಮ್ಬಡಂ ಮಾಡಿದರ್ ಪುರಾತನಕವಿಗಳ್ ‖ that in Kannaḍa which (according to the opinion of some) is wholly insufficient with regard to (its) words, (there is) jattâṇa and bĕdaṇḍĕ, the ancient poets have proved by (their) renowned poetical works that now still exist. See § 284 (under dative ಕುಲಕಂ ಚಲಕ್ಕಂ); § 287, under 2 (ಎರಡು ಸಮಾಸಪದಕ್ಕಂ); § 287, under 3 (ಎರಡು ಮಿಝ್ಗಂ). *Cf.* § 302, 4.

18, (gamana, *i. e.* going to, the point toward which movement is directed, *e. g.* ಅವನು ಊರಿಗೆ ಹೋದನು, he went to the town; ನದಿಗಳು ಸಮುದ್ರಕ್ಕೆ ಹರಿಯುತ್ತವೆ, rivers flow into the sea; ರಾಮನು ವನಕ್ಕೆ ನಡಿದನು, Râma walked to the forest).

19, [arghya, *i. e.* price or exchange, *e. g.* ಹತ್ತು ರೂಪಾಯಿಗೆ ಇದನ್ನು ಕೊಟ್ಟೆನು, I gave this for ten rupees; ದುಡ್ಡಿಗೆ ಪಂಚೇರು, five sêrs for a duḍḍu;

ಅಫೀಮು ಬಹಳ ತುಟ್ಟಿ, ಏಳೆಂಟು ರೂಪಾಯಿಗೆ ಒನ್ದು ಸೇರು ಮಾರುತ್ತದೆ, opium (is) very dear, one sêr is sold for seven or eight rupees; ಎಷ್ಟಕ್ಕೆ ಕೊಡುತ್ತೀರಿ, for how much will you give (it)? ಎರಡು ರೂಪಾಯಿಗೆ ಕೊಡುತ್ತೇನೆ, I will give (it) for two rupees]. *Cf.* § 302, 7.

20, (mâtra, *i. e.* mereness, the one thing and no more, *e. g.* ಹೆಸರಿಗೆ ಅರಸನು, a king only as to name; ಮಾತಿಗೆ ಜಾಣನು, a wise man only as to words; *cf.* § 352, 4, *b*).

21, (dikku, *i. e.* direction, *e. g.* ಧಾರವಾಡಕ್ಕೆ ಬೆಳಗಾವಿ ಉತ್ತರ, Belgaum (is) to the north of Dharwar; *cf.* § 352, 4, *a.* 3).

22, [dûra, *i. e.* distance, *e. g.* ಧಾರವಾಡಕ್ಕೆ ಬೆಳಗಾವಿ ಹದಿನಾರು ಹರದಾರಿ ಅದೆ, Belgaum is sixteen haradâris from Dharwar; ಈವೂರಿಗೆ ಆವೂರು ಹರದಾರಿ, that village (is) three miles from this village; ಬೆಂಗಳೂರಿಗೂ ಮೈಸೂರಿಗೂ ಎಷ್ಟು ದೂರ, what (is) the distance between Bangalore and Mysore? *cf.* § 352, 4, *a.* 4].

23, šakti, *i. e.* power, *e. g.* ಮಲ್ಲಂಗೆ ಮಲ್ಲಂ ಶಕ್ತಂ, a wrestler (is) a match for a wrestler; ಅತಂಗೀತಂ ಸಮರ್ಥಂ, this man is able to mate with that man (Šabdânušâsana).

24, asûyĕ, *i. e.* detraction, *e. g.* ಧರ್ಮಂಗೆ ಕೌರವನ್ ಅಸೂಯೆಗೆಯ್ವಂ, the Kaurava takes away from the reputation of Dharma; ರಾಮಂಗೆ ರಾವಣಂ ದೋಷವನ್ ಆರೋಪಿಸಿದಂ, Râvaṇa ascribes vice to Râma (Šabdânušâsaná).

25, drôha, *i. e.* mischief, *e. g.* ಅರಸಂಗೀತಂ ದ್ರೋಹಿ, this man (is) a traitor to the king; ಒಡೆಯಂಗಪಕಾರಿ ದಾಸೇರಂ, the servant does ill to (his) master (Šabdânušâsana).

26, svâhâ, svadhâ, vashaṭkâra, *i. e.* the three ritual invocations of hail and prayer, *e. g.* ಅಗ್ನಿಗೆ ಸ್ವಾಹಾಕಾರಂ, hail to Agni! ಪಿತೃಗಳ್ಗೆ ಸ್ವಧಾಕಾರಂ, benison to the manes! ಇನ್ದ್ರಂಗೆ ವಷಟ್ಕಾರಂ, vashaṭ to Indra! (Šabdânušâsana).

27, tâdarthya, *i. e.* sake, purpose, material cause. *e. g.* ಮೋಕ್ಷಕ್ಕೆ ತತ್ತ್ವಜ್ಞಾನಂ, for final liberation knowledge of the truth (is necessary); ಕುಣ್ಡಲಕ್ಕೆ ಚಿನ್ನಂ, for an earring gold (is taken); ತೇರ್ಗೆ ಮರಂ, for a chariot wood (is required); ಅವಘಾತಕ್ಕೊನಕೆ, for pounding a pestle (is required) (Šabdânušâsana).

28, utpâta, *i. e.* portents, *e. g.* ಬರಕ್ಕೆ (lit. regarding famine) ಬೆಳ್ಮಿಂಚು, white flashes of lightning (portend) famine; ಲೋಕನಾಶಕ್ಕೆ ಕಪ್ಪೆಯ ಜಣ್ಡೆಕೆ, frogs' tufts (portend) the ruin of the world; ಬಿರುಬಿಸಿಲ್ಗೆ ಕೆಮ್ಮಿಂಚು, red flashes of lightning (portend) excessive heat of the sun (Šabdânušâsana).

29, [ಕಾಲ, *i. e.* time (*cf.* § 302, 2. 7; 303, 1, *a;* § 346, 7; § 352, 4, *a.* 5. 6, *c*), *e.g.* ಇನ್ದಿಗೆ, to-day; ಸಾಯಂಕಾಲಕ್ಕೆ, in the evening; ಎರಡು ವರ್ಷಕ್ಕೆ, for two years; ಬರುವ ತಿಂಗಳಿಗೆ, next month; ಏಳು ಗಣ್ಟೆಗೆ, at seven o'clock].

30, (ಯೋಗ್ಯತೆ, *i. e.* deserving state, *e. g.* ಮಾನಕ್ಕೆ ತಕ್ಕವನು, he who deserves honour; ತರಹರಿಸಲಾರಿದವಳು ಮರಣಕ್ಕೆ ಪಾತ್ರಳು, she who cannot bear patiently deserves death).

31, (ಭೇದ, *i.e.* difference, *e. g.* ಇದಕ್ಕೂ ಅದಕ್ಕೂ ಬಹು ಹೆಚ್ಚುಕಡಿಮೆ, (there is) a great difference betwixt this and that; *cf.* § 352, 4, *a.* 2).

32, (ಕಾರಣ, *i. e.* cause, purpose, end, see §§ 302, 7; 352, 4, *a.* 11; *e. g.* ಯಾತಕ್ಕೆ ಬನ್ದೆ, why didst thou come? ಕೆಲಸಕ್ಕೆ ಬನ್ದೆನು, I came on business; ನೋಡುವದಕ್ಕೆ ಹೋದೆನು, I went to see).

Remarks.

1, In § 316 it is stated that 'to have', 'to possess' is expressed by ಉಳ್, etc. preceded by the dative case.

2, Regarding adverbs used with the dative see § 282 under dative.

3, Some verbs are often used with the dative, *e.g.* ಸೂರ್ಯನಿನ್ದ ನಮಗೆ ಬೆಳಕು ಬಿಸಲು ದೊರೆಯುತ್ತದೆ, from the sun we get light and heat; ಸಭ್ಯ ಆಕಳು ನಮ್ಮ ಒಡೆಯನು ಬಡವನಿದ್ದದರಿನ್ದ ನನಗೆ ಹೊಟ್ಟೆ ತುಮ್ಬಾ ಮೇವು ದೊರಕುವದಿಲ್ಲ ಎನ್ದು ಹೇಳಿತು, the tame cow said "because my master is poor, I do not get sufficient food to fill my stomach". ನನಗೆ ಸಿಕ್ಕಿತು, I found (it). ನನಗೆ ತಿಳಿಯದು, I know not. ಅವನಿಗೆ ಹುಚ್ಚು ಹಿಡಿಯಿತು, he went mad.

349. In sentences in which the ablative case (apâdâna, *cf.* § 352, 2, *d.* 4, *a*) is used, the following specific meanings are considered to be expressed by it: —

1, apâdâna, *i. e.* (simple) separation from, coming from, going away from, *e.g.* ಮರದತ್ತಣಿಂ ಪಣ್ಣುದಿರ್ದುವು, ripe fruits fell from the tree; ಗಿರಿಯತ್ತಣಿಂ ಕಲ್ಲುರುಳ್ದುವು, stones rolled down from the mountain; ಕೆಱೆಯತ್ತಣಿಂ ಬನ್ದಂ, he came from the tank; ಓಡುವ ಕುದುರೆಯತ್ತಣಿಂ ಬಿದ್ದಂ, he fell from (his) horse which was running; ಪರಿವ ಬಣ್ಡಿಯತ್ತಣಿನ್ದುರುಳ್ದಂ, he rolled from the cart which was moving rapidly; ಉಪಾಧ್ಯಾಯನತ್ತಣಿಂ ಮಱೆಯಾದಂ, he hid himself from the teacher; ಗುರುಗಳತ್ತಣಿಂ ಕೆಲಸ್ಸೊಕ್ಕಂ, he went out of the way of the guru; ಮುಗಿಲತ್ತಣಿಂ ಮಿಂಚು ಮಿಂಚಿತು, a flash of lightning flashed from the cloud.

2, bhaya, *i. e.* fear (*cf.* § 348, 6; § 352, 4, *a.* 6), *e.g.* ಅರಸನತ್ತಣಿಂ ದಾಟಿ ಬನ್ದುದು, an inroad arose from the king; ಪುಲಿಯತ್ತಣಿನ್ದಂಜಿದಂ, he was afraid of the tiger; ಪುಲಿಯತ್ತಣಿಂ ಭೀತಿ, fear (proceeding) from a tiger; ಪಾಪದತ್ತಣಿಂ ಪೆಳಱು, anxiety (coming) from sin.

3, svîkâra, *i. e.* adoption, making one's own, (acquiring for one's self), *e. g.* ಸ್ವಾಮಿಯತ್ತಣಿಂ ನಿರ್ವಾಹಮ್ ಆದುದು, from (his) king the achievement (of his object) was got; ಉಪಾಧ್ಯಾಯನತ್ತಣಿಂ ವಿದ್ಯೆಯನ್ ಇರ್ಕುಳಿಗೊಣ್ಡಂ, he acquired knowledge from (his) teacher.

4, ishṭa, *i. e.* agreeableness, pleasure (*cf.* § 352, 4, *a.* 7), *e. g.* ರಮ್ಭೆಯತ್ತಣಿಂ ಸುಖಂ ಪ್ರಾಪ್ತಿಸಿದುದು, from Rambhĕ pleasure was obtained; ಪಾಪದತ್ತಣಿಂ ರಕ್ಷಿಸಿದಂ, he saved from sin; ಬಱದತ್ತಣಿಂ ಸಲಹಿದಂ, he saved from famine.

5, anishṭa, *i. e.* disagreeableness (*cf.* § 352, 4, *a.* 8), *e. g.* ಪಗೆಯತ್ತಣಿಂ ಬನ್ಧನಂ ಬನ್ದುದು, imprisonment came from the enemy; ಪಾಪದತ್ತಣಿಂ ಮೋಹಿಸಿದಂ, he suffered bewilderment from sin.

6, hêtu, *i. e.* cause, means, *e. g.* ಉದ್ಯೋಗದತ್ತಣಿಂ ಸಿರಿ ಬನ್ದುದು, wealth came from office. *Cf.* § 348, 10; § 352, 4, *a.* 9.

7, udaya, *i. e.* springing from, originating (*cf.* § 352, 4, *a.* 10), *e. g.* ಸದ್ವಂಶದತ್ತಣಿಂ ಪುಟ್ಟಿದಂ, he sprang from a good family; ಹಿಮವತ್ಪರ್ವತದತ್ತಣಿಂ ಗಂಗೆ ಪುಟ್ಟಿತ್ತು, the Ganges rose from the Himavat mountain; ಬೀಜದತ್ತಣಿನ್ದಂಕುರಮ್ ಆದುದು, the sprout arose from the seed; ಶೃಂಗದತ್ತಣಿಂ ಶರಮ್ ಆದುದು, the water proceeded from the top of the mountain.

8, gurutva, pĕrmĕ, *i. e.* dignity, age (in comparison), *e. g.* ಕೃಷ್ಣನತ್ತಣಿಂ ಬಲಭದ್ರಂ ಪಿರಿಯಂ, Balabhadra (is) older than Kṛishṇa; ಅರ್ಜುನನತ್ತಣಿಂ ವಾಸುದೇವನ್ ಅಧಿಕಂ, Vâsudêva (is) more excellent than Arjuna; ನಕುಲನತ್ತಣಿಂ ಸಹದೇವಂ ಕಿಱಿಯಂ, Sahadêva (is) younger than Nakula; ಆತನತ್ತಣಿನ್ದೀತಂ ಪಟು, this man (is) smarter than that man. *Cf.* §§ 343, 2, *a*; 343, 3; 348, 7; 350, 2, *a—c*.

350. In sentences in which the locative case (adhikaraṇa, âdhâra, *cf.* § 352, 3. 5, *c.* 6, *a*) is used, the following specific meanings are considered to be expressed by it:—

1, adhikaraṇa, âdhâra, *i. e.* (simple) relation to site, place, *e. g.* ಪಾಸಿನೊಳ್ ನಿದ್ರೆಗೆಯ್ದಂ, he slept on the bed; ಪಱಿಗೋಲೊಳ್ ಕುಳ್ಳಿರ್ದಂ, he sat down in the basket-boat; ಮನ್ದಿರದೊಳ್ ತುಱುಗಳ್, the cows (are) in the house; ಮರದ ಹರಿಯಾಣದೊಳ್ ಉಣ್ಡಂ, he ate from a plate of wood; ಬಿಮ್ಬದೊಳ್ ತೇಜಂ, (there is) splendour in the disk of the sun; ಅಲರೊಳ್ ಬೆಳ್ಪು, (there is) white colour in the flower; ತಾವರೆಯೊಳ್ ಪುಟ್ಟಿದಂ, he was born in a lotus (or sprung from a lotus); [ಮನೆಯಲ್ಲಿದ್ದಾನೆ, he is in the house; ಅಡವಿಯಲ್ಲಿ ಅನ್ನವನ್ನಟ್ಟರು, they cooked rice in the jungle; ಮೆಯ್ಯಲ್ಲಿ ಕಸುವದೆ, (there) is strength in (his) body].

2, nirdhâraṇa, *i. e.* specifying one out of many (comparison, see § 343, 4. 5; § 352, 1, *c*).

a) as to quality (guṇa), *e. g.* ದೇವರೊಳ್ ನಿರ್ದೋಷಿಯಾಪ್ತಂ, a fit one among princes (or the fittest one of princes is) the guiltless one; ರತ್ನಂಗಳೊಳ್ ಮಾಣಿಕ್ಯಮ್ ಉತ್ತಮಂ, among jewels the ruby (is) precious; ತುಱುಗಳೊಳ್ ಕಾರಾಕಳ್ ಪಾಲುಳ್ಳುದು, among cows the black cow (is) that which has (most) milk; ವಸ್ತ್ರದೊಳ್ ಬೆಳ್ಪಟ್ಟೆಯೊಳ್ಳಿತ್ತು, among cloth white cloth (is) good;

b) as to action or being (kriyĕ), *e.g.* ಪರಿಕಾಱರೊಳ್ ಈತಂ ಕಾಲ್ವಲ್ಲಿದಂ, among the runners this man (is) a strong-footed one (or this man is the most strong-footed one of the runners); ಕಾದುವರೊಳ್ ಈತಂ ಮೆಯ್ವಲಿ, among those who fight this man (is) a strong-bodied one; ಅವರೊಳ್ ಓಡುವಂ ಕಾಲ್ಪೇಗ, among them he who runs (is) a swift-footed one; ಪಣ್ಗಳೊಳ್ ಬೀೞ್ವುದು ತನಿವಣ್, among ripe fruits that which drops (from the tree is) a mature fruit (or the most mature fruit of ripe fruits is that which drops from the tree);

c) as to race (jâti), *e. g.* ಮಾನವರೊಳ್ ಪುರುಷರ್ ಉತ್ತಮರ್, among men males (are) chiefs (or males are the most eminent of men); ಪುರುಷರೊಳ್ ಕ್ಷತ್ರಿಯರ್ ಶೂರರ್, among males Kshatriyas (are) valiant men.

3, dravya, *i. e.* a fit object (considered by itself), *e. g.* ಇವರೊಳ್ ಈತನ್ ಎಮ್ಮಾತಂ, among these persons this one (is) ours; ಅವರೊಳ್ ಆತಂ ಕಲಿ, among those persons this one (is) the hero (Šabdânušâsana).

4, pûjyasâdhunipuṇa, *i. e.* the introduction of persons who are good to praiseworthy people or are skilful in praiseworthy things, *e. g.* ತಾಯೊಳ್ ಸಾಧು, (he is) kind to (his) mother; ತಾಯೊಳ್ ಒಳ್ಳಿದಂ, (he is) good to (his) mother; ಗುರುವಿನೊಳ್ ಸಹಜಂ, (he is) true to (his) guru; ಪೂಜೆಯೊಳ್ ಜಾಣಂ, (he is) proficient in adoration; ಚಿತ್ರದೊಳ್ ಕುಶಲಂ, (he is) expert in (drawing) pictures (Šabdânušâsana).

5, vishaya, *i. e.* a peculiar province or place, *e. g.* ಕಿವಿಯೊಳ್ ಪಚಿರ್ದಂ, he whispered in the ear; ಮೊಗನೊಳ್ ನೇಲ್ದಂ, he was suspended by (his) mouth [o. r.—ಮೆಲ್ದಂ, he chewed with (his) mouth].

6, vyâpaka, *i. e.* inherent property or substance (*cf.* No. 1), *e. g.* ಪೂವಿನೊಳ್ ಕಮ್ಪು, (there is) fragrance in flowers; ಕರ್ಬಿನೊಳ್ ರಸಂ, (there is) juice in the sugar-cane; ಎಳ್ಳೊಳ್ ಎಣ್ಣೆ, (there is) oil in the oil-plant; ಪಾಲೊಳ್ ಮಧುರಂ, (there is) sweetness in milk.

7, vyavahâra, *i.e.* engaging in, conduct or action in, *e.g.* ತಪದೊಳ್ ನೆಗಳ್ದಂ, he engaged in austerities; ವೀರದೊಳ್ ಎಸೆದಂ, he distinguished himself in (the department of) valour.

8, kâla, *i.e.* time (*cf.* §§ 348, 29; 352, 6, *a.* 6, *c*), *e.g.* ವಸನ್ತದೊಳ್ ಮಾವು ಬನ್ದುದು, mangoes appeared in spring; ಶರದೊಳ್ ದಿಗ್ವಿಜಯಮ್ ಉಚಿತಂ, universal conquest (is) proper in autumn; (ಒನ್ದು ತಿಂಗಳಲ್ಲಿ ವ್ಯಾಕರಣ ಓದಿದನು, he read through the grammar in one month; ಒನ್ದು ದಿನದಲ್ಲಿ ಕೆಲಸವಾಗುತ್ತದೆ, in one day the work will be done).

9, upâdâna, *i.e.* material cause (*cf.* § 347, 4), *e.g.* ಮರದೊಳ್ ಸಮೆದಂಕವಣೆಯನ್ ಏಱಿದಂ, he ascended the decorated seat that was made of wood; [ಮೊಸರಲೆ ಮಾಡಿದದು, that which (they) have made even of curdled milk].

10, [karaṇa, *i. e.* means, *e. g.* ಕಾಲಲ್ಲಿ ನಡೆಯುತ್ತೇವೆ, we walk by means of (our) feet; ಕಣ್ಣಲ್ಲಿ ನೋಡುತ್ತೇವೆ, we see with (our) eyes].

351. **The genitive case** that is not classed with the six kârakas (see § 344), **expresses the connection** (sambandha) **of nouns to nouns** (*cf.* § 352, 5, *a*; for adverbs with the genitive see § 282), which connection is of the following kinds:—

1, svâmisambandha, *i. e.* connection of ownership, *e. g.* ಊರೊಡೆಯಂ, the chief of the town; ನಾಡೊಡೆಯಂ, the chief of the district; (ಅರಸುಗಳ ಬೀಡಾರ, the house of the king; ರಾಯರ ಕುದುರೆ, the horse of the râja; ಹುಡುಗರ ಪುಸ್ತಕ, the books of the boys; ಕುಮ್ಬಾರನ ಹೆಣ್ಡತಿ, the wife of the potter).

2, kulasambandha, *i. e.* connection of family or caste, *e. g.* ಎಮ್ಮ ಸೊಮ್ಮು, the property of us (*i. e.* our property); ಎಮ್ಮ ಮೋಱೆ, our face; ಎಮ್ಮಳಿಯಂ, our son-in-law; ಎಮ್ಮ ತಮ್ಮಂ, our younger brother; (ಶೂದ್ರನ ಮಗನು, a Śûdra's son; ಬಣಜಿಗನ ಮಗಳು, a merchant's daughter).

3, jâtisambandha, *i.e.* connection of genus, class or kind, *e.g.* ಆನೆಯ ಘಟೆ, a troop of elephants; ಕುದುರೆಯ ಥಟ್ಟು, a multitude of horses; ಗಿಳಿಯ ಪಿಣ್ಡು, a flock of parrots; ಅಲರ ಕಮ್ಪು, the fragrance of flowers; ಕಣ್ಣ ಬೆಳ್ಪು, the white of the eye; (ಹುಣಸಿಯ ಹಣ್ಣು, the ripe fruit of the tamarind; ಬಾಳೆಯ ಕಾಯಿ, the fruit of the plantain; ವೀಳ್ಯದೆಲೆ, the leaf of the betel plant; ನಾಯಿಯ ಮರಿ, a dog's puppy; ಕೋೞಿಯ ಕೂಗು, the cry of cocks).

4, avayavasambandha, *i. e.* connection of membership, *e. g.* ಮರದ ಕೊಮ್ಬು, the branch of a tree; ಪೂವಿನೆಸಳ್, the petal of a flower; ಕೊಡೆಯ ಕಾವು, the stick of an umbrella.

5, lakshaṇasambandha, *i. e.* connection of distinctive marks, *e. g.* ಟೊಪ್ಪಿಯ ಮಾನಿಸಂ, a man with a cap; ತತ್ತಳದ ರಾವುತಂ, a horseman of perplexity (*i. e.* a perplexed horseman, o. r. ತತ್ಥಳದ or ತತ್ತಳದ ರಾವುತಂ); ಸಿನ್ಧು ದೇಶದ ಕುದುರೆ, a horse of Sindh; (ಕಸುವಿನಾಳು, a person of power, a powerful person; ದರ್ಪದ ಬಣ್ಟನು, a proud soldier; ಹಿತದ ಉಪದೇಶ, friendly advice).

6, sannidhânasambandha, *i. e.* connection of proximity or vicinity, *e. g.* ಕೆಱೆಯ ಕೋಡಿ, an outlet (in the proximity) of a tank; ಊರ ಮುನ್ದು, the place in front of a town; ಅದಱ ಕೆಲಂ, the vicinity of that (*i. e.* its vicinity).

7, saṁsparšasambandha, *i. e.* connection of close contact, *e. g.* ಕಳದ ತಳಿರ್, young foliage on a threshing floor; ನೀರ ಹಾವಸೆ, duck-weed on water; ತೋಳ ಬನ್ದಿ, an ornamental tie on the arm.

8, sambandhasambandha, *i. e.* connection of connection (occurring when two genitives precede a noun), *e. g.* ನೊಸಲ ಕಣ್ಣ ದೇವಂ, the god of an eye of the forehead (*i. e.* the god who has an eye on the forehead); ತೋಳ ಬಾಳ ಕಾನ್ತಿ, the lustre of the sword of the arm; ಹರಿಯ ಪೊಕ್ಕುೞ ತಾವರೆ, the lotus of the navel of Hari.

9, šêshasambandha, *i. e.* connection of remainder or rest, *e. g.* ಬಳ್ಳ ದಱಿ, the substance that remains in a baḷḷa; ಅದಱ ಮಱಿ, the young one (which was left) to it.

10, vikârasambandha, *i. e.* connection of change of form, *e. g.* ಪೊನ್ನ ಕೋಲ್, a staff of gold; (ಚಿನ್ನದುಂಗರ, a ring of gold).

11, (sthalasambandha, *i. e.* connection of place, *e. g.* ಅಡವಿಯ ಪರವಾಸ, sojourning in the forest; ಕಾಶಿಯ ವಾಸ, dwelling in Kâši; ಮನೆಯ ಊಟ, dinner at one's house).

Remark.

It may be stated here that **several genitives, one after the other, in connection with only one noun,** are sometimes used in the following manner (from which use will also appear that the conjunctions ಉಂ, etc. are never suffixed to the genitive, see § 284):—

ಕೀರದ ಹಂಸದ ಪಿಕದ ಚ
ಕೋರದ ಚಕ್ರಾಹ್ವಯದನ್ತೆ ಮಾಡಿದ ಗರುಡೋ |
ದ್ಗಾರದ ಮುತ್ತಿನ ನೀಲದ
ಹೀರದ ಮಾಣಿಕದ ಪೊಳೆವ ಜೀರ್ಕೊೞವಿಗಳಂ || 125 ||

ತಮ ತಮಗೆ ಕಳೆದು ಕೊಣ್ಡು ವಿವಿಧಗನ್ಧಜಳಂಗಳಿನ್ ಒರ್ವರೊರ್ವರ ಮೇಲೆ ಸಿವ್ಪಿಸುವಾಗಳ್ (Ćandraprabhâpurâṇa VII). They discharged the shining syringes of emeralds, pearls, sapphires, diamonds (and) rubies which (artificers) had made (*i. e.* which had been made, see § 315, 2, under *k*) like parrots, swans, cuckoos, partridges (and) ruddy geese, against themselves, and besprinkled one another with water of various fragrance.

ಮಧುರವಾಣಿಯ ಕೃತಜ್ಞನ ದಾನಪರನ ಪರ
ವಧುವಿನೊಲ್ಮೆಯ ಬೇಟೆಗೊಳಗಾಗದನ ಮಾನ
ನಿಧಿಯೆನಿಸುವನ ತೀರ್ಥಸಂಗತನ ಸಲೆ ಕೂಟಸಾಕ್ಷ್ಯವಂ ನುಡಿಯದವನಾ |
ವಿಧಿಕರ್ಮದ ಮಾಡ್ಕೆಯಂ ಮಾಜದಾತನ ವ
ಸುಧೆಯೊಳ್ ಇಷ್ಟಾರ್ಥಪೂರ್ತಿಯ ನೆಗೞ್ಚುವನ ಬಹು
ವಿಧಧರ್ಮಂಗಳಂ ರಚಿಸುವನ ಮನೆಯೊಳ್ ಇನ್ದಿರೆ ಬಿಡದೆ ನೆಲಸಿರ್ಪಳೂ || 67 in Jaimini v ||.

The goddess of fortune continually remains in the house of him who utters friendly words, is grateful, is intent upon giving, is kind to others' wives, is not addicted to chase, is rich is honour, associates with worthy persons, never utters false witness, does proper works, does not hide (his) doings, engages in abundant agreeable things on earth (and) performs various virtuous acts.

Compare also ಕೆಯ್ಯ ಕಾಲ ಎಲ್ವು, the bone of the arm (and) of the leg (*i. e.* the radius of the arm and the skin-bone, Halâyudha). ರಾಮನ ಕೃಷ್ಣನ ಮಕ್ಕಳನ್ನು ತೋಱಿಸು, show (me) the children of Râma (and) Kṛishṇa; ನಿನ್ನಾ ಅವನಾ ದ್ವೇಷವದೆ, there is enmity between thee (and) him (Nuḍigaṭṭu).

352. The seven cases sometimes change places (*cf.* also § 253, 1, *a. b*), *viz.*

1, *a*) **the genitive** stands for the nominative, *e. g.* ನಿಶ್ಶಂಕೆಯಿಂ ನೃಪನ ಪೇೞ್ದಿ and ಚಿತ್ರಭವಗೃಹದ ಸೊಂಕೆ stand for ನಿಶ್ಶಂಕೆಯಿಂ ನೃಪಂ ಪೇೞ್ದಿ and ಚಿತ್ರಭವಗೃಹಂ ಸೊಂಕೆ.

The author of the present grammar considers this statement of Kêšava to be erroneous, as the genitives ನೃಪನ and ಗೃಹದ stand before the nouns ಪೇೞ್ದಿ and ಸೊಂಕೆ; see §§ 188. (365).

The Šabdânušâsana has the instance ನಿನ್ನ ಬನ್ದಯ್ for ನೀಂ ಬನ್ದಯ್, thou camest, the proof for the correctness of which must be left to Bhaṭṭâkalaṅka dêva.

b) the genitive stands for the accusative, *e. g.* ಎಲವೊ, ನೀನ್ ಎನ್ನ ಕೊನ್ದಯ್ and ತೆಂಕನಾಡ ಮಱೆಯುಳ್ಕೆನ್ದುಂ ಮನಂ ಬರ್ಕುಮೆ stand for ಎಲವೊ, ನೀನ್ ಎನ್ನಂ ಕೊನ್ದಯ್, O thou killedst me, and ತೆಂಕನಾಡಂ ಮಱೆಯುಳ್ಕೆನ್ದುಂ

ಮನಂ ಬರ್ಕುಮೆ, does it ever come to (my) mind to forget the southern country?

The author of the present grammar thinks that ಎನ್ನ and ನಾಡ are accusatives with final ಅ, as he has indicated in § 117, *a*, 2; 122, *a*, 2.

c) the genitive stands for the locative (in comparison), *e.g.* ಚಾಗಿಗಳ ಬಲ್ಲಹಂ stands for ಚಾಗಿಗಳೊಳ್ ಬಲ್ಲಹಂ, a supreme one among liberal persons; ಈವರ ದೇವಂ for ಈವರೊಳ್ ದೇವಂ, a prince among donors; ರಸಿಕರ ಚಕ್ರವರ್ತಿ for ರಸಿಕರೊಳ್ ಚಕ್ರವರ್ತಿ, a king among the witty. See § 343, 5 and *cf.* § 350, 2, *a*.

2, *a*) **the accusative** stands for the nominative (*cf.* No. 6, *b*), *e.g.* ನುಣ್ಪನುಳ್ಳಂ stands for ನುಣ್ಪುಳ್ಳಂ (resting on ಉಳ್ meaning also 'to possess'), one who possesses fineness. The Šabdânušâsana has also the instance: ದೇವದತ್ತನನ್ ಇರ್ದಂ, instead of ದೇವದತ್ತನ್ ಇರ್ದಂ. *Cf.* §§ 346. 348, 12.

b) the accusative stands for the instrumental, *e.g.* ಪೂವಿನ್ ಅರ್ಚಿಸಿದಂ, he worshipped with flowers, stands for ಪೂವನ್ ಅರ್ಚಿಸಿದಂ, he presented flowers in worship. See § 347.

c) the accusative stands for the dative (*cf.* No. 5, *b*), *e. g.* ಪೊನ್ನಂ ಬಡ್ಡಿಯುಂ ಕೊಟ್ಟಂ stands for ಪೊನ್ನಂ ಬಡ್ಡಿಗೆ ಕೊಟ್ಟಂ, he lent gold coins on interest; ಲೋಕಮನ್ ಅಧಿಕಂ for ಲೋಕಕ್ಕಧಿಕಂ, the greatest of all (this second sentence is from the Šabdânušâsana; *cf.* § 348, 7); (ದೇವರನ್ನು ವನ್ದಿಸುತ್ತೇನೆ for ದೇವರಿಗೆ ವನ್ದಿಸುತ್ತೇನೆ; ಪಾದವನ್ನು ಎಱಗುತ್ತೇನೆ for ಪಾದಕ್ಕೆ ಎಱಗುತ್ತೇನೆ; ಅರಸನನ್ನು ಮಱೆ ಹೊಕ್ಕನು for ಅರಸನಿಗೆ ಮಱೆ ಹೊಕ್ಕನು; ಮೋಕ್ಷವನ್ನು ಚಿನ್ತಿಸು for ಮೋಕ್ಷಕ್ಕೆ ಚಿನ್ತಿಸು; thus also ಪರದ್ರವ್ಯವನ್ನು ಆಶಿಸ ಬೇಡ; ತಲೆಯನ್ನು ಅಡರಿದಳು; ಮರವನ್ನು ಏಱಿದನು; ನನ್ನನ್ನು ಬಯ್ಯುತ್ತಾನೆ; ಊರನ್ನು ಸೇರಿದನು).

d) the accusative stands for the ablative, *e.g.* ಮಾಣವಕನಂ ಕಾರ್ಯಮಂ ಬೆಸಗೊಣ್ಡಂ, he demanded business of the lad, for ಮಾಣವಕನತ್ತಣಿಂ ಕಾರ್ಯಮಂ ಬೆಸಗೊಣ್ಡಂ. See § 349.

3, **the locative** stands for the instrumental, *e.g.* ಕೊಡಲಿಯೊಳ್ ಕಡಿದಂ stands for ಕೊಡಲಿಯಿಂ ಕಡಿದಂ, he cut with the axe; ಗದೆಯೊಳ್ ಪೊಯ್ದಂ for ಗದೆಯಿಂ ಪೊಯ್ದಂ; ಕಿವಿಯೊಳ್ ಕೇಳ್ದಂ for ಕಿವಿಯಿಂ ಕೇಳ್ದಂ; ಕುಡುಗೋಲೊಳ್ ಕೊಯ್ದಂ for ಕುಡುಗೋಲಿಂ ಕೊಯ್ದಂ. See § 350.

4, *a*) **the instrumental** stands for the ablative (*cf.* § 117, *a*, 5; see § 349; § 343 ablative and instrumental in comparison; § 302, 1 instrumental for 'since'; § 282 adverbs with the instrumental).

1. in simple apâdâna, *e. g.* ಕೆಱೆಯಿಂ ಬನ್ದಂ stands for ಕೆಱೆಯತ್ತಣಿಂ ಬನ್ದಂ, he came from the tank; ಕರಿಶಿರದಿಂ ಮುತ್ತುಕ್ಕುವು for ಕರಿಶಿರದತ್ತಣಿಂ ಮುತ್ತುಕ್ಕುವು, from the head of the elephant pearls dropped; ಮರದಿನ್ದೆಲೆ ಬಿಱ್ದುದು for ಮರದತ್ತಣಿನ್ದೆಲೆ ಬಿಱ್ದುದು, a leaf fell from the tree. ಅಲಿವರಲ್ಗಳುಮ್ ಇನ್ದ್ರಗೋಪಮುಂ ಸೂಸಿದುವಭ್ರದಿಂ. ತಿಳಿಗೊಳದಿನ್ದೆ ಪಾಱಿದುವು ಹಂಸಕುಳಂ. (ಊರಿನ್ದ ಬನ್ದನು; ಉಪ್ಪರಿಗೆಯಿನ್ದ ಇೞಿದನು; ಗಂಗೆ ಹಿಮಾಲಯದಿನ್ದ ಹರಿಯುತ್ತದೆ.)

ಮತ್ತಹಸ್ತಿಗಳ ಮಸ್ತಕದಿಂ ಬಿದಿರಿಂ ಫಣೀ
ನ್ದ್ರೋತ್ತಮಾಂಗದಿನ್ ಅಗುರ್ವಿಪ ಪನ್ನಿಯ ಕೋಡ್ಗಳಿಂ ।
ಪತ್ತುವಿಟ್ಟಗನಿಕಾಯದೊಳ್ ಒಕ್ಕಿಳಮುತ್ತನಾ
ಯ್ವುತ್ತಮಿರ್ಪ ಶಬರವಿಪ್ರಿಯಕಾಮಿನಿಯರ್ಕಳಿಂ ॥ by the beloved women of the Šabaras who were gathering the fine pearls which were loosened from the heads of the mad elephants, from the bamboos, from the heads of the cobras (and) from the tusks of the formidable hogs, and dropped on the massy rocks....

2. [in bhêda, *i. e.* difference (*cf.* § 348, 31), *e. g.* ಅದಱಿನ್ದ ಇದು ಬೇಱೆ, this (is) different from that].

3. (in dikku, *i. e.* direction, quarter, *e. g.* ಧಾರವಾಡದಿನ್ದ ಬೆಳಗಾವಿ ಬಡಗಲು, Belgaum (is) to the north of Dharwar: *cf.* § 348, 21).

4. (in dûra, *i. e.* distance, *e. g.* ಆ ಹಳ್ಳಿಯು ಇಲ್ಲಿನ್ದ ಐದು ಮೈಲು ಅದೆ, that village is five miles from this place; ಊರಿನ್ದ ಅಡವಿ ಒನ್ದು ಕೂಗಳತೆ ಅದೆ, the jungle is a loud cry distant from the town; *cf.* § 348, 22).

5. [in kâla, *i. e.* time, *e. g.* ಬಹುಕಾಲದಿನ್ದ ತಮ್ಮ ದರ್ಶನವಾಯಿತು, it is long since you visited (me); ಚಿಕ್ಕನ್ದಿನಿನ್ದ ಅವನು ದರಿದ್ರನು, he (is) poor from (his) youth; *cf.* § 302, 1; § 348, 29].

6. (in bhaya, *i.e.* fear, *e.g.* ಹುಲಿಯಿನ್ದ ಅಂಜಿದನು, he was afraid of the tiger; *cf.* § 349, 2).

7. (in ishṭa, *i. e.* agreeableness, pleasure, *e. g.* ನನ್ನನ್ನು ಪಾಪದಿನ್ದ ರಕ್ಷಿಸಿದನು, he saved me from sin; *cf.* § 349, 4).

8. (in anishṭa, *i. e.* disagreeableness, *e. g.* ವೈರಿಯಿನ್ದ ಬನ್ಧನವಾಯಿತು, imprisonment came from the enemy; *cf.* § 349, 3).

9. (in hêtu, *i. e.* cause, means, *e. g.* ಉದ್ಯೋಗದಿನ್ದ ಸಿರಿ ಬನ್ತು, wealth came from office; ವಿದ್ಯೆಯಿನ್ದ ವಿನಯ ಬರುತ್ತದೆ, from learning comes good behaviour; *cf.* § 349, 6).

10. [in udaya, *i. e.* springing from, originating (*cf.* § 349, 7), *e. g.* ಬೀಜದಿನ್ದ ಅಂಕುರವಾಗುತ್ತದೆ, the sprout arises from seed; ಲಕ್ಷ್ಮಿಯಿನ್ದ ಕಾಮನು ಹುಟ್ಟಿದನು, Kâma was born of Lakshmî].

11. [in ಕಾರಣ, cause, reason, see §§ 302, 7; 348, 32; *cf.* also:— ಜ್ಞಾನದಿನ್ದ ವೃದ್ಧನು, on account of (his) wisdom (he is already) a full-grown person; ಆಚಾರದಿನ್ದ ಪವಿತ್ರನು, on account of (his) right conduct (he is) a good person].

b) [the instrumental stands for the dative, *e.g.* ಹೆಸರಿನಿನ್ದ ಅರಸನು for ಹೆಸರಿಗೆ ಅರಸನು, a king (only) in name; *cf.* § 348, 20. Observe also: ಜನಿವಾರದಿನ್ದ ಬ್ರಾಹ್ಮಣನು, (he is) a Brâhmaṇa (only) for (his) sacrificial thread; ಜಟೆಯಿನ್ದ ತಾಪಸನು, (he is) an ascetic (only) for (his) matted hair; ಮಾತಿನಿನ್ದ ಸಾತ್ವಿಕನು, (he is) a gentle person (only) in (his) words].

5, *a*) the dative stands for the genitive, *e.g.* ನಾಡಿಗೊಡೆಯಂ stands for ನಾಡೊಡೆಯಂ, the chief of the district; ಕೊಡೆಗೊಡೆಯಂ for ಕೊಡೆಯೊಡೆಯಂ, the lord of the umbrella; ಎರ್ದೆಗಾಣ್ಮಂ for ಎರ್ದೆಯಾಣ್ಮಂ, a heart's ruler; ಜಗಕ್ಕೊಡೆಯಂ for ಜಗದೊಡೆಯಂ, the lord of the world; (ಲೋಕಕ್ಕೆ ತನ್ದೆ for ಲೋಕದ ತನ್ದೆ).

b) the dative stands for the accusative (*cf.* No. 2, *c*), *e.g.* ಶಿಷ್ಯಂಗೆ ಕಲ್ಪಿಸಿದಂ stands for ಶಿಷ್ಯನಂ ಕಲ್ಪಿಸಿದಂ, he ordered the pupil; ಆಕೆಗೆ ತಿಳಿಪಿದಂ for ಆಕೆಯಂ ತಿಳಿಪಿದಂ, he informed her; (ದೇವರಿಗೆ ವನ್ದಿಸುತ್ತೇನೆ for ದೇವರನ್ನು ವನ್ದಿಸುತ್ತೇನೆ; ಪಾದಕ್ಕೆ ಎಱಗುತ್ತೇನೆ for ಪಾದವನ್ನು ಎಱಗುತ್ತೇನೆ; thus also ಅರಸನಿಗೆ ಮಱಿ ಹೊಕ್ಕನು; ಮೋಕ್ಷಕ್ಕೆ ಚಿನ್ತಿಸು; ಪರದ್ರವ್ಯಕ್ಕೆ ಆಶಿಸ ಬೇಡ; ತಲೆಗೆ ಅಡರಿದಳು; ಮರಕ್ಕೆ ಏಱಿದನು; ನನಗೆ ಬಯ್ಯುತ್ತಾನೆ; ಊರಿಗೆ ಸೇರಿದನು; ಆರಿಗಾದರೂ ಪೂರ್ವಕರ್ಮ ಬಿಡದು, see § 291).

c) the dative stands for the locative (*cf.* § 350, 1. 6), *e.g.* ತಾವರೆಗೆ ಪುಟ್ಟಿದಂ stands for ತಾವರೆಯೊಳ್ ಪುಟ್ಟಿದಂ, he sprang from a lotus; ಬಿಮ್ಬಕ್ಕೆ ತೇಜಂ for ಬಿಮ್ಬದೊಳ್ ತೇಜಂ, (there is) splendour in the disk of the sun; ಅಲರ್ಗೆ ಬೆಳ್ಪು for ಅಲರೊಳ್ ಬೆಳ್ಪು, (there is) white colour in the flower; ಎಳ್ಗೆಣ್ಣೆ for ಎಳ್ಳೊಳ್ ಎಣ್ಣೆ, (there is) oil in the oil-plant; (ಈ ಊರಿಗೆ ನಾಲ್ಕು ಕೆಱೆಗಳುಣ್ಟು for ಈ ಊರಲ್ಲಿ ನಾಲ್ಕು ಕೆಱೆಗಳುಣ್ಟು; ಮೂರ್ಖರಿಗೆ ಬುದ್ಧಿಯಿಲ್ಲ for ಮೂರ್ಖರಲ್ಲಿ ಬುದ್ಧಿಯಿಲ್ಲ).

6, *a*) the nominative stands for the locative (*cf.* No. 6, *c*), *e.g.* ಒನ್ದು ದಿವಸಂ ಬನ್ದಂ for ಒನ್ದು ದಿವಸದೊಳ್ ಬನ್ದಂ, he came in one day.

b) the nominative stands for the accusative (*cf.* No, 2, *c*), *e.g.* ಒನ್ದು ವರ್ಷಮ್ ಇರ್ದಂ stands for ಒನ್ದು ವರ್ಷಮನ್ ಇರ್ದಂ, he stayed one year; ಘಟಂ ಮಾಡಿದಂ for ಘಟಮಂ ಮಾಡಿದಂ he made a water-vessel (the first instance is from the Śabdamaṇidarpaṇa, the second one from the Śabdânuśâsana).

There may be adduced the following ancient additional instances (see § 120, *a*, 2): — ನುಡಿವೊಡೆಲ್ಲರುಂ ಮಾತಱಿಯರ್, if (they) speak, all of them do not know (proper) words [Šabdamaṇidarpaṇa sub sûtra 250 where the Mûḍabidar MS. has ಮುಳಿವೊಡೆಲ್ಲರುಂ ಮುನ್ದಱಿಯರ್, if (they) grow passionate, they do not know what is to come]. ಮಗನೆ, ಮಗನೆ, ನೀನ್ ಒಳ್ಳಿತು ಗೆಯ್ದುಯ್, O son, O son, thou didst what is good (Šabdânušâsana s. sûtra 399). ಪಶು ಕಱೆಯಲ್ ಬನ್ದಂ, he came to milk the cow; ರಮಣಿ ನೋಡಲ್ ಬನ್ದಂ, he came to see the woman (Šabdânušâsana). ಪೊಲನಱಿಯದ ನೆಲನಱಿಯದ ಕೆಲನಱಿಯದ ಮಿಗದ ಮೂಱು ವಿಧವಱಿಯದ (ಮನುಷ್ಯಂ), (a person) who did not know the direction, who did not know the place, who did not know the side, who did not know the three ways of beasts (Šmd. p. 127). See also § 339, 5 (ಕುಂಕುಮವಾರಿ ಕುಪ್ಪಳಿಸಿ), § 362, 2, *b* (ತಿದಿಯೊತ್ತುವ).

In the modern dialect it is very common to use the crude base of a noun for the accusative, *e. g.* ಕೆಲಸ ಬಿಡು; ಊಟ ಮಾಡು; ಬುದ್ಧಿ ಹೇಳು; ತುರಿ ಮಾಡು; ಮಾತು ಕಲಿಸು; ಗೂಡು ಕಟ್ಟು; ಎಣ್ಣೆ ಹೂಸು; ಮನೆ ಮಾಡು.

c) [the nominative is used to express time instead of the dative, etc. (*cf.* §§ 348, 29; 350, 8, etc.; and No. 6, *a*), *e. g.* ಹೋದ ಶನಿವಾರ ಬನ್ದನು, he came last Saturday; ಬೃಹಸ್ಪತಿವಾರ ದೊರೆಗಳು ಪುಸ್ತಕಗಳನ್ನು ಇನಾಮು ಕೊಡುವದಕ್ಕೆ ಬರುತ್ತಾರೆ, on Thursday the gentleman will come to make a present of books; ಎಣ್ಟು ದಿನ ನಾನು ಸಾಲೆಗೆ ಹೋಗಲಾರಿದೆ ಮನೆಯಲ್ಲಿಯೇ ನಿನ್ತು ಕೊಣ್ಡೆನು, eight days (or for eight days) I could not go to school and remained even at home; ಅವನು ಇಲ್ಲಿ ಎರಡು ವರುಷ ಇದ್ದನು, he lived here two (or for two) years; ಹಬ್ಬದ ದಿವಸ ಮುಂಜಾನೇ ಬರುವನು, early on the day of the feast he will come; ಈ ಹೊತ್ತು, to-day; ಇನ್ದು, to-day; ಹಗಲಿರುಳು, by day and night; ಈ ದಿವಸ, on this day; ಸೋಮವಾರ ದಿವಸ, on Monday; ಒನ್ದು ದಿವಸ, one day, on a certain day].

353. The instances in § **345** *seq.*, as far as they are not in parenthesis, are taken chiefly from the ancient dialect (as it appears in the Šabdamaṇidarpaṇa, Šabdânušâsana, etc.), which regarding the meaning, use and interchange of the cases does not materially differ from the mediæval and modern one. That there is some difference concerning the form of the seven cases in the three dialects, has been shown in § 100 *seq.* The instances of the modern dialect in parenthesis belong mostly to a small Kannaḍa grammar of the Southern Mahratta country, called Nuḍigaṭṭu.

354. Some special rules regarding the use of the singular and plural of nouns, etc. in or without sentences are to be given, *viz.*

I. **The singular stands or may stand for the plural in nouns.** *Cf.* § 133.

1, For the plural that conveys the meaning of a pair (yugaḷa) the singular is used, *e. g.* for ಪದಯುಗಂಗಳ್ there occurs ಪದಯುಗಂ, a couple of verse-lines.

2, Further, the singular is used instead of the plural in âvishṭa-liṅga, *i. e.* when the base of a noun (in an inflected state) refers to a noun in the plural which comprises more things than a pair, *e. g.* ವೇದಂಗಳ್ ಪ್ರಮಾಣಂ (for ವೇದಂಗಳ್ ಪ್ರಮಾಣಂಗಳ್), the (four) vêdas (are) proof;— or when it refers to a number of nouns which are connected by the conjunction ಉಂ, *e. g.* ಪ್ರತಿಭೆಯುಮ್ ಅಭ್ಯಾಸಮುಂ ವಿದ್ವತ್ಸೇವೆಯುಂ ಕಾವ್ಯಪರಿಚಯಮುಂ ಕವಿತೆಗೆ ಕಾರಣಂ (for... ಕಾರಣಂಗಳ್), genius, exercise, the service of the learned and the acquaintance with poems (are) the means for poetical composition.

(That the interrogative pronoun ಏನ್ which has no form of the plural, may get the meaning of the plural, appears in § 262.)

3, An optional use of the singular for the plural occurs regarding nouns of race, species or kind (jâti), such as ಕಾಲಾಳ್, ಆನೆ, ಕುದುರೆ, ಎರಲೆ, ಪುಲ್ಲೆ, ಎಱ್ತು (ಎತ್ತು), ಗಿಳಿ, ಹಂಸೆ, ಸೋಗೆ, ಕೋಗಿಲೆ, ತುಮ್ಬಿ, ಕೋೞಿ, ಪಲ್ (ಹಲ್ಲು), ಕಱಿವೆ, ಪೂ, etc., *e. g.* ಕಾಲಾಳ್ or ಕಾಲಾಳ್ಗಳ್, foot-soldiers, ಆನೆ or ಆನೆಗಳ್, elephants; similarly also ಕಣ್ಣಾಲಿ or ಕಣ್ಣಾಲಿ, the pupil of the eye. See § 355, I, 3. 4. But

a) If a jâti noun in the singular is preceded by an adjective which is, so to say, its kâraka (*i. e.* determinating the case and number of the noun, *cf.* § 355, IV, 5), it always has the meaning of the singular, *e. g.* ಇನ್ತುಟಾನೆ, such an elephant; ಇನ್ತುಟು ಕುದುರೆ, such a horse; (ನೇರಿತ್ತು ಬೆರಲ್, a straight finger; ಚಲೋದು ಮೋಱೆ, a beautiful face).

b) If jâti nouns stand in the singular and are preceded by an adjective in the plural, they always convey the meaning of the plural, *e. g.* ನೇರಿದುವು ಬೆರಲ್, straight fingers; ತೋರಿದುವು ಜಘನಂ, big buttocks; ಬೆಟ್ಟಿದುವು ಮೊಲೆ, stout breasts.

c) Observe the following sentences in which, either by a preceding noun in the plural or by a following demonstrative pronoun in the plural, the plural number of a jâti noun is indicated:— ಗೂಡಿನೊಳಗೆ ಕೆಲವು ತತ್ತಿಗಳು ಇದ್ದವು, ಹೆಣ್ಣುಗುಬ್ಬಿ ತತ್ತೀ (*i. e.* ತತ್ತಿಗಳನ್ನು) ಬಿಟ್ಟು ಹೊಱಗೆ ಹಾಱಿ ಹೋಯಿತು. ಮಗನು ಅನ್ನದ್ದೇನು— ಕೋಣೆಯೊಳಗೆ ಮಾವಿನ ಹಣ್ಣು (*i. e.* ಮಾವಿನ ಹಣ್ಣುಗಳನ್ನು)

ಇಡಲಿಕ್ಕೆ ಹೋದೆನು; ಅದಕ್ಕೆ ತನ್ದೆ ಅನ್ದದ್ದೇನು — ಮಾವಿನ ಹಣ್ಣು (*i. e.* ಮಾವಿನ ಹಣ್ಣುಗಳು)? ಅವು ನಿನಗೆ ಎಲ್ಲಿನ್ದ ಬನ್ದವು?

4, An optional use of the singular for the plural further takes place when objects are to be counted (saṅkhyêya, saṅkhyâvastu), *e. g.* ಪತ್ತು ದೆಸೆ or ಪತ್ತು ದೆಸೆಗಳ್, the ten points of the compass; ಮೂಱು ಲೋಕಂ or ಮೂಱು ಲೋಕಂಗಳ್, the (mentioned) three worlds; ಮೂಱು ಲಿಂಗಂ or ಮೂಱು ಲಿಂಗಗಳ್, the (mentioned) three genders; ನಾಲ್ಕು ಯುಗಂ or ನಾಲ್ಕು ಯುಗಂಗಳ್, the (mentioned) four ages of the world; ಈರೇೞು ಲೋಕಂ or ಈರೇೞು ಲೋಕಂಗಳ್, the fourteen worlds; ಈರಯ್ದುವಸ್ಥೆ or ಈರಯ್ದುವಸ್ಥೆಗಳ್, the ten states or conditions; (ನಾಲ್ಕು ತಿಂಗಳು or ನಾಲ್ಕು ತಿಂಗಳುಗಳು, four months; ನಾಲ್ಕು ತಿಂಗಳು ಆದವು or ನಾಲ್ಕು ತಿಂಗಳುಗಳು ಆದವು, it is four months).

5, An optional use of the singular for the plural further takes place when numerals are counted (saṅkhyâna, saṅkhyêya), *e. g.* ಒನ್ದು ನಾಲ್ಕು or ಒನ್ದು ನಾಲ್ಕುಗಳ್, one fours (*i. e.* four); ಈರಯ್ದು or ಈರಯ್ದುಗಳ್, two fives (*i. e.* ten); ಪತ್ತು ನೂಱು or ಪತ್ತು ನೂಱುಗಳ್, ten hundreds (*i. e.* one thousand). *Cf.* § 278, 1.

6, An optional use of the singular for the plural further takes place with regard to nouns of quality (bhâva), such as ಕೂರ್ಪು, ಕರ್ಪು, *e. g.* ಕಣ್ಗಳ ಕೂರ್ಪು or ಕಣ್ಗಳ ಕೂರ್ಪುಗಳ್, the penetrating looks of the eyes; ಪೂಗಳ ಬೆಳ್ಪು or ಪೂಗಳ ಬೆಳ್ಪುಗಳ್; ಕುರುಳ್ಗಳ ಕರ್ಪು or ಕುರುಳ್ಗಳ ಕರ್ಪುಗಳ್.

II. The plural of nouns stands for the singular

1, in spontaneous respect (*i. e.* in respect that proceeds alone from natural feeling, ayatnakṛitagurutva, prayatnam alladirpa gurutva), *e. g.* ಎಮ್ಮ ದೇವತೆಗಳ್, our deity; ಎಮ್ಮ ತನ್ದೆಗಳ್, our father; ಎಮ್ಮ ತಾಯ್ಗಳ್, our mother; ಎಮ್ಮಯ್ಯಂಗಳ್, our master; (ದೇವರ್ಗೆ ಪೊಡಮಟ್ಟಂ, he made obeisance to the king). *Cf.* §§ 257. 258. 261. 268.

The modern dialect when referring to 'God' uses ದೇವರು (see § 355, I, 1).

2, in (considering) the excellence of gurus, munîśvaras, etc. (and speaking or writing of them), *e. g.* ಗುರುಗಳ್, guru; ಸ್ವಾಮಿಗಳ್, master (lord or guru);

ಶ್ರೀಮತ್ಸಮಸ್ತಭದ್ರ
ಸ್ವಾಮಿಗಳ, ಜಗತ್ಪ್ರಸಿದ್ಧಕವಿಪರಮೇಷ್ಠಿ ।
ಸ್ವಾಮಿಗಳ, ಪೂಜ್ಯಪಾದ
ಸ್ವಾಮಿಗಳ ಪಾದಂಗಳ್ ಈಗೆ ಶಾಶ್ವತಪದಮಂ ॥ may the feet of

the illustrious svâmi Samantabhadra, of the world-famed poet svâmi Paramêshṭhi (and) of svâmi Pûjyapâda give perpetual protection.

3, Instead of the singular ತ್ರಿಭುವನಂ, the three worlds, its plural ತ್ರಿಭುವನಂಗಳ್ has been used in Kannaḍa.

4, If two or more nouns in the singular connected by ಉಂ (ಊ), 'and' (§ 284) are formed into a dvandva compound (§ 250), the plural is generally used, *e.g.* ಮರನುಂ ಗಿಡುವುಂ become ಮರಗಿಡುಗಳ್, trees and shrubs, ತನ್ದೆಯುಂ ತಾಯುಂ become ತನ್ದೆತಾಯ್ಗಳ್, father and mother, ರಾಮನುಂ ಲಕ್ಷ್ಮಣನುಂ become ರಾಮಲಕ್ಷ್ಮಣರ್, Râma and Lakshmaṇa, ಮರನುಂ ಗಿಡುವುಂ ಬಳ್ಳಿಯುಂ ಪುಲ್ಲುಂ ಪೊದಱುಂ ಪಕ್ಕಿಯುಂ ಮಿಗಮುಂ become ಮರಗಿಡುಬಳ್ಳಿಪುಲ್ಪೊದಱುಪಕ್ಕಿಮಿಗಂಗಳ್, trees, shrubs, creepers, grass, bushes, birds and antelopes; ಬಕನುಂ ಕಂಸನುಂ ಕೇಶಿಯುಂ become ಬಕಕಂಸಕೇಶಿಗಳ್, *e.g.* ಆವಂ ಬಕಕಂಸಕೇಶಿಗಳಂ ಅದಟಲೆದಂ, who subdued Baka, Kaṁsa and Kêśi?

Likewise in the modern dialect there frequently are sentences like the following:—ವಿದ್ಯೆಬುದ್ಧಿಗಳನ್ನು ದಡ್ಡರು ಮಾತ್ರ ಹೞಿಯುತ್ತಾರೆ, only stupid persons revile knowledge (and) wisdom; ಕಾಶಿರಾಯನಿಗೆ ರಾಮಕೃಷ್ಣರೆಮ್ಬುವರಿಬ್ಬರು ಗಣ್ಡುಮಕ್ಕಳು, Kâśirâja (had) two sons, Râma (and) Kṛishṇa; ಹಿರಿಕಿಱಿಯರು, old (and) young persons; ನಮ್ಮ ಕಾಗದಲೆಕ್ಕಣಿಕೆಪುಸ್ತಕಅಱಿವೆಗಳನ್ನು ಬಹು ಸ್ವಚ್ಛವಾಗಿ ಇಟ್ಟುಕೊಳ್ಳ ತಕ್ಕದು, it is proper to keep (our) paper, pens, books (and) clothes so that they remain very clean; ತಾಯಿತನ್ದೆಗುರುಯಜಮಾನರು ಹೇೞಿದ ಕೆಲಸವನ್ನು ಕೂಡಲೇ ಮಾಡ ಬೇಕು, (we) must do at once the work which (our) mother, father, teacher (and) master order (us to do); ಕುದುರೆಯೆತ್ತುಕೋಣಗಳು ಬಣ್ಡಿ ಎೞೆಯುತ್ತವೆ, horses, oxen (and) buffaloes draw carriages; ಎಮ್ಮೆಯಾಕಳುಗಳು ಹಾಲು ಹಿಣ್ಡುತ್ತವೆ, female buffaloes (and) cows give milk.

Exceptionally also the singular is used instead of the plural, as appears from § 250; thus there occurs in the modern dialect *e.g.* ಹುಡುಗರು ತಮ್ಮ ತಾಯಿತನ್ದೆಗುರು ಹೇೞಿದ ಮಾತು ಕೇಳ ಬೇಕು, boys must listen to the words told (them) by their mothers, fathers (and) teachers[1].

---

[1] It may be stated here that occasionally ಉಂ (ಊ) is omitted, see end of § 284; § 355, III, 2; § 355, IV, 5; § 357, 2, *d*, and compare also the following verse:—

ವಿಧುವಿಲ್ಲದಿರುಳ್, ತನ್ನಯ
ವಧುವಿಲ್ಲದ ಲೀಲೆ, ಮಧುರಮಧುವಿಲ್ಲದ ಪೂ, ।
ದಧಿಯಿಲ್ಲದುಣಿಸದೆಂತುದೋ
ಬುಧರಿಲ್ಲದ ಸಭೆ, ಸರಸ್ವತೀಮಣಿಹಾರಾ? ॥ will a night without the moon, a play without one's own wife, a flower without sweet nectar, a meal without curds (and) a congregation without intelligent persons be pleasant, Sarasvatimaṇihârâ?—The modern

Remarks.

a) If in the modern dialect two or more nouns occur one after the other without ಊ in the singular or promiscuously in both numbers, their plural is indicated by a demonstrative pronoun in the plural added to them with the proper inflection, *e.g.* ಅರಳೆ ಹಾಲು ಇವು ಬಿಳೇ ಬಣ್ಣದವು, dressed cotton (and) milk (are) of a white colour; ಎತ್ತು ಆಕಳು ಕೋಣ ಎಮ್ಮೆ ಇವುಗಳಿಗೆ ದನ ಅನ್ನುತ್ತಾರೆ, oxen, cows, male buffaloes (and) female buffaloes are called cattle. ಕೌರವನು ಅವನ ಗುರುಗಳು ತಮ್ಮನ್ದಿರು ಮಿತ್ರರು ಆ ಮಿತ್ರರ ಹಿತಚಿನ್ತಕರು ಇವರೆಲ್ಲರನ್ನು ಪಾಣ್ಡವರು ಜಯಿಸಿದರು, the Pâṇḍavas overcame the Kaurava, his gurus, (his) younger brothers, (his) friends (and) them who desired the welfare of those friends. Similarly the mediæval dialect has *e.g.* ಪಾದ ದೇವಭಟ್ಟಾರಕ ಈ ಮೂಱುಂ ಕಡೆಯೊಳು ಪೂಜಾವಚನಂ (see § 287 under 2).

b) If (especially in the ancient and mediæval dialect) two or more nouns are enumerated without ಉಂ or ಊ as mere terms, and ಮೊದಲಾದ, 'having become the first', 'and so forth', 'etc.', is placed at the end, a demonstrative pronoun in the plural (always neuter also when masculine or feminine terms are concerned) follows the nouns and another one in the plural is suffixed to ಮೊದಲಾದ (the first pronoun being sometimes omitted), *e.g.* ಶಿವ ಶಂಕರ ರಾಮ ಭೀಮ ಅರಸ ಇವು (ಶಬ್ದಗಳು) ಮೊದಲಾದುವು, Śiva, Śaṅkara, Râma, Bhîma, king, etc.; ಖಳಿಲೆನೆ ಛಳಿಲೆನೆ ಘಳಿಲೆನೆ ಇವು ಮೊದಲಾದುವು ಮಹಾಪ್ರಾಣಾನುಕರಣಂಗಳ್, khaḻilĕnĕ, čhaḻilĕnĕ, ghaḻilĕnĕ, etc. (are) imitative sounds with hard breathing; ಉರ್ದು ಕಡಲೆ ತೊಗರಿ ಗೋದುವೆ ಹೆಸಱು ಮೊದಲಾದುವನ್ ಇಕ್ಕಿ ಅಟ್ಟ ಕೂೞ್, food prepared of urdu, kaḍalĕ, tŏgari, gôduvĕ, hĕsaṟu, etc.; ಆಕಳ ಹಾಲು ಮೊಸರು ಮೊದಲಾದವೆಲ್ಲಂ ಗವ್ಯಮ್ ಎನಿಸುಗು,

---

dialect has *e.g.* ನೀತಿಯನೀತಿ ತಿಳಿಯದವನೇ ಪಶುವು, he who does not know justice (and) injustice (is) a beast. ಎಚ್ಚರದಲ್ಲಿ ಕನಸಿನಲ್ಲಿ ಗಾಢನಿದ್ರೆಯಲ್ಲಿ ನಿನ್ನನ್ನು ದೇವರು ಕಾಯುತ್ತಾನೆ, God protects thee in (thy) waking, dreaming (and) soundly sleeping.

The following additional verses may be quoted from the Śabdamaṇidarpaṇa:—

ವೇದವಿದಂ ಕಾಲತ್ರಯ
ವೇದಿ ಬಹುಶ್ರುತನ್ ಅಥರ್ವಕುಶಲಂ ಶುಭದಂ |
ಶೋದಯನ್ ಉತ್ತಮನ್ ಆಶೀ
ರ್ವಾದಪರಂ ಪರಹಿತಂ ಪುರೋಹಿತನಕ್ಕುಂ ||
ಮನುವಿನ ಮಾರ್ಗಂ ಸುರಗುರು
ವಿನದೀಪ್ತಿ ಪವಮಾನಸೂನುವಿನದ್ಧಯತಿ ಪೆ |
ಮ್ಪಿನೊಳೆಸೆವ ಕರ್ಣನೊಳ್ಪಿ
ತನಗದು ನಿಜವಾಗೆ ನೆಗಳ್ದನಾ ವಿಧುವಿಳೆಯೊಳ್ ||. See also the half verse in § 272, 2 (ನಿನತು ಚಲಮ್ etc.) and the verse in § 364 (ಪಾಡುವ ತುಮ್ಬಿ etc.).

milk of cows, curds, etc. are called, gavya. ಎಲೆ ಕಾಯಿ ಮೊದಲಾದವಂ ಮೊಸರಲ್ಲಿ ಕಲಸಿದುದು, leaves, fruits, etc. mixed with curdled milk.

In the modern dialect ಮುನ್ತಾದ is more generally used instead of ಮೊದಲಾದ in such a case, in the following manner:—ಬಂಗಾರ ಹಿತ್ತಾಳಿ ಬೇಗಡಿ ಮುನ್ತಾದವುಗಳು; ಚಿನ್ನ ಬೆಳ್ಳಿ ತಾಮ್ರ ಕಬ್ಬಿಣ ಮುನ್ತಾದವುಗಳು; ಮನುಷ್ಯ ಪಶು ಪಕ್ಷಿ ಗಿಡ ಭೂಮಿ ಆಕಾಶ ಸೂರ್ಯ ಚನ್ದ್ರ ನಕ್ಷತ್ರ ಮುನ್ತಾದವುಗಳನ್ನು ದೇವರು ಹುಟ್ಟಿಸಿದನು; ಸೇಕದಾರ ಮಾಮಲೇದಾರ ಮುನ್ತಾದವರು; ಹೆಣ್ಡತಿ ಮಕ್ಕಳು ಸೊಸೆನ್ದಿರು ಮೊಮ್ಮಕ್ಕಳು ಆಶ್ರಿತರು ಆಳುಮಕ್ಕಳು ಮುನ್ತಾದವರು.

If a noun follows ಮೊದಲಾದ or ಮುನ್ತಾದ, the way is as follows:—ಹರಿವೆ ಗಡಿಗೆ ಹರಿವಾಣ ಮೊದಲಾದ ಪಾತ್ರೆಗಳು; ಬೇಳೆ ಅಕ್ಕಿ ಜೋಳ ಮುನ್ತಾದ ಕಾಳುಗಳು.

Occasionally the pronoun suffixed to ಮೊದಲಾದ (or ಮುನ್ತಾದ) may stand in the singular, *e. g.* ಅಜಾಗರೂಕತೆ ಅವಿವೇಕ ಮುನ್ತಾದದು.

Sometimes only a single noun precedes ಮುನ್ತಾದ, *e. g.* ಒನ್ದು ಜಾತಿಯ ಚಿರ್ಚ ಕೊಳಿಕು ಮಾಂಸ ಮುನ್ತಾದ್ದನ್ನು ತಿನ್ನುತ್ತದೆ, a kind of leopard eats decayed flesh (and) other things. ಹೆಜಿವರ ಪುಸ್ತಕ ಮುನ್ತಾದವುಗಳನ್ನು ಕದ್ದು ಕೊಣ್ಡರೆ.

III. The plural of pronouns stands for the singular.

1, Where two words are connected by the conjunction ಉಂ, 'and', and both are demonstrative pronouns, if they are referred to and are to be expressed by one demonstrative pronoun, the second one has to stand in the plural, preponderating as to form and gender, *e. g.* ಆತನುಮ್ ಈತನುಂ become ಇವರ್, ಈತನುಂ ಊತನುಂ ಉವರ್, ಆಕೆಯುಮ್ ಈಕೆಯುಂ ಇವರ್, ಆಕೆಯುಮ್ ಆತನುಂ ಅವರ್, ಆತನುಂ ಅದುವುಂ ಅವು, ಅದುವುಮ್ ಆಕೆಯುಂ ಅವರ್.

2, When two words are connected by the conjunction ಉಂ, and one is a noun and the other a demonstrative pronoun, if they are referred to and are to be expressed by one word, the plural of the pronoun has to occur, preponderating as to gender, *e. g.* ಕುದುರೆಯುಂ ಆತನುಂ become ಅವರ್, ಅದುಂ ಕುದುರೆಯುಂ ಅವು, ಲತೆಯುಮ್ ಈಕೆಯುಂ ಇವರ್, ಪೂವುಮ್ ಉದುಂ ಉವು.

3, When two words are connected by the conjunction ಉಂ, and are personal or reflexive pronouns, if they are referred to and are to be expressed by one word, the second pronoun has to be in the plural, *e. g.* ತಾನುಂ ನೀನುಂ become ನೀಮ್, ನೀನುಮ್ ಆನುಂ ಆಮ್.

Where two words are connected by the conjunction ಉಂ, and the first one is a noun and the second one a personal or reflexive pronoun, if they are referred to and are to be expressed by one word, the pronoun has to be in the plural, *e. g.* ಜಿನದತ್ತನುಮ್ ಆನುಂ become ಆಮ್, ಯಜ್ಞದತ್ತನುಂ ನೀನುಂ ನೀಮ್, ವಿಷ್ಣುಮಿತ್ರನುಂ ತಾನುಂ ತಾಮ್.

355. Peculiarities regarding the use of the singular and plural of verbs in a sentence are the following:—

I. On the use of the singular or plural of verbs in connection with nouns.

1, **If ದೇವರು, 'God', the honorific plural of** ದೇವ (see § 354, II, 1), is used by people of the present day (*cf.* § 258 where instances of prayer are given), they put the verb in the singular, *e.g.* ದೇವರಿದ್ದಾನೆ, (there) is God; ದೇವರು ಮಳೆಯನ್ನು ಉಣ್ಟು ಮಾಡುತ್ತಾನೆ, God causes it to rain; ದೇವರು ಲೋಕವನ್ನು ಹುಟ್ಟಿಸಿದನು, God created the world; ದೇವರು ನಿನಗೆ ಕಲ್ಯಾಣ ಮಾಡ್ಯಾನು, God may make thee happy; ದೇವರು ದೊಡ್ಡವನು, God (is) great; ನಾವು ಇರುವ ಭೂಮಣ್ಡಲವನ್ನು ಮಾಡಿದವನು ದೇವರೇ, ಎಲ್ಲಾ ವಸ್ತುಗಳು ಆತನಿನ್ದಲೇ ಆಗಿವೆ; ನೋಡು, ದೇವರು ಎನ್ಥಾ ಜ್ಞಾನಿಯು, ಎನ್ಥಾ ಸಮರ್ಥನು, ಎನ್ಥಾ ಒಳ್ಳೆಯವನು, even God has made the terrestrial globe on which we are; all things have become even through Him; look, how wise, how powerful, how good God (is)! Regarding the use of the singular of a demonstrative pronoun referring to ದೇವರು, observe also the following instance: ದೇವರಿಗೆ ಅಂಜಿಕೊಣ್ಡು ಯಾವಾಗಲೂ ಒಳ್ಳೇ ರೀತಿಯಿನ್ದ ನಡೆದರೆ ಆತನು ನಮಗೆ ಸಹಾಯ ಮಾಡುವನು (see § 341 under 'to fear').

Exceptionally, however, a person says ದೇವರಿದ್ದಾರೆ.

If ದೇವರು is used instead of ದೆವ್ವ, as is occasionally done in vulgar speech, the verb is also put in the singular, *e. g.* ಅವನ ಮೆಯ್ಯಲ್ಲಿ ದೇವರು ಬರುತ್ತದೆ, an evil spirit enters his body.

2, If a person is addressed in the vocative singular, the verb may stand in the plural, *e. g.* ದೇವಾಸುರಮಂ (o. r. ದಿವಾಸುರಮಂ) ಕೇಳಿರೆ, ದೇವ, O king, did you (or do you) not ask the kingly Asura? ಅಱಿಯಿರ್ ನೀನುಮ್ ಆಮುಮ್ ಒಡನೋಡಿದೆವೆಮ್ಬುದನ್, ಅಣ್ಣ (o. r. ಅಣ್ಣಾ), O elder brother, do you not know that you and we ran together?

Such is especially the case in disgustful conduct, *i. e.* in order to ridicule a person for such conduct, when the personal pronouns relating to him also stand in the plural, *e. g.*

ಬಡವಾದಿರ್, ಅರಸ! ಕಾಲೊಳ್
ನಡೆಹಪಿರ್; ಒಡನಾರುಮ್ ಇಲ್ಲ; ಕಟಿಲೆಗಳೇಂ ನಿ |
ಮ್ಮಡಿಯೊಳಗೆ? ಪಡುವ ದೇಗುಲ
ದೆಡೆಯಾವುದು? ಕುಡದ ನಿಮಗಮ್ ಈಯೆಡಱಾಯ್ತೇ? || O king,

you have become poor; you walk on foor; nobody is with you; why (are) small thorny twigs in your pouch? what (is) the place of the temple where you repose? Could have befallen even you who do not give (alms), this indigency?

[It seems as if the small grammar called Nuḍigaṭṭu, wants to express a similar thing, when it says that if an act of the subject is improper (hŏlla), the verb may stand in the third person plural instead of the second person. Its instances are the following—ನೀವು ಅರಸರಾದ ಮೇಲೆ ಕಣ್ಣಲ್ಲಿ ತಿರುಗುವರೆ, after you have become king, should they (*i. e.* you) roam about *ad libitum*? ಅರಸಾ, ನೀನು ಮರುಳಾಗುವರೆ, O king, should they (*i. e.* shouldst) thou become bewildered? ನೀನು ಹೀಗೆ ಮಾಡುತ್ತಾರೆ, do they (*i. e.* doest) thou make thus?]

3, If a noun of race, species or kind, *i. e.* a jâti noun (see § 354, I, 3) as subject is in the singular, it conveys the meaning of the plural, whenever it is connected with a verb in the plural, *e. g.* ಆನೆ ನೂಂಕಿದುವು (=ಆನೆಗಳ್ ನೂಂಕಿದುವು), the elephants pushed; ಕುದುರೆಯೇಱಿದುವು, the horses ascended; ಕಾಲಾಳ್ ಕವಿದುವು, the foot-soldiers attacked; ಎತ್ತು ಪೋದುವು, the oxen went; ಬೆರಲ್ ತೋರಿದುವು, the fingers (are) big; ನುಡಿ ಸೂರುಳ್ಗಳ್, the words (are) imprecating; ಕಲ್ಲು ಒಡೆದವು; ಕಲ್ಲು ಬೀೞುತ್ತವೆ; ಆಳು ಬನ್ದವು; ಬೆರಳು ಮುಱಿದವು; ಮಿಂಚಿನ ಕಡೆಗೆ ನೋಡಿದರೆ ಕಣ್ಣೇ ಕುಕ್ಕುತ್ತವೆ;—also when preceded by ಆ or ಈ (§ 264), *e. g.* ಆಯೆರಲೆ ಪೋದುವು, those deer went; ಈಯೆರಲೆ ಬನ್ದುವು, these antelopes came.

It is not uncommon in the modern dialect to use the singular of some jâti nouns which seem to allow no plural meaning in the respective sentences, with the verb in the plural, *e. g.* ನೀರು ಉಕ್ಕುತ್ತಾ ಅವೆ, the water is boiling; ಅದನ್ನು ನೋಡಿದರೆ ಬಾಯಲ್ಲಿ ನೀರು ಬರುತ್ತವೆ, if (one) sees that, water comes to the mouth (*i. e.* one's mouth waters); ಇವರನ್ನು ನೋಡುವಾಗ ಕಣ್ಣೀರು ಬರುತ್ತವೆ, when (I) see them, eye-water comes (*i. e.* I shed tears); ನೀರು ಹರಿಯುತ್ತವೆ, the water runs; ತೆಂಗಿನ ಎಳೆಗಾಯೊಳಗಿನ ನೀರು ಬಹು ಸವಿ ಇರುತ್ತವೆ, the water in a young cocoanut is very sweet;—ಅಕ್ಕಿ ತುಟ್ಟಿಯಾದವು, rice became dear; ಇಲ್ಲಿ ಅಕ್ಕಿ ಅವೆ, ಅನ್ನ ಮಾಡು, here is rice, cook (it);—ಕಾಳು ಬಹಳ ತುಟ್ಟಿಯಾದವು, corn became very dear;—ಮಜ್ಜಿಗೆ ಹುಳಿ ಹುಳಿ ಇರುತ್ತವೆ, buttermilk is very sour; ಮಜ್ಜಿಗೆ ಚೆಲ್ಲಿದವು, buttermilk was spilt;—ಜ್ವರ ಬರುತ್ತವೆ, fever comes; ನಿನ್ನೆ ಜ್ವರ ಬನ್ದಿದ್ದವು, yesterday fever had come; ಜ್ವರ ನಿನ್ತವು, fever ceased;—ಆ ಮೋಡಗಳಿನ್ದ ಮೞೆ ಬೀೞುತ್ತವೆ, rain falls from those clouds;—ಬಳುತರುಗಳಂ ಚಿವುಟಿದೊಡೆ ಪಾಲ್ ಉಗುವವೇ, if (he) cut devotees with (his) nails, will milk come forth? (this sentence is from the mediæval dialect).

On the other hand we find *e. g.* ನೀರ್ ತಿಳಿದುದು, the water became clear; ತಿಳಿದುವು ನೀರ್ಗಳ್, the waters (in tanks, etc.) became clear; ಮೞೆಯ ನೀರಿಂ ಬೆಳೆವ ಭೂಮಿ, land (the crop of) which grows by means of the water of rain; ಕಣ್ತುಮ್ಬ ನೀರು ತನ್ದನು, he brought water so that (his) eyes filled (*i. e.* his eyes became full of tears); ನೀರು ಹರಿಯುತ್ತದೆ, the water runs; ಅವ್ವಾ, ಕುಡಿಯುವದಕ್ಕೆ ನೀರು ಕೊಡು, O mother, give (me) water to drink; ಮೞೆಯ ನೀರು ಬಿಟ್ಟು, ಮಂಜಿನ ನೀರಿಗೆ ಕೆಯ್ ಒಡ್ಡಿದ ಹಾಗೆ, he left the water of rain and held the joined palms of the hand to the water of dew (*i. e.* so as to catch the water of dew);—ಮಜ್ಜಿಗೆ ಚೆಲ್ಲಿತು, buttermilk was spilt;—ದೇಹಜ್ವರವನ್ ಈಗಳೆ ಕಿಡಿಸು, ಸದ್ಗುರುವೇ, O excellent guru, at once remove the fever of (my) body!—ಮೞೆಯಿಲ್ಲದ ಪಯ್ರು ಮಾತೆಯಿಲ್ಲದ ಕೂಸು, a young crop without rain (is like) a motherless child;—ಆ ಗಿಡಕ್ಕೆ ಚೂರಿಯಿನ್ದ ಕಚ್ಚು ಹಾಕಿದರೆ ಒಳಗಿನ್ದ ಬೆಳ್ಳನ್ನ ಹಾಲು ಬರುತ್ತದೆ, if (one) makes incisions with a knife into that tree, white milk will come forth.

4, If however a jâti noun as subject stands in the singular and is connected with a verb in the singular, it always conveys the meaning of the singular, *e. g.* ನಡೆದುದು ಹಂಸೆ, a (or the) swan walked; ಕೇಗಿದುದು ಸೋಗೆ, a (or the) peacock cried; ಪಾಡಿದುದು ತುಮ್ಬಿ, a (or the) black bee hummed; ಕೞವೆ ಬೆಳೆದುದು, the (crop of) kaḻavĕ grew; ಗೋದಿ ಕೆಟ್ಟುದು, the wheat was destroyed; ಧಾನ್ಯಂ ಪೆರ್ಚಿತು, the corn increased; ಬೆರಲ್ ತೋರಿತ್ತು, the finger (is) big; ನುಡಿ ಸೂರುಳ್, the word (is) imprecating.

5, Also where the noun is no jâti noun, it occasionally happens that such a noun as subject is used in the singular in the sense of the plural, in which case the verb is to be in the plural, *e. g.* ಮನಂ ಸಂಚಲಮ್ ಆದುವು, the minds became fickle.

6, An optional use of the plural of the verb may take place, if some neuter nouns in the singular are combined by the conjunction ಊ (ಉಂ), 'and', *e. g.* ವಿದ್ಯೆಯಿನ್ದ ಜ್ಞಾನವೂ ಜ್ಞಾನದಿನ್ದ ಯೋಗ್ಯತೆಯೂ ಯೋಗ್ಯತೆಯಿನ್ದ ಮಾನವೂ ದೊರೆಯುತ್ತದೆ or ದೊರೆಯುತ್ತವೆ, by learning wisdom is obtained, by wisdom propriety, by propriety honour.

II. On the use of the plural of verbs in connection with pronouns.

1, If some pronouns as subjects of a sentence are joined together by the conjunction ಉಂ (ಊ), and the last one is ಆನ್ (ಆಂ, ನಾನ್, ನಾನು), I, the first person plural of the verb is used or the 'I' has the pre-eminence (mukhyatva), *e.g.* ಆತನುಂ ನೀನುಮ್ ಆನುಂ ಪೋಟಿಗಾಗಿರ್ದೆವುರ್ವೀಪತಿಗೆ ಪಿಸು

ಣರಿಂ, he and thou and I were not connected with the slanderers of (lit. as regards) the king. ಅವನೂ ನೀನೂ ನಾನೂ ಹೋದೆವು.

If the pronouns are in reversed order, the same takes place, *e. g.* ನೀನುಮ್ ಆತನುಮ್ ಆನುಂ ಮಣಿಕೂಟನಗರಕ್ಕೆ ಪೋಪೆವು, thou and he and I shall go to the town of Maṇikûṭa; ಆತನುಮ್ ಆನುಂ ನೀನುಂ ಕಜ್ಜದ ತೆಱನ್ ಅಱಿದು ಪೇೞ್ದೆವು, he and I and thou knew and told the manner of the affair; ಆನುಂ ನೀನುಮ್ ಆತನುಂ ಬೆಸಕೆಯ್ವೆವು, I and thou and he shall worship.

2, If two pronouns as subjects are joined by the conjunction ಉಂ (ಊ), and the second one is ನೀನ್ (ನೀಂ, ನೀನು), thou, the second person plural of the verb is used or 'thou' has the pre-eminence, *e. g.* ಆತನುಂ ನೀನುಂ ಕೂಡಿದಿರ್ ಅಪ್ಪೊಡೆಯಾಹವಕ್ಕೆ ಕಿಚ್ಚುಂ ಗಾಳಿಯುಂ ಕೂಡಿದನ್ತೆ, he and thou joined; when (it) happened, (it was) as if fire and wind joined for battle. ಅವನೂ ನೀನೂ ಹೋದಿರಿ.

If the two pronouns are in reversed order, the same takes place, *e.g.* ನಾಳಿನ ದಿನದೊಳ್ ನೀನುಮ್ ಆತನುಂ ಕೂಡಿದಪಿರ್, to-morrow thou and he will join.

III. On the use of the plural of the verb, especially of its gender, when combined with nouns of different gender.

1, If nouns of different gender are joined together by the conjunction ಉಂ (ಊ), that noun which comes last, is the chief one, and the verb in the plural has to conform itself to it as to gender, *e. g.* ಸೇನೆಯುಮ್ ಅರಸಿಯುಮ್ ಅರಸನುಂ ಬನ್ದರ್, the army and the queen and the king came; ಆನೆಯುಮ್ ಅರಸನುಮ್ ಅರಸಿಯುಂ ಬನ್ದರ್, the elephant (or the elephants) and the king and the queen came; ಅರಸನುಮ್ ಅರಸಿಯುಂ ಬನ್ದರ್, the king and the queen came; ಅರಸನುಮ್ ಅರಸಿಯುಂ ಚತುರಂಗಬಲಮುಂ ಬನ್ದುವು, the king and the queen and the complete army came; ಸೇನೆಯೂ ರಾಜನೂ ರಾಣಿಯೂ ಬನ್ದರು; ರಾಜನೂ ರಾಣಿಯೂ ಸೇನೆಯೂ ಬನ್ದವು.

2, If some neuter (here compound) nouns in the nominative singular (without the conjunction ಉಂ, see § 354, II, 4, foot-note) precede the verb, this has to stand in the neuter form of the plural at the end of them, all the nouns having to be supplied (adhyâhârya, see § 357, 2, *b*) for it, *e.g.*

ಅವತಂಸೋತ್ಪಲತಾಡನಂ ಕನಕಕಾಂಚೀಬನ್ಧನಂ ನೂಪುರಾ
ರವಝುಂಕಾರಿತಚಾರುವಾಮಚರಣಾಘಾತಂ ಚಲದ್ಭ್ರೂಲತಾ |
ಗ್ರವಿಭಾಗೋತ್ಕಟತರ್ಜನಂ ತರಲತಾತಾಮ್ರಾಧರಂ ಚಕ್ರಿಗಿ
ತ್ತುವಲಮ್ಪಂ. . . . . || the beating of the blue lotus-

garland, the band of the gold-zone, the striking of the pleasant left foot with the anklet's sound, the excessive threatening of the points of the moving-about creeper-like eyebrows (and) the tremulous red lower lip (of the woman) gave pleasure to the king.

IV. On the use of the singular and plural of Saṁskṛita adjectives and their agreement with nouns.

1, If a Saṁskṛita adjective is preceded by a neuter noun in the plural (see § 103 about Kannaḍa gender), it may stand in the singular, *e.g.* ಮಹೇನ್ದ್ರಮಹದೈಶ್ವರ್ಯಂಗಳ್ ಇವೆಲ್ಲಮ್ ಅಧ್ರುವಂ, the great riches of the great Indra these all (are) impermanent.

2, If a Saṁkṛita noun in the singular is followed by an adjective in the plural, it gets a plural meaning, *e.g.* ಐಶ್ವರ್ಯಮ್ ಅಧ್ರುವಂಗಳ್, riches (are) impermanent.

3, If a Saṁskṛita adjective precedes a neuter noun in the plural, it may stand in the plural, *e.g.* ಗರ್ಜಿಸೆ ಜಲದನಿಭಂಗಳ್ ಗಜಂಗಳ್, when the cloud-resembling elephants roared. See an instance in § 313, 4 (ಅಣಿಯುರಮ್ ಎಸೆದೊಪ್ಪಿರ್ಪುವು etc.).

4, Regarding Saṁskṛita adjectives and their use in general (and regarding so-called Kannaḍa adjectives and their use) see §§ 273. 274. 275.

5, If Saṁskṛita adjectives (viśêshaṇapadas, appositional nouns, without the conjunction ಉಂ, see § 354, II, 4, foot-note) in the nominative precede their ruling noun (kârakapada, *cf.* § 354, I, 3, *a*), they receive, in construing (anvayisuvalli, *cf.* 357, 3), the case of that noun, *e.g.*

ವೀರನ್ ಉದಾರಂ ಶುಚಿ ಗ
ಮ್ಭೀರಂ ನಯಶಾಲಿ ಕೆಯ್ದುವೊತ್ತರ ದೇವಂ ।
ಗಾರ್ ಎಱಗರ್ ನೃಪತುಂಗಂ
ಗೆ. . . . . ॥ of which the construction (anvaya) is:— ವೀರಂಗೆ ಉದಾರಂಗೆ ಗಮ್ಭೀರಂಗೆ ನಯಶಾಲಿಗೆ ಕೆಯ್ದುವೊತ್ತರ ದೇವಂಗೆ ನೃಪತುಂಗಂಗೆ ಆರ್ ಎಱಗರ್, to Nṛipatuṅga, to the hero, to the liberal one, to the pure one, to the profound one, to him who possesses political wisdom; to him who is the lord of them who carry weapons who will not make obeisance? ಸಂಗತಸತ್ವರಂ ಕುರುರಾಜಂ ಕರ್ಣಂಗೆ, of which the construction is:— ಸಂಗತಸತ್ವರಂಗೆ ಕುರುರಾಜಂಗೆ ಕರ್ಣಂಗೆ, to Karṇa, to the quick one in friendship, to the king of the Kurus.

356. On the order of words in sentences.

I. From the simple sentences quoted in §§ 345. 346. 347. 348. 349. 350, it appears that the nominative (subject), the accusative (object), the instrumental, the dative, the ablative and the locative precede the verb or that **the verb stands at the end.** In § 350, 8 there is a sentence in which the order is: locative, subject, verb; and in § 350, 9 one in which the order is: locative, the relative past participle connected with it, accusative, verb. § 351 shows that the genitive precedes the noun with which it is connected. § 352, 4, *a* adduces two instances in which the order is: (instrumental or) ablative, subject, verb, and two in which the order is: (instrumental or) ablative, verb, and exceptionally the subject at the end.

Sentences in which the order is: subject, object, verb, are *e.g.* ದಾರಿಗರ್ ಊರಂ ಸಾರಿದರ್. ಎಮ್ಮೆ ಹಾಲನ್ನು ಹಿಣ್ಡುತ್ತವೆ.

The vocative begins a sentence, or stands at its end, *e.g.* ರಾಯ, ಕೇಳ್!— ಅಪ್ಪಾ, ನಾನು ಆ ಕುದುರೇ ಮೇಲೆ ಕೂತು ಕೊಳ್ಳಲೀ?— ಎಲಾ ತಮ್ಮಾ, ನೋಡು!— ಕೇಳ್, ಎಲೆ ನೃಪಾಲ!— ಹೋಗು, ತಂಗೀ!— ಇಷ್ಟು ಅವಸರವು ಯಾಕೋ, ರಾಮಾ?

II. **The following instances, quoted from the prose of the modern dialect, will serve to show the order of words, when there are more component parts in sentences than subject, object and verb;** it must however not be expected to find uniformity, as every author is apt to use more or less slight variations according to circumstances.

1, **Regarding the accusative:**— ನಿನ್ನನ್ನು ಯಾರೂ ಹತ್ತರ ಬರಗೊಡುವದಿಲ್ಲ.— ಆ ಎಮ್ಮೆ ದಿನಾಲು ಎರಡು ತಪ್ಪಿಗೆ ಹಾಲನ್ನು ಕಱೆಯುತ್ತಿತ್ತು.— ಈ ಹುಡಿಗೆ ಒನ್ದು ಎಳ್ಳು ಕಾಳಿಷ್ಟು ಎರಡನೆಯವರ ಮಾತನ್ನು ಕೇಳುವದಿಲ್ಲ.

2, **Regarding the instrumental:**— ಕಣ್ಣುಗಳಿನ್ದ ನಾವು ವಸ್ತುಗಳನ್ನು ನೋಡುತ್ತೇವೆ; ಕೆಯ್ಗಳಿನ್ದ ನಾವು ಒಡಿವೆಗಳನ್ನು ಹಿಡಿಯುತ್ತೇವೆ.— ಬಿಸಿನೀರಿನ್ದ ನನ್ನನ್ನು ಆಗಾಗ್ಗೆ ಎಱೆಯುತ್ತಿದ್ದಳು.

3, **Regarding the dative:**— ನೀನು ನಿನ್ನ ತಾಯಿತನ್ದೆಗಳಿಗೆ ಸನ್ಮಾನ ಮಾಡು!— ಆಕೆ ನಮ್ಮ ಸೋದರಮಾವನ ಮನೆಗೆ ನಿನ್ನೆ ಹೋಗಿದ್ಧಾಳೆ.— ದೇವರು ಎಲ್ಲರಿಗೂ ಎರಡೆರಡು ಕಣ್ಣುಗಳನ್ನು ಕೊಟ್ಟಿದ್ಧಾನೆ.— ನಾನು ನಾಳೆ ಮುಂಜಾನೇ ನಮ್ಮ ಚಿಗವ್ವನ ಮನೆಗೆ ಹೋಟೀನು.— ಆಕೆ ನನಗೆ, ಹಬ್ಬಕ್ಕೆ ಒನ್ದು ಅಂಗೀ ಹೊಲಿಸಿ ಕೊಡುತ್ತೇನೆನ್ದು, ಹೇೞಿದ್ಧಾಳೆ.— ಮಿಾನುಗಳು ತತ್ತೀ ಇಡುತ್ತವೆ; ಅವುಗಳಿಗೆ ತಮ್ಮನ್ನೂ ತಮ್ಮ ತತ್ತಿಗಳನ್ನೂ ಸಂರಕ್ಷಿಸಿ ಕೊಳ್ಳುವಷ್ಟು ಹುಟ್ಟುಬುದ್ಧಿಯುಣ್ಟು.— ಇದು ನನಗೆ ಬಂಗಾರದನ್ತೆ ಕಾಣುತ್ತದೆ.— ನನ್ನ ಕಾಲಿಗೆ ಕುಡುಗೋಲು ತಾಕಿತು.— ಎಲ್ಲಿಗಾದರೂ ಆಡಲಿಕ್ಕೆ ಹೋಗುವ.

4, **Regarding the ablative (in the form of the instrumental):**—ಒನ್ದು ದಿನ ಅವನು ಸಾಲೆಯಿನ್ದ ಮನೆಗೆ ಬನ್ದ ಬಱಿಕ ಅವನ ತನ್ದೆ ಅವನಿಗೆ ನಾಲ್ಕು ದುಡ್ಡು ಕೊಟ್ಟನು.—ಬುದ್ಧಿವನ್ತರು ಕೆಟ್ಟ ನಡತೆಯುವರಿನ್ದ ದೂರ ಇರುವರು.—ಈ ಹೆಮ್ಮೆ ಬಹು ದಿವಸದಿನ್ದ ಇತ್ತು.—ಪಟ್ಣದಿನ್ದ ಹೆಚ್ಚು ಕಡಿಮೆ ಎರಡು ಹರದಾರಿ ಹೋದನು.

5, **Regarding the locative:**—ಆನೆಗಳು ಏಶಿಯಖಣ್ಡದಲ್ಲಿಯೂ ಅಫ್ರಿಕಖಣ್ಡದಲ್ಲಿಯೂ ಇರುತ್ತವೆ.—ಒಬ್ಬ ಸವುಕಾರನು ವ್ಯಾಪಾರದೊಳಗೆ ಎಲ್ಲ ಹಣವನ್ನು ಕಳ ಕೊಣ್ಡನು.—ವಿಜಾಪುರಪಟ್ಟಣವು ಈಗ ಕಲಾದಗಿ ಜಿಲ್ಲೆಯೊಳಗೆ ಒನ್ದು ಮುಖ್ಯಗ್ರಾಮವದೆ; ಇದಱಲ್ಲಿ ೧೨,೯೩೫ ಜನರ ವಸ್ತಿಯುಣ್ಟು.—ಒನ್ದೆರಡು ತಿಂಗಳೊಳಗೆ ನಿನಗೆ ನನ್ನನ್ತೆ ಬರೆಯಲಿಕ್ಕೆ ಬನ್ದೀತು.—ವಸನ್ತಕಾಲದಲ್ಲಿ ಒನ್ದು ದಿನ ಮೂಱುಸಂಜೆಯ ಮುನ್ದೆ ಗೋಪಿನಾಥಶಾಸ್ತ್ರಿಯು ತನ್ನ ಮನೆಯ ಮುನ್ದೆ ಕಟ್ಟೆಯ ಮೇಲೆ ಚಾಪೇ ಹಾಸಿ ಕೊಣ್ಡು, ವರ್ತಮಾನಪತ್ರವನ್ನು ಓದುತ್ತ ಕೂತಿದ್ದನು.—ಆ ಕಾಗದದ ಮೇಲೆ ನಾನು ದಸರೆಯ ಹಬ್ಬದಲ್ಲಿ ಪುಸ್ತೀ ಬರೆಯುತ್ತೇನೆ.—ಒನ್ದು ಹಳ್ಳಿಯಲ್ಲಿ ಮುರಿಗೆಪ್ಪಸೆಟ್ಟಿ ಎಮ್ಬುವನೊಬ್ಬ ಬಣಜಿಗನು ಇದ್ದನು.—ಒಬ್ಬ ಗವಳಿಗನ ಬಱಿಯಲ್ಲಿ ಒನ್ದು ಎಮ್ಮೆ ಇತ್ತು.—ಗೂಡಿನೊಗೆ ಕೆಲವು ತತ್ತಿಗಳು ಇದ್ದವು.—ನನ್ನ ಸನ್ದುಕದಲ್ಲಿ ಒನ್ದು ಕಲ್ಲಂಗಡೀ ಹಣ್ಣು ಅದೆ.

6, **Regarding site (expressed by adverbs):**—ಒಬ್ಬ ಕುಱುಬನ ಹತ್ತರ ಹಲವು ಕುಱಿಗಳು ಇದ್ದವು.—ನಿನ್ನ ಸಂಗಡ ಒಬ್ಬ ಆಳು ಬರುವನು.—ಈ ಚಾಪೆಯ ಮೇಲೆ ತುಸು ಕೂಡ್ರು.—ಊರ ಹೊಱಗೆ ನಮ್ಮ ತೋಟಕ್ಕೆ ಬಾ!

7, **Regarding time:**—ಆ ಬಱಿಕ ಕಲ್ಲೊಳಗಿನ್ದ ಕಬ್ಬಿಣ ಸೋಸಿ ತೆಗೆಯ ಬೇಕು.—ಒನ್ದು ದಿನ ಒನ್ದು ಬೆಕ್ಕೂ ಒನ್ದು ನರಿಯೂ ಕೂಡಿ ಕೂತವು.—ಹೊತ್ತ್ಮುಣ್ಟಲೆ ಮನೆಗೆ ಹೋಗಲಿಕ್ಕೆ ನಮಗೆ ಅಪ್ಪಣೆ ಕೊಟ್ಟರು.—ಇನ್ದಿನಿನ್ದ ನೀನು ನಮ್ಮ ಸಾಲೆಗೆ ದಿನಾಲು ಬರುತ್ತ ಬಾ!—ಬೆಕ್ಕಿನ ಮಱಿಗಳು ಹುಟ್ಟಿದ ಬಱಿಕ ಕೆಲವು ದಿವಸಗಳ ವರೆಗೆ ಕಣ್ಣು ತೆಱೆಯುವದಿಲ್ಲ.—ಟೊಂಗಿಯನ್ನು ಕಡಿಯುವಾಗ ನನ್ನ ಕಾಲಿಗೆ ಕುಡುಗೋಲು ತಾಕಿತು.—ಸಾಯುವ ತನಕ (ಆ ಕೆಲಸ) ಮಾಡಿದರೂ ತೀರದು.—ಕಟ್ಲೆ ತುಮ್ಬಿದ ಮೇಲೆ ಜಣಮಾತ್ರಮಿರಲಿಲ್ಲ. (*Cf.* ದಿನಾಲು above sub No. 1; ಆಗಾಗ್ಗೆ s. No. 2; ನಿನ್ನೆ, ನಾಳೆ s. No. 3; ಬಹುದಿವಸದಿನ್ದ s. No. 4; ಈಗ, ಒನ್ದು ದಿನ s. No. 5; ಎನ್ದಿಗೂ, ಯಾವಾಗಲೂ further on s. No. 8; ನಾಳೆ s. No. 9; ಒನ್ದು ದಿನ s. No. 11.)

8, **Regarding reason and purpose:**—ಅದಱಿ ತುಸುಕ ತೊತ್ತಾಯಿತು.—ಪ್ರಾಣಿಗಳು ಯಾವಾಗಲೂ ತಮ್ಮ ಆಹಾರ ದೊರಕಿಸುವದಕ್ಕೋಸ್ಕರ ತಿರುಗಾಡುತ್ತವೆ.—ನಮ್ಮ ಹಿತದ ಸಲುವಾಗಿಯೇ ಅಯ್ಯನವರು ನಮಗೆ ಹೇೞುತ್ತಾರೆ.—ಯಾವದಾದರೊನ್ದು ಕೆಟ್ಟ ರೂಢಿ ಬಿದ್ದ ಬಱಿಕ ಅದು ಬೇಗ ಬಿಡುವದಿಲ್ಲ, ಆ ಕಾರಣ ಮೊದಲೇ ಉತ್ತಮರೀತಿಯನ್ನು ಹಿಡಿಯ ಬೇಕು.—(ದೇವರನ್ನು) ನಮ್ಬಿದವರಿಗೆ ಆತನು ತಾಯಿತನ್ದೆಗಳಿಗಿನ್ತ ಹೆಚ್ಚಿನ ಆಪ್ತನು; ಆದದಱಿನ್ದ ಆತನನ್ನು ನಾವೆಲ್ಲರೂ ಎನ್ದಿಗೂ ಮಱೆಯ ಬಾರದು.

9, Regarding **condition**:— ಮೊಸರು ಕಡೆದರೆ ಬೆಣ್ಣೆ ಬರುವದು.— ನಿನ್ನ ಹಿರಿಯರ ಮಾನ ಕಾಯ್ದರೆ ಮುನ್ದೆ ನಿನ್ನ ಮಕ್ಕಳು ನಿನ್ನ ಮಾನ ಕಾಯುವರು.— ನಿನ್ನ ಕೂಡಾ ನಾಳೆ ಬನ್ದರೆ ನನ್ನದು ನಾಲ್ಕು ದಿವಸದ ಓದು ನಿಲ್ಲುತ್ತದೆ.— ಪ್ರತಿದಿನ ನೇಮದಿನ್ದ ಕೆಲಸ ಮಾಡಿದರೆ ದೊಡ್ಡ ದೊಡ್ಡ ಮನೆಯನ್ನು ಒಬ್ಬನೇ ಕಟ್ಟಿ ಮುಗಿಸ ಬಹುದು.

10, Regarding **the verbs** ಎನ್, ಅನ್ (ಎನ್ನು, ಅನ್ನು) see § 332.

11, Regarding **past participles** (or gerunds, § 154 *seq.*): — ಗಣಪತಿಯ ಉಡಿಯಲ್ಲಿ ಕಡ್ಲೆ ಉಣ್ಟೆನ್ದು ತಿಳಿದು, ಆ ಕುದುರೆಯು ತಿನ್ನಲಿಕ್ಕೆ ಬನ್ತು.— ಆ ಹಾಲು ಮಾರಿಕೊಣ್ಡು, ಅವನು ಹೊಟ್ಟೇ ತುಮ್ಬಿ ಕೊಳ್ಳುತ್ತಿದ್ದನು.— ತಾಯಿ ಒನ್ದು ದಿನ ಗಡಿಗೆಯೊಳಗಿನ್ದ ಬೆಲ್ಲ ತೆಗೆಯುತ್ತಿದ್ದಳು; ಅದನ್ನು ಕಣ್ಡು, ಶಿವು, ಅವ್ವಾ ನನಗೆ ಬಹಳ ಬೆಲ್ಲಾ ಕೊಡು ಎನ್ದು, ಆಕೆಯ ಬಳಿಗೆ ಓಡುತ್ತ ಹೋದನು.— ಕೆಲಸ ಬಿಟ್ಟು, ತಾಯಿ ನಿನ್ನನ್ನು ಎತ್ತಿ, ಅವಚಿಕೊಣ್ಡು, ನಿನಗೆ ಮೊಲೆ ಕೊಡುತ್ತಿದ್ದಳು.— ಅದನ್ನು ಕಣ್ಡು, ಅವನು ಅತ್ತನು.— ಆ ರೂಪಾಯಿ ತಕ್ಕೊಣ್ಡು, ಆ ಅರಬನು ಕುದುರೆಯ ಕಡೆಗೆ ನೋಡಿದನು.— ತನ್ದೆಯ ಮಾತು ಕೇಳಿ, ತುಸು ಹೊತ್ತು ವಿಚಾರ ಮಾಡಿ, ಭೀಮನು, ಅಪ್ಪಾ ದಯ ಮಾಡಿ ಅಷ್ಟು ತಿಳಿಸಿ ಹೇಳಿರಿ! ಅನ್ದನು.— ವರ್ತಕನನ್ನು ನೋಡಿ, ಫಕೀರನು, ನೀವು ಒನ್ದು ಒಣ್ಟೆಯನ್ನು ಕಳ ಕೊಣ್ಡನ್ತೆ ತೋರುತ್ತದೆ ಎನ್ದು, ಅನ್ದನು.— ಈ ಮೇರೆಗೆ ಆ ಪಣ್ಡಿತನ ಅಪೂರ್ವಸಯ್ತ್ರಣೆಯನ್ನು ನೋಡಿ, ಶಿಷ್ಯನು ಬಹಳ ಬೆರಗಾದನು.

(Regarding **the present participle** see *e.g.* the ancient sentence in § 339, 5: ಒಡ್ಡೊಡ್ಡೊಡ್ಡೆನುತೊಡ್ಡಿ etc.)

12, Regarding **questions**:— ನಮ್ಮ ಕುದುರೆ ಎಲ್ಲಿ ಅದೆ? ಅದರ ಮೇಲೆ ನಾನು ಯಾವಾಗ ಕೂಡ್ರ ಬೇಕು?— ದೊರೆಗಳು ಎನ್ದು ಊರಿಗೆ ಹೋಗುತ್ತಾರೆ?— ಸಾಲೆಯಲ್ಲಿ ಏನು ಕಲಿಯುತ್ತೀ?— ಈ ಕಾಗದವನ್ನು ನೀನು ಎಲ್ಲಿನ್ದ ತನ್ದಿ?— ನೀನು ಯಾರಯ್ಯಾ?— ಅದೇನು ಕೆಲಸ?— ಈ ತಮ್ಬಿಗೆ ಯಾತರದು?— ಇಷ್ಟು ತ್ವರೆ ಯಾಕೆ?— ಗಂಗಾ, ಈ ಹೊತ್ತು ಯಾಕೆ ಬಹಳ ಸಿಂಗಾರಾಗಿದ್ಧಿ?— ಯಾಕಾಗ ವಲ್ಲದು?— ಸೃಷ್ಟಪದಾರ್ಥಗಳಲ್ಲಿ ಮುಖ್ಯ ಮೂರು ಕೋಟಿಗಳು ಯಾವವು?— ನಿನ್ನ ವರ್ಗದಲ್ಲಿ ಎಷ್ಟು ಹುಡುಗರು ಅವೆ?— ಸುಣ್ಣದ ಬಣ್ಣ ಎನ್ಥಾದು?— ಆ ನೊಣವನ್ನು ಏನು ಮಾಡುತ್ತೀ?— ತಾವು ಬನ್ದ ಕಾರಣ ಏನು?— ತಾವು ಹೋಗುವದು ಎಲ್ಲಿಗೆ?— ಈ ಊರಿಗೆ ದೊರೆಗಳು ಬನ್ದು ಎಷ್ಟು ದಿವಸ ಆಯಿತು?— ನಿನ್ನೆ ಯಾವ ವಾರ?— ನೀನು ಸಾಲೆಗೆ ಹೋಗ ಹತ್ತಿ ಎಷ್ಟು ತಿಂಗಳು ಆಯಿತು?— ಮಜ್ಜಿಗೆಯ ರುಚಿ ಹ್ಯಾಗೆ?— ಕಾಯದೆ ನೀ ಭಕ್ತನ ಬಿಟ್ಟರೆ ನಾ ಮಾಡುವದೇನು?— ಬಂಗಾರಕ್ಕೂ ಹಿತ್ತಾಳಿಗೂ ಹೆಚ್ಚು ಕಡಿಮೆ ಏನು?— ನಿನ್ನ ವಯಸು ಎಷ್ಟು (how old art thou)? Regarding questions see also §§ 265. 271. 283.

13, Regarding **exclamations**:— ಈ ಹುಡುಗಿ ಎಷ್ಟು ಹೊಲಸು ಕಾಣಿಸುತ್ತದೆ!— ಉಟ್ಟ ದಟ್ಟಿ ಎಷ್ಟು ಮಾಸಿದೆ!— ಗುಡ್ಡದ ಮೇಲೆ ಎಷ್ಟೋ ಜನರು ಅಡ್ಡಾಡುತ್ತಾರೆ!— ನನ್ನ ಹತ್ತರ ಎನ್ಥಾ ಚಲೋ ಕಾಗದ!— ತಮ್ಮಾ, ನೋಡು, ಇದು ಎನ್ಥಾ ಚಲೋ ಕುದುರೆ ಹೋಗು

ತ್ತದೆ! — ರಾಮಾ, ಈ ಆಕಳು ಎಷ್ಟ ಚಂದವದೆ! — ಆಕಳ ಕುತ್ತಿಗೆಯ ಕೆಳಗೆ ಮೆತ್ತನ್ನ ತೊಗಲು ಹ್ಯಾಗೆ ಜೋತಾಡುತ್ತದೆ! — ಆಕಳ ತೊರೆದ ಮೊಲೆಗಳು ಹ್ಯಾಗೆ ಕಾಣಿಸುತ್ತವೆ!

III. As the works of the ancient dialect are principally in verse, it is obvious that the order of words in them often varies considerably. Kêšava, the grammarian, also wrote his Šabdamaṇidarpaṇa in verse, and says in it that, as the words in the verses of his grammar may be in irregular order on account of the requirements of alliteration (prâsa), poetical measure (čhandas) and construction (anvaya), he has added an explanation in prose (vṛitti) to each verse, to which explanations we must refer our readers regarding his order of words in prose.

Here follow some quotations made by Kêšava from ancient poems which we give in order to show something of the license taken by their authors as to the order of words: —

1, **The subject is placed after the verb,** *e.g.* ಕೆಳಱಿ ಹಯಂಗಳ್, ಗರ್ಜಿಸೆ ಜಳದನಿಭಂಗಳ್ ಗಜಂಗಳ್, when the horses neighed (and) when the cloud-resembling elephants roared. ತಿದಿಯೊತ್ತುವ ಕಮ್ಮಱಿವ್ಪೊಲ್ ಇರ್ದಂ ಭೀಮಂ, Bhîma was like blacksmith who plied the bellows. ಬಾರಿಸಿದುವು ಬಿಡದೆ ಜಡೆದು ವನದೇವತೆಗಳ್, the sylvan deities continually menaced and checked. ನೆಗಟ್ದಿನ್ ಆ ವಿಭುವಿಳೆಯೊಳ್, that king was famous on the earth. ಪಡೆದಂ ಪದ್ಮಜನಿ ಜಗತ್ರಯಮಂ, Brahmâ obtained the three worlds. ಮುತ್ತುದು ನೇಸಱ ತೇಜಂ, ಸತ್ತುದು ದಾವಾಗ್ನಿ, the sunshine increased, the forest-conflagration died away. ಅಱಿದಳ್ ಪಾಣ್ಡುತನೂಜರ ತೆಱನ್ ಎಲ್ಲವನ್ ಈಕೆ, this woman knew the whole manner of the sons of Pâṇḍu. ನಯದಿನ್ದೆ ಬೀಸುಗುಂ ಗನ್ಧವಹಂ, the wind blew gently. ಅರ್ಕೇನ್ದುಗಳಂ ತವೆ ನುಂಗಿರ್ದುದು ಕತ್ತಲೆ, darkness had quite swallowed up the sun and moon. ಆ ಪುರದೊಳ್ ಇರ್ಪನ್ ಇನಕುಲದೀಪಂ ವಿಪುಲಪ್ರತಾಪಂ, in that town (there) is the light of the solar race, one of great valour. ಬೆಕ್ಕಸವ್ಪಟ್ಟು ಬಾಯಂ ಬಿಟ್ಟರ್ ಭೀಷ್ಮರ್, Bhîshma was astonished and cried 'ah'. ಪಸರಿಸಿದತ್ತು ಮೂಡದೆಸೆಯೊಳ್ ಬೆಳಗೆಂಪು, a dazzling red colour spread about in the east. ನಡೆದುದು ಹಂಸೆ, the swan walked.

2, **The accusative is placed after the verb,** *e.g.* ಕುರುಪತಿಯಂ ವಿಷ್ಣು ಬೇಡಿದಂ ಧರೆಯರೆಯಂ, Vishṇu asked the king of the Kurus for the half of (his) land. ತಾನ್ ಎಚ್ಚಂ ಪೊಚ್ಚಮ್ ಅಲ್ಲದರಿವಾಹಿನಿಯಂ, he shot arrows at the enemy's army (or river) that was no river. ಆವ್ ಅಱಿವ್ಪೊಡಮ್ ಉಸಿರಲ್ ಅಮ್ಮೆವಾಳ್ದನ ಗತಿಯಂ, though we know (it), we cannot tell (you) the condition of the ruler. ಒರ್ವನೆ ಗೆಲ್ದಂ ಕಿರೀಟಿ ಕೌರವಬಲಮಂ, Arjuna quite alone overcame the force of the Kauravas. ಮುಜುಂಗುವಿನಂ ಮಾಣದೆಚ್ಚನ್ ಅರಿವಾಹಿನಿಯುಂ, till (he, or when he) suffered distress, he shot arrows at the enemy's army.

3, **The dative is placed after the accusative and also after the verb,** *e. g.* ದೇವತೆಯರ್ ಮೆಚ್ಚಿ ವರವನ್ ಅರಸಂಗಿತ್ತರ್, the gods were pleased and gave a boon to the king. ಗಿರಿಯುಂ ಕರಿಯುಂ ನಿಲ್ಲವು ಪವಿಮುಖದ ಕೋಟ್ಗಿವ್ ಆತನ ಬಾಳ್ಗಂ, the mountains and the elephants do not stand the point of the thunderbolt's head and his sword.

Observe also the following verse (*cf.* § 241):—

ಬನ್ನಿಯ ತರು ಡಕ್ಕೆಗೆ, ಸುರ
ಹೊನ್ನೆಯ ತರು ಡಮರುಗಕ್ಕೆ, ಕರುವಿಡಿದಿರ್ಪಾ ।
ಚೆನ್ನಂಗಿಯ ತರು ಡಾಣೆಗೆ,
ಹೊನ್ನಂ ಕುಡುವೆಡೆಗೆ ಕಲ್ಪತರು, ಡಾಕರಸಾ! ॥

4, **The genitive is placed after the noun it is connected with,** *e. g.* ಕಾಲಾಗ್ನಿರುದ್ರನ್ ಎನಿಸಿದುದು ತೋಳ ಬಾಳ್ ತೈಲಪನಾ, the sword of the arm of Tailapa caused itself to be called Rudra, the fire that is to destroy the world. ಆನೆಯ ಮೇಲೆಯುಮ್ ಆಳ ಮೇಲೆಯುಂ ಕುದುರೆಯ ಮೇಲೆಯುಂ ಪರಿದುದು ಗಜಂ ಭುವನೈಕರಾಮನಾ, the elephant of Bhuvanaikarâma ran upon the elephants, and upon the warriors, and upon the horses.

5, Regarding time observe *e.g.* ಕುಕ್ಕೂಕೂ ಎನ್ದು, ಕೋಟಿ ಕೂಗಿದುವಾಗಳ್.

357. As the words in the metrical compositions of the ancient dialect are combined strictly to the rules of euphonic junction (§ 213 *seq.*) and therefore are separated with some difficulty by a common reader, it has been thought necessary by commentators when commenting on verse, first to offer a **padaččhêda** or resolving a verse into its elementary parts, as has been done *e. g.* by the commentator on the Šabdamaṇi-darpaṇa. Thereupon an **anvaya** (*cf.* No. 3 of this §) or arrangement of the words in their prose-order, without regard to euphonic junction, is adduced by them, and then they give the **ṭiku** or explanation. The grammarian Kêšava, as told in § 356, III, wrote an explanation in prose on his sûtras in verse himself.

In reading poetry the following remarks of Kêšava are to be noticed:—

1, **It is required to use adhyârôpa,** *i. e.* attributing or assigning, with nêya, *i. e.* logical inference, *e. g.* in the half-verse

ಆರಕ್ತಮ್ ಆಗಿ ನೇಟಿಲ
ದೊರೆಯುನ್ ಅನುಕರಿಪು ದಾದುದಾಗಸಂ । the sky became reddish

and became equal in appearance to (the colour of a ripe fruit of) the *Eugenia jambolana,* one has to assign as the cause the redness of evening and not red dust, though also red dust might (under circumstances) be assigned as the cause. If **adhyârôpa** becomes wanting in precision (asamartha), being referable to two or more things, there is no (definite) nêya (possible, as perhaps in the half-verse quoted above).

Adhyârôpa is also needed regarding the six kârakas and the genitive (§ 344) in verses like the following one: —

ಕಡುಗಲಿ. ಸೆಣಸುವ ಭಟರಾರ್?
ಒಡೆಯಂಗತಿಹಿತವರಾರ್? ಧುರಕ್ಕೊದಗುವರಾರ್? ।
ತೊಡರ್ದೊಡೆ ಭಂಗಂ ಬರ್ಕುಂ.
ಸಡಗರಮಿದು. ಜಯಮೆ ಮೆಱೆವುದಱಿ ಬೊಪ್ಪಲನಂ! ॥

wherein ಆತಂ, the nominative, is to be attributed to ಕಡುಗಲಿ; ಆತನಂ, the accusative, to ಸೆಣಸುವ ಭಟರಾರ್; ಆತನಿಂ, the instrumental, to ಒಡೆಯಂಗತಿಹಿತವರಾರ್; ಆತಂಗೆ, the dative, to ಧುರಕ್ಕೊದಗುವರಾರ್; ಆತನತ್ತಣಿಂ, the ablative, to ತೊಡರ್ದೊಡೆ ಭಂಗಂ ಬರ್ಕುಂ; ಆತನ, the genitive, to ಸಡಗರಮಿದು; ಆತನೊಳ್, the locative, to ಜಯಮೆ ಮೆಱೆವುದು: (He is) a great hero. What warriors do envy (him)? Who (are all) they that (through him became) intimate friends to (our) king? Who will come to war (against him)? If (they) attack (him), defeat will come (from him). This (is) the grandeur (of him). Indeed victory will appear (in him). Know Bŏppala!

2, **It is required to use adhyâhâra,** *i. e.* supplying, which refers

a) to the kâraka, in this case the kartṛi or subject (§§ 344, 1; 345), or also to a predicate of the subject, *e. g.* ಏಕೆ? ನಿರ್ವಹಣಕ್ಕೆ ಸಲ್ಗುಮೊ, ಪೂಣ್ದೊಡಂ ಕೃತಿಬನ್ಧಮುಂ?, in which case ಕೃತಿಬನ್ಧಂ is to be supplied (adyâhârya) as subject: Why? will it (the kṛitibandhaṁ, ever) be accomplished, though (you) have promised the composition of the poem? — ಕರ್ಣನುಂ ದಾನಿ, ಮೇಣ್ ಈತನುಂ, in which case ದಾನಿ is to be supplied: Karṇa (is) a liberal person and this man too (is a dâni).

b) to the kriyĕ or verb, *e. g.* ಪುರುಷೋತ್ತಮಂ ಮನುಷ್ಯಮಾತ್ರಮೆ?, in which case ಅಲ್ಲಂ is to be supplied: (Is) Purushôttama a mere man? (no, he is not, allaṁ). — ಧೃತರಾಷ್ಟ್ರಂ ನುಡಿದಾರ್ತನೆ? ಹರಿ ಭರಂಗೆಯ್ದಾರ್ತನೆ? in which case ಆಱಿಂ (ಆಱಿರ್) is to be supplied: (Is) Dhṛitarâshṭra able, when he speaks? (is) Hari able, when he hastens? (no, they are not able).

(See ಅಧ್ಯಾಹಾರ್ಯ also in §§ 355, III, 2; 358.)

c) to the adverb ಎ of doubt, *e. g.* ಉಜಿಸಿಮಂಜಿಮೆ? ಬೆರ್ಚಿಮೆ? ಬೆಸಕೆಯಿಗೆ ಮೆ, ದೇವ?, in which case the final ಎ of ಉಜಿಸಿಮೆ which has disappeared in the initial ಅ of ಅಂಜಿಮೆ on account of euphonic junction, is to be supplied: Shall we not hesitate? shall we not fear? shall we not be frightened? shall we not bow to the injunction, O king?

d) to the conjunction ಉಂ, *e. g.* ಆಯುಂ ಸಿರಿ ತಾಯುಂ ತನ್ದೆ ಕಣ್ಣುಂ ಗತಿಯೆನಿಸಿದಪಂ ಸಿಂಹಸೇನಕ್ಷಿತೀಶಂ, in which case ಉಂ is to be supplied for ಸಿರಿ, ತನ್ದೆ and ಗತಿ: King Siṁhasêna causes himself to be called (our) life and wealth and mother and father and eye and refuge. (See § 354, II, 4, foot-note.)

e) to vâkyadîpaka, *i. e.* the clearing up (of the meaning) of a sentence, *e. g.* ಆತನುಮ್ ಅವನುಂ ಬನ್ದಂ, in which case, in order to show that each one (pratyêka) came, ಬನ್ದಂ is to be supplied; ಆತನುಂ ಬನ್ದನ್ ಅವನುಂ ಬನ್ದಂ, that person came and that person came.

3, **It is needed to use proper construction of words** (vâkyânvaya, *cf.* the beginning of the present § and § 355, IV, 5) **regarding ಅವಂ, ಅವಳ್, ಅದು, ಆವಳ್, ಆವಳ್, ಅವ್ರುದು,** that is to say regarding their use in so-called relative sentences.

ಅವಂ, ಅವಳ್, ಅದು (and their plurals) are anvayasvatantras, *i. e.* independent of another word, *e. g.* ಪೊನ್ನುಳ್ಳವನೆ ಕುಲೀನಂ, he who has gold, (is) well born, in which case one cannot say ಆವಂ ಪೊನ್ನುಳ್ಳವನೆ ಕುಲೀನಂ; ಸೊಬಗುಳ್ಳವಳೆ ಪೆಣ್, she who possesses beauty (is) a woman, and not ಆವಳ್ ಸೊಬಗುಳ್ಳವಳೆ ಪೆಣ್; ರೂಢಿಯನುಳ್ಳುದೆ ಲೇಸು, that which has customary usage, (is) fit, and not ಆವುದು ರೂಢಿಯನುಳ್ಳದುವೆ ಲೇಸು.

ಆವಂ, ಆವಳ್, ಆವುದು (and their plurals) are anvayaparatantras, *i. e.* dependent on another word, *e. g.* ಆವನ್ ಅಧಿಕ ಪುಣ್ಯನ್ ಅವನೆ ಸೇವ್ಯಂ, who (is) very virtuous, even he (is) to be served; ಆವಳ್ ಪತಿವ್ರತೆ ಅವಳ್ ಮಾನ್ಯೆ, who (is) a woman faithful to her husband, she (is) to be honoured; ಆವುದು ಚೆಲ್ವಾದುದದು ದರ್ಶನೀಯಂ, what (is) beautiful, it (is) worthy to be seen. See §§ 267. 316, 1. 330.

Also ತಾನ್ (and its plural) Kêšava classes with the anvayaparatantras, as it is to be followed by a demonstrative pronoun which shows its gender, *e. g.* ತಾನ್ ಅವಂ ಚದುರಂ, he (is) a clever man; ತಾನ್ ಅವಳ್ ಚದುರೆ, she (is) a clever woman; ತಾನ್ ಅದು ಪಿರಿದು, that (is) a large thing.

About ತಾಂ (ತಾನ್, ತಾನು, ತಾ) §§ 256. 259.

358. In § 357, 2 the grammarian Kêśava's rules about **adhyâhâra** or supplying have been given; it remains to be shown how it is **to be** used **also** elsewhere, that is to say **where pronouns (or their respective nouns or 'one') are to be supplied** (see *e. g.* § 254, 2, *a—d*; § 315, 2, *k. l*).

This can be best shown by citing some instances, putting into parenthesis the words to be supplied, *viz.*

ಪೇೞ್ದ ವಿಭಕ್ತಿಗಳ್, the terminations which (I) have mentioned. ವಾಕ್ಕೆಮ್ಬ ದೇವಿ, the goddess whom (people) call speech. ಹೊಲಿದ ದಾರ ಹಱಿದು ವಾಲೆಗಳು ಉಚ್ಚುವವು, the threads which (people) have sewed, will be torn and the leaves become loose (see § 315, *k. l*). ಕೞ್ತೆಯೆನ್ದು ಗರ್ದಭಂ, kaḻte (people) having said (is) a donkey (*i. e.* kaḻtĕ means a donkey, see § 332). ನುಡಿವೊಡೆಲ್ಲರುಂ ಮಾತಱಿಯರ್, if (they) speak, all of them do not know (proper) words (see § 314). ತೆರಳೆಯ ಹುೞು ಮುಕುಲಾಕಾರದಿನ್ದ ಮಾಡಿದುದ ಬಿಡಿಸಿ ನೆಯ್ದ ಸೀರೆ, a cloth which (they) have woven after separating what silk-worms have made in the form of buds. ಆನೆಯ ಹಿಡಿಯಲೋಸ್ಕರ ಮಾಡಿದ ಕಪ್ಪುಗುೞಿ, a pit which (people) have made for catching elephants. ಹೆಬ್ಬೊಟ್ಟು ಸುಟ್ಟುಮ್ಬೆ ಕೂಡಿ ಅಳದರೆ ಪ್ರಾದೇಶ ಎನಿಸುಗು, if (one) measures (a span) with both the thumb and forefinger, it is called a prâdêśa. ಹೋಗ ಬಾರದ ಬಟ್ಟೆ, a road which (people) are unable to go. ಪೊಯ್ದ ಬೞಿ, a place (of the body) to which (somebody) has applied a blow. ಪಡುವ ದೇಗುಲದೆಡೆಯಾವುದು, what (is) the place of the temple where (you) rest? ಹೋದರೆ ಒನ್ದು ಕಲ್ಲು, ಬನ್ದರೆ ಒನ್ದು ಹಣ್ಣು, if (it) goes, (it is) a stone, if (it) comes, (it is) a ripe fruit (*i.e.* what goes in one's giving, is a mere stone; what comes for it, is a ripe fruit). ಬರುವಾಗ ಹುಲಿಯ ಹಾಗೆ, ಹೋಗುವಾಗ ಇಲಿಯ ಹಾಗೆ, when (he) comes, (he is) like a tiger; when (he) goes, (he is) like a mouse. ನಿನ್ನ ಕೂಡಾ ನಾಳೆ ಬನ್ದರೆ ನನ್ನದು ನಾಲ್ಕು ದಿವಸದ ಓದು ನಿಲ್ಲುತ್ತದೆ, if (I) come with thee to-morrow, my study will be interrupted for four days. ಹಾಗೆ ನಡೆದರೆ ಕೆಟ್ಟು ಹೋಗುವಿ, if (thou) behavest thus, thou wilt be ruined. ಮೊಸರು ಕಡೆದರೆ ಬೆಣ್ಣೆ ಬರುವದು, if (one) churns curds, butter is produced. ಬೆಣ್ಡುಬತ್ತಾಸು ಕೊಣ್ಡರೆ ತಿನ್ದು ಹೋಗುತ್ತದೆ, if (I) buy sweetmeats, they will be eaten. ಎಲೇ ಮಗನೇ, ಜನರ ಕೂಡ ಗೆಳೆತನ ಮಾಡಿದರೆ ಬಹು ಎಚ್ಚಱಿದಿನ್ದ ಮಾಡಬೇಕು, O son, if (thou) wantest to form friendship with people, (thou) must do so with much caution. ಅಣ್ಣತಮ್ಮನ್ದಿರ ಕೂಡ ಪ್ರೀತಿಯಿನ್ದ ನಡಕೊಳ್ಳಬೇಕು, (we) must converse in love with (our) brothers. ಮಾತು ಕಲಿಸಿದರೆ ಗಿಳಿಗಳು ಬೇಗ ಕಲಿಯುತ್ತವೆ, if (you) teach (them) words, parrots will quickly learn (them). See *e. g.* also §§ 302, 7 (ಯಾಕನ್ದರೆ). 314 (the conditional). 323 (ಏನೆನ್ದೊಡೆ, etc.). 326 (ಎನ್ತೆನ್ದೊಡೆ, etc.). 332. 333 (ಎನ್ದರೆ, etc.).

ತಾಯೊಳ್ ಒಳ್ಳಿದಂ, (he is) good to (his) mother. ಗುರು ಶಿಷ್ಯನಂ ವ್ಯಾಕರಣಮನ್ ಓದಿಸಿದಂ, the teacher caused (his) disciple to read the grammar. ದಯ ಮಾಡಿ ಮನೆತನಕ ಬರ್ರಿ, please come as far as (my) house. ಯಜಮಾನನು ಕೆಯ್ ಕಾಲು ತೊಳ ಕೊಳ್ಳಲಿಕ್ಕೆ ಎದ್ದನು, the master stood up to wash (his) hands and feet. ಆ ಹೆಂಗಸು ತಲೆಯ ಮೇಲೆ ಏನು ಹೊತ್ತು ಕೊಣ್ಡು ಬರುತ್ತಾಳೆ, what does that woman carry on (her) head? ತಂಗಿಗೆ ವರನ್ ಈತನೆನ್ದು, ಮದನಂ ತಿಳಿದಂ, Madana perceived "this man (is) a suitable husband for (my) younger sister". ಕಱು ತಾಯ ಬೞಿಯನ್ ಉೞಿಯದು, a calf does not leave the company of (its) mother. ಗುರುವಿನನ್ತೆ ಶಿಷ್ಯ, the pupil (is) like (his) spiritual teacher. ಕಣ್ಣಲ್ಲಿ ನೋಡುತ್ತೇವೆ, we see with (our) eyes.

ನೀನು ಆಱು ತಿಂಗಳುಗಳ ಕೆಳಗೆ ಕೊಡ ಬೇಕಾಗಿತ್ತು, you ought to have given (it, *i. e.* the money) six months ago. ಆ ವೈದನು, ಯಾಕೆ ತಕ್ಕೊಳ್ಳುವದಿಲ್ಲ ಎನ್ದು, ಕೇಳಲು, when that physician asked "why will you not take (them, *i. e.* the medicines)?" The grammar called Nuḍigaṭṭu adduces also the following instances:— ಅವನು ಉತ್ತಮನು, ಹೊಡೆಯ ಬೇಡ, he (is) a good fellow, do not beat (him). ಬ್ರಾಹ್ಮಣನು ಸಾತ್ವಿಕನಿದ್ದಾನೆ, ಹತ್ತು ರೂಪಾಯಿ ಕೊಡು, the Brâhmaṇa is an honest man, give (him) ten rupees. ಸಪ್ಪನ್ನ ಹಾಲು ನನಗೆ ಸೇರುವದಿಲ್ಲ, ಸಕ್ಕರೆಯ ಹಾಕು, insipid milk does not agree with me; put (some) sugar (into it)! ಈ ಕೊಡಲಿ ಹದನಾಗಿದೆ, ಕಟ್ಟಿಗೆಯ ಕಡಿ, this axe is sharp; cut the wood (with it)!

359. In § 275 there are various instances of the modern dialect in which the verb ಇರು, to be, is the verb of a sentence, *e. g.* ಆನೆಗಳು ಕಪ್ಪು ಇರುತ್ತವೆ, elephants are black; ಚಾಕು ಚಲೋದು ಅದೆ, the penknife is beautiful; ಆ ಸ್ತ್ರೀಯರು ಚಿಕ್ಕವರಿದ್ದಾರೆ, those women are small; ಹೂಗಳು ಹಸರು ಅವೆ, the flowers are green. On the other hand we find there various instances in which the verb ಇರು is omitted, *e. g.* ಅವನು ಚಲೋ ಹುಡುಗನು, he (is) a nice boy; ಅವನ ಮನೆ ದೊಡ್ಡದು, his house (is) large; etc. From such instances it might appear as if the insertion and omission of the verb ಇರು were arbitrary.

But the above instances belong to the present modern dialect; in the ancient and mediæval dialect the verb ಇರ್ (ಇರು) is always understood and never expressed, if it is a mere copula to connect a subject with its predicate, *e. g.* ಅವನ್ ಒಳ್ಳಿದಂ, he (is) a good man. ಅವಳ್ ಒಳ್ಳಿದಳ್, she (is) a good woman. ಇವಳ್ ದೇವರ ತೊೞ್ತು, she (is) the king's maid-servant. ಪಾಲ್ ಬಿಳಿದು, milk (is) white. ಅವರ್ ಬಲ್ಲಿದರ್, they (are) able persons. ಅವು ಪಿರಿಯುವು, they (the pearls, are) large. ನಾನ್ ಆಳ್, I (am) a servant. ಆಳ್ ಇವಂ, he (is) a servant. ನೀಂ ಕಾಮಂ, thou (art) Kâma. ಆಂ ಗೌರಿ, I (am) Gauri. ರತ್ನಂಗಳೊಳ್ ಮಾಣಿಕ್ಯಮ್ ಉತ್ತಮಂ, among jewels the ruby (is) precious. ಮಾನವರೊಳ್ ಪುರುಷರ್ ಉತ್ತಮರ್, among men males (are) chiefs (see § 350, 2, *a. b. c*; § 354, I, 2; § 348, 5. 7;. § 349, 8; § 357, 3). ಚಾಗದೊಳ್ ಈತಂ ಮಾನ್ಧಾತಂ, this man as to generosity (is) a Mândhâta. ತಾಯೊರ್ವಳ್, ತನ್ದೆ ಬೇಱೆ, the mother (is) one (*i. e.* the same), the father (is) different. ಆರ್ತೀ ತುರಂಗಂ, whose horse (is) this? ನೀನಾರ ಮಗಳ್, whose daughter (art) thou? Instances like these are the rule and quite idiomatic.

In sentences like the following Kannaḍa people would also nowadays scarcely use the verb ಇರು:—ಇವರು ಯಾರು, who (are) these persons? ಈಕೆ ಯಾರ ಹೆಣ್ಡತಿ, whose wife (is) she? ಯಾವಾಕೆ ನಿಮ್ಮಕ್ಕ, which (is) your elder sister? ಇವರು ನಿಮ್ಮ ತಾಯಿಯುವರು, ಅಲ್ಲವೋ, this (is) your mother; is she not? ಅವರು ಅಣ್ಣತಮ್ಮನ್ದಿರು, they (are) brothers.

In the following instance of the present modern dialect also the past tense of the verb ಇರು, when a mere copula, is to be understood:—ಆರ್ಯರ ಮೂಲ ಭಾಷೆ ಸಂಸ್ಕೃತವು; ಅದಱಿನ್ದ ಮುನ್ದೆ ಹಲವು ಭಾಷೆಗಳು ಹುಟ್ಟಿದವು, the original language of the Âryas (was) Saṁskṛita; from that, in course of time, several languages came into existence.

360. It is a different thing, if the verb 'to be' is not a mere copula, but expresses 'to exist', 'to be', 'to have', when the verbs ಉಳ್, ಇರ್ (ಇರು) and the forms ಅಯ್ತು, ಆದೆ, ಇದೆ, ಅವೆ, ಇವೆ, are used (see §§ 196. 316, 1. 2), *e.g.*

ನೀನುಳ್ಳೊಡುಣ್ಟು ರಾಜ್ಯಂ;
ನೀನುಳ್ಳೊಡೆ ಪಟ್ಟಮ್ ಉಣ್ಟು, ಪೇಳಿಗೆಯುಣ್ಟು; |
ನೀನುಳ್ಳೊಡುಣ್ಟು ಬೆಳ್ಗೊಡೆ;
ನೀನಿಲ್ಲದಿವೆಲ್ಲಮ್ ಒಳವೆ, ಭಾನುತನೂಜಾ? || if thou art, (there) is an empire; if thou art, (there) are the insignia of royalty and (there) are boxes (with money); if thou art, (there) is the white umbrella; if thou art (or be) not, will all these (things) exist?

ಪಣಮ್ ಉಣ್ಟು, (there) is money. ಕುದುರೆಗಳ್ ಒಳವು, (there) are horses. ಜಸಮ್ ಉಣ್ಟೀತಂಗೆ, (there) is fame to him (*i. e.* he has fame). ಅವರ್ ಒಳರ್,

they are present. ಬನದುತ್ತರದಿಗ್ಭಾಗದೊಳ್ ಅಂಜನಗಿರಿಯೆಮ್ಬ ಪರ್ವತಮ್ ಉಣ್ಟು, to the north of that forest (there) is the mountain of Añjanagiri. ಆ ಮನೆಯ ಹತ್ತಿರ ಒನ್ದು ಬಾವಿ ಉಣ್ಟು, (there) is a well near that house. ದೋಣಿಯಲ್ಲಿ ಒಬ್ಬನೇ ಇದ್ದನು, (there) was even one man in the boat. ಈ ಅಡವಿಯಲ್ಲಿ ಬಹಳ ಹುಲಿಗಳಿವೆ, (there) are many tigers in this jungle. ದೇವರಿದ್ದಾನೆ, (there) is God. ಆ ಗೃಹಸ್ಥನ ಸಂಗಡ ಬಹಳ ಮನ್ದಿ ಸೇವಕರಿದ್ದರು, (there) were many servants with that gentleman. ಆ ಬಾವಿಯೊಳಗೆ ನೀರು ಇಲ್ಲ, (there) is no water in the well. ತಾಯಿಗಿನ್ತ ಹಿತವರಿಲ್ಲ, ಸಕ್ಕರೆಗಿನ್ತ ಸವಿಯಿಲ್ಲ, (there) are no greater benefactors than a mother, (there) is nothing sweeter than sugar. ಗೃಹದೊಳ್ ಇರ್ದಪಳ್, she is in the house. ಎನ್ನೆವರಂ ಸಿರಿ ತಮಗುಣ್ಟನ್ನೆವರಂ ಸೇವ್ಯರಲ್ತೆ ಖಳರುಂ, as long as they possess riches, will not also scoundrels be honourable persons?

In such instances the verb ಉಳ್, etc. are often also not expressed, *e. g.* ಪೂವಿನೊಳ್ ಕಮ್ಪು, (there is) fragrance in flowers. ಅಲರೊಳ್ ಬೆಳ್ಪು, (there s) white colour in the flower. ಪಾಲೊಳ್ ಮಧುರಂ, (there is) sweetness in milk. ಬಿಮ್ಬದೊಳ್ ತೇಜಂ, (there is) splendour in the disk of the sun. ಸನ್ಧಿಯೆಣ್ಟು ಶಬ್ದಮಣಿದರ್ಪಣದೊಳ್ (there are) eight chapters in the Śabdamaṇidarpaṇa. ಗುರುವಿನೊಳ್ ಸಹಜಂ, (he is) true to (his) guru. ಪೂಜೆಯೊಳ್ ಜಾಣಂ, (he is) proficient in adoration. ಬೆಕ್ಕಿಗೆ ಆಟ, ಇಲಿಗೆ ಪ್ರಾಣಸಂಕಟ, for the cat (it is) play, for the mouse (it is) extreme distress. ಬಂಗಾರಕ್ಕಿನ್ತ ಜ್ಞಾನವು ಹೆಚ್ಚಿನದು, knowledge (is) superior to gold. ಅಲ್ಲಿ ಬಹಳ ಮನ್ದಿ ಆಟಗಾರರು, (there were) many players there.

It will have been observed from the above sentences that the English terms **'there', 'there is', 'there are', 'there were', etc.,** used to begin sentences, **cannot be expressed in Kannaḍa,** to which may be added *e. g.* ಆತಂಗಮ್ ಆಕೆಗಂ ವಿಖ್ಯಾತಯಶಂ ಪುಟ್ಟಿದಂ, (there) was born to him and to her Vikhyâtayaśa. ಅರಸಣತ್ತಣಿಂ ದಾಟಿ ಬನ್ದುದು, (there) occurred an inroad from the side of the king.

Notice also the following: ನಾನು ಇದ್ದೇನೆ or ನಾನೇ, it is I. ನಾವು ಇದ್ದೇವೆ or ನಾವೇ, it is we. ಅವರಲ್ಲ, ನಾವೇ ಹಾಗೆ ಅನ್ನುತ್ತೇವೆ, it is we, not they, who say so. ಹುಡುಗಿ ಇದ್ದಾಳೆ or ಹುಡುಗಿ, it is a girl.

361. In §§ 154—170 the forms of **the past verbal participle** have been given (*cf.* ಇಲ್ಲದೆ, ಅಲ್ಲದೆ in § 338, and the repetition of verbs in § 339).

It is used

1, **in simple succession of actions**, the actions having the same subject, *e. g.* ಒಸೆದು ಕೊಟ್ಟಂ, he was delighted (and) gave. ಮೆಚ್ಚಿ ಪೊಗಟ್ದಂ, he was pleased (and) praised. ಪಾಡಿ ಕುಣಿದಂ, he sang (and) danced. ಬೇಡಿ ಕೊಣ್ಡಂ, he begged (and) received. ಅಱಸಿ ಕಣ್ಡಂ, he sought (and) found. ನೋಡಿ ಮಣಿದಂ, he saw (and) made obeisance. ಉಣ್ಡೊಱಗಿದಂ, he ate (and) went to sleep. ಕುಡಿದುಗುಳ್ದಂ, he drank (and) spit. ಮಿಸ್ದುಣ್ಡು ಕುಡಿದು ಮಗುಳ್ದಂ, he bathed, ate, drank (and) turned back. ಮಾಲವದೇಶಮುಂ ಕಿಡಿಸಿ ತದ್ಧಾರಾ ಪುರಸ್ತ್ರೀಯರಂ ತೊೞ್ತಿರ್ ಮಾಡಿದಂ, he ruined the country of Mâlava (and) made the women of its (town of) Dhârâpura (his) maid-servants. ಪೊಮ್ಮಱಿವೊಲ್ ಪೊಳೆದು ಪಾಱ ಪೋದಂ ಶ್ವೇತಂ, like a gold-coloured young antelope the white (horse) rolled about, sprang (and) went. ನಾನು ಮನೆಗೆ ಹೋಗಿ ಉಣ್ಡು ಪುಸ್ತಕಗಳನ್ನು ತಕ್ಕೊಣ್ಡು ಬರುತ್ತೇನೆ, I go home, eat, take (my) books (and) come. ಊಟಾ ಮಾಡಿ ಬರುತ್ತೇನೆ, I will eat (and) come. ಸಮುದ್ರ ದೊಳಗಿನ ನೀರು ಬಿಸಲಿಗೆ ಕಾದು ಉಗಿಯಾಗಿ ಮೇಲಕ್ಕೆ ಹೋಗಿ ಆಕಾಶದೊಳಗೆ ಒಟ್ಟು ಗೂಡಿ ಮೋಡಗಳು ಆಗುತ್ತವೆ, the water in the sea is heated by the sunshine, becomes vapour, rises up, joins together in the air (and) becomes clouds. ಮೊಸರು ಕಡೆದು ಮಜ್ಜಿಗೆಯನ್ನು ಮಾಡುತ್ತಾರೆ, they churn curds (and) make buttermilk. ಗೞವಿಡಿದಾಡುವಂ, he seizes the pole (and) plays. ಮಾಡದೆ ಪೋದಂ, he did not make (it and) went. ಓಡದೆ ಕಾದಿ ಗೆದ್ದನು, he did not run away, fought (and) overcame.

(It will be seen that in translating the past participle the verb finite in combination with 'and' has been used.)

2, **in manner**, the actions having the same subject, *e. g.* ಕುಸಿದು ನಡೆದಂ, he walked stoopingly. ನಡೆದು ಬನ್ದಂ, he came on foot. ಬಿಗಿದು ಕಟ್ಟಿದಂ, he tied (it) firmly. ಸಂಗ್ರಹಿಸಿ ಬರೆದಂ, he wrote (it) in an abridged way. ಟಿಪ್ಪ ಣಿಸಿ ಬರೆದಂ, he wrote (it) commentatorially. ತಿಳಿಯದೆ ಮಾತಾಡ ಬಾರದು, do not speak without understanding.

3, **in means**, the actions having the same subject, *e. g.* ತಿರಿದುಣ್ಡಂ, he ate by wandering in quest of alms. ಬೇಡಿ ಕೊಣ್ಡು ತಿನ್ನ ಬಹುದು, ಕದ್ದು ಕೊಣ್ಡು ತಿನ್ನ ಬಾರದು, (one) may eat by begging, (but one) ought not to live by stealing. ದನಗಳನ್ನು ಹೊಡೆದು ಓಡಿಸಿದನು, he drove the cattle away by beating.

4, **in cause**, the actions having the same subject, *e. g.* ಅಱಯದೆ ಕೆಟ್ಟಂ, because he did not know, he was ruined. ಹುಡುಗನು ಓದದೆ ಕೆಟ್ಟನು, the boy was ruined, because he did not study. ಗಣ್ಡನು ಕೂತು ಕೆಟ್ಟ, ಹೆಂಗಸು ತಿರಿಗಿ ಕೆಟ್ಟಳು, the husband was ruined, because he sat (lazily); the woman was ruined, because she rambled about. ಮಳೆಗೆ ಹೆದಱಿ ಹೊೞಿಗೆ ಹಾಱಿದ ಹಾಗೆ, as if (one) springs into the river, because he is afraid of the rain.

When a different subject from that of the last verb occurs, it is used chiefly

1, **in cause,** *e.g.* ಪೆಣನಂ ಕಣ್ಡು ದುಃಖಮ್ ಆದುದು, grief originated, because (he) saw the corpse. ಪ್ರಿಯಳಂ ಕಣ್ಡು ಸುಖಮ್ ಆದುದು, joy originated, because (he) saw the beloved woman. ಗಾಳಿ ಬೀಸಿ ಮರದಿನ್ದ ಹಣ್ಣು ಬಿತ್ತು, because the wind blew, (there) fell a ripe fruit from the tree. ಹಣ ಹೋಗಿ ಬಡವನಾದನು, because (his) money went, he became poor. ಹಾವು ಕಚ್ಚಿ ವಿಷವೇಱಿ ಅರಸನು ಸತ್ತನು, the king died, because a snake bit (him), and the poison rose (to his head). ಉದ್ದ ಮರದ ತುದಿಯನ್ ಏಱಿ ಕೆಯ್ ತಪ್ಪಿ ಬಿದ್ದು ಸತ್ತನ್ತೆ, as if (a man) ascended the top of a high tree, fell down, because his hand slipped, and died. ಫಲಾ ನೋಡದೆ ಕೆಟ್ಟಿತು, ಹೊಲಾ ಮಾಡದೆ ಕೆಟ್ಟಿತು, because nobody took care of the fruit, it was spoiled; because nobody cultivated the field, it was ruined. ಸೀಸದ ಲೆಕ್ಕಣಿಕೆ ಬರೆದು ಸವೆಯಿತು, the lead-pencil wore, because (people) wrote (with it). ಅವನು ಬೇನೆ ಬನ್ದು ಸತ್ತನು, he died, because disease attacked (him). ಅವನ ಒಲ್ಲಿಯ ಸೆಱಗು ತಾಕಿ ಅಲ್ಲಿಟ್ಟಿದ್ದ ಕುಣ್ಡದೊಳಗಿನ ಗಿಡದ ಹೂವು ಕೆಳಗೆ ಬಿತ್ತು, the flower of a shrub which was put there in a pot, fell down, because the end of his garment touched it.

2, **in lapse of time,** *e.g.* ಅವನು ಹೋಗಿ ಅಯ್ದು ದಿವಸ ಆಯಿತು, it is five days since he went. ಅರಸನು ಬನ್ದು ಒನ್ದು ತಿಂಗಳಾಯಿತು, it is a month since the king came.

362. The forms of the **present verbal participle** are adduced in §§ 172. 173. **It expresses**

1, **contemporaneous action,** *e.g.* ನಗುತುಂ ಬನ್ದಂ, he came laughing. ಕರೆಯುತುಂ ಪೋದಂ, he went calling. ಕಾದುತ್ತುಂ ಬನ್ದಂ, he came fighting. ಜಡಿಯುತ್ತುಂ ಪೊಡೆದಂ, he beat chiding. ಕೆತ್ತುತ್ತೆ ಕಡಿದಂ, he cut chipping. ಪರಸುತ್ತೆ ಬನ್ದಂ, he came blessing. ಮಿಱುಗುತೆ ಪೋದಂ, he went shining. ನಗುತ್ತ ಹೇೞಿದನು, he spoke laughing. ಓಡುತ್ತ ಹೋಗುವವನು ಎಡವಿ ಬಿದ್ದಾನು, he who goes running may stumble (and) fall. ನಗುತ್ತ ತಿನ್ನುತ್ತ ಹರಟುತ್ತಾನೆ, he prates (whilst) laughing (and) eating. ರಾಮನು ಹಾಡುತ್ತ ಬಾಱಿಸುತ್ತ ನಗುತ್ತ ಕುಣಿಯುತ್ತಾನೆ, Râma dances singing, playing a musical instrument (and) laughing. ಅಪ್ಪಾ, ನೋಡು! ಅತ್ತಕಡೆಯಿನ್ದ ಕೋಲು ಊಱುತ್ತ ಒಬ್ಬ ಮುದುಕನು ಬರು

ತ್ತಾನೆ, see, father! from that side (there) comes an old man putting down (his) stick on the ground (at every step to support himself).

2, **continuation** (*cf.* § 339, 6)

a) in the present tense (see § 313, 1).

b) in the imperfect (see § 313, 2), *e.g.* ಇಸುತಿರ್ದಂ, he was shooting (arrows). ಉಣ್ಣುತಮ್ ಇರ್ದಂ, he was eating. ನಿನ್ನನ್ ಆಂ ಕೂಡಿ ನೋಡಿ ಕಾಣದಿನ್ನೆವರಂ ಚಿನ್ತಿಸುತಿರ್ದೆಂ, both of us looked about, did not see thee (and) were in anxiety (as to thee) up to this moment.

ಮದಗಜವೆರಡಱ ಬಾಲದ
ಮೊದಲಂ ಪಿಡಿದೆತ್ತಿ ನುರ್ಗುತ್ತಿರೆಯಾ ।
ಸ್ಯದಿನ್ ಒಗುವ ರಕ್ತಮ್ ಉರಿಯೆನೆ
ತಿದಿಯೊತ್ತುವ ಕಮ್ಮಱವೊಲಿರ್ದಂ ಭೀಮಂ ॥ Bhîma seized the end of the tails of the two furious elephants, (and) whilst he crushed (them), was like a blacksmith who plied the bellows, the blood that came forth from (their) mouth being the flame. ಗಣಪತಿಯು ತನ್ನ ಕುದುರೆಯನ್ನು ಹುಡುಕುತ್ತಾ ನಡೆದನು, Gaṇapati walked seeking his horse.

c) in the future (see § 313, 3).

When in the modern dialect the present participle has its own subject, it suffixes the vowels ಎ or ಇ combined with a euphonic ಲ್ (see §§ 282. 285. 286), *e.g.* ವಸನ್ತ ಬರುತ್ತಲೆ ಕೋಗಿಲೆ ಉಲಿಯುತ್ತದೆ, the cuckoo cries even spring coming (*i.e.* at the very time when spring comes, as soon as spring comes). ಮಡದಿಸುತರ ಮಮಕಾರಕೆ ನೀ ಮನ ಒಡಬಡುತಲಿ ನಗುತಿರ ಬೇಡ, do not laugh on account of love for (your) wife and son, (your) heart even taking pleasure (in them).

363. The forms of the **past relative participle** are given in §§ 175—179. *Cf.* § 254.

It is used to take the place of the relative pronouns in other languages, *e.g.* ಪಾಡಿದಂ, he who sang; ಪೋದಂ, he who went; ಬೇಡಿದಳ್, she who begged; ಬಗೆದಾತಂ, he who considered; ಪೀರ್ದುದು, it that drank; ಏೞ್ವರ್, those who rise; ಆಡಿದ ಪೊಲಂ, a place in which (people) played; ಕೊಟ್ಟ ವಸ್ತು, a (or the) thing which (somebody) had given; ಮೊಳೆತ ಪುಲ್, the grass which had germinated; ಕಲ್ತ ಪಾಠಂ, the lesson which (somebody) had learned; ಪೊಯ್ದ ಬೞಿ, the place (of the body) to which (somebody) applied a blow; ಆದ ವಿಷ್ಣು, Vishṇu who had become; ಮಾಡದ ಕೆಯ್, a field which nobody cultivates; ಕಿಡದ ಪಕ್ಷಂ, in case that (something) should not be destroyed; ತೀರದ ಕಜ್ಜಂ, an affair that does not end; ಅಲ್ಲದ ಕಾರ್ಯಂ, an affair which is not proper; ಬಿಗಿದ ಮಿಳಿ, a strap which has been tightened; ಬೇಡಿದ ದಾನಂ, a gift which has been asked for; ಕುತ್ತಮ್ ಓಸರಿಸಿದಂ, he whose affliction was removed; ಪುತ್ರನು ಹುಟ್ಟದವರು, they to whom a son has not been born; ಕೊಮ್ಬು ಮುಱಿದೆತ್ತು, an ox whose horns are broken. *Cf.* § 267.

About its use before adverbs (postpositions, § 212, 6) see § 282.

364. The forms of the present and future relative participles are given in §§ 180—186. *Cf.* § 254.

They are used in the same way as the relative past participle (also before adverbs, see §§ 282. 365), *e.g.* ಉಳ್ಳಂ, he who is or has (see §§ 185. 316); ಅಱಿವಳ್, she who knows or will know (see § 186); ಕೂಡುವ ಪುಳಿಲ್, a sand-bank that is accumulating; ತೂಗುವ ಸೊಡರ್, a lamp that hangs; ಪೊಯ್ವ ಮೞೆ, a rain which dashes; ಬೀಸುವ ಚಾಮರಂ, a chowrie which (somebody) waves; ಬೆಳೆವ ತೆನೆ, an ear of corn that grows; ಪೊಡೆವ ಭೇರಿ, a kettle-drum that (somebody) beats; ಪೂರಯ್ಸುವ ಶಂಖಂ, a conch-shell that (somedody) blows; ಪರಿವ ತೊಱೆ, a stream that runs; ಪಿಡಿವ ಕಹಳೆ, a trumpet which (somebody) applies to his mouth for blowing; ಪೊಣ್ಮುವ ಘರ್ಮಜಲಂಗಳ್, perspiration which comes forth (see § 253, 2, *d*); ಪೊರೆವಂ, he that nourishes or will nourish; ಸೋವಾಳೆ, a woman who scares away (see § 254). ಹಿಣ್ಡಿ ಕೊಳ್ಳುವ ಹೊತ್ತು ಆಯಿತು, the time in which (the cows) are milked, has come. See §§ 273. 330, and *cf.* § 267. An additonal instance is:—

ಪಾಡುವ ತುಮ್ಬಿ ತೀಡುವೆಲರ್ ಆಡುವ ಸೋಗೆ ಕೊಳಂಗಳೊಳ್ ತುಳುಂ
ಕಾಡುವ ಬಾೞೆ ಕೋಡುವ ಪುಳಿಲ್ ಸಲೆ ಕೂಡುವ ಕೊಂಟೆ ಮುಟ್ಟೆ ಮು |
ದ್ದಾಡುವ ಜಕ್ಕವಕ್ಕಿ ನಲಿದಾಡುವ ಕನ್ನಡವಕ್ಕಿ ಮುದ್ದುಮಾ
ತಾಡುವ ಜಾಣವಕ್ಕಿ ನಡೆ ನೋಡುವರ್ಗೆಱ್ಱಿಯನ್ ಉಣ್ಬು ಮಾಡುಗಂ || the black bees which hum, the wind which blows, the leaves of palms which wave about, the plantains which fluctuate in (the water of) the ponds, the small islands (in the river) which are cool, the herons which do meet together, the ruddy geese which mutually touch and kiss, the parrots which play about, the clever birds which utter pleasant words cause much pleasure to those who look on.

After one or more preceding past participles the present-future relative participle is often used, giving it or them so to say the sense of the present, *e.g.* ನೀಳ್ದಲರ್ವ ಬಾಲಂ, a tail which is long and extends itself.

ಎಡಱಿದರನ್ ಅಟ್ಟಿ ಮೋದುವ ಪಡಿಯಱಗಟ್ಟಿಗೆಗಳ್, the doorkeepers' sticks which drive away and strike those who are dishonest. ತನ್ನೊಳ್ ಪಳಂಚಿ ಕಿಡುಗುಟ್ಟಿ ತಪ್ಪುವಮ್ಬುಗಳರವಂ, the speed of the arrows that touch, knock against him (and) miss (their deadly aim). ದುರ್ಬಲರಾದವರು ಬಲಿಷ್ಠರ ಕೆಯ್ ಹಿಡಿದು ನಿಲ್ಲಿಸಿ ಕೇಳುವಷ್ಟು ಸಾಮರ್ಥ್ಯ ಸಾಲದೇ ಇರುವದಱಿಂದ ಅವರೇನು ಮಾಡಿದರೂ ಸುಮ್ಮಗೆ ತಾಳಿಕೊಣ್ಡು ಹೋಗ ಬೇಕಾಗುತ್ತದೆ, because weak persons have not sufficient power to seize the hand of very strong persons, to stop (them and) demand (their rights), they are obliged to bear quietly whatsoever those do.

It is still to be mentioned that occasionally present relative participles are put in an uninterrupted series one after another, *e. g.* ಗಱಿವಿಡಿದಾಡುವ ದೀವಿಗೆವಿಡಿವೆಲೆವರದಾಡುವನೊಳ್ ಅಟಿಗಪ್ರತ್ಯಯಮ್ ಅಕ್ಕುಂ, the suffix aṭiga is used (regarding) a man who seizes a pole (and) plays, (regarding) one who bears (or uses to bear) a lamp, (and) regarding one who carries on a betel-leaf trade.

ತಿವಿವ ಮರಳ್ಚುವಬ್ಬರಿಪ ವಗರ್ವಿಪ ಬೊಬ್ಬಿಱಿವಾರ್ವ ಸಾರ್ವ ಮೇಣ್
ಕವಿವ ಕಡಂಗುವಿಟ್ಟಣಿಪ ಸುತ್ತುವ ನಿಲ್ವ ಗೆಲ್ವ ಪೊ ।
ಣ್ಮುವ ಪುಟವೇಱ್ವ ಪಾಯ್ವ ಮಿಗೆ ಪೊಯ್ವ ತೊಡಂಕುವ ತೋಟಿಗೆಯ್ವ ಕೂಂ
ಕುವ ನೆಱೆ ನೂಂಕುವೇೞ್ಗೆಯ ಬಲಂ ಬಗೆಗೊಣ್ಡುದು ತತ್ಕುಮಾರನಾ ॥ that (king's) son's grand army which was piercing, causing to retreat, whooping, behaving proudly, shouting, crying aloud, coming near, and attacking, striving, crowding, surrounding, closing with, standing, gaining the victory, coming forth, jumping up, advancing, beating excessively, getting entangled, struggling, rising (and) pushing in a good manner, attracted the attention.

365. The forms and signification of the infinitive appear in § 187. 188. Here follow some instances:—ಉಣಲ್ ಬನ್ದಂ, he came to eat. ತರಲ್ ಪೋದಂ, he went to bring. ಆವ ಜಗಮಂ ಸಾಧಿಸಲ್ ಪೋದಯ್? ಪೇೞ್, ಎಲೆ ವಿದ್ಯಾಧರಚಕ್ರವರ್ತಿ, which world doest thou go to subdue? Tell, O Vidyâdharačakravarti! ನುಡಿಯಲ್ಕೆ ಬನ್ದಂ, he came to speak. ಬಿತ್ತರಿಸಲ್ಕೆವೇೞ್ ಸುವರ್ಣೋತ್ಕರಮಂ, tell to make large the heap of gold! ಮಾಡಲ್ ದಕ್ಷಂ, he (is) clever to make. ನೋಡಲ್ ಸಮರ್ಥಂ, he (is) suitable to examine. ಉಣಲ್ ಒಳ್ಳಿತು, it (is) good to eat. ನೋಡಲ್ ಸಮಯಂ, it (is) time to see. ಪೋಗಲ್ ಪೊತ್ತು, it (is) time to go. ಉಡವೇೞ್ (or ಉಡಲ್ವೇೞ್), tell (him) to put on clothes. ತರವೇೞ್ (or ತರಲ್ವೇೞ್) ಸನ್ನದ್ಧವಾಜಿಸಾಧನಮಂ, tell to bring the force of well equipped horses. ಉಪದ್ರವಮಂ ಮಾಡ ಬೇಡ (or ಮಾಡಲ್ ಬೇಡ), do not cause trouble. ಆಗಲು ಬೇಡಿದುದು, that is fit (or about) to become. ಹುಡುಗರು ಅರ್ಥವನ್ನು ಗ್ರಹಿಸಲಾಱರು, the boys cannot understand the meaning. ನೀಚರು ಹಾದಿಗೆ ಬರಲೊಲ್ಲರು, mean persons will not come to the (proper) way. ನಾನು ಊರಿಗೆ ಹೋಗಲಿಕ್ಕೆ ಬೇಕು, it is necessary for me to go to the town. ಹೊತ್ತುಣ್ಟಲೆ ಮನೆಗೆ ಹೋಗಲಿಕ್ಕೆ ನಮಗೆ ಅಪ್ಪಣೆ ಕೊಟ್ಟರು, they ordered us to go home early. ನನಗೆ ಓದಲಿಕ್ಕೆ ಬರುತ್ತದೆ, I can read. ತಾವು ರಕ್ಷಿಸ ಬೇಕು, you must deliver. ನೀವು ಒಳಗೆ ಬರ ಬಹುದು, you may come in. ತಾವು ಇನ್ಥ ಮಾತುಗಳನ್ನು ಆಡ ಬಾರದು, you must not utter such words. ಅವರು ಇಲ್ಲಿಗೆ ಬರ ತಕ್ಕದು, it is proper for them to come here. See § 315 (concerning the passive); § 316, 3 *seq.*

The locative-infinitive (satisaptami; satyartha, see Šabdamaṇidarpaṇa under its sûtra 133) has been touched upon in §§ 187, 4; 188, remark; 286. It is the infinitive with the final vowel ಎ (see also the passive in § 315 wherein it is used, and § 352, 1, *a*). According to the grammarian Kêšava it is used when there are two subjects (ubhayakartṛi, Šabdamaṇidarpaṇa under sûtra 249), *e. g.* ಗಾಯಕಂ ಪಾಡೆ ದೇವಂ ಮೆಚ್ಚಿದಂ, when the singer sang, the king was pleased (lit. the singer a singing, the king was pleased). ಪಾತ್ರಪಾಡೆ ಪಾದಕಂ ಬಾಜಿಸಿದಂ, when the actor played, the musician sounded (his) musical instrument. ವನ್ದಿ ಪೊಗೞೆ ಚಾಗಿ ಕೊಟ್ಟಂ, when the bard praised, the liberal man gave. ಬರೆ ಕಣ್ಡಂ, when (he) came, (the king) saw (him). . ನೆಲನ್ ಅದಿರೆ ನೋಟಕರ್ ಕಣ್ಣಲಸೆ ಮನಂಗೊರಗೆ, when the earth quaked, when the spectators' eyes became tired (and) when the mind was afflicted.

"Some authors", Kêšava says, "do not hesitate to use ಅಲ್ instead (of ಎ), but that is not proper", and adduces the following instances as wrong (abaddha):— ಪಾದಪದ್ಮಂಗಳನ್ ಒತ್ತುತ್ತಿರಲ್ ಶೂದ್ರಿಕಪತಿ ಸುಖಾಸೀನನಾಗಿರ್ದನ್ ಆಗಳ್, when (they) shampooed (his) lotus-like feet, king Šûdrika was then comfortably seated. ಬಯ್ಗಿನ ಕೆಮ್ಬಿಸಿಲ್ ಎಳಸಲ್ ಎಸೆದುವಾಶ್ರಮತರುಗಳ್, when (they) desired the purple sunshine of evening, the trees of the hermitage appeared (see § 120, *a*, 2).

Kêšava remarks that in the above instances ಅಲೊಡಂ (ಅಲ್+ಒಡಂ) would have been right (šuddha), for which he gives the following instances:— ವಸನ್ತಂ ಬರಲೊಡಂ ಕೋಗಿಲೆಯುಲಿಗುಂ, when spring came, the cuckoo sang. ಗಾಳಿ ಬೀಸಲೊಡನ್ ಎಲೆ ಕಟಿಲ್ದುವು, when the wind blew, leaves dropped down.

According to that grammarian substitutes (âdêšas, as to use) for ಎ are ಇನಂ, ಇನೆಗಂ, ಉದುಂ (ಉದು+ಉಂ), ಅನ್ನಂ, ಅನ್ನೆಗಂ, ಅಲೊಡಂ and also ಅಲೊಡನೆ (ಅಲ್+ಒಡಂ+ಎ), *e.g.* ಕಾಮಕರಂ ಕರಮ್ ಅಡಂಗಿ ಸುರ್ಗಪ್ಪಿನೆಗಂ ಕಾವುದನ್ ಅಡಂಗೆವೊಯ್ದಂ, when (his) pride hides itself (and) is crushed completely, Skanda beats him so that he becomes ashamed. ಅವಧಿ ಬರ್ಪಿನೆಗಂ ಸಯ್ರಿಸಿದಂ, when extremity comes, he bears (it) patiently. ಬರಪೇೞ್ ಎಮ್ಬುದುಮ್ ಅಂಜನಾಚಲದ ವೊಲ್ ಕಣ್ಗೊಪ್ಪಿ ಬರ್ಪಮ್ಬುಜೋದರನಂ, when (he) said "tell Vishṇu to come (him) who appears (and) is coming (there) like the Añjanâčala!" ನಿನ್ನಿನೆಯನ ಪೞಿಕ್ಕೆಯೊಳ್ ಇರೆನ್ದು ಸಖಿ ತೊಲಗುವುದುಂ, when the female companion said "remain near thy beloved one", and went away. ಓಲಗಂ ಪರೆವುದುಮ್ ಆಲೋಚನೆಗೆ ಪೊಕ್ಕಂ, when the assembly dispersed, he began to consider. (See § 286.) ಉದ್ದವಿರ್ದನ್ ನೆಗೆವನ್ನಂ ಪೊಯ್ಯಲೆನ್ದವ್ವಳಿಪುದು, when he who is on high jumps down, jump upon (him) in order to beat (him)! ಬರಮ್ಬಡೆವನ್ನವರ್ ಆರಾಧಿಸಿದಂ, so that (his son) may receive a boon, he worships. ಗಂಗೆಯ ಮಡುಗಳನ್ ಅಡಹಡಿಸಿ ಪುಗುವಿನಂ ಭಯವಶದಿಂ, when from fear (he) rushes forward (and) enters the pools of the Ganges. ಇದಿರ್ವರ್ಪಿನಮ್ ಅಪ್ಪಿ ಕೊಣ್ಡಂ, when he comes to meet (him), he embraces (him). ಈವನ್ನೆಗಮ್ ಇರ್ದಂ, so that (the king) may give, he remains. ಒಲೆಯೊಡನೆ ಮುತ್ತುಂಗಾಲೊಳ್ ನರೆ ಬರ್ಪನ್ನೆಗಮ್ ಇರ್, be together with the fire-place when in (thy) old age grey hair grows. ಕುರುಕುಲಾಧಿಪಂ ನುಡಿಯಲೊಡಂ, when the chief of the Kuru race spoke. ಪಾವಸೆ ಕಿಡಲೊಡಂ ನೀರ್ ತಿಳಿದುದು, when the duck-weed was destroyed, the water became clear (see § 286). ಬರಲೊಡನೆ ಕೊಟ್ಟಂ, when (he) came, he gave (him something).

Kêšava remarks that ಅನ್ನೆಗಂ, ಅನ್ನಂ, ಇನೆಗಂ, ಇನಂ use to express the present and future, ಉದುಂ, ಅಲೊಡಂ the past, and according to this his remark the sentences quoted above have been translated.

Concerning Kêšava's rule as to the use of the infinitive with final ಎ the observation may be made that Bhaṭṭâkalaṅka, the author of the Šabdânušâsana, does not take notice of it, because he quotes (as it seems) the following sentences regarding the use of ಅಲ್ without raising any objection:—ಗಾಯಕಂ ಪಾಡಲ್ ಅರಸಂ ಮೆಚ್ಚಿದಂ, when the singer sang, the king was pleased. ಅರ್ಥಿ ಬೇಡಲ್ ದಾನಿಯಿತ್ತಂ, when the beggar begged, the liberal man gave. ನೇಸಱ್ ಮೂಡಲ್ ಕತ್ತಲೆ ಪೋದುದು, when the sun rose, darkness went.

In the modern dialect there is no particular rule regarding the use of ಅಲು (= ಅಲ್), although it is also employed to express 'when', *e. g.* ಕೇಳಲು, when (he, she, etc.) asked (lit. an asking). ಒಪ್ಪಿ ಕೊಳ್ಳಲು, when (he, she, etc.) assented. ಎನಲು, when (he, she, etc.) said. ಧರ್ಮನು ರಾಜ್ಯವ ಆಳುತ್ತಿರಲು ಪ್ರಜೆಗಳು ಸುಖದಿನ್ದಿದ್ದರು, when Dharma was ruling the kingdom, (his) subjects were happy. ನೀನು ಬರಲು ನಾನು ಹೋಗುತ್ತೇನೆ, when thou comest, I shall go. It is however more common to suffix ಆಗಿ (the past participle of ಆಗು) to ಅಲು, *e.g.* ಕೇಳಲಾಗಿ, a hearing having become, *i. e.* when (he, she, etc.) heard; ಮಾಡಲಾಗಿ, ಆಳುತ್ತಿರಲಾಗಿ.

In § 188 it has been shown that the so-called infinitives ending in ಎ, ಅಲ್, ಅಲು originally are verbal nouns. In modern poetry the form with ಎ occurs occasionally; see *e. g.* the verse from the Dâsapadas quoted in § 366 under remark *a*.

366. About the conjugation of verbs, (nouns, pronouns and adjectives) in the present, future and past see §§ 189-204.

Some instances are — ವಸನ್ತರಾಜನ್ ಎಯ್ತಿನ್ದಪನ್, ಇನ್ದು ನಾಳೆ ಬರ್ದುಕಿಲ್ಲ ವಿಯೋಗಿಗೆ, the king of spring comes; to-day (and) to-morrow (there) is no life for him who is separated from (his wife and other dear ones). ನುಂಗುವುವುಮ್ ಒಳವುದಧಿಯೊಳ್ ಮಹಾಮತ್ಸ್ಯಂಗಳ್, there are also devouring large fishes in the ocean. ನೀನುಳ್ಳೊಡುಣ್ಟು ಬೆಳ್ಗೊಡೆ, if thou art, the white umbrella is. ನಿಮ್ಮ ದೊರೆಗೆ ಬೋಲ್ತಿಯರ್ ಒಳರೇ, are there (any) deities like you? ಅಂಜಿಸಿದಂ ಮೂಲೋಕಮಂ ತಾರಕಂ, Târaka frightened the three worlds. ಜಗುನೆಯ ತಡಿಯಲ್ಲಿ ತುಱುಗಳಂ ಮೇಯಿಸಿದಂ, he caused the kine to eat grass on the banks of the Yamunâ. ಘೃತಾಹುತಿವಡೆದನಲನನ್ತೆ ದಳ್ಳಿಸಿದಂ, he increased in force like fire that has obtained an oblation of ghee. ಅಱಿದಳ್ ಪಾಣ್ದುತನೂಜರ ತೆಱನೆಲ್ಲಮನ್ ಈಕೆ, this woman knew the whole state of the sons of Pâṇḍu.

ಆನ್ ಅಱಿವೆಂ, ಪೃಥೆಯಱಿವಳ್,
ದಾನವರಿಪುವಱಿವನ್ ಅರ್ಕನ್ ಅಱಿವಂ, ದಿವ್ಯ ।
ಜ್ಞಾನಿಸಹದೇವನ್ ಅಱಿವಂ;
ನೀನ್ ಆರ್ಗೆನ್ದಾರುಮ್ ಅಱಿಯರ್, ಅಂಗಾಧಿಪತೀ? ‖ I shall know, Prithĕ will know, Krishṇa will know, the sun (or Indra) will know, the very wise person Sahadêva will know; thou to whom (didst thou make known)? When will nobody know, king of Aṅga?

ತನಿವಣ್ಣಂ ಲಂಚಮ್ ಈವೆಂ ಪುರುಳಿ ನಿನಗೆ ಪೂಗೊಂಚಲಂ ಬೇಗದಿನ್ದಂ
ನಿನಗೀವೆಂ ತುಮ್ಬಿ ಕೆನ್ದಾವರೆಯ ಮಿಸುಪ ಮೆಲ್ಮೊಗ್ಗೆಯಂ ಮಾಣದೆನ್ದುಂ।
ನಿನಗೀವೆಂ ಹಂಸೆ ಕಮ್ಪಂ ನಿನಗೊಸಯಿಸುವೆಂ ಕೂಡೆ ತಂಗಾಳಿಯೆನ್ನೋ
ಪನನ್ ಇನ್ದಾರಯ್ದು ತನ್ದೆನ್ನೊಡನಿರಿಸಿದೊಡೆನ್ದಾಕೆ ಮಾತಾಡುತಿರ್ಪಳ್ || She was saying "I will give thee a fully ripe fruit as a present, O female parrot, quickly I will give thee a bunch of flowers, O black bee, ever without stopping I will give thee a soft shining bud of the red lotus, O swan, and I will give thee fragrance, O cool wind, if to-day (you) search, bring and place my lover near me".

ಮುಟ್ಟಿತು ಮುಟ್ಟದು ದಿವಮಂ
ಮೆಟ್ಟಿತು ಮೆಟ್ಟದು ರಸಾತಲಾಗ್ರಮನ್ ಎಮ್ಬೊಲ್ ।
ಬಿಟ್ಟಳಮ್ ಆಗಿರೆ ದಿವಿಜರ
ದಿಟ್ಟಿಗೆ ಸೊಗಯಿಪುದು ಮುನ್ದೆ ಮನ್ದರಶೈಲಂ || In front the mountain Mandara appeared to the eyes of the deities in such hugeness that (they) said: "did it touch (or) did it not touch heaven? did it place down (or) did it not place down (its) foot on the top of Rasâtala?" ಈಶ್ವರನ ಮನಮ್ ಅಲ್ಲಾಡಿತ್ತೋಡಿತ್ತು ಕಿನ್ನರಸೈನ್ಯಂ, Îśvara's mind became agitated, the army of the Kinnaras ran away. ಪಸರಿಸಿದತ್ತು ಮೂಡದೆಸೆಯೊಳ್ ಬೆಳರ್ಗೆಮ್ಪು, a dazzlingly red colour spread about in the east. ಪುದಿದತ್ತು ಪ್ರಕಾಶಂ, lustre came in.

ಅಸವಸದಿಂ ಪಳಗೆಯ್ವಂ
ಕಸಮಂ ಸೋದಿಸದೆ ಬಿತ್ತಿದೊಕ್ಕಲಿಗನ ಪೋಲ್ ।
ಪಸಿಯಂ ನೋಡಿ ತಲೋದರಿ
ಬಿಸುಸುಯ್ಯುಂ ಬಯ್ಗುಮ್ ಇನ್ತು ಮಾಡಿದ ಬಿದಿಯಂ || With haste he will make a crop like a farmer who does not remove the weeds (and) sows; the wife examines the young plants, sighs deeply (and) reviles the way in which (he) has done it. ಭೂವಲಯಾಧಿಪಂ ನುಡಿಗುಮ್ ಆ ದೂತಂಗೆ ಸ್ವಚಿತ್ತಗತಾರ್ಥಮಂ, the king told the messenger the meaning contained in his own mind. ಕೋಗಿಲೆಯುಲಿಗುಂ ನಯದಿನ್ದೆ ಬೀಸುಗುಂ ಗನ್ಧವಹಂ, the cuckoo cried nicely, the wind blew. ಅರ್ಕೇನ್ದುಗಳಂ ತವೆ ನುಂಗಿರ್ದುಂ ಕತ್ತಲೆ ಸಿಡಿಲ್ಗಳೆಱಗುಗುಂ, darkness had quite swallowed sun and moon, thunder-bolts came down. ಈ ಯೋಗದೊಳ್ ಆವ ರೋಗಮುಮಂ ಪರಿಹರಿಕುಂ, in this manner (he) will remove whatsoever sickness. ಪಾಲಿಕ್ಕುಂ ಜಗವೆಲ್ಲವಂ ಕಮಲಭವಂ, Brahmâ rules the whole world.

ತರ್ದುಗಳ್ ಅಱಿಗುಂ ಬಱಿಟಿಯೊ
ಳ್ ಉರ್ದಿ ನೆಲಾವರೆಯ ಬೇರನ್ ಆಮಲಕಮುಮಂ ।

ಬರ್ದಿಲಿಮಿಂಚಿಯ ರಸದೊಳ್

ನಿರ್ದಯೆಯಿನೊದ್ದರಸಿ ಪೂಸೆ ದಿನಪಂಚಕದೊಳ್ || Ringworm will disappear in five days when (one) rubs (it) with dried cow-dung, rubs, in a merciless manner, the root of Senna and also *Emblic myrobalan* in the juice of a well-matured lemon, and applies (this medicament to it).

Remarks.

a) In § 195 the contingent future of the modern dialect (the Nuḍigaṭṭu calls it saṁśayârthakriyâpada) has been introduced. Here follow some additional instances:—ಅವರು ನಾಳೆ ಬನ್ನಾರು, they may come to-morrow. ಓಡುತ್ತ ಹೋಗುವವನು ಎಡವಿ ಬಿದ್ದಾನು, he who goes running may stumble (and) fall. ಹುಲಿ ಸಿಂಹವನ್ನು ಎದುರಿಸೀತು, a tiger may withstand a lion. ರಾಯರ ಮನೆಯಲ್ಲಿ ಊಟ ಸಿಕ್ಕೀತು, in the king's house a dinner may be obtained. ಅವನು ಈಗ ಬರುತ್ತಿದ್ದಾನು, he may be coming now.

ಸತ್ಯದ ಧರ್ಮವ ನಿತ್ಯವು ಬೋಧಿಸೆ ತೊತ್ತಿನ ಮನಸಿಂಗೆ ಸೊಗಸೀತೇ?
ತತ್ವದ ಅರ್ಥ ವಿಚಿತ್ರದಿ ಪೇಳಿಲು ಕತ್ತೆಯ ಮನಸಿಂಗೆ ತಿಳಿದೀತೇ? |
ಪುತ್ತಳಿಬೊಮ್ಮೆಯ ಚಿತ್ರದಿ ಬರೆದಿರೆ ಮುತ್ತು ಕೊಟ್ಟರೆ ಮಾತಾಡೀತೇ?
ಕತ್ತುರಿತಿಲಕವನ್ ಒತ್ತಿ ಫಣೆಯೊಳ್ ಇಡೆ ಅರ್ತಿಯ ತೋಱದೆ ಇದ್ದೀತೇ? ||

Dâsapada 9 || When (one) teaches (her) the duty of truth continually, could it be pleasant to the mind of a female servant? When (one) tells (it) the real nature of the soul manifoldly, could it be known to the mind of a donkey? When (one) has drawn a figure of pure gold, if (one) kisses (it), could it speak? When (one) applies a mark of musk to the forehead, will it possibly not cause a nice appearance?

b) The past tense, as remarked in § 194, is not unfrequently used for the present or future, *e. g.* ಅಯ್ಯೊ, ನಾನು ಸತ್ತೆನು, alas, I die (or shall die). ಕೊಟ್ಟೆನು ಕೊಟ್ಟೆನೆನ್ದು ತಿಳಿ, know I shall certainly give. ನಾನು ಬನ್ದೆನು, ನೀವು ಮುನ್ದೆ ನಡೆಯಿರಿ, I come, walk on! ಅಡಿಗೆಯಾಯಿತು, ಎಲೆ ಹಾಕಿರಿ, dinner will (soon) be ready; put the leaves (used as plates)! ಮಾತು ಬಲ್ಲವ ಮಾಣಿಕ ತನ್ದ, ಮಾತು ಅಱಿಯದವ ಜಗಳ ತನ್ದ, he who knows (proper) words, brings a ruby; (but) he who does not know (proper) words, brings quarrel. (It may be mentioned here that sometimes the English 'is' is expressed by ಆಯಿತು, it became or has become, *e. g.* ಹೊತ್ತಾಯಿತು, it is late. ಬೆಳಗಾಯಿತು, it is morning. ಸಾಯಂಕಾಲವಾಯಿತು, it is evening. ಎಷ್ಟು ಗಣ್ಟೆಯಾಯಿತು, what o'clock is it? ಒನ್ದು ಗಣ್ಟೆಯಾಯಿತು, it is one o'clock. ಆಱು ವರೆ ಗಣ್ಟೆಯಾ

ಯಿತು, it is half past six o'clock. ಹನ್ನೆರಡು ಕಾಲು ಗಣ್ಟೆಯಾಯಿತು, it is a quarter past twelve. ಕಾಲು ಕಡಿಮೆ ಹತ್ತು ಗಣ್ಟೆಯಾಯಿತು, it is a quarter to ten; but ಅಯ್ದಕ್ಕೆ ನಾಲ್ಕು ಮಿನಿಟು ಕಡಿಮೆ ಅವೆ, it is four minutes to five.)

c) **The present tense may be used for the future,** *e. g.*

ಬನದೊಳಗೆ ಪೋಗಿ ಪೊಸಪೂ

ವಿನ ಗೊಂಚಲನ್, ಅಕ್ಕ, ನಿನಗೆ ತರ್ಪೆಂ. . . । I go into the garden (and) bring (for ತರ್ಪೆಂ, I shall bring) thee, sister, a bunch of fresh flowers (see § 215, 5, *b*).

The Kannaḍa grammar Nuḍigaṭṭu says that in speaking (ಬಾಯ್ಮಾತು) the form of the future does not occur (in modern Kannaḍa), in its stead the present is used, *e. g.* for ರಾಯರು ನಾಳೆ ಬರುವರು people say ರಾಯರು ನಾಳೆ ಬರುತ್ತಾರೆ.

Also when in the modern dialect the meaning of **'to use'** is expressed either by the simple future tense, as ಬ್ರಾಹ್ಮಣರು ದಿನಾಲು ಸ್ನಾನ ಮಾಡುವರು, people say ಬ್ರಾಹ್ಮಣರು ದಿನಾಲು ಸ್ನಾನ ಮಾಡುತ್ತಾರೆ, or by the continuative future tense, as ಬ್ರಾಹ್ಮಣರು ನಿತ್ಯದಲ್ಲಿ ಸ್ನಾನ ಮಾಡುತ್ತಿರುವರು, they say ಬ್ರಾಹ್ಮಣರು ನಿತ್ಯದಲ್ಲಿ ಸ್ನಾನ ಮಾಡುತ್ತಿರುತ್ತಾರೆ (see § 313, 3).

A few additional sentences are:—ನಾಳೆ ಹೋಗುತ್ತೇನೆ, I shall go to-morrow. ನೀರು ಬೇಕಾದರೆ ಕೊಡುತ್ತೇನೆ, if (you) want water, I shall give (you some). ನೀವು ಬರುವ ತನಕ ನಿನ್ತಿರುತ್ತೇನೆ, I shall stay till you come. ನಿನ್ನ ಕೂಡಾ ನಾಳೆ ಬನ್ದರೆ ನನ್ನದು ನಾಲ್ಕು ದಿವಸದ ಓದು ನಿಲ್ಲುತ್ತದೆ, if (I) come with thee to-morrow, my study will be interrupted for four days.

367. The forms of **the imperative** appear in § 205—208.[1]

The following **instances** may be given:—

Singular.

ಆನ್ ಇದಂ ಮಾಳ್ಪೆಂ, let me do it!

ಪಾಡೆಲೆ ತುಮ್ಬಿ! ಬಗ್ಗಿಸೆಲೆ ಕೋಗಿಲೆ! ತೀಡೆಲೆ ಗನ್ಧವಾಹ! hum, O black bee! cry, O cuckoo! blow, O wind! ಹರಿ, ಕೇಳ್, hear, Hari!

---

[1] It may be remarked that according to the Śabdânuśâsana the imperative with final ಗೆ, etc. includes âśis, blessing, benediction; vidhi, ordering; nimantraṇa, bidding; âmantraṇa, calling; adhyêshaṇa, soliciting; sampraśna, questioning about or considering what is to be done; prêshaṇa, urging (an inferior); vijñâpana, begging (a superior); âjñâpana, directing (to follow a rule); prârthanâ, praying.

ವಾಯಸದನ್ತೆ ನೋಡು! ಬಕನನ್ತಿರೆ ಮೆಲ್ಲನೆ ಮೆಟ್ಟು! ಕಚ್ಛಪೋ
ಪಾಯದಡಂಗು! ನಿಲ್ ಭ್ರಮರಿವೋಲ್! ಭ್ರಮಿಯನ್ತಿರೆ ಬೆಚ್ಚರಾಗು! ಖ |
ಡ್ಗಾಯುಧಚಾಪಮಂ ಪೊಳೆವ ಮಿಂಚನೆ ಪೋಲ್ತಿರೆ ಬೀಸು! ನೀಂ ಖಳ
ನ್ಯಾಯದಿನೆಲ್ಲಮಂ ನೆಱೆಯೆ ಕಲ್ತುಪದೇಶಕನಾಗು ಲೋಕದೊಳ್! || Look like a crow! Step slowly like a crane! Hide with the stratagem of a tortoise! Stand like a spinning top (?)! Be roaming like a bee! Swing the sword-weapon-bow (?) whilst resembling a shining flash of lightning! In the manner of a scoundrel learn all well (and) become a teacher in the world! ನೀನ್ ಇರು or ನೀನ್ ಇರ್, be thou!

ಇರು, ಮಗಳೆ (o. r. ಮರುಳೆ)! ಶುಷ್ಕವೈಯಾ
ಕರಣಾಂಗಂ ಶುಷ್ಕತಾರ್ಕಿಕಂಗಂ ಬೆಳ್ಳ |
ಕ್ಕರಿಗಂಗಂ ವಿಷಯಮೆ ಕಾ
ವ್ಯರತುನಮ್ ಅತಿಚತುರಕವಿಕದಮ್ಬಕವಿಷಯಂ? || Remain, O daughter! Have the vain grammarian and the vain disputant and the rustic as their aim excellent poems which are (only) the aim of the mass of very clever poets?

ಕೊಳ್ಕೊಳ್ಳೆನ್ದೊಡನೊಡನೆಯೆ
ತುಳ್ಕುವ ಯುವತಿಯರ ಕರಪರಿಚ್ಯುತಸಲಿಲಂ |
ಗಳ್ಕೊಳೆ ಬಿಡಿಕೆದಱುವ ಕಿಂ
ಜಳ್ಕದಿನ್ ಆದುದು ಸರೋವರಂ ಕಪಿಶಜಳಂ || When the pond took the waters that fell from the hands of the young women who said "take! take!" and all at once sprinkled, it became reddish-brown water on account of the filaments (of lotus flowers) that became loose and were scattered about. ತಮ್ಮಾ, ಇಲ್ಲಿಗೆ ಬಾ, brother, come here! ತಂಗೀ, ಊಟಕ್ಕೆ ನಡೆ, sister, go to dine! ಮಗಳೇ, ಸುಖದಿನ್ದ ಇರು, daughter, be joyful! ದೇವಾ, ನನ್ನನ್ನು ಉದ್ಧರಿಸು, God, save me!

ಬಾರ, ಮರಾಳಿಕಾಗಮನೆ! ನೋಡ, ಚಕೋರವಿಲೋಲನೇತ್ರೆ! come thou who walkest like a female swan! see thou who hast the fickle eye of a partridge! ನೀನ್ ಇರ, be thou!

ಅವಧರಿಪುದು ಬಿನ್ನಪಮಂ, listen (thou) to (my) respectful petition! ರಕ್ಷಿಪುದೆನ್ನಂ, save (thou) me! ಮಗುೞೆ ಬೇೞ್ವುದೆ ಬೇೞ್ವುದು, even pray (thou), pray (thou) again!

ಅವಂ ಕುಡುಗೆ, may he give! ಅವಂ ತರ್ಕೆ, let him (or may he) bring! ದೇವರಂ ಪೂಜಿಸುಗೆ ಬುಧಂ, let the wise man worship the gods! ಸಂಜೆಯೊಳ್ ನಿಯಮಮಂ ಮಾಡುಗೆ, let him perform the religious observance in the evening! ಬುಭುಕ್ಷು ಭೋಜನಂಗೆಯ್ಗೆ, may the hungry man eat! ಉಪಾಧ್ಯಾಯಂ ಮಾಣವಕನನ್ ಓದಿಸುಗೆ, let the teacher instruct the boy in the šâstras! ಪುತ್ರಂ ವ್ಯಾಕರಣಮನ್ ಓದುಗೆ, ಮೇಣ್ ವೇದಮನ್ ಓದುಗೆ, the son may read the grammar, or he may read the vêda! ಬಣ್ಬನ್ ಊಟಿಗಂಗೆಯ್ಗೆ, let the servant work! ಅರಸನ್ ಇದಂ ಮಾಡುಗೆ, may the king do this! ಪ್ರಜೆಯಿನ್ತು ಮಾಡುಗೆ, let the people do thus! ಎಮಗೀತಂ ಭಿಕ್ಷುಮಂ ಕುಡುಗೆ, may this man give us alms! ನರನಾಥನ್ ಆ ತೆಱಿದಿಂ ಪೆರ್ಚಿಕ್ಕೆ ದೇಶಂಗಳಂ, may the king cause the countries to thrive in that manner! ವೇದದೊಳ್ ಒನ್ದಿದಾಯು ನಿನಗಕ್ಕೆ ಬೇಗಂ, may soon the life that is usual in the vêda, become thine! ದೇವರು ನಿನಗೆ ದಯ ಮಾಡಲಿ, may God have compassion on thee! ಅವನು ಒಳಗೆ ಬರಲಿ, let him come in! (see § 316, 10. 14).

ಜಿನನ್ ಎಮಗೆ ಸುಖಮಂ ಮಾಱ್ಪಿದು, may the Jina give us joy!

Plural.

ಅನಿಬರುಮ್ ಒನ್ದಾಗಿ ತಾಗುವಂ ಫಾಲ್ಗುಣನೊಳ್, let us altogether attack Phâlguṇa! ಆಮ್ ಎಲ್ಲರುಮ್ ಈಗಳ್ ಅಶ್ವಮೇಧಂಗೆಯ್ವಂ, let all of us now perform a horse-sacrifice! ಏಗೆಯ್ವಂ, what shall we do? ಇನ್ನು ಮನೆಗೆ ಹೋಗೋಣ, let us now go to (our) house! ತನ್ದೆಯಪ್ಪಣೆಯನ್ನು ಕೇಳುವ, let us ask the permission of (our) father!

ವ್ಯಾಳದನ್ತಿಕುಳಮಂ ಸಮ ಕಟ್ಟಿಂ, make ye ready the troop of beasts (and) elephants! ಗುರುಗಳಿರಾ, ಮುದದಿನ್ ಎಮಗೆ ಬೆಸಸಿಂ ಕಥೆಯಂ, O guru, delightfully communicate a story to us! ಮಕ್ಕಳಿರಾ, ನಿತ್ಯದಲ್ಲಿ ದೇವರನ್ನು ಹೊಗಳಿರಿ, O children, praise God continually! ಅಣ್ಣಾ, ಇಲ್ಲಿ ಬನ್ನಿರಿ, O brother, come here! ಸ್ವಾಮಿಾ, ತಾವು ಕೂತು ಕೊಳ್ಳಿರಿ, O sir, sit down! ನೋಡಿ ನೀವು, see ye!

ನೀಮ್ ಎಮಗಭೀಷ್ಟಮನ್ ಈವುದು, give ye us the desired object! ನೀಮ್ ಇದಂ ಮಾಱ್ಪಿದು, make you this!

ಅವರ್ ಮಾೞ್ಕೆ, may they (or let them) do (it)! ತತ್ವಮಂ ನಮ್ಬುಗೆ ವಿಬುಧರ್, may the wise put their trust in true knowledge! ಎಮ್ಮ ಮಗಂಗಿವರ್ ಪೆಣ್ಣಂ ಕುಡುಗೆ, may they give a female to our son! ಅವರು ಬರೆಯಲಿ, may they (or let them) write!

ತಾಮ್ ಇದಂ ಮಾಱ್ಪಿದು, let them do this! ಅವರು ಹೋಗುವದು, let them go!

368. The forms of the **conjugated negative** are given in §§ 209. 210; *cf.* § 316, 5. 6. 8. 9. Regarding **bhâvavaćanas combined with ಇಲ್ಲ** see §§ 209 298. 299. 316, 2. 13; *cf.* § 254, remark 1.

Here follow **some modern instances:**—ಅವರು ಈಗ ಬಾರರು, they do not come now. ಯುಧಿಷ್ಠಿರನ ಸದಾಚಾರವನ್ನು ಎಷ್ಟು ವರ್ಣಿಸಲಿ? ಅವನು ತನ್ನ ವೈರಿಗಾದರೂ ಬಿಱುನುಡಿಗಳನ್ನು ಆಡನು, ಪರಸ್ತ್ರೀಯರನ್ನು ಪಾಪದೃಷ್ಟಿಯಿನ್ದ ನೋಡನು ಇತ್ಯಾದಿ, how much shall I praise the virtuous conduct of Yudhishṭhira? He did not utter abusive words even against his enemies, he did not look at the wives of others with a wicked eye, etc. ಇನ್ನು ನಾನು ಬಾೞೆನು, I shall live no longer. ದೊರೆಯ ರಥವಾದರೂ ಎಣ್ಣೆಯಿಲ್ಲದೆ ತಿರಗದು, even the king's chariot does not go without oil. ದೇವರು ವರಾ ಕೊಟ್ಟರೂ ಪೂಜಾರಿ ವರಾ ಕೊಡನು, though God gives a boon, the officiating priest does not give the boon. ದೇವರಿಗೆ ತಿಳಿಯದ ಹಾಗೆ ಮಾಡುವದು ಎನ್ದಿಗೂ ನಮ್ಮಿನ್ದಾಗದು, acting without God's knowledge is never possible for us. ಅವನಿನ್ದ ಇಷ್ಟು ಭಾರವ ಹೊರೋಣವಾಗದು, he cannot bear such a load. ರಾಮನು ಊರಿಗೆ ಹೋಗುವದಿಲ್ಲ, Râma does not go abroad. ಭ್ರಾನ್ತಿ ಹೋದರೂ ಭಯ ಹೋಗಲಿಲ್ಲ, though (his) bewilderment goes, (his) fear has not gone. ನಾನು ಏನೂ ಅನ್ನಲಿಲ್ಲ, I have said nothing.

XXVII. On words corrupted from Saṁskṛita.

369. The Kannaḍa language consists

1, of words that are peculiar to the country (**dêśiyas**) or are pure Kannaḍa (aččagannaḍa, which are represented by fat types in the Mangalore Dictionary),

2, of words that have been borrowed from Saṁskṛita without any alteration (**samasaṁskṛitas**, see § 70),

3, of words that have been more or less corrupted from Saṁskṛita (**apabhraṁśas or tadbhavas**, see §§ 74. 79. 81. 82. 84—89. 218. 219. 223. 273. 370), regarding which it is to be remarked that they may also (in speaking or writing) be used in their original form,

4, of some words (about 21) that exist in Kannaḍa as well as in Saṁskṛita (**tatsamas**, see § 71, and compounds with them, § 252, 3) or are as it were Kannaḍa and Saṁskṛita.

Of these four kinds of words the language was made up at the time of the grammarian Kêśava and his learned predecessors.

Afterwards during the reign of the Musulmans many Hindusthâni terms were introduced, and also Mahratti words became naturalised in Kannaḍa.

370. Saṁskṛita words which only change their finals when naturalised or used as declinable bases in Kannaḍa, have been introduced in §§ 74—79. 81. 82. 84—89.

Saṁskṛita words which undergo further, so to say more essential changes when adopted by Kannaḍa people, *i.e.* the real **apabhraṁśas or tadbhavas**, are now to be considered. It will be sufficient for learning the way of their formation from the following alphabetical list in which all the Tadbhavas especially mentioned by Kêśava as such (about 800) are included, the terms in parenthesis denoting the original Saṁskṛita terms. Final ಅ of Saṁskṛita words is represented by ಎ.

ಅಕ್ಕರ (ಅಕ್ಷರ); ಅಗಸೆ (ಅತಸಿ); ಅಗುೞಿ (ಅರ್ಗಲ); ಅಗ್ಗ (ಅರ್ಘ); ಅಗ್ಗಿ (ಅಗ್ನಿ); ಅಂಕುಸ (ಅಂಕುಶ); ಅಂಗಣ (ಅಂಕನ or ಅಂಗನ); ಅಚ್ಚ (ಅಚ್ಛ or ಅಛ್ಯ); ಅಚ್ಚನೆ (ಅರ್ಚನೆ); ಅಚ್ಚರಸಿ (ಅಪ್ಸರಸಿ); ಅಚ್ಚರಿ (ಆಶ್ಚರ್ಯ); ಅಚ್ಚಿ (ಅಕ್ಷಿ); ಅಚ್ಚು (ಅಕ್ಷ); ಅಜ್ಜ (ಆರ್ಯ); ಅಂಚೆ (ಹಂಸೆ); ಅಟ್ಟವೆ (ಅಷ್ಟಮಿ); ಅಡವಿ (ಅಟವಿ); ಅದ್ದ (ಅರ್ಧ); ಅದ್ದಿಕ (ಅಧ್ಯಕ್ಷ); ಅನ್ತ (ಅನ್ತ್ರಃ); ಅನ್ದಳ (ಆನ್ದೋಲ); ಅನ್ದುಗೆ (ಅನ್ದುಕ); ಅನ್ನೆಯ (ಅನ್ಯಾಯ); ಅಮರ್ದು (ಅಮೃತ); ಅಮಾಸೆ (ಅಮಾವಾಸ್ಯೆ); ಅಯೊಗ (ಅಯೋಗ್ರ); ಅರುಹ (ಅರ್ಹ); ಅಲಸುಗೆ (ಆಲಸ್ಯಕ); ಅಲುಪ (ಅಲ್ಪ); ಅವಣ (ಅವನ); ಅವತೆ (ಅವಸ್ಥೆ); ಅವರೆ (ಅಸುರೆ; *cf.* ಆವರೆ); ಅವಸೆ (ಅಮಾವಾಸ್ಯೆ; *cf.* ಅಮಾಸೆ); ಅಸಡಿ or ಆಸಡಿ (ಆಷಾಢ); ಅಸನಿ (ಅಶನಿ); ಅಸುಗೆ (ಅಶೋಕ or ಅಶೋಕೆ); ಅಳಕ (ಅಲೇಖ); ಅೞಿಗೆ (ಅಲಿಕ); — ಆಕರುಸನ (ಆಕರ್ಷಣ); ಆಕಾಸ (ಆಕಾಶ; *cf.* ಆಗಸ); ಆಗರ (ಆಕರ); ಆಗಸ (ಆಕಾಶ); ಆಗಾರ (ಆಕಾರ; *cf.* ಆರ); ಆಂಗಿರ (ಆಂಗಿರಸ); ಆಡಸೊಗೆ (ಆಟರೂಷಕ); ಆಣೆ (ಆಜ್ಞೆ); ಆಮಿಸ (ಆಮಿಷ); ಆಯಿಸ (ಆಯುಷ್ಯ); ಆರ (ಆಕಾರ); ಆರ (ಆಗಾರ); ಆರಮ್ಬ (ಆರಮ್ಭ); ಆರವೆ (ಆರಾಮ); ಆವರೆ (ಅಮರೆ); ಆಸಡಿ, see ಅಸಡಿ; — ಇಂಗಳ (ಅಂಗಾರ); ಇಂಗು (ಹಿಂಗು); ಇಂಗುಲಿಕ (ಹಿಂಗುಲಿಕ); ಇಚ್ಚೆ (ಇಚ್ಛೆ); ಇಟ್ಟಗೆ (ಇಷ್ಟಕ); ಇನ್ದರ (ಇನ್ದ್ರ); — ಈಸರ (ಈಶ್ವರ); — ಉಗ್ಗಟ (ಉತ್ಕಟ); ಉಂಗುಟ or ಉಂಗುಟ್ಟ (ಅಂಗುಷ್ಠ); ಉಜ್ಜವಣೆ (ಉದ್ಯಾಪನ); ಉಜ್ಜಳ (ಉಜ್ಜ್ವಲ); ಉಜ್ಜುಗ (ಉದ್ಯೋಗ); ಉಜ್ಜೆಣಿ (ಉಜ್ಜಯನಿ); ಉತ್ತರಿಗೆ (ಉತ್ತರೀಯಕ); ಉದ್ದ (ಉಚ್ಚ); ಉಪ್ಪಡ (ಉತ್ಪಟ); ಉಮ್ಮತ or ಉಮ್ಮತ್ತ (ಉನ್ಮತ್ತ); ಉಮ್ಮೆ (ಉಷ್ಮೆ); — ಎಕ್ಕ (ಏಕ); ಎರ್ಕೆ (ಅರ್ಕ); ಎಳೆ (ಇಲೆ); — ಏಳಗ (ಏಡಕ); — ಒಟ್ಟೆ (ಉಷ್ಟ್ರ); — ಓಗ (ಓಘ); ಓಳಿಗೆ (ಓಲಿಕೆ); — ಔಸದ (ಔಷಧ); — ಕಂಸಾಳ (ಕಾಂಸ್ಯತಾಲ); ಕಕ್ಕಸ (ಕರ್ಕಶ); ಕಂಕರಿ (ಖಂಕರಿ); ಕಚ್ಚ (ಕಕ್ಷ); ಕಜಾಕ (ಖಜಾಖ); ಕಜ್ಜ (ಕಾರ್ಯ); ಕಜ್ಜಿ (ಖರ್ಜು); ಕಂಚಿ (ಕಾಂಚಿ); ಕಂಚು (ಕಾಂಸ್ಯ); ಕಟುರ (ಕಠೋರ); ಕಟ್ಟ (ಕಷ್ಟ); ಕಡ (ಕಟ); ಕಡಗ (ಕಟಕ); ಕಡ್ಡಿ (ಕಾಷ್ಠ); ಕಣಿ (ಖನಿ); ಕಣ್ಟ (ಕಣ್ಠ); ಕಣ್ಟಿಕೆ or ಕಣ್ಟಿಗೆ (ಕಣ್ಠಿಕೆ); ಕಣ್ಟಿಯ (ಕಣ್ಟಕ); ಕಣ್ಡ (ಕಾಣ್ಡ); ಕತೆ (ಕಥೆ); ಕತ್ತರಿ (ಕರ್ತರಿ); ಕತ್ತುರಿ (ಕಸ್ತೂರಿ); ಕದಿರ (ಖದಿರ; *cf.* ಕಯ್ರ); ಕನ್ತೆ (ಕನ್ಥೆ); ಕನ್ನ (ಕರ್ಣ); ಕನ್ನಡ (ಕರ್ಣಾಟಕ);

ಕನ್ನಿಕೆ (ಕನ್ಯಕೆ); ಕಪ (ಕಫ); ಕಪ್ಪಡ (ಕರ್ಪಟ); ಕಪ್ಪುರ (ಕರ್ಪೂರ); ಕಬ್ಬ (ಕಾವ್ಯ); ಕಮ್ಬಳಿ (ಕಮ್ಬಲ); ಕಮ್ಮ (ಕರ್ಮ); ಕಮ್ಮಿ (ಕರ್ಮಿ); ಕಯ್ರ or ಕೈರ (ಖದಿರ); ಕರ (ಖರ); ಕರಗಸ (ಕ್ರಕಚ); ಕರಡಗೆ (ಕರಣ್ಡಕ); ಕರಮ್ಬ (ಕದಮ್ಬ); ಕವ (ಕ್ರಮ); ಕವಳ (ಕಬಲ); ಕವಿಂಜಳ or ಕವಿಂಜು (ಕಪಿಂಜಲ); ಕವಿಲೆ (ಕಪಿಲೆ); ಕವುಂಗು (ಕ್ರಮುಕ); ಕಸಾಯ (ಕಷಾಯ); ಕಳ (ಖಲ); ಕಳಸ (ಕಲಶ); ಕಱಿವೆ (ಕಲಮ); ಕಾಗೆ (ಕಾಕ); ಕಾರ (ಕ್ಷಾರ); ಕಾರಿಗೆ or ಗಾರಿಗೆ (ಖಾತಿಕೆ); ಕಾಸ (ಖಾಸ); ಕಾಸಾಯ (ಕಾಷಾಯ); ಕಾಸೆ or ಕಾಸಿ (ಕಾಶಾ); ಕಾಳೆ (ಕಹಲೆ); ಕಿಳ್ (ಖಿಲ್ವ); ಕೀರ (ಕ್ಷೀರ); ಕೀಲ್ (ಕೀಲ); ಕುಕ್ಕೆ (ಕುಕ್ಷಿ); ಕುಂಕುವ (ಕುಂಕುಮ); ಕುಣ್ಟ (ಕುಣ್ಠ); ಕುಪ್ಪಸ (ಕೂರ್ಪಾಸ); ಕುಮ್ಬ (ಕುಪ್ಯ); ಕುಮ್ಬಳ (ಕೂಷ್ಮಾಣ್ಡ); ಕುರ (ಖುರ); ಕುವರ (ಕುಮಾರ; *cf.* ಕೋರ); ಕುಸುಮ್ಬೆ (ಕುಸುಮ್ಭ); ಕೂವ (ಕೂಪ); ಕೂಱ್ (ಕ್ರೂರ); ಕೇಣಿ (ಕ್ರೇಣಿ); ಕೇವಣ (ಕ್ಷೇಪಣ); ಕೈದವ (ಕೈತವ); ಕೈರ=ಕಯ್ರ; ಕೊಂಚೆ (ಕ್ರೌಂಚ); ಕೊಟ್ಟ (ಕೋಷ್ಠ); ಕೊಡಲಿ (ಕುಠಾರ); ಕೊಡಸಿಗೆ (ಕುಟಜಕ); ಕೊಣ್ಡ (ಕುಣ್ಡ); ಕೊತ್ತುಮ್ಬರಿ (ಕುಸ್ತುಮ್ಬುರು); ಕೊನ್ತ (ಕುನ್ತ); ಕೊಯಕ (ಕುಹಕ); ಕೋಗಿಲೆ (ಕೋಕಿಲ); ಕೋಟೆ or ಕೋಣ್ಟೆ (ಕೋಟ್ಟ); ಕೋಡಿ (ಕೋಟಿ); ಕೋಡು (ಕೂಟ); ಕೋಣ್ (ಕೋಣ); ಕೋರ (ಕುಮಾರ); ಕೋವಣ (ಕೌಪೀನ); ಕೋಱಿ (ಕುಕ್ಕುಟ); — ಗಜೆ (ಗದೆ); ಗಂಜಿ (ಕಾಂಜಿ); ಗಡಗೆ (ಘಟಕ); ಗಡೆ (ಘಟಿ); ಗಣ್ಟು (ಗ್ರನ್ಥಿ); ಗಣ್ಟೆ (ಘಣ್ಟೆ); ಗದಕಿ (ಕೃತಕಿ); ಗನ್ತ (ಗ್ರನ್ಥ); ಗರಣ (ಗ್ರಹಣ); ಗರ್ಗರ (ಘರ್ಘರ); ಗಳನ್ತಿಗೆ (ಗಲನ್ತಿಕೆ); ಗಱಿಗೆ (ಘಟಿಕೆ); ಗಾಜು (ಕಾಚ); ಗಾಡ (ಗಾಢ); ಗಾನ (ಗಹನ); ಗಾರಿಗೆ, see ಕಾರಿಗೆ; ಗಾವ or ಗಾವೆ (ಗ್ರಾಮ); ಗಾವಿಲ (ಗ್ರಾವಿಣ); ಗಾಹೆ (ಗಾಥೆ); ಗಿರಿಗಟ (ಗಿರ್ಗಟ); ಗಿರಿಸ (ಗಿರಿಶ); ಗುಜ್ಜರ (ಗುರ್ಜರ); ಗುಡಿ (ಕುಟಿ); ಗುಣ್ಟಿಗೆ (ಘುಣ್ಟಿಕೆ); ಗುತ್ತ (ಗುಪ್ತ); ಗುದ್ದಲಿ (ಕುದ್ದಾಲ); ಗುಮ್ಬಸ (ಗುಮ್ಫನ); ಗುಳ (ಗುಡ); ಗುಳಿಗೆ (ಘುಟಿಕೆ); ಗೂಗೆ (ಘೂಕ); ಗೋಟ್ಟಿ (ಗೋಷ್ಠಿ); ಗೋಡೆ (ಕೋಟೆ); ಗೋದುವೆ (ಗೋಧೂಮ); ಗೋರಟೆ or ಗೋರಣ್ಟೆ (ಕುರುಣ್ಟ); ಗೋವಳ (ಗೋಪಾಲ); ಗೋಸಣೆ (ಗೋಷಣೆ); ಗೋಱಿ, o. r. ಘೋಱಿ (ಘೋಟ); ಗೋಱಿಗೆ, o. r. ಘೋಱಿಗೆ (ಘೋಟಿಕೆ); ಗೌಳ (ಗೌಡ); — ಘಟ್ಟಣೆ (ಘಟ್ಟಣ); — ಚಕ್ಕ (ಚಕ್ರ); ಚಕ್ಕುಲಿ (ಶಷ್ಕುಲಿ); ಚಟ್ಟಿ (ಷಷ್ಠಿ); ಚದುರ (ಚತುರ); ಚನ್ದ (ಛನ್ದ); ಚನ್ದ (ಚನ್ದ್ರ); ಚರಿಗೆ (ಚರ್ಯೆ); ಚವಿ (ಛವಿ); ಚಾನ್ದಸ (ಛಾನ್ದಸ); ಚಾವಳ (ಚಾಪಲ); ಚಾವುಣ್ಡೆ (ಚಾಮುಣ್ಡೆ); ಚಿಕರಿ (ಶಿಖರಿ); ಚಿಕಿಜ್ಜೆ (ಚಿಕಿತ್ಸೆ); ಚಿತ್ತ (ಚಿತ್ರ); ಚಿನ್ನ (ಛಿಹ್ನ); ಚಿನ್ನ (ಛಿನ್ನ); ಚಿಪ್ಪ (ಶಿಲ್ಪ); ಚಿಪ್ಪಿಗ (ಶಿಲ್ಪಿಕ); ಚೌ (ಚತುಃ); — ಜಗನ (ಜಘನ); ಜಗ (ಜಗತ್); ಜಗಳೆ (ಝುಗಟೆ, o. r. ಝುಗಡೆ); ಜಗುನೆ (ಯಮುನೆ); ಜಂಕೆ (ಝುಂಕೆ); ಜಂಜು (ಝುಂಝೂ); ಜಡಿತಿ (ಝುಟಿತಿ); ಜಡೆ (ಜಟೆ); ಜತನ (ಯತ್ನ); ಜತಿ (ಯತಿ); ಜನ್ತ (ದನ್ತ); ಜನ್ತ (ಯನ್ತ್ರ); ಜನ್ನ (ಯಜ್ಞ); ಜಮಳ (ಯಮಲ; *cf.* ಜವಳ); ಜಮ್ಪ (ಝುಮ್ಪ); ಜರ (ಜ್ವರ); ಜವ (ಯಮ); ಜವಣ (ಜೇಮನ; *cf.* ಜೇವಣ); ಜವನಿಕೆ (ಯವನಿಕೆ); ಜವಳ (ಯಮಲ); ಜವಳಿ (ಯಮಲಿ or ಯಮಲ); ಜವೆ (ಯವೆ); ಜವ್ವನ (ಯೌವನ); ಜಸ

(ಯಶ); ಜಸೋಯೆ (ಯಶೋದೆ); ಜಾಣ್ (ಜ್ಞಾನ); ಜಾತ್ರೆ (ಯಾತ್ರೆ); ಜಾದಿ (ಜಾತಿ); ಜಾದು (ಧಾತು); ಜಾಣ (ಧ್ಯಾನ); ಜಾಳೆ (ಜ್ವಾಲೆ); ಜಿಗುಳಿ or ಜಿಗುಳೆ (ಜಲೂಕೆ); ಜಿಣ್ಣ, o. r. ಜೀಣ್ಣ (ಜೀರ್ಣ); ಜೀರಗೆ, o. r. ಜೀರಿಗೆ (ಜೀರಕ); ಜೀವಗ (ಜೀವಕ); ಜುಕುತಿ or ಜುಗುತಿ (ಯುಕ್ತಿ; cf. ಜುತ್ತಿ); ಜುಗ (ಯುಗ); ಜುಗುಮ (ಯುಗ್ಮ); ಜುತ್ತಿ (ಯುಕ್ತಿ); ಜುದ್ದ (ಯುದ್ಧ); ಜೂಜು, see ಜೂದು; ಜೂದು, o. r. ಜೂಜು (ದ್ಯೂತ); ಜೇಟಿ (ಜೇಷ್ಟಿ); ಜೇವಣ (ಜೇಮನ); ಜೊಣ್ಣ (ಜ್ಯೋತ್ಸ್ನ); ಜೋಗ (ಯೋಗ); ಜೋಗಿ (ಯೋಗಿ); ಜೋಣ್ಣಿಗ (ಝೋಣ್ಣಿಗ?); ಜೋತಿ (ಜ್ಯೋತಿ); ಜೋಯಿಸ (ಜ್ಯೋತಿಷ); ಜೋಸ (ಜೋಷ);— ಝುಲ್ಲಱಿ (ಝುಲ್ಲರಿ); ಝುಳ (ಝುಲೆ); ಝುಳಕ, or perhaps ಝುಟಿಕ (ಝುಲಕ್ಕೆ);— ಡಕ್ಕೆ (ಢಕ್ಕೆ); ಡಮರುಗ or ಡವರುಗ (ಡಮರುಕ); ಡೆಂಕೆ (ಢೆಂಕೆ);— ತಡ (ತಟ); ತಡಿ (ತಟಿ); ತದಿಗೆ (ತೃತೀಯೆ); ತನ್ತುರ (ತನ್ತ್ರ); ತನ್ದೆ (ತಾತ); ತಪಸಿ (ತಪಸ್ವಿ; cf. ತವಸಿ); ತಮ್ಬುಲ (ತಾಮ್ಬೂಲ); ತರಂಗು (ತರಂಗ); ತರಣ (ತ್ರಾಣ); ತರಸ (ತ್ರಾಸ); ತರ್ದುರ (ದರ್ದುರ); ತವಸಿ (ತಪಸ್ವಿ); ತಳ (ಸ್ಥಲ); ತಾಣ (ಸ್ಥಾನ); ತಾಪಣೆ (ಸ್ಥಾಪನ); ತಾಱ (ತಾಲ); ತಿ (ತ್ರಿ); ತಿಕ್ಕ (ತೀಕ್ಷ್ಣ); ತಿಗ (ತ್ರಿಕ); ತಿಣ (ತೃಣ); ತಿಬ್ಬ (ತೀವ್ರ); ತಿಮಿತ (ಸ್ತಿಮಿತ); ತುಚ್ಛ (ತುಚ್ಛ್ಯ); ತುತಿ (ಸ್ತುತಿ); ತುರಿತ (ತ್ವರಿತ); ತೂಳ (ಸ್ಥೂಲ); ತೆಲ್ಲಿಗ (ತೈಲಿಕ); ತೊಣ್ಡೆ (ತುಣ್ಡಿ); ತೊವರಿ (ತುವರಿ); ತೊಳಚಿ or ತೊಳಚೆ (ತುಲಸಿ); ತೋಮ (ಸ್ತೋಮ);— ದಣ್ಟು (ದಣ್ಡ); ದನ (ಧನ); ದನಿ (ಧ್ವನಿ); ದಪ್ಪ (ದರ್ಪ); ದಮ್ಮ or ಧಮ್ಮ (ಧರ್ಮ); ದಮ್ಮಾಣಿ (ಧರ್ಮಪಾನೀಯ); ದರ (ದ್ವಾರ); ದರುಸನ (ದರ್ಶನ); ದಸೆ (ದಶೆ); ದಾಡೆ (ದಂಷ್ಟ್ರ); ದಾರ (ದ್ವಾರ); ದಾರೆ (ಧಾರೆ); ದಾವು (ಧಾಮ); ದಾಳಿಮ್ಬ (ದಾಡಿಮ); ದಾಟಿ (ಧಾಟಿ); ದೀಕೆ (ದೀಕ್ಷೆ); ದೀಪ (ದ್ವೀಪ); ದೀವಿ (ದ್ವೀಪ); ದೀವಿಗೆ (ದೀಪಿಕೆ); ದು (ದ್ವಿ); ದುಗ (ದ್ವಿಕ); ದುಗುಲ (ದುಕೂಲ); ದುಜ್ಜೋದನ (ದುರ್ಯೋಧನ); ದುಟ್ಟ (ದುಷ್ಟ); ದೂ (ದ್ವಿ); ದೂದಿ (ದೂತಿ); ದೂಪ (ಧೂಪ); ದೂವೆ (ಧೂಮ); ದೂಸಣ or ದೂಸಣೆ (ದೂಷಣ); ದೂಸರ (ಧೂಸರ); ದೂಳಿ (ಧೂಲಿ); ದೆವಸ (ದಿವಸ); ದೆಸೆ (ದಿಶೆ); ದೋಣ (ದ್ರೋಣ); ದೋಣಿ (ದ್ರೋಣಿ); ದೋಸ (ದೋಷ); ದೋಹ (ದ್ರೋಹ);— ಧಮ್ಮ (ಧರ್ಮ, see ದಮ್ಮ);— ನಕ (ನಖ); ನಚ್ಚಣಿ (ನರ್ತಕಿ); ನಟ್ಟಿ (ನಷ್ಟಿ); ನಾಮಿ (ನವಮಿ); ನಾಯ (ನ್ಯಾಯ; cf. ನೇಯ); ನಾಱಿ (ನಾಡಿ); ನಾಱಿಗೆ (ನಾಡಿಕೆ); ನಿಗಣ್ಟು (ನಿಘಣ್ಟು); ನಿಚ್ಚ (ನಿತ್ಯ); ನಿಚ್ಚಲ, ನಿಚ್ಚಳ (ನಿಶ್ಚಲ); ನಿಚ್ಚಿನ್ತ (ನಿಶ್ಚಿನ್ತ); ನಿಟ್ಟುರ (ನಿಷ್ಠುರ); ನಿಟ್ಟೆ (ನಿಷ್ಠೆ); ನಿದಾನ (ನಿಧಾನ); ನಿದಿ (ನಿಧಿ); ನಿದ್ದೆ (ನಿದ್ರೆ); ನಿಬುದ್ದಿ (ನಿರ್ಬುದ್ಧಿ; cf. ನಿಬ್ಬುದ್ದಿ); ನಿಬ್ಬನ್ದಿಗ (ನಿರ್ಬನ್ಧಿಕ); ನಿಬ್ಬುದ್ದಿ (ನಿರ್ಬುದ್ಧಿ); ನಿಮಿಸ (ನಿಮಿಷ); ನಿಮ್ಮಳ (ನಿರ್ಮಲ); ನಿರವ (ನಿರೂಪ); ನಿಸಾದಿ (ನಿಷಾದಿ); ನಿಸಿ (ನಿಶೆ); ನಿಸ್ಸಂಕ (ನಿಶ್ಶಂಕ); ನೀರ್ (ನೀರ); ನೂನ (ನ್ಯೂನ); ನೆತ್ತ (ನೇತ್ರ); ನೇಮ (ನಿಯಮ); ನೇಯ (ನ್ಯಾಯ); ನೊಗ (ಯುಗ);— ಪಕ್ಕ (ಪಕ್ಷ); ಪಕ್ಕಿ (ಪಕ್ಷಿ); ಪಗರಣ (ಪ್ರಕರಣ); ಪಖ್ಖಾಳ (ಪ್ರಕ್ಷಾಲ); ಪಜ್ಜಳ (ಪ್ರಜ್ವಲ); ಪಜ್ಜೆ or ಹೆಜ್ಜೆ (ಪದ್ಧತಿ); ಪಂಚವೆ (ಪಂಚಮಿ); ಪಟ್ಟಣ (ಪತ್ತನ); ಪಟ್ಟಿಗೆ (ಪಟ್ಟಿಕೆ); ಪಡ (ಪಟ); ಪಡಗು (ಪಡಹು?); ಪಡಡಕ್ಕೆ (ಪದಡಕ್ಕೆ); ಪಡಿ (ಪ್ರತಿ; cf. ಪಱಿ); ಪಡಿಚನ್ದ (ಪ್ರತಿಛನ್ದ);

ಪಣಿ (ಫಣಿ); ಪತ (ಪಥ); ಪತ್ತ (ಪತ್ರ); ಪತ್ತಿ (ಪತ್ರ); ಪದುಮ (ಪದ್ಮ); ಪಯ (ಪದ), ಪಯಣ (ಪ್ರಯಾಣ); ಪರಸು (ಪರಶು); ಪರಿಕೆ (ಪರೀಕ್ಷೆ); ಪರಿಕೆ or ಪರಿಗೆ (ಪರಿಖೆ); ಪರುಸ (ಸ್ಪರ್ಶ); ಪಲುಗುಣ (ಫಲ್ಗುನ); ಪಲ್ಲಣ, see ಹಲ್ಲಣ; ಪವಣ್ (ಪ್ರಮಾಣ); ಪಸದನ or ಹಸದನ (ಪ್ರಸಾಧನ); ಪಸು (ಪಶು); ಪಳ (ಫಲ); ಪಳಿಕ (ಸ್ಫಟಿಕ); ಪಳಿಕು or ಪಳುಕು (ಸ್ಫಟಿಕ); ಪಱಿ (ಪ್ರತಿ; *cf.* ಪಡಿ); ಪಾಗದ (ಪ್ರಾಕೃತ); ಪಾಗಲ್ or ಪಾಗಲ (ಪ್ರಾಕಾರ); ಪಾಣಿಯ (ಪಾನೀಯ); ಪಾದರಿ or ಹಾದರಿ (ಪಾಟಲ); ಪಾಯ (ಪಾದ); ಪಾಲುಗುಣ (ಫಾಲ್ಗುನ); ಪಾವುಗೆ or ಹಾವುಗೆ (ಪಾದುಕ); ಪಾಸ (ಪಾಶ; *cf.* ಹಾಸ); ಪಾಸಣ್ಡಿ (ಪಾಷಣ್ಡಿ); ಪಾಸಾಣ (ಪಾಷಾಣ); ಪಾಸಾಣ್ಡಿ (ಪಾಷಣ್ಡಿ); ಪಾಲ or ಪಾಳ (ಫಾಲ); ಪಿಟ್ಟು or ಹಿಟ್ಟು (ಪಿಷ್ಟ); ಪಿಣ್ಡಿಗೆ (ಪಿಣ್ಡಿಕೆ); ಪಿಣ್ಡಿವಾಳ (ಭಿಣ್ಡಿವಾಲ); ಪಿಣ್ಡು or ಹಿಣ್ಡು (ಪಿಣ್ಡ); ಪಿಸುಣ (ಪಿಶುನ; *cf.* ಹಿಸುಣ); ಪೀಱಿಗೆ, o. r. ಪೇಱಿಗೆ (ಪೀಠಿಕೆ, o. r. ಪೇಠಿಕೆ); ಪುಗ್ಗಿ (ಫುರ್ಗಿ?); ಪುತ್ತಳಿ, or perhaps ಪುತ್ತಱಿ (ಪುತ್ರಿಕೆ); ಪುತ್ತಿಗೆ (ಪುತ್ರಿಕೆ); ಪುರ (ಪೂರ); ಪುಳ (ಸ್ಫುಟ); ಪುಱಿಲ್ (ಪುಲಿನ); ಪೂರಿಗೆ (ಪೂರಿಕೆ); ಪೆಕ್ಕಣ (ಪ್ರೇಕ್ಷಣ); ಪೆಟ್ಟಿಗೆ (ಪೇಟಿಕೆ; *cf.* ಪೇಳಿಗೆ); ಪೆಟ್ಟು (ಪೇಟ); ಪೇನ (ಫೇನ); ಪೇಳಿ, or perhaps ಪೇಱಿ (ಫೇಲಿ, ಫೇಲೆ?); ಪೇಳಿಗೆ (ಪೇಟಿಕೆ); ಪೊತ್ತಗೆ (ಪುಸ್ತಕ); ಪೋಳಿಗೆ, see ಹೋಳಿಗೆ; ಪೌರುಸ (ಪೌರುಷ); ಪ್ರಹರಣೆ (ಪ್ರಹರಣ);—ಬಕುತಿ (ಭಕ್ತಿ); ಬಗ್ಗ (ವರ್ಗ); ಬಗ್ಗ (ವ್ಯಾಘ್ರ); ಬಚ್ಚಳೆ or ಬಚ್ಚಣೆ (ವತ್ಸಲೆ); ಬಜೆ (ವಚೆ); ಬಂಚ (ವಂಶ); ಬಂಚನೆ (ವಂಚನೆ); ಬಂಜೆ (ವನ್ಧ್ಯೆ); ಬಟ್ಟ (ಭ್ರಷ್ಟ); ಬಡಗಿ or ಬಡ್ಡಗಿ (ವರ್ಧಕಿ); ಬಣ್ಟ (ವಣ್ಠ); ಬಣ್ಡ or ಭಣ್ಡ (ಭಾಣ್ಡ); ಬಣ್ಣ (ವರ್ಣ); ಬತ್ತಿ (ವರ್ತಿ); ಬದ್ದವಣ (ವರ್ಧಮಾನ); ಬನ್ದ (ಬನ್ಧ); ಬನ್ದುಗೆ (ಬನ್ಧೂಕ); ಬಬ್ಬರ (ಬರ್ಬರ; *cf.* ಬೊಬ್ಬುಲಿ); ಬರಿಸ (ವರ್ಷ); ಬರ್ಮ (ಬ್ರಹ್ಮ; *cf.* ಬೊಮ್ಮ); ಬಲ್ಲಹ (ವಲ್ಲಭ); ಬವರ (ಭ್ರಮರ); ಬವಿ (ಭವಿ); ಬಸದಿ (ವಸತಿ); ಬಸನ್ತ (ವಸನ್ತ); ಬಸವ (ವೃಷಭ); ಬಸೆ (ವಸೆ); ಬಳೆ (ವಲಯ); ಬಾಜನೆ (ವಾಚನೆ); ಬಾಡು (ವಾಟ); ಬಾದು (ವಾದ); ಬಾರ (ದ್ವಾರ); ಬಾವಿ (ವಾಪಿ); ಬಾಸನ್ತಿ (ವಾಸನ್ತಿ); ಬಾಸೆ (ಭಾಷೆ); ಬಾಳ (ವಾಲ); ಬಿಕ್ಕೆ (ಭಿಕ್ಷೆ); ಬಿಂಗ (ಭೃಂಗ); ಬಿಂಗಾರ or ಬಿಂಗಾರಿ (ಭೃಂಗಾರ); ಬಿಚ್ಚಣ್ಡ (ವಿಚ್ಛನ್ದ); ಬಿಚ್ಚನ್ದ (ವಿಚ್ಛನ್ದ); ಬಿಚ್ಚು (ಭಿಕ್ಷು); ಬಿಜ್ಜೆ (ವಿದ್ಯೆ); ಬಿಜ್ಜೋದರ (ವಿದ್ಯಾಧರ); ಬಿಂಜ (ವಿನ್ಧ್ಯ); ಬಿತ್ತರ (ವಿಸ್ತಾರ); ಬಿದಿ (ವಿಧಿ); ಬಿದಿಗೆ (ದ್ವಿತೀಯೆ); ಬಿನ್ದ (ವೃನ್ದ); ಬಿನ್ನಣ (ವಿಜ್ಞಾನ); ಬಿನ್ನಣಿ (ವಿಜ್ಞಾನಿ); ಬಿನ್ನಪ or ಬಿನ್ನಹ (ವಿಜ್ಞಾಪನ); ಬಿಯದ (ವ್ಯಾಧ); ಬಿಯದಿ (ವ್ಯಾಧಿ); ಬಿಯಸಂಗ (ವ್ಯಾಸಂಗ); ಬಿಯಳ (ವ್ಯಾಲ); ಬಿಸ (ವಿಷ); ಬೀಣೆ (ವೀಣೆ); ಬೀದಿ (ವೀಥಿ); ಬೀಮ (ಭೀಮ; *cf.* ಬೀವ); ಬೀರ (ವೀರ); ಬೀವ (ಭೀಮ); ಬುದ (ಬುಧ); ಬೂದಿ (ಭೂತಿ); ಬೂವಿ (ಭೂಮಿ); ಬೆಜ್ಜ (ವೈದ್ಯ); ಬೆಂಜನ (ವ್ಯಂಜನ); ಬೆತಿರೇಕ (ವ್ಯತಿರೇಕ); ಬೆತೆ (ವ್ಯಥೆ); ಬೆತ್ತ (ವೇತ್ರ); ಬೆನಕ (ವಿನಾಯಕ); ಬೆಲ್ಲವತ್ತ (ಬಿಲ್ವಪತ್ರ); ಬೇಗ (ವೇಗ); ಬೇದನೆ (ವೇದನೆ); ಬೇರ (ವೈರ); ಬೇರಿ (ಭೇರಿ); ಬೇಸಗೆ (ವೈಶಾಖ; *cf.* ವೈಸಾಗ); ಬೇಹಾರ (ವ್ಯವಹಾರ); ಬೈಕ (ಭೈಕ್ಷ); ಬೈರವ (ಭೈರವ); ಬೊಜಂಗ (ಭುಜಂಗ); ಬೊಬ್ಬುಲಿ (ಬರ್ಬರ, ಬರ್ಬೂರ); ಬೊಮ್ಮ (ಬ್ರಹ್ಮ); ಬೋಗ (ಭೋಗ); ಬೋಗಿ

(ಭೋಗಿ);— ಭಣ್ಡ, see ಬಣ್ಡ; ಭೈತ್ರ (ಬಹಿತ್ರ);— ಮಕ್ಕಡ or ಮಂಕಡ (ಮರ್ಕಟ); ಮಕ್ಕರಿ
(ಮಸ್ಕರಿ); ಮಗುಡ (ಮಕುಟ); ಮಚ್ಚ (ಮಛ್ಯ); ಮಚ್ಚರ (ಮಚ್ಛರ); ಮಚ್ಚು (ಮಕ್ಷಿ);
ಮಂಜಿಟಿಗೆ or ಮಂಜಿಟ್ಟಿಗೆ (ಮಂಜಿಷ್ಠಕ); ಮಟ (ಮಠ); ಮಡ (ಮಠ); ಮಣ್ಡ (ಮಣ್ಠ);
ಮಣ್ಡಿಗೆ (ಮಣ್ಡಕ); ಮದ್ದಳೆ (ಮರ್ದಲ); ಮನ್ತ (ಮನ್ಥ); ಮನ್ತಣಿ (ಮನ್ಥನಿ); ಮನ್ತ್ರ
(ಮನ್ತ್ರಿ); ಮನ್ತ್ರರ (ಮನ್ತ್ರ); ಮನ್ನಱಿ (ಮನ್ಯಾಲಿ); ಮಯಣ (ಮದನ); ಮರುಗ (ಮರು
ವಕ); ಮಲ್ಲಿಗೆ (ಮಲ್ಲಿಕೆ); ಮಸಣ (ಶ್ಮಶಾನ); ಮಸಿ (ಮಷಿ); ಮಱಿಗೆ (ಮರಿಕೆ); ಮಾ
(ಮಹತ್); ಮಯ್ಸಿ, see ಮೈಸಿ; ಮಾಗಿ (ಮಾಘ); ಮಾಡ (ಮಾಟ); ಮಾಣಿಕ (ಮಾಣಿಕ್ಯ);
ಮಾತ (ಮಹನ್ತ); ಮಾನಸ (ಮಾನುಷ್ಯ); ಮಾನಿಸ (ಮಾನುಷ್ಯ); ಮಿಗ (ಮೃಗ); ಮಿತಿಳೆ
(ಮಿಥಿಲೆ); ಮಿತ್ತು or ಮಿಱ್ತು (ಮೃತ್ಯು); ಮೀನ್ (ಮೀನ); ಮುಕ (ಮುಖ; *cf.* ಮೊಗ);
ಮುಕುತಿ (ಮುಕ್ತಿ); ಮುಗುಳ್ (ಮುಕುಲ); ಮುಟ್ಟಿಗೆ (ಮುಷ್ಟಿಕೆ); ಮುದ್ದಿಗೆ (ವೃದ್ಧೀಕೆ);
ಮುದ್ದಿಗೆ (ಮುದ್ರಿಕೆ); ಮುಷ್ಟಿಗೆ (ಮುಷ್ಟಿಕೆ); ಮೆಳಸು [ಮೆಱಿಸು], ಮೆಣಸು (ಮರಿಚ);
ಮೇಣ್ಟಿ or ಮೆಣ್ಟಿ (ಮೇಠಿ, o.r. ಮೇಧಿ); ಮೇಸ (ಮೇಷ); ಮೈಮೆ (ಮಹಿಮೆ); ಮೈಸಿ or
ಮಯ್ಸಿ (ಮಹಿಷಿ); ಮೊಗ (ಮುಖ); ಮೊದೆ (ಮುಂಜ); ಮೋಡ (ಮೂಢ); ಮೋರ
(ಮಯೂರ);— ಯುಗುಮ (ಯುಗ್ಮ);— ರಕ್ಕಸ (ರಾಕ್ಷಸ); ರಕ್ಕೆ (ರಕ್ಷೆ); ರಗಳೆ (ರಘಟೆ);
ರತುನ (ರತ್ನ; *cf.* ರನ್ನ); ರನ್ನ (ರತ್ನ); ರಮ್ಬೆ (ರಮ್ಭೆ); ರಸೆಯನ or ರಸಯನ (ರಸಾಯನ);
ರಾಯ (ರಾಜ); ರಾಸಿ (ರಾಶಿ); ರಿಜು (ಋಜು); ರಿಣ (ಋಣ); ರಿತು (ಋತು); ರಿಸಿ (ಋಷಿ);
ರೂಡಿ (ರೂಢಿ); ರೂಪು or ರೂವು (ರೂಪ); ರೋವ (ರೋಮ);— ಲಕುಮಣ (ಲಕ್ಷ್ಮಣ);
ಲಕುಮಿ (ಲಕ್ಷ್ಮಿ); ಲಕ್ಕ (ಲಕ್ಷ); ಲಕ್ಕಣ (ಲಕ್ಷಣ); ಲಗುಡ (ಲಕುಟ); ಲಗುನ (ಲಗ್ನ);
ಲಗ್ಗಿಗ or ಲಗ್ಗಿಕ (ಲಾಗ್ನಿಕ); ಲಚ್ಚಣ (ಲಾಂಛನ); ಲಮ್ಬಣ (ಲಮ್ಬನ); ಲಮ್ಬಳ, or
perhaps ಲಮ್ಬಱ (ಲಮ್ಪಟ); ಲಾಮಚ or ಲಾಮಜ್ಜ (ಲಾಮಜ್ಜ); ಲಾಱ (ಲಾಟ);
ಲಾಱಬಾಸೆಗ (ಲಾಟಭಾಷಿಕ); ಲೆಪ್ಪ (ಲೇಪ್ಯ); ಲೋಬ (ಲೋಭ);— ವಂಕ (ವಕ್ರ); ವತ್ತಿ
(ವರ್ತಿ); ವರಾಳ (ವರಾಟ); ವಳಿಗೆ, or perhaps also ವಱಿಗೆ (ವಟಿಕೆ); ವಾಸ (ವಾಂಶ್ಯ);
ವಾಸುಗಿ (ವಾಸುಕಿ); ವಾಹಳಿ (ವಾಹ್ಯಾಲಿ); ವಾಳಿ (ವಾಹ್ಯಾಲಿ); ವಿಕ್ಕಿರ (ವಿಷ್ಕಿರ); ವಿತೆ
(ವೃಥೆ); ವಿತ್ತಿ (ವೃತ್ತಿ); ವಿದ್ದಿ (ವೃದ್ಧಿ); ವಿಲಸ (ವಿಲಾಸ); ವಿವನ್ದ (ವಿಬನ್ಧ); ವಿಸ (ವಿಷ, *cf.*
ಬಿಸ); ವಿಸಯ (ವಿಷಯ); ವಿಳಂಗ (ವಿಡಂಗ); ವೀಳಿಗೆ (ವೀಟಿಕೆ); ವೇಸ (ವೇಷ); ವೈಸಾಗ
(ವೈಶಾಖ; *cf.* ಬೇಸಗೆ); ವೈಹಾಳಿ or ವೈಹ್ಯಾಳಿ (ವಾಹ್ಯಾಲಿ);— ಸಂಸಯ (ಸಂಶಯ);
ಸಕುನ (ಶಕುನ); ಸಕುನಿ (ಶಕುನಿ); ಸಕ್ಕದ (ಸಂಸ್ಕೃತ); ಸಕ್ಕರೆ (ಶರ್ಕರೆ); ಸಕ್ಕಿ (ಸಾಕ್ಷಿ; *cf.*
ಸಾಕ್ಕಿ); ಸಗ್ಗ (ಸರ್ಗ); ಸಂಕ (ಶಂಖ); ಸಂಕರ (ಶಂಕರ); ಸಂಕಲೆ (ಶೃಂಖಲ); ಸಂಕು
(ಶಂಕು); ಸಂಕೆ (ಶಂಕೆ); ಸಂಗ (ಸಂಘ); ಸಂಗಡ (ಸಂಘಾತ); ಸಂಗವ (ಸಂಗಮ); ಸಂಜೆ
(ಸನ್ಧ್ಯೆ); ಸಟೆ (ಶಠೆ); ಸಣಿ (ಶನಿ); ಸಣ್ಡ (ಷಣ್ಡ); ಸಣ್ಣ (ಸನ್ನ); ಸತ್ತವಿ or ಸತ್ತವೆ (ಸಪ್ತ
ಮಿ); ಸತ್ತಿಗೆ (ಛತ್ರಿಕೆ); ಸತ್ತುಗ (ಸತ್ವಕ); ಸನ್ತಸ (ಸನ್ತೋಷ); ಸನ್ತೆ (ಸಂಸ್ಥಾ); ಸನ್ದು
(ಸನ್ಧಿ); ಸನ್ನಣ (ಸನ್ನಾಹ); ಸಪ್ಪಳ, o.r. ಸಪ್ಪಳ (ಸತ್ಫಲ); ಸಬುದ (ಶಬ್ದ); ಸಬ್ಬ (ಸರ್ವ);
ಸಮ್ಬರ (ಸಮ್ಭಾರ); ಸಮ್ಬರ (ಶಮ್ಬರ); ಸಮ್ಬಳ (ಶಮ್ಬಲ); ಸಮ್ಬು (ಶಮ್ಭು); ಸಮ್ಮ

(ಚರ್ಮ); ಸಯಮ್ಬು (ಸ್ವಯಮ್ಭು); ಸರ (ಸ್ವರ); ಸರ (ಶರ); ಸರದ (ಶರದ); ಸರಸತಿ (ಸರಸ್ವತಿ); ಸರುಸಪ (ಸರ್ಷಪ; *cf.* ಸಾಸವೆ); ಸರೂಪ (ಸ್ವರೂಪ); ಸಲಗೆ (ಶಲಾಕೆ); ಸವ (ಶಬ); ಸವ (ಶ್ರಮ); ಸವಗ (ಸವೋಘ); ಸವಣ (ಕ್ಷಪಣ and ಶ್ರವಣ); ಸಸಿ (ಶಶಿ); ಸಸಿ (ಸಸ್ಯ); ಸಾ (ಸಹ); ಸಾಕ್ಕಿ (ಸಾಕ್ಷಿ); ಸಾಣ or ಸಾಣೆ (ಶಾಣ); ಸಾತಿ (ಸ್ವಾತಿ); ಸಾದನೆ (ಸಾಧನ); ಸಾನ (ಶ್ವಾನ); ಸಾನ್ತಿ (ಶಾನ್ತಿ); ಸಾಪ (ಶಾಪ); ಸಾಮ (ಶ್ಯಾಮ); ಸಾಮಿ (ಸ್ವಾಮಿ); ಸಾರಿದ (ಶಾರಿದ); ಸಾರೀರ (ಶಾರೀರ); ಸಾಲಣ (ಶಾಲಣ); ಸಾಲೆ (ಶಾಲೆ); ಸಾವನ್ತ (ಸಾಮನ್ತ); ಸಾವೆ (ಶ್ಯಾಮ); ಸಾಸ (ಸಾಹಸ); ಸಾಸತ (ಶಾಶ್ವತ); ಸಾಸವೆ (ಸರ್ಷಪ); ಸಿಂಗ (ಸಿಂಹ); ಸಿಂಗಾರ (ಶೃಂಗಾರ); ಸಿಂಗಿ (ಶೃಂಗಿ); ಸಿಟ್ಟಿ (ಸೃಷ್ಟಿ); ಸಿನ್ದುರ (ಸಿನ್ಧುರ); ಸಿರ (ಶಿರ); ಸಿರಿ (ಶ್ರೀ); ಸಿರಿಯ (ಶ್ರೀ); ಸಿವಿಗೆ (ಶಿಬಿಕೆ); ಸಿವೆ (ಶಿವೆ); ಸೀತ (ಶೀತ); ಸೀರೆ (ಚೀರ); ಸೀಲ್ (ಶೀಲ); ಸೀವರ (ಶೀಕರ); ಸೀಸಕ (ಶೀರ್ಷಕ); ಸುಗ್ಗಿ? (ಸುಗಿ?); ಸುಚಿ (ಶುಚಿ); ಸುಣ್ಟಿ (ಶುಣ್ಠಿ); ಸುಣ್ಣ (ಚೂರ್ಣ); ಸುತ್ತಿ (ಶುಕ್ತಿ); ಸುತ್ತಿಗೆ (ಸೂತ್ರಿಕೆ); ಸುದ್ದಿ (ಶುದ್ಧಿ); ಸುಬ (ಶುಭ); ಸುಮ್ಬ (ಶುಮ್ಭ); ಸುರಿಗೆ (ಛುರಿಕೆ); ಸುಲ್ or ಸುಲು (ಶುಲ್ವ); ಸುಳ (ಶೂಲ; *cf.* ಸೂಳ); ಸೂಕುಮ (ಸೂಕ್ಷ್ಮ); ಸೂಜಿ (ಶೂಚಿ); ಸೂವ (ಸೂಪ); ಸೂಳ (ಶೂಲ); ಸೆಜ್ಜೆ (ಶಯ್ಯೆ); ಸೆನ್ದವ (ಸೈನ್ಧವ; *cf.* ಸೈನ್ದವ); ಸೆನ್ದುರ (ಸಿನ್ಧೂರ); ಸೆಲೆ (ಶಿಲೆ); ಸೇಣಿ (ಶ್ರೇಣಿ); ಸೇತ (ಶ್ವೇತ); ಸೇಮ (ಕ್ಷೇಮ); ಸೇಸ (ಶೇಷ); ಸೇಸೆ (ಶೇಷೆ); ಸೈನ್ದವ (ಸೈನ್ಧವ); ಸೈವ (ಶೈವ); ಸೊಕ or ಸೊಗ (ಸುಖ); ಸೊಣಗ (ಶುನಕ); ಸೊದೆ (ಸುಧೆ); ಸೊನ್ನೆ (ಸ್ವರ್ಣ); ಸೊನ್ನೆ (ಶೂನ್ಯ); ಸೊಬಗು (ಶುಭಗ); ಸೊರಟ (ಸೌರಾಷ್ಟ್ರ); ಸೊಸೆ (ಸ್ನುಷೆ); ಸೋಣಿ (ಶ್ರೋಣಿ); ಸೋವಾಸಿಣಿ (ಸುವಾಸಿನಿ); ಸೌರಿ (ಶೌರಿ);— ಹಗ್ಗ (ಪ್ರಗ್ರಹ); ಹಗ್ಗಿ (ಅಗ್ನಿ); ಹಂಜರ (ಪಂಜರ); ಹಟ್ಟಿಗೆ (ಪಟ್ಟಿಕೆ); ಹಡಲಗೆ (ಪಟಲಕ); ಹಣಿತೆ (ಪ್ರಣೀತೆ); ಹಣ್ಡ (ಪಣ್ಡ); ಹತ್ತ (ಹಸ್ತ); ಹದಿಟೆ or ಹದಿಡೆ (ಪ್ರತಿಷ್ಠೆ); ಹದಿಬತೆ or ಹದಿಬದೆ (ಪತಿವ್ರತೆ); ಹಸ್ತ (ಪಸ್ಥ); ಹಬು (ಪ್ರಭು); ಹಬೆ (ಪ್ರಭೆ); ಹರಣ (ಪ್ರಾಣ); ಹರಯ (ಪ್ರಾಯಃ); ಹರವಸ (ಪರವಶ); ಹರುಸ (ಹರ್ಷ); ಹಲಗೆ (ಫಲಕ); ಹಲ್ಲಣ or ಪಲ್ಲಣ (ಪಲ್ಯಯನ); ಹಸದನ, see ಪಸದನ; ಹಸರ (ಪ್ರಸರ); ಹಾದರಿ (ಪಾಟಲ, *cf.* ಪಾದರಿ); ಹಾವುಗೆ (ಪಾದುಕ, *cf.* ಪಾವುಗೆ); ಹಾಸ (ಪಾಶ, *cf.* ಪಾಸ); ಹಿಟ್ಟು (ಪಿಷ್ಟ, *cf.* ಹಿಟ್ಟು); ಹಿಣ್ಡು (ಪಿಣ್ಡ, *cf.* ಪಿಣ್ಡು); ಹಿಪ್ಪಲಿ (ಪಿಪ್ಪಲಿ); ಹಿವ (ಹಿಮ); ಹಿಸುಣ (ಪಿಶುನ, *cf.* ಪಿಸುಣ); ಹುಬ್ಬೆ (ಪೂರ್ವೆ); ಹುರ (ಪುರ); ಹೆಕ್ಕೆ or ಹಿಕ್ಕೆ (ಸ್ಫಿಕ್ಕೆ); ಹೆಜ್ಜೆ (ಪದ್ಧತಿ, *cf.* ಪಜ್ಜೆ); ಹೆಟ್ಟ (ಹೃಷ್ಟ); ಹೆಡಗೆ (ಪಿಟಕ, ಏಡಕ); ಹೆದೆಯ (ಹೃದಯ); ಹೇರಿಗ (ಹೇರಿಕ); ಹೈತಿಗ or ಹೈತಿಗೆ (ಪೈತೃಕ); ಹೊಕ್ಕರಣೆ (ಪುಷ್ಕರಿಣಿ); ಹೊತ್ತಗೆ (ಪುಸ್ತಕ, *cf.* ಪೊತ್ತಗೆ); ಹೊನ್ನೆ (ಪರ್ಣ); ಹೋಳಿಗೆ, or perhaps ಹೋಲಿಗೆ (ಸ್ಫೋಟಕ, *cf.* ಪೋಳಿಗೆ).

Regarding compounds with them see § 252, 4 *seq.*

In the Šabdânušâsana there are the following additional tadbhavas:—

ಅಕ್ಖೋಳ (ಆಕ್ಷೋಟ); ಅಗಸೆ (ಅಗಸ್ತ್ಯ); ಅಚ್ಚರಸೆ (ಅಪ್ಸರಸ್); ಅಬಸಂಗ (ಅಭಿಷ್ವಂಗ); ಆರ (ಹಾರ); ಇಂಗಲಿಕ (ಹಿಂಗುಲಕ); ಉಗ್ಗಡ (ಉತ್ಕಟ); ಉತ್ತಡೆ (ಉತ್ಪಟ);

ಉಬ್ಬಟೆ (ಉತ್ಪಾಟ); ಉಬ್ಬೆ (ಊಷ್ಮ); ಎಕ್ಕೆ (or ಎಱಿಕ್ಕೆ? ಅರ್ಕ); ಏಯಾರಸಿ (ಏಕಾದಶಿ); ಕವಿ (ಕಪಿ); ಕಾವ (ಕಾಮ); ಕಿಷ್ಣ (ಕೃಷ್ಣ); ಕೀರ್ (ಕೀರ); ಕುಯಕ (ಕುಹಕ); ಕೂರ್ (ಕೂರ); ಗಟೆ (ಘಟೆ); ಚನ್ದಿರ (ಚನ್ದ್ರ); ಚನ್ನ (ಛನ್ನ); ಚೌತಿ (ಚತುರ್ಥಿ); ಚೌದಸೆ (ಚತುರ್ದಶಿ); ಜಗಳ (ಝಕಟ); ಜಂಗೆ (ಝಂಕೆ); ಜಟ್ಟಿ (ಜ್ಯೇಷ್ಠ); ಜಮ್ಪೆ (ಝಮ್ಪೆ); ಜಸ (ಝಷ); ಜಾಗ (ಯಾಗ); ಜಾವ (ಯಾಮ); ಜಾವಕ (ಯಾವಕ); ಜಾವಳ (ಚಾಪಲ); ತಣ್ಡಿಲ (ಸ್ಥಣ್ಡಿಲ); ತಿತಿ (ಸ್ಥಿತಿ); ತೇರಸೆ (ತ್ರಯೋದಶಿ); ದಡ (ತಟ); ದರೆ (ಧರೆ); ದಸವೆ (ದಶಮಿ); ದಾವು (ದಾಮ); ದಿಡ (ದೃಢ); ದುಗ್ಗ (ದುರ್ಗ); ದೆವ್ವ (ದೈವ); ನಚ್ಚಣ (ನರ್ತನ); ನೊದೆ (ಮುಂಜ); ಪಕ್ಕಾಳನ (ಪ್ರಕ್ಷಾಲನ); ಪರಸನ (ಪ್ರಶ್ನ); ಪರಿಸಂಗ (ಪರಿಷ್ವಂಗ); ಪಾಗರ (ಪ್ರಾಕಾರ); ಪಾಡಿವ (ಪ್ರತಿಪದ್); ಪಾಳಿಲ್ (ಪಾಲೀನ); ಬಪ್ಪ (ವಪ್ರ); ಬಯ (ಭಯ); ಬರತ (ವ್ರತ); ಬಾದಸೆ (ದ್ವಾದಶಿ); ಬಿಲಸ (ವಿಲಾಸ); ಮನ್ದಿರ (ಮನ್ತ್ರ); ಮನ್ನಣೆ (ಮನ್ಯತೆ); ಮಾಗ (ಮಾಘ); ಮಾಳರ (ಮಾತರ); ಮಿದ್ದಿಗೆ (ಮೃದ್ವಿಕೆ); ಮೂಡೆ (ಮೂತ); ಮೋಜನ (ಮೋಚನ); ಯತನ (ಯತ್ನ); ಯುಕುತಿ (ಯುಕ್ತಿ); ರಿದ್ದಿ (ಋದ್ಧಿ); ರಿಸಬ (ಋಷಭ); ರುತು (ಋತು); ಲಚ್ಚಿ (ಲಕ್ಷ್ಮಿ); ಲಮ್ಬಳಿಗೆ (ಲಾಮ್ಪತ್ಯ); ವನ್ದನ (ಬನ್ಧನ); ವಿವಾದ (ವಿಬಾಧ); ವೀಳೆಯ (ವೀಟಿಕೆ); ಸಂವ (ಶಮ್ಭು); ಸಂಜಯ (ಸಂಚಯ); ಸನ್ನೆ (ಸಂಜ್ಞೆ); ಸಬು (ಸ್ವಭೂ); ಸಯ (ಶ್ರೀಯ); ಸರಮ (ಶ್ರಮ); ಸಾಜ (ಸಹಜ); ಸಾದಕ (ಸಾಧಕ); ಸಿಂಗರ (ಶೃಂಗಾರ); ಸೀಲೆ (ಶೀಲೆ); ಸುಟ್ಟಿ (ಸೃಷ್ಟಿ); ಸೇಲೆ (ಚೇಲ); ಸೊಚ್ಚ (ಸ್ವಚ್ಛ); ಸೊಬಗು (ಸೌಭಾಗ್ಯ); ಸೋಬೆ (ಶೋಭೆ); ಹತ್ತಿಗೆ (ಪತ್ರಿಕೆ); ಹಿದಯ (ಹೃದಯ); ಹಿರಿ (ಹ್ರೀ); ಹೀವರ (ಪೀವರ). Of these 91 tadbhavas twenty-eight (*viz.* ಅರ, ಉಗ್ಗಡ, ಕಾವ, ಕುಯಕ, ಚನ್ದಿರ, ಚೌತಿ, ಜಾಗ, ಜಾವ, ತಿತಿ, ತೇರಸೆ [as ತೇರಸಿ], ದಡ, ದರೆ, ದಸವೆ [as ದಸವಿ], ದಿಡ, ದುಗ್ಗ, ದೆವ್ವ, ನಚ್ಚಣ, ನೊದೆ, ಪಾಡಿವ, ಯತನ, ಯುಕುತಿ, ರುತು, ಲಚ್ಚಿ, ವೀಳೆಯ, ಸನ್ನೆ, ಸಾಜ, ಸಿಂಗರ, ಸೇಲೆ) are in the Dictionary. See also the Śabdânuśâsana's words with ಱ in § 231.

It must not be thought that the tadbhavas mentioned by Kêšava in the above list and the Šabdânušâsana, are all which Kannaḍa contains; Kêšava himself knew more, *e. g.* ಪಱಿಯಿಗೆ, ಪಱಿಹ, etc. There are many others, as the Dictionary will show. It may be said that most of the tadbhavas are used in conversation by all classes of Kannaḍa people.

XXVIII. On the doubling of consonants.

371. As in Saṁskṛita so also in Kannaḍa a doubling of consonants takes place which properly does not belong to the department of grammar. It is now found mostly in ancient inscriptions (śâsanas), more or less also in ancient manuscripts.

The grammarian Kêšava teaches such doubling in the following instances in all of which it is optional:—

1, in the dative plural where ಗೆ is preceded by ರ್, *e. g.* ದೇವರ್ಗ್ಗೆ, ಎರೆವರ್ಗ್ಗೆ (§ 119, *a,* dative), ಸ್ತ್ರೀಯರ್ಗ್ಗೆ (§ 132, *a,* dative; § 240, 5);

2, in the past participle formed by ದು preceded by ರ್, *e. g.* ಪೇರ್ದ್ದು, ಸೋರ್ದ್ದು, ಅಮರ್ದ್ದು, ಒಸರ್ದ್ದು (§ 155);

3, in the present-future relative participle, if ವ and ಪ are preceded by ರ್ or ಱ್, *e. g.* ಅಲರ್ವ್ವ; ಕುಳಿರ್ವ್ವ, ಕೊನರ್ವ್ವ (§ 180, 1), ಅಡರ್ವ್ವ, ಉದಿರ್ವ್ವ, ಅಡರ್ಪ್ಪ, ಉದಿರ್ಪ್ಪ (§ 183, 10), ಇರ್ಪ್ಪ, ತರ್ಪ್ಪ, ಅರ್ಪ್ಪ, ತೋರ್ಪ್ಪ (§ 183, 1. 2); and also, if that is not the case, *e. g.* ತೊಳಪ್ಪ, ಬೆಳಪ್ಪ, ಎನಿಪ್ಪ, ತರಿಪ್ಪ (§ 183, 7. 8);

4, in compounds after a rêpha, *e. g.* ನೀರ್ಗ್ಗಜ್ಜು, ಊರ್ವ್ವೇಲಿ (§ 246, *a*), and also when there are no compounds, *e. g.* ಬೇರ್ಪ್ಪಱಿದುದು, ನೀರ್ತ್ತಿಳಿದುದು (§ 246, *a*).

His other rules regarding the doubling of consonants (§ 109, *a,* dative ಕ್ಕೆ for ಕೆ; § 194 ಅಪ್ಪೆಂ etc. for ಅಪೆಂ etc. in the present tense; § 198, 3 ಇತ್ತು for ಇತು in the past tense; § 203 ಕ್ಕುಂ for ಕುಂ in the present, future and past tenses; § 205 ಕ್ಕೆ for ಕೆ in the imperative; 215, 7, *d* the doubling of ನ್, ಣ್, ಲ್, ಯ್, ಳ್ in declinable bases; § 215, 7, *e* that of ಯ್ in certain verbal themes; § 215, 7, *f* that of ನ್, ಣ್, ಲ್, ಯ್, ಳ್ in the negative; § 248, 3 where a following consonant is doubled after ಮು; and § 273 ಅಗಲಿತ್ತು for ಅಗಲಿತು, etc.) belong to the sphere of grammar.

Bhaṭṭâkalaṅka in his grammar Šabdânušâsana (sûtra 65 *seq.*) expatiates on the doubling of consonants, giving *e. g.* the following instances:—

ಕುಳಿರ್ಕ್ಕೋಡುಗುಂ, ಇವರ್ಖ್ಖಣ್ಡಿಸಿದರ್, ಊರ್ಗ್ಗಳ್, ಸುರರ್ಘ್ಘನಮಹಿಮರ್, ಜಿನರ್ಜ್ಜವನಪಣ್ಡಿತರ್, ಬುಧರ್ಚ್ಚದುರರ್, ಇವರ್ಛ್ಛಾತ್ರರ್, ಸುರರ್ಜ್ಜಯಿಸಿದರ್, ಅಲರ್ಝ್ಝಷಕೇತನಂಗೆ, ಅವರ್ಞ್ಞಕಾರಮನ್ ಉಚ್ಚರಿಸಿದರ್, ಬುಧರ್ಟ್ಟೀಕಿಸಿದರ್, ಭಟರ್ಠ್ಠಣದೊಳ್, ಬಡಗರ್ಡ್ಡೊಮ್ಬರ್, ಸುಡಿವರ್ಢ್ಢಾಳಕರ್, ಅವರ್ಣ್ಣಕಾರಂ ಬರೆದರ್, ಸೂತರ್ತ್ತನ್ದರ್, ಪರರ್ಥ್ಥಟ್ಟುತಾರಾದರ್, ನೃಪರ್ದ್ದಾನಶೂರರ್, ವಣಿಜರ್ಧ್ಧನವನ್ತರ್, ಪಣ್ಡಿತರ್ನ್ನೀತಿವನ್ತರ್, ಇವರ್ಪ್ಪಣ್ಡಿತರ್, ಅಲರ್ಫ್ಫಲಮ್ ಆದುದು, ಬಸ್ದರ್ಬ್ಬಟ್ಟೆಗರ್, ಸತಿಯರ್ಭ್ಭೀರುಗಳ್, ಚಪಲೆಯರ್ಮ್ಮಾನಿನಿಯರ್, ನಪುಂಸಕರ್ಷ್ಷಣ್ಡರ್, ಋಷಿಯರ್ಸ್ಸಾಧುಗಳ್;— ಕಲ್ಕ್ಕಡಿಯಾದುದು, ನಿಲ್ತ್ತಂ, ಬಲ್ಸ್ಸಾಹಸಿ,

ಮುಳ್ಡೊಂಗಲ್, ಜಾಳ್ತನಂ, ಕಳ್ಗಡಿದಂ;—ಬರಿಸಿಪ್ಪ್ರಧಾನರಂ, ಕಣ್ದುಕ್ಕ್ಷತ್ರಿಯರಂ, ಇದುಸ್ಸ್ವಾದು, ಅದುವ್ವ್ಯವಸಾಯಂ;—ಬಲ್ಲ್ಯತನಂ, ಮೇಲ್ಲ್ಪ್ರಸ್ನಂ, ಬಲ್ಲಿಣ್ದಂ, ಕಲ್ವ್ವಾೞಿ;—ಒಳ್ಳ್ಯತನಂ, ಒಳ್ಪ್ರಸ್ನಂ, ಒಳ್ವ್ವಣಿಗೆ;—ಎಸಳ್ವ್ವಳಿ, ಸುಸುಳ್ವ್ವಾಗಿಲ್;—ನೇಸರ್ವ್ವೋರ್ಗಲ್, ಬಾಸುೞ್ವ್ವೋರ್ಗಲ್, ನೇಸರ್ದ್ದಾರ್ಗಣಂ, ಬಾಸುೞ್ಗ್ಗಿಣ್ಪು;—ಪೊಱಮಾರ್ಗ್ಗಣ್ಟೆ, ಪೊಱಮಾರ್ದ್ದನಂ, ಗಱಿಗೊೞ್ಜ್ಜಿರಿ (o. r. ಗಱಿಗೊೞ್ಜ್ಜಾರಿ), ಒಳನಾೞ್ಜ್ಜಿಗಳಂ;—ಇರ್ದ್ದುರ್, ಒರ್ಗ್ಗೇರ್ಣ್, ಮುಳ್ಗ್ಗೊಂಚಲ್, ಅಗೞ್ದ್ದ, ಅರಲ್ದ್ದ, ಅರಲ್ದ್ದೋರ್ಣ್ಪಂ, ಚಿಗುರ್ತ್ತುರ್, ಬಿಗುರ್ತ್ತುರ್, ಮುಗುಳ್ತ್ತು, ಅಗೞ್ತ್ತು, ಮಿಸಪೊಣರ್ಗ್ಗಂಗೆಯೊಳ್, ಅವಳ್ಗ್ಗಡಿಕಾರ್ತ್ತಿ, ಇವರ್ದ್ದಕ್ಷರ್, ಇವಳ್ದ್ದಕ್ಷಾಯಣಿ, ಬುಧರ್ವ್ವಿಶಿಷ್ಟರ್, ಪೊಗೞ್ವ್ವಾಸವನಂ, ಕುಡಿದರ್ಜ್ಜನ್ನಮಂ, ಪೊಗೞ್ಜ್ಜಾನಕಿಯಂ;—ಕೊನರ್ಗ್ಗೆ, ಅದಿರ್ಗ್ಗೆ, ಎಸಳ್ಗ್ಗೆ, ಪೊಗೞ್ಗ್ಗೆ, ಸುರರ್ಗ್ಗಳ್, ಎಸಳ್ಗ್ಗಳ್, ಉಸಿರ್ದ್ದರ್, ಉಗುೞ್ದ್ದಯ್, ಉಸಿರ್ದ್ದಪೆಂ, ಪೊಗೞ್ದ್ದಪೆಂ, ಕಿಸುರ್ವ್ವಯ್, ತೆಗೞ್ವ್ವೆಂ, ಒಸರ್ಗ್ಗುಂ, ಮಗುೞ್ಗ್ಗುಂ;—ತಾಯ್ವಿರ್ಗ್ಗೆ, ತಾಯ್ದಿರ್ಗ್ಗಳ್, ಕಣ್ಮಲರ್ದ್ದಯ್, ಕಣ್ಮಲರ್ದ್ದಪಯ್, ಕಣ್ಮಲರ್ವ್ವಯ್, ಕಣ್ಮಲರ್ಗ್ಗುಂ, ಬಾಸುೞ್ಗ್ಗೆ, ಬಾಸುೞ್ಗ್ಗಳ್, ಸೂರುಳ್ಗ್ಗೆ, ಸೂರುಳ್ಗ್ಗುಂ;—ಪೊಱಮಾರ್ಗ್ಗೆ, ಪೊಱಮಾರ್ಗ್ಗಳ್, ಒಳಸೋರ್ಗ್ಗೆ, ಒಳಸೋರ್ಗ್ಗಳ್, ಒಳಸೋರ್ದ್ದಂ, ಒಳಸೋರ್ದ್ದಪಂ, ಒಳಸೋರ್ದ್ದಪಯ್, ಒಳಸೋರ್ವ್ವಂ, ಒಳಸೋರ್ಗ್ಗುಂ, ನೆಲದಾೞ್ಗ್ಗೆ, ನೆಲದಾೞ್ಗ್ಗಳ್, ನೆಲೆಬಾೞ್ಗ್ಗೆ, ನೆಲೆಬಾೞ್ಗ್ಗಳ್, ನೆಲೆಬಾೞ್ದ್ದಂ, ನೆಲೆಬಾೞ್ದ್ದಪಂ, ನೆಲೆಬಾೞ್ವ್ವಂ, ನೆಲೆಬಾೞ್ಗ್ಗುಂ;—ಮುಳ್ಗ್ಗೆ, ಮುಳ್ಗ್ಗಳ್, ಕಳ್ಗ್ಗೆ, ಕಳ್ಗ್ಗಳ್, ಕಳ್ದ್ದಂ, ಕಳ್ದ್ದಪಂ, ಕಳ್ವ್ವಂ, ಕಳ್ಗ್ಗುಂ;—ಬಿಸಿಲ್ಗ್ಗೆ, ಬಿಸಿಲ್ಗ್ಗಳ್, ಕವಲ್ಗ್ಗೆ, ಕವಲ್ಗ್ಗಳ್, ಕವಲ್ದ್ದುದು, ಕವಲ್ದ್ದಪ್ಪುದು, ಕವಲ್ವ್ವಂ, ಕವಲ್ಗ್ಗುಂ;—ಅಲರ್ಗ್ಗೋರಟೆಯಾ, ಪೊಗೞ್ಗ್ಗಂಗೇಯನಂ, ಪಾರ್ವ್ವರ್ದ್ದಾನಪ್ರಿಯರ್, ಮುಗುಳ್ದ್ದಳಿವ್ಪದ, ಜಿನರ್ವ್ವನ್ದ್ಯರ್;—ಕಾದಲರ್ಗ್ಗೆ, ಕಾದಲರ್ಗ್ಗಳ್;—ನೀರ್ದ್ದಾಣಮ್ ಎನೆದುದು; ಬನ್ದಿನ್ನೀರ್ಂ;—ನೇಸರ್ಬ್ಬಟ್ಟೆ, ಜೇಸನ್ನುಡಿ, ನೂರ್ಚ್ಛಾಸಿರಂ, ಬಸುರ್ಬ್ಬಡವಾದುದು;—ಬೆದರ್ಗ್ಗಣ್ಟೆ, ಕೆದರ್ತ್ತಲೆ;—ತೋರ್ತ್ತಾಣಂ, ಮಾರ್ಗ್ಗಣ್ಟೆ;—ಮಾರ್ಕ್ಕೋರ್ಲ್, ಬೇರ್ತ್ತಡೆ, ಬೇರ್ಪ್ಪಟ್ಟಂ, ನೀರ್ಗ್ಗಣ್ಡೆ, ಕೂರ್ಗ್ಗಲಿ;—ನೀರ್ವ್ವೋಯ್ದಂ, ಜೇರ್ವ್ವರಸಿ, ನೀರ್ಮ್ಮಜ್ಜಿಗೆ, ಇರ್ಬ್ಬಾಳ್, ಇರ್ಮ್ಮನೆ;—ಇರ್ಚ್ಛವಡಿ, ಇರ್ಚ್ಛಾವಡಿ, ಇರ್ಚ್ಛಿಂಗು, ಒರ್ಚ್ಛೇರ್ಗಣ್;—ಒರ್ಕ್ಕಯ್, ಇರ್ಪ್ಪಾನಿ;—ಇರ್ಚ್ಛಾಸಿರಂ, ಒರ್ಚ್ಛಾಸಿರಂ;—ಒರ್ವ್ವಂ, ಒರ್ವ್ವಳ್.

Professor Max Müller gives the following instances on the doubling of consonants in Saṁskṛita in his 'A Sanskrit Grammar for Beginners'

p. 59:—ಅರ್ಕ್ಕ (for ಅರ್ಕ), ಬ್ರಹ್ಮ್ಮನ್ (for ಬ್ರಹ್ಮನ್), ವರ್ದ್ಧನ (for ವರ್ಧನ), ದರ್ಶ್ಶ್ಯತೇ (for ದರ್ಶ್ಯತೇ, it is shown).

His general remarks are as follows:—"According to some grammarians any consonants except r and h, followed by another consonant and preceded by a vowel, may be doubled; likewise any consonant preceded by r or h, these letters being themselves preceded by a vowel. As no practical object is obtained by this practice, it is best, with (the grammarian) Šâkalya, to discontinue it throughout."

372. An alphabetically arranged list of words (compounds and others) which are contained in various places of the Šabdânušâsana, the numbers referring to the sûtras under which they are found. When a word is explained in the Šabdânušâsana, the explanation in that grammar's generally Saṁskṛita form is adduced immediately after it in the list. If a mere number is added, it denotes that the meaning of the term is not given by Bhaṭṭâkalaṅka and is not known to the author of the present grammar.

ಅಕ್ಕೋೞ್. Tadbhava of ಅಕ್ಕೋಟ. 160.— ಅಗಸಗಿತಿ. A washerwoman. 190.— ಅಂಕಂಗಾಱ. A warrior. See under ಸಮರಂಗಾಱ.— ಅಂಘವಣೆ. 80. *Cf.* ಅಂಗವಣೆ in Dictionary?— ಅಚ್ಚಳ. ಚರ್ಮಕ್ರಿಯಾ ತುರಂಗಾದಿಸಜ್ಜೀಕರಣಂ ವಾ. Working in leather or skins; the making ready or decorating horses etc. 425.— ಅಚ್ಚಳಾಯ್ತ. A man who is at the head of, or engaged in, ಅಚ್ಚಳ. 425.— ಅಚ್ಚಳಿಗ. = ಅಚ್ಚಳಾಯ್ತ. 425.— ಅಂಚಿಕೆ. 80. (Tbh. of ಅಂಶುಕ?).— ಅಟಮಟ. ಪರೇಷಾಂ ಭೇದಕಾರಿವಚನಂ. Producing dissension or disunion of others. 407.— ಅಟಮಟಿಗ. A man who practices ಅಟಮಟ. 407.— ಅಟ್ಟವಣೆ. 67. (*Cf.* ಅಟ್ಟವಣೆ in Dictionary?).— ಅಡಪತ್ತಿ. A female who carries her mistress' betel-nut pouch. 200.— ಅಡಿಯಟ್ಟೆ. The lower part of a spear. 348.— ಅಡುಕುೞಿ. ಪಚನಶೀಲಃ. A man who practices cooking. 545.— ಅಡುಗಿಗ. A man who cooks. 410.— ಅಡುೞಿಗ. = ಅಡುಗಿಗ. 410.— ಅಣೆಪ. The act of touching, etc. 561.— ಅಣ್ಣುಕ. 441.— ಅತ್ತಣ್ಗೆ. Dative of ಅತ್ತ. 265.— ಅದವಱಲ್. Grief, page 101 in the following verse: ಪಱಮುಱವಾಱಿಡಿ ಸೆಱೆಯುದವಱಲ್ ಅೞಲ್ ಎಡೞಿಯಂ ಛಲಿಂಚೆ ಮಾಂಜಲ್ ಲಂಚಂ । ಕಳವು ಪಿಸುಣ್ ಪಸಿವು ಬಱಂ ಪೞಿವೞಿವಲಸೊಲಸು ಕುತ್ತಮ್ ಇಲ್ಲ ನಾಡೊಳ್ ‖ There is no pillage, enmity, captivity, grief, weeping, and poverty, cheat (?), fraud, bribery, theft, slander, hunger, famine, blame, destruction, weariness, trembling, sickness in that district.— ಅನಿಮಿಸ. Tbh. of ಅನಿಮಿಷ. 138.— ಅನುಲ್ಲಂಘ್ಯ. Not to be passed beyond; not to be disregarded. 441.— ಅನ್ನುಕ. 80.— ಅನ್ನುಟು. ತಥಾ. In that manner, so, thus. 437.— ಅಬಿಸಂಗ. Tbh. of ಅಭಿಷ್ವಂಗ. 151.— ಅಮಳ್ವಾಸು. A joint-bed. 73.— ಅರಮಗಳ್. A king's daughter. 248.— ಅರಲ್ದೋಟ. A flower-garden.

73.—ಅರಲ್ಮನೆ. A flower-bud. 95.—ಅರಹನ್ತ. Tbh. of ಅರ್ಹನ್ತ. 147.—ಅರುಹ. Tbh. of ಅರ್ಹ. 147.—ಅರಿಹನ್ತ.=ಅರಹನ್ತ. 147.—ಅರೆಪ. Grinding, etc. 561.—ಅಱುಮೊೞ. Six cubits. 355.—ಅಲರ್ಗಣ್ಣನ್ತ. A male who has a flower-like eye. 402.—ಅಲರ್ಗೋರಂಟೆ. A flowering amaranth or barleria. 74.—ಅಲರ್ದೋರ್ಗೊಂಬ್ಬ.=ಅರಲ್ದೋರ್ಗೊಂಬ್ಬ. 73.—ಅವಸರಾಯ್ತ. A woman who is hasty from necessity. 195.—ಅವಸರಾಯ್ತೆ.=ಅವಸರಾಯ್ತ. 195.—ಅವು. 473. 515. (It appears there as a verb together with ತವು).—ಅವುಕುೞ. 473.—ಅವ್ವೞ. 67.—ಅಱುಜನ. ಕ್ಷುದ್ರಜನಃ. A vile man. 296.—ಆಕ್ಷೋಳ. Tbh. of ಆಕ್ಷೋಟ. 140.—ಆಗಡ. ತದಾ. At that time. 19. 20. (*Cf.* ಆಗಡು in Dictionary).—ಆಟಕಾಱ. A male addicted to play. 423.—ಆಟಕಾಱಿಕೆ. Addiction to play. 431.—ಆನುಂ. ಪಕ್ಷಾನ್ತರಾರ್ಥಃ. Either-or. 20.—ಆನೆಗುಲಿ. ಸಿಂಹಃ. An elephant-killer: a lion.—ಆನ್ಕೆ. Leaving upon, etc. 557.—ಆಯ್ಮಗೆ. ನಿರ್ಭರಾರ್ಥಃ. Vehemently, etc. 20.—ಆಯ್ಮನೆ.=ಆಯ್ಮಗೆ. 20.—ಆಯ್ಕೆ. Selecting. 556.—ಆಯ್ತ. ಅಧಿಕೃತಃ ಪ್ರಪ್ರಾಪ್ತಾಧಿಕಾರಃ. Placed at the head of, etc.; being engaged in or occupied with; etc. 425.—ಆರ್ಮ್ಮ. (ಆರ್ಮ). An able, great man, 88. 352 in the following verse: ಕೊರ್ಮೆಯಿನ್ ಆ ಮುನಿಯುಂ ಕಣ್ಡಾರ್ಮ್ಮಂ ನೀನ್ ಅಲ್ಲದಿಲ್ಲ ಪೆಱತೆನ್ದರಸಂ । ಮೂವರ್ಮ ಬಲವನ್ದು ನುತಿಸಿ ಪಲವರ್ಮ ತುೞಿಲ್ಗೆಯ್ದು ಭಕ್ತಿಯಿಂ ಬೆಸಗೊಣ್ಡಂ ॥.—ಆಱ್ಕುೞ (*i. e.* ಆಡ್ಕುೞ). ಕ್ರೀಡನಸ್ವಭಾವಃ. A male who is inclined to play. 545.—ಆೞ್ತ. Sinking in a fluid, etc. 140.—ಇಂಘಾರಿಗೆ. 80. (A sweet cake?).—ಇಟ್ಟೞ. In a crowd: greatly. In a verse under 65, and in one under 193.—ಇತ್ತಣ್ಗೆ. Dative of ಇತ್ತ. 265.—ಇನ್ತುಟು. ಇತ್ಥಂ. Thus, in this manner. 437.—ಇನ್ಮಗೆ. A smile. 95.—ಇನ್ನಿವಮ್ಮಾವು (o. r. ಇನ್ನವಮ್ಮಾವು). A sweet mango. 55.—ಇಕರ್ಮಱುಗೊಳ್. In the sentence ಉಪಾಧ್ಯಾಯನತ್ತಣಿಂ ವಿದ್ಯೆಯುಮ್ ಇಕರ್ಮಱುಗೊಣ್ಡಂ. 221.—ಇರ್ಚವಡಿ. Two pairs. 93. 94.—ಇರ್ಚಾವಡಿ. Two choultries. 93.—ಇರ್ಚೆಱಂಗು. Two ends of a garment. 93.—ಇರ್ಪಾನಿ. 90. 101. (Two armies?, see ಪಾನಿ).—ಇರ್ಮೊನೆ. Two points. 92.—ಇಲಿಗುಲಿ. ಆಖುಭುಕ್. A rat-killer: a cat. 547.—ಈತ. Giving (ಈವುದು). 579.—ಈನ್ತ. Bringing forth young (ಈಮ್ಬುದು). 579.—ಉಕ್ಕಿನ್ದೊಱೆ. A rising river (ಉಕ್ಕುವುದು ತೊಱೆ). 333.—ಉಜ್ಜುಗಿ. Tbh. of ಉದ್ಯೋಗಿ. See ಬಲ್ಲುಜುಗಿ.—ಉಣ್ಕೆ. Eating. 557.—ಉಣ್ಡಲಿಗೆ. In the sentence ಬೆಸ ಕೆಂಗುಣ್ಡಲಿಗೆಯುೞ್ತ. 214.—ಉತ್ಪಾಟ. Pulling up by the roots, destroying; a disease of the external ear. See ಉಬ್ಬಟೆ.—ಉನ್ತು. ಕಥಂ (?). How? in what manner? 437.—ಉನ್ತುಟು.=ಉನ್ತು. 437.—ಉನ್ತೆ. 1.=ಉನ್ತು. 437.—ಉನ್ತೆ. 2. ತೂಷ್ಣೀಂ. Silently, quietly. 437.—ಉನ್ನತತನ. The state of being high. 431.—ಉಪವಾಸಿಗ. A man who abstains from food. 407.—ಉಬ್ಬಟೆ. Tbh. of ಉತ್ಪಾಟ. 160.—ಉಶನಸ್ಸು. Tbh. of ಉಶನಸ್. 133.—ಉಷ್ಟು. So much as this in an intermediate manner. 441.—ಉೞಿಗ. ಕರ್ತಾ. A suffix to denote a maker of. 410.—ಉಱುಕಲ್. 140.—ಉಱುಕೆಱ. 140.—ಉಱುಲ. 140.—ಉಱ್ಕು. 140.—ಊಟಿಗ. A great eater. 415.—ಊಟವಣಿಗ.=ಊಟಿಗ. 415.—ಊಟವಣಿಗಿತಿ. Feminine of ಊಟವಣಿಗ. 196.—ಊಸು.=ಉಷ್ಟು. 441.—ಊಳ್ಕೆ. Crying out, etc. 558.—ಎಕ್ಕರಾಸಿ. Tbh. of ಏಕರಾಶಿ. 375.—ಎಗ್ಗೆ. A stupid etc. female. 197.—ಎಣಿಸಿಸು. To cause to reckon, etc. 541.—ಎಣ್ಗಾವುದ. Eight gâvudas. 351.—ಎಣ್ಮೆ. ಚತುರೋ ವಾರಾನ್. Eight times. 351.—ಎನ್ತುಟು. ಕಥಂ. How? in what manner? 439.—ಎನ್ತೆ.=ಎನ್ತುಟು. 439.—ಎರಡನೆಯುಳ್. A second female. Plural ಎರಡನೆಯುಳ್ವಿರ್. 185.—ಎರಲುಣಿ. ವಾಯುಭುಜ್. A wind-eater: a snake.

546. — ಎರಡುಸ್ಸಾರಿ. Two times. 313. — ಎರಡುಸ್ಸಾಳ್. Two knives or swords. 359. — ಎಮ್ಮೆ. A female buffalo. 444. — ಎಲವು or ಎಲವೋ. A particle used in smaraṇa, viċâra and âmantraṇa. 21. — ಎಸಳ್ಗನ್ದ. The fragrance of flower-leaves. 73. — ಎಸಳ್ಹಾಸೆ. A mat of (or for) petals. 73. — ಎಸಳ್ತಾಣ. A place of petals. 73. — ಎಸಳ್ವಳೆ. A ring of petals. 72. — ಎಳಗರು. A young calf. 87. — ಎಳಮುಯ್ಯಾಪಿನ್ಡು. A herd of young kine. 87. — ಎಱ್ಕೆ. (ಅರ್ಕ, ಎಕ್ಕೆ). The gigantic swallow-wort. 140. 160. — ಎಱ್ಗು. 140. — ಎತ್ತು. 140. (Standing up?). — ಎತ್ತರದಿಟ್ಟಿ. An upward look, a high view. 332. — ಏಕರಾಶಿ. A heap, a crowd. See ಎಕ್ಕರಾಸಿ. — ಏಯಾರಸಿ. Tbh. of ಏಕಾದಶಿ. The eleventh day. 160. — ಏಱುಗಾವುಡ. Seven gâvudas. 356. — ಏಱುಗಯ್ಯ. ಸಪ್ತಹಸ್ತಃ. A male who has seven hands. 356. — ಏಱುಕೆ. ಸಪ್ತವಾರಾನ್. Seven times. 356. — ಒಗುತೆ. Bursting forth, etc. Plural ಒಗುತೆಗಳ್. 560. — ಒಡಲೇೞ್ಗೆ. Rising, etc. of the body. 335. — ಒಡ್ಡಾರ. 67. — ಒರೆಪ. Pulling or rubbing. 561. — ಒಱಗಾತಿ. A female sheath-maker. 201. — ಒಕ್ಕೆಯ್. One hand. 90. 101. — ಒಕ್ಕೋಲ್. One stick; one arrow. 101. — ಒಗೇಣ್. One span; one sword. 73. — ಒಚೆರಂಗು. One end of a garment. 94. — ಒಛ್ಛಾಸಿರ. One thousand. 94. — ಒತಲೆ. One head. 358. — ಒಲಸು. Trembling. See under ಅದವಲ್. — ಒಳ ಕೆಯ್ಸು. In a verse on page 78 beginning ಅರಲ. — ಒಳ ತೋಟ. An inner garden. 101. — ಒಳ ನಾಡುಗಳ. A quarrel of the inland country. 73. — ಒಳ. 566. (A verb from which ಒಳವು is derived). — ಒಳವು. 566. — ಒಳ್ಪನ್ನ. A good pearl. 71. — ಒಳ್ಪಾವಣಿಗೆ. 71. — ಒಳ್ಪಾರ. A fine string of pearls. 333. — ಒಳ್ಗಂಗನ್ನಡ. Good Kannaḍa. 55. — ಒಳ್ಬುರಿಜ. A male who has been born in a good village. 420. — ಒಳ್ಬೂರಿಗ. A male who belongs to, or has been born in, a good village. 419. — ಓಡುಂಜಗಳ. A fight in which one runs. 344. — ಓದುಕುಳಿ. A person addicted to reading. 140. — ಓವು. Loving. 573. — ಓಲಗಕಾತಿ. A female servant, in the sentence ಅರಮಗನ್ ಇರ್ಪ ಓಲಗದ ಓಲಗಕಾತಿಯರ್ ಎಲ್ಲರ್ ಓಪ್ಪಿದರ್. 34. — ಓಲೆಕಾಱಿಕೆ. The business of a ôlêkâṟa. 431. — ಕಂಚುಗಾಱಿಕೆ. = ಕಂಚಗಾಱಿಕೆ in Dictionary. 431. — ಕಂಚುವಡಿಗ. ಕಾಂಸ್ಯಕಾರಃ. A brazier. 416. — ಕಟ್ಟುಕ. ಕಟ್ಟು ಇತಿ ಅನುಲ್ಲಂಘ್ಯೋ ನಿರ್ಣಯಃ । ತತ್ ಕುರ್ವನ್. A male who makes a decision that is not to be disregarded. 441. — ಕಟ್ಟೆಲ್ವು. A strong bone. 339. — ಕಡಿಕ. A strong, or rough, man. 403. — ಕಡುಗಾಡಿ. Great gracefulness. 340. — ಕಡುಚೋಜಿಗ. A great wonder. 93. — ಕಡುರಾಗ. Excessive love, etc. 296. — ಕಣ್ಗುರುಡ. A male who is blind of the eyes. 301. — ಕಣ್ಬಯ. Tbh. of ಕಣ್ವಕ. 160. See however ಕಣ್ಬೆಯುದರ. — ಕಣ್ಬಿಸು. To be angry with, in the sentence ನಲ್ಲಂಗಿನಿಯಳ್ ಕಣ್ಬಿಸಿದಳ್. 214. — ಕಣ್ಬೆಯುದರ. Tbh. of ಕಣ್ವಕದ್ವಾರ. 378. — ಕಣ್ಬೆಯದಾರ. = ಕಣ್ಬೆಯುದರ. 378. — ಕಣ್ಬೆಯಬಾರ. = ಕಣ್ಬೆಯುದರ. 378. — ಕಣ್ಣನೊಡ್ಡಬಲಿ. ಚಕ್ಷುರ್ಗೋಲಕಂ. An eye-ball. 346. — ಕಣ್ಣುಮ್ಮಾಳೆ (ಕಣ್ಣುಮ್ಮಾಬ್?). 55. — ಕಣ್ಣೆಯ್ದಲ್. A water-lily-like eye. 95. — ಕಣ್ಬಾಪೆ. The pupil of the eye. 89. — ಕಣ್ಬನ್ತ. A male who has eyes. 403. — ಕದಿರ್ವಳ. A man who has ears of corn, etc. 73. — ಕನ್ಡಾಯ. 80. — ಕನ್ನಡಿಜ. A man born in the Kannaḍa country. 420. 421. — ಕನ್ನಡಿತಿ. A Kannaḍa woman. 190. — ಕಬ್ಬಿಳಿಗ. A poet. 410. — ಕಮ್ಪುಣಿ. ಗನ್ಧಲಿಟ್. A fragrance-sucker. 308. 546. — ಕಮ್ಮಟಿತಿ. The wife of a blacksmith, etc. 199. — ಕಮ್ಮಿಗ. ಕರ್ಮಕರ್ತಾ. A male who does any act or work. 412. — ಕರಹಡಿಜ. A man born in the country of

Karahâḍa. 420.— ಕರಹಡಿಚಿ. A woman born in Karahâḍa. 196.— ಕರಹಾಡಿಗ. A man who resides in, or has been born in, Karahâḍa. 419.— ಕರಿಕ. ಕರಿಮುಣ್ಪದರ್ಕ್ಕೆ ಕರಿಕಂ ವಸ್ತ್ರಂ ಕಮ್ಬಳವುಮ್ ಅನ್ನದ್ ವಾ. Black colour, (as that of) cloth, blankets, etc.; one who has a black colour, one who is black. 402. 403.— ಕರಿಕವನ್ತ. A man who has a black colour. 402.— ಕರಿಕಿ. A female who is black. 194.— ಕರು. ಕರು ಶಬ್ದಃ ಸುವರ್ಣರಜತಾದಿಲೋಹಮಯಪ್ರತಿಮಾದಿನಿರ್ಮಾಣಕೇ ರಸೇ ನಿಷೇಚನಾರ್ಥಂ ಸಿಕ್ಥಾದಿಕೃತಪ್ರತಿಕೃತಿ ವಾಚೀ | ಗೃಹಾದಿನಿರ್ಮಾಣಕೇ ಸುಲಗ್ನಸ್ಥಾಪಿತಪ್ರಥಮಸ್ತಮ್ಭವಾಚೀ ವಾ. The word ಕರು denotes a likeness (or form) made of bee's wax etc. (surrounded with clay) in order to pour out (the metal) in a fluid state (into the form), when one makes statues of gold, silver and other metals (*i. e.* a mould); or at the construction of a house, etc. it denotes the first (or principal) post erected at an auspicious time. 296. See ಗುಣ ಕರು.— ಕರ್ಗಣ್ಟೆ. 344. (Could it be ಕರ್ಗಣ್ಟಿ? *Cf.* ಬಿದರ್ಗಣ್ಟೆ under ಬಿದರ್ಗಣ್ಟಿ?).— ಕರ್ಮಡು. A black pool. 334.— ಕಲಹಡಿ. 330, in the sentence ನಾಡೆಲಿ ಕಲಹಡಿ; (perhaps = a ಕಲಹಾಡಿ, a quarrelsome female).— ಕಲಿಚ. ಕಾಲೊಳ್ ಪುಟ್ಟಿದಂ, ಶೂದ್ರಃ. Who has been born from the feet, a Śûdra. 420.— ಕಲ್ಲಾಕಲ್ಲಿ. A mutual fighting with stones. 331.— ಕಲ್ಲಾಯ್ತ. A superintendent of (precious) stones. 425.— ಕಲ್ಲುಗ. = ಕಲ್ಲಾಯ್ತ. 425.— ಕಲ್ಬಾಳೆ. A plantain hard as a stone. 70.— ಕಲ್ಸರಿ. Stone-rain. 93.— ಕವಡು. 569. (A verbal theme from which ಕವಡಿಕೆ comes).— ಕವಲ್ಗೋಲೆ. A forked horn of a bow. 83.— ಕಾಡುಗಾಣ್ or ಕಾಡುಂಗಾಣ್. To see a wilderness. 380.— ಕಾಯ್ಗುಳಿ. A person addicted to take pods. 414.— ಕಾಯ್ತು. Fruit having developed. Plural ಕಾಯ್ತುಂಗಳ್. 553.— ಕಾಲೂರ್. ಗ್ರಾಮಃ. A village. 419.— ಕಾಲೂರಿಗ. A man who resides in, or is born in, a village. 419.— ಕಾಲ್ಗುಣ್ಟ. A male lame in one leg or in the legs. 301.— ಕಾಲ್ಗೆರೆ. A tank with a channel. 305.— ಕಾಲ್ವನ್ತ. A man who has feet. 403.— ಕಾಲ್ವೇಗಿ. A fleet person. 223.— ಕಾರ್ಬೊಡೆ. A black belly (?). 91.— ಕಿಚ್ಚುಗಣ್ಣ. ಅಗ್ನಿಲೋಚನಃ. A male who has eyes like fire. 311.— ಕಿತ್ತಡಕಿಲ್. A small pile. 53.— ಕಿತ್ತೀಳೆ. ಕಿಱುದೀಳೆ. A small orange. 337.— ಕಿನ್ನಟ್ಟೆ. Low condition, etc. 368.— ಕಿಱುಕೆ. Making close, etc. 557.— ಕಿಱುಗೋಲ್. A small stick or arrow. 87.— ಕಿಸ್ಣ. Tbh. of ಕೃಷ್ಣ. 158.— ಕಿಸುದಳಿರ್. Red new leaves. 343.— ಕಿಟಕಿಟನೆ or ಕಿಳಕಿಳನೆ. A certain imitative sound. 140.— ಕಿಡಲ್. Uprooting, etc., that may stand for ಕೀಱುಲ್. 478.— ಕಿಟಿಲನೆ or ಕಿಳಿಲನೆ. A certain imitative sound. 140.— ಕೀಟ್ಕೀಱು. 368.— ಕೀೞ್ವೊಟ್ಟೆ. The abdomen. 90. 368.— ಕೀೞ್ವೊಲ್ಲಿಗೆ. An inexact solligĕ. 93.— ಕುಕ್ಕೆ. Tbh. of ಕುಕ್ಷಿ. 110.— ಕುಡುಗೋಲ್ಗೊಯ್. To cut with the sickle. 300.— ಕುದಿಪ. Boiling. Plural ಕುದಿಪಂಗಳ್. 562.— ಕುಮ್ಬಱತಿ. A potter-female. 199.— ಕುಮ್ಬಱಿತಿ. = ಕುಮ್ಬಱತಿ. 198.— ಕುಮ್ಬಿಗ. ಕುಮ್ಭಕಾರ. A potter. 412.— ಕುಮ್ಭಗಾಱ. A potter. 384.— ಕುಱುಗೆಯ್ಯ. A male who has a small hand or small hands. 97.— ಕುಱುಮನೆ. A small house. 369.— ಕುಸಿ. ಭಯೇನ ಲಜ್ಜಯಾ ವಾ ಉತ್ಸಾಹವಿಕಲಂ ಚೇತಃ. A mind deprived of strength by fear or shame. 441.— ಕುಸಿಕ. A man whose mind is deprived of strength by fear or shame. 441.— ಕುಸಿಗೊರಲಿ. A woman with a short neck. 328.— ಕುಳಿ. A suffix used in ಶೀಲ, ಸ್ವಭಾವ and ಪ್ರಕೃತಿ. 545.— ಕೂಸ್ಕೆ. Bending. 557.— ಕೂರಿತೆ. Sharpness. See under ಸಮರಂಗಾಱ.— ಕೂ ರ್ಗಲಿ. A sharp warrior. 90.— ಕೂರ್ಗತ್ತಿ. A sharp knife or sword. 345.— ಕೂರ್ಗಣೆ.

= ಕೂೞ್ಕಲೆ. 90. — ಕೂೞ್ಗಟ್ಟೆ. A structure where boiled rice is to be had (?). 90. — ಕೆಂಗಣ್ಣೆ. A female with red eyes. 111. — ಕೆಂಗಾಯ್. A red unripe fruit. 342. — ಕೆಚ್ಚಕ್ಕಿ. A red kind of rice. 343. — ಕೆಚ್ಚಾನೆ. A reddish elephant. 343. — ಕೆಚ್ಚುರಿ. A red flame. 343. — ಕೆಚ್ಚೋಲೆ. A red cadjan leaf, etc. 341. — ಕೆಂಜಂಜೆ. A purple twilight. 343. — ಕೆದಱುದಲೆ. A dishevelled head of hair. 83. — ಕೆದರ್ದಲೆ. = ಕೆದಱುದಲೆ. 83. — ಕೆನ್ದೆಂಗು. ರಕ್ತಚೋಚಃ. The red cocoanut tree (= ಚೆನ್ದೆಂಗು); (or a red plantain). 341. 342. — ಕೆನ್ನಕ್ಕಿ. = ಕೆಚ್ಚಕ್ಕಿ. 343. — ಕೆನ್ನುರಿ. = ಕೆಚ್ಚುರಿ. 343. — ಕೆಪ್ಪೆ. A deaf female. 197. — ಕೆಮ್ಬಿತ್ತು. A red seed, in a verse under 193; see it under ಮಾಗ್ಗಟ್ಟೆ. — ಕೆಮ್ಬೊನ್. ನಿಷ್ಟಪ್ತಕಾಂಚನಂ. Burnished gold. 341. *Cf.* ಚೆಮ್ಬೊನ್ in Dictionary. — ಕೆಮ್ಮಿಂಚು. A red lightning, in the instance ಬಿಱುವಿಸಿಲ್ಗೆ ಕೆಮ್ಮಿಂಚು. 218. — ಕೆಯ್ದುವಗಿತಿ. A female weapon-maker, a woman of the weapon-makers. 192. — ಕೆಯ್ಯೋಡು. A handy earthen pan. 305. — ಕೆಲವೆರ್ಮೆ. A few times. 441. — ಕೆಳೆಯತನ. Companionship, etc. 432. — ಕೆಱು. 140. — ಕೆಱ್. 140. — ಕೇಗುಂಚೊಗೆ. A crying peacock. 344. — ಕೇಸಣ. Tbh. of ಕ್ಷೇಪಣ. 155. — ಕೇಳ್ವೆ. 67. — ಕೊಂಕಣಿಗಿತಿ. A Concan Brâhmaṇa female. 190. — ಕೊಂಕುದಾಣೆ. A crooked staff. 379. — ಕೊಂಕುಬ್ದಾಣೆ. = ಕೊಂಕುದಾಣೆ. 379. — ಕೊಂಕುವುರ್ಬು. A bent eyebrow. 372. — ಕೊಡಲಿಗಡಿ. To cut with an axe. 300. — ಕೊರಲ್ಗಱೆ. A stain on the throat. 305. — ಕೊಲ್ಲಟ. ಲಂಘನಾದ್ಯಾಶ್ಚರ್ಯಕಾರೀ ವಿದ್ಯಾ. Jumping and other surprising art. 441. — ಕೊಲ್ಲಱ್. 140. — ಕೋಡಿನೀರ್. ತಟಾಕಪ್ರಾನ್ತೋದಕ. Water from the end of a tank. 82. — ಕೋಲಾಕೋಲಿ. ಕೋಲಿಂ ಕೋಲಿಂ ಪೊಯ್ಯುವುದು ಆದ ಯುದ್ಧದೊಳ್ ಅದು. A fight in which they mutually strike one another with sticks. 331. — ಕೋಡ್ಗೊನೆ. ಶೃಂಗಾಗ್ರಂ. The top of a mountain. 82. — ಕ್ರೀಡನ. Playing, sporting. See ಅಬ್ಬುಳಿ. — ಕ್ಷತ್ರಿಯಿತಿ. A woman of the Kshatriyas. 190. — ಖೂಳ. 140. — ಗಜ್ಜುಕ. 67. — ಗಟೆ. Tbh. of ಘಟೆ. 143. — ಗಣಿವ. ಗಣಿತಶಾಸ್ತ್ರಂ. Tbh. of ಗಣಿತ. 408. — ಗಣಿದಿಗ. A man versed in arithmetic. 408. — ಗಣ್ಡುತನ. Valiantness. See under ಸಮರಂಗಾಱ. — ಗತಕ. Tbh. of ಕೃತಕ. 160. — ಗತಕಿ. A false woman. 329. *Cf.* ಗದಕಿ in Dictionary. — ಗನ್ಧಿಗಿತಿ. A female seller of perfumes. 192. — ಗರ. See under ಗರವಟಿಗ. — ಗರತಿತನ. The state of a decent woman. 430. — ಗರವಟ. See under ಗರವಟಿಗ. — ಗರವಟಿಗ. ಗರ ಇತಿ ಜಲಯನ್ತ್ರವಿಶೇಷಃ ತತ್ರ ನಿಯುಕ್ತಃ. A man who is engaged in (the business of) a certain water-engine. ಅಥವಾ ಗರವಟ ಇತಿ ದುರ್ಗಾದೌ ಪ್ರಹರೇ ಪ್ರಹರೇ ಪರ್ಯಟನಾದಿನಾ ಕ್ರಿಯಮಾಣೋ ರಕ್ಷಾವಿಶೇಷಃ ತತ್ರನಿಯುಕ್ತಃ. Or one who is engaged in the guarding which is made in a fort, etc. by wandering about from watch to watch, etc. 441. — ಗರ್ಮುಗು. ಕುಬೇರಾಕ್ಷೀ. The plant *Bignonia suaveolens*. 76. — ಗವೀ. A cow. See ಚಕಿತಗವೀ, ತ್ರಿಗವೀ. — ಗಱಿಗುಟಿಗ. A man who bruises bamboo rods, etc. 548. — ಗಱಿಗೂೞ್. Boiled rice of the stick (*i. e.* boiled rice which has been turned with a stick?). 89. — ಗಱಿಗೂೞ್ಪುರಿ (o. r. ಗಱಿಗೂಱ್ಪುರಿ). 73. — ಗಱಿವಟಿಗ. ಗಱಿ ಇತಿ ಲಂಘನಾದ್ಯಾಶ್ಚರ್ಯಕರೀ ವಿದ್ಯೋಪಕರಣಂ ತದ್ ಉಪಜೀವೀ ಸ ಏವ. A Dŏmba. 441. — ಗಾಡಿಕಾಱ. A charming man, in the instance ನೀಂ ಗಾಡಿಕಾಱಂ. 80. — ಗಾಣಿಗಿತಿ. The wife of an oil-maker. 190. — ಗಿಡುಗಡಿ. To cut a tree. 380. — ಗಿಡುಗಾಯ್. The unripe fruit of a tree. 380. — ಗಿಡುಂಗಡಿ. = ಗಿಡುಗಡಿ. 380. — ಗಿಱ್ಱನೆ. ಪರಿಭ್ರಮಣಾರ್ಥಃ. With a whirl, etc. 20. — ಗುಣಕೆಱು. ಗುಣಾನಾಂ ಪ್ರಥಮಸೃಷ್ಟಿಃ. The most excellent of properties. 296. See ಕೆಱು. — ಗುದ್ದು. Cuffing. Plural

ಗರ್ದುಗಳ್. 552. — ಗುೞ. ಗೃಹ್ಣಂ. A seizer or taker. 414. — ಗುಜ್ಜಕಲ್. 140. — ಗೂಡಾರ. Tbh. of ಗೂಢಾಗಾರ. 378. — ಗೃಹ್ಣತ್. (ಗೃಹ್ಣನ್, ಗೃಹ್ಣತೀ, ಗೃಹ್ಣತ್). Seizing, taking, accepting; using, putting on; etc. 414. — ಗೆಲ್ಲಗಾಱ. A gainer or winner. 383. — ಗೇಣಂಜುರಿಗೆ. A knife (of the length) of a span. 55. — ಗೇಣ್ನೆೞ. The length of a span. 95. — ಗೊಬಸು. 140. — ಗೋಣನ್ನಾಳಿ. A tubular vessel of the throat. 346. (*Cf.* ಗೋನಾಳಿ, ಗೋಮುನಾಳಿ in Dictionary). — ಗೋಣ್ಣಾಳಿ. = ಗೋಣನ್ನಾಳಿ. 346. — ಗೋಮುಹ. Tbh. of ಗೋದುಹ್. 129. — ಗೌಡಿ. A female servant. 240. (See ಗವುಡಿ in Dictionary). — ಗೌಳಿ. Tbh. of ಗೌಡಿ. 140. — ಘಾಂರಿಗೆ. (= ಗಾಂರಿಗೆ or ಘಾರಿಗೆ in Dictionary?). See ಇಂಘಾರಿಗೆ. — ಚಕಿತಗವಿ. A frightened cow. See ಬೆದರ್ಗನ್ತಿ. — ಚಟ್ಟು. ಶ್ರೀಖಣ್ಡಕುಂಕುಮಾದಿಗನ್ಧದ್ರವ್ಯಕರ್ದಮಕೃತಸ್ಥಾಸಕವಚನಂ. A term for the perfuming (of the body) which is performed with an unguent of sandal, saffron and other fragrant substances. 441. — ಚಟ್ಟುಕ. ತತ್ಕರ್ತನ್. A man who performs that perfuming. 441. (*Cf.* ಚಟ್ಟಿಜ in Dictionary). — ಚನ್ದ್ರಮಸ್ಸು. Tbh. of ಚನ್ದ್ರಮಸ್. 133. — ಚಪ್ಪಟಿ. 140. — ಚಿನ್ನಮ್ಮಣೆ. A golden seat. 55. — ಚಿವುಡಿಕೆ. Cutting off with the nails, etc. 570. — ಚೆಂಗಾಯ್. = ಕೆಂಗಾಯ್. 342. — ಚೆಚ್ಚರ. ವ್ಯಕ್ತಾರ್ಥಂ. Manifestly, clearly. 20. — ಚೆಂಜಂಜೆ. = ಕೆಂಜಂಜೆ. 343. — ಚೆಲ್ವತನ. Beauty. 430. — ಚೆಳಿ. 105. — ಚೌಡಿ. 105. (A crested female? or *cf.* ಚವುಡಿ in Dictionary?). — ಚೌತ. Tbh. of ಚತುರ್ಥ. 376. — ಚೌತಯ. Tbh. of ಚತುಷ್ಟಯ. 376. — ಚೌದಸಿ. Tbh. of ಚತುರ್ದಶಿ. 160. — ಚೌಪದಿಗ. A man who makes čaupadas. 410. ಚೌಪದಮುಳಿಗ. = ಚೌಪದಿಗ. 410. — ಚೌಭಾಗಿ. Sharing in, or entitled to, a fourth part. 376. — ಚೌವಿಧ. Four-fold; of four kinds, in four ways. 376. — ಛಲಿಂಚಿ. Deceit (?). See under ಅವಪಬಲ್. — ಜಗಳ. Tbh. of ಝಕಟ. 143. — ಜಗಳಜಾಣ. A male who is clever in quarrels. 292. — ಜಗಳವನ್ತ. A quarrelsome male. 402. — ಜಂಗೆ. Tbh. of ಝಂಕೆ. 143. — ಜನ್ನವಿರವನ್ತ. A man who has a sacrificial cord. 402. — ಜಮ್ಪೆ. Tbh. of ಝಮ್ಪೆ. 143. — ಜಸವನ್ತ. A man who has fame. 402. — ಜಳಜ. Tbh. of ಜಲಜ. 140. — ಜಾಣವಕ್ಕಿ. In a verse on page 77. *Cf.* ಜಾನವಕ್ಕಿ in Dictionary. — ಜಾವಕ. Tbh. of ಯಾಮಕ. 141. — ಜಾಱುಗೆ. 140. — ಜೂಜುಗಾರ್ತಿ. A female gambler. 201. — ಜೂದುಗ. A male gambler. 384. — ಜೂದುಜಾಣ. A man who is expert in gambling. 305. — ಜೇಱ್. 140. — ಜೋಗಿತಿ. A female yôgi. 202. — ಜೋಱುಗೆ. 140. — ಜ್ಯಾಯ. Tbh. of ಜ್ಯಾಯಸ್. 134. — ಜ್ಯಾಯಸ್ಸು. = ಜ್ಯಾಯ. 134. — ಝಕಟ. = ಜಗಳ. 143. 402. (Is ಝಕಟ in Saṁskṛita Dictionaries?). — ಝಮ್ಪೆ. A spring, a jump; springing, jumping. — ಝುಮ್ಮನೆ. An imitative sound, in the instance ಝುಮ್ಮನೆ ಒಸರ್ದು. 20. — ಡಾಣಾಡಾಣಿ. A mutual fight with clubs. 331. — ಡಾಣೆ. In the instance ತೂಗುವ ಡಾಣೆ. 531. See ತೂಗುಡ್ಡಾಣೆ. — ಡಾಳಕ. In the instance ನಿಱ ಡಾಳಕಂ. 80. *Cf.* ಢಾಳಕಂ? — ಡೊಕ್ಕಗೆ. A kind of adverb. 49. — ಡೊಕ್ಕನೆ. = ಡೊಕ್ಕಗೆ. 49. — ಢಾಳಕ. The bearer of a banner (?), in the instance ಸುಡಿದರ್ ಢಾಳಕರ್. 65. — ತಕ್ಷಣ. Cutting, paring, planing; a cutter an abrador; the divisor employed in certain computations. 533. — ತಟ್ಟುಕ. = ಚಟ್ಟುಕ. 441. — ತಡ ಬಡ. ವಾಕ್ಯಮ್ಲಾನಾರ್ಥಃ. Bluntness or perplexity of speech. 20. — ತಣ್ಡಿಲ. Tbh. of ಸ್ಥಣ್ಡಿಲ. 149. — ತನ್ದರಿ. Tbh. of ತನ್ದ್ರಿ. 147. — ತನ್ದ್ರಿ. = ತನ್ದರಿ. 147. — ತನ್ದುರಿ. = ತನ್ದರಿ. 147. — ತಮಬ್. 140. — ತರ್ಕವೆ. Bringing. Plural ತರ್ಕವೆಗಳ್. 572. — ತಲೆವಡಿಕೆ. Joining head to head. 570. — ತಳಮಳ. ನಿರ್ಣಯವಾಚಿ. Decisively, certainly.

20. — ತಳಿಪ. Sprinkling, etc. Plural ತಳಿಪಂಗಳ್. 562. — ತಳಿರ್ಗೆಮ್ಪು. The redness of young leaves. 73. — ತಱಿ. 140. — ತಾಱುಗೆ. Becoming dry, etc. 565. — ತಾಱುವರ. The tree *Terminalia bellerica*. 82. — ತಾರ್ಕಣಿಸು. 90, in the verse ಬೇರ್ಕೆಯ್ದುರೆಬರನ್ ಅವರೊಳ್ ಕೂರ್ಕಲಿಗಳನ್ ಆತ್ಮನಿಕಟದೊಳ್ ಮಿಕ್ಕವರಂ । ತಾರ್ಕಣಿಸಿ ಸಮರಕೇಳಿಗೆ ಸೂರ್ಕಡಿಗಡಿದಂ ನೃಪಾಲಕಂ ರಿಪುಬಲಮಂ ॥. — ತಾಳಿಗೆ. Suffering, etc. 565. — ತಾಡ್ or ತಾಡು. The palm (and other plants or trees). Plural ತಾಡ್ಗಳ್ or ತಾಡುಗಳ್. 140. 193. (See the verse quoted under ಪಾಡ್ಗಟ್ಟಿ). — ತಾಡುಗಿ. A woman engaged in (gaining her livelihood by the produce of) the palmyra tree. 193. — ತಾಡುಗಿತಿ. = ತಾಡುಗಿ. 193. — ತಿಗ. = ತೀಗ. 378. — ತಿಗುಣ್ಡ. Tbh. of ತ್ರಿಕುಣ್ಡ. 376. — ತಿಟ್ಟಗೆ. ತಿಟ್ಟನೆ. 49. See ತಿಟ್ಟನೆ in Dictionary. — ತಿವಣ್ಡೆ. Tbh. of ತ್ರಿವಣ್ಡೆ. 376. — ತಿಮೊಗ. Tbh. of ತ್ರಿಮುಖ. 376. — ತಿಱುಕೆ. Bartering, etc. 557. — ತಿಱ್ಱಗೆ. ಪರಿಭ್ರಮಣಾರ್ಥಃ. Whirlingly, etc. 20. — ತಿಹುರಾನ್ತಕ. Tbh. of ತ್ರಿಪುರಾನ್ತಕ. 296. — ತಿಳಿತು. What is thin or delicate. See ತಿಳಿತುಬಸುಱು. — ತಿಳಿತುಬಸುಱು. ತೆಳ್ಪುವ್ವಸುಱ್. 55. — ತಿಳಿಪ. Becoming clear, etc. Plural ತಿಳಿಪಂಗಳ್. 562. — ತಿಳಿವೆಳಗು. Bright lustre. See the third verse on page 100. — ತೀಗ. = ತಿಗ. Tbh. of ತ್ರಿಕ. 378. — ತುಡ್ಬೆ. A wicked, etc. female. 197. — ತುರವ್ವೆ (?). See ತುರುವಪ್ಪೆ. — ತುರುವಪ್ಪೆ. Tbh. of ತುರವ್ವೆ. 160. — ತುಱುಗಾಡು. A jungle for kine (to graze). 87. — ತೂಗುದಣ್ಡೆ. An oscillating staff. 344. — ತೆಗೆಪ. Taking. 561. — ತೆಮಱ್. 140. — ತೆರಪೊನ್. A mass of gold. 332. — ತೆಬ್ಬರ. 80. (*Cf.* ತೆಬ್ಬೆ in Dictionary ?). — ತೆಳ್ವಸುರ್. Tender green grass. 66. — ತೆಳ್ವೆಳಗು. Delicate lustre. In a verse on page 100. — ತೆಳ್ಪುವ್ವಸುಱ್. A thin or delicate belly. 55. 347. — ತೇನಂ. ತೇನತೇನಂ. ಅದೃಢಾರ್ಥೇ ಏತೌ. In an unfirm etc. manner. 20. — ತೇಪೆ. 197. (It is a term for a certain female). — ತೇರಸಿ. Tbh. of ತ್ರಯೋದಶಿ. 160. — ತೇರ್ಮರ. A tree (used) for a chariot. 302. — ತೇಱ್. ತೇಱು. Plural ತೇಱ್ಗಳ್ or ತೇಱುಗಳ್. 85. — ತೊಟ್ಟಗೆ. ನಿರ್ಭರಾರ್ಥಃ. Excessively, etc. 20. — ತೊಡೆಪ. Smearing, etc. 561. — ತೊನೆಪ. Swinging, etc. 561. — ತೊಮ್ಬರ್. ನವಪುರುಷಾಃ ಸ್ತ್ರಿಯೋ ವಾ. Nine persons. 361. — ತೊಮ್ಮೆ. ನವವಾರಾನ್. Nine times. 361. — ತೊಯ್ತ. Becoming wet, etc. Plural ತೊಯ್ತಂಗಳ್. 553. — ತೊಳಪ. Shining, etc. ತೊಳಪಂಗಳ್. 562. — ತೊಱ್. 140. — ತೋಟಿಗಿತಿ. A female florist. 191. — ತೋರಿಕ. A big male. 403. — ತೋಱ್ತಾಣ. A place of appearing. 87. — ತೋಱ್. 140. — ತೋಱು. 140. — ತ್ರಿಕುಣ್ಡ. Having three pits (?). 376. — ತ್ರಿಗವೀ. Three cows. See ಮೂಱಾವು. — ತ್ರಿಮುಖ. Three faced; name of an Arhat. — ತ್ವರಣ. Making haste. 534. — ತ್ವಷ್ಟಾರ. Tbh. of ತ್ವಷ್ಟೃ. 124. — ಥಟ್ಟುತಾರು. Page 65 in the instance ಪರರ್ ಥಟ್ಟುತಾರಾದರ್. *Cf.* ತಾಱುಥಟ್ಟು in Dictionary. — ಥಟ್ಟುಱು. 140. — ದಣಿಯಿಸು. To satisfy, in the verse under 474. — ದಣ್ಡವನ್ತ. Having a stick, etc. 402. — ದಮ್ಮಾಣಿ. Tbh. of ದ್ರಮ್ಮಾಣಿ. ದ್ರಮ್ಮಂ ನಾಣಕವಿಶೇಷಃ ಟಂಕಶಾಲಾ ಇತ್ಯರ್ಥಃ. A mint. 378. — ದಲ್ಲಿಱ. 140. — ದವಸಿಗ. A man who sells corn. 405. — ದಸವೆ. Tbh. of ದಶಮಿ. 160. — ದಱವುಱ. 140. — ದಾನಶೂರ. A very liberal man. 65. — ದಿಣ್ಣ. ದಿಣ್ಣ ಇತಿ ಭಯವಿವೇಕವಿಧುರಪುರುಷವಪುರ್ಬಲಂ. The (savage) bodily power of a man who is without fear and deliberation. 441. — ದಿಣ್ಣಕ. ತದ್ವಾನ್. A man who is possessed of that (*i. e.* ದಿಣ್ಣ), a wild or savage man. 441. — ದೀವಾಳಿಗೆ. Tbh. of ದೀಪಾವಳಿಕೆ. 378. — ದೀವ್ಯತ್ (ದೀವ್ಯನ್). Playing, sporting. See ನಾವಿಲ. — ದುಜಾವ. Tbh. of ದ್ವಿಯಾಮ. 377. — ದುತಯ. Tbh. of ದ್ವಿತಯ. 377. — ದುತೀಯ. Tbh. of ದ್ವಿತೀಯ. 377. — ದುಮುಖ. Tbh. of ದ್ವಿಮುಖ. 377. — ದೂಗ. Tbb. of

ದ್ವಿಕ. 378. — ದೂಜಾವ. = ದುಜಾವ. 377. — ದೂತಯ. = ದುತಯ. 377. — ದೂಶೀಯ. = ದುಶೀಯ. 377. — ದೂಮುಕ. = ದುಮುಕ. 377. — ದೇವಡಿಗಿತ್ತಿ. A female who worships an idol. 111. — ದೇವಿಗ. ದೇವರಂ ಮಾಡುವಂ. A man who makes idols. 410. — ದೇವುಳಿಗ. = ದೇವಿಗ. 410. — ದೇವುಳಿಗಿತಿ. A woman who makes idols. 192. — ದೇವೇಜ್. Sacrificing to the gods. — ದೇವೇಜ. Tbh. of ದೇವೇಜ್. 129. — ದೋಷವನ್ತ. A man in whom faults are. 402. — ದ್ರಮ್ಮ. See under ದಮ್ಮಣಿ. A certain coin, a drachma. — ದ್ವಿಯಾಮ. Two night watches. — ದ್ವಾರಿಗ. A doorkeeper. 418. — ಧನಂಗುಳ. A person who is addicted to receive money, etc. 383. — ಧನವನ್ತೆ. A rich woman. 402. — ಧತಾರ. Tbh. of ಧತೃ. 123. — ಧತೃ. Holding, bearing, supporting; a bearer, supporter, preservor. — ಧಾಳಿ. 466, in a verse. (*Cf.* ದಾಟು in Dictionary ?). — ನಗೆಕಾಱ. ಹಾಸ್ಯೇ ಪ್ರಾಢಂ ಉದ್ಯುಕ್ತೋ ವಾ. A man who is proficient in laughter (or jest) or addicted to it. 423. — ನಗೆಕಾತಿ. A female who is proficient in laughter (or jest) or addicted to it. 201. — ನನ್ದಿಕೆ. Being extinguished, etc. Plural ನನ್ದಿಕೆಗಳ್. 568. — ನಮಿಯಿಸು. To bow, etc. 534. — ನರಗಟ್ಟು. A muscle bundle (?). 332. — ನಸಿಕ. A man who has ನಸೆ, *q. v.* 441. — ನಸುಮುಳಿಸು. Slight anger. 101. — ನಸುವಿರಿದು. Small power, etc. 91. — ನಸೆ. ನಸೆ ಇತಿ ವಯಸಾ ವ್ಯಾಧಿನಾ ಕೃತ್ರಿಮವಿಷೇಣ ವಾ ಜೀರ್ಣಂ ಗಾತ್ರಂ. A body become decrepit by old age, sickness or artificially made poison. 441. — ನಾರ್. ಓಷಧಿಃ. A plant, a herb. 424. — ನಾರುಗ. ತತ್ಪ್ರಯೋಗಾದಾ. A man who uses herbs, etc. 424. — ನಾರುಗಿ. A woman who uses herbs, etc. 193. — ನಾರುಗಿತಿ. = ನಾರುಗಿ. 193. — ನಾಲ್ಗಾವುದ. Four gâvudas. 351. — ನಾಲ್ಗೆಯ್ಯ. A male with four hands. 53. — ನಾಲ್ದಲೆಯ. A male with four heads. 97. — ನಾಲ್ಭುಜ. A male with four arms. 294. — ನಾವಿಲ. ನಾವಾ ದೀವ್ಯನ್, ನಾವಿಕಃ. A navigator. 441. — ನಾಡಱ್. 140. (*Cf.* ನೇಡಲ್ in Dictionary ?). — ನಾಡಿಕ್ಕಿಡು. A district to be ruined. ನಾಡಿಕ್ಕಿಟ್ಟುದು, the district was ruined. 82. — ನಾಡತ್ತೂಲೆ. A district-weight, etc. 90. — ನಿಚ್ಚಟ. Not false, firm, in the sentence ದೇಹಮನ್ ಎನ್ತು ನಿಚ್ಚಟಂ ನಮ್ಬಿದಪಯ್ or ನಮ್ಬಿದಪೋ. 461. — ನಿಟ್ಟಾಯ. ನಿಡಿದು ಆಯ. A long extent (?). 339. — ನಿಡಿಯುನ್ದಲೆ. A long or large head. 345. — ನಿಡುಗಣ್ಣಾಲಿ. The pupil of a long eye. 53. — ನಿಡುಗಣ್ಣೆ. A female with long eyes. 29. 194. — ನಿಡುಗಾಲ್. A long foot. 327. — ನಿಡುಚಾಲ್. A long row. 93. — ನಿಡುಜಡೆಯಳ್. A female with long braided tresses. 328. — ನಿಡುಮೆಯ್ಯ. A man with a long body. 53. — ನಿಡುಮ್ಬು. 80. — ನಿಡುವಣೆಯ. A man with a long forehead. 328. — ನಿಡುವೆನ್ನ. A man with a long back. 329. — ನಿಡುವೆರಲಿ. A female with long fingers. 29. 194. — ನಿಡುಸೂಲ್. A long pregnancy. 87. — ನಿಯಮಿಗ. A man who practises or observes religious observances. 401. 407. — ನಿರವ. Tbh. of ನಿರೂಪ. 160. — ನೀರ್ಗಣ್ಡಿ. ಜಲನಿರ್ಗಮನದ್ವಾರಂ. The opening through which water goes out. 90. — ನೀರ್ದೊಳೆ. ನೀರಿಂ ತೊಳೆ. To wash with water. 292. — ನೀರ್ಮಜ್ಜಿಗೆ. Buttermilk diluted with water. 92. — ನೀರ್ಮಡುದಾಣ. The place of a water-pool. 87. — ನೀರ್ವಟಿಗ. ನೀರ್ ಇತಿ ಜಲಂ ತದಭ್ಯಾಸಶೀಲಃ । ತರಣ್ಯಾದಿನಾ ತೇನ ವಿನಾಪಿ ವಾ ಸದ್ಯಾದ್ಯುತ್ತರಣಶೀಲಃ. A man who is in the habit of practising with water: one whose habit is to cross rivers etc. on rafts or also otherwise. 441. — ನುಣ್ದೊಡೆಯ. A man with soft thighs. 328. — ನುಣ್ದೊಡೆಯಳ್. A woman with soft thighs. 182. — ನುಸುಳ್ಮಾವಣಿಗೆ. 72. — ನುಸುಳ್ವಾಗಿಲ್. A door (which is so narrow that) one has to squeeze through. 72. —

ನೆನೆಪ. Bearing in mind, etc. 561. — ನೆಮಱ್. 140. — ನೆರವಾನಿಸ. A neighbouring man, etc. 332. — ನೆಲವಿಡಿ. To seize land, etc. 381. — ನೆಲವಿಡಿ. = ನೆಲವಿಡಿ. 381. — ನೆಲೆಬಾೞ್. A firm condition of life. 74. — ನೆಯ್ಗಱ. 140. — ನೇಷ್ಟಾರ. Tbh. of ನೇಷ್ಟೃ. 124. — ನೇಷ್ಟೃ. One of the chief officiating priests at a Sôma sacrifice. — ನೇಸರ್ದಾಣ. A sunny place. 73. — ನೇಸರ್ಬಟ್ಟೆ. The disk of the sun. 82. — ನೊಣೆಪ. Swallowing. 561. — ನೊೞ್. (ನೊಱ್?). A verbal theme from which ನೊೞವು (ನೊಱವು?) comes. 569. — ನೊೞಗಾಡು. A wilderness (full) of flies. 332. — ನೊಱವು. 140. — ನೋಡು. Seeing, sight, etc. Plural ನೋಡುಗಳ್. 549. — ನೌಮಿ. Tbh. of ನವಮಿ. 160. — ಪಕ್ಕಗೆ or ಪಕ್ಕನೆ. See ಪಕ್ಕನೆ in Dictionary. 49. — ಪಕ್ಕಿಗೂಡು. A bird's nest. 304. — ಪಕ್ಖಾಳನ. Tbh. of ಪ್ರಕ್ಷಾಲನ. 160. — ಪಗಲಾಣ್ಮ. The sun. 537. — ಪಂಗಾಯ್. ಶಲಾಟುಃ. Green, unripe fruit. 341. — ಪಂಚತಯ. Fivefold, having five parts or limbs. 376. — ಪಟ್ಟಣಿಗ. A man who resides in, or has been born in, a town. 419. — ಪಟ್ಟಸಾಲಿಗಿತಿ. A female silk-weaver. 192. — ಪಟ್ಟಸಾಲಿತಿ. = ಪಟ್ಟಸಾಲಿಗಿತಿ. 202. — ಪಟ್ಟು. ಪಟ್ಟುಶಬ್ದಃ ಪಕ್ಷವಚನಃ. A side, a faction. 441. — ಪಟ್ಟುಕ. ತತ್ (*i. e.* ಪಟ್ಟು) ಕುರ್ವನ್, ಪಕ್ಷಪಾತಿ. A partisan. 441. — ಪಡಿಸಣ. Tbh. of ಪ್ರತಿಸ್ಥಾನ. 407. — ಪಡಿಸಣಿಗ. ಭುಜಿಷ್ಯಃ. A man who eats the remainder of the food left by his master: a servant. 407. — ಪಡೆವಳ್ತಿ. A female commander of an army. 200. — ಪಣಂಗುೞ. A man who receives money (as a bribe?). 414. — ಪಣ್ಕೆ. Ripe fruit being produced. 557. — ಪಣ್ಗುೞ. A man who receives ripe fruits (as a bribe?). 414. — ಪಣ್ಣಾಣಿ. 80. — ಪದಯಿಲ. ಪದಂ ಸ್ಥಾನಂ ಸನ್ದರ್ಭವಿಶೇಷೋ ವಾ । ತತ್ಕುರ್ವನ್. A man who makes a dwelling place or abode; one who makes verses. 441. — ಪದಿರ್, in ಕೂಡಲ್ ಪದಿರ್, a variety of sounds to join (?). 585. — ಪನ್ತ. Tbh. of ಪನ್ಥ. A path, a road. 142. — ಪನ್ಥಾನ. Tbh. of ಪಥಿನ್. A path, a road. 130. — ಪನ್ನತ. 431. — ಪನ್ನತತನ. 431. — ಪಯುನ್. = ಹಯುನು in Dictionary. See ಬತ್ತುನ್ಪಯುನ್. — ಪಯಿನ್ನೂಱು. ಹತ್ತು ನೂಱು. ದಶಶತಂ. Ten hundred, a thousand. 363. — ಪಯಿಮ್ಬರ್. Ten persons. 363. — ಪಯಿಮ್ಮೆ. ದಶವಾರಾನ್. Ten times. 363. — ಪಯ್ಕನೆ. ಶೀಘ್ರಾರ್ಥಃ. Quickly. 20. — ಪರಲುಗ. A pearl-merchant. 424. — ಪರಸನ. Tbh. of ಪ್ರಶ್ನೆ. 147. — ಪರಿಸಂಗ. Tbh. of ಪರಿಷ್ವಂಗ. 151. — ಪಱೆಗ. A drummer. 416. — ಪಱೆವಡಿಗ. = ಪಱೆಗ. 416. — ಪಲಗೆದೆಱೆಯ. A man with a board-like chest. 328. — ಪಲ್ಯಾಣ. Tbh. of ಪಲ್ಯಯನ. 160. — ಪಸಱ್. 140. — ಪಾಕಿಗ. ಪಾಕಕರ್ತಾ. A man who cooks, etc. 410. — ಪಾಕುೞಗ. = ಪಾಕಿಗ. 410. 411. — ಪಾಕುೞಗಿತಿ. A woman who cooks, etc. 192. — ಪಾಡುಗ. A singer. 384. — ಪಾಣೆಯುವರ. Tbh. of ಪಾನೀಯದ್ವಾರ. 378. — ಪಾಣೆಯದಾರ. = ಪಾಣೆಯುವರ. 378. — ಪಾನಿ. See ಇಪಾರ್ನಿ. (Is Tamiḷ ಪಾನಿ = ಪಡೆ, an army, meant?). — ಪಾಯ್ತ. Jumping, etc. Plural ಪಾಯ್ತಂಗಳ್. 553. — ಪಾಱು. Fighting. See ಪಾಱುವೆಣ್. (*Cf.* Tamiḷ ಪಾಱು, to fight). — ಪಾಱುವೆಣ್. ಕಲಹಶೀಲಾ ಸ್ತ್ರೀ. A woman addicted to quarrel. 82. — ಪಾಱುಡು. A jumping iguana (?). 82. — ಪಾರ್ವತಿ. A Brâhmaṇa woman. 202. — ಪಾರ್ವನ್ತಿ. = ಪಾರ್ವತಿ. 202. — ಪಾವಡಿಗಿತಿ. A female of the caste of snake-catchers. 192. — ಪಾವುಗುಲಿ. A snake-killer: a mungoose; a peacock. 547. — ಪಾವುಣಿ. A snake-eater: a peacock. 546. — ಪಾವುವಟ್ಟ. A male with a snake-ornament. 441. (*Cf.* ತೊಟ್ಟ). — ಪಾೞಲ್. Tbh. of ಪಾಠೀನ. 140. 160. — ಪಿಂಜಱಂಗು. The hind end of a garment. 93. — ಪಿನ್ದಲೆ. The back of the head. 349. — ಪಿಪ್ಪಲಿಗ. A seller of long pepper. 409. — ಪೀೞಕೆ. Tbh. of ಪೀಠಿಕೆ. 140. 160. —

ಪುರೂರವಸ್ಸು. Tbh. of ಪುರೂರವಸ್. 133. — ಪುಸಿಬಾದಿ. A speaker of lies. 329. — ಪೂಣ್ಕೆ. Fixing, as an arrow; admitting, etc. 557. — ಪೂವಡಿಗಿತಿ. A female florist. 192. — ಪೆಡಗಾಲ್. A hind leg. 369. — ಪೆಣ್ಡತಿವನ್ತ. One who has a wife. 402. — ಪೆಣ್ಣುಗ. ಪೆಣ್ಣೊಳ್ ಪ್ರವಣಂ ವ್ಯಾಪೃತಂ ಮೇಣ್. A man addicted to, or occupied about, women. 424. — ಪೆಱೆನೊಸಲ. A man with a moon-like forehead. 327. — ಪೆಱೆನೊಸಲೆಯಳ್. A woman with a moon-like forehead. 182. 328. 330. — ಪೆಱಱು. 140. — ಪೇಱಿವಾಂಸ. 132. — ಪೇಱುಗೆ. In a verse under 140 (page 100): — ಬಾಱಿಯೊಳ್ ಅರಿಗಳನ್ ಅಳಱಿಸಿ ಪಾಱಿಯೊಳ್ ಅಳವಡಿಸಿ ನೆಲನರಾವಂ ಕರೆವಾ । ಕೇಱಿಯೊಳೆ ನಲಿದು ತನ್ನಯ ಪೇಱುಗೆಯುಂ ನೆಱೆಯೆ ನೆರೆಪಿದಂ ಧರಣೀಶಂ ॥. — ಪೊಗುತೆ. Entering, etc. Plural ಪೊಗತೆಗಳ್. 560. — ಪೊಚ್ಚ. ನದೀವಚನಂ ಆಭರಣವಾಚ್ಯಪಿ ಪೊಚ್ಚಶಬ್ದೋಽಸ್ತಿ. 1, a river; 2, an ornament (*cf.* ಪಾವುಪಚ್ಚ; ಪಚ್ಚ in Dictionary). 311. — ಪೊಚ್ಚವಚ್ಚ. An ornamental dress. 441. — ಪೊಂಜೆಳ. A golden staff. 93. — ಪೊಟ್ಟೆವನ್ತ. A male who has a (big) belly, in the instance ಪೊಟ್ಟೆವನ್ತಂ ಜನಕಂ. 402. — ಪೊಣರಿಸು. To cause to fight, in the instance ಪೊಣರಿಸಿದನ್ ಆನೆಯುಂ ಜೋದಂ. 537. — ಪೊಣರ್ಚಿಸು. To cause (somebody) to make (something) fight, in the instance ಪೊಣರ್ಚಿಸಿದನ್ ಆನೆಯುಂ ಮಾವಟಿಗನಿನ್ ಅರಸಂ. 541. — ಪೊಣರ್ಚು. = ಪೊಣರಿಸು, in the instance ಪೊಣರ್ಚಿದನ್ ಆನೆಯುಂ ಜೋದಂ. 537. — ಪೊನ್ದಗಡು. A sheet of gold. 93. — ಪೊನ್ದಿಕೆ. Joining, etc. Plural ಪೊನ್ದಿಕೆಗಳ್. 568. — ಪೊನ್ನಂಗಲ್. A golden stone. 55. — ಪೊನ್ನುಗ. A man who is addicted to, and busy with acquiring, gold. 424. — ಪೊಪ್ಪಳ. 67. — ಪೊಯ್ಯುಳ್. Beating; a blow. Plural ಪೊಯ್ಯುಗಳ್. 555. — ಪೊರೆಪ. Nourishing, etc. 561. ಪೊಱಕಟ್ಟು. An outer tie, etc. 101. — ಪೊಱಕೆಯ್. The upper part of the hand. 101. — ಪೊಱಕೋಟೆ. An outer fort. 101. — ಪೊಱಮಾರ್ಗಣ್ಣೆ. ಪೊಱಮಾಱಿನ ಗಣ್ಣೆ. A swelling at the posteriors. 73. — ಪೊಱಮಾರ್ದನ. Cows of flight (?). 73. — ಪೊಱುಕೆ. Bearing on the head, etc. 557. — ಪೊಸ ಆನೆ. A wonderful elephant. 46. — ಪೊಸ ಚಾವಡಿ. A new choultry. 91. — ಪೊಸ ಚಿಗುರಿ. A beautiful antelope. 93. — ಪೊಸ ಜವಳ. New cloth. 91. — ಪೊಸ ತೊಲೆ. A new balance, etc. 101. — ಪೊಸ ತೋಟ. A new garden. 101. — ಪೊಸ ಬಿಡುಮುತ್ತು. Fine loose pearls. 87. — ಪೊಸ ಬೀಡು. A new camp. 87. — ಪೊಸ ಮಡು. A new pool. 87. — ಪೊಸ ಮಾಡ್ಕಟ್ಟೆ. A new artificial structure. 87. — ಪೊಸವ್ವಳ್. A new woman. 169. — ಪೊಸವೆಟ್ಟ. A wonderful mountain. 92. — ಪೊಸ ಸಕ್ಕರೆ. Beautiful sugar. 89. — ಪೊಱಗು. (A verb from which ಪೊಱವು comes). — ಪೊಱವು. 140. Plural ಪೊಱವುಗಳ್. 574. — ಪೋಚ. Name of a man. 80. — ಪೋಳಿಗೆ. Tbh. of ಸ್ಫೋಟಿಕ. 160. — ಪೋಱ್. Used as verb intransitive in the sentence ಪೋಱ್ಯುಂ ಬಳ್ಗರಿಗಳ್ ಅಸ್ಸ ವಜ್ರಾಹತಿಯಿಂ. 463. — ಪೋಱ್ಗಿದಱ್. Parts to be scattered. 193 (in a verse). — ಪೌವಗೆ. ಭಯಾಕಸ್ಮಿಕಾರ್ಥೆ. Oh! woe to me!; unexpectedly. 20. — ಪ್ರತಿಗ್ರನ್ಥಿ. See ಸೂಡಿಗಣ್ಣು. — ಪ್ರತಿಸ್ಥಾನ. ಯತ್ರ ಸ್ಥಾನೇ ಸ್ವಾಮಿ ಭುಕ್ತ್ವೋತ್ಥಾಯ ಗತಸ್ ತತ್ಸ್ಥಾನ ಏವೋಪವಿಶ್ಯ ತದುಚ್ಛಿಷ್ಟಭೋಜನಂ ಪ್ರತಿಸ್ಥಾನಮ್ ಉಚ್ಯತೇ. Pratisthâna denotes the eating of the remainder (of the dinner) of him (*i. e.* of the master), one (who does so) sitting down in the very same place in which the master has eaten, risen and gone. 407. — ಪ್ರಧಾನಿತಿ. A female of noble birth. 191. — ಬಗೆಕಾತಿ. A mindful woman. 201. — ಬಗ್ಗನ್ದೊವಲ್. A tiger-skin. 379. — ಬಂಗಳಿಚ. A man of Bangâḷa. 420. — ಬಟ್ಟಮೊಲೆಯಳ್. A woman with round breasts. 328. — ಬಟ್ಟೆಗ. A man on the road, a traveller, in the instance ಬಿಸಿಲ್ ಬಟ್ಟೆಗನಂ ಬಱಲಿಸಿತ್ತು. 536. — ಬಡಕಿ. A female who beats; or a lean female.

29. — ಬಡಗಣಳ್. A woman of the north. 182. — ಬಡಿಗೊಳ್. To take a cudgel. 380. — ಬಡಿಸಿಸು. To cause to make beat, in the instance ಬಡಿಸಿಸಿದಳ್ ಸೊಸೆಯಿನ್ದತ್ತೆ. 541. — ಬಣಜು. 80. (Tbh. of ವಣಿಜ್, trade?). — ಬಣಂಜು. = ಬಣಜು. 80. — ಬತಿ. 329. (Tbh. of ವೃತಿ? *cf.* ಬರತ). — ಬತ್ತುವ್ವುಯನ್. ಬತ್ತುವುದು ಪಯನ್. Water, milk, etc. drying up. 333. 344. — ಬನಜ. ಬಾನೊಳ್ ಪುಟ್ಟಿದುದು, ಮೇಘಜ್ಯೋತಿಃ. What is born in the sky: a flash of lightning. 420. — ಬಯ್ಕನೆ. ಶೀಘ್ರಾರ್ಥಃ. Quickly. 20. — ಬಯ್ಗು. ಬಯ್ಗಿಯೊಳ್, ಬಯ್ಗಿಯಲ್ಲಿ. In the evening. 278. — ಬರತ. Tbh. of ವ್ರತ. 147. — ಬರವಟ್ಟೆ. A road whereon (somebody or something) comes. 332. — ಬಱಿಕಾಲ್. A naked foot. 101. — ಬಱುವ್ವ. A vain man. 172. — ಬಱುವ್ವಳ್. A vain woman. 172. — ಬಱುವಳ್. = ಬಱುವ್ವಳ್. 172. — ಬರ್ಕುಮೆ. Coming. Plural ಬರ್ಕುಮೆಗಳ್. 572. — ಬಲ್ಗಿರಿ. A big mountain. 463. — ಬಲ್ಗೆಯ್ಯ. A man with a strong hand. 331. — ಬಲ್ಯತನ. Strong effort. 66. — ಬಲ್ಲಣ್ಣ. A great villain. 66. — ಬಲ್ಲುಜುಗಿ. A man of great exertion, etc. 329. — ಬಲ್ಸಾಹಸಿ. A great valiant man. 66. — ಬಲ್ಪಾಂಸೆ. Abundant duck-weed. 66. — ಬಳಪವ್ವಿಡಿ. To seize the pot-stone pencil. 298. — ಬಳಪವಿಡಿ. = ಬಳಪವ್ವಿಡಿ. 381. — ಬಳೆಗಾಱಿಕೆ. The making and selling of bracelets. 431. — ಬಱುವೆಳಗು. A regular lustre, in a verse under 140. — ಬಱ್ತು. Living (?). 140. — ಬಱ್ತಲೆ. 140. — ಬಱ್ತೆಳಗು. Living, steady lustre, in a verse under 140. — ಬಾಗರಣ. Tbh. of ವ್ಯಾಕರಣ. 408. — ಬಾಗರಣಿಗ. A grammarian. 408. — ಬಾಗಿಲಿಗ. A doorkeeper. 418. — ಬಾಗಿಲಾಯ್ತು. = ಬಾಗಿಲಿಗ. 425. — ಬಾಗುಳಿ. Tbh. of ವಾಗುರೆ. 140. — ಬಾದಸೆ. Tbh. of ದ್ವಾದಶಿ. 160. — ಬಾದಿ. = ವಾದಿ. See ಪುಸಿಬಾದಿ. — ಬಾನಂಗುಱಿ. ಗಗನಗರ್ತಃ. A hollow of the sky. 346. — ಬಾನಿಗ. One who resides, or is born, in the sky. 419. — ಬಾಸುಬ್ಬುಣ್ಬ. The swelling of a wale. 73. — ಬಾಱ್. = ಬಾಡು, flesh, in ಬಾಱ್ವವಿಯಾದುದು. 82. — ಬಾೞ್ದಾಣ. A place of living. 90. — ಬಾೞ್ದಱುವಿಣ್ಡು. A happy living herd of kine. 87. — ಬಿಂಗಳಿ. Tbh. of ಭೃಂಗಾರಿ. 140. — ಬಿಜಯಂಗೆಯ್. In the second verse under 468. — ಬಿಮ್ಮಗೆ. ತೂಷ್ಣೀಂ. Silently, quietly. 20. — ಬಿಮ್ಮನೆ. = ಬಿಮ್ಮಗೆ. 20. — ಬಿಱುವಜ್ಜ. A rough manner or custom. 369. — ಬಿಱುವಜ್ಜೆಯ. A man of rough manners. 369. — ಬಿೞ್ದನೆ. Stiffly, in ಬಿೞ್ದನೆ ಬೀಗು. 20. — ಬಿಳಸ. Tbh. of ವಿಲಾಸ. 160. — ಬಿಳಾಳ. Tbh. of ಬಿಡಾಲ. 140. — ಬಿಳಿಕ. A white man. 403. — ಬಿಳಿಕಿ. A white woman. 194. — ಬಿಳಿಯ. A whitish male. Instance ಬಿಳಿಯಂ ಬಗ್ಗಂ. 102. — ಬಿಳಿಯಳ್. A white female. ಬಿಳಿಯಳ್ ಸರಸ್ವತಿ. 102. Plural ಬಿಳಿಯಳ್ದಿರ್. 884. — ಬಿಳರ್. (A certain verb). 507. (*Cf.* ಬೆಳರ್ in Dictionary?). — ಬಿೞ್ಕು. 140. *Cf.* ಬಿಕ್ಕು in Dictionary? — ಬಿೞ್ಕುಳಿಸು. 538. *Cf.* ಬಿಕ್ಕುಳಿಸು in Dictionary? — ಬೀಡುವ್ವೊಗು. To enter an abode, etc. 380. — ಬೀಡುಪೊಗು. = ಬಿಡುವ್ವೊಗು. 380. — ಬೀಣಿಗ. A lute-player. 406. — ಬೀವ. Tbh. of ಭೀಮ. 144. — ಬೀೞ್. = ಬೀಡು, of which the plural is ಬೀಡುಗಳ್, ಬೀೞ್ಕಳ್ or ಬೀೞ್ಗಳ್. 233. — ಬೀಱುಸ್ಥಾಣ. A halting place. 55. *Cf.* ಬೀಱುತ್ತಾಣ. — ಬೀಱುತ್ತಾಣ. ಬೀಡುತಾಣ, ಶಿಬಿರ. A camp. 87. — ಬೀೞ್ಲಕಾರ. The consonant ೞ. 66. — ಬುಗತಿ. Tbh. of ಭುಕ್ತಿ. 147. — ಬುಗುತಿ. = ಬುಗತಿ. 147. — ಬೂತು. ಭಣ್ಡಿಮಾ. Deception, fraud (?). 415. — ಬೂತುಗ. ತಮುಪಜೀವೀ. A man living on deception (?). 415. — ಬೂತುಗಿ. A woman living on deception (?). 193. — ಬೂತುಗಿತಿ. = ಬೂತುಗಿ. 193. — ಬೂತುವಣಿಗ = ಬೂತುಗ. 415. — ಬೆಂಗದಿರ್. ಸೂರ್ಯಕಿರಣಃ. A sunbeam. 341. — ಬೆಂಗಲ್. ಸೂರ್ಯಕಾನ್ತೋಪಲಃ. The sun-stone: crystal. 342. — ಬೆಚ್ಚ. Hot. See ಬೆಚ್ಚಗೂೞ್, ಬೆಚ್ಚುರಿ. — ಬೆಚ್ಚಗೂೞ್. Hot rice. 343. — ಬೆಚ್ಚರ. ವ್ಯಕ್ತಾರ್ಥಃ. Manifestly, clearly. 20. — ಬೆಚ್ಚುರಿ. A hot flame. 343. —

ಬಿಚ್ಚೋಡು. A hot potsherd. 336. 341. 343. — ಬೆಟ್ಟವಳ್. A fierce female. 102. — ಬೆಟ್ಟುಗಾಡು. A hill-jungle. 379. — ಬೆಟ್ಟುಂಗಾಡು. = ಬೆಟ್ಟುಗಾಡು. 379. — ಬೆಟ್ಟುವಟ್ಟೆ. A hill-stream, or a hill-path. 379. — ಬೆಟ್ಟುವೊಲ್. = ಬೆಟ್ಟುವಟ್ಟೆ. 379. — ಬೆಣ್ಣೆ. 80. — ಬೆದರುಗಣ್ಣಿ. (Originally ಬೆದುರುಗಣ್ಣಿ). = ಬೆದರ್ಗಣ್ಣಿ. 83. — ಬೆದರುಡು. A frightened iguana (?). 82. — ಬೆದರ್ಗಣ್ಣಿ. (Originally ಬೆದರ್ಗಣ್ಣಿ). ಚಕಿತಗವೀ. A frightened cow. 83. — ಬೆನ್ದೊವಲ್. The skin of the back. 80. — ಬೆನ್ನುರಿ. A hot flame. 343. — ಬೆನ್ನೋಡು. = ಬಿಚ್ಚೋಡು. 343. — ಬೆಮ್ಬೂದಿ. ಕೋಷ್ಣಭಸ್ಮ. Hot ashes. 341. — ಬೆಳ್ಗರಿ (or ಬೆಳ್ಪರಿ). A rain of white colour. 93. — ಬೆಳ್ಪದ (or ಬೆಳ್ಪಳ). ಭಯಚಕಿತಾರ್ಥಃ. Frightened from fear, etc. 20. — ಬೆಳ್ಪಟ್ಟೆ. White cloth. 223. 347. — ಬೆಳ್ಳಗಸೆ. White flax. 336. — ಬೆಳ್ಳೆ. A white female. 197. — ಬೆಱಪು. 140. — ಬೆಱ್. 140. — ಬೇರುಗಿ. A woman who deals in, or sells, roots. 193. — ಬೇರುಗಿತಿ. — ಬೇರುಗಿ. 193. — ಬೇರ್ತಡೆ. An impediment of roots, etc. 90. — ಬೇಸು. Hotness. See ಬೇಸುರಿ, ಬೇಸೋಡು. — ಬೇಸುರಿ. A hot flame. 334. 343. — ಬೇಸೋಡು. A hot potsherd. 343. — ಬೇಹಾರಿ. A trader. 329. — ಬೇಹುಚವರ. A man clever in spying. 305. — ಬೊನ್ದು. ಜೀರ್ಣಮಲಿನವಸ್ತ್ರಖಣ್ಡಕಟಾದಿದ್ರವ್ಯವಚನಃ. An old dirty piece of cloth, mat and other things. 441. — ಬೊನ್ದುಕ. ತದ್ (ಬೊನ್ದು) ಗೃಹ್ಣನ್. A man who puts on an old dirty piece of cloth, etc. 441. — ಬೊಳ್ಳೆ. A vociferous woman (?). 197. — ಬೊಱ್. 140. — ಬೊಱ್. 140. — ಬ್ರಾಹ್ಮಣಗಿತಿ. A Brâhmaṇa female. 28. 190. — ಭಣ್ಡಿಮೆ. Deception, fraud (?). See ಬೂತು. — ಮಜ್ಝ. 60. *Cf.* ಮಜ್ಝಸಾರ in Dictionary. — ಮಡಿವಳ್ತಿ. A washerwoman. 200. — ಮಡುನೀರ್. Water of a pool. 380. — ಮಡುವಿಪ್ಪಾಱ್. To fall into a pool. 380. — ಮಡುವೀೞ್. = ಮಡುವಿಪ್ಪಾೞ್. 380. — ಮಣಿತ. Bending, etc. ಮಣಿವುದು. 579. Plural ಮಣಿತಂಗಳ್. 554. — ಮಣ್ಮುಱ್. 140. See ಮಣ್ಮುಱ್ in Dictionary. — ಮದನವತಿಗ. ಮದನವತೀವೃತ್ತವಿಶೇಷಕರ್ತಾ. A man who composes the madanavati metre. 412. — ಮಧುಲಿಹ. Tbh. of ಮಧುಲಿಹ್. 129. — ಮನೆಸರಕು. The articles of a house. 89. — ಮರಕುಟಿಗ. ಪಕ್ಷಿವಿಶೇಷೋ ದಾರುತಕ್ಷಾ ವಾ. A wood-pecker; a wood-cutter, a carpenter. 548. — ಮರಗಡಿ. To cut a tree or wood. 382. — ಮರಂಗಡಿ. = ಮರಗಡಿ. 382. — ಮರುಳ್ನಗೆಗ. A foolish laugher. 66. — ಮರ್ದುಗೂೞ್. Rice with a drug in it. 379. — ಮರ್ದುಂಗೂೞ್. = ಮರ್ದುಗೂೞ್. 379. — ಮುಱ್ಗ. 140. — ಮಾಗ. Tbh. of ಮಾಘ. 143. — ಮಾಂಕರಣೆ. Disregard. See under ಸಮರಂಗಾಱ. — ಮಾಂಗದಿರ್. The splendour of a mango. 348. — ಮಾಂಚಳೆ. A small branch of a mango tree. 348. — ಮಾಂಜೊಮ್ಪು. A cluster of mangoes. 348. — ಮಾಣ್ದೊಡೆ. 348. — ಮಾತುಗಿ. A talkative woman. 193. — ಮಾತುಗಿತಿ. = ಮಾತುಗಿ. 193. — ಮಾತುವಣಿಗ. A talkative man. 415. — ಮಾಮುಗುಳ್. An opening bud of a mango. 332. — ಮಾಮೊಗ್ಗು. The flower of a mango. 348. — ಮಾಮೊಣರ್. A couple of mangoes. 348. — ಮಾರಿಗ. ಮಾರಿಯಂ ಪೂಜಿಸುವಂ. A man who worships Mâri. 413. — ಮಾಱುಡು. Another iguana (?). 82. — ಮಾರೋಗ್. A staff that measures a fathom. 90. — ಮಾಲೆವಡಿಗ. ಮಾಲಾಕಾರಃ. A male florist. 416. — ಮಾಲೆವಡಿಗಿತಿ. A female florist. 192. — ಮಾವಣಿಗೆ. See ಒಳ್ಮಾವಣಿಗೆ, ನುಸುಳ್ಮಾವಣಿಗೆ. — ಮಾಳರ. Tbh. of ಮಾಲರ. 160. — ಮಾಳಲ. = ಮಾಳರ. 140. — ಮಾಱಿಡು. 488. — ಮಾಡ್ಕಟ್ಟೆ. An artificial structure. See ಪೊಸ. — ಮಾಡ್ಕುಳಿ. ಮಾಡ್ಪುದು ಶೀಲಮ್ ಈತಂಗೆ. A man addicted to making, etc. 545. — ಮಾಡ್ಗಟ್ಟೆ. 140. = ಮಾಡ್ಕಟ್ಟೆ. See also the following verse under 193: —
ಮಾಡ್ಗಟ್ಟೆಗಳ್ ಇರ್ತಡಿಯೊಳ್ ಸೀಳ್ಗಾಯ್ಗಳ್ ಬೀಗಿ ಬೆಳೆದು ಕೆಮ್ಮಿತ್ತುಗಳಿಂ । ಪೊಟ್ಗದಿರೆ ದಾಳಿಮ್ಬದ ತಾಱ್ಗಳ್ ನಿಟ್ಟಿವರ ದಿಟ್ಟಿಗಿಟ್ಟಳಮ್ ಎಸೆಗುಂ ॥ — ಮಾಡ್ತೊಱೆ. An artificial stream. 87. —

ಮಿಗುತೆ. Becoming great, etc. Plural ಮಿಗತೆಗಳ್. 560. — ಮಿಂಚುಮಿಳ್ಳುಬು. A fire-fly, etc. 344. — ಮಿತ್ತು. Past participle of ಮಿದಿ. 482. 506. — ಮಿದಿಪ. Pounding. Plural ಮಿದಿಪಂಗಳ್. 562. — ಮಿದ್ದಿಗೆ. Tbh. of ಮೃದ್ವೀಕೆ. 160. — ಮಿಳಿ. (A certain verb). 566. — ಮಿಳಿವು. A bhâva noun of ಮಿಳಿ. 566. — ಮೀಂಗುಲಿ. ಧೀವರಃ ಪಕ್ಷಿವಿಶೇಷೋ ವಾ. A fisherman; a crane. 547. — ಮುಕ. Tbh. of ಮುಖ. See ದುಮುಕ. — ಮುಕತಿ. Tbh. of ಮುಕ್ತಿ. 147. — ಮುಕ್ಕುಳಿಸಿಸು. To cause to rinse the mouth with water and spit it out, etc. Instance: — ಮುಕ್ಕುಳಿಸಿಸಿದಂ ರೋಗಿಯಿಂ ಬಜ್ಜಂ. 541. — ಮುಕ್ಕೋಡಿ. Three crores, etc. 101. — ಮುಕ್ಕ್ರೋಶ. Three kos. 68. — ಮುಗುಳ್ತೆ. Closing, etc. 559. — ಮುಗುಳ್ದಾಳಿಮ್ಬ. A budding pomegranate. 74. — ಮುಗುಳ್ಗೊಂಚಲ್. A cluster of buds. 73. — ಮುಚ್ಚೆಟ್ಟಿ. Three bankers, etc. (?). 94. — ಮುಚ್ಚಾವಡಿ. Three choultries. 93. — ಮುಚ್ಚೆರಂಗು. Three ends of a garment. 93. — ಮುಚ್ಛತ್ರ. Three halting places for travellers, etc. 68. — ಮುಚ್ಚಾಸಿರ. Three thousand. 94. — ಮುಚ್ಚೋಡಿಸ. 94. — ಮುಣ್ಟು. ಧಾರ್ಷ್ಟ್ಯಂ. Violence, audacity, etc. 423. — ಮುಣ್ಡುಕಾಱ. A man disposed to violence, etc. 423. — ಮುತ್ತಲೆ. ಮೂಱುತಲೆ. Three heads. 360. — ಮುತ್ತಳೆ. Three ties, etc. 101. — ಮುದುಡುಗಣ್ಬು. ಆಮೂಲಾಗ್ರಗ್ರನ್ಥಿ. A knot from the root to the top. 83. — ಮುದುಙ್ಗಣ್ಬು. = ಮುದುಡುಗಣ್ಬು. 83. — ಮುಪ್ಪಾದೇಶ. Three spans. 68. — ಮುಮ್ಬಿಸಿಲ್. The first sunshine of the morning. 536. — ಮುಯ್ಮೆ. ತ್ರೀನ್ ವಾರಾನ್. Three times, thrice. 360. — ಮುಯ್ಯಾಱಡಿ. Eighteen feet; (or three humble bees). 68. — ಮುಯ್ಯಾಳ್. Three servants, etc. 68. — ಮುಯ್ವರ್. Three persons. 360. — ಮುವ್ವರ್. = ಮುಯ್ವರ್. 354. — ಮುಳ್ಗೊಂಚಲ್. A cluster of thorns. 73. — ಮುಳ್ಚೀರೆ (or ಮುಳ್ಸೀರೆ). A prickly garment. 93. — ಮುಳ್ದೊಂಗಲ್. A bundle or cluster of thorns. 66. — ಮುಳ್ಬಾಗಿಲ್. A door of thorns. 72. — ಮುಳ್ಸೆಱಂಗು. Prickly ends of a garment. 93. — ಮುಱುಂಗಿಸು. To immerse (*v. tr.*) to let go down, etc., in the instance ಬಟ್ಟಗಂ ಗಟ್ಟದೊಳ್ ಪೊಡ್ತಂ ಮುಱುಂಗಿಸಿದಂ. 536. — ಮುಱ್ಬು. 140. — ಮೂಗುಡ್ಡೆ. Three heaps. 353. — ಮೂಗೆಯ್ಯ. A male with three hands. 97. — ಮೂಗೊಡೆ. Three parasols. 353. — ಮೂಚೋಟು. Three spans. 353. — ಮೂಡಣಳ್. A female of the east. 140. — ಮೂದಲೆಯ. A male with three heads. 352. — ಮೂಱಾವು. ತ್ರಿಗವೀ. Three cows. 352. — ಮೂಱುಕೆಯ್ಯ. = ಮೂಗೆಯ್ಯ. 97. — ಮೂಱುದಲೆಯ. = ಮೂದಲೆಯ. 352. — ಮೂರ್ಮಡಿ. Thrice. 88. — ಮೆಣ್ಪೆ. Tbh. of ಮೇಖಿ. 160. See ಮೇಣ್ಪೆ in Dictionary. — ಮೆಣಸಿಗ. A seller of black pepper. 409. — ಮೆಯ್ದೊವಲ್. The skin of the body. 89. — ಮೆಲಿಸು. To cause to chew. 62. — ಮೆಲ್ಗೆಯ್ಯ. A man with a soft hand. 331. — ಮೆಲ್ಮೊಗ್ಗೆ. A tender bud, in a verse under 442. — ಮೆಲ್ಲಿದಳ್. A gentle, etc. woman. 59. — ಮೆಲ್ಲೆರ್ದೆಯ. A man with a kind heart. 14. — ಮೆಲ್ಲೆರ್ದೆಯಳ್. A woman with a kind heart. 182. — ಮೆಳಸು. ಮರಿಚಂ. Black pepper. 140. — ಮೆೞ್. 140. — ಮೇಲುರಿಚ. A man who has been born in a superior village or town. 420. — ಮೇಲೂರ್. A superior village or town. 420. — ಮೇಲ್ರನ್ನ. A precious pearl. 66. — ಮೆಲ್ವಣ್ಣ. An excellent colour. 92. — ಮೇಲ್ಮಾತು. An excellent word. 92. — ಮೊಗೆಪ. Scooping, etc. 561. — ಮೊೞ್. 140. — ಮೋಜನ. Tbh. of ಮೋಚನ. 143. — ಮೋದಿಕೆ. Striking, etc. ಮೋದುವುದು. 579. Plural ಮೋದಿಕೆಗಳ್. 569. — ಮೋದು. Striking, etc. Plural ಮೋದುಗಳ್. 549. — ಮೋಸಕಾಱ. A deceiver, etc. 423. — ರಕ್ಕೆವನ್ತ. A man who is guarded; one who guards. Instance: — ರಕ್ಕೆವನ್ತಂ ಗರುಡಂ. 402. — ರಸಯಣ. Tbh. of ರಸಾಯನ. 160. — ರಾವುತರಾಯ. ತುರುಗಾರೂಢರಾಜಃ. A chief of horsemen. 295.—ರಾಬಾಕಟಾ. 140.—ರಿದ್ಧಿ. Tbh. of ಋದ್ಧಿ. 159.—ರುಂಚೆ. (A feminine noun). 197.—ಲೋಡಗ. A laugher, etc. See ಮರುಳೊತ್ತಡಗ.—ಲಂಚಗ. ಲಂಚದಿಂ ಜೀವಿಸುವಂ. A man who lives by taking bribes. 401. 415.—ಲಂಚಗಿ. A woman who takes bribes. 193.—ಲಂಚಗಿತಿ.= ಲಂಚಗಿ. 193.—ಲಂಚವಣಿಗೆ. = ಲಂಚಗಿ. 196.—ಲಜೆ. A deeply designing woman. 197.—ಲಮ್ಪಳಿಕೆ. 140. (= ಲಮ್ಪಳಿಗೆ ?).—ಲಮ್ಪಳಿಗೆ. Tbh. of ಲಾಮ್ಪಟ್ಯ. 160.—ಲಾವ್ಪಟ್ಯ. Lasciviousness, lustiness, lewdness, dissoluteness.—ವಗ್ಗ. Tbh. of ವರ್ಗ. 153.—ವಣ್ಚೆ. 80. (*Cf.* ಒಣ್ಚೆ in Dictionary ?).—ವರಳಿಚ. A man born in Varâḷa. 420.—ವಲಂ. ಸ್ಫುಟಾರ್ಥಃ. Clearly, manifestly. 20.—ವಲ್ಲಂ. = ವಲಂ. 20.—ವಿತರಣಿಸು. To pass over, etc. 59.—ವಿಧುಗಾಣ್. To see the moon. 382.—ವಿಧುಂಗಾಣ್. = ವಿಧುಗಾಣ್. 382.—ವಿಸವನ್ತ. That has poison. Instance:—ವಿಸವನ್ತಂ ಸೇಸಂ. 402.—ವೆಲಂ. ಸ್ಫುಟಾರ್ಥಃ. Manifestly. 20.—ವೈಯಾಳಿ. Tbh. of ವಾಹ್ಯಾಳಿ. 140.—ವ್ರೀಳೆ. Tbh. of ವ್ರೀಡೆ. 140.—ಸಂವ. Tbh. of ಶಮ್ಬ. 140.—ಸಣು. = ಸಣ್ಣು. 441.—ಸಣುಕ. = ಸಣ್ಣುಕ. 441.—ಸಣ್ಣು. ಸಣುಸಣ್ಣುಶಬ್ದೌ ಕುಬ್ಜವಾಮನಾವಯವವಿಶೇಷವಚನೌ. Two words which denote the particular limbs of a hump-backed and dwarfish man. 441.—ಸಣ್ಣುಕ. (A man who is small:) a man who is hump-backed or dwarfish. 441.—ಸತ್ತಿಗೆವನ್ತ. A man with an umbrella. 402.—ಸದುಮ. Tbh. of ಸದ್ಮ. 147.—ಸಪ್ಪಳ. Tbh. of ಸಷ್ಫಲ. 160.—ಸಮರಂಗಾಬಿ. A combatant, in the following verse under 384:—ಅಂಕೆಂಗಾಬಿನ ಗಣ್ಡುತನಂ ಕೊರಿತೆ ತುಮುಲಯುದ್ಧದೊಳ್ ಪಟುಭಟರಂ | ನೂಂಕುವ ಸಮರಂಗಾಬಿನ ಮೂಂಕರಣೆಯೆ ಗಣ್ಡುತನದ ತಿರುಳೆನಿಪ್ಪುದು ‖ a warrior's valiantness, sharpness, even the disregard of the combatant who pushes away fierce soldiers in a vehement fight one has to call the essence of valiantness.—ಸರವಣ್ಡಿಗ. Tbh. of ಸ್ವರಬನ್ಧಕ. 406. A man who binds, confines or checks the voice or tone(?).—ಸರವಣ್ಡಿಗಿತಿ. A female saravaṇḍiga. 192.—ಸರಿಸವ. Tbh. of ಸರ್ಷಪ. 147.—ಸಸಿದೋಣ್ಟ. A garden of young plants, etc., in a verse under 193.—ಸಸಿಸೇಖರ. Tbh. of ಶಶಿಶೇಖರ. 138.—ಸಳಿಳ. Tbh. of ಸಲಿಲ. 139.—ಸಾದಕ. Tbh. of ಸಾಧಕ. 143.—ಸಾಲ್ಗುಳಿ. ಋಣಶೀಲಃ. A man addicted to contracting debts. 545.—ಸಾಲ್ಗರುದಾಣ. A place where calves are in a row or in rows. 87.—ಸಾಸಿರ್ದಲೆಯ. A male with a thousand heads. 356.—ಸಾಸಿದೋಳ. A male with a thousand arms. 356.—ಸಿಗ್ಗನೆ. With the sound of splitting, in the sentence ಸಿಗ್ಗನೆ ಸಿಗಿದು. 20.—ಸಿರಿದರ, ಸಿರಿದಾರ, ಸಿರಿಬಾರ. Tbh. of ಶ್ರೀದ್ವಾರ. 378. *Cf.* ಸಿರಿಯುದರ, etc. in Dictionary, and ಸೀಯುದರ, etc.—ಸಿರಿರಾಮ. Tbh. of ಶ್ರೀರಾಮ. 296.—ಸಿಳ್ಗ. 140, in a verse near the end.—ಸೀಯುದರ, ಸೀಯುದಾರ, ಸೀಯುಬಾರ. = ಸಿರಿದರ, etc. 378.—ಸೀಱುಡು. 82. A screaming iguana (?).—ಸೀಲೆ. Tbh. of ಶೀಲೆ. A female who is disposed to, etc. 160.—ಸೀಳುಂಗಲ್ಲ. A split cheek. 55.—ಸೀಳ್ಗಾಯ್. A split capsula, 193 in a verse.—ಸೀಳ್ವೊಟ್ಟೆ. A split abdomen. 91.—ಸುಗಿತ. Fearing; tearing off. Plural ಸುಗಿತಂಗಳ್. 554.—ಸುಂಕಿಗಿತಿ. A female collector of customs. 191.—ಸುಟ್ಟಿ. Tbh. of ಸೃಷ್ಟಿ. 160.—ಸುಯ್ತ. Breathing, etc. Plural ಸುಯ್ತಂಗಳ್. 553.—ಸುರ್ಕುಂಗುರುಳಿ. A woman with curled hair. 194.—ಸುಬ್ಬನೆ. With the sound of pouring, dropping, etc., in the instance ಸುಬ್ಬನೆ ಸುರಿದು. 20.—ಸೂಡಿಗಣ್ಬು. ಪ್ರತಿಗ್ರನ್ಥಿಃ. 82.—ಸೂಯಾಣ. Tbh. of ಸೂಪಸ್ಥಾನಂ, ಮಹಾನಸಂ. A cook's place, a cooking place, a kitchen. 378.—ಸೂಟ್. ವಾರಂ ನಿವೇದನಂ ವಾ. A time, a turn;—making known, announcing, proclaiming, apprising, publishing, relating, communication;

information; representation; delivering, giving, entrusting; an offering, oblation; dedication. 425.—ಸೂೞಾಯ್ತ. ಸೂೞೊಳ್ ಅಧಿಕೃತಂ. A man appointed to proclaiming, etc. 425.—ಸೂೞಾಯ್ತಿ. A female ಸೂೞಾಯ್ತ. 195.—ಸೂೞುಗ = ಸೂೞಾಯ್ತ. 425.—ಸೆಟ್ಟಿತಿ. A female banker, etc. 190. 200.—ಸೆದ್ದು. 67.—ಸೆೞವು. 140.—ಸೆೞಸು. 140.—ಸೇನೆವೞ or ಸೇನೆವಳ್ಳ. A general. 426.—ಸೇನ್ದು. Drawing water out. 569.—ಸೊಚ್ಚ. Tbh. of ಸ್ವಚ್ಛ. 160.—ಸೊಮ್ಮುೞಿ. 140 (where ಪೊಮ್ಮುೞಿ is separately adduced).—ಸೊಬರ್. 80.—ಸೊಸೆಮುದ್ದು. A kiss, or the affection, of a daughter-in-law. 101.—ಸ್ಫಿಕ್ಕೆ. See ಹಿಕ್ಕೆ.—ಸ್ಮರ್ತಾರ. Tbh. of ಸ್ಮರ್ತೃ. 123.—ಸ್ಮರ್ತೃ. One who remembers or recollects.—ಸ್ವರಬನ್ಧಕ. See ಸರವಡ್ಡಿಗ.—ಹಟ್ಟಿಗೆ. Tbh. of ಪಟ್ಟಿಕೆ. 145.—ಹತ್ತಿಗೆ. Tbh. of ಪತ್ರಿಕೆ. 154.—ಹದಿಡೆ. Tbh. of ಪ್ರತಿಷ್ಠೆ. 160.—ಹರಡಿಕೆ. Scratching; spreading. 569.—ಹರ್ತಾರ. Tbh. of ಹರ್ತೃ. 123.—ಹಸದನ. Tbh. of ಪ್ರಸಾಧನ. 160.—ಹಾಂಸೆ. See ಬಲ್ಹಾಂಸೆ.—ಹಿದಯ. Tbh. of ಹೃದಯ. 160.—ಹಿಕ್ಕೆ. Tbh. of ಸ್ಫಿಕ್ಕೆ (ಸ್ಫಿಕ್ಕ್ಯ). 150.—ಹೀವರ. Tbh. of ಪೀವರ. 145.—ಹೆಲ್ಲ. ಹೆಲ್ಲಶಬ್ದಕ್ ಶರೀರಾರ್ಥಃ ಪುರಶ್ಚೂಡಾರ್ಥೋ ವಾ. 1, The body; 2, the front tuft of hair. 312.—ಹೆಲ್ಲಾಹೆಲ್ಲಿ. ಹೆಲ್ಲಮಂ ಹೆಲ್ಲಮಂ ಮೆಟ್ಟಿ ಮಾಱ್ಪ ಯುದ್ಧಂ. 1, A fight in which they mutually trample on the body of each other. ಹೆಲ್ಲಮಂ ಹೆಲ್ಲಮನ್ ಓರೊನ್ದಂ ಪಿಡಿವುದಾವ ಯುದ್ಧದೊಳ್ ಅದು. 2, A fight in which they mutually seize the front tuft of hair of each other. 312.

INDEX.

The numbers refer to the pages.

I. Kannaḍa and Saṁskṛita letters, syllables and words,

wherever required with due diacritical signs.

2. Indexical words in English.

CORRECTIONS AND ADDITIONS.

Page 2, note, *read* Kharôshṭi *for* Khanôshṭi.

P. 5, line 32, read ೞ್ for ಱ್.

P. 6, l. 29, *read* ṛi *for* ṛî.

P. 7, l. 11, *read* bottom *for* botom.

P. 8, l. 16, *read* sub letter *for* sub-letter.

P. 10, l. 24 (under Present Malayâḷa), *read* lṛî *for* lṛ.

P. 11, l. 17, read ಅ ಅ for ಅ ಅ.

P. 11, l. 26, read 216 for 217.

P. 11, l. 35, read 19 for 18.

P. 15, l. 11, read ೞ್ for ಱ್.

P. 16, l. 2, *read* gala *for* galla.

P. 16, l. 18, *read* ananunâsika *for* anunâsika.

P. 19, l. 11, *read* ṭlṛi *for* ṭlri.

P. 26, l. 24, read ನಾಱು for ಸಾಱು.

P. 26, l. 34, add, § 151, *a*, 4.

P. 26, l. 35, read 24 for 34.

P. 27, l. 2, remove § 151, *a*, 4.

P. 28, l. 35, read ಮುಱುಗು for ಮುೞುಗು.

P. 29, l. 19, read ಎ for ಏ.

P. 31, l. 34, read ಅ for ಲ.

P. 32, l. 17, read ಸೃಜ್ for ಸ್ರಿಜ್.

P. 33, l. 20 *after* ಎನಿತು, *read*, and also ಎಲ್ಲದು.

P. 35, l. 18, *read* is *for* are.

P. 35, l. 25, read ಮುಟ್ಟಗ for ಮಟ್ಟಗ.

P. 37, l. 19, *read* (see No. 8, *b*) *for* (see No. 8, remark).

P. 37, l. 20, *read* same *for* sume.

P. 38, l. 29, note 1, read (ಸವರ್ಣ, ವಿಶ್ವ) for (ಸವರ್ಣ ವಿಶ್ವ).

P. 38, l. 42, note 2, read ಈಗ for ಇಗ.

P. 39, l. 12, read 253, 2, *d* for 253, 2, *c*.

P. 40, l. 29, put a stop after ತೊೞಲ್ಗರ್, and read (See 102, 9).

P. 42, l. 24, put , for ;

P. 44, l. 30, *put a comma after* therefore.

P. 45, l. 8, read ಗ್ಲಾವ್ for ಗಾವ್.

P. 47, l. 28, put (after accusative.

P. 47, l. 37, read ನಾಡ for ನಾಟ.

P. 48, l. 4, *read* dialect *for* dialects.

P. 49, l. 1, read ಇಷ್ಠಂ for ಇಷ್ಣಂ.

P. 49, l. 18, *read* are *for* and.

P. 53, l. 28, read ಕೆಮ್ಮಿಸಿಲೆಳಸಲ್ for ಕೆಮ್ಮ್ಬಿಸಿಲೆಳಸಲ್, and remove ; before it.

P. 54, l. 8, read ಕುರುಳ for ಕುರುಶ.

P. 55, l. 9, *read* dialect *for* dialects.

P. 57. l. 2, read 371 for 370.

P. 59, l. 7, read ಅವುದಟೊಳ್ for ಅವುದ ಟೊಳ್.

P. 60, l. 31, *read* ಉ of *for* of ಉ.

P. 65, l. 19, remove ಸ್ವಕರ್ತೃಗಳೊಳ್.

P. 65, l. 32, remove ಸ್ವಕರ್ತೃವಿನಲ್ಲಿ.

P. 66, l. 22, add ಸ್ವಕರ್ತೃಗಳೊಳ್.

P. 66, after l. 26, add, 7, Loc. ಇನಲ್ಲಿ, *e. g.* ಸ್ವಕರ್ತೃವಿನಲ್ಲಿ.

P. 71, l. 26, read ಓರೆಗಿತ್ತಿಯು for ಓವೆಗಿತ್ತಿಯು.

P. 72, l. 36, remove letter *c*.

P. 73, l. 14, read ಎಲ್ಲಮುಂ for ಎಲಮುಂ.

P. 74, l. 6, put) after the plural.

P. 76, l. 24, *read* Malayâḷa *for* Malyâḷa.

P. 83, l. 29, read ಞ for ಱ್ and ಅಞ್ಚ for ಅಟ್ಟ.

P. 83, l. 40, *read* dialects *for* dialect.

P. 85, l. 40, read 131, *a*, *b* for 131, *b*, *c*.

P. 88, l. 11, *remove* (*before* as.

P. 88, l. 26, put a comma after ವರ್ತಮಾನ.

P. 92, l. 26, add ನಿರ್ಣಯಿಸು after ಓಲಗಿಸು.

P. 92, l. 29, remove ನಿರ್ಣಯಿಸು.

P. 93, l. 4, *add*, Curious formations are ಖಣ್ಡ್ರಿಸು (in śâsanas ಕಣ್ಡರಿಸು) and ಚೇತರಿಸು from ಖಣ್ಡರಣೆ or ಕಣ್ಡರಣೆ, cutting, engraving, and ಚೇತರಣೆ.

P. 98, l. 31, *read* must have been ಬೆರಣ್ಟು.

P. 102, l. 19, read ನಡ ನಡ ನಡಗು for ನಡ ನಡ ನಡುಗು.

P. 102, l. 35, read ಅಳ್ಕು for ಆಳ್ಕು.

P. 103, foot-note, *read* Dr. J. F. Fleet *for* Dr. I. F. Fleet.

P. 104, l. 10, read ಮೆಟ್ಟ್ದು.

P. 111, l. 27, read ಅವಾಚ್ಯಲಿಂಗ for ಎವಾಚ್ಯ ಲಿಂಗ.

P. 111, l. 28, put a comma after ಪಾಡಿದಳ್.

P. 111, l. 29, after ಪಾಡಿದರ್ read ಪಾಡಿದುವು for ಪಾಡಿದುದು.

P. 118, l. 2, *read* ಆಪ (of ಆಜ್) appears in this paragraph under No. 2 *for* ಆಪ (of ಅಬ್) appears in the paragraph under No. 1.

P. 118, l. 8, read ತೂಂಕಡಿಪ for ತೂಂಕಡಿ.

P. 120, l. 17, *remove* (of an ಉಳ್ವು) *and read* (of an ಉಳ್ಪು; see page 114, remark).

P. 120, l. 29, *add*, It may be thought that at least in some of the above mentioned instances, *e.g.* in ಬೀಸುವ, simply a euphonic ವ್ may have been inserted to form the genitive.

P. 127, l. 14, read 254 for 253.

P. 129, l. 26, read ಕೇಳ್ದಪ್ಪುವು for ಕೇಳಪ್ಪುವು.

P. 141, l. 28, read (ಬೇ + ಯ್ + ಇತು) for (ಬೆ + ಯ್ + ಇತು), and l. 29, read (ಮೇ + ಯ್ + ಇತು) for ಮೆ + ಯ್ + ಇತು).

P. 142, l. 17, read ಆಯ್ for ಅಯ್.

P. 142, l. 30, read ಅದ for ಆದ.

P. 145, l. 10, read ಆಪ್ಪಾರ್ for ಅಪ್ಪಾರ್.

P. 147, l. 32, remark, *remove* § §.

P. 149, l. 38, read ಪೊಲ್ಗೆ for ಪೊಬ್ಗೆ.

P. 150, l. 13, read ಪಾಳಿಕೆ for ವಾಳಿಕೆ.

P. 151, l. 19, remove the comma after ಆಂ.

P. 158, l. 5, *put* (*before* I have not seen.

P. 160, l. 8, remove the comma after ಬಾರ್.

P. 161, l. 24, *read* yet to be *for* yet be.

P. 164, l. 33, *after* ಪಿನ್ದು, behind, *read* med.

P. 165, l. 8, *include within the brackets* ಹಿಂದೆ, behind (*d*, med., mod.).

P. 167, l. 17, *read* 109, *a*, 7 *for* 109 *a*, 5; *and* l. 32, *put a semicolon after* (see sub ಅಡೆ).

P. 168, l. 15, read 316, 5 for 318, 5.

P. 169, l. 18, put a comma after ಭೋರ್ for the semicolon.

P. 169, l. 25, read ಅರೆ ಉಬ್ for ಅರೆ ಉಬ್.

P. 171, l. 32, read ಅ for ಆ.

P. 172, l. 11, read ಜ್ಯಾಯೊಳ್ for ಜಾಯೊಳ್.

P. 174, l. 6, read § 96 for § 97.

P. 176, l. 7, read ಕೇಡಾಯಿತೆ for ಕೊಡಾ ಯಿತೆ.

P. 176, l. 12, *remove* 6.

P. 177, l. 35, *read* in *for* see.

P. 182, l. 5, read ಪಿತ್ರ್ಯಾಣ for ಪಿತೃಣ.

P. 182, l. 35, read ತನು + ಛಾಯೆ for ತನು + ಚ್ಛಾಯೆ.

P. 184, l. 27, *read* ತಪಸ್ + ಫಲ *for* ತಪಸ್, + ಫಲ; and l. 29, *read* (or ತಪಶ್ಶೀಲ) *for* (ತಪಶೀಲ).

P. 188, l. 25, *insert* this *before* Nâra-siṁha.

P. 193, l. 4, *add*, *Cf.* § 372.

P. 193, l. 8, read ಕಾಡುಕಿಚ್ಚು for ಕಡುಕಿಚ್ಚು.

P. 193, l. 22, remove the parenthesis of ಎಲರ್.

P. 194, l. 35, read ಪ್ಲುತ for ಪುತ.

P. 195, l. 22, *read* yamaka *for* vamaka.

P. 200, l. 15, *read* 205, 1, 3rd person, *a* *for* 205, 1, *d*.

P. 201, l. 16, read ಬದಿಕೆಗ for ಬಡಿಕೆಗ, and l. 21, put a stop for the comma after (ಬಯ್).

P. 204, l. 33, read ಮೇಲುರಿಚೆ for ಮೆಲುರಿಚೆ.

P. 205, l. 35, read ಗಟಿಕಾಱ for ಗೆಟಿಕಾಱ.

P. 206, l. 27, *read* ಪ್ರಹರೇ ಪ್ರಹರೇ *for* ಪ್ರಹ ರೇ, *and after* l. 28, *add*, See page 446.

P. 214, l. 28, read ಗಣ್ಡವಸದನಂ for ಗಣ್ಡವ ಸದನ.

P. 214, l. 31, read ಮಲ್ಲಮುರಾನ್ತಕಂ for ಮ ಲಮುರಾನ್ತಕಂ.

P. 216, l. 9, *put a quotation mark after* (arthavyakti).

P. 219, l. 6, *read* played *for* sang.

P. 233, l. 15, compound ಅಧಿಕ and ಪುಣ್ಯನ್.

P. 235, l. 1, *put* for *after* used.

P. 238, l. 25, read ಏತಱ for ಏತರ.

P. 239, l. 10, *remove the stop after* genitives.

P. 240, l. 13, *read* that *for* this.

P. 247, l. 13, *read* (see § 355, I, 3).

P. 249, l. 8, read ತೀರ for ತೀರಾ.

P. 251, l. 8, *read* of the uvula *for* of the eyes.

P. 253, l. 28, read ಏಱುಸಾವಿರ for ಏೞುಸಾವಿರ.

P. 255, l. 27 and 28, read ಕೋಷ್ಠಕ for ಕೋಷ್ಟಕ.

P. 259, l. 11, read ಇಮ್ಮೆ for ಇಮೆ.

P. 264, l. 29, *read* of the becoming then *for* of the coming then.

P. 265, l. 1, remove the semicolon after ಬಗ್ಗೆ, and put a comma for it.

P. 265, l. 21, *read* ಲ್ (or ಅಲ್) *for* ಅಲ್; *and* l. 22, § 362, 2, *c*) *for* 362, after *c*).

P. 271, l. 24, *put* mango *in parenthesis.*

P. 273, l. 32, read ಪದ್ಮೋದರಂಗೆ for ಪದೋ ದರಂಗೆ.

P. 276, l. 33, read ಹಾರುವನ for ಹಾಱುವನ.

P. 285, l. 25, read ಅಲ್, ಅಲು for ಅಲು.

P. 291, l. 3, *read* a euphonic ವ್.

P. 294, l. 17, read ದಿರಾಗಮು ವಿರಾಗಮುಂಗಳ್ಗ for ವಿರಾಗಮು ವಿರಾಗಮುಂಗಳ್ಗ.

P. 297, l. 10, read ಖಳರುಂ for ಬಳರುಂ.

P. 298, l. 7, *read* dative *for* genitive; *and* l. 25, *read* upon thee *for* upon you.

P. 304, l. 17, *put a semicolon after* fellow.

P. 306, l. 14, read ಓರೊರ್ವರ್ ಓರೊರ್ವರ for ಓರೊರ್ವರ್ ಓರೊರ್ವರ್.

P. 309, l. 29, read ದಿನೊತ್ತೊಮ್ಮೊಮ್ಮೆ for ದಿನೊದ್ದೊಮ್ಮೊಮ್ಮೆ; and l. 32, read ಅಕ್ಕ್ಯವನ್ for ಅಕ್ಕ್ಯಂ.

P. 312, l. 24, *put* but *in parenthesis*; *and* l. 25, *read* if one is a sensualist *for* if one (is) a sensualist.

P. 317, l. 27, read ಬರುವದರ್ಕೊಳಗೆ for ಬಱು ವದರ್ಕೊಳಗೆ; and l. 35, read ಬರೆದಿರುವಿ for ಬರೆದಿರುವಿರಿ.

P. 319, l. 1 and 2, *read* having caused to make was, *i. e.* had caused to make or had made; *and* l. 10, *insert* ಮಯೂಖ *after* ನೀಹಾರ.

P. 320, l. 28, *add*, Let it be expressly stated here with regard to ಪಳಂಚಿನ ಪೊಡೆ that ಒಡೆ is attached also to the participial form used for the formation of the present tense (see § 194) in the ancient dialect.

P. 322, l. 3, *read* we *for* (you), *and* l. 4, *read* us *for* you.

P. 328, l. 7, read ಚತುರ್ಥೀಗಳ್ for ಚತರ್ಥೀ ಗಳ್.

P. 329, l. 1, *read* ಗೃಹಸ್ಥನಂ *and* gṛihastha; *and* l. 10, ಹುಲ್ಲುಗಳಿನ್ದ *for* ಹಲ್ಲುಗಳಿನ್ದ.

P. 332, l. 4, *insert* large *after* swallowing.

P. 334, l. 29, read ನೋಯಿಸದನ್ತೆ for ನೋ ಯಿಸನ್ತೆ.

P. 335, l. 5, read ಹುಲ್ಲು for ಹಲ್ಲು.

P. 343, l. 10, read ಲಿಂಗಂಗಳಿರೆ for ಅಂಗಂ ಗಳಿರೆ.

P. 345, l. 11, read ಉ, ಊ for ಉ.

P. 346, l. 31, read ಮಾಱಾಟಕ್ಕೆ for ಮಱಾಟ ಕ್ಕೆ; and l. 34, remove ದೊಡ್ಡ.

P. 350, l. 16 and 17, read ಬೊಱಿಸಿ for ಬೊಱಿಸಿ.

P. 356, l. 28, read ಇರ್ದ್ದಿನಿಸ್ದ for ಇನಿನಿಂದ.

P. 358, l. 4, read ಅದೆಯುನ್ತೆ for ಅದೆಯೆನ್ತೆ.

P. 365, l. 7, read ಅದುವಾದುದು for ಅದುದಾ ದುದಂ.

P. 367, l. 9, read ಚೀಱಾಡುತ್ತಾರೆ for ಚೀ ಆಡುತ್ತಾರೆ.

P. 370, l. 33, read ಕೊಣ್ಡು ಕೊಣ್ಡು for ಕೊಣ್ಡು.

P. 377, l. 1, read ಮೇಱುವಿಂಗೀತನ್ for ಮೇ ಱುವೆಂಗೀತನ್.

P. 382, l. 28, *add*, *Cf.* § 352, 6, *b*.

P. 383, l. 24, *read* treatise *for* treaty.

P. 384, l. 7, *read* kartṛi *for* kartri.

P. 393, l. 6, *read* (Čandraprabhapurâṇa) *for* (Čandraprabhâpurâṇa).

P. 396, l. 9, *add*, *Cf.* 347, 8.

P. 396, l. 31, *read* No. 2, *a for* No. 2, *c*.

P. 396, l. 35, *add*, *Cf.* 346, 7.

P. 397, l. 17, *read* 350, 8, *for* 350, 8, etc.

P. 397, l. 27 and 33, *read* parenthesis and brackets.

P. 400, l. 19, *read* our *for* (our).

P. 402, l. 14, read ಕೊಡಕೆ for ಕೊಟಕು; and l. 33, add 4.

P. 403, l. 34, read ನಡೆದಪಿರ್ for ನಡೆಹಪಿರ್.

P. 408, l. 10, *read* and one *for* and two.

P. 411, l. 17, *read* like a blacksmith; *and* l. 35, *read* ಗೆಲ್ಗುಂ *for* ಗೆಲ್ವುಂ.

P. 412, l. 1, *read* ಮಱುಗುವಿನಂ *for* ಮುಱು ಗುವಿನಂ; *and* l. 2, *read* he incessantly shot.

P. 413, l. 6, *remove* as perhaps in the half-verse quoted above.

P. 414, l. 17, read ಅವನ್ for ಅವಳ್.

P. 418, l. 15, *read* is *for* s; and l. 27, read ಅರಸನತ್ತಣಿಂ for ಅರಸಣತ್ತಣಿಂ.

P. 422, l. 11, after 185 insert 186; and l. 24, read ಕೊಂಚೆ for ಕೊಂಚ.

P. 423, l. 16, remove ವ before ಗರ್ವಿಸ; and l. 17, insert ಪತ್ತುವ after ಸುತ್ತುವ.

P. 424, l. 19, read ವಾದಕಂ for ಪಾದಕಂ.

P. 426, l. 29, put a comma before ಅರ್ಕನ್.

P. 431, l. 15, read ಅವುರ್ for ಅವುರ್.

P. 434, l. 14, add § 71 to ಕೋಟೆ, where it appears as a ತತ್ಸಮ term.

P. 435, l. 5, read (ಜ್ಯೇಷ್ಠ) for (ಚೇಷ್ಟೆ).

P. 438, l. 14, read ಸಿನ್ದುರ (ಸಿನ್ಧೂರ) for ಸೆನ್ದುರ (ಸಿನ್ಧೂರ); and l. 24, read *cf.* ಪಿಟ್ಟು for *cf.* ಹಿಟ್ಟು.

P. 441, l. 1 and 2, read ಇದುಸ್ಸಾದು for ಇದುಸ್ಸಾದು; l. 10, read ತಾಯ್ವಿ for ತಾ ಯ್ದಿ; and l. 21, read ನೀವ್ವೋಗಯ್ದಂ for ನೀವ್ವೊಯ್ದಂ.

P. 442, *under* 372, *add* — Through the favour of Mr. B. Lewis Rice the following "Explanation of some of the words contained in Rev. Kittel's list" kindly prepared by his Munshi, was forwarded to the author, and is given here as far as the explanations are not conjectural, viz.

ಉಱಾಲ. A bird of omen. ಉಱಾಲವೆನ್ದೊನ್ದು ಶಕುನದ ಪಕ್ಷಿ (Karṇâṭakasañjîvana). — ಎಙ್ಗ. A fool. The old spelling of ಎಗ್ಗ. — ಕೊಙ್ಗಟ್ಟಿ. Rice and a hollow made for the reception of pepper-water, etc. — ಕೆಱ. The same as ಕೆಳಗು in the Dictionary. — ಕೇಳ್ವಿ. The act of hearing. There is a game in cards called ಕೇಳ್ವಿ (or ಕೇಳುವೆ) ಒದವೆ. — ಖೂಱ. = ಕೂಱ. ಖೂ ಱನ್ ಎಗ್ಗಂ (Karṇâṭakasañjîvana). — ಘು ಱುಮ್ಮನೆ. Imitation of the sound produced when plunging into water. — ಚಪ್ಪಱ. ಚಪ್ಪಱಾಯೆನಲ್ಕೆ ಚಪ್ಪಟೆ (Karṇâṭakasañjîvana). — ತೇಱ್. ತೇಱು. As a verb

(= ತೀರು 2 of the Dictionary) it means 'to succeed etc.' ತೀಱಿದನೆನೆ ಪುಷ್ಟಿಯಾದಂ (Karṇâṭaka nighaṇṭu). ತೀಱಲ್. ತೀಱು as a noun (= ತೀರು 3) means 'success'. ತೀಗರ್ಗಳ್ = successes.—ದಬಪ್ಪೞ. = ಬಲ್ಲೂಱ್ (Karṇâṭakasañjîvana).—ನೊಳ್ (= ನೋಳ್ of the Dictionary). ನೊಳ್ದನೆನೆ ಮುನ್ದೆ ಪೋದಂ (Karṇâṭakasañjîvana). ಪದಿರ್. ಕೂಡಲ್ (ಎನೆ) ಪದಿರ್ appears to mean ಪದಿರ್ (is) success (ಕೂಡಲ್).—ಪಾಱುಡು, ಬೆದಱುಡು, ಮಾಱುಡು, ಸೀಱುಡು. ಪಾಯುಡು, etc. are compounds of ಪಾಱು, etc. with ಉಡು, a well-known animal. ಸೀಱುಡು of the Dictionary seems to mean some animal rather than 'a cascade'; it may be the correct form of the modern ಜೀರುಂಡೆ. (ಜೀಱುಂಡೆ of the Dictionary?).—ಪೆಬಪು. Lameness.—ಪೇಚಿವಾಂಸ. One who has cooked (from ಪಚ್, to cook).—ಪೊಬಪು. ಪೊಬಪು ಸಾಮಾನ್ಯಾಕೃತಿಗೆ ಸಂಜ್ಞಕಂ. (*Cf.* ಪೊಬಕು in the Dictionary).—ಬಿಳಲ್. A clear mistake for ಬಿಳಲ್, to get pendent roots.—ಭಣ್ಡಿಮೆ (ಭಣ್ಡಿಮಾ). Buffoonery (from Samskṛita ಭಣ್ಡ + ಇಮಾ).—ರುಂಚಿ. The same as the second part of ದಪ್ರುಂಚಿ.—ಸಿಗ್ಗ. Tadbhava of ಶಿಗ್ಗ.

P. 442, l. 35, read ಅಭಿಷ್ವಂಗ for ಅಭಿಷ್ಟಂಗ.

P. 443, l. 6, read ಅವು = ಅವಿ (Šabdânušâsana sûtra 473. 480. 513).

P. 445, l. 24, *read* a black, or bad, belly; l. 32, *read* sŏllige *for* sollige; *and* l. 35, *read* ಕುಮ್ಮುಗಾಱ.

P. 446, l. 37, *read* Ḍŏmba *for* Dŏmba.

P. 449, l. 37, read ಸದ್ಯಾದ್ಯುತ್ತರಣಶೀಲಃ for ಸದ್ಯಾದ್ಯುತ್ತರಣಶೀಲಃ.

P. 452, l. 32, read ಬೀಡುವೆಬ್ಬುಗು for ಬಿಡುವೆಬ್ಬುಗು.

P. 453, l. 2, read ಬೆಟ್ಟುಂಗಾಡು for ಬೆಟ್ಟುಂಗಾಡು; and l. 13, read ಬೇಹುಚದುರ for ಬೇಹುಚದರ.

P. 455, l. 34, read ಸೀಳ್ಪೊಟ್ಟೆ for ಸೀಲ್ಪೊಟ್ಟೆ.

P. 456, l. 4, read ಸೆಬಪು and ಸೆಬಸು; and l. 13, read ಪುರಶ್ಶೂಡಾಘೋರ್ಗವಾ.